MW00353356

UNIVERSITY CASEBOOK SERIES

CASES, COMMENT, QUESTIONS

CRIMINAL PROCESS

SEVENTH EDITION

by

LLOYD L. WEINREB
Dane Professor of Law, Harvard University

FOUNDATION PRESS
NEW YORK, NEW YORK
2004

THOMSON
WEST™

395 Hudson Street
New York, NY 10014
Phone Toll Free 1–877–888–1330
Fax (212) 367–6799
fdpress.com

Printed in the United States of America

ISBN 1–58778–738–5

PREFACE

The objective of this book is to provide a model of criminal process in this country by a close examination of federal law and practice. In its major premises federal criminal process is representative of criminal process in the states. Details and nomenclature vary widely, but the problems and their solution are in general remarkably uniform. The influence of federal law on the states and the dispersion of federal law make it apt as a model; the peculiar features of federal crime are softened by cases in the District of Columbia where all crime is federal.

Because the subject of study is criminal process generally and not federal criminal procedure, some issues, such as the problems created by the relationships of the states to each other and to the federal government, are largely disregarded. The broad outline of much of criminal process is a constitutional matter, and much of the material here concerns constitutional decisions of the Supreme Court and other courts. Again, the focus is the nature of the process established by such decisions, not the ways of constitutional adjudication. Except as they bear on criminal process, discussions in the opinions of precedent, jurisdictional matters, and constitutional law generally are omitted.

While it seems to me that investigation and prosecution of crime are separable for purposes of study from the rest of criminal process, I would not have that taken as an indication that I think the rest is less important. In particular, the law's disregard of what happens to a person after he is convicted of a crime compared with its close attention to the methods by which he is convicted seems to me greatly mistaken. At two points, in Chapter 8 on Bail and the section Nature of the Penalty in Chapter 15 on Sentence and Judgment, I have included a small suggestion of the issues about jails and prisons.

For the most part, the process studied here is concerned with serious crimes. If numbers of individuals (or crimes) alone are considered, the emphasis should be on minor crime, and what has been called the "low-level" criminal process. The number of misdemeanors, of which the largest part involve drunkenness and related offenses, vastly exceeds the number of felonies. Certainly we should not allow the process in these cases to remain below the level of our vision; in almost every respect, low-level criminal process is a challenge to the principles we profess and should make us wary of accepting our professions of principle without skepticism. It is composed too little of our aspirations, however, and too much of failings that we all acknowledge as failings to be useful as a model of the criminal process.

Notes have been numbered consecutively through the book to 653. Footnotes are numbered consecutively in each chapter. I have generally omitted footnotes in reproduced materials. Those which appear are renumbered but are in the original materials unless the footnote number is enclosed in brackets. In Supreme Court cases, separate opinions of Justices that are not reproduced are indicated in a footnote at the end, along with the votes of the Justices who did not join one of the reproduced opinions. I have corrected obvious typographical and similar errors and have made a few other small changes in reproduced materials not affecting their sense.

Experience with previous editions suggests that I should make the following comment. It is generally not my assumption that students will go to the reports to read the opinions in the large number of cases that are described briefly or are cited following questions in the notes. Such notes are intended primarily to provide factual variations on themes presented in the main cases and materials, as problems for discussion or reflection. Usually, resort to the opinions will provide authority for some result but not otherwise add substantially to the material in the book.

Preparing this seventh edition, I am impressed by how well the general conception for the book has stood up over the past 35 years. The "revolution in criminal procedure" that was supposed to have taken place in the decade of the '60s is now well in the past and, if there was indeed a revolution, there has since been something of a counter-revolution. For all that, it is remarkable how little the broad contours of criminal process have changed. In any case, it seems to me now, as it did then, that if one's primary interest is criminal process—the procedures by which crimes are investigated and criminals prosecuted—there is no better course than to follow the process from beginning to end and to pick up constitutional and statutory issues and so forth where and as they arise in the process. So also, it still seems to me that it is useful for students to see the forms by which various investigative steps and procedural matters are carried out, even if the forms have little content of their own. And it seems to me now, as then, that the issues of professional ethics and strategy that confront lawyers for the prosecution or defense should be integrated into material that sets forth the relevant law.

I am grateful to the American Bar Association for permission to reproduce the excerpt from the ABA Standards for Criminal Justice, Pleas of Guilty (3d ed. 1999) that appears on p. 746; the excerpts from the ABA Standards for Criminal Justice, Prosecution Function and Defense Function (3d ed. 1993) that appear on pp. 1004, 1014, and 1017; the excerpts from the Model Rules of Professional Conduct (2004) that appear on pp. 1005 and 1025; and the excerpt from the ABA Standards for Criminal Justice, The Function of the Trial Judge (3d ed. 2000) that appears on p. 1027.

Police forms were provided by the Boston Police Department. Some of the police forms were prepared for the Boston Police Department by Comnetix Computer Systems, Inc. Robert Layfield, Director of Police Sales for

Comnetix, kindly allowed me to use sample forms on which his name and picture appear for demonstration purposes. Forms used in the federal courts were provided by the Office of the Clerk of the United States District Court for the District of Massachusetts.

Lawrence Heftman, while a student at Harvard Law School, gave me substantial research and editorial assistance for this edition. Melinda Eakin was responsible for copy editing and for preparation of the manuscript in all its stages; her assistance was invaluable. As in the past, I am grateful to Raymond S. Andrews ("Sherwood") who did the illustrations.

LLOYD L. WEINREB

June 2004

*

SUMMARY OF CONTENTS

*

TABLE OF CONTENTS

PART TWO. PROSECUTION

*

TABLE OF CASES

Principal cases are in bold type. Non-principal cases are in roman type. References are to Pages.

CASES, COMMENT, QUESTIONS

CRIMINAL PROCESS

*

PART ONE

INVESTIGATION

A crime is committed. How should the criminal process—official response to crime—begin? Consider the following cases:

(1) A policeman walking a beat at night stumbles across a man's body on the sidewalk. The man has been shot to death.

(2) A policeman walking a beat at night hears the burglar alarm of a jewelry store. When he arrives at the store no one is in sight. The store window is broken.

(3) A policeman walking a beat at night hears the burglar alarm of a jewelry store. As he arrives at the store, a woman rushes out the door.

(4) A policeman walking a beat at night hears a scream and the sound of a gun being fired. He goes to the place from which the sounds came and sees people rushing out of a house.

(5) An accountant reports to the president of a bank that there is a recurrent shortage in the daily cash receipts of one of the tellers.

(6) A tax examiner reports to her superior that a bank president has apparently understated his income on tax returns for the past three years.

(7) A bank president calls her husband on the telephone to report that their son has been kidnapped.

(8) The wife of a bank president tells him that for the past several weeks she has received anonymous threatening telephone calls.

(9) A woman reports to the police that her husband has beaten her up.

In each of the cases, a crime has apparently been committed. What should happen next? So far as the policemen know, the same crime has been committed in cases (2) and (3). Should the two policemen act alike? Why (not)? In cases (3), (5), (6), and (9) the identity of the apparent criminal is known. Should the official action taken in each case be the same? Why (not)?

What should be accomplished at the beginning of the criminal process? Who should be advised that the process has "begun"? Who should be asked to participate? Or required to participate? Why?

Contrast the cases above with some of the following situations:

(1) A mother finds her small son standing on a chair and, in violation of her strict rule, reaching into the cookie jar.

(2) A woman finds the housekeeper taking a nip from a bottle in the liquor cabinet.

(3) A student discovers her roommate in the act of stealing her class notes.

(4) A student discovers that his class notes are missing and suspects strongly that his roommate has taken them.

(5) A private on guard duty sees a prisoner climbing the camp fence.

(6) An army officer leading an attack on the enemy sees one of his men running away to the rear.

(7) A policeman sees a car parked in a "no parking" zone on a quiet Sunday when traffic is slight.

Is there any official function that *must* be performed before it can be said that criminal process has begun?

Boston Police
INCIDENT REPORT

HANDPRINT

ORIGINAL ☐ SUPPLEMENTARY ☐

01. KEY SITUATIONS ☐ DRUGS ☐ LICENSED PREMISES ☐ ELDERLY ☐ JUVENILE ☐ COMMUNITY DISORDERS ☐ DOMESTIC ☐ OTHER | 02. COMPLAINT NO. | 03. REPORT DIST. | CLEARANCE DIST | PAGE | OF

04. TYPE OF INCIDENT | 05. CRIME CODE | 06. STATUS ☐ INACTIVE ☐ UNFOUNDED ☐ ARREST ☐ UNDER 18 ☐ EXCEPT CL ☐ UNDER 18 | 07. DATE OF OCCUR. A | B

08. LOCATION OF INCIDENT (NO STREET) (INTERSECTION-ALPHA ORDER) | APT. | 09. DISPATCH TIME ☐ A ☐ P | 10. TIME OF OCCUR A ☐ A ☐ P | B ☐ A ☐ P

11. VICTIM-COMP. (LAST, FIRST, MI) | 12. PHONE | 13. SEX ☐ M ☐ F | 14. RACE | 15. MARITAL STATUS ☐ MARRIED ☐ UNMARRIED

16. ADDRESS (NO., STREET, CITY AND STATE IF OTHER THAN BOSTON OR MASS.) | APT. | OCCUPATION | 17. AGE | 18. D.O.B.

19. PERSON REPORTING (IF DIFFERENT THAN ABOVE) | 20. ADDRESS | APT. | 21. PHONE

PERSON INTERVIEWED	AGE	LOCATION OF INTERVIEW	APT NO.	HOME ADDRESS	APT.	TEL RES / BUS
						TEL RES / BUS
						TEL RES / BUS

PERSONS

24. ☐ ARREST ☐ WARRANT ☐ MISSING ☐ SUMMONS ☐ SUSPECT | 25. NAME (LAST, FIRST, MI) | 26. S.S. NO. | 27. BOOKING NO. | 28. PHOTO NO. | 29. ALIAS

30. WARRANT NO | 31. ADDRESS | 32. SEX ☐ M ☐ F | 33. RACE | 34. AGE | 35. HEIGHT | 36. D.O.B.

37. SPECIAL CHARACTERISTICS (INCLUDING CLOTHING) | 38. WEIGHT | 39. BUILD | 40. HAIR | 41. EYES

VEHICLES

43. ☐ STOLEN ☐ RECOV. ☐ LV. SCENE ☐ ABAND. ☐ IN CUST. ☐ TOWED ☐ USED IN CRIME ☐ OTHER | 44. REG. STATE NO. | 45. PLATE TYPE YEAR (EXP.) | 46. MODEL

47. VEHICLE MAKE-YEAR | 48. VEHICLE NO. | 49. STYLE | 50. COLOR (TOP-BOTTOM)

51. OPERATOR'S NAME | 52. LICENSE NO. | 53. OPERATOR'S ADDRESS

54. OWNER'S NAME | 55. OWNER'S ADDRESS

PROPERTY

57. TYPE OF PROPERTY	58. SERIAL OR I-DENTI-GUARD NO.	59. BRAND NAME-DESCRIPTION	60. MODEL	61. VALUE	62. UCR	63. RECOV.

MO

65. TYPE OF WEAPON-TOOL | 66. NEIGHBORHOOD | 67. TYPE OF BUILDING | 68. PLACE OF ENTRY

69. WEATHER | 70. LIGHTING | 71. TRANSPORTIRRON OF SUSPECT (CAR, FOOT, MBTA, ETC.) | 72. VICTIM'S ACTIVITY

73. UNUSUAL ACTIONS AND STATEMENTS OF PERPETRATOR | RELATIONSHIP TO VICTIM

BLOCK NO. | 76. NARRATIVE AND ADDITIONAL INFORMATION

77. UNIT ASSIGNED | 78. TOUR UF DUTY | 79. REPORTING OFFICER'S SIGNATURE | 80. REPORTING OFFICER'S ID | 81. PARTNER'S ID | F.I. ☐ YES ☐ NO

82. DATE OF REPORT | 83. SPECIAL UNITS NOTIFIED (REPORTING) | TELETYPE NO.

84. TIME COMPLETED ☐ A ☐ P | 85. SIGNATURE OF PATROL SUPERVISOR | 86. PAT. SUP. ID | 87. SIGNATURE DUTY SUPERVISOR | 88. DUTY SUP. ID

BPD Form 1.1 Revised 85

HEADQUARTER'S COPY

CHAPTER 1

ARREST

Complaint

FEDERAL RULES OF CRIMINAL PROCEDURE

Rule 3

THE COMPLAINT

The complaint is a written statement of the essential facts constituting the offense charged. It must be made under oath before a magistrate judge or, if none is reasonably available, before a state or local judicial officer.

Rule 4

ARREST WARRANT OR SUMMONS ON A COMPLAINT

(a) Issuance. If the complaint or one or more affidavits filed with the complaint establish probable cause to believe that an offense has been committed and that the defendant committed it, the judge must issue an arrest warrant to an officer authorized to execute it. At the request of an attorney for the government, the judge must issue a summons, instead of a warrant, to a person authorized to serve it. A judge may issue more than one warrant or summons on the same complaint. If a defendant fails to appear in response to a summons, a judge may, and upon request of an attorney for the government must, issue a warrant.

(b) Form.

(1) *Warrant.* A warrant must:

(A) contain the defendant's name or, if it is unknown, a name or description by which the defendant can be identified with reasonable certainty;

(B) describe the offense charged in the complaint;

(C) command that the defendant be arrested and brought without unnecessary delay before a magistrate judge or, if none is reasonably available, before a state or local judicial officer; and

(D) be signed by a judge.

(2) *Summons.* A summons must be in the same form as a warrant except that it must require the defendant to appear before a magistrate judge at a stated time and place.

(c) Execution or Service, and Return.

(1) *By Whom.* Only a marshal or other authorized officer may execute a warrant. Any person authorized to serve a summons in a federal civil action may serve a summons.

(2) *Location.* A warrant may be executed, or a summons served, within the jurisdiction of the United States or anywhere else a federal statute authorizes an arrest.

(3) *Manner.*

(A) A warrant is executed by arresting the defendant. Upon arrest, an officer possessing the warrant must show it to the defendant. If the officer does not possess the warrant, the officer must inform the defendant of the warrant's existence and of the offense charged and, at the defendant's request, must show the warrant to the defendant as soon as possible.

(B) A summons is served on an individual defendant:

(i) by delivering a copy to the defendant personally; or

(ii) by leaving a copy at the defendant's residence or usual place of abode with a person of suitable age and discretion residing at that location and by mailing a copy to the defendant's last known address.

(C) A summons is served on an organization by delivering a copy to an officer, to a managing or general agent, or to another agent appointed or legally authorized to receive service of process. A copy must also be mailed to the organization's last known address within the district or to its principal place of business elsewhere in the United States.

(4) *Return.*

(A) After executing a warrant, the officer must return it to the judge before whom the defendant is brought in accordance with Rule 5. At the request of an attorney for the government, an unexecuted warrant must be brought back to and canceled by a magistrate judge or, if none is reasonably available, by a state or local judicial officer.

(B) The person to whom a summons was delivered for service must return it on or before the return day.

(C) At the request of an attorney for the government, a judge may deliver an unexecuted warrant, an unserved summons, or a copy of the warrant or summons to the marshal or other authorized person for execution or service.

If the complaint (and accompanying affidavits) must show probable cause "to believe that an offense has been committed and that the defendant committed it," it is apparent that the criminal process is well under way when the complaint is filed. The investigatory stage of the process, if not complete, has advanced to the point where officials have concluded that a crime has been committed, have identified a person who they are prepared to assert has probably committed it, and are able to show a basis for their assertion. The filing of a complaint that satisfies the requirements of Rule 4 may occur long after the commission of a crime, after police and prosecutorial officials have performed a variety of functions that may impose substantially on the person charged in the complaint or on others. Should officials who are investigating the commission of a crime but are not prepared to make a complaint showing probable cause be required to file an official statement that (they believe) a crime has occurred or that they are investigating the conduct of a specific person or persons in connection with the crime? Why (not)? If so, what form should "filing" take? With or without filing, should the officials be required to notify anyone that the investigation is taking place?

Giordenello v. United States

357 U.S. 480, 78 S.Ct. 1245, 2 L.Ed.2d 1503 (1958)

■ MR. JUSTICE HARLAN delivered the opinion of the Court.

Petitioner was convicted of the unlawful purchase of narcotics, see 26 U.S.C. (Supp. V) § 4704, after a trial without a jury before the Federal District Court for the Southern District of Texas. A divided Court of Appeals affirmed. . . . We granted certiorari to consider petitioner's challenge to the legality of his arrest and the admissibility in evidence of the narcotics seized from his person at the time of the arrest. . . .

Agent Finley of the Federal Bureau of Narcotics obtained a warrant for the arrest of petitioner from the United States Commissioner in Houston, Texas, on January 26, 1956. This warrant, issued under Rules 3 and 4 of the Federal Rules of Criminal Procedure . . . was based on a written complaint, sworn to by Finley, which read in part:

> The undersigned complainant [Finley] being duly sworn states: That on or about January 26, 1956, at Houston, Texas in the Southern District of Texas, Veto Giordenello did receive, conceal, etc., narcotic drugs, to-wit: heroin hydrochloride with knowledge of unlawful importation; in violation of Section 174, Title 21, United States Code.
>
> And the complainant further states that he believes that ______ ______ are material witnesses in relation to this charge.

About 6 o'clock in the afternoon of the following day, January 27, Finley saw petitioner drive up to his residence in a car and enter the house. He emerged shortly thereafter and drove away in the same car, closely followed in a second car by a person described by Finley as a "well-known police character." Finley pursued the cars until they stopped near another residence which was entered by petitioner. When petitioner left this residence, carrying a brown paper bag in his hand, and proceeded towards his car, Finley executed the arrest warrant and seized the bag, which proved to contain a mixture of heroin and other substances. Although warned of his privilege to remain silent, petitioner promptly admitted purchasing the heroin in Chicago and transporting it to Houston.

. . .

Petitioner challenges the sufficiency of the warrant on two grounds: (1) that the complaint on which the warrant was issued was inadequate because the complaining officer, Finley, relied exclusively upon hearsay information rather than personal knowledge in executing the complaint; and (2) that the complaint was in any event defective in that it in effect recited no more than the elements of the crime charged, namely the concealment of heroin with knowledge of its illegal importation in violation of 21 U.S.C. § 174.

It appears from Finley's testimony at the hearing on the suppression motion that until the warrant was issued on January 26 his suspicions of petitioner's guilt derived entirely from information given him by law enforcement officers and other persons in Houston, none of whom either appeared before the Commissioner or submitted affidavits. But we need not decide whether a warrant may be issued solely on hearsay information, for in any event we find this complaint defective in not providing a sufficient basis upon which a finding of probable cause could be made.

Criminal Rules 3 and 4 provide that an arrest warrant shall be issued only upon a written and sworn complaint (1) setting forth "the essential facts constituting the offense charged," and (2) showing "that there is probable cause to believe that [such] an offense has been committed and that the defendant has committed it. . . ." The provisions of these Rules must be read in light of the constitutional requirements they implement. The language of the Fourth Amendment, that ". . . no Warrants shall issue, but upon probable cause, supported by Oath or affirmation, and particularly describing . . . the persons or things to be seized," of course applies to arrest as well as search warrants. . . . The protection afforded by these Rules, when they are viewed against their constitutional background, is that the inferences from the facts which lead to the complaint "be drawn by a neutral and detached magistrate instead of being judged by the officer engaged in the often competitive enterprise of ferreting out crime." Johnson v. United States, 333 U.S. 10, 14. The purpose of the complaint, then, is to enable the appropriate magistrate, here a Commissioner, to determine whether the "probable cause" required to support a warrant exists. The Commissioner must judge for himself the persuasiveness of the facts relied on by a complaining officer to show probable cause. He should not accept without question the complainant's mere conclusion that the person whose arrest is sought has committed a crime.

When the complaint in this case is judged with these considerations in mind, it is clear that it does not pass muster because it does not provide any basis for the Commissioner's determination under Rule 4 that probable cause existed. The complaint contains no affirmative allegation that the affiant spoke with personal knowledge of the matters contained therein; it does not indicate any sources for the complainant's belief; and it does not set forth any other sufficient basis upon which a finding of probable cause could be made. We think these deficiencies could not be cured by the Commissioner's reliance upon a presumption that the complaint was made on the personal knowledge of the complaining officer. The insubstantiality of such an argument is illustrated by the facts of this very case, for Finley's testimony at the suppression hearing clearly showed that he had no personal knowledge of the matters on which his charge was based. In these circumstances, it is difficult to understand how the Commissioner could be expected to assess independently the probability that petitioner committed the crime charged. Indeed, if this complaint were upheld, the substantive requirements would be completely read out of Rule 4, and the complaint would be of only formal significance, entitled to perfunctory approval by the Commissioner. This would not comport with the protective purposes which a complaint is designed to achieve.

. . .[1]

Jaben v. United States

381 U.S. 214, 85 S.Ct. 1365, 14 L.Ed.2d 345 (1965)

[The petitioner Jaben was prosecuted for wilfully attempting to evade federal income taxes. The statute of limitations on that offense required that an indictment be obtained within six years after its commission, but provided that if a complaint were filed within that period the government should have an additional nine months after the complaint was filed within which to obtain an indictment. Internal Revenue Code of 1954, § 6531. On the day before the period expired, the government filed a complaint against Jaben:

> The undersigned complainant, being duly sworn, states:
>
> That he is a Special Agent of the Internal Revenue Service and, in the performance of the duties imposed on him by law, he has conducted an investigation of the Federal income tax liability of Max Jaben for the calendar year 1956, by examining the said taxpayer's tax return for the year 1956 and other years; by identifying and interviewing third parties with whom the said taxpayer did business; by consulting public and private records reflecting the said taxpayer's income; and by interviewing third persons having knowledge of the said taxpayer's financial condition.

[1] Justice Clark wrote a dissenting opinion, which Justice Burton and Justice Whittaker joined.

That based on the aforesaid investigation, the complainant has personal knowledge that on or about the 16th day of April, 1957, at Kansas City, Missouri, in the Western District of Missouri, Max Jaben did unlawfully and wilfully attempt to evade and defeat the income taxes due and owing by him to the United States of America for the calendar year 1956, by filing and causing to be filed with the District Director of Internal Revenue for the District of Kansas City, Missouri, at Kansas City, Missouri, a false and fraudulent income tax return, wherein he stated that his taxable income for the calendar year 1956 was $17,665.31, and that the amount of tax due and owing thereon was the sum of $6,017.32, when in fact his taxable income for the said calendar year was the sum of $40,001.76 upon which said taxable income he owed to the United States of America an income tax of $14,562.99.

[Signed] David A. Thompson

Special Agent

Internal Revenue Service
Kansas City, Missouri.

The commissioner before whom the complaint was filed determined that there was probable cause to believe that Jaben had committed the offense and issued a summons ordering Jaben to appear one month later for a preliminary examination on the complaint. Before the hearing was held, after the six-year period had expired but within the nine-month extension if it were applicable, the grand jury returned an indictment. Jaben moved to dismiss the indictment on the ground that, the complaint being invalid for failure to show probable cause, the indictment was untimely.]

■ MR. JUSTICE HARLAN delivered the opinion of the Court.

. . .

Under the Government's interpretation of § 6531, probable cause is not relevant to the complaint's ability to initiate the extension of the limitation period. Section 6531 provides that the nine-month extension is brought into play "[w]here a complaint is instituted before a commissioner of the United States" within the six-year period of limitations. . . . Rule 3 of the Federal Rules of Criminal Procedure defines a complaint as

> . . . a written statement of the essential facts constituting the offense charged. It shall be made upon oath before a commissioner or other officer empowered to commit persons charged with offenses against the United States.

Since the Government's complaint stated the essential facts constituting the offense of attempted tax evasion and was made upon oath before a

Commissioner, the Government contends that regardless of the complaint's adequacy for any other purposes, it was valid for the purpose of triggering the nine-month extension of the limitation period whether or not it showed probable cause. The Government would, thus, totally ignore the further steps in the complaint procedure required by Rules 4 and 5. Indeed it follows from its position that once having filed a complaint, the Government need not further pursue the complaint procedure at all, and, in the event that the defendant pressed for a preliminary hearing and obtained a dismissal of the complaint, that the Government could nonetheless rely upon the complaint as having extended the limitation period.

We do not accept the Government's interpretation. Its effort to look solely to Rule 3 and ignore the requirements of the Rules that follow would deprive the institution of the complaint before the Commissioner of any independent meaning which might rationally have led Congress to fasten upon it as the method for initiating the nine-month extension. The Commissioner's function, on that view, would be merely to rubber-stamp the complaint. The Government seeks to give his role importance in its version of § 6531 by pointing out that he would administer the oath, receive the complaint, and make sure that it stated facts constituting the offense (a requirement which would be met by a charge in the words of the statute); but surely these matters are essentially formalities. The argument ignores the fact that the Commissioner's basic functions under the Rules are to make the judgment that probable cause exists and to warn defendants of their rights. Furthermore, if we do not look beyond Rule 3, there is no provision for notifying the defendant that he has been charged and the period of limitations extended. (Indeed, it is not until we reach Rule 4 that we find a requirement that the complaint must show who it was that committed the offense.) Notice to a criminal defendant is usually achieved by service upon him of the summons or arrest warrant provided for in Rule 4. Neither is appropriate absent a judgment by the Commissioner that the complaint shows probable cause, and no other form of notice is specified by the Rules.

More basically, the evident statutory purpose of the nine-month extension provision is to afford the Government an opportunity to indict criminal tax offenders in the event that a grand jury is not in session at the end of the normal limitation period. This is confirmed by the immediate precursor of the present section which provided for an extension "until the discharge of the grand jury at its next session within the district." I.R.C. 1939 § 3748(a). Clearly the statute was not meant to grant the Government greater time in which to make its case (a result which could have been accomplished simply by making the normal period of limitation six years and nine months), but rather was intended to deal with the situation in which the Government has its case made within the normal limitation period but cannot obtain an indictment because of the grand jury schedule. The Government's interpretation does not reflect this statutory intention, for it provides no safeguard whatever to prevent the Government from filing a complaint at a time when it does not have its case made, and then using the nine-month period to make it.

The better view of § 6531 is that the complaint, to initiate the time extension, must be adequate to begin effectively the criminal process prescribed by the Federal Criminal Rules. It must be sufficient to justify the next steps in the process—those of notifying the defendant and bringing him before the Commissioner for a preliminary hearing. To do so the complaint must satisfy the probable cause requirement of Rule 4. Furthermore, we think that the Government must proceed through the further steps of the complaint procedure by affording the defendant a preliminary hearing as required by Rule 5, unless before the preliminary hearing is held, the grand jury supersedes the complaint procedure by returning an indictment. This interpretation of the statute reflects its purpose by insuring that within a reasonable time following the filing of the complaint, either the Commissioner will decide whether there is sufficient cause to bind the defendant over for grand jury action, or the grand jury itself will have decided whether or not to indict. A dismissal of the complaint before the indictment is returned would vitiate the time extension.

In this case the Government obtained a superseding indictment before any preliminary hearing took place. Under the interpretation which we have adopted it follows that if the complaint satisfied the requirements of Rules 3 and 4, in particular the probable cause standard of Rule 4, then the nine-month extension had come into play and had not been cut off by any later dismissal of the complaint. We turn then to the question whether the complaint showed probable cause.

. . .

Petitioner argues that the complaint is basically indistinguishable from that which the Court found wanting in Giordenello v. United States, 357 U.S. 480. . . .

The complaints there and here are materially distinguishable. Information in a complaint alleging the commission of a crime falls into two categories: (1) that information which, if true, would directly indicate commission of the crime charged, and (2) that which relates to the source of the directly incriminating information. The *Giordenello* complaint gave no source information whatsoever. Its directly incriminating information consisted merely of an allegation in the words of the statute, and even then incomplete, supplemented by "on or about January 26, 1956, at Houston." If the *Jaben* complaint were as barren, it would have stated simply that "on or about April 16, 1957, at Kansas City, Missouri, Jaben willfully filed a false income tax return." In fact, it gave dollars-and-cents figures for the amounts which allegedly should have been returned and the amounts actually returned. As to sources, the affiant indicated that he, in his official capacity, had personally conducted an investigation in the course of which he had examined the taxpayer's returns for 1956 and other years, interviewed third persons with whom the taxpayer did business and others having knowledge of his financial condition, and consulted public and private records reflecting the taxpayer's income; and that the conclusion that Jaben had committed the offense was based upon this investigation.

Beyond the substance of the complaint there is a material distinction in the nature of the offense charged. Some offenses are subject to putative establishment by blunt and concise factual allegations, e.g., "*A* saw narcotics in *B*'s possession," whereas "*A* and *B* file a false tax return" does not mean very much in a tax evasion case. Establishment of grounds for belief that the offense of tax evasion has been committed often requires a reconstruction of the taxpayer's income from many individually unrevealing facts which are not susceptible of a concise statement in a complaint. Furthermore, unlike narcotics informants, for example, whose credibility may often be suspect, the sources in this tax evasion case are much less likely to produce false or untrustworthy information. Thus, whereas some supporting information concerning the credibility of informants in narcotics cases or other common garden varieties of crime may be required, such information is not so necessary in the context of the case before us.

Giordenello v. United States, supra, and Aguilar v. Texas, 378 U.S. 108, established that a magistrate is intended to make a neutral judgment that resort to further criminal process is justified. A complaint must provide a foundation for that judgment. It must provide the affiant's answer to the magistrate's hypothetical question, "What makes you think that the defendant committed the offense charged?" This does not reflect a requirement that the Commissioner ignore the credibility of the complaining witness. There is a difference between disbelieving the affiant and requiring him to indicate some basis for his allegations. Obviously any reliance upon factual allegations necessarily entails some degree of reliance upon the credibility of the source. . . . Nor does it indicate that each factual allegation which the affiant puts forth must be independently documented, or that each and every fact which contributed to his conclusions be spelled out in the complaint. . . . It simply requires that enough information be presented to the Commissioner to enable him to make the judgment that the charges are not capricious and are sufficiently supported to justify bringing into play the further steps of the criminal process.

In this instance the issue of probable cause comes down to the adequacy of the basis given for the allegation that petitioner's income was $40,001.76 instead of the $17,665.31 he had reported. This is not the type of fact that can be physically observed. The amount of petitioner's income could only be determined by examining records and interviewing third persons familiar with petitioner's financial condition. . . . Here the affiant, a Special Agent of the Internal Revenue Service, swore that he had conducted just such an investigation and thereafter swore that he had personal knowledge as to petitioner's actual income. In such circumstances, the magistrate would be justified in accepting the agent's judgment of what he "saw" without requiring him to bring the records and persons to court, to list and total the items of unreported income or to otherwise explain how petitioner's actual income was calculated.

We conclude that the challenged count of this indictment is not time-barred.

. . .[2]

Giordenello was prosecuted for the purchase of narcotics. Jaben was prosecuted for tax evasion. In *Jaben*, the Court says that "there is a material distinction in the nature of the offense charged" in the two cases, p. 12 above, which has a bearing on how the issue of probable cause is treated. Does the nature of the offenses also have a bearing on what official steps should be taken if there is probable cause to believe that the crime was committed? What official steps were taken in each case after the complaint was filed? Is the difference justified by the facts so far as they appear in the reports of the cases?

---

1. Rule 4(a), p. 4 above, provides that probable cause may be established in "one or more affidavits filed with the complaint." When *Giordenello* and *Jaben* were decided, there was no reference in the rule to affidavits accompanying the complaint. If affidavits are used to show probable cause, does the complaint as such effectively begin the criminal process in any significant sense?

2. Do the federal rules authorize the making of a complaint that does not itself or in accompanying affidavits show "probable cause to believe that an offense has been committed and that the defendant committed it"? Should a magistrate refuse to accept such a complaint for filing? If he accepts it, what should he do with it? Where and how should he "file" it? Is there any reason why anyone should want to file such a complaint?

3. The Fourth Amendment requires that warrants be "supported by oath or affirmation." "The nearly unanimous view is that the Fourth Amendment requires that only information related to the magistrate on oath or affirmation is competent upon which to base a finding of probable cause; that unsworn oral statements may not form a basis for that decision." Frazier v. Roberts, 441 F.2d 1224, 1227 (8th Cir.1971).

[2] Justice White wrote an opinion concurring in the judgment, which Justice Black joined. Justice Goldberg wrote an opinion concurring in part and dissenting in part, which Chief Justice Warren and Justice Douglas joined.

AO91 (Rev. 8/01) Criminal Complaint

UNITED STATES DISTRICT COURT

____________________ DISTRICT OF ____________________

UNITED STATES OF AMERICA
V.

CRIMINAL COMPLAINT

Case Number:

(Name and Address of Defendant)

I, the undersigned complainant state that the following is true and correct to the best of my knowledge and belief. On or about __________ (Date) in __________ County, in the __________ District of __________ defendant(s) did,

(Track Statutory Language of Offense)

in violation of Title ______ United States Code, Section(s) __________ .

I further state that I am a(n) __________ (Official Title) and that this complaint is based on the following facts:

Continued on the attached sheet and made a part of this complaint: ☐ Yes ☐ No

____
Signature of Complainant

____
Printed Name of Complainant

Sworn to before me and signed in my presence,

____________________ at ____________________
Date City State

____________________ ____________________
Name of Judicial Officer Title of Judicial Officer Signature of Judicial Officer

Rules 3 and 4 require that the sworn support for an arrest warrant, whether the complaint or accompanying affidavits, be in writing. "It is clear that the Fourth Amendment permits the warrant-issuing magistrate to consider sworn oral testimony supplementing a duly executed affidavit to determine whether there is probable cause upon which to issue a search [and presumably an arrest] warrant." *Frazier*, 441 F.2d at 1226. Accord United States v. Clyburn, 24 F.3d 613, 617 (4th Cir.1994). Rule 41(d)(2)(B) provides for the issuance of a search warrant on the basis of sworn oral testimony "if doing so is reasonable under the circumstances." See p. 178 below.

In Stewart v. Abraham, 275 F.3d 220 (3d Cir.2001), the court held that the Fourth Amendment does not bar the immediate rearrest of a person on probable cause following a preliminary examination at which a magistrate dismissed a complaint charging the same offense for lack of probable cause and ordered the person released from custody. The court noted that the information on which the second complaint was based might be different from the evidence that was presented at the preliminary examination and that under the state law the standard of probable cause for issuance of a complaint was different from the standard for upholding a complaint at a preliminary examination.

4. Who issues a warrant? Rule 3 requires that the complaint be made before a magistrate judge or a state or local judicial officer. Rule 4(b)(1)(D) provides that an arrest warrant shall be "signed by a judge."

Magistrate judges are appointed by the judges of the United States district courts and are ordinarily to be members of the bar for at least five years. A full-time magistrate judge is appointed for a renewable term of eight years, a part-time magistrate judge for a renewable term of four years. 28 U.S.C. § 631. See generally 28 U.S.C. §§ 631–639.

Is the issuance of a warrant *constitutionally* a judicial function? In Coolidge v. New Hampshire, 403 U.S. 443 (1971), the Court held that the Fourth Amendment prohibited the Attorney General of the state from issuing a search warrant. The Court observed that at the time he issued the warrant, the Attorney General "was actively in charge of the investigation and later was to be chief prosecutor at the trial." Quoting language from Johnson v. United States, 333 U.S. 10, 13–14 (1948), the Court said that a prosecutor was not the "neutral and detached magistrate" that the Constitution requires. "Prosecutors and policemen simply cannot be asked to maintain the requisite neutrality with regard to their own investigations—the 'competitive enterprise [of ferreting out crime]' that must rightly engage their single-minded attention." *Coolidge*, 403 U.S. at 450. Under state law, the Attorney General was a justice of the peace and authorized to issue the warrant.

AO 442 (Rev. 10/03) Warrant for Arrest

UNITED STATES DISTRICT COURT

______________________ District of ______________________

UNITED STATES OF AMERICA

V.

WARRANT FOR ARREST

Case Number:

To: The United States Marshal
and any Authorized United States Officer

YOU ARE HEREBY COMMANDED to arrest ______________________
Name

and bring him or her forthwith to the nearest magistrate judge to answer a(n)

☐ Indictment ☐ Information ☐ Complaint ☐ Order of court ☐ Probation Violation Petition ☐ Supervised Release Violation Petition ☐ Violation Notice

charging him or her with (brief description of offense)

in violation of Title ________ United States Code, Section(s) ______________

Name of Issuing Officer	Signature of Issuing Officer
Title of Issuing Officer	Date and Location

RETURN		
This warrant was received and executed with the arrest of the above-named defendant at		
DATE RECEIVED	NAME AND TITLE OF ARRESTING OFFICER	SIGNATURE OF ARRESTING OFFICER
DATE OF ARREST		

AO 442 (Rev. 10/03) Warrant for Arrest

THE FOLLOWING IS FURNISHED FOR INFORMATION ONLY:

DEFENDANT'S NAME: ______________________________

ALIAS: ______________________________

LAST KNOWN RESIDENCE: ______________________________

LAST KNOWN EMPLOYMENT: ______________________________

PLACE OF BIRTH: ______________________________

DATE OF BIRTH: ______________________________

SOCIAL SECURITY NUMBER: ______________________________

HEIGHT: ______________ WEIGHT: ______________

SEX: ______________ RACE: ______________

HAIR: ______________ EYES: ______________

SCARS, TATTOOS, OTHER DISTINGUISHING MARKS: ______________________________

____

____

FBI NUMBER: ______________________________

COMPLETE DESCRIPTION OF AUTO: ______________________________

____

INVESTIGATIVE AGENCY AND ADDRESS: ______________________________

____

____

____

While a warrant must be issued by someone "independent of the police or prosecution," he need not in all cases be a judge or a lawyer. In Shadwick v. City of Tampa, 407 U.S. 345 (1972), the Court upheld issuance by a clerk of the municipal court of an arrest warrant for "impaired driving" in violation of a municipal ordinance. The clerk was a civil servant; he was not a lawyer. The Court concluded that clerks of the municipal court met the two prongs of the test of authority to issue a warrant: the person who issues it "must be neutral and detached, and he must be capable of determining whether probable cause exists for the requested arrest or search." Reference in prior cases to a "magistrate" or "judicial officer" implied only that. Id. at 348. (The Court indicated that its holding did not necessarily extend to the issuance of warrants in more serious cases or to authorization of an official "entirely outside the sphere of the judicial branch" to issue warrants.) See generally Gerstein v. Pugh, 420 U.S. 103, 117–18 (1975), p. 522 below. In Connally v. Georgia, 429 U.S. 245 (1977), the Court held that an unsalaried justice of the peace who received a fee for each search warrant that he issued but no fee for rejecting an application for a warrant was not the "neutral and detached" officer required by the Constitution, because of the "element of personal financial gain" in the issuance of a warrant.

In State v. Ruotolo, 247 A.2d 1 (N.J.1968), the court said that a deputy court clerk could issue an arrest warrant on the basis of a complaint made before him by the defendant's wife charging the defendant with nonsupport, a misdemeanor. "By its very nature probable cause is a standard which can be applied by laymen, so long as they exercise reasonable caution. It is a practical, non-technical concept, not requiring the complex weighing of factual and legal considerations which is the judge's daily task." Id. at 5.

To the contrary, in State ex rel. Duhn v. Tahash, 147 N.W.2d 382 (Minn.1966), the Supreme Court of Minnesota (relying on *Giordenello*, p. 6 above) held that a deputy clerk could not issue a warrant based on a complaint charging a felony. In State v. Paulick, 151 N.W.2d 591 (Minn. 1967), the court extended *Duhn* to a prosecution for violation of a traffic ordinance:

> It occurs to us that in initiating and prosecuting charges which are misdemeanors the grave consequences to the accused resulting from a wrongful arrest far outweigh the potential harm to the community in requiring something more than the peremptory issuance of a warrant by a clerk untrained in the law. The harm to an accused arrested in his home or at his place of work, the humiliation and embarrassment to his family, and the fact he has a record of arrest, however unjust, are consequences difficult to measure. . . . However conscientious and impartial may be the clerk of Hennepin County Municipal Court who supervised the execution of the complaint and issued the warrant on behalf of the village of Minnetonka, his background and experience we can assume are not in the law. It is highly improbable that he was qualified to determine whether the complaint and warrant met consti-

> tutional standards. It is with the greatest difficulty that we envision his refusing to issue a warrant upon the complaint of a state highway patrolman. These are functions which the judiciary cannot delegate, since they require both a knowledge of the law and the authority to grant or refuse the request of law-enforcement officers to initiate criminal procedures. . . .

Id. at 597–98.

To the same effect, see Caulk v. Municipal Court, 243 A.2d 707 (Del.1968). Whether those decisions survive *Shadwick*, above, may be doubted, but they have not been overruled.

5. Whether or not the approval of a prosecuting official is sufficient for the filing of a complaint and issuance of an arrest warrant, should his approval be *necessary*? An early draft of the American Law Institute's Model Code of Pre-Arraignment Procedure provided that, with some specific exceptions, a complaint shall be issued "only by a prosecuting attorney having jurisdiction over the prosecution of the offense and shall be filed only with his approval." ALI § 6.02(1) (Tent.Draft No. 1, 1966). The Draft provided also that a judicial officer might permit the filing of a complaint "if, after hearing the complainant and the prosecuting attorney, he finds there is reasonable cause to believe that the person named in the complaint has committed the offense charged." § 6.02(3). Procedures for the filing of a complaint are not included in the Model Code of Pre-Arraignment Procedure as finally adopted. See ALI, A Model Code of Pre-Arraignment Procedure § 130.2(1)(b), (6) (1975).

6. Whatever may be the requirements of the Constitution and the procedure formally prescribed by state law, in most cases "the prosecutor alone makes the effective warrant decision." Miller & Tiffany, "Prosecutor Dominance of the Warrant Decision: A Study of Current Practices," 1964 Wash. U. L.Q. 1, 4. The courts and magistrates have generally recognized the prosecutor's control of the prosecutorial function and his "greater capacity to make the initial decision correctly." Id. at 12. The result is a tacit division of labor by which the police (who, in the case of minor crimes, commonly also serve a prosecutorial role) and prosecutor have primary responsibility for the initiation of the criminal process, and the judiciary asserts its responsibility as the case develops for trial.

Whose judgment that a person should be charged with a crime is more likely to be correct, the magistrate's or the prosecutor's? Whose judgment that a person should not be charged is more likely to be correct?

How realistic is the Court's insistence on the judgment of a "neutral and detached magistrate," *Coolidge*, p. 15 above? Does the observable fact that the magistrate's judgment is commonly a perfunctory approval of the prosecutorial decision suggest that the current practice should be reformed or that the standard set by the Court is inappropriate to the functions being performed? Or does the procedure of applying for the magistrate's "rubber stamp" serve a purpose even if it is almost always given?

7. Does *Giordenello* require a magisterial judgment for issuance of a summons (as in *Jaben*) as well as an arrest warrant? In United States v. Greenberg, 320 F.2d 467 (9th Cir.1963), the court concluded that it does, at least under the scheme of the federal rules, which leaves the choice of warrant or summons to the attorney for the government. See Rule 4(a). "[I]nsofar as a defendant is concerned, there is but little distinction between the issuance of a warrant or a summons. If he fails to respond to a summons, a warrant of arrest may issue. If he appears in response to the summons, in most instances he is required to post bail or suffer arrest and detention until a determination has been made by the Commissioner in respect to the charges pending against him." 320 F.2d at 471.

8. Once an arrest warrant has been issued, how quickly must it be executed? "[O]rdinarily there is no legal requirement that a warrant of arrest must be executed immediately or at the first opportunity. . . . While its execution should not be unreasonably delayed there may be perfectly valid reasons why further investigation should be made before the drastic step is taken of arresting a citizen on a criminal charge. Certainly there is no constitutional right to be arrested promptly or otherwise." United States v. Joines, 258 F.2d 471, 472–73 (3d Cir.1958). Accord United States v. Drake, 655 F.2d 1025 (10th Cir.1981). See Hoffa v. United States, 385 U.S. 293, 310 (1966), in which the Court observed that "there is no constitutional right to be arrested." In what circumstances would it be appropriate for law enforcement officials to file a complaint and obtain issuance of an arrest warrant and then to delay execution of the warrant in order to investigate further?

"Police officials are required to use diligence in the execution of arrest warrants. They may not hold one unexecuted for an unreasonable period of time in the hope that they may ultimately find the defendant in a house or other building which they would like to search, but which they could not lawfully search except as an incident of a lawful arrest. Agents are not required to neglect all other investigatory and enforcement activity in order to execute every arrest warrant, however, and sixteen days' delay in executing an arrest warrant upon one whose residential address was not definitely known is far from unreasonable on its face. Moreover, such agents are entitled to proceed with some circumspection, so that the fact of their search for a defendant is not disclosed to him at a time when he may flee successfully." United States v. Weaver, 384 F.2d 879, 880–81 (4th Cir.1967).

AO83 (Rev. 10/03) Summons in a Criminal Case

UNITED STATES DISTRICT COURT

_______________ DISTRICT OF _______________

UNITED STATES OF AMERICA
V.

SUMMONS IN A CRIMINAL CASE

Case Number:

(Name and Address of Defendant)

YOU ARE HEREBY SUMMONED to appear before the United States District Court at the place, date and time set forth below.

Place	Room
Before:	Date and Time

To answer a(n)
☐ Indictment ☐ Information ☐ Complaint ☐ Probation Violation Petition ☐ Supervised Release Violation Petition ☐ Violation Notice

Charging you with a violation of Title _______________ United States Code, Section(s) _______________

Brief description of offense:

_______________ _______________
Signature of Issuing Officer Date

____
Name and Title of Issuing Officer

In Godfrey v. United States, 358 F.2d 850, 852 (D.C.Cir.1966), the court said that if there is delay in filing a complaint in order "to advance the public interest in effective law enforcement,"[3] there is a special obligation to make the arrest quickly after the arrest warrant is issued; "the disadvantage to the accused inherent in the deliberate preference accorded the public interest in the one period should not be compounded by a failure to exercise appropriate diligence in the other." "[E]very time there is delay in the making of the arrest and there is a search made as incidental to the arrest, the law enforcement officers take the risk that they will be charged with using the arrest as a mere pretext for the search. . . . In other words, the delay in making the arrest is one of the factors to be taken into consideration when the time comes for a judicial determination of the question of whether or not the search was 'reasonable.'" Carlo v. United States, 286 F.2d 841, 846 (2d Cir.1961).

9. An arrest made in good-faith reliance on an ordinance later declared unconstitutional is valid, and evidence seized in a search incident to the arrest should not be suppressed. Michigan v. DeFillippo, 443 U.S. 31 (1979) (6–3). "The enactment of a law forecloses speculation by enforcement officers concerning its constitutionality—with the possible exception of a law so grossly and flagrantly unconstitutional that any person of reasonable prudence would be bound to see its flaws." Id. at 38. See Sandul v. Larion, 119 F.3d 1250 (6th Cir.1997) (First Amendment rights; *DeFillippo* found not applicable).

Arrest Without a Warrant

United States v. Watson

423 U.S. 411, 96 S.Ct. 820, 46 L.Ed.2d 598 (1976)

■ MR. JUSTICE WHITE delivered the opinion of the Court.

This case presents questions under the Fourth Amendment as to the legality of a warrantless arrest and of an ensuing search of the arrestee's automobile carried out with his purported consent.

I

The relevant events began on August 17, 1972, when an informant, one Khoury, telephoned a postal inspector informing him that respondent Watson was in possession of a stolen credit card and had asked Khoury to cooperate in using the card to their mutual advantage. On five to 10 previous occasions Khoury had provided the inspector with reliable infor-

3. For example, when an undercover agent has a basis for a complaint but is not ready to "surface." See Ross v. United States, 349 F.2d 210 (D.C.Cir.1965).

mation on postal inspection matters, some involving Watson. Later that day Khoury delivered the card to the inspector. On learning that Watson had agreed to furnish additional cards, the inspector asked Khoury to arrange to meet with Watson. Khoury did so, a meeting being scheduled for August 22. Watson canceled that engagement, but at noon on August 23, Khoury met with Watson at a restaurant designated by the latter. Khoury had been instructed that if Watson had additional stolen credit cards, Khoury was to give a designated signal. The signal was given, the officers closed in, and Watson was forthwith arrested. He was removed from the restaurant to the street where he was given the warnings required by Miranda v. Arizona, 384 U.S. 436 (1966). A search having revealed that Watson had no credit cards on his person, the inspector asked if he could look inside Watson's car, which was standing within view. Watson said, "Go ahead," and repeated these words when the inspector cautioned that "[i]f I find anything, it is going to go against you." Using keys furnished by Watson, the inspector entered the car and found under the floor mat an envelope containing two credit cards in the names of other persons. These cards were the basis for two counts of a four-count indictment charging Watson with possessing stolen mail in violation of 18 U.S.C. § 1708.

Prior to trial, Watson moved to suppress the cards, claiming that his arrest was illegal for want of probable cause and an arrest warrant and that his consent to search the car was involuntary and ineffective because he had not been told that he could withhold consent. The motion was denied, and Watson was convicted of illegally possessing the two cards seized from his car.

A divided panel of the Court of Appeals for the Ninth Circuit reversed . . . ruling that the admission in evidence of the two credit cards found in the car was prohibited by the Fourth Amendment. In reaching this judgment, the court decided two issues in Watson's favor. First, notwithstanding its agreement with the District Court that Khoury was reliable and that there was probable cause for arresting Watson, the court held the arrest unconstitutional because the postal inspector had failed to secure an arrest warrant although he concededly had time to do so. Second, based on the totality of the circumstances, one of which was the illegality of the arrest, the court held Watson's consent to search had been coerced and hence was not a valid ground for the warrantless search of the automobile. We granted certiorari. . . .

II

A major part of the Court of Appeals' opinion was its holding that Watson's warrantless arrest violated the Fourth Amendment. Although it did not expressly do so, it may have intended to overturn the conviction on the independent ground that the two credit cards were the inadmissible fruits of an unconstitutional arrest. . . . However that may be, the Court of Appeals treated the illegality of Watson's arrest as an important factor in determining the voluntariness of his consent to search his car. We therefore deal first with the arrest issue.

Contrary to the Court of Appeals' view, Watson's arrest was not invalid because executed without a warrant. Title 18 U.S.C. § 3061(a)(3) expressly empowers the Board of Governors of the Postal Service to authorize Postal Service officers and employees "performing duties related to the inspection of postal matters" to

> make arrests without warrant for felonies cognizable under the laws of the United States if they have reasonable grounds to believe that the person to be arrested has committed or is committing such a felony.

By regulation, 39 CFR § 232.5(a)(3) (1975), and in identical language, the Board of Governors has exercised that power and authorized warrantless arrests. Because there was probable cause in this case to believe that Watson had violated § 1708, the inspector and his subordinates, in arresting Watson, were acting strictly in accordance with the governing statute and regulations. The effect of the judgment of the Court of Appeals was to invalidate the statute as applied in this case and as applied to all the situations where a court fails to find exigent circumstances justifying a warrantless arrest. We reverse that judgment.

Under the Fourth Amendment, the people are to be "secure in their persons, houses, papers, and effects, against unreasonable searches and seizures . . . and no Warrants shall issue, but upon probable cause. . . ." Section 3061 represents a judgment by Congress that it is not unreasonable under the Fourth Amendment for postal inspectors to arrest without a warrant provided they have probable cause to do so. This was not an isolated or quixotic judgment of the legislative branch. Other federal law enforcement officers have been expressly authorized by statute for many years to make felony arrests on probable cause but without a warrant. This is true of United States marshals . . . and of agents of the Federal Bureau of Investigation . . . the Drug Enforcement Administration . . . the Secret Service . . . and the Customs Service. . . .

Because there is a "strong presumption of constitutionality due to an Act of Congress, especially when it turns on what is 'reasonable,' " "[o]bviously the Court should be reluctant to decide that a search thus authorized by Congress was unreasonable and that the Act was therefore unconstitutional." United States v. Di Re, 332 U.S. 581, 585 (1948). Moreover, there is nothing in the Court's prior cases indicating that under the Fourth Amendment a warrant is required to make a valid arrest for a felony. Indeed, the relevant prior decisions are uniformly to the contrary.

. . .

The cases construing the Fourth Amendment thus reflect the ancient common-law rule that a peace officer was permitted to arrest without a warrant for a misdemeanor or felony committed in his presence as well as for a felony not committed in his presence if there was reasonable ground for making the arrest. . . . This has also been the prevailing rule under state constitutions and statutes. . . .

The balance struck by the common law in generally authorizing felony arrests on probable cause, but without a warrant, has survived substantially intact. It appears in almost all of the States in the form of express statutory authorization. . . .

This is the rule Congress has long directed its principal law enforcement officers to follow. Congress has plainly decided against conditioning warrantless arrest power on proof of exigent circumstances. Law enforcement officers may find it wise to seek arrest warrants where practicable to do so, and their judgments about probable cause may be more readily accepted where backed by a warrant issued by a magistrate. . . . But we decline to transform this judicial preference into a constitutional rule when the judgment of the Nation and Congress has for so long been to authorize warrantless public arrests on probable cause rather than to encumber criminal prosecutions with endless litigation with respect to the existence of exigent circumstances, whether it was practicable to get a warrant, whether the suspect was about to flee, and the like.

Watson's arrest did not violate the Fourth Amendment, and the Court of Appeals erred in holding to the contrary.

. . .

[The Court concluded further that Watson's consent to the search was valid.]

. . .[4]

---

10. In United States v. Santana, 427 U.S. 38 (1976), police officers went to the defendant's house to arrest her. When they arrived, she was standing in the doorway. As they approached, she retreated into the vestibule, where they made the arrest. The Court held that the arrest without a warrant was lawful.

> In Warden v. Hayden, 387 U.S. 294 (1967) [p. 242 note 134 below], we recognized the right of police, who had probable cause to believe that an armed robber had entered a house a few minutes before, to make a warrantless entry to arrest the robber and to search for weapons. This case, involving a true "hot pursuit," is clearly governed by *Warden*; the need to act quickly here is even greater than in that case while the intrusion is much less. . . .
>
> We thus conclude that a suspect may not defeat an arrest which has been set in motion in a public place, and is therefore proper under *Watson*, by the expedient of escaping to a private place. . . .

427 U.S. at 42–43. See Fontenot v. Cormier, 56 F.3d 669 (5th Cir.1995) (*Santana* applied); cf. Joyce v. Town of Tewksbury, Mass., 112 F.3d 19 (1st Cir.1997) (police pursued person standing inside door of third person's house into house; *Santana* noted).

---

[4] Justice Powell wrote a concurring opinion. Justice Stewart concurred in the result. Justice Marshall wrote a dissenting opinion, which Justice Brennan joined.

Draper v. United States

358 U.S. 307, 79 S.Ct. 329, 3 L.Ed.2d 327 (1959)

[Petitioner was convicted of knowingly concealing and transporting narcotic drugs. Before trial he moved to suppress evidence seized from him at the time of his arrest. He contended that his arrest, without a warrant, was without probable cause and unlawful, and therefore that the search of his person and seizure of the evidence incident to the arrest were unlawful. The district court denied the motion and the evidence was used against him at the trial. The court of appeals affirmed his conviction.]

■ MR. JUSTICE WHITTAKER delivered the opinion of the Court.

. . .

The evidence offered at the hearing on the motion to suppress was not substantially disputed. It established that one Marsh, a federal narcotic agent with 29 years' experience, was stationed at Denver; that one Hereford had been engaged as a "special employee" of the Bureau of Narcotics at Denver for about six months, and from time to time gave information to Marsh regarding violations of the narcotic laws, for which Hereford was paid small sums of money, and that Marsh had always found the information given by Hereford to be accurate and reliable. On September 3, 1956, Hereford told Marsh that James Draper (petitioner) recently had taken up abode at a stated address in Denver and "was peddling narcotics to several addicts" in that city. Four days later, on September 7, Hereford told Marsh "that Draper had gone to Chicago the day before [September 6] by train [and] that he was going to bring back three ounces of heroin [and] that he would return to Denver either on the morning of the 8th of September or the morning of the 9th of September also by train." Hereford also gave Marsh a detailed physical description of Draper and of the clothing he was wearing,[5] and said that he would be carrying "a tan zipper bag," and that he habitually "walked real fast."

On the morning of September 8, Marsh and a Denver police officer went to the Denver Union Station and kept watch over all incoming trains from Chicago, but they did not see anyone fitting the description that Hereford had given. Repeating the process on the morning of September 9, they saw a person, having the exact physical attributes and wearing the precise clothing described by Hereford, alight from an incoming Chicago train and start walking "fast" toward the exit. He was carrying a tan zipper bag in his right hand and the left was thrust in his raincoat pocket. Marsh, accompanied by the police officer, overtook, stopped and arrested him. They then searched him and found the two "envelopes containing heroin" clutched in his left hand in his raincoat pocket, and found the syringe in the tan zipper bag. Marsh then took him (petitioner) into custody. Hereford died four days after the arrest and therefore did not testify at the hearing on the motion.

5. Hereford told Marsh that Draper was a Negro of light brown complexion, 27 years of age, 5 feet 8 inches tall, weighed about 160 pounds, and that he was wearing a light colored raincoat, brown slacks and black shoes.

26 U.S.C. (Supp. V) § 7607, added by § 104(a) of the Narcotic Control Act of 1956, 70 Stat. 570, provides, in pertinent part:

> The Commissioner . . . and agents, of the Bureau of Narcotics . . . may— . . .
>
> . . .
>
> (2) make arrests without warrant for violations of any law of the United States relating to narcotic drugs . . . where the violation is committed in the presence of the person making the arrest or where such person has reasonable grounds to believe that the person to be arrested has committed or is committing such violation.

The crucial question for us then is whether knowledge of the related facts and circumstances gave Marsh "probable cause" within the meaning of the Fourth Amendment, and "reasonable grounds" within the meaning of § 104(a), supra,[6] to believe that petitioner had committed or was committing a violation of the narcotic laws. If it did, the arrest, though without a warrant, was lawful and the subsequent search of petitioner's person and the seizure of the found heroin were validly made incident to a lawful arrest, and therefore the motion to suppress was properly overruled and the heroin was competently received in evidence at the trial. . . .

Petitioner does not dispute this analysis of the question for decision. Rather, he contends (1) that the information given by Hereford to Marsh was "hearsay" and, because hearsay is not legally competent evidence in a criminal trial, could not legally have been considered, but should have been put out of mind, by Marsh in assessing whether he had "probable cause" and "reasonable grounds" to arrest petitioner without a warrant, and (2) that, even if hearsay could lawfully have been considered, Marsh's information should be held insufficient to show "probable cause" and "reasonable grounds" to believe that petitioner had violated or was violating the narcotic laws and to justify his arrest without a warrant.

Considering the first contention, we find petitioner entirely in error. Brinegar v. United States, 338 U.S. 160, 172–73, has settled the question the other way. There, in a similar situation, the convict contended "that the factors relating to inadmissibility of the evidence [for] *purposes of proving guilt at the trial*, deprive[d] the evidence as a whole of sufficiency to show probable cause for the search. . . ." Id., at 172. (Emphasis added.) But this Court, rejecting that contention, said: "[T]he so-called distinction places a wholly unwarranted emphasis upon the criterion of admissibility in evidence, to prove the accused's guilt, of the facts relied upon to show probable cause. That emphasis, we think, goes much too far in confusing and disregarding the difference between what is required to prove guilt in a criminal case and what is required to show probable cause for arrest or search. It approaches requiring (if it does not in practical effect require) proof sufficient to establish guilt in order to substantiate the existence of

6. The terms "probable cause" as used in the Fourth Amendment and "reasonable grounds" as used in § 104(a) of the Narcotic Control Act, 70 Stat. 570, are substantial equivalents of the same meaning. . . .

probable cause. There is a large difference between the two things to be proved [guilt and probable cause], as well as between the tribunals which determine them, and therefore a like difference in the *quanta* and modes of proof required to establish them." 338 U.S., at 172–73.

Nor can we agree with petitioner's second contention that Marsh's information was insufficient to show probable cause and reasonable grounds to believe that petitioner had violated or was violating the narcotic laws and to justify his arrest without a warrant. The information given to narcotic agent Marsh by "special employee" Hereford may have been hearsay to Marsh, but coming from one employed for that purpose and whose information had always been found accurate and reliable, it is clear that Marsh would have been derelict in his duties had he not pursued it. And when, in pursuing that information, he saw a man, having the exact physical attributes and wearing the precise clothing and carrying the tan zipper bag that Hereford had described, alight from one of the very trains from the very place stated by Hereford and start to walk at a "fast" pace toward the station exit, Marsh had personally verified every facet of the information given him by Hereford except whether petitioner had accomplished his mission and had the three ounces of heroin on his person or in his bag. And surely, with every other bit of Hereford's information being thus personally verified, Marsh had "reasonable grounds" to believe that the remaining unverified bit of Hereford's information—that Draper would have the heroin with him—was likewise true.

"In dealing with probable cause, . . . as the very name implies, we deal with probabilities. These are not technical; they are the factual and practical considerations of everyday life on which reasonable and prudent men, not legal technicians, act." Brinegar v. United States, supra, at 175. Probable cause exists where "the facts and circumstances within [the arresting officers'] knowledge and of which they had reasonably trustworthy information [are] sufficient in themselves to warrant a man of reasonable caution in the belief that" an offense has been or is being committed. Carroll v. United States, 267 U.S. 132, 162.

We believe that, under the facts and circumstances here, Marsh had probable cause and reasonable grounds to believe that petitioner was committing a violation of the laws of the United States relating to narcotic drugs at the time he arrested him. The arrest was therefore lawful, and the subsequent search and seizure, having been made incident to that lawful arrest, were likewise valid. It follows that petitioner's motion to suppress was properly denied and that the seized heroin was competent evidence lawfully received at the trial.

■ MR. JUSTICE DOUGLAS, dissenting.

Decisions under the Fourth Amendment, taken in the long view, have not given the protection to the citizen which the letter and spirit of the Amendment would seem to require. One reason, I think, is that wherever a culprit is caught red-handed, as in leading Fourth Amendment cases, it is difficult to adopt and enforce a rule that would turn him loose. A rule protective of law-abiding citizens is not apt to flourish where its advocates are usually criminals. Yet the rule we fashion is for the innocent and guilty alike. If the word of the informer on which the present arrest was made is sufficient to make the arrest legal, his word would also protect the police who, acting on it, hauled the innocent citizen off to jail.

Of course, the education we receive from mystery stories and television shows teaches that what happened in this case is efficient police work. The police are tipped off that a man carrying narcotics will step off the morning train. A man meeting the precise description does alight from the train. No warrant for his arrest has been—or, as I see it, could then be—obtained. Yet he is arrested; and narcotics are found in his pocket and a syringe in the bag he carried. This is the familiar pattern of crime detection which has been dinned into public consciousness as the correct and efficient one. It is, however, a distorted reflection of the constitutional system under which we are supposed to live.

With all due deference, the arrest made here on the mere word of an informer violated the spirit of the Fourth Amendment and the requirement of the law, 26 U.S.C. (Supp. V) § 7607, governing arrests in narcotics cases. . . . The arresting officers did not have a bit of evidence, known to them and as to which they could take an oath had they gone to a magistrate for a warrant, that petitioner had committed any crime. The arresting officers did not know the grounds on which the informer based his conclusion; nor did they seek to find out what they were. They acted solely on the informer's word. In my view that was not enough.

The rule which permits arrest for felonies, as distinguished from misdemeanors, if there are reasonable grounds for believing a crime has been or is being committed . . . grew out of the need to protect the public safety by making prompt arrests. . . . Yet, apart from those cases where the crime is committed in the presence of the officer, arrests without warrants, like searches without warrants, are the exception, not the rule in our society. . . .

. . .

The Court is quite correct in saying that proof of "reasonable grounds" for believing a crime was being committed need not be proof admissible at the trial. It could be inferences from suspicious acts, e.g., consort with known peddlers, the surreptitious passing of a package, an intercepted message suggesting criminal activities, or any number of such events coming to the knowledge of the officer. . . . But, if he takes the law into his own hands and does not seek the protection of a warrant, he must act on some evidence known to him. The law goes far to protect the citizen. Even suspicious acts observed by the officers may be as consistent with innocence as with guilt. That is not enough, for even the guilty may not be implicated on suspicion alone. . . . The reason is, as I have said, that the standard set by the Constitution and by the statute is one that will protect both the officer and the citizen. For if the officer acts with "probable cause" or on "reasonable grounds," he is protected even though the citizen is innocent. . . .

Here the officers had no evidence—apart from the mere word of an informer—that petitioner was committing a crime. The fact that petitioner walked fast and carried a tan zipper bag was not evidence of any crime. The officers knew nothing except what they had been told by the informer. If they went to a magistrate to get a warrant of arrest and relied solely on the report of the informer, it is not conceivable to me that one would be granted. . . . For they could not present to the magistrate any of the facts which the informer may have had. They could swear only to the fact that the informer had made the accusation. They could swear to no evidence that lay in their own knowledge. They could present, on information and belief, no facts which the informer disclosed. No magistrate could issue a warrant on the mere word of an officer, without more. . . . We are not justified in lowering the standard when an arrest is made without a warrant and allowing the officers more leeway than we grant the magistrate.

With all deference I think we break with tradition when we sustain this arrest. We said in United States v. Di Re, [332 U.S. 581 (1948)], at 595, "a search is not to be made legal by what it turns up. In law it is good or bad when it starts and does not change character from its success." In this case it was only after the arrest and search were made that there was a shred of evidence known to the officers that a crime was in the process of being committed.

---

11. In Smith v. Ohio, 494 U.S. 541 (1990), the Court emphasized the point made by Justice Douglas at the end of his opinion in *Draper*: an arrest cannot be justified by what is found in a search incident to the arrest. "The exception for searches incident to arrest permits the police to search a lawfully arrested person and areas within his immediate control. . . . [I]t does not permit the police to search any citizen without a warrant or probable cause so long as an arrest immediately follows." Id. at 543.

12. "[T]here are at least two means by which the credibility of an informant may be established. One is by corroborating external circumstances occurring in the course of the very case that is at issue, as happened in the Draper case. . . . The other is the fact that on prior occasions in other cases the informant has given information which turned out to be reliable." Costello v. United States, 324 F.2d 260, 262 (9th Cir.1963). How significant were the "corroborating external circumstances" in *Draper*? See Illinois v. Gates, 462 U.S. 213 (1983), p. 180 below.

13.

> It is notorious that the narcotics informer is often himself involved in the narcotics traffic and is often paid for his information in cash, narcotics, immunity from prosecution, or lenient punishment. . . .
>
> The reliability of such persons is obviously suspect. The fact that their information may have produced convictions in the past does not justify taking their reports on faith. . . . [T]he present informer practice amounts to condoning felonies on condition that the confessed or suspected felon brings about the conviction of others. Under such

stimulation it is to be expected that the informer will not infrequently reach for shadowy leads, or even seek to incriminate the innocent. The practice of paying fees to the informer for the cases he makes may also be expected, from time to time, to induce him to lure non-users into the drug habit and then entrap them into law violations.

For such reasons, the law has wisely circumscribed the use of informers' reports as a basis for making arrest. It has required a showing of reliability of the information and some corroboration by facts within the arresting officer's own knowledge. Such corroboration may be obtained by placing the suspect under surveillance and observing whether his behavior—e.g., making contact with persons known to be in the trade, or surreptitious passing of a package—tends to support the informer's story.

How much personal knowledge the policeman must have before making the arrest cannot be determined for all cases. Since circumstances vary, the rule must be stated in terms of what is reasonably inferable from the particular circumstances by a prudent police officer. . . . It would appear from *Draper* [v. United States, 358 U.S. 307 (1959)] that when a reliable informer tells an officer that an individual has left town to buy narcotics and is returning by train at a certain time, the policeman's observation of his return is enough to justify an arrest without a warrant.

When deprivation of liberty by arrest is justified by a combination of an informer's report and a policeman's own observations, the less the policeman is required to observe, the more significant becomes the informer's report. Since observation of so commonplace an act as coming home by train is enough, in combination with the report of an informer, to justify an arrest, the only significant limitation of the informer's power to cause an arrest is the requirement of reliability. The requirement that the informer be reliable stands as the only effective legal safeguard against false denunciations by irresponsible individuals who may be motivated by self-interest, spite, or even paranoia. The only other safeguard which remains rests not on law but on the good will of the police officer.

Jones v. United States, 266 F.2d 924, 928–29 (D.C.Cir.1959) (Bazelon, J.).

14. "We have discovered no case that extends this requirement [of evidence that an informant's information is credible or that he is reliable] to the identified bystander or victim-eyewitness to a crime, and now hold that no such requirement need be met. The rationale behind requiring a showing of credibility and reliability is to prevent searches based upon an unknown informant's tip that may not reflect anything more than idle rumor or irresponsible conjecture. Thus, without the establishment of the probability of reliability, a 'neutral and detached magistrate' could not adequately assess the probative value of the tip in exercising his judgment as to the existence of probable cause. Many informants are intimately involved with the persons informed upon and with the illegal conduct at hand, and this circumstance could also affect their credibility. None of

Boston Police Department
Arrest Booking Form

Report Date: 02/10/1997 11:55:19
Booking Status: COMPLETED
Printed By: Dahlbeck, Joseph W

District: 09 Cell Number: 5
Charges: Breaking And Entering (Residence)
Court: Boston Municipal UCR Code:
Docket #: WA 123145-0000

Master Name: Pomeroy, Arnold, George DOB: 03/17/1956
Location Of Arrest: 7 Warren Ave

Booking Name: Layfield, Robert, Arthur
Alias: Pomeroy, Raymond, Allen
Address: Apt 23, 312 Evergreen CR , Boston, MA.

Booking Number: 95-000316-04 Incident Number: CR Number: 000001-80
Booking Date: 02/10/1997 11:25 Arrest Date: 03/17/1995 14:00 RA Number:

Sex: Male
Race: White Non-Hispanic
Date Of Birth: 06/09/1942
Place Of Birth: Boston, MA, USA
Marital Status: Separated
Mother Name: Jones, Hazel K
Father Name: Layfield, Arthur

Height: 5' 11"
Weight: 200 lbs
Build: Medium
Eye Color: Brown
Hair Color: Dark
Complexion: Medium

Occupation: Welder
Employer / School:
Emp/School Address:
Social Sec. Number: 100104100
Operators License: S02489647
State:

Phone Used: YES
Examined at Hospital: NO
Breathalizer Used: NO
Scars / Marks /:
Tattoos:
Clothing Desc:

Arresting Officer:	BPD	09566	Joseph W Dahlbeck
Booking Officer:	BPD	10127	Sean P Scannell
Informed Of Rights:	BPD	09566	Joseph W Dahlbeck
Placed In Cell By:	BPD	10427	Claudio R McKenzie
Searched By:	BPD	10427	Claudio R McKenzie

Arresting Partner ID: 10427
Unit: 123
Transporting Unit: 123

Cautions:

Booking Comments:
none

Visible Injuries:
Any injuries would be listed in this area

JUVENILE INFORMATION

Person Notified:
Address:
Notified By: BPD
Relationship:
Phone:
Juv. Prob. Officer:
Notified Date / Time:

Bail Set By:
Bailed By:
Amount:

I Selected the Bail Comm.

Signature Of Prisoner

BOP Check:
Suicide Check:
BOP Warrant:
BOP Court:

Signature of Duty Supervisor

these considerations is present in the eyewitness situation. . . . Such observers are seldom involved with the miscreants or the crime. Eyewitnesses by definition are not passing along idle rumor, for they either have been the victims of the crime or have otherwise seen some portion of it." United States v. Bell, 457 F.2d 1231, 1238–39 (5th Cir.1972).

15. "[T]he arresting officer testified that he was informed by a lieutenant from the Criminal Investigation Bureau that an anonymous phone call had been received informing the lieutenant that a described man named Bernie Horowitz was then shaping up for work at the mail room of the New York Times Building and had in his possession a brown paper bag containing stolen United States savings bonds and pornographic literature; that he found the defendant at the mail room of the Times Building, identified himself as a police officer, asked the defendant his name and obtained a brown paper bag which the defendant carried containing United States savings bonds in the name of Anthony Cardone which were later identified as having been stolen." The description that was given of Horowitz was that he "was over six feet tall, weighed more than 200 pounds, and was known as 'Mr. Clean' because of the lack of hair on his head." People v. Horowitz, 233 N.E.2d 453, 453–54 (N.Y.1967). Was Horowitz's arrest lawful?

16.

On September 22, 1961, at about 3:45 A.M., the defendant and two other men were stopped by two uniformed Baltimore City police officers while riding in a 1960 Oldsmobile, bearing Maryland license number AL29–32. The officers got out of the police car, drew their pistols, placed the defendant and the others under arrest, told them to put their hands on the dashboard, and held them in that position until their sergeant arrived. Then, the defendant and the other occupants were ordered out of the car and were subjected to a search, in the course of which the arresting officers discovered in the right jacket pocket of the defendant a small package wrapped in green paper, the contents of which were later identified as heroin. In a subsequent search at police headquarters, a similar package, the contents of which were also later identified as heroin, was found in the defendant's sock.

Officer Snead, one of the arresting officers, testified that the reason he stopped the vehicle the defendant was driving was that he had received a teletype message on his patrol car radio to stop a vehicle matching the description of the Oldsmobile, with Maryland tags number AL29–32, in which were two colored occupants who were suspected of illegally possessing narcotics, that he had not been informed of and did not know the defendant's name or his description, and that at no time did he see the defendant violate any law.

The instruction to stop the vehicle which the defendant was driving, on which the arresting officers relied in making their arrest, was placed on teletype at approximately 12:30 A.M. September 22, by the Maryland State Police at the request of one Greenfeld, a federal agent who was acting upon information which had been relayed to him in Baltimore by Federal narcotics agents in New York who had had the defendant under surveillance as a result of information passed on to them by a special employee (an informant). The New York agents both

> testified that they had not observed the defendant violate any law nor had their special employee, who merely had heard that the defendant had narcotics in his possession which he was taking back to Baltimore. Agent Greenfeld testified that based on the information he had received from New York, his evaluation thereof, and a conversation with Captain Carroll of the Baltimore Police Narcotics Squad as to the local narcotics activities of the defendant, he "believed" that the defendant was bringing narcotics to Baltimore.

Stanley v. State, 186 A.2d 478, 479–80 (Md.1962). Was the arrest constitutionally valid?

"The police department of a large metropolis does not and can not operate on a segmented basis with each officer acting separately and independently of each other and detached from the central headquarters. There must be cooperation, co-ordination and direction, with some central control and exchange of information." Miller v. United States, 356 F.2d 63, 67 (5th Cir.1966). When the basis of an arrest is "the collective information of the police rather than that of only the officer who performs the act of arresting," Smith v. United States, 358 F.2d 833, 835 (D.C.Cir.1966), what should be the test?

17. Whiteley v. Warden, 401 U.S. 560 (1971). Relying on a police bulletin, an officer arrested Whiteley. It turned out that the warrant for Whiteley's arrest on which the bulletin was based was invalid. The Court rejected the argument that the arresting officer nevertheless had probable cause for the arrest because he was entitled to rely on the bulletin. "Certainly police officers called upon to aid other officers in executing arrest warrants are entitled to assume that the officers requesting aid offered the magistrate the information requisite to support an independent judicial assessment of probable cause. Where, however, the contrary turns out to be true, an otherwise illegal arrest cannot be insulated from challenge by the decision of the instigating officer to rely on fellow officers to make the arrest." Id. at 568. The precedential value of Whiteley v. Warden, insofar as application of the exclusionary rule is concerned, was questioned in Arizona v. Evans, 514 U.S. 1 (1995) (6–3), p. 150 note 81 below. Cf. United States v. Hensley, 469 U.S. 221 (1985), p. 125 note 69 below.

Beck v. Ohio

379 U.S. 89, 85 S.Ct. 223, 13 L.Ed.2d 142 (1964)

■ MR. JUSTICE STEWART delivered the opinion of the Court.

On the afternoon of November 10, 1961, the petitioner, William Beck, was driving his automobile in the vicinity of East 115th Street and Beulah Avenue in Cleveland, Ohio. Cleveland police officers accosted him, identified themselves, and ordered him to pull over to the curb. The officers possessed neither an arrest warrant nor a search warrant. Placing him under arrest, they searched his car but found nothing of interest. They then took him to a nearby police station where they searched his person and found an envelope containing a number of clearing house slips "beneath the sock of his leg." The petitioner was subsequently charged in the Cleveland Municipal Court with possession of clearing house slips in violation of a state criminal statute. . . .

. . .

[Before trial, the petitioner moved to suppress the clearing house slips. The motion was denied. The slips were admitted in evidence at trial and he was convicted. The Ohio courts affirmed the conviction; admission of the slips was upheld on the ground that the search was incident to a lawful arrest and therefore valid.]

There are limits to the permissible scope of a warrantless search incident to a lawful arrest, but we proceed on the premise that, if the arrest itself was lawful, those limits were not exceeded here. . . . The constitutional validity of the search in this case, then, must depend upon the constitutional validity of the petitioner's arrest. Whether that arrest was constitutionally valid depends in turn upon whether, at the moment the arrest was made, the officers had probable cause to make it—whether at that moment the facts and circumstances within their knowledge and of which they had reasonably trustworthy information were sufficient to warrant a prudent man in believing that the petitioner had committed or was committing an offense. . . . "The rule of probable cause is a practical, nontechnical conception affording the best compromise that has been found for accommodating . . . often opposing interests. Requiring more would unduly hamper lawful enforcement. To allow less would be to leave law-abiding citizens at the mercy of the officers' whim or caprice." Brinegar v. United States, [338 U.S. 160 (1949)], at 176.

. . .

The record is meager, consisting only of the testimony of one of the arresting officers, given at the hearing on the motion to suppress. As to the officer's own knowledge of the petitioner before the arrest, the record shows no more than that the officer "had a police picture of him and knew what he looked like," and that the officer knew that the petitioner had "a record in connection with clearing house and scheme of chance." Beyond that, the officer testified only that he had "information" that he had "heard reports," that "someone specifically did relate that information," and that he "knew who that person was." There is nowhere in the record any indication of what "information" or "reports" the officer had received or, beyond what has been set out above, from what source the "information" and "reports" had come. The officer testified that when he left the station house, "I had in mind looking for [the petitioner] in the area of East 115th Street and Beulah, stopping him if I did see him make a stop in that area." But the officer testified to nothing that would indicate that any informer had said that the petitioner could be found at that time and place. . . . And the record does not show that the officers saw the petitioner "stop" before they arrested him, or that they saw, heard, smelled, or otherwise perceived anything else to give them ground for belief that the petitioner had acted or was then acting unlawfully.

No decision of this Court has upheld the constitutional validity of a warrantless arrest with support so scant as this record presents. The respondent relies upon Draper v. United States, 358 U.S. 307. But in that case the record showed that a named special employee of narcotics agents who had on numerous occasions given reliable information had told the arresting officer that the defendant, whom he described minutely, had taken up residence at a stated address and was selling narcotics to addicts in Denver. The informer further had told the officer that the defendant was going to Chicago to obtain narcotics and would be returning to Denver on one of two trains from Chicago, which event in fact took place. In complete contrast, the record in this case does not contain a single objective fact to support a belief by the officers that the petitioner was engaged in criminal activity at the time they arrested him.

An arrest without a warrant bypasses the safeguards provided by an objective predetermination of probable cause, and substitutes instead the far less reliable procedure of an after-the-event justification for the arrest or search, too likely to be subtly influenced by the familiar shortcomings of hindsight judgment. "Whether or not the requirements of reliability and particularity of the information on which an officer may act are more stringent where an arrest warrant is absent, they surely cannot be less stringent than where an arrest warrant is obtained. Otherwise, a principal incentive now existing for the procurement of arrest warrants would be destroyed." Wong Sun v. United States, 371 U.S. 471, 479–80. Yet even in cases where warrants were obtained, the Court has held that the Constitution demands a greater showing of probable cause than can be found in the present record. . . .

When the constitutional validity of an arrest is challenged, it is the function of a court to determine whether the facts available to the officers at the moment of the arrest would "warrant a man of reasonable caution in the belief" that an offense has been committed. Carroll v. United States, 267 U.S. 132, 162. If the court is not informed of the facts upon which the arresting officers acted, it cannot properly discharge that function. All that the trial court was told in this case was that the officers knew what the petitioner looked like and knew that he had a previous record of arrests or convictions for violations of the clearing house law. Beyond that, the arresting officer who testified said no more than that someone (he did not say who) had told him something (he did not say what) about the petitioner. We do not hold that the officer's knowledge of the petitioner's physical appearance and previous record was either inadmissible or entirely irrelevant upon the issue of probable cause. . . . But to hold that knowledge of either or both of these facts constituted probable cause would be to hold that anyone with a previous criminal record could be arrested at will.

It is possible that an informer did in fact relate information to the police officer in this case which constituted probable cause for the petitioner's arrest. But when the constitutional validity of that arrest was challenged, it was incumbent upon the prosecution to show with considerably more specificity than was shown in this case what the informer actually said, and why the officer thought the information was credible. We may assume that the officers acted in good faith in arresting the petitioner. But "good faith on the part of the arresting officers is not enough." Henry v. United States, 361 U.S. 98, 102. If subjective good faith alone were the test, the protections of the Fourth Amendment would evaporate, and the people would be "secure in their persons, houses, papers, and effects," only in the discretion of the police.

. . .[7]

18.

The pertinent circumstances are those of the moment, the actual ones. Officers patrolling the streets at night do not prearrange the setting. They do not schedule their steps in the calm of an office. Things just happen. They are required as a matter of duty to act as reasonably prudent men would act under the circumstances as those circumstances happen. . . .

Among the other pertinent circumstances is the qualification and function of the person making the arrest. The standard is a reasonable, cautious and prudent man. But the question is whether the person making the arrest had probable cause. Probable cause is not a philosophical concept existing in a vacuum; it is a practical and factual matter. A fact which spells reasonable cause to a doctor may make no impression on a carpenter, and vice versa. Did the person who made the arrest, if a reasonable and prudent man, have probable cause? An officer experienced in the narcotics traffic may find probable cause in the smell of drugs and the appearance of paraphernalia which to the lay eye is without significance. His action is not measured by what might be probable cause to an untrained civilian passerby. When a peace officer makes the arrest the standard means a reasonable, cautious and prudent peace officer. The question is what constituted probable cause in the eyes of a reasonable, cautious and prudent peace officer under the circumstances of the moment.

Bell v. United States, 254 F.2d 82, 85–86 (D.C.Cir.1958).

19.

Shortly after midnight on a February morning in 1966, Grady Johnson and Henry Ussery, while walking along a sidewalk, were attacked by several men. A wallet, a watch and a small sum of money were taken from Johnson, and a watch and a penknife from Ussery. Within a few minutes, police officers, responding to a reported shooting

[7] Justice Clark wrote a dissenting opinion, which Justice Black joined. Justice Harlan also wrote a dissenting opinion.

> in the same block, arrived at the scene. Soon gathered there, too, were a number of spectators, among whom our appellant was standing.
>
> Ussery, bruised and bleeding about his face, informed Officers Arthur G. Delaney and Rudolph Scipio of the attack, and pointed to appellant—a stranger to him—as one of the robbers. Though somewhat excited, and admittedly having been drinking prior to the incident, Ussery insisted that he was positive in his identification.
>
> Officer Scipio then approached appellant and inquired as to what he was doing in the area. Appellant replied that he had just left a party, and was taking a walk to get some fresh air. The officer then informed appellant of Ussery's accusation, which appellant denied, and proceeded to arrest him. A concomitant search uncovered on appellant's person the watch taken from Johnson, and the watch and penknife stolen from Ussery.

Pendergrast v. United States, 416 F.2d 776 (D.C.Cir.1969). Were the arrest and search incident to it lawful?

20.

> In essence, the testimony of the arresting officers was that they had been specially assigned to look for the perpetrator of a series of day-time housebreakings that had taken place in a particular area in Northeast Washington. They said that the Police Department had broadcast many descriptions of the suspect ("lookouts"), the latest having been issued on the day prior to the arrest. The lookouts—based on information received from complaining witnesses—described the suspect as a "brown-skinned" colored man about "five feet seven" or "five feet eight" in height, about 150 pounds in weight, "very neatly" dressed, wearing a "gray topcoat," sometimes said to have a "half-belt" in the back, or a "black topcoat," and a "brown" or "gray" hat. His age was variously described as "middle teens," "late teens," "19, 21, 22," or "22–24." The look-outs, issued from time to time over a period of months, referred to each of a series of crimes of common pattern, all having been committed by someone who forced open the front doors of houses, with some instrument, in the daylight hours.
>
> On the day in question, shortly before noon, the officers, who were in plain clothes, were driving an unmarked car down one of the streets in the area where the crimes had occurred. They saw Ellis approach on foot from the opposite direction. They testified they were mindful of the descriptions given in the look-outs, and that Ellis appeared to them to be the wanted man: he was "brown-skinned," "around five seven or five eight" in height, from "a hundred forty-five to a hundred and fifty" pounds in weight, "very neatly dressed," wearing a "gray topcoat with a half-belt in the back," and a "brown" hat, and was estimated to be "between twenty-two and twenty-five" years old.
>
> The officers drove on a short distance, turned their car around, and waited. They saw Ellis go up on the porch of a house, knock on the door, stand there looking "around the area" for a "few minutes," then

> return to the street and walk back toward the direction from which he had come. As Ellis approached, the officers hailed him and asked him to come to their car, saying that they were police officers. They got out of the car, and asked Ellis his name. He gave it. He was then asked, "Do you have any identification?" The answer was in the negative. Ellis appeared nervous; he "dropped his money . . . chewing gum, cigarettes, and so forth on the ground." The officers "asked him twice to take his hand out of his pocket." However, he "kept his right hand in his coat pocket and his arm close against his side." One of the officers "patted him and found a bulge in his inside pocket on the righthand side." The officers then searched him, and found certain items which were later used against him.

Ellis v. United States, 264 F.2d 372, 373–74 (D.C.Cir.1959). The use against Ellis of the items found on his person was permissible only if the search was incident to a lawful arrest. Were the items properly admitted in evidence?

21.

> At 2:00 A.M. on November 9, 1962, the Old Hickory Barbecue Restaurant in Southeast Washington was robbed. A police lookout, based on descriptions of three robbers given by the witnesses at the restaurant, was broadcast. Private Fallin, the arresting officer, testified that the lookout contained "a general description of three colored males." Forty-five minutes after receiving the first lookout, Fallin testified, he received another call to respond to South Capitol and Howard Streets. There he found a taxi driver and more police. The cab driver told Fallin that a suspicious-acting person had fled from his cab as he drove into the Esso station on that corner. Fallin proceeded to track with his dog behind the Esso station in what appeared to be an abandoned area. After searching almost an hour, however, the dog was injured and the tracking operation was discontinued.
>
> On returning to his cruiser, Fallin testified, he met his partner. His partner told him that a man had just come out of the general area where he was searching and was at that time walking down the highway. Fallin, with his partner, then approached this man, who turned out to be Gatlin, and arrested him at approximately 3:40 A.M.

Gatlin v. United States, 326 F.2d 666, 668–70 (D.C.Cir.1963). Was Gatlin arrested lawfully?

22. Although a reasonable mistake of fact may furnish an objective basis for reasonable suspicion or probable cause, a mistake of law, however reasonable, cannot. Furthermore, the good faith exception to the exclusionary rule, see p. 148 below, does not extend to a mistake of law. United States v. Chanthasouxat, 342 F.3d 1271 (11th Cir. 2003). Cf. Illinois v. Rodriguez, p. 169 below.

23. In Ornelas v. United States, 517 U.S. 690 (1996) (8–1), the Court considered the standard for appellate review of a determination that there is either reasonable suspicion (justifying an investigative stop, see pp. 100–117 below) or probable cause. It said:

> Articulating precisely what "reasonable suspicion" and "probable cause" mean is not possible. They are commonsense, nontechnical conceptions that deal with "the factual and practical considerations of everyday life on which reasonable and prudent men, not legal technicians, act." Illinois v. Gates, 462 U.S. 213, 231 (1983) (quoting Brinegar v. United States, 338 U.S. 160, 176 (1949)) . . . As such, the standards are "not readily, or even usefully, reduced to a neat set of legal rules." *Gates*, supra, at 232. We have described reasonable suspicion simply as "a particularized and objective basis" for suspecting the person stopped of criminal activity, United States v. Cortez, 449 U.S. 411, 417–18 (1981), and probable cause to search as existing where the known facts and circumstances are sufficient to warrant a man of reasonable prudence in the belief that contraband or evidence of a crime will be found. . . . We have cautioned that these two legal principles are not "finely-tuned standards," comparable to the standards of proof beyond a reasonable doubt or of proof by a preponderance of the evidence. *Gates*, supra, at 235. They are instead fluid concepts that take their substantive content from the particular contexts in which the standards are being assessed. . . .
>
> The principal components of a determination of reasonable suspicion or probable cause will be the events which occurred leading up to the stop or search, and then the decision whether these historical facts, viewed from the standpoint of an objectively reasonable police officer, amount to reasonable suspicion or to probable cause. The first part of the analysis involves only a determination of historical facts, but the second is a mixed question of law and fact: "[T]he historical facts are admitted or established, the rule of law is undisputed, and the issue is whether the facts satisfy the [relevant] statutory [or constitutional] standard, or to put it another way, whether the rule of law as applied to the established facts is or is not violated." Pullman-Standard v. Swint, 456 U.S. 273, 289, n.19 (1982).
>
> We think independent appellate review of these ultimate determinations of reasonable suspicion and probable cause is consistent with the position we have taken in past cases. We have never, when reviewing a probable-cause or reasonable-suspicion determination ourselves, expressly deferred to the trial court's determination. . . . A policy of sweeping deference would permit, "[i]n the absence of any significant difference in the facts," "the Fourth Amendment's incidence [to] tur[n] on whether different trial judges draw general conclusions that the facts are sufficient or insufficient to constitute probable cause." *Brinegar*, supra, at 171. Such varied results would be inconsistent with the idea of a unitary system of law. This, if a matter-of-course, would be unacceptable.
>
> In addition, the legal rules for probable cause and reasonable suspicion acquire content only through application. Independent re-

> view is therefore necessary if appellate courts are to maintain control of, and to clarify the legal principles. . . .
>
> Finally, de novo review tends to unify precedent and will come closer to providing law enforcement officers with a defined "set of rules which, in most instances, makes it possible to reach a correct determination beforehand as to whether an invasion of privacy is justified in the interest of law enforcement." New York v. Belton, 453 U.S. 454, 458 (1981). . . .
>
> . . .
>
> We therefore hold that as a general matter determinations of reasonable suspicion and probable cause should be reviewed de novo on appeal. Having said this, we hasten to point out that a reviewing court should take care both to review findings of historical fact only for clear error and to give due weight to inferences drawn from those facts by resident judges and local law enforcement officers.
>
> A trial judge views the facts of a particular case in light of the distinctive features and events of the community; likewise a police officer views the facts through the lens of his police experience and expertise. The background facts provide a context for the historical facts, and when seen together yield inferences that deserve deference. . . . The background facts, though rarely the subject of explicit findings, inform the judge's assessment of the historical facts.
>
> In a similar vein, our cases have recognized that a police officer may draw inferences based on his own experience in deciding whether probable cause exists. . . . An appeals court should give due weight to a trial court's finding that the officer was credible and the inference was reasonable.

517 U.S. at 696–700.

The Court revisited *Ornelas* in United States v. Arvizu, 534 U.S. 266 (2002), as it applies to reasonable suspicion. It said that a court should not reduce the "totality of the circumstances" test to a rigid formula and indicated considerable deference to the trained judgment of the officer who makes a stop.

24. The temporary detention of a motorist who the arresting officer has probable cause to believe has committed a civil traffic violation does not violate the Fourth Amendment even if the officer's reliance on the traffic violation was pretextual (the officer was seeking evidence of some unrelated crime) and the stop was not objectively reasonable (it deviated substantially from ordinary police practice). Having probable cause, the stop is reasonable under the Fourth Amendment, without more. Whren v. United States, 517 U.S. 806 (1996).

The Court extended the holding of *Whren* to a full custodial arrest, rather than a traffic stop, in Arkansas v. Sullivan, 532 U.S. 769 (2001) (per curiam). See United States v. Castro, 166 F.3d 728 (5th Cir. 1999) (en banc) (pretextual arrest for speeding and seat belt violations followed by impoundment and search of vehicle, at behest of narcotics investigators; *Whren* applied).

In the preceding cases, would the police officer who made the arrest have been derelict in his duty if he had *not* done so? If the officer in any of the cases should not have made the arrest, was there something else that he should have done?

---

25. Probable cause. The Supreme Court has not developed the concept of probable cause significantly beyond its expression in Carroll v. United States, 267 U.S. 132 (1925), and Brinegar v. United States, 338 U.S. 160 (1949), the most important portions of which are quoted in the opinion in *Draper*, p. 26 above. The statements in those cases were restatements of existing law without much clarification. See, e.g., Husty v. United States, 282 U.S. 694, 700–701 (1931); Dumbra v. United States, 268 U.S. 435, 441 (1925); Stacey v. Emery, 97 U.S. 642, 645 (1878).

If the primary function of a formula which expresses the standard of "probable cause" is to advise law enforcement officials of the circumstances in which they may arrest (or search)—an assumption which is by no means apparent from the cases—can you do any better than the Court has done in framing a formula? Putting aside the adequacy of the Court's formulation of the standard, do you have a clear understanding of why the standard is what it is? Has the Court expressed and explained the values which led it to permit the arrest in *Draper* but not *Beck*?

26. "Whether or not the requirements of reliability and particularity of the information on which an officer may act are more stringent where an arrest warrant is absent, they surely cannot be less stringent than where an arrest warrant is obtained. Otherwise, a principal incentive now existing for the procurement of arrest warrants would be destroyed." Wong Sun v. United States, 371 U.S. 471, 479–80 (1963).

Is the Court's statement in *Wong Sun*, above, persuasive? What might be the response to the argument that police would not obtain warrants if to do so they had to have stronger evidence than to arrest without a warrant? Consider United States v. Watson, 423 U.S. 411 (1976), p. 22 above.

Although the Court has often expressed a preference for an arrest or search pursuant to a warrant rather than without a warrant, e.g. Illinois v. Gates, 462 U.S. 213, 236 (1983); United States v. Ventresca, 380 U.S. 102 (1965), it has also emphasized in many cases that the Fourth Amendment requires only that an arrest or search be "reasonable" and that failure to obtain a warrant is not itself indicative of unreasonableness. E.g., Illinois v. Rodriguez, 497 U.S. 177 (1990); Chambers v. Maroney, 399 U.S. 42 (1970). One might conclude from such cases that the preference for a warrant is in practice not very strong.

The Requirement of a Warrant

A warrantless arrest is not invalid simply because the arresting officer failed to take advantage of an opportunity to obtain a warrant. In Trupiano v. United States, 334 U.S. 699, 705 (1948), the Court said: "The absence of a warrant of arrest, even though there was sufficient time to obtain one, does not destroy the validity of an arrest under these circumstances [felony committed in the presence of the arresting officer]. Warrants of arrest are designed to meet the dangers of unlimited and unreasonable arrests of persons who are not at the moment committing any crime. Those dangers, obviously, are not present where a felony plainly occurs before the eyes of an officer of the law at a place where he is lawfully present. Common sense then dictates that an arrest in that situation is valid despite the failure to obtain a warrant of arrest."

The same rule, that a warrant is not required to make an arrest, applies to a minor criminal offense. Atwater v. City of Lago Vista, 532 U.S. 318 (2001) (5–4) (misdemeanor seat belt violation punishable only by fine).

The intimation in *Trupiano* that if there is time a warrant must be obtained to arrest for a crime *not* being committed in the presence of the arresting officer has not been developed. See United States v. Watson, 423 U.S. 411 (1976). Should such a requirement be imposed? Why (not)? See generally the dissenting opinion of Justice White in Chimel v. California, 395 U.S. 752, 770 (1969), p. 215 note 122 below.

---

27. If an arrest is made pursuant to a warrant that is subsequently found to be invalid, can it be sustained as an arrest without a warrant, if there was probable cause to arrest? The answer generally has been that it is. See Chimel v. California, 395 U.S. 752 (1969), p. 205 below; Giordenello v. United States, 357 U.S. 480, 487–88 (1958). In light of this rule, how much force have the requirements of an arrest warrant other than the existence of probable cause? What reasons are there for or against upholding an arrest on this basis?

28. Shortly after he was advised by police radio to be on the lookout for two suspects in a holdup earlier that night, a police officer saw two people in a car parked in a private parking lot. The broadcast descriptions of the suspects and the car they were driving corresponded generally to the officer's observations. Suspecting that they were the wanted men but believing (as he testified later) that there was not probable cause for their arrest on the holdup charge, the officer arrested the two men for vagrancy. The facts known to the officer did furnish probable cause to arrest the men for the holdup. There was not probable cause for their arrest for vagrancy. Is evidence found in a search of the car incident to the arrest admissible against the two men? See Ricehill v. Brewer, 459 F.2d 537 (8th Cir.1972); Klingler v. United States, 409 F.2d 299 (8th Cir.1969). Is Whren v. United States, 517 U.S. 806 (1996), p. 41 note 24 above, controlling?

Payton v. New York

445 U.S. 573, 100 S.Ct. 1371, 63 L.Ed.2d 639 (1980)

■ MR. JUSTICE STEVENS delivered the opinion of the Court.

These appeals challenge the constitutionality of New York statutes that authorize police officers to enter a private residence without a warrant and with force, if necessary, to make a routine felony arrest.

. . .

. . . We now . . . hold that the Fourth Amendment to the United States Constitution, made applicable to the States by the Fourteenth Amendment . . . prohibits the police from making a warrantless and nonconsensual entry into a suspect's home in order to make a routine felony arrest.

. . .

I

On January 14, 1970, after two days of intensive investigation, New York detectives had assembled evidence sufficient to establish probable cause to believe that Theodore Payton had murdered the manager of a gas station two days earlier. At about 7:30 a.m. on January 15, six officers went to Payton's apartment in the Bronx, intending to arrest him. They had not obtained a warrant. Although light and music emanated from the apartment, there was no response to their knock on the metal door. They summoned emergency assistance and, about 30 minutes later, used crowbars to break open the door and enter the apartment. No one was there. In plain view, however, was a .30-caliber shell casing that was seized and later admitted into evidence at Payton's murder trial.

In due course Payton surrendered to the police, was indicted for murder, and moved to suppress the evidence taken from his apartment. The trial judge held that the warrantless and forcible entry was authorized by the New York Code of Criminal Procedure, and that the evidence in plain view was properly seized. He found that exigent circumstances justified the officers' failure to announce their purpose before entering the apartment as required by the statute. He had no occasion, however, to decide whether those circumstances also would have justified the failure to obtain a warrant, because he concluded that the warrantless entry was adequately supported by the statute without regard to the circumstances. . . .

On March 14, 1974, Obie Riddick was arrested for the commission of two armed robberies that had occurred in 1971. He had been identified by the victims in June of 1973, and in January 1974 the police had learned his address. They did not obtain a warrant for his arrest. At about noon on March 14, a detective, accompanied by three other officers, knocked on the door of the Queens house where Riddick was living. When his young son opened the door, they could see Riddick sitting in bed covered by a sheet. They entered the house and placed him under arrest. Before permitting him to dress, they opened a chest of drawers two feet from the bed in search of weapons and found narcotics and related paraphernalia. Riddick was subsequently indicted on narcotics charges. At a suppression hearing, the trial judge held that the warrantless entry into his home was authorized by the revised New York statute, and that the search of the immediate area was reasonable under Chimel v. California, 395 U.S. 752. . . .

The New York Court of Appeals, in a single opinion, affirmed the convictions of both Payton and Riddick. . . .

. . .

Before addressing the narrow question presented by these appeals, we put to one side other related problems that are *not* presented today. Although it is arguable that the warrantless entry to effect Payton's arrest might have been justified by exigent circumstances, none of the New York courts relied on any such justification. The Court of Appeals majority treated both Payton's and Riddick's cases as involving routine arrests in which there was ample time to obtain a warrant, and we will do the same. Accordingly, we have no occasion to consider the sort of emergency or dangerous situation, described in our cases as "exigent circumstances," that would justify a warrantless entry into a home for the purpose of either arrest or search.

Nor do these cases raise any question concerning the authority of the police, without either a search or arrest warrant, to enter a third party's home to arrest a suspect. The police broke into Payton's apartment intending to arrest Payton and they arrested Riddick in his own dwelling. We also note that in neither case is it argued that the police lacked probable cause to believe that the suspect was at home when they entered. Finally, in both cases we are dealing with entries into homes made without the consent of any occupant. In *Payton*, the police used crowbars to break down the door and in *Riddick*, although his three-year-old son answered the door, the police entered before Riddick had an opportunity either to object or to consent.

II

It is familiar history that indiscriminate searches and seizures conducted under the authority of "general warrants" were the immediate evils that motivated the framing and adoption of the Fourth Amendment.

Indeed, as originally proposed in the House of Representatives, the draft contained only one clause, which directly imposed limitations on the issuance of warrants, but imposed no express restrictions on warrantless searches or seizures. As it was ultimately adopted, however, the Amendment contained two separate clauses, the first protecting the basic right to be free from unreasonable searches and seizures and the second requiring that warrants be particular and supported by probable cause. . . .

It is thus perfectly clear that the evil the Amendment was designed to prevent was broader than the abuse of a general warrant. Unreasonable searches or seizures conducted without any warrant at all are condemned by the plain language of the first clause of the Amendment. Almost a century ago the Court stated in resounding terms that the principles reflected in the Amendment "reached farther than the concrete form" of the specific cases that gave it birth, and "apply to all invasions on the part of the Government and its employés of the sanctity of a man's home and the privacies of life." Boyd v. United States, 116 U.S. 616, 630. Without pausing to consider whether that broad language may require some qualification, it is sufficient to note that the warrantless arrest of a person is a species of seizure required by the Amendment to be reasonable. . . .

The simple language of the Amendment applies equally to seizures of persons and to seizures of property. Our analysis in this case may therefore properly commence with rules that have been well established in Fourth Amendment litigation involving tangible items. As the Court reiterated just a few years ago, the "physical entry of the home is the chief evil against which the wording of the Fourth Amendment is directed." United States v. United States District Court, 407 U.S. 297, 313. And we have long adhered to the view that the warrant procedure minimizes the danger of needless intrusions of that sort.

It is a "basic principle of Fourth Amendment law" that searches and seizures inside a home without a warrant are presumptively unreasonable. Yet it is also well settled that objects such as weapons or contraband found in a public place may be seized by the police without a warrant. The seizure of property in plain view involves no invasion of privacy and is presumptively reasonable, assuming that there is probable cause to associate the property with criminal activity. . . .

. . .

The majority of the New York Court of Appeals, however, suggested that there is a substantial difference in the relative intrusiveness of an entry to search for property and an entry to search for a person. . . . It is true that the area that may legally be searched is broader when executing a search warrant than when executing an arrest warrant in the home. . . . This difference may be more theoretical than real, however, because the police may need to check the entire premises for safety reasons, and sometimes they ignore the restrictions on searches incident to arrest.

But the critical point is that any differences in the intrusiveness of entries to search and entries to arrest are merely ones of degree rather than kind. The two intrusions share this fundamental characteristic: the breach of the entrance to an individual's home. The Fourth Amendment protects the individual's privacy in a variety of settings. In none is the zone of privacy more clearly defined than when bounded by the unambiguous physical dimensions of an individual's home—a zone that finds its roots in clear and specific constitutional terms: "The right of the people to be secure in their . . . houses . . . shall not be violated." That language unequivocally establishes the proposition that "[a]t the very core [of the Fourth Amendment] stands the right of a man to retreat into his own home and there be free from unreasonable governmental intrusion." Silverman v. United States, 365 U.S. 505, 511. In terms that apply equally to seizures of property and to seizures of persons, the Fourth Amendment has drawn a firm line at the entrance to the house. Absent exigent circumstances, that threshold may not reasonably be crossed without a warrant.

III

Without contending that United States v. Watson, [423 U.S. 411 (1976)], decided the question presented by these appeals, New York argues that the reasons that support the Watson holding require a similar result here. In *Watson* the Court relied on (a) the well-settled common-law rule that a warrantless arrest in a public place is valid if the arresting officer had probable cause to believe the suspect is a felon; (b) the clear consensus among the States adhering to that well settled common-law rule; and (c) the expression of the judgment of Congress that such an arrest is "reasonable." We consider each of these reasons as it applies to a warrantless entry into a home for the purpose of making a routine felony arrest.

A

An examination of the common-law understanding of an officer's authority to arrest sheds light on the obviously relevant, if not entirely dispositive, consideration of what the Framers of the Amendment might have thought to be reasonable. . . .

A study of the common law on the question whether a constable had the authority to make warrantless arrests in the home on mere suspicion of a felony—as distinguished from an officer's right to arrest for a crime committed in his presence—reveals a surprising lack of judicial decisions and a deep divergence among scholars.

. . .

[T]he common-law rule on warrantless home arrests was not as clear as the rule on arrests in public places. . . . [T]he weight of authority as it appeared to the Framers was to the effect that a warrant was required, or at the minimum that there were substantial risks in proceeding without one. The common-law sources display a sensitivity to privacy interests that could not have been lost on the Framers. The zealous and frequent repetition of the adage that a "man's house is his castle," made it abundantly clear that both in England and in the Colonies "the freedom of one's house" was one of the most vital elements of English liberty.[8]

Thus, our study of the relevant common law does not provide the same guidance that was present in *Watson*. Whereas the rule concerning the validity of an arrest in a public place was supported by cases directly in point and by the unanimous views of the commentators, we have found no direct authority supporting forcible entries into a home to make a routine arrest and the weight of the scholarly opinion is somewhat to the contrary. Indeed, the absence of any 17th or 18th century English cases directly in point, together with the unequivocal endorsement of the tenet that "a man's house is his castle," strongly suggests that the prevailing practice was not to make such arrests except in hot pursuit or when authorized by a warrant. . . . In all events, the issue is not one that can be said to have been definitively settled by the common law at the time the Fourth Amendment was adopted.

B

A majority of the States that have taken a position on the question permit warrantless entry into the home to arrest even in the absence of exigent circumstances. At this time, 24 States permit such warrantless entries; 15 States clearly prohibit them, though 3 States do so on federal constitutional grounds alone; and 11 States have apparently taken no position on the question.

But these current figures reflect a significant decline during the last decade in the number of States permitting warrantless entries for arrest. . . .

A longstanding, widespread practice is not immune from constitutional scrutiny. But neither is it to be lightly brushed aside. This is particularly so when the constitutional standard is as amorphous as the word "reasonable," and when custom and contemporary norms necessarily play such a large role in the constitutional analysis. In this case, although the weight of state-law authority is clear, there is by no means the kind of virtual unanimity on this question that was present in United States v. Watson, with regard to warrantless arrests in public places. . . . Only 24 of the 50 States currently sanction warrantless entries into the home to arrest . . . and there is an obvious declining trend. . . .

C

No congressional determination that warrantless entries into the home are "reasonable" has been called to our attention. None of the federal statutes cited in the *Watson* opinion reflects any such legislative judgment. Thus, that support for the *Watson* holding finds no counterpart in this case. . . .

8. . . . 2 Legal Papers of John Adams 142 (L. Wroth and H. Zobel ed. 1965).

[N]either history nor this Nation's experience requires us to disregard the overriding respect for the sanctity of the home that has been embedded in our traditions since the origins of the Republic.

IV

The parties have argued at some length about the practical consequences of a warrant requirement as a precondition to a felony arrest in the home. In the absence of any evidence that effective law enforcement has suffered in those States that already have such a requirement . . . we are inclined to view such arguments with skepticism. More fundamentally, however, such arguments of policy must give way to a constitutional command that we consider to be unequivocal.

Finally, we note the State's suggestion that only a search warrant based on probable cause to believe the suspect is at home at a given time can adequately protect the privacy interests at stake, and since such a warrant requirement is manifestly impractical, there need be no warrant of any kind. We find this ingenious argument unpersuasive. It is true that an arrest warrant requirement may afford less protection than a search warrant requirement, but it will suffice to interpose the magistrate's determination of probable cause between the zealous officer and the citizen. If there is sufficient evidence of a citizen's participation in a felony to persuade a judicial officer that his arrest is justified, it is constitutionally reasonable to require him to open his doors to the officers of the law. Thus, for Fourth Amendment purposes, an arrest warrant founded on probable cause implicitly carries with it the limited authority to enter a dwelling in which the suspect lives when there is reason to believe the suspect is within.

Because no arrest warrant was obtained in either of these cases, the judgments must be reversed. . . .

. . .[9]

---

29. *Payton* is applied in Kirk v. Louisiana, 536 U.S. 635 (2002) (per curiam). See Valdez v. McPheters, 172 F.3d 1220 (10th Cir.1999), holding that an arrest warrant is sufficient to authorize entry of a house in order to make an arrest only if the arresting officers reasonably believe that the person resides there and is within.

30. In Welsh v. Wisconsin, 466 U.S. 740 (1984) (6–2), the Supreme Court gave a partial answer to the question left open in *Payton*: What exigent circumstances justify a warrantless entry into a home to make an arrest? Police, having probable cause to believe that the defendant had been driving while drunk, arrested him in his home without a warrant. A

[9] Justice Blackmun wrote a concurring opinion. Justice White wrote a dissenting opinion, which Chief Justice Burger and Justice Rehnquist joined. Justice Rehnquist also wrote a dissenting opinion.

first offense of drunk driving was a noncriminal violation. The Court held that the Fourth Amendment prohibited an entry to arrest in those circumstances. It said that "it is difficult to conceive of a warrantless home arrest that would not be unreasonable under the Fourth Amendment when the underlying offense is extremely minor."

In view of the nature of the offense, the Court said, it was immaterial that evidence, the alcohol content of the defendant's blood, might imminently be lost. "[A]n important factor to be considered when determining whether any exigency exists is the gravity of the underlying offense for which the arrest is being made. Moreover, although no exigency is created simply because there is probable cause to believe that a serious crime has been committed . . . application of the exigent-circumstances exception in the context of a home entry should rarely be sanctioned when there is probable cause to believe that only a minor offense . . . has been committed." Id. at 753.

See United States v. Gray, 626 F.2d 102 (9th Cir.1980) (drug offenses; warrantless entry to arrest in exigent circumstances upheld); United States v. Campbell, 581 F.2d 22 (2d Cir.1978) (armed robbery; same). Compare United States v. Santana, 427 U.S. 38 (1976), p. 25 note 10 above.

See New York v. Harris, 495 U.S. 14 (1990), p. 81 below.

31. Premises of third persons. In the absence of an emergency or consent to the entry, the Fourth Amendment requires a *search* warrant to enter the home of a third person in order to arrest a person for whom the police have an arrest warrant. Steagald v. United States, 451 U.S. 204 (1981) (7–2).

> [W]hile an arrest warrant and a search warrant both serve to subject the probable cause determination of the police to judicial review, the interests protected by the two warrants differ. An arrest warrant is issued by a magistrate upon a showing that probable cause exists to believe that the subject of the warrant has committed an offense and thus the warrant primarily serves to protect an individual from an unreasonable seizure. A search warrant, in contrast, is issued upon a showing of probable cause to believe that the legitimate object of a search is located in a particular place and therefore safeguards an individual's interest in the privacy of his home and possessions against the unjustified intrusion of the police.
>
> . . . Because an arrest warrant authorizes the police to deprive a person of his liberty, it necessarily also authorizes a limited invasion of that person's privacy interest when it is necessary to arrest him in his home. This analysis, however, is plainly inapplicable when the police seek to use an arrest warrant as legal authority to enter the home of a third party to conduct a search. Such a warrant embodies no judicial determination whatsoever regarding the person whose home is to be searched. Because it does not authorize the police to deprive the third person of his liberty, it cannot embody any derivative authority to deprive this person of his interest in the privacy of his home. Such a

> deprivation must instead be based on an independent showing that a legitimate object of a search is located in the third party's home. We have consistently held however, that such a determination is the province of the magistrate, and not that of the police officer.

Id. at 212–13, 214–15 n.7.

In United States v. Underwood, 717 F.2d 482 (9th Cir.1983), the defendant was arrested in the home of another person, where he was an overnight guest. Having a warrant for his arrest and information that he was in the house, officers entered the house without a search warrant and arrested him. Upholding the arrest, the court said that *Payton* rather than *Steagald* controlled. It reasoned that the person arrested had no greater rights in the home of a third person than in his own, so that if an arrest warrant sufficed in the latter case it sufficed also in the former. *Steagald* was distinguished on the ground that there it was the third person whose home was entered who objected to the search. Accord United States v. Buckner, 717 F.2d 297 (6th Cir.1983).

32. Is Lewis v. United States, p. 304 below, consistent with *Payton*? See United States v. White, 660 F.2d 1178 (7th Cir.1981). Consider note 172, following the opinion in *Lewis*, p. 307 below.

"Arrest"

Rios v. United States

364 U.S. 253, 80 S.Ct. 1431, 4 L.Ed.2d 1688 (1960)

■ MR. JUSTICE STEWART delivered the opinion of the Court.

An indictment filed in the United States District Court for the Southern District of California charged the petitioner with unlawful receipt and concealment of narcotics in violation of 21 U.S.C. § 174. . . .

At about ten o'clock on the night of February 18, 1957, two Los Angeles police officers, dressed in plain clothes and riding in an unmarked car, observed a taxicab standing in a parking lot next to an apartment house at the corner of First and Flower Streets in Los Angeles. The neighborhood had a reputation for "narcotics activity." The officers saw the petitioner look up and down the street, walk across the lot, and get into the cab. Neither officer had ever before seen the petitioner, and neither of them had any idea of his identity. Except for the reputation of the neighborhood, neither officer had received information of any kind to suggest that someone might be engaged in criminal activity at that time and place. They were not searching for a participant in any previous crime. They were in possession of no arrest or search warrants.

The taxicab drove away, and the officers followed it in their car for a distance of about two miles through the city. At the intersection of First and State Streets the cab stopped for a traffic light. The two officers alighted from their car and approached on foot to opposite sides of the cab. One of the officers identified himself as a policeman. In the next minute there occurred a rapid succession of events. The cab door was opened; the petitioner dropped a recognizable package of narcotics to the floor of the vehicle; one of the officers grabbed the petitioner as he alighted from the cab; the other officer retrieved the package; and the first officer drew his revolver.

The precise chronology of all that happened is not clear in the record. In their original arrest report the police stated that the petitioner dropped the package only after one of the officers had opened the cab door. In testifying later, this officer said that he saw the defendant drop the package before the door of the cab was opened. The taxi driver gave a substantially different version of what occurred. He stated that one of the officers drew his revolver and "took hold of the defendant's arm while he was still in the cab."

. . .

[The package of narcotics was turned over to federal authorities and was admitted in evidence at the petitioner's trial.]

. . . The seizure can survive constitutional inhibition only upon a showing that the surrounding facts brought it within one of the exceptions to the rule that a search must rest upon a search warrant. . . . Here justification is primarily sought upon the claim that the search was an incident to a lawful arrest. Yet upon no possible view of the circumstances revealed in the testimony of the Los Angeles officers could it be said that there existed probable cause for an arrest at the time the officers decided to alight from their car and approach the taxi in which the petitioner was riding. . . . This the Government concedes.

If, therefore, the arrest occurred when the officers took their positions at the doors of the taxicab, then nothing that happened thereafter could make that arrest lawful, or justify a search as its incident. . . . But the Government argues that the policemen approached the standing taxi only for the purpose of routine interrogation, and that they had no intent to detain the petitioner beyond the momentary requirements of such a mission. If the petitioner thereafter voluntarily revealed the package of narcotics to the officers' view, a lawful arrest could then have been supported by their reasonable cause to believe that a felony was being committed in their presence. The validity of the search thus turns upon the narrow question of when the arrest occurred, and the answer to that question depends upon an evaluation of the conflicting testimony of those who were there that night.

The judgment is vacated, and the case is remanded to the District Court for further proceedings consistent with this opinion.

. . .[10]

---

192 F.Supp. 888 (S.D.Cal.1961)

■ HALL, CHIEF JUDGE.

. . .

Without extended discussion I now resolve such conflicts in the testimony as there are, and find the facts concerning the arrest and the seizure of the narcotics to be as follows:

(1) That Officers Beckman and Grace were lawfully making a routine surveillance of the taxicab and its occupants, and for the purpose of making a routine interrogation, they approached the taxicab but did not stop or detain it until after the commission of a crime by the defendant in the officers' sight and presence;

(2) That the taxicab in which the defendant was riding was not stopped by the officers;

(3) That it stopped for a traffic light at a brightly-lighted intersection;

(4) That while the taxicab was thus stopped, Officer Beckman approached the taxicab on the right side and Officer Grace approached it on the left;

(5) That Officer Beckman flashed his flashlight on his badge, exhibiting it to the driver and to the defendant who was sitting in the back seat, to identify himself, and he did identify himself orally as a police officer;

(6) That after, and almost simultaneous with, such identification, the officer saw the defendant, and the defendant did, voluntarily take from his pocket a rubber contraceptive of a light color which appeared to the officer to be filled with a light powder, and defendant voluntarily dropped it to the floor of the cab;

(7) That immediately thereafter the defendant and Officer Beckman simultaneously reached for the door of the taxicab, and both opened the door;

(8) That defendant alighted from the cab, and he was not pulled or forced out of it by either officer; and that thereupon, and not before, Officer Beckman announced that defendant was under arrest on suspicion of narcotics; and thereupon, and not before, the defendant was under arrest;

(9) That the time transpiring between the time Officer Beckman identified himself as above set forth and the time when defendant was out of the cab was about one minute;

[10] Justice Frankfurter wrote a dissenting opinion which Justice Clark, Justice Harlan, and Justice Whittaker joined. Justice Harlan wrote a memorandum which Justice Clark and Justice Whittaker joined.

(10) That within seconds after defendant got out of the taxicab, Officer Grace retrieved the contraceptive containing the heroin from the floor of the taxicab where the defendant had placed it by dropping it there;

(11) That by voluntarily dropping the package of narcotics to the floor and getting out of the cab, the defendant voluntarily gave up possession thereof;

(12) That Officer Beckman had had more than four years experience working the Narcotic Detail in Los Angeles, and had made over 400 arrests;

(13) That it was known to him that a common method of carrying heroin is to carry it in a rubber contraceptive;

(14) That under those circumstances and the "testimony of the officer's own senses," (Burks v. United States, 9 Cir., 287 F.2d 117, and cases therein cited), in light of his experience, when he saw defendant take a contraceptive from his pocket and drop it to the floor of the taxicab, and when he observed the nature of the object, he had reasonable cause to believe that contraceptive contained heroin, and reasonable cause to, in good faith, believe that defendant had committed a felony in his presence, viz.: violation of the State and Federal Penal Statutes relating to narcotics.

From the foregoing, I conclude as a matter of law, that the arrest was lawful, the search and seizure were reasonable and lawful, and if conducted by federal officers, the arrest and search and seizure would have been reasonable and lawful, and the arrest and search and seizure did not violate the defendant's immunity from unreasonable searches and seizures under the Fourth Amendment, and would not have done so if conducted by federal officers.

The motion of the defendant to suppress the evidence is denied. . . .

. . .

---

33. In a footnote in *Rios*, above, the Court noted: "The petitioner later broke free from the policeman's grasp and ran into an alley. There the officer apprehended him after shooting him in the back." 364 U.S. at 256 n.1.[11]

---

11. See also Abel v. United States, 362 U.S. 217 (1960), in which the Court carefully treated the seizure of evidence as an incident to the petitioner's arrest and mentioned only in passing the facts that following his arrest in New York he was "taken by airplane to a detention center for aliens in Texas" and kept there "for several weeks until arrested upon the charge of conspiracy to commit espionage for which he was brought to trial," id. at 225. The Court's studious attention to the precise moment when an arrest occurs and comparative disregard of other more substantial interferences with the person in some situations has led one commentator to observe that "by focusing judicial attention upon the search and seizure aspects of police procedures, the rule [requiring the exclusion of evidence obtained unlawfully] tends to create an impression that other forms of police

When a police officer believes that he has the authority to make an arrest and exercises (or, if he is mistaken, purports to exercise) his authority, there is ordinarily no difficulty in concluding that an "arrest" has been made. Difficulty arises when the officer intends not to arrest but to take action having some, but (necessarily, since the intention is lacking) not all, the characteristics of the paradigm. In such cases, one can try to draw the line between arrests and nonarrests more and more precisely, and then attribute to all the instances labeled "arrest" the significance and consequences of the paradigm. Or one can proceed by comparing the paradigm and a particular instance and noting the similarities and differences, and then noting what consequences are at stake and what it is about the paradigm that leads to that consequence and why, and finally deciding whether the particular instance sufficiently resembles the paradigm in the relevant respect. One may answer the question, "Is this an arrest?" with the question, "Why do you want to know?" or with the answer, equally incomplete, "It all depends," or "It is and it isn't." Once the difficulty is presented as raising the question, "Is this an arrest?" however, there may be pressure to avoid incomplete answers in favor of an answer which tends to construct a platonic ideal against which actual instances can be measured.

Even if one can assert with confidence that there is no ideal "arrest," and that "really" at stake is a complex of related acts, it is not clear that the second of the two approaches is the best one for the law. The law may have to deal with some "givens," such as language of special significance and historically fixed meaning, in this case the language of the Fourth Amendment. Also, the law is not the process or product of intellectual inquiry wherever it may lead; it is intended to help us to accomplish certain objectives. In this case, one might ask whether relatively simple rules reflected in simple, direct language (or even the appearance of simple rules) might not achieve the objectives of arrest practice better than a more subtle analysis.

---

34. In the following cases, when did the arrest occur?

(i)

At 5:30 A.M., on July 22, 1959, a uniformed police officer was walking his beat when he observed the defendant attempting to flag a taxicab. The defendant was carrying what appeared to be a sack and from it an electrical cord was dragging on the ground. The officer stopped the defendant, asked him where he was coming from and what his name was. The defendant replied that he was coming from a party and stated his name. Upon the request of the officer, the defendant

illegality, however seriously they may invade personal rights and liberty, are of lesser importance." Barrett, "Personal Rights, Property Rights, and the Fourth Amendment," 1960 Sup. Ct. Rev. 46, 55–56.

took from his wallet a selective service card which corroborated the defendant's oral identification. The officer testified that, "walking my beat all night long, I did not observe any party anywhere." However, at this point, no crime had been reported to the officer and he had observed none. No warrant for the arrest of the defendant was outstanding.

The officer then asked the defendant to accompany him to a police call box which was about one block away. When the defendant inquired whether he was under arrest, the officer replied, "No, you are just being detained." At the call box, the defendant seated himself on the record player contained in the sack (a pillow case) and the officer put in his call. He inquired whether there had been any reported housebreakings (up to that time he was not aware that a crime had been committed) and was told there had not been. He then requested the dispatch of a scout car to the area, when, by coincidence, a scout car appeared. At this point, the defendant fled from the scene, leaving the property behind. He was apprehended one week later. . . .

United States v. Mitchell, 179 F.Supp. 636, 637 (D.D.C.1959).

(ii)

On March 26, 1959, around 10 a.m., Officers Dorrell and Fesler went to a warehouse where defendant was employed. After speaking to the foreman, the latter called defendant from a box car which had been pulled up alongside of the building. Defendant walked over to the officers where he was shown their identification cards and told "[W]e are police officers. We would like to talk to you." Defendant then said "[J]ust a minute," turned and started to walk back toward the box car. Officer Dorrell took hold of defendant's arm and said, "[W]e would like to talk to you now." The officer did not pull or shove the defendant who then turned back around; the officer let go of his arm. Defendant then walked towards the door, together with the two officers, through the warehouse, outside under a roofed portion of a platform. Although Sergeant Fesler thought that as defendant turned around Officer Dorrell suggested to him that they go outside "to get away from the other people inside there," the officers did not "walk" him outside the warehouse, did not in any way physically touch him as they walked out together, did not tell him to go outside, and said nothing to him while walking before they reached the outside of the warehouse. Standing on the outside platform, Officer Dorrell asked him if he was using narcotics, which defendant denied; then if he was selling them, and defendant said "no." The officer then said to him, "[W]ell, then, you don't mind if we look through your pockets, do you?" and defendant answered "[N]o, go ahead and search me if you want to. I don't have anything on me." Whereupon Officer Dorrell searched him and found in defendant's right hand shirt pocket three capsules of heroin. Defendant told the officers the capsules contained heroin and he had bought them for

> his own use for $20; but denied having an outfit. They then told him he was under arrest and handcuffed him.

People v. Zavaleta, 6 Cal.Rptr. 166, 167 (Dist.Ct.App.1960). See People v. Haven, 381 P.2d 927 (Cal.1963) (*Zavaleta* disapproved).

(iii)

> Harry Hobson, a policeman of the Santa Barbara police force, was informed by a man named Pembleton that he had been the victim of a robbery and that the robber drove a " '49 or '50 Chevy two-door dropped down in the back end"; that the robber was about 5 feet 10 inches tall, weighed about 150 pounds, was dark complexioned and had dark curly hair. Pembleton told Officer Hobson that the man, later identified by Pembleton, struck him, knocked him down, struck him several times while he was on the ground, and that while he was in the latter position he felt his wallet being pulled out of his pocket and that the robber then ran away.
>
> The next day Officer Hobson, in ordinary street clothes, saw the defendant through a porch screen at an address on Haley Street in Santa Barbara and asked him to come out. When the defendant complied with the request Hobson then identified himself as being from the police department and asked the defendant if he would go to the police station with him and "be checked out on a robbery case." The defendant stated that he would do so and Hobson asked him if he would drive his own car. Defendant stated that he had no driver's license, but that Hobson could drive defendant's car and that he would go with him. Hobson then drove the defendant's automobile with defendant riding therein to the police station.
>
> At the police station parking lot Hobson asked the defendant if he could search defendant's car and defendant answered, "Yes, go ahead." Hobson opened the door on the driver's side of the automobile and upon looking under the front seat found a 14-inch billy club with a wooden handle and a leather thong attached thereto, used for wrapping around the wrist. Hobson then asked defendant, "What is this?" and defendant answered that it was a billy club and said further, "I was hoping you wouldn't find that." Hobson inquired as to how long it had been in the automobile and was told by the defendant, "It's been in there about five months." The defendant was then arrested. . . .

People v. Hood, 309 P.2d 135, 136 (Cal.Dist.Ct.App.1957).

Would your answer to the question when the arrest occurred in any of the cases be different if the issue to be decided was not whether evidence obtained pursuant to the arrest could be used against the defendant but rather (1) whether the defendant was entitled to use force to resist the arrest; (2) whether the police officer was entitled to use force to effect the arrest; (3) whether the police officer was liable for false arrest; (4) whether the police officer was required to file an arrest report; (5) whether the police officer was required to carry out a directive that all persons who are arrested shall be brought to the station house for fingerprinting and then brought before a magistrate?

California v. Hodari D.

499 U.S. 621, 111 S.Ct. 1547, 113 L.Ed.2d 690 (1991)

■ JUSTICE SCALIA delivered the opinion of the Court.

Late one evening in April 1988, Officers Brian McColgin and Jerry Pertoso were on patrol in a high-crime area of Oakland, California. They were dressed in street clothes but wearing jackets with "Police" embossed on both front and back. Their unmarked car proceeded west on Foothill Boulevard, and turned south onto 63rd Avenue. As they rounded the corner, they saw four or five youths huddled around a small red car parked at the curb. When the youths saw the officers' car approaching they apparently panicked, and took flight. The respondent here, Hodari D., and one companion ran west through an alley; the others fled south. The red car also headed south, at a high rate of speed.

The officers were suspicious and gave chase. McColgin remained in the car and continued south on 63rd Avenue; Pertoso left the car, ran back north along 63rd, then west on Foothill Boulevard, and turned south onto 62nd Avenue. Hodari, meanwhile, emerged from the alley onto 62nd and ran north. Looking behind as he ran, he did not turn and see Pertoso until the officer was almost upon him, whereupon he tossed away what appeared to be a small rock. A moment later, Pertoso tackled Hodari, handcuffed him, and radioed for assistance. Hodari was found to be carrying $130 in cash and a pager; and the rock he had discarded was found to be crack cocaine.

In the juvenile proceeding brought against him, Hodari moved to suppress the evidence relating to the cocaine. The court denied the motion without opinion. The California Court of Appeal reversed, holding that Hodari had been "seized" when he saw Officer Pertoso running towards him, that this seizure was unreasonable under the Fourth Amendment, and that the evidence of cocaine had to be suppressed as the fruit of that illegal seizure. The California Supreme Court denied the State's application for review. We granted certiorari. . . .

As this case comes to us, the only issue presented is whether, at the time he dropped the drugs, Hodari had been "seized" within the meaning of the Fourth Amendment.[12] If so, respondent argues, the drugs were the

12. California conceded below that Officer Pertoso did not have the "reasonable suspicion" required to justify stopping Hodari, see Terry v. Ohio, 392 U.S. 1 (1968). That it would be unreasonable to stop, for brief inquiry, young men who scatter in panic upon the mere sighting of the police is not self-evident, and arguably contradicts proverbial common sense. See Proverbs 28:1 ("The wicked flee when no man pursueth"). We do not decide that point here, but rely entirely upon the State's concession.

fruit of that seizure and the evidence concerning them was properly excluded. If not, the drugs were abandoned by Hodari and lawfully recovered by the police, and the evidence should have been admitted. (In addition, of course, Pertoso's seeing the rock of cocaine, at least if he recognized it as such, would provide reasonable suspicion for the unquestioned seizure that occurred when he tackled Hodari. . . .)

We have long understood that the Fourth Amendment's protection against "unreasonable . . . seizures" includes seizure of the person. . . . From the time of the founding to the present, the word "seizure" has meant a "taking possession," 2 N. Webster, An American Dictionary of the English Language 67 (1828). . . . For most purposes at common law, the word connoted not merely grasping, or applying physical force to, the animate or inanimate object in question, but actually bringing it within physical control. . . . To constitute an arrest, however—the quintessential "seizure of the person" under our Fourth Amendment jurisprudence—the mere grasping or application of physical force with lawful authority, whether or not it succeeded in subduing the arrestee, was sufficient. . . .

To say that an arrest is effected by the slightest application of physical force, despite the arrestee's escape, is not to say that for Fourth Amendment purposes there is a *continuing* arrest during the period of fugitivity. If, for example, Pertoso had laid his hands upon Hodari to arrest him, but Hodari had broken away and had *then* cast away the cocaine, it would hardly be realistic to say that that disclosure had been made during the course of an arrest. . . . The present case, however, is even one step further removed. It does not involve the application of any physical force; Hodari was untouched by Officer Pertoso at the time he discarded the cocaine. His defense relies instead upon the proposition that a seizure occurs "when the officer, by means of physical force *or show of authority*, has in some way restrained the liberty of a citizen." Terry v. Ohio, 392 U.S. 1, 19, n.16 (1968) (emphasis added). Hodari contends (and we accept as true for purposes of this decision) that Pertoso's pursuit qualified as a "show of authority" calling upon Hodari to halt. The narrow question before us is whether, with respect to a show of authority as with respect to application of physical force, a seizure occurs even though the subject does not yield. We hold that it does not.

The language of the Fourth Amendment, of course, cannot sustain respondent's contention. The word "seizure" readily bears the meaning of a laying on of hands or application of physical force to restrain movement, even when it is ultimately unsuccessful. ("She seized the purse-snatcher, but he broke out of her grasp.") It does not remotely apply, however, to the prospect of a policeman yelling "Stop, in the name of the law!" at a fleeing form that continues to flee. That is no seizure. Nor can the result respondent wishes to achieve be produced—indirectly, as it were—by suggesting that Pertoso's uncomplied-with show of authority was a common-law arrest, and then appealing to the principle that all common-law arrests are seizures. An arrest requires *either* physical force (as described above) or, where that is absent, *submission* to the assertion of authority. . . .

We do not think it desirable, even as a policy matter, to stretch the Fourth Amendment beyond its words and beyond the meaning of arrest, as respondent urges. Street pursuits always place the public at some risk, and compliance with police orders to stop should therefore be encouraged. Only a few of those orders, we must presume, will be without adequate basis, and since the addressee has no ready means of identifying the deficient ones it almost invariably is the responsible course to comply. Unlawful orders will not be deterred, moreover, by sanctioning through the exclusionary rule those of them that are *not* obeyed. Since policemen do not command "Stop!" expecting to be ignored, or give chase hoping to be outrun, it fully suffices to apply the deterrent to their genuine, successful seizures.

Respondent contends that his position is sustained by the so-called *Mendenhall test*, formulated by Justice Stewart's opinion in United States v. Mendenhall, 446 U.S. 544, 554 (1980), and adopted by the Court in later cases . . . : "A person has been 'seized' within the meaning of the Fourth Amendment only if, in view of all the circumstances surrounding the incident, a reasonable person would have believed that he was not free to leave." 446 U.S., at 554. . . . In seeking to rely upon that test here, respondent fails to read it carefully. It says that a person has been seized "only if," not that he has been seized "whenever"; it states a *necessary*, but not a *sufficient* condition for seizure—or, more precisely, for seizure effected through a "show of authority." *Mendenhall* establishes that the test for existence of a "show of authority" is an objective one: not whether the citizen perceived that he was being ordered to restrict his movement, but whether the officer's words and actions would have conveyed that to a reasonable person. Application of this objective test was the basis for our decision in the other case principally relied upon by respondent, [Michigan v.] *Chesternut*, [486 U.S. 567 (1988)], where we concluded that the police cruiser's slow following of the defendant did not convey the message that he was not free to disregard the police and go about his business. We did not address in *Chesternut*, however, the question whether, if the *Mendenhall* test was met—if the message that the defendant was not free to leave *had* been conveyed—a Fourth Amendment seizure would have occurred. . . .

. . .

In sum, assuming that Pertoso's pursuit in the present case constituted a "show of authority" enjoining Hodari to halt, since Hodari did not comply with that injunction he was not seized until he was tackled. The cocaine abandoned while he was running was in this case not the fruit of a seizure, and his motion to exclude evidence of it was properly denied. . . .

. . .[13]

---

[13] Justice Stevens wrote a dissenting opinion, which Justice Marshall joined.

35. Applying Terry v. Ohio, p. 100 below, the Court held that a person's "unprovoked flight" from approaching police officers in an area known for narcotics activity furnished reasonable suspicion justifying a *Terry* stop. Illinois v. Wardlow, 528 U.S. 119, 124 (2000) (5–4).

36. Rejecting the analysis of the Court in *Hodari D.*, the Supreme Court of New Jersey observed: "We are not satisfied as the Supreme Court was . . . that the biblical observation that '[t]he wicked flee when no man pursueth' " [p. 58 n.12 above] "is a satisfactory explanation of why a young man in a contemporary urban setting might run at the sight of the police." State v. Tucker, 642 A.2d 401, 407 (N.J.1994).

In State v. Young, 957 P.2d 681 (Wash.1998), the Supreme Court of Washington rejected *Hodari D.* and said that under state law the test was not whether a person has actually been seized but whether a reasonable person would have felt that he was free to leave. Other state cases following or rejecting *Hodari D.* are cited.

The Manner of Arrest

Tennessee v. Garner

471 U.S. 1, 105 S.Ct. 1694, 85 L.Ed.2d 1 (1985)

■ JUSTICE WHITE delivered the opinion of the Court.

This case requires us to determine the constitutionality of the use of deadly force to prevent the escape of an apparently unarmed suspected felon. We conclude that such force may not be used unless it is necessary to prevent the escape and the officer has probable cause to believe that the suspect poses a significant threat of death or serious physical injury to the officer or others.

I

At about 10:45 p.m. on October 3, 1974, Memphis Police Officers Elton Hymon and Leslie Wright were dispatched to answer a "prowler inside call." Upon arriving at the scene they saw a woman standing on her porch and gesturing toward the adjacent house. She told them she had heard glass breaking and that "they" or "someone" was breaking in next door. While Wright radioed the dispatcher to say that they were on the scene, Hymon went behind the house. He heard a door slam and saw someone run across the backyard. The fleeing suspect, who was appellee-respondent's decedent, Edward Garner, stopped at a 6-feet-high chain link fence at the edge of the yard. With the aid of a flashlight, Hymon was able to see Garner's face and hands. He saw no sign of a weapon, and, though not certain, was "reasonably sure" and "figured" that Garner was unarmed.

App. 41, 56; Record 219. He thought Garner was 17 or 18 years old and about 5′5″ or 5′7″ tall. While Garner was crouched at the base of the fence, Hymon called out "police, halt" and took a few steps toward him. Garner then began to climb over the fence. Convinced that if Garner made it over the fence he would elude capture, Hymon shot him. The bullet hit Garner in the back of the head. Garner was taken by ambulance to a hospital, where he died on the operating table. Ten dollars and a purse taken from the house were found on his body.

In using deadly force to prevent the escape, Hymon was acting under the authority of a Tennessee statute and pursuant to Police Department policy. The statute provides that "[i]f, after notice of the intention to arrest the defendant, he either flee or forcibly resist, the officer may use all the necessary means to effect the arrest." Tenn.Code Ann. § 40–7–108 (1982).[14] The Department policy was slightly more restrictive than the statute, but still allowed the use of deadly force in cases of burglary. . . . The incident was reviewed by the Memphis Police Firearms Review Board and presented to a grand jury. Neither took any action. . . .

Garner's father then brought this action in the Federal District Court for the Western District of Tennessee, seeking damages under 42 U.S.C. § 1983 for asserted violations of Garner's constitutional rights. The complaint . . . named as defendants Officer Hymon, the Police Department, its Director, and the Mayor and city of Memphis. After a 3-day bench trial, the District Court entered judgment for all defendants. . . . It . . . concluded that Hymon's actions were authorized by the Tennessee statute, which in turn was constitutional. Hymon had employed the only reasonable and practicable means of preventing Garner's escape. Garner had "recklessly and heedlessly attempted to vault over the fence to escape, thereby assuming the risk of being fired upon." App. to Pet. for Cert. A10.

. . .

The Court of Appeals reversed and remanded. 710 F.2d 240 (1983). It reasoned that the killing of a fleeing suspect is a "seizure" under the Fourth Amendment, and is therefore constitutional only if "reasonable." The Tennessee statute failed as applied to this case because it did not adequately limit the use of deadly force by distinguishing between felonies of different magnitudes—"the facts, as found, did not justify the use of deadly force under the Fourth Amendment." Id., at 246. Officers cannot resort to deadly force unless they "have probable cause . . . to believe that the suspect [has committed a felony and] poses a threat to the safety of the officers or a danger to the community if left at large." Ibid.

The State of Tennessee, which had intervened to defend the statute, see 28 U.S.C. § 2403(b), appealed to this Court. The city filed a petition for certiorari. We noted probable jurisdiction in the appeal and granted the petition. . . .

14. Although the statute does not say so explicitly, Tennessee law forbids the use of deadly force in the arrest of a misdemeanant. See Johnson v. State, 114 S.W.2d 819 (1938).

II

Whenever an officer restrains the freedom of a person to walk away, he has seized that person. . . . While it is not always clear just when minimal police interference becomes a seizure . . . there can be no question that apprehension by the use of deadly force is a seizure subject to the reasonableness requirement of the Fourth Amendment.

A

A police officer may arrest a person if he has probable cause to believe that person committed a crime. . . . Petitioners and appellant argue that if this requirement is satisfied the Fourth Amendment has nothing to say about how that seizure is made. This submission ignores the many cases in which this Court, by balancing the extent of the intrusion against the need for it, has examined the reasonableness of the manner in which a search or seizure is conducted. To determine the constitutionality of a seizure "[w]e must balance the nature and quality of the intrusion on the individual's Fourth Amendment interests against the importance of the governmental interests alleged to justify the intrusion." United States v. Place, 462 U.S. 696, 703 (1983). . . . Because one of the factors is the extent of the intrusion, it is plain that reasonableness depends on not only when a seizure is made, but also how it is carried out. . . .

. . .

B

The . . . balancing process . . . demonstrates that, notwithstanding probable cause to seize a suspect, an officer may not always do so by killing him. The intrusiveness of a seizure by means of deadly force is unmatched. The suspect's fundamental interest in his own life need not be elaborated upon. The use of deadly force also frustrates the interest of the individual, and of society, in judicial determination of guilt and punishment. Against these interests are ranged governmental interests in effective law enforcement. It is argued that overall violence will be reduced by encouraging the peaceful submission of suspects who know that they may be shot if they flee. Effectiveness in making arrests requires the resort to deadly force, or at least the meaningful threat thereof. "Being able to arrest such individuals is a condition precedent to the state's entire system of law enforcement." Brief for Petitioners 14.

Without in any way disparaging the importance of these goals, we are not convinced that the use of deadly force is a sufficiently productive means of accomplishing them to justify the killing of nonviolent suspects. . . . The use of deadly force is a self-defeating way of apprehending a suspect and so setting the criminal justice mechanism in motion. If successful, it guarantees that that mechanism will not be set in motion. And while the meaningful threat of deadly force might be thought to lead to the arrest of more live suspects by discouraging escape attempts, the presently available evidence does not support this thesis. The fact is that a majority of police departments in this country have forbidden the use of deadly force against nonviolent suspects. . . . If those charged with the enforcement of the criminal law have abjured the use of deadly force in arresting nondangerous felons, there is a substantial basis for doubting that the use of such force is an essential attribute of the arrest power in all felony cases. . . . Petitioners and appellant have not persuaded us that shooting nondangerous fleeing suspects is so vital as to outweigh the suspect's interest in his own life.

The use of deadly force to prevent the escape of all felony suspects, whatever the circumstances, is constitutionally unreasonable. It is not better that all felony suspects die than that they escape. Where the suspect poses no immediate threat to the officer and no threat to others, the harm resulting from failing to apprehend him does not justify the use of deadly force to do so. It is no doubt unfortunate when a suspect who is in sight escapes, but the fact that the police arrive a little late or are a little slower afoot does not always justify killing the suspect. A police officer may not seize an unarmed, nondangerous suspect by shooting him dead. The Tennessee statute is unconstitutional insofar as it authorizes the use of deadly force against such fleeing suspects.

It is not, however, unconstitutional on its face. Where the officer has probable cause to believe that the suspect poses a threat of serious physical harm, either to the officer or to others, it is not constitutionally unreasonable to prevent escape by using deadly force. Thus, if the suspect threatens the officer with a weapon or there is probable cause to believe that he has committed a crime involving the infliction or threatened infliction of serious physical harm, deadly force may be used if necessary to prevent escape, and if, where feasible, some warning has been given. As applied in such circumstances, the Tennessee statute would pass constitutional muster.

III

A

It is insisted that the Fourth Amendment must be construed in light of the common-law rule, which allowed the use of whatever force was necessary to effect the arrest of a fleeing felon, though not a misdemeanant. . . . Most American jurisdictions also imposed a flat prohibition against the use of deadly force to stop a fleeing misdemeanant, coupled with a general privilege to use such force to stop a fleeing felon. . . .

The State and city argue that because this was the prevailing rule at the time of the adoption of the Fourth Amendment and for some time thereafter, and is still in force in some States, use of deadly force against a fleeing felon must be "reasonable." It is true that this Court has often looked to the common law in evaluating the reasonableness, for Fourth Amendment purposes, of police activity. . . . On the other hand, it "has not simply frozen into constitutional law those law enforcement practices that existed at the time of the Fourth Amendment's passage." Payton v. New York, 445 U.S. 573, 591, n.33 (1980). Because of sweeping change in the legal and technological context, reliance on the common-law rule in this case would be a mistaken literalism that ignores the purposes of a historical inquiry.

B

It has been pointed out many times that the common-law rule is best understood in light of the fact that it arose at a time when virtually all felonies were punishable by death. . . . Courts have also justified the common-law rule by emphasizing the relative dangerousness of felons. . . .

Neither of these justifications makes sense today. Almost all crimes formerly punishable by death no longer are or can be. . . . And while in earlier times "the gulf between the felonies and the minor offences was broad and deep," 2 [F.] Pollock & [F.] Maitland [The History of English Law (2d ed. 1909)] 467, n.3 . . . today the distinction is minor and often arbitrary. Many crimes classified as misdemeanors, or nonexistent, at common law are now felonies. . . . These changes have undermined the concept, which was questionable to begin with, that use of deadly force against a fleeing felon is merely a speedier execution of someone who has already forfeited his life. They have also made the assumption that a "felon" is more dangerous than a misdemeanant untenable. Indeed, numerous misdemeanors involve conduct more dangerous than many felonies.

There is an additional reason why the common-law rule cannot be directly translated to the present day. The common-law rule developed at a time when weapons were rudimentary. Deadly force could be inflicted almost solely in a hand-to-hand struggle during which, necessarily, the safety of the arresting officer was at risk. Handguns were not carried by police officers until the latter half of the last century. . . . Only then did it become possible to use deadly force from a distance as a means of apprehension. As a practical matter, the use of deadly force under the standard articulation of the common-law rule has an altogether different meaning—and harsher consequences—now than in past centuries. . . .

One other aspect of the common-law rule bears emphasis. It forbids the use of deadly force to apprehend a misdemeanant, condemning such action as disproportionately severe. . . .

In short, though the common law pedigree of Tennessee's rule is pure on its face, changes in the legal and technological context mean the rule is distorted almost beyond recognition when literally applied.

C

In evaluating the reasonableness of police procedures under the Fourth Amendment, we have also looked to prevailing rules in individual jurisdictions. . . . The rules in the States are varied. . . .

It cannot be said that there is a constant or overwhelming trend away from the common-law rule. . . . Nonetheless, the long-term movement has been away from the rule that deadly force may be used against any fleeing felon, and that remains the rule in less than half the States.

This trend is more evident and impressive when viewed in light of the policies adopted by the police departments themselves. Overwhelmingly, these are more restrictive than the common-law rule. . . . A 1974 study reported that the police department regulations in a majority of the large cities of the United States allowed the firing of a weapon only when a felon presented a threat of death or serious bodily harm. . . . Overall, only 7.5% of departmental and municipal policies explicitly permit the use of deadly force against any felon; 86.8% explicitly do not. . . . In light of the rules adopted by those who must actually administer them, the older and fading common-law view is a dubious indicium of the constitutionality of the Tennessee statute now before us.

D

Actual departmental policies are important for an additional reason. We would hesitate to declare a police practice of long standing "unreasonable" if doing so would severely hamper effective law enforcement. But the indications are to the contrary. There has been no suggestion that crime has worsened in any way in jurisdictions that have adopted, by legislation or departmental policy, rules similar to that announced today. . . . [T]he obvious state interests in apprehension are not sufficiently served to warrant the use of lethal weapons against all fleeing felons. . . .

Nor do we agree with petitioners and appellant that the rule we have adopted requires the police to make impossible, split-second evaluations of unknowable facts. . . . We do not deny the practical difficulties of attempting to assess the suspect's dangerousness. However, similarly difficult judgments must be made by the police in equally uncertain circumstances. . . . Nor is there any indication that in States that allow the use of deadly force only against dangerous suspects . . . the standard has been difficult to apply or has led to a rash of litigation involving inappropriate second-guessing of police officers' split-second decisions. Moreover, the highly technical felony/misdemeanor distinction is equally, if not more, difficult to apply in the field. An officer is in no position to know, for example, the precise value of property stolen, or whether the crime was a first or second offense. Finally, as noted above, this claim must be viewed with suspicion in light of the similar self-imposed limitations of so many police departments.

IV

. . .

[T]he Court of Appeals . . . held that "the facts, as found, did not justify the use of deadly force." 710 F.2d, at 246. We agree. Officer Hymon could not reasonably have believed that Garner—young, slight, and unarmed—posed any threat. Indeed, Hymon never attempted to justify his actions on any basis other than the need to prevent an escape. The District Court stated in passing that "[t]he facts of this case did not indicate to Officer Hymon that Garner was 'nondangerous.'" App. to Pet. for Cert. A34. This conclusion is not explained, and seems to be based solely on the fact that Garner had broken into a house at night. However, the fact that Garner was a suspected burglar could not, without regard to the other circumstances, automatically justify the use of deadly force. Hymon did not have probable cause to believe that Garner, whom he correctly believed to be unarmed, posed any physical danger to himself or others.

. . . While we agree that burglary is a serious crime, we cannot agree that it is so dangerous as automatically to justify the use of deadly force. The FBI classifies burglary as a "property" rather than a "violent" crime. . . . Although the armed burglar would present a different situation, the fact that an unarmed suspect has broken into a dwelling at night does not automatically mean he is physically dangerous. This case demonstrates as much. . . . In fact, the available statistics demonstrate that burglaries only rarely involve physical violence. During the 10-year period from 1973–1982, only 3.8% of all burglaries involved violent crime. . . .

V

. . . We hold that the statute is invalid insofar as it purported to give Hymon the authority to act as he did. . . .

. . .[15]

---

37. *Garner* was applied in Pruitt v. City of Montgomery, Alabama, 771 F.2d 1475 (11th Cir.1985) (use of deadly force not justified). Compare Ryder v. City of Topeka, 814 F.2d 1412, 1419 n.16 (10th Cir.1987) (use of deadly force justified), in which the court rejected the suggestion in *Pruitt* that an officer has probable cause to believe a suspect poses a serious threat to his person *only* if the suspect displays a weapon. See generally City of Los Angeles v. Lyons, 461 U.S. 95 (1983) (5–4), in which the defendant sought an injunction restraining Los Angeles police officers from using a "chokehold" on arrested persons who do not appear to be threatening the immediate use of deadly force. A majority of the Court concluded that the federal courts lacked jurisdiction to grant the injunction in the circumstances of the case.

A police officer's high-speed automobile chase to apprehend a suspected offender which results in the latter's death does not violate his substantive right not to be deprived of life without due process, even if the officer's pursuit is deliberately or recklessly indifferent to life. Such a claim would be substantiated only if the officer had "a purpose to cause harm unrelated to the legitimate object of arrest." County of Sacramento v. Lewis, 523 U.S. 833 (1998).

---

[15] Justice O'Connor wrote a dissenting opinion, which Chief Justice Burger and Justice Rehnquist joined.

Wilson v. Arkansas

514 U.S. 927, 115 S.Ct. 1914, 131 L.Ed.2d 976 (1995)

■ JUSTICE THOMAS delivered the opinion of the Court.

At the time of the framing, the common law of search and seizure recognized a law enforcement officer's authority to break open the doors of a dwelling, but generally indicated that he first ought to announce his presence and authority. In this case, we hold that this common-law "knock and announce" principle forms a part of the reasonableness inquiry under the Fourth Amendment.

I

During November and December 1992, petitioner Sharlene Wilson made a series of narcotics sales to an informant acting at the direction of the Arkansas State Police. In late November, the informant purchased marijuana and methamphetamine at the home that petitioner shared with Bryson Jacobs. On December 30, the informant telephoned petitioner at her home and arranged to meet her at a local store to buy some marijuana. According to testimony presented below, petitioner produced a semiautomatic pistol at this meeting and waved it in the informant's face, threatening to kill her if she turned out to be working for the police. Petitioner then sold the informant a bag of marijuana.

The next day, police officers applied for and obtained warrants to search petitioner's home and to arrest both petitioner and Jacobs. Affidavits filed in support of the warrants set forth the details of the narcotics transactions and stated that Jacobs had previously been convicted of arson and firebombing. The search was conducted later that afternoon. Police officers found the main door to petitioner's home open. While opening an unlocked screen door and entering the residence, they identified themselves as police officers and stated that they had a warrant. Once inside the home, the officers seized marijuana, methamphetamine, valium, narcotics paraphernalia, a gun, and ammunition. They also found petitioner in the bathroom, flushing marijuana down the toilet. Petitioner and Jacobs were arrested and charged with delivery of marijuana, delivery of methamphetamine, possession of drug paraphernalia, and possession of marijuana.

Before trial, petitioner filed a motion to suppress the evidence seized during the search. Petitioner asserted that the search was invalid on various grounds, including that the officers had failed to "knock and announce" before entering her home. The trial court summarily denied the suppression motion. After a jury trial, petitioner was convicted of all charges and sentenced to 32 years in prison.

The Arkansas Supreme Court affirmed petitioner's conviction on appeal. . . .

We granted certiorari to resolve the conflict among the lower courts as to whether the common-law knock-and-announce principle forms a part of the Fourth Amendment reasonableness inquiry. . . . We hold that it does, and accordingly reverse and remand.

II

The Fourth Amendment to the Constitution protects "[t]he right of the people to be secure in their persons, houses, papers, and effects, against unreasonable searches and seizures." In evaluating the scope of this right, we have looked to the traditional protections against unreasonable searches and seizures afforded by the common law at the time of the framing. . . . "Although the underlying command of the Fourth Amendment is always that searches and seizures be reasonable," New Jersey v. T.L.O., 469 U.S. 325, 337 (1985), our effort to give content to this term may be guided by the meaning ascribed to it by the Framers of the Amendment. An examination of the common law of search and seizure leaves no doubt that the reasonableness of a search of a dwelling may depend in part on whether law enforcement officers announced their presence and authority prior to entering.

Although the common law generally protected a man's house as "his castle of defence and asylum," 3 W. Blackstone, Commentaries *288 (hereinafter Blackstone), common-law courts long have held that "when the King is party, the sheriff (if the doors be not open) may break the party's house, either to arrest him, or to do other execution of the K[ing]'s process, if otherwise he cannot enter." Semayne's Case, 5 Co.Rep. 91a, 91b, 77 Eng.Rep. 194, 195 (K.B. 1603). To this rule, however, common-law courts appended an important qualification:

> But before he breaks it, he ought to signify the cause of his coming, and to make request to open doors . . . for the law without a default in the owner abhors the destruction or breaking of any house (which is for the habitation and safety of man) by which great damage and inconvenience might ensue to the party, when no default is in him; for perhaps he did not know of the process, of which, if he had notice, it is to be presumed that he would obey it. . . .

Ibid., 77 Eng.Rep., at 195–96.

. . .

Several prominent founding-era commentators agreed on this basic principle. . . .

The common-law knock-and-announce principle was woven quickly into the fabric of early American law. Most of the States that ratified the Fourth Amendment had enacted constitutional provisions or statutes generally incorporating English common law . . . and a few States had enacted statutes specifically embracing the common-law view that the breaking of the door of a dwelling was permitted once admittance was refused. . . . Early American courts similarly embraced the common-law knock-and-announce principle. . . .

Our own cases have acknowledged that the common-law principle of announcement is "embedded in Anglo–American law," Miller v. United States, 357 U.S. 301, 313 (1958), but we have never squarely held that this principle is an element of the reasonableness inquiry under the Fourth Amendment. We now so hold. Given the longstanding common-law endorsement of the practice of announcement, we have little doubt that the Framers of the Fourth Amendment thought that the method of an officer's entry into a dwelling was among the factors to be considered in assessing the reasonableness of a search or seizure. Contrary to the decision below, we hold that in some circumstances an officer's unannounced entry into a home might be unreasonable under the Fourth Amendment.

This is not to say, of course, that every entry must be preceded by an announcement. The Fourth Amendment's flexible requirement of reasonableness should not be read to mandate a rigid rule of announcement that ignores countervailing law enforcement interests. As even petitioner concedes, the common-law principle of announcement was never stated as an inflexible rule requiring announcement under all circumstances. . . .

. . .

Thus, because the common-law rule was justified in part by the belief that announcement generally would avoid "the destruction or breaking of any house . . . by which great damage and inconvenience might ensue," Semayne's Case, supra, at 91b, 77 Eng.Rep., at 196, courts acknowledged that the presumption in favor of announcement would yield under circumstances presenting a threat of physical violence. . . . Similarly, courts held that an officer may dispense with announcement in cases where a prisoner escapes from him and retreats to his dwelling. . . . Proof of "demand and refusal" was deemed unnecessary in such cases because it would be a "senseless ceremony" to require an officer in pursuit of a recently escaped arrestee to make an announcement prior to breaking the door to retake him. . . . Finally, courts have indicated that unannounced entry may be justified where police officers have reason to believe that evidence would likely be destroyed if advance notice were given. . . .

We need not attempt a comprehensive catalog of the relevant countervailing factors here. For now, we leave to the lower courts the task of determining the circumstances under which an unannounced entry is reasonable under the Fourth Amendment. We simply hold that although a search or seizure of a dwelling might be constitutionally defective if police officers enter without prior announcement, law enforcement interests may also establish the reasonableness of an unannounced entry.

III

Respondent contends that the judgment below should be affirmed because the unannounced entry in this case was justified for two reasons. First, respondent argues that police officers reasonably believed that a prior announcement would have placed them in peril, given their knowledge that petitioner had threatened a government informant with a semiautomatic weapon and that Mr. Jacobs had previously been convicted of arson and firebombing. Second, respondent suggests that prior announcement would have produced an unreasonable risk that petitioner would destroy easily disposable narcotics evidence.

These considerations may well provide the necessary justification for the unannounced entry in this case. Because the Arkansas Supreme Court did not address their sufficiency, however, we remand to allow the state courts to make any necessary findings of fact and to make the determination of reasonableness in the first instance. . . .

. . .

---

38. Applying Wilson v. Arkansas, in Richards v. Wisconsin, 520 U.S. 385 (1997), the Court held that the Fourth Amendment does not permit a blanket exception to the knock-and-announce rule for a category of crimes (narcotics felonies). The Court concluded nevertheless that a no-knock entry was justified by the particular circumstances. See Ingram v. City of Columbus, 185 F.3d 579 (6th Cir.1999) (circumstances did not justify exception to knock-and-announce rule).

39. In United States v. Banks, 540 U.S. ___ (2003), the Court held that a 15–20 second wait after the police knocked and announced their authority was long enough to permit a forcible entry, in the circumstances of the case. The police had gone to the defendant's apartment with a warrant to search for drugs. After waiting 15–20 seconds, they broke open the front door. The defendant testified that he was in the shower and had heard nothing before the door was broken open. The Court said that the critical inquiry was whether the police had reason to fear the destruction of evidence on the basis of what they knew, not whether the person inside had in fact heard them or whether there was time for him to get to the door. Since someone wanting to dispose of drugs could do so by flushing them down the toilet or sink within as little as 15–20 seconds, the police acted reasonably in not waiting longer.

40. "An unannounced intrusion into a dwelling . . . is no less an unannounced intrusion whether officers break down a door, force open a chain lock or a partially open door, open a locked door by use of a passkey, or . . . open a closed but unlocked door." Sabbath v. United States, 391 U.S. 585, 590 (1968). In United States v. Beale, 445 F.2d 977 (5th Cir.1971), the court observed that *Sabbath* applied only where at least minimal force was used "in the sense of physical action by the officer to remove the barrier that prevents his entry," and "left undisturbed the existent distinction between entry where some force is employed and entry where force is not an element at all." On that basis, the court concluded that the requirement of notice of authority and purpose did not apply to an entry by deception. Accord, e.g., United States v. Raines, 536 F.2d 796, 800 (8th Cir.1976): "A police entry into a private home by invitation without force, though the invitation be obtained by ruse, is not a breaking and does not invoke the common law requirement of prior announcement of authority and purpose, codified in § 3109." See United States v. Lopez, 475 F.2d 537 (7th Cir.1973), in which federal agents waited outside the defendant's motel room until the door was opened and immediately entered to arrest the occupants.

We raised the hue and cry and chased the Shire, but he seems to have disappeared into thin eyre.

41. Police officials were admitted to the defendant's home by his young son; they told him they were gas inspectors and asked to wait for his father's return. About twenty minutes later the defendant came home and was arrested on the back porch. The defendant was believed to have participated in an armed robbery in the course of which a policeman had been shot; news that an accomplice had been arrested a short time before had been broadcast on the radio. Was the arrest lawful? See People v. Macias, 234 N.E.2d 783 (Ill.1968).

42. If there would have been no necessity to break and enter in order to arrest but for the police officers' deliberate failure to arrest the defendant before he entered his home, does the necessity justify the entry? Does the reason why the police failed to arrest earlier make a difference? See McKnight v. United States, 183 F.2d 977 (D.C.Cir.1950), with which compare United States v. Drake, 655 F.2d 1025 (10th Cir.1981). See note 8, p. 20 above.

43. Is the requirement of notice applicable to an entry for a purpose other than to make an arrest?

> [T]he police officer on radio patrol duty received a "radio run" to the effect that there was a "disorderly man at 404 West 115th Street." He proceeded to a rooming (converted apartment) house at this address where he was met by the night manager. The officer heard "shouting, screaming, clapping of hands" and the manager stated "that that had been going on for several evenings."

> The manager then directed the police officer and a fellow officer to a fifth floor "apartment," evidently a division of the converted apartment house. The noise was coming from this apartment. As the officer knocked on the door, the shouting stopped, and a male voice inside said three times: "Wait a minute. Wait a minute, I'm not dressed." After a minute's wait, the officer directed the manager to open the door with his passkey. Upon opening the door they saw defendant standing in the middle of the room, stripped to the waist, and wet with perspiration. He was holding "a syringe, an eye dropper, with a needle on the end of it, in his right hand." When defendant saw the three men, he threw the contraband under a bed and the officer placed him under arrest.

People v. Gallmon, 227 N.E.2d 284, 285–86 (N.Y.1967). If "the officer did not come to the premises or to the apartment to make an arrest . . . [but] had responded to a call from the manager of a rooming house to investigate an unusual, noisy disturbance," id. at 286, was the arrest lawful?

44. Federal law and state law. To what extent can the states determine for themselves when and how an arrest should be made? In Ker v. California, 374 U.S. 23, 31 (1963), the Supreme Court said that the Constitution required "no total obliteration of state laws relating to arrests and searches in favor of federal law."

"This Court's long-established recognition that standards of reasonableness under the Fourth Amendment are not susceptible of Procrustean application is carried forward when that Amendment's proscriptions are enforced against the States through the Fourteenth Amendment. . . . The States are not . . . precluded from developing workable rules governing arrests, searches and seizures to meet 'the practical demands of effective criminal investigation and law enforcement' in the States, provided that those rules do not violate the constitutional proscription of unreasonable searches and seizures and the concomitant command that evidence so seized is inadmissible against one who has standing to complain. . . . Such a standard implies no derogation of uniformity in applying federal constitutional guarantees but is only a recognition that conditions and circumstances vary just as do investigative and enforcement techniques." Id. at 33–34.

While a state may not allow an arrest based on less than probable cause, it may require more. The usual rule, derived from the common law, is that a police officer can arrest a person without a warrant if he has reasonable grounds (in effect, probable cause) to believe that the person has committed a felony or if the person has committed a misdemeanor in the officer's presence. In the absence of applicable federal law, the law of the state in which an arrest occurs determines the validity of the arrest for federal law. United States v. Di Re, 332 U.S. 581, 589 (1948). See, e.g., United States v. Thompson, 356 F.2d 216, 223–24 (2d Cir.1965); cf. Sabbath v. United States, 380 F.2d 108 (9th Cir.1967) (method of entry to arrest by federal officers for federal offense is a matter of federal law), rev'd on other grounds, 391 U.S. 585 (1968). See also United States v. Mahoney, 712 F.2d 956 (5th Cir.1983) (application, in federal court, of good-faith exception to exclusionary rule to evidence obtained by state officers is a matter of federal law).

If evidence is obtained pursuant to an arrest that is unlawful under state law but not unconstitutional—i.e., an arrest that the state could constitutionally have authorized—is the Fourth Amendment's prohibition against *unreasonable* searches and seizures violated, so that the rule requiring exclusion of evidence obtained in violation of the defendant's constitutional rights is applicable? If state law determines the lawfulness of the arrest, does a violation of the law make the arrest constitutionally unreasonable? In *Di Re*, above, the Court indicated that, at least in a federal court, the answer is that it does. See United States v. Mota, 982 F.2d 1384 (9th Cir.1993) (*Di Re* applied). Some other cases, however, have held otherwise. See, e.g., United States v. Walker, 960 F.2d 409 (5th Cir.1992).

Cases generally hold that a nonconstitutional violation of a state law affecting some matter other than the amount of evidence needed to make an arrest does not call for application of the *Di Re* principle. E.g., United States v. Hall, 543 F.2d 1229 (9th Cir.1976) (arrest based on wiretap lawful under federal law but not state law, which would have required suppression of evidence); United States v. Dudek, 530 F.2d 684 (6th Cir.1976) (failure to comply with state requirement of prompt return and verified inventory following search).

See State v. Bridges, 925 P.2d 357 (1996). In that case, Hawaii police obtained the cooperation of California police in the investigation of a drug conspiracy, because some of the events involved in the conspiracy occurred in California. The California police used audio and video recording equipment to obtain evidence against the defendants that was relevant to their prosecution in Hawaii. The equipment did not violate the federal Constitution or the law of California but would have violated the law of Hawaii if it had occurred there. In an opinion thoroughly discussing the reasons for the exclusion of illegally obtained evidence and citing cases in other jurisdictions, the court held that the evidence should not be excluded in the Hawaii prosecution.

Consequences of an Unlawful Arrest

Ker v. Illinois

119 U.S. 436, 7 S.Ct. 225, 30 L.Ed. 421 (1886)

[Ker was convicted of larceny in the Illinois courts. He alleged that he had been in Lima, Peru and that a warrant for his extradition had been issued, but that, without presenting the warrant, the person who was directed to receive him into custody from the Peruvian authorities had forcibly arrested him and transported him to Illinois.]

■ MR. JUSTICE MILLER delivered the opinion of the court.

. . .

. . . It is contended . . . that the proceedings in the arrest in Peru, and the extradition and delivery to the authorities of Cook County, were not "due process of law," and we may suppose, although it is not so alleged, that this reference is to that clause of Article XIV of the Amendments to the Constitution of the United States which declares that no State shall deprive any person of life, liberty, or property "without due process of law." The "due process of law" here guaranteed is complied with when the party is regularly indicted by the proper grand jury in the State court, has a trial according to the forms and modes prescribed for such trials, and when, in that trial and proceedings, he is deprived of no rights to which he is lawfully entitled. We do not intend to say that there may not be proceedings previous to the trial, in regard to which the prisoner could invoke in some manner the provisions of this clause of the Constitution, but, for mere irregularities in the manner in which he may be brought into the custody of the law, we do not think he is entitled to say that he should not be tried at all for the crime with which he is charged in a regular indictment. He may be arrested for a very heinous offence by persons without any warrant, or without any previous complaint, and brought before a proper officer, and this may be in some sense said to be "without due process of law." But it would hardly be claimed, that after the case had been investigated and the defendant held by the proper authorities to answer for the crime, he could plead that he was first arrested "without due process of law." So here, when found within the jurisdiction of the State of Illinois and liable to answer for a crime against the laws of that State, unless there was some positive provision of the Constitution or of the laws of this country violated in bringing him into court, it is not easy to see how he can say that he is there "without due process of law," within the meaning of the constitutional provision.

. . .

The question of how far his forcible seizure in another country, and transfer by violence, force, or fraud, to this country, could be made available to resist trial in the State court, for the offence now charged upon him, is one which we do not feel called upon to decide, for in that transaction we do not see that the Constitution, or laws, or treaties, of the United States guarantee him any protection. There are authorities of the highest respectability which hold that such forcible abduction is no sufficient reason why the party should not answer when brought within the jurisdiction of the court which has the right to try him, for such an offence, and presents no valid objection to his trial in such court. . . .

. . .

---

45. In Frisbie v. Collins, 342 U.S. 519 (1952), Collins sought his release by a petition for habeas corpus from a Michigan state prison, where he was serving a life sentence for murder. He alleged that "while he was living in Chicago, Michigan officers forcibly seized, handcuffed, blackjacked and took him to Michigan." He claimed that his trial and conviction in such circumstances denied him due process of law and violated the Federal Kidnapping Act, 18 U.S.C. § 1201, and that the conviction was therefore a nullity. The claim was rejected.

"This Court has never departed from the rule announced in Ker v. Illinois, 119 U.S. 436, 444, that the power of a court to try a person for crime is not impaired by the fact that he had been brought within the court's jurisdiction by reason of a 'forcible abduction.' No persuasive reasons are now presented to justify overruling this line of cases. They rest on the sound basis that due process of law is satisfied when one present in court is convicted of crime after having been fairly apprized of the charges against him and after a fair trial in accordance with constitutional procedural safeguards. There is nothing in the Constitution that requires a court to permit a guilty person rightfully convicted to escape justice because he was brought to trial against his will." Frisbie v. Collins, 342 U.S. at 522. The Court noted the severe penalties prescribed for kidnapping and concluded that the statute did not include "a sanction barring a state from prosecuting persons wrongfully brought to it by its officers." Id. at 523.

The Court applied *Ker* in United States v. Alvarez-Machain, 504 U.S. 655 (1992) (6–3). The defendant, a citizen and resident of Mexico, was indicted in the United States for the kidnapping and murder of a federal narcotics agent. Federal agents abducted him in Mexico and brought him into the United States, where he was arrested. He claimed that the federal court lacked jurisdiction to try him because his abduction violated an extradition treaty between the United States and Mexico. The Court held that although the treaty established procedures for extradition, it did not prohibit other methods of obtaining a wanted person's presence and that the treaty had not been violated.

46. Some inroad on *Ker* and Frisbie v. Collins was made in United States v. Toscanino, 500 F.2d 267 (2d Cir.1974). The defendant, who was convicted of a narcotics offense in New York, alleged that American agents kidnapped him in Uruguay, brought him to Brazil and tortured him there, and finally brought him to the United States to be prosecuted.

Observing that cases decided since Frisbie v. Collins had "eroded" its holding, the court said: "[W]e view due process as now requiring a court to divest itself of jurisdiction over the person of a defendant where it has been acquired as the result of the government's deliberate, unnecessary and unreasonable invasion of the accused's constitutional rights. This conclusion represents but an extension of the well-recognized power of federal courts in the civil context to decline to exercise jurisdiction over a defendant whose presence has been secured by force or fraud." Id. at 275. The case on which the court relied primarily is Rochin v. California, 342 U.S. 165 (1952), p. 351 below. Those cases, it said, indicated that due process was concerned not only with a fair trial but also with the conduct of law enforcement authorities before trial. In the end, however, the court appeared to rely not (or not only) on a constitutional ruling but on its "supervisory power over the administration of criminal justice in the district courts within our jurisdiction," 500 F.2d at 276. (*Ker* and Frisbie v. Collins were distinguished further on the ground that those cases did not involve violation of a treaty, as *Toscanino* did.)

The case was remanded with instructions to conduct an evidentiary hearing if, in response to the government's denial, the defendant was able to offer "some credible supporting evidence" of his allegations, 500 F.2d at 281. On remand, the district court concluded that the defendant did not submit any credible evidence to support his claim that United States officials were involved in his abduction or torture, and declined to hold an evidentiary hearing. 398 F.Supp. 916 (E.D.N.Y.1975).

Toscanino was limited in United States ex rel. Lujan v. Gengler, 510 F.2d 62 (2d Cir.1975), in which the defendant was abducted in Bolivia and brought to the United States where he was arrested: "[I]n recognizing that *Ker* and *Frisbie* no longer provided a carte blanche to government agents bringing defendants from abroad to the United States by the use of torture, brutality and similar outrageous conduct, we did not intend to suggest that *any* irregularity in the circumstances of a defendant's arrival in the jurisdiction would vitiate the proceedings of the criminal court. In holding that *Ker* and *Frisbie* must yield to the extent they were inconsistent with the Supreme Court's more recent pronouncements we scarcely could have meant to eviscerate the *Ker–Frisbie* rule, which the Supreme Court has never felt impelled to disavow." 510 F.2d at 65.

"[A]bsent a set of incidents like that in *Toscanino*, not every violation by prosecution or police is so egregious that *Rochin* and its progeny require nullification of the indictment." Id. at 65, 66. The court noted also the absence of a violation of international law in this case, since there was no allegation of a protest by another nation.

Except for *Toscanino*, the courts of appeals have regularly applied the *Ker–Frisbie* rule. E.g., United States v. Matta-Ballesteros, 71 F.3d 754 (9th Cir.1995); Matta-Ballesteros v. Henman, 896 F.2d 255 (7th Cir.1990) (additional cases cited). Frisbie v. Collins was cited with approval in *Alvarez-Machain*, note 45 above. Also, in Gerstein v. Pugh, 420 U.S. 103, 119 (1975), the Court declared that its ruling, see p. 522 below, marked no "retreat from the established rule that illegal arrest or detention does not void a subsequent conviction," id. at 525.

47. As Frisbie v. Collins, note 45 above, indicates, a person illegally arrested is not entitled to be released on habeas corpus if there is legal cause for his detention. "Where it appears that sufficient ground for detention exists a prisoner will not be discharged for defects in the original arrest or commitment." Stallings v. Splain, 253 U.S. 339, 343 (1920). "The invalidity of [an arrest] warrant is not comparable to the invalidity of an indictment. A person may not be punished for a crime without a formal and sufficient accusation even if he voluntarily submits to the jurisdiction of the court. . . . But a false arrest does not necessarily deprive the court of jurisdiction of the proceeding in which it was made." Albrecht v. United States, 273 U.S. 1, 8 (1927). In Kelly v. Griffin, 241 U.S. 6 (1916), Chicago police arrested the defendant. On the following day, a complaint was made before the U.S. commissioner, a warrant was issued, and the defendant was turned over to the U.S. marshal. The Court rejected the defendant's claim that if his arrest were illegal, he was entitled to be released before the federal warrant could be executed. "[H]owever illegal the arrest by the Chicago police it does not follow that the taking of the appellant's body by the marshal under the warrant . . . was void. The action of the officers of the State or city did not affect the jurisdiction of the Commissioner of the United States. . . . [T]he appellant came within reach of the Commissioner's warrant by his own choice, and the most that can be said is that the effective exercise of authority was made easier by what had been done. It was not even argued that the appellant was entitled to a chance to escape before either of the warrants could be executed. This proceeding is not a fox hunt. But merely to be declared free in a room with the marshal standing at the door having another warrant in his hand would be an empty form." Id. at 12–13.

48. How does the rule that a court's jurisdiction over a defendant does not depend at all on the manner in which he was brought before the court comport with the result in Rochin v. California, 342 U.S. 165 (1952), p. 351 below, in which, relying on the Due Process Clause, the Court reversed a conviction based in part on indubitably reliable evidence (morphine capsules recovered from the defendant's stomach by "stomach pumping") because the evidence had been obtained by conduct that "shocks the conscience," id. at 172. *Rochin* was one of the cases on which the court relied in *Toscanino*, see note 46, p. 76 above. See United States v. Hart, 409

F.2d 221 (10th Cir.1969) (brutality by police is not itself a bar to prosecution).

Evidence Obtained as the Result of an Unlawful Arrest (Wong Sun v. United States)

---

49. In Wong Sun v. United States, 371 U.S. 471 (1963), the Court made it clear that the rule excluding from use at trial evidence that was obtained in violation of the defendant's constitutional rights, see p. 145 below, applies to evidence of all kinds that is the "fruit" of an unlawful (i.e. unconstitutional) arrest.

> The exclusionary rule has traditionally barred from trial physical, tangible materials obtained either during or as a direct result of an unlawful invasion. It follows from our holding in Silverman v. United States, 365 U.S. 505, that the Fourth Amendment may protect against the overhearing of verbal statements as well as against the more traditional seizure of "papers and effects." Similarly, testimony as to matters observed during an unlawful invasion has been excluded in order to enforce the basic constitutional policies. . . . Thus, verbal evidence which derives . . . immediately from an unlawful entry and an unauthorized arrest . . . is no less the "fruit" of official illegality than the more common tangible fruits of the unwarranted intrusion. . . . Nor do the policies underlying the exclusionary rule invite any logical distinction between physical and verbal evidence. Either in terms of deterring lawless conduct by federal officers . . . or of closing the doors of the federal courts to any use of evidence unconstitutionally obtained . . . the danger in relaxing the exclusionary rules in the case of verbal evidence would seem too great to warrant introducing such a distinction.

371 U.S. at 485–86.

The Court declined to hold that any evidence which would not have been discovered *but for* an illegal arrest must be suppressed. It said that "the more apt question in such a case is 'whether, granting establishment of the primary illegality, the evidence to which instant objection is made has been come at by exploitation of that illegality or instead by means sufficiently distinguishable to be purged of the primary taint,' Maguire, Evidence of Guilt 221 (1959)." On that basis it concluded that a confession made several days after a defendant had been unlawfully arrested, been released and lawfully arraigned, when he returned voluntarily to make the statement, was not "tainted" by the illegality of the arrest and was admissible at trial. Id. at 488, 491.

The courts have generally asked two questions to determine whether evidence is tainted by an unlawful arrest. One is whether, despite the arrest, the evidence was the product of "a clear act of free will on the part of the defendant," Rogers v. United States, 330 F.2d 535, 541 (5th Cir. 1964). See United States v. Hoffman, 385 F.2d 501, 504 (7th Cir.1967), in which the court referred to "the exercise of those attributes of will, perception, memory and volition unique to the individual human personality which serve to distinguish the evidentiary character of a witness from the relative immutability of inanimate evidence."

The Court relied on the "free will" test in Brown v. Illinois, 422 U.S. 590 (1975), in which, following an illegal arrest, the defendant was given the *Miranda* warnings (see Miranda v. Arizona, p. 417 below) and subsequently made incriminating statements. The Court rejected the conclusion that the giving of the warnings automatically broke the connection between the illegal arrest and the statements. Otherwise, it said, illegal arrests for investigation "would be encouraged by the knowledge that evidence derived therefrom could well be made admissible at trial by the simple expedient of giving *Miranda* warnings." 422 U.S. at 602. It said further: "The question whether a confession is the product of a free will under *Wong Sun* must be answered on the facts of each case. No single fact is dispositive. The workings of the human mind are too complex, and the possibilities of misconduct too diverse, to permit protection of the Fourth Amendment to turn on such a talismanic test. The *Miranda* warnings are an important factor, to be sure, in determining whether the confession is obtained by exploitation of an illegal arrest. But they are not the only factor to be considered. The temporal proximity of the arrest and the confession, the presence of intervening circumstances . . . and, particularly, the purpose and flagrancy of the official misconduct are all relevant." Id. at 603–604. Compare the suggestion in Collins v. Beto, 348 F.2d 823, 828 (5th Cir. 1965), that "the best and perhaps the only way" to purge the taint of an illegal arrest and render admissible statements made during the ensuing detention is "to afford the suspect an effective opportunity to obtain the assistance of counsel." See Rawlings v. Kentucky, 448 U.S. 98, 106–10 (1980). Cf. United States v. Bailey, 691 F.2d 1009 (11th Cir.1982) (unlawful arrest provoked criminal response furnishing basis for second lawful arrest; search pursuant to latter arrest upheld).

The other question that is asked is whether the evidence was the product of "deliberate exploitation" by the police of the primary illegality. Copeland v. United States, 343 F.2d 287, 291 (D.C.Cir.1964) (evidence admissible); see United States v. Pimental, 645 F.2d 85 (1st Cir.1981) (evidence admissible); United States ex rel. Gockley v. Myers, 450 F.2d 232 (3d Cir.1971) (evidence inadmissible). In that connection, see Nix v. Williams, p. 147 note 77 below, holding that evidence that the police would inevitably have discovered without any illegal conduct on their part need not be excluded because the police were in fact led to it by such conduct.

In United States v. Ceccolini, 435 U.S. 268 (1978), the Court reversed a judgment that a witness's testimony be excluded under *Wong Sun* because the government was led to the witness by an illegal search. A police officer had looked into an envelope in a shop operated by the defendant, where the officer was taking a "break," and had discovered policy slips. He asked the witness, who worked in the store, who owned the envelope; she told him that the defendant owned it and had instructed her to give it to someone.

The officer reported this fact to an FBI agent investigating gambling operations in the area. Four months later, the agent interviewed the witness. She spoke willingly, incriminating the defendant, and she later testified against him at trial. The Court said that the witness's willingness to testify had a bearing on the connection required by *Wong Sun* between the illegality and the evidence to be excluded: "[E]valuated properly, the degree of free will necessary to dissipate the taint will very likely be found more often in the case of live-witness testimony than other kinds of evidence." Furthermore, were the *Wong Sun* rule applied to exclude the testimony of a witness whenever the government was led to him by an illegal act, the exclusion "would perpetually disable a witness from testifying about relevant and material facts, regardless of how unrelated such testimony might be to the purpose of the originally illegal search or the evidence discovered thereby. . . . [S]ince the cost of excluding live-witness testimony often will be greater [than the cost of excluding particular tangible evidence], a closer, more direct link between the illegality and that kind of testimony is required." The Court concluded that "the exclusionary rule should be invoked with much greater reluctance where the claim is based on a causal relationship between a constitutional violation and the discovery of a live witness than when a similar claim is advanced to support suppression of an inanimate object." Id. at 276–78, 280.

See United States v. Leonardi, 623 F.2d 746 (2d Cir.1980) (*Ceccolini* applied). *Ceccolini* is distinguished in United States v. Scios, 590 F.2d 956 (D.C.Cir.1978); the majority opinion and especially the dissenting opinion of Judge Wilkey contain extended discussions of the "taint" issue.

In New York v. Harris, 495 U.S. 14 (1990) (5–4), the Court held that a person's arrest in his home without a warrant, in violation of *Payton*, p. 44 above, did not require the exclusion of a statement he made while in custody following the arrest. Although Harris's statement was the product of his arrest, it was not the product of unlawful custody, since there was probable cause for his arrest; nor was it a product of his having been arrested in his home rather than elsewhere. *Payton*, the Court said, "was designed to protect the physical integrity of the home; it was not intended to grant criminal suspects, like Harris, protection for statements made outside their premises where the police have probable cause to arrest the suspect for committing a crime." Id. at 17. See also United States v. Crews, 445 U.S. 463 (1980), in which the Court held that a witness's courtroom identification of the defendant was independent of the defendant's illegal arrest, so that exclusion of the identification was not required.

50. Consider the following cases:

(i) The defendant was arrested unlawfully on a charge of robbery. Clothing that he was wearing at the time of his arrest was used in a lineup at which he was identified by the victim of the robbery.

(ii) The defendants were arrested during the night and detained unlawfully. At noon the next day the body of a man was discovered. From that point the police had probable cause to arrest the defendants on a charge of murder. Several hours later the defendants' clothing was taken from them for laboratory examinations, which disclosed blood and other incriminating matter on the clothing. The results of the examinations were introduced in evidence against them.

(iii) The police received information that the defendant had committed a rape. They unlawfully entered his house in his absence and found his work badge, by which they discovered where he worked. They then went to his place of work and arrested him. They examined his clothing, and the clothing and the results of the examination were introduced in evidence against him. The defendant claimed that at the time of his arrest he was about to destroy the clothing.

(iv) The defendants parked a car which they were driving in a motel parking lot. A security officer of the motel became suspicious; unlawfully, he arrested and detained them in their automobile for investigation, and called the police. Within a few minutes the police obtained a report on the license number of the car, the license plate being in plain view, and learned that the car was stolen. Testimony that the defendants were driving a stolen car was introduced at their trial for unlawful interstate transportation of a stolen motor vehicle.

(v) The defendant was arrested unlawfully. While he was being driven to the station house in a police car, he stuffed some papers under the back seat. They were retrieved and introduced in evidence against him.

Was the use of the evidence in these cases consistent with Wong Sun? See (i) Miller v. Eklund, 364 F.2d 976 (9th Cir.1966); (ii) Hancock v. Nelson, 363 F.2d 249 (1st Cir.1966); (iii) Leek v. Maryland, 353 F.2d 526 (4th Cir.1965); (iv) United States v. Ruffin, 389 F.2d 76 (7th Cir.1968); also, United States v. Kennedy, 457 F.2d 63 (10th Cir.1972); (v) United States v. Barber, 557 F.2d 628 (8th Cir.1977).

51. The "*McNabb–Mallory* rule." Rule 5(a), Fed.R.Crim.P., provides that a person who is arrested shall be taken "without unnecessary delay" before a magistrate judge or a state or local judicial officer. In McNabb v. United States, 318 U.S. 332 (1943), decided before promulgation of the rules, the Court held that incriminating statements made by a defendant during a period of unlawful detention between his arrest and presentation before a magistrate could not be used against him at trial. It said that the detention of arrested persons for questioning before presenting them for commitment is "a procedure which is wholly incompatible with the vital but very restricted duties of the investigating and arresting officers of the Government." Id. at 342. The Court's holding was not constitutionally based; rather, it was an exercise of the Court's "supervision of the administration of justice in the federal courts." Id. at 340.

In Mallory v. United States, 354 U.S. 449 (1957), the Court reaffirmed this ruling, basing it this time on Rule 5(a). It said that, although the duty to bring arrested persons before a committing magistrate "without unnecessary delay" did not call for "mechanical or automatic obedience," it allowed "arresting officers little more leeway than the interval between arrest and the ordinary administrative steps required to bring a suspect before the nearest available magistrate." Id. at 453, 455. Since neither *McNabb* nor *Mallory* was a constitutional holding, it has been assumed that the states are not obliged to follow the rule there announced. E.g., State v. Stubbs, 407 P.2d 215 (Kan.1965).

In *Mallory*, the Court said: "Circumstances may justify a brief delay between arrest and arraignment, as for instance, where the story volunteered by the accused is susceptible of quick verification through third parties." 354 U.S. at 455. A delay of 26 hours between arrest and arraignment was found not to be "unnecessary" for purposes of the *McNabb–Mallory* rule, in United States v. Collins, 462 F.2d 792 (2d Cir.1972): "We have consistently held that delays for purposes of routine processing—here a total of 3 hours and 15 minutes spent at the 105th Precinct, FBI headquarters and Assistant United States Attorney Puccio's office—or for overnight lodging—here the 11½ hours in the Manhattan House of Detention—do not constitute unnecessary delay within the *McNabb–Mallory* rule. . . . Of the remaining 9½ hours, 3½ hours, the time spent in transit, was clearly necessary to move Collins through the complexities of the combined federal-state system, ½ hour was necessary to establish his identity and 5½ hours were consumed in particularizing a voluntarily given confession. No part of these detention periods was unnecessary. The conduct of the FBI and the New York City Police Department was at all times directed to processing Collins as expeditiously as possible for arraignment." *Collins*, 462 F.2d at 795–96. See also United States v. Marrero, 450 F.2d 373 (2d Cir.1971) (delay from 8:00 p.m. until noon on following day was not unreasonable); Pettyjohn v. United States, 419 F.2d 651 (D.C.Cir. 1969) (seven hours delay after defendant's arrest late at night was not unreasonable). Rule 5(a) does not prevent federal authorities from questioning a person in state custody before he is presented to a federal magistrate, so long as the state custody is not at the instance of the federal authorities. E.g., Barnett v. United States, 384 F.2d 848 (5th Cir.1967).

In *Pettyjohn*, the defendant gave the police a confession after being advised of his Miranda rights (see p. 417 below). The court said that by agreeing to speak after being advised of his rights to silence and to consult an attorney the defendant had also waived his right to be brought before a magistrate as soon as possible. "Surely the law does not allow a person to voluntarily discuss the crime to which he has just confessed for a period of some twenty minutes and then claim on appeal that the twenty minute period during which they spoke constituted a prejudicial delay in violation of his right to rapid arraignment." 419 F.2d at 656. *Pettyjohn* was followed (over a dissent) in United States v. Poole, 495 F.2d 115 (D.C.Cir.1974); the relationship between *McNabb–Mallory* and *Miranda* is thoroughly discussed in the several opinions. See also United States v. Salamanca, 990 F.2d 629 (D.C.Cir.1993); United States v. Duvall, 537 F.2d 15, 23–26 (2d Cir.1976).

A federal statute enacted in 1968 provides in effect that a delay of six hours before a person is brought before a magistrate does not by itself require exclusion of a confession obtained during that period. 18 U.S.C. § 3501(c). In United States v. Alvarez-Sanchez, 511 U.S. 350 (1994), the Court said that this provision has no application to a detention by state

Boston Police Department
Prisoner Booking Form

Report Date: 05/09/1997 13:12:49
Booking Status: COMPLETED
Printed By: Dahlbeck, Joseph W

Booking Name: Layfield
First: Robert
Middle: Arthur
Address: Apt 23, 312 Evergreen CR , Boston, MA.
Sex: Male
Race: White Non-Hispanic
Date of Birth: 06/09/1942

District: 09
Booking Number: 95-000316-04
Incident Number: 95-1000000
Arrest Date: 03/17/1995 14:00
Booking Date: 02/10/1997 11:25
Charges: Breaking & Entering N/T, Poss cl B

Miranda Warning

Before asking you any questions, it is my duty to advise you of your rights:

- **You have the right to remain silent;**
- **If you choose to speak, anything you say may be used against you in a court of law or other proceeding;**
- **You have the right to consult with a lawyer before answering any questions and you may have him present with you during questioning;**
- **If you cannot afford a lawyer and you want one, a lawyer will be provided for you by the Commonwealth without cost to you;**
- **You may also waive the right to counsel and your right to remain silent and you may answer any question or make any statement you wish. If you decide to answer any questions you may stop any time to consult with a lawyer.**

Do you understand what I have told you?

Yes, I understand

Informed of Rights By Officer:

09566	Joseph W Dahlbeck

Signature of Prisoner

Signature of Officer

Prisoner Property

Money: $ 36.25 **Property Storage Number:** 5

Property: timex watch, gold ring, pocket knife,

Acknowledgement of property items being held

Signature of Prisoner

Telephone Used: YES
Breathalyzer Used: NO
Examined at Hospital: NO

Visible Injuries:
Any injuries would be listed in this area

officials for a violation of state law, so long as there is no collusion with federal officials. It declined to consider whether the effect of § 3501(c), when it applied, is to require exclusion on grounds of delay of incriminating statements made outside the six-hour "safe harbor" or only to prohibit suppression on such grounds of incriminating statements made within that period. See United States v. Perez, 733 F.2d 1026 (2d Cir.1984) (court has discretion to exclude confession solely on ground of delay of more than six hours, if unreasonable).

Even if there is unreasonable delay before a person is brought before a magistrate, a statement need not be excluded if it is made within the period while the delay is not unreasonable. United States v. Martinez-Gallegos, 807 F.2d 868 (9th Cir.1987). See generally United States v. Rubio, 709 F.2d 146 (2d Cir.1983).

Although a violation of *McNabb–Mallory* is not itself a violation of the person's constitutional rights, a prolonged detention after arrest may be. See Coleman v. Frantz, 754 F.2d 719 (7th Cir.1985) (detention for 18 days). See generally Sanders v. City of Houston, 543 F.Supp. 694 (S.D.Tex.1982); Dommer v. Hatcher, 427 F.Supp. 1040 (N.D.Ind.1975), rev'd in part, 653 F.2d 289 (7th Cir.1981); Lively v. Cullinane, 451 F.Supp. 1000 (D.D.C. 1978), all discussing the time that police are allowed to complete booking and investigative procedures.

If a person is arrested without a warrant or indictment, the Fourth Amendment requires that he be brought promptly before a judicial officer for a determination of probable cause. Gerstein v. Pugh, 420 U.S. 103 (1975), p. 522 below. This requirement is ordinarily satisfied if the determination is made within 48 hours. County of Riverside v. McLaughlin, 500 U.S. 44 (1991), p. 527 below. This constitutional requirement is distinct from the *McNabb–Mallory* rule, which is nonconstitutional and applies to arrests on a warrant as well as arrests without a warrant, but the two are closely related.

Civil Remedies

---

52. In Ker v. Illinois, 119 U.S. 436 (1886), p. 74 above, the Court noted that its conclusion did not leave Ker or the Peruvian government "without remedy for his unauthorized seizure within its territory." Peru could seek extradition of Ker's abductor and try him for violation of its laws. Ker could sue his abductor "in an action of trespass and false imprisonment, and the facts [alleged] . . . would without doubt sustain the action. Whether he could recover a sum sufficient to justify the action would probably depend on moral aspects of the case," which the Court did not consider. 119 U.S. at 444.[16]

16. In Mulligan v. Schlachter, 389 F.2d 231 (6th Cir.1968), the complainant sought damages under the Civil Rights Act, see note 53 below, for an alleged arrest and seizure of his property without probable cause, on a charge of murder for which he was subsequently tried and convicted. The court said: "[A] trial does not necessarily provide adequate recompense for constitutional depriva-

The "moral aspects" of such cases have not often been favorable to civil recovery. Persons arrested illegally typically are not "respectable citizens" and find it difficult to prove significant injury to their reputation, which would be the basis for recovery of substantial damages. Juries do not readily favor a person who has been arrested, albeit unlawfully, over a policeman who was "only doing his duty." It has been suggested that tort liability might be an effective means of controlling police illegality, if there were (1) government liability for the illegal acts of individual police officers,[17] (2) minimum liquidated damages, and (3) restriction of defenses based on reputation, etc. which keep potential plaintiffs out of court. Foote, "Tort Remedies for Police Violations of Individual Rights," 39 Minn. L. Rev. 493, 514–16 (1955).

53. 42 U.S.C. § 1983. In Monroe v. Pape, 365 U.S. 167 (1961), the petitioners brought an action for violation of their constitutional rights, in which they claimed damages under the Civil Rights Act of 1871, R.S. § 1979, 42 U.S.C. § 1983: "Every person who, under color of any statute, ordinance, regulation, custom, or usage, of any State or Territory, subjects, or causes to be subjected, any citizen of the United States or other person within the jurisdiction thereof to the deprivation of any rights, privileges, or immunities secured by the Constitution and laws, shall be liable to the party injured in an action at law, suit in equity, or other proper proceeding for redress." The complaint alleged that without an arrest or search warrant "13 Chicago police officers broke into petitioners' home in the early morning, routed them from bed, made them stand naked in the living room, and ransacked every room, emptying drawers and ripping mattress covers"; "that Mr. Monroe was then taken to the police station and detained on 'open' charges for 10 hours, while he was interrogated about a two-day-old murder, that he was not taken before a magistrate, though one was accessible, that he was not permitted to call his family or attorney, [and] that he was subsequently released without criminal charges being preferred against him." 365 U.S. at 169.

The Court held that the complaint stated a cause of action, since there were alleged "facts constituting a deprivation under color of state authority of a right guaranteed by the Fourteenth Amendment." A purpose of the statute was "to provide a federal remedy where the state remedy, though adequate in theory, was not available in practice"; it was, therefore, irrelevant that the petitioners might also have a remedy under state tort law and that the state remedy had not been sought first and refused. Id. at 171, 174.

Aside from the observation in another context that § 1983 "should be read against the background of tort liability that makes a man responsible for the natural consequences of his actions," id. at 187, the Court left unclear what were the elements of the legal wrong that the plaintiffs had

tions. . . . While considerations of state-federal comity and judicial efficiency may dictate that a civil rights action be dismissed when the alleged deprivation has been examined fully during a state criminal trial or has been waived by the complainant, the simple fact of an unreversed state conviction cannot by itself require dismissal." Id. at 232–33.

17. Some states have provisions for indemnification of police officers who are held liable for damages arising out of the performance of their duties. E.g., Wis.Stat. § 895.46(1)(a).

suffered and what was the measure of damages that they should recover. With respect both to liability and to defenses to liability, the courts have, for the most part, applied the law of torts of the state in which the wrong occurred. But there are qualifications to that general approach.

Summarizing case law since Monroe v. Pape, the Court has said: "Our general approach to questions of immunity under § 1983 is by now well established. Although the statute on its face admits of no immunities, we have read it 'in harmony with general principles of tort immunities and defenses rather than in derogation of them.' Imbler v. Pachtman, 424 U.S. 409, 418 (1976). Our initial inquiry is whether an official claiming immunity under § 1983 can point to a common-law counterpart to the privilege he asserts. Tower v. Glover, 467 U.S. 914 (1984). If 'an official was accorded immunity from tort actions at common law when the Civil Rights Act was enacted in 1871, the Court next considers whether § 1983's history or purposes nonetheless counsel against recognizing the same immunity in § 1983 actions.' Id., at 920. Thus, while we look to the common law for guidance, we do not assume that Congress intended to incorporate every common-law immunity into § 1983 in unaltered form." Malley v. Briggs, 475 U.S. 335, 338 (1986).

Concerning the statute of limitations applicable to § 1983 actions, see Garcia v. Wilson, 731 F.2d 640 (10th Cir.1984), aff'd, 471 U.S. 261 (1985), concluding that "every section 1983 claim is in essence an action for injury to personal rights" and holding that all such claims will be so characterized for purposes of the statute of limitations. The opinion reviews cases in other circuits.

The liability of police officers for an unlawful arrest and actions taken in the wake of an arrest is a major issue under § 1983. In Pierson v. Ray, 386 U.S. 547 (1967), the Court held that police officers are not liable under § 1983 for making an illegal arrest if "they acted in good faith and with probable cause"; "a policeman's lot is not so unhappy that he must choose between being charged with dereliction of duty if he does not arrest when he has probable cause, and being mulcted in damages if he does." Id. at 555. Since the policemen who were defendants claimed to have acted in good faith with probable cause pursuant to a statute later found to be invalid, the Court was not called upon to decide whether a policeman was liable if he acted in good faith *without* probable cause. Subsequent cases, however, have established that an officer who acts reasonably and in good faith with respect to probable cause does have immunity. In Anderson v. Creighton, 483 U.S. 635, 641 (1987) (6–3), the Court said: "[I]t is inevitable that law enforcement officials will in some cases reasonably but mistakenly conclude that probable cause is present, and . . . in such cases those officials—like other officials who act in ways they reasonably believe to be lawful—should not be held personally liable." To the same effect, see Hunter v. Bryant, 502 U.S. 224 (1991) (6–2).

It is generally held that a police officer who negligently but in good faith seeks and obtains a search warrant on an insufficient affidavit is not liable under § 1983. E.g., Stadium Films, Inc. v. Baillargeon, 542 F.2d 577, 578 (1st Cir.1976): "Under the prevailing view in this country, a peace officer may not be held liable in damages for making negligent errors of law in seeking or executing a search warrant." On the other hand, the issuance of a warrant does not by itself preclude liability of the officer who applied for the warrant. The officer is liable despite the magistrate's issuance of the warrant "if, on an objective basis, it is obvious that no reasonably competent officer would have concluded that a warrant should issue." Malley v. Briggs, 475 U.S. 335, 341 (1986) (7–2).

A claim that police officers used excessive force in making an arrest or other seizure of the person is tested by a standard of objective reasonableness under the Fourth Amendment rather than a standard of substantive due process. Graham v. Connor, 490 U.S. 386 (1989). See Saucier v. Katz, 533 U.S. 194 (2001). In Jenkins v. Averett, 424 F.2d 1228 (4th Cir.1970), the plaintiff had been chased by the police for six blocks and was then shot in the leg. He was not subsequently charged with any crime. The court held that the plaintiff was entitled to recover under § 1983, even if the shot was not intentionally fired. It said that the plaintiff had been subjected "to the reckless use of excessive force" amounting to "gross and culpable conduct." Since that was sufficient to support a claim for assault and battery under state law, it was sufficient under federal law also: "if intent is required, it may be supplied, for federal purposes, by gross and culpable negligence, just as it was supplied in the common law cause of action." The court went on to say that "bad motive or evil intent" was not generally a necessary element of a claim under § 1983. Id. at 1232. The court held also that damages of $448, covering the plaintiff's out-of-pocket expenses, were inadequate and that he should be compensated for pain and suffering.

In Baker v. McCollan, 443 U.S. 137 (1979) (6–3), the plaintiff alleged that he had been arrested pursuant to a warrant intended for another person and was detained for several days before the mistake was discovered and he was released. The warrant itself was facially valid. Observing that the plaintiff might have a tort action for false imprisonment under state law, the Court held that, there having been no violation of a constitutional right, he did not have a cause of action under § 1983. Compare Coleman v. Frantz, p. 85 above. To the same effect as Baker v. McCollan, see Street v. Surdyka, 492 F.2d 368 (4th Cir.1974). The plaintiff was arrested without a warrant for a misdemeanor not committed in the arresting officer's presence. Assuming that the arrest violated state law and might give rise to an action for false arrest under common law but that the arrest was not unconstitutional (there having been probable cause), the court held that the plaintiff had no cause of action under § 1983. See also Allen v. Eicher, 295 F.Supp. 1184, 1185 (D.Md.1969), holding that an interrogation in violation of Miranda v. Arizona, p. 417 below, and the subsequent trial use in the complainant's criminal trial of his statements during the interrogation did not constitute a cause of action under the Civil Rights Act: "*Miranda* does not per se make an interrogation which violates its precepts into an actionable tort. Unlike an illegal arrest, or an illegal search or seizure, an improper interrogation is not itself a tort." 295 F.Supp. at 1185–86.

In Pritchard v. Perry, 508 F.2d 423 (4th Cir.1975), the court rejected the defendant's claim that the plaintiff could not recover under § 1983, because his arrest and detention had been brief and without injury to him.

It said: "That an infringement of personal liberty such as follows from an unconstitutional arrest has resulted in but a short period of restraint or has involved no physical injury may go in mitigation of damages but it manifestly cannot immunize the constitutional deprivation or abort an aggrieved plaintiff's right of action under Section 1983. The enabling statute was not so considered at the time of its enactment nor has it since been authoritatively construed. There is no justification for the incorporation of a *de minimis* rule by way of a limitation on the right of action by an individual for an admitted violation of constitutional rights. There is no warrant for any separation of constitutional rights into redressable rights and non-redressable rights, of major and minor unconstitutional deprivations, and Section 1983 makes no such distinction and authorizes no such separation." Id. at 425.

In Monroe v. Pape, above, the Court held that Congress had not intended to make municipalities liable for their officers' violations of the Civil Rights Act, and upheld the dismissal of the complaint against the City of Chicago. That holding was overruled in Monell v. Department of Social Services of the City of New York, 436 U.S. 658 (1978) (7–2). The Court concluded that local governing bodies can be sued directly for relief, where the allegedly unconstitutional action executes or implements official policy adopted by the body or governmental "custom." Liability cannot, however, be based solely on the tortious conduct of an employee under a doctrine of *respondeat superior*.

"Proof of a single incident of unconstitutional activity is not sufficient to impose liability under *Monell*, unless proof of the incident includes proof that it was caused by an existing, unconstitutional municipal policy, which policy can be attributed to a municipal policymaker. Otherwise the existence of the unconstitutional policy, and its origin, must be separately proved." City of Oklahoma City v. Tuttle, 471 U.S. 808, 823 (1985) (7–1). The question, when there is a policy and when an independent action by an employee, is discussed in City of St. Louis v. Praprotnik, 485 U.S. 112 (1988) (7–1). Compare Grandstaff v. City of Borger, 767 F.2d 161 (5th Cir.1985) (municipality liable), with Carter v. District of Columbia, 795 F.2d 116 (D.C.Cir.1986) (municipality not liable), and Vippolis v. Village of Haverstraw, 768 F.2d 40 (2d Cir.1985) (same).

In City of Canton v. Harris, 489 U.S. 378 (1989) (6–3), the Court held that a municipality might be liable under § 1983 for an injury due to inadequate police training, but only if the failure to train reflected a deliberate or conscious choice that amounted to a municipal policy. See Parker v. District of Columbia, 850 F.2d 708 (D.C.Cir.1988) (inadequate police training; municipal liability upheld); Spell v. McDaniel, 824 F.2d 1380 (4th Cir.1987) (same).

Municipalities do not have a "qualified immunity" from liability based on the good faith of the officials involved. Owen v. City of Independence, 445 U.S. 622 (1980) (5–4). They are, however, immune from punitive damages under § 1983. City of Newport v. Fact Concerts, Inc., 453 U.S. 247 (1981) (6–3). *Monell* notwithstanding, it remains the law that neither a state nor state officials acting in their official capacity are "persons" who may be sued under § 1983. Will v. Michigan Department of State Police, 491 U.S. 58 (1989) (5–4).

In Pierson v. Ray, above, the Court said also that § 1983 did not remove judges' traditional immunity for acts within their office, 386 U.S. at 553–55, as it had held earlier that legislators retained immunity under the statute for acts within their office, Tenney v. Brandhove, 341 U.S. 367 (1951). A court reporter does not share judges' absolute immunity for performance of the judicial function and has only qualified immunity for failing to produce a transcript for a federal criminal trial. Antoine v. Byers & Anderson, Inc., 508 U.S. 429 (1993).

A prosecutor's absolute immunity from liability under § 1983 for actions taken in his prosecutorial role was affirmed in Imbler v. Pachtman, 424 U.S. 409 (1976). The Court noted that under the common law a prosecutor had absolute immunity from suits for malicious prosecution. It said further:

> A prosecutor is duty bound to exercise his best judgment both in deciding which suits to bring and in conducting them in court. The public trust of the prosecutor's office would suffer if he were constrained in making every decision by the consequences in terms of his own potential liability in a suit for damages. Such suits could be expected with some frequency, for a defendant often will transform his resentment at being prosecuted into the ascription of improper and malicious actions to the State's advocate. . . . Further, if the prosecutor could be made to answer in court each time such a person charged him with wrongdoing, his energy and attention would be diverted from the pressing duty of enforcing the criminal law.
>
> Moreover, suits that survived the pleadings would pose substantial danger of liability even to the honest prosecutor. The prosecutor's possible knowledge of a witness' falsehoods, the materiality of evidence not revealed to the defense, the propriety of a closing argument, and—ultimately in every case—the likelihood that prosecutorial misconduct so infected a trial as to deny due process, are typical of issues with which judges struggle in actions for post-trial relief, sometimes to differing conclusions. The presentation of such issues in a § 1983 action often would require a virtual retrial of the criminal offense in a new forum, and the resolution of some technical issues by the lay jury. It is fair to say, we think, that the honest prosecutor would face greater difficulty in meeting the standards of qualified immunity than other executive or administrative officials. Frequently acting under serious constraints of time and even information, a prosecutor inevitably makes many decisions that could engender colorable claims of constitutional deprivation. Defending these decisions, often years after they were made, could impose unique and intolerable burdens upon a prosecutor responsible annually for hundreds of indictments and trials. . . .

> The affording of only a qualified immunity to the prosecutor also could have an adverse effect upon the functioning of the criminal justice system. Attaining the system's goal of accurately determining guilt or innocence requires that both the prosecution and the defense have wide discretion in the conduct of the trial and the presentation of evidence. The veracity of witnesses in criminal cases frequently is subject to doubt before and after they testify, as is illustrated by the history of this case. If prosecutors were hampered in exercising their judgment as to the use of such witnesses by concern about resulting personal liability, the triers of fact in criminal cases often would be denied relevant evidence.
>
> The ultimate fairness of the operation of the system itself could be weakened by subjecting prosecutors to § 1983 liability. Various post-trial procedures are available to determine whether an accused has received a fair trial. These procedures include the remedial powers of the trial judge, appellate review, and state and federal post-conviction collateral remedies. In all of these the attention of the reviewing judge or tribunal is focused primarily on whether there was a fair trial under law. This focus should not be blurred by even the subconscious knowledge that a post-trial decision in favor of the accused might result in the prosecutor's being called upon to respond in damages for his error or mistaken judgment.
>
> We conclude that the considerations outlined above dictate the same absolute immunity under § 1983 that the prosecutor enjoys at common law. To be sure, this immunity does leave the genuinely wronged defendant without civil redress against a prosecutor whose malicious or dishonest action deprives him of liberty. But the alternative of qualifying a prosecutor's immunity would disserve the broader public interest. It would prevent the vigorous and fearless performance of the prosecutor's duty that is essential to the proper functioning of the criminal justice system. Moreover, it often would prejudice defendants in criminal cases by skewing post-conviction judicial decisions that should be made with the sole purpose of insuring justice.

424 U.S. at 424–28.

The Court confined its holding to the prosecutor's prosecutorial functions ("initiating a prosecution and . . . presenting the State's case") and declined to consider "whether like or similar reasons require immunity for those aspects of the prosecutor's responsibility that cast him in the role of an administrator or investigative officer rather than that of an advocate." Id. at 430–31.

Following *Imbler*, the Court held that a prosecutor's participation as lawyer for the state in a hearing to determine whether there is probable cause for issuance of a search warrant is covered by absolute prosecutorial immunity, but that such immunity does not extend to the function of giving legal advice to the police in the investigative stage of a criminal proceeding; with respect to the latter, a prosecutor has only qualified (good faith) immunity. Burns v. Reed, 500 U.S. 478 (1991). Nor does a prosecutor have absolute immunity if he makes an affidavit to support an application for an arrest warrant, because he is there functioning not as an advocate but as a complaining witness, Kalina v. Fletcher, 522 U.S. 118 (1997). Prosecutors were held not to have absolute immunity from liability for alleged preindictment fabrication of false evidence, inasmuch as the alleged acts occurred while the prosecutors were acting as investigators rather than as advocates. Buckley v. Fitzsimmons, 509 U.S. 259 (1993) (5–4). Similarly, in Briggs v. Goodwin, 569 F.2d 10 (D.C.Cir.1977), the court held that a prosecutor who was presenting witnesses to a grand jury as part of an investigation of certain violations of federal law was functioning in an "investigative" capacity rather than as an advocate, and therefore did not have the absolute immunity granted by *Imbler*. Nor are a prosecutor's allegedly false statements to the press covered by absolute immunity. "Comments to the media," the Court said, "have no functional tie to the judicial process just because they are made by a prosecutor." *Buckley*, above, 509 U.S. at 277.

Prosecutors who withheld exculpatory evidence that was discovered following the defendants' convictions for murder but while direct appeals were pending did not have absolute immunity. The prosecutors were not personally involved in the post-conviction proceedings and were not then acting as prosecutors. Houston v. Partee, 978 F.2d 362 (7th Cir.1992).

In Scheuer v. Rhodes, 416 U.S. 232 (1974), the estates of three students killed during the disturbance at Kent State University in 1970 sought damages under § 1983 against the Governor and other officers of the State of Ohio, officers and members of the National Guard, and the president of the university. The court held that the defendants did not have absolute executive immunity from suit, but had an immunity that is "qualified or limited," so that their liability depended on all the circumstances. "[I]n varying scope, a qualified immunity is available to officers of the executive branch of government, the variation being dependent upon the scope of discretion and responsibilities of the office and all the circumstances as they reasonably appeared at the time of the action on which liability is sought to be based. It is the existence of reasonable grounds for the belief formed at the time and in light of all the circumstances, coupled with good-faith belief, that affords a basis for qualified immunity of executive officers for acts performed in the course of official conduct." Id. at 239, 247–48.

The rationale of *Scheuer* was applied in Apton v. Wilson, 506 F.2d 83 (D.C.Cir.1974), an action for alleged violations of constitutional rights occurring during the "Mayday Demonstrations" in Washington in 1970; the named defendants included the Attorney General and other high officials in the Department of Justice, the Chief of Police, and other police officers. In both cases, the disposition was to remand for further proceedings; the courts did not have facts before them with which to decide whether the defendants did have immunity in the circumstances of the case.

Relying on *Scheuer* and related cases, the court, in Bryan v. Jones, 530 F.2d 1210 (5th Cir.1976), held that in a § 1983 action for false imprisonment, the defense of official immunity is available to a jailer acting in reasonable good faith. Qualified immunity of prison officials is not available for unconstitutional acts if officials had fair warning that the acts were unconstitutional, even in a novel factual situation. Hope v. Pelzer, 536 U.S. 730 (2002) (6–3). "[P]rivate prison guards, unlike those who work directly for the government, do not enjoy immunity from suit in a § 1983 case." Richardson v. McKnight, 521 U.S. 399 (1997) (5–4).

It has been held that court-appointed defense counsel and public defenders acting in their capacity as lawyers also have absolute immunity from suit under § 1983. E.g., Robinson v. Bergstrom, 579 F.2d 401 (7th Cir.1978); Minns v. Paul, 542 F.2d 899 (4th Cir.1976). In *Minns*, the court said that there were two reasons for such immunity: "(a) the need to recruit and hold able lawyers to represent indigents—both full and part-time public defenders, as well as private practitioners appointed by courts to represent individual defendants or litigants, and (b) the need to encourage counsel in the full exercise of professionalism, i.e., the unfettered discretion, in the light of their training and experience, to decline to press the frivolous, to assign priorities between indigent litigants, and to make strategic decisions with regard to a single litigant as to how best his interests may be advanced." Id. at 901. The court added that the latter consideration was particularly compelling when counsel is supplied by the state, since the lawyer may have no control over which clients he will accept and "the client has no economic incentive for eschewing frivolous claims." Id. at 902. That conclusion is considerably undermined by Ferri v. Ackerman, 444 U.S. 193, 204 (1979), below, in which the Court said that since "a defense counsel's principal responsibility is to serve the individual interests of his client," it was not necessary to insulate him entirely from the risk of a claim against him by the client. See White v. Bloom, 621 F.2d 276, 280 (8th Cir.1980), stating that after Ferri v. Ackerman, the position taken in *Robinson* and *Minns* is "no longer tenable."

In any event, it is generally held that defense counsel, whether appointed or retained, is not acting under color of state law, as required by § 1983, but is acting as a private attorney. E.g., United States ex rel. Simmons v. Zibilich, 542 F.2d 259 (5th Cir.1976). "The lack of state action for volunteer court-appointed counsel follows from the nature of the attorney-client relationship. . . . The court-appointed attorney, like any retained counsel, serves his client. He represents the client, not the state. The ancillary facts that the court has a hand in providing counsel, and that the attorney selection board in Orleans Parish obtains its authority from statute, do not alter the attorney-client relationship. That relationship is our concern here." Id. at 261. The Court has held also that a public defender who represents an indigent defendant in a state criminal proceeding does not act "under color of state law." Polk County v. Dodson, 454 U.S. 312 (1981) (8–1). The Court said that a public defender's function rather than his employment relationship with the state is determinative. A public defender's function is defined by "the same standards of competence and integrity as a private lawyer" and requires the "exercise of independent judgment on behalf of the client." Id. at 321.

Public defenders have no immunity from liability under § 1983, however, for intentional misconduct such as a conspiracy with state officials to violate federal constitutional rights. Tower v. Glover, 467 U.S. 914 (1984). (With respect to the holding of Polk County v. Dodson, above, an otherwise private person acts "under color of state law" if he engages in a conspiracy with state officials to violate federal rights. Dennis v. Sparks, 449 U.S. 24 (1980).) See also Ferri v. Ackerman, 444 U.S. 193 (1979), holding that an attorney appointed to represent an indigent defendant in a federal criminal trial does not, as a matter of federal law, have absolute immunity in a state malpractice suit brought against him by his former client.

Government witnesses, like other witnesses, have an absolute immunity from a convicted defendant's suit under § 1983 for damages for having given perjured testimony at the defendant's trial. Briscoe v. LaHue, 460 U.S. 325 (1983) (6–3). The witnesses in question were police officers. The Court observed that the principle of Pierson v. Ray (judges) and Imbler v. Pachtman (prosecutors), above, applied also to witnesses, "who perform a somewhat different function in the trial process but whose participation in bringing the litigation to a just—or possibly unjust—conclusion is equally indispensable." 460 U.S. at 345.

54. "[A] jury may be permitted to assess punitive damages in an action under § 1983 when the defendant's conduct is shown to be motivated by evil motive or intent, or when it involves reckless or callous indifference to the federally protected rights of others." Smith v. Wade, 461 U.S. 30, 56 (1983) (5–4).

55. In an action under § 1983 charging that the defendant police officers made an unlawful entry into the plaintiff's apartment and assaulted him, the district judge found that there had been an unlawful entry but not an assault, and that the plaintiff did not suffer physical or emotional damage. The judge awarded damages of $500 which he described as "nominal damages." On appeal, the court said that the award was improper. "If a compensable injury has been shown, compensatory damages must be given; if not, nominal damages should not be used to compensate plaintiff in any substantial manner, since he has shown no right to such compensation. We do not accept those decisions that have awarded as nominal damages more than a token amount. Five hundred dollars charged against an individual police officer is no mere token." The court went on to say that substantial damages could be awarded as compensation "for actual, though wholly impalpable injuries," such as "an intangible loss of civil rights or purely mental suffering." Magnett v. Pelletier, 488 F.2d 33 (1st Cir.1973).

"[I]n order to recover damages for allegedly unconstitutional conviction or imprisonment, or for other harm caused by actions whose unlawfulness would render a conviction or sentence invalid, a § 1983 plaintiff must prove that the conviction or sentence has been reversed on direct appeal, expunged by executive order, declared invalid by a state tribunal authorized to make such determination, or called into question by a federal court's issuance of a writ of habeas corpus, 28 U.S.C. § 2254. A claim for damages bearing that relationship to a conviction or sentence that has *not* been so invalidated is not cognizable under § 1983. Thus, when a state prisoner seeks damages in a § 1983 suit, the district court must consider whether a judgment in favor of the plaintiff would necessarily imply the invalidity of his conviction or sentence; if it would, the complaint must be dismissed unless the plaintiff can demonstrate that the conviction or sentence has already been invalidated. But if the district court determines that the plaintiff's action, even if successful, will *not* demonstrate the invalidity of any outstanding criminal judgment against the plaintiff, the action should be allowed to proceed, in the absence of some other bar to the suit.'' Heck v. Humphrey, 512 U.S. 477, 486–87 (1994).

56. Bivens v. Six Unknown Named Agents of Federal Bureau of Narcotics, 403 U.S. 388 (1971). Section 1983 provides no remedy for violation of constitutional rights by federal officials. In *Bivens*, the Supreme Court held that the violation of rights protected by the Fourth Amendment by a federal agent acting under color of his authority gives rise to a federal cause of action. The person whose rights are violated is entitled to recover money damages for any injuries he suffered as a result of the violation.

On remand, the court of appeals held that federal police officers, such as FBI agents, have no immunity from actions for damages based on a violation of constitutional rights. With respect to liability, the court said: ''[T]o prevail the police officer need not allege and prove probable cause in the constitutional sense. The standard governing police conduct is composed of two elements, the first is subjective and the second is objective. Thus the officer must allege and prove not only that he believed, in good faith, that his conduct was lawful, but also that his belief was reasonable. And so we hold that it is a defense to allege and prove good faith and reasonable belief in the validity of the arrest and search and in the necessity for carrying out the arrest and search in the way the arrest was made and the search was conducted. We think, as a matter of constitutional law and as a matter of common sense, a law enforcement officer is entitled to protection.'' 456 F.2d 1339, 1348 (2d Cir.1972).

As a general matter, the rules applicable to actions under § 1983, p. 86 note 53 above, are applicable also to actions against federal officers under *Bivens*. See, e.g., Brawer v. Horowitz, 535 F.2d 830 (3d Cir.1976) (federal prosecutors have the same immunity as state prosecutors).

57. Arrest records. Can a person who is arrested and subsequently released without charges being filed or following dismissal of the charges or an acquittal have his arrest record and fingerprints and photographs made at the time of his arrest suppressed? The FBI maintains an elaborate system for the accumulation and retrieval of arrest records and fingerprints of persons arrested on federal or state charges. See Utz v. Cullinane, 520 F.2d 467, 480–82 (D.C.Cir.1975); Menard v. Saxbe, 498 F.2d 1017, 1020–22 (D.C.Cir.1974). Local and state police departments maintain their own files.

In *Menard*, the appellant sued to compel removal from the FBI files of an arrest record including his fingerprints. He had been arrested and detained by the California police, who later released him without charges. The district court found that there had been probable cause for the arrest. Expungement of the record was denied. On appeal from the district court's order the court of appeals held that Menard was entitled to an order directing the FBI to remove his record from its criminal files. The court noted the variety of disabilities that may flow from an arrest record.

> There is an undoubted "social stigma" involved in an arrest record. "[I]t is common knowledge that a man with an arrest record is much more apt to be subject to police scrutiny—the first to be questioned and the last eliminated as a suspect to an investigation."[18] Existence of a record may burden a decision whether to testify at trial. And records of arrest are used by judges in making decisions as to sentencing, whether to grant bail, or whether to release pending appeal.
>
> The arrest record is used outside the field of criminal justice. Most significant is its use in connection with subsequent inquiries on applications for employment and licenses to engage in certain fields of work. An arrest record often proves to be a substantial barrier to employment.

498 F.2d at 1024.

The court said that ordinarily an action to expunge an arrest record should be brought against the local police agency that made the arrest. With respect to the FBI, the court said that "the FBI's function of maintaining and disseminating criminal identification records and files carries with it as a corollary the responsibility to discharge this function reliably and responsibly and without unnecessary harm to individuals whose rights have been invaded. The FBI cannot take the position that it is a mere passive recipient of records received from others, when it in fact energizes those records by maintaining a system of criminal files and disseminating the criminal records widely, acting in effect as a step-up transformer that puts into the system a capacity for both good and harm." Id. at 1026. Having been informed by the local police that there was no basis for Menard's arrest, the FBI had no authority to retain his record in its criminal files along with arrest records. The court's decision was based on its interpretation of the statute (28 U.S.C. § 534) authorizing the FBI to maintain identification files.

In Tarlton v. Saxbe, 507 F.2d 1116 (D.C.Cir.1974), the court of appeals indicated that the FBI's duty went beyond expungement of arrest records later reported to it as incorrect and included some more general duty to prevent dissemination of inaccurate arrest and conviction records. The court recognized the practical difficulties that such an affirmative duty might impose on the FBI, and remanded to the district court for an inquiry into its appropriate nature and scope. The court noted that the FBI could not reasonably be required to resolve a factual or legal conflict between arresting authorities and the person arrested, nor to guarantee the accuracy of its files. The district court's findings and orders, which include a description of the FBI's practices, appear at 407 F.Supp. 1083 (D.D.C.1976). See generally Utz v. Cullinane, above (transmission of local arrest records to FBI).

The rulings in *Menard* and *Tarlton* are unusual. Where there is no claim that the police conduct in making the arrest was abusive or that

18. Davidson v. Dill, 503 P.2d 157, 159 (Colo.1972).

Boston Police Department
Mugshot Form

Report Date: 05/09/1997 12:57:24
Booking Status: COMPLETED
Printed By: Dahlbeck, Joseph W

Master Name: **Pomeroy, Arnold, George**
Booking Name: Layfield, Robert, Arthur
Address: Apt 23, 312 Evergreen CR , Boston, MA.
Charges: Breaking & Entering N/T, Poss cl B

Sex: Male
Date of Birth: 06/09/1942
Height: 5' 11"
Weight: 200 **lbs**
Eye Color: Brown
Hair Color: Dark Brown
Race: White Non-Hispanic
Booking No: 95-000316-04
Booking Date: 02/10/1997 11:25
Incident Number: 95-1000000
BPD CR No: 000001-80
State Tracking No: 1234567890123
FBI No: 1234567890

Boston Police Department
Mugshot Form

Report Date: 05/09/1997 12:57:24
Booking Status: COMPLETED
Printed By: Dahlbeck, Joseph W

Master Name: **Pomeroy, Arnold, George**
Booking Name: Layfield, Robert, Arthur
Address: Apt 23, 312 Evergreen CR , Boston, MA.
Charges: Breaking & Entering N/T, Poss cl B

Sex: Male
Date of Birth: 06/09/1942
Height: 5' 11"
Weight: 200 **lbs**
Eye Color: Brown
Hair Color: Dark Brown
Race: White Non-Hispanic
Booking No: 95-000316-04
Booking Date: 02/10/1997 11:25
Incident Number: 95-1000000
BPD CR No: 000001-80
State Tracking No: 1234567890123
FBI No: 1234567890

Boston Police Department
Fingerprint Scratch Pad

Report Date: 05/16/1997 12:30:38
Printed by: Joseph W Dahlbeck

Booking Number: 95-000318-04 Criminal Record Number: 967132-80 Booking Name: Layfield, Robert, Arthur there was an intention to make improper use of the arrest record, expungement has generally not been ordered. "[A]n acquittal, standing alone, is not in itself sufficient to warrant an expunction of an arrest record." United States v. Linn, 513 F.2d 925, 927–28 (10th Cir.1975). In Herschel v. Dyra, 365 F.2d 17, 20 (7th Cir.1966), the court said: "We think that under the obligations which the Chicago Police Department has in maintaining the public safety and welfare in Chicago, the Superintendent of Police is justified and, indeed, duty-bound to compile and retain arrest records of all persons arrested, and that the execution of that policy does not violate plaintiff's right of privacy." To the same effect, see, e.g., United States v. Schnitzer, 567 F.2d 536 (2d Cir.1977). But see Kowall v. United States, 53 F.R.D. 211 (W.D.Mich.1971) (expungement order upheld). For an example of a case in which improper conduct in making the arrests was the basis of the demand for expungement, see Sullivan v. Murphy, 478 F.2d 938 (D.C.Cir.1973) (case remanded to district court for fashioning of remedy). See also Bilick v. Dudley, 356 F.Supp. 945 (S.D.N.Y.1973) (arrests without probable cause and in violation of First Amendment rights; expungement ordered).

The subject of expungement of records maintained by the executive branch of government is discussed thoroughly in Sealed Appellant v. Sealed Appellee, 130 F.3d 695 (5th Cir.1997). The appellee had been convicted of wire fraud and conspiracy. The conviction was subsequently set aside because of error in the jury instructions, and he was not retried. Six years later, alleging that records of his conviction interfered with his professional law-enforcement activities, he filed a petition for expungement of all records of his convictions. The court said that "[t]here is no constitutional basis for a 'right to expungement.' " Id. at 699. "To have standing, a party claiming expungement of executive branch records must make a showing of more than mere burden. Unlike a person asking for expungement of judicial records—over which the court has supervisory powers—the claimant must show an affirmative rights violation by executive branch officers or agencies to justify the intrusion into the executive's affairs. This injury must be such that no other remedy would afford relief." Id. at 697. The court concluded that the district court's expungement order was an abuse of discretion.

In United States v. Doe, 730 F.2d 1529 (D.C.Cir.1984), the court held that the provision of the Federal Youth Corrections Act for setting aside a conviction requires that court records disclosing a conviction be sealed and available only to judicial, administrative, and law enforcement officials in the performance of their duties. But see United States v. Doe, 732 F.2d 229 (1st Cir.1984).

Compare Paul v. Davis, 424 U.S. 693 (1976) (5–3), in which the plaintiff's name and photograph appeared on a flyer describing "active shoplifters" that the police distributed to local merchants. He had been charged with shoplifting, but the case had been filed without a disposition. Observing that the plaintiff might well have a claim for defamation under state law, the Court concluded that he nevertheless did not have any claim under 42 U.S.C. § 1983 for deprivation of a constitutional right, in particular a denial of due process of law.

CHAPTER 2

STOP (AND FRISK)

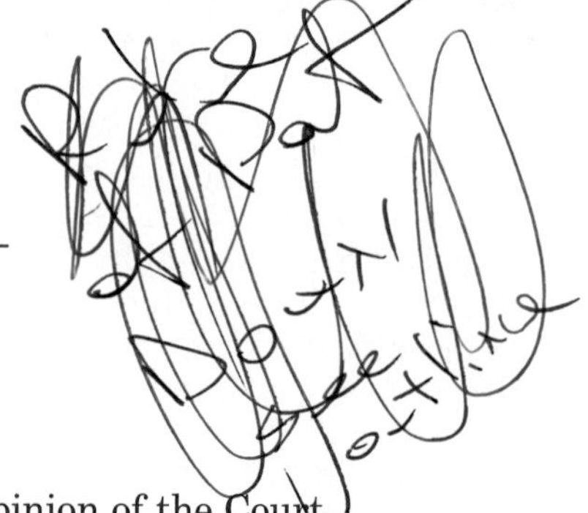

Terry v. Ohio

392 U.S. 1, 88 S.Ct. 1868, 20 L.Ed.2d 889 (1968)

■ MR. CHIEF JUSTICE WARREN delivered the opinion of the Court.

This case presents serious questions concerning the role of the Fourth Amendment in the confrontation on the street between the citizen and the policeman investigating suspicious circumstances.

Petitioner Terry was convicted of carrying a concealed weapon and sentenced to the statutorily prescribed term of one to three years in the penitentiary. Following the denial of a pretrial motion to suppress, the prosecution introduced in evidence two revolvers and a number of bullets seized from Terry and a codefendant, Richard Chilton, by Cleveland Police Detective Martin McFadden. At the hearing on the motion to suppress this evidence, Officer McFadden testified that while he was patrolling in plain clothes in downtown Cleveland at approximately 2:30 in the afternoon of October 31, 1963, his attention was attracted by two men, Chilton and Terry, standing on the corner of Huron Road and Euclid Avenue. He had never seen the two men before, and he was unable to say precisely what first drew his eye to them. However, he testified that he had been a policeman for 39 years and a detective for 35 and that he had been assigned to patrol this vicinity of downtown Cleveland for shoplifters and pickpockets for 30 years. He explained that he had developed routine habits of observation over the years and that he would "stand and watch people or walk and watch people at many intervals of the day." He added: "Now, in this case when I looked over they didn't look right to me at the time."

His interest aroused, Officer McFadden took up a post of observation in the entrance to a store 300 to 400 feet away from the two men. "I get more purpose to watch them when I seen their movements," he testified. He saw one of the men leave the other one and walk southwest on Huron Road, past some stores. The man paused for a moment and looked in a store window, then walked on a short distance, turned around and walked back toward the corner, pausing once again to look in the same store window. He rejoined his companion at the corner, and the two conferred briefly. Then the second man went through the same series of motions, strolling down Huron Road, looking in the same window, walking on a short distance, turning back, peering in the store window again, and returning to confer with the first man at the corner. The two men repeated this ritual alternately between five and six times apiece—in all, roughly a dozen trips. At one point, while the two were standing together on the corner, a third man approached them and engaged them briefly in conversation. This man then left the two others and walked west on Euclid Avenue. Chilton and Terry resumed their measured pacing, peering, and conferring. After this had gone on for 10 to 12 minutes, the two men walked off together, heading west on Euclid Avenue, following the path taken earlier by the third man.

By this time Officer McFadden had become thoroughly suspicious. He testified that after observing their elaborately casual and oft-repeated reconnaissance of the store window on Huron Road, he suspected the two men of "casing a job, a stick-up," and that he considered it his duty as a police officer to investigate further. He added that he feared "they may have a gun." Thus, Officer McFadden followed Chilton and Terry and saw them stop in front of Zucker's store to talk to the same man who had conferred with them earlier on the street corner. Deciding that the situation was ripe for direct action, Officer McFadden approached the three men, identified himself as a police officer and asked for their names. At this point his knowledge was confined to what he had observed. He was not acquainted with any of the three men by name or by sight, and he had received no information concerning them from any other source. When the men "mumbled something" in response to his inquiries, Officer McFadden grabbed petitioner Terry, spun him around so that they were facing the other two, with Terry between McFadden and the others, and patted down the outside of his clothing. In the left breast pocket of Terry's overcoat Officer McFadden felt a pistol. He reached inside the overcoat pocket, but was unable to remove the gun. At this point, keeping Terry between himself and the others, the officer ordered all three men to enter Zucker's store. As they went in, he removed Terry's overcoat completely, removed a .38-caliber revolver from the pocket and ordered all three men to face the wall with their hands raised. Officer McFadden proceeded to pat down the outer clothing of Chilton and the third man, Katz. He discovered another revolver in the outer pocket of Chilton's overcoat, but no weapons were found on Katz. The officer testified that he only patted the men down to see whether they had weapons, and that he did not put his hands beneath the outer garments of either Terry or Chilton until he felt their guns. So far as appears from the record, he never placed his hands beneath Katz' outer garments. Officer McFadden seized Chilton's gun, asked the proprietor of the store to call a police wagon, and took all three men to the station, where Chilton and Terry were formally charged with carrying concealed weapons.

On the motion to suppress the guns the prosecution took the position that they had been seized following a search incident to a lawful arrest. The trial court rejected this theory, stating that it "would be stretching the facts beyond reasonable comprehension" to find that Officer McFadden had had probable cause to arrest the men before he patted them down for weapons. However, the court denied the defendants' motion on the ground that Officer McFadden, on the basis of his experience, "had reasonable cause to believe . . . that the defendants were conducting themselves suspiciously, and some interrogation should be made of their action." Purely for his own protection, the court held, the officer had the right to pat down the outer clothing of these men, who he had reasonable cause to believe might be armed. The court distinguished between an investigatory "stop" and an arrest, and between a "frisk" of the outer clothing for weapons and a full-blown search for evidence of crime. The frisk, it held, was essential to the proper performance of the officer's investigatory duties, for without it "the answer to the police officer may be a bullet, and a loaded pistol discovered during the frisk is admissible."

After the court denied their motion to suppress, Chilton and Terry waived jury trial and pleaded not guilty. The court adjudged them guilty, and the Court of Appeals for the Eighth Judicial District, Cuyahoga County, affirmed. . . . The Supreme Court of Ohio dismissed their appeal on the ground that no "substantial constitutional question" was involved. We granted certiorari . . . to determine whether the admission of the revolvers in evidence violated petitioner's rights under the Fourth Amendment, made applicable to the States by the Fourteenth. . . . We affirm the conviction.

I

The Fourth Amendment provides that "the right of the people to be secure in their persons, houses, papers, and effects, against unreasonable searches and seizures, shall not be violated. . . ." This inestimable right of personal security belongs as much to the citizen on the streets of our cities as to the homeowner closeted in his study to dispose of his secret affairs. . . . We have recently held that "the Fourth Amendment protects people, not places," Katz v. United States, 389 U.S. 347, 351 (1967), and whenever an individual may harbor a reasonable "expectation of privacy," id., at 361 (Mr. Justice Harlan, concurring), he is entitled to be free from unreasonable governmental intrusion. Of course, the specific content and incidents of this right must be shaped by the context in which it is asserted. For "what the Constitution forbids is not all searches and seizures, but unreasonable searches and seizures." Elkins v. United States, 364 U.S. 206, 222 (1960). Unquestionably petitioner was entitled to the protection of the Fourth Amendment as he walked down the street in Cleveland. . . . The question is whether in all the circumstances of this on-the-street encounter, his right to personal security was violated by an unreasonable search and seizure.

We would be less than candid if we did not acknowledge that this question thrusts to the fore difficult and troublesome issues regarding a sensitive area of police activity—issues which have never before been squarely presented to this Court. Reflective of the tensions involved are the practical and constitutional arguments pressed with great vigor on both sides of the public debate over the power of the police to "stop and frisk"—as it is sometimes euphemistically termed—suspicious persons.

On the one hand, it is frequently argued that in dealing with the rapidly unfolding and often dangerous situations on city streets the police are in need of an escalating set of flexible responses, graduated in relation to the amount of information they possess. For this purpose it is urged that distinctions should be made between a "stop" and an "arrest" (or a "seizure" of a person), and between a "frisk" and a "search." Thus, it is argued, the police should be allowed to "stop" a person and detain him briefly for questioning upon suspicion that he may be connected with criminal activity. Upon suspicion that the person may be armed, the police should have the power to "frisk" him for weapons. If the "stop" and the "frisk" give rise to probable cause to believe that the suspect has committed a crime, then the police should be empowered to make a formal "arrest," and a full incident "search" of the person. This scheme is justified in part upon the notion that a "stop" and a "frisk" amount to a mere "minor inconvenience and petty indignity," which can properly be imposed upon the citizen in the interest of effective law enforcement on the basis of a police officer's suspicion.

On the other side the argument is made that the authority of the police must be strictly circumscribed by the law of arrest and search as it has developed to date in the traditional jurisprudence of the Fourth Amendment. It is contended with some force that there is not—and cannot be—a variety of police activity which does not depend solely upon the voluntary cooperation of the citizen and yet which stops short of an arrest based upon probable cause to make such an arrest. The heart of the Fourth Amendment, the argument runs, is a severe requirement of specific justification for any intrusion upon protected personal security, coupled with a highly developed system of judicial controls to enforce upon the agents of the State the commands of the Constitution. Acquiescence by the courts in the compulsion inherent in the field interrogation practices at issue here, it is urged, would constitute an abdication of judicial control over, and indeed an encouragement of, substantial interference with liberty and personal security by police officers whose judgment is necessarily colored by their primary involvement in "the often competitive enterprise of ferreting out crime." Johnson v. United States, 333 U.S. 10, 14 (1948). This, it is argued, can only serve to exacerbate police-community tensions in the crowded centers of our Nation's cities.

In this context we approach the issues in this case mindful of the limitations of the judicial function in controlling the myriad daily situations in which policemen and citizens confront each other on the street. The State has characterized the issue here as "the right of a police officer . . . to make an on-the-street stop, interrogate and pat down for weapons (known in street vernacular as 'stop and frisk')." But this is only partly accurate. For the issue is not the abstract propriety of the police conduct, but the admissibility against petitioner of the evidence uncovered by the search and seizure. Ever since its inception, the rule excluding evidence seized in violation of the Fourth Amendment has been recognized as a principal mode of discouraging lawless police conduct. . . . Thus its major thrust is a deterrent one . . . and experience has taught that it is the only effective deterrent to police misconduct in the criminal context, and that without it the constitutional guarantee against unreasonable searches and seizures would be a mere "form of words." Mapp v. Ohio, 367 U.S. 643, 655 (1961). The rule also serves another vital function—"the imperative of judicial integrity." Elkins v. United States, 364 U.S. 206, 222 (1960). Courts which sit under our Constitution cannot and will not be made party to lawless invasions of the constitutional rights of citizens by permitting unhindered governmental use of the fruits of such invasions. Thus in our system evidentiary rulings provide the context in which the judicial process of inclusion and exclusion approves some conduct as comporting with constitutional guarantees and disapproves other actions by state agents. A ruling admitting evidence in a criminal trial, we recognize, has the necessary effect of legitimizing the conduct which produced the evidence, while an application of the exclusionary rule withholds the constitutional imprimatur.

The exclusionary rule has its limitations, however, as a tool of judicial control. It cannot properly be invoked to exclude the products of legitimate police investigative techniques on the ground that much conduct which is closely similar involves unwarranted intrusions upon constitutional protections. Moreover, in some contexts the rule is ineffective as a deterrent. Street encounters between citizens and police officers are incredibly rich in diversity. They range from wholly friendly exchanges of pleasantries or mutually useful information to hostile confrontations of armed men involving arrests, or injuries, or loss of life. Moreover, hostile confrontations are not all of a piece. Some of them begin in a friendly enough manner, only to take a different turn upon the injection of some unexpected element into the conversation. Encounters are initiated by the police for a wide variety of purposes, some of which are wholly unrelated to a desire to prosecute for crime. Doubtless some police "field interrogation" conduct violates the Fourth Amendment. But a stern refusal by this Court to condone such activity does not necessarily render it responsive to the exclusionary rule. Regardless of how effective the rule may be where obtaining convictions is an important objective of the police, it is powerless to deter invasions of constitutionally guaranteed rights where the police either have no interest in prosecuting or are willing to forgo successful prosecution in the interest of serving some other goal.

Proper adjudication of cases in which the exclusionary rule is invoked demands a constant awareness of these limitations. The wholesale harassment by certain elements of the police community, of which minority groups, particularly Negroes, frequently complain, will not be stopped by the exclusion of any evidence from any criminal trial. Yet a rigid and unthinking application of the exclusionary rule, in futile protest against practices which it can never be used effectively to control, may exact a high toll in human injury and frustration of efforts to prevent crime. No judicial opinion can comprehend the protean variety of the street encounter, and we can only judge the facts of the case before us. Nothing we say today is to be taken as indicating approval of police conduct outside the legitimate investigative sphere. Under our decision, courts still retain their traditional responsibility to guard against police conduct which is overbearing or harassing, or which trenches upon personal security without the objective evidentiary justification which the Constitution requires. When such conduct is identified, it must be condemned by the judiciary and its fruits must be excluded from evidence in criminal trials. And, of course, our approval of legitimate and restrained investigative conduct undertaken on the basis of ample factual justification should in no way discourage the employment of other remedies than the exclusionary rule to curtail abuses for which that sanction may prove inappropriate.

Having thus roughly sketched the perimeters of the constitutional debate over the limits on police investigative conduct in general and the background against which this case presents itself, we turn our attention to the quite narrow question posed by the facts before us: whether it is always unreasonable for a policeman to seize a person and subject him to a limited search for weapons unless there is probable cause for an arrest. Given the narrowness of this question, we have no occasion to canvass in detail the constitutional limitations upon the scope of a policeman's power when he confronts a citizen without probable cause to arrest him.

II

Our first task is to establish at what point in this encounter the Fourth Amendment becomes relevant. That is, we must decide whether and when Officer McFadden "seized" Terry and whether and when he conducted a "search." There is some suggestion in the use of such terms as "stop" and "frisk" that such police conduct is outside the purview of the Fourth Amendment because neither action rises to the level of a "search" or "seizure" within the meaning of the Constitution. We emphatically reject this notion. It is quite plain that the Fourth Amendment governs "seizures" of the person which do not eventuate in a trip to the station house and prosecution for crime—"arrests" in traditional terminology. It must be recognized that whenever a police officer accosts an individual and restrains his freedom to walk away, he has "seized" that person. And it is nothing less than sheer torture of the English language to suggest that a careful exploration of the outer surfaces of a person's clothing all over his or her body in an attempt to find weapons is not a "search." Moreover, it is simply fantastic to urge that such a procedure performed in public by a policeman while the citizen stands helpless, perhaps facing a wall with his hands raised, is a "petty indignity." It is a serious intrusion upon the sanctity of the person, which may inflict great indignity and arouse strong resentment, and it is not to be undertaken lightly.

The danger in the logic which proceeds upon distinctions between a "stop" and an "arrest," or "seizure" of the person, and between a "frisk" and a "search" is twofold. It seeks to isolate from constitutional scrutiny the initial stages of the contact between the policeman and the citizen. And by suggesting a rigid all-or-nothing model of justification and regulation under the Amendment, it obscures the utility of limitations upon the scope, as well as the initiation, of police action as a means of constitutional regulation. This Court has held in the past that a search which is reasonable at its inception may violate the Fourth Amendment by virtue of its intolerable intensity and scope. . . . The scope of the search must be "strictly tied to and justified by" the circumstances which rendered its initiation permissible. Warden v. Hayden, 387 U.S. 294, 310 (1967) (Mr. Justice Fortas, concurring). . . .

The distinctions of classical "stop-and-frisk" theory thus serve to divert attention from the central inquiry under the Fourth Amendment—the reasonableness in all the circumstances of the particular governmental invasion of a citizen's personal security. "Search" and "seizure" are not talismans. We therefore reject the notions that the Fourth Amendment does not come into play at all as a limitation upon police conduct if the officers stop short of something called a "technical arrest" or a "full-blown search."

In this case there can be no question, then, that Officer McFadden "seized" petitioner and subjected him to a "search" when he took hold of him and patted down the outer surfaces of his clothing. We must decide whether at that point it was reasonable for Officer McFadden to have interfered with petitioner's personal security as he did.[1] And in determining whether the seizure and search were "unreasonable" our inquiry is a dual one—whether the officer's action was justified at its inception, and whether it was reasonably related in scope to the circumstances which justified the interference in the first place.

III

If this case involved police conduct subject to the Warrant Clause of the Fourth Amendment, we would have to ascertain whether "probable cause" existed to justify the search and seizure which took place. However, that is not the case. We do not retreat from our holdings that the police must, whenever practicable, obtain advance judicial approval of searches and seizures through the warrant procedure . . . or that in most instances failure to comply with the warrant requirement can only be excused by exigent circumstances. . . . But we deal here with an entire rubric of police conduct—necessarily swift action predicated upon the on-the-spot observations of the officer on the beat—which historically has not been, and as a practical matter could not be, subjected to the warrant procedure. Instead, the conduct involved in this case must be tested by the Fourth Amendment's general proscription against unreasonable searches and seizures.

Nonetheless, the notions which underlie both the warrant procedure and the requirement of probable cause remain fully relevant in this context. In order to assess the reasonableness of Officer McFadden's

1. We thus decide nothing today concerning the constitutional propriety of an investigative "seizure" upon less than probable cause for purposes of "detention" and/or interrogation. Obviously, not all personal intercourse between policemen and citizens involves "seizures" of persons. Only when the officer, by means of physical force or show of authority, has in some way restrained the liberty of a citizen may we conclude that a "seizure" has occurred. We cannot tell with any certainty upon this record whether any such "seizure" took place here prior to Officer McFadden's initiation of physical contact for purposes of searching Terry for weapons, and we thus may assume that up to that point no intrusion upon constitutionally protected rights had occurred.

conduct as a general proposition, it is necessary "first to focus upon the governmental interest which allegedly justifies official intrusion upon the constitutionally protected interests of the private citizen," for there is "no ready test for determining reasonableness other than by balancing the need to search [or seize] against the invasion which the search [or seizure] entails." Camara v. Municipal Court, 387 U.S. 523, 534–35, 536–37 (1967). And in justifying the particular intrusion the police officer must be able to point to specific and articulable facts which, taken together with rational inferences from those facts, reasonably warrant that intrusion. The scheme of the Fourth Amendment becomes meaningful only when it is assured that at some point the conduct of those charged with enforcing the laws can be subjected to the more detached, neutral scrutiny of a judge who must evaluate the reasonableness of a particular search or seizure in light of the particular circumstances. And in making that assessment it is imperative that the facts be judged against an objective standard: would the facts available to the officer at the moment of the seizure or the search "warrant a man of reasonable caution in the belief" that the action taken was appropriate? . . . Anything less would invite intrusions upon constitutionally guaranteed rights based on nothing more substantial than inarticulate hunches, a result this Court has consistently refused to sanction. . . . And simple " 'good faith on the part of the arresting officer is not enough.' . . . If subjective good faith alone were the test, the protections of the Fourth Amendment would evaporate, and the people would be 'secure in their persons, houses, papers, and effects,' only in the discretion of the police." Beck v. Ohio [379 U.S. 89 (1964)], at 97.

Applying these principles to this case, we consider first the nature and extent of the governmental interests involved. One general interest is of course that of effective crime prevention and detection; it is this interest which underlies the recognition that a police officer may in appropriate circumstances and in an appropriate manner approach a person for purposes of investigating possibly criminal behavior even though there is no probable cause to make an arrest. It was this legitimate investigative function officer McFadden was discharging when he decided to approach petitioner and his companions. He had observed Terry, Chilton, and Katz go through a series of acts, each of them perhaps innocent in itself, but which taken together warranted further investigation. There is nothing unusual in two men standing together on a street corner, perhaps waiting for someone. Nor is there anything suspicious about people in such circumstances strolling up and down the street, singly or in pairs. Store windows, moreover, are made to be looked in. But the story is quite different where, as here, two men hover about a street corner for an extended period of time, at the end of which it becomes apparent that they are not waiting for anyone or anything; where these men pace alternately along an identical route, pausing to stare in the same store window roughly 24 times; where each completion of this route is followed immediately by a conference between the two men on the corner; where they are joined in one of these conferences by a third man who leaves swiftly; and where the two men finally follow the third and rejoin him a couple of blocks away. It would have been poor police work indeed for an officer of 30 years' experience in the detection of thievery from stores in this same neighborhood to have failed to investigate this behavior further.

The crux of this case, however, is not the propriety of Officer McFadden's taking steps to investigate petitioner's suspicious behavior, but rather, whether there was justification for McFadden's invasion of Terry's personal security by searching him for weapons in the course of that investigation. We are now concerned with more than the governmental interest in investigating crime; in addition, there is the more immediate interest of the police officer in taking steps to assure himself that the person with whom he is dealing is not armed with a weapon that could unexpectedly and fatally be used against him. Certainly it would be unreasonable to require that police officers take unnecessary risks in the performance of their duties. American criminals have a long tradition of armed violence, and every year in this country many law enforcement officers are killed in the line of duty, and thousands more are wounded. Virtually all of these deaths and a substantial portion of the injuries are inflicted with guns and knives.

In view of these facts, we cannot blind ourselves to the need for law enforcement officers to protect themselves and other prospective victims of violence in situations where they may lack probable cause for an arrest. When an officer is justified in believing that the individual whose suspicious behavior he is investigating at close range is armed and presently dangerous to the officer or to others, it would appear to be clearly unreasonable to deny the officer the power to take necessary measures to determine whether the person is in fact carrying a weapon and to neutralize the threat of physical harm.

We must still consider, however, the nature and quality of the intrusion on individual rights which must be accepted if police officers are to be conceded the right to search for weapons in situations where probable cause to arrest for crime is lacking. Even a limited search of the outer clothing for weapons constitutes a severe, though brief, intrusion upon cherished personal security, and it must surely be an annoying, frightening, and perhaps humiliating experience. Petitioner contends that such an intrusion is permissible only incident to a lawful arrest, either for a crime involving the possession of weapons or for a crime the commission of which led the officer to investigate in the first place. However, this argument must be closely examined.

Petitioner does not argue that a police officer should refrain from making any investigation of suspicious circumstances until such time as he has probable cause to make an arrest; nor does he deny that police officers in properly discharging their investigative function may find themselves confronting persons who might well be armed and dangerous. Moreover, he does not say that an officer is always unjustified in searching a suspect to discover weapons. Rather, he says it is unreasonable for the policeman to take that step until such time as the situation evolves to a point where there is probable cause to make an arrest. When that point has been reached, petitioner would concede the officer's right to conduct a search of the suspect for weapons, fruits or instrumentalities of the crime, or "mere" evidence, incident to the arrest.

There are two weaknesses in this line of reasoning, however. First, it fails to take account of traditional limitations upon the scope of searches, and thus recognizes no distinction in purpose, character, and extent between a search incident to an arrest and a limited search for weapons. The former, although justified in part by the acknowledged necessity to protect the arresting officer from assault with a concealed weapon . . . is also justified on other grounds . . . and can therefore involve a relatively extensive exploration of the person. A search for weapons in the absence of probable cause to arrest, however, must, like any other search, be strictly circumscribed by the exigencies which justify its initiation. . . . Thus it must be limited to that which is necessary for the discovery of weapons which might be used to harm the officer or others nearby, and may realistically be characterized as something less than a "full" search, even though it remains a serious intrusion.

A second, and related, objection to petitioner's argument is that it assumes that the law of arrest has already worked out the balance between the particular interests involved here—the neutralization of danger to the policeman in the investigative circumstance and the sanctity of the individual. But this is not so. An arrest is a wholly different kind of intrusion upon individual freedom from a limited search for weapons, and the interests each is designed to serve are likewise quite different. An arrest is the initial stage of a criminal prosecution. It is intended to vindicate society's interest in having its laws obeyed, and it is inevitably accompanied by future interference with the individual's freedom of movement, whether or not trial or conviction ultimately follows. The protective search for weapons, on the other hand, constitutes a brief, though far from inconsiderable, intrusion upon the sanctity of the person. It does not follow that because an officer may lawfully arrest a person only when he is apprised of facts sufficient to warrant a belief that the person has committed or is committing a crime, the officer is equally unjustified, absent that kind of evidence, in making any intrusions short of an arrest. Moreover, a perfectly reasonable apprehension of danger may arise long before the officer is possessed of adequate information to justify taking a person into custody for the purpose of prosecuting him for a crime. Petitioner's reliance on cases which have worked out standards of reasonableness with regard to "seizures" constituting arrests and searches incident thereto is thus misplaced. It assumes that the interests sought to be vindicated and the invasions of personal security may be equated in the two cases, and thereby ignores a vital aspect of the analysis of the reasonableness of particular types of conduct under the Fourth Amendment. . . .

Our evaluation of the proper balance that has to be struck in this type of case leads us to conclude that there must be a narrowly drawn authority to permit a reasonable search for weapons for the protection of the police officer, where he has reason to believe that he is dealing with an armed and dangerous individual, regardless of whether he has probable cause to arrest the individual for a crime. The officer need not be absolutely certain that the individual is armed; the issue is whether a reasonably prudent man in the circumstances would be warranted in the belief that his safety or that of others was in danger. . . . And in determining whether the officer acted reasonably in such circumstances, due weight must be given, not to his inchoate and unparticularized suspicion or "hunch," but to the specific reasonable inferences which he is entitled to draw from the facts in light of his experience. . . .

IV

We must now examine the conduct of Officer McFadden in this case to determine whether his search and seizure of petitioner were reasonable, both at their inception and as conducted. He had observed Terry, together with Chilton and another man, acting in a manner he took to be preface to a "stick-up." We think on the facts and circumstances Officer McFadden detailed before the trial judge a reasonably prudent man would have been warranted in believing petitioner was armed and thus presented a threat to the officer's safety while he was investigating his suspicious behavior. The actions of Terry and Chilton were consistent with McFadden's hypothesis that these men were contemplating a daylight robbery—which, it is reasonable to assume, would be likely to involve the use of weapons—and nothing in their conduct from the time he first noticed them until the time he confronted them and identified himself as a police officer gave him sufficient reason to negate that hypothesis. Although the trio had departed the original scene, there was nothing to indicate abandonment of an intent to commit a robbery at some point. Thus, when Officer McFadden approached the three men gathered before the display window at Zucker's store he had observed enough to make it quite reasonable to fear that they were armed; nothing in their response to his hailing them, identifying himself as a police officer, and asking their names served to dispel that reasonable belief. We cannot say his decision at that point to seize Terry and pat his clothing for weapons was the product of a volatile or inventive imagination, or was undertaken simply as an act of harassment; the record evidences the tempered act of a policeman who in the course of an investigation had to make a quick decision as to how to protect himself and others from possible danger, and took limited steps to do so.

The manner in which the seizure and search were conducted is, of course, as vital a part of the inquiry as whether they were warranted at all. The Fourth Amendment proceeds as much by limitations upon the scope of governmental action as by imposing preconditions upon its initiation. . . . The entire deterrent purpose of the rule excluding evidence seized in violation of the Fourth Amendment rests on the assumption that "limitations upon the fruit to be gathered tend to limit the quest itself." United States v. Poller, 43 F.2d 911, 914 (C.A.2d Cir.1930). . . . Thus, evidence may not be introduced if it was discovered by means of a seizure and search which were not reasonably related in scope to the justification for their initiation. . . .

We need not develop at length in this case, however, the limitations which the Fourth Amendment places upon a protective seizure and search for weapons. These limitations will have to be developed in the concrete factual circumstances of individual cases. . . . Suffice it to note that such a search, unlike a search without a warrant incident to a lawful arrest, is not justified by any need to prevent the disappearance or destruction of evidence of crime. . . . The sole justification of the search in the present situation is the protection of the police officer and others nearby, and it must therefore be confined in scope to an intrusion reasonably designed to discover guns, knives, clubs, or other hidden instruments for the assault of the police officer.

The scope of the search in this case presents no serious problem in light of these standards. Officer McFadden patted down the outer clothing of petitioner and his two companions. He did not place his hands in their pockets or under the outer surface of their garments until he had felt weapons, and then he merely reached for and removed the guns. He never did invade Katz' person beyond the outer surfaces of his clothes, since he discovered nothing in his pat-down which might have been a weapon. Officer McFadden confined his search strictly to what was minimally necessary to learn whether the men were armed and to disarm them once he discovered the weapons. He did not conduct a general exploratory search for whatever evidence of criminal activity he might find.

V

We conclude that the revolver seized from Terry was properly admitted in evidence against him. At the time he seized petitioner and searched him for weapons, Officer McFadden had reasonable grounds to believe that petitioner was armed and dangerous, and it was necessary for the protection of himself and others to take swift measures to discover the true facts and neutralize the threat of harm if it materialized. The policeman carefully restricted his search to what was appropriate to the discovery of the particular items which he sought. Each case of this sort will, of course, have to be decided on its own facts. We merely hold today that where a police officer observes unusual conduct which leads him reasonably to conclude in light of his experience that criminal activity may be afoot and that the persons with whom he is dealing may be armed and presently dangerous; where in the course of investigating this behavior he identifies himself as a policeman and makes reasonable inquiries; and where nothing in the initial stages of the encounter serves to dispel his reasonable fear for his own or others' safety, he is entitled for the protection of himself and others in the area to conduct a carefully limited search of the outer clothing of such persons in an attempt to discover weapons which might be used to assault him. Such a search is a reasonable search under the Fourth Amendment, and any weapons seized may properly be introduced in evidence against the person from whom they were taken.

■ MR. JUSTICE HARLAN, concurring.

While I unreservedly agree with the Court's ultimate holding in this case, I am constrained to fill in a few gaps, as I see them, in its opinion. I do this because what is said by this Court today will serve as initial guidelines for law enforcement authorities and courts throughout the land as this important new field of law develops.

A police officer's right to make an on-the-street "stop" and an accompanying "frisk" for weapons is of course bounded by the protections afforded by the Fourth and Fourteenth Amendments. The Court holds, and I agree, that while the right does not depend upon possession by the officer of a valid warrant, nor upon the existence of probable cause, such activities must be reasonable under the circumstances as the officer credibly relates them in court. Since the question in this and most cases is whether evidence produced by a frisk is admissible, the problem is to determine what makes a frisk reasonable.

If the State of Ohio were to provide that police officers could, on articulable suspicion less than probable cause, forcibly frisk and disarm persons thought to be carrying concealed weapons, I would have little doubt that action taken pursuant to such authority could be constitutionally reasonable. Concealed weapons create an immediate and severe danger to the public, and though that danger might not warrant routine general weapons checks, it could well warrant action on less than a "probability." I mention this line of analysis because I think it vital to point out that it cannot be applied in this case. On the record before us Ohio has not clothed its policemen with routine authority to frisk and disarm on suspicion; in the absence of state authority, policemen have no more right to "pat down" the outer clothing of passers-by, or of persons to whom they address casual questions, than does any other citizen. Consequently, the Ohio courts did not rest the constitutionality of this frisk upon any general authority in Officer McFadden to take reasonable steps to protect the citizenry, including himself, from dangerous weapons.

The state courts held, instead, that when an officer is lawfully confronting a possibly hostile person in the line of duty he has a right, springing only from the necessity of the situation and not from any broader right to disarm, to frisk for his own protection. This holding, with which I agree and with which I think the Court agrees, offers the only satisfactory basis I can think of for affirming this conviction. The holding has, however, two logical corollaries that I do not think the Court has fully expressed.

In the first place, if the frisk is justified in order to protect the officer during an encounter with a citizen, the officer must first have constitutional grounds to insist on an encounter, to make a *forcible* stop. Any person, including a policeman, is at liberty to avoid a person he considers dangerous. If and when a policeman has a right instead to disarm such a person for his own protection, he must first have a right not to avoid him but to be in his presence. That right must be more than the liberty (again, possessed by every citizen) to address questions to other persons, for ordinarily the person addressed has an equal right to ignore his interrogator and walk away; he certainly need not submit to a frisk for the questioner's protection. I would make it perfectly clear that the right to frisk in this case depends upon the reasonableness of a forcible stop to investigate a suspected crime.

Where such a stop is reasonable, however, the right to frisk must be immediate and automatic if the reason for the stop is, as here, an articulable suspicion of a crime of violence. Just as a full search incident to a lawful arrest requires no additional justification, a limited frisk incident to a lawful stop must often be rapid and routine. There is no reason why an officer, rightfully but forcibly confronting a person suspected of a serious crime, should have to ask one question and take the risk that the answer might be a bullet.

The facts of this case are illustrative of a proper stop and an incident frisk. Officer McFadden had no probable cause to arrest Terry for anything, but he had observed circumstances that would reasonably lead an experienced, prudent policeman to suspect that Terry was about to engage in burglary or robbery. His justifiable suspicion afforded a proper constitutional basis for accosting Terry, restraining his liberty of movement briefly, and addressing questions to him, and Officer McFadden did so. When he did, he had no reason whatever to suppose that Terry might be armed, apart from the fact that he suspected him of planning a violent crime. McFadden asked Terry his name, to which Terry "mumbled something." Whereupon McFadden, without asking Terry to speak louder and without giving him any chance to explain his presence or his actions, forcibly frisked him.

I would affirm this conviction for what I believe to be the same reasons the Court relies on. I would, however, make explicit what I think is implicit in affirmance on the present facts. Officer McFadden's right to interrupt Terry's freedom of movement and invade his privacy arose only because circumstances warranted forcing an encounter with Terry in an effort to prevent or investigate a crime. Once that forced encounter was justified, however, the officer's right to take suitable measures for his own safety followed automatically.

Upon the foregoing premises, I join the opinion of the Court.[2]

Adams v. Williams

407 U.S. 143, 92 S.Ct. 1921, 32 L.Ed.2d 612 (1972)

■ MR. JUSTICE REHNQUIST delivered the opinion of the Court.

Respondent Robert Williams was convicted in a Connecticut state court of illegal possession of a handgun found during a "stop and frisk," as well

[2] Justice White also wrote a concurring opinion. Justice Black noted his concurrence in the opinion of the Court with specific reservations. Justice Douglas wrote a dissenting opinion.

as of possession of heroin that was found during a full search incident to his weapons arrest. After respondent's conviction was affirmed by the Supreme Court of Connecticut . . . this Court denied certiorari. . . . Williams' petition for federal habeas corpus relief was denied by the District Court and by a divided panel of the Second Circuit . . . but on rehearing en banc the Court of Appeals granted relief. . . . That court held that evidence introduced at Williams' trial had been obtained by an unlawful search of his person and car, and thus the state court judgments of conviction should be set aside. Since we conclude that the policeman's actions here conformed to the standards this Court laid down in Terry v. Ohio, 392 U.S. 1 (1968), we reverse.

Police Sgt. John Connolly was alone early in the morning on car patrol duty in a high-crime area of Bridgeport, Connecticut. At approximately 2:15 a.m. a person known to Sgt. Connolly approached his cruiser and informed him that an individual seated in a nearby vehicle was carrying narcotics and had a gun at his waist.

After calling for assistance on his car radio, Sgt. Connolly approached the vehicle to investigate the informant's report. Connolly tapped on the car window and asked the occupant, Robert Williams, to open the door. When Williams rolled down the window instead, the sergeant reached into the car and removed a fully loaded revolver from Williams' waistband. The gun had not been visible to Connolly from outside the car, but it was in precisely the place indicated by the informant. Williams was then arrested by Connolly for unlawful possession of the pistol. A search incident to that arrest was conducted after other officers arrived. They found substantial quantities of heroin on Williams' person and in the car, and they found a machete and a second revolver hidden in the automobile.

Respondent contends that the initial seizure of his pistol, upon which rested the later search and seizure of other weapons and narcotics, was not justified by the informant's tip to Sgt. Connolly. He claims that absent a more reliable informant, or some corroboration of the tip, the policeman's actions were unreasonable under the standards set forth in Terry v. Ohio, supra.

In *Terry* this Court recognized that "a police officer may in appropriate circumstances and in an appropriate manner approach a person for purposes of investigating possibly criminal behavior even though there is no probable cause to make an arrest." Id., at 22. The Fourth Amendment does not require a policeman who lacks the precise level of information necessary for probable cause to arrest to simply shrug his shoulders and allow a crime to occur or a criminal to escape. On the contrary, *Terry* recognizes that it may be the essence of good police work to adopt an intermediate response. See id., at 23. A brief stop of a suspicious individual, in order to determine his identity or to maintain the status quo momentarily while obtaining more information, may be most reasonable in light of the facts known to the officer at the time. Id., at 21–22. . . .

The Court recognized in *Terry* that the policeman making a reasonable investigatory stop should not be denied the opportunity to protect himself from attack by a hostile suspect. "When an officer is justified in believing that the individual whose suspicious behavior he is investigating at close range is armed and presently dangerous to the officer or to others," he may conduct a limited protective search for concealed weapons. 392 U.S., at 24. The purpose of this limited search is not to discover evidence of crime, but to allow the officer to pursue his investigation without fear of violence, and thus the frisk for weapons might be equally necessary and reasonable, whether or not carrying a concealed weapon violated any applicable state law. So long as the officer is entitled to make a forcible stop,[3] and has reason to believe that the suspect is armed and dangerous, he may conduct a weapons search limited in scope to this protective purpose. Id., at 30.

Applying these principles to the present case, we believe that Sgt. Connolly acted justifiably in responding to his informant's tip. The informant was known to him personally and had provided him with information in the past. This is a stronger case than obtains in the case of an anonymous telephone tip. The informant here came forward personally to give information that was immediately verifiable at the scene. Indeed, under Connecticut law, the informant might have been subject to immediate arrest for making a false complaint had Sgt. Connolly's investigation proved the tip incorrect. Thus, while the Court's decisions indicate that this informant's unverified tip may have been insufficient for a narcotics arrest or search warrant . . . the information carried enough indicia of reliability to justify the officer's forcible stop of Williams.

In reaching this conclusion, we reject respondent's argument that reasonable cause for a stop and frisk can only be based on the officer's personal observation, rather than on information supplied by another person. Informants' tips, like all other clues and evidence coming to a policeman on the scene, may vary greatly in their value and reliability. One simple rule will not cover every situation. Some tips, completely lacking in indicia of reliability, would either warrant no police response or require further investigation before a forcible stop of a suspect would be authorized. But in some situations—for example, when the victim of a street crime seeks immediate police aid and gives a description of his assailant, or when a credible informant warns of a specific impending crime—the subtleties of the hearsay rule should not thwart an appropriate police response.

While properly investigating the activity of a person who was reported to be carrying narcotics and a concealed weapon and who was sitting alone in a car in a high-crime area at 2:15 in the morning, Sgt. Connolly had ample reason to fear for his safety. When Williams rolled down his window, rather than complying with the policeman's request to step out of the car so that his movements could more easily be seen, the revolver allegedly at Williams' waist became an even greater threat. Under these circumstances the policeman's action in reaching to the spot where the gun was thought

3. Petitioner does not contend that Williams acted voluntarily in rolling down the window of his car.

to be hidden constituted a limited intrusion designed to insure his safety, and we conclude that it was reasonable. The loaded gun seized as a result of this intrusion was therefore admissible at Williams' trial. Terry v. Ohio, 392 U.S., at 30.

Once Sgt. Connolly had found the gun precisely where the informant had predicted, probable cause existed to arrest Williams for unlawful possession of the weapon. Probable cause to arrest depends "upon whether, at the moment the arrest was made . . . the facts and circumstances within [the arresting officers'] knowledge and of which they had reasonably trustworthy information were sufficient to warrant a prudent man in believing that the [suspect] had committed or was committing an offense." Beck v. Ohio, 379 U.S. 89, 91 (1964). In the present case the policeman found Williams in possession of a gun in precisely the place predicted by the informant. This tended to corroborate the reliability of the informant's further report of narcotics and, together with the surrounding circumstances, certainly suggested no lawful explanation for possession of the gun. Probable cause does not require the same type of specific evidence of each element of the offense as would be needed to support a conviction. . . . Rather, the court will evaluate generally the circumstances at the time of the arrest to decide if the officer had probable cause for his action. . . .

Under the circumstances surrounding Williams' possession of the gun seized by Sgt. Connolly, the arrest on the weapons charge was supported by probable cause, and the search of his person and of the car incident to that arrest was lawful. . . . The fruits of the search were therefore properly admitted at Williams' trial, and the Court of Appeals erred in reaching a contrary conclusion.

. . .[4]

---

58. An anonymous tip was held to provide sufficient basis for a stop of a person driving in a car in Alabama v. White, 496 U.S. 325 (1990) (6–3). The Court said:

> Reasonable suspicion is a less demanding standard than probable cause not only in the sense that reasonable suspicion can be established with information that is different in quantity or content than that required to establish probable cause, but also in the sense that reasonable suspicion can arise from information that is less reliable than that required to show probable cause.

Id. at 330. In this case, the Court said, "under the totality of the circumstances the anonymous tip, as corroborated, exhibited sufficient indicia of reliability to justify the investigatory stop of the respondent's car." Id. at 338.

[4] Justice Douglas wrote a dissenting opinion, which Justice Marshall joined. Justice Brennan wrote a dissenting opinion. Justice Marshall wrote a dissenting opinion, which Justice Douglas joined.

White is distinguished in Florida v. J.L., 529 U.S. 266 (2000), in which the Court held that an anonymous tip that a person is carrying a gun is not by itself sufficient to justify a stop and frisk. The Court declined to adopt a "firearm exception" that would authorize a stop and frisk if a tip alleged that a person was illegally carrying a gun, even if the tip would otherwise be insufficient.

59. In *Terry*, the Court said that "whenever a police officer accosts an individual and restrains his freedom to walk away, he has 'seized' that person," p. 105 above. Whether or not a seizure has occurred depends on all the circumstances of the particular case. Michigan v. Chesternut, 486 U.S. 567 (1988). In *Chesternut*, the Court concluded that the police conduct—accelerating a patrol car to catch up with the defendant, who was on foot, and then briefly driving alongside him, in a city neighborhood—did not constitute a seizure. See also California v. Hodari D., p. 58 above.

The question has arisen often in the context of a stop of an airline passenger suspected of carrying narcotics. See the various opinions in Florida v. Royer, 460 U.S. 491 (1983) (5–4), and United States v. Mendenhall, 446 U.S. 544 (1980) (5–4). In *Mendenhall*, the police actions were upheld; in *Royer*, they were not. For additional cases involving the stop of an airline passenger, see, e.g., United States v. Borys, 766 F.2d 304 (7th Cir.1985) (brief stop of defendant at airport and 75-minute seizure of his luggage upheld); United States v. Wilson, 953 F.2d 116 (4th Cir.1991) (prolonged, persistent questioning of disembarking airline passenger who had plainly indicated unwillingness to engage in further conversation was seizure under Fourth Amendment); United States v. Moore, 675 F.2d 802 (6th Cir.1982); United States v. Black, 675 F.2d 129 (7th Cir.1982). In United States v. Wylie, 569 F.2d 62 (D.C.Cir.1977), distinguishing between a "contact," which leaves the person accosted by a policeman free to walk away, and a "stop," the court said that the crucial consideration when there is no explicit show of force is whether the person reasonably believed he was not free to walk away. See United States v. Jordan, 958 F.2d 1085 (D.C.Cir.1992) (defendant was seized within meaning of Fourth Amendment when officer took and retained his driver's license and thereby prevented him from going about his business).

Terry also requires courts to distinguish between an investigative stop, which does not require probable cause, and an arrest, which does. The distinction is discussed in the majority and dissenting opinions in United States v. White, 648 F.2d 29 (D.C.Cir.1981), in which officers stopped an automobile and with guns drawn ordered the occupants to get out. The majority concluded that the police action was an investigative stop. See also, to the same effect, United States v. Merritt, 695 F.2d 1263 (10th Cir.1982), and United States v. Jackson, 652 F.2d 244 (2d Cir.1981). But see United States v. Morin, 665 F.2d 765 (5th Cir.1982) (successive stops of airline passenger based on same information "strongly indicate" an arrest); United States v. Ceballos, 654 F.2d 177 (2d Cir.1981) (arrest). See also United States v. Chaidez, 919 F.2d 1193 (7th Cir.1990) (police actions falling between stop and arrest upheld as reasonable, albeit without probable cause).

Brief questioning during a temporary detention not amounting to an arrest is not custodial interrogation and does not have to be preceded by *Miranda* warnings, see p. 417 below, even if there is probable cause for an arrest. United States v. Woods, 720 F.2d 1022 (9th Cir.1983).

60. *Terry* was extended to the search of a car for dangerous weapons after the driver has stepped out of the car, in Michigan v. Long, 463 U.S. 1032 (1983) (6–3). The same test that is applied to the protective frisk of the person under *Terry* may authorize a protective search of the interior of the car.

The New York Court of Appeals disapproved the reasoning of *Long* and reached a different rule under the state constitution in People v. Torres, 543 N.E.2d 61 (N.Y.1989). The court observed that "it is unrealistic to assume . . . that having been stopped and questioned without incident, a suspect who is about to be released and permitted to proceed on his way would, upon reentry into his vehicle, reach for a concealed weapon and threaten the departing police officer's safety." Id. at 65. See also United States v. Barlin, 686 F.2d 81 (2d Cir.1982) (search of handbag).

Cf. Ybarra v. Illinois, 444 U.S. 85 (1979) (6–3), in which the Court declined to uphold a frisk of the patron of a tavern that police were searching pursuant to a valid search warrant; the Court noted that there were no specific facts indicating that the patron was connected with criminal activity or might be inclined to assault the police. But see generally United States v. Bonds, 829 F.2d 1072 (11th Cir.1987) (stop and frisk distinguished; frisk upheld).

61. In United States v. Place, 462 U.S. 696 (1983), the Court relied on the principles of *Terry* and succeeding cases to uphold the authority of law enforcement personnel briefly to detain personal luggage for exposure to a trained narcotic detection dog on the basis of reasonable suspicion, not amounting to probable cause, that the luggage contains narcotics. The very limited nature of the intrusion on privacy, the Court said, justifies the lessened requirement for the procedure. With respect to the nature of the intrusion, "the canine sniff is sui generis. We are aware of no other investigative procedure that is so limited both in the manner in which the information is obtained and in the content of the information revealed by the procedure." Id. at 707. In the actual case, however, the Court concluded that the duration and circumstances of the detention exceeded what was permitted.

Place is distinguished in B.C. v. Plumas Unified School District, 192 F.3d 1260 (9th Cir.1999), in which school authorities required students to pass in front of a dog trained to sniff for drugs. Saying that a dog sniff of one's person is offensive, the court held that the sniff violated the plaintiff's reasonable expectation of privacy and constituted a search. *Place* is distinguished also in United States v. Thomas, 757 F.2d 1359 (2d Cir.1985) (using trained dog to sniff contents of private premises). See also Bond v.

United States, 529 U.S. 334 (2000) (7–2) (law officer's manipulation of luggage of bus passenger, which passenger had placed on rack above his seat, was a search that violated the passenger's rights under the Fourth Amendment).

62.

On September 5, 1975, New York City Policeman Saverio Alesi was patrolling in uniform on Eighth Avenue between 42d and 45th Streets. At approximately 3:00 P.M. he observed appellee Magda talking with another man on the north side of 43d Street just west of Eighth Avenue. They were about thirty to thirty-five feet from Alesi, who was standing on the southwest corner of the intersection.

As Alesi watched the two men, he saw them exchange something. Although he could not see exactly what had changed hands, he did see that each man gave and received something simultaneously. After the exchange, the unidentified participant looked in the officer's direction. Immediately after doing so, he turned away in a "rapid motion" and proceeded west on 43d Street. Meanwhile, Magda crossed 43d Street at an angle and started down Eighth Avenue toward 42d Street. As he passed, Alesi tapped him on the shoulder and asked him to stop. Magda turned to face Alesi and slowed his pace but continued down Eighth Avenue, walking backwards. The two men proceeded in this fashion for several steps, covering about ten feet before they both stopped.

Alesi inquired about what had taken place on 43d Street, and at first Magda said that nothing had happened. When asked a second time, Magda replied, "All right. I bought a marijuana cigarette for a dollar," and produced the cigarette from his inside coat pocket. Alesi placed him under arrest and walked him back to 43d Street in a vain attempt to find the other man. Alesi then searched Magda and, upon discovering an unloaded handgun and a robbery demand note, took him to the police station and booked him on gun and drug charges. Subsequent investigation by the FBI linked the note with a robbery at the United Mutual Savings Bank in New York City and resulted in the instant indictment.

The area in which Alesi first observed Magda had "a high incidence of narcotics dealing." United States v. Magda, 547 F.2d 756, 757 (2d Cir. 1976). Alesi had been a policeman for 11 years, a foot patrolman for about three and thereafter a motorcycle policeman. He had been a foot patrolman in the area of the stop for six months, during which he had witnessed two narcotics arrests. Was his conduct lawful?

63.

About 2:50 A.M. on July 2, 1966, Sergeant Bergin, while in the vicinity of Commonwealth Avenue, Brookline, observed the defendant walking on Crowninshield Road to Commonwealth Avenue. There had been several breaking and entering incidents in the neighborhood, but none had been reported that night. The officer stopped the defendant and inquired about his identity and purpose for being abroad. The

> defendant identified himself and stated that he was walking from Boston to visit a friend who lived on Commonwealth Avenue in Brookline. When questioned as to the route he was taking, the defendant replied that "he had felt like taking a walk." Observing that the defendant was carrying a paper bag with the name of "Mal's Department Store" on the outside, the officer asked if he might examine its contents, and the defendant readily assented. The bag contained new articles of clothing, consisting of underwear and socks, and a sales slip bearing the date of June 28. The defendant informed the officer that he had purchased the articles on the preceding day, July 1. Because the items of clothing were apparently not of the defendant's size, the officer became suspicious and frisked him to determine if he was carrying any weapons. The frisk consisted of the officer quickly running his hands over the defendant's clothing. He discovered, in the small of the defendant's back and tucked under his shirt and belt, a screwdriver, the shaft of which was seven inches long; it was not new and had paint marks on both the shaft and handle. The defendant said he had bought the screwdriver along with the clothing at Mal's Department Store. The defendant was thereupon arrested and taken to the police station where a thorough search was made. He was charged with possession of burglarious instruments.

Commonwealth v. Matthews, 244 N.E.2d 908, 909 (Mass.1969). Is the screwdriver admissible in evidence against the defendant?

64.

> At 12:15 a.m. on the morning of October 15, 1972, Kenneth Steck, a police officer assigned to the Tactical Patrol Force of the New York Police Department, was working the 6:00 p.m. to 2:00 a.m. tour of duty, assigned to patrol by foot a certain section of Brooklyn. While walking his beat on a street illuminated by ordinary street lamps and devoid of pedestrian traffic, he and his partner noticed someone walking on the same side of the street in their direction. When the solitary figure of the defendant, Louis De Bour, was within 30 or 40 feet of the uniformed officers he crossed the street. The two policemen followed suit and when De Bour reached them Officer Steck inquired as to what he was doing in the neighborhood. De Bour, clearly but nervously, answered that he had just parked his car and was going to a friend's house.
>
> The patrolman then asked De Bour for identification. As he was answering that he had none, Officer Steck noticed a slight waist-high bulge in defendant's jacket. At this point the policeman asked De Bour to unzipper his coat. When De Bour complied with this request Officer Steck observed a revolver protruding from his waistband. The loaded weapon was removed from behind his waistband and he was arrested for possession of the gun.
>
> At the suppression hearing Officer Steck testified to the above facts noting that the encounter lasted "a few minutes." On cross-

> examination, Officer Steck stated that at the time he believed defendant might have been involved with narcotics and crossed the street to avoid apprehension. On the other hand the defendant testified that he never saw the police until they crossed the street in front of him and that he continued walking straight ahead. He stated that the police asked him where he was going and also whether he had any dope in his pockets. He answered that he had been visiting at his mother's home with relatives. De Bour further testified that during this encounter, Steck's partner proceeded to pat his clothing and two or three minutes later Steck found the gun and fired it in order to see whether it was operable.

People v. De Bour, 352 N.E.2d 562, 565 (N.Y.1976). Were the police officers' stop of De Bour and subsequent actions lawful?

65. "On September 10, 1968, Seattle police officers were alerted by police broadcast to pick up two men in a 1964 Pontiac convertible. A warrant had been issued for the arrest of one of the men, Bobby Ray Bush. Officers apprehended the car and, as they did not know which man was Bush, they arrested both Bush and his companion, appellant. The officers in the course of the arrest patted down appellant and, finding a pistol and ammunition, arrested him for carrying a concealed weapon." Hurst v. United States, 425 F.2d 177 (9th Cir.1970). Was the police conduct lawful?

66.

> Part of the difficulty in developing a rule for frisks is that the policeman, assuming his good faith, will be acting on a subjective standard—his own immediate sense of risk to himself—while the court testing his action for purposes of admissibility will be acting on an objective standard—what a reasonably prudent policeman in his position would do after weighing the risks of harm from possible hidden weapons presented by the particular known circumstances against our society's aversion to physical intrusions on the person of a free man. . . . Where the standard of action—necessarily almost unreflective and reflexive—is to be tested after the event by a non-congruent rational test, the deterrent effect of the rule must perforce become less than complete. . . .
>
> Yet the objective rule does have some useful prophylactic effect. . . . At the very least it provides some insurance against dishonesty by the policeman who does not in fact have reason to suspect that the subject is armed, but who would be willing to fabricate his remembered emotions to validate a productive frisk. . . . And guarding against this danger becomes particularly important if, as we believe, a proper frisk permits seizure of nonweapon contraband. Moreover, the objective rule signals to the public at large that, to the extent possible, courts do what they can to maintain constitutional protections as more than mere verbal symbols.
>
> The standard of probability which is required to justify intrusions at the "frisk" level has been variously stated. . . .

. . .

> We need not now determine which verbal formulation of the standard is correct. For our purposes there is a common denominator. A reviewing court must: (1) determine the objective evidence then available to the law enforcement officer and (2) decide what level of probability existed that the individual was armed and about to engage in dangerous conduct; it must then rule whether that level of probability justified the "frisk" in light of (3) the manner in which the frisk was conducted as bearing on the resentment it might justifiably arouse in the person frisked (assuming he is not about to engage in criminal conduct) and the community and (4) the risk to the officer and the community of not disarming the individual at once.

United States v. Lopez, 328 F.Supp. 1077, 1095–97 (E.D.N.Y.1971). See United States v. Sigmond-Ballesteros, 285 F.3d 1117 (9th Cir.2002) (rejecting various alleged grounds for reasonable suspicion justifying stop of motor vehicle).

67. The "plain feel" rule, analogous to the plain view doctrine, see Horton v. California, 496 U.S. 128 (1990), p. 197 below, is upheld in Minnesota v. Dickerson, 508 U.S. 366, 375–76 (1993): "If a police officer lawfully pats down a suspect's outer clothing and feels an object whose contour or mass makes its identity immediately apparent, there has been no invasion of the suspect's privacy beyond that already authorized by the officer's search for weapons; if the object is contraband, its warrantless seizure would be justified by the same practical considerations that inhere in the plain view context."

Brown v. Texas

443 U.S. 47, 99 S.Ct. 2637, 61 L.Ed.2d 357 (1979)

■ MR. CHIEF JUSTICE BURGER delivered the opinion of the Court.

This appeal presents the question whether appellant was validly convicted for refusing to comply with a policeman's demand that he identify himself pursuant to a provision of the Texas Penal Code which makes it a crime to refuse such identification on request.

I

At 12:45 on the afternoon of December 9, 1977, officers Venegas and Sotelo of the El Paso Police Department were cruising in a patrol car. They observed appellant and another man walking in opposite directions away from one another in an alley. Although the two men were a few feet apart when they first were seen, officer Venegas later testified that both officers believed the two had been together or were about to meet until the patrol car appeared.

The car entered the alley, and officer Venegas got out and asked appellant to identify himself and explain what he was doing there. The other man was not questioned or detained. The officer testified that he stopped appellant because the situation "looked suspicious and we had never seen that subject in that area before." The area of El Paso where appellant was stopped has a high incidence of drug traffic. However, the officers did not claim to suspect appellant of any specific misconduct, nor did they have any reason to believe that he was armed.

Appellant refused to identify himself and angrily asserted that the officers had no right to stop him. Officer Venegas replied that he was in a "high drug problem area"; officer Sotelo then "frisked" appellant, but found nothing.

When appellant continued to refuse to identify himself, he was arrested for violation of Texas Penal Code Ann. § 38.02(a), which makes it a criminal act for a person to refuse to give his name and address to an officer "who has lawfully stopped him and requested the information." Following the arrest the officers searched appellant; nothing untoward was found.

While being taken to the El Paso County Jail appellant identified himself. Nonetheless, he was held in custody and charged with violating § 38.02(a). When he was booked he was routinely searched a third time. Appellant was convicted in the El Paso Municipal Court and fined $20 plus court costs for violation of § 38.02. He then exercised his right under Texas law to a trial *de novo* in the El Paso County Court. There, he moved to set aside the information on the ground that § 38.02(a) of the Texas Penal Code violated the First, Fourth, and Fifth Amendments and was unconstitutionally vague in violation of the Fourteenth Amendment. The motion was denied. Appellant waived jury, and the court convicted him and imposed a fine of $45 plus court costs.

. . . On appeal here we noted probable jurisdiction. . . . We reverse.

II

When the officers detained appellant for the purpose of requiring him to identify himself, they performed a seizure of his person subject to the requirements of the Fourth Amendment. In convicting appellant, the County Court necessarily found as a matter of fact that the officers "lawfully stopped" appellant. . . . The Fourth Amendment, of course, "applies to all seizures of the person, including seizures that involve only a brief detention short of traditional arrest." Davis v. Mississippi, 394 U.S. 721 (1969); Terry v. Ohio, 392 U.S. 1, 16–19 (1968). "[W]henever a police officer accosts an individual and restrains his freedom to walk away, he has 'seized' that person," id., at 16, and the Fourth Amendment requires that the seizure be "reasonable." United States v. Brignoni-Ponce, 422 U.S. 873, 878 (1975).

The reasonableness of seizures that are less intrusive than a traditional arrest . . . depends "on a balance between the public interest and the individual's right to personal security free from arbitrary interference by law officers." Pennsylvania v. Mimms, 434 U.S. 106, 109 (1977). . . . Consideration of the constitutionality of such seizures involves a weighing of the gravity of the public concerns served by the seizure, the degree to which the seizure advances the public interest, and the severity of the interference with individual liberty. . . .

A central concern in balancing these competing considerations in a variety of settings has been to assure that an individual's reasonable expectation of privacy is not subject to arbitrary invasions solely at the unfettered discretion of officers in the field. . . . To this end, the Fourth Amendment requires that a seizure must be based on specific, objective facts indicating that society's legitimate interests require the seizure of the particular individual, or that the seizure must be carried out pursuant to a plan embodying explicit, neutral limitations on the conduct of individual officers. . . .

The State does not contend that appellant was stopped pursuant to a practice embodying neutral criteria, but rather maintains that the officers were justified in stopping appellant because they had a "reasonable, articulable suspicion that a crime had just been, was being, or was about to be committed." We have recognized that in some circumstances an officer may detain a suspect briefly for questioning although he does not have "probable cause" to believe that the suspect is involved in criminal activity, as is required for a traditional arrest. . . . However, we have required the officers to have a reasonable suspicion, based on objective facts, that the individual is involved in criminal activity. . . .

The flaw in the State's case is that none of the circumstances preceding the officers' detention of appellant justified a reasonable suspicion that he was involved in criminal conduct. Officer Venegas testified at appellant's trial that the situation in the alley "looked suspicious," but he was unable to point to any facts supporting that conclusion.[5] There is no indication in the record that it was unusual for people to be in the alley. The fact that appellant was in a neighborhood frequented by drug users, standing alone, is not a basis for concluding that appellant himself was engaged in criminal conduct. In short, the appellant's activity was no different from the activity of other pedestrians in that neighborhood. When pressed, officer Venegas acknowledged that the only reason he stopped appellant was to ascertain his identity. The record suggests an understandable desire to assert a police presence; however that purpose does not negate Fourth Amendment guarantees.

In the absence of any basis for suspecting appellant of misconduct, the balance between the public interest and appellant's right to personal security and privacy tilts in favor of freedom from police interference. The Texas statute under which appellant was stopped and required to identify

5. This situation is to be distinguished from the observations of a trained, experienced police officer who is able to perceive and articulate meaning in given conduct which would be wholly innocent to the untrained observer. . . .

himself is designed to advance a weighty social objective in large metropolitan centers: prevention of crime. But even assuming that purpose is served to some degree by stopping and demanding identification from an individual without any specific basis for believing he is involved in criminal activity, the guarantees of the Fourth Amendment do not allow it. When such a stop is not based on objective criteria, the risk of arbitrary and abusive police practices exceeds tolerable limits. . . .

The application of Texas Penal Code Ann. § 38.02 to detain appellant and require him to identify himself violated the Fourth Amendment because the officers lacked any reasonable suspicion to believe appellant was engaged or had engaged in criminal conduct. Accordingly, appellant may not be punished for refusing to identify himself, and the conviction is reversed.

. . .

---

68. The investigative stop of a vehicle for 20 minutes, on the basis of a reasonable and articulable suspicion that the occupants were engaged in transporting marijuana is permissible under the Fourth Amendment. United States v. Sharpe, 470 U.S. 675 (1985) (7–2). The Court declined to say what period of time would be too long to count as an investigative stop. It is necessary "to consider the law enforcement purposes to be served by the stop as well as the time reasonably needed to effectuate those purposes. . . . Much as a 'bright line' rule would be desirable, in evaluating whether an investigative detention is unreasonable, common sense and ordinary human experience must govern over rigid criteria." Id. at 685.

In United States v. Brigham, 343 F.3d 490 (5th Cir. 2003), the court held that questioning the driver and passengers of a vehicle for eight minutes after a valid traffic stop about matters unrelated to the stop violated their rights under the Fourth Amendment. The court observed that a computer check on a driver's license and registration is permissible and that questioning while the computer check is carried out is permissible, if it does not prolong the detention. Here, however, the questioning preceded a computer check and, therefore, prolonged the detention.

69. A brief stop and detention of a person who is suspected of having been involved in a completed crime may be lawful even though there is not probable cause for his arrest. In United States v. Hensley, 469 U.S. 221 (1985), a police department issued a "flyer" asking that the defendant be held for investigation of a robbery, if he were located. The flyer was distributed to other nearby police departments in the area. An officer in another department who was aware of the flyer stopped the defendant and called headquarters to determine whether a warrant for his arrest had been issued. During the brief detention that followed, evidence was discovered that furnished an independent basis for his arrest.

The Court held that, even though the department issuing the flyer lacked probable cause for the defendant's arrest, the brief stop was lawful. It acknowledged that the situation was different from one like *Terry*, in

Boston Police DEPARTMENT CIRCULAR #: POSTER GENERATED BY: Dahlbeck, Joseph W

WANTED

FOR DEMONSTRATION ONLY

Pomeroy, Arnold, George

LAST KNOWN ADDRESS: Apt 23, 312 Evergreen CR , Boston, MA.
DOB: 03/17/1956
HEIGHT: 5' 11"
WEIGHT: 200
BUILD: Medium
RACE: White Non-Hispanic
COMPLEXION: Medium
SEX: Male
EYES: Brown
HAIR: Dark Brown
CAUTION FLAGS: ARMED

COURT: Boston Municipal Ct
DOCKET #: 95cr87469
INCIDENT #: 953258933

ALIASES: Raymond Allen Pomeroy, Rocko

Right Thumb
0 9 U 000 12
22 17 U 000 14

ARMED

Please Contact Area A-1 Detectives 343-0000

YOU CAN HELP THE BOSTON POLICE DEPARTMENT BY CALLING THE CRIME STOPPERS UNIT. IF YOUR INFORMATION LEADS TO THE ARREST AND INDICTMENT OF ANY VIOLENT FELONY OFFENDER YOU CAN RECEIVE A REWARD UP TO $1,000.00

1-(800) 494-TIPS

CALLERS REMAIN ANONYMOUS

which the stop is for investigation of suspected ongoing criminal activity. Nevertheless,

> where police have been unable to locate a person suspected of involvement in a past crime, the ability to briefly stop that person, ask questions, or check identification in the absence of probable cause promotes the strong government interest in solving crimes and bringing offenders to justice. Restraining police action until after probable cause is obtained would not only hinder the investigation, but might also enable the suspect to flee in the interim and to remain at large. Particularly in the context of felonies or crimes involving a threat to public safety, it is in the public interest that the crime be solved and the suspect detained as promptly as possible. The law enforcement interests at stake in these circumstances outweigh the individual's interest to be free of a stop and detention that is no more extensive than permissible in the investigation of imminent or ongoing crimes.
>
> [I]f police have a reasonable suspicion, grounded in specific and articulable facts that a person they encounter was involved in or is wanted in connection with a completed felony, then a *Terry* stop may be made to investigate that suspicion.

Id. at 229. The Court added that the officer who stopped the defendant was entitled to rely on the flyer issued by the other department and was not required himself to have knowledge of facts justifying the stop. It is enough if the police who issue such a flyer have a basis justifying the action taken.

Florida v. Bostick

501 U.S. 429, 111 S.Ct. 2382, 115 L.Ed.2d 389 (1991)

■ JUSTICE O'CONNOR delivered the opinion of the Court.

We have held that the Fourth Amendment permits police officers to approach individuals at random in airport lobbies and other public places to ask them questions and to request consent to search their luggage, so long as a reasonable person would understand that he or she could refuse to cooperate. This case requires us to determine whether the same rule applies to police encounters that take place on a bus.

I

Drug interdiction efforts have led to the use of police surveillance at airports, train stations, and bus depots. Law enforcement officers stationed at such locations routinely approach individuals, either randomly or because they suspect in some vague way that the individuals may be engaged in criminal activity, and ask them potentially incriminating questions. Broward County has adopted such a program. County Sheriff's Department officers routinely board buses at scheduled stops and ask passengers for permission to search their luggage.

In this case, two officers discovered cocaine when they searched a suitcase belonging to Terrance Bostick. The underlying facts of the search are in dispute, but the Florida Supreme Court, whose decision we review here, stated explicitly the factual premise for its decision:

> Two officers, complete with badges, insignia and one of them holding a recognizable zipper pouch, containing a pistol, boarded a bus bound from Miami to Atlanta during a stopover in Fort Lauderdale. Eyeing the passengers, the officers admittedly without articulable suspicion, picked out the defendant passenger and asked to inspect his ticket and identification. The ticket, from Miami to Atlanta, matched the defendant's identification and both were immediately returned to him as unremarkable. However, the two police officers persisted and explained their presence as narcotics agents on the lookout for illegal drugs. In pursuit of that aim, they then requested the defendant's consent to search his luggage. Needless to say, there is a conflict in the evidence about whether the defendant consented to the search of the second bag in which the contraband was found and as to whether he was informed of his right to refuse consent. However, any conflict must be resolved in favor of the state, it being a question of fact decided by the trial judge.

554 So.2d 1153, 1154–55 (1989), quoting 510 So.2d 321, 322 (Fla.App.1987) (Letts, J., dissenting in part).

Two facts are particularly worth noting. First, the police specifically advised Bostick that he had the right to refuse consent. Bostick appears to have disputed the point, but, as the Florida Supreme Court noted explicitly, the trial court resolved this evidentiary conflict in the State's favor. Second, at no time did the officers threaten Bostick with a gun. The Florida Supreme Court indicated that one officer carried a zipper pouch containing a pistol—the equivalent of carrying a gun in a holster—but the court did not suggest that the gun was ever removed from its pouch, pointed at Bostick, or otherwise used in a threatening manner. The dissent's characterization of the officers as "gun-wielding inquisitor[s]," post, at 9, is colorful, but lacks any basis in fact.

Bostick was arrested and charged with trafficking in cocaine. He moved to suppress the cocaine on the grounds that it had been seized in violation of his Fourth Amendment rights. The trial court denied the motion but made no factual findings. Bostick subsequently entered a plea of guilty, but reserved the right to appeal the denial of the motion to suppress.

The Florida District Court of Appeal affirmed, but considered the issue sufficiently important that it certified a question to the Florida Supreme Court. 510 So.2d, at 322. The Supreme Court reasoned that Bostick had been seized because a reasonable passenger in his situation would not have felt free to leave the bus to avoid questioning by the police. . . . It rephrased and answered the certified question so as to make the bus setting dispositive in every case. It ruled categorically that " 'an impermissible seizure result[s] when police mount a drug search on buses during scheduled stops and question boarded passengers without articulable reasons for doing so, thereby obtaining consent to search the passengers' luggage.' " Ibid. The Florida Supreme Court thus adopted a per se rule that the Broward County Sheriff's practice of "working the buses" is unconstitutional. The result of this decision is that police in Florida, as elsewhere, may approach persons at random in most public places, ask them questions and seek consent to a search . . . but they may not engage in the same behavior on a bus. . . . We granted certiorari . . . to determine whether the Florida Supreme Court's per se rule is consistent with our Fourth Amendment jurisprudence.

II

The sole issue presented for our review is whether a police encounter on a bus of the type described above necessarily constitutes a "seizure" within the meaning of the Fourth Amendment. The State concedes, and we accept for purposes of this decision, that the officers lacked the reasonable suspicion required to justify a seizure and that, if a seizure took place, the drugs found in Bostick's suitcase must be suppressed as tainted fruit.

Our cases make it clear that a seizure does not occur simply because a police officer approaches an individual and asks a few questions. So long as a reasonable person would feel free "to disregard the police and go about his business," California v. Hodari D., 499 U.S. 621, 628 (1991), the encounter is consensual and no reasonable suspicion is required. The encounter will not trigger Fourth Amendment scrutiny unless it loses its consensual nature. . . .

[W]e have held repeatedly that mere police questioning does not constitute a seizure. . . .

There is no doubt that if this same encounter had taken place before Bostick boarded the bus or in the lobby of the bus terminal, it would not rise to the level of a seizure. The Court has dealt with similar encounters in airports and has found them to be "the sort of consensual encounter[s] that implicat[e] no Fourth Amendment interest." Florida v. Rodriguez, 469 U.S. 1, 5–6 (1984). We have stated that even when officers have no basis for suspecting a particular individual, they may generally ask questions of that individual . . . ask to examine the individual's identification . . . and request consent to search his or her luggage . . . as long as the police do not convey a message that compliance with their requests is required.

Bostick insists that this case is different because it took place in the cramped confines of a bus. A police encounter is much more intimidating in this setting, he argues, because police tower over a seated passenger and there is little room to move around. Bostick claims to find support in language from Michigan v. Chesternut, 486 U.S. 567, 573 (1988), and other cases, indicating that a seizure occurs when a reasonable person would believe that he or she is not "free to leave." Bostick maintains that a reasonable bus passenger would not have felt free to leave under the circumstances of this case because there is nowhere to go on a bus. Also, the bus was about to depart. Had Bostick disembarked, he would have risked being stranded and losing whatever baggage he had locked away in the luggage compartment.

The Florida Supreme Court found this argument persuasive, so much so that it adopted a per se rule prohibiting the police from randomly boarding buses as a means of drug interdiction. The state court erred, however, in focusing on whether Bostick was "free to leave" rather than on the principle that those words were intended to capture. When police attempt to question a person who is walking down the street or through an airport lobby, it makes sense to inquire whether a reasonable person would feel free to continue walking. But when the person is seated on a bus and has no desire to leave, the degree to which a reasonable person would feel that he or she could leave is not an accurate measure of the coercive effect of the encounter.

Here, for example, the mere fact that Bostick did not feel free to leave the bus does not mean that the police seized him. Bostick was a passenger on a bus that was scheduled to depart. He would not have felt free to leave the bus even if the police had not been present. Bostick's movements were "confined" in a sense, but this was the natural result of his decision to take the bus; it says nothing about whether or not the police conduct at issue was coercive.

. . .

. . . Bostick's freedom of movement was restricted by a factor independent of police conduct—i.e., by his being a passenger on a bus. Accordingly, the "free to leave" analysis on which Bostick relies is inapplicable. In such a situation, the appropriate inquiry is whether a reasonable person would feel free to decline the officers' requests or otherwise terminate the encounter. This formulation follows logically from prior cases and breaks no new ground. We have said before that the crucial test is whether, taking into account all of the circumstances surrounding the encounter, the police conduct would "have communicated to a reasonable person that he was not at liberty to ignore the police presence and go about his business." *Chesternut*, supra, at 569. . . . Where the encounter takes place is one factor, but it is not the only one. And, as the Solicitor General correctly observes, an individual may decline an officer's request without fearing prosecution. . . . We have consistently held that a refusal to cooperate, without more, does not furnish the minimal level of objective justification needed for a detention or seizure. . . .

The facts of this case, as described by the Florida Supreme Court, leave some doubt whether a seizure occurred. Two officers walked up to Bostick on the bus, asked him a few questions, and asked if they could search his bags. As we have explained, no seizure occurs when police ask questions of an individual, ask to examine the individual's identification, and request consent to search his or her luggage—so long as the officers do not convey a message that compliance with their requests is required. Here, the facts recited by the Florida Supreme Court indicate that the officers did not point guns at Bostick or otherwise threaten him and that they specifically advised Bostick that he could refuse consent.

Nevertheless, we refrain from deciding whether or not a seizure occurred in this case. The trial court made no express findings of fact, and the Florida Supreme Court rested its decision on a single fact—that the encounter took place on a bus—rather than on the totality of the circumstances. We remand so that the Florida courts may evaluate the seizure question under the correct legal standard. . . .

. . .

We adhere to the rule that, in order to determine whether a particular encounter constitutes a seizure, a court must consider all the circumstances surrounding the encounter to determine whether the police conduct would have communicated to a reasonable person that the person was not free to decline the officers' requests or otherwise terminate the encounter. That rule applies to encounters that take place on a city street or in an airport lobby, and it applies equally to encounters on a bus. The Florida Supreme Court erred in adopting a per se rule.

. . .

■ JUSTICE MARSHALL, with whom JUSTICE BLACKMUN and JUSTICE STEVENS join, dissenting.

. . .

I

At issue in this case is a "new and increasingly common tactic in the war on drugs": the suspicionless police sweep of buses in interstate or intrastate travel. . . . Typically under this technique, a group of state or federal officers will board a bus while it is stopped at an intermediate point on its route. Often displaying badges, weapons or other indicia of authority, the officers identify themselves and announce their purpose to intercept drug traffickers. They proceed to approach individual passengers, requesting them to show identification, produce their tickets, and explain the purpose of their travels. Never do the officers advise the passengers that they are free not to speak with the officers. An "interview" of this type ordinarily culminates in a request for consent to search the passenger's luggage. . . .

These sweeps are conducted in "dragnet" style. The police admittedly act without an "articulable suspicion" in deciding which buses to board and which passengers to approach for interviewing. By proceeding systematically in this fashion, the police are able to engage in a tremendously high volume of searches. . . . The percentage of successful drug interdictions is low. . . .

To put it mildly, these sweeps "are inconvenient, intrusive, and intimidating." United States v. Chandler, 744 F.Supp. [333 (D.D.C.1990)], at 335. They occur within cramped confines, with officers typically placing themselves in between the passenger selected for an interview and the exit of the bus. . . . Because the bus is only temporarily stationed at a point short of its destination, the passengers are in no position to leave as a means of evading the officers' questioning. Undoubtedly, such a sweep holds up the progress of the bus. . . . Thus, this "new and increasingly common tactic," United States v. Lewis, 921 F.2d [1294 (D.C.App. 1990)], at 1295, burdens the experience of traveling by bus with a degree of governmental interference to which, until now, our society has been proudly unaccustomed. . . .

. . .

The question for this Court, then, is whether the suspicionless, dragnet-style sweep of buses in intrastate and interstate travel is consistent with the Fourth Amendment. The majority suggests that this latest tactic in the drug war is perfectly compatible with the Constitution. I disagree.

II

. . .

[The facts in this case] exhibit all of the elements of coercion associated with a typical bus sweep. Two officers boarded the Greyhound bus on which respondent was a passenger while the bus, en route from Miami to Atlanta, was on a brief stop to pick up passengers in Fort Lauderdale. The officers made a visible display of their badges and wore bright green "raid" jackets bearing the insignia of the Broward County Sheriff's Department; one held a gun in a recognizable weapons pouch. . . . These facts alone constitute an intimidating "show of authority." See Michigan v. Chesternut, 486 U.S. 567, 575 (1988). . . . Once on board, the officers approached respondent, who was sitting in the back of the bus, identified themselves as narcotics officers and began to question him. . . . One officer stood in front of respondent's seat, partially blocking the narrow aisle through which respondent would have been required to pass to reach the exit of the bus. . . .

. . .

. . . Apart from trying to accommodate the officers, respondent had only two options. First, he could have remained seated while obstinately refusing to respond to the officers' questioning. But in light of the intimidating show of authority that the officers made upon boarding the bus, respondent reasonably could have believed that such behavior would only arouse the officers' suspicions and intensify their interrogation. Indeed, officers who carry out bus sweeps like the one at issue here frequently admit that this is the effect of a passenger's refusal to cooperate. . . . The majority's observation that a mere refusal to answer questions, "without more," does not give rise to a reasonable basis for seizing a passenger, ante, at 437, is utterly beside the point, because a passenger unadvised of his rights and otherwise unversed in constitutional law *has no reason to know* that the police cannot hold his refusal to cooperate against him.

Second, respondent could have tried to escape the officers' presence by leaving the bus altogether. But because doing so would have required respondent to squeeze past the gun-wielding inquisitor who was blocking the aisle of the bus, this hardly seems like a course that respondent reasonably would have viewed as available to him. . . . Our decisions recognize the obvious point . . . that the choice of the police to "display" their weapons during an encounter exerts significant coercive pressure on the confronted citizen. . . . We have never suggested that the police must go so far as to put a citizen in immediate apprehension of *being shot* before a court can take account of the intimidating effect of being questioned by an officer with weapon in hand.

Even if respondent had perceived that the officers would *let* him leave the bus, moreover, he could not reasonably have been expected to resort to this means of evading their intrusive questioning. For so far as respondent knew, the bus' departure from the terminal was imminent. Unlike a person approached by the police on the street . . . or at a bus or airport terminal after reaching his destination . . . a passenger approached by the police at an intermediate point in a long bus journey cannot simply leave the scene and repair to a safe haven to avoid unwanted probing by law-enforcement officials. The vulnerability that an intrastate or interstate traveler experiences when confronted by the police outside of his "own familiar territory" surely aggravates the coercive quality of such an encounter. . . .

. . .

Rather than requiring the police to justify the coercive tactics employed here, the majority blames respondent for his own sensation of constraint. The majority concedes that respondent "did not feel free to leave the bus" as a means of breaking off the interrogation by the Broward County officers. Ante, at 436. But this experience of confinement, the majority explains, "was the natural result of *his* decision to take the bus." Ibid. (emphasis added). Thus, in the majority's view, because respondent's "freedom of movement was restricted by a factor independent of police conduct—i.e., by his being a passenger on a bus," ante, at 436, respondent was not seized for purposes of the Fourth Amendment.

This reasoning borders on sophism and trivializes the values that underlie the Fourth Amendment. Obviously, a person's "voluntary decision" to place himself in a room with only one exit does not authorize the police to force an encounter upon him by placing themselves in front of the exit. It is no more acceptable for the police to force an encounter on a person by exploiting his "voluntary decision" to expose himself to perfectly legitimate personal or social constraints. By consciously deciding to single out persons who have undertaken interstate or intrastate travel, officers who conduct suspicionless, dragnet-style sweeps put passengers to the choice of cooperating or of exiting their buses and possibly being stranded in unfamiliar locations. It is exactly because this "choice" is no "choice" at all that police engage in this technique.

In my view, the Fourth Amendment clearly condemns the suspicionless, dragnet-style sweep of intrastate or interstate buses. Withdrawing this particular weapon from the government's drug-war arsenal would hardly leave the police without any means of combatting the use of buses as instrumentalities of the drug trade. The police would remain free, for example, to approach passengers whom they have a reasonable, articulable basis to suspect of criminal wrongdoing. Alternatively, they could continue to confront passengers without suspicion so long as they took simple stops, like advising the passengers confronted of their right to decline to be questioned, to dispel the aura of coercion and intimidation that pervades such encounters. There is no reason to expect that such requirements would render the Nation's buses law-enforcement-free zones.

. . .

---

70. When police officers approach a passenger on a bus to ask questions and request his consent to a search, the failure to advise him that he does not need to cooperate does not of itself require the suppression of his responses and any evidence found in the search. Rather, whether the passenger was seized before answering the questions and whether he consented to the search depends on all the circumstances. United States v. Drayton, 536 U.S. 194 (2002) (6–3) (admission of evidence upheld).

In United States v. Stephens, 206 F.3d 914 (9th Cir. 2000), narcotics agents became suspicious of the defendant when they observed him in a bus terminal and watched as he boarded a bus and placed his bag in an overhead compartment. When the bus was scheduled to depart, they boarded the bus and announced that they were conducting a routine narcotics investigation and would like to talk to the passengers but that anyone was free to leave. In response to a question, the defendant said that he had no carry-on baggage. The agents removed the bag that he had carried on and asked if anyone owned it. When the bag was not claimed, they removed it and opened it. It contained narcotics. The court concluded that the defendant had abandoned the bag but that the abandonment was involuntary and the result of an unlawful seizure. It said that the agents' announcement and conduct indicated to passengers that they had only two choices: to cooperate with the agents or to get off the bus, which would itself have created suspicion. In view of all the circumstances, the court concluded that the defendant had been seized.

71.

> One has an undoubted right to resist an unlawful arrest, and courts will uphold the right of resistance in proper cases. But courts will hardly penalize failure to display a spirit of resistance or to hold futile debates on legal issues in the public highway with an officer of the law. A layman may not find it expedient to hazard resistance on his own judgment of the law at a time when he cannot know what information, correct or incorrect, the officers may be acting upon. It is likely to end in fruitless and unseemly controversy in a public street, if not in an additional charge of resisting an officer. . . .
>
> It is the right of one placed under arrest to submit to custody and to reserve his defenses for the neutral tribunals erected by the law for the purpose of judging his case. An inference of probable cause from a failure to engage in discussion of the merits of the charge with arresting officers is unwarranted. Probable cause cannot be found from submissiveness, and the presumption of innocence is not lost or impaired by neglect to argue with a policeman. It is the officer's responsi-

> bility to know what he is arresting for, and why, and one in the unhappy plight of being taken into custody is not required to test the legality of the arrest before the officer who is making it.

United States v. Di Re, 332 U.S. 581, 594–95 (1948).

Does the same reasoning apply to a person who is stopped but not arrested by a police officer? To what extent can an officer rely on a person's unresponsiveness or uncooperativeness as a basis for determining that he should be detained further or arrested? Does it make any difference in this connection whether the person is required to stop if told to do so by an officer or can only be asked to stop by the officer?

72. In Immigration and Naturalization Service v. Delgado, 466 U.S. 210 (1984) (7–2), the Court upheld an INS practice of "factory surveys," pursuant to which agents of the INS enter a factory, briefly question workers about their status in this country, and, if the questions arouse no suspicion, move on. If a worker acknowledges that he is an alien or his responses to the questions are unsatisfactory, he is asked to produce immigration papers. The INS conducted the surveys in question pursuant to warrants obtained on probable cause to believe that illegally resident aliens were employed in the factories, and in one case without a warrant but with the employer's consent. During the survey, workers were free to move around the factory. Agents were posted at the exits to the factories; otherwise there was no indication that workers were not free to leave after answering questions or without answering them.

The Court said:

> Although we have yet to rule directly on whether mere questioning of an individual by a police official, without more, can amount to a seizure under the Fourth Amendment . . . interrogation relating to one's identity or a request for identification by the police does not, by itself, constitute a Fourth Amendment seizure. . . .
>
> [P]olice questioning, by itself, is unlikely to result in a Fourth Amendment violation. While most citizens will respond to a police request, the fact that people do so, and do so without being told they are free not to respond, hardly eliminates the consensual nature of the response. . . . Unless the circumstances of the encounter are so intimidating as to demonstrate that a reasonable person would have believed he was not free to leave if he had not responded, one cannot say that the questioning resulted in a detention under the Fourth Amendment. But if the person refuses to answer and the police take additional steps . . . to obtain an answer, then the Fourth Amendment imposes some minimal level of objective justification to validate the detention or seizure.

466 U.S. at 216–17. The Court relied on *Delgado* in *Bostick*, p. 127 above, 501 U.S. at 436.

73. Should a policeman have authority to stop (and frisk) a person for questioning if he has no reason to believe that the person has himself committed a crime but believes that he has information concerning a crime? Suppose, for example, that a witness to a street holdup is anxious to leave the scene of the crime. Should a police officer be able to require him to remain? Or to give his name and address? Or to answer questions? If so, what should be the consequences of the person's refusal to do so?

Roadblock

Michigan Department of State Police v. Sitz

496 U.S. 444, 110 S.Ct. 2481, 110 L.Ed.2d 412 (1990)

■ CHIEF JUSTICE REHNQUIST delivered the opinion of the Court.

This case poses the question whether a State's use of highway sobriety checkpoints violates the Fourth and Fourteenth Amendments to the United States Constitution. We hold that it does not and therefore reverse the contrary holding of the Court of Appeals of Michigan.

Petitioners, the Michigan Department of State Police and its director, established a sobriety checkpoint pilot program in early 1986. The director appointed a Sobriety Checkpoint Advisory Committee comprising representatives of the State Police force, local police forces, state prosecutors, and the University of Michigan Transportation Research Institute. Pursuant to its charge, the advisory committee created guidelines setting forth procedures governing checkpoint operations, site selection, and publicity.

Under the guidelines, checkpoints would be set up at selected sites along state roads. All vehicles passing through a checkpoint would be stopped and their drivers briefly examined for signs of intoxication. In cases where a checkpoint officer detected signs of intoxication, the motorist would be directed to a location out of the traffic flow where an officer would check the motorist's driver's license and car registration and, if warranted, conduct further sobriety tests. Should the field tests and the officer's observations suggest that the driver was intoxicated, an arrest would be made. All other drivers would be permitted to resume their journey immediately.

The first—and to date the only—sobriety checkpoint operated under the program was conducted in Saginaw County with the assistance of the Saginaw County Sheriff's Department. During the 75-minute duration of the checkpoint's operation, 126 vehicles passed through the checkpoint. The average delay for each vehicle was approximately 25 seconds. Two drivers were detained for field sobriety testing, and one of the two was arrested for driving under the influence of alcohol. A third driver who drove through without stopping was pulled over by an officer in an observation vehicle and arrested for driving under the influence.

On the day before the operation of the Saginaw County checkpoint, respondents filed a complaint in the Circuit Court of Wayne County seeking declaratory and injunctive relief from potential subjection to the checkpoints. Each of the respondents "is a licensed driver in the State of Michigan . . . who regularly travels throughout the State in his automobile." See Complaint, App. 3a–4a. During pretrial proceedings, petitioners agreed to delay further implementation of the checkpoint program pending the outcome of this litigation.

After the trial, at which the court heard extensive testimony concerning, inter alia, the "effectiveness" of highway sobriety checkpoint programs, the court ruled that the Michigan program violated the Fourth Amendment and Art. 1, § 11, of the Michigan Constitution. . . . On appeal, the Michigan Court of Appeals affirmed the holding that the program violated the Fourth Amendment. . . . [W]e granted certiorari. . . .

To decide this case, the trial court performed a balancing test derived from our opinion in Brown v. Texas, 443 U.S. 47 (1979). . . .

. . .

Petitioners concede, correctly in our view, that a Fourth Amendment "seizure" occurs when a vehicle is stopped at a checkpoint. . . . The question thus becomes whether such seizures are "reasonable" under the Fourth Amendment.

It is important to recognize what our inquiry is *not* about. No allegations are before us of unreasonable treatment of any person after an actual detention at a particular checkpoint. . . . As pursued in the lower courts, the instant action challenges only the use of sobriety checkpoints generally. We address only the initial stop of each motorist passing through a checkpoint and the associated preliminary questioning and observation by checkpoint officers. Detention of particular motorists for more extensive field sobriety testing may require satisfaction of an individualized suspicion standard. . . .

No one can seriously dispute the magnitude of the drunken driving problem or the States' interest in eradicating it. Media reports of alcohol-related death and mutilation on the Nation's roads are legion. The anecdotal is confirmed by the statistical. . . .

Conversely, the weight bearing on the other scale—the measure of the intrusion on motorists stopped briefly at sobriety checkpoints—is slight. . . . The trial court and the Court of Appeals, thus, accurately gauged the "objective" intrusion, measured by the duration of the seizure and the intensity of the investigation, as minimal. . . .

With respect to what it perceived to be the "subjective" intrusion on motorists, however, the Court of Appeals found such intrusion substantial. . . . The court first affirmed the trial court's finding that the guidelines governing checkpoint operation minimize the discretion of the officers on the scene. But the court also agreed with the trial court's conclusion that the checkpoints have the potential to generate fear and surprise in motorists. This was so because the record failed to demonstrate that approaching motorists would be aware of their option to make U-turns or turnoffs to avoid the checkpoints. On that basis, the court deemed the subjective intrusion from the checkpoints unreasonable. . . .

We believe the Michigan courts misread our cases concerning the degree of "subjective intrusion" and the potential for generating fear and surprise. The "fear and surprise" to be considered are not the natural fear of one who has been drinking over the prospect of being stopped at a sobriety checkpoint but, rather, the fear and surprise engendered in law abiding motorists by the nature of the stop. . . . Here, checkpoints are selected pursuant to the guidelines, and uniformed police officers stop every approaching vehicle. . . .

The Court of Appeals went on to consider as part of the balancing analysis the "effectiveness" of the proposed checkpoint program. Based on extensive testimony in the trial record, the court concluded that the checkpoint program failed the "effectiveness" part of the test, and that this failure materially discounted petitioners' strong interest in implementing the program. We think the Court of Appeals was wrong on this point as well.

The actual language from Brown v. Texas, upon which the Michigan courts based their evaluation of "effectiveness," describes the balancing factor as "the degree to which the seizure advances the public interest." 443 U.S., at 51. This passage from *Brown* was not meant to transfer from politically accountable officials to the courts the decision as to which among reasonable alternative law enforcement techniques should be employed to deal with a serious public danger. Experts in police science might disagree over which of several methods of apprehending drunken drivers is preferable as an ideal. But for purposes of Fourth Amendment analysis, the choice among such reasonable alternatives remains with the governmental officials who have a unique understanding of, and a responsibility for, limited public resources, including a finite number of police officers. . . .

In Delaware v. Prouse, [440 U.S. 648 (1979)], we disapproved random stops made by Delaware Highway Patrol officers in an effort to apprehend unlicensed drivers and unsafe vehicles. We observed that *no* empirical evidence indicated that such stops would be an effective means of promoting roadway safety and said that "[i]t seems common sense that the percentage of all drivers on the road who are driving without a license is very small and that the number of licensed drivers who will be stopped in order to find one unlicensed operator will be large indeed." Id., at 659–660. We observed that the random stops involved the "kind of standardless and unconstrained discretion [which] is the evil the Court has discerned when in previous cases it has insisted that the discretion of the official in the field be circumscribed, at least to some extent." Id., at 661. We went on to state that our holding did not "cast doubt on the permissibility of roadside truck weigh-stations and inspection checkpoints, at which some vehicles may be subject to further detention for safety and regulatory inspection than are others." Id., at 663, n.26.

Unlike *Prouse*, this case involves neither a complete absence of empirical data nor a challenge to random highway stops. During the operation of the Saginaw County checkpoint, the detention of the 126 vehicles that entered the checkpoint resulted in the arrest of two drunken drivers. Stated as a percentage, approximately 1.6 percent of the drivers passing through the checkpoint were arrested for alcohol impairment. In addition, an expert witness testified at the trial that experience in other States demonstrated that, on the whole, sobriety checkpoints resulted in drunken driving arrests of around 1 percent of all motorists stopped. . . .

In sum, the balance of the State's interest in preventing drunken driving, the extent to which this system can reasonably be said to advance that interest, and the degree of intrusion upon individual motorists who are briefly stopped, weighs in favor of the state program. We therefore hold that it is consistent with the Fourth Amendment. The judgment of the Michigan Court of Appeals is accordingly reversed, and the cause is remanded for further proceedings not inconsistent with this opinion.

. . . [6]

---

74. Distinguishing *Sitz*, the Court held that a highway checkpoint program, the primary purpose of which was narcotics interdiction, violated the Fourth Amendment. City of Indianapolis v. Edmond, 531 U.S. 32 (2000) (6–3). It said:

> Of course, there are circumstances that may justify a law enforcement checkpoint, where the primary purpose would otherwise, but for some emergency, relate to ordinary crime control. For example, as the Court of Appeals noted, the Fourth Amendment would almost certainly permit an appropriately tailored roadblock set up to thwart an imminent terrorist attack or to catch a dangerous criminal who is likely to flee by way of a particular route. . . . The exigencies created by these scenarios are far removed from the circumstances under which authorities might simply stop cars as a matter of course to see if there just happens to be a felon leaving the jurisdiction. While we do not limit the purposes that may justify a checkpoint program to any rigid set of categories, we decline to approve a program whose primary purpose is ultimately indistinguishable from the general interest in crime control.
>
> . . .
>
> Our holding also does not affect the validity of border searches or searches at places like airports and government buildings, where the

[6] Justice Blackmun wrote an opinion concurring in the judgment. Justice Brennan wrote a dissenting opinion, which Justice Marshall joined. Justice Stevens also wrote a dissenting opinion, part of which Justice Brennan and Justice Marshall joined.

On remand, the Michigan Court of Appeals held that the roadblock violated the state constitution's prohibition against unreasonable seizures. Sitz v. Department of State Police, 485 N.W. 2d 135 (Mich.App. 1992).

need for such measures to ensure public safety can be particularly acute. Nor does our opinion speak to other intrusions aimed primarily at purposes beyond the general interest in crime control. Our holding also does not impair the ability of police officers to act appropriately upon information that they properly learn during a checkpoint stop justified by a lawful primary purpose, even where such action may result in the arrest of a motorist for an offense unrelated to that purpose. Finally, we caution that the purpose inquiry in this context is to be conducted only at the programmatic level and is not an invitation to probe the minds of individual officers acting at the scene.

Id. at 44, 47–48.

Edmond was distinguished in Illinois v. Lidster, 540 U.S. ___ (2004). In *Lidster*, the police set up a traffic checkpoint near the scene of a hit-and-run accident, in order to ask persons in the cars whether they had any information about the accident. Such "information seeking" highway stops are not presumptively unconstitutional, the Court said. Rather, their reasonableness under the Fourth Amendment must be judged on the basis of the particular circumstances. On that basis, the Court said that the brief stops in this case were constitutional.

75. In United States v. Brignoni-Ponce, 422 U.S. 873 (1975), two officers of the Border Patrol pursued the car driven by Brignoni-Ponce and stopped it near the Mexican border in Southern California; their only reason for doing so was that the three occupants appeared to be of Mexican descent. They questioned him and his passengers about their citizenship and arrested all three when they learned that the passengers were aliens who had entered illegally. On appeal from their convictions, the government claimed that the stop was pursuant to the Border Patrol's statutory authority, since in the border area "a person's apparent Mexican ancestry alone justifies belief that he or she is an alien," id. at 877. While conceding the importance and difficulty of enforcing the immigration law, the Court denied the broad authority sought:

> [B]ecause of the importance of the governmental interest at stake, the minimal intrusion of a brief stop, and the absence of practical alternatives for policing the border, we hold that when an officer's observations lead him reasonably to suspect that a particular vehicle may contain aliens who are illegally in the country, he may stop the car briefly and investigate the circumstances that provoke suspicion. As in *Terry* [v. Ohio, 392 U.S. 1 (1968)], the stop and inquiry must be "reasonably related in scope to the justification for their initiation." 392 U.S., at 29. The officer may question the driver and passengers about their citizenship and immigration status, and he may ask them to explain suspicious circumstances, but any further detention or search must be based on consent or probable cause.
>
> We are unwilling to let the Border Patrol dispense entirely with the requirement that officers must have a reasonable suspicion to justify roving-patrol stops. In the context of border area stops, the

> reasonableness requirement of the Fourth Amendment demands something more than the broad and unlimited discretion sought by the Government. Roads near the border carry not only aliens seeking to enter the country illegally, but a large volume of legitimate traffic as well. . . . To approve roving-patrol stops of all vehicles in the border area, without any suspicion that a particular vehicle is carrying illegal immigrants, would subject the residents of these and other areas to potentially unlimited interference with their use of the highways, solely at the discretion of Border Patrol officers. . . .
>
> We are not convinced that the legitimate needs of law enforcement require this degree of interference with lawful traffic. . . . [T]he nature of illegal alien traffic and the characteristics of smuggling operations tend to generate articulable grounds for identifying violators. Consequently, a requirement of reasonable suspicion for stops allows the Government adequate means of guarding the public interest and also protects residents of the border areas from indiscriminate official interference. Under the circumstances, and even though the intrusion incident to a stop is modest, we conclude that it is not "reasonable" under the Fourth Amendment to make such stops on a random basis.

Brignoni-Ponce, 422 U.S. at 881–83.

Brief, routine stops at a permanent checkpoint away from the border were upheld in United States v. Martinez-Fuerte, 428 U.S. 543 (1976) (7–2). The Court said that a brief stop for questioning was permissible even in the absence of any basis for stopping a particular car and that some cars could be directed to a secondary inspection area for further brief inquiry into the residence status of the occupants without the "reasonable suspicion" required for a roving-patrol stop; such further inquiry could be made "largely on the basis of apparent Mexican ancestry," id. at 563. The Court balanced the minimal invasion of private interests against the strong public interest in controlling unlawful immigration and the success of the checkpoint at serving that objective. See also United States v. Cortez, 449 U.S. 411 (1981) (stop of vehicle reasonably believed to be carrying illegal aliens upheld).

In Delaware v. Prouse, 440 U.S. 648 (1979) (8–1), a police officer stopped a car for what he called a "routine" stop; he said that he had observed no violation or suspicious activity but, being on patrol and not "answering any complaints," decided to pull the car over for a license and registration check. When the car was stopped, the officer smelled marijuana smoke and seized marijuana in plain view on the floor of the car. The Court emphasized the entire lack of standards regulating the stop and observed: "When there is not probable cause to believe that a driver is violating any one of the multitude of applicable traffic and equipment regulations—or other articulable basis amounting to reasonable suspicion that the driver is unlicensed or his vehicle unregistered—we cannot conceive of any legitimate basis upon which a patrolman could decide that stopping a particular driver for a spot check would be more productive than stopping any other driver." Id. at 661.

The Court held: "Except in those situations in which there is at least articulable and reasonable suspicion that a motorist is unlicensed or that an automobile is not registered, or that either the vehicle or an occupant is otherwise subject to seizure for violation of law, stopping an automobile and detaining the driver in order to check his driver's license and the registration of the automobile are unreasonable under the Fourth Amendment. This holding does not preclude the . . . States from developing methods for spot checks that involve less intrusion or that do not involve the unconstrained exercise of discretion. Questioning of all oncoming traffic at roadblock-type stops is one possible alternative. We hold only that persons in automobiles on public roadways may not for that reason alone have their travel and privacy interfered with at the unbridled discretion of police officers." Id. at 663.

In Pennsylvania v. Mimms, 434 U.S. 106 (1977) (per curiam; 6–3), the Court held that a police officer who has lawfully directed a driver to stop his automobile, in this case because the license plate had expired, needs no additional basis of suspicion before ordering the driver to get out of the car. The Court said that the potential danger to the officer, both from armed drivers and from oncoming traffic, outweighs the "de minimis" additional intrusion on the driver's personal liberty.

The Court extended its reasoning in *Mimms* to passengers in a car that has been lawfully stopped, in Maryland v. Wilson, 519 U.S. 408 (1997) (7–2). It said: "[D]anger to an officer from a traffic stop is likely to be greater when there are passengers in addition to the driver in the stopped car. While there is not the same basis for ordering the passengers out of the car as there is for ordering the driver out, the additional intrusion on the passenger is minimal. We therefore hold that an officer making a traffic stop may order passengers to get out of the car pending completion of the stop." Id. at 414–15. Cf. Michigan v. Summers, 452 U.S. 692 (1981), p. 195 note 108 below.

CHAPTER 3

SEARCH

"The right of the people to be secure in their persons, houses, papers, and effects, against unreasonable searches and seizures, shall not be violated, and no warrants shall issue, but upon probable cause, supported by oath or affirmation, and particularly describing the place to be searched, and the persons or things to be seized." U.S. Constitution amend. IV.

[The Amendment] took its origin in the determination of the framers of the Amendments to the Federal Constitution to provide for that instrument a Bill of Rights, securing to the American people, among other things, those safeguards which had grown up in England to protect the people from unreasonable searches and seizures, such as were permitted under the general warrants issued under authority of the Government by which there had been invasions of the home and privacy of the citizens and the seizure of their private papers in support of charges, real or imaginary, made against them. Such practices had also received sanction under warrants and seizures under the so-called writs of assistance, issued in the American colonies. . . . Resistance to these practices had established the principle which was enacted into the fundamental law in the Fourth Amendment, that a man's house was his castle and not to be invaded by any general authority to search and seize his goods and papers. . . .

The effect of the Fourth Amendment is to put the courts of the United States and Federal officials, in the exercise of their power and authority, under limitations and restraints as to the exercise of such power and authority, and to forever secure the people, their persons, houses, papers and effects against all unreasonable searches and seizures under the guise of law. This protection reaches all alike, whether accused of crime or not, and the duty of giving to it force and effect is obligatory upon all entrusted under our Federal system with the enforcement of the laws. The tendency of those who execute the criminal laws of the country to obtain conviction by means of unlawful seizures and enforced confessions, the latter often obtained after subjecting accused persons to unwarranted practices destructive of rights secured by the Federal Constitution, should find no sanction in the judgments of the courts which are charged at all times with the support of the Constitution and to which people of all conditions have a right to appeal for the maintenance of such fundamental rights.

Weeks v. United States, 232 U.S. 383, 390, 391–92 (1914). The Court held that evidence obtained by a search and seizure which violated the defendant's rights under the Fourth Amendment was inadmissible in evidence against him in a federal court.

The security of one's privacy against arbitrary intrusion by the police—which is at the core of the Fourth Amendment—is basic to a free society. It is therefore implicit in "the concept of ordered liberty" and as such enforceable against the States through the Due Process Clause. The knock at the door, whether by day or by night, as a prelude to a search, without authority of law but solely on the authority of the police, did not need the commentary of recent history to be condemned as inconsistent with the conception of human rights enshrined in the history and the basic constitutional documents of English-speaking peoples.

Accordingly, we have no hesitation in saying that were a State affirmatively to sanction such police incursion into privacy it would run counter to the guaranty of the Fourteenth Amendment. But the ways of enforcing such a basic right raise questions of a different order. How such arbitrary conduct should be checked, what remedies against it should be afforded, the means by which the right should be made effective, are all questions that are not to be so dogmatically answered as to preclude the varying solutions which spring from an allowable range of judgment on issues not susceptible of quantitative solution.

In Weeks v. United States, [232 U.S. 383 (1914)], this Court held that in a federal prosecution the Fourth Amendment barred the use of evidence secured through an illegal search and seizure. This ruling was made for the first time in 1914. It was not derived from the explicit requirements of the Fourth Amendment; it was not based on legislation expressing Congressional policy in the enforcement of the Constitution. The decision was a matter of judicial implication. Since then it has been frequently applied and we stoutly adhere to it. But the immediate question is whether the basic right to protection against arbitrary intrusion by the police demands the exclusion of logically relevant evidence obtained by an unreasonable search and seizure because, in a federal prosecution for a federal crime, it would be excluded. As a matter of inherent reason, one would suppose this to be an issue as to which men with complete devotion to the protection of the right of privacy might give different answers. When we find that in fact most of the English-speaking world does not regard as vital to such protection the exclusion of evidence thus obtained, we must hesitate to treat this remedy as an essential ingredient of the right. The contrariety of views of the States is particularly impressive in view of the careful reconsideration which they have given the problem in the light of the *Weeks* decision.[1]

. . .

The jurisdictions which have rejected the *Weeks* doctrine have not left the right to privacy without other means of protection. Indeed, the exclusion of evidence is a remedy which directly serves only to protect those upon whose person or premises something incriminating has been found. We cannot, therefore, regard it as a departure from basic standards to remand such persons, together with those who emerge scatheless from a search, to the remedies of private action and such protection as the internal discipline of the police, under the eyes of an alert public opinion, may afford. Granting that in practice the exclusion of evidence may be an effective way of deterring unreasonable searches, it is not for this Court to condemn as falling below the minimal standards assured by the Due Process Clause a State's reliance upon other methods which, if consistently enforced, would be equally effective. . . . We cannot brush aside the experience of States which deem the incidence of such conduct by the police too slight to call for a deterrent remedy not by way of disciplinary measures but by overriding the relevant rules of evidence. There are, moreover, reasons for excluding evidence unreasonably obtained by the federal police which are less compelling in the case of police under State or local authority. The public opinion of a community can far more effectively be exerted against oppressive conduct on the part of police directly responsible to the community itself than can local opinion, sporadically aroused, be brought to bear upon remote authority pervasively exerted throughout the country.

We hold, therefore, that in a prosecution in a State court for a State crime the Fourteenth Amendment does not forbid the admission of evidence obtained by an unreasonable search and seizure.

Wolf v. Colorado, 338 U.S. 25, 27–33 (1949).

Today we once again examine *Wolf*'s constitutional documentation of the right to privacy free from unreasonable state intrusion, and, after its dozen years on our books, are led by it to close the only courtroom door remaining open to evidence secured by official lawlessness in flagrant abuse of that basic right, reserved to all persons as a specific guarantee against that very same unlawful conduct. We hold that all evidence obtained by searches and seizures in violation of the Constitution is, by that same authority, inadmissible in a state court.

Since the Fourth Amendment's right of privacy has been declared enforceable against the States through the Due Process Clause of the

[1] The Court's analysis of state cases indicated that 47 states had considered the *Weeks* doctrine since the decision of that case, and that 31 states rejected the doctrine and 16 accepted it. The analysis of state cases is detailed in an appendix to the Court's opinion, 338 U.S. at 33.

"Nice weather we're having, eh Mulligan?"

Fourteenth, it is enforceable against them by the same sanction of exclusion as is used against the Federal Government. Were it otherwise, then just as without the *Weeks* [v. United States, 232 U.S. 383 (1914)] rule the assurance against unreasonable federal searches and seizures would be "a form of words," valueless and undeserving of mention in a perpetual charter of inestimable human liberties, so too, without that rule the freedom from state invasions of privacy would be so ephemeral and so neatly severed from its conceptual nexus with the freedom from all brutish means of coercing evidence as not to merit this Court's high regard as a freedom "implicit in the concept of ordered liberty." At the time that the Court held in *Wolf* that the Amendment was applicable to the States through the Due Process Clause, the cases of this Court, as we have seen, had steadfastly held that as to federal officers the Fourth Amendment included the exclusion of the evidence seized in violation of its provisions. Even *Wolf* "stoutly adhered" to that proposition. The right to privacy, when conceded operatively enforceable against the States, was not susceptible of destruction by avulsion of the sanction upon which its protection and enjoyment had always been deemed dependent under the *Boyd* [v. United States, 116 U.S. 616 (1886)], *Weeks* and *Silverthorne* [Lumber Co. v. United States, 251 U.S. 385 (1920)] cases. Therefore, in extending the substantive protections of due process to all constitutionally unreasonable searches—state or federal—it was logically and constitutionally necessary that the exclusion doctrine—an essential part of the right to privacy—be also insisted upon as an essential ingredient of the right newly recognized by the *Wolf* case. In short, the admission of the new constitutional right by *Wolf* could not consistently tolerate denial of its most important constitutional privilege, namely, the exclusion of the evidence which an accused had been forced to give by reason of the unlawful seizure. To hold otherwise is to grant the right but in reality to withhold its privilege and enjoyment.

Mapp v. Ohio, 367 U.S. 643, 654–56 (1961). See Bivens v. Six Unknown Named Agents of Federal Bureau of Narcotics, 403 U.S. 388 (1971), p. 95 note 56 above.[2]

---

76. In Walder v. United States, 347 U.S. 62 (1954), the Court held that illegally obtained evidence can be used by the prosecution to impeach the credibility of the defendant's own testimony. The defendant had testified that he had never possessed narcotics. The prosecution was permitted to introduce into evidence narcotics obtained by an illegal search.

Walder was applied in United States v. Havens, 446 U.S. 620, 627–28 (1980) (5–4), in which the Court held that "a defendant's statements made in response to proper cross-examination reasonably suggested by the defendant's direct examination are subject to otherwise proper impeachment by the government, albeit by evidence that has been illegally obtained that is inadmissible on the government's direct case, or otherwise, as substantive evidence of guilt." The majority in *Havens* emphasized the importance of "arriving at the truth" in a criminal trial and concluded that that interest outweighed the incremental furthering of the ends served by the exclusionary rule if evidence were excluded in these circumstances. Id. at 626–27. The dissenting Justices argued that the majority's rule allowed the prosecutor to lay the basis for admission of otherwise excluded evidence by structuring his questions on cross-examination accordingly.

In James v. Illinois, 493 U.S. 307 (1990) (5–4), however, the Court held that the *Walder* exception to the exclusionary rule does not extend to the use of illegally obtained evidence to impeach testimony of a defense witness other than the defendant. In *James*, the evidence in question was statements of the defendant that he made while he was unlawfully arrested.

77. Inevitable discovery. In Nix v. Williams, 467 U.S. 431 (1984) (7–2), drawing on the rule that police illegality does not require the exclusion of evidence that has been obtained "by means wholly indepen-

2. In a civil drug forfeiture proceeding (pursuant to 21 U.S.C § 881(a)(7)), the Due Process Clause requires that before real property is seized, the property owner be given notice and an opportunity to be heard, unless there are exigent circumstances establishing a need for immediate seizure. United States v. James Daniel Good Real Property, 510 U.S. 43 (1993) (5–4). The Court observed: "While the Fourth Amendment places limits on the Government's power to seize property for purposes of forfeiture, it does not provide the sole measure of constitutional protection that must be afforded property owners in forfeiture proceedings." Id. at 495–96.

dent of any constitutional violation," id. at 443, the Court held that evidence to which the police are led by such a violation need not be excluded if "it would ultimately or inevitably have been discovered even if no violation of any constitutional or statutory provision had taken place," id. at 434. In Nix v. Williams, the police were led to the body of a murder victim by the defendant, in response to police conduct that violated his right to counsel under the Sixth Amendment. Finding that teams searching for the body were closing in on the location where it was concealed and would inevitably have found it in the same condition in which it was actually found, the Court held that evidence obtained thereby was properly admitted.

Nix v. Williams was applied in United States v. Cherry, 759 F.2d 1196 (5th Cir.1985) (some evidence admitted, some excluded). The court said that in order for the "inevitable discovery" exception to apply, "the prosecution must demonstrate both a reasonable probability that the evidence would have been discovered in the absence of police misconduct and that the government was actively pursuing a substantial alternate line of investigation at the time of the constitutional violation." Id. at 1205–1206. Otherwise, the court said, the exception would encourage the police to engage in illegal conduct. "In certain circumstances, however, such as when the hypothetical independent source comes into being only after the misconduct, the absence of a strong deterrent interest may warrant the application of the inevitable discovery exception without a showing of active pursuit by the government in order to ensure that the government is not unjustifiably disadvantaged by the police misconduct." Id. at 1206.

See United States v. Silvestri, 787 F.2d 736 (1st Cir.1986), discussing *Cherry* and other cases, and concluding: "Our review of these cases reveals that there are three basic concerns which surface in an inevitable discovery analysis: are the legal means truly independent; are both the use of the legal means and the discovery by that means truly inevitable; and does the application of the inevitable discovery exception either provide an incentive for police misconduct or significantly weaken fourth amendment protection?" Id. at 774. In *Silvestri*, the court considered cases in which police make a search and seize items prior to obtaining a warrant that authorized the search and seizure. It concluded that the warrant application process need not have been initiated at the time the search occurs but that there must have been probable cause for the issuance of a warrant at that time.

See Murray v. United States, 487 U.S. 533 (1988) (4–3), p. 190 note 104 below.

---

78. Good-faith exception. In United States v. Leon, 468 U.S. 897, 900 (1984) (6–3), the Court held that the exclusionary rule does not "bar the use in the prosecution's case in chief of evidence obtained by officers acting in reasonable reliance on a search warrant issued by a detached and neutral magistrate but ultimately found to be unsupported by probable cause."

The Court first repeated prior statements that the use of evidence obtained in violation of the Fourth Amendment is not itself a violation of the Amendment and that the exclusion of such evidence is not a cure for the violation itself but rather a judicial measure to deter violations. Therefore, it said, application of the exclusionary rule depends on "weighing the costs and benefits." The principle cost of excluding "inherently trustworthy tangible evidence" is that it interferes "with the criminal justice system's truth-finding function," with the result "that some guilty defendants may go free or receive reduced sentences as a result of favorable plea bargains." Id. at 907. The Court referred to prior cases, see note 83 p. 151 below, in which it had found that the costs of applying the exclusionary rule exceeded the benefits.

The Court considered the benefit that might be derived from evidence obtained pursuant to a warrant and concluded "that the marginal or nonexistent benefits produced by suppressing evidence obtained in objectively reasonable reliance on a subsequently invalidated search warrant cannot justify the substantial cost of exclusion," id. at 922. The exclusion of evidence, it said, remained "an appropriate remedy if the magistrate or judge issuing a warrant was misled by information in an affidavit that the affiant knew was false or would have known was false except for his reckless disregard of the truth," or "where the issuing magistrate wholly abandoned his judicial role," or if a warrant were altogether lacking in indicia of probable cause or were "facially deficient." Id. at 923. In such cases, an officer relying on the warrant would not be acting in an objectively reasonable manner.

In a dissenting opinion, which Justice Marshall joined, Justice Brennan said that the majority's ruling was the "*pièce de résistance*" of "the Court's gradual but determined strangulation of the [exclusionary] rule." Id. at 928–29. The majority's cost/benefit analysis, he said, gave "an illusion of technical precision and ineluctability," id. at 929, but was a product of "inherently unstable compounds of intuition, hunches, and occasional pieces of partial and often inconclusive data," id. at 942. "[T]he entire enterprise of attempting to assess the benefits and costs of the exclusionary rule in various contexts is a virtually impossible task for the judiciary to perform honestly or accurately." Id.

Justice Brennan rejected the majority's view of the exclusionary rule as a deterrent measure separate from the Fourth Amendment itself. "Because seizures are executed principally to secure evidence, and because such evidence generally has utility in our legal system only in the context of a trial supervised by a judge, it is apparent that the admission of illegally obtained evidence implicates the same constitutional concerns as the initial seizure of that evidence." Id. at 933.

The good-faith exception was applied also in a companion case to *Leon*, Massachusetts v. Sheppard, 468 U.S. 981 (1984) (7–2).

79. With respect to probable cause for issuance of a warrant, does the Court's test of objective reasonableness have the effect that there is a "discount" on the amount of evidence that is required for issuance of a warrant? For cases applying *Leon*, see, e.g., United States v. Thomas, 263 F.3d 805 (8th Cir.2001) (warrant invalid because it contained incorrect address; exclusion not required); United States v. Weaver, 99 F.3d 1372 (6th Cir.1996) (reasonably prudent officer would have sought more corroboration of probable cause, and officer did not, therefore, rely on warrant in good faith); United States v. Merida, 765 F.2d 1205 (5th Cir.1985) ("inadequate showing of nexus between items sought and location to be searched"; exclusion not required); United States v. Savoca, 761 F.2d 292 (6th Cir. 1985) (no probable cause; exclusion not required); United States v. Strand, 761 F.2d 449 (8th Cir.1985) (seized items not included in warrant; exclusion required); United States v. Merchant, 760 F.2d 963 (9th Cir.1985) (warrantless search based on subterfuge that person was on probation; exclusion required).

The good-faith exception to the exclusionary rule was extended to a warrantless administrative search pursuant to a statute subsequently declared invalid under the Fourth Amendment, in Illinois v. Krull, 480 U.S. 340 (1987) (5–4).

80. After the decision in *Leon*, it was feared by those who agreed with the dissenting opinion that the good-faith exception would be extended to searches without a warrant, e.g., a search incident to an arrest, see Chimel v. California, 395 U.S. 752 (1969), p. 205 below. That has not happened. But cf. Illinois v. Rodriguez, 497 U.S. 177 (1990), p. 169 below.

81. The exclusionary rule does not apply to "evidence seized in violation of the Fourth Amendment by an officer who acted in reliance on a police record indicating the existence of an outstanding arrest warrant—a record that is later determined to be erroneous," if the source of the error is a clerical error of a court employee and not the fault of the police. Arizona v. Evans, 514 U.S. 1 (1995) (7–2).

82. Observing that "the grant of motions to suppress evidence obtained pursuant to defective search warrants is relatively uncommon and apparently poses no significant obstacle to law-enforcement efforts" and stating its view that "the good-faith exception will ultimately reduce respect for and compliance with the probable-cause standard," the New Jersey Supreme Court rejected the *Leon* rule as inapplicable to the State constitution's provision against unreasonable search and seizure. State v. Novembrino, 519 A.2d 820 (N.J.1987). The good-faith exception is rejected also in State v. Marsala, 579 A.2d 58 (Conn.1990); State v. Gutierrez, 863 P.2d 1052 (N.M.1993); Commonwealth v. Edmunds, 586 A.2d 887 (Pa. 1991); and State v. Oakes, 598 A.2d 119 (Vt.1991). In *Gutierrez*, the court noted that seven other states had rejected the exception, including, in addition to those mentioned, Idaho, New York, and North Carolina. 863 P.2d at 1068 n.10.

83. In United States v. Calandra, 414 U.S. 338 (1974) (6–3), the Supreme Court held that the exclusionary rule announced in *Mapp*, p. 145 above, does not apply to evidence presented to a grand jury. It said:

> The exclusionary rule was adopted to effectuate the Fourth Amendment right of all citizens "to be secure in their houses, papers, and effects, against unreasonable searches and seizures...." Under this rule, evidence obtained in violation of the Fourth Amendment cannot be used in a criminal proceeding against the victim of the illegal search and seizure. . . . This prohibition applies as well to the fruits of the illegally seized evidence. . . .
>
> The purpose of the exclusionary rule is not to redress the injury to the privacy of the search victim. . . . Instead, the rule's prime purpose is to deter future unlawful police conduct and thereby effectuate the guarantee of the Fourth Amendment against unreasonable search and seizures. . . . In sum, the rule is a judicially-created remedy designed to safeguard Fourth Amendment rights generally through its deterrent effect, rather than a personal constitutional right of the party aggrieved.
>
> Despite its broad deterrent purpose, the exclusionary rule has never been interpreted to proscribe the use of illegally-seized evidence in all proceedings or against all persons. As with any remedial device, the application of the rule has been restricted to those areas where its remedial objectives are thought most efficaciously served.

Id. at 347.

The Court concluded that application of the exclusionary rule "would seriously impede the grand jury" and that "any incremental deterrent effect which might be achieved by extending the rule to grand jury proceedings is uncertain at best." Id. at 349, 351. In a dissenting opinion joined by Justice Douglas and Justice Marshall, Justice Brennan observed: "For the first time, the Court today discounts to the point of extinction the vital function of the [exclusionary] rule to insure that the judiciary avoids even the slightest appearance of sanctioning illegal government conduct." Id. at 360.

Extending *Calandra*, in United States v. Puglia, 8 F.3d 478 (7th Cir.1993), the court of appeals held that the use in a grand jury proceeding of evidence that had previously been suppressed does not require dismissal of an indictment.

The application of the exclusionary rule was limited again, in United States v. Janis, 428 U.S. 433 (1976) (5–3). The Court there ruled that evidence unlawfully obtained (in good faith) by state criminal law enforcement officials and turned over to federal officials need not be excluded in a federal tax proceeding. Concluding that whatever deterrent effect such an application of the rule might have was outweighed by the social costs of excluding the evidence, the Court held that "the judicially created exclusionary rule should not be extended to forbid the use in the civil proceeding of one sovereign of evidence seized by a criminal law enforcement agent of another sovereign," id. at 459–60. See Wolf v. Commissioner of Internal Revenue, 13 F.3d 189 (6th Cir.1993) (*Janis* applied). The exclusionary rule does not apply in civil deportation hearings, Immigration and Naturalization Service v. Lopez-Mendoza, 468 U.S. 1032 (1984) (5–4), or in parole revocation hearings, Pennsylvania Board of Probation and Parole v. Scott, 524 U.S. 357 (1998) (5–4).

84. In Stone v. Powell, 428 U.S. 465 (1976), the Court limited the availability of collateral federal proceedings to contest the validity of a state criminal conviction on the ground that unconstitutionally obtained evidence was introduced at the trial. See note 434, p. 877 below.

85. The Fourth Amendment does not apply to a search and seizure by United States officials of property owned by a nonresident alien and located in a foreign country. United States v. Verdugo-Urquidez, 494 U.S. 259 (1990) (6–3). See also United States v. Mount, 757 F.2d 1315 (D.C.Cir.1985) (exclusionary rule not applicable to search conducted abroad by foreign officials; additional cases cited).

Consent

Stoner v. California

376 U.S. 483, 84 S.Ct. 889, 11 L.Ed.2d 856 (1964)

■ MR. JUSTICE STEWART delivered the opinion of the Court.

The petitioner was convicted of armed robbery after a jury trial in the Superior Court of Los Angeles County, California. At the trial several articles which had been found by police officers in a search of the petitioner's hotel room during his absence were admitted into evidence over his objection. A District Court of Appeal of California affirmed the conviction, and the Supreme Court of California denied further review. We granted certiorari, limiting review "to the question of whether evidence was admitted which had been obtained by an unlawful search and seizure." 374 U.S. 826. For the reasons which follow, we conclude that the petitioner's conviction must be set aside.

The essential facts are not in dispute. On the night of October 25, 1960, the Budget Town Food Market in Monrovia, California, was robbed by two men, one of whom was described by eyewitnesses as carrying a gun and wearing horn-rimmed glasses and a grey jacket. Soon after the robbery a checkbook belonging to the petitioner was found in an adjacent parking lot and turned over to the police. Two of the stubs in the checkbook indicated that checks had been drawn to the order of the Mayfair Hotel in Pomona, California. Pursuing this lead, the officers learned from the Police Department of Pomona that the petitioner had a previous criminal record, and they obtained from the Pomona police a photograph of the petitioner. They showed the photograph to the two eyewitnesses to the robbery, who both stated that the picture looked like the man who had carried the gun. On the basis of this information the officers went to the Mayfair Hotel in Pomona at about 10 o'clock on the night of October 27. They had neither search nor arrest warrants. There then transpired the following events, as later recounted by one of the officers:

> We approached the desk, the night clerk, and asked him if there was a party by the name of Joey L. Stoner living at the hotel. He checked his records and stated "Yes, there is." And we asked him what room he was in. He stated he was in Room 404 but he was out at this time.
>
> We asked him how he knew that he was out. He stated that the hotel regulations required that the key to the room would be placed in the mail box each time they left the hotel. The key was in the mail box, that he therefore knew he was out of the room.
>
> We asked him if he would give us permission to enter the room, explaining our reasons for this.
>
> Q. What reasons did you explain to the clerk?
>
> A. We explained that we were there to make an arrest of a man who had possibly committed a robbery in the City of Monrovia, and that we were concerned about the fact that he had a weapon. He stated "In this case, I will be more than happy to give you permission and I will take you directly to the room."
>
> Q. Is that what the clerk told you?
>
> A. Yes, sir.
>
> Q. What else happened?
>
> A. We left one detective in the lobby, and Detective Oliver, Officer Collins, and myself, along with the night clerk, got on the elevator and proceeded to the fourth floor, and went to Room 404. The night clerk placed a key in the lock, unlocked the door, and says, "Be my guest."

The officers entered and made a thorough search of the room and its contents. They found a pair of horn-rimmed glasses and a grey jacket in the room, and a .45-caliber automatic pistol with a clip and several cartridges in the bottom of a bureau drawer. The petitioner was arrested two days later in Las Vegas, Nevada. He waived extradition and was returned to California for trial on the charge of armed robbery. The gun, the cartridges and clip, the horn-rimmed glasses, and the grey jacket were all used as evidence against him at his trial.

The search of the petitioner's room by the police officers was conducted without a warrant of any kind, and it therefore "can survive constitutional inhibition only upon a showing that the surrounding facts brought it within one of the exceptions to the rule that a search must rest upon a search warrant. [. . .]" Rios v. United States, 364 U.S. 253, 261. . . .

[T]he respondent has made no argument that the search can be justified as an incident to the petitioner's arrest. Instead, the argument is made that the search of the hotel room, although conducted without the petitioner's consent, was lawful because it was conducted with the consent of the hotel clerk. We find this argument unpersuasive.

Even if it be assumed that a state law which gave a hotel proprietor blanket authority to authorize the police to search the rooms of the hotel's guests could survive constitutional challenge, there is no intimation in the California cases cited by the respondent that California has any such law. Nor is there any substance to the claim that the search was reasonable because the police, relying upon the night clerk's expressions of consent, had a reasonable basis for the belief that the clerk had authority to consent to the search. Our decisions make clear that the rights protected by the Fourth Amendment are not to be eroded by strained applications of the law of agency or by unrealistic doctrines of "apparent authority." . . .

It is important to bear in mind that it was the petitioner's constitutional right which was at stake here, and not the night clerk's nor the hotel's. It was a right, therefore, which only the petitioner could waive by word or deed, either directly or through an agent. It is true that the night clerk clearly and unambiguously consented to the search. But there is nothing in the record to indicate that the police had any basis whatsoever to believe that the night clerk had been authorized by the petitioner to permit the police to search the petitioner's room.

At least twice this Court has explicitly refused to permit an otherwise unlawful police search of a hotel room to rest upon consent of the hotel proprietor. Lustig v. United States, 338 U.S. 74; United States v. Jeffers, 342 U.S. 48. In *Lustig* the manager of a hotel allowed police to enter and search a room without a warrant in the occupant's absence, and the search was held unconstitutional. In *Jeffers* the assistant manager allowed a similar search, and that search was likewise held unconstitutional.

It is true, as was said in *Jeffers*, that when a person engages a hotel room he undoubtedly gives "implied or express permission" to "such persons as maids, janitors or repairmen" to enter his room "in the performance of their duties." 342 U.S., at 51. But the conduct of the night clerk and the police in the present case was of an entirely different order. In a closely analogous situation the Court has held that a search by police officers of a house occupied by a tenant invaded the tenant's constitutional right, even though the search was authorized by the owner of the house, who presumably had not only apparent but actual authority to enter the house for some purposes, such as to "view waste." Chapman v. United States, 365 U.S. 610. The Court pointed out that the officers' purpose in entering was not to view waste but to search for distilling equipment, and concluded that to uphold such a search without a warrant would leave tenants' homes secure only in the discretion of their landlords.

No less than a tenant of a house, or the occupant of a room in a boarding house . . . a guest in a hotel room is entitled to constitutional protection against unreasonable searches and seizures. . . . That protection would disappear if it were left to depend upon the unfettered discretion of an employee of the hotel. It follows that this search without a warrant was unlawful. Since evidence obtained through the search was admitted at the trial, the judgment must be reversed. . . .

. . .[3]

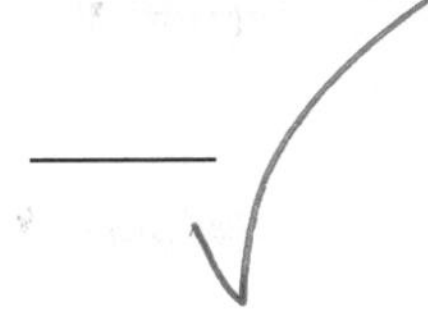

Schneckloth v. Bustamonte

412 U.S. 218, 93 S.Ct. 2041, 36 L.Ed.2d 854 (1973)

■ MR. JUSTICE STEWART delivered the opinion of the Court.

It is well settled under the Fourth and Fourteenth Amendments that a search conducted without a warrant issued upon probable cause is "per se unreasonable . . . subject only to a few specifically established and well-delineated exceptions." Katz v. United States, 389 U.S. 347, 357. . . . It is equally well settled that one of the specifically established exceptions to the requirements of both a warrant and probable cause is a search that is conducted pursuant to consent. . . . The constitutional question in the present case concerns the definition of "consent" in this Fourth and Fourteenth Amendment context.

I

The respondent was brought to trial in a California court upon a charge of possessing a check with intent to defraud. He moved to suppress the introduction of certain material as evidence against him on the ground that the material had been acquired through an unconstitutional search and seizure. In response to the motion, the trial judge conducted an evidentiary hearing where it was established that the material in question had been acquired by the State under the following circumstances:

While on routine patrol in Sunnyvale, California, at approximately 2:40 in the morning, Police Officer James Rand stopped an automobile when he observed that one headlight and its license plate light were burned out. Six men were in the vehicle. Joe Alcala and the respondent, Robert Bustamonte, were in the front seat with Joe Gonzales, the driver. Three older men were seated in the rear. When, in response to the policeman's question, Gonzales could not produce a driver's license, Officer Rand asked if any of the other five had any evidence of identification. Only Alcala produced a license, and he explained that the car was his brother's. After the six occupants had stepped out of the car at the officer's request and after two additional policemen had arrived, Officer Rand asked Alcala if he could search the car. Alcala replied, "Sure, go ahead." Prior to the search no one was threatened with arrest and, according to Officer Rand's uncontradicted testimony, it "was all very congenial at this time." Gonzales testified that Alcala actually helped in the search of the car, by opening the

[3] Justice Harlan wrote an opinion concurring in part and dissenting in part.

trunk and glove compartment. In Gonzales' words: "[T]he police officer asked Joe [Alcala], he goes, 'Does the trunk open?' And Joe said, 'Yes.' He went to the car and got the keys and opened up the trunk." Wadded up under the left rear seat, the police officers found three checks that had previously been stolen from a car wash.

The trial judge denied the motion to suppress, and the checks in question were admitted in evidence at Bustamonte's trial. On the basis of this and other evidence he was convicted. . . .

Thereafter, the respondent sought a writ of habeas corpus in a federal district court. It was denied. On appeal, the Court of Appeals for the Ninth Circuit . . . set aside the District Court's order. . . . The appellate court reasoned that a consent was a waiver of a person's Fourth and Fourteenth Amendment rights, and that the State was under an obligation to demonstrate, not only that the consent had been uncoerced, but that it had been given with an understanding that it could be freely and effectively withheld. Consent could not be found, the court held, solely from the absence of coercion and a verbal expression of assent. Since the District Court had not determined that Alcala had known that his consent could have been withheld and that he could have refused to have his vehicle searched, the Court of Appeals vacated the order denying the writ and remanded the case for further proceedings. We granted certiorari to determine whether the Fourth and Fourteenth Amendments require the showing thought necessary by the Court of Appeals. . . .

II

It is important to make it clear at the outset what is not involved in this case. The respondent concedes that a search conducted pursuant to a valid consent is constitutionally permissible. . . . And similarly the State concedes that "[w]hen a prosecutor seeks to rely upon consent to justify the lawfulness of a search, he has the burden of proving that the consent was, in fact, freely and voluntarily given." Bumper v. North Carolina, 391 U.S. 543, 548. . . .

The precise question in this case, then, is what must the prosecution prove to demonstrate that a consent was "voluntarily" given. And upon that question there is a square conflict of views between the state and federal courts that have reviewed the search involved in the case before us. The Court of Appeals for the Ninth Circuit concluded that it is an essential part of the State's initial burden to prove that a person knows he has a right to refuse consent. The California courts have followed the rule that voluntariness is a question of fact to be determined from the totality of all the circumstances, and that the state of a defendant's knowledge is only one factor to be taken into account in assessing the voluntariness of a consent. . . .

A

The most extensive judicial exposition of the meaning of "voluntariness" has been developed in those cases in which the Court has had to determine the "voluntariness" of a defendant's confession for purposes of the Fourteenth Amendment. . . . It is to that body of case law to which we turn for initial guidance on the meaning of "voluntariness" in the present context.

Those cases yield no talismanic definition of "voluntariness," mechanically applicable to the host of situations where the question has arisen. . . . [N]either linguistics nor epistemology will provide a ready definition of the meaning of "voluntariness."

Rather, "voluntariness" has reflected an accommodation of the complex of values implicated in police questioning of a suspect. At one end of the spectrum is the acknowledged need for police questioning as a tool for the effective enforcement of criminal laws. . . . Without such investigation, those who were innocent might be falsely accused, those who were guilty might wholly escape prosecution, and many crimes would go unsolved. In short, the security of all would be diminished. . . . At the other end of the spectrum is the set of values reflecting society's deeply felt belief that the criminal law cannot be used as an instrument of unfairness, and that the possibility of unfair and even brutal police tactics poses a real and serious threat to civilized notions of justice. "[I]n cases involving involuntary confessions, this Court enforces the strongly felt attitude of our society that important human values are sacrificed where an agency of the government, in the course of securing a conviction, wrings a confession out of an accused against his will." Blackburn v. Alabama, 361 U.S. 199, 206–207. . . .

This Court's decisions reflect a frank recognition that the Constitution requires the sacrifice of neither security nor liberty. The Due Process Clause does not mandate that the police forgo all questioning, nor that they be given carte blanche to extract what they can from a suspect. "The ultimate test remains that which has been the only clearly established test in Anglo–American courts for two hundred years: the test of voluntariness. Is the confession the product of an essentially free and unconstrained choice by its maker? If it is, if he has willed to confess, it may be used against him. If it is not, if his will has been overborne and his capacity for self-determination critically impaired, the use of his confession offends due process." Culombe v. Connecticut, [367 U.S. 568 (1961)], at 602.

In determining whether a defendant's will was overborne in a particular case, the Court has assessed the totality of all the surrounding circumstances—both the characteristics of the accused and the details of the interrogation. Some of the factors taken into account have included the youth of the accused . . . his lack of education . . . or his low intelligence . . . the lack of any advice to the accused of his constitutional rights . . . the length of detention . . . the repeated and prolonged nature of the questioning . . . and the use of physical punishment such as the deprivation of food or sleep. . . . In all of these cases, the Court determined the factual circumstances surrounding the confession, assessed the psychological impact on the accused, and evaluated the legal significance of how the accused reacted. . . .

The significant fact about all of these decisions is that none of them turned on the presence or absence of a single controlling criterion; each reflected a careful scrutiny of all the surrounding circumstances. . . . In none of them did the Court rule that the Due Process Clause required the prosecution to prove as part of its initial burden that the defendant knew he had a right to refuse to answer the questions that were put. While the state of the accused's mind, and the failure of the police to advise the accused of his rights, were certainly factors to be evaluated in assessing the "voluntariness" of an accused's responses, they were not in and of themselves determinative. . . .

B

Similar considerations lead us to agree with the courts of California that the question whether a consent to a search was in fact "voluntary" or was the product of duress or coercion, express or implied, is a question of fact to be determined from the totality of all the circumstances. While knowledge of the right to refuse consent is one factor to be taken into account, the government need not establish such knowledge as the sine qua non of an effective consent. As with police questioning, two competing concerns must be accommodated in determining the meaning of a "voluntary" consent—the legitimate need for such searches and the equally important requirement of assuring the absence of coercion.

In situations where the police have some evidence of illicit activity, but lack probable cause to arrest or search, a search authorized by a valid consent may be the only means of obtaining important and reliable evidence. In the present case for example, while the police had reason to stop the car for traffic violations, the State does not contend that there was probable cause to search the vehicle or that the search was incident to a valid arrest of any of the occupants. Yet, the search yielded tangible evidence that served as a basis for a prosecution, and provided some assurance that others, wholly innocent of the crime, were not mistakenly brought to trial. And in those cases where there is probable cause to arrest or search, but where the police lack a warrant, a consent search may still be valuable. If the search is conducted and proves fruitless, that in itself may convince the police that an arrest with its possible stigma and embarrassment is unnecessary, or that a far more extensive search pursuant to a warrant is not justified. In short, a search pursuant to consent may result in considerably less inconvenience for the subject of the search, and, properly conducted, is a constitutionally permissible and wholly legitimate aspect of effective police activity.

But the Fourth and Fourteenth Amendments require that a consent not be coerced, by explicit or implicit means, by implied threat or covert force. For, no matter how subtly the coercion were applied, the resulting "consent" would be no more than a pretext for the unjustified police intrusion against which the Fourth Amendment is directed. . . .

The problem of reconciling the recognized legitimacy of consent searches with the requirement that they be free from any aspect of official coercion cannot be resolved by any infallible touchstone. To approve such searches without the most careful scrutiny would sanction the possibility of official coercion; to place artificial restrictions upon such searches would jeopardize their basic validity. Just as was true with confessions, the requirement of a "voluntary" consent reflects a fair accommodation of the constitutional requirements involved. In examining all the surrounding circumstances to determine if in fact the consent to search was coerced, account must be taken of subtly coercive police questions, as well as the possibly vulnerable subjective state of the person who consents. Those searches that are the product of police coercion can thus be filtered out without undermining the continuing validity of consent searches. In sum, there is no reason for us to depart in the area of consent searches, from the traditional definition of "voluntariness."

The approach of the Court of Appeals for the Ninth Circuit finds no support in any of our decisions that have attempted to define the meaning of "voluntariness." Its ruling, that the State must affirmatively prove that the subject of the search knew that he had a right to refuse consent, would, in practice, create serious doubt whether consent searches could continue to be conducted. . . . [W]here there was no evidence of any coercion, explicit or implicit, the prosecution would nevertheless be unable to demonstrate that the subject of the search in fact had known of his right to refuse consent.

The very object of the inquiry—the nature of a person's subjective understanding—underlines the difficulty of the prosecution's burden under the rule applied by the Court of Appeals in this case. Any defendant who was the subject of a search authorized solely by his consent could effectively frustrate the introduction into evidence of the fruits of that search by simply failing to testify that he in fact knew he could refuse to consent. . . .

One alternative that would go far toward proving that the subject of a search did know he had a right to refuse consent would be to advise him of that right before eliciting his consent. That, however, is a suggestion that has been almost universally repudiated by both federal and state courts, and, we think, rightly so. For it would be thoroughly impractical to impose on the normal consent search the detailed requirements of an effective warning. Consent searches are part of the standard investigatory techniques of law enforcement agencies. They normally occur on the highway, or in a person's home or office, and under informal and unstructured conditions. The circumstances that prompt the initial request to search may develop quickly or be a logical extension of investigative police questioning. The police may seek to investigate further suspicious circumstances or to follow up leads developed in questioning persons at the scene of a crime. These situations are a far cry from the structured atmosphere of a trial where, assisted by counsel if he chooses, a defendant is informed of his trial rights. . . . And, while surely a closer question, these situations are still immeasurably far removed from "custodial interrogation" where, in Miranda v. Arizona [384 U.S. 436 (1966)] we found that the Constitution required certain now familiar warnings as a prerequisite to police interrogation. . . .

Consequently, we cannot accept the position of the Court of Appeals in this case that proof of knowledge of the right to refuse consent is a necessary prerequisite to demonstrating a "voluntary" consent. Rather, it is only by analyzing all the circumstances of an individual consent that it can be ascertained whether in fact it was voluntary or coerced. It is this careful sifting of the unique facts and circumstances of each case that is evidenced in our prior decisions involving consent searches.

. . .

[I]f under all the circumstances it has appeared that the consent was not given voluntarily—that it was coerced by threats or force, or granted only in submission to a claim of lawful authority—then we have found the consent invalid and the search unreasonable. . . .

. . .

In short, neither this Court's prior cases, nor the traditional definition of "voluntariness" requires proof of knowledge of a right to refuse as the sine qua non of an effective consent to a search.

. . .

D

Much of what has already been said disposes of the argument that the Court's decision in the *Miranda* case requires the conclusion that knowledge of a right to refuse is an indispensable element of a valid consent. The considerations that informed the Court's holding in *Miranda* are simply inapplicable in the present case. In *Miranda* the Court found that the techniques of police questioning and the nature of custodial surroundings produce an inherently coercive situation. . . .

In this case, there is no evidence of any inherently coercive tactics—either from the nature of the police questioning or the environment in which it took place. Indeed, since consent searches will normally occur on a person's own familiar territory, the specter of incommunicado police interrogation in some remote station house is simply inapposite. There is no reason to believe, under circumstances such as are present here, that the response to a policeman's question is presumptively coerced; and there is, therefore, no reason to reject the traditional test for determining the voluntariness of a person's response. . . .

It is also argued that the failure to require the Government to establish knowledge as a prerequisite to a valid consent, will relegate the Fourth Amendment to the special province of "the sophisticated, the knowledgeable and the privileged." We cannot agree. The traditional definition of voluntariness we accept today has always taken into account evidence of minimal schooling, low intelligence, and the lack of any effective warnings to a person of his rights; and the voluntariness of any statement taken under those conditions has been carefully scrutinized to determine whether it was in fact voluntarily given.

E

Our decision today is a narrow one. We hold only that when the subject of a search is not in custody and the State attempts to justify a search on the basis of his consent, the Fourth and Fourteenth Amendments require that it demonstrate that the consent was in fact voluntarily given, and not the result of duress or coercion, express or implied. Voluntariness is a question of fact to be determined from all the circumstances, and while the subject's knowledge of a right to refuse is a factor to be taken into account, the prosecution is not required to demonstrate such knowledge as a prerequisite to establishing a voluntary consent. Because the California courts followed these principles in affirming the respondent's conviction, and because the Court of Appeals for the Ninth Circuit in remanding for an evidentiary hearing required more, its judgment must be reversed.

. . .[4]

---

86. The test of whether consent to a search is voluntary that the Court elaborated in Schneckloth v. Bustamonte, above, is applied in United States v. Watson, 423 U.S. 411 (1976), the facts of which are given above, p. 22. Holding that the consent was given voluntarily, the Court said: "There were no promises made to . . . [Watson] and no indication of more subtle forms of coercion that might flaw his judgment. He had been arrested and was in custody, but his consent was given while on a public street, not in the confines of the police station. Moreover, the fact of custody alone has never been enough in itself to demonstrate a coerced confession or consent to search. Similarly, under *Schneckloth*, the absence of proof that Watson knew he could withhold his consent, though it may be a factor in the overall judgment, is not to be given controlling significance. There is no indication in this record that Watson was a newcomer to the law, mentally deficient, or unable in the face of a custodial arrest to exercise a free choice. He was given *Miranda* warnings and was further cautioned that the results of the search of his car could be used against him. He persisted in his consent." Id. at 424–25. See Ohio v. Robinette, 519 U.S. 33 (1996) (8–1).

87. A person's general consent to a search of his car may extend to closed containers within the car. "A suspect may of course delimit as he chooses the scope of the search to which he consents. But if his consent would reasonably be understood to extend to a particular container, the Fourth Amendment provides no grounds for requiring a more explicit authorization." Florida v. Jimeno, 500 U.S. 248 (1991) (7–2).

[4] Justice Blackmun wrote a concurring opinion. Justice Powell also wrote a concurring opinion, which Chief Justice Burger and Justice Rehnquist joined. Justice Douglas, Justice Brennan, and Justice Marshall wrote dissenting opinions.

In Schneckloth v. Bustamonte, consent to the search of the car was held to include a search "under the left rear seat" where three wadded checks were found. Even if the conclusion that Alcala's consent was voluntarily given is accepted, does it follow that his answer, "Sure, go ahead," in response to the officer's asking if he could search the car included the place where the checks were found? If so, on what basis? Compare United States v. Ibarra, 948 F.2d 903 (5th Cir.1991), in which consent to the search of a house was held to include search of an attic, the entrance to which was inside a bedroom closet and was boarded up; police knocked out the boards with a sledgehammer.

Why is it that a man who truly consents, in the fullest sense, to a search of premises cannot later complain that the search violates his rights under the Fourth Amendment? Is it enough to say simply that he has "waived" his rights? If the search turns out to be against the man's interest, *why* does his consent constitute a "waiver"?

---

88. "[N]o sane man who denies his guilt would actually be willing that policemen search his room for contraband which is certain to be discovered. It follows that when police identify themselves as such, search a room, and find contraband in it, the occupant's words or signs of acquiescence in the search, accompanied by denial of guilt, do not show consent; at least in the absence of some extraordinary circumstance, such as ignorance that contraband is present." Higgins v. United States, 209 F.2d 819, 820 (D.C.Cir.1954). To the same effect, that it "defies ordinary common sense" that a person who is carrying incriminating evidence would consent to a search of his person, see United States v. Viale, 312 F.2d 595, 601 (2d Cir.1963).

On the other hand:

> [The defendant] argues that since it is incredible he would freely have consented to a search which he knew would disclose incriminating evidence, his words of consent should be considered an involuntary submission to authority and therefore insufficient to waive a constitutional right. Acceptance of this contention would mean that expressions of consent could relieve officers of the need of obtaining a warrant only when the speaker was not aware that the search would disclose damaging evidence—a fact usually not within the officers' knowledge. Such a ruling not only would almost destroy the principle permitting a search on consent but would enable experienced criminals to lay traps for officers who, relying on the words of consent, failed to secure a search warrant that would have been theirs for the asking. Where . . . no force or deception was either used or threatened, we see no reason why a court should disregard a suspect's expression of

> consent simply because efficient and lawful investigation and his own attempt to avoid apprehension had produced a situation where he could hardly avoid giving it.

United States v. Gorman, 355 F.2d 151, 158–59 (2d Cir.1965). "Bowing to events, even if one is not happy about them, is not the same thing as being coerced." Robbins v. MacKenzie, 364 F.2d 45, 50 (1st Cir.1966). See United States v. Lace, 669 F.2d 46, 52–53 (2d Cir.1982): "The consent to a search by one who realizes that the jig is up and a search warrant will issue in any event is similar to a plea of guilty by one who believes that he will be convicted if he stands trial. . . . His act does not become involuntary simply because the consequences would have been the same if he refused."

The issue whether a defendant's own (alleged) consent to a search was effective arises only if he later contests the use of evidence discovered during the search. Would it be a sound rule of constitutional law that consent is never an effective basis for a search without a warrant if there is time to obtain a warrant? Why (not)? Would it be a sound rule of police practice that police should never ask for consent to search without a warrant unless there is no time to obtain one?

---

89. A state regulation authorizing a probation officer to search a probationer's home without a warrant, if there are reasonable grounds to believe that he has contraband on the premises, including items prohibited by the terms of probation, does not violate the Fourth Amendment. The special needs of the probation system justify departure from the requirements of a warrant and probable cause. The regulation authorizing the search satisfies the requirement of reasonableness. Griffin v. Wisconsin, 483 U.S. 868 (1987) (5–4).

A warrantless search (supported by reasonable suspicion) of the premises of a person sentenced to probation for a drug offense, whose probation was expressly conditional on his submission to a search by a law enforcement officer at any time, is valid. United States v. Knights, 534 U.S. 112 (2001). The Court said that, viewing the totality of the circumstances, the fact that a person is on probation alters the balance by which the reasonableness of the search is assessed. It both increases the likelihood that the person is violating the law and, as a form of criminal punishment, somewhat reduces the person's liberty and, therefore, his expectation of privacy. See United States v. Reyes, 283 F.3d 446 (2d Cir.2002), stating that a person on probation has a "significantly diminished" expectation of privacy with respect to supervision by a probation officer and rejecting the "stalking horse" theory that if a probation officer acts at the behest of law enforcement authorities, the usual Fourth Amendment standards apply.

Consent of Another

---

90. In *Stoner*, p. 152 above, the Court concluded that the hotel clerk's consent did not authorize the police to search the defendant's hotel room. Further, as noted in the opinion, although the owner of premises who has leased them to another may have authority to enter the premises for a variety of purposes, he does not generally have authority to consent to a search by police for evidence that incriminates his tenant. Chapman v. United States, 365 U.S. 610 (1961). So also, an employer does not have authority to consent to a search of a desk that has been assigned for the exclusive use of an employee. United States v. Blok, 188 F.2d 1019 (D.C.Cir.1951). Could an employer retain such authority by advising each employee that although his desk was otherwise for his exclusive use, the employer retained authority at will to search it himself or allow others to search it?

In what circumstances *does* the consent of one person authorize a search of premises and the evidentiary use against another person of items found in the search?

Suppose Stoner had hidden his pistol in a flower pot in the hotel lobby. If the police had searched the lobby with the consent of the hotel management and found the pistol, could it have been used in evidence against Stoner? Why (not)?

---

91. The defendant rented a small wooden shack from Stein. He arranged with Stein that Stein would receive deliveries for him and gave Stein a key to the shack so that deliveries could be stored inside. Postal authorities became suspicious of the defendant's activities, and inspectors questioned Stein, who unlocked the shack and invited the inspectors to examine its contents. The search led to evidence that incriminated the defendant, who was prosecuted for mail fraud. Did Stein's possession of a key and unwitting involvement in the defendant's unlawful activity give him authority to allow the postal inspectors to enter and search the shack? For a similar case, see United States v. Diggs, 544 F.2d 116 (3d Cir.1976), in which the defendant's wife gave a locked metal box to her uncle for safekeeping. He became suspicious and asked FBI agents to open it. They did so and found money taken in a recent bank robbery.

92. A person's consent to a general search of a computer does not authorize a search of the files of another joint user of the computer, whose files are protected by a password to which the consenting person does not have access. Trulock v. Freeh, 275 F.3d 391 (4th Cir.2001). The court likened the protected files to a locked footlocker.

93. If one person who shares the use of premises with another consents to a search of a portion of the premises used in common by both and the search reveals evidence that incriminates the other person, can the evidence be seized and used against him?

In United States v. Matlock, 415 U.S. 164 (1974), the Court upheld the validity of a woman's consent to the search of a room in which she had been living together with the defendant. The Court said that "the consent of one who possesses common authority over premises or effects is valid as against the absent, nonconsenting person with whom that authority is shared." Id. at 170.

On what does "common authority" depend?

"Common authority is, of course, not to be implied from the mere property interest a third party has in the property. The authority which justifies the third-party consent does not rest upon the law of property, with its attendant historical and legal refinements . . . but rests rather on mutual use of the property by persons generally having joint access or control for most purposes, so that it is reasonable to recognize that any of the co-inhabitants has the right to permit the inspection in his own right and that the others have assumed the risk that one of their number might permit the common area to be searched." Id. at 171 n.7.

See Frazier v. Cupp, 394 U.S. 731 (1969), upholding the authority of a "joint user" of a duffel bag to consent to a search that revealed evidence against the defendant, the other user.

For a variety of situations in which the courts found authority to consent by someone other than the defendant, see United States v. Buettner-Janusch, 646 F.2d 759 (2d Cir.1981) (research assistant and professional colleague with access to premises); United States v. Gargiso, 456 F.2d 584 (2d Cir.1972) (highest officer of company at scene of search); United States v. Cataldo, 433 F.2d 38 (2d Cir.1970) (roommate's consent effective as to defendant's separate bedroom); Drummond v. United States, 350 F.2d 983 (8th Cir.1965) (coconspirator using premises in common with owner); Burge v. United States, 342 F.2d 408 (9th Cir.1965) (owner's consent effective against house guest); United States v. Sferas, 210 F.2d 69 (7th Cir.1954) (consent of one partner to search of partnership premises effective against other partner); Calhoun v. United States, 172 F.2d 457, 458 (5th Cir.1949) (consent of "owner and master of the house" effective against one who has only permission to use a room "whenever he happened to be there").

Matlock has been applied to the search of a suitcase belonging to the defendant and being carried by her companion while they boarded an airplane; the court said that the defendant "granted her companion sufficient control over the suitcase so that it is reasonable to conclude that she assumed the risk that he might permit it to be searched at the airport check point." United States v. Canada, 527 F.2d 1374, 1379 (9th Cir.1975).

In United States v. Heisman, 503 F.2d 1284 (8th Cir.1974), the court held that a cotenant who had a legal right to enter a portion of premises used by the defendant but not a factual "possessory right" could not validly consent to a search there. See also United States v. Harris, 534 F.2d 95 (7th Cir.1976) (consent of occasional visitor inadequate).

94.

> The right of one party to consent to a search which affects the interest of another derives from the consenting party's equal right of possession or control of the same premises or property as the other. Such cases fall into three classes. In one class a party having a joint right of control consents to a search directed only at himself and not at the other, but it discloses evidence harmful to the other. A second class consists of those cases in which one having a joint right of control consents to a search which he knows is directed at the other although he does so in the independent exercise of his right of joint control. The justification of the search in both these classes of cases results from the impossibility of severing the joint right of control and the undesirability of permitting the exercise of the right of one to be limited by the right of the other. . . .
>
> A new and intruding element which has not been isolated heretofore may be said to distinguish a third class of cases. This element is the consenting party's agreement to the search out of motives of hostility to the other, made with the intent to harm him by an antagonistic consent. Where it is possible to identify this element a serious question would arise whether the right to consent is not spent when it reaches this point of deliberate antagonistic intrusion on the rights of the other who has an equal right to possession or control. This would be especially true where a wife intentionally acts against her husband's interest, since she would not be acting in harmony with the marital relationship from which her joint right of ownership or control is derived, but in antagonism to it.

United States ex rel. Cabey v. Mazurkiewicz, 431 F.2d 839, 842–43 (3d Cir.1970).

In *Matlock*, above, the court referred to the "*absent*, nonconsenting person" (emphasis added). Suppose joint occupants of premises are both present when the police ask to make a search. If the occupants have "equal rights" in the premises, is the consent of one of the occupants sufficient to authorize the search despite the objection of the other? In United States v. Sumlin, 567 F.2d 684 (6th Cir.1977), the court said yes. The defendant was arrested at an apartment in which he was a joint occupant with one Alexander, in whose name the apartment was leased. After the arrest, the defendant was asked for permission to search the apartment, which he refused. The arresting officers then obtained permission to search from Alexander. The defendant did not ask Alexander to withhold her consent.

The court said that the defendant's presence while the search was made without his consent was not constitutionally significant. It noted that in *Matlock* the defendant had just been arrested in the yard of the place that was searched pursuant to the consent of a third person. United States v. Morning, 64 F.3d 531 (9th Cir.1995), is to the same effect. "[T]he primary factor is the defendant's reasonable expectations under the circumstances. Those expectations must include the risk that a co-occupant will allow someone to enter, even if the defendant does not approve of the entry. The risks to property or privacy interests are not substantially lessened because of the defendant's own lack of consent. Although there is always the fond hope that a co-occupant will follow one's known wishes, the risks remain. A defendant cannot expect sole exclusionary authority unless he lives alone, or at least has a special and private space within the joint residence." Id. at 536. Accord United States v. Flores, 172 F.3d 695 (9th Cir.1999); United States v. Rith, 164 F.3d 1323 (10th Cir.1999); J.L. Foti Construction Co. v. Donovan, 786 F.2d 714 (6th Cir.1986) (administrative search).

Other courts have taken a different view. In State v. Leach, 782 P.2d 1035, 1040 (Wash.1989), the Washington Supreme Court said: "Where the police have obtained consent to search from an individual possessing, at best, equal control over the premises, that consent remains valid against a cohabitant, who also possesses equal control, only while the cohabitant is absent. However, should the cohabitant be present and able to object, the police must also obtain the cohabitant's consent. Any other rule exalts expediency over an individual's Fourth Amendment guarantees." Similarly, in Randolph v. State, 590 S.E.2d 834 (Ga.Ct.App.2003), the court said: "*Matlock* and its progeny stand for the proposition that, in the absence of evidence to the contrary, there is a presumption that a co-occupant has waived his right of privacy as to other co-occupants. However, when police are confronted with an unequivocal assertion of that co-occupant's Fourth Amendment right, such presumption cannot stand. After all, the right involved is the right to be free from police intrusion, not the right to invite police into one's home." Id. at 838. See United States v. Impink, 728 F.2d 1228, 1234 (9th Cir.1984).

In view of the facts that the defendant in *Matlock* had just been arrested in the yard and the officers knew that he lived in the house, was the rule about absent nonconsenting persons, on which the Court relied, really dispositive?

Is there a basis in the Fourth Amendment for the principle that the consent of one joint occupant to a search is effective against other occupants if they are absent but not if they are present? If so, could a joint occupant avoid that principle by expressly stating to other joint occupants (with "equal rights" in the premises) that he did not consent to any searches without a warrant? Why (not)?

---

95. The family home. It is generally the rule that the consent of one spouse to a search of the family home is effective against the other, absent spouse. E.g., United States v. Duran, 957 F.2d 499, 505 (7th Cir.1992): "[A] spouse presumptively has authority to consent to a search of all areas of the homestead; the nonconsenting spouse may rebut this presumption only by showing that the consenting spouse was denied access to the particular area searched." Do you agree with the statement in *Cabey*, p. 166 note 94 above, that if spouses are antagonistic to one another, the authority of either to consent to a search of joint premises is affected? In Kelley v. State, 197 S.W.2d 545 (Tenn.1946), for example, a woman asked the police to come to her house to arrest her husband for assaulting her and when they arrived led them to contraband which he had concealed in the house. Applying the theory that the validity of the woman's consent depended on an agency relationship with her husband, the court created an "angry wife" exception to the rule upholding third-party consent and invalidated the search. Fifty years later, in State v. Bartram, 925 S.W.2d 227 (1996), the court overruled *Kelley*. It said that the agency theory was no longer regarded as the basis for a spouse's consent, which rested simply on the spouse's common, independent authority over the premises.

Is the consent of a parent in whose home a child is living effective against the child? In State v. Kinderman, 136 N.W.2d 577 (Minn.1965), shortly after the defendant had been arrested on a charge of robbery and while he was still in custody, police officers went to his home and obtained his father's permission to make a search. The house was owned by the father; the defendant, who was 22 years old, occupied a bedroom on the second floor. The court upheld the admission in evidence of a gun found in a closet in the defendant's bedroom and items of defendant's clothing found in the basement. It said: "We can agree that the father's 'house' may also be that of the child, but if a man's house is still his castle in which his rights are superior to the state, those rights should also be superior to the rights of children who live in his house. We cannot agree that a child, whether he be dependent or emancipated (defendant was 22 years of age at the time of his arrest), has the same constitutional rights of privacy in the family home which he might have in a rented hotel room." Id. at 580. To the same effect, relying on the parent's "proprietary interest in the house . . . undiminished by any kind of a less-than-fee interest" of the defendant, see Maxwell v. Stephens, 348 F.2d 325, 336–37 (8th Cir.1965). Accord, e.g., United States v. Rith, 164 F.3d 1323 (10th Cir.1999); United States v. Peterson, 524 F.2d 167, 178–81 (4th Cir.1975). Would the same reasoning be applicable if the defendant were at home and objected to the search?

Contrary to the above cases, in People v. Nunn, 304 N.E.2d 81 (Ill.1973), the court held that the 19-year-old defendant had a reasonable expectation of privacy in a room in his mother's house that he kept locked, and that her consent to a search of the room was not effective. See State v. Kieffer, 577 N.W.2d 352 (Wis.1998) (father-in-law, who owned house, lacked authority to consent). Compare United States v. Block, 590 F.2d 535 (4th Cir.1978) (mother's consent authorized search of son's room in her house but not of locked trunk in room).

Suppose the defendant and his mother live as tenants or guests in a house owned by his sister. Does the mother have authority to consent to a search of the defendant's room (and a bureau used by the defendant)? See Reeves v. Warden, 346 F.2d 915 (4th Cir.1965). In Holzhey v. United States, 223 F.2d 823 (5th Cir.1955), the defendant lived in the home of her son-in-law and daughter. Did they have authority to consent to a search of a part of the home used primarily by the defendant? Is it relevant that the defendant made "occasional" small payments of rent?

Does a housekeeper who is alone in the house when police arrive have authority to consent to a search of parts of the house which she regularly enters for housekeeping purposes? See Cunningham v. Heinze, 352 F.2d 1 (9th Cir.1965). See also United States v. Dearing, 9 F.3d 1428 (9th Cir.1993) (live-in caretaker of handicapped child lacked actual or apparent authority to authorize search of homeowner's bedroom); People v. Misquez, 313 P.2d 206 (Cal.Dist.Ct.App.1957) (babysitter); People v. Carswell, 308 P.2d 852 (Cal.Dist.Ct.App.1957) (housepainter). In United States v. Jones, 335 F.3d 527 (6th Cir.2003), after having arrested the defendant in his car and asked him for and been refused permission to search his residence, police went to the residence and asked a handyman who was there for permission to search, which he gave. The court held that the handyman's consent was not effective. "Although . . . an employee does in some instances have sufficient authority to consent to entry into or a search of the employer's residence, the lesser, and necessarily derivative, interest of the employee cannot override the greater interest of the owner. When the primary occupant has denied permission to enter and conduct a search, his employee does not have the authority to override that denial." Id. at 531.

---

96. The defendant loaned his automobile to a friend who wanted to "take his young daughter . . . for a ride around town." Does his friend, while still in possession of the car, have authority to consent to a search of the automobile for evidence that incriminates the defendant? Does the extent of the search make a difference? See United States v. Eldridge, 302 F.2d 463 (4th Cir.1962). If the defendant leaves a locked briefcase in the home of a friend and the friend turns it over to the police, may they, without a warrant, force it open and search it if they have probable cause to believe that it contains narcotics? See Sartain v. United States, 303 F.2d 859 (9th Cir.1962). Compare Corngold v. United States, 367 F.2d 1 (9th Cir.1966) (package delivered to airline for transportation).

Illinois v. Rodriguez

497 U.S. 177, 110 S.Ct. 2793, 111 L.Ed.2d 148 (1990)

■ JUSTICE SCALIA delivered the opinion of the Court.

In United States v. Matlock, 415 U.S. 164 (1974), this Court reaffirmed that a warrantless entry and search by law enforcement officers does not violate the Fourth Amendment's proscription of "unreasonable searches and seizures" if the officers have obtained the consent of a third party who possesses common authority over the premises. The present case presents an issue we expressly reserved in *Matlock*, see id., at 177, n.14: whether a warrantless entry is valid when based upon the consent of a third party whom the police, at the time of the entry, reasonably believe to possess common authority over the premises, but who in fact does not do so.

I

Respondent Edward Rodriguez was arrested in his apartment by law enforcement officers and charged with possession of illegal drugs. The police gained entry to the apartment with the consent and assistance of Gail Fischer, who had lived there with respondent for several months. The relevant facts leading to the arrest are as follows.

On July 26, 1985, police were summoned to the residence of Dorothy Jackson on South Wolcott in Chicago. They were met by Ms. Jackson's daughter, Gail Fischer, who showed signs of a severe beating. She told the officers that she had been assaulted by respondent Edward Rodriguez earlier that day in an apartment on South California. Fischer stated that Rodriguez was then asleep in the apartment, and she consented to travel there with the police in order to unlock the door with her key so that the officers could enter and arrest him. During this conversation, Fischer several times referred to the apartment on South California as "our" apartment, and said that she had clothes and furniture there. It is unclear whether she indicated that she currently lived at the apartment, or only that she used to live there.

The police officers drove to the apartment on South California, accompanied by Fischer. They did not obtain an arrest warrant for Rodriguez, nor did they seek a search warrant for the apartment. At the apartment, Fischer unlocked the door with her key and gave the officers permission to enter. They moved through the door into the living room, where they observed in plain view drug paraphernalia and containers filled with white powder that they believed (correctly, as later analysis showed) to be cocaine. They proceeded to the bedroom, where they found Rodriguez asleep and discovered additional containers of white powder in two open attaché cases. The officers arrested Rodriguez and seized the drugs and related paraphernalia.

Rodriguez was charged with possession of a controlled substance with intent to deliver. He moved to suppress all evidence seized at the time of his arrest, claiming that Fischer had vacated the apartment several weeks earlier and had no authority to consent to the entry. The Cook County Circuit Court granted the motion, holding that at the time she consented to the entry Fischer did not have common authority over the apartment. The Court concluded that Fischer was not a "usual resident" but rather an "infrequent visitor" at the apartment on South California, based upon its findings that Fischer's name was not on the lease, that she did not contribute to the rent, that she was not allowed to invite others to the apartment on her own, that she did not have access to the apartment when respondent was away, and that she had moved some of her possessions from the apartment. The Circuit Court also rejected the State's contention that, even if Fischer did not possess common authority over the premises, there was no Fourth Amendment violation if the police *reasonably believed* at the time of their entry that Fischer possessed the authority to consent.

The Appellate Court of Illinois affirmed the Circuit Court in all respects. . . . [W]e granted certiorari. . . .

II

The Fourth Amendment generally prohibits the warrantless entry of a person's home, whether to make an arrest or to search for specific objects. . . . The prohibition does not apply, however, to situations in which voluntary consent has been obtained, either from the individual whose property is searched . . . or from a third party who possesses common authority over the premises. . . . The State of Illinois contends that that exception applies in the present case.

As we stated in *Matlock*, 415 U.S., at 171, n.7, "[c]ommon authority" rests "on mutual use of the property by persons generally having joint access or control for most purposes. . . ." The burden of establishing that common authority rests upon the State. On the basis of this record, it is clear that burden was not sustained. . . . To the contrary, the Appellate Court's determination of no common authority over the apartment was obviously correct.

III

A

The State contends that, even if Fischer did not in fact have authority to give consent, it suffices to validate the entry that the law enforcement officers reasonably believed she did. . . .

. . .

B

On the merits of the issue, respondent asserts that permitting a reasonable belief of common authority to validate an entry would cause a defendant's Fourth Amendment rights to be "vicariously waived." Brief for Respondent 32. We disagree.

We have been unyielding in our insistence that a defendant's waiver of his trial rights cannot be given effect unless it is "knowing" and "intelligent." Colorado v. Spring, 479 U.S. 564, 574–75 (1987). . . . But one must make a distinction between, on the one hand, trial rights that *derive* from the violation of constitutional guarantees and, on the other hand, the nature of those constitutional guarantees themselves. . . .

What Rodriguez is assured by the trial right of the exclusionary rule, where it applies, is that no evidence seized in violation of the Fourth Amendment will be introduced at his trial unless he consents. What he is assured by the Fourth Amendment itself, however, is not that no government search of his house will occur unless he consents; but that no such search will occur that is "unreasonable." U.S. Const., Amdt. 4. There are various elements, of course, that can make a search of a person's house "reasonable"—one of which is the consent of the person or his cotenant. The essence of respondent's argument is that we should impose upon this element a requirement that we have not imposed upon other elements that regularly compel government officers to exercise judgment regarding the facts: namely, the requirement that their judgment be not only responsible but correct.

The fundamental objective that alone validates all unconsented governmental searches is, of course, the seizure of persons who have committed or are about to commit crimes, or of evidence related to crimes. But "reasonableness," with respect to this necessary element, does not demand that the government be factually correct in its assessment that that is what a search will produce. Warrants need only be supported by "probable cause," which demands no more than a proper "assessment of probabilities in particular factual contexts...." Illinois v. Gates, 462 U.S. 213, 232 (1983). . . .

Another element often, though not invariably, required in order to render an unconsented search "reasonable" is, of course, that the officer be authorized by a valid warrant. Here also we have not held that "reasonableness" precludes error with respect to those factual judgments that law enforcement officials are expected to make. . . .

. . .

. . . It is apparent that in order to satisfy the "reasonableness" requirement of the Fourth Amendment, what is generally demanded of the many factual determinations that must regularly be made by agents of the government—whether the magistrate issuing a warrant, the police officer executing a warrant, or the police officer conducting a search or seizure under one of the exceptions to the warrant requirement—is not that they always be correct, but that they always be reasonable. . . .

We see no reason to depart from this general rule with respect to facts bearing upon the authority to consent to a search. Whether the basis for such authority exists is the sort of recurring factual question to which law enforcement officials must be expected to apply their judgment; and all the Fourth Amendment requires is that they answer it reasonably. The Constitution is no more violated when officers enter without a warrant because they reasonably (though erroneously) believe that the person who has consented to their entry is a resident of the premises, than it is violated when they enter without a warrant because they reasonably (though erroneously) believe they are in pursuit of a violent felon who is about to escape. . . .

. . .

[W]hat we hold today does not suggest that law enforcement officers may always accept a person's invitation to enter premises. Even when the invitation is accompanied by an explicit assertion that the person lives there, the surrounding circumstances could conceivably be such that a reasonable person would doubt its truth and not act upon it without further inquiry. As with other factual determinations bearing upon search and seizure, determination of consent to enter must "be judged against an objective standard: would the facts available to the officer at the moment . . . 'warrant a man of reasonable caution in the belief?' " that the consenting party had authority over the premises? Terry v. Ohio, 392 U.S. 1, 21–22 (1968). If not, then warrantless entry without further inquiry is unlawful unless authority actually exists. But if so, the search is valid.

■ JUSTICE MARSHALL, with whom JUSTICE BRENNAN and JUSTICE STEVENS join, dissenting.

. . .

The baseline for the reasonableness of a search or seizure in the home is the presence of a warrant. . . . Because the sole law enforcement purpose underlying third-party consent searches is avoiding the inconvenience of securing a warrant, a departure from the warrant requirement is not justified simply because an officer reasonably believes a third party has consented to a search of the defendant's home. . . .

. . .

Unlike searches conducted pursuant to the recognized exceptions to the warrant requirement . . . third-party consent searches are not based on an exigency and therefore serve no compelling social goal. Police officers, when faced with the choice of relying on consent by a third party or securing a warrant, should secure a warrant, and must therefore accept the risk of error should they instead choose to rely on consent.

. . .

A search conducted pursuant to an officer's reasonable but mistaken belief that a third party had authority to consent is . . . on an entirely different constitutional footing from one based on the consent of a third party who in fact has such authority. Even if the officers reasonably believed that Fischer had authority to consent, she did not, and Rodriguez's expectation of privacy was therefore undiminished. Rodriguez accordingly can challenge the warrantless intrusion into his home as a violation of the Fourth Amendment. . . .

. . .

Acknowledging that the third party in this case lacked authority to consent, the majority seeks to rely on cases suggesting that reasonable but mistaken factual judgments by police will not invalidate otherwise reasonable searches. . . .

[T]he possibility of factual error is built into the probable cause standard, and such a standard, by its very definition, will in some cases result in the arrest of a suspect who has not actually committed a crime. Because probable cause defines the reasonableness of searches and seizures outside of the home, a search is reasonable under the Fourth Amendment whenever that standard is met, notwithstanding the possibility of "mistakes" on the part of police. . . . In contrast, our cases have already struck the balance against warrantless home intrusions in the absence of an exigency. . . . Because reasonable factual errors by law enforcement officers will not validate unreasonable searches, the reasonableness of the officer's mistaken belief that the third party had authority to consent is irrelevant.

. . .

---

97. Would "a state law which gave a hotel proprietor blanket authority to authorize the police to search the rooms of the hotel's guests . . . survive constitutional challenge," *Stoner*, p. 152 above? If so, could state law also give the manager of an apartment building such authority? The manager of a public housing project? If not, why not? Compare United States v. Biswell, 406 U.S. 311 (1972), in which the Court upheld the warrantless search, authorized by federal statute, of a gun dealer's storeroom.

98.

On the morning of February 28, 1968, the Dean of Men of Troy State University was called to the office of the Chief of Police of Troy, Alabama, to discuss "the drug problem" at the University. Two State narcotic agents and two student informers from Troy State University were also present. Later on that same day, the Dean of Men was called to the city police station for another meeting; at this time he was informed by the officers that they had sufficient evidence that marijuana was in the dormitory rooms of certain Troy State students and that they desired the cooperation of University officials in searching these rooms. The police officers were advised by the Dean of Men that they would receive the full cooperation of the University officials in searching for the marijuana. The informers, whose identities have not yet been disclosed, provided the police officers with names of students whose rooms were to be searched. Still later on that same day (which was during the week of final examinations at the University and was to be followed by a week-long holiday) the law enforcement officers, accompanied by some of the University officials, searched six or seven dormitory rooms located in two separate residence halls. The rooms of both Piazzola and Marinshaw were searched without search warrants and without their consent. Present during the search of the room occupied by Marinshaw were two State narcotic agents, the University security officer, and a counselor of the residence hall where Marinshaw's room was located. Piazzola's room was searched twice. Present during the first search were two State narcotic agents and a University

> official; no evidence was found at this time. The second search of Piazzola's room, which disclosed the incriminating evidence, was conducted solely by the State and City police officials.
>
> At the time of the seizure the University had in effect the following regulation: "The college reserves the right to enter rooms for inspection purposes. If the administration deems it necessary, the room may be searched and the occupant required to open his personal baggage and any other personal material which is sealed." Each of the petitioners was familiar with this regulation. After the search of the petitioners' rooms and the discovery of the marijuana, they were arrested, and the State criminal prosecutions and convictions ensued.

Piazzola v. Watkins, 442 F.2d 284, 286 (5th Cir.1971). Were the searches lawful?

99. The Fourth Amendment's prohibition against unreasonable searches and seizures applies to searches of students conducted by school officials. New Jersey v. T.L.O., 469 U.S. 325 (1985) (6–3). However, the standard of reasonableness is not as stringent as the standard applied to law enforcement officers in the conduct of criminal investigations. The Court said:

> How, then, should we strike the balance between the schoolchild's legitimate expectations of privacy and the school's equally legitimate need to maintain an environment in which learning can take place? It is evident that the school setting requires some easing of the restrictions to which searches by public authorities are ordinarily subject. The warrant requirement, in particular, is unsuited to the school environment: requiring a teacher to obtain a warrant before searching a child suspected of an infraction of school rules (or of the criminal law) would unduly interfere with the maintenance of the swift and informal disciplinary procedures needed in the schools. Just as we have in other cases dispensed with the warrant requirement when "the burden of obtaining a warrant is likely to frustrate the governmental purpose behind the search," Camara v. Municipal Court, 387 U.S. [523 (1967)], at 532–33, we hold today that school officials need not obtain a warrant before searching a student who is under their authority.
>
> The school setting also requires some modification of the level of suspicion of illicit activity needed to justify a search. Ordinarily, a search—even one that may permissibly be carried out without a warrant—must be based upon "probable cause" to believe that a violation of the law has occurred. . . . However, "probable cause" is not an irreducible requirement of a valid search. . . . Where a careful balancing of governmental and private interests suggests that the public interest is best served by a Fourth Amendment standard of reasonableness that stops short of probable cause, we have not hesitated to adopt such a standard.
>
> We join the majority of courts that have examined this issue in concluding that the accommodation of the privacy interests of school-

> children with the substantial need of teachers and administrators for freedom to maintain order in the schools does not require strict adherence to the requirement that searches be based on probable cause to believe that the subject of the search has violated or is violating the law. Rather, the legality of a search of a student should depend simply on the reasonableness, under all the circumstances, of the search. Determining the reasonableness of any search involves a twofold inquiry: first, one must consider "whether the . . . action was justified at its inception," Terry v. Ohio, 392 U.S. [1 (1968)], at 20; second, one must determine whether the search as actually conducted "was reasonably related in scope to the circumstances which justified the interference in the first place," ibid. Under ordinary circumstances, a search of a student by a teacher or other school official will be "justified at its inception" when there are reasonable grounds for suspecting that the search will turn up evidence that the student has violated or is violating either the law or the rules of the school. Such a search will be permissible in its scope when the measures adopted are reasonably related to the objectives of the search and not excessively intrusive in light of the age and sex of the student and the nature of the infraction.
>
> This standard will, we trust, neither unduly burden the efforts of school authorities to maintain order in their schools nor authorize unrestrained intrusions upon the privacy of schoolchildren. By focusing attention on the question of reasonableness, the standard will spare teachers and school administrators the necessity of schooling themselves in the niceties of probable cause and permit them to regulate their conduct according to the dictates of reason and common sense. At the same time, the reasonableness standard should ensure that the interests of students will be invaded no more than is necessary to achieve the legitimate end of preserving order in the school.

469 U.S. at 340–43.

In an opinion concurring in part and dissenting in part, Justice Brennan argued that, although the warrant requirement was not applicable, the standard of probable cause should be retained. In an opinion concurring in part and dissenting in part, Justice Stevens argued that a warrantless search of students by school officials should be restricted to cases in which there is reason to believe that the search will uncover "*evidence that the student is violating the law or engaging in conduct that is seriously disruptive of school order, or the educational process.*" Id. at 378. The Court's rule, he urged, would unnecessarily allow school officials to search for evidence of violation of minor school regulations. (Justice Marshall joined both opinions.)

The Fourth Amendment does not prohibit a program of random testing for drugs by urinalysis of public school students who participate voluntarily in interscholastic athletics. Vernonia School District 47J v. Acton, 515 U.S. 646 (1995) (6–3).

Search Warrant

FEDERAL RULES OF CRIMINAL PROCEDURE

Rule 41

SEARCH AND SEIZURE

(a) Scope and Definitions.

(1) *Scope.* This rule does not modify any statute regulating search or seizure, or the issuance and execution of a search warrant in special circumstances.

(2) *Definitions.* The following definitions apply under this rule:

(A) "Property" includes documents, books, papers, any other tangible objects, and information.

(B) "Daytime" means the hours between 6:00 a.m. and 10:00 p.m. according to local time.

(C) "Federal law enforcement officer" means a government agent (other than an attorney for the government) who is engaged in enforcing the criminal laws and is within any category of officers authorized by the Attorney General to request a search warrant.

(b) Authority to Issue a Warrant. At the request of a federal law enforcement officer or an attorney for the government:

(1) a magistrate judge with authority in the district—or if none is reasonably available, a judge of a state court of record in the district—has authority to issue a warrant to search for and seize a person or property located within the district;

(2) a magistrate judge with authority in the district has authority to issue a warrant for a person or property outside the district if the person or property is located within the district when the warrant is issued but might move or be moved outside the district before the warrant is executed; and

(3) a magistrate judge—in an investigation of domestic terrorism or international terrorism (as defined in 18 U.S.C. § 2331)—having authority in any district in which activities related to the terrorism may have occurred, may issue a warrant for a person or property within or outside that district.

(c) Persons or Property Subject to Search or Seizure. A warrant may be issued for any of the following:

(1) evidence of a crime;

(2) contraband, fruits of crime, or other items illegally possessed;

(3) property designed for use, intended for use, or used in committing a crime; or

(4) a person to be arrested or a person who is unlawfully restrained.

(d) Obtaining a Warrant.

(1) *Probable Cause.* After receiving an affidavit or other information, a magistrate judge or a judge of a state court of record must issue the warrant if there is probable cause to search for and seize a person or property under Rule 41(c).

(2) *Requesting a Warrant in the Presence of a Judge.*

(A) *Warrant on an Affidavit.* When a federal law enforcement officer or an attorney for the government presents an affidavit in support of a warrant, the judge may require the affiant to appear personally and may examine under oath the affiant and any witness the affiant produces.

(B) *Warrant on Sworn Testimony.* The judge may wholly or partially dispense with a written affidavit and base a warrant on sworn testimony if doing so is reasonable under the circumstances.

(C) *Recording Testimony.* Testimony taken in support of a warrant must be recorded by a court reporter or by a suitable recording device, and the judge must file the transcript or recording with the clerk, along with any affidavit.

(3) *Requesting a Warrant by Telephonic or Other Means.*

(A) *In General.* A magistrate judge may issue a warrant based on information communicated by telephone or other appropriate means, including facsimile transmission.

(B) *Recording Testimony.* Upon learning that an applicant is requesting a warrant, a magistrate judge must:

(i) place under oath the applicant and any person on whose testimony the application is based; and

(ii) make a verbatim record of the conversation with a suitable recording device, if available, or by a court reporter, or in writing.

(C) *Certifying Testimony.* The magistrate judge must have any recording or court reporter's notes transcribed, certify the transcription's accuracy, and file a copy of the record and the transcription with the clerk. Any written verbatim record must be signed by the magistrate judge and filed with the clerk.

(D) *Suppression Limited.* Absent a finding of bad faith, evidence obtained from a warrant issued under Rule 41(d)(3)(A) is not subject to suppression on the ground that issuing the warrant in that manner was unreasonable under the circumstances.

(e) Issuing the Warrant.

(1) *In General.* The magistrate judge or a judge of a state court of record must issue the warrant to an officer authorized to execute it.

(2) *Contents of the Warrant.* The warrant must identify the person or property to be searched, identify any person or property to be seized, and designate the magistrate judge to whom it must be returned. The warrant must command the officer to:

(A) execute the warrant within a specified time no longer than 10 days;

(B) execute the warrant during the daytime, unless the judge for good cause expressly authorizes execution at another time; and

(C) return the warrant to the magistrate judge designated in the warrant.

(3) *Warrant by Telephonic or Other Means.* If a magistrate judge decides to proceed under Rule 41(d)(3)(A), the following additional procedures apply:

(A) *Preparing a Proposed Duplicate Original Warrant.* The applicant must prepare a "proposed duplicate original warrant" and must read or otherwise transmit the contents of that document verbatim to the magistrate judge.

(B) *Preparing an Original Warrant.* The magistrate judge must enter the contents of the proposed duplicate original warrant into an original warrant.

(C) *Modifications.* The magistrate judge may direct the applicant to modify the proposed duplicate original warrant. In that case, the judge must also modify the original warrant.

(D) *Signing the Original Warrant and the Duplicate Original Warrant.* Upon determining to issue the warrant, the magistrate judge must immediately sign the original warrant, enter on its face the exact time it issued, and direct the applicant to sign the judge's name on the duplicate original warrant.

(f) Executing and Returning the Warrant.

(1) *Noting the Time.* The officer executing the warrant must enter on its face the exact date and time it is executed.

(2) *Inventory.* An officer present during the execution of the warrant must prepare and verify an inventory of any property seized. The officer must do so in the presence of another officer and the person from whom, or from whose premises, the property was taken. If either one is not present, the officer must prepare and verify the inventory in the presence of at least one other credible person.

(3) *Receipt.* The officer executing the warrant must:

(A) give a copy of the warrant and a receipt for the property taken to the person from whom, or from whose premises, the property was taken; or

(B) leave a copy of the warrant and receipt at the place where the officer took the property.

(4) *Return.* The officer executing the warrant must promptly return it—together with a copy of the inventory—to the magistrate judge designated on the warrant. The judge must, on request, give a copy of the inventory to the person from whom, or from whose premises, the property was taken and to the applicant for the warrant.

(g) Motion to Return Property. A person aggrieved by an unlawful search and seizure of property or by the deprivation of property may move for the property's return. The motion must be filed in the district where the property was seized. The court must receive evidence on any factual issue necessary to decide the motion. If it grants the motion, the court must return the property to the movant, but may impose reasonable conditions to protect access to the property and its use in later proceedings.

(h) Motion to Suppress. A defendant may move to suppress evidence in the court where the trial will occur, as Rule 12 provides.

(i) Forwarding Papers to the Clerk. The magistrate judge to whom the warrant is returned must attach to the warrant a copy of the return, of the inventory, and of all other related papers and must deliver them to the clerk in the district where the property was seized.

---

100. In the absence of special circumstances, Rule 41(d) requires an officer executing a warrant to give a copy of the warrant to the person whose premises are to be searched, if present, before the search is executed. United States v. Gantt, 194 F.3d 987 (9th Cir.1999) (deliberate violation of Rule 41(d) required suppression of evidence).

It is a violation of the Fourth Amendment for police who are executing a search warrant to allow members of the media or other persons to accompany them into the premises to be searched, if their presence is not in aid of execution of the warrant. Wilson v. Layne, 526 U.S. 603 (1999). (The Court (8–1) held also, however, that since the law was not clearly established at the time of the search, police officers who permitted members of the media to accompany them were entitled to qualified immunity as defendants in a lawsuit under 42 U.S.C. § 1983, charging them with a violation of the rights of the persons whose home was searched.)

Illinois v. Gates

462 U.S. 213, 103 S.Ct. 2317, 76 L.Ed.2d 527 (1983)

■ JUSTICE REHNQUIST delivered the opinion of the Court.

Respondents Lance and Susan Gates were indicted for violation of state drug laws after police officers, executing a search warrant, discovered marihuana and other contraband in their automobile and home. Prior to trial the Gateses moved to suppress evidence seized during this search. The

Illinois Supreme Court affirmed the decisions of lower state courts granting the motion. . . . It held that the affidavit submitted in support of the State's application for a warrant to search the Gateses' property was inadequate under this Court's decisions in Aguilar v. Texas, 378 U.S. 108 (1964) and Spinelli v. United States, 393 U.S. 410 (1969).

We granted certiorari to consider the application of the Fourth Amendment to a magistrate's issuance of a search warrant on the basis of a partially corroborated anonymous informant's tip. . . .

. . .

. . . A chronological statement of events usefully introduces the issues at stake. Bloomingdale, Ill., is a suburb of Chicago located in Du Page County. On May 3, 1978, the Bloomingdale Police Department received by mail an anonymous handwritten letter which read as follows:

> This letter is to inform you that you have a couple in your town who strictly make their living on selling drugs. They are Sue and Lance Gates, they live on Greenway, off Bloomingdale Rd. in the condominiums. Most of their buys are done in Florida. Sue his wife drives their car to Florida, where she leaves it to be loaded up with drugs, then Lance flys down and drives it back. Sue flys back after she drops the car off in Florida. May 3 she is driving down there again and Lance will be flying down in a few days to drive it back. At the time Lance drives the car back he has the trunk loaded with over $100,000.00 in drugs. Presently they have over $100,000.00 worth of drugs in their basement.
>
> They brag about the fact they never have to work, and make their entire living on pushers.
>
> I guarantee if you watch them carefully you will make a big catch. They are friends with some big drugs dealers, who visit their house often.
>
> Lance & Susan Gates
>
> Greenway
>
> in Condominiums

The letter was referred by the Chief of Police of the Bloomingdale Police Department to Detective Mader, who decided to pursue the tip. Mader learned, from the office of the Illinois Secretary of State, that an Illinois driver's license had been issued to one Lance Gates, residing at a stated address in Bloomingdale. He contacted a confidential informant, whose examination of certain financial records revealed a more recent address for the Gateses, and he also learned from a police officer assigned to O'Hare Airport that "L. Gates" had made a reservation on Eastern Airlines flight 245 to West Palm Beach, Fla., scheduled to depart from Chicago on May 5 at 4:15 p.m.

Mader then made arrangements with an agent of the Drug Enforcement Administration for surveillance of the May 5 Eastern Airlines flight. The agent later reported to Mader that Gates had boarded the flight, and that federal agents in Florida had observed him arrive in West Palm Beach and take a taxi to the nearby Holiday Inn. They also reported that Gates went to a room registered to one Susan Gates and that, at 7:00 o'clock the next morning, Gates and an unidentified woman left the motel in a Mercury bearing Illinois license plates and drove northbound on an interstate frequently used by travelers to the Chicago area. In addition, the DEA agent informed Mader that the license plate number on the Mercury was registered to a Hornet station wagon owned by Gates. The agent also advised Mader that the driving time between West Palm Beach and Bloomingdale was approximately 22 to 24 hours.

Mader signed an affidavit setting forth the foregoing facts, and submitted it to a judge of the Circuit Court of Du Page County, together with a copy of the anonymous letter. The judge of that court thereupon issued a search warrant for the Gateses' residence and for their automobile. The judge, in deciding to issue the warrant, could have determined that the *modus operandi* of the Gateses had been substantially corroborated. As the anonymous letter predicted, Lance Gates had flown from Chicago to West Palm Beach late in the afternoon of May 5th, had checked into a hotel room registered in the name of his wife, and, at 7:00 o'clock the following morning, had headed north, accompanied by an unidentified woman, out of West Palm Beach on an interstate highway used by travelers from South Florida to Chicago in an automobile bearing a license plate issued to him.

At 5:15 a.m. on March 7th, only 36 hours after he had flown out of Chicago, Lance Gates, and his wife, returned to their home in Bloomingdale, driving the car in which they had left West Palm Beach some 22 hours earlier. The Bloomingdale police were awaiting them, searched the trunk of the Mercury, and uncovered approximately 350 pounds of marihuana. A search of the Gateses' home revealed marihuana, weapons, and other contraband. The Illinois Circuit Court ordered suppression of all these items, on the ground that the affidavit submitted to the Circuit Judge failed to support the necessary determination of probable cause to believe that the Gateses' automobile and home contained the contraband in question. This decision was affirmed in turn by the Illinois Appellate Court . . . and by a divided vote of the Supreme Court of Illinois. . . .

The Illinois Supreme Court concluded—and we are inclined to agree—that, standing alone, the anonymous letter sent to the Bloomingdale Police Department would not provide the basis for a magistrate's determination that there was probable cause to believe contraband would be found in the Gateses' car and home. The letter provides virtually nothing from which one might conclude that its author is either honest or his information reliable; likewise, the letter gives absolutely no indication of the basis for the writer's predictions regarding the Gateses' criminal activities. Something more was required, then, before a magistrate could conclude that there was probable cause to believe that contraband would be found in the Gateses' home and car. . . .

The Illinois Supreme Court also properly recognized that Detective Mader's affidavit might be capable of supplementing the anonymous letter with information sufficient to permit a determination of probable cause. . . . In holding that the affidavit in fact did not contain sufficient additional information to sustain a determination of probable cause, the

Illinois court applied a "two-pronged test," derived from our decision in Spinelli v. United States, 393 U.S. 410 (1969). The Illinois Supreme Court, like some others, apparently understood *Spinelli* as requiring that the anonymous letter satisfy each of two independent requirements before it could be relied on. . . . According to this view, the letter, as supplemented by Mader's affidavit, first had to adequately reveal the "basis of knowledge" of the letterwriter—the particular means by which he came by the information given in his report. Second, it had to provide facts sufficiently establishing either the "veracity" of the affiant's informant, or, alternatively, the "reliability" of the informant's report in this particular case.

The Illinois court, alluding to an elaborate set of legal rules that have developed among various lower courts to enforce the "two-pronged test," found that the test had not been satisfied. First, the "veracity" prong was not satisfied because, "[t]here was simply no basis [for] conclud[ing] that the anonymous person [who wrote the letter to the Bloomingdale Police Department] was credible." . . . The court indicated that corroboration by police of details contained in the letter might never satisfy the "veracity" prong, and in any event, could not do so if, as in the present case, only "innocent" details are corroborated. . . . In addition, the letter gave no indication of the basis of its writer's knowledge of the Gateses' activities. The Illinois court understood *Spinelli* as permitting the detail contained in a tip to be used to infer that the informant had a reliable basis for his statements, but it thought that the anonymous letter failed to provide sufficient detail to permit such an inference. Thus, it concluded that no showing of probable cause had been made.

We agree with the Illinois Supreme Court that an informant's "veracity," "reliability," and "basis of knowledge" are all highly relevant in determining the value of his report. We do not agree, however, that these elements should be understood as entirely separate and independent requirements to be rigidly exacted in every case, which the opinion of the Supreme Court of Illinois would imply. Rather, as detailed below, they should be understood simply as closely intertwined issues that may usefully illuminate the common-sense, practical question whether there is "probable cause" to believe that contraband or evidence is located in a particular place.

III

This totality-of-the-circumstances approach is far more consistent with our prior treatment of probable cause than is any rigid demand that specific "tests" be satisfied by every informant's tip. Perhaps the central teaching of our decisions bearing on the probable cause standard is that it is a "practical, nontechnical conception." Brinegar v. United States, 338 U.S. 160, 176 (1949). "In dealing with probable cause . . . as the very name implies, we deal with probabilities. These are not technical; they are the factual and practical considerations of everyday life on which reasonable and prudent men, not legal technicians, act." Id., at 175. . . .

[P]robable cause is a fluid concept—turning on the assessment of probabilities in particular factual contexts—not readily, or even usefully, reduced to a neat set of legal rules. Informants' tips doubtless come in many shapes and sizes from many different types of persons. . . . Rigid legal rules are ill-suited to an area of such diversity. . . .

Moreover, the "two-pronged test" directs analysis into two largely independent channels—the informant's "veracity" or "reliability" and his "basis of knowledge." . . . There are persuasive arguments against according these two elements such independent status. Instead, they are better understood as relevant considerations in the totality-of-the-circumstances analysis that traditionally has guided probable cause determinations: a deficiency in one may be compensated for, in determining the overall reliability of a tip, by a strong showing as to the other, or by some other indicia of reliability. . . .

If, for example, a particular informant is known for the unusual reliability of his predictions of certain types of criminal activities in a locality, his failure, in a particular case, to thoroughly set forth the basis of his knowledge surely should not serve as an absolute bar to a finding of probable cause based on his tip. . . . Likewise, if an unquestionably honest citizen comes forward with a report of criminal activity—which if fabricated would subject him to criminal liability—we have found rigorous scrutiny of the basis of his knowledge unnecessary. . . . Conversely, even if we entertain some doubt as to an informant's motives, his explicit and detailed description of alleged wrongdoing, along with a statement that the event was observed first-hand, entitles his tip to greater weight than might otherwise be the case. Unlike a totality-of-the-circumstances analysis, which permits a balanced assessment of the relative weights of all the various indicia of reliability (and unreliability) attending an informant's tip, the "two-pronged test" has encouraged an excessively technical dissection of informants' tips, with undue attention being focused on isolated issues that cannot sensibly be divorced from the other facts presented to the magistrate.

. . .

We also have recognized that affidavits "are normally drafted by nonlawyers in the midst and haste of a criminal investigation. Technical requirements of elaborate specificity once exacted under common law pleading have no proper place in this area." United States v. Ventresca, supra, 380 U.S. 102, 108 (1965). Likewise, search and arrest warrants long have been issued by persons who are neither lawyers nor judges, and who certainly do not remain abreast of each judicial refinement of the nature of "probable cause." . . . The rigorous inquiry into the *Spinelli* prongs and the complex superstructure of evidentiary and analytical rules that some have seen implicit in our *Spinelli* decision, cannot be reconciled with the fact that many warrants are—quite properly . . . issued on the basis of nontechnical, common-sense judgments of laymen applying a standard less demanding than those used in more formal legal proceedings. Likewise, given the informal, often hurried context in which it must be applied, the "built-in subtleties," Stanley v. State, 313 A.2d 847, 860 (1974), of the "two-pronged test" are particularly unlikely to assist magistrates in determining probable cause.

Similarly, we have repeatedly said that after-the-fact scrutiny by courts of the sufficiency of an affidavit should not take the form of de novo review. A magistrate's "determination of probable cause should be paid great deference by reviewing courts." *Spinelli*, supra, at 419. "A grudging or negative attitude by reviewing courts toward warrants," *Ventresca*, 380 U.S., at 108, is inconsistent with the Fourth Amendment's strong preference for searches conducted pursuant to a warrant; "courts should not invalidate warrant[s] by interpreting affidavit[s] in a hypertechnical, rather than a commonsense, manner." Id., at 109.

If the affidavits submitted by police officers are subjected to the type of scrutiny some courts have deemed appropriate, police might well resort to warrantless searches, with the hope of relying on consent or some other exception to the Warrant Clause that might develop at the time of the search. In addition, the possession of a warrant by officers conducting an arrest or search greatly reduces the perception of unlawful or intrusive police conduct, by assuring "the individual whose property is searched or seized of the lawful authority of the executing officer, his need to search, and the limits of his power to search." United States v. Chadwick, 433 U.S. 1, 9 (1977). . . .

. . . The strictures that inevitably accompany the "two-pronged test" cannot avoid seriously impeding the task of law enforcement. . . . If, as the Illinois Supreme Court apparently thought, that test must be rigorously applied in every case, anonymous tips would be of greatly diminished value in police work. Ordinary citizens, like ordinary witnesses . . . generally do not provide extensive recitations of the basis of their everyday observations. Likewise, as the Illinois Supreme Court observed in this case, the veracity of persons supplying anonymous tips is by hypothesis largely unknown, and unknowable. As a result, anonymous tips seldom could survive a rigorous application of either of the *Spinelli* prongs. Yet, such tips, particularly when supplemented by independent police investigation, frequently contribute to the solution of otherwise "perfect crimes." While a conscientious assessment of the basis for crediting such tips is required by the Fourth Amendment, a standard that leaves virtually no place for anonymous citizen informants is not.

For all these reasons, we conclude that it is wiser to abandon the "two-pronged test" established by our decisions in *Aguilar* and *Spinelli*. In its place we reaffirm the totality-of-the-circumstances analysis that traditionally has informed probable cause determinations. . . . The task of the issuing magistrate is simply to make a practical, common-sense decision whether, given all the circumstances set forth in the affidavit before him, including the "veracity" and "basis of knowledge" of persons supplying hearsay information, there is a fair probability that contraband or evidence of a crime will be found in a particular place. And the duty of a reviewing court is simply to ensure that the magistrate had a "substantial basis for . . . conclud[ing]" that probable cause existed. Jones v. United States, 362 U.S. [257 (1960)], at 271. We are convinced that this flexible, easily applied standard will better achieve the accommodation of public and private interests that the Fourth Amendment requires than does the approach that has developed from *Aguilar* and *Spinelli.*

. . .

IV

Our decisions applying the totality-of-the-circumstances analysis outlined above have consistently recognized the value of corroboration of details of an informant's tip by independent police work. In Jones v. United States, 362 U.S., at 269, we held that an affidavit relying on hearsay "is not to be deemed insufficient on that score, so long as a substantial basis for crediting the hearsay is presented." We went on to say that even in making a warrantless arrest an officer "may rely upon information received through an informant, rather than upon his direct observations, so long as the informant's statement is reasonably corroborated by other matters within the officer's knowledge." Ibid. Likewise, we recognized the probative value of corroborative efforts of police officials in *Aguilar*—the source of the "two-pronged test"—by observing that if the police had made some effort to corroborate the informant's report at issue, "an entirely different case" would have been presented. *Aguilar*, 378 U.S., at 109, n.1.

Our decision in Draper v. United States, 358 U.S. 307 (1959), however, is the classic case on the value of corroborative efforts of police officials. There, an informant named Hereford reported that Draper would arrive in Denver on a train from Chicago on one of two days, and that he would be carrying a quantity of heroin. The informant also supplied a fairly detailed physical description of Draper, and predicted that he would be wearing a light colored raincoat, brown slacks and black shoes, and would be walking "real fast." Id. at 309. Hereford gave no indication of the basis for his information.

On one of the stated dates police officers observed a man matching this description exit a train arriving from Chicago; his attire and luggage matched Hereford's report and he was walking rapidly. We explained in *Draper* that, by this point in his investigation, the arresting officer "had personally verified every facet of the information given him by Hereford except whether petitioner had accomplished his mission and had the three ounces of heroin on his person or in his bag. And surely, with every other bit of Hereford's information being thus personally verified, [the officer] had 'reasonable grounds' to believe that the remaining unverified bit of Hereford's information—that Draper would have the heroin with him—was likewise true," id., at 313.

The showing of probable cause in the present case was fully as compelling as that in *Draper*. Even standing alone, the facts obtained through the independent investigation of Mader and the DEA at least suggested that the Gateses were involved in drug trafficking. In addition to being a popular vacation site, Florida is well-known as a source of narcotics and other illegal drugs. . . . Lance Gates' flight to Palm Beach, his brief, overnight stay in a motel, and apparent immediate return north to Chicago in the family car, conveniently awaiting him in West Palm Beach, is as suggestive of a prearranged drug run, as it is of an ordinary vacation trip.

In addition, the magistrate could rely on the anonymous letter, which had been corroborated in major part by Mader's efforts—just as had occurred in *Draper*.[5] The Supreme Court of Illinois reasoned that *Draper* involved an informant who had given reliable information on previous occasions, while the honesty and reliability of the anonymous informant in this case were unknown to the Bloomingdale police. While this distinction might be an apt one at the time the Police Department received the anonymous letter, it became far less significant after Mader's independent investigative work occurred. The corroboration of the letter's predictions that the Gates' car would be in Florida, that Lance Gates would fly to Florida in the next day or so, and that he would drive the car north toward Bloomingdale all indicated, albeit not with certainty, that the informant's other assertions also were true. "[B]ecause an informant is right about some things, he is more probably right about other facts," *Spinelli*, 393 U.S., at 427 (White, J., concurring)—including the claim regarding the Gateses' illegal activity. This may well not be the type of "reliability" or "veracity" necessary to satisfy some views of the "veracity prong" of *Spinelli*, but we think it suffices for the practical, common-sense judgment called for in making a probable-cause determination. It is enough, for purposes of assessing probable cause, that "[c]orroboration through other sources of information reduced the chances of a reckless or prevaricating tale," thus providing "a substantial basis for crediting the hearsay." Jones v. United States, 362 U.S., at 269, 271.

Finally, the anonymous letter contained a range of details relating not just to easily obtained facts and conditions existing at the time of the tip, but to future actions of third parties ordinarily not easily predicted. The letterwriter's accurate information as to the travel plans of each of the Gateses was of a character likely obtained only from the Gateses themselves, or from someone familiar with their not entirely ordinary travel

5. The Illinois Supreme Court thought that the verification of details contained in the anonymous letter in this case amounted only to "[t]he corroboration of innocent activity," 423 N.E.2d 887, 893 (1981), and that this was insufficient to support a finding of probable cause. We are inclined to agree, however, with the observation of Justice Moran in his dissenting opinion that "[i]n this case, just as in *Draper*, seemingly innocent activity became suspicious in the light of the initial tip." 423 N.E.2d, at 896. And it bears noting that *all* of the corroborating detail established in *Draper*, supra, was of entirely innocent activity—a fact later pointed out by the Court. . . .

This is perfectly reasonable. As discussed previously, probable cause requires only a probability or substantial chance of criminal activity, not an actual showing of such activity. By hypothesis, therefore, innocent behavior frequently will provide the basis for a showing of probable cause; to require otherwise would be to *sub silentio* impose a drastically more rigorous definition of probable cause than the security of our citizens demands. We think the Illinois court attempted a too rigid classification of the types of conduct that may be relied upon in seeking to demonstrate probable cause. . . . In making a determination of probable cause the relevant inquiry is not whether particular conduct is "innocent" or "guilty," but the degree of suspicion that attaches to particular types of non-criminal acts.

plans. If the informant had access to accurate information of this type a magistrate could properly conclude that it was not unlikely that he also had access to reliable information of the Gateses' alleged illegal activities. Of course, the Gateses' travel plans might have been learned from a talkative neighbor or travel agent; under the "two-pronged test" developed from *Spinelli*, the character of the details in the anonymous letter might well not permit a sufficiently clear inference regarding the letterwriter's "basis of knowledge." But, as discussed previously, supra, at 235, probable cause does not demand the certainty we associate with formal trials. It is enough that there was a fair probability that the writer of the anonymous letter had obtained his entire story either from the Gateses or someone they trusted. And corroboration of major portions of the letter's predictions provides just this probability. It is apparent, therefore, that the judge issuing the warrant had a "substantial basis for . . . conclud[ing]" that probable cause to search the Gateses' home and car existed. The judgment of the Supreme Court of Illinois therefore must be reversed.[6]

101.

Probable cause—the area between bare suspicion and virtual certainty—describes not a point but a zone, within which the graver the crime the more latitude the police must be allowed. The shooting of seven persons (four fatally) by a team of criminals in the space of two hours is about as grave a crisis as a local police department will encounter. The police must be allowed more leeway in resolving it than when they are investigating the theft of a bicycle. Especially when a multiple murderer is at large in circumstances suggesting that he may be about to kill again, the interest in public safety is paramount.

It is true that the gravity of the crime and the threat of its imminent repetition usually are discussed in relation to the existence of an emergency justifying a search or arrest without a warrant . . . rather than in relation to probable cause for the search or arrest. But there is some judicial recognition of the latter relation. . . . The amount of information that prudent police will collect before deciding to make a search or an arrest, and hence the amount of probable cause they will have, is a function of the gravity of the crime, and especially the danger of its imminent repetition. If a multiple murderer is at large, the police must compress their investigation and make the decision to search or arrest on less information than if they could investigate at their leisure.

Llaguno v. Mingey, 763 F.2d 1560, 1565–66 (7th Cir.1985).

102. It is generally assumed that the standards of "probable cause" for an arrest and for a search are alike. The Court has cited search cases to explain the meaning of probable cause in arrest cases, see, e.g., Beck v.

[6] Justice White wrote an opinion concurring in the judgment. Justice Brennan wrote a dissenting opinion, which Justice Marshall joined. Justice Stevens wrote a dissenting opinion, which Justice Brennan joined.

AO106 (Rev. 7/87) Affidavit for Search Warrant

UNITED STATES DISTRICT COURT

_______________ DISTRICT OF _______________

In the Matter of the Search of
(Name, address or brief description of person, property or premises to be searched)

APPLICATION AND AFFIDAVIT FOR SEARCH WARRANT

Case Number:

I, _______________ being duly sworn depose and say:

I am a(n) _______________ and have reason to believe
Official Title

that ☐ on the person of or ☐ on the property or premises known as (name, description and/or location)

in the _______________ District of _______________

there is now concealed a certain person or property, namely (describe the person or property to be seized)

which is (state one or more bases for search and seizure set forth under Rule 41(b) of the Federal Rules of Criminal Procedure)

concerning a violation of Title ________ United States code, Section(s) _______________

The facts to support a finding of Probable Cause are as follows:

Continued on the attached sheet and made a part hereof: ☐ Yes ☐ No

____
Signature of Affiant

Sworn to before me and subscribed in my presence,

_______________ at _______________
Date City State

_______________ _______________
Name of Judicial Officer Title of Judicial Officer Signature of Judicial Officer

Ohio, 379 U.S. 89 (1964), and the reverse, see, e.g., Aguilar v. Texas, 378 U.S. 108 (1964). (But see Johnson v. United States, 333 U.S. 10 (1948), in which the Court suggested that evidence that might have justified a search was insufficient to justify an arrest.) Is it a sufficient explanation for the convergence of these standards that "the language of the Fourth Amendment, that '. . . no Warrants shall issue, but upon probable cause, supported by Oath or affirmation, and particularly describing . . . the persons or things to be seized,' of course applies to arrest as well as search warrants," Giordenello v. United States, 357 U.S. 480, 485–86 (1958)? Or that a lawful arrest may permit an otherwise unlawful search, see pp. 205–228 below? Or that it is often not clear whether the police conduct being evaluated is "really" a search or an arrest? See, e.g., Brinegar v. United States, 338 U.S. 160 (1949). Are there relevant differences between an arrest and a search which suggest that a different amount and/or kind of information should be required to authorize each? If so, are the differences such that a different standard for each can meaningfully and usefully be expressed?

103. In Commonwealth v. White, 371 N.E.2d 777 (Mass.1977), the court held that statements obtained in violation of the *Miranda* requirements cannot be used as the basis of probable cause for issuance of a search warrant. The court relied on earlier cases holding that evidence obtained in violation of the Fourth Amendment cannot be used as the basis for a search warrant and that statements obtained in violation of *Miranda* cannot be considered in determining whether there is probable cause for an arrest. *White* was affirmed without opinion, by an equally divided Court. 439 U.S. 280 (1978).

104. Evidence obtained in the course of a search pursuant to a valid search warrant is not inadmissible because the same evidence had been discovered in the course of a prior illegal search, provided that the warrant was obtained on the basis of information wholly independent of the prior illegality. Murray v. United States, 487 U.S. 533 (1988) (4–3).

105. Premises of a third person. In Zurcher v. Stanford Daily, 436 U.S. 547 (1978) (5–3), police secured a warrant to search the offices of a student newspaper for photographs that might be evidence of a crime. There was no claim that the newspaper staff was at all involved in the crime. In an action under 42 U.S.C. § 1983, the lower court held that a warrant to search for materials in the possession of one who is not himself suspected of a crime could not be issued unless there was probable cause to believe that a subpoena *duces tecum* would be impracticable and that the possessor would not obey a court order that the material be preserved. The court also held that where the innocent possessor is a newspaper, special First Amendment interests are involved and require a clear showing that the warrant is necessary.

The Supreme Court reversed. Referring to past cases, it held that the fact that the possessor of seizable material was himself innocent is immaterial to the issuance of a warrant. Nor does the fact that the possessor is a newspaper require more than scrupulous observance of the Fourth Amendment's requirements.

The Justice Department has issued guidelines for federal agents' use of search warrants to obtain documentary evidence from innocent third parties. These guidelines allow use of a warrant only if less intrusive means like a subpoena would jeopardize the availability or usefulness of the materials sought. Special, stricter limitations are placed on use of a warrant that might intrude on a confidential relationship, for example when the third party is a lawyer or physician.

106. The Fourth Amendment authorizes the issuance only of search warrants "particularly describing the place to be searched." How particular must the description be?

The "place to be searched" is usually regarded as one premises or residential unit, however large or small, whether it is composed of multiple buildings, on one hand, or several units are contained within a single building, on the other. "For purposes of the Fourth Amendment, two or more apartments in the same building stand on the same footing as two or more houses. A single warrant cannot describe an entire building when cause is shown for searching only one apartment." Moore v. United States, 461 F.2d 1236, 1238 (D.C.Cir.1972). Accord United States v. Busk, 693 F.2d 28 (3d Cir.1982). See generally United States v. Votteller, 544 F.2d 1355, 1362–64 (6th Cir.1976), and cases cited.

A warrant authorizing the search of the apartment on the third floor of a building did not violate the particularity requirement of the Warrant Clause because it turned out that, unknown to the officers at the time the warrant was issued, there were two apartments on the floor and the officers had probable cause to search only one. Since the officers acted in accordance with the warrant and the facts as they believed them to be and ceased to search the second apartment when they realized that it was a separate unit, their presence in the latter was not a violation of the occupant's rights. Maryland v. Garrison, 480 U.S. 79 (1987) (6–3). See also United States v. Williams, 917 F.2d 1088 (8th Cir.1990) (officers obtained search warrant for rooming house reasonably believing it was a single family dwelling; search upheld).

107. Government agents obtained a warrant to search the premises of the Hillside Press, which was owned by the appellant and his brother. During the search, they found on the floor under a desk a briefcase that they had seen the appellant carry into the office a short while before. They searched the briefcase and found evidence incriminating the appellant. He moved to suppress the evidence on the ground that the briefcase was his personal property and was not covered by the warrant. The motion was denied. On appeal, the judgment was affirmed. United States v. Micheli, 487 F.2d 429 (1st Cir.1973). The court said:

> [W]e do not mean to suggest that anything found on the premises would necessarily fall within the scope of a warrant to search premises. Nor would we imply that the result would be different if, when the officers entered, appellant was physically holding the briefcase. To allow our decision to be interpreted as giving carte blanche to seize any objects reposing within premises covered by a warrant would be a disservice to law enforcement officials, individuals who may find their personal privacy invaded by a premises search warrant, and courts which must rule on suppression motions. Without attempting to write in black letters, we think some confusion may be spared by setting forth our rationale in deciding this case.

AO 93 (Rev. 8/98) Search Warrant

UNITED STATES DISTRICT COURT

_______________ District of _______________

In the Matter of the Search of
(Name, address or brief description of person or property to be searched)

SEARCH WARRANT

Case Number:

TO: _______________ and any Authorized Officer of the United States

Affidavit(s) having been made before me by _______________ who has reason to believe
Affiant

that ☐ on the person of, or ☐ on the premises known as (name, description and/or location)

in the _______________ District of _______________ there is now concealed a certain person or property, namely (describe the person or property)

I am satisfied that the affidavit(s) and any record testimony establish probable cause to believe that the person or property so described is now concealed on the person or premises above-described and establish grounds for the issuance of this warrant.

YOU ARE HEREBY COMMANDED to search on or before _______________
Date

(not to exceed 10 days) the person or place named above for the person or property specified, serving this warrant and making the search ☐ in the daytime — 6:00 AM to 10:00 P.M. ☐ at anytime in the day or night as I find reasonable cause has been established and if the person or property be found there to seize same, leaving a copy of this warrant and receipt for the person or property taken, and prepare a written inventory of the person or property seized and promptly return this warrant to _______________ as required by law.
U.S. Judge or Magistrate

_______________ at _______________
Date and Time Issued — City and State

_______________ _______________
Name and Title of Judicial Officer — Signature of Judicial Officer

AO 93 (Rev. 8/98) Search Warrant (Reverse)

RETURN		Case Number:
DATE WARRANT RECEIVED	DATE AND TIME WARRANT EXECUTED	COPY OF WARRANT AND RECEIPT FOR ITEMS LEFT WITH
INVENTORY MADE IN THE PRESENCE OF		
INVENTORY OF PERSON OR PROPERTY TAKEN PURSUANT TO THE WARRANT		

CERTIFICATION

I swear that this inventory is a true and detailed account of the person or property taken by me on the warrant.

____

Subscribed, sworn to, and returned before me this date.

______________________________ U.S. Judge or Magistrate

______________ Date

Had appellant been a doctor on call at the Press and had the agents reason to know that the briefcase belonged to him, we would not reach the result we do here. We are not helped, in distinguishing these two situations, by the general proposition that a warrant to search premises does not permit a personal search of one who merely happens to be present at the time. For the question is: what is a personal search? A search of clothing currently worn is plainly within the ambit of a personal search and outside the scope of a warrant to search the premises. But a personal effect such as a briefcase, carried on to the premises and then tucked under a desk, does not clearly fall either within the realm of a personal search or a search of the premises. While the articulation of guiding principle may result in a line drawn with a stub of chalk rather than with a draftsman's pen, we nevertheless think principle exists.

Some courts approach the quest for principle by immunizing from a search under sanction of a premises warrant any item within the physical possession of an individual on the premises. . . . This has the virtue of precision but suffers from being at once too broad and too narrow. It is too broad in that a search warrant could be frustrated to the extent that there are hands inside the premises to pick up objects before the door is opened by the police. . . .

A focus on actual physical possession is too narrow, however, in that it would leave vulnerable many personal effects, such as wallets, purses, cases, or overcoats, which are often set down upon chairs or counters, hung on racks, or checked for convenient storage. The Fourth Amendment's basic interest in protecting privacy . . . and avoiding unreasonable governmental intrusions . . . is hardly furthered by making its applicability hinge upon whether the individual happens to be holding or wearing his personal belongings after he chances into a place where a search is underway. . . .

In determining to what extent a recognizable personal effect not currently worn, but apparently temporarily put down, such as a briefcase, falls outside the scope of a warrant to search the premises, we would be better advised to examine the relationship between the person and the place. . . . It should not be assumed that whatever is found on the premises described in the warrant necessarily falls within the proper scope of the search; rather, it is necessary to examine why a person's belongings happen to be on the premises. . . . [T]he protective boundary established by requiring a search warrant should encompass those extensions of a person which he reasonably seeks to preserve as private, regardless of where he may be.

[T]he problem we are discussing is a narrow one, falling between two primary rules, one permitting searches of premises, the other prohibiting searches of person. In this interstitial area where the literal application of either primary rule would frustrate the legitimate interests of either the police or the individual, we think it more consistent with the Fourth Amendment that searches of the personal effects of visitors to premises be appraised by reference to the reasonable expectations of privacy which visitors bring to premises rather than by attributing significance to a literal coup de main.

> Our basic rationale for deciding that appellant's briefcase fell within the scope of the warrant to search the premises does not, therefore, rest upon the fact that at the time of the search his briefcase was out of his physical possession. Rather, we base our decision on the fact that, as co-owner of the Hillside Press, appellant was not in the position of a mere visitor or passerby who suddenly found his belongings vulnerable to a search of the premises. He had a special relation to the place, which meant that it could reasonably be expected that some of his personal belongings would be there. Thus, the showing of probable cause and necessity which was required prior to the initial intrusion into his office reasonably comprehended within its scope those personal articles, such as his briefcase, which might be lying about the office. The search of the briefcase, under these circumstances, was properly carried out within the scope of the warrant.

487 F.2d at 430–32. Compare Commonwealth v. Snow, 298 N.E.2d 804 (Mass.1973) (search of customer's coat on rack in barber shop).

108. Persons on the premises. In Ybarra v. Illinois, 444 U.S. 85 (1979) (6–3), police executed a valid warrant to search a tavern for evidence of narcotics offenses. During the search, the police frisked about a dozen patrons who were present. Narcotics were found on the person of the defendant. The Court held that the warrant to search the premises did not allow a search of the person of those who were present, who had "individualized [constitutional] protection . . . separate and distinct from the Fourth and Fourteenth Amendment protection possessed by the proprietor of the tavern." Id. at 91–92. The Court apparently allowed the possibility of a warrant to search premises as well as unnamed persons found on the premises, provided there was probable cause for such a search. Id. at 92 n.4. Compare United States v. Barlin, 686 F.2d 81 (2d Cir.1982) (search of handbag of person present while search is conducted upheld).

The Court has held, however, that officers executing a valid warrant to search for contraband have authority to detain the occupants of the premises while a proper search is conducted. Michigan v. Summers, 452 U.S. 692 (1981) (6–3). Referring to "stop" cases like Terry v. Ohio, p. 100 above, the Court said that these are "such limited intrusions on the personal security of those detained and are justified by such substantial law enforcement interests that they may be made on less than probable cause, so long as police have an articulable basis for suspecting criminal activity." 452 U.S. at 699. Among the "law enforcement interests" that the Court mentioned are "preventing flight in the event that incriminating evidence is found," "minimizing the risk of harm to the officers," and facilitating "the orderly completion of the search." Id. at 702–703.

The Court concluded: "If the evidence that a citizen's residence is harboring contraband is sufficient to persuade a judicial officer that an invasion of the citizen's privacy is justified, it is constitutionally reasonable to require that citizen to remain while officers of the law execute a valid warrant to search his home. Thus, for Fourth Amendment purposes, we hold that a warrant to search for contraband founded on probable cause implicitly carries with it the limited authority to detain the occupants of the premises while a proper search is conducted." Id. at 704–705. The Court observed that it did not decide whether the same result would be reached if a warrant authorized a search only for evidence.

Applying Michigan v. Summers, in Burchett v. Kiefer, 310 F.3d 937 (6th Cir.2002), the court held that police executing a search warrant may detain a person who approaches but does not go on the property and flees when the police tell him to get on the ground, for the duration of the search.

109. The Fourth Amendment requires that warrants "particularly" describe "the persons or things to be seized." In Marron v. United States, 275 U.S. 192, 196 (1927), the Court said: "The requirement that warrants shall particularly describe the things to be seized makes general searches under them impossible and prevents the seizure of one thing under a warrant describing another. As to what is to be taken, nothing is left to the discretion of the officer executing the warrant."

A warrant that fails to describe the things to be seized is invalid and is not saved by the fact that the application for the warrant described the things to be seized. Groh v. Ramirez, 540 U.S. ___ (2004) (7–2). The Court indicated that a warrant might incorporate some other document by reference, but the warrant in this case did not do so. A search pursuant to such a warrant is unconstitutional even if, in fact, the officers who conducted the search confined it to the items that were listed in the application.

See Lo-Ji Sales, Inc. v. New York, 442 U.S. 319 (1979) (warrant to search generally for obscene materials too broad); Stanford v. Texas, 379 U.S. 476 (1965) (warrant to search for books, records and other written material "concerning the Communist Party of Texas" too broad); United States v. Cardwell, 680 F.2d 75 (9th Cir.1982) (warrant to search for business records too broad); United States v. Klein, 565 F.2d 183 (1st Cir.1977) (generic description of sound tapes, which failed to distinguish ones to be seized from others, was too broad); United States v. Jarvis, 560 F.2d 494 (2d Cir.1977) ("John Doe" arrest warrant invalid even though person identified by "extrinsic evidence"); VonderAhe v. Howland, 508 F.2d 364 (9th Cir.1974) (warrant to seize "fiscal records" too broad).

See generally Andresen v. Maryland, 427 U.S. 463, 479–82 (1976), in which the Court observed: "We recognize that there are grave dangers inherent in executing a warrant authorizing a search and seizure of a person's papers that are not necessarily present in executing a warrant to search for physical objects whose relevance is more easily ascertainable. In searches for papers, it is certain that some innocuous documents will be examined, at least cursorily, in order to determine whether they are, in fact, among those papers authorized to be seized. Similar dangers, of course, are present in executing a warrant for the 'seizure' of telephone conversations. In both kinds of searches, responsible officials, including judicial officials, must take care to assure that they are conducted in a manner that minimizes unwarranted intrusions upon privacy." Id. at 482 n.11.

The good-faith exception to the exclusionary rule, see note 78, p. 148 above, was applied to an overbroad warrant in United States v. Maxwell, 920 F.2d 1028 (D.C.Cir.1990). But see United States v. George, 975 F.2d 72 (2d Cir.1992).

In United States v. Stefonek, 179 F.3d 1030 (7th Cir.1999), the court concluded that a warrant specifying the things to be seized as "evidence of crime" did not meet the particularity requirement, but that since the affidavit accompanying the application for the warrant contained an adequate specification and the agents executing the warrant knew the specification and complied with it, suppression of the evidence seized was not necessary. The court said that advising the person whose premises are searched of the scope of the search was a secondary purpose of the particularity requirement.

Horton v. California

496 U.S. 128, 110 S.Ct. 2301, 110 L.Ed.2d 112 (1990)

■ JUSTICE STEVENS delivered the opinion of the Court.

In this case we revisit an issue that was considered, but not conclusively resolved, in Coolidge v. New Hampshire, 403 U.S. 443 (1971): Whether the warrantless seizure of evidence of crime in plain view is prohibited by the Fourth Amendment if the discovery of the evidence was not inadvertent. We conclude that even though inadvertence is a characteristic of most legitimate "plain view" seizures, it is not a necessary condition.

I

Petitioner was convicted of the armed robbery of Erwin Wallaker, the treasurer of the San Jose Coin Club. When Wallaker returned to his home after the Club's annual show, he entered his garage and was accosted by two masked men, one armed with a machine gun and the other with an electrical shocking device, sometimes referred to as a "stun gun." The two men shocked Wallaker, bound and handcuffed him, and robbed him of jewelry and cash. During the encounter sufficient conversation took place to enable Wallaker subsequently to identify petitioner's distinctive voice. His identification was partially corroborated by a witness who saw the robbers leaving the scene and by evidence that petitioner had attended the coin show.

Sergeant LaRault, an experienced police officer, investigated the crime and determined that there was probable cause to search petitioner's home for the proceeds of the robbery and for the weapons used by the robbers. His affidavit for a search warrant referred to police reports that described the weapons as well as the proceeds, but the warrant issued by the Magistrate only authorized a search for the proceeds, including three specifically described rings.

Pursuant to the warrant, LaRault searched petitioner's residence, but he did not find the stolen property. During the course of the search, however, he discovered the weapons in plain view and seized them. Specifically, he seized an Uzi machine gun, a .38-caliber revolver, two stun guns, a handcuff key, a San Jose Coin Club advertising brochure, and a few items of clothing identified by the victim. LaRault testified that while he was searching for the rings, he also was interested in finding other evidence connecting petitioner to the robbery. Thus, the seized evidence was not discovered "inadvertently."

The trial court refused to suppress the evidence found in petitioner's home and, after a jury trial, petitioner was found guilty and sentenced to prison. The California Court of Appeal affirmed. . . . It rejected petitioner's argument that our decision in *Coolidge* required suppression of the seized evidence that had not been listed in the warrant because its discovery was not inadvertent. . . . The California Supreme Court denied petitioner's request for review. . . .

Because the California courts' interpretation of the "plain view" doctrine conflicts with the view of other courts, and because the unresolved issue is important, we granted certiorari. . . .

II

. . .

The right to security in person and property protected by the Fourth Amendment may be invaded in quite different ways by searches and seizures. A search compromises the individual interest in privacy; a seizure deprives the individual of dominion over his or her person or property. . . . The "plain-view" doctrine is often considered an exception to the general rule that warrantless searches are presumptively unreasonable, but this characterization overlooks the important difference between searches and seizures. If an article is already in plain view, neither its observation nor its seizure would involve any invasion of privacy. . . . A seizure of the article, however, would obviously invade the owner's possessory interest. . . . If "plain view" justifies an exception from an otherwise applicable warrant requirement, therefore, it must be an exception that is addressed to the concerns that are implicated by seizures rather than by searches.

The criteria that generally guide "plain view" seizures were set forth in Coolidge v. New Hampshire, 403 U.S. 443 (1971). The Court held that the police, in seizing two automobiles parked in plain view on the defendant's driveway in the course of arresting the defendant, violated the Fourth Amendment. Accordingly, particles of gun powder that had been subsequently found in vacuum sweepings from one of the cars could not be introduced in evidence against the defendant. The State endeavored to justify the seizure of the automobiles, and their subsequent search at the police station, on four different grounds, including the "plain-view" doctrine. The scope of that doctrine as it had developed in earlier cases was fairly summarized in these three paragraphs from Justice Stewart's opinion:

> It is well established that under certain circumstances the police may seize evidence in plain view without a warrant. But it is important to keep in mind that, in the vast majority of cases, *any* evidence seized by

the police will be in plain-view, at least at the moment of seizure. The problem with the "plain-view" doctrine has been to identify the circumstances in which plain view has legal significance rather than being simply the normal concomitant of any search, legal or illegal.

An example of the applicability of the "plain-view" doctrine is the situation in which the police have a warrant to search a given area for specified objects, and in the course of the search come across some other article of incriminating character. [. . .] Where the initial intrusion that brings the police within plain view of such an article is supported, not by a warrant, but by one of the recognized exceptions to the warrant requirement, the seizure is also legitimate. Thus the police may inadvertently come across evidence while in "hot pursuit" of a fleeing suspect. [. . .] And an object that comes into view during a search incident to arrest that is appropriately limited in scope under existing law may be seized without a warrant. [. . .] Finally, the "plain-view" doctrine has been applied where a police officer is not searching for evidence against the accused, but nonetheless inadvertently comes across an incriminating object. [. . .]

What the "plain-view" cases have in common is that the police officer in each of them had a prior justification for an intrusion in the course of which he came inadvertently across a piece of evidence incriminating the accused. The doctrine serves to supplement the prior justification—whether it be a warrant for another object, hot pursuit, search incident to lawful arrest, to some other legitimate reason for being present unconnected with a search directed against the accused—and permits the warrantless seizure. Of course, the extension of the original justification is legitimate only where it is immediately apparent to the police that they have evidence before them; the "plain-view" doctrine may not be used to extend a general exploratory search from one object to another until something incriminating at last emerges.

Id., at 465–66 (footnote omitted). Justice Stewart then described the two limitations on the doctrine that he found implicit in its rationale: First, "that plain view *alone* is never enough to justify the warrantless seizure of evidence, id., at 468; and second, that 'the discovery of evidence in plain view must be inadvertent.' " Id., at 469.

Justice Stewart's analysis of the "plain-view" doctrine did not command a majority, and a plurality of the Court has since made clear that the discussion is "not a binding precedent." Texas v. Brown, 460 U.S. 730, 737 (1983) (opinion of Rehnquist, J.). . . .

. . .

II

Justice Stewart concluded that the inadvertence requirement was necessary to avoid a violation of the express constitutional requirement that a valid warrant must particularly describe the things to be seized. He explained:

> The rationale of the exception to the warrant requirement, as just stated, is that a plain-view seizure will not turn an initially valid (and therefore limited) search into a "general" one, while the inconvenience of procuring a warrant to cover an inadvertent discovery is great. But where the discovery is anticipated, where the police know in advance the location of the evidence and intend to seize it, the situation is altogether different. The requirement of a warrant to seize imposes no inconvenience whatever, or at least none which is constitutionally cognizable in a legal system that regards warrantless searches as "per se unreasonable" in the absence of "exigent circumstances."
>
> If the initial intrusion is bottomed upon a warrant that fails to mention a particular object, though the police know its location and intend to seize it, then there is a violation of the express constitutional requirement of "Warrants . . . particularly describing . . . [the] things to be seized."

403 U.S., at 469–71.

We find two flaws in this reasoning. First, evenhanded law enforcement is best achieved by the application of objective standards of conduct, rather than standards that depend upon the subjective state of mind of the officer. The fact that an officer is interested in an item of evidence and fully expects to find it in the course of a search should not invalidate its seizure if the search is confined in area and duration by the terms of a warrant or a valid exception to the warrant requirement. If the officer has knowledge approaching certainty that the item will be found, we see no reason why he or she would deliberately omit a particular description of the item to be seized from the application for a search warrant. Specification of the additional item could only permit the officer to expand the scope of the search. On the other hand, if he or she has a valid warrant to search for one item and merely a suspicion concerning the second, whether or not it amounts to probable cause, we fail to see why that suspicion should immunize the second item from seizure if it is found during a lawful search for the first. The hypothetical case put by Justice White in his dissenting opinion in *Coolidge* is instructive:

> Let us suppose officers secure a warrant to search a house for a rifle. While staying well within the range of a rifle search, they discover two photographs of the murder victim, both in plain sight in the bedroom. Assume also that the discovery of the one photograph was inadvertent but finding the other was anticipated. The Court would permit the seizure of only one of the photographs. But in terms of the "minor" peril to Fourth Amendment values there is surely no difference between these two photographs: the interference with possession is the same in each case and the officers' appraisal of the photograph they expected to see is no less reliable than their judgment about the other. And in both situations the actual inconvenience and danger to evidence remain identical if the officers must depart and secure a warrant.

Id., at 516.

Second, the suggestion that the inadvertence requirement is necessary to prevent the police from conducting general searches, or from converting specific warrants into general warrants, is not persuasive because that interest is already served by the requirements that no warrant issue unless it "particularly describ[es] the place to be searched and the persons or things to be seized," . . . and that a warrantless search be circumscribed by the exigencies which justify its initiation. . . . Scrupulous adherence to these requirements serves the interests in limiting the area and duration of the search that the inadvertence requirement inadequately protects. Once those commands have been satisfied and the officer has a lawful right of access, however, no additional Fourth Amendment interest is furthered by requiring that the discovery of evidence be inadvertent. If the scope of the search exceeds that permitted by the terms of a validly issued warrant or the character of the relevant exception from the warrant requirement, the subsequent seizure is unconstitutional without more. . . .

In this case, the scope of the search was not enlarged in the slightest by the omission of any reference to the weapons in the warrant. Indeed, if the three rings and other items named in the warrant had been found at the outset—or if petitioner had them in his possession and had responded to the warrant by producing them immediately—no search for weapons could have taken place. . . .

As we have already suggested, by hypothesis the seizure of an object in plain view does not involve an intrusion on privacy. If the interest in privacy has been invaded, the violation must have occurred before the object came into plain view and there is no need for an inadvertence limitation on seizures to condemn it. The prohibition against general searches and general warrants serves primarily as a protection against unjustified intrusions on privacy. But reliance on privacy concerns that support that prohibition is misplaced when the inquiry concerns the scope of an exception that merely authorizes an officer with a lawful right of access to an item to seize it without a warrant.

In this case the items seized from petitioner's home were discovered during a lawful search authorized by a valid warrant. When they were discovered, it was immediately apparent to the officer that they constituted incriminating evidence. He had probable cause, not only to obtain a warrant to search for the stolen property, but also to believe that the weapons and handguns had been used in the crime he was investigating. The search was authorized by the warrant; the seizure was authorized by the "plain-view" doctrine. The judgment is affirmed.

. . .[7]

---

110. In Arizona v. Hicks, 480 U.S. 321 (1987) (6–3), the Court rejected the argument that the plain-view doctrine authorized police to *move* an object in order to examine it more closely. The Court said: "[T]aking action, unrelated to the objectives of the authorized intrusion, which exposed to view concealed portions of the apartment or its contents, did produce a new invasion of respondent's privacy unjustified by the

[7] Justice Brennan wrote a dissenting opinion, which Justice Marshall joined.

AO 93A (Rev. 5/85) Search Warrant Upon Oral Testimony

UNITED STATES DISTRICT COURT

______________________ District of ______________________

In the Matter of the Search of
(Name, address or brief description of person or property to be searched)

SEARCH WARRANT UPON ORAL TESTIMONY

Case Number:

TO: ______________________ and any Authorized Officer of the United States

Sworn oral testimony has been communicated to me by ______________________
Affiant

that ☐ on the person of, or ☐ on the premises known as (name, description and/or location)

in the ______________________ District of ______________________ there is now concealed a certain person or property, namely (describe the person or property)

I am satisfied that the circumstances are such as to make it reasonable to dispense with a written affidavit and that there is probable cause to believe that the property or person so described is concealed on the person or premises above described and that grounds for application for issuance of the search warrant exist as communicated orally to me in a sworn statement which has been recorded electronically, stenographically, or in long-hand and upon the return of the warrant, will be transcribed, certified as accurate and attached hereto.

YOU ARE HEREBY COMMANDED to search on or before ______________________
Date

the person or place named above for the person or property specified, serving this warrant and making the search ☐ in the day-time — 6:00 AM to 10:00 PM ☐ at anytime in the day or night as I find reasonable cause has been established and if the person or property be found there to seize same, leaving a copy of this warrant and receipt for the person or property taken, and prepare a written inventory of the person or property seized and promptly return this warrant to ______________________
U.S. Judge or Magistrate Judge

as required by law.

______________________ at ______________________
Date and Time Issued City and State

______________________ ______________________
Name and Title of Judicial Officer Signature of Judicial Officer

I certify that on ______________________ at ______________________
Date Time

______________________ orally authorized the
U.S. Judge or Magistrate Judge

issuance and execution of a search warrant conforming to all the foregoing terms.

______________________ ______________________ ______________________
Name of affiant Signature of affiant Exact time warrant

exigent circumstance that validated the entry." Id. at 325. The police had moved stereo equipment, which they suspected, but did not have probable cause to believe, was stolen, in order to read its serial numbers.

111. Rule 41(e)(2)(A) provides that a warrant "must command the officer to . . . execute the warrant within a specified time no longer than 10 days." So long as the warrant is executed within that period, the officer may presumably choose a time that will facilitate an arrest. See note 8, p. 20 above.

112. Rule 41(e)(1) provides that a warrant must be issued "to an officer authorized to execute it." Referring to a comparable provision in an earlier version of the rule, in United States v. Soriano, 482 F.2d 469, 478 (5th Cir.1973), the court said that the requirement protected "several important interests. . . . [O]ne of its functions is to fix responsibility in the event the warrant is not executed. Also, it enables the magistrate to make a presearch determination that an appropriate officer will serve the warrant. It assists the person whose premises are to be searched in ensuring that the search will be made by an authorized officer and not by an imposter. And it provides a record so that, if necessary, the judicial processes can make a post-search determination that the search was conducted by an authorized officer." Where, however, there was only "technical noncompliance" with the requirement and "the magistrate knew in advance who was to serve the warrant, and the designated officer indeed served it," id. at 479, the search was not invalid.

113. Rule 41(e)(2)(B) provides that a warrant must ordinarily be executed during the daytime. Is there any requirement that a warrant be executed, if practicable, while the occupant of the premises is at home? See United States v. Gervato, 474 F.2d 40 (3d Cir.1973), concluding that there is not. In Payne v. United States, 508 F.2d 1391, 1394 (5th Cir.1975), the court followed *Gervato*, saying that notwithstanding the "knock-and-announce" requirement, see Wilson v. Arkansas p. 68 above, "forcible entry pursuant to a search warrant of unoccupied premises is not per se a violation of the Fourth Amendment." "The statutory requirements of judicial supervision based on probable cause, the requisites of specificity in describing the premises and the items to be seized, and the delivery of a written inventory of the items taken to the occupant or other competent person provide adequate safeguards against potential abuse and sufficiently limit police discretion."

114. Rule 41(f)(4) provides that "[t]he officer executing the warrant must promptly return it—together with a copy of the inventory—to the magistrate judge designated on the warrant." The failure to make a prompt return was held not to be "constitutionally significant" and, therefore, not to require suppression of evidence obtained pursuant to a valid warrant, in United States v. Hall, 505 F.2d 961 (3d Cir.1974). To the same effect, see United States v. Dudek, 530 F.2d 684 (6th Cir.1976) (cases cited). In *Hall*, the court said that suppression was required only if the defendant showed prejudice from the violation of the rule.

115. Suppose a defendant attacks a search warrant on the ground that the affidavits supporting the warrant are false. The Court considered the procedure for making such an attack and the circumstances in which an affidavit's falsity invalidates a warrant in Franks v. Delaware, 438 U.S.

154 (1978) (7–2). It concluded that, in order to avoid having to conduct a hearing without sufficient cause, a "substantial preliminary showing" of falsity is required.

> [W]here the defendant makes a substantial preliminary showing that a false statement knowingly and intentionally, or with reckless disregard for the truth, was included by the affiant in the warrant affidavit, and if the allegedly false statement is necessary to the finding of probable cause, the Fourth Amendment requires that a hearing be held at the defendant's request. In the event that at that hearing the allegation of perjury or reckless disregard is established by the defendant by a preponderance of the evidence, and, with the affidavit's false material set to one side, the affidavit's remaining content is insufficient to establish probable cause, the search warrant must be voided and the fruits of the search excluded to the same extent as if probable cause was lacking on the face of the affidavit.
>
> . . .
>
> . . . There is, of course, a presumption of validity with respect to the affidavit supporting the search warrant. To mandate an evidentiary hearing, the challenger's attack must be more than conclusory and must be supported by more than a mere desire to cross-examine. There must be allegations of deliberate falsehood or of reckless disregard for the truth, and those allegations must be accompanied by an offer of proof. They should point out specifically the portion of the warrant affidavit that is claimed to be false; and they should be accompanied by a statement of supporting reasons. Affidavits or sworn or otherwise reliable statements of witnesses should be furnished, or their absence satisfactorily explained. Allegations of negligence or innocent mistake are insufficient. The deliberate falsity or reckless disregard whose impeachment is permitted today is only that of the affiant, not of any nongovernmental informant. Finally, if these requirements are met, and if, when material that is the subject of the alleged falsity or reckless disregard is set to one side, there remains sufficient content in the warrant affidavit to support a finding of probable cause, no hearing is required. On the other hand, if the remaining content is insufficient, the defendant is entitled, under the Fourth and Fourteenth Amendments, to his hearing. Whether he will prevail at that hearing is, of course, another issue.

Id. at 155–56, 171–72.

Franks was applied in United States v. Stanert, 762 F.2d 775 (9th Cir.1985) (defendant's preliminary showing required evidentiary hearing); United States v. Namer, 680 F.2d 1088 (5th Cir.1982) (search warrant invalid); United States v. Cortina, 630 F.2d 1207 (7th Cir.1980) (same).

Without a Warrant

Chimel v. California

395 U.S. 752, 89 S.Ct. 2034, 23 L.Ed.2d 685 (1969)

■ MR. JUSTICE STEWART delivered the opinion of the Court.

This case raises basic questions concerning the permissible scope under the Fourth Amendment of a search incident to a lawful arrest.

The relevant facts are essentially undisputed. Late in the afternoon of September 13, 1965, three police officers arrived at the Santa Ana, California, home of the petitioner with a warrant authorizing his arrest for the burglary of a coin shop. The officers knocked on the door, identified themselves to the petitioner's wife, and asked if they might come inside. She ushered them into the house, where they waited 10 or 15 minutes until the petitioner returned home from work. When the petitioner entered the house, one of the officers handed him the arrest warrant and asked for permission to "look around." The petitioner objected, but was advised that "on the basis of the lawful arrest," the officers would nonetheless conduct a search. No search warrant had been issued.

Accompanied by the petitioner's wife, the officers then looked through the entire three-bedroom house, including the attic, the garage, and a small workshop. In some rooms the search was relatively cursory. In the master bedroom and sewing room, however, the officers directed the petitioner's wife to open drawers and "to physically move contents of the drawers from side to side so that [they] might view any items that would have come from [the] burglary." After completing the search, they seized numerous items—primarily coins, but also several medals, tokens, and a few other objects. The entire search took between 45 minutes and an hour.

At the petitioner's subsequent state trial on two charges of burglary, the items taken from his house were admitted into evidence against him, over his objection that they had been unconstitutionally seized. He was convicted, and the judgments of conviction were affirmed by both the California District Court of Appeal . . . and the California Supreme Court. . . . Both courts accepted the petitioner's contention that the arrest warrant was invalid because the supporting affidavit was set out in conclusory terms, but held that since the arresting officers had procured the warrant "in good faith," and since in any event they had had sufficient information to constitute probable cause for the petitioner's arrest, that arrest had been lawful. From this conclusion the appellate courts went on to hold that the search of the petitioner's home had been justified, despite the absence of a search warrant, on the ground that it had been incident to a valid arrest. We granted certiorari in order to consider the petitioner's substantial constitutional claims. . . .

Without deciding the question, we proceed on the hypothesis that the California courts were correct in holding that the arrest of the petitioner was valid under the Constitution. This brings us directly to the question whether the warrantless search of the petitioner's entire house can be constitutionally justified as incident to that arrest. The decisions of this

Court bearing upon that question have been far from consistent, as even the most cursory review makes evident.

. . .

[I]n Harris v. United States, 331 U.S. 145, decided in 1947 . . . officers had obtained a warrant for Harris' arrest on the basis of his alleged involvement with the cashing and interstate transportation of a forged check. He was arrested in the living room of his four-room apartment, and in an attempt to recover two canceled checks thought to have been used in effecting the forgery, the officers undertook a thorough search of the entire apartment. Inside a desk drawer they found a sealed envelope marked "George Harris, personal papers." The envelope, which was then torn open, was found to contain altered selective service documents, and those documents were used to secure Harris' conviction for violating the Selective Training and Service Act of 1940. The Court rejected Harris' Fourth Amendment claim, sustaining the search as "incident to arrest." Id., at 151.

Only a year after *Harris*, however, the pendulum swung again. In Trupiano v. United States, 334 U.S. 699, agents raided the site of an illicit distillery, saw one of several conspirators operating the still, and arrested him, contemporaneously "seiz[ing] the illicit distillery." Id., at 702. The Court held that the arrest and others made subsequently had been valid, but that the unexplained failure of the agents to procure a search warrant—in spite of the fact that they had had more than enough time before the raid to do so—rendered the search unlawful. The opinion stated:

> It is a cardinal rule that, in seizing goods and articles, law enforcement agents must secure and use search warrants wherever reasonably practicable. . . . This rule rests upon the desirability of having magistrates rather than police officers determine when searches and seizures are permissible and what limitations should be placed upon such activities. . . . To provide the necessary security against unreasonable intrusions upon the private lives of individuals, the framers of the Fourth Amendment required adherence to judicial processes wherever possible. And subsequent history has confirmed the wisdom of that requirement.
>
> . . .
>
> A search or seizure without a warrant as an incident to a lawful arrest has always been considered to be a strictly limited right. It grows out of the inherent necessities of the situation at the time of the arrest. But there must be something more in the way of necessity than merely a lawful arrest.

Id., at 705, 708.

In 1950, two years after *Trupiano*, came United States v. Rabinowitz, 339 U.S. 56, the decision upon which California primarily relies in the case now before us. In *Rabinowitz*, federal authorities had been informed that the defendant was dealing in stamps bearing forged overprints. On the basis of that information they secured a warrant for his arrest, which they

executed at his one-room business office. At the time of the arrest, the officers "searched the desk, safe, and file cabinets in the office for about an hour and a half," id., at 59, and seized 573 stamps with forged overprints. The stamps were admitted into evidence at the defendant's trial, and this Court affirmed his conviction, rejecting the contention that the warrantless search had been unlawful. The Court held that the search in its entirety fell within the principle giving law enforcement authorities "[t]he right 'to search the place where the arrest is made in order to find and seize things connected with the crime. . . .' " Id., at 61. *Harris* was regarded as "ample authority" for that conclusion. Id., at 63. The opinion rejected the rule of *Trupiano* that "in seizing goods and articles, law enforcement agents must secure and use search warrants wherever reasonably practicable." The test, said the Court, "is not whether it is reasonable to procure a search warrant, but whether the search was reasonable." Id., at 66.

Rabinowitz has come to stand for the proposition, inter alia, that a warrantless search "incident to a lawful arrest" may generally extend to the area that is considered to be in the "possession" or under the "control" of the person arrested. And it was on the basis of that proposition that the California courts upheld the search of the petitioner's entire house in this case. That doctrine, however, at least in the broad sense in which it was applied by the California courts in this case, can withstand neither historical nor rational analysis.

Even limited to its own facts, the *Rabinowitz* decision was, as we have seen, hardly founded on an unimpeachable line of authority. . . .

Nor is the rationale by which the State seeks here to sustain the search of the petitioner's house supported by a reasoned view of the background and purpose of the Fourth Amendment. Mr. Justice Frankfurter wisely pointed out in his *Rabinowitz* dissent that the Amendment's proscription of "unreasonable searches and seizures" must be read in light of "the history that gave rise to the words"—a history of "abuses so deeply felt by the Colonies as to be one of the potent causes of the Revolution. . . ." 339 U.S., at 69. The Amendment was in large part a reaction to the general warrants and warrantless searches that had so alienated the colonists and had helped speed the movement for independence. In the scheme of the Amendment, therefore, the requirement that "no Warrants shall issue, but upon probable cause," plays a crucial part. As the Court put it in McDonald v. United States, 335 U.S. 451:

> We are not dealing with formalities. The presence of a search warrant serves a high function. Absent some grave emergency, the Fourth Amendment has interposed a magistrate between the citizen and the police. This was done not to shield criminals nor to make the home a safe haven for illegal activities. It was done so that an objective mind might weigh the need to invade that privacy in order to enforce the law. The right of privacy was deemed too precious to entrust to the discretion of those whose job is the detection of crime and the arrest of criminals. . . . And so the Constitution requires a magistrate to pass on the desires of the police before they violate the privacy of the home.

> We cannot be true to that constitutional requirement and excuse the absence of a search warrant without a showing by those who seek exemption from the constitutional mandate that the exigencies of the situation made that course imperative.

Id., at 455–56. . . . Clearly, the general requirement that a search warrant be obtained is not lightly to be dispensed with, and "the burden is on those seeking [an] exemption [from the requirement] to show the need for it. . . . " United States v. Jeffers, 342 U.S. 48, 51.

Only last Term in Terry v. Ohio, 392 U.S. 1, we emphasized that "the police must, whenever practicable, obtain advance judicial approval of searches and seizures through the warrant procedure," id., at 20, and that "[t]he scope of [a] search must be 'strictly tied to and justified by' the circumstances which rendered its initiation permissible." Id., at 19. . . .

A similar analysis underlies the "search incident to arrest" principle, and marks its proper extent. When an arrest is made, it is reasonable for the arresting officer to search the person arrested in order to remove any weapons that the latter might seek to use in order to resist arrest or effect his escape. Otherwise, the officer's safety might well be endangered, and the arrest itself frustrated. In addition, it is entirely reasonable for the arresting officer to search for and seize any evidence on the arrestee's person in order to prevent its concealment or destruction. And the area into which an arrestee might reach in order to grab a weapon or evidentiary items must, of course, be governed by a like rule. A gun on a table or in a drawer in front of one who is arrested can be as dangerous to the arresting officer as one concealed in the clothing of the person arrested. There is ample justification, therefore, for a search of the arrestee's person and the area "within his immediate control"—construing that phrase to mean the area from within which he might gain possession of a weapon or destructible evidence.

There is no comparable justification, however, for routinely searching rooms other than that in which an arrest occurs—or, for that matter, for searching through all the desk drawers or other closed or concealed areas in that room itself. Such searches, in the absence of well-recognized exceptions, may be made only under the authority of a search warrant. The "adherence to judicial processes" mandated by the Fourth Amendment requires no less.

. . .

It is argued in the present case that it is "reasonable" to search a man's house when he is arrested in it. But that argument is founded on little more than a subjective view regarding the acceptability of certain sorts of police conduct, and not on considerations relevant to Fourth Amendment interests. Under such an unconfined analysis, Fourth Amendment protection in this area would approach the evaporation point. It is not easy to explain why, for instance, it is less subjectively "reasonable" to search a man's house when he is arrested on his front lawn—or just down the street—than it is when he happens to be in the house at the time of arrest. As Mr. Justice Frankfurter put it:

> To say that the search must be reasonable is to require some criterion of reason. It is no guide at all either for a jury or for district judges or the police to say that an "unreasonable search" is forbidden—that the search must be reasonable. What is the test of reason which makes a search reasonable? The test is the reason underlying and expressed by the Fourth Amendment: the history and the experience which it embodies and the safeguards afforded by it against the evils to which it was a response.

United States v. Rabinowitz, 339 U.S., at 83 (dissenting opinion). Thus, although "[t]he recurring questions of the reasonableness of searches" depend upon "the facts and circumstances—the total atmosphere of the case," id., at 63, 66 (opinion of the Court), those facts and circumstances must be viewed in the light of established Fourth Amendment principles.

It would be possible, of course, to draw a line between *Rabinowitz* and *Harris* on the one hand, and this case on the other. For *Rabinowitz* involved a single room, and *Harris* a four-room apartment, while in the case before us an entire house was searched. But such a distinction would be highly artificial. The rationale that allowed the searches and seizures in *Rabinowitz* and *Harris* would allow the searches and seizures in this case. No consideration relevant to the Fourth Amendment suggests any point of rational limitation, once the search is allowed to go beyond the area from which the person arrested might obtain weapons or evidentiary items. The only reasoned distinction is one between a search of the person arrested and the area within his reach on the one hand, and more extensive searches on the other.

The petitioner correctly points out that one result of decisions such as *Rabinowitz* and *Harris* is to give law enforcement officials the opportunity to engage in searches not justified by probable cause, by the simple expedient of arranging to arrest suspects at home rather than elsewhere. We do not suggest that the petitioner is necessarily correct in his assertion that such a strategy was utilized here, but the fact remains that had he been arrested earlier in the day, at his place of employment rather than at home, no search of his house could have been made without a search warrant. In any event, even apart from the possibility of such police tactics, the general point so forcefully made by Judge Learned Hand in United States v. Kirschenblatt, 16 F.2d 202, remains:

> After arresting a man in his house, to rummage at will among his papers in search of whatever will convict him, appears to us to be indistinguishable from what might be done under a general warrant; indeed, the warrant would give more protection, for presumably it must be issued by a magistrate. True, by hypothesis the power would not exist if the supposed offender were not found on the premises; but it is small consolation to know that one's papers are safe only so long as one is not at home.

Id., at 203.

Rabinowitz and *Harris* have been the subject of critical commentary for many years, and have been relied upon less and less in our own decisions. It is time, for the reasons we have stated, to hold that on their own facts, and insofar as the principles they stand for are inconsistent with those that we have endorsed today, they are no longer to be followed.

Application of sound Fourth Amendment principles to the facts of this case produces a clear result. The search here went far beyond the petitioner's person and the area from within which he might have obtained either a weapon or something that could have been used as evidence against him. There was no constitutional justification, in the absence of a search warrant, for extending the search beyond that area. The scope of the search was, therefore, "unreasonable" under the Fourth and Fourteenth Amendments, and the petitioner's conviction cannot stand.[8]

---

116. As the Court acknowledged in *Chimel*, above, the course of decisions concerning the scope of a valid search "incident to an arrest" has not been unwavering. In addition to the cases cited, see Weeks v. United States, 232 U.S. 383 (1914); Carroll v. United States, 267 U.S. 132 (1925); Agnello v. United States, 269 U.S. 20 (1925); Marron v. United States, 275 U.S. 192 (1927); Go-Bart Importing Co. v. United States, 282 U.S. 344 (1931); United States v. Lefkowitz, 285 U.S. 452 (1932), all discussed elsewhere in the Court's opinion in *Chimel*. See also Kremen v. United States, 353 U.S. 346 (1957); Abel v. United States, 362 U.S. 217 (1960).

117. How should *Chimel* be applied to items on the defendant's person at the time of his arrest that are themselves containers of other items? Such things include small containers carried by almost everyone, like a wallet or pocketbook, as well as large containers, like a briefcase or suitcase.

In United States v. Simpson, 453 F.2d 1028 (10th Cir.1972), for example, the defendant was arrested on a warrant charging him with possession and transportation of explosives. At the time of his arrest his wallet, found in his pocket, was searched and someone else's selective service documents were found. Simpson was prosecuted for the unlawful possession of the documents. His motion to suppress the documents was denied. The court said:

> The general rule is that incident to a lawful arrest, a search without a warrant may be made of portable personal effects in the immediate possession of the person arrested. The discovery during a search of a totally unrelated object which provides grounds for prosecution of a crime different than that which the accused was arrested for does not render the search invalid. . . . We observe that although the

[8] Justice Harlan wrote a concurring opinion. Justice White wrote a dissenting opinion, see note 122, p. 215 below, which Justice Black joined.

> general rule approved here does not require specific justification on a case-to-case basis, we take notice that knives and other small weapons can be secreted in wallets and that cards and addresses may disclose names of those who may have conspired with the person searched in the commission of the crime charged.

Id. at 1031. The reference to "personal property not immediately associated with the person," in *Chadwick*, p. 212 note 119 below, is evidently intended to refer to cases of this kind.

See, e.g., United States v. Harrison, 461 F.2d 1127 (5th Cir.1972). The defendant was arrested pursuant to a warrant charging him with parole violations. He was found lying on a mattress in his apartment. After arresting him, FBI agents found a wallet inside a cigar box on a table next to the mattress. There were documents in the wallet linking the defendant to new crimes. Relying on *Chimel*, the court upheld the use of the documents against him.

Is there any reason why the police should not remove a wallet and similar containers without searching them? Does *Chimel* on its own terms authorize the search of a wallet of an arrested person after it has been taken from his possession?

118. A group of about eight narcotics agents arrested the appellant Becker in his apartment at around midnight.

> Appellant was sitting on a couch in the living-dining room area of his apartment watching television. He was directed to stand next to a wall with his hands up against it. This location was approximately 12 feet from the corner of the couch where Becker was first seen, and was the nearest wall space free of furniture or openings. The arresting agent testified that he had no handcuffs and finally secured Becker with a belt. He stated that appellant kept turning around and "wasn't being real cooperative." Some four or five minutes elapsed before the prisoner was secured. Another agent who was in the same room said that Becker refused to follow orders—that he continued to turn around, kept his hands down instead of up and was constantly moving in a direction other than where he was told to remain. He described appellant's conduct as "resisting" and said it was almost five minutes before the resistance ended.
>
> There was a desk-type table three to five feet from where appellant was standing and the L.S.D. tablets were found in one of its drawers which had been closed. The agent who discovered the drugs stated, "There was a time when I secured the chest to make sure there were no weapons." He said that when Becker had been subdued the other agent searched the prisoner while he checked the surrounding area for weapons. This witness testified that he had put his gun away before he began his search for weapons and that he was "no longer threatened by the situation." However, since Becker had not been tied with the belt at that time, he considered that there was "still a potential danger." It was admitted that Becker never tried to use physical force

> on any agent. . . . [T]he agent who subdued Becker stated that he was searching him when the pills were found and that he did not believe he had put the belt on appellant's arms at that time.

United States v. Becker, 485 F.2d 51, 53 (6th Cir.1973).

Was the search of the table drawer permitted under *Chimel*?

In United States v. Myers, 308 F.3d 251 (3d Cir.2002), the court considered at length the permissible scope of a search incident to an arrest. Distinguishing the search of the passenger compartment of an automobile after the driver's arrest, which is governed by the *Belton* rule (p. 214 note 121) the court said that a search incident to an arrest is "reasonable" under the Fourth Amendment only "when it is confined to, and controlled by, the circumstances that warrant the intrusion," 308 F.3d at 266. Noting that the defendant, who was handcuffed behind his back, lying face down, and watched by two armed police officers, would have to have been an acrobat or Houdini to gain access to a school bag lying a few feet from him, the court held that a search of the bag by a third police officer was not permissible. See United States v. Griffith, 537 F.2d 900, 904 (7th Cir.1976), in which the court said: "Once a suspect is under the control of arresting officers, the area of permissible search under *Chimel* is narrowed accordingly." The area which the officers could search was not enlarged by the fact that they allowed the person whom they arrested to move freely about the room while getting dressed. "They did not have the right to create a situation which gave them a pretext for searching beyond the area of defendant's immediate control."

In People v. Fitzpatrick, 300 N.E.2d 139 (N.Y.1973), however, the court held that "the authorized 'grabbable' area" under *Chimel* included a closet in which the defendant had been hiding, so that the police could search the closet after the defendant had been removed from the closet, handcuffed, and taken out of the room into the hall, where the police advised him of his rights and questioned him briefly before returning to the closet to search it. In a ruling similar to *Fitzpatrick*, the court held that a search incident to an arrest could be conducted after the defendant had been handcuffed and removed from the room, in United States v. Turner, 926 F.2d 883 (9th Cir.1991). The court said that since the area searched was under the arrested person's immediate control at the moment of arrest and could have been searched then, it was reasonable to delay the search for a few minutes for the officers' safety. Does the reasoning of *Chimel* support that conclusion? See, to the same effect, United States v. Abdul-Saboor, 85 F.3d 664, 668 (D.C.Cir.1996) (area subject to "incident" search is not literally area within defendant's control but turns on "whether the arrest and search are so separated in time or by intervening events that the latter cannot fairly be said to have been incident to the former").

119. In United States v. Chadwick, 433 U.S. 1 (1977), the Court upheld a ruling that federal agents could not make a warrantless search of a heavy, locked footlocker that the defendants had placed in the trunk of a car just before their arrest. "Once law enforcement officers have reduced luggage or other personal property not immediately associated with the person of the arrestee to their exclusive control, and there is no longer any danger that the arrestee might gain access to the property to seize a weapon or destroy evidence, a search of that property is no longer an incident of the arrest." Id. at 15.

In United States v. Eatherton, 519 F.2d 603 (1st Cir.1975), decided before *Chadwick*, the court upheld the search of a briefcase carried by the defendant, who was arrested on the street and dropped the briefcase to the ground, as he was ordered; before searching the briefcase, the arresting officers handcuffed the defendant behind his back and placed him in their car. The court said that while "a briefcase may be a different order of container from a cigarette box, it is not easy to rest a principled articulation of the reach of the fourth amendment upon the distinction." Declining to rely on such "gossamer distinctions," the court concluded also that the cases indicated no difference between searching such a container if it were removed from the defendant's person and searching it after it had been dropped to the ground in response to a command. Id. at 610. In United States v. Schleis, 582 F.2d 1166 (8th Cir.1978), however, the court applied *Chadwick* and invalidated the stationhouse search of a locked briefcase taken from the defendant at the time of his arrest.

In United States v. Burnette, 698 F.2d 1038 (9th Cir.1983), a police officer seized and searched the defendant's purse at the time of her arrest. The search was lawful as an incident of the arrest. Later, at the station the purse was searched more thoroughly and incriminating evidence was found. Reasoning that the initial search reduced the defendant's expectation of privacy, the court concluded that the subsequent search was lawful. "[O]nce an item in an individual's possession has been lawfully seized and searched, subsequent searches of that item, so long as it remains in the legitimate uninterrupted possession of the police, may be conducted without a warrant." Id. at 1038. Cf. United States v. Edwards, 415 U.S. 800 (1974), p. 221 below. With *Burnette*, compare United States v. Monclavo-Cruz, 662 F.2d 1285 (9th Cir.1981), in which the court held that the warrantless search of a woman's purse an hour after the woman had been arrested and the purse had been seized from the car in which she had been riding was not lawful.

Chadwick evidently distinguishes between "personal property . . . immediately associated with the person" and other kinds of containers in the possession of a person who is arrested, the former being subject to a full search incident to the arrest and the latter not. What does the quoted phrase mean? Is it equivalent to the common distinction in ordinary language between things carried "on the person" and things carried "by the person"? What justification is there, under *Chimel* or otherwise, for such a distinction?

120. Customs officials opened a large, locked metal container that was shipped to the United States from abroad. Marijuana was found inside. Following the practice of "controlled delivery" in order to determine the owner of the container, the officials resealed the container and delivered it to the addressee. After the delivery, they maintained close but imperfect surveillance over the container. Before they could obtain a warrant to seize the container, the person to whom delivery was made left his apartment with it. The officials arrested him, seized the container, and reopened it at the police station. The marijuana inside was seized.

The Court held that the second warrantless seizure and search were lawful, since there was not a "substantial likelihood" that the contents of the container had been changed between the first and second searches. "It is obvious that the privacy interest in the contents of a container diminishes with respect to a container that law enforcement authorities have already lawfully opened and found to contain illicit drugs. No protected privacy interest remains in contraband in a container once government officers lawfully have opened that container and identified its contents as illegal. The simple act of resealing the container to enable the police to make a controlled delivery does not operate to revive or restore the lawfully invaded privacy rights." Illinois v. Andreas, 463 U.S. 765, 771 (1983) (7–2).

Compare Walter v. United States, 447 U.S. 649 (1980) (5–4), holding that government agents, having lawfully obtained possession of films that they believed to be obscene, were required to obtain a warrant before screening the films. With *Walter*, compare United States v. Passaro, 624 F.2d 938 (9th Cir.1980), upholding the search of an arrested person's wallet and photocopying of a document found in the wallet unrelated to the crime for which he was arrested.

121. In New York v. Belton, 453 U.S. 454 (1981) (6–3), the Court held that a search incident to a lawful custodial arrest of the occupant of an automobile can extend to the entire passenger compartment of the automobile, including all containers, closed or open, within it. "Container," the Court said, includes "any object capable of holding another object," including the glove compartment, luggage, boxes, clothing, etc. Id. at 460 n.4. Quoting *Chimel*, the Court based its conclusion on "the generalization that articles inside the relatively narrow compass of the passenger compartment of an automobile are in fact generally, even if not inevitably, within 'the area into which an arrestee might reach in order to grab a weapon or evidentiary item.' " Id. at 460.

Belton authorizes a search of the passenger compartment of a vehicle after the occupant has been ordered out and arrested, handcuffed, and placed in the back of a police car. E.g., United States v. McLaughlin, 170 F.3d 889 (9th Cir.1999) (search lawful although driver had already been removed from scene); United States v. Doward, 41 F.3d 789 (1st Cir.1994). Generally confirming this line of reasoning, the Court held that a *Belton* search is lawful if the police officer does not initiate contact until the occupant of an automobile has left it, provided that he left it "recently" and is still in close proximity to it. Thornton v. United States, 541 U.S. ___ (2004) (7–2). The Court said that in those circumstances the justifications for a warrantless arrest that were stated in *Chimel*—"to remove any weapon the arrestee might seek to use to resist arrest or to escape, and . . . to prevent the concealment or destruction of evidence," id. at ___—remains applicable. In a separate opinion, Justice Scalia argued that the rationale of *Chimel* does not justify a search in those circumstances. Rather, he said, if the officer has reasonable grounds to believe that evidence relevant to the crime for which the person has been arrested will be found in the automobile, a search is justified under the pre-*Chimel* rationale of United States v. Rabinowitz, p. 206 above. 541 U.S. at ___ (opinion concurring in the judgment).

Belton evidently sets up a potential conflict with *Chadwick*, p. ___ note 119 above. Why should a container be more subject to search if it is found as an incident of the arrest of the occupant of a car than if a person is arrested while carrying it? See note 129, p. 235 below.

122. In a dissenting opinion in *Chimel*, above, Justice White argued: "An arrest itself may often create an emergency situation making it impracticable to obtain a warrant before embarking on a related search. Again assuming that there is probable cause to search premises at the spot where a suspect is arrested, it seems to me unreasonable to require the police to leave the scene in order to obtain a search warrant when they are already legally there to make a valid arrest, and when there must almost always be a strong possibility that confederates of the arrested man will in the meanwhile remove the items for which the police have probable cause to search. This must so often be the case that it seems to me as unreasonable to require a warrant for a search of the premises as to require a warrant for search of the person and his very immediate surroundings." 395 U.S. at 773–74.

Assuming, as the majority in *Chimel* concluded, that Justice White's factual assertions are an insufficient basis for a rule generally allowing searches of premises where an arrest occurs, does *Chimel* allow justification of a warrantless search of premises in particular cases if the police have special reason to believe that evidence (or, more particularly, contraband or stolen goods) is on the premises and will be removed before a warrant can be obtained? If not, what action can the police take in such cases to prevent removal of the items in question?

In a footnote to its opinion in *Chimel*, the Court said: "Our holding today is of course entirely consistent with the recognized principle that, assuming the existence of probable cause, automobiles and other vehicles may be searched without warrants 'where it is not practicable to secure a warrant because the vehicle can be quickly moved out of the locality or jurisdiction in which the warrant must be sought.' Carroll v. United States, 267 U.S. 132, 153 ..." 395 U.S. at 764 n.9. In view of the Court's rejection of Justice White's argument, are *Chimel* and *Carroll* "entirely consistent"?

Compare Vale v. Louisiana, 399 U.S. 30 (1970), p. 226 below, with Chambers v. Maroney, 399 U.S. 42 (1970), p. 228 below, which the Court decided on the same day.

123. A police officer arrested the defendant's roommate and accompanied him to his room for him to get identification. Waiting at the door of the room, the officer saw what appeared to be marijuana inside. He entered the room, confirmed that what he had seen was marijuana, and seized it. The defendant was subsequently prosecuted for possession of the marijuana. Holding that the entry into the room was lawful, the Court said:

> [I]t is not "unreasonable" under the Fourth Amendment for a police officer, as a matter of routine, to monitor the movements of an arrested person, as his judgment dictates, following the arrest. The officer's need to ensure his own safety—as well as the integrity of the arrest—is compelling. Such surveillance is not an impermissible invasion of the privacy or personal liberty of an individual who has been arrested.

Washington v. Chrisman, 455 U.S. 1, 7 (1982) (6–3).

124. A search of the person incident to an arrest for a traffic offense, for which the arrestee is taken into custody, was upheld in United States v. Robinson, 414 U.S. 218 (1973) (6–3). Robinson was stopped and arrested for driving without a license. The arresting officer patted him down and felt an object in Robinson's coat pocket. He reached into the pocket and removed the object, which turned out to be a crumpled cigarette packet. He opened the packet and found narcotics, for possession of which Robinson was prosecuted. The Court distinguished a search of the person from a search of the area surrounding the person. The former, the Court said, as an incident of a lawful arrest, had never been questioned. In particular, a search of the person is not limited to the "frisk" authorized by Terry v. Ohio, p. 100 above.

> The justification or reason for the authority to search incident to a lawful arrest rests quite as much on the need to disarm the suspect in order to take him into custody as it does on the need to preserve evidence on his person for later use at trial. . . . The standards traditionally governing a search incident to lawful arrest are not, therefore, commuted to the stricter *Terry* standards by the absence of probable fruits or further evidence of the particular crime for which the arrest is made.
>
> Nor are we inclined, on the basis of what seems to us to be a rather speculative judgment, to qualify the breadth of the general authority to search incident to a lawful custodial arrest on an assumption that persons arrested for the offense of driving while their license has been revoked are less likely to be possessed of dangerous weapons than are those arrested for other crimes. It is scarcely open to doubt that the danger to an officer is far greater in the case of the extended exposure which follows the taking of a suspect into custody and transporting him to the police station than in the case of the relatively fleeting contact resulting from the typical *Terry*-type stop. This is an adequate basis for treating all custodial arrests alike for purposes of search justification.
>
> But quite apart from these distinctions . . . [we do not agree] that there must be litigated in each case the issue of whether or not there was present one of the reasons supporting the authority for a search of

> the person incident to a lawful arrest. We do not think the long line of authorities of this Court dating back to *Weeks* [v. United States, 232 U.S. 383 (1914)], nor what we can glean from the history of practice in this country and in England, requires such a case by case adjudication. A police officer's determination as to how and where to search the person of a suspect whom he has arrested is necessarily a quick ad hoc judgment which the Fourth Amendment does not require to be broken down in each instance into an analysis of each step in the search. The authority to search the person incident to a lawful custodial arrest, while based upon the need to disarm and to discover evidence, does not depend on what a court may later decide was the probability in a particular arrest situation that weapons or evidence would in fact be found upon the person of the suspect. A custodial arrest of a suspect based on probable cause is a reasonable intrusion under the Fourth Amendment; that intrusion being lawful, a search incident to the arrest requires no additional justification. It is the fact of the lawful arrest which establishes the authority to search, and we hold that in the case of a lawful custodial arrest a full search of the person is not only an exception to the warrant requirement of the Fourth Amendment, but is also a "reasonable" search under that Amendment.

414 U.S. at 234–35.

In Knowles v. Iowa, 525 U.S. 113 (1998), the Court apparently regarded *Robinson* as authorizing a search not only of the person of someone who is arrested for a traffic offense but also of the car, as an incident of the arrest. See id. at 118. However, in *Knowles* the Court declined to apply that rule if a person is stopped for a traffic offense and issued a citation, instead of being arrested. The Court said that in such a case the risk to the officer is less and there is no concern about the destruction of evidence, so a general "bright-line rule" as in *Robinson* was inapt.

The courts in several states have rejected the reasoning of *Robinson*, on the basis of the state constitution. In Zehrung v. State, 569 P.2d 189, 199–200 (Alaska 1977), for example, the court said: "[A]bsent specific articulable facts justifying the intrusion . . . a warrantless search incident to an arrest, other than for weapons, is unreasonable and therefore violative of the Alaska Constitution if the charge on which the arrest is made is not one, evidence of which could be concealed on the person." (On a petition for rehearing, the ruling was later qualified.) The court said that the stated rule "should normally be followed unless exigencies demand a different course of action." 573 P.2d 858 (Alaska 1978). To the same effect, see People v. Brisendine, 531 P.2d 1099 (Cal.1975); People v. Clyne, 541 P.2d 71 (Colo.1975); State v. Kaluna, 520 P.2d 51 (Haw.1974).

125. Protective sweep. In Maryland v. Buie, 494 U.S. 325, 327 (1990) (7–2), the Court upheld the practice of a "protective sweep": "a quick and limited search of premises, incident to an arrest and conducted to protect the safety of police officers or others . . . narrowly confined to a cursory visual inspection of those places in which a person might be hiding." The Court said that the reasoning that justified a frisk on the street in Terry v. Ohio, p. 100 above, and the search of a car in Michigan v. Long, p. 118 note 60 above, also justified a protective sweep. "In the instant case, there is an analogous interest of the officers in taking steps to assure themselves that the house in which a suspect is being or has just been arrested is not harboring other persons who are dangerous and who could unexpectedly launch an attack. The risk of danger in the context of an arrest in the home is as great as, if not greater than, it is in an on-the-street or roadside investigatory encounter. A *Terry* or *Long* frisk occurs before a police-citizen confrontation has escalated to the point of arrest. A protective sweep, in contrast, occurs as an adjunct to the serious step of taking a person into custody for the purpose of prosecuting him for a crime. Moreover, unlike an encounter on the street or along a highway, an in-home arrest puts the officer at the disadvantage of being on his adversary's 'turf.' An ambush in a confined setting of unknown configuration is more to be feared than it is in open, more familiar surroundings." 494 U.S. at 333.

The Court held that when an arrest is made inside a house or other premises, the arresting officers can

> as a precautionary matter and without probable cause or reasonable suspicion, look in closets and other spaces immediately adjoining the place of arrest from which an attack could be immediately launched. Beyond that . . . there must be articulable facts which, taken together with the rational inferences from those facts, would warrant a reasonably prudent officer in believing that the area to be swept harbors an individual posing a danger to those on the arrest scene. . . .
>
> [S]uch a protective sweep, aimed at protecting the arresting officers, if justified by the circumstances, is nevertheless not a full search of the premises, but may extend only to a cursory inspection of those spaces where a person may be found. The sweep lasts no longer than is necessary to dispel the reasonable suspicion of danger and in any event no longer than it takes to complete the arrest and depart the premises.

Id. at 334–36.

Justice Brennan, dissenting, observed that the Court for the first time had dispensed with the requirement of a warrant and probable cause inside private premises. Id. at 339.

Compare the majority and dissenting opinions in Vale v. Louisiana, p. 226 below.

See United States v. Biggs, 70 F.3d 913 (6th Cir.1995) (arrest of defendant in parking lot justified protective sweep of motel room); United States v. Ford, 56 F.3d 265 (D.C.Cir.1995) (search under mattress and behind window shades exceeded permissible scope of protective sweep).

Cupp v. Murphy

412 U.S. 291, 93 S.Ct. 2000, 36 L.Ed.2d 900 (1973)

■ MR. JUSTICE STEWART delivered the opinion of the Court.

The respondent, Daniel Murphy, was convicted by a jury in an Oregon court of the second-degree murder of his wife. The victim died by strangulation in her home in the city of Portland, and abrasions and lacerations were found on her throat. There was no sign of a break-in or robbery. Word of the murder was sent to the respondent, who was not then living with his wife. Upon receiving the message, Murphy promptly telephoned the Portland police and voluntarily came into Portland for questioning. Shortly after the respondent's arrival at the station house, where he was met by retained counsel, the police noticed a dark spot on the respondent's finger. Suspecting that the spot might be dried blood and knowing that evidence of strangulation is often found under the assailant's fingernails, the police asked Murphy if they could take a sample of scrapings from his fingernails. He refused. Under protest and without a warrant, the police proceeded to take the samples, which turned out to contain traces of skin and blood cells, and fabric from the victim's nightgown. This incriminating evidence was admitted at the trial.

The respondent appealed his conviction, claiming that the fingernail scrapings were the product of an unconstitutional search under the Fourth and Fourteenth Amendments. The Oregon Court of Appeals affirmed the conviction . . . and we denied certiorari. . . . Murphy then commenced the present action for federal habeas corpus relief. The District Court, in an unreported decision, denied the habeas petition, and the Court of Appeals for the Ninth Circuit reversed. . . . The Court of Appeals assumed the presence of probable cause to search or arrest, but held that in the absence of an arrest or other exigent circumstances, the search was unconstitutional. . . . We granted certiorari . . . to consider the constitutional question presented.

. . .

It is . . . undisputed that the police did not obtain an arrest warrant or formally "arrest" the respondent, as that term is understood under Oregon law. The respondent was detained only long enough to take the fingernail scrapings, and was not formally "arrested" until approximately one month later. Nevertheless, the detention of the respondent against his will constituted a seizure of his person, and the Fourth Amendment guarantee of freedom from "unreasonable searches and seizures" is clearly implicated. . . . As the Court said in Davis v. Mississippi, 394 U.S. 721, 726–27, "Nothing is more clear than that the Fourth Amendment was meant to prevent wholesale intrusions upon the personal security of our citizenry, whether these intrusions be termed 'arrests' or 'investigatory detentions.'"

In *Davis*, the Court held that fingerprints obtained during the brief detention of persons seized in a police dragnet procedure, without probable cause, were inadmissible in evidence. Though the Court recognized that fingerprinting "involves none of the probing into an individual's private life and thoughts that marks an interrogation or search," 394 U.S., at 727, the Court held the stationhouse detention in that case to be violative of the Fourth and Fourteenth Amendments. "Investigatory seizures would subject unlimited numbers of innocent persons to the harassment and ignominy incident to involuntary detention," id., at 726.

The respondent in this case, like Davis, was briefly detained at the station house. Yet here, there was . . . probable cause to believe that the respondent had committed the murder. The vice of the detention in *Davis* is therefore absent in the case before us. . . .

The inquiry does not end here, however, because Murphy was subjected to a search as well as a seizure of his person. Unlike the fingerprinting in *Davis*, the voice exemplar obtained in United States v. Dionisio, [410 U.S. 1 (1973)], or the handwriting exemplar obtained in United States v. Mara, 410 U.S. 19, the search of the respondent's fingernails went beyond mere "physical characteristics . . . constantly exposed to the public," United States v. Dionisio, supra, at 14, and constituted the type of "severe, though brief, intrusion upon cherished personal security" that is subject to constitutional scrutiny. Terry v. Ohio, [392 U.S. 1 (1968)], at 24–25.

We believe this search was constitutionally permissible under the principles of Chimel v. California, 395 U.S. 752. *Chimel* stands in a long line of cases recognizing an exception to the warrant requirement when a search is incident to a valid arrest. . . . The basis for this exception is that when an arrest is made, it is reasonable for a police officer to expect the arrestee to use any weapons he may have and to attempt to destroy any incriminating evidence then in his possession. . . . The Court recognized in *Chimel* that the scope of a warrantless search must be commensurate with the rationale that excepts the search from the warrant requirement. Thus, a warrantless search incident to arrest, the Court held in *Chimel*, must be limited to the area "into which an arrestee might reach." 395 U.S., at 763.

Where there is no formal arrest, as in the case before us, a person might well be less hostile to the police and less likely to take conspicuous, immediate steps to destroy incriminating evidence on his person. Since he knows he is going to be released, he might be likely instead to be concerned with diverting attention away from himself. Accordingly, we do not hold that a full *Chimel* search would have been justified in this case without a formal arrest and without a warrant. But the respondent was not subjected to such a search.

At the time Murphy was being detained at the station house, he was obviously aware of the detectives' suspicions. Though he did not have the full warning of official suspicion that a formal arrest provides, Murphy was sufficiently apprised of his suspected role in the crime to motivate him to attempt to destroy what evidence he could without attracting further attention. Testimony at trial indicated that after he refused to consent to the taking of fingernail samples, he put his hands behind his back and appeared to rub them together. He then put his hands in his pockets, and a "metallic sound, such as keys or change rattling" was heard. The rationale of *Chimel*, in these circumstances, justified the police in subjecting him to the very limited search necessary to preserve the highly evanescent evidence they found under his fingernails. . . .

On the facts of this case, considering the existence of probable cause, the very limited intrusion undertaken incident to the station house detention, and the ready destructibility of the evidence, we cannot say that this search violated the Fourth and Fourteenth Amendments. Accordingly, the judgment of the Court of Appeals is reversed.[9]

United States v. Edwards

415 U.S. 800, 94 S.Ct. 1234, 39 L.Ed.2d 771 (1974)

■ MR. JUSTICE WHITE delivered the opinion of the Court.

The question here is whether the Fourth Amendment should be extended to exclude from evidence certain clothing taken from respondent Edwards while he was in custody at the city jail approximately 10 hours after his arrest.

Shortly after 11 p.m. on May 31, 1970, respondent Edwards was lawfully arrested on the streets of Lebanon, Ohio, and charged with attempting to break into that city's Post Office. He was taken to the local jail and placed in a cell. Contemporaneously or shortly thereafter, investigation at the scene revealed that the attempted entry had been made through a wooden window which apparently had been pried up with a pry bar, leaving paint chips on the window sill and wire mesh screen. The next morning, trousers and a T-shirt were purchased for Edwards to substitute for the clothing which he had been wearing at the time of and since his arrest. His clothing was then taken from him and held as evidence. Examination of the clothing revealed paint chips matching the samples that had been taken from the window. This evidence and his clothing were received at trial over Edwards' objection that neither the clothing nor the results of its examination were admissible because the warrantless seizure of his clothing was invalid under the Fourth Amendment.

The Court of Appeals reversed. Expressly disagreeing with two other courts of appeals, it held that although the arrest was lawful and probable cause existed to believe that paint chips would be discovered on petitioner's clothing, the warrantless seizure of the clothing carried out "after the administrative process and mechanics of arrest have come to a halt" was nevertheless unconstitutional under the Fourth Amendment. United States v. Edwards, 474 F.2d 1206, 1211 (CA6 1973). We granted certiorari . . .

[9] Justice Marshall wrote a concurring opinion. Justice Blackmun wrote a brief concurring opinion which Chief Justice Burger joined. Justice Powell wrote a brief concurring opinion which Chief Justice Burger and Justice Rehnquist joined. Justice White noted that he thought the issue of probable cause remained open on remand. Justice Douglas and Justice Brennan wrote opinions dissenting in part.

and now conclude that the Fourth Amendment should not be extended to invalidate the search and seizure in the circumstances of this case.

The prevailing rule under the Fourth Amendment that searches and seizures may not be made without a warrant is subject to various exceptions. One of them permits warrantless searches incident to custodial arrests . . . and has traditionally been justified by the reasonableness of searching for weapons, instruments of escape and evidence of crime when a person is taken into official custody and lawfully detained. . . .

It is also plain that searches and seizures that could be made on the spot at the time of arrest may legally be conducted later when the accused arrives at the place of detention. If need be, Abel v. United States, 362 U.S. 217 (1960), settled this question. There the defendant was arrested at his hotel, but the belongings taken with him to the place of detention were searched there. In sustaining the search, the Court noted that a valid search of the property could have been made at the place of arrest and perceived little difference

> when the accused decides to take the property with him, for the search of it to occur instead at the first place of detention when the accused arrives there, especially as the search of the property carried by the accused to the place of detention has additional justification, similar to those which justify search of the person of one who is arrested.

Id., at 239. The Courts of Appeals have followed this same rule, holding that both the person and the property in his immediate possession may be searched at the station house after the arrest has occurred at another place and if evidence of crime is discovered, it may be seized and admitted in evidence. Nor is there any doubt that clothing or other belongings may be seized upon arrival of the accused at the place of detention and later subjected to laboratory analysis or that the test results are admissible at trial.

Conceding all this, the Court of Appeals in this case nevertheless held that a warrant is required where the search occurs after the administrative mechanics of arrest have been completed and the prisoner is incarcerated. But even on these terms, it seems to us that the normal processes incident to arrest and custody had not been completed when Edwards was placed in his cell on the night of May 31. With or without probable cause, the authorities were entitled at that point in time not only to search Edwards' clothing but also to take it from him and keep it in official custody. There was testimony that this was the standard practice in this city. The police were also entitled to take from Edwards any evidence of the crime in his immediate possession, including his clothing. And the Court of Appeals acknowledged that contemporaneously with or shortly after the time Edwards went to his cell, the police had probable cause to believe that the articles of clothing he wore were themselves material evidence of the crime for which he had been arrested. . . . But it was late at night; no substitute clothing was then available for Edwards to wear, and it would certainly have been unreasonable for the police to have stripped petitioner of his clothing and left him exposed in his cell throughout the night. . . . When the substitutes were purchased the next morning, the clothing he had been wearing at the time of arrest was taken from him and subjected to laboratory analysis. This was no more than taking from petitioner the effects in his immediate possession that constituted evidence of crime. This was and is a normal incident of a custodial arrest, and reasonable delay in effectuating it does not change the fact that Edwards was no more imposed upon than he could have been at the time and place of the arrest or immediately upon arrival at the place of detention. The police did no more on June 1 than they were entitled to do incident to the usual custodial arrest and incarceration.

Other closely related considerations sustain the examination of the clothing in this case. It must be remembered that on both May 31 and June 1 the police had lawful custody of Edwards and necessarily of the clothing he wore. When it became apparent that the articles of clothing were evidence of the crime for which Edwards was being held, the police were entitled to take, examine, and preserve them for use as evidence, just as they are normally permitted to seize evidence of crime when it is lawfully encountered. . . . Surely, the clothes could have been brushed down and vacuumed while Edwards had them on in the cell, and it was similarly reasonable to take and examine them as the police did, particularly in view of the existence of probable cause linking the clothes to the crime. Indeed, it is difficult to perceive what is unreasonable about the police examining and holding as evidence those personal effects of the accused that they already have in their lawful custody as the result of a lawful arrest.

. . .

[O]nce the defendant is lawfully arrested and is in custody, the effects in his possession at the place of detention that were subject to search at the time and place of his arrest may lawfully be searched and seized without a warrant even though a substantial period of time has elapsed between the arrest and subsequent administrative processing on the one hand and the taking of the property for use as evidence on the other. This is true where the clothing or effects are immediately seized upon arrival at the jail, held under the defendant's name in the "property room" of the jail and at a later time searched and taken for use at the subsequent criminal trial. The result is the same where the property is not physically taken from the defendant until sometime after his incarceration.

In upholding this search and seizure, we do not conclude that the warrant clause of the Fourth Amendment is never applicable to post-arrest seizures of the effects of an arrestee.[10] But we do think that the Court of

10. Holding the Warrant Clause inapplicable in the circumstances present here does not leave law enforcement officials subject to no restraints. This type of police conduct "must [still] be tested by the Fourth Amendment's general proscription against unreasonable searches and seizures." Terry v. Ohio, 392 U.S. 1, 20 (1968). But the Court of Appeals here conceded that probable cause existed for the search and seizure of petitioner's clothing, and petitioner complains only that a warrant should have been secured. We thus have no occasion to express a view concerning those circumstances surrounding custodial searches incident to incarceration which might "violate the dictates of reason

Appeals for the First Circuit captured the essence of situations like these when it said in United States v. DeLeo, 422 F.2d [487 (1st Cir.1970)] at 493 (footnote omitted):

> While the legal arrest of a person should not destroy the privacy of his premises, it does—for at least a reasonable time and to a reasonable extent—take his own privacy out of the realm of protection from police interest in weapons, means of escape and evidence.

The judgment of the Court of Appeals is reversed.

So ordered.

■ MR. JUSTICE STEWART, with whom MR. JUSTICE DOUGLAS, MR. JUSTICE BRENNAN, and MR. JUSTICE MARSHALL join, dissenting.

The Court says that the question before us "is whether the Fourth Amendment should be extended" to prohibit the warrantless seizure of Edwards' clothing. I think, on the contrary, that the real question in this case is whether the Fourth Amendment is to be ignored. For in my view the judgment of the Court of Appeals can be reversed only by disregarding established Fourth Amendment principles firmly embodied in many previous decisions of this Court.

As the Court has repeatedly emphasized in the past, "the most basic constitutional rule in this area is that 'searches conducted outside the judicial process, without prior approval by judge or magistrate, are per se unreasonable under the Fourth Amendment—subject only to a few specifically established and well-delineated exceptions.'" Coolidge v. New Hampshire, 403 U.S. 443, 454–55. . . . Since it is conceded here that the seizure of Edwards' clothing was not made pursuant to a warrant, the question becomes whether the Government has met its burden of showing that the circumstances of this seizure brought it within one of the "jealously and carefully drawn"[11] exceptions to the warrant requirement.

The Court finds a warrant unnecessary in this case because of the custodial arrest of the respondent. It is of course well-settled that the Fourth Amendment permits a warrantless search or seizure incident to a constitutionally valid custodial arrest. . . . But the mere fact of an arrest does not allow the police to engage in warrantless searches of unlimited geographic or temporal scope. Rather, the search must be spatially limited to the person of the arrestee and the area within his reach . . . and must, as to time, be "substantially contemporaneous with the arrest," Stoner v. California, 376 U.S. 483, 486. . . .

Under the facts of this case, I am unable to agree with the Court's holding that the search was "incident" to Edwards' custodial arrest. The search here occurred fully 10 hours after he was arrested, at a time when the administrative processing and mechanics of arrest had long since come

either because of their number or their manner of perpetration." Charles v. United States, 278 F.2d 386, 389 (9th Cir. 1960). . . .

11. Jones v. United States, 357 U.S. 493, 499.

to an end. His clothes were not seized as part of an "inventory" of a prisoner's effects, nor were they taken pursuant to a routine exchange of civilian clothes for jail garb. And the considerations that typically justify a warrantless search incident to a lawful arrest were wholly absent here. . . .

Accordingly, I see no justification for dispensing with the warrant requirement here. The police had ample time to seek a warrant, and no exigent circumstances were present to excuse their failure to do so. Unless the exceptions to the warrant requirement are to be "enthroned into the rule," United States v. Rabinowitz, 339 U.S. 56, 80 (Frankfurter, J., dissenting), this is precisely the sort of situation where the Fourth Amendment requires a magistrate's prior approval for a search.

The Court says that the relevant question is "not whether it was reasonable to procure a search warrant, but whether the search itself was reasonable." Ante, at 807. Precisely such a view, however, was explicitly rejected in Chimel v. California, 395 U.S. [752 (1969)], at 764–65, where the Court characterized the argument as "founded on little more than a subjective view regarding the acceptability of certain sorts of police conduct, and not on considerations relevant to Fourth Amendment interests." . . .

The intrusion here was hardly a shocking one, and it cannot be said that the police acted in bad faith. The Fourth Amendment, however, was not designed to apply only to situations where the intrusion is massive and the violation of privacy shockingly flagrant. . . .

Because I believe that the Court today unjustifiably departs from well-settled constitutional principles, I respectfully dissent.

---

126. An inventory search of "property found on the person or in the possession of an arrested person who is to be jailed" was upheld in Illinois v. Lafayette, 462 U.S. 640 (1983). The Court mentioned the risks that a person's property would be stolen, that he would make a false claim that property was missing, and that he would injure himself or others. "Examining all the items removed from the arrestee's person or possession and listing or inventorying them is an entirely reasonable administrative procedure. It is immaterial whether the police actually fear any particular package or container; the need to protect against such risks arises independent of a particular officer's subjective concerns." Id. at 646. Responding to the suggestion that the interests of the police could be protected in a less intrusive way, such as allowing an arrested person to place his belongings in a secure locker, the Court said: "Perhaps so, but the real question is not what 'could have been achieved,' but whether the Fourth Amendment *requires* such steps; it is not our function to write a manual on administering routine, neutral procedures of the station house. Our role is to assure against violations of the Constitution." Id. at 647.

In Zehrung v. State, 569 P.2d 189 (Alaska 1977), modified, 573 P.2d 858 (1978), the court limited the authority to make an "inventory search" of a person who is taken into custody: "[W]hen one is arrested and brought to a jail for a minor offense for which bail has already been set in a bail schedule, he should be allowed a reasonable opportunity to attempt to raise bail before being subjected to the remand and booking procedures and the incident inventory search." 569 P.2d at 195.

See Mary Beth G. v. City of Chicago, 723 F.2d 1263 (7th Cir.1983) (policy of conducting strip search of all women arrested for misdemeanors prior to detention in city lockup is unconstitutional).

Vale v. Louisiana

399 U.S. 30, 90 S.Ct. 1969, 26 L.Ed.2d 409 (1970)

■ MR. JUSTICE STEWART delivered the opinion of the Court.

The appellant, Donald Vale, was convicted in a Louisiana court on a charge of possessing heroin and was sentenced as a multiple offender to 15 years' imprisonment at hard labor. The Louisiana Supreme Court affirmed the conviction, rejecting the claim that evidence introduced at the trial was the product of an unlawful search and seizure. . . .

The evidence adduced at the pretrial hearing on a motion to suppress showed that on April 24, 1967, officers possessing two warrants for Vale's arrest and having information that he was residing at a specified address proceeded there in an unmarked car and set up a surveillance of the house. The evidence of what then took place was summarized by the Louisiana Supreme Court as follows:

> After approximately 15 minutes the officers observed a green 1958 Chevrolet drive up and sound the horn and after backing into a parking place, again blew the horn. At this juncture Donald Vale, who was well known to Officer Brady, having arrested him twice in the previous month, was seen coming out of the house and walk up to the passenger side of the Chevrolet where he had a close brief conversation with the driver; and after looking up and down the street returned inside of the house. Within a few minutes he reappeared on the porch, and again cautiously looked up and down the street before proceeding to the passenger side of the Chevrolet, leaning through the window. From this the officers were convinced a narcotics sale had taken place. They returned to their car and immediately drove toward Donald Vale, and as they reached within approximately three cars lengths from the accused, (Donald Vale) he looked up and, obviously recognizing the officers, turned around, walking quickly toward the house. At the same time the driver of the Chevrolet started to make his getaway when the car was blocked by the police vehicle. The three officers promptly alighted from the car, whereupon Officers Soule and Laumann called

> to Donald Vale to stop as he reached the front steps of the house, telling him he was under arrest. Officer Brady at the same time, seeing the driver of the Chevrolet, Arizzio Saucier, whom the officers knew to be a narcotic addict, place something hurriedly in his mouth, immediately placed him under arrest and joined his co-officers. Because of the transaction they had just observed they informed Donald Vale they were going to search the house, and thereupon advised him of his constitutional rights. After they all entered the front room, Officer Laumann made a cursory inspection of the house to ascertain if anyone else was present and within about three minutes Mrs. Vale and James Vale, mother and brother of Donald Vale, returned home carrying groceries and were informed of the arrest and impending search.

215 So.2d, at 815 (footnote omitted). The search of a rear bedroom revealed a quantity of narcotics.

The Louisiana Supreme Court held that the search of the house did not violate the Fourth Amendment because it occurred "in the immediate vicinity of the arrest" of Donald Vale and was "substantially contemporaneous therewith. . . ." 215 So.2d, at 816. We cannot agree. Last Term in Chimel v. California, 395 U.S. 752, we held that when the search of a dwelling is sought to be justified as incident to a lawful arrest, it must constitutionally be confined to the area within the arrestee's reach at the time of his arrest—"the area from within which he might gain possession of a weapon or destructible evidence." 395 U.S., at 763. But even if *Chimel* is not accorded retroactive effect—a question on which we do not now express an opinion—no precedent of this Court can sustain the constitutional validity of the search in the case before us.

A search may be incident to an arrest " 'only if it is substantially contemporaneous with the arrest and is confined to the *immediate* vicinity of the arrest.' " Shipley v. California, 395 U.S. 818, 819. . . . If a search of a house is to be upheld as incident to an arrest, that arrest must take place *inside* the house . . . not somewhere outside—whether two blocks away . . . twenty feet away . . . or on the sidewalk near the front steps. "Belief, however well founded, that an article sought is concealed in a dwelling house furnishes no justification for a search of that place without a warrant." Agnello v. United States [269 U.S. 20 (1925)], at 33. That basic rule "has never been questioned in this Court." Stoner v. California [376 U.S. 483 (1964)], at 487 n.5.

The Louisiana Supreme Court thought the search independently supportable because it involved narcotics, which are easily removed, hidden, or destroyed. It would be unreasonable, the Louisiana court concluded, "to require the officers under the facts of the case to first secure a search warrant before searching the premises, as time is of the essence inasmuch as the officers never know whether there is anyone on the premises to be searched who could very easily destroy the evidence." 215 So.2d, at 816. Such a rationale could not apply to the present case, since by their own account the arresting officers satisfied themselves that no one else was in the house when they first entered the premises. But entirely apart from that point, our past decisions make clear that only in "a few specifically established and well-delineated" situations, Katz v. United States, 389 U.S. 347, 357, may a warrantless search of a dwelling withstand constitutional scrutiny, even though the authorities have probable cause to conduct it. The burden rests on the State to show the existence of such an exceptional situation. . . . And the record before us discloses none.

. . .

The officers were able to procure two warrants for Vale's arrest. They also had information that he was residing at the address where they found him. There is thus no reason, so far as anything before us appears, to suppose that it was impracticable for them to obtain a search warrant as well. . . . We decline to hold that an arrest on the street can provide its own "exigent circumstance" so as to justify a warrantless search of the arrestee's house.

The Louisiana courts committed constitutional error in admitting into evidence the fruits of the illegal search. . . .

. . .[12]

---

127. Having accompanied the defendant's wife to their trailer home, police officers were told by her that he had drugs inside. They asked him if they could search, and he said no. An officer then went to get a search warrant. The defendant having by then come onto the porch, the other officer allowed him to reenter the trailer only under the officer's observation. The former officer returned with a search warrant within two hours. A search uncovered marijuana. The Court held that in light of the circumstances and the need to prevent the destruction of evidence, the police conduct was reasonable and not a violation of the Fourth Amendment. Illinois v. McArthur, 531 U.S. 326 (2001) (8–1).

Chambers v. Maroney

399 U.S. 42, 90 S.Ct. 1975, 26 L.Ed.2d 419 (1970)

■ MR. JUSTICE WHITE delivered the opinion of the Court.

The principal question in this case concerns the admissibility of evidence seized from an automobile, in which petitioner was riding at the time of his arrest, after the automobile was taken to a police station and was there thoroughly searched without a warrant. The Court of Appeals for the Third Circuit found no violation of petitioner's Fourth Amendment rights. We affirm.

[12] Justice Black wrote a dissenting opinion, which Chief Justice Burger joined.

I

During the night of May 20, 1963, a Gulf service station in North Braddock, Pennsylvania, was robbed by two men, each of whom carried and displayed a gun. The robbers took the currency from the cash register; the service station attendant, one Stephen Kovacich, was directed to place the coins in his right-hand glove, which was then taken by the robbers. Two teen-agers, who had earlier noticed a blue compact station wagon circling the block in the vicinity of the Gulf station, then saw the station wagon speed away from a parking lot close to the Gulf station. About the same time, they learned that the Gulf station had been robbed. They reported to police, who arrived immediately, that four men were in the station wagon and one was wearing a green sweater. Kovacich told the police that one of the men who robbed him was wearing a green sweater and the other was wearing a trench coat. A description of the car and the two robbers was broadcast over the police radio. Within an hour, a light blue compact station wagon answering the description and carrying four men was stopped by the police about two miles from the Gulf station. Petitioner was one of the men in the station wagon. He was wearing a green sweater and there was a trench coat in the car. The occupants were arrested and the car was driven to the police station. In the course of a thorough search of the car at the station, the police found concealed in a compartment under the dashboard two .38-caliber revolvers (one loaded with dumdum bullets), a right-hand glove containing small change, and certain cards bearing the name of Raymond Havicon, the attendant at a Boron service station in McKeesport, Pennsylvania, who had been robbed at gunpoint on May 13, 1963. In the course of a warrant-authorized search of petitioner's home the day after petitioner's arrest, police found and seized certain .38-caliber ammunition, including some dumdum bullets similar to those found in one of the guns taken from the station wagon.

Petitioner was indicted for both robberies. His first trial ended in a mistrial but he was convicted of both robberies at the second trial. Both Kovacich and Havicon identified petitioner as one of the robbers. The materials taken from the station wagon were introduced into evidence, Kovacich identifying his glove and Havicon the cards taken in the May 13 robbery. The bullets seized at petitioner's house were also introduced over objections of petitioner's counsel. Petitioner was sentenced to a term of four to eight years' imprisonment for the May 13 robbery and to a term of two to seven years' imprisonment for the May 20 robbery, the sentences to run consecutively. Petitioner did not take a direct appeal from these convictions. In 1965, petitioner sought a writ of habeas corpus in the state court, which denied the writ after a brief evidentiary hearing; the denial of the writ was affirmed on appeal in the Pennsylvania appellate courts. Habeas corpus proceedings were then commenced in the United States District Court for the Western District of Pennsylvania. An order to show cause was issued. Based on the State's response and the state court record, the petition for habeas corpus was denied without a hearing. The Court of Appeals for the Third Circuit affirmed . . . and we granted certiorari. . . .

II

We pass quickly the claim that the search of the automobile was the fruit of an unlawful arrest. Both the courts below thought the arresting officers had probable cause to make the arrest. We agree. Having talked to the teen-age observers and to the victim Kovacich, the police had ample cause to stop a light blue compact station wagon carrying four men and to arrest the occupants, one of whom was wearing a green sweater and one of whom had a trench coat with him in the car.[13]

Even so, the search that produced the incriminating evidence was made at the police station some time after the arrest and cannot be justified as a search incident to an arrest: "Once an accused is under arrest and in custody, then a search made at another place, without a warrant, is simply not incident to the arrest." Preston v. United States, 376 U.S. 364, 367 (1964). . . . [T]he reasons that have been thought sufficient to justify warrantless searches carried out in connection with an arrest no longer obtain when the accused is safely in custody at the station house.

There are, however, alternative grounds arguably justifying the search of the car in this case. . . . Here . . . the police had probable cause to believe that the robbers, carrying guns and the fruits of the crime, had fled the scene in a light blue compact station wagon which would be carrying four men, one wearing a green sweater and another wearing a trench coat. As the state courts correctly held, there was probable cause to arrest the occupants of the station wagon that the officers stopped; just as obviously was there probable cause to search the car for guns and stolen money.

In terms of the circumstances justifying a warrantless search, the Court has long distinguished between an automobile and a home or office. In Carroll v. United States, 267 U.S. 132 (1925), the issue was the admissibility in evidence of contraband liquor seized in a warrantless search of a car on the highway. After surveying the law from the time of the adoption of the Fourth Amendment onward, the Court held that automobiles and other conveyances may be searched without a warrant in circumstances that would not justify the search without a warrant of a house or an office, provided that there is probable cause to believe that the car contains articles that the officers are entitled to seize. The Court expressed its holding as follows:

> We have made a somewhat extended reference to these statutes to show that the guaranty of freedom from unreasonable searches and seizures by the Fourth Amendment has been construed, practically since the beginning of the Government, as recognizing a necessary difference between a search of a store, dwelling house or other structure in respect of which a proper official warrant readily may be obtained, and a search of a ship, motor boat, wagon or automobile, for

13. In any event, as we point out below, the validity of an arrest is not necessarily determinative of the right to search a car if there is probable cause to make the search. Here, as will be true in many cases, the circumstances justifying the arrest are also those furnishing probable cause for the search.

> contraband goods, where it is not practicable to secure a warrant because the vehicle can be quickly moved out of the locality or jurisdiction in which the warrant must be sought.
>
> Having thus established that contraband goods concealed and illegally transported in an automobile or other vehicle may be searched for without a warrant, we come now to consider under what circumstances such search may be made. . . . [T]hose lawfully within the country, entitled to use the public highways, have a right to free passage without interruption or search unless there is known to a competent official authorized to search, probable cause for believing that their vehicles are carrying contraband or illegal merchandise. . . .
>
> . . .
>
> The measure of legality of such a seizure is, therefore, that the seizing officer shall have reasonable or probable cause for believing that the automobile which he stops and seizes has contraband liquor therein which is being illegally transported.

267 U.S., at 153–54, 155–56. The Court also noted that the search of an auto on probable cause proceeds on a theory wholly different from that justifying the search incident to an arrest:

> The right to search and the validity of the seizure are not dependent on the right to arrest. They are dependent on the reasonable cause the seizing officer has for belief that the contents of the automobile offend against the law.

267 U.S., at 158–59. Finding that there was probable cause for the search and seizure at issue before it, the Court affirmed the convictions.

. . .

Neither *Carroll*, supra, nor other cases in this Court require or suggest that in every conceivable circumstance the search of an auto even with probable cause may be made without the extra protection for privacy that a warrant affords. But the circumstances that furnish probable cause to search a particular auto for particular articles are most often unforeseeable; moreover, the opportunity to search is fleeting since a car is readily movable. Where this is true, as in *Carroll* and the case before us now, if an effective search is to be made at any time, either the search must be made immediately without a warrant or the car itself must be seized and held without a warrant for whatever period is necessary to obtain a warrant for the search.[14]

In enforcing the Fourth Amendment's prohibition against unreasonable searches and seizures, the Court has insisted upon probable cause as a minimum requirement for a reasonable search permitted by the Constitu-

14. Following the car until a warrant can be obtained seems an impractical alternative since, among other things, the car may be taken out of the jurisdiction. Tracing the car and searching it hours or days later would of course permit instruments or fruits of crime to be removed from the car before the search.

tion. As a general rule, it has also required the judgment of a magistrate on the probable-cause issue and the issuance of a warrant before a search is made. Only in exigent circumstances will the judgment of the police as to probable cause serve as a sufficient authorization for a search. *Carroll*, supra, holds a search warrant unnecessary where there is probable cause to search an automobile stopped on the highway; the car is movable, the occupants are alerted, and the car's contents may never be found again if a warrant must be obtained. Hence an immediate search is constitutionally permissible.

Arguably, because of the preference for a magistrate's judgment, only the immobilization of the car should be permitted until a search warrant is obtained; arguably, only the "lesser" intrusion is permissible until the magistrate authorizes the "greater." But which is the "greater" and which the "lesser" intrusion is itself a debatable question and the answer may depend on a variety of circumstances. For constitutional purposes, we see no difference between on the one hand seizing and holding a car before presenting the probable cause issue to a magistrate and on the other hand carrying out an immediate search without a warrant. Given probable cause to search, either course is reasonable under the Fourth Amendment.

On the facts before us, the blue station wagon could have been searched on the spot when it was stopped since there was probable cause to search and it was a fleeting target for a search. The probable-cause factor still obtained at the station house and so did the mobility of the car unless the Fourth Amendment permits a warrantless seizure of the car and the denial of its use to anyone until a warrant is secured. In that event there is little to choose in terms of practical consequences between an immediate search without a warrant and the car's immobilization until a warrant is obtained.[15] The same consequences may not follow where there is unforeseeable cause to search a house. Compare Vale v. Louisiana, ante, p. 30. But as *Carroll*, supra, held, for the purposes of the Fourth Amendment there is a constitutional difference between houses and cars.

. . .

■ MR. JUSTICE HARLAN, concurring in part and dissenting in part.

. . .

In sustaining the search of the automobile I believe the Court ignores the framework of our past decisions circumscribing the scope of permissible search without a warrant. The Court has long read the Fourth Amendment's proscription of "unreasonable" searches as imposing a general principle that a search without a warrant is not justified by the mere knowledge by the searching officers of facts showing probable cause. The "general requirement that a search warrant be obtained" is basic to the

15. It was not unreasonable in this case to take the car to the station house. All occupants in the car were arrested in a dark parking lot in the middle of the night. A careful search at that point was impractical and perhaps not safe for the officers, and it would serve the owner's convenience and the safety of his car to have the vehicle and the keys together at the station house.

Amendment's protection of privacy, and " 'the burden is on those seeking [an] exemption . . . to show the need for it.' " E.g., Chimel v. California, 395 U.S. 752, 762 (1969). . . .

Fidelity to this established principle requires that, where exceptions are made to accommodate the exigencies of particular situations, those exceptions be no broader than necessitated by the circumstances presented. For example, the Court has recognized that an arrest creates an emergency situation justifying a warrantless search of the arrestee's person and of "the area from within which he might gain possession of a weapon or destructible evidence"; however, because the exigency giving rise to this exception extends only that far, the search may go no further. . . . Similarly we held in Terry v. Ohio, 392 U.S. 1 (1968), that a warrantless search in a "stop and frisk" situation must "be strictly circumscribed by the exigencies which justify its initiation." Id., at 26. Any intrusion beyond what is necessary for the personal safety of the officer or others nearby is forbidden.

Where officers have probable cause to search a vehicle on a public way, a further limited exception to the warrant requirement is reasonable because "the vehicle can be quickly moved out of the locality or jurisdiction in which the warrant must be sought." Carroll v. United States, 267 U.S. 132, 153 (1925). Because the officers might be deprived of valuable evidence if required to obtain a warrant before effecting any search or seizure, I agree with the Court that they should be permitted to take the steps necessary to preserve evidence and to make a search possible. . . . The Court holds that those steps include making a warrantless search of the entire vehicle on the highway—a conclusion reached by the Court in *Carroll* without discussion—and indeed appears to go further and to condone the removal of the car to the police station for a warrantless search there at the convenience of the police. I cannot agree that this result is consistent with our insistence in other areas that departures from the warrant requirement strictly conform to the exigency presented.

The Court concedes that the police could prevent removal of the evidence by temporarily seizing the car for the time necessary to obtain a warrant. It does not dispute that such a course would fully protect the interests of effective law enforcement; rather it states that whether temporary seizure is a "lesser" intrusion than warrantless search "is itself a debatable question and the answer may depend on a variety of circumstances." Ante, at 51–52.[16] I believe it clear that a warrantless search involves the greater sacrifice of Fourth Amendment values.

16. The Court, unable to decide whether search or temporary seizure is the "lesser" intrusion, in this case authorizes both. The Court concludes that it was reasonable for the police to take the car to the station, where they searched it once to no avail. The searching officers then entered the station, interrogated petitioner and the car's owner, and returned later for another search of the car—this one successful. At all times the car and its contents were secure against removal or destruction. Nevertheless, the Court approves the searches without even an inquiry into the officers' ability promptly to take their case before a magistrate.

The Fourth Amendment proscribes, to be sure, unreasonable "seizures" as well as "searches." However, in the circumstances in which this problem is likely to occur, the lesser intrusion will almost always be the simple seizure of the car for the period—perhaps a day—necessary to enable the officers to obtain a search warrant. In the first place, as this case shows, the very facts establishing probable cause to search will often also justify arrest of the occupants of the vehicle. Since the occupants themselves are to be taken into custody, they will suffer minimal further inconvenience from the temporary immobilization of their vehicle. Even where no arrests are made, persons who wish to avoid a search—either to protect their privacy or to conceal incriminating evidence—will almost certainly prefer a brief loss of the use of the vehicle in exchange for the opportunity to have a magistrate pass upon the justification for the search. To be sure, one can conceive of instances in which the occupant, having nothing to hide and lacking concern for the privacy of the automobile, would be more deeply offended by a temporary immobilization of his vehicle than by a prompt search of it. However, such a person always remains free to consent to an immediate search, thus avoiding any delay. Where consent is not forthcoming, the occupants of the car have an interest in privacy that is protected by the Fourth Amendment even where the circumstances justify a temporary seizure. . . . The Court's endorsement of a warrantless invasion of that privacy where another course would suffice is simply inconsistent with our repeated stress on the Fourth Amendment's mandate of " 'adherence to judicial processes.' " E.g., Katz v. United States, 389 U.S. [347 (1967)], at 357.[17]

. . .[18]

---

128. The Court has confirmed the rule of *Chambers*, that probable cause alone authorizes the search of a car and that a warrant need not be obtained, even if there is time to do so, on several occasions. E.g., Maryland v. Dyson, 527 U.S. 465 (1999) (per curiam); Pennsylvania v. Labron, 518 U.S. 938 (1996) (7–2); Texas v. White, 423 U.S. 67 (1975) (7–2).

The Supreme Court of Connecticut has rejected the rule of *Chambers*. "In light of our demonstrated constitutional preference for warrants and our concomitant obligation narrowly to describe exceptions to the state constitutional warrant requirement, we conclude that a warrantless automobile search supported by probable cause, but conducted after the auto-

17. Circumstances might arise in which it would be impracticable to immobilize the car for the time required to obtain a warrant—for example, where a single police officer must take arrested suspects to the station, and has no way of protecting the suspects' car during his absence. In such situations it might be wholly reasonable to perform an on-the-spot search based on probable cause. However, where nothing in the situation makes impracticable the obtaining of a warrant, I cannot joint the Court in shunting aside that vital Fourth Amendment safeguard.

[18] Justice Stewart wrote a brief concurring opinion.

mobile has been impounded at the police station, violates article first, § 7, of the Connecticut constitution." State v. Miller, 630 A.2d 1315, 1326 (Conn.1993).

129. If the police have authority to search an automobile without a search warrant under the rationale of *Chambers*, the search can be as broad as a search pursuant to a warrant. United States v. Ross, 456 U.S. 798 (1982) (6–3). "The scope of a warrantless search based on probable cause is no narrower—and no broader—than the scope of a search authorized by a warrant supported by probable cause. Only the prior approval of the magistrate is waived; the search otherwise is as the magistrate could authorize." Id. at 823. More particularly, the Court said that containers within the automobile that might hold the items to be seized can be opened and searched. "When a legitimate search is under way, and when its purpose and its limits have been precisely defined, nice distinctions between closets, drawers, and containers, in the case of a home, or between glove compartments, upholstered seats, trunks, and wrapped packages, in the case of a vehicle, must give way to the interest in the prompt and efficient completion of the task at hand." Id. at 821. However, the Court noted its statement in *Chadwick*, p. 212 note 119 above, that the "automobile exception" could not be extended to other movable containers, like luggage, found in a public place. Id. at 811–12.

The search authorized by *Ross* includes containers that belong to a passenger or to someone not present in the car when it is stopped. Wyoming v. Houghton, 526 U.S. 295 (1999) (6–3).

For a time after *Ross* was decided, the Court distinguished between probable cause to search a car and probable cause to search a container within a car. In the latter situation, the Court said, not *Ross* but *Chadwick* prevailed. Yet, if the basis of the search was not *Chambers* but *Belton*, p. 214 note 121 above, *Chadwick* was inapplicable. The confusion that resulted is described in California v. Acevedo, 500 U.S. 565 (1991). Concluding that a uniform rule was desirable, the Court held in *Acevedo* that (the rule of *Belton* aside) whether there is probable cause to search a car or probable cause to search a container within a car, if the container is lawfully seized, it may be searched without a warrant. (It remains true, however, that if the police have probable cause to search only the container and not the car, *Ross* does not authorize a search of the car beyond what is necessary to find the container.) Aside from opting for a clear rule in the case of containers found in a car, *Acevedo* does little to resolve the tension between *Chadwick*, on one hand, and *Belton* and *Ross*, on the other.

If police officials remove containers from a vehicle pursuant to *Ross*, the search of the containers authorized by *Ross* need not take place immediately; in the absence of any particular claim that the delay affected the defendant's privacy interests, a warrantless search of the containers three days after their removal from the searched vehicles is not unreasonable. United States v. Johns, 469 U.S. 478 (1985) (7–2).

130. The "automobile exception" to the requirement of a search warrant was applied to a "Dodge Mini Motor Home" parked in a city lot, in California v. Carney, 471 U.S. 386 (1985) (6–3). Summarizing the rationale for the exception, the Court said:

> In short, the pervasive schemes of regulation, which necessarily lead to reduced expectations of privacy, and the exigencies attendant to ready mobility justify searches without prior recourse to the authority of a magistrate so long as the overriding standard of probable cause is met.
>
> When a vehicle is being used on the highways, or if it is readily capable of such use and is found stationary in a place not regularly used for residential purposes—temporary or otherwise—the two justifications for the vehicle exception come into play. First, the vehicle is obviously readily mobile by the turn of a switch key, if not actually moving. Second, there is a reduced expectation of privacy stemming from its use as a licensed motor vehicle subject to a range of police regulation inapplicable to a fixed dwelling. At least in these circumstances, the overriding societal interests in effective law enforcement justify an immediate search before the vehicle and its occupants become unavailable.

Id. at 392–93.

That was so, the Court concluded, even though the defendant's vehicle "possessed some, if not many of the attributes of a home." Id. at 393. The Court added that it did "not pass on the application of the vehicle exception to a motor home that is situated in a way or place that objectively indicates that it is being used as a residence. Among the factors that might be relevant in determining whether a warrant would be required in such a circumstance is its location, whether the vehicle is readily mobile or instead, for instance, elevated on blocks, whether the vehicle is licensed, whether it is connected to utilities, and whether it has convenient access to a public road." Id. at 394 n.3.

Carney was applied to an unattended motor home parked in a driveway, in United States v. Markham, 844 F.2d 366 (6th Cir.1988).

131. The Court held that there was not a violation of the Fourth Amendment when a police officer opened a car door to move papers obstructing his view of the Vehicle Identification Number on the dashboard, in New York v. Class, 475 U.S. 106 (5–4). The officer stopped the driver of the car for a traffic offense. After the driver got out of the car, the officer opened the car door to look for the VIN on the door jamb. He found none. Federal law requires that the VIN be either on the door jamb or on the dashboard, visible from outside the car. The officer reached into the car to move papers from the area of the dashboard where the VIN is located. Doing so, he saw a gun hidden under the seat. The Court upheld the seizure of the gun. The Court said that in the circumstances—the requirement that the VIN be visible from the outside, the minimal intrusion, the basis for stopping the driver initially, and the possible risk to the officer if he had asked the driver to re-enter the car to expose the VIN—the officer's action was reasonable. Cf. Arizona v. Hicks, 480 U.S. 321 (1987), p. 201 note 110 above.

South Dakota v. Opperman

428 U.S. 364, 96 S.Ct. 3092, 49 L.Ed.2d 1000 (1976)

■ Mr. Chief Justice Burger delivered the opinion of the Court.

We review the judgment of the Supreme Court of South Dakota, holding that local police violated the Fourth Amendment to the Federal Constitution, as applicable to the States under the Fourteenth Amendment, when they conducted a routine inventory search of an automobile lawfully impounded by police for violations of municipal parking ordinances.

(1)

Local ordinances prohibit parking in certain areas of downtown Vermillion, S.D., between the hours of 2 a.m. and 6 a.m. During the early morning hours of December 10, 1973, a Vermillion police officer observed respondent's unoccupied vehicle illegally parked in the restricted zone. At approximately 3 a.m., the officer issued an overtime parking ticket and placed it on the car's windshield. The citation warned:

"Vehicles in violation of any parking ordinance may be towed from the area."

At approximately 10 o'clock on the same morning, another officer issued a second ticket for an overtime parking violation. These circumstances were routinely reported to police headquarters, and after the vehicle was inspected, the car was towed to the city impound lot.

From outside the car at the impound lot, a police officer observed a watch on the dashboard and other items of personal property located on the back seat and back floorboard. At the officer's direction, the car door was then unlocked and, using a standard inventory form pursuant to standard police procedures, the officer inventoried the contents of the car, including the contents of the glove compartment, which was unlocked. There he found marihuana contained in a plastic bag. All items, including the contraband, were removed to the police department for safekeeping. During the late afternoon of December 10, respondent appeared at the police department to claim his property. The marihuana was retained by police.

Respondent was subsequently arrested on charges of possession of marihuana. His motion to suppress the evidence yielded by the inventory search was denied; he was convicted after a jury trial and sentenced to a fine of $100 and 14 days' incarceration in the county jail. On appeal, the Supreme Court of South Dakota reversed the conviction. The court concluded that the evidence had been obtained in violation of the Fourth Amendment prohibition against unreasonable searches and seizures. We granted certiorari . . . and we reverse.

(2)

This Court has traditionally drawn a distinction between automobiles and homes or offices in relation to the Fourth Amendment. Although automobiles are "effects" and thus within the reach of the Fourth Amendment . . . warrantless examinations of automobiles have been upheld in circumstances in which a search of a home or office would not. . . .

The reason for this well-settled distinction is twofold. First, the inherent mobility of automobiles creates circumstances of such exigency that, as a practical necessity, rigorous enforcement of the warrant requirement is impossible. . . . But the Court has also upheld warrantless searches where no immediate danger was presented that the car would be removed from the jurisdiction. . . . Besides the element of mobility, less rigorous warrant requirements govern because the expectation of privacy with respect to one's automobile is significantly less than that relating to one's home or office. In discharging their varied responsibilities for ensuring the public safety, law enforcement officials are necessarily brought into frequent contact with automobiles. Most of this contact is distinctly noncriminal in nature. . . . Automobiles, unlike homes, are subjected to pervasive and continuing governmental regulation and controls, including periodic inspection and licensing requirements. As an everyday occurrence, police stop and examine vehicles when license plates or inspection stickers have expired, or if other violations, such as exhaust fumes or excessive noise, are noted, or if headlights or other safety equipment are not in proper working order.

The expectation of privacy as to automobiles is further diminished by the obviously public nature of automobile travel. . . .

In the interests of public safety and as part of what the Court has called "community caretaking functions," Cady v. Dombrowski, [413 U.S. 433 (1973)] at 441, automobiles are frequently taken into police custody. Vehicle accidents present one such occasion. To permit the uninterrupted flow of traffic and in some circumstances to preserve evidence, disabled or damaged vehicles will often be removed from the highways or streets at the behest of police engaged solely in caretaking and traffic-control activities. Police will also frequently remove and impound automobiles which violate parking ordinances and which thereby jeopardize both the public safety and the efficient movement of vehicular traffic. The authority of police to seize and remove from the streets vehicles impeding traffic or threatening public safety and convenience is beyond challenge.

When vehicles are impounded, local police departments generally follow a routine practice of securing and inventorying the automobiles' contents. These procedures developed in response to three distinct needs: the protection of the owner's property while it remains in police custody . . . the protection of the police against claims or disputes over lost or stolen property . . . and the protection of the police from potential danger. . . . The practice has been viewed as essential to respond to incidents of theft or vandalism. . . . In addition, police frequently attempt to determine whether a vehicle has been stolen and thereafter abandoned.

These caretaking procedures have almost uniformly been upheld by the state courts, which by virtue of the localized nature of traffic regulation have had considerable occasion to deal with the issue. Applying the Fourth Amendment standard of "reasonableness," the state courts have overwhelmingly concluded that, even if an inventory is characterized as a "search," the intrusion is constitutionally permissible. . . .

The majority of the Federal Courts of Appeals have likewise sustained inventory procedures as reasonable police intrusions. . . . These cases have recognized that standard inventories often include an examination of the glove compartment, since it is a customary place for documents of ownership and registration . . . as well as a place for the temporary storage of valuables.

(3)

The decisions of this Court point unmistakably to the conclusion reached by both federal and state courts that inventories pursuant to standard police procedures are reasonable. . . .

In applying the reasonableness standard adopted by the Framers, this Court has consistently sustained police intrusions into automobiles impounded or otherwise in lawful police custody where the process is aimed at securing or protecting the car and its contents. In Cooper v. California [386 U.S. 58 (1967)], the Court upheld the inventory of a car impounded under the authority of a state forfeiture statute. Even though the inventory was conducted in a distinctly criminal setting and carried out a week after the car had been impounded, the Court nonetheless found that the car search, including examination of the glove compartment where contraband was found, was reasonable under the circumstances. This conclusion was reached despite the fact that no warrant had issued and probable cause to search for the contraband in the vehicle had not been established. The Court said in language explicitly applicable here:

> It would be unreasonable to hold that the police, having to retain the car in their custody for such a length of time, had no right, even for their own protection, to search it.

386 U.S., at 61–62.

In the following Term, the Court in Harris v. United States, 390 U.S. 234 (1968), upheld the introduction of evidence, seized by an officer who, after conducting an inventory search of a car and while taking means to safeguard it, observed a car registration card lying on the metal stripping of the car door. Rejecting the argument that a warrant was necessary, the Court held that the intrusion was justifiable since it was "taken to protect the car while it was in police custody." Id., at 236.

Finally, in Cady v. Dombrowski, supra, the Court upheld a warrantless search of an automobile towed to a private garage even though no probable cause existed to believe that the vehicle contained fruits of a crime. The sole justification for the warrantless incursion was that it was incident to the caretaking function of the local police to protect the community's safety. Indeed, the protective search was instituted solely because local police "were under the impression" that the incapacitated driver, a Chicago police officer, was required to carry his service revolver at all times; the police had reasonable grounds to believe a weapon might be in the car, and thus available to vandals. 413 U.S., at 436. The Court carefully noted that the protective search was carried out in accordance with *standard procedures* in the local police department, ibid., a factor tending to ensure that the intrusion would be limited in scope to the extent necessary to carry out the caretaking function. . . .

The holdings in *Cooper*, *Harris*, and *Cady* point the way to the correct resolution of this case. None of the three cases, of course, involves the precise situation presented here; but, as in all Fourth Amendment cases, we are obliged to look to all the facts and circumstances of this case in light of the principles set forth in these prior decisions. . . .

The Vermillion police were indisputably engaged in a caretaking search of a lawfully impounded automobile. . . . The inventory was conducted only after the car had been impounded for multiple parking violations. The owner, having left his car illegally parked for an extended period, and thus subject to impoundment, was not present to make other arrangements for the safekeeping of his belongings. The inventory itself was prompted by the presence in plain view of a number of valuables inside the car. As in *Cady*, there is no suggestion whatever that this standard procedure, essentially like that followed throughout the country, was a pretext concealing an investigatory police motive.

On this record we conclude that in following standard police procedures, prevailing throughout the country and approved by the overwhelming majority of courts, the conduct of the police was not "unreasonable" under the Fourth Amendment.

The judgment of the South Dakota Supreme Court is therefore reversed, and the case is remanded for further proceedings not inconsistent with this opinion.[19]

---

132. "[A]n inventory search must not be a ruse for a general rummaging in order to discover incriminating evidence. The policy or practice governing inventory searches should be designed to produce an inventory."

[19] Justice Powell wrote a concurring opinion. Justice Marshall wrote a dissenting opinion, which Justice Brennan and Justice Stewart joined. Justice White also dissented, and filed a brief statement indicating his agreement with most of the "analysis and conclusions" of Justice Marshall.

On remand, the South Dakota Supreme Court concluded that the search had violated a provision of the state constitution "almost identical" to the Fourth Amendment and, therefore, that the evidence should have been suppressed. State v. Opperman, 247 N.W.2d 673 (S.D.1976). Subsequently, in State v. Flittie, 425 N.W.2d 1 (S.D.1988), although adhering to its own view in the *Opperman* case itself, the South Dakota court reviewed with considerable approval the Supreme Court's rulings about inventory searches.

Although police officers conducting an inventory cannot have "uncanalized discretion," they need not be required to conduct the inventory "in a totally mechanical 'all or nothing' fashion. . . . The allowance of the exercise of judgment based on concerns related to the purpose of an inventory search does not violate the Fourth Amendment." Florida v. Wells, 495 U.S. 1, 4 (1990). See United States v. Castro, 129 F.3d 752 (5th Cir.1997) (purported inventory search following stop for traffic offense was not routine but was for investigative purpose; evidence suppressed).

The Court relied on *Opperman* and Illinois v. Lafayette, p. 225 note 126 above, to uphold an on-site inventory search of a van, after the driver was arrested for drunk driving. In the course of the search, an officer opened a closed backpack behind the front seat, removed a nylon bag containing metal canisters, and opened the canisters, in which he found drugs, drug paraphernalia, and cash. In an outside zippered pouch of the backpack, he found a sealed envelope containing cash. The Court held that the seizure of the above items was lawful, as part of a "reasonable" inventory search carried out in good faith pursuant to police regulations, whether or not another procedure might equally have served the functions of the search with less invasion of privacy. Colorado v. Bertine, 479 U.S. 367 (1987) (7–2). In United States v. Andrews, 22 F.3d 1328, 1335 (5th Cir.1994), the court held that a page-by-page examination of a notebook as part of an inventory search, "to determine whether valuables might be found between its pages," was permissible. See also United States v. Khoury, 901 F.2d 948 (11th Cir.1990), holding that as part of the inventory search of a car, police officers could flip through a spiral notebook found in a briefcase in the trunk of the car in order to determine if it was valuable or contained anything of value, without examining it further.

Inventory searches that deviate from standard procedures have been invalidated. After the defendant's car was involved in a collision, he was taken into custody for traffic offenses, including driving without a proper license. The truck was impounded and searched at a service station away from the scene of the collision. During an inventory search, cocaine was found behind a door panel. The court held that searching behind a door panel was not standard procedure and could not be justified as an inventory search. Nor could the search, conducted away from the scene of the arrest, be justified as incident to it, or as performance of a "community caretaking" function. United States v. Lugo, 978 F.2d 631 (10th Cir.1992). See also United States v. Duguay, 93 F.3d 346 (7th Cir.1996) (inventory search invalid because not pursuant to standard procedure).

133. "[W]here police assumed custody of defendant's automobile for no legitimate state purpose other than safekeeping, and where defendant had arranged for alternative means, not shown to be unreasonable, for the safekeeping of his property, impoundment of defendant's automobile was unreasonable and, therefore, the concomitant inventory was an unreasonable search under the Fourth Amendment." State v. Goodrich, 256 N.W.2d 506, 507 (Minn.1977).

"[C]ontraband discovered in the course of an inventory conducted without first permitting vehicle occupants to utilize available alternative means of safeguarding their property is inadmissible as evidence in a criminal prosecution. Such police conduct amounts to an unreasonable and unwarranted intrusion into the privacy interests of occupants in contravention of the Fourth Amendment...." State v. Mangold, 414 A.2d 1312, 1313 (N.J.1980). In *Mangold*, the inventory was made of a vehicle at the scene of an accident in which it was involved, while the occupants were still present.

134. Hot pursuit.

About 8 a.m. on March 17, 1962, an armed robber entered the business premises of the Diamond Cab Company in Baltimore, Maryland. He took some $363 and ran. Two cab drivers in the vicinity, attracted by shouts of "Holdup," followed the man to 2111 Cocoa Lane. One driver notified the company dispatcher by radio that the man was a Negro about 5′8″ tall, wearing a light cap and dark jacket, and that he had entered the house on Cocoa Lane. The dispatcher relayed the information to police who were proceeding to the scene of the robbery. Within minutes, police arrived at the house in a number of patrol cars. An officer knocked and announced their presence. Mrs. Hayden answered, and the officers told her they believed that a robber had entered the house, and asked to search the house. She offered no objection.

The officers spread out through the first and second floors and the cellar in search of the robber. Hayden was found in an upstairs bedroom feigning sleep. He was arrested when the officers on the first floor and in the cellar reported that no other man was in the house. Meanwhile an officer was attracted to an adjoining bathroom by the noise of running water, and discovered a shotgun and a pistol in a flush tank; another officer who, according to the District Court, "was searching the cellar for a man or the money" found in a washing machine a jacket and trousers of the type the fleeing man was said to have worn. A clip of ammunition for the pistol and a cap were found under the mattress of Hayden's bed, and ammunition for the shotgun was found in a bureau drawer in Hayden's room. All these items of evidence were introduced against respondent at his trial.

. . .

We agree with the Court of Appeals that neither the entry without warrant to search for the robber, nor the search for him without warrant was invalid. Under the circumstances of this case, "the exigencies of the situation made that course imperative." McDonald v. United States, 335 U.S. 451, 456. The police were informed that an armed robbery had taken place, and that the suspect had entered 2111 Cocoa Lane less than five minutes before they reached it. They acted reasonably when they entered the house and began to search for a man of the description they had been given and for weapons which he had used in the robbery or might use against them. The Fourth Amendment does not require police officers to delay in the course of an investigation if to do so would gravely endanger their lives or the lives of others. Speed here was essential, and only a thorough search of the house for persons and weapons could have insured that Hayden was the only man present and that the police had control of all weapons which could be used against them or to effect an escape.

We do not rely upon Harris v. United States, [331 U.S. 145 (1947)], in sustaining the validity of the search. The principal issue in *Harris* was whether the search there could properly be regarded as incident to the lawful arrest, since Harris was in custody before the search was made and the evidence seized. Here, the seizures occurred prior to or immediately contemporaneous with Hayden's arrest, as part of an effort to find a suspected felon, armed, within the house into which he had run only minutes before the police arrived. The permissible scope of search must, therefore, at the least, be as broad as may reasonably be necessary to prevent the dangers that the suspect at large in the house may resist or escape.

It is argued that, while the weapons, ammunition, and cap may have been seized in the course of a search for weapons, the officer who seized the clothing was searching neither for the suspect nor for weapons when he looked into the washing machine in which he found the clothing. But even if we assume, although we do not decide, that the exigent circumstances in this case made lawful a search without warrant only for the suspect or his weapons, it cannot be said on this record that the officer who found the clothes in the washing machine was not searching for weapons. He testified that he was searching for the man or the money, but his failure to state explicitly that he was searching for weapons, in the absence of a specific question to that effect, can hardly be accorded controlling weight. He knew that the robber was armed and he did not know that some weapons had been found at the time he opened the machine. In these circumstances the inference that he was in fact also looking for weapons is fully justified.

Warden, Maryland Penitentiary v. Hayden, 387 U.S. 294, 297–300 (1967).[20]

135. The "hot pursuit" that justified an entry to search without a warrant in Warden v. Hayden, p. 242 note 134 above, is an example of the general rule that the requirement of a warrant does not apply in an emergency ("exigent circumstances") provided that the emergency was not created or readily avoidable by official action. See, e.g., Llaguno v. Mingey, 763 F.2d 1560 (7th Cir.1985) (search for killer); United States v. McEachin, 670 F.2d 1139 (D.C.Cir.1981) (entry to prevent removal or destruction of evidence); United States v. Robinson, 533 F.2d 578 (D.C.Cir.1975) (search of unoccupied parked car believed to have been used in robbery an hour earlier, to obtain information to apprehend robbers); United States v. Goldenstein, 456 F.2d 1006 (8th Cir.1972) (person needing assistance). In United States v. Beltran, 917 F.2d 641 (1st Cir.1990) the Court said that

20. For another aspect of this case, see p. 246 below.

the emergency requiring an entry without a warrant was due to the failure of police to obtain a warrant while there was time and held that the search was unlawful.

See also United States v. Hand, 516 F.2d 472 (5th Cir.1975), in which "exigent circumstances" were held to authorize a search of the defendant's handbags, which she had left in her employer's office, for evidence of embezzlement. The defendant was not under arrest and was not present in the office when the bags were searched, but she had indicated that she was going to remove them. The court relied primarily on Chambers v. Maroney, p. 228 above. Accord United States v. De La Fuente, 548 F.2d 528 (5th Cir.1977) (suitcase carried by airline passenger could be searched after he checked it and was allowed to board, as alternative to detaining it until warrant was obtained). Are such decisions consistent with United States v. Chadwick, 433 U.S. 1 (1977), p. 212 note 119 above? In Ingram v. City of Columbus, 185 F.3d 579 (6th Cir.1999), the court said that officers entering premises pursuant to exigent circumstances do not have general authority to handcuff occupants and detain them at gunpoint.

The "exigent circumstances" rule is not without limits. In Mincey v. Arizona, 437 U.S. 385 (1978), the Court rejected its application to create a general "murder-scene exception" to requirements of the Fourth Amendment. *Mincey* was confirmed in Flippo v. West Virginia, 528 U.S. 11 (1999) (per curiam). *Mincey* was applied in Thompson v. Louisiana, 469 U.S. 17 (1984) (per curiam). See also Welsh v. Wisconsin, 466 U.S. 740 (1984), p. 49 note 30 above.

136. Postal authorities having a basis for suspicion may temporarily detain packages (first class mail) to investigate and to obtain a warrant for a search of the packages. United States v. Van Leeuwen, 397 U.S. 249 (1970). See United States v. Martell, 654 F.2d 1356 (9th Cir.1981) (brief detention of luggage; *Van Leeuwen* applied).

Van Leeuwen is distinguished in United States v. Hunt, 496 F.2d 888 (5th Cir.1974), in which the court held that the temporary removal of allegedly obscene materials and their delivery to a magistrate for a hearing on obscenity constituted a seizure within the meaning of the Fourth Amendment. The court noted that in *Van Leeuwen*, the packages were "merely removed . . . from the normal flow of the mails" and later replaced "to proceed on to their destination," while in *Hunt* the seizure involved items in the defendant's possession. Id. at 893.

137. Administrative searches. Commercial premises in a closely regulated industry may be subject to administrative searches without a search warrant. In New York v. Burger, 482 U.S. 691 (1987) (6–3), the Court upheld a statute authorizing the warrantless search of automobile junkyards. The administrative search was permissible, the Court said, even though the ultimate purpose of the regulatory scheme was prevention of crime and searches under it might disclose evidence of crime; nor was it significant that police officers rather than administrative officials conducted the search.

"Searches and seizures by government employers or supervisors of the private property of their employees . . . are subject to the restraints of the Fourth Amendment." O'Connor v. Ortega, 480 U.S. 709, 715 (1987) (5–4). *Ortega* involved a search by state hospital officials of the office of a physician employed by the hospital. The search was conducted in the wake of an investigation of alleged misconduct by the physician. Although all members of the Court agreed that the Fourth Amendment applies in this general context, there was no clear majority view about what the Amendment requires. The extent of an employee's "reasonable expectation of privacy" is affected by "the operational realities of the workplace," id. at 717, as well as the actual practices at the workplace. A majority of the Court concluded that a warrant is not required to search for a "work-related purpose," id. at 722; nor does the requirement of probable cause apply. Four members of the Court concluded that "public employer intrusions on the constitutionally protected privacy interests of government employees for noninvestigatory, work-related purposes, as well as for investigation of work-related misconduct, should be judged by the standard of reasonableness under all the circumstances." Id. at 725–26. A fifth Justice (Justice Scalia) concluded that "government searches to retrieve work-related materials or to investigate violations of workplace rules—searches of the sort that are regarded as reasonable and normal in the private-employer context—do not violate the Fourth Amendment." Id. at 732 (opinion concurring in the judgment). Four dissenting Justices concluded that in the absence of "special need" dictated by the purpose to be achieved, id. at 741–43, the ordinary requirements of a warrant and probable cause should apply. See Schowengerdt v. General Dynamics Corp., 823 F.2d 1328 (9th Cir.1987) (*Ortega* applied).

Federal regulations requiring blood and urine tests of railroad employees who are involved in certain train accidents and authorizing railroads to administer breath and urine tests to employees who violate certain safety rules were upheld in Skinner v. Railway Labor Executives' Association, 489 U.S. 602 (1989) (7–2). The regulations were promulgated to control widespread alcohol and drug abuse among the employees. The Court noted that the regulations were a safety measure and not intended to aid prosecution of the employees. It said that imposing a warrant requirement would significantly hinder the objectives of the testing program without adding to the protection afforded by the regulations themselves. In a companion case, National Treasury Employees Union v. Von Raab, 489 U.S. 656 (1989) (5–4), the Court upheld the U.S. Customs Service's program requiring drug tests by urinalysis of employees seeking assignment to positions involving the interdiction of drugs or the carrying of firearms. The Court remanded the case for determination whether, as applied to employees seeking assignment to positions involving the handling of classified information, the program identified the category of employees covered so as to include only employees likely to gain access to sensitive material.

A state statute authorizing a blood alcohol test of any motorist who is in an accident involving death or serious injury was declared invalid in Commonwealth v. Kohl, 615 A.2d 308 (Pa.1992), because, the court said, there was no special need to dispense with the warrant and probable cause requirements, as there was in *Skinner*; the test program involved here was solely to help the state prosecute drunk drivers.

See United States v. Attson, 900 F.2d 1427 (9th Cir.1990), holding that a doctor employed by the federal government in a public hospital was not subject to the requirements for search and seizure under the Fourth Amendment when he took a blood sample for medical reasons from a patient who was a criminal suspect.

Seizure

Warden, Maryland Penitentiary v. Hayden

387 U.S. 294, 87 S.Ct. 1642, 18 L.Ed.2d 782 (1967)

■ MR. JUSTICE BRENNAN delivered the opinion of the Court.

We review in this case the validity of the proposition that there is under the Fourth Amendment a "distinction between merely evidentiary materials, on the one hand, which may not be seized either under the authority of a search warrant or during the course of a search incident to arrest, and on the other hand, those objects which may validly be seized including the instrumentalities and means by which a crime is committed, the fruits of crime such as stolen property, weapons by which escape of the person arrested might be effected, and property the possession of which is a crime."[21]

A Maryland court sitting without a jury convicted respondent of armed robbery. Items of his clothing, a cap, jacket, and trousers, among other things, were seized during a search of his home, and were admitted in evidence without objection. After unsuccessful state court proceedings, he sought and was denied federal habeas corpus relief in the District Court for Maryland. A divided panel of the Court of Appeals believed that Harris v. United States, 331 U.S. 145, 154, sustained the validity of the search, but held that respondent was correct in his contention that the clothing seized was improperly admitted in evidence because the items had "evidential value only" and therefore were not lawfully subject to seizure. We granted certiorari. . . . We reverse.

. . .

[The facts and the first part of the Court's opinion, in which the Court concluded that the search of the defendant's home was lawful, are given in note 134, p. 242 above.]

21. Harris v. United States, 331 U.S. 145, 154 [(1947)].

We come, then, to the question whether, even though the search was lawful, the Court of Appeals was correct in holding that the seizure and introduction of the items of clothing violated the Fourth Amendment because they are "mere evidence." The distinction made by some of our cases between seizure of items of evidential value only and seizure of instrumentalities, fruits, or contraband has been criticized by courts and commentators. . . . We today reject the distinction as based on premises no longer accepted as rules governing the application of the Fourth Amendment.

. . .

Nothing in the language of the Fourth Amendment supports the distinction between "mere evidence" and instrumentalities, fruits of crime, or contraband. On its face, the provision assures the "right of the people to be secure in their persons, houses, papers, and effects . . ." without regard to the use to which any of these things are applied. This "right of the people" is certainly unrelated to the "mere evidence" limitation. Privacy is disturbed no more by a search directed to a purely evidentiary object than it is by a search directed to an instrumentality, fruit, or contraband. A magistrate can intervene in both situations, and the requirements of probable cause and specificity can be preserved intact. Moreover, nothing in the nature of property seized as evidence renders it more private than property seized, for example, as an instrumentality; quite the opposite may be true. Indeed, the distinction is wholly irrational, since, depending on the circumstances, the same "papers and effects" may be "mere evidence" in one case and "instrumentality" in another. . . .

In Gouled v. United States, 255 U.S. 298, 309, the Court said that search warrants "may not be used as a means of gaining access to a man's house or office and papers solely for the purpose of making search to secure evidence to be used against him in a criminal or penal proceeding. . . ." The Court derived from Boyd v. United States, [116 U.S. 616 (1886)], the proposition that warrants "may be resorted to only when a primary right to such search and seizure may be found in the interest which the public or the complainant may have in the property to be seized, or in the right to the possession of it, or when a valid exercise of the police power renders possession of the property by the accused unlawful and provides that it may be taken," 255 U.S., at 309; that is, when the property is an instrumentality or fruit of crime, or contraband. Since it was "impossible to say, on the record . . . that the Government had any interest" in the papers involved "other than as evidence against the accused . . ." "to permit them to be used in evidence would be, in effect, as ruled in the *Boyd* case, to compel the defendant to become a witness against himself." Id., at 311.

The items of clothing involved in this case are not "testimonial" or "communicative" in nature, and their introduction therefore did not compel respondent to become a witness against himself in violation of the Fifth Amendment. Schmerber v. California, 384 U.S. 757. This case thus does not require that we consider whether there are items of evidential value whose very nature precludes them from being the object of a reasonable search and seizure.

The Fourth Amendment ruling in *Gouled* was based upon the dual, related premises that historically the right to search for and seize property depended upon the assertion by the Government of a valid claim of superior interest, and that it was not enough that the purpose of the search and seizure was to obtain evidence to use in apprehending and convicting criminals. . . . Thus stolen property—the fruits of crime—was always subject to seizure. And the power to search for stolen property was gradually extended to cover "any property which the private citizen was not permitted to possess," which included instrumentalities of crime (because of the early notion that items used in crime were forfeited to the State) and contraband. Kaplan, "Search and Seizure: A No-Man's Land in the Criminal Law," 49 Calif. L. Rev. 474, 475. No separate governmental interest in seizing evidence to apprehend and convict criminals was recognized; it was required that some property interest be asserted. The remedial structure also reflected these dual premises. Trespass, replevin, and the other means of redress for persons aggrieved by searches and seizures, depended upon proof of a superior property interest. And since a lawful seizure presupposed a superior claim, it was inconceivable that a person could recover property lawfully seized. . . .

The premise that property interests control the right of the Government to search and seize has been discredited. Searches and seizures may be "unreasonable" within the Fourth Amendment even though the Government asserts a superior property interest at common law. We have recognized that the principal object of the Fourth Amendment is the protection of privacy rather than property, and have increasingly discarded fictional and procedural barriers rested on property concepts. . . .

The development of search and seizure law . . . is replete with examples of the transformation in substantive law brought about through the interaction of the felt need to protect privacy from unreasonable invasions and the flexibility in rulemaking made possible by the remedy of exclusion. . . .

The premise in *Gouled* that government may not seize evidence simply for the purpose of proving crime has likewise been discredited. The requirement that the Government assert in addition some property interest in material it seizes has long been a fiction, obscuring the reality that government has an interest in solving crime. *Schmerber* settled the proposition that it is reasonable, within the terms of the Fourth Amendment, to conduct otherwise permissible searches for the purpose of obtaining evidence which would aid in apprehending and convicting criminals. The requirements of the Fourth Amendment can secure the same protection of privacy whether the search is for "mere evidence" or for fruits, instrumentalities or contraband. There must, of course, be a nexus—automatically provided in the case of fruits, instrumentalities or contraband—between the item to be seized and criminal behavior. Thus in the case of "mere evidence," probable cause must be examined in terms of cause to believe that the evidence sought will aid in a particular apprehension or conviction. In so doing, consideration of police purposes will be required. . . . But no such problem is presented in this case. The clothes found in the washing machine matched the description of those worn by the robber and the police therefore could reasonably believe that the items would aid in the identification of the culprit.

The remedy of suppression, moreover, which made possible protection of privacy from unreasonable searches without regard to proof of a superior property interest, likewise provides the procedural device necessary for allowing otherwise permissible searches and seizures conducted solely to obtain evidence of crime. For just as the suppression of evidence does not entail a declaration of superior property interest in the person aggrieved, thereby enabling him to suppress evidence unlawfully seized despite his inability to demonstrate such an interest (as with fruits, instrumentalities, contraband), the refusal to suppress evidence carries no declaration of superior property interest in the State, and should thereby enable the State to introduce evidence lawfully seized despite its inability to demonstrate such an interest. And, unlike the situation at common law, the owner of property would not be rendered remediless if "mere evidence" could lawfully be seized to prove crime. For just as the suppression of evidence does not in itself necessarily entitle the aggrieved person to its return (as, for example, contraband), the introduction of "mere evidence" does not in itself entitle the State to its retention. Where public officials "unlawfully seize or *hold* a citizen's realty or chattels, recoverable by appropriate action at law or in equity . . ." the true owner may "bring his possessory action to reclaim that which is wrongfully withheld." Land v. Dollar, 330 U.S. 731, 738. (Emphasis added.)

The survival of the *Gouled* distinction is attributable more to chance than considered judgment. Legislation has helped perpetuate it. Thus, Congress has never authorized the issuance of search warrants for the seizure of mere evidence of crime. . . . *Gouled* concluded, needlessly it appears, that the Constitution virtually limited searches and seizures to these categories. After *Gouled*, pressure to test this conclusion was slow to mount. Rule 41(b) of the Federal Rules of Criminal Procedure incorporated the *Gouled* categories as limitations on federal authorities to issue warrants and Mapp v. Ohio, 367 U.S. 643, only recently made the "mere evidence" rule a problem in the state courts. Pressure against the rule in the federal courts has taken the form rather of broadening the categories of evidence subject to seizure, thereby creating considerable confusion in the law. . . .

The rationale most frequently suggested for the rule preventing the seizure of evidence is that "limitations upon the fruit to be gathered tend to limit the quest itself." United States v. Poller, 43 F.2d 911, 914 (C.A.2d Cir.1930). But privacy "would be just as well served by a restriction on search to the even-numbered days of the month. . . . And it would have the extra advantage of avoiding hair-splitting questions. . . ." *Kaplan*, at 479. The "mere evidence" limitation has spawned exceptions so numerous and confusion so great, in fact, that it is questionable whether it affords meaningful protection. But if its rejection does enlarge the area of permissible searches, the intrusions are nevertheless made after fulfilling the probable cause and particularity requirements of the Fourth Amendment and after the intervention of "a neutral and detached magistrate. . . ." Johnson v. United States, 333 U.S. 10, 14. The Fourth Amendment allows intrusions upon privacy under these circumstances, and there is no viable reason to distinguish intrusions to secure "mere evidence" from intrusions to secure fruits, instrumentalities, or contraband.

The judgment of the Court of Appeals is

Reversed.[22]

---

138. In 1968 Congress implemented the decision in Warden v. Hayden, above, in the Omnibus Crime Control & Safe Streets Act, § 1401(a), 82 Stat. 238, which amended Title 18 U.S.C. by adding § 3103a: "Additional grounds for issuing warrant. . . . [A] warrant may be issued to search for and seize any property that constitutes evidence of a criminal offense in violation of the laws of the United States." A similar provision has been incorporated in Rule 41(c)(1), see p. 177 above.

Was the ruling in *Gouled* concerned with seizures or the scope of a search? Or was it concerned with the *occasion* for a search? Is it so obviously true that from a privacy perspective there is no reason to distinguish a search for evidence from a search for the fruits or instrumentalities of a crime or contraband?

139. If police officials intend to use recovered stolen property in evidence against the thief and retain it pending the trial over the objection of the victim of the theft (who, aside from destroying the chain of custody, wants to use it in a way that will make it unavailable as evidence) is the property " 'wrongfully withheld,' " p. 249 above? If so, is the Court's

[22] Justice Fortas wrote a concurring opinion which Chief Justice Warren joined. Justice Black concurred in the result. Justice Douglas wrote a dissenting opinion.

observation that there is a "possessory action," id., to recover the property sufficient? Is the situation different if the owner of the property who wants its return (and is entitled to its return) is the thief? Suppose Hayden had demanded the return of his cap, jacket and trousers before trial?

Rule 41(g) provides for a "motion to return property," to be filed in the district where the property was seized. If, following a hearing on any factual issues, the motion is granted, the property must be returned to the movant, but the court "may impose reasonable conditions to protect access to the property and its use in later proceedings." See United States v. Wilson, 540 F.2d 1100, 1103–1104 (D.C.Cir.1976): "[I]t is fundamental to the integrity of the criminal justice process that property . . . against which no Government claim lies, be returned promptly to its rightful owner"; "the district court, once its need for the property has terminated, has both the jurisdiction and the duty to return the contested property here regardless and independently of the validity or invalidity of the underlying search and seizure." In United States v. Palmer, 565 F.2d 1063 (9th Cir.1977), the court ordered that money seized from a convicted bank robber, which the government offered in evidence at trial, should be returned to him rather than to the government, absent any claim of ownership adverse to his.

The warrantless seizure from a public place of a car that the police have probable cause to believe is forfeitable contraband is not a violation of the Fourth Amendment. Florida v. White, 526 U.S. 559 (1999) (7–2). The car was subject to forfeiture under a state statute because it had been used in drug transactions.

140. Andresen v. Maryland, 427 U.S. 463 (1976) (7–2). The question left open in Warden v. Hayden, see p. 248 above, whether the privilege against self-incrimination may inhibit the seizure of items if the seizure is lawful under the Fourth Amendment has been answered in the negative. In Andresen v. Maryland, investigators made a search on a warrant of the defendant's offices. The Court held that the privilege against self-incrimination did not require the suppression of incriminating records containing statements made by the defendant that were seized during the search.

> [I]n this case, petitioner was not asked to say or to do anything. The records seized contained statements that petitioner had voluntarily committed to writing. The search for and seizure of these records were conducted by law enforcement personnel. Finally, when these records were introduced at trial, they were authenticated by a handwriting expert, not by petitioner. Any compulsion of petitioner to speak, other than the inherent psychological pressure to respond at trial to unfavorable evidence, was not present.
>
> This case thus falls within the principle stated by Mr. Justice Holmes: "A party is privileged from producing the evidence but not

AO 109 (Rev. 2/90) Seizure Warrant

UNITED STATES DISTRICT COURT

_______________ District of _______________

In the Matter of the Seizure of
(Address or brief description of property or premises to be seized)

SEIZURE WARRANT

CASE NUMBER:

TO: _______________ and any Authorized Officer of the United States

Affidavit(s) having been made before me by _______________ who has reason to
Affiant

believe that in the _______________ District of _______________ there is now certain property which is subject to forfeiture to the United States, namely (describe the property to be seized)

I am satisfied that the affidavit(s) and any recorded testimony establish probable cause to believe that the property so described is subject to seizure and that grounds exist for the issuance of this seizure warrant.

YOU ARE HEREBY COMMANDED to seize within 10 days the property specified, serving this warrant and making the seizure ☐ (in the daytime—6:00 A.M. to 10:00 P.M.) ☐ (at any time in the day or night as I find reasonable cause has been established), leaving a copy of this warrant and receipt for the property seized, and prepare a written inventory of the property seized and promptly return this warrant to _______________ as required by law.
U.S. Judge or Magistrate

_______________ at _______________
Date and Time Issued | City | State

_______________ _______________
Name of Judicial Officer | Title of Judicial Officer | Signature of Judicial Officer

from its production." Johnson v. United States, 228 U.S. 457, 458 (1913). This principle recognizes that the protection afforded by the Self-Incrimination Clause of the Fifth Amendment "adheres basically to the person, not to information that may incriminate him." Couch v. United States, 409 U.S. [322 (1973)], at 328. Thus, although the Fifth Amendment may protect an individual from complying with a subpoena for the production of his personal records in his possession because the very act of protection may constitute a compulsory authentication of incriminating information . . . a seizure of the same materials by law enforcement officers differs in a crucial respect—the individual against whom the search is directed is not required to aid in the discovery, production, or authentication of incriminating evidence.

. . .

[A] contrary determination would prohibit the admission of evidence traditionally used in criminal cases and traditionally admissible despite the Fifth Amendment. For example, it would bar the admission of an accused's gambling records in a prosecution for gambling; a note given temporarily to a bank teller during a robbery and subsequently seized in the accused's automobile or home in a prosecution for bank robbery; and incriminating notes prepared, but not sent, by an accused in a kidnaping or blackmail prosecution.

We find a useful analogy to the Fifth Amendment question in those cases that deal with the "seizure" of oral communications. As the Court has explained, "[t]he constitutional privilege against self-incrimination . . . is designed to prevent the use of legal process to force from the lips of the accused individual the evidence necessary to convict him or to force him to produce and authenticate any personal documents or effects that might incriminate him." Bellis v. United States, 417 U.S. [85 (1974)], at 88, quoting United States v. White, 322 U.S. [694 (1944)] at 698. The significant aspect of this principle was apparent and applied in Hoffa v. United States, 385 U.S. 293 (1966), where the Court rejected the contention that an informant's "seizure" of the accused's conversation with him, and his subsequent testimony at trial concerning that conversation, violated the Fifth Amendment. The rationale was that, although the accused's statements may have been elicited by the informant for the purpose of gathering evidence against him, they were made voluntarily. We see no reasoned distinction to be made between the compulsion upon the accused in that case and the compulsion in this one. In each, the communication, whether oral or written, was made voluntarily. The fact that seizure was

> contemporaneous with the communication in *Hoffa* but subsequent to the communication here does not affect the question whether the accused was compelled to speak.
>
> Finally, we do not believe that permitting the introduction into evidence of a person's business records seized during an otherwise lawful search would offend or undermine any of the policies undergirding the privilege. Murphy v. Waterfront Commission, 378 U.S. 52, 55 (1964).
>
> In this case, petitioner, at the time he recorded his communication, at the time of the search, and at the time the records were admitted at trial, was not subjected to "the cruel trilemma of self-accusation, perjury or contempt." Ibid. Indeed, he was never required to say or to do anything under penalty of sanction. Similarly, permitting the admission of the records in question does not convert our accusatorial system of justice into an inquisitorial system. . . . Further, the search for and seizure of business records pose no danger greater than that inherent in every search that evidence will be "elicited by inhumane treatment and abuses." 378 U.S., at 55. In this case, the statements seized were voluntarily committed to paper before the police arrived to search for them, and petitioner was not treated discourteously during the search. Also, the "good cause" to "disturb," ibid., petitioner was independently determined by the judge who issued the warrants; and the State bore the burden of executing them. Finally, there is no chance, in this case, of petitioner's statements being self-deprecatory and untrustworthy because they were extracted from him—they were already in existence and had been made voluntarily.

427 U.S. at 473–77.

141. While the defendant was in police custody, police officers visited his home to speak to his wife about the crime of which he was suspected. During the course of the interview, she gave the officers guns and clothing belonging to her husband. Coolidge v. New Hampshire, 403 U.S. 443 (1971). The Court rejected his claim that their receiving the items without his permission constituted an unlawful search and seizure:

> The first branch of the petitioner's argument is that when Mrs. Coolidge brought out the guns and clothing, and then handed them over to the police, she was acting as an "instrument" of the officials, complying with a "demand" made by them. Consequently, it is argued, Coolidge was the victim of a search and seizure within the constitutional meaning of those terms. Since we cannot accept this interpretation of the facts, we need not consider the petitioner's further argument that Mrs. Coolidge could not or did not "waive" her husband's constitutional protection against unreasonable searches and seizures.
>
> Had Mrs. Coolidge, wholly on her own initiative, sought out her husband's guns and clothing and then taken them to the police station to be used as evidence against him, there can be no doubt under

existing law that the articles would later have been admissible in evidence. . . . The question presented here is whether the conduct of the police officers at the Coolidge house was such as to make her actions their actions for purposes of the Fourth and Fourteenth Amendments and their attendant exclusionary rules. The test, as the petitioner's argument suggests, is whether Mrs. Coolidge, in light of all the circumstances of the case, must be regarded as having acted as an "instrument" or agent of the state when she produced her husband's belongings. . . .

In a situation like the one before us there no doubt always exist forces pushing the spouse to cooperate with the police. Among these are the simple but often powerful convention of openness and honesty, the fear that secretive behavior will intensify suspicion, and uncertainty as to what course is most likely to be helpful to the absent spouse. But there is nothing constitutionally suspect in the existence, without more, of these incentives to full disclosure or active cooperation with the police. The exclusionary rules were fashioned "to prevent, not to repair," and their target is official misconduct. They are "to compel respect for the constitutional guaranty in the only effectively available way—by removing the incentive to disregard it." Elkins v. United States, 364 U.S. 206, 217. But it is no part of the policy underlying the Fourth and Fourteenth Amendments to discourage citizens from aiding to the utmost of their ability in the apprehension of criminals. If, then, the exclusionary rule is properly applicable to the evidence taken from the Coolidge house on the night of February 2, it must be upon the basis that some type of unconstitutional police conduct occurred.

Yet it cannot be said that the police should have obtained a warrant for the guns and clothing before they set out to visit Mrs. Coolidge, since they had no intention of rummaging around among Coolidge's effects or of dispossessing him of any of his property. Nor can it be said that they should have obtained Coolidge's permission for a seizure they did not intend to make. There was nothing to compel them to announce to the suspect that they intended to question his wife about his movements on the night of the disappearance or about the theft from his employer. Once Mrs. Coolidge had admitted them, the policemen were surely acting normally and properly when they asked her, as they had asked those questioned earlier in the investigation, including Coolidge himself, about any guns there might be in the house. The question concerning the clothes Coolidge had been wearing on the night of the disappearance was logical and in no way coercive. Indeed, one might doubt the competence of the officers involved had they not asked exactly the questions they did ask. And surely when Mrs. Coolidge of her own accord produced the guns and clothes for inspection, rather than simply describing them, it was not incumbent on the police to stop her or avert their eyes.

> The crux of the petitioner's argument must be that when Mrs. Coolidge asked the policemen whether they wanted the guns, they should have replied that they could not take them, or have first telephoned Coolidge at the police station and asked his permission to take them, or have asked her whether she had been authorized by her husband to release them. Instead, after one policeman had declined the offer, the other turned and said, "We might as well take them," to which Mrs. Coolidge replied, "If you would like them, you may take them."
>
> In assessing the claim that this course of conduct amounted to a search and seizure, it is well to keep in mind that Mrs. Coolidge described her own motive as that of clearing her husband, and that she believed that she had nothing to hide. She had seen her husband himself produce his guns for two other policemen earlier in the week, and there is nothing to indicate that she realized that he had offered only three of them for inspection on that occasion. The two officers who questioned her behaved, as her own testimony shows, with perfect courtesy. There is not the slightest implication of an attempt on their part to coerce or dominate her, or, for that matter, to direct her actions by the more subtle techniques of suggestion that are available to officials in circumstances like these. To hold that the conduct of the police here was a search and seizure would be to hold, in effect, that a criminal suspect has constitutional protection against the adverse consequences of a spontaneous, good-faith effort by his wife to clear him of suspicion.

Coolidge, 403 U.S. at 487–90.

In United States v. Sherwin, 539 F.2d 1 (9th Cir.1976), the manager of a trucking company turned over to the FBI books contained in a shipment that he believed to be obscene. Following the reasoning in *Coolidge*, above, the court said that in a case of this kind "only the fact of consent is relevant, not whether it was properly authorized." Further, "the private person's legal authority to approve a transfer of objects found in a private search has no bearing on whether his relinquishment of those objects to the government is coerced or voluntary. . . . If a transfer is voluntary, then it is not a seizure and the fourth amendment's reasonableness standard is simply inapplicable." Id. at 7–8. See also United States v. Black, 767 F.2d 1334 (9th Cir. 1985) (surrender of business records by former employee and friend).

142. Employees of a private freight carrier opened a damaged package and found plastic bags containing a white powder concealed inside a tube. They notified federal narcotics agents. An agent removed the bags from the tube, opened them, and took a trace of the powder. He performed a field test on the powder, which was cocaine. The Court held that the agent's actions did not violate the Fourth Amendment. The inspection and removal of the plastic bags only confirmed information he had already obtained from the carrier's employees, whose action was a private search; they violated no additional expectation of privacy. The seizure of the bags without a warrant was lawful, since there was probable cause to believe that they contained contraband. The test was permissible since it could disclose only one further fact, whether or not the powder was cocaine, and did not invade any legitimate interest in privacy. United States v. Jacobsen, 466 U.S. 109 (1984) (7–2). Cf. Walter v. United States, 447 U.S. 649 (1980) (5–4), p. 214 above.

143. After the defendant had been taken into custody on a charge of murder, the police learned that he had left a suit of clothes at the cleaners shortly after the murder occurred. At their request, the proprietor of the cleaning establishment turned the suit over to them. It revealed evidence incriminating the defendant. The police had no warrant, nor did they have the defendant's permission to seize the suit. Clarke v. Neil, 427 F.2d 1322 (6th Cir.1970). Was the evidence admissible?

Standing

Rakas v. Illinois

439 U.S. 128, 99 S.Ct. 421, 58 L.Ed.2d 387 (1978)

■ MR. JUSTICE REHNQUIST delivered the opinion of the Court.

Petitioners were convicted of armed robbery in the Circuit Court of Kankakee County, Ill., and their convictions were affirmed on appeal. At their trial, the prosecution offered into evidence a sawed-off rifle and rifle shells that had been seized by police during a search of an automobile in which petitioners had been passengers. Neither petitioner is the owner of the automobile and neither has ever asserted that he owned the rifle or shells seized. The Illinois Appellate Court held that petitioners lacked standing to object to the allegedly unlawful search and seizure and denied their motion to suppress the evidence. We granted certiorari in light of the obvious importance of the issues raised to the administration of criminal justice . . . and now affirm.

I

Because we are not here concerned with the issue of probable cause, a brief description of the events leading to the search of the automobile will suffice. A police officer on a routine patrol received a radio call notifying him of a robbery of a clothing store in Bourbonnais, Ill., and describing the getaway car. Shortly thereafter, the officer spotted an automobile which he thought might be the getaway car. After following the car for some time and after the arrival of assistance, he and several other officers stopped the vehicle. The occupants of the automobile, petitioners and two female companions, were ordered out of the car and after the occupants had left the car, two officers searched the interior of the vehicle. They discovered a box of rifle shells in the glove compartment, which had been locked, and a sawed-off rifle under the front passenger seat. . . . After discovering the rifle and the shells, the officers took petitioners to the station and placed them under arrest.

Before trial petitioners moved to suppress the rifle and shells seized from the car on the ground that the search violated the Fourth and Fourteenth Amendments. They conceded that they did not own the automobile and were simply passengers; the owner of the car had been the driver of the vehicle at the time of the search. Nor did they assert that they owned the rifle or the shells seized. The prosecutor challenged petitioners' standing to object to the lawfulness of the search of the car because neither the car, the shells nor the rifle belonged to them. The trial court agreed that petitioners lacked standing and denied the motion to suppress the evidence. . . . In view of this holding, the court did not determine whether there was probable cause for the search and seizure. On appeal after petitioners' conviction, the Appellate Court of Illinois, Third Judicial District, affirmed the trial court's denial of petitioners' motion to suppress because it held that "without a proprietary or other similar interest in an automobile, a mere passenger therein lacks standing to challenge the legality of the search of the vehicle." 360 N.E.2d 1252, 1253 (1977). . . .

The Illinois Supreme Court denied petitioners leave to appeal.

II

Petitioners first urge us to relax or broaden the rule of standing enunciated in Jones v. United States, 362 U.S. 257 (1960), so that any criminal defendant at whom a search was "directed" would have standing to contest the legality of that search and object to the admission at trial of evidence obtained as a result of the search. Alternatively, petitioners argue that they have standing to object to the search under *Jones* because they were "legitimately on [the] premises" at the time of the search.

The concept of standing discussed in *Jones* focuses on whether the person seeking to challenge the legality of a search as a basis for suppressing evidence was himself the "victim" of the search or seizure. Id., at 261. Adoption of the so-called "target" theory advanced by petitioners would in effect permit a defendant to assert that a violation of the Fourth Amendment rights of a third party entitled him to have evidence suppressed at his trial. If we reject petitioners' request for a broadened rule of standing such as this, and reaffirm the holding of *Jones* and other cases that Fourth Amendment rights are personal rights that may not be asserted vicariously, we will have occasion to re-examine the "standing" terminology emphasized in *Jones*. For we are not at all sure that the determination of a motion to suppress is materially aided by labeling the inquiry identified in *Jones* as one of standing, rather than simply recognizing it as one involving the substantive question of whether or not the proponent of the motion to suppress has had his own Fourth Amendment rights infringed by the search and seizure which he seeks to challenge. We shall therefore consider in turn petitioners' target theory, the necessity for continued adherence to the notion of standing discussed in *Jones* as a concept that is theoretically distinct from the merits of a defendant's Fourth Amendment claim, and finally, the proper disposition of petitioners' ultimate claim in this case.

A

We decline to extend the rule of standing in Fourth Amendment cases in the manner suggested by petitioners. As we stated in Alderman v. United States, 394 U.S. 165 (1969), "Fourth Amendment rights are personal rights which, like some other constitutional rights, may not be vicariously asserted." Id., at 174. . . . A person who is aggrieved by an illegal search and seizure only through the introduction of damaging evidence secured by a search of a third person's premises or property has not had any of his Fourth Amendment rights infringed. . . . And since the exclusionary rule is an attempt to effectuate the guaranties of the Fourth Amendment . . . it is proper to permit only defendants whose Fourth Amendment rights have been violated to benefit from the rule's protections. . . . There is no reason to think that a party whose rights have been infringed will not, if evidence is used against him, have ample motivation to move to suppress it. . . . Even if such a person is not a defendant in the action, he may be able to recover damages for the violation of his Fourth Amendment rights . . . or seek redress under state law for invasion of privacy or trespass.

. . .

Conferring standing to raise vicarious Fourth Amendment claims would necessarily mean a more widespread invocation of the exclusionary rule during criminal trials. The Court's opinion in *Alderman* counseled against such an extension of the exclusionary rule:

> The deterrent values of preventing the incrimination of those whose rights the police have violated have been considered sufficient to justify the suppression of probative evidence even though the case against the defendant is weakened or destroyed. We adhere to that judgment. But we are not convinced that the additional benefits of extending the exclusionary rule to other defendants would justify further encroachment upon the public interest in prosecuting those accused of crime and having them acquitted or convicted on the basis of all the evidence which exposes the truth.

394 U.S., at 174–75. Each time the exclusionary rule is applied it exacts a substantial social cost for the vindication of Fourth Amendment rights. Relevant and reliable evidence is kept from the trier of fact and the search for truth at trial is deflected. . . . Since our cases generally have held that one whose Fourth Amendment rights are violated may successfully suppress evidence obtained in the course of an illegal search and seizure, misgivings as to the benefit of enlarging the class of persons who may invoke that rule are properly considered when deciding whether to expand standing to assert Fourth Amendment violations.

B

Had we accepted petitioners' request to allow persons other than those whose own Fourth Amendment rights were violated by a challenged search and seizure to suppress evidence obtained in the course of such police activity, it would be appropriate to retain *Jones*' use of standing in Fourth Amendment analysis. Under petitioners' target theory, a court could determine that a defendant had standing to invoke the exclusionary rule without having to inquire into the substantive question of whether the challenged search or seizure violated the Fourth Amendment rights of that particular defendant. However, having rejected petitioners' target theory and reaffirmed the principle that the "rights assured by the Fourth Amendment are personal rights, [which] . . . may be enforced by exclusion of evidence only at the instance of one whose own protection was infringed by the search and seizure," Simmons v. United States, 390 U.S. [377 (1968)], at 389, the question necessarily arises whether it serves any useful analytical purpose to consider this principle a matter of standing, distinct from the merits of a defendant's Fourth Amendment claim. We can think of no decided cases from this Court that would have come out differently had we concluded, as we do now, that the type of standing requirement discussed in *Jones* and reaffirmed today is more properly subsumed under substantive Fourth Amendment doctrine. Rigorous application of the principle that the rights secured by this Amendment are personal, in place of a notion of "standing," will produce no additional situations in which evidence must be excluded. The inquiry under either approach is the same. But we think the better analysis forthrightly focuses on the extent of a particular defendant's rights under the Fourth Amendment, rather than on any theoretically separate, but invariably intertwined concept of standing. . . .

It should be emphasized that nothing we say here casts the least doubt on cases which recognize that, as a general proposition, the issue of standing involves two inquiries: first, whether the proponent of a particular legal right has alleged "injury in fact," and, second, whether the proponent is asserting his own legal rights and interests rather than basing his claim for relief upon the rights of third parties. . . . But this Court's long history of insistence that Fourth Amendment rights are personal in nature has already answered many of these traditional standing inquiries, and we think that definition of those rights is more properly placed within the purview of substantive Fourth Amendment law than within that of standing. . . .

Analyzed in these terms, the question is whether the challenged search or seizure violated the Fourth Amendment rights of a criminal defendant who seeks to exclude the evidence obtained during it. That inquiry in turn requires a determination of whether the disputed search and seizure has infringed an interest of the defendant which the Fourth Amendment was designed to protect. We are under no illusion that by dispensing with the rubric of standing used in *Jones* we have rendered any simpler the determination of whether the proponent of a motion to suppress is entitled to contest the legality of a search and seizure. But by frankly recognizing that this aspect of the analysis belongs more properly under the heading of substantive Fourth Amendment doctrine than under the heading of standing, we think the decision of this issue will rest on sounder logical footing.

C

Here petitioners, who were passengers occupying a car which they neither owned nor leased, seek to analogize their position to that of the defendant in Jones v. United States, 362 U.S. 257 (1960). In *Jones*, petitioner was present at the time of the search of an apartment which was owned by a friend. The friend had given Jones permission to use the apartment and a key to it, with which Jones had admitted himself on the day of the search. He had a suit and shirt at the apartment and had slept there "maybe a night," but his home was elsewhere. At the time of the search, Jones was the only occupant of the apartment because the lessee was away for a period of several days. Id., at 259. Under these circumstances, this Court stated that while one wrongfully on the premises could not move to suppress evidence obtained as a result of searching them,[23] "anyone legitimately on premises where a search occurs may challenge its legality." 362 U.S., at 267. Petitioners argue that their occupancy of the automobile in question was comparable to that of Jones in the apartment and that they therefore have standing to contest the legality of the search—or as we have rephrased the inquiry, that they, like Jones, had their Fourth Amendment rights violated by the search.

We do not question the conclusion in *Jones* that the defendant in that case suffered a violation of his personal Fourth Amendment rights if the search in question was unlawful. Nonetheless, we believe that the phrase "legitimately on premises" coined in *Jones* creates too broad a gauge for measurement of Fourth Amendment rights. For example, applied literally, this statement would permit a casual visitor who has never seen, or been permitted to visit, the basement of another's house to object to a search of the basement if the visitor happened to be in the kitchen of the house at the time of the search. Likewise, a casual visitor who walks into a house one minute before a search of the house commences and leaves one minute after the search ends would be able to contest the legality of the search.

23. The Court in Jones was quite careful to note that "wrongful" presence at the scene of a search would not enable a defendant to object to the legality of the search. 362 U.S., at 267. . . . Despite this clear statement in *Jones*, several lower courts inexplicably have held that a person present in a stolen automobile at the time of a search may object to the lawfulness of the search of the automobile. . . .

The first visitor would have absolutely no interest or legitimate expectation of privacy in the basement, the second would have none in the house, and it advances no purpose served by the Fourth Amendment to permit either of them to object to the lawfulness of the search.[24]

We think that *Jones* on its facts merely stands for the unremarkable proposition that a person can have a legally sufficient interest in a place other than his own home so that the Fourth Amendment protects him from unreasonable governmental intrusion into that place. . . . In defining the scope of that interest, we adhere to the view expressed in *Jones* and echoed in later cases that arcane distinctions developed in property and tort law between guests, licensees, invitees, and the like, ought not to control. . . . But the *Jones* statement that a person need only be "legitimately on premises" in order to challenge the validity of the search of a dwelling place cannot be taken in its full sweep beyond the facts of that case.

Katz v. United States, 389 U.S. 347 (1967), provides guidance in defining the scope of the interest protected by the Fourth Amendment. In the course of repudiating the doctrine . . . that if police officers had not been guilty of a common-law trespass they were not prohibited by the Fourth Amendment from eavesdropping, the Court in *Katz* held that capacity to claim the protection of the Fourth Amendment depends not upon a property right in the invaded place but upon whether the person who claims the protection of the Amendment has a legitimate expectation of privacy in the invaded place. . . . Viewed in this manner, the holding in *Jones* can best be explained by the fact that Jones had a legitimate expectation of privacy in the premises he was using and therefore could claim the protection of the Fourth Amendment with respect to a governmental invasion of those premises, even though his "interest" in those premises might not have been a recognized property interest at common law.[25] . . .

24. This is not to say that such visitors could not contest the lawfulness of the seizure of evidence or the search if their own property were seized during the search.

25. Obviously, however, a "legitimate" expectation of privacy by definition means more than a subjective expectation of not being discovered. A burglar plying his trade in a summer cabin during the off season may have a thoroughly justified subjective expectation of privacy, but it is not one which the law recognizes as "legitimate." His presence, in the words of *Jones*, 362 U.S., at 267, is "wrongful"; his expectation is not "one that society is prepared to recognize as 'reasonable.' " Katz v. United States, 389 U.S. 347, 361 (1967) (Harlan, J., concurring). And it would, of course, be merely tautological to fall back on the notion that those expectations of privacy which are legitimate depend primarily on cases deciding exclusionary rule issues in criminal cases. Legitimation of expectations of privacy by law must have a source outside of the Fourth Amendment, either by reference to concepts of real or personal property law or to understandings that are recognized and permitted by society. One of the main rights attaching to property is the right to exclude others . . . and one who owns or lawfully possesses or controls property will in all likelihood have a legitimate expectation of privacy by virtue of this right to exclude. Expectations of privacy protected by the Fourth Amendment, of course, need not be based on a common-law interest in real or personal property, or on the invasion of such an interest. These ideas were rejected both in *Jones*, supra, and *Katz*, supra. But by focusing on legitimate expectations of privacy in Fourth Amendment jurisprudence, the Court

Our Brother White in dissent expresses the view that by rejecting the phrase "legitimately on [the] premises" as the appropriate measure of Fourth Amendment rights, we are abandoning a thoroughly workable, "bright line" test in favor of a less certain analysis of whether the facts of a particular case give rise to a legitimate expectation of privacy. Post, at 168. If "legitimately on premises" were the successful litmus test of Fourth Amendment rights that he assumes it is, his approach would have at least the merit of easy application, whatever it lacked in fidelity to the history and purposes of the Fourth Amendment. But a reading of lower court cases that have applied the phrase "legitimately on premises," and of the dissent itself, reveals that this expression is not a shorthand summary for a bright line rule which somehow encapsulates the "core" of the Fourth Amendment's protections.

. . .

. . . In abandoning "legitimately on premises" for the doctrine that we announce today, we are not forsaking a time-tested and workable rule, which has produced consistent results when applied, solely for the sake of fidelity to the values underlying the Fourth Amendment. We also are rejecting blind adherence to a phrase which at most has superficial clarity and which conceals underneath that thin veneer all of the problems of line drawing which must be faced in any conscientious effort to apply the Fourth Amendment. Where the factual premises for a rule are so generally prevalent that little would be lost and much would be gained by abandoning case-by-case analysis, we have not hesitated to do so. . . . But the phrase "legitimately on premises" has not shown to be an easily applicable measure of Fourth Amendment rights so much as it has proved to be simply a label placed by the courts on results which have not been subjected to careful analysis. We would not wish to be understood as saying that legitimate presence on the premises is irrelevant to one's expectation of privacy, but it cannot be deemed controlling.

D

Judged by the foregoing analysis, petitioners' claims must fail. They asserted neither a property nor a possessory interest in the automobile, nor an interest in the property seized. And as we have previously indicated, the fact that they were "legitimately on [the] premises" in the sense that they were in the car with the permission of its owner is not determinative of whether they had a legitimate expectation of privacy in the particular areas of the automobile searched. It is unnecessary for us to decide here whether

has not altogether abandoned use of property concepts in determining the presence or absence of the privacy interests protected by that Amendment. No better demonstration of this proposition exists than the decision in Alderman v. United States, 394 U.S. 165 (1969), where the Court held that an individual's property interest in his own home was so great as to allow him to object to electronic surveillance of conversations emanating from his home, even though he himself was not a party to the conversations. On the other hand, even a property interest in premises may not be sufficient to establish a legitimate expectation of privacy with respect to particular items located on the premises or activity conducted thereon. . . .

the same expectations of privacy are warranted in a car as would be justified in a dwelling place in analogous circumstances. We have on numerous occasions pointed out that cars are not to be treated identically with houses or apartments for Fourth Amendment purposes. . . . But here petitioners' claim is one which would fail even in an analogous situation in a dwelling place since they made no showing that they had any legitimate expectation of privacy in the glove compartment or area under the seat of the car in which they were merely passengers. Like the trunk of an automobile, these are areas in which a passenger *qua* passenger simply would not normally have a legitimate expectation of privacy. . . .

Jones v. United States, 362 U.S. 257 (1960) and Katz v. United States, 389 U.S. 347 (1967), involved significantly different factual circumstances. Jones not only had permission to use the apartment of his friend, but had a key to the apartment with which he admitted himself on the day of the search and kept possessions in the apartment. Except with respect to his friend, Jones had complete dominion and control over the apartment and could exclude others from it. Likewise in *Katz*, the defendant occupied the telephone booth, shut the door behind him to exclude all others and paid the toll, which "entitled [him] to assume that the words he utter[ed] into the mouthpiece would not be broadcast to the world." 389 U.S., at 352. Katz and Jones could legitimately expect privacy in the areas which were the subject of the search and seizure they sought to contest. No such showing was made by these petitioners with respect to those portions of the automobile which were searched and from which incriminating evidence was seized.

III

The Illinois courts were therefore correct in concluding that it was unnecessary to decide whether the search of the car might have violated the rights secured to someone else by the Fourth and Fourteenth Amendments to the United States Constitution. Since it did not violate any rights of these petitioners their judgment of conviction is

Affirmed.[26]

---

144. *Rakas* is applied in United States v. Lochan, 674 F.2d 960 (1st Cir.1982), in which the defendant was driving a friend's car on a long trip, in the company of the friend. The court concluded that the defendant lacked standing to object to a search of the car. To the same effect, see United States v. Jefferson, 925 F.2d 1242 (10th Cir.1991) (nonowner driver and nonowner passenger lack standing, when owner also present as passenger). See also United States v. Carter, 14 F.3d 1150 (6th Cir. 1994) (evidence suppressed against owner of vehicle but not against passenger).

[26] Justice Powell wrote a concurring opinion, which Chief Justice Burger joined. Justice White wrote a dissenting opinion, which Justice Brennan, Justice Marshall, and Justice Stevens joined.

In United States v. Twilley, 222 F.3d 1092 (9th Cir.2000), the court said that although the defendant, as a passenger in a car, had no standing to challenge the search of the car, he had standing to challenge the initial stop. Furthermore, because the initial stop violated the Fourth Amendment, the items seized would be suppressed as fruit of the poisonous tree. Accord, United States v. Kimball, 25 F.3d 1 (1st Cir.1994).

In United States v. Dall, 608 F.2d 910 (1st Cir.1979), the defendant loaned his pickup truck, which was fitted with a "camper cap," to someone else, who was stopped for speeding in another state. The driver produced the out-of-state registration for the car and identified its owner, but did not have a driver's license. For that reason, the police impounded the vehicle; they called the owner, who confirmed the driver's story, and told him that he would have to come to pick up the truck, which he later did. Pursuant to established practice for impounded vehicles, the police opened the locked camper cap and inventoried the contents. Evidence found in the truck was later used against the defendant. Upholding admission of the evidence, the court of appeals said that the defendant's ownership of the truck was "not enough to establish a reasonable and legitimate expectation of privacy" in the circumstances, and that he therefore lacked standing to challenge the search. The expectation of privacy, it said, attached to the driver's possession and not the owner's title.

Minnesota v. Olson

495 U.S. 91, 110 S.Ct. 1684, 109 L.Ed.2d 85 (1990)

■ JUSTICE WHITE delivered the opinion of the Court.

The police in this case made a warrantless, nonconsensual entry into a house where respondent Robert Olson was an overnight guest and arrested him. The issue is whether the arrest violated Olson's Fourth Amendment rights. We hold that it did.

I

Shortly before 6 a.m. on Saturday, July 18, 1987, a lone gunman robbed an Amoco gasoline station in Minneapolis, Minnesota, and fatally shot the station manager. A police officer heard the police dispatcher report and suspected Joseph Ecker. The officer and his partner drove immediately to Ecker's home, arriving at about the same time that an Oldsmobile arrived. The driver of the Oldsmobile took evasive action, and the car spun out of control and came to a stop. Two men fled the car on foot. Ecker, who was later identified as the gunman, was captured shortly thereafter inside his home. The second man escaped.

Inside the abandoned Oldsmobile, police found a sack of money and the murder weapon. They also found a title certificate with the name Rob Olson crossed out as a secured party, a letter addressed to a Roger R. Olson of 3151 Johnson Street, and a videotape rental receipt made out to Rob Olson and dated two days earlier. The police verified that a Robert Olson lived at 3151 Johnson Street.

The next morning, Sunday, July 19, a woman identifying herself as Dianna Murphy called the police and said that a man by the name of Rob drove the car in which the gas-station killer left the scene and that Rob was planning to leave town by bus. About noon, the same woman called again, gave her address and phone number, and said that a man named Rob had told a Maria and two other women, Louanne and Julie, that he was the driver in the Amoco robbery. The caller stated that Louanne was Julie's mother and that the two women lived at 2406 Fillmore Northeast. The detective-in-charge who took the second phone call sent police officers to 2406 Fillmore to check out Louanne and Julie. When police arrived they determined that the dwelling was a duplex and that Louanne Bergstrom and her daughter Julie lived in the upper unit but were not home. Police spoke to Louanne's mother, Helen Niederhoffer, who lived in the lower unit. She confirmed that a Rob Olson had been staying upstairs but was not then in the unit. She promised to call the police when Olson returned. At 2 p.m., a pickup order, or "probable cause arrest bulletin," was issued for Olson's arrest. The police were instructed to stay away from the duplex.

At approximately 2:45 p.m., Niederhoffer called police and said Olson had returned. The detective-in-charge instructed police officers to go to the house and surround it. He then telephoned Julie from headquarters and told her Rob should come out of the house. The detective heard a male voice say "tell them I left." Julie stated that Rob had left, whereupon at 3 p.m. the detective ordered the police to enter the house. Without seeking permission and with weapons drawn, the police entered the upper unit and found respondent hiding in a closet. Less than an hour after his arrest, respondent made an inculpatory statement at police headquarters.

The Hennepin County trial court held a hearing and denied respondent's motion to suppress his statement. . . . The statement was admitted into evidence at Olson's trial, and he was convicted on one count of first-degree murder, three counts of armed robbery, and three counts of second-degree assault. On appeal, the Minnesota Supreme Court reversed. . . . The court ruled that respondent had a sufficient interest in the Bergstrom home to challenge the legality of his warrantless arrest there, that the arrest was illegal because there were no exigent circumstances to justify a warrantless entry, and that respondent's statement was tainted by that illegality and should have been suppressed. Because the admission of the statement was not harmless beyond reasonable doubt, the court reversed Olson's conviction and remanded for a new trial.

We granted the State's petition for certiorari . . . and now affirm.

II

It was held in Payton v. New York, 445 U.S. 573 (1980), that a suspect should not be arrested in his house without an arrest warrant, even though there is probable cause to arrest him. The purpose of the decision was not to protect the person of the suspect but to protect his home from entry in the absence of a magistrate's finding of probable cause. In this case, the court below held that Olson's warrantless arrest was illegal because he had a sufficient connection with the premises to be treated like a householder. The State challenges that conclusion.

Since the decision in Katz v. United States, 389 U.S. 347 (1967), it has been the law that "capacity to claim the protection of the Fourth Amendment depends . . . upon whether the person who claims the protection of the Amendment has a legitimate expectation of privacy in the invaded place." Rakas v. Illinois, 439 U.S. 128, 143 (1978). A subjective expectation of privacy is legitimate if it is " 'one that society is prepared to recognize as "reasonable," ' " id., at 143–44, n.12, quoting Katz, supra, at 361 (Harlan, J., concurring).

The State argues that Olson's relationship to the premises does not satisfy the 12 factors which in its view determine whether a dwelling is a "home."[27] Aside from the fact that it is based on the mistaken premise that a place must be one's "home" in order for one to have a legitimate expectation of privacy there, the State's proposed test is needlessly complex. We need go no further than to conclude, as we do, that Olson's status as an overnight guest is alone enough to show that he had an expectation of privacy in the home that society is prepared to recognize as reasonable.

As recognized by the Minnesota Supreme Court, the facts of this case are similar to those in Jones v. United States, 362 U.S. 257 (1960). In *Jones*, the defendant was arrested in a friend's apartment during the execution of a search warrant and sought to challenge the warrant as not supported by probable cause.

> [Jones] testified that the apartment belonged to a friend, Evans, who had given him the use of it, and a key, with which [Jones] had admitted himself on the day of the arrest. On cross-examination [Jones] testified that he had a suit and shirt at the apartment, that his home was elsewhere, that he paid nothing for the use of the apart-

27. The 12 factors are:

(1) the visitor has some property rights in the dwelling;

(2) the visitor is related by blood or marriage to the owner or lessor of the dwelling;

(3) the visitor receives mail at the dwelling or has his name on the door;

(4) the visitor has a key to the dwelling;

(5) the visitor maintains regular or continuous presence in the dwelling, especially sleeping there regularly;

(6) the visitor contributes to the upkeep of the dwelling, either monetarily or otherwise;

(7) the visitor has been present at the dwelling for a substantial length of time prior to the arrest;

(8) the visitor stores his clothes or other possessions in the dwelling;

(9) the visitor has been granted by the owner exclusive use of a particular area of the dwelling;

(10) the visitor has the right to exclude other persons from the dwelling;

(11) the visitor is allowed to remain in the dwelling when the owner is absent;

(12) the visitor has taken precautions to develop and maintain his privacy in the dwelling.

Brief for Petitioner 21.

> ment, that Evans had let him use it "as a friend," that he had slept there "maybe a night," and that at the time of the search Evans had been away in Philadelphia for about five days.

Id., at 259.[28]

The Court ruled that Jones could challenge the search of the apartment because he was "legitimately on [the] premises," id., at 267. Although the "legitimately on [the] premises" standard was rejected in *Rakas* as too broad, 439 U.S., at 142–48, the *Rakas* Court explicitly reaffirmed the factual holding in *Jones*. . . . *Rakas* thus recognized that, as an overnight guest, Jones was much more than just legitimately on the premises.

The distinctions relied on by the State between this case and *Jones* are not legally determinative. The State emphasizes that in this case Olson was never left alone in the duplex or given a key, whereas in *Jones* the owner of the apartment was away and Jones had a key with which he could come and go and admit and exclude others. . . . We do not understand *Rakas*, however, to hold that an overnight guest can never have a legitimate expectation of privacy except when his host is away and he has a key, or that only when those facts are present may an overnight guest assert the "unremarkable proposition," id., at 142, that a person may have a sufficient interest in a place other than his home to enable him to be free in that place from unreasonable searches and seizures.

To hold that an overnight guest has a legitimate expectation of privacy in his host's home merely recognizes the everyday expectations of privacy that we all share. Staying overnight in another's home is a longstanding social custom that serves functions recognized as valuable by society. We stay in others' homes when we travel to a strange city for business or pleasure, when we visit our parents, children, or more distant relatives out of town, when we are in between jobs or homes, or when we house-sit for a friend. We will all be hosts and we will all be guests many times in our lives. From either perspective, we think that society recognizes that a houseguest has a legitimate expectation of privacy in his host's home.

From the overnight guest's perspective, he seeks shelter in another's home precisely because it provides him with privacy, a place where he and his possessions will not be disturbed by anyone but his host and those his host allows inside. We are at our most vulnerable when we are asleep because we cannot monitor our own safety or the security of our belongings. It is for this reason that, although we may spend all day in public places, when we cannot sleep in our own home we seek out another private place to sleep, whether it be a hotel room, or the home of a friend. Society expects at least as much privacy in these places as in a telephone booth—"a temporarily private place whose momentary occupants' expectations of freedom from intrusion are recognized as reasonable," *Katz*, 389 U.S., at 361 (Harlan, J., concurring).

28. Olson, who had been staying at Ecker's home for several days before the robbery, spent the night of the robbery on the floor of the Bergstroms' home with their permission. He had a change of clothes with him at the duplex.

That the guest has a host who has ultimate control of the house is not inconsistent with the guest having a legitimate expectation of privacy. The houseguest is there with the permission of his host, who is willing to share his house and his privacy with his guest. It is unlikely that the guest will be confined to a restricted area of the house; and when the host is away or asleep, the guest will have a measure of control over the premises. The host may admit or exclude from the house as he prefers, but it is unlikely that he will admit someone who wants to see or meet with the guest over the objection of the guest. On the other hand, few houseguests will invite others to visit them while they are guests without consulting their hosts; but the latter, who have the authority to exclude despite the wishes of the guest, will often be accommodating. The point is that hosts will more likely than not respect the privacy interests of their guests, who are entitled to a legitimate expectation of privacy despite the fact that they have no legal interest in the premises and do not have the legal authority to determine who may or may not enter the household. If the untrammeled power to admit and exclude were essential to Fourth Amendment protection, an adult daughter temporarily living in the home of her parents would have no legitimate expectation of privacy because her right to admit or exclude would be subject to her parents' veto.

Because respondent's expectation of privacy in the Bergstrom home was rooted in "understandings that are recognized and permitted by society," *Rakas*, supra, at 144, n.12, it was legitimate, and respondent can claim the protection of the Fourth Amendment.

. . .

[The Court upheld the "fact-specific" finding that there were not exigent circumstances justifying the warrantless entry.]

We therefore affirm the judgment of the Minnesota Supreme Court.

. . .[29]

---

145. In United States v. Haydel, 649 F.2d 1152, modified 664 F.2d 84 (5th Cir.1981), the court, applying *Rakas*, concluded that the defendant had a legitimate expectation of privacy in his parents' home, where he kept papers and clothing, and occasionally remained overnight, and that he had standing to contest a search. Supposing that, if his parents had consented to the search while he was absent, the search would have been lawful, see note 95, p. 168 above, does that have a bearing on the question of standing?

In People v. Moreno, 3 Cal.Rptr.2d 66, 69 (Ct.App.1992), the court concluded that since a babysitter "as a general rule . . . is in exclusive charge of the child and the premises," a babysitter has standing to challenge a search of the premises while sitting. If that is correct, is it for

[29] Justice Stevens wrote a concurring opinion. Justice Kennedy wrote a brief concurring opinion. Chief Justice Rehnquist and Justice Blackmun dissented.

the reason given by the court? Does the babysitter have authority to consent to a search of the premises?

In United States v. Padilla, 508 U.S. 77 (1993) (per curiam), the Court rejected a rule developed in the Ninth Circuit that a co-conspirator who, in virtue of the conspiracy has joint control and supervision over a searched place, has standing to contest the search. Co-conspirators, the Court said, may have standing based on their expectations and interests, but the fact of the conspiracy by itself makes no difference.

In State v. Stott, 794 A.2d 120 (N.J.2002), the court held that a patient in a psychiatric hospital has a reasonable expectation of privacy in the portion of a shared room occupied by him.

146. A federal agent posing as a dealer in narcotics arranged to purchase narcotics from the defendant. The transaction took place in a motel room rented by the agent. According to plan, while the transaction was in progress, other agents entered the room with a key and by breaking the night latch that the defendant had fastened. The agents seized the narcotics and arrested the defendant. Are the narcotics admissible in evidence against him? See Garza-Fuentes v. United States, 400 F.2d 219 (5th Cir.1968).

147. Before *Rakas* was decided, in United States v. Carriger, 541 F.2d 545, 549 (6th Cir.1976) (other cases cited), the court held that the tenant of an apartment building has "a reasonable expectation of privacy in the common areas of the building not open to the general public," and therefore has standing to object to an entry into the building by stealth. Cf. United States v. Fluker, 543 F.2d 709 (9th Cir.1976). But see, e.g., United States v. Cruz Pagan, 537 F.2d 554 (1st Cir.1976) (persons residing in multidwelling apartment house or condominium do not have a reasonable expectation of privacy in "well traveled common areas" such as a common garage; entry into garage involved no Fourth Amendment right of such persons). Cf. United States v. Kelly, 551 F.2d 760 (8th Cir.1977). Are such cases affected by *Rakas*?

148. In United States v. Gamez-Orduño, 235 F.3d 453 (9th Cir.2000), the defendants, who were smuggling drugs, stayed overnight in a trailer at the invitation of the occupant. The court held that, as overnight guests, they had standing under *Olson* to contest the search of the trailer, notwithstanding their illegal business. Compare Minnesota v. Carter, below.

149. The defendant was employed in a federal agency. He had his own office and a computer with internet access. His employer announced a policy that the internet was to be used only for official business and specifically prohibiting viewing unlawful materials. Employees were told that "electronic audits" would be conducted to ensure compliance, which would include inspection of employees' internet activity. Suspecting that the defendant was viewing and downloading pornographic material, the employer examined his computer files. The court held that in view of the announced policy, the defendant did not have a legitimate expectation of privacy in the search of his computer. United States v. Simons, 206 F.3d 392 (4th Cir.2000).

Minnesota v. Carter

525 U.S. 83, 119 S.Ct. 469, 142 L.Ed.2d 373 (1998)

■ CHIEF JUSTICE REHNQUIST delivered the opinion of the Court.

Respondents and the lessee of an apartment were sitting in one of its rooms, bagging cocaine. While so engaged they were observed by a police officer, who looked through a drawn window blind. The Supreme Court of Minnesota held that the officer's viewing was a search which violated respondents' Fourth Amendment rights. We hold that no such violation occurred.

James Thielen, a police officer in the Twin Cities suburb of Eagan, Minnesota, went to an apartment building to investigate a tip from a confidential informant. The informant said that he had walked by the window of a ground-floor apartment and had seen people putting a white powder into bags. The officer looked in the same window through a gap in the closed blind and observed the bagging operation for several minutes. He then notified headquarters, which began preparing affidavits for a search warrant while he returned to the apartment building. When two men left the building in a previously identified Cadillac, the police stopped the car. Inside were respondents Carter and Johns. As the police opened the door of the car to let Johns out, the observed a black zippered pouch and a handgun, later determined to be loaded, on the vehicle's floor. Carter and Johns were arrested, and a later police search of the vehicle the next day discovered pagers, a scale, and 47 grams of cocaine in plastic sandwich bags.

After seizing the car, the police returned to Apartment 103 and arrested the occupant, Kimberly Thompson, who is not a party to this appeal. A search of the apartment pursuant to a warrant revealed cocaine residue on the kitchen table and plastic baggies similar to those found in the Cadillac. Thielen identified Carter, Johns, and Thompson as the three people he had observed placing the powder into baggies. The police later learned that while Thompson was the lessee of the apartment, Carter and Johns lived in Chicago and had come to the apartment for the sole purpose of packaging the cocaine. Carter and Johns had never been to the apartment before and were only in the apartment for approximately 2½ hours. In return for the use of the apartment, Carter and Johns had given Thompson one-eighth of an ounce of the cocaine.

Carter and Johns were charged with conspiracy to commit controlled substance crime in the first degree and aiding and abetting in a controlled substance crime in the first degree. . . . They moved to suppress all evidence obtained from the apartment and the Cadillac, as well as to suppress several post-arrest incriminating statements they had made. They argued that Thielen's initial observation of their drug packaging activities was an unreasonable search in violation of the Fourth Amendment and that all evidence obtained as a result of this unreasonable search was inadmissible as fruit of the poisonous tree. The Minnesota trial court held that since, unlike the defendant in Minnesota v. Olson, 495 U.S. 91 (1990), Carter and Johns were not overnight social guests but temporary out-of-state visitors, they were not entitled to claim the protection of the Fourth Amendment against the government intrusion into the apartment. The trial court also concluded that Thielen's observation was not a search within the meaning of the Fourth Amendment. After a trial, Carter and Johns were each convicted of both offenses. . . .

A divided Minnesota Supreme Court reversed, holding that respondents had "standing" to claim the protection of the Fourth Amendment because they had " 'a legitimate expectation of privacy in the invaded place.' " 569 N.W.2d 169, 174 (1997) (quoting Rakas v. Illinois, 439 U.S. 128, 143 (1978)). The court noted that even though "society does not recognize as valuable the task of bagging cocaine, we conclude that society does recognize as valuable the right of property owners or leaseholders to invite persons into the privacy of their homes to conduct a common task, be it legal or illegal activity. We, therefore, hold that [respondents] had standing to bring [their] motion to suppress the evidence gathered as a result of Thielen's observations." 569 N.W.2d, at 176. . . . Based upon its conclusion that the respondents had "standing" to raise their Fourth Amendment claims, the court went on to hold that Thielen's observation constituted a search of the apartment under the Fourth Amendment, and that the search was unreasonable. Id., at 176–79. We granted certiorari . . . and now reverse.

The Minnesota courts analyzed whether respondents had a legitimate expectation of privacy under the rubric of "standing" doctrine, an analysis which this Court expressly rejected 20 years ago in *Rakas*. 439 U.S., at 139–40. In that case, we held that automobile passengers could not assert the protection of the Fourth Amendment against the seizure of incriminating evidence from a vehicle where they owned neither the vehicle nor the evidence. Ibid. Central to our analysis was the idea that in determining whether a defendant is able to show the violation of his (and not someone else's) Fourth Amendment rights, the "definition of those rights is more than within that of standing." 439 U.S., at 140. Thus, we held that in order to claim the protection of the Fourth Amendment, a defendant must demonstrate that he personally has an expectation of privacy in the place searched, and that his expectation is reasonable; i.e., one which has "a source outside of the Fourth Amendment, either by reference to concepts of real or personal property law or to understandings that are recognized and permitted by society." Id., at 143–44, and n.12. . . .

The Fourth Amendment . . . protects persons against unreasonable searches of "their persons [and] houses" and thus indicates that the Fourth Amendment is a personal right that must be invoked by an individual. See Katz v. United States, 389 U.S. 347, 351 (1967) ("[T]he Fourth Amendment protects people, not places"). But the extent to which the Fourth Amendment protects people may depend upon where those people are. We have held that "capacity to claim the protection of the Fourth Amendment depends . . . upon whether the person who claims the protection of the Amendment has a legitimate expectation of privacy in the invaded place." *Rakas*, supra, at 143. . . .

The text of the Amendment suggest that its protections extend only to people in "their" houses. But we have held that in some circumstances a person may have a legitimate expectation of privacy in the house of someone else. In Minnesota v. Olson, 495 U.S. 91 (1990), for example, we decided that an overnight guest in a house had the sort of expectation of privacy that the Fourth Amendment protects. . . .

. . . Thus an overnight guest in a home may claim the protection of the Fourth Amendment, but one who is merely present with the consent of the householder may not.

Respondents here were obviously not overnight guests, but were essentially present for a business transaction and were only in the home a matters of hours. There is no suggestion that they had a previous relationship with Thompson, or that there was any other purpose to their visit. Nor was there anything similar to the overnight guest relationship in *Olson* to suggest a degree of acceptance into the household. While the apartment was a dwelling place for Thompson, it was for these respondents simply a place to do business.

Property used for commercial purposes is treated differently for Fourth Amendment purposes than residential property. "An expectation of privacy in commercial premises, however, is different from, and indeed less than, a similar expectation in an individual's home." New York v. Burger, 482 U.S. 691, 700 (1987). And while it was a "home" in which respondents were present, it was not their home. Similarly, the Court has held that in some circumstances a worker can claim Fourth Amendment protection over his own workplace. See, e.g., O'Connor v. Ortega, 480 U.S. 709 (1987). But there is no indication that respondents in this case had nearly as significant a connection to Thompson's apartment as the worker in *O'Connor* had to his own private office. See id. at 716–17.

If we regard the overnight guest in Minnesota v. Olson as typifying those who may claim the protection of the Fourth Amendment in the home of another, and one merely "legitimately on the premises" as typifying those who may not do so, the present case is obviously somewhere in between. But the purely commercial nature of the transaction engaged in here, the relatively short period of time on the premises, and the lack of any previous connection between respondents and the householder, all lead us to conclude that respondents' situation is closer to that of one simply permitted on the premises. We therefore hold that any search which may have occurred did not violate their Fourth Amendment rights.

Because we conclude that respondents had no legitimate expectation of privacy in the apartment, we need not decide whether the police officer's observation constituted a "search." The judgment of the Supreme Court of Minnesota is accordingly reversed, and the cause is remanded for proceedings not inconsistent with this opinion.

■ JUSTICE SCALIA, with whom JUSTICE THOMAS joins, concurring.

I join the opinion of the Court because I believe it accurately applies our recent case law, including Minnesota v. Olson, 495 U.S. 91 (1990). I write separately to express my view that case law—like the submissions of the parties in this case—gives short shrift to the text of the Fourth Amendment, and to the well and long understood meaning of that text. Specifically, it leaps to apply the fuzzy standard of "legitimate expectation of privacy"—a consideration that is often relevant to whether a search or seizure covered by the Fourth Amendment is "unreasonable"—to the threshold question whether a search or seizure covered by the Fourth Amendment *has occurred*. If that latter question is addressed first and analyzed under the text of the Constitution as traditionally understood, the present case is not remotely difficult.

The Fourth Amendment protects "[t]he right of the people to be secure in *their* persons, houses, papers, and effects, against unreasonable searches and seizures...." U.S. Const., Amdt 4 (emphasis added). It must be acknowledged that the phrase "their . . . houses" in this provision is, in isolation, ambiguous. It could mean "their respective houses," so that the protection extends to each person only in his own house. But it could also mean "their respective and each other's houses," so that each person would be protected even when visiting the house of someone else. As today's opinion for the Court suggests, however, ante, at 88–90, it is not linguistically possible to give the provision the latter, expansive interpretation with respect to "houses" without giving it the same interpretation with respect to the nouns that are parallel to "houses"—"persons, . . . papers, and effects"—which would give me a constitutional right not to have your person unreasonably searched. This is so absurd that it has to my knowledge never been contemplated. The obvious meaning of the provision is that *each* person has the right to be secure against unreasonable searches and seizures in *his own* person, house, papers, and effects.

The Founding-era materials that I have examined confirm that this was the understood meaning. . . .

. . .

Of course this is not to say that the Fourth Amendment protects only the Lord of the Manor who holds his estate in fee simple. People call a house "their" home when legal title is in the bank, when they rent it, and even when they merely occupy it rent-free—*so long as they actually live there*. . . .

. . . [I]n deciding the question presented today we write upon a slate that is far from clean. . . . We went to the absolute limit of what text and tradition permit in Minnesota v. Olson, 495 U.S. 91 (1990), when we protected a mere overnight guest against an unreasonable search of his hosts' apartment. But whereas it is plausible to regard a person's overnight lodging as at least his "temporary" residence, it is entirely impossible to give that characterization to an apartment that he uses to package cocaine. Respondents here were not searched in "their . . . hous[e]" under any interpretation of the phrase that bears the remotest relationship to the well understood meaning of the Fourth Amendment.

. . .

■ JUSTICE KENNEDY, concurring.

I join the Court's opinion, for its reasoning is consistent with my view that almost all social guests have a legitimate expectation of privacy, and hence protection against unreasonable searches, in their host's home.

. . .

The homeowner's right to privacy is not at issue in this case. The Court does not reach the question whether the officer's unaided observations of Thompson's apartment constituted a search. If there was in fact a search, however, then Thompson had a right to object to the unlawful police surveillance of her apartment and the right to suppress any evidence disclosed by the search. Similarly, if the police had entered her home without a search warrant to arrest respondents, Thompson's own privacy interests would be violated and she could presumably bring an action under 42 U.S.C. § 1983 or an action for trespass. Our cases establish, however, that respondents have no independent privacy right, the violation of which results in exclusion of evidence against them, unless they can establish a meaningful connection to Thompson's apartment.

The settled rule is that the requisite connection is an expectation of privacy that society recognizes as reasonable. Katz v. United States, 389 U.S. 347, 361 (1967) (Harlan, J., concurring). The application of that rule involves consideration of the kind of place in which the individual claims the privacy interest and what expectations of privacy are traditional and well recognized. Ibid. I would expect that most, if not all, social guests legitimately expect that, in accordance with social custom, the homeowner will exercise her discretion to include or exclude others for the guests' benefit. As we recognized in Minnesota v. Olson, 495 U.S. 91 (1990), where these social expectations exist—as in the case of an overnight guest—they are sufficient to create a legitimate expectation of privacy, even in the absence of any property right to exclude others. In this respect, the dissent must be correct that the reasonable expectations of the owner are shared, to some extent, by the guest. This analysis suggests that, as a general rule, social guests will have an expectation of privacy in their host's home. That is not the case before us, however.

In this case respondents have established nothing more than a fleeting and insubstantial connection with Thompson's home. For all that appears in the record, respondents used Thompson's home simply as a convenient processing station, their purpose involving nothing more than the mechanical act of chopping and packaging a substance for distribution. There is no suggestion that respondents engaged in confidential communications with Thompson about their transaction. Respondents had not been to Thompson's apartment before, and they left it even before their arrest. The Minnesota Supreme Court, which overturned respondents' convictions, acknowledged that respondents could not be fairly characterized as Thompson's "guests." 569 N.W.2d 169, 175–76 (1997). . . .

If respondents here had been visiting homes, each for a minute or two, to drop off a bag of cocaine and were apprehended by a policeman wrongfully present in the nineteenth home; or if they had left the goods at a home where they were not staying and the police had seized the goods in their absence, we would have said that *Rakas* compels rejection of any privacy interest respondents might assert. So it does here, given that respondents have established no meaningful tie or connection to the owner, the owner's home, or the owner's expectation of privacy.

■ JUSTICE GINSBURG, with whom JUSTICE STEVENS and JUSTICE SOUTER join, dissenting.

The Court's decision undermines not only the security of short-term guests, but also the security of the home resident herself. In my view, when a homeowner or lessor personally invites a guest into her home to share in a common endeavor, whether it be for conversation, to engage in leisure activities, or for business purposes licit or illicit, that guest should share his host's shelter against unreasonable searches and seizures.

. . . I would here decide only the case of the homeowner who chooses to share the privacy of her home and her company with a guest, and would not reach classroom hypotheticals like the milkman or pizza deliverer.

My concern centers on an individual's choice to share her home and her associations there with persons she selects. Our decisions indicate that people have a reasonable expectation of privacy in their homes in part because they have the prerogative to exclude others. . . . The power to exclude implies the power to include. . . . Our Fourth Amendment decisions should reflect these complementary prerogatives.

A homedweller places her own privacy at risk, the Court's approach indicates, when she opens her home to others, uncertain whether the duration of their stay, their purpose, and their "acceptance into the household" will earn protection. Ante, at 90. . . . Human frailty suggests that today's decision will tempt police to pry into private dwellings without warrant, to find evidence incriminating guests who do not rest there through the night. . . . *Rakas* [v. Illinois, 439 U.S. 128 (1978)] tolerates that temptation with respect to automobile searches. . . . I see no impelling reason to extend this risk into the home. . . . As I see it, people are not genuinely "secure in their . . . houses . . . against unreasonable searches and seizures," U.S. Const., Amdt. 4, if their invitations to others increase the risk of unwarranted governmental peering and prying into their dwelling places.

Through the host's invitation, the guest gains a reasonable expectation of privacy in the home. Minnesota v. Olson, 495 U.S. 91 (1990), so held with respect to an overnight guest. The logic of that decision extends to shorter term guests as well. . . . Visiting the home of a friend, relative, or business associate, whatever the time of day, "serves functions recognized as valuable by society." *Olson*, 495 U.S., at 98. One need not remain overnight to anticipate privacy in another's home, "a place where [the guest] and his possessions will not be disturbed by anyone but his host and those his host allows inside." Id., at 99. In sum, when a homeowner chooses to share the privacy of her home and her company with a short-term guest, the twofold requirement "emerg[ing] from prior decisions" has been satisfied: Both host and guest "have exhibited an actual (subjective) expectation of privacy"; that "expectation [is] one [our] society is prepared to recognize as 'reasonable.' " Katz v. United States, 389 U.S. 347, 361 (1967) (Harlan, J., concurring).

As the Solicitor General acknowledged, the illegality of the host–guest conduct, the fact that they were partners in crime, would not alter the analysis. See Tr. of Oral Arg. 22–23. . . . Indeed, it must be this way. If the illegality of the activity made constitutional an otherwise unconstitutional search, such Fourth Amendment protection, reserved for the innocent only, would have little force in regulating police behavior toward either the innocent or the guilty.

Our leading decision in *Katz* is key to my view of this case. There, we ruled that the Government violated the petitioner's Fourth Amendment rights when it electronically recorded him transmitting wagering information while he was inside a public telephone booth. 389 U.S., at 353. . . .

The Court's decision in this case veers sharply from the path marked in *Katz*. I do not agree that we have a more reasonable expectation of privacy when we place a business call to a person's home from a public telephone booth on the side of the street . . . than when we actually enter that person's premises to engage in a common endeavor.

. . .[30]

---

150. The opinion in Jones v. United States, 362 U.S. 257 (1960), which was the principal discussion of standing by the Supreme Court before *Rakas*, had announced a rule of "automatic standing," to the effect that if possession of a seized item is the basis of the crime charged, the defendant had standing to contest the search and seizure without any further demonstration that a protected interest in privacy was affected by the search. Such a rule was necessary, the Court said, lest the government take contradictory positions by asserting the defendant's possession in its case in chief and contesting it in opposition to the motion to suppress.

[30] Justice Breyer wrote an opinion concurring in the judgment. He agreed with Justice Ginsburg, dissenting, that the defendants could claim the protection of the Fourth Amendment, but, on the basis of his own reading of the factual record, he concluded that the police officer's actions were not an unlawful search.

The dilemma that a defendant would otherwise have faced was alleviated in Simmons v. United States, 390 U.S. 377 (1968). The Court there held that "when a defendant testifies in support of a motion to suppress evidence on Fourth Amendment grounds, his testimony may not thereafter be admitted against him at trial on the issue of guilt unless he makes no objection." Id. at 394.[31] After *Simmons*, the *Jones* rule of automatic standing (which had commonly been applied if possession was a significant element, even if not an "essential" one, of the prosecution's case) was questioned. In a footnote in *Rakas*, 439 U.S. at 135 n.4, the Court noted that it had not decided whether the rule survived *Simmons*.

The Court decided the question and rejected the *Jones* rule, in United States v. Salvucci, 448 U.S. 83 (1980) (7–2). Noting the effect of *Simmons*, the Court said that the other aspect of *Jones*, that the government ought not take contradictory positions, was eliminated by recognition that possession of a seized good is not itself sufficient to establish a Fourth Amendment interest. Referring to its reasoning in *Rakas*, the Court said: "We simply decline to use possession of a seized good as a substitute for a factual finding that the owner of the good had a legitimate expectation of privacy in the area searched." Id. at 92.

Some state courts have disagreed with the Court's reasoning in *Rakas* and, relying on state constitutional provisions, have retained the rule of automatic standing. State v. Alston, 440 A.2d 1311 (N.J.1981); Commonwealth v. Sell, 470 A.2d 457 (Pa.1983). (In contrast, California, which had not required standing at all to contest an allegedly unlawful search, see People v. Martin, 290 P.2d 855 (Cal.1955), abrogated the *Martin* rule by an initiative measure providing that "relevant evidence shall not be excluded in any criminal proceeding." See In re Lance W., 694 P.2d 744 (Cal.1985).)

151. In Rawlings v. Kentucky, 448 U.S. 98 (1980) (5–2–2), the Court held that the defendant did not have a sufficient legitimate expectation of privacy to contest the legality of a search of his friend's purse, in which police found narcotics owned by him. Both the defendant and his friend were present when the purse was found and searched. The defendant had known his friend for only a few days and had not previously had access to her purse, he was aware that another person had access to the purse, and

31. *Simmons* was distinguished in United States v. Kahan, 415 U.S. 239 (1974), in which the Court rejected the defendant's claim that the admission at his criminal trial of false statements in his application for the appointment of counsel violated his privilege against self-incrimination and right to counsel. Citing Harris v. New York, 401 U.S. 222 (1971), p. 479 below, the Court said: "The protective shield of Simmons is not to be converted into a license for false representations on the issue of indigency free from the risk that the claimant will be held accountable for his falsehood." 415 U.S., at 243.

Simmons notwithstanding, "the government may call to testify at trial a third-party witness called by the defendant at a pretrial suppression hearing whose testimony at that hearing was favorable to the defendant's motion to establish standing and whose identity was not previously known to the government, but whose testimony to the same effect at trial inculpated the defendant." United States v. Boruff, 870 F.2d 316, 318 (5th Cir. 1989). The court reasoned that a defendant's privilege against self-incrimination is not involved when another person testifies in his behalf at a suppression hearing.

the circumstances of the transaction did not suggest that the defendant was taking precautions to maintain his privacy. His ownership of the seized items, while relevant, was insufficient by itself to create the necessary interest under the Fourth Amendment. Justice Marshall wrote a dissenting opinion, which Justice Brennan joined, in which he argued that a property interest in a seized item is enough to confer standing to challenge the legality of the search in which it was found and seized.

Many possessions are themselves containers, the opening and examining the contents of which may be a substantial invasion of privacy. After *Rakas*, are there any circumstances in which a property interest (possession or ownership) establishes rights under the Fourth Amendment without reference to any privacy interest? Or is a property interest significant only as an indication of a privacy interest? How ought Justice Rehnquist's allusion in *Rakas*, p. 262 n.24 above, to the seizure of a visitor's property be understood?

152. In United States v. Kelly, 529 F.2d 1365 (8th Cir.1976), decided before *Rakas*, books and magazines were shipped to the defendant by United Parcel Service. While they were in the possession of UPS, they were seized by federal officials. The government argued that the defendant had no standing to contest the seizure, since he was not on the premises when the seizure occurred, alleged no interest in the premises, and was not charged with an offense of which possession of the seized evidence was an element. Upholding the defendant's standing, the court of appeals said:

> Logically, a person's protectible expectation of privacy must extend both to places *and objects*. A contrary conclusion would emasculate the plain language of the Fourth Amendment, which protects "papers" and "effects." . . .
>
> In the instant case, it is clear that Thomas Kelly was the sole victim of the government's investigation and the one against whom the search or seizure was directed. . . . The packages from which the books and magazines were taken were addressed to Century News. Appellant Kelly is the sole owner of Century News. . . . No other individuals, including employees of Sovereign News, the shipper and distributor of the materials, were prosecuted.
>
> Furthermore, Kelly maintained more than a marginal proprietary interest in the packages of books and magazines. . . . The packages were consigned to Century News, in other words Thomas Kelly; many of the books and magazines were ultimately delivered to Kelly; and Kelly wrote Sovereign News and obtained credit for shortages.
>
> These same facts support the conclusion that appellant was entitled to a reasonable expectation of privacy in the packages of books and magazines. . . . The government contends that appellant had no legitimate expectation of privacy since the packages were mailed C.O.D. to Century News and because a common carrier has a right to inspect packages. The government emphasizes that Kelly did not come into possession and had no right to possession until he had paid for the

> shipments. The contentions of the government, however, are too firmly tied to concepts of traditional property law, and a defendant's expectation of privacy should not be deemed unreasonable merely because he had not yet paid postage nor because of a right of the UPS to inspect packages. . . .
>
> The denial of standing to appellant would subject Kelly to contradictory assertions of power by the government. . . . Appellant has been convicted of the knowing *use* of an interstate carrier for the transportation of obscene materials. The government has attempted to show that Kelly exercised dominion and control over interstate shipments of purportedly obscene books at the time of their seizure and simultaneously has contended that Kelly does not have a sufficient interest to challenge the search or seizure of the same materials. Proper administration of criminal justice should not include such contradictory assertions of governmental power.

Id. at 1369–71.

Is the result in *Kelly* affected by *Rakas*?

153. The defendants employed a private detective agency to conduct electronic surveillance of various houses. Working with an electronics expert, the agency installed the necessary devices on telephone poles and in automobiles parked near the target houses. The agency edited the tape recordings that they obtained to exclude extraneous conversations and gave the master tapes to the defendants. The defendants paid all the expenses of the surveillance including the cost of the equipment. After the surveillance had been in operation for some time, one of the agency's employees was arrested in his car as he was leaving the location of the surveillance. In the back of the car the police found a tape recorder. At the police station, they played the tapes. Do the defendants have standing to challenge the seizure of the tapes or the playing of them? Does it make a difference who was the owner of the tapes, the defendants or the detective agency? See United States v. Hunt, 505 F.2d 931 (5th Cir.1974). See also United States v. Lisk, 522 F.2d 228 (7th Cir.1975), in which an explosive bomb belonging to the defendant was seized by police from the trunk of a friend's car; the defendant had no interest in the car but retained ownership of the bomb, which the friend was to return to him whenever the defendant asked for it. Assuming that the search of the car was unlawful, can the defendant obtain suppression of the bomb as evidence against him?

154. The importance of the standing requirement was reaffirmed in United States v. Payner, 447 U.S. 727 (1980) (6–3). There, the district court had suppressed evidence obtained in violation of a third person's constitutional rights, on the basis that, despite the defendant's lack of standing, the government's purposeful violation of the other person's constitutional rights required suppression of the evidence as an exercise of the court's inherent supervisory power. The Supreme Court reversed. It said that the balance of interests involved in the application of the exclusionary rule included the requirement of standing, and that the supervisory power should not be used to subvert that balance.

With *Payner*, compare Waring v. State, 670 P.2d 357, 363 (Alaska 1983), holding that under state law "a defendant has standing to assert the violation of a co-defendant's fourth amendment rights if he or she can show (1) that a police officer obtained the evidence as a result of gross or shocking misconduct, or (2) that the officer deliberately violated a co-defendant's rights."

155. United States v. Miller, 425 U.S. 435 (1976) (7–2). A grand jury subpoenaed from two banks records of the accounts of the defendant in connection with a tax investigation. The banks were required to maintain the records by federal law. The defendant was subsequently prosecuted and moved to suppress the records on the ground that they had been illegally seized, because the subpoenas were defective. The Court held that the defendant had no interest in the records that was protected by the Fourth Amendment and accordingly had no standing to challenge their production under the subpoenas. It said that a depositor's checks and deposit slips were not "confidential communications" but negotiable business instruments, and rejected the argument that the statutory requirement that the banks maintain the records gave the defendant a special constitutional claim. The records, it said, belonged to the banks and contained information voluntarily communicated by the defendant. "This Court has held repeatedly that the Fourth Amendment does not prohibit the obtaining of information revealed to a third party and conveyed by him to Government authorities, even if the information is revealed on the assumption that it will be used only for a limited purpose and the confidence placed in the third party will not be betrayed." Id. at 443.

Outer Boundaries of Search and Seizure

156.

Two police officers found appellant unconscious on a public street; they called an ambulance when they could not rouse him. One officer searched appellant in order to secure identification if possible and then to prepare a report for the hospital concerning the sick man. In the process, he examined the appellant's pockets, did not find identifying material, but found 15 cellophane envelopes containing a white powder which at the time appeared to the officer to be narcotics, packaged as he had observed contraband narcotics on other occasions.

After the arrival of the ambulance crew who attended the appellant, the latter regained consciousness and was taken to the police station where a capsule, containing a white powder similar to that in the cellophane envelopes, was found on his person. Subsequent laboratory analysis confirmed the officer's original tentative conclusion that the white substance was narcotics.

Vauss v. United States, 370 F.2d 250, 251 (D.C.Cir.1966). Can the narcotics be used in evidence against the appellant? If so, on what basis?

Winston v. Lee

470 U.S. 753, 105 S.Ct. 1611, 84 L.Ed.2d 662 (1985)

■ JUSTICE BRENNAN delivered the opinion of the Court.

Schmerber v. California, 384 U.S. 757 (1966), held, inter alia, that a State may, over the suspect's protest, have a physician extract blood from a person suspected of drunken driving without violation of the suspect's right secured by the Fourth Amendment not to be subjected to unreasonable searches and seizures. However, *Schmerber* cautioned: "That we today hold that the Constitution does not forbid the States' minor intrusions into an individual's body under stringently limited conditions in no way indicates that it permits more substantial intrusions, or intrusions under other conditions." Id., at 772. In this case, the Commonwealth of Virginia seeks to compel the respondent Rudolph Lee, who is suspected of attempting to commit armed robbery, to undergo a surgical procedure under a general anesthetic for removal of a bullet lodged in his chest. Petitioners allege that the bullet will provide evidence of respondent's guilt or innocence. We conclude that the procedure sought here is an example of the "more substantial intrusion" cautioned against in *Schmerber*, and hold that to permit the procedure would violate respondent's right to be secure in his person guaranteed by the Fourth Amendment.

I

A

At approximately 1 a.m. on July 18, 1982, Ralph E. Watkinson was closing his shop for the night. As he was locking the door, he observed someone armed with a gun coming toward him from across the street. Watkinson was also armed and when he drew his gun, the other person told him to freeze. Watkinson then fired at the other person, who returned his fire. Watkinson was hit in the legs, while the other individual, who appeared to be wounded in his left side, ran from the scene. The police arrived on the scene shortly thereafter, and Watkinson was taken by ambulance to the emergency room of the Medical College of Virginia (MCV) Hospital.

Approximately 20 minutes later, police officers responding to another call found respondent eight blocks from where the earlier shooting occurred. Respondent was suffering from a gunshot wound to his left chest area and told the police that he had been shot when two individuals attempted to rob him. An ambulance took respondent to the MCV Hospital.

Watkinson was still in the MCV emergency room and, when respondent entered that room, said "[t]hat's the man that shot me." App. 14. After an investigation, the police decided that respondent's story of having been himself the victim of a robbery was untrue and charged respondent with attempted robbery, malicious wounding, and two counts of using a firearm in the commission of a felony.

B

The Commonwealth shortly thereafter moved in state court for an order directing respondent to undergo surgery to remove an object thought to be a bullet lodged under his left collarbone. . . .

. . .

[J]ust before the surgery was scheduled, the surgeon ordered that X rays be taken of respondent's chest. The X rays revealed that the bullet was in fact lodged two and one-half to three centimeters (approximately one inch) deep in muscular tissue in respondent's chest, substantially deeper than had been thought when the state court granted the motion to compel surgery. The surgeon now believed that a general anesthetic would be desirable for medical reasons.

. . . After an evidentiary hearing, the District Court enjoined the threatened surgery. . . . A divided panel of the Court of Appeals for the Fourth Circuit affirmed. . . . We granted certiorari . . . to consider whether a State may consistently with the Fourth Amendment compel a suspect to undergo surgery of this kind in a search for evidence of a crime.

II

The Fourth Amendment protects "expectations of privacy," see Katz v. United States, 389 U.S. 347 (1967)—the individual's legitimate expectations that in certain places and at certain times he has "the right to be let alone—the most comprehensive of rights and the right most valued by civilized men." Olmstead v. United States, 277 U.S. 438, 478 (1928) (Brandeis, J., dissenting). Putting to one side the procedural protections of the warrant requirement, the Fourth Amendment generally protects the "security" of "persons, houses, papers, and effects" against official intrusions up to the point where the community's need for evidence surmounts a specified standard, ordinarily "probable cause." Beyond this point, it is ordinarily justifiable for the community to demand that the individual give up some part of his interest in privacy and security to advance the community's vital interests in law enforcement; such a search is generally "reasonable" in the Amendment's terms.

A compelled surgical intrusion into an individual's body for evidence, however, implicates expectations of privacy and security of such magnitude that the intrusion may be "unreasonable" even if likely to produce evidence of a crime. In Schmerber v. California, 384 U.S. 757 (1966), we addressed a claim that the State had breached the Fourth Amendment's protection of the "right of the people to be secure in their *persons* . . . against unreasonable searches and seizures" (emphasis added) when it compelled an individual suspected of drunken driving to undergo a blood test. . . .

. . .

. . . The intrusion perhaps implicated Schmerber's most personal and deep-rooted expectations of privacy, and the Court recognized that Fourth Amendment analysis thus required a discerning inquiry into the facts and circumstances to determine whether the intrusion was justifiable. The Fourth Amendment neither forbids nor permits all such intrusions; rather, the Amendment's "proper function is to constrain, not against all intrusions as such, but against intrusions which are not justified in the circumstances, or which are made in an improper manner." Id., at 768.

The reasonableness of surgical intrusions beneath the skin depends on a case-by-case approach, in which the individual's interests in privacy and security are weighed against society's interests in conducting the procedure. In a given case, the question whether the community's need for evidence outweighs the substantial privacy interests at stake is a delicate one admitting of few categorical answers. We believe that *Schmerber*, however, provides the appropriate framework of analysis for such cases.

Schmerber recognized that the ordinary requirements of the Fourth Amendment would be the threshold requirements for conducting this kind of surgical search and seizure. We noted the importance of probable cause. . . . And we pointed out: "Search warrants are ordinarily required for searches of dwellings, and, absent an emergency, no less could be required where intrusions into the human body are concerned. . . . The importance of informed, detached and deliberate determinations of the issue whether or not to invade another's body in search of evidence of guilt is indisputable and great." Id., at 770.

Beyond these standards, *Schmerber*'s inquiry considered a number of other factors in determining the "reasonableness" of the blood test. A crucial factor in analyzing the magnitude of the intrusion in *Schmerber* is the extent to which the procedure may threaten the safety or health of the individual. . . . Notwithstanding the existence of probable cause, a search for evidence of a crime may be unjustifiable if it endangers the life or health of the suspect.

Another factor is the extent of intrusion upon the individual's dignitary interests in personal privacy and bodily integrity. . . .

Weighed against these individual interests is the community's interest in fairly and accurately determining guilt or innocence. This interest is of course of great importance. . . . In *Schmerber*, we concluded that this state interest was sufficient to justify the intrusion, and the compelled blood test was thus "reasonable" for Fourth Amendment purposes.

III

Applying the *Schmerber* balancing test in this case, we believe that the Court of Appeals reached the correct result. The Commonwealth plainly had probable cause to conduct the search. In addition, all parties apparently agree that respondent has had a full measure of procedural protections and has been able fully to litigate the difficult medical and legal questions necessarily involved in analyzing the reasonableness of a surgical incision of this magnitude. Our inquiry therefore must focus on the extent of the intrusion on respondent's privacy interests and on the State's need for the evidence.

The threats to the health or safety of respondent posed by the surgery are the subject of sharp dispute between the parties. Before the new revelations of October 18, the District Court found that the procedure could be carried out "with virtually no risk to [respondent]." 551 F.Supp., at 252. On rehearing, however, with new evidence before it, the District Court held that "the risks previously involved have increased in magnitude even as new risks are being added." Id., at 260.

The Court of Appeals examined the medical evidence in the record and found that respondent would suffer some risks associated with the surgical procedure. One surgeon had testified that the difficulty of discovering the exact location of the bullet "could require extensive probing and retracting of the muscle tissue," carrying with it "the concomitant risks of injury to the muscle as well as injury to the nerves, blood vessels and other tissue in the chest and pleural cavity." 717 F.2d at 900. The court further noted that "the greater intrusion and the larger incisions increase the risks of infection." Ibid. Moreover, there was conflict in the testimony concerning the nature and the scope of the operation. One surgeon stated that it would take 15–20 minutes, while another predicted the procedure could take up to two and one-half hours. . . . The court properly took the resulting uncertainty about the medical risks into account.

Both lower courts in this case believed that the proposed surgery, which for purely medical reasons required the use of a general anesthetic, would be an "extensive" intrusion on respondent's personal privacy and bodily integrity. . . . When conducted with the consent of the patient, surgery requiring general anesthesia is not necessarily demeaning or intrusive. In such a case, the surgeon is carrying out the patient's own will concerning the patient's body and the patient's right to privacy is therefore preserved. In this case, however, the Court of Appeals noted that the Commonwealth proposes to take control of respondent's body, to "drug this citizen—not yet convicted of a criminal offense—with narcotics and barbiturates into a state of unconsciousness," id., at 901, and then to search beneath his skin for evidence of a crime. This kind of surgery involves a virtually total divestment of respondent's ordinary control over surgical probing beneath his skin.

The other part of the balance concerns the Commonwealth's need to intrude into respondent's body to retrieve the bullet. The Commonwealth claims to need the bullet to demonstrate that it was fired from Watkinson's gun, which in turn would show that respondent was the robber who confronted Watkinson. However, although we recognize the difficulty of making determinations in advance as to the strength of the case against respondent, petitioners' assertions of a compelling need for the bullet are hardly persuasive. The very circumstances relied on in this case to demonstrate probable cause to believe that evidence will be found tend to vitiate the Commonwealth's need to compel respondent to undergo surgery. The Commonwealth has available substantial additional evidence that respondent was the individual who accosted Watkinson on the night of the robbery. No party in this case suggests that Watkinson's entirely spontaneous identification of respondent at the hospital would be inadmissible. In addition, petitioners can no doubt prove that Watkinson was found a few blocks from Watkinson's store shortly after the incident took place. And petitioners can certainly show that the location of the bullet (under respondent's left collarbone) seems to correlate with Watkinson's report that the robber "jerked" to the left. App. 13. The fact that the Commonwealth has available such substantial evidence of the origin of the bullet restricts the need for the Commonwealth to compel respondent to undergo the contemplated surgery.

In weighing the various factors in this case, we therefore reach the same conclusion as the courts below. The operation sought will intrude substantially on respondent's protected interests. The medical risks of the operation, although apparently not extremely severe, are a subject of considerable dispute; the very uncertainty militates against finding the operation to be "reasonable." In addition, the intrusion on respondent's privacy interests entailed by the operation can only be characterized as severe. On the other hand, although the bullet may turn out to be useful to the Commonwealth in prosecuting respondent, the Commonwealth has failed to demonstrate a compelling need for it. We believe that in these circumstances the Commonwealth has failed to demonstrate that it would be "reasonable" under the terms of the Fourth Amendment to search for evidence of this crime by means of the contemplated surgery.

IV

The Fourth Amendment is a vital safeguard of the right of the citizen to be free from unreasonable governmental intrusions into any area in which he has a reasonable expectation of privacy. Where the Court has found a lesser expectation of privacy . . . or where the search involves a minimal intrusion on privacy interests . . . the Court has held that the Fourth Amendment's protections are correspondingly less stringent. Conversely, however, the Fourth Amendment's command that searches be "reasonable" requires that when the State seeks to intrude upon an area in which our society recognizes a significantly heightened privacy interest, a more substantial justification is required to make the search "reasonable." Applying these principles, we hold that the proposed search in this case would be "unreasonable" under the Fourth Amendment.

Affirmed.[32]

---

[32] Chief Justice Burger wrote a brief concurring opinion. Justice Blackmun and Justice Rehnquist concurred in the judgment.

157. The defendant, accompanied by his brother and father, entered the Tucson Medical Center for treatment of a gunshot wound. A statute required medical personnel to notify the police of requests for treatment of wounds that might have resulted from criminal acts. The local police were notified of defendant's request for treatment. "The doctor removed a bullet from defendant's head and shortly thereafter he turned to a small group of men in the emergency room including policemen and detectives, held out the bullet which he had removed from defendant's head, and said something to the effect that 'I believe you want this object?' He then handed the bullet to the investigator from the Pima County Sheriff's office." The bullet proved to have been fired from the gun of a person who shot at an unknown assailant the night before. State v. Turner, 416 P.2d 409, 410 (Ariz.1966). Is the bullet admissible against the defendant over his objection at his trial for assault with intent to commit murder? See also People v. Capra, 216 N.E.2d 610 (N.Y.1966).

If after arresting a person the police take him to the hospital for treatment of wounds, may they, without a warrant, obtain from the hospital samples of blood extracted for typing purposes in preparation for a transfusion? May they arrange for a nurse to comb his hair and obtain hair samples for later use in evidence against him? See Commonwealth v. Gordon, 246 A.2d 325 (Pa.1968). See generally note 202, p. 363 below. If a person detained in jail is given a routine haircut as "an ordinary barbering incident" and, without the person's knowledge, at the request of the FBI the barber preserves hair clippings in an envelope and gives them to the FBI, can the clippings and laboratory analysis of them be used against him? See United States v. Cox, 428 F.2d 683 (7th Cir.1970).

158. "[A]n entry to fight a fire requires no warrant, and . . . once in the building, officials may remain there for a reasonable time to investigate the cause of the blaze. Thereafter, additional entries to investigate the cause of the fire must be made pursuant to the warrant procedures governing administrative searches." Michigan v. Tyler, 436 U.S. 499, 511 (1978) (7–1).

The holding of Michigan v. Tyler is elaborated in Michigan v. Clifford, 464 U.S. 287 (1984) (5–4):

> Except in certain carefully defined classes of cases, the nonconsensual entry and search of property are governed by the warrant requirement of the Fourth and Fourteenth Amendments. The constitutionality of warrantless and nonconsensual entries onto fire-damaged premises, therefore, normally turns on several factors: whether there are legitimate privacy interests in the fire-damaged property that are protected by the Fourth Amendment; whether exigent circumstances justify the government intrusion regardless of any reasonable expectations of privacy; and, whether the object of the search is to determine the cause of the fire or to gather evidence of criminal activity.

. . . Privacy expectations will vary with the type of property, the amount of fire damage, the prior and continued use of the premises, and in some cases the owner's efforts to secure it against intruders. Some fires may be so devastating that no reasonable privacy interests remain in the ash and ruins, regardless of the owner's subjective expectations. The test essentially is an objective one. . . . If reasonable privacy interests remain in the fire-damaged property, the warrant requirement applies, and any official entry must be made pursuant to a warrant in the absence of consent or exigent circumstances.

A burning building of course creates an exigency that justifies a warrantless entry by fire officials to fight the blaze. Moreover, in *Tyler* we held that once in the building, officials need no warrant to *remain* for "a reasonable time to investigate the cause of a blaze after it has been extinguished." 436 U.S., at 510. Where, however, reasonable expectations of privacy remain in the fire-damaged property, additional investigations begun after the fire has been extinguished and fire and police officials have left the scene, generally must be made pursuant to a warrant or the identification of some new exigency.

The aftermath of a fire often presents exigencies that will not tolerate the delay necessary to obtain a warrant or to secure the owner's consent to inspect fire-damaged premises. Because determining the cause and origin of a fire serves a compelling public interest, the warrant requirement does not apply in such cases.

If a warrant is necessary, the object of the search determines the type of warrant required. If the primary object is to determine the cause and origin of a recent fire, an administrative warrant will suffice. To obtain such a warrant, fire officials need show only that a fire of undetermined origin has occurred on the premises, that the scope of the proposed search is reasonable and will not intrude unnecessarily on the fire victim's privacy, and that the search will be executed at a reasonable and convenient time.

If the primary object of the search is to gather evidence of criminal activity, a criminal search warrant may be obtained only on a showing of probable cause to believe that relevant evidence will be found in the place to be searched. If evidence of criminal activity is discovered during the course of a valid administrative search, it may be seized under the "plain view" doctrine. . . . This evidence then may be used to establish probable cause to obtain a criminal search warrant. Fire officials may not, however, rely on this evidence to expand the scope of their administrative search without first making a successful showing of probable cause to an independent judicial officer.

The object of the search is important even if exigent circumstances exist. Circumstances that justify a warrantless search for the cause of a fire may not justify a search to gather evidence of criminal activity once that cause has been determined. If, for example, the administrative search is justified by the immediate need to ensure against rekindling, the scope of the search may be no broader than reasonably

> necessary to achieve its end. A search to gather evidence of criminal activity not in plain view must be made pursuant to a criminal warrant upon a traditional showing of probable cause.

464 U.S. at 291–95.

See Steigler v. Anderson, 496 F.2d 793 (3d Cir.1974) (investigation of the scene immediately after fire was extinguished was justified by exigent circumstances); State v. Hansen, 286 N.W.2d 163 (Iowa 1979) (investigation on day following fire, without warrant, not justified). See also Marshall v. Barlow's, Inc., 436 U.S. 307 (1978) (5–3) (holding unconstitutional a provision of the Occupational Safety and Health Act that authorized agents of the Secretary of Labor to inspect work areas for safety hazards and violations of OSHA regulations without a search warrant or comparable process).

159. Border search.

> Both Congress and the courts have long appreciated the peculiar problems faced by customs officials in policing our extensive national borders and our numerous, large international port facilities. . . . Realization of customs officials' special problems has resulted not only in the courts' giving the broadest interpretation compatible with our constitutional principles in construing the statutory powers of customs officers . . . but also has resulted in the application of special standards when the legality of a stop, search, and seizure made by a customs official at or near our borders or international port facilities has been challenged. . . .
>
> A customs officer has the unique power to stop a person at an international entry point and to conduct a "border search" without having a search warrant or even having a probable cause to believe the person has committed a crime. . . . Typically, mere suspicion of possible illegal activity within their jurisdiction is enough "cause" to permit a customs officer to stop and search a person. . . . This is not to say that the restrictions of the Fourth Amendment that searches and seizures may not be unreasonable are inapplicable to border stops and searches conducted by customs officials. On the contrary, border stops and searches, like all stops and searches by public officials, are restricted by the requirement that they be reasonable . . . but what is reasonable, of course, will depend on all the facts of a particular case. . . .
>
> A customs officer's unique power to conduct a "border search" is coextensive with the limits of our international border areas, and a search and seizure within these areas by a customs officer, reasonable enough under these circumstances, could perhaps be challenged as violative of the Fourth Amendment if conducted by different officials elsewhere. The term "border area" in this context, is elastic . . . ; the precise limits of the border area depend on the particular factual situation presented by the case raising the issue. For our purposes, it need only be said that "border area" reasonably includes not only

> actual land border checkpoints but also the checkpoints at all international ports of entry and a reasonable extended geographic area in the immediate vicinity of any entry point.

United States v. Glaziou, 402 F.2d 8, 12–13 (2d Cir.1968).

In Almeida-Sanchez v. United States, 413 U.S. 266 (1973) (5–4), the government argued that a search of the defendant's car by a "roving patrol," about 25 miles from the border, constituted a border search and was therefore lawful despite the absence of consent or probable cause. The search was part of the Border Patrol's effort to prevent the illegal entry of aliens. Although conceding that a "routine border search" can be conducted not only at the border but also at its "functional equivalents," such as "an established station near the border, at a point marking the confluence of two or more roads that extend from the border," id. at 272–73, a majority of the Court held that the search was unlawful. *Almeida-Sanchez* was followed in United States v. Ortiz, 422 U.S. 891 (1975), in which the search was made at a traffic checkpoint 66 miles from the border on a main highway; the Border Patrol screened cars passing the checkpoint and stopped only a small number of them, those that aroused their suspicion. Cf. note 75, p. 140 above.

Applying the border exception to the usual requirements of the Fourth Amendment, the Supreme Court has upheld a federal statute authorizing customs officials to search incoming international mail, whether packages or letters, if they have "reasonable cause to suspect" that they contain illegally imported matter. United States v. Ramsey, 431 U.S. 606 (1977) (6–3). See also United States v. Montoya de Hernandez, 473 U.S. 531 (1985), discussed in note 195, p. 354 below.

160. Airline searches. In the wake of September 11, 2001, the inspection and search of passengers and their baggage before they board an airplane has been greatly intensified. Whether that change will be permanent or will be reversed when (and if) the danger of terrorist attacks diminishes remains to be seen. Even earlier, a number of less catastrophic hijackings had led airlines to adopt a variety of measures to prevent hijacking or danger to the occupants of a plane in flight. In United States v. Cyzewski, 484 F.2d 509 (5th Cir.1973), the defendants were identified as potential hijackers according to a confidential "Behavior Pattern Profile" of the Federal Aviation Agency. Federal marshals accosted them at the boarding area and asked for identification. When they said that their identification papers were in their luggage, the luggage was retrieved from the plane. Before the luggage was produced, the defendants produced identification from their pockets, which showed that they had purchased their tickets under false names. They refused to allow their luggage to be inspected but agreed to pass before a magnetometer which tested for metal objects. The magnetometer indicated that one of the defendants had a metal object in his suitcase. He said that the only metal objects were buckles on his shoes, and he placed his hand in the suitcase to remove the shoes. A marshal grabbed the bag at that point, opened it, and searched it. He found a bag of marijuana.

Was the seizure lawful? If so, on what basis?

In United States v. Edwards, 498 F.2d 496, 498 (2d Cir.1974), the court observed that "a consensus does seem to be emerging that an airport search is not to be condemned as violating the Fourth Amendment simply because it does not precisely fit into one of the previously recognized categories for dispensing with a search warrant, but only if the search is 'unreasonable' on the facts." The subject of airline searches is discussed extensively in United States v. Albarado, 495 F.2d 799 (2d Cir.1974), citing many additional cases, id. at 801 n.1. See generally note 59, p. 117 above.

161. The Fourth Amendment does not prohibit customs officials from boarding a vessel in waters leading to the open sea in order to check its documentation, pursuant to federal statutory authority; no specific, articulable suspicion is necessary. The difference in the circumstances between this situation and the stop of an automobile on a highway and the difference in the need for and the nature of documentation in the two situations justify the difference in outcome from cases involving a border check of an automobile. United States v. Villamonte-Marquez, 462 U.S. 579 (1983) (6–3).

162. Electronic tracking devices. In United States v. Knotts, 460 U.S. 276 (1983), the Court upheld the use of an electronic beeper placed inside a drum of chemicals to track a car containing the drum on public roads and to locate the drum on the defendant's premises. The beeper was placed in the drum with the consent of the company that sold it. The Court said that all that the investigating agents learned from the beeper could have been observed by ordinary visual surveillance and that all that the beeper did was to enhance their ordinary "sensory faculties." There was, therefore, no invasion of a legitimate expectation of privacy.

In United States v. Karo, 468 U.S. 705 (1984), the Court answered questions left unresolved by *Knotts*. First, the Court held (6–3) that the transfer of a container in which an electronic tracking device has been installed with the consent of the owner to a buyer having no knowledge of the device is not a search and seizure within the meaning of the Fourth Amendment. Second, the Court held that monitoring the device while it is on private premises not open to visual surveillance violates the Fourth Amendment rights of persons who have a justifiable interest in the privacy of the premises. (Justices O'Connor and Rehnquist would have limited the violation of Fourth Amendment rights to persons having a privacy interest in the container itself.) The usual requirement of a warrant is applicable.

For other similar cases, see United States v. McIver, 186 F.3d 1119 (9th Cir.1999) (device placed on underside of car); United States v. Michael, 645 F.2d 252 (5th Cir.1981) (device attached to van); United States v. Conroy, 589 F.2d 1258 (5th Cir.1979) (device placed on board ship by person with permission to be there); United States v. Pretzinger, 542 F.2d 517 (9th Cir.1976) (device attached to airplane); United States v. Emery, 541 F.2d 887 (1st Cir.1976) (device inserted in package of contraband before mail delivery).

163. Upholding the authority of prison officials to make random searches of prison cells and to seize "any articles, which, in their view, disserve legitimate institutional interests," the Court held that "the Fourth Amendment has no applicability to a prison cell." Hudson v. Palmer, 468 U.S. 517, 528 n.8, 536 (1984) (5–4). "[S]ociety is not prepared to recognize as legitimate any subjective expectation of privacy that a prisoner might have in his prison cell. . . . The recognition of privacy rights for prisoners in their individual cells simply cannot be reconciled with the concept of incarceration and the needs and objectives of penal institutions." Id. at 526.

In United States v. Cohen, 796 F.2d 20 (2d Cir.1986), the court held that, notwithstanding Hudson v. Palmer, a person detained pending trial is protected by the Fourth Amendment against a search of his cell initiated by the prosecution in an effort to obtain evidence. It said that in *Hudson*, the Court "did not contemplate a cell search intended solely to bolster the prosecution's case against a pre-trial detainee awaiting his day in court" and having nothing to do with security or other institutional concerns. Id. at 23.

Abandoned Property

After the defendant had vacated his hotel room, federal agents searched the room with the permission of the management. Their express purpose was to find evidence of crimes committed by the defendant. They found incriminating evidence in a wastepaper basket. Upholding the seizure and use of the evidence against the defendant, the Court said: "[P]etitioner had abandoned these articles. He had thrown them away. So far as he was concerned, they were *bona vacantia*. There can be nothing unlawful in the Government's appropriation of such abandoned property." Abel v. United States, 362 U.S. 217, 241 (1960).

California v. Greenwood

486 U.S. 35, 108 S.Ct. 1625, 100 L.Ed.2d 30 (1988)

■ JUSTICE WHITE delivered the opinion of the Court.

The issue here is whether the Fourth Amendment prohibits the warrantless search and seizure of garbage left for collection outside the curtilage of a home. We conclude, in accordance with the vast majority of lower courts that have addressed the issue, that it does not.

I

In early 1984, Investigator Jenny Stracner of the Laguna Beach Police Department received information indicating that respondent Greenwood might be engaged in narcotics trafficking. Stracner learned that a criminal suspect had informed a federal drug-enforcement agent in February 1984 that a truck filled with illegal drugs was en route to the Laguna Beach address at which Greenwood resided. In addition, a neighbor complained of heavy vehicular traffic late at night in front of Greenwood's single-family home. The neighbor reported that the vehicles remained at Greenwood's house for only a few minutes.

Stracner sought to investigate this information by conducting a surveillance of Greenwood's home. She observed several vehicles make brief stops at the house during the late-night and early-morning hours, and she followed a truck from the house to a residence that had previously been under investigation as a narcotics trafficking location.

On April 6, 1984, Stracner asked the neighborhood's regular trash collector to pick up the plastic garbage bags that Greenwood had left on the curb in front of his house and to turn the bags over to her without mixing their contents with garbage from other houses. The trash collector cleaned his truck bin of other refuse, collected the garbage bags from the street in front of Greenwood's house, and turned the bags over to Stracner. The officer searched through the rubbish and found items indicative of narcotics use. She recited the information that she had gleaned from the trash search in an affidavit in support of a warrant to search Greenwood's home.

Police officers encountered both respondents at the house later that day when they arrived to execute the warrant. The police discovered quantities of cocaine and hashish during their search of the house. Respondents were arrested on felony narcotics charges. They subsequently posted bail.

The police continued to receive reports of many late-night visitors to the Greenwood house. On May 4, Investigator Robert Rahaeuser obtained Greenwood's garbage from the regular trash collector in the same manner as had Stracner. The garbage again contained evidence of narcotics use.

Rahaeuser secured another search warrant for Greenwood's home based on the information from the second trash search. The police found more narcotics and evidence of narcotics trafficking when they executed the warrant. Greenwood was again arrested.

The Superior Court dismissed the charges against respondents. . . . The court found that the police would not have had probable cause to search the Greenwood home without the evidence obtained from the trash searches.

. . .

. . . We granted certiorari . . . and now reverse.

II

The warrantless search and seizure of the garbage bags left at the curb outside the Greenwood house would violate the Fourth Amendment only if respondents manifested a subjective expectation of privacy in their garbage that society accepts as objectively reasonable. . . . Respondents do not disagree with this standard.

They assert, however, that they had, and exhibited, an expectation of privacy with respect to the trash that was searched by the police: The trash, which was placed on the street for collection at a fixed time, was contained in opaque plastic bags, which the garbage collector was expected to pick up, mingle with the trash of others, and deposit at the garbage dump. The trash was only temporarily on the street, and there was little likelihood that it would be inspected by anyone.

It may well be that respondents did not expect that the contents of their garbage bags would become known to the police or other members of the public. An expectation of privacy does not give rise to Fourth Amendment protection, however, unless society is prepared to accept that expectation as objectively reasonable.

Here, we conclude that respondents exposed their garbage to the public sufficiently to defeat their claim to Fourth Amendment protection. It is common knowledge that plastic garbage bags left on or at the side of a public street are readily accessible to animals, children, scavengers, snoops, and other members of the public. . . . Moreover, respondents placed their refuse at the curb for the express purpose of conveying it to a third party, the trash collector, who might himself have sorted through respondents' trash or permitted others, such as the police, to do so. Accordingly, having deposited their garbage "in an area particularly suited for public inspection and, in a manner of speaking, public consumption, for the express purpose of having strangers take it," United States v. Reicherter, 647 F.2d 397, 399 (CA3 1981), respondents could have had no reasonable expectation of privacy in the inculpatory items that they discarded.

Furthermore, as we have held, the police cannot reasonably be expected to avert their eyes from evidence of criminal activity that could have been observed by any member of the public. . . .

. . .

Our conclusion that society would not accept as reasonable respondents' claim to an expectation of privacy in trash left for collection in an area accessible to the public is reinforced by the unanimous rejection of similar claims by the Federal Courts of Appeals. . . . In addition, of those state appellate courts that have considered the issue, the vast majority have held that the police may conduct warrantless searches and seizures of garbage discarded in public areas. . . .[33]

33. Given that the dissenters are among the tiny minority of judges whose views are contrary to ours, we are distinctly unimpressed with the dissent's prediction that "society will be shocked to learn" of today's decision. Post, at 46.

. . .

[The Court rejected the respondents' further arguments that their expectation of privacy in the trash should be deemed reasonable because a search of the trash was illegal under state law and that the Due Process Clause required California to apply the exclusionary rule to a search in violation of state law.]

The judgment of the California Court of Appeal is therefore reversed, and this case is remanded for further proceedings not inconsistent with this opinion.

. . .

■ JUSTICE BRENNAN, with whom JUSTICE MARSHALL joins, dissenting.

Every week for two months, and at least once more a month later, the Laguna Beach police clawed through the trash that respondent Greenwood left in opaque, sealed bags on the curb outside his home. . . . Complete strangers minutely scrutinized their bounty, undoubtedly dredging up intimate details of Greenwood's private life and habits. The intrusions proceeded without a warrant, and no court before or since has concluded that the police acted on probable cause to believe Greenwood was engaged in any criminal activity.

Scrutiny of another's trash is contrary to commonly accepted notions of civilized behavior. I suspect, therefore, that members of our society will be shocked to learn that the Court, the ultimate guarantor of liberty, deems unreasonable our expectation that the aspects of our private lives that are concealed safely in a trash bag will not become public.

. . .

A single bag of trash testifies eloquently to the eating, reading, and recreational habits of the person who produced it. A search of trash, like a search of the bedroom, can relate intimate details about sexual practices, health, and personal hygiene. Like rifling through desk drawers or intercepting phone calls, rummaging through trash can divulge the target's financial and professional status, political affiliations and inclinations, private thoughts, personal relationships, and romantic interests. It cannot be doubted that a sealed trash bag harbors telling evidence of the "intimate activity associated with the 'sanctity of a man's home and the privacies of life,' " which the Fourth Amendment is designed to protect. Oliver v. United States, 466 U.S. 170, 180 (1984) (quoting Boyd v. United States, 116 U.S. 616, 630 (1886)). . . .

The Court properly rejects the State's attempt to distinguish trash searches from other searches on the theory that trash is abandoned and therefore not entitled to an expectation of privacy. . . . In evaluating the reasonableness of Greenwood's expectation that his sealed trash bags would not be invaded, the Court has held that we must look to "understandings that are recognized and permitted by society."[34] Most of us, I believe, would

34. Rakas v. Illinois, 439 U.S. 128, 143–44, n.12 (1978). . . .

be incensed to discover a meddler—whether a neighbor, a reporter, or a detective—scrutinizing our sealed trash containers to discover some detail of our personal lives. . . .

. . .

Had Greenwood flaunted his intimate activity by strewing his trash all over the curb for all to see, or had some nongovernmental intruder invaded his privacy and done the same, I could accept the Court's conclusion that an expectation of privacy would have been unreasonable. Similarly, had police searching the city dump run across incriminating evidence that, despite commingling with the trash of others, still retained its identity as Greenwood's, we would have a different case. But all that Greenwood "exposed . . . to the public," ante, at 40, were the exteriors of several opaque, sealed containers. Until the bags were opened by police, they hid their contents from the public's view. . . . Faithful application of the warrant requirement does not require police to "avert their eyes from evidence of criminal activity that could have been observed by any member of the public." Rather, it only requires them to adhere to norms of privacy that members of the public plainly acknowledge.

The mere *possibility* that unwelcome meddlers *might* open and rummage through the containers does not negate the expectation of privacy in its contents any more than the possibility of a burglary negates an expectation of privacy in the home; or the possibility of a private intrusion negates an expectation of privacy in an unopened package; or the possibility that an operator will listen in on a telephone conversation negates an expectation of privacy in the words spoken on the telephone. . . .

Nor is it dispositive that "respondents placed their refuse at the curb for the express purpose of conveying it to a third party . . . who might himself have sorted through respondents' trash or permitted others, such as police, to do so." Ante, at 40. In the first place, Greenwood can hardly be faulted for leaving trash on his curb when a county ordinance commanded him to do so . . . and prohibited him from disposing of it in any other way. . . . Unlike in other circumstances where privacy is compromised, Greenwood could not "avoid exposing personal belongings . . . by simply leaving them at home." *O'Connor* [v. Ortega, 480 U.S. 709 (1987)], at 725. More importantly, even the voluntary relinquishment of possession or control over an effect does not necessarily amount to a relinquishment of a privacy expectation in it. Were it otherwise, a letter or package would lose all Fourth Amendment protection when placed in a mail box or other depository with the "express purpose" of entrusting it to the postal officer or a private carrier. . . .

III

In holding that the warrantless search of Greenwood's trash was consistent with the Fourth Amendment, the Court paints a grim picture of our society. It depicts a society in which local authorities may command their citizens to dispose of their personal effects in the manner least protective of the "sanctity of [the] home and the privacies of life," Boyd v.

United States, 116 U.S., at 630, and then monitor them arbitrarily and without judicial oversight—a society that is not prepared to recognize as reasonable an individual's expectation of privacy in the most private of personal effects sealed in an opaque container and disposed of in a manner designed to commingle it imminently and inextricably with the trash of others. . . .

---

164. In United States v. Hedrick, 922 F.2d 396 (7th Cir.1991), the court held that the defendant had no reasonable expectation of privacy in garbage cans left on the driveway within the curtilage for trash pickup. It observed: "As a general rule, the reasonableness of the expectation [of privacy] will increase as the garbage gets closer to the garage or house." Id. at 400. See United States v. Redmon, 117 F.3d 1036 (7th Cir.1997). See United States v. Long, 176 F.3d 1304 (10th Cir.1999) (same; trash bags placed on top of camper-trailer on defendant's property, near property line).

Greenwood was applied to shredded documents placed in trash bags, in United States v. Scott, 975 F.2d 927 (1st Cir.1992). The documents had been reduced to 5/32 inch strips, which IRS agents recovered from trash bags and "painstakingly pieced together," id. at 928. The court said:

> The fact that the abandoned property was partially destroyed by shredding, although constituting evidence of appellee's subjective desire or hope that the contents be unintelligible to third parties, does not change the fact that it is as a result of appellee's own actions that the shredded evidence was placed in the public domain. . . .
>
> What we have here is a failed attempt at secrecy by reason of underestimation of police resourcefulness, not invasion of constitutionally protected privacy. . . .
>
> Appellee here thought that reducing the documents to 5/32 inch pieces made them undecipherable. It turned out he was wrong. He is in no better position than the citizen who merely tears up a document by hand and discards the pieces onto the sidewalk. Can there be any doubt that the police are allowed to pick up the pieces from the sidewalk for use of the contents against that person? Should the mere use of more sophisticated "higher" technology in attempting destruction of the pieces of paper grant higher constitutional protection to this failed attempt at secrecy? We think not.

Id. at 929, 930.

165. The Supreme Court of the State of Washington declined to follow *Greenwood* and found that the warrantless search of defendant's trash violated the state constitution, in State v. Boland, 800 P.2d 1112 (Wash.1990). The Supreme Court of New Hampshire has ruled similarly, State v. Goss, 834 A.2d 316 (2003), as has the Supreme Court of New Jersey, State v. Hempele, 576 A.2d 793 (N.J.1990). Before *Greenwood* was decided, the Supreme Court of Hawaii had held that the state constitution prohibited the police from searching without a warrant trash placed in trash bags on private property. State v. Tanaka, 701 P.2d 1274 (Haw.1985).

166.

Defendant rented a room at the Eugene Hotel. The Eugene Police Department was informed by employees of the hotel that they suspected defendant of using narcotics. Detective Matoon of the Eugene Police Department went to the hotel and made inquiry of the manager of the hotel and other employees concerning defendant's activities. Matoon, learning that defendant was occupying room 705 went up to the seventh floor of the hotel where he enlisted the help of two maids who were in the process of cleaning and making ready the rooms on that floor. He asked them to keep the trash from room 705 separate from the trash collected from the other rooms. He explained to them that he thought that defendant was using narcotics and that he wanted to examine the trash taken from the room for narcotics. More specifically, he instructed them to look for "homemade cigarettes." During this time the hotel manager came up to the seventh floor and instructed the maids to commence cleaning room 705. The maids went into the room at approximately 2:30 p.m. and began cleaning the room. They deposited all items which they regarded as waste or trash and brought them out in a flat cardboard box to Matoon. If they had followed their usual procedure, they would have dumped the trash into a bag on their cleaning cart.

Matoon examined the contents of the receptacle brought to him while the maids returned to room 705 and resumed their cleaning. They then found on the floor between the bed and a chair a cigarette butt wrapped in a cardboard cover of a matchbook. They decided that this was what the officer was looking for so they brought it out to him. Matoon tentatively identified the butt as containing marijuana.

State v. Purvis, 438 P.2d 1002, 1002–1003 (Or.1968).

Assuming that Matoon asked the maids to remove, and they did remove, only what they would have removed in the customary course of their work, is the cigarette butt containing marijuana admissible in evidence against the defendant?

167. Open fields. In Hester v. United States, 265 U.S. 57, 59 (1924), the Supreme Court held that a trespass on open land did not itself constitute an unreasonable search or make a seizure unreasonable, and said: "[T]he special protection accorded by the Fourth Amendment to the people in their 'persons, houses, papers, and effects,' is not extended to the open fields. The distinction between the latter and the house is as old as the common law." In contrast to open fields, the "curtilage" of a dwelling is protected. *Hester* was reaffirmed in Oliver v. United States, 466 U.S. 170 (1984) (6–3). In *Oliver*, the Court said that "the curtilage is the area to which extends the intimate activity associated with the 'sanctity of a man's home and the privacies of life,' Boyd v. United States, 116 U.S. 616, 630

(1886), and therefore has been considered part of the home itself for Fourth Amendment purposes." 466 U.S. at 180. The curtilage is defined "by reference to the factors that determine whether an individual reasonably may expect that an area immediately adjacent to the home will remain private." Id.

> No single factor determines whether an individual legitimately may claim under the Fourth Amendment that a place should be free of government intrusion not authorized by warrant. . . . In assessing the degree to which a search infringes upon individual privacy, the Court has given weight to such factors as the intention of the Framers of the Fourth Amendment . . . the uses to which the individual has put a location . . . and our societal understanding that certain areas deserve the most scrupulous protection from government invasion. . . . These factors are equally relevant to determining whether the government's intrusion upon open fields without a warrant or probable cause violates reasonable expectations of privacy and is therefore a search proscribed by the Amendment.
>
> In this light, the rule of Hester v. United States . . . that we reaffirm today, may be understood as providing that an individual may not legitimately demand privacy for activities conducted out of doors in fields, except in the area immediately surrounding the home. . . . This rule is true to the conception of the right to privacy embodied in the Fourth Amendment. The Amendment reflects the recognition of the Founders that certain enclaves should be free from arbitrary government interference. For example, the Court since the enactment of the Fourth Amendment has stressed "the overriding respect for the sanctity of the home that has been embedded in our traditions since the origins of the Republic." Payton v. New York [445 U.S. 573 (1980)], at 601. . . .
>
> In contrast, open fields do not provide the setting for those intimate activities that the Amendment is intended to shelter from government interference or surveillance. There is no societal interest in protecting the privacy of those activities, such as the cultivation of crops, that occur in open fields. Moreover, as a practical matter these lands usually are accessible to the public and the police in ways that a home, an office or commercial structure would not be. It is not generally true that fences or no trespassing signs effectively bar the public from viewing open fields in rural areas. And . . . the public and police lawfully may survey lands from the air. For these reasons, the asserted expectation of privacy in open fields is not an expectation that "society recognizes as reasonable."

466 U.S. at 177–79.

In United States v. Dunn, 480 U.S. 294, 301 (1987) (7–2), the Court said that the extent of a home's curtilage is based on four factors: "the proximity of the area claimed to be curtilage to the home, whether the area is included within an enclosure surrounding the home, the nature of the uses to which the area is put, and the steps taken by the resident to protect the area from observation by people passing by." Those factors, the Court said, do not yield a "finely tuned formula"; they "are useful analytical tools only to the degree that, in any given case, they bear upon the centrally relevant consideration—whether the area in question is so intimately tied to the home itself that it should be placed under the home's 'umbrella' of Fourth Amendment protection." Applying these factors, the Court concluded that a barn located 50 yards from a fence surrounding the defendant's house and 60 yards from the house itself was not within the curtilage. The Court held also that, under *Oliver*, the interior of the barn was not constitutionally protected, independently of the house, from being observed by police standing in the open fields outside it.

See Dow Chemical Co. v. United States, 476 U.S. 227 (1986) (5–4). The Environmental Protection Agency employed a commercial aerial photographer to fly over the defendant's industrial complex, which extended over 2000 acres, and to photograph equipment and installations open to view from above. The Court said that the area photographed "can perhaps be seen as falling somewhere between 'open fields' and curtilage, but lacking some of the critical characteristics of both." Id. at 236. It concluded that although the area might be protected from some forms of sophisticated technological surveillance, it was not protected from the aerial photography. See note 191, p. 342 below.

Unofficial Conduct

---

168. Burdeau v. McDowell, 256 U.S. 465, 475–76 (1921):

The Fourth Amendment gives protection against unlawful searches and seizures, and . . . its protection applies to governmental action. Its origin and history clearly show that it was intended as a restraint upon the activities of sovereign authority, and was not intended to be a limitation upon other than governmental agencies; as against such authority it was the purpose of the Fourth Amendment to secure the citizen in the right of unmolested occupation of his dwelling and the possession of his property, subject to the right of seizure by process duly issued.

[P]apers having come into the possession of the Government without a violation of petitioner's rights by governmental authority, we see no reason why the fact that individuals, unconnected with the Government, may have wrongfully taken them, should prevent them from being held for use in prosecuting an offense where the documents are of an incriminatory character.

Justice Brandeis dissented:

> That the court would restore the papers to plaintiff if they were still in the thief's possession is not questioned. That it has power to control the disposition of these stolen papers, although they have passed into the possession of the law officer, is also not questioned. But it is said that no provision of the Constitution requires their surrender and that the papers could have been subpoenaed. This may be true. Still I cannot believe that action of a public official is necessarily lawful, because it does not violate constitutional prohibitions and because the same result might have been attained by other and proper means. At the foundation of our civil liberty lies the principle which denies to government officials an exceptional position before the law and which subjects them to the same rules of conduct that are commands to the citizen. And in the development of our liberty insistence upon procedural regularity has been a large factor. Respect for law will not be advanced by resort, in its enforcement, to means which shock the common man's sense of decency and fair play.

Id. at 477.

The principle of Burdeau v. McDowell has frequently been applied. E.g., United States v. Knoll, 16 F.3d 1313 (2d Cir.1994); Meister v. Commissioner, 504 F.2d 505 (3d Cir.1974) (taxpayer's records stolen by bookkeeper); Barnes v. United States, 373 F.2d 517 (5th Cir.1967) (motel owner).

"A private search in which the government is in no respect involved—either directly as a participant or indirectly as an encourager—is not subject to the Fourth Amendment because the private actor is motivated in whole or in part by a unilateral desire to aid in the enforcement of the law." United States v. Gumerlock, 590 F.2d 794, 800 (9th Cir.1979).

Searches of baggage by airline personnel have presented a recurring problem. "In the absence of the requisite government sanction—whether by explicit authorization or comparable degree of involvement—searches of cargo by common carriers resulting in the discovery and seizure of contraband which form the basis for subsequent criminal proceedings are private rather than governmental and thus not subject to the strictures of the Fourth Amendment. . . . Such searches, whether founded on common law right or conducted pursuant to tariff, do not differ for Fourth Amendment purposes from private searches: the evidence so obtained is not subject to exclusion under the Fourth Amendment because it was not discovered by government officers." United States v. Fannon, 556 F.2d 961, 963 (9th Cir.1977). Despite the principle enunciated, the court concluded that federal legislation authorizing airlines to condition transportation of persons or property on consent to searches for dangerous substances conferred on carriers "a governmental function sufficient to subject its conduct to constitutional limitations." Id. at 964. The court declined to say fully what was constitutionally required in these circumstances but said that at least "reasonable notice to the shipper that search is a condition of carriage" was required. Id. at 965.

For examples of cases in which the involvement of government agents was too great for the conduct in question to escape application of the Fourth Amendment, see United States v. Newton, 510 F.2d 1149 (7th Cir.1975); Corngold v. United States, 367 F.2d 1 (9th Cir.1966). See also United States v. Haes, 551 F.2d 767 (8th Cir.1977) (air freight); Knoll Associates, Inc. v. Federal Trade Commission, 397 F.2d 530 (7th Cir.1968) (corporate documents stolen by private person to aid government and with its approval).

In United States v. Bomengo, 580 F.2d 173 (5th Cir.1978), persons employed by an apartment complex entered the defendant's apartment in his absence to locate the source of a water leak. While they were inspecting, they saw guns with silencers attached in plain view and summoned the police. The police entered the apartment and saw the guns, then went away and obtained a search warrant for their seizure. The court said that "a police view subsequent to a search conducted by private citizens does not constitute a 'search' within the meaning of the Fourth Amendment so long as the view is confined to the scope and product of the initial search," id. at 175, and held that the initial view leading the police to obtain a warrant was not improper. See United States v. Runyan, 275 F.3d 449 (5th Cir.2001), appeal after remand, 290 F.3d 223 (2002), discussing the permissible scope of a warrantless police search following a private search, reported to the police, of the same premises or containers.

169.

In December 1982, defendant Lambert hired Diana Hall to be his housekeeper. Hall claims that Lambert and his friends openly used illegal drugs in the house. Beginning in May 1982, Hall approached the Federal Bureau of Investigation (FBI) and provided information about Lambert's drug activities. Hall concedes that the FBI paid her some expense money but she insists that her decision to go to the FBI was not motivated by money. Rather, she claims that she acted because of her concerns about the negative effects of drug use, particularly on young people, and her worry about Lambert's health. Over the course of the following year, Hall contacted the FBI approximately 25 times concerning Lambert's activities.

During several of her meetings with the FBI, Hall brought items which she had taken from the Lambert home. These items included test tubes, pills and other drug paraphernalia, as well as check stubs and phone bills which Hall thought might be related to Lambert's drug transactions. She insisted that these items had been discarded or abandoned by Lambert and that she had picked them up while performing her housekeeping duties.

Hall emphasized that the FBI never asked her to retrieve any items from Lambert's house or even suggested that this would be helpful to them. Agent Bill Welsh confirmed this during his testimony before the court. In fact, Hall and Welsh both testified that, after she had expressed a desire to search Lambert's closed safe and his garage, the FBI agents specifically told her *not* to do so.

In November 1982, defendant Block visited Lambert at his home and stayed for a few days in a basement bedroom. During that time, several other persons visited the home and a meeting took place in the basement. Hall, who was working upstairs, smelled chemical odors coming from the basement. She believed that the odors were caused by cocaine being cut or purified. The next day, as she was cleaning the basement, Hall went into a closet and discovered a small football-sized object. Next to it was a thermos. The thermos contained a white powder. Suspecting cocaine, Hall brought a sample from the thermos to the FBI. She emphasized that the FBI had not asked her to search for drugs or to bring this item to its office. The FBI analyzed the powder in its crime lab and determined that it was indeed cocaine.

United States v. Lambert, 771 F.2d 83, 86–87 (6th Cir.1985).

Lambert was prosecuted for drug offenses. Are the items taken from his home by Hall admissible in evidence against him?

170. Burglars entered the Genivivas' home and stole an amount of money. The burglars were arrested and the money was recovered and turned over to local police as evidence. If the police turn the money over to agents of the Internal Revenue Service, can it be used as evidence in a prosecution of the Genivivas for income tax evasion? See Geniviva v. Bingler, 206 F.Supp. 81 (W.D.Pa.1961).

171. In a divorce action, should evidence of the wife's adultery, which the husband obtained by an illegal forcible entry into her home in the company of private investigators, be admitted at the trial? See Sackler v. Sackler, 203 N.E.2d 481 (N.Y.1964), with which compare Williams v. Williams, 221 N.E.2d 622 (Ohio Ct.Com.Pl.1966). Compare Honeycutt v. Aetna Insurance Co., 510 F.2d 340 (7th Cir.1975), an action on an insurance claim in which the defendant insurance company introduced evidence of arson obtained during an unlawful search by state officials. The court of appeals concluded that "the Fourth and Fourteenth Amendments do *not* require in civil cases that the exclusionary rule be extended to situations where private parties seek to introduce evidence obtained through unauthorized searches made by state officials." Id. at 348.

CHAPTER 4

INFORMERS, EAVESDROPPING, WIRETAPPING

Lewis v. United States

385 U.S. 206, 87 S.Ct. 424, 17 L.Ed.2d 312 (1966)

■ MR. CHIEF JUSTICE WARREN delivered the opinion of the Court.

The question for resolution here is whether the Fourth Amendment was violated when a federal narcotics agent, by misrepresenting his identity and stating his willingness to purchase narcotics, was invited into petitioner's home where an unlawful narcotics transaction was consummated and the narcotics were thereafter introduced at petitioner's criminal trial over his objection. We hold that under the facts of this case it was not. Those facts are not disputed and may be briefly stated as follows:

On December 3, 1964, Edward Cass, an undercover federal narcotics agent, telephoned petitioner's home to inquire about the possibility of purchasing marihuana. Cass, who previously had not met or dealt with petitioner, falsely identified himself as one "Jimmy the Pollack [*sic*]" and stated that a mutual friend had told him petitioner might be able to supply marihuana. In response, petitioner said, "Yes. I believe, Jimmy, I can take care of you," and then directed Cass to his home where, it was indicated, a sale of marihuana would occur. Cass drove to petitioner's home, knocked on the door, identified himself as "Jim," and was admitted. After discussing the possibility of regular future dealings at a discounted price, petitioner led Cass to a package located on the front porch of his home. Cass gave petitioner $50, took the package, and left the premises. The package contained five bags of marihuana. On December 17, 1964, a similar transaction took place, beginning with a phone conversation in which Cass identified himself as "Jimmy the Pollack" and ending with an invited visit by Cass to petitioner's home where a second sale of marihuana occurred. Once again, Cass paid petitioner $50, but this time he received in return a package containing six bags of marihuana.

Petitioner was arrested on April 27, 1965, and charged by a two-count indictment with violations of the narcotics laws relating to transfers of marihuana. 26 U.S.C. § 4742(a). A pretrial motion to suppress as evidence the marihuana and the conversations between petitioner and the agent was denied, and they were introduced at the trial. The District Court, sitting without a jury, convicted petitioner on both counts and imposed concurrent five-year penitentiary sentences. The Court of Appeals for the First Circuit affirmed . . . and we granted certiorari. . . .

Petitioner does not argue that he was entrapped, as he could not on the facts of this case; nor does he contend that a search of his home was made or that anything other than the purchased narcotics was taken away. His only contentions are that, in the absence of a warrant, any official intrusion upon the privacy of a home constitutes a Fourth Amendment violation and that the fact the suspect invited the intrusion cannot be held a waiver when the invitation was induced by fraud and deception.

Both petitioner and the Government recognize the necessity for some undercover police activity and both concede that the particular circumstances of each case govern the admissibility of evidence obtained by stratagem or deception. Indeed, it has long been acknowledged by the decisions of this Court . . . that, in the detection of many types of crime, the Government is entitled to use decoys and to conceal the identity of its agents. The various protections of the Bill of Rights, of course, provide checks upon such official deception for the protection of the individual. . . .

Petitioner argues that the Government overstepped the constitutional bounds in this case and places principal reliance on Gouled v. United States, 255 U.S. 298 (1921).[1] But a short statement of that case will demonstrate how misplaced his reliance is. There, a business acquaintance of the petitioner, acting under orders of federal officers, obtained entry into the petitioner's office by falsely representing that he intended only to pay a social visit. In the petitioner's absence, however, the intruder secretly ransacked the office and seized certain private papers of an incriminating nature. This Court had no difficulty concluding that the Fourth Amendment had been violated by the secret and general ransacking, notwithstanding that the initial intrusion was occasioned by a fraudulently obtained invitation rather than by force or stealth.

In the instant case, on the other hand, the petitioner invited the undercover agent to his home for the specific purpose of executing a felonious sale of narcotics. Petitioner's only concern was whether the agent was a willing purchaser who could pay the agreed price. Indeed, in order to convince the agent that his patronage at petitioner's home was desired, petitioner told him that if he became a regular customer there, he would in the future receive an extra bag of marihuana at no additional cost; and in fact petitioner did hand over an extra bag at a second sale which was consummated at the same place and in precisely the same manner. During neither of his visits to petitioner's home did the agent see, hear, or take anything that was not contemplated, and in fact intended, by petitioner as a necessary part of his illegal business. Were we to hold the deceptions of the agent in this case constitutionally prohibited, we would come near to a rule that the use of undercover agents in any manner is virtually unconsti-

[1] The aspect of *Gouled* discussed here is separate from that considered in connection with Warden v. Hayden, 387 U.S. 294 (1967), p. 246 above.

tutional per se. Such a rule would, for example, severely hamper the Government in ferreting out those organized criminal activities that are characterized by covert dealings with victims who either cannot or do not protest. A prime example is provided by the narcotics traffic.

The fact that the undercover agent entered petitioner's home does not compel a different conclusion. Without question, the home is accorded the full range of Fourth Amendment protections. . . . But when, as here, the home is converted into a commercial center to which outsiders are invited for purposes of transacting unlawful business, that business is entitled to no greater sanctity than if it were carried on in a store, a garage, a car, or on the street. A government agent, in the same manner as a private person, may accept an invitation to do business and may enter upon the premises for the very purposes contemplated by the occupant. Of course, this does not mean that, whenever entry is obtained by invitation and the locus is characterized as a place of business, an agent is authorized to conduct a general search for incriminating materials; a citation to the *Gouled* case, supra, is sufficient to dispose of that contention.

. . . The instant . . . case has been well summarized by the Government at the conclusion of its brief as follows:

> In short, this case involves the exercise of no governmental power to intrude upon protected premises; the visitor was invited and willingly admitted by the suspect. It concerns no design on the part of a government agent to observe or hear what was happening in the privacy of a home; the suspect chose the location where the transaction took place. It presents no question of the invasion of the privacy of a dwelling; the only statements repeated were those that were willingly made to the agent and the only things taken were the packets of marihuana voluntarily transferred to him. The pretense resulted in no breach of privacy; it merely encouraged the suspect to say things which he was willing and anxious to say to anyone who would be interested in purchasing marihuana.

Further elaboration is not necessary. The judgment is

Affirmed.

■ MR. JUSTICE DOUGLAS, dissenting.

. . .

We are here concerned with the manner in which government agents enter private homes. In *Lewis* the undercover agent appeared as a prospective customer. Tomorrow he may be a policeman disguised as the grocery deliveryman or telephone repairman, or even a health inspector. . . .

. . .

Entering another's home in disguise to obtain evidence is a "search" that should bring into play all the protective features of the Fourth Amendment. When the agent in *Lewis* had reason for believing that petitioner possessed narcotics, a search warrant should have been obtained.

Almost every home is at times used for purposes other than eating, sleeping, and social activities. Are the sanctity of the home and its privacy stripped away whenever it is used for business? . . . I think not. A home is still a sanctuary, however the owner may use it. There is no reason why an owner's Fourth Amendment rights cannot include the right to open up his house to limited classes of people. And, when a homeowner invites a friend or business acquaintance into his home, he opens his house to a friend or acquaintance, not a government spy.

This does not mean he can make his sanctuary invasion-proof against government agents. The Constitution has provided a way whereby the home can lawfully be invaded, and that is with a search warrant. Where, as here, there is enough evidence to get a warrant to make a search I would not allow the Fourth Amendment to be short-circuited.

We downgrade the Fourth Amendment when we forgive noncompliance with its mandate and allow these easier methods of the police to thrive.

A householder who admits a government agent, knowing that he is such, waives of course any right of privacy. One who invites or admits an old "friend" takes, I think, the risk that the "friend" will tattle and disclose confidences or that the Government will wheedle them out of him. The case for me, however, is different when government plays an ignoble role of "planting" an agent in one's living room or uses fraud and deception in getting him there. These practices are at war with the constitutional standards of privacy which are parts of our choicest tradition.

. . .[2]

---

172. What precisely is the principle established by *Lewis*? Is any entry pursuant to an invitation permissible under the Fourth Amendment despite the official's concealment of his official capacity, provided that he does only what he was invited inside to do? How should the Court's phrase "the very purposes contemplated by the occupant," p. 306 above, be understood? (In one obvious sense, Cass's purpose in entering could not have been more opposed to the purpose for which Lewis invited him in.) In United States v. Guidry, 534 F.2d 1220 (6th Cir.1976), for example, a federal agent who suspected that the defendants were engaged in counterfeiting arranged to pose as the "helper" of a service representative of a printing company when the latter made a call at the defendants' house. The service representative told the defendants that he was there to look at the printing press, which they wanted to sell. While he was in the house, the agent observed the press and removed from it a piece of paper with green ink. Was the agent's observation of the press lawful? The removal of the paper? See also United States v. Ressler, 536 F.2d 208 (7th Cir.1976).

[2] Justice Brennan wrote a concurring opinion, which Justice Fortas joined.

How important in *Lewis* is the fact that the purpose for which Cass was invited to enter was itself illegal? Suppose, as Justice Douglas imagined, p. 306 above, a police officer posed as a telephone repairman and observed nothing except what a repairman would inevitably observe and would, therefore, be expected to observe. In *Guidry*, above, the purpose of the service representative's visit was entirely lawful. See also United States v. Wagner, 884 F.2d 1090 (8th Cir.1989), in which an officer posed as a UPS delivery man, and United States v. Alvarez, 812 F.2d 668 (11th Cir.1987), in which agents posed as bank representatives seeking information for a "merchant questionnaire." In United States v. Giraldo, 743 F.Supp. 152 (E.D.N.Y.1990), the court held that entry obtained by an agent's representation that she was a gas company worker checking for a gas leak was unlawful, because the purported purpose of the visit gave the defendant no effective choice to deny entry.

Does it make any difference that the purpose of the entry is a business transaction? Suppose Lewis had invited Cass to his house and told him that he was going to give him a gift of marijuana.

For an extreme application of *Lewis*, see U.S. v. Baldwin, 621 F.2d 251, 632 F.2d 1 (6th Cir.1980). In that case, an undercover agent obtained employment as handyman and chauffeur in the home of a person who was under investigation. The agent lived there for six months, during which period he found and removed material that was used as evidence against his employer.

173. The defendant was convicted of tax offenses. The evidence against him included microfilms of records that the defendant voluntarily made available to an IRS agent who was conducting an audit of the defendant's returns at the request of the Organized Crime and Racketeering Section of the Department of Justice. The court of appeals found that "the agent's failure to apprise the appellant of the obvious criminal nature of this investigation was a sneaky deliberate deception." United States v. Tweel, 550 F.2d 297, 299 (5th Cir.1977). Should the evidence have been admitted? Compare United States v. Davis, 749 F.2d 292 (5th Cir.1985) ("mere failure to warn an individual that an investigation might result in criminal charges does not constitute fraud, deceit or trickery").

174. The defendant was indicted for income tax evasion. Thereafter, on several occasions an accountant who had prepared the defendant's tax returns for many years and had prepared net worth schedules for the defendant at the request of his counsel came alone and voluntarily to the United States Attorney's office. He was interviewed by government counsel and agents of the Internal Revenue Service and voluntarily turned over to them his file on the defendant, which included the net worth schedules. The government had prepared its own net worth schedules for use at trial, with which it compared the schedules prepared for the defendant. Defense counsel was promptly advised of the disclosures. The matter was called to the court's attention before trial by the defendant's motion to suppress. United States v. Mancuso, 378 F.2d 612 (4th Cir.1967). Were any rights of the defendant infringed? If so, what action should the court have taken?

175. In Weatherford v. Bursey, 429 U.S. 545 (1977) (7–2), an undercover government agent who, as an agent, had been involved in a crime with the defendant was arrested with him in order to maintain his cover. During the pretrial period, the agent met with the defendant and the defendant's lawyer on two occasions when the trial was discussed. The agent did not initiate the meetings, nor did he discuss what happened at them with the prosecutor. He appeared at the trial as a witness for the prosecution. The Court concluded that there had been no denial of the right to counsel in those circumstances. Nothing having been communicated to the prosecution, the defense was not hampered in any way. Furthermore, there was no purposeful intrusion into the attorney-client relationship, and the intrusion that took place was necessitated by the nature of undercover work. Compare Hoffa v. United States, 385 U.S. 293, 304–309 (1966); United States v. Valencia, 541 F.2d 618 (6th Cir.1976) (attorney's secretary was government informant; indictment dismissed).

See United States v. Mastroianni, 749 F.2d 900 (1st Cir.1984). A government informant was invited to attend a meeting of the defendants with defense counsel. The court of appeals upheld the district court's finding that the informant's attendance at the meeting was not a deliberate intrusion into the defense camp and was permissible to maintain the informant's "cover." After the meeting, the informant was "debriefed" by the government and revealed confidential matter that he had heard at the defense meeting. The court of appeals upheld the district court's finding that the government had met its high burden of showing that the defendants were not prejudiced by the informant's disclosures. See also United States v. Melvin, 650 F.2d 641 (5th Cir.1981) (inter alia, applying reasoning of *Morrison*, p. 1015 note 516 below).

176. Is it permissible for the government to employ informers on a "contingent fee" basis, the fee being based on a government agent's estimate of the value of their services? Does it matter whether the government is seeking evidence against a particular defendant? Or whether it has agreed to pay for evidence of a crime already committed rather than a crime expected to be committed? See United States v. Cervantes-Pacheco, 800 F.2d 452 (5th Cir.1986), overruling a prior decision to the contrary and stating the general rule that contingent fee arrangements are, within limits, permissible.

Katz v. United States

389 U.S. 347, 88 S.Ct. 507, 19 L.Ed.2d 576 (1967)

■ MR. JUSTICE STEWART delivered the opinion of the Court.

The petitioner was convicted in the District Court for the Southern District of California under an eight-count indictment charging him with transmitting wagering information by telephone from Los Angeles to

Miami and Boston, in violation of a federal statute. At trial the Government was permitted, over the petitioner's objection, to introduce evidence of the petitioner's end of telephone conversations, overheard by FBI agents who had attached an electronic listening and recording device to the outside of the public telephone booth from which he had placed his calls. In affirming his conviction, the Court of Appeals rejected the contention that the recordings had been obtained in violation of the Fourth Amendment, because "[t]here was no physical entrance into the area occupied by [the petitioner]."[3] We granted certiorari in order to consider the constitutional questions thus presented.

The petitioner has phrased those questions as follows:

> A. Whether a public telephone booth is a constitutionally protected area so that evidence obtained by attaching an electronic listening recording device to the top of such a booth is obtained in violation of the right to privacy of the user of the booth.
>
> B. Whether physical penetration of a constitutionally protected area is necessary before a search and seizure can be said to be violative of the Fourth Amendment to the United States Constitution.

We decline to adopt this formulation of the issues. In the first place, the correct solution of Fourth Amendment problems is not necessarily promoted by incantation of the phrase "constitutionally protected area." Secondly, the Fourth Amendment cannot be translated into a general constitutional "right to privacy." That Amendment protects individual privacy against certain kinds of governmental intrusion, but its protections go further, and often have nothing to do with privacy at all. Other provisions of the Constitution protect personal privacy from other forms of governmental invasion. But the protection of a person's *general* right to privacy—his right to be let alone by other people—is, like the protection of his property and of his very life, left largely to the law of the individual States.

Because of the misleading way the issues have been formulated, the parties have attached great significance to the characterization of the telephone booth from which the petitioner placed his calls. The petitioner has strenuously argued that the booth was a "constitutionally protected area." The Government has maintained with equal vigor that it was not. But this effort to decide whether or not a given "area," viewed in the abstract, is "constitutionally protected" deflects attention from the problem presented by this case. For the Fourth Amendment protects people, not places. What a person knowingly exposes to the public, even in his own home or office, is not a subject of Fourth Amendment protection. . . . But what he seeks to preserve as private, even in an area accessible to the public, may be constitutionally protected. . . .

The Government stresses the fact that the telephone booth from which the petitioner made his calls was constructed partly of glass, so that he was

3. 369 F.2d 130, 134.

as visible after he entered it as he would have been if he had remained outside. But what he sought to exclude when he entered the booth was not the intruding eye—it was the uninvited ear. He did not shed his right to do so simply because he made his calls from a place where he might be seen. No less than an individual in a business office, in a friend's apartment, or in a taxicab, a person in a telephone booth may rely upon the protection of the Fourth Amendment. One who occupies it, shuts the door behind him, and pays the toll that permits him to place a call is surely entitled to assume that the words he utters into the mouthpiece will not be broadcast to the world. To read the Constitution more narrowly is to ignore the vital role that the public telephone has come to play in private communication.

The Government contends, however, that the activities of its agents in this case should not be tested by Fourth Amendment requirements, for the surveillance technique they employed involved no physical penetration of the telephone booth from which the petitioner placed his calls. It is true that the absence of such penetration was at one time thought to foreclose further Fourth Amendment inquiry, Olmstead v. United States, 277 U.S. 438, 457, 464, 466; Goldman v. United States, 316 U.S. 129, 134–36, for that Amendment was thought to limit only searches and seizures of tangible property. But "[t]he premise that property interests control the right of the Government to search and seize has been discredited." Warden v. Hayden, 387 U.S. 294, 304. Thus, although a closely divided Court supposed in *Olmstead* that surveillance without any trespass and without the seizure of any material object fell outside the ambit of the Constitution, we have since departed from the narrow view on which that decision rested. Indeed, we have expressly held that the Fourth Amendment governs not only the seizure of tangible items, but extends as well to the recording of oral statements, overheard without any "technical trespass under . . . local property law." Silverman v. United States, 365 U.S. 505, 511. Once this much is acknowledged, and once it is recognized that the Fourth Amendment protects people—and not simply "areas"—against unreasonable searches and seizures, it becomes clear that the reach of that Amendment cannot turn upon the presence or absence of a physical intrusion into any given enclosure.

We conclude that the underpinnings of *Olmstead* and *Goldman* have been so eroded by our subsequent decisions that the "trespass" doctrine there enunciated can no longer be regarded as controlling. The Government's activities in electronically listening to and recording the petitioner's words violated the privacy upon which he justifiably relied while using the telephone booth and thus constituted a "search and seizure" within the meaning of the Fourth Amendment. The fact that the electronic device employed to achieve that end did not happen to penetrate the wall of the booth can have no constitutional significance.

The question remaining for decision, then, is whether the search and seizure conducted in this case complied with constitutional standards. In that regard, the Government's position is that its agents acted in an entirely defensible manner: They did not begin their electronic surveillance until investigation of the petitioner's activities had established a strong probability that he was using the telephone in question to transmit gambling information to persons in other States, in violation of federal law. Moreover, the surveillance was limited, both in scope and in duration, to the specific purpose of establishing the contents of the petitioner's unlawful telephonic communications. The agents confined their surveillance to the brief periods during which he used the telephone booth,[4] and they took great care to overhear only the conversations of the petitioner himself.

Accepting this account of the Government's actions as accurate, it is clear that this surveillance was so narrowly circumscribed that a duly authorized magistrate properly notified of the need for such investigation, specifically informed of the basis on which it was to proceed, and clearly apprised of the precise intrusion it would entail, could constitutionally have authorized, with appropriate safeguards, the very limited search and seizure that the Government asserts in fact took place. Only last Term we sustained the validity of such an authorization, holding that, under sufficiently "precise and discriminate circumstances," a federal court may empower government agents to employ a concealed electronic device "for the narrow and particularized purpose of ascertaining the truth of the . . . allegations" of a "detailed factual affidavit alleging the commission of a specific criminal offense." Osborn v. United States, 385 U.S. 323, 329–30. Discussing that holding, the Court in Berger v. New York, 388 U.S. 41, said that "the order authorizing the use of the electronic device" in *Osborn* "afforded similar protections to those . . . of conventional warrants authorizing the seizure of tangible evidence." Through those protections, "no greater invasion of privacy was permitted than was necessary under the circumstances." Id., at 57. Here, too, a similar judicial order could have accommodated "the legitimate needs of law enforcement"[5] by authorizing the carefully limited use of electronic surveillance.

The Government urges that, because its agents relied upon the decisions in *Olmstead* and *Goldman*, and because they did no more here than they might properly have done with prior judicial sanction, we should retroactively validate their conduct. That we cannot do. It is apparent that the agents in this case acted with restraint. Yet the inescapable fact is that this restraint was imposed by the agents themselves, not by a judicial officer. They were not required, before commencing the search, to present their estimate of probable cause for detached scrutiny by a neutral magistrate. They were not compelled, during the conduct of the search itself, to observe precise limits established in advance by a specific court order. Nor

4. Based upon their previous visual observations of the petitioner, the agents correctly predicted that he would use the telephone booth for several minutes at approximately the same time each morning. The petitioner was subjected to electronic surveillance only during this predetermined period. Six recordings, averaging some three minutes each, were obtained and admitted in evidence. They preserved the petitioner's end of conversations concerning the placing of bets and the receipt of wagering information.

5. Lopez v. United States, 373 U.S. 427, 464 (dissenting opinion of Mr. Justice Brennan).

were they directed, after the search had been completed, to notify the authorizing magistrate in detail of all that had been seized. In the absence of such safeguards, this Court has never sustained a search upon the sole ground that officers reasonably expected to find evidence of a particular crime and voluntarily confined their activities to the least intrusive means consistent with that end. Searches conducted without warrants have been held unlawful "notwithstanding facts unquestionably showing probable cause," Agnello v. United States, 269 U.S. 20, 33, for the Constitution requires "that the deliberate, impartial judgment of a judicial officer . . . be interposed between the citizen and the police. . . ." Wong Sun v. United States, 371 U.S. 471, 481–82. "Over and again this Court has emphasized that the mandate of the [Fourth] Amendment requires adherence to judicial processes," United States v. Jeffers, 342 U.S. 48, 51, and that searches conducted outside the judicial process, without prior approval by judge or magistrate, are per se unreasonable under the Fourth Amendment—subject only to a few specifically established and well-delineated exceptions.

It is difficult to imagine how any of those exceptions could ever apply to the sort of search and seizure involved in this case. Even electronic surveillance substantially contemporaneous with an individual's arrest could hardly be deemed an "incident" of that arrest. Nor could the use of electronic surveillance without prior authorization be justified on grounds of "hot pursuit." And, of course, the very nature of electronic surveillance precludes its use pursuant to the suspect's consent.

The Government does not question these basic principles. Rather, it urges the creation of a new exception to cover this case. It argues that surveillance of a telephone booth should be exempted from the usual requirement of advance authorization by a magistrate upon a showing of probable cause. We cannot agree. Omission of such authorization

> bypasses the safeguards provided by an objective predetermination of probable cause, and substitutes instead the far less reliable procedure of an after-the-event justification for the . . . search, too likely to be subtly influenced by the familiar shortcomings of hindsight judgment.

Beck v. Ohio, 379 U.S. 89, 96. And bypassing a neutral predetermination of the scope of a search leaves individuals secure from Fourth Amendment violations "only in the discretion of the police." Id., at 97.

These considerations do not vanish when the search in question is transferred from the setting of a home, an office, or a hotel room to that of a telephone booth. Wherever a man may be, he is entitled to know that he will remain free from unreasonable searches and seizures. The government agents here ignored "the procedure of antecedent justification . . . that is central to the Fourth Amendment,"[6] a procedure that we hold to be a

6. See Osborn v. United States, 385 U.S. 323, 330.

constitutional precondition of the kind of electronic surveillance involved in this case. Because the surveillance here failed to meet that condition, and because it led to the petitioner's conviction, the judgment must be reversed.

. . .[7]

---

177. Observing that most people are aware that the telephone numbers dialed from a telephone may be recorded by the telephone company for a variety of purposes, the Supreme Court held that the use on a private telephone of a pen register, which mechanically records dialed numbers without overhearing conversations, was not a search within the meaning of the Fourth Amendment. Smith v. Maryland, 442 U.S. 735 (1979) (5–3).

Congress has enacted legislation regulating the installation and use of a pen register. The new provisions, with certain exceptions, prohibit installation or use of a pen register without a court order. An attorney for the government or a state investigative or law enforcement officer may apply to a court for an order authorizing the installation and use of a pen register, which order may be issued ex parte for not more than 60 days. 18 U.S.C. §§ 3121–3126.

178. In United States v. United States District Court for the Eastern District of Michigan, 407 U.S. 297 (1972), the Court rejected the government's claim that the need to investigate in order to protect domestic security allowed the Attorney General to authorize electronic surveillance without a warrant. The Court stated that its opinion was applicable to domestic security only and not to matters involving foreign nations. It noted also that different procedures might be reasonable in connection with domestic security matters than were used in ordinary criminal cases.

179. In Dalia v. United States, 441 U.S. 238 (1979) (5–4), the Court considered the problem of entries into private premises to install an electronic surveillance device pursuant to an order under 18 U.S.C. §§ 2510–2522, p. 326 below. The Court held that "the Fourth Amendment does not prohibit per se a covert entry performed for the purpose of installing otherwise legal electronic bugging equipment." 441 U.S. at 248. Further, the Court concluded that Congress had intended to include authorization to make such an entry within the power conferred on the courts by the statute and that a judicial order authorizing surveillance, which complied with the requirements for a search warrant under the Fourth Amendment, does not need to include explicit authorization for the entry. See United States v. Villegas, 899 F.2d 1324 (2d Cir.1990) (warrant for covert entry to take photographs without seizing any property upheld).

---

[7] Justice Douglas wrote a concurring opinion, which Justice Brennan joined. Justice Harlan and Justice White also wrote concurring opinions. Justice Black wrote a dissenting opinion.

United States v. White

401 U.S. 745, 91 S.Ct. 1122, 28 L.Ed.2d 453 (1971)

■ MR. JUSTICE WHITE announced the judgment of the Court and an opinion in which THE CHIEF JUSTICE, MR. JUSTICE STEWART, and MR. JUSTICE BLACKMUN join.

In 1966, respondent James A. White was tried and convicted under two consolidated indictments charging various illegal transactions in narcotics violative of 26 U.S.C. § 4705(a) and 21 U.S.C. § 174. He was fined and sentenced as a second offender to 25-year concurrent sentences. The issue before us is whether the Fourth Amendment bars from evidence the testimony of governmental agents who related certain conversations which had occurred between defendant White and a government informant, Harvey Jackson, and which the agents overheard by monitoring the frequency of a radio transmitter carried by Jackson and concealed on his person. On four occasions the conversations took place in Jackson's home; each of these conversations was overheard by an agent concealed in a kitchen closet with Jackson's consent and by a second agent outside the house using a radio receiver. Four other conversations—one in respondent's home, one in a restaurant, and two in Jackson's car—were overheard by the use of radio equipment. The prosecution was unable to locate and produce Jackson at the trial and the trial court overruled objections to the testimony of the agents who conducted the electronic surveillance. The jury returned a guilty verdict and defendant appealed.

The Court of Appeals read Katz v. United States, 389 U.S. 347 (1967), as . . . interpreting the Fourth Amendment to forbid the introduction of the agents' testimony in the circumstances of this case. Accordingly, the court reversed. . . . In our view, the Court of Appeals misinterpreted both the *Katz* case and the Fourth Amendment. . . .

I

Until Katz v. United States, neither wiretapping nor electronic eavesdropping violated a defendant's Fourth Amendment rights "unless there has been an official search and seizure of his person, or such a seizure of his papers or his tangible material effects, or an actual physical invasion of his house 'or curtilage' for the purpose of making a seizure." Olmstead v. United States, 277 U.S. 438, 466 (1928); Goldman v. United States, 316 U.S. 129, 135–36 (1942). But where "eavesdropping was accomplished by means of an unauthorized physical penetration into the premises occupied" by the defendant, although falling short of a "technical trespass under the local property law," the Fourth Amendment was violated and any evidence of what was seen and heard, as well as tangible objects seized, was considered the inadmissible fruit of an unlawful invasion. Silverman v. United States, 365 U.S. 505, 509, 511 (1961). . . .

Katz v. United States, however, finally swept away doctrines that electronic eavesdropping is permissible under the Fourth Amendment unless physical invasion of a constitutionally protected area produced the challenged evidence. In that case government agents, without petitioner's consent or knowledge, attached a listening device to the outside of a public telephone booth and recorded the defendant's end of his telephone conversations. In declaring the recordings inadmissible in evidence in the absence of a warrant authorizing the surveillance, the Court overruled *Olmstead* and *Goldman* and held that the absence of physical intrusion into the telephone booth did not justify using electronic devices in listening to and recording Katz' words, thereby violating the privacy on which he justifiably relied while using the telephone in those circumstances.

The Court of Appeals understood *Katz* to render inadmissible against White the agents' testimony concerning conversations that Jackson broadcast to them. We cannot agree. *Katz* involved no revelation to the Government by a party to conversations with the defendant nor did the Court indicate in any way that a defendant has a justifiable and constitutionally protected expectation that a person with whom he is conversing will not then or later reveal the conversation to the police.

Hoffa v. United States, 385 U.S. 293 (1966), which was left undisturbed by *Katz*, held that however strongly a defendant may trust an apparent colleague, his expectations in this respect are not protected by the Fourth Amendment when it turns out that the colleague is a government agent regularly communicating with the authorities. In these circumstances, "no interest legitimately protected by the Fourth Amendment is involved," for that amendment affords no protection to "a wrongdoer's misplaced belief that a person to whom he voluntarily confides his wrongdoing will not reveal it." Hoffa v. United States, at 302. No warrant to "search and seize" is required in such circumstances, nor is it when the Government sends to defendant's home a secret agent who conceals his identity and makes a purchase of narcotics from the accused, Lewis v. United States, 385 U.S. 206 (1966), or when the same agent, unbeknown to the defendant, carries electronic equipment to record the defendant's words and the evidence so gathered is later offered in evidence. Lopez v. United States, 373 U.S. 427 (1963).

Conceding that *Hoffa*, *Lewis*, and *Lopez* remained unaffected by *Katz*, the Court of Appeals nevertheless read both *Katz* and the Fourth Amendment to require a different result if the agent not only records his conversations with the defendant but instantaneously transmits them electronically to other agents equipped with radio receivers. Where this occurs, the Court of Appeals held, the Fourth Amendment is violated and the testimony of the listening agents must be excluded from evidence.

. . .

Concededly a police agent who conceals his police connections may write down for official use his conversations with a defendant and testify concerning them, without a warrant authorizing his encounters with the defendant and without otherwise violating the latter's Fourth Amendment rights. . . . For constitutional purposes, no different result is required if the agent instead of immediately reporting and transcribing his conversations with defendant, either (1) simultaneously records them with electronic equipment which he is carrying on his person . . . (2) or carries radio equipment which simultaneously transmits the conversations either to recording equipment located elsewhere or to other agents monitoring the transmitting frequency. . . . If the conduct and revelations of an agent operating without electronic equipment do not invade the defendant's constitutionally justifiable expectations of privacy, neither does a simultaneous recording of the same conversations made by the agent or by others from transmissions received from the agent to whom the defendant is talking and whose trustworthiness the defendant necessarily risks.

Our problem is not what the privacy expectations of particular defendants in particular situations may be or the extent to which they may in fact have relied on the discretion of their companions. Very probably, individual defendants neither know nor suspect that their colleagues have gone or will go to the police or are carrying recorders or transmitters. Otherwise, conversation would cease and our problem with these encounters would be nonexistent or far different from those now before us. Our problem, in terms of the principles announced in *Katz*, is what expectations of privacy are constitutionally "justifiable"—what expectations the Fourth Amendment will protect in the absence of a warrant. So far, the law permits the frustration of actual expectations of privacy by permitting authorities to use the testimony of those associates who for one reason or another have determined to turn to the police, as well as by authorizing the use of informants in the manner exemplified by *Hoffa* and *Lewis*. If the law gives no protection to the wrongdoer whose trusted accomplice is or becomes a police agent, neither should it protect him when that same agent has recorded or transmitted the conversations which are later offered in evidence to prove the State's case. . . .

Inescapably, one contemplating illegal activities must realize and risk that his companions may be reporting to the police. If he sufficiently doubts their trustworthiness, the association will very probably end or never materialize. But if he has no doubts, or allays them, or risks what doubt he has, the risk is his. In terms of what his course will be, what he will or will not do or say, we are unpersuaded that he would distinguish between probable informers on the one hand and probable informers with transmitters on the other. Given the possibility or probability that one of his colleagues is cooperating with the police, it is only speculation to assert that the defendant's utterances would be substantially different or his sense of security any less if he also thought it possible that the suspected colleague is wired for sound. At least there is no persuasive evidence that the difference in this respect between the electronically equipped and the unequipped agent is substantial enough to require discrete constitutional recognition, particularly under the Fourth Amendment which is ruled by fluid concepts of "reasonableness."

Nor should we be too ready to erect constitutional barriers to relevant and probative evidence which is also accurate and reliable. An electronic recording will many times produce a more reliable rendition of what a defendant has said than will the unaided memory of a police agent. It may also be that with the recording in existence it is less likely that the informant will change his mind, less chance that threat or injury will suppress unfavorable evidence and less chance that cross-examination will confound the testimony. Considerations like these obviously do not favor the defendant, but we are not prepared to hold that a defendant who has no constitutional right to exclude the informer's unaided testimony nevertheless has a Fourth Amendment privilege against a more accurate version of the events in question.

It is thus untenable to consider the activities and reports of the police agent himself, though acting without a warrant, to be a "reasonable" investigative effort and lawful under the Fourth Amendment but to view the same agent with a recorder or transmitter as conducting an "unreasonable" and unconstitutional search and seizure. Our opinion is currently shared by Congress and the Executive Branch, Title III, Omnibus Crime Control and Safe Streets Act of 1968, 82 Stat. 212, 18 U.S.C. § 2510 et seq. (1964 ed., Supp. V), and the American Bar Association. Project on Standards for Criminal Justice, Electronic Surveillance § 4.1 (Approved Draft 1971). It is also the result reached by prior cases in this Court. . . .

No different result should obtain where, as in . . . the instant case, the informer disappears and is unavailable at trial; for the issue of whether specified events on a certain day violate the Fourth Amendment should not be determined by what later happens to the informer. His unavailability at trial and proffering the testimony of other agents may raise evidentiary problems or pose issues of prosecutorial misconduct with respect to the informer's disappearance, but they do not appear critical to deciding whether prior events invaded the defendant's Fourth Amendment rights.

. . .

The judgment of the Court of Appeals is reversed.

. . .

■ MR. JUSTICE HARLAN, dissenting.

. . .

Before turning to matters of precedent and policy, several preliminary observations should be made. We deal here with the constitutional validity of instantaneous third-party electronic eavesdropping, conducted by federal law enforcement officers, without any prior judicial approval of the technique utilized, but with the consent and cooperation of a participant in the conversation, and where the substance of the matter electronically overheard is related in a federal criminal trial by those who eavesdropped as direct, not merely corroborative, evidence of the guilt of the nonconsenting party. The magnitude of the issue at hand is evidenced not simply by the obvious doctrinal difficulty of weighing such activity in the Fourth Amendment balance, but also, and more importantly, by the prevalence of police utilization of this technique. . . .

. . .

[T]he decisions of this Court . . . establish sound general principles for application of the Fourth Amendment. . . . I have already traced some of these principles . . . : that verbal communication is protected by the Fourth Amendment, that the reasonableness of a search does not depend on the presence or absence of a trespass, and that the Fourth Amendment is principally concerned with protecting interests of privacy, rather than property rights.

Especially when other recent Fourth Amendment decisions, not otherwise so immediately relevant, are read with those already discussed, the primacy of an additional general principle becomes equally evident: official investigatory action that impinges on privacy must typically, in order to be constitutionally permissible, be subjected to the warrant requirement. . . .

. . .

The impact of the practice of third-party bugging, must, I think, be considered such as to undermine that confidence and sense of security in dealing with one another that is characteristic of individual relationships between citizens in a free society. It goes beyond the impact on privacy occasioned by the ordinary type of "informer" investigation upheld in *Lewis* and *Hoffa*. The argument of the plurality opinion, to the effect that it is irrelevant whether secrets are revealed by the mere tattletale or the transistor, ignores the differences occasioned by third-party monitoring and recording which insures full and accurate disclosure of all that is said, free of the possibility of error and oversight that inheres in human reporting.

Authority is hardly required to support the proposition that words would be measured a good deal more carefully and communication inhibited if one expected his conversations were being transmitted and transcribed. Were third-party bugging a prevalent practice, it might well smother that spontaneity—reflected in frivolous, impetuous, sacrilegious, and defiant discourse—that liberates daily life. Much off-hand exchange is easily forgotten and one may count on the obscurity of his remarks, protected by the very fact of a limited audience, and the likelihood that the listener will either overlook or forget what is said, as well as the listener's inability to reformulate a conversation without having to contend with a documented record.[8] All these values are sacrificed by a rule of law that

8. From the same standpoint it may also be thought that electronic recording by an informer of a face-to-face conversation with a criminal suspect, as in *Lopez* [v. United States, 373 U.S. 427 (1963)], should be differentiated from third-party monitoring, as in . . . the case before us, in that the latter assures revelation to the Government by obviating the possibility that the informer may be tempted to renege in his undertaking to pass on to the Government all that he has learned. While the continuing vitality of *Lopez* is not drawn directly into question by this case, candor compels me to acknowledge that the views expressed in this opinion may impinge upon that part of the reasoning in *Lopez* which suggested that a suspect has no right to anticipate unreliable testimony. I am now persuaded that such an approach misconceives the basic issue, focusing, as it does, on the interests of a particular individual rather than evaluating the impact of a practice on the sense of security that is the true concern of the Fourth Amendment's protection of privacy. Distinctions do, however, exist between *Lopez*, where a known government agent uses a recording device, and this case which involves third-party overhearing.

permits official monitoring of private discourse limited only by the need to locate a willing assistant.

. . .

Finally, it is too easy to forget—and, hence, too often forgotten—that the issue here is whether to interpose a search warrant procedure between law enforcement agencies engaging in electronic eavesdropping and the public generally. By casting its "risk analysis" solely in terms of the expectations and risks that "wrongdoers" or "one contemplating illegal activities" ought to bear, the plurality opinion, I think, misses the mark entirely. . . . The interest . . . [that the majority] fails to protect is the expectation of the ordinary citizen, who has never engaged in illegal conduct in his life, that he may carry on his private discourse freely, openly, and spontaneously without measuring his every word against the connotations it might carry when instantaneously heard by others unknown to him and unfamiliar with his situation or analyzed in a cold, formal record played days, months, or years after the conversation. Interposition of a warrant requirement is designed not to shield "wrongdoers," but to secure a measure of privacy and a sense of personal security throughout our society.

The Fourth Amendment does, of course, leave room for the employment of modern technology in criminal law enforcement, but in the stream of current developments in Fourth Amendment law I think it must be held that third-party electronic monitoring, subject only to the self-restraint of law enforcement officials, has no place in our society.

. . .[9]

---

180. *White* and Lopez v. United States, 373 U.S. 427 (1963), which is discussed in *White*, are affirmed in United States v. Caceres, 440 U.S. 741 (1979) (7–2). There, an agent of the Internal Revenue Service secretly transmitted conversations with the defendant, without obtaining authorization as required by IRS regulations. Recordings of the conversations were offered in evidence against the defendant, but were excluded by the district court. The Court held that the failure to follow the regulations, which were not constitutionally required, did not require suppression of the evidence.

181. The reasoning in *White* was applied to telephonic eavesdropping and recording with the consent of one of the parties to the conversation, in United States v. Bonanno, 487 F.2d 654 (2d Cir.1973), and, over a strong

However unlikely that the participant recorder will not play his tapes, the fact of the matter is that in a third-party situation the intrusion is instantaneous. Moreover, differences in the prior relationship between the investigator and the suspect may provide a focus for future distinctions. . . .

[9] Justice Brennan wrote an opinion concurring in the result. Justice Black noted his concurrence in the result. Justice Douglas and Justice Marshall also wrote dissenting opinions.

dissent, in Holmes v. Burr, 486 F.2d 55 (9th Cir.1973). Suppose the person consenting to the tap owns the telephone but is not a party to the conversation. See United States v. San Martin, 469 F.2d 5 (2d Cir.1972) (question raised but not decided); cf. United States v. Pui Kan Lam, 483 F.2d 1202 (2d Cir.1973).

The Supreme Court of Vermont has held that a police officer's secret recording of a conversation he had with a person in the person's own home, without a judicially authorized warrant, violated the person's rights under the state constitution. State v. Geraw, 795 A.2d 1219 (2002). The court relied heavily on Justice Harlan's dissenting opinion in *White* and emphasized that the location of the recorded conversation may make a difference; the home, it said, is a place where the expectation of privacy is at its highest. The court observed further that the fact that the person spoke freely to the police officer does not indicate that he had no expectation of privacy so far as recording is concerned; otherwise the officer would not have recorded secretly. Relying on their state constitutions, Alaska and Massachusetts have also rejected *White*. State v. Glass, 583 P.2d 872 (Alaska 1978); Commonwealth v. Blood, 507 N.E.2d 1029 (Mass.1987).

182. United States v. Longoria, 177 F.3d 1179 (10th Cir.1999). The defendant conversed in Spanish with his codefendants while they were together with a government informant in the latter's shop. The informant secretly recorded the conversations, which were later introduced in evidence. The defendant believed that the informant did not understand Spanish. The defendant claimed that he had a "reasonable expectation of privacy" and therefore, that the conversations were "oral communications" protected from disclosure under 18 U.S.C. §§ 2510(2), 2515. The court held that, despite his belief that the informant did not speak Spanish, his expectation of privacy was not one that society is prepared to accept as reasonable.

183. Police officers installed audio and video recording equipment in the hotel suite of the defendant, with the cooperation of a person who rented the suite for the defendant's use. The equipment was installed before the defendant's arrival. The officers monitored conversations between the defendant and the other person, in which the defendant incriminated himself. The officers monitored activity in the corridor outside the suite and turned on the equipment only when the person cooperating with them was in the suite. United States v. Lee, 359 F.3d 194 (3d Cir.2004). In those circumstances, the court said, the rules applicable to monitoring a conversation between a consenting person and another apply. It made no difference that the equipment was installed in the room rather than being carried by the consenting person.

184. Who has standing to object to the introduction of evidence obtained by unlawful eavesdropping? In Alderman v. United States, 394 U.S. 165, 176 (1969) (5–2–1) the Court said: "[A]ny petitioner would be entitled to the suppression of government evidence originating in electronic surveillance violative of his own Fourth Amendment right to be free of unreasonable searches and seizures. Such violation would occur if the United States unlawfully overheard conversations of a petitioner himself or conversations occurring on his premises, whether or not he was present or participated in those conversations."

This was the conclusion of Chief Justice Warren and Justices White (who wrote the opinion) and Brennan. Justices Douglas and Fortas believed that standing should be extended also to "a person concerning whom an investigation involving illegal electronic surveillance has been conducted," 394 U.S. at 201, whether or not he participated in the monitored conversation or it occurred on his premises. (That position is rejected generally in the Court's discussion of the "target" theory of standing in Rakas v. Illinois, 439 U.S. 128 (1978), pp. 258–62 above.)

Justices Harlan and Stewart believed that a person should not have standing to object to introduction of an overheard conversation in which he did not participate even if the conversation occurred on his premises. In an opinion concurring in part and dissenting in part, Justice Harlan said:

> There is a very simple reason why the traditional law of standing permits the owner of the premises to exclude a tangible object illegally seized on his property, despite the fact that he does not own the particular object taken by the police. Even though he does not have title to the object, the owner of the premises is in possession of it—and we have held that a property interest of even less substance is a sufficient predicate for standing under the Fourth Amendment. . . . This simple rationale does not, however, justify granting standing to the property owner with regard to third-party conversations. The absent property owner does not have a property interest of any sort in a conversation in which he did not participate. The words that were spoken are gone beyond recall.
>
> Consequently, in order to justify the traditional rule, one must argue, as does the majority, that the owner of the premises should be granted standing because the bugged third-party conversations are "fruits" of the police's infringement of the owner's property rights. The "fruits" theory, however, does not necessarily fit when the police overhear private conversations in violation of the Fourth Amendment. As Katz v. United States, 389 U.S. 347, 352–53 (1967), squarely holds, the right to the privacy of one's conversation does not hinge on whether the Government has committed a technical trespass upon the premises on which the conversations took place. Olmstead v. New York, 277 U.S. 438 (1928), is no longer the law. If in fact there has been no trespass upon the premises, I do not understand how traditional theory permits the owner to complain if a conversation is overheard in which he did not participate. Certainly the owner cannot suppress records of such conversations on the ground that they are the "fruits" of an unconstitutional invasion of his property rights. . . .
>
> It is true, of course, that the "fruits" theory would require a different result if the police used a listening device which did physically trespass upon the accused's premises. But the fact that this theory

depends completely on the presence or absence of a technical trespass only serves to show that the entire theoretical basis of standing law must be reconsidered in the area of conversational privacy. For we have not buried *Olmstead,* so far as it dealt with the substance of Fourth Amendment rights, only to give it new life in the law of standing. Instead, we should reject traditional property concepts entirely, and reinterpret standing law in the light of the substantive principles developed in *Katz.* Standing should be granted to every person who participates in a conversation he legitimately expects will remain private—for it is such persons that *Katz* protects. On the other hand, property owners should not be permitted to assert a Fourth Amendment claim in this area if we are to respect the principle, whose vitality the Court has now once again reaffirmed, which establishes "the general rule that Fourth Amendment rights are personal rights which . . . may not be vicariously asserted." Ante, at 174. For granting property owners standing does not permit them to vindicate intrusions upon their *own* privacy, but simply permits criminal defendants to intrude into the private lives of others.

The following hypothetical suggests the paradoxical quality of the Court's rule. Imagine that I own an office building and permit a friend of mine, Smith, to use one of the vacant offices without charge. Smith uses the office to have a private talk with a third person, Jones. The next day, I ask my friend to tell me what Jones had said in the office I had given him. Smith replies that the conversation was private, and that what was said was "none of your business." Can it be that I could properly feel aggrieved because the conversation occurred on my property? It would make no sense if I were to reply to Smith: "*My privacy* has been infringed if you do not tell me what was said, for I own the *property*!" It is precisely the other way around—Smith is telling me that when he and Jones had talked together, they had a legitimate expectation that their conversation would remain secret, even from me as the property owner.

Now suppose that I had placed a listening device in the office I had given to Smith, without telling him. Could anyone doubt that I would be guilty of an outrageous violation of the privacy of Smith and Jones if I then listened to what they had said? It would be ludicrous to defend my conduct on the ground that I, after all, was the owner of the office building. The case does not stand differently if I am accused of a crime and demand the right to hear the Smith–Jones conversation which the police had monitored. The Government doubtless has violated the privacy of Smith and Jones, but their privacy would be violated *further* if the conversation were also made available to me.

In the field of conversational privacy, the Fourth Amendment protects persons, not places. . . . And a man can only be in one place at one time. If the privacy of his conversation is respected at that place, he may engage in all those activities for which that privacy is an essential prerequisite. His privacy is not at all disturbed by the fact that other people in other places cannot speak without the fear of being overheard. That fact may be profoundly disturbing to the man whose privacy remains intact. But it remains a fact about *other* people's privacy. . . .

. . .

The Court's response seems to be that the Fourth Amendment protects "houses" as well as "persons." But this is simply to treat private conversations as if they were pieces of tangible *property*. Since an individual cannot carry his possessions with him wherever he goes, the Fourth Amendment protects a person's "house" so that his personal possessions may be kept out of the Government's easy reach. In contrast, a man must necessarily carry his voice around with him, and cannot leave it at home even if he wished. When a man is not at home, he cannot converse there. There is thus no need to protect a man's "house" in order to protect *his* right to engage in private conversation. Consequently, the Court has not increased the scope of an accused's *personal* privacy by holding that the police have unconstitutionally invaded his "house" by putting a "bug" there. Houses don't speak; only people do. The police only have violated the *privacy* of those persons whose conversations are overheard.

I entirely agree, however, that if the police see a person's tangible property while committing their trespass, they may not constitutionally use this knowledge either to obtain a search warrant or to gain a conviction. Since a man has no choice but to leave the bulk of his physical possessions in his "house," the Fourth Amendment must protect his "house" in this way or else the immunity of his personal possessions from arbitrary search could not be assured. Thus if an individual's personal *possessions* are to be protected at all, they must be protected in his house; but a person's private *conversations* are protected as much as is possible when he can complain as to any conversation in which he personally participated. To go further and protect other conversations occurring on his property is simply to give the householder the right to complain as to the Government's treatment of others.

Alderman, 394 U.S. at 189–95.

Responding to Justice Harlan's argument, Justice White said:

If the police make an unwarranted search of a house and seize tangible property belonging to third parties—even a transcript of a third-party conversation—the homeowner may object to its use against him, not because he had any interest in the seized items as "effects" protected by the Fourth Amendment, but because they were the fruits of an unauthorized search of his house, which is itself expressly protected by the Fourth Amendment. Nothing seen or found on the premises may legally form the basis for an arrest or search warrant or for testimony at the homeowner's trial, since the prosecution would be using the fruits of a Fourth Amendment violation. . . .

The Court has characteristically applied the same rule where an unauthorized electronic surveillance is carried out by physical invasion of the premises. This much the dissent frankly concedes. Like physical evidence which might be seized, overheard conversations are fruits of an illegal entry and are inadmissible in evidence. . . .

Because the Court has now decided that the Fourth Amendment protects a person's private conversations as well as his private premises . . . the dissent would discard the concept that private conversations overheard through an illegal entry into a private place must be excluded as the fruits of a Fourth Amendment violation. Although officers without a valid warrant may not search a house for physical evidence or incriminating information, whether the owner is present or away, the dissent would permit them to enter that house without consent and without a warrant, install a listening device and use any overheard third-party conversations against the owner in a criminal case, in spite of the obvious violation of his Fourth Amendment right to be secure in his own dwelling. Even if the owner is present on his premises during the surveillance, he would have no complaint unless his own conversations were offered or used against him. Information from a telephone tap or from the microphone in the kitchen or in the rooms of guests or children would be freely usable as long as the homeowner's own conversations are not monitored and used against him. Indeed, if the police, instead of installing a device, secreted themselves on the premises, they could neither testify about nor use against the owner anything they saw or carried away, but would be free to use against him everything they overheard except his own conversations. And should police overhear third parties describing narcotics which they have discovered in the owner's desk drawer, the police could not then open the drawer and seize the narcotics, but they could secure a warrant on the basis of what they had heard and forthwith seize the narcotics pursuant to that warrant.

These views we do not accept. We adhere to the established view in this Court that the right to be secure in one's house against unauthorized intrusion is not limited to protection against a policeman viewing or seizing tangible property—"papers" and "effects." Otherwise, the express security for the home provided by the Fourth Amendment would approach redundancy. The rights of the owner of the premises are as clearly invaded when the police enter and install a listening device in his house as they are when the entry is made to undertake a warrantless search for tangible property; and the prosecution as surely employs the fruits of an illegal search of the home when it offers overheard third-party conversations as it does when it introduces tangible evidence belonging not to the homeowner but to others.

394 U.S. at 176–80.

185. What interest in the premises is necessary for standing to object to a conversation in which one did not participate? In *Alderman*, the Court expressed no opinion on that question, 394 U.S. at 168 n.1; see id. at 191–92 (opinion of Harlan, J.).

---

18 U.S.C. §§ 2510–2522

In 1968 as part of the Omnibus Crime Control and Safe Streets Act, Congress enacted very broad prohibitions against wiretapping and eavesdropping by the use of eavesdropping devices. The prohibitions cover the interception, disclosure, or other use of wire or oral communications, as well as the manufacture, distribution, possession and advertising of devices intended to be used for the unlawful interception of communications. Unlawfully intercepted communications and their fruits were declared inadmissible in all governmental proceedings. 18 U.S.C. § 2515. A civil cause of action was provided for persons whose communications were unlawfully intercepted, disclosed, or used. 18 U.S.C. §§ 2510–2515, 2520.

The prohibitions are subject to equally broad exceptions, which allow wiretapping and eavesdropping for the purpose of law enforcement. The provisions for authorization of wiretapping or eavesdropping and prescribing how it is to be carried out are given below.

---

§ 2516. Authorization for interception of wire, oral, or electronic commuications

(1) The Attorney General, Deputy Attorney General, Associate Attorney General, or any Assistant Attorney General, any acting Assistant Attorney General, or any Deputy Assistant Attorney General or acting Deputy Assistant Attorney General in the Criminal Division specially designated by the Attorney General, may authorize an application to a Federal judge of competent jurisdiction for, and such judge may grant in conformity with section 2518 of this chapter an order authorizing or approving the interception of wire or oral communications by the Federal Bureau of Investigation, or a Federal agency having responsibility for the investigation of the offense as to which the application is made, when such interception may provide or has provided evidence of—

(a) any offense punishable by death or by imprisonment for more than one year under sections 2274 through 2277 of title 42 of the United States Code (relating to the enforcement of the Atomic Energy Act of 1954), section 2284 of title 42 of the United States Code (relating to sabotage of nuclear facilities or fuel), or under the following chapters of this title: chapter 37 (relating to espionage), chapter 55 (relating to kidnapping) chapter 90 (relating to protection of trade secrets), chapter 105 (relating to treason), chapter 102 (relating to riots), chapter 65 (relating to malicious mischief), chapter 111 (relating to destruction of vessels), or chapter 81 (relating to piracy);

(b) a violation of section 186 or section 501(c) of title 29, United States Code (dealing with restrictions on payments and loans to labor organizations), or any offense which involves murder, kidnapping, robbery, or extortion, and which is punishable under this title;

(c) any offense which is punishable under the following sections of this title: section 201 (bribery of public officials and witnesses), section 215 (relating to bribery of bank officials), section 224 (bribery in sporting contests), subsection (d), (e), (f), (g), (h), or (i) of section 844 (unlawful use of explosives), section 1032 (relating to concealment of assets), section 1084 (transmission of wagering information), section 751 (relating to escape), section 1014 (relating to loans and credit applications generally; renewals and discounts), sections 1503, 1512, and 1513 (influencing or injuring an officer, juror, or witness generally), section 1510 (obstruction of criminal investigations), section 1511 (obstruction of State or local law enforcement), section 1591 (sex trafficking of children by force, fraud, or coercion), section 1751 (Presidential and Presidential staff assassination, kidnapping, and assault), section 1951 (interference with commerce by threats or violence), section 1952 (interstate and foreign travel or transportation in aid of racketeering enterprises), section 1958 (relating to use of interstate commerce facilities in the commission of murder for hire), section 1959 (relating to violent crimes in aid of racketeering activity), section 1954 (offer, acceptance, or solicitation to influence operations of employee benefit plan), section 1955 (prohibition of business enterprises of gambling), section 1956 (laundering of monetary instruments), section 1957 (relating to engaging in monetary transactions in property derived from specified unlawful activity), section 659 (theft from interstate shipment), section 664 (embezzlement from pension and welfare funds), section 1343 (fraud by wire, radio, or television), section 1344 (relating to bank fraud), sections 2251 and 2252 (sexual exploitation of children), section 2251A (selling or buying of children), section 2252A (relating to material constituting or containing child pornography), section 1466A (relating to child obscenity), section 2260 (production of sexually explicit depictions of a minor for importation into the United States), sections 2421, 2422, 2433, and 2425 (relating to transportation for illegal sexual activity and related crimes), sections 2312, 2313, 2314, and 2315 (interstate transportation of stolen property), section 2321 (relating to trafficking in certain motor vehicles or motor vehicle parts), section 1203 (relating to hostage taking), section 1029 (relating to fraud and related activity in connection with access devices), section 3146 (relating to penalty for failure to appear), section 3521(b)(3) (relating to witness relocation and assistance), section 32 (relating to destruction of aircraft or aircraft facilities), section 1963 (violations with respect to racketeer influenced and corrupt organizations), section 115 (relating to threatening or retaliating against a Federal official), section 1341 (relating to mail fraud), a felony violation of section 1030 (relating to computer fraud and abuse), section 351 (violations with respect to congressional, Cabinet, or Supreme Court assassinations, kidnapping, and assault), section 831 (relating to prohibited transactions involving nuclear materials), section 33 (relating to destruction of motor vehicles or motor vehicle facilities), section 175 (relating to biological weapons), section 1992 (relating to wrecking trains), a felony violation of section 1028 (relating to production of false identification documentation), section 1425 (relating to the procurement of citizenship or nationalization unlawfully), section 1426 (relating to the reproduction of naturalization or citizenship papers), section 1427 (relating to the sale of naturalization or citizenship papers), section 1541 (relating to passport issuance without authority), section 1542 (relating to false statements in passport applications), section 1543 (relating to forgery or false use of passports), section 1544 (relating to misuse of passports), or section 1546 (relating to fraud and misuse of visas, permits, and other documents);

(d) any offense involving counterfeiting punishable under section 471, 472, or 473 of this title;

(e) any offense involving fraud connected with a case under title 11 or the manufacture, importation, receiving, concealment, buying, selling, or otherwise dealing in narcotic drugs, marihuana, or other dangerous drugs, punishable under any law of the United States;

(f) any offense including extortionate credit transactions under sections 892, 893, or 894 of this title;

(g) a violation of section 5322 of title 31, United States Code (dealing with the reporting of currency transactions);

(h) any felony violation of sections 2511 and 2512 (relating to interception and disclosure of certain communications and to certain intercepting devices) of this title;

(i) any felony violation of chapter 71 (relating to obscenity) of this title;

(j) any violation of section 60123(b) (relating to destruction of a natural gas pipeline) or section 46502 (relating to aircraft piracy) of title 49;

(k) any criminal violation of section 2778 of title 22 (relating to the Arms Export Control Act);

(l) the location of any fugitive from justice from an offense described in this section;

(m) a violation of section 274, 277, or 278 of the Immigration and Nationality Act (8 U.S.C. 1324, 1327, or 1328) (relating to the smuggling of aliens);

(n) any felony violation of sections 922 and 924 of title 18, United States Code (relating to firearms); or

(o) any violation of section 5861 of the Internal Revenue Code of 1986 (relating to firearms); or

(p) a felony violation of section 1028 (relating to production of false identification documents), section 1542 (relating to false statements in passport applications), section 1546 (relating to fraud and misuse of visas, permits, and other documents) of this title or a violation of section 274, 277, or 278 of the Immigration and Nationality Act (relating to the smuggling of aliens); or

(q) any criminal violation of section 229 (relating to chemical weapons); or sections 2332, 2332a, 2332b, 2332d, 2332f, 2339A, 2339B, or 2339C of this title (relating to terrorism); or

(r) any conspiracy to commit any offense described in any subparagraph of this paragraph.

(2) The principal prosecuting attorney of any State, or the principal prosecuting attorney of any political subdivision thereof, if such attorney is authorized by a statute of that State to make application to a State court judge of competent jurisdiction for an order authorizing or approving the interception of wire, oral, or electronic communications, may apply to such judge for, and such judge may grant in conformity with section 2518 of this chapter and with the applicable State statute an order authorizing, or approving the interception of wire, oral, or electronic communications by investigative or law enforcement officers having responsibility for the investigation of the offense as to which the application is made, when such interception may provide or has provided evidence of the commission of the offense of murder, kidnapping, gambling, robbery, bribery, extortion, or dealing in narcotic drugs, marihuana or other dangerous drugs, or other crime dangerous to life, limb, or property, and punishable by imprisonment for more than one year, designated in any applicable State statute authorizing such interception, or any conspiracy to commit any of the foregoing offenses.

(3) Any attorney for the Government (as such term is defined for the purposes of the Federal Rules of Criminal Procedure) may authorize an application to a Federal judge of competent jurisdiction for, and such judge may grant, in conformity with section 2518 of this title, an order authorizing or approving the interception of electronic communications by an investigative or law enforcement officer having responsibility for the investigation of the offense as to which the application is made, when such interception may provide or has provided evidence of any Federal felony.

§ 2517. Authorization for disclosure and use of intercepted wire, oral, or electronic communications

(1) Any investigative or law enforcement officer who, by any means authorized by this chapter, has obtained knowledge of the contents of any wire, oral, or electronic communication, or evidence derived therefrom, may disclose such contents to another investigative or law enforcement officer to

the extent that such disclosure is appropriate to the proper performance of the official duties of the officer making or receiving the disclosure.

(2) Any investigative or law enforcement officer who, by any means authorized by this chapter, has obtained knowledge of the contents of any wire, oral, or electronic communication or evidence derived therefrom may use such contents to the extent such use is appropriate to the proper performance of his official duties.

(3) Any person who has received, by any means authorized by this chapter, any information concerning a wire, oral, or electronic communication, or evidence derived therefrom intercepted in accordance with the provisions of this chapter may disclose the contents of that communication or such derivative evidence while giving testimony under oath or affirmation in any proceeding held under the authority of the United States or of any State or political subdivision thereof.

(4) No otherwise privileged wire, oral, or electronic communication intercepted in accordance with, or in violation of, the provisions of this chapter shall lose its privileged character.

(5) When an investigative or law enforcement officer, while engaged in intercepting wire, oral, or electronic communications in the manner authorized herein, intercepts wire, oral, or electronic communications relating to offenses other than those specified in the order of authorization or approval, the contents thereof, and evidence derived therefrom, may be disclosed or used as provided in subsections (1) and (2) of this section. Such contents and any evidence derived therefrom may be used under subsection (3) of this section when authorized or approved by a judge of competent jurisdiction where such judge finds on subsequent application that the contents were otherwise intercepted in accordance with the provisions of this chapter. Such application shall be made as soon as practicable.

(6) Any investigative or law enforcement officer, or attorney for the Government, who by any means authorized by this chapter, has obtained knowledge of the contents of any wire, oral, or electronic communication, or evidence derived therefrom, may disclose such contents to any other Federal law enforcement, intelligence, protective, immigration, national defense, or national security official to the extent that such contents include foreign intelligence or counterintelligence (as defined in section 3 of the National Security Act of 1947), or foreign intelligence information (as defined in subsection (19) of section 2510 of this title), to assist the official who is to receive that information in the performance of his official duties. Any Federal official who receives information pursuant to this provision may use that information only as necessary in the conduct of that person's official duties subject to any limitations on the unauthorized disclosure of such information.

(7) Any investigative or law enforcement officer, or other Federal official in carrying out official duties as such Federal official, who by any means authorized by this chapter, has obtained knowledge of the contents of any wire, oral, or electronic communication, or evidence derived there-

from, may disclose such contents or derivative evidence to a foreign investigative or law enforcement officer to the extent that such disclosure is appropriate to the proper performance of the official duties of the officer making or receiving the disclosure, and foreign investigative or law enforcement officers may use or disclose such contents or derivative evidence to the extent such use or disclosure is appropriate to the proper performance of their official duties.

(8) Any investigative or law enforcement officer, or other Federal official in carrying out official duties as such Federal official, who by any means authorized by this chapter, has obtained knowledge of the contents of any wire, oral, or electronic communication, or evidence derived therefrom, may disclose such contents or derivative evidence to any appropriate Federal, State, local, or foreign government official to the extent that such contents or derivative evidence reveals a threat of actual or potential attack or other grave hostile acts of a foreign power or an agent of a foreign power, domestic or international sabotage, domestic or international terrorism, or clandestine intelligence gathering activities by an intelligence service or network of a foreign power or by an agent of a foreign power, within the United States or elsewhere, for the purpose of preventing or responding to such a threat. Any official who receives information pursuant to this provision may use that information only as necessary in the conduct of that person's official duties subject to any limitations on the unauthorized disclosure of such information, and any State, local, or foreign official who receives information pursuant to this provision may use that information only consistent with such guidelines as the Attorney General and Director of Central Intelligence shall jointly issue.

§ 2518. Procedure for interception of wire, oral, or electronic communications

(1) Each application for an order authorizing or approving the interception of a wire, oral, or electronic communication under this chapter shall be made in writing upon oath or affirmation to a judge of competent jurisdiction and shall state the applicant's authority to make such application. Each application shall include the following information:

(a) the identity of the investigative or law enforcement officer making the application, and the officer authorizing the application;

(b) a full and complete statement of the facts and circumstances relied upon by the applicant, to justify his belief that an order should be issued, including (i) details as to the particular offense that has been, is being, or is about to be committed, (ii) except as provided in subsection (11), a particular description of the nature and location of the facilities from which or the place where the communication is to be intercepted, (iii) a particular description of the type of communications sought to be intercepted, (iv) the identity of the person, if known, committing the offense and whose communications are to be intercepted;

(c) a full and complete statement as to whether or not other investigative procedures have been tried and failed or why they reasonably appear to be unlikely to succeed if tried or to be too dangerous;

(d) a statement of the period of time for which the interception is required to be maintained. If the nature of the investigation is such that the authorization for interception should not automatically terminate when the described type of communication has been first obtained, a particular description of facts establishing probable cause to believe that additional communications of the same type will occur thereafter;

(e) a full and complete statement of the facts concerning all previous applications known to the individual authorizing and making the application, made to any judge for authorization to intercept, or for approval of interceptions of, wire, oral, or electronic communications involving any of the same persons, facilities or places specified in the application, and the action taken by the judge on each such application; and

(f) where the application is for the extension of an order, a statement setting forth the results thus far obtained from the interception, or a reasonable explanation of the failure to obtain such results.

(2) The judge may require the applicant to furnish additional testimony or documentary evidence in support of the application.

(3) Upon such application the judge may enter an ex parte order, as requested or as modified, authorizing or approving interception of wire, oral, or electronic communications within the territorial jurisdiction of the court in which the judge is sitting (and outside that jurisdiction but within the United States in the case of a mobile interception device authorized by a Federal court within such jurisdiction), if the judge determines on the basis of the facts submitted by the applicant that—

(a) there is probable cause for belief that an individual is committing, has committed, or is about to commit a particular offense enumerated in section 2516 of this chapter;

(b) there is probable cause for belief that particular communications concerning that offense will be obtained through such interception;

(c) normal investigative procedures have been tried and have failed or reasonably appear to be unlikely to succeed if tried or to be too dangerous;

(d) except as provided in subsection (11), there is probable cause for belief that the facilities from which, or the place where, the wire, oral, or electronic communications are to be intercepted are being used, or are about to be used, in connection with the commission of such offense, or are leased to, listed in the name of, or commonly used by such person.

(4) Each order authorizing or approving the interception of any wire, oral, or electronic communication under this chapter shall specify—

(a) the identity of the person, if known, whose communications are to be intercepted;

(b) the nature and location of the communications facilities as to which, or the place where, authority to intercept is granted;

(c) a particular description of the type of communication sought to be intercepted, and a statement of the particular offense to which it relates;

(d) the identity of the agency authorized to intercept the communications, and of the person authorizing the application; and

(e) the period of time during which such interception is authorized, including a statement as to whether or not the interception shall automatically terminate when the described communication has been first obtained.

An order authorizing the interception of a wire, oral, or electronic communication under this chapter shall, upon request of the applicant, direct that a provider of wire or electronic communication service, landlord, custodian or other person shall furnish the applicant forthwith all information, facilities, and technical assistance necessary to accomplish the interception unobtrusively and with a minimum of interference with the services that such service provider, landlord, custodian, or person is according the person whose communications are to be intercepted. Any provider of wire or electronic communication service, landlord, custodian or other person furnishing such facilities or technical assistance shall be compensated therefor by the applicant for reasonable expenses incurred in providing such facilities or assistance. Pursuant to section 2522 of this chapter, an order may also be issued to enforce the assistance capability and capacity requirements under the Communications Assistance for Law Enforcement Act.

(5) No order entered under this section may authorize or approve the interception of any wire, oral, or electronic communication for any period longer than is necessary to achieve the objective of the authorization, nor in any event longer than thirty days. Such thirty-day period begins on the earlier of the day on which the investigative or law enforcement officer first begins to conduct an interception under the order or ten days after the order is entered. Extensions of an order may be granted, but only upon application for an extension made in accordance with subsection (1) of this section and the court making the findings required by subsection (3) of this section. The period of extension shall be no longer than the authorizing judge deems necessary to achieve the purposes for which it was granted and in no event for longer than thirty days. Every order and extension thereof shall contain a provision that the authorization to intercept shall be executed as soon as practicable, shall be conducted in such a way as to minimize the interception of communications not otherwise subject to interception under this chapter, and must terminate upon attainment of the authorized objective, or in any event in thirty days. In the event the

intercepted communication is in a code or foreign language, and an expert in that foreign language or code is not reasonably available during the interception period, minimization may be accomplished as soon as practicable after such interception. An interception under this chapter may be conducted in whole or in part by Government personnel, or by an individual operating under a contract with the Government, acting under the supervision of an investigative or law enforcement officer authorized to conduct the interception.

(6) Whenever an order authorizing interception is entered pursuant to this chapter, the order may require reports to be made to the judge who issued the order showing what progress has been made toward achievement of the authorized objective and the need for continued interception. Such reports shall be made at such intervals as the judge may require.

(7) Notwithstanding any other provision of this chapter, any investigative or law enforcement officer, specially designated by the Attorney General, the Deputy Attorney General, the Associate Attorney General or by the principal prosecuting attorney of any State or subdivision thereof acting pursuant to a statute of that State, who reasonably determines that—

(a) an emergency situation exists that involves—

(i) immediate danger of death or serious physical injury to any person,

(ii) conspiratorial activities threatening the national security interest, or

(iii) conspiratorial activities characteristic of organized crime,

that requires a wire, oral, or electronic communication to be intercepted before an order authorizing such interception can, with due diligence, be obtained, and

(b) there are grounds upon which an order could be entered under this chapter to authorize such interception,

may intercept such wire, oral, or electronic communication if an application for an order approving the interception is made in accordance with this section within forty-eight hours after the interception has occurred, or begins to occur. In the absence of an order, such interception shall immediately terminate when the communication sought is obtained or when the application for the order is denied, whichever is earlier. In the event such application for approval is denied, or in any other case where the interception is terminated without an order having been issued, the contents of any wire, oral, or electronic communication intercepted shall be treated as having been obtained in violation of this chapter, and an inventory shall be served as provided for in subsection (d) of this section on the person named in the application.

(8)(a) The contents of any wire, oral, or electronic communication intercepted by any means authorized by this chapter shall, if possible, be recorded on tape or wire or other comparable device. The recording of the contents of any wire, oral, or electronic communication under this subsection shall be done in such way as will protect the recording from editing or other alterations. Immediately upon the expiration of the period of the order, or extensions thereof, such recordings shall be made available to the judge issuing such order and sealed under his directions. Custody of the recordings shall be wherever the judge orders. They shall not be destroyed except upon an order of the issuing or denying judge and in any event shall be kept for ten years. Duplicate recordings may be made for use or disclosure pursuant to the provisions of subsections (1) and (2) of section 2517 of this chapter for investigations. The presence of the seal provided for by this subsection, or a satisfactory explanation for the absence thereof, shall be a prerequisite for the use or disclosure of the contents of any wire, oral, or electronic communication or evidence derived therefrom under subsection (3) of section 2517.

(b) Applications made and orders granted under this chapter shall be sealed by the judge. Custody of the applications and orders shall be wherever the judge directs. Such applications and orders shall be disclosed only upon a showing of good cause before a judge of competent jurisdiction and shall not be destroyed except on order of the issuing or denying judge, and in any event shall be kept for ten years.

(c) Any violation of the provisions of this subsection may be punished as contempt of the issuing or denying judge.

(d) Within a reasonable time but not later than ninety days after the filing of an application for an order of approval under section 2518(7)(b) which is denied or the termination of the period of an order or extensions thereof, the issuing or denying judge shall cause to be served, on the persons named in the order or the application, and such other parties to intercepted communications as the judge may determine in his discretion that is in the interest of justice, an inventory which shall include notice of—

(1) the fact of the entry of the order or the application;

(2) the date of the entry and the period of authorized, approved or disapproved interception, or the denial of the application; and

(3) the fact that during the period wire, oral, or electronic communications were or were not intercepted.

The judge, upon the filing of a motion, may in his discretion make available to such person or his counsel for inspection such portions of the intercepted communications, applications and orders as the judge determines to be in the interest of justice. On an ex parte showing of good cause to a judge of competent jurisdiction the serving of the inventory required by this subsection may be postponed.

(9) The contents of any wire, oral, or electronic communication intercepted pursuant to this chapter or evidence derived therefrom shall not be received in evidence or otherwise disclosed in any trial, hearing, or other proceeding in a Federal or State court unless each party, not less than ten days before the trial, hearing, or proceeding, has been furnished with a

copy of the court order, and accompanying application, under which the interception was authorized or approved. This ten-day period may be waived by the judge if he finds that it was not possible to furnish the party with the above information ten days before the trial, hearing, or proceeding and that the party will not be prejudiced by the delay in receiving such information.

(10)(a) Any aggrieved person in any trial, hearing, or proceeding in or before any court, department, officer, agency, regulatory body, or other authority of the United States, a State, or a political subdivision thereof, may move to suppress the contents of any wire or oral communication intercepted pursuant to this chapter, or evidence derived therefrom, on the grounds that—

(i) the communication was unlawfully intercepted;

(ii) the order of authorization or approval under which it was intercepted is insufficient on its face; or

(iii) the interception was not made in conformity with the order of authorization or approval.

Such motion shall be made before the trial, hearing, or proceeding unless there was no opportunity to make such motion or the person was not aware of the grounds of the motion. If the motion is granted, the contents of the intercepted wire or oral communication, or evidence derived therefrom, shall be treated as having been obtained in violation of this chapter. The judge, upon the filing of such motion by the aggrieved person, may in his discretion make available to the aggrieved person or his counsel for inspection such portions of the intercepted communication or evidence derived therefrom as the judge determines to be in the interests of justice.

(b) In addition to any other right to appeal, the United States shall have the right to appeal from an order granting a motion to suppress made under paragraph (a) of this subsection, or the denial of an application for an order of approval, if the United States attorney shall certify to the judge or other official granting such motion or denying such application that the appeal is not taken for purposes of delay. Such appeal shall be taken within thirty days after the date the order was entered and shall be diligently prosecuted.

(c) The remedies and sanctions described in this chapter with respect to the interception of electronic communications are the only judicial remedies and sanctions for nonconstitutional violations of this chapter involving such communications.

(11) The requirements of subsections (1)(b)(ii) and (3)(d) of this section relating to the specification of the facilities from which, or the place where, the communication is to be intercepted do not apply if—

(a) in the case of an application with respect to the interception of an oral communication—

(i) the application is by a Federal investigative or law enforcement officer and is approved by the Attorney General, the Deputy

Attorney General, the Associate Attorney General, an Assistant Attorney General, or an acting Assistant Attorney General;

(ii) the application contains a full and complete statement as to why such specification is not practical and identifies the person committing the offense and whose communications are to be intercepted; and

(iii) the judge finds that such specification is not practical; and

(b) in the case of an application with respect to a wire or electronic communication—

(i) the application is by a Federal investigative or law enforcement officer and is approved by the Attorney General, the Deputy Attorney General, the Associate Attorney General, an Assistant Attorney General, or an acting Assistant Attorney General;

(ii) the application identifies the person believed to be committing the offense and whose communications are to be intercepted and the applicant makes a showing that there is probable cause to believe that the person's actions could have the effect of thwarting interception from a specified facility;

(iii) the judge finds that such showing has been adequately made; and

(iv) the order authorizing or approving the interception is limited to interception only for such time as it is reasonable to presume that the person identified in the application is or was reasonably proximate to the instrument through which such communication will be or was transmitted.

(12) An interception of a communication under an order with respect to which the requirements of subsections (1)(b)(ii) and (3)(d) of this section do not apply by reason of subsection (11)(a) shall not begin until the place where the communication is to be intercepted is ascertained by the person implementing the interception order. A provider of wire or electronic communications service that has received an order as provided for in subsection (11)(b) may move the court to modify or quash the order on the ground that its assistance with respect to the interception cannot be performed in a timely or reasonable fashion. The court, upon notice to the government, shall decide such a motion expeditiously.

§ 2519. Reports concerning intercepted wire, oral, or electronic communications

(1) Within thirty days after the expiration of an order (or each extension thereof) entered under section 2518, or the denial of an order approving an interception, the issuing or denying judge shall report to the Administrative Office of the United States Courts—

(a) the fact that an order or extension was applied for;

(b) the kind of order or extension applied for (including whether or not the order was an order with respect to which the requirements of sections 2518(1)(b)(ii) and 2518(3)(d) of this title did not apply by reason of section 2518(11) of this title);

(c) the fact that the order or extension was granted as applied for, was modified, or was denied;

(d) the period of interceptions authorized by the order, and the number and duration of any extensions of the order;

(e) the offense specified in the order or application, or extension of an order;

(f) the identity of the applying investigative or law enforcement officer and agency making the application and the person authorizing the application; and

(g) the nature of the facilities from which or the place where communications were to be intercepted.

(2) In January of each year the Attorney General, an Assistant Attorney General specially designated by the Attorney General, or the principal prosecuting attorney of a State, or the principal prosecuting attorney for any political subdivision of a State, shall report to the Administrative Office of the United States Courts—

(a) the information required by paragraphs (a) through (g) of subsection (1) of this section with respect to each application for an order or extension made during the preceding calendar year;

(b) a general description of the interceptions made under such order or extension, including (i) the approximate nature and frequency of incriminating communications intercepted, (ii) the approximate nature and frequency of other communications intercepted, (iii) the approximate number of persons whose communications were intercepted, (iv) the number of orders in which encryption was encountered and whether such encryption prevented law enforcement from obtaining the plain text of communications, intercepted pursuant to such order, and (v) the approximate nature, amount, and cost of the manpower and other resources used in the interceptions;

(c) the number of arrests resulting from interceptions made under such order or extension, and the offenses for which arrests were made;

(d) the number of trials resulting from such interceptions;

(e) the number of motions to suppress made with respect to such interceptions, and the number granted or denied;

(f) the number of convictions resulting from such interceptions and the offenses for which the convictions were obtained and a general assessment of the importance of the interceptions; and

(g) the information required by paragraphs (b) through (f) of this subsection with respect to orders or extensions obtained in a preceding calendar year.

(3) In April of each year the Director of the Administrative Office of the United States Courts shall transmit to the Congress a full and complete report concerning the number of applications for orders authorizing or approving the interception of wire, oral, or electronic communications pursuant to this chapter and the number of orders and extensions granted or denied pursuant to this chapter during the preceding calendar year. Such report shall include a summary and analysis of the data required to be filed with the Administrative Office by subsections (1) and (2) of this section. The Director of the Administrative Office of the United States Courts is authorized to issue binding regulations dealing with the content and form of the reports required to be filed by subsections (1) and (2) of this section.

---

186. How restrictive are the provisions authorizing wiretapping and eavesdropping for law enforcement? Section 2516, for example, restricts their use to the investigation of specific crimes. Are there any crimes that law enforcement officials are likely to want to investigate by these means that are not included?

Section 2518 provides elaborate procedures to apply for an authorization to wiretap or eavesdrop. How much do they regulate the practice? Aside from requiring probable cause, § 2518(3), do they do much more than impose a considerable burden of documentation?

Section 2518(5) provides that an authorization may cover a period up to 30 days and allows an extension for an additional 30 days. Aside from that, the principal substantive limitation is the proviso that the wiretapping or eavesdropping "shall be conducted in such a way as to minimize the interception of communications not otherwise subject to interception." The proviso is construed in Scott v. United States, 436 U.S. 128 (1978) (7–2). The Court said that the test of whether the requirement has been met is not the eavesdropping agents' "good faith" effort to minimize but an objective assessment of the agents' conduct in all the circumstances. Among the relevant circumstances, the Court said, were the percentage of nonpertinent calls (although there were situations where a high percentage of such calls might reasonably be intercepted), the nature of the crime being investigated, the type of use to which the telephone is normally put, and the ability of the intercepting agents to develop categories of calls that need not be intercepted. The Court upheld a telephone wiretap, in which all calls were intercepted. About 40% of the calls were related to the investigation for which the wiretap was sought. Many of the other calls were short and unimportant, such as wrong numbers, calls to persons who were unavailable, etc. In the circumstances, the Court concluded, the agents conducting the wiretap were unable to develop a category of innocent calls that they could avoid intercepting in their entirety.

Look again at *Katz*, p. 309 above. Consider the specific facts of that case and the circumstances in which the Court said eavesdropping would be permissible. Do the provisions of the federal statute comport with the Court's reasoning? What about the provision for 30 days plus 30 days during which electronic surveillance can be maintained?

In United States v. Koyomejian, 970 F.2d 536 (9th Cir.1992), the court said that the statute regulates aural surveillance and has no application to silent video surveillance.

187. Section 2518(1)(b)(iv) requires the government to include in a wiretap or eavesdropping application "the identity of the person, if known, committing the offense and whose communications are to be intercepted." In United States v. Kahn, 415 U.S. 143 (1974) (6–3), the Court said that the government is not required to name anyone unless it knows both that the person is committing the offense and that his communications will be intercepted. It is not required to ascertain in advance whether a person whom it does not know to be committing the offense but whose communications will be intercepted may not be within the first category as well. The government is, however, required to name all persons whom it knows to be within both categories. The statute is not satisfied by providing only the name of the "principal target," usually the person whose telephone is monitored. United States v. Donovan, 429 U.S. 413 (1977).

Section 2518(8)(d) provides for an inventory notice to be served on persons named in the authorization order or application, which must indicate that there was an application, the period of any authorized wiretap or eavesdrop, and whether any conversations were intercepted. The judge who issued or denied the order has discretion to require service on other parties to intercepted communications "in the interest of justice." In *Donovan*, above, the Court held that the government has an obligation to furnish information about persons in the latter category sufficient to enable the judge to exercise her discretion.

Failure to meet either of the above requirements does not require suppression of evidence obtained pursuant to an otherwise valid order. *Donovan*, above (6–3).

Section 2516(1) designates specific officials in the Department of Justice who may authorize an application for a wiretap or eavesdropping order. In United States v. Giordano, 416 U.S. 505 (1974), the Court said that no other persons (in particular, the Attorney General's Executive Assistant) may authorize an application, and that evidence secured pursuant to an order issued in response to an application not so authorized must be suppressed.

The requirement of § 2518(8)(a) that recordings be immediately sealed and the provision that a failure to meet the requirement must be satisfactorily explained in order for the recording to be used or disclosed are discussed in United States v. Ojeda Rios, 495 U.S. 257 (1990) (6–3).

188. In In re Grand Jury, 111 F.3d 1066 (3d Cir.1997), the court held, notwithstanding the general rule that proceedings before a grand jury are not subject to supervision by the courts, see United States v. Williams, 504 U.S. 36 (1992), p. 682 below, that a person whose conversation was intercepted by a private illegal wiretap has standing to quash a subpoena directing the person who placed the wiretap to produce the tape of the conversation. The court observed: "We do not believe Congress intended the grand jury and the courts to use their respective powers to compel violations of the federal anti-wiretapping statute." 111 F.3d at 1076.

189. Having probable cause to believe that persons who had rented a motel room were engaged in a narcotics operation, police officials sought to rent an adjoining room. There being none available, the motel clerk, whom they had told of their investigation, moved the suspects to another room and rented an adjoining one to the officials. Using no special devices, the officials overheard conversations, sometimes while sitting on the bed in the middle of their room and sometimes by lying prone on the floor a few inches from a crack between the door and the carpet. Are the overheard conversations admissible? See United States v. Fisch, 474 F.2d 1071 (9th Cir.1973). See also United States v. Agapito, 620 F.2d 324 (2d Cir.1980).

Can a government agent testify to what he sees and hears through an open bathroom window while standing behind a motel unit in a parking lot? See Ponce v. Craven, 409 F.2d 621 (9th Cir.1969).

See United States v. Johnson, 561 F.2d 832 (D.C.Cir.1977), in which a police officer stepped a few feet onto the grass outside a house in order to look through a basement window. The police had received a tip that narcotics activities could be seen through the window. Characterizing the intrusion as a "technical trespass," the court concluded that in the circumstances of the case, there was no violation of the Fourth Amendment. See also United States v. Wheeler, 641 F.2d 1321 (9th Cir.1981); United States v. Llanes, 398 F.2d 880 (2d Cir.1968); Texas v. Gonzales, 388 F.2d 145 (5th Cir.1968).

190.

> On the night of April 6, 1967, federal investigators for the Alcohol Tax Unit of the Internal Revenue Service, acting upon information received from an unnamed informant, who they stated was a "reliable" source of information, went upon the farm of one Marzett, a co-defendant of appellant, and took up positions for observation of a house and shed from a distance. With the aid of binoculars, they observed through an open door the three defendants operating a still inside the shed, appellant in particular being recognized. They also watched the defendants load bottles of distilled spirits from the shed into a 1957 Ford automobile, and then saw the Ford leave the premises followed by a 1965 Chevrolet driven by appellant. The investigators followed the two cars for several miles, never losing sight of them, and then stopped and searched the cars and arrested the occupants. During the search, seventy-four gallons of non-taxpaid distilled spirits were found in the Ford. Thereafter, the investigators secured a warrant for search of the Marzett premises, which search took place that same night and revealed two distilleries, 1,400 gallons of mash, other miscel-

laneous distilling apparatus and eighteen gallons of non-taxpaid distilled spirits.

Fullbright v. United States, 392 F.2d 432, 433 (10th Cir.1968). Can the defendants' arrest and the search of the cars validly be based on the information learned by the observation of the house and shed? See also United States v. Whaley, 779 F.2d 585 (11th Cir.1986) (binoculars used to see conduct inside house that could be seen also with naked eye from location not generally accessible to public; search upheld); United States v. Taborda, 635 F.2d 131 (2d Cir.1980) (surveillance of interior of premises by telescope impermissible).

191. In California v. Ciraolo, 476 U.S. 207 (1986) (5–4), the Court held that "naked-eye" observation of a fenced-in area within the curtilage of the defendant's home, from an airplane flying at an altitude of a thousand feet, did not violate his rights under the Fourth Amendment. Police officers suspected that marijuana was being grown. They flew over the area in order to inspect it. The Court said that even though the defendant had exhibited an expectation of privacy, the expectation that he was protected from observation of this kind "in a physically nonintrusive manner" was "unreasonable and is not an expectation that society is prepared to honor." "Any member of the public flying in this airspace who glanced down could have seen everything that these officers observed." Id. at 209. It is immaterial, the Court said, that the officers flew over the area for the purpose of observing it in the course of criminal investigation. Accord Florida v. Riley, 488 U.S. 445 (1989) (5–4) (surveillance from helicopter flying at 400 feet).

See also Dow Chemical Co. v. United States, 476 U.S. 227 (1986) (5–4), p. 298 note 167 above, in which the Court held that sophisticated aerial photography of unenclosed parts of an industrial complex, which was closely guarded from ordinary observation, did not violate the Fourth Amendment. The holding was apparently based both on the nature of the premises observed, which the Court said were not clearly curtilage or open fields, and the method of observation. It intimated that more intrusive or unusual methods of observation "not generally available to the public" might have been a prohibited search. Id. at 238.

Kyllo v. United States

533 U.S. 27, 121 S.Ct. 2038, 150 L.Ed.2d 94 (2001)

■ JUSTICE SCALIA delivered the opinion of the Court.

This case presents the question whether the use of a thermal-imaging device aimed at a private home from a public street to detect relative amounts of heat within the home constitutes a "search" within the meaning of the Fourth Amendment.

I

In 1991 Agent William Elliott of the United States Department of the Interior came to suspect that marijuana was being grown in the home belonging to petitioner Danny Kyllo, part of a triplex on Rhododendron Drive in Florence, Oregon. Indoor marijuana growth typically requires high-intensity lamps. In order to determine whether an amount of heat was emanating from petitioner's home consistent with the use of such lamps, at 3:20 a.m. on January 16, 1992, Agent Elliott and Dan Haas used an Agema Thermovision 210 thermal imager to scan the triplex. Thermal imagers detect infrared radiation, which virtually all objects emit but which is not visible to the naked eye. The imager converts radiation into images based on relative warmth—black is cool, white is hot, shades of gray connote relative differences; in that respect, it operates somewhat like a video camera showing heat images. The scan of Kyllo's home took only a few minutes and was performed from the passenger seat of Agent Elliott's vehicle across the street from the front of the house and also from the street in back of the house. The scan showed that the roof over the garage and a side wall of petitioner's home were relatively hot compared to the rest of the home and substantially warmer than neighboring homes in the triplex. Agent Elliott concluded that petitioner was using halide lights to grow marijuana in his house, which indeed he was. Based on tips from informants, utility bills, and the thermal imaging, a Federal Magistrate Judge issued a warrant authorizing a search of petitioner's home, and the agents found an indoor growing operation involving more than 100 plants. Petitioner was indicted on one count of manufacturing marijuana, in violation of 21 U.S.C. § 841(a)(1). He unsuccessfully moved to suppress the evidence seized from his home and then entered a conditional guilty plea.

The Court of Appeals for the Ninth Circuit remanded the case for an evidentiary hearing regarding the intrusiveness of thermal imagine. On remand the District Court found that the Agema 210 "is a non-intrusive device which emits no rays or beams and shows a crude visual image of the heat being radiated from the outside of the house"; it "did not show any people or activity within the walls of the structure"; "[t]he device used cannot penetrate walls or windows to reveal conversations or human activities"; and "[n]o intimate details of the home were observed." Supp. App. to Pet. for Cert. 39–40. Based on these findings, the District Court upheld the validity of the warrant that relied in part upon the thermal imaging, and reaffirmed its denial of the motion to suppress. A divided Court of Appeals . . . affirmed, 190 F.3d 1041 (1999), with Judge Noonan dissenting. The court held that petitioner had shown no subjective expectation of privacy because he had made no attempt to conceal the heat escaping from his home . . . and even if he had, there was no objectively reasonable expectation of privacy because the imager "did not expose any intimate details of Kyllo's life," only "amorphous 'hot spots' on the roof and exterior wall," id. at 1047. We granted certiorari. . . .

II

The Fourth Amendment provides that "[t]he right of the people to be secure in their persons, houses, papers, and effects, against unreasonable searches and seizures, shall not be violated." "At the very core" of the Fourth Amendment "stands the right of a man to retreat into his own home and there be free from unreasonable governmental intrusion." Silverman v. United States, 365 U.S. 505, 511 (1961). With few exceptions, the question whether a warrantless search of a home is reasonable and hence constitutional must be answered no. . . .

On the other hand, the antecedent question of whether or not a Fourth Amendment "search" has occurred is not so simple under our precedent. The permissibility of ordinary visual surveillance of a home used to be clear because, well into the 20th century, our Fourth Amendment jurisprudence was tied to common-law trespass. . . . We have since decoupled violation of a person's Fourth Amendment rights from trespassory violation of his property . . . but the lawfulness of warrantless visual surveillance of a home has still been preserved. . . .

One might think that the new validating rationale would be that examining the portion of a house that is in plain public view, while it is a "search" despite the absence of trespass, is not an "unreasonable" one under the Fourth Amendment. . . . But in fact we have held that visual observation is no "search" at all—perhaps in order to preserve somewhat more intact our doctrine that warrantless searches are presumptively unconstitutional. . . . In assessing when a search is not a search, we have applied somewhat in reverse the principle first enunciated in Katz v. United States, 389 U.S. 347 (1967). *Katz* involved eavesdropping by means of an electronic listening device placed on the outside of a telephone booth—a location not within the catalog ("persons, houses, papers, and effects") that the Fourth Amendment protects against unreasonable searches. We held that the Fourth Amendment nonetheless protected Katz from the warrantless eavesdropping because he "justifiably relied" upon the privacy of the telephone booth. Id., at 353. As Justice Harlan's oft-quoted concurrence described it, a Fourth Amendment search occurs when the government violates a subjective expectation of privacy that society recognizes as reasonable. See id., at 361. We have subsequently applied this principle to hold that a Fourth Amendment search does *not* occur—even when the explicitly protected location of a *house* is concerned—unless "the individual manifested a subjective expectation of privacy in the object of the challenged search," and "society [is] willing to recognize that the expectation as reasonable." [California v.] *Ciraolo*, [476 U.S. 207 (1986)], at 211. . . .

The present case involves officers on a public street engaged in more than naked-eye surveillance of a home. We have previously reserved judgment as to how much technological enhancement of ordinary perception from such a vantage point, if any, is too much. . . .

III

It would be foolish to contend that the degree of privacy secured to citizens by the Fourth Amendment has been entirely unaffected by the advance of technology. For example, as the cases discussed above make clear, the technology enabling human flight has exposed to public view (and hence, we have said, to official observation) uncovered portions of the house and its curtilage that once were private. . . . The question we confront today is what limits there are upon this power of technology to shrink the realm of guaranteed privacy.

The *Katz* test—whether the individual has an expectation of privacy that society is prepared to recognize as reasonable—has often been criticized as circular, and hence subjective and unpredictable. . . . While it may be difficult to refine *Katz* when the search of areas such as telephone booths, automobiles, or even the curtilage and uncovered portions of residences are at issue, in the case of the search of the interior of homes—the prototypical and hence most commonly litigated area of protected privacy—there is a ready criterion, with roots deep in the common law, of the minimal expectation of privacy that *exists*, and that is acknowledged to be *reasonable*. To withdraw protection of this minimum expectation would be to permit police technology to erode the privacy guaranteed by the Fourth Amendment. We think that obtaining by sense-enhancing technology any information regarding the interior of the home that could not otherwise have been obtained without physical "intrusion into a constitutionally protected area," *Silverman* [v. United States], 365 U.S. [505 (1961)], at 512, constitutes a search—at least where (as here) the technology in question is not in general public use. This assures preservation of that degree of privacy against government that existed when the Fourth Amendment was adopted. On the basis of this criterion, the information obtained by the thermal imager in this case was the product of a search.

The Government maintains, however, that the thermal imaging must be upheld because it detected "only heat radiating from the external surface of the house," Brief for United States 26. The dissent makes this its leading point . . . contending that there is a fundamental difference between what it calls "off-the-wall" observations and "through-the-wall surveillance." But just as a thermal imager captures only heat emanating from a house, so also a powerful directional microphone picks up only sound emanating from a house—and a satellite capable of scanning from many miles away would pick up only visible light emanating from a house. We rejected such a mechanical interpretation of the Fourth Amendment in *Katz*, where the eavesdropping device picked up only sound waves that reached the exterior of the phone booth. Reversing that approach would leave the homeowner at the mercy of advancing technology—including imaging technology that could discern all human activity in the home. While the technology used in the present case was relatively crude, the rule we adopt must take account of more sophisticated systems that are already in use or in development. The dissent's reliance on the distinction between "off-the-wall" and "through-the-wall" observation is entirely incompatible with the dissent's belief, which we discuss below, that thermal-imaging observations of the intimate details of a home are impermissible. The most sophisticated thermal imaging devices continue to measure heat "off-the-wall" rather than "through-the-wall"; the dissent's disapproval of those more sophisticated thermal-imaging devices . . . is an acknowledgement that there is no substance to this distinction. As for the dissent's extraordinary assertion that anything learned through "an inference" cannot be a search . . . that would validate even the "through-the-wall" technologies that the dissent purports to disapprove. Surely the dissent does not believe that the through-the-wall radar or ultrasound technology produces an 8–by–10 Kodak glossy that needs no analysis (i.e., the making of inferences). . . .

The Government also contends that the thermal imaging was constitutional because it did not "detect private activities occurring in private areas," Brief for United States 22. It points out that in *Dow Chemical* we observed that the enhanced aerial photography did not reveal any "intimate details." [Dow Chemical Co. v. United States,] 476 U.S. [227 (1986)], at 238. *Dow Chemical*, however, involved enhanced aerial photography of an industrial complex, which does not share the Fourth Amendment sanctity of the home. . . . In the home, our cases show, *all* details are intimate details, because the entire area is held safe from prying government eyes. . . .

Limiting the prohibition of thermal imaging to "intimate details" would not only be wrong in principle; it would be impractical in application, failing to provide "a workable accommodation between the needs of law enforcement and the interest protected by the Fourth Amendment," Oliver v. United States, 466 U.S. 170, 181 (1984). To begin with, there is no necessary connection between the sophistication of the surveillance equipment and the "intimacy" of the details that it observes—which means that one cannot say (and the police cannot be assured) that the use of the relatively crude equipment at issue here will always be lawful. The Agema Thermovision 210 might disclose, for example, at what hour each night the lady of the house takes her daily sauna and bath—a detail that many would consider "intimate"; and a much more sophisticated system might detect nothing more intimate than the fact that someone left a closet light on. We could not, in other words, develop a rule approving only that through-the-wall surveillance which identifies objects no smaller than 36 by 36 inches, but would have to develop a jurisprudence specifying which home activities are "intimate" and which are not. And even when (if ever) that jurisprudence were fully developed, no police officer would be able to know *in advance* whether his through-the-wall surveillance picks up "intimate" details—and thus would be unable to know in advance whether it is constitutional.

. . .

We have said that the Fourth Amendment draws "a firm line at the entrance to the house," *Payton* [v. New York], 455 U.S. [573 (1980)], at 590. That line, we think, must be not only firm but bright—which requires clear specification of those methods of surveillance that require a warrant. While it is certainly possible to conclude from the videotape of the thermal imaging that occurred in this case that no "significant" compromise of the homeowner's privacy has occurred, we must take the long view, from the original meaning of the Fourth Amendment forward. . . . Where, as here, the Government uses a device that is not in general public use, to explore details of the home that would previously have been unknowable without physical intrusion, the surveillance is a "search" and is presumptively unreasonable without a warrant.

. . .

■ JUSTICE STEVENS, with whom THE CHIEF JUSTICE, JUSTICE O'CONNOR, and JUSTICE KENNEDY join, dissenting.

There is, in my judgment, a distinction of constitutional magnitude between "through-the-wall surveillance" that gives the observer or listener direct access to information in a private area, on the one hand, and the thought processes used to draw inferences from information in the public domain, on the other hand. The Court has crafted a rule that purports to deal with direct observations of the inside of the home, but the case before us merely involves indirect deductions from "off-the-wall" surveillance, that is, observations of the exterior of the home. Those observations were made with a fairly primitive thermal imager that gathered data exposed on the outside of petitioner's home but did not invade any constitutionally protected interest in privacy. Moreover, I believe that the supposedly "bright-line" rule the Court has created in response to its concerns about future technological developments is unnecessary, unwise, and inconsistent with the Fourth Amendment.

I

There is no need for the Court to craft a new rule to decide this case, as it is controlled by established principles from our Fourth Amendment jurisprudence. One of those core principles, of course, is that "searches and seizures *inside a home* without a warrant are presumptively unreasonable." Payton v. New York, 445 U.S. 573, 586 (1980) (emphasis added). But it is equally well settled that searches and seizures of property in plain view are presumptively reasonable. . . . Whether that property is residential or commercial, the basic principle is the same: " 'What a person knowingly exposes to the public, even in his own home or office, is not a subject of Fourth Amendment protection.' " California v. Ciraolo, 476 U.S. 207, 213 (1986) (quoting Katz v. United States, 389 U.S. 347, 351 (1967)). . . . That is the principle implicated here.

While the Court "[t]akes the long view" and decides this case based largely on the potential of yet-to-be-developed technology that might allow "through-the-wall surveillance," ante, at 38–40 . . . this case involves nothing more than off-the-wall surveillance by law enforcement officers to gather information exposed to the general public from the outside of petitioner's home. All that the infrared camera did in this case was passively measure heat emitted from the exterior surfaces of petitioner's home; all that those measurements showed were relative differences in emission levels, vaguely indicating that some areas of the roof and outside walls were warmer than others. As still images from the infrared scans show . . . no details regarding the interior of petitioner's home were revealed. Unlike an x-ray scan, or other possible "through-the-wall" techniques, the detection of infrared radiation emanating from the home did not accomplish "an unauthorized physical penetration into the premises," Silverman v. United States, 365 U.S. 505, 509 (1961), nor did it "obtain information that it could not have obtained by observation from outside the curtilage of the house," United States v. Karo, 468 U.S. 705, 715 (1984).

Indeed, the ordinary use of the senses might enable a neighbor or passerby to notice the heat emanating from a building, particularly if it is vented, as was the case here. Additionally, any member of the public might notice that one part of a house is warmer than another part or a nearby building if, for example, rainwater evaporates or snow melts at different rates across its surfaces. Such use of the senses would not convert into an unreasonable search if, instead, an adjoining neighbor allowed an officer onto her property with a sensitive thermometer. Nor, in my view, does such observation become an unreasonable search if made from a distance with the aid of a device that merely discloses that the exterior of one house, or one area of the house, is much warmer than another. Nothing more occurred in this case.

Thus the notion that heat emissions from the outside of a dwelling is a private matter implicating the protections of the Fourth Amendment (the text of which guarantees the right of people "to be secure *in* their . . . houses" against unreasonable searches and seizures (emphasis added)) is not only unprecedented but also quite difficult to take seriously. Heat waves, like aromas that are generated in a kitchen, or in a laboratory or opium den, enter the public domain if and when they leave a building. A subjective expectation that they would remain private is not only implausible but also surely not "one that society is prepared to recognize as 'reasonable.'" *Katz*, 389 U.S., at 361 (Harlan, J., concurring).

To be sure, the homeowner has a reasonable expectation of privacy concerning what takes place within the home, and the Fourth Amendment's protection against physical invasions of the home should apply to their functional equivalent. But the equipment in this case did not penetrate the walls of petitioner's home, and while it did pick up "details of the home" that were exposed to the public, ante, at 38, it did not obtain "any information regarding the *interior* of the home," ante, at 40 (emphasis added). In the Court's own words, based on what the thermal imager "showed" regarding the outside of petitioner's home, the officers "concluded" that petitioner was engaging in illegal activity inside the home. Ante, at 30. It would be quite absurd to characterize their thought processes as "searches," regardless of whether they inferred (rightly) that petitioner was growing marijuana in his house, or (wrongly) that "the lady of the house [was taking] her daily sauna and bath." Ante, at 38. . . . For the first time in its history, the Court assumes that an inference can amount to a Fourth Amendment violation. See ante, at 36–37.

Notwithstanding the implications of today's decision, there is a strong public interest in avoiding constitutional litigation over the monitoring of emissions from homes, and over the inferences drawn from such monitoring. Just as "the police cannot reasonably be expected to avert their eyes from evidence of criminal activity that could have been observed by any member of the public," [California v.] *Greenwood*, 486 U.S. [35 (1988)], at 41, so too public official should not have to avert their senses or their equipment from detecting emissions in the public domain such as excessive heat, traces of smoke, suspicious odors, odorless gases, airborne particulates, or radioactive emissions, any of which could identify hazards to the community. In my judgment, monitoring such emissions with "sense-enhancing technology," ante, at 34, and drawing useful conclusions from such monitoring, is an entirely reasonable public service.

On the other hand, the countervailing privacy interest is at best trivial. After all, homes generally are insulated to keep heat in, rather than to prevent the detection of heat going out, and it does not seem to me that society will suffer from a rule requiring the rare homeowner who both intends to engage in uncommon activities that produce extraordinary amounts of heat, and wishes to conceal that production from outsiders, to make sure that the surrounding area is well insulated. . . . The interest in concealing the heat escaping from one's house pales in significance to "the chief evil against which the wording of the Fourth Amendment is directed," the "physical entry of the home," United States v. United States Dist. Court for Eastern Dist. of Mich., 407 U.S. 297, 313 (1972), and it is hard to believe that it is an interest the Framers sought to protect in our Constitution.

Since what was involved in this case was nothing more than drawing inferences from off-the-wall surveillance, rather than any "through-the-wall" surveillance, the officers' conduct did not amount to a search and was perfectly reasonable.

II

Instead of trying to answer the question whether the use of the thermal imager in this case was even arguably unreasonable, the court has fashioned a rule that is intended to provide essential guidance for the day when "more sophisticated systems" gain the "ability to 'see' through walls and other opaque barriers." Ante, at 35, and n.3. . . . As I have suggested, I would not erect a constitutional impediment to the use of sense-enhancing technology unless it provides its user with the functional equivalent of actual presence in the area being searched.

. . .

Although the Court is properly and commendably concerned about the threats to privacy that may flow from advances in the technology available to the law enforcement profession, it has unfortunately failed to heed the tried and true counsel of judicial restraint. Instead of concentrating on the rather mundane issue that is actually presented by the case before it, the Court has endeavored to craft an all-encompassing rule for the future. It would be far wiser to give legislators an unimpeded opportunity to grapple with these emerging issues rather than to shackle them with prematurely devised constitutional constraints.

. . .

---

192. Is evidence obtained by a "mail cover," in which, at the request of a government agency, post office employees record and transmit to the agency information on the outside of mail to a particular individual, such as the name and address of the sender, admissible in evidence against the person "covered"? Against the senders? See United States v. Choate, 576 F.2d 165 (9th Cir.1978); Cohen v. United States, 378 F.2d 751, 759–60 (9th Cir.1967).

193.

> Agents of the Federal Bureau of Investigation kept plaintiff and his home, together with his relatives, friends and associates, under constant surveillance and observation at his home twenty-four hours per day. . . .
>
> . . .
>
> . . . Agents of the Federal Bureau of Investigation followed the plaintiff, Sam Giancana, and members of his family as he went about his private affairs and went to the home of Mrs. Rose Flood where plaintiff and members of his family went to visit. Agents of the Federal Bureau of Investigation remained outside of the home of Rose Flood flashing the lights of their vehicles as signals and maintaining constant surveillance of the home of Rose Flood while the plaintiff Sam Giancana was in and about said residence.
>
> . . . Agents of the Federal Bureau of Investigation followed the plaintiff Sam Giancana to the golf club where he patronizes [sic] and remained close to him and those with whom he played golf so that Agents of the Federal Bureau of Investigation numbering from two to four were directly behind plaintiff and his friends as they played golf, being immediately the next foursome following plaintiff and the group with which he was playing golf.
>
> [T]he number of vehicles which the . . . [F.B.I.] maintained in and about the home of the plaintiff Sam Giancana at 1147 South Wenonah Street, Village of Oak Park, Illinois, numbered variously from two to as many as five each with two Agents of the Federal Bureau of Investigation for the purpose of maintaining constant twenty-four hour a day observation and surveillance of the plaintiff and his home and to follow him as he went about his private affairs.

Giancana v. Johnson, 335 F.2d 366, 370, n.1 (7th Cir.1964) (findings of the district court).

Were the constitutional rights of the plaintiff violated?

CHAPTER 5

Examination and Identification

Rochin v. California

342 U.S. 165, 72 S.Ct. 205, 96 L.Ed. 183 (1952)

■ Mr. Justice Frankfurter delivered the opinion of the Court.

Having "some information that [the petitioner] was selling narcotics," three deputy sheriffs of the County of Los Angeles, on the morning of July 1, 1949, made for the two-story dwelling house in which Rochin lived with his mother, common-law wife, brothers and sisters. Finding the outside door open, they entered and then forced open the door to Rochin's room on the second floor. Inside they found petitioner sitting partly dressed on the side of the bed, upon which his wife was lying. On a "night stand" beside the bed the deputies spied two capsules. When asked "Whose stuff is this?" Rochin seized the capsules and put them in his mouth. A struggle ensued, in the course of which the three officers "jumped upon him" and attempted to extract the capsules. The force they applied proved unavailing against Rochin's resistance. He was handcuffed and taken to a hospital. At the direction of one of the officers a doctor forced an emetic solution through a tube into Rochin's stomach against his will. This "stomach pumping" produced vomiting. In the vomited matter were found two capsules which proved to contain morphine.

Rochin was brought to trial before a California Superior Court, sitting without a jury, on the charge of possessing "a preparation of morphine" in violation of the California Health and Safety Code, 1947, § 11500. Rochin was convicted and sentenced to sixty days' imprisonment. The chief evidence against him was the two capsules. They were admitted over petitioner's objection, although the means of obtaining them was frankly set forth in the testimony by one of the deputies substantially as here narrated.

On appeal, the District Court of Appeal affirmed the conviction. . . . The Supreme Court of California denied without opinion Rochin's petition for a hearing. . . .

This Court granted certiorari . . . because a serious question is raised as to the limitations which the Due Process Clause of the Fourteenth Amendment imposes on the conduct of criminal proceedings by the States.

. . .

[The Court's general discussion of the Due Process Clause and of due process of law is omitted.]

[W]e are compelled to conclude that the proceedings by which this conviction was obtained do more than offend some fastidious squeamishness or private sentimentalism about combatting crime too energetically. This is conduct that shocks the conscience. Illegally breaking into the privacy of the petitioner, the struggle to open his mouth and remove what was there, the forcible extraction of his stomach's contents—this course of proceeding by agents of government to obtain evidence is bound to offend even hardened sensibilities. They are methods too close to the rack and the screw to permit of constitutional differentiation.

It has long since ceased to be true that due process of law is heedless of the means by which otherwise relevant and credible evidence is obtained. This was not true even before the series of recent cases enforced the constitutional principle that the States may not base convictions upon confessions, however much verified, obtained by coercion. These decisions are not arbitrary exceptions to the comprehensive right of States to fashion their own rules of evidence for criminal trials. They are not sports in our constitutional law but applications of a general principle. They are only instances of the general requirement that States in their prosecutions respect certain decencies of civilized conduct. Due process of law, as a historic and generative principle, precludes defining, and thereby confining, these standards of conduct more precisely than to say that convictions cannot be brought about by methods that offend "a sense of justice." See Mr. Chief Justice Hughes, speaking for a unanimous Court in Brown v. Mississippi, 297 U.S. 278, 285–86. It would be a stultification of the responsibility which the course of constitutional history has cast upon this Court to hold that in order to convict a man the police cannot extract by force what is in his mind but can extract what is in his stomach.

To attempt in this case to distinguish what lawyers call "real evidence" from verbal evidence is to ignore the reasons for excluding coerced confessions. Use of involuntary verbal confessions in State criminal trials is constitutionally obnoxious not only because of their unreliability. They are inadmissible under the Due Process Clause even though statements contained in them may be independently established as true. Coerced confessions offend the community's sense of fair play and decency. So here, to sanction the brutal conduct which naturally enough was condemned by the court whose judgment is before us, would be to afford brutality the cloak of law. Nothing would be more calculated to discredit law and thereby to brutalize the temper of a society.

In deciding this case we do not heedlessly bring into question decisions in many States dealing with essentially different, even if related, problems. We therefore put to one side cases which have arisen in the State courts through use of modern methods and devices for discovering wrongdoers and bringing them to book. It does not fairly represent these decisions to suggest that they legalize force so brutal and so offensive to human dignity in securing evidence from a suspect as is revealed by this record. Indeed the California Supreme Court has not sanctioned this mode of securing a conviction. It merely exercised its discretion to decline a review of the conviction. All the California judges who have expressed themselves in this case have condemned the conduct in the strongest language.

We are not unmindful that hypothetical situations can be conjured up, shading imperceptibly from the circumstances of this case and by gradations producing practical differences despite seemingly logical extensions. But the Constitution is "intended to preserve practical and substantial rights, not to maintain theories." Davis v. Mills, 194 U.S. 451, 457.

On the facts of this case the conviction of the petitioner has been obtained by methods that offend the Due Process Clause. The judgment below must be

Reversed.[1]

---

194. The "shock the conscience" test of *Rochin*, above, has not generally been favored by the Court. In Irvine v. California, 347 U.S. 128 (1954) (5–4), the Court concluded over strong protest that repeated illegal, surreptitious entries into the petitioner's home and installation in the bedroom and elsewhere of eavesdropping devices did not shock the conscience. The absence of coercion was apparently the feature that distinguished *Rochin*, see id. at 133. And in Breithaupt v. Abram, 352 U.S. 432 (1957), the Court rejected an argument that the withdrawal of a blood sample by a hypodermic needle from an unconscious man in order to perform a blood alcohol test shocked the conscience. The Court said:

> [T]here is nothing "brutal" or "offensive" in the taking of a sample of blood when done, as in this case, under the protective eye of a physician. To be sure, the driver here was unconscious when the blood was taken, but the absence of conscious consent, without more, does not necessarily render the taking a violation of a constitutional right; and certainly the test as administered here would not be considered offensive by even the most delicate. Furthermore, due process is not measured by the yardstick of personal reaction or the sphygmogram of the most sensitive person, but by that whole community sense of "decency and fairness" that has been woven by common experience into the fabric of acceptable conduct. It is on this bedrock that this Court has established the concept of due process. The blood test procedure has become routine in our everyday life. It is a ritual for those going into the military service as well as those applying for marriage licenses. Many colleges require such tests before permitting entrance and literally millions of us have voluntarily gone through the same, though a longer, routine in becoming blood donors. Likewise, we note that a majority of our States have either enacted statutes in some form authorizing tests of this nature or permit findings so obtained to be admitted in evidence. We therefore conclude that a blood test taken by a skilled technician is not such "conduct that shocks the con-

[1] Justice Black and Justice Douglas wrote concurring opinions.

> science," *Rochin*, [342 U.S.] at 172, nor such a method of obtaining evidence that it offends a "sense of justice," Brown v. Mississippi, 297 U.S. 278, 285–86 (1936). This is not to say that the indiscriminate taking of blood under different conditions or by those not competent to do so may not amount to such "brutality" as would come under the *Rochin* rule. The chief law-enforcement officer of New Mexico, while at the Bar of this Court, assured us that every proper medical precaution is afforded an accused from whom blood is taken.

352 U.S. at 435–38.

In State v. Thompson, 505 N.W.2d 673, 675, 676 (Neb.1993), citing other cases, the court held that use of a choke hold ("lateral vascular neck restraint") that rendered a person unconscious for about ten seconds, in order to extract narcotic substances "between the size of a pinhead and a pea" from his mouth, was not an unreasonable search or otherwise unconstitutional. The *Rochin* "outrageous conduct" test is discussed in the context of alleged entrapment, in United States v. Tucker, 28 F.3d 1420 (6th Cir.1994), and United States v. Santana, 6 F.3d 1 (1st Cir.1993).

195. The problem of controlling illegal importation of goods, particularly narcotics, by swallowing them or concealing them in a body cavity has led the courts to allow as part of a "border search," see note 159, p. 289 above, the "stomach pump" device employed in *Rochin*, above, and body probes. E.g., United States v. Ogberaha, 771 F.2d 655 (2d Cir.1985) (reasonable suspicion is sufficient to justify search of body cavity); United States v. Aman, 624 F.2d 911 (9th Cir.1980) ("clear indication" required to justify search of body cavity). See generally United States v. Nelson, 36 F.3d 758 (8th Cir.1994) (evidence obtained by search of body cavity, not at border and in absence of exigent circumstances, suppressed).

Emphasizing the government's "plenary authority" to conduct routine searches at the border, without any requirement of probable cause or a warrant, the Supreme Court has held that "the detention of a traveler at the border, beyond the scope of a routine customs search and inspection, is justified at its inception if customs agents, considering all the facts surrounding the traveler and her trip, reasonably suspect that the traveler is smuggling contraband in her alimentary canal." United States v. Montoya de Hernandez, 473 U.S. 531, 541 (1985) (7–2). In that case, border authorities suspected that the defendant was carrying narcotics in her alimentary canal. She was detained and asked if she would undergo an x-ray at a hospital. After some discussion, she refused. She was given the option of returning to Colombia, her point of embarkation, by the first available flight, to which she agreed; but no flight was immediately available. She was then told that she would be detained unless she was x-rayed or she had moved her bowels and her stool was inspected. She was detained incommunicado and under observation until 16 hours after her plane had landed. Customs officers then sought a court order authorizing an x-ray and rectal examination, which was obtained about eight hours later. (The defendant had asserted that she was pregnant. The x-ray was made conditional on a negative result of a pregnancy test.) Balloons containing narcotics were removed from the defendant during a rectal examination; later she excreted additional balloons. An x-ray was not performed, although the pregnancy test later turned out to be negative. Conceding that the investigative detention in this case was longer than any that had previously been approved on the basis of reasonable suspicion and that the detention was "long, uncomfortable, indeed, humiliating," id. at 544, the Court concluded that, nevertheless, in view of the special responsibilities of customs officials to protect the border, it was permissible in the circumstances.

See also United States v. Couch, 688 F.2d 599 (9th Cir.1982) (x-ray of abdominal region at border upheld); Yanez v. Romero, 619 F.2d 851 (10th Cir.1980) (urine sample obtained by threat to use catheter held admissible).

Schmerber v. California

384 U.S. 757, 86 S.Ct. 1826, 16 L.Ed.2d 908 (1966)

■ MR. JUSTICE BRENNAN delivered the opinion of the Court.

Petitioner was convicted in Los Angeles Municipal Court of the criminal offense of driving an automobile while under the influence of intoxicating liquor. He had been arrested at a hospital while receiving treatment for injuries suffered in an accident involving the automobile that he had apparently been driving. At the direction of a police officer, a blood sample was then withdrawn from petitioner's body by a physician at the hospital. The chemical analysis of this sample revealed a percent by weight of alcohol in his blood at the time of the offense which indicated intoxication, and the report of this analysis was admitted in evidence at the trial. Petitioner objected to receipt of this evidence of the analysis on the ground that the blood had been withdrawn despite his refusal, on the advice of his counsel, to consent to the test. He contended that in that circumstance the withdrawal of the blood and the admission of the analysis in evidence denied him due process of law under the Fourteenth Amendment, as well as specific guarantees of the Bill of Rights secured against the States by that Amendment: his privilege against self-incrimination under the Fifth Amendment; his right to counsel under the Sixth Amendment; and his right not to be subjected to unreasonable searches and seizures in violation of the Fourth Amendment. The Appellate Department of the California Superior Court rejected these contentions and affirmed the conviction. . . .

We affirm.

I.

The Due Process Clause Claim.

Breithaupt [v. Abram, 352 U.S. 432 (1957)] was also a case in which police officers caused blood to be withdrawn from the driver of an automobile involved in an accident, and in which there was ample justification for the officer's conclusion that the driver was under the influence of alcohol. There, as here, the extraction was made by a physician in a simple, medically acceptable manner in a hospital environment. There, however, the driver was unconscious at the time the blood was withdrawn and hence had no opportunity to object to the procedure. We affirmed the conviction there resulting from the use of the test in evidence, holding that under such circumstances the withdrawal did not offend "that 'sense of justice' of which we spoke in Rochin v. California, 342 U.S. 165." 352 U.S., at 435. *Breithaupt* thus requires the rejection of petitioner's due process argument, and nothing in the circumstances of this case[2] or in supervening events persuades us that this aspect of *Breithaupt* should be overruled.

II.

The Privilege Against Self-Incrimination Claim.

Breithaupt summarily rejected an argument that the withdrawal of blood and the admission of the analysis report involved in that state case violated the Fifth Amendment privilege of any person not to "be compelled in any criminal case to be a witness against himself," citing Twining v. New Jersey, 211 U.S. 78. But that case, holding that the protections of the Fourteenth Amendment do not embrace this Fifth Amendment privilege, has been succeeded by Malloy v. Hogan, 378 U.S. 1, 8. We there held that "[t]he Fourteenth Amendment secures against state invasion the same privilege that the Fifth Amendment guarantees against federal infringement—the right of a person to remain silent unless he chooses to speak in the unfettered exercise of his own will, and to suffer no penalty . . . for such silence." We therefore must now decide whether the withdrawal of the blood and admission in evidence of the analysis involved in this case violated petitioner's privilege. We hold that the privilege protects an accused only from being compelled to testify against himself, or otherwise provide the State with evidence of a testimonial or communicative nature, and that the withdrawal of blood and use of the analysis in question in this case did not involve compulsion to these ends.

It could not be denied that in requiring petitioner to submit to the withdrawal and chemical analysis of his blood the State compelled him to submit to an attempt to discover evidence that might be used to prosecute him for a criminal offense. He submitted only after the police officer rejected his objection and directed the physician to proceed. The officer's direction to the physician to administer the test over petitioner's objection constituted compulsion for the purposes of the privilege. The critical question then, is whether petitioner was thus compelled "to be a witness against himself."

2. We "cannot see that it should make any difference whether one states unequivocally that he objects or resorts to physical violence in protest or is in such condition that he is unable to protest." Breithaupt v. Abram, 352 U.S., at 441 (Warren, C.J., dissenting). It would be a different case if the police initiated the violence, refused to respect a reasonable request to undergo a different form of testing, or responded to resistance with inappropriate force. Compare the discussion at Part IV, infra.

If the scope of the privilege coincided with the complex of values it helps to protect, we might be obliged to conclude that the privilege was violated. In Miranda v. Arizona, [384 U.S. 436 (1966)] at 460, the Court said of the interests protected by the privilege: "All these policies point to one overriding thought: the constitutional foundation underlying the privilege is the respect a government—state or federal—must accord to the dignity and integrity of its citizens. To maintain a 'fair state-individual balance,' to require the government 'to shoulder the entire load' . . . to respect the inviolability of the human personality, our accusatory system of criminal justice demands that the government seeking to punish an individual produce the evidence against him by its own independent labors, rather than by the cruel, simple expedient of compelling it from his own mouth." The withdrawal of blood necessarily involves puncturing the skin for extraction, and the percent by weight of alcohol in that blood, as established by chemical analysis, is evidence of criminal guilt. Compelled submission fails on one view to respect the "inviolability of the human personality." Moreover, since it enables the State to rely on evidence forced from the accused, the compulsion violates at least one meaning of the requirement that the State procure the evidence against an accused "by its own independent labors."

As the passage in *Miranda* implicitly recognizes, however, the privilege has never been given the full scope which the values it helps to protect suggest. History and a long line of authorities in lower courts have consistently limited its protection to situations in which the State seeks to submerge those values by obtaining the evidence against an accused through "the cruel, simple expedient of compelling it from his own mouth. . . . In sum, the privilege is fulfilled only when the person is guaranteed the right 'to remain silent unless he chooses to speak in the unfettered exercise of his own will.'" Ibid. The leading case in this Court is Holt v. United States, 218 U.S. 245. There the question was whether evidence was admissible that the accused, prior to trial and over his protest, put on a blouse that fitted him. It was contended that compelling the accused to submit to the demand that he model the blouse violated the privilege. Mr. Justice Holmes, speaking for the Court, rejected the argument as "based upon an extravagant extension of the Fifth Amendment," and went on to say: "[T]he prohibition of compelling a man in a criminal court to be witness against himself is a prohibition of the use of physical or moral compulsion to extort communications from him, not an exclusion of his body as evidence when it may be material. The objection in principle would forbid a jury to look at a prisoner and compare his features with a photograph in proof." 218 U.S., at 252–53.

It is clear that the protection of the privilege reaches an accused's communications, whatever form they might take, and the compulsion of responses which are also communications, for example, compliance with a subpoena to produce one's papers. . . . On the other hand, both federal and state courts have usually held that it offers no protection against compulsion to submit to fingerprinting, photographing, or measurements, to write or speak for identification, to appear in court, to stand, to assume a stance, to walk, or to make a particular gesture. The distinction which has emerged, often expressed in different ways, is that the privilege is a bar against compelling "communications" or "testimony," but that compulsion which makes a suspect or accused the source of "real or physical evidence" does not violate it.

Although we agree that this distinction is a helpful framework for analysis, we are not to be understood to agree with past applications in all instances. There will be many cases in which such a distinction is not readily drawn. Some tests seemingly directed to obtain "physical evidence," for example, lie detector tests measuring changes in body function during interrogation, may actually be directed to eliciting responses which are essentially testimonial. To compel a person to submit to testing in which an effort will be made to determine his guilt or innocence on the basis of physiological responses, whether willed or not, is to evoke the spirit and history of the Fifth Amendment. Such situations call to mind the principle that the protection of the privilege "is as broad as the mischief against which it seeks to guard," Counselman v. Hitchcock, 142 U.S. 547, 562.

In the present case, however, no such problem of application is presented. Not even a shadow of testimonial compulsion upon or enforced communication by the accused was involved either in the extraction or in the chemical analysis. Petitioner's testimonial capacities were in no way implicated; indeed, his participation, except as a donor, was irrelevant to the results of the test, which depend on chemical analysis and on that alone. Since the blood test evidence, although an incriminating product of compulsion, was neither petitioner's testimony nor evidence relating to some communicative act or writing by the petitioner, it was not inadmissible on privilege grounds.

III.

The Right to Counsel Claim.

This conclusion also answers petitioner's claim that, in compelling him to submit to the test in face of the fact that his objection was made on the advice of counsel, he was denied his Sixth Amendment right to the assistance of counsel. Since petitioner was not entitled to assert the privilege, he has no greater right because counsel erroneously advised him that he could assert it. His claim is strictly limited to the failure of the police to respect his wish, reinforced by counsel's advice, to be left inviolate. No issue of counsel's ability to assist petitioner in respect of any rights he did possess is presented. The limited claim thus made must be rejected.

IV.

The Search and Seizure Claim.

. . . The question is squarely presented . . . whether the chemical analysis introduced in evidence in this case should have been excluded as the product of an unconstitutional search and seizure.

The overriding function of the Fourth Amendment is to protect personal privacy and dignity against unwarranted intrusion by the State. . . .

The values protected by the Fourth Amendment thus substantially overlap those the Fifth Amendment helps to protect. History and precedent have required that we today reject the claim that the Self-Incrimination Clause of the Fifth Amendment requires the human body in all circumstances to be held inviolate against state expeditions seeking evidence of crime. But if compulsory administration of a blood test does not implicate the Fifth Amendment, it plainly involves the broadly conceived reach of a search and seizure under the Fourth Amendment. That Amendment expressly provides that "[t]he right of the people to be secure in their *persons*, houses, papers, and effects, against unreasonable searches and seizures, shall not be violated. . . ." (Emphasis added.) It could not reasonably be argued, and indeed respondent does not argue, that the administration of the blood test in this case was free of the constraints of the Fourth Amendment. Such testing procedures plainly constitute searches of "persons," and depend antecedently upon seizures of "persons," within the meaning of that Amendment.

Because we are dealing with intrusions into the human body rather than with state interferences with property relationships or private papers—"houses, papers, and effects"—we write on a clean slate. Limitations on the kinds of property which may be seized under warrant, as distinct from the procedures for search and the permissible scope of search, are not instructive in this context. We begin with the assumption that once the privilege against self-incrimination has been found not to bar compelled intrusions into the body for blood to be analyzed for alcohol content, the Fourth Amendment's proper function is to constrain, not against all intrusions as such, but against intrusions which are not justified in the circumstances, or which are made in an improper manner. In other words, the questions we must decide in this case are whether the police were justified in requiring petitioner to submit to the blood test, and whether the means and procedures employed in taking his blood respected relevant Fourth Amendment standards of reasonableness.

In this case, as will often be true when charges of driving under the influence of alcohol are pressed, these questions arise in the context of an arrest made by an officer without a warrant. Here, there was plainly probable cause for the officer to arrest petitioner and charge him with driving an automobile while under the influence of intoxicating liquor. The police officer who arrived at the scene shortly after the accident smelled liquor on petitioner's breath, and testified that petitioner's eyes were "bloodshot, watery, sort of a glassy appearance." The officer saw petitioner again at the hospital, within two hours of the accident. There he noticed similar symptoms of drunkenness. He thereupon informed petitioner "that he was under arrest and that he was entitled to the services of an attorney, and that he could remain silent, and that anything that he told me would be used against him in evidence."

While early cases suggest that there is an unrestricted "right on the part of the Government, always recognized under English and American law, to search the person of the accused when legally arrested to discover and seize the fruits or evidences of crime," Weeks v. United States, 232 U.S. 383, 392 . . . the mere fact of a lawful arrest does not end our inquiry. The suggestion of these cases apparently rests on two factors—first, there may be more immediate danger of concealed weapons or of destruction of evidence under the direct control of the accused . . . ; second, once a search of the arrested person for weapons is permitted, it would be both impractical and unnecessary to enforcement of the Fourth Amendment's purpose to attempt to confine the search to those objects alone. . . . Whatever the validity of these considerations in general, they have little applicability with respect to searches involving intrusions beyond the body's surface. The interests in human dignity and privacy which the Fourth Amendment protects forbid any such intrusions on the mere chance that desired evidence might be obtained. In the absence of a clear indication that in fact such evidence will be found, these fundamental human interests require law officers to suffer the risk that such evidence may disappear unless there is an immediate search.

Although the facts which established probable cause to arrest in this case also suggested the required relevance and likely success of a test of petitioner's blood for alcohol, the question remains whether the arresting officer was permitted to draw these inferences himself, or was required instead to procure a warrant before proceeding with the test. Search warrants are ordinarily required for searches of dwellings, and, absent an emergency, no less could be required where intrusions into the human body are concerned. The requirement that a warrant be obtained is a requirement that the inferences to support the search "be drawn by a neutral and detached magistrate instead of being judged by the officer engaged in the often competitive enterprise of ferreting out crime." Johnson v. United States, 333 U.S. 10, 13–14. . . . The importance of informed, detached and deliberate determinations of the issue whether or not to invade another's body in search of evidence of guilt is indisputable and great.

The officer in the present case, however, might reasonably have believed that he was confronted with an emergency, in which the delay necessary to obtain a warrant, under the circumstances, threatened "the destruction of evidence," Preston v. United States, 376 U.S. 364, 367. We are told that the percentage of alcohol in the blood begins to diminish shortly after drinking stops, as the body functions to eliminate it from the system. Particularly in a case such as this, where time had to be taken to bring the accused to a hospital and to investigate the scene of the accident, there was no time to seek out a magistrate and secure a warrant. Given these special facts, we conclude that the attempt to secure evidence of blood-alcohol content in this case was an appropriate incident to petitioner's arrest.

Similarly, we are satisfied that the test chosen to measure petitioner's blood-alcohol level was a reasonable one. Extraction of blood samples for testing is a highly effective means of determining the degree to which a person is under the influence of alcohol. . . . Such tests are a commonplace in these days of periodic physical examinations and experience with them teaches that the quantity of blood extracted is minimal, and that for most people the procedure involves virtually no risk, trauma, or pain. Petitioner is not one of the few who on grounds of fear, concern for health, or religious scruple might prefer some other means of testing, such as the "breathalyzer" test petitioner refused. . . . We need not decide whether such wishes would have to be respected.

Finally, the record shows that the test was performed in a reasonable manner. Petitioner's blood was taken by a physician in a hospital environment according to accepted medical practices. We are thus not presented with the serious questions which would arise if a search involving use of a medical technique, even of the most rudimentary sort, were made by other than medical personnel or in other than a medical environment—for example, if it were administered by police in the privacy of the stationhouse. To tolerate searches under these conditions might be to invite an unjustified element of personal risk of infection and pain.

We thus conclude that the present record shows no violation of petitioner's right under the Fourth and Fourteenth Amendments to be free of unreasonable searches and seizures. It bears repeating, however, that we reach this judgment only on the facts of the present record. The integrity of an individual's person is a cherished value of our society. That we today hold that the Constitution does not forbid the States minor intrusions into an individual's body under stringently limited conditions in no way indicates that it permits more substantial intrusions, or intrusions under other conditions.

Affirmed.[3]

---

196. In United States v. Montoya de Hernandez, 473 U.S. 531, 540 (1985) (7–2), discussed in note 195, p. 354 above, the Supreme Court observed that the reference in *Schmerber* to a "clear indication" that evidence will be found, p. 360 above, was "used to indicate the necessity for particularized suspicion that the evidence sought might be found within the body of the individual, rather than as enunciating still a third Fourth Amendment threshold between 'reasonable suspicion' and 'probable cause.' "

197. *Schmerber*, p. 356 n.2, seems to indicate that the use of "appropriate" force to make a person submit to a blood test or another such procedure is permissible, provided that the procedure itself is one that can be required. Is that proposition sound? In Hammer v. Gross, 932 F.2d 842 (9th Cir.1991), the court upheld the use of reasonable force to obtain a

[3] Justice Harlan wrote a brief concurring opinion, which Justice Stewart joined. Justice Black wrote a dissenting opinion, which Justice Douglas joined. Chief Justice Warren, Justice Douglas and Justice Fortas also wrote brief dissenting opinions.

blood sample from a driver suspected of drunk driving. The evidence was suppressed in State v. Ravotto, 777 A.2d 301 (N.J.2001), because unreasonable force was used.

198. The DNA Analysis Backlog Elimination Act of 2000, 42 U.S.C. § 14135a, requires persons in federal custody or on parole, probation or supervised release to provide a DNA sample, to be turned over to the FBI for analysis, the results of which are put in a data bank. All the states have enacted similar legislation mandating DNA testing and storage of the results for some similar group of persons. The data obtained by state and federal officials is kept in a unified data bank and made available to law enforcement officials. In United States v. Kincade, 345 F.3d 1095 (9th Cir.2003), vacated and rehearing granted, 354 F.3d 1000 (2004), the court held that the Fourth Amendment does not permit the involuntary extraction of blood to obtain a DNA sample, unless it is supported by individualized reasonable suspicion.

199. Relying on *Schmerber*, the Supreme Court of South Dakota held that the taking of a urine sample of an arrested person without her consent did not violate the defendant's rights under the Fourth Amendment. State v. Hanson, 588 N.W.2d 885 (S.D.1999).

In State v. Holt, 156 N.W.2d 884 (Iowa 1968), the defendant, who had been arrested for drunk driving, refused to take a blood test or a urine test at the police station. With respect to the blood test, he said that he refused to take the test because he had frequently been stuck with needles and hated them. The court held that testimony of his refusal was properly admitted in evidence against him.

In *Schmerber*, the Court declined to say whether, if a method of testing is generally proper and "for most people . . . involves virtually no risk, trauma, or pain," the wishes of "the few who on grounds of fear, concern for health, or religious scruple might prefer some other means of testing . . . have to be respected," p. 361. Should unusual squeamishness be a sufficient basis for requiring police not to employ a method of testing in a particular case?

200. In United States v. Chapel, 55 F.3d 1416 (9th Cir.1995) (en banc), noting that *Schmerber* required probable cause to arrest before a blood sample may be taken, the court held that a formal arrest before (or soon after) the blood sample is taken is not essential. In Matter of Lavigne, 641 N.E.2d 1328 (Mass.1994), the court held that a search warrant, issued after a hearing, can authorize the compelled extraction of a blood sample from a person not under arrest, to obtain evidence of a crime. So also, in Matter of Abe A., 437 N.E.2d 265 (N.Y.1982), it was held that a court may order a suspect not under arrest to furnish a blood sample, provided that there is probable cause to believe he has committed a crime, there is a "clear indication" that relevant material evidence will be obtained, and a safe, reliable method is used.

201. A Massachusetts statute prescribing an automatic 90-day suspension of the driver's license of someone who is lawfully arrested for drunken driving and refuses to take a breathalyzer test was sustained, against the claim that such suspension without a prior opportunity for a hearing is unconstitutional, in Mackey v. Montrym, 443 U.S. 1 (1979) (5–4). *Mackey* was followed in Illinois v. Batchelder, 463 U.S. 1112 (1983) (6–3).

The introduction at trial of evidence that the defendant refused to take a blood alcohol test after a police officer lawfully asked him to do so is not a violation of the privilege against self-incrimination. South Dakota v. Neville, 459 U.S. 553 (1983) (7–2).

202. Can a suspect be required to undress so that police can examine his body for scars? See McFarland v. United States, 150 F.2d 593 (D.C.Cir. 1945). Can he be required to shave before he appears in a lineup? See United States v. Crouch, 478 F.Supp. 867 (E.D.Cal.1979). See also United States v. Brown, 920 F.2d 1212 (5th Cir.1991) (defendant required to dye hair as it was alleged to be at time of crime, before appearing in lineup); United States v. Valenzuela, 722 F.2d 1431 (9th Cir.1983) (defendant required to be clean shaven at trial to facilitate identification). Are photographs of his body admissible in evidence over his objection? See People v. Smith, 298 P.2d 540 (Cal.Dist.Ct.App.1956). Are hairs clipped from the defendant's head over his protest while he is in custody admissible in evidence against him? See United States v. Anderson, 739 F.2d 1254 (7th Cir.1984) (taking of hair from scalp and beard pursuant to search warrant upheld); United States v. Weir, 657 F.2d 1005 (8th Cir.1981) (clipping strands of hair from head, beard, and moustache of arrested persons was "so minor . . . [that] fourth amendment rights were not implicated").

203. Fingerprints. As the Court indicated in *Schmerber*, above, claims that the taking of fingerprints over objection violates the privilege against self-incrimination have been rejected. E.g., United States v. Kelly, 55 F.2d 67 (2d Cir.1932). See also United States v. Richardson, 388 F.2d 842 (6th Cir.1968) (examination of hands under ultraviolet light for fluorescein power dusted on stolen goods). Nor have the courts accepted the claims, made by "respectable" defendants (for example, in antitrust cases) that the requirement of fingerprinting as to them was a punishment, e.g., United States v. Krapf, 285 F.2d 647, 650–51 (3d Cir.1960), or was an unconstitutional invasion of their privacy, United States v. Laub Baking Co., 283 F.Supp. 217 (N.D.Ohio 1968). In In re Reardon, 445 F.2d 798 (1st Cir.1971), the court ruled that if the defendant failed to comply with the district court's order to furnish a palmprint, his bail would be revoked.

204. Handwriting. In Gilbert v. California, 388 U.S. 263 (1967), the Court ruled that the taking of handwriting exemplars from a defendant following his arrest and their use against him, all without his consent, did not violate his privilege against self-incrimination. Following *Schmerber*, the Court said: "A mere handwriting exemplar, in contrast to the content of what is written, like the voice or body itself, is an identifying physical characteristic outside its protection." Id. at 266–67.[4]

4. The Court concluded also that "the taking of the exemplars was not a 'critical' stage of the criminal proceedings entitling petitioner to the assistance of counsel. . . .

Dissenting from this portion of the Court's opinion, Justice Fortas observed:

> Unlike blood, handwriting cannot be extracted by a doctor from an accused's veins while the accused is subjected to physical restraint, which *Schmerber* permits. So presumably, on the basis of the Court's decision, trial courts may hold an accused in contempt and keep him in jail—indefinitely—until he gives a handwriting exemplar.
>
> This decision goes beyond *Schmerber*. Here the accused, in the absence of any warning that he has a right to counsel, is compelled to cooperate, not merely to submit; to engage in a volitional act, not merely to suffer the inevitable consequences of arrest and state custody; to take affirmative action which may not merely identify him, but tie him directly to the crime.

Gilbert, 388 U.S. at 291–92.

In United States v. Doe, 405 F.2d 436 (2d Cir.1968), the court held that a witness who refused to comply with a court order to furnish exemplars for a grand jury could be punished by a commitment for contempt and, if he persisted in refusing and was subsequently indicted, his refusal could be considered by the jury at his trial.[5] Accord United States v. Knight, 607 F.2d 1172 (5th Cir.1979) (instructions to jury on refusal to furnish exemplar upheld); United States v. Nix, 465 F.2d 90 (5th Cir.1972). In United States v. Stembridge, 477 F.2d 874 (5th Cir.1973), the court held that the prosecutor could introduce expert testimony at the trial to explain the difference between a robbery note and the defendant's exemplars. A defendant may not, however, be required to give a handwriting sample by writing to dictation, because his spelling of the words dictated would be testimonial evidence. United States v. Campbell, 732 F.2d 1017 (1st Cir. 1984).

In United States v. Euge, 444 U.S. 707 (1980) (6–3), the Court upheld the authority of the IRS to require a person being investigated for tax liability to furnish a handwriting exemplar, under its authority to issue a summons for a person to appear and produce papers and records, etc., 26 U.S.C. § 7602.

205. Voice. In United States v. Wade, 388 U.S. 218 (1967), p. 369 below, the Court again relied on *Schmerber*, above, and held that an accused could be compelled "to speak within hearing distance of the witnesses, even to utter words purportedly uttered by the robber"; in such

[T]here is minimal risk that the absence of counsel might derogate from his right to a fair trial. . . . If, for some reason, an unrepresentative exemplar is taken, this can be brought out and corrected through the adversary process at trial since the accused can make an unlimited number of additional exemplars for analysis and comparison by government and defense handwriting experts."

388 U.S. at 267. See United States v. Wade, p. 369 below.

5. The witness was ordered committed for 30 days. The court of appeals indicated, contrary to Justice Fortas's speculation in *Gilbert*, that an indefinite commitment might be excessive and violate due process. 405 F.2d at 438–39.

a case, the accused is "required to use his voice as an identifying physical characteristic, not to speak his guilt." 338 U.S. at 222–23. See United States v. Leone, 823 F.2d 246 (8th Cir.1987) (defendant required to speak incriminating words recorded on tape before jury). Compare Palmer v. Peyton, 359 F.2d 199 (4th Cir.1966), in which the court held that the method used to obtain a voice identification (without a lineup) was so unreliable that its admission in evidence violated fundamental standards of due process.

Justice Fortas dissented from this portion of the Court's opinion in *Wade*:

> In my view . . . the accused may not be compelled in a lineup to speak the words uttered by the person who committed the crime. I am confident that it could not be compelled in court. It cannot be compelled in a lineup. It is more than passive, mute assistance to the eyes of the victim or of witnesses. It is the kind of volitional act—the kind of forced cooperation by the accused—which is within the historical perimeter of the privilege against compelled self-incrimination.
>
> Our history and tradition teach and command that an accused may stand mute. The privilege means just that; not less than that. According to the Court, an accused may be jailed—indefinitely—until he is willing to say, for an identifying audience, whatever was said in the course of the commission of the crime. Presumably this would include, "Your money or your life"—or perhaps, words of assault in a rape case. This is intolerable under our constitutional system.
>
> . . .
>
> . . . *Schmerber*, which authorized the forced extraction of blood from the veins of an unwilling human being, did not compel the person actively to cooperate—to accuse himself by a volitional act which differs only in degree from compelling him to act out the crime, which, I assume, would be rebuffed by the Court. It is the latter feature which places the compelled utterance by the accused squarely within the history and noble purpose of the Fifth Amendment's commandment.

388 U.S. at 260–61.

206. The complexity of the testimonial–nontestimonial distinction that the Court used in *Schmerber* to resolve the defendant's claim under the Fifth Amendment privilege against compulsory self-incrimination is indicated in Pennsylvania v. Muniz, 496 U.S. 582 (1990). The defendant was driving on the highway and was stopped by a patrol officer, who had reason to believe that the defendant was drunk. The officer asked him to perform three standard field sobriety tests (e.g., walk a straight line), which he performed badly. He told the officer that he did badly because he had been drinking. He was arrested and brought to a station for booking. During booking, which was videotaped, he was asked routine questions about his name, address, age, etc., and asked also whether he knew the date of his sixth birthday. He stumbled over questions about his address and age and said that he did not remember the date of his sixth birthday.

He was again asked to perform the sobriety tests, which he performed badly, attempting again to explain his bad performance. He was asked to take a breathalyzer test, which, after asking some questions and commenting about his state of drunkenness, he refused to do. No *Miranda* warnings were given until then.

The Court held that evidence about the defendant's slurring of speech and lack of muscular coordination was nontestimonial and therefore admissible. The answer to the question whether he knew the date of his sixth birthday, however, required a testimonial response; its incriminating significance lay not in its delivery but in its content. The defendant's responses to the routine booking questions and his remarks in the course of the sobriety tests and responses to the request that he take a breathalyzer test were also testimonial; but, the Court said, the former were admissible under a "routine booking exception" to the *Miranda* requirements and the latter were admissible because they were not in response to custodial interrogation. (On the *Miranda* aspects of the case, see note 240, p. 437 below.)

207. In Estelle v. Smith, 451 U.S. 454 (1981), the defendant was indicted for murder. Before trial, the court ordered a psychiatric examination to determine whether he was competent to stand trial. He was subsequently tried and convicted. At the sentencing proceeding, the psychiatrist who had examined the defendant gave testimony based on the examination, which supported the state's request for the death penalty. The defendant was sentenced to death.

The Court held that this use of the psychiatrist's testimony violated the defendant's privilege against compulsory self-incrimination and his right to counsel. As to the privilege, the Court said: "A criminal defendant, who neither initiates a psychiatric evaluation nor attempts to introduce any psychiatric evidence, may not be compelled to respond to a psychiatrist if his statements can be used against him at a capital sentencing proceeding. Because respondent did not voluntarily consent to the pretrial psychiatric examination after being informed of his right to remain silent and the possible use of his statements, the State could not rely on what he said to . . . [the psychiatrist] to establish his future dangerousness." Id. at 468. The Court noted that if the defendant had refused to answer questions, the competency examination could have proceeded on the condition that the results of the examination would be used only for that purpose. With respect to the right to counsel, the Court said that, having already been indicted, the defendant had the right to be assisted by counsel before deciding whether to submit to the competency examination.

Estelle v. Smith was distinguished in Buchanan v. Kentucky, 483 U.S. 402 (1987) (7–2), in which the defense counsel had requested the psychiatric evaluation and the prosecutor used a report of the evaluation to rebut evidence presented by the defense. See also United States v. Byers, 740 F.2d 1104, 1115 (D.C.Cir.1984), in which the court held that "when a defendant raises the defense of insanity, he may constitutionally be subjected to compulsory examination by court-appointed or government psychiatrists without the necessity of recording; and when he introduces into evidence psychiatric testimony to support his insanity defense, testimony of those examining psychiatrists may be received (on that issue) as well." The court rejected also a claim that the defendant's right to counsel was violated because his lawyer was not permitted to attend psychiatric staff conferences leading to an evaluation of the defendant subsequently used at his trial. The majority and dissenting opinions canvass the issues thoroughly and cite other federal cases. Estelle v. Smith is distinguished also in Penry v. Johnson, 532 U.S. 782 (2001), in which a witness referred to a psychiatric examination of the defendant prepared at the request of defense counsel in a previous unrelated case, to determine the defendant's competence to stand trial. The psychiatrist concluded that the defendant would be dangerous if released. Among the distinguishing factors, the court noted that Penry himself had made his mental condition an issue in the earlier trial and the current one, whereas in *Estelle*, the trial court had called for the examination and had chosen the examining psychiatrist; that the prosecutor elicited the testimony about the psychiatric examination during cross-examination of a defense witness, whereas in *Estelle* it had been elicited during the prosecution's affirmative case; and that in *Estelle* it was clear at the time of the psychiatric examination that future dangerousness would be an issue at trial, which was not so in this case. The Court declined to say whether these distinctions affected the merits of the defendant's Fifth Amendment claim. It said only that, for purposes of the defendant's habeas corpus petition, it was not unreasonable for the lower court to conclude that they did.

Estelle v. Smith was *not* followed in Allen v. Illinois, 478 U.S. 364 (1986) (5–4), in which, collaterally to criminal charges, the state brought proceedings to have the petitioner declared a sexually dangerous person and committed. In those proceedings, he was ordered to submit to psychiatric examinations. The testimony of the psychiatrists was introduced at the trial to determine whether the petitioner should be committed, over his objection that their information had been obtained in violation of his privilege against compulsory self-incrimination. The Court upheld the order of commitment. It said that since the state's purpose is treatment and not punishment, sexually dangerous person proceedings are noncriminal in nature and the privilege is not involved, even though the proceedings are initiated only after criminal charges are brought and in many procedural respects resemble a criminal trial.

208. The courts have generally held that the results of lie-detector tests are too unreliable to be admissible in evidence, nor is testimony that the defendant was willing or unwilling to take a test admissible. See, however, United States v. Oliver, 525 F.2d 731 (8th Cir.1975), in which the court upheld the admission of test results over the defendant's objection, because, before submitting to the test, for which the government had paid on the defendant's motion, he had agreed to admission of the results whatever they might be. The court rejected the defendant's claim that he was compelled to agree to their admission as the condition of his motion being granted. Lie-detector tests are discussed at length in Commonwealth v. Juvenile (No. 1), 313 N.E.2d 120 (Mass.1974), in which a rule like the result in *Oliver* is approved. Fifteen years later, the Massachusetts court observed that its expectation that polygraphy would gain general scientific acceptance had not materialized, and it ruled that "polygraphic evidence, with or without pretest stipulation, is inadmissible in criminal trials . . . either for substantive purposes or for corroboration or impeachment of testimony." Commonwealth v. Mendes, 547 N.E.2d 35, 41 (Mass.1989) (cases in other jurisdictions cited). See also People v. Barbara, 255 N.W.2d 171 (Mich.1977), in which the court concluded that the results of a test should continue to be inadmissible at trial but may be considered by the court in a hearing on a motion for a new trial. Lie-detector tests are discussed in United States v. Scheffer, 523 U.S. 303 (1998) (8–1), holding that a provision of the Military Rules of Evidence that makes polygraph evidence inadmissible in court-martial proceedings does not unconstitutionally restrict the right to make a defense.

The Court's disposition of cases involving evidence obtained by various kinds of examinations of the defendant is based on its holding and analysis of the Fifth Amendment claim in Schmerber v. California, p. 355 above (which in turn relies heavily on phrases borrowed from Miranda v. Arizona, p. 417 below). The Court's holding is that "the privilege [against self-incrimination] protects an accused only from being compelled to testify against himself, or otherwise provide the State with evidence of a testimonial or communicative nature," p. 356 above. Apparently conceding that the distinction is not always clear-cut, the Court asserted nevertheless that it provides "a helpful framework for analysis," p. 358 above.

How helpful is it? (Does the Court itself make much use of it as an analytic tool in *Schmerber*?) Why should the government, in aid of a criminal prosecution, be allowed to require that a man exhibit himself before others or speak or write, to make an impression of lines on the tips of his fingers, and to extract blood, but not be able to require that he answer questions? (How much of a factor is the comparative reliability of the evidence obtained by each technique?) In all of the situations some degree of cooperation by the defendant is needed. Equally in all of them, that the defendant is "required" to cooperate does not necessarily mean that physical force can be used to overcome his refusal to do so. (But see note 197, p. 361 above.) What interest(s) of the defendant is invaded by compelled testimony but not the other practices? (The Court acknowledges that at least the extraction of blood involves the same "complex of values" as questioning, p. 357 above.) What is the relevance in this context of the distinction between testimonial (or communicative) and nontestimonial evidence? Is it clear what the distinction is?

What is the point of the Court's observation that Schmerber's "participation, except as a donor" was irrelevant to the results of the test. Since it was Schmerber's blood that was tested, his participation as a donor was altogether crucial. Why does the Court have a difficult time with lie detector tests? How does an involuntary physiological response, see p. 358 above, which reveals guilt or innocence differ from chemical analysis of one's blood which reveals guilt or innocence?

Would there be significant value in rules that applied more literally the policy that "the government seeking to punish an individual produce the evidence against him by its own independent labors," p. 357 above, and prohibited all "use" of the defendant to procure evidence against himself after he has been taken into custody?

Lineups

United States v. Wade

388 U.S. 218, 87 S.Ct. 1926, 18 L.Ed.2d 1149 (1967)

■ MR. JUSTICE BRENNAN delivered the opinion of the Court.

The question here is whether courtroom identifications of an accused at trial are to be excluded from evidence because the accused was exhibited to the witnesses before trial at a post-indictment lineup conducted for identification purposes without notice to and in the absence of the accused's appointed counsel.

The federally insured bank in Eustace, Texas, was robbed on September 21, 1964. A man with a small strip of tape on each side of his face entered the bank, pointed a pistol at the female cashier and the vice president, the only persons in the bank at the time, and forced them to fill a pillowcase with the bank's money. The man then drove away with an accomplice who had been waiting in a stolen car outside the bank. On March 23, 1965, an indictment was returned against respondent, Wade, and two others for conspiring to rob the bank, and against Wade and the accomplice for the robbery itself. Wade was arrested on April 2, and counsel was appointed to represent him on April 26. Fifteen days later an FBI agent, without notice to Wade's lawyer, arranged to have the two bank employees observe a lineup made up of Wade and five or six other prisoners and conducted in a courtroom of the local county courthouse. Each person in the line wore strips of tape such as allegedly worn by the robber and upon direction each said something like "put the money in the bag," the words allegedly uttered by the robber. Both bank employees identified Wade in the lineup as the bank robber.

At trial, the two employees, when asked on direct examination if the robber was in the courtroom, pointed to Wade. The prior lineup identification was then elicited from both employees on cross-examination. At the close of testimony, Wade's counsel moved for a judgment of acquittal or, alternatively, to strike the bank officials' courtroom identifications on the ground that conduct of the lineup, without notice to and in the absence of his appointed counsel, violated his Fifth Amendment privilege against self-incrimination and his Sixth Amendment right to the assistance of counsel. The motion was denied, and Wade was convicted. The Court of Appeals for the Fifth Circuit reversed the conviction and ordered a new trial at which the in-court identification evidence was to be excluded, holding that, though the lineup did not violate Wade's Fifth Amendment rights, "the lineup, held as it was, in the absence of counsel, already chosen to represent appellant, was a violation of his Sixth Amendment rights . . ." 358 F.2d 557, 560. . . .

I.

Neither the lineup itself nor anything shown by this record that Wade was required to do in the lineup violated his privilege against self-incrimination. We have only recently reaffirmed that the privilege "protects an accused only from being compelled to testify against himself, or otherwise provide the State with evidence of a testimonial or communicative nature. . . ." Schmerber v. California, 384 U.S. 757, 761. . . .

. . .

[I]t deserves emphasis that this case presents no question of the admissibility in evidence of anything Wade said or did at the lineup which implicates his privilege. The Government offered no such evidence as part of its case, and what came out about the lineup proceedings on Wade's cross-examination of the bank employees involved no violation of Wade's privilege.

II.

The fact that the lineup involved no violation of Wade's privilege against self-incrimination does not, however, dispose of his contention that the courtroom identifications should have been excluded because the lineup was conducted without notice to and in the absence of his counsel. Our rejection of the right to counsel claim in Schmerber rested on our conclusion in that case that "[n]o issue of counsel's ability to assist petitioner in respect of any rights he did possess is presented." 384 U.S., at 766. In contrast, in this case it is urged that the assistance of counsel at the lineup was indispensable to protect Wade's most basic right as a criminal defendant—his right to a fair trial at which the witnesses against him might be meaningfully cross-examined.

[The Sixth Amendment] reads: "In all criminal prosecutions, the accused shall enjoy the right . . . to have the Assistance of Counsel *for his defence*." (Emphasis supplied.) The plain wording of this guarantee thus encompasses counsel's assistance whenever necessary to assure a meaningful "defence."

. . .

[I]n addition to counsel's presence at trial, the accused is guaranteed that he need not stand alone against the State at any stage of the prosecution, formal or informal, in court or out, where counsel's absence might derogate from the accused's right to a fair trial. The security of that right is as much the aim of the right to counsel as it is of the other guarantees of the Sixth Amendment—the right of the accused to a speedy and public trial by an impartial jury, his right to be informed of the nature and cause of the accusation, and his right to be confronted with the witnesses against him and to have compulsory process for obtaining witnesses in his favor. The presence of counsel at such critical confrontations, as at the trial itself, operates to assure that the accused's interests will be protected consistently with our adversary theory of criminal prosecution. . . .

In sum . . . [we are required to] scrutinize any pretrial confrontation of the accused to determine whether the presence of his counsel is necessary to preserve the defendant's basic right to a fair trial as affected by his right meaningfully to cross-examine the witnesses against him and to have effective assistance of counsel at the trial itself. It calls upon us to analyze whether potential substantial prejudice to defendant's rights inheres in the particular confrontation and the ability of counsel to help avoid that prejudice.

III.

The Government characterizes the lineup as a mere preparatory step in the gathering of the prosecution's evidence, not different—for Sixth Amendment purposes—from various other preparatory steps, such as systematized or scientific analyzing of the accused's fingerprints, blood sample, clothing, hair, and the like. We think there are differences which preclude such stages being characterized as critical stages at which the accused has the right to the presence of his counsel. Knowledge of the techniques of science and technology is sufficiently available, and the variables in techniques few enough, that the accused has the opportunity for a meaningful confrontation of the Government's case at trial through the ordinary processes of cross-examination of the Government's expert witnesses and the presentation of the evidence of his own experts. The denial of a right to have his counsel present at such analyses does not therefore violate the Sixth Amendment; they are not critical stages since there is minimal risk that his counsel's absence at such stages might derogate from his right to a fair trial.

IV.

But the confrontation compelled by the State between the accused and the victim or witnesses to a crime to elicit identification evidence is peculiarly riddled with innumerable dangers and variable factors which might seriously, even crucially, derogate from a fair trial. The vagaries of eyewitness identification are well-known; the annals of criminal law are rife with instances of mistaken identification. . . . A major factor contributing to the high incidence of miscarriage of justice from mistaken identification has been the degree of suggestion inherent in the manner in which the prosecution presents the suspect to witnesses for pretrial identification. . . . Suggestion can be created intentionally or unintentionally in many subtle ways. And the dangers for the suspect are particularly grave when the witness' opportunity for observation was insubstantial, and thus his susceptibility to suggestion the greatest.

Moreover, "[i]t is a matter of common experience that, once a witness has picked out the accused at the line-up, he is not likely to go back on his word later on, so that in practice the issue of identity may (in the absence of other relevant evidence) for all practical purposes be determined there and then, before the trial."[6]

The pretrial confrontation for purpose of identification may take the form of a lineup, also known as an "identification parade" or "showup," as in the present case, or presentation of the suspect alone to the witness. . . . It is obvious that risks of suggestion attend either form of confrontation and increase the dangers inhering in eyewitness identification. But as is the case with secret interrogations, there is serious difficulty in depicting what transpires at lineups and other forms of identification confrontations. . . . For the same reasons, the defense can seldom reconstruct the manner and mode of lineup identification for judge or jury at trial. Those participating in a lineup with the accused may often be police officers; in any event, the participants' names are rarely recorded or divulged at trial. The impediments to an objective observation are increased when the victim is the witness. Lineups are prevalent in rape and robbery prosecutions and present a particular hazard that a victim's understandable outrage may excite vengeful or spiteful motives. In any event, neither witnesses nor line-up participants are apt to be alert for conditions prejudicial to the suspect. And if they were, it would likely be of scant benefit to the suspect since neither witnesses nor lineup participants are likely to be schooled in the detection of suggestive influences. Improper influences may go undetected by a suspect, guilty or not, who experiences the emotional tension which we might expect in one being confronted with potential accusers. Even when he does observe abuse, if he has a criminal record he may be reluctant to take the stand and open up the admission of prior convictions. Moreover, any protestations by the suspect of the fairness of the lineup made at trial are likely to be in vain; the jury's choice is between the accused's unsupported version and that of the police officers present. In short, the accused's inability effectively to reconstruct at trial any unfairness that occurred at the lineup may deprive him of his only opportunity meaningfully to attack the credibility of the witness' courtroom identification.

What facts have been disclosed in specific cases about the conduct of pretrial confrontations for identification illustrate both the potential for substantial prejudice to the accused at that stage and the need for its

6. Williams & Hammelmann, Identification Parades, Part I, [1963] Crim. L. Rev. 479, 482.

revelation at trial. . . . [S]tate reports, in the course of describing prior identifications admitted as evidence of guilt, reveal numerous instances of suggestive procedures, for example, that all in the lineup but the suspect were known to the identifying witness, that the other participants in a lineup were grossly dissimilar in appearance to the suspect, that only the suspect was required to wear distinctive clothing which the culprit allegedly wore, that the witness is told by the police that they have caught the culprit after which the defendant is brought before the witness alone or is viewed in jail, that the suspect is pointed out before or during a lineup, and that the participants in the lineup are asked to try on an article of clothing which fits only the suspect.

The potential for improper influence is illustrated by the circumstances, insofar as they appear, surrounding the prior identifications in the three cases we decide today. In the present case, the testimony of the identifying witnesses elicited on cross-examination revealed that those witnesses were taken to the courthouse and seated in the courtroom to await assembly of the lineup. The courtroom faced on a hallway observable to the witnesses through an open door. The cashier testified that she saw Wade "standing in the hall" within sight of an FBI agent. Five or six other prisoners later appeared in the hall. The vice president testified that he saw a person in the hall in the custody of the agent who "resembled the person that we identified as the one that had entered the bank."

The lineup in *Gilbert* [v. California, 388 U.S. 263 (1967)] was conducted in an auditorium in which some 100 witnesses to several alleged state and federal robberies charged to Gilbert made wholesale identifications of Gilbert as the robber in each other's presence, a procedure said to be fraught with dangers of suggestion. And the vice of suggestion created by the identification in *Stovall* [v. Denno, 388 U.S. 293 (1967)], was the presentation to the witness of the suspect alone handcuffed to police officers. It is hard to imagine a situation more clearly conveying the suggestion to the witness that the one presented is believed guilty by the police. . . .

The few cases that have surfaced therefore reveal the existence of a process attended with hazards of serious unfairness to the criminal accused and strongly suggest the plight of the more numerous defendants who are unable to ferret out suggestive influences in the secrecy of the confrontation. We do not assume that these risks are the result of police procedures intentionally designed to prejudice an accused. Rather we assume they derive from the dangers inherent in eyewitness identification and the suggestibility inherent in the context of the pretrial identification. . . .

Insofar as the accused's conviction may rest on a courtroom identification in fact the fruit of a suspect pretrial identification which the accused is helpless to subject to effective scrutiny at trial, the accused is deprived of that right of cross-examination which is an essential safeguard to his right to confront the witnesses against him. . . . And even though cross-examination is a precious safeguard to a fair trial, it cannot be viewed as an absolute assurance of accuracy and reliability. Thus in the present context, where so many variables and pitfalls exist, the first line of defense must be the prevention of unfairness and the lessening of the hazards of eyewitness identification at the lineup itself. The trial which might determine the accused's fate may well not be that in the courtroom but that at the pretrial confrontation, with the State aligned against the accused, the witness the sole jury, and the accused unprotected against the overreaching, intentional or unintentional, and with little or no effective appeal from the judgment there rendered by the witness—"that's the man."

Since it appears that there is grave potential for prejudice, intentional or not, in the pretrial lineup, which may not be capable of reconstruction at trial, and since presence of counsel itself can often avert prejudice and assure a meaningful confrontation at trial, there can be little doubt that for Wade the post-indictment lineup was a critical stage of the prosecution at which he was "as much entitled to such aid [of counsel] . . . as at the trial itself." Powell v. Alabama, 287 U.S. 45, 57. Thus both Wade and his counsel should have been notified of the impending lineup, and counsel's presence should have been a requisite to conduct of the lineup, absent an "intelligent waiver." . . . No substantial countervailing policy considerations have been advanced against the requirement of the presence of counsel. Concern is expressed that the requirement will forestall prompt identifications and result in obstruction of the confrontations. As for the first, we note that in the two cases in which the right to counsel is today held to apply, counsel had already been appointed and no argument is made in either case that notice to counsel would have prejudicially delayed the confrontations. Moreover, we leave open the question whether the presence of substitute counsel might not suffice where notification and presence of the suspect's own counsel would result in prejudicial delay. And to refuse to recognize the right to counsel for fear that counsel will obstruct the course of justice is contrary to the basic assumptions upon which this Court has operated in Sixth Amendment cases. . . . In our view counsel can hardly impede legitimate law enforcement; on the contrary, for the reasons expressed, law enforcement may be assisted by preventing the infiltration of taint in the prosecution's identification evidence. That result cannot help the guilty avoid conviction but can only help assure that the right man has been brought to justice.

Legislative or other regulations, such as those of local police departments, which eliminate the risks of abuse and unintentional suggestion at lineup proceedings and the impediments to meaningful confrontation at trial may also remove the basis for regarding the stage as "critical." But neither Congress nor the federal authorities have seen fit to provide a solution. What we hold today "in no way creates a constitutional straitjacket which will handicap sound efforts at reform, nor is it intended to have this effect." Miranda v. Arizona [384 U.S. 436 (1996)], at 467.

V.

We come now to the question whether the denial of Wade's motion to strike the courtroom identification by the bank witnesses at trial because of the absence of his counsel at the lineup required . . . the grant of a new trial at which such evidence is to be excluded. We do not think this disposition can be justified without first giving the Government the opportunity to establish by clear and convincing evidence that the in-court identifications were based upon observations of the suspect other than the lineup identification. . . . Where, as here, the admissibility of evidence of the lineup identification itself is not involved, a per se rule of exclusion of courtroom identification would be unjustified. . . . A rule limited solely to the exclusion of testimony concerning identification at the lineup itself, without regard to admissibility of the courtroom identification, would render the right to counsel an empty one. The lineup is most often used, as in the present case, to crystallize the witnesses' identification of the defendant for future reference. We have already noted that the lineup identification will have that effect. The State may then rest upon the witnesses' unequivocal courtroom identification, and not mention the pretrial identification as part of the State's case at trial. Counsel is then in the predicament in which Wade's counsel found himself—realizing that possible unfairness at the lineup may be the sole means of attack upon the unequivocal courtroom identification, and having to probe in the dark in an attempt to discover and reveal unfairness, while bolstering the government witness' courtroom identification by bringing out and dwelling upon his prior identification. Since counsel's presence at the lineup would equip him to attack not only the lineup identification but the courtroom identification as well, limiting the impact of violation of the right to counsel to exclusion of evidence only of identification at the lineup itself disregards a critical element of that right.

We think it follows that the proper test to be applied in these situations is that quoted in Wong Sun v. United States, 371 U.S. 471, 488, " '[W]hether, granting establishment of the primary illegality, the evidence to which instant objection is made has been come at by exploitation of that illegality or instead by means sufficiently distinguishable to be purged of the primary taint.' Maguire, Evidence of Guilt 221 (1959)." . . . Application of this test in the present context requires consideration of various factors; for example, the prior opportunity to observe the alleged criminal act, the existence of any discrepancy between any pre-lineup description and the defendant's actual description, any identification prior to lineup of another person, the identification by picture of the defendant prior to the lineup, failure to identify the defendant on a prior occasion, and the lapse of time between the alleged act and the lineup identification. It is also relevant to consider those facts which, despite the absence of counsel, are disclosed concerning the conduct of the lineup.

. . .

[The Court concluded that the court of appeals had not applied the proper test, stated above, for exclusion of the in-court identifications and remanded the case for further proceedings.][7]

---

[7] Justice Clark wrote a brief concurring opinion. Justice Black wrote an opinion dissenting in part and concurring in part. Justice White also wrote an opinion dissenting in

209. In an opinion dissenting in part and concurring in part in *Wade*, above, Justice Black said: "The 'tainted fruit' determination required by the Court involves more than considerable difficulty. I think it is practically impossible. How is a witness capable of probing the recesses of his mind to draw a sharp line between a courtroom identification due exclusively to an earlier lineup and a courtroom identification due to memory not based on the lineup? What kind of 'clear and convincing evidence' can the prosecution offer to prove upon what particular events memories resulting in an in-court identification rest?" 388 U.S. at 248. Justice White, dissenting in part and concurring in part, agreed that if the state wanted to free a courtroom identification from an earlier improperly obtained identification, it had "a heavy burden . . . and probably an impossible one. To all intents and purposes, courtroom identifications are barred if pretrial identifications have occurred without counsel being present." Id. at 251.

210. Gilbert v. California, 388 U.S. 263 (1967), was decided with *Wade*. The Court there held that "a per se exclusionary rule" was applicable to testimony of an identification at a lineup that failed to meet the standards set in *Wade*; only such a rule, the Court said, "can be an effective sanction to assure that law enforcement authorities will respect the accused's constitutional right to the presence of his counsel at the critical lineup." Id. at 273.

211. *Wade*'s requirement of the presence of counsel applies only to the actual confrontation between a witness and the accused, and not to a conference between the witness and the prosecutor following the confrontation. United States v. Bierey, 588 F.2d 620 (8th Cir.1978) (other cases cited).

212. The defendant was arrested for car theft. He was assigned counsel and directed to appear for arraignment two weeks later. Before the arraignment, a detective who was investigating a robbery committed a month earlier learned that the defendant fit a description of one of the robbers. The detective arranged for a victim of the robbery to be present at the arraignment, and she identified the defendant, who was subsequently convicted of the robbery. The lawyer assigned to him for the car theft case was present at the arraignment when the identification was made. Did the defendant have any Sixth Amendment right to counsel in connection with the identification? See Boyd v. Henderson, 555 F.2d 56 (2d Cir.1977).

213. Also decided with *Wade*, Stovall v. Denno, 388 U.S. 293 (1967), established that *Wade* would not be applied retroactively. The Court observed, however, that past convictions based on an identification could be attacked on the ground that the method by which identification of the defendant was obtained "was so unnecessarily suggestive and conducive to irreparable mistaken identification that he was denied due process of law."

part and concurring in part, which Justice Harlan and Justice Stewart joined. Justice Fortas wrote an opinion concurring in part and dissenting in part, which Chief Justice Warren and Justice Douglas joined; see note 205, p. 364 above.

Id. at 302. In *Stovall*, the Court found that the defendant, who had been brought alone to a hospital where he was identified by one of his victims, had not been denied due process in "the totality of the circumstances," particularly that "an immediate hospital confrontation was imperative," id.

The Court applied *Stovall* in Foster v. California, 394 U.S. 440 (1969), and concluded that the facts presented "a compelling example of unfair lineup procedures," id. at 442. The petitioner Foster and others were charged with the armed robbery of a Western Union office.

> Except for the robbers themselves, the only witness to the crime was Joseph David, the late night manager of the Western Union office. After Foster had been arrested, David was called to the police station to view a lineup. There were three men in the lineup. One was petitioner. He is a tall man; close to six feet in height. The other two men were short—five feet, five or six inches. Petitioner wore a leather jacket which David said was similar to the one he had seen underneath the coveralls worn by the robber. After seeing this lineup, David could not positively identify petitioner as the robber. He "thought" he was the man, but he was not sure. David then asked to speak to petitioner, and petitioner was brought into an office and sat across from David at a table. Except for prosecuting officials there was no one else in the room. Even after this one-to-one confrontation David still was uncertain whether petitioner was one of the robbers: "truthfully—I was not sure," he testified at trial. A week or 10 days later, the police arranged for David to view a second lineup. There were five men in that lineup. Petitioner was the only person in the second lineup who had appeared in the first lineup. This time David was "convinced" petitioner was the man.
>
> At trial, David testified to his identification of petitioner in the lineups, as summarized above. He also repeated his identification of petitioner in the courtroom. The only other evidence against petitioner which concerned the particular robbery with which he was charged was the testimony of the alleged accomplice Clay.

The Court concluded that "the pretrial confrontations clearly were so arranged as to make the resulting identifications virtually inevitable." Id. at 441–43.

The Court considered the standards that apply in such cases again, in Neil v. Biggers, 409 U.S. 188 (1972). It said:

> Some general guidelines emerge . . . as to the relationship between suggestiveness and misidentification. It is, first of all, apparent that the primary evil to be avoided is "a very substantial likelihood of irreparable misidentification." Simmons v. United States, 390 U.S., at 384. While the phrase was coined as a standard for determining whether an in-court identification would be admissible in the wake of a suggestive out-of-court identification, with the deletion of "irreparable" it serves equally well as a standard for the admissibility of testimony concerning the out-of-court identification itself. It is the

> likelihood of misidentification which violates a defendant's right to due process, and it is this which was the basis of the exclusion of evidence in *Foster*. Suggestive confrontations are disapproved because they increase the likelihood of misidentification, and unnecessarily suggestive ones are condemned for the further reason that the increased chance of misidentification is gratuitous. But as *Stovall* makes clear, the admission of evidence of a showup without more does not violate due process.
>
> What is less clear from our cases is whether . . . unnecessary suggestiveness alone requires the exclusion of evidence. While we are inclined to agree with the courts below that the police did not exhaust all possibilities in seeking persons physically comparable to respondent, we do not think that the evidence must therefore be excluded. The purpose of a strict rule barring evidence of unnecessarily suggestive confrontations would be to deter the police from using a less reliable procedure where a more reliable one may be available, not because in every instance the admission of evidence of such a confrontation offends due process.

Id. at 198–99.

In Manson v. Brathwaite, 432 U.S. 98, 114 (1977) (7–2), the Court reaffirmed that "reliability is the linchpin in determining the admissibility of identification testimony" under the Due Process Clause and that pretrial identification evidence obtained by an unnecessarily suggestive procedure need not be excluded automatically, The factors to be considered in determining reliability "include the opportunity of the witness to view the criminal at the time of the crime, the witness' degree of attention, the accuracy of his prior description of the criminal, the level of certainty demonstrated at the confrontation, and the time between the crime and the confrontation," against which "is to be weighed the corrupting effect of the suggestive identification itself." Id. See, e.g., United States v. Emanuele, 51 F.3d 1123 (3d Cir.1995) (witness's viewing of defendant outside courtroom in shackles and accompanied by marshals was impermissibly suggestive; subsequent identification of defendant in court violated due process); Thigpen v. Cory, 804 F.2d 893 (6th Cir.1986) (use of identification violated due process); Solomon v. Smith, 645 F.2d 1179 (2d Cir.1981) (use of identification violated due process and right to counsel).

Kirby v. Illinois

406 U.S. 682, 92 S.Ct. 1877, 32 L.Ed.2d 411 (1972)

■ MR. JUSTICE STEWART announced the judgment of the Court and an opinion in which THE CHIEF JUSTICE, MR. JUSTICE BLACKMUN, and MR. JUSTICE REHNQUIST join.

. . . In the present case we are asked to extend the *Wade–Gilbert* per se exclusionary rule to identification testimony based upon a police station showup that took place *before* the defendant had been indicted or otherwise formally charged with any criminal offense.

On February 21, 1968, a man named Willie Shard reported to the Chicago police that the previous day two men had robbed him on a Chicago street of a wallet containing, among other things, traveler's checks and a Social Security card. On February 22, two police officers stopped the petitioner and a companion, Ralph Bean, on West Madison Street in Chicago.[8] When asked for identification, the petitioner produced a wallet that contained three traveler's checks and a Social Security card, all bearing the name of Willie Shard. Papers with Shard's name on them were also found in Bean's possession. When asked to explain his possession of Shard's property, the petitioner first said that the traveler's checks were "play money," and then told the officers that he had won them in a crap game. The officers then arrested the petitioner and Bean and took them to a police station.

Only after arriving at the police station, and checking the records there, did the arresting officers learn of the Shard robbery. A police car was then dispatched to Shard's place of employment, where it picked up Shard and brought him to the police station. Immediately upon entering the room in the police station where the petitioner and Bean were seated at a table, Shard positively identified them as the men who had robbed him two days earlier. No lawyer was present in the room, and neither the petitioner nor Bean had asked for legal assistance, or been advised of any right to the presence of counsel.

More than six weeks later, the petitioner and Bean were indicted for the robbery of Willie Shard. Upon arraignment, counsel was appointed to represent them, and they pleaded not guilty. A pretrial motion to suppress Shard's identification testimony was denied, and at the trial Shard testified as a witness for the prosecution. In his testimony he described his identification of the two men at the police station on February 22, and identified them again in the courtroom as the men who had robbed him on February 20. He was cross-examined at length regarding the circumstances of his identification of the two defendants. . . . The jury found both defendants guilty, and the petitioner's conviction was affirmed on appeal. . . . The Illinois appellate court held that the admission of Shard's testimony was not error, relying upon an earlier decision of the Illinois Supreme Court . . . holding that the *Wade–Gilbert* per se exclusionary rule is not applicable to pre-indictment confrontations. We granted certiorari, limited to this question. . . .

8. The officers stopped the petitioner and his companion because they thought the petitioner was a man named Hampton, who was "wanted" in connection with an unrelated criminal offense. The legitimacy of this stop and the subsequent arrest is not before us.

I

We note at the outset that the constitutional privilege against compulsory self-incrimination is in no way implicated here. The Court emphatically rejected the claimed applicability of that constitutional guarantee in *Wade* itself. . . .

. . .

The *Wade–Gilbert* exclusionary rule, by contrast, stems from a quite different constitutional guarantee—the guarantee of the right to counsel contained in the Sixth and Fourteenth Amendments. Unless all semblance of principled constitutional adjudication is to be abandoned, therefore, it is to the decisions construing that guarantee that we must look in determining the present controversy.

In a line of constitutional cases in this Court stemming back to the Court's landmark opinion in Powell v. Alabama, 287 U.S. 45, it has been firmly established that a person's Sixth and Fourteenth Amendment right to counsel attaches only at or after the time that adversary judicial proceedings have been initiated against him. . . .

This is not to say that a defendant in a criminal case has a constitutional right to counsel only at the trial itself. The *Powell* case makes clear that the right attaches at the time of arraignment, and the Court has recently held that it exists also at the time of a preliminary hearing. . . . But the point is that, while members of the Court have differed as to existence of the right to counsel in the contexts of some of the above cases, *all* of those cases have involved points of time at or after the initiation of adversary judicial criminal proceedings—whether by way of formal charge, preliminary hearing, indictment, information, or arraignment.

The only seeming deviation from this long line of constitutional decisions was Escobedo v. Illinois, 378 U.S. 478. But *Escobedo* is not apposite here for two distinct reasons. First, the Court in retrospect perceived that the "prime purpose" of *Escobedo* was not to vindicate the constitutional right to counsel as such, but, like *Miranda*, "to guarantee full effectuation of the privilege against self-incrimination. . . ." Johnson v. New Jersey, 384 U.S. 719, 729. Secondly, and perhaps even more important for purely practical purposes, the Court has limited the holding of *Escobedo* to its own facts . . . and those facts are not remotely akin to the facts of the case before us.

The initiation of judicial criminal proceedings is far from a mere formalism. It is the starting point of our whole system of adversary criminal justice. For it is only then that the government has committed itself to prosecute, and only then that the adverse positions of government and defendant have solidified. It is then that a defendant finds himself faced with the prosecutorial forces of organized society, and immersed in the intricacies of substantive and procedural criminal law. It is this point, therefore, that marks the commencement of the "criminal prosecutions" to which alone the explicit guarantees of the Sixth Amendment are applicable. . . .

In this case we are asked to import into a routine police investigation an absolute constitutional guarantee historically and rationally applicable only after the onset of formal prosecutorial proceedings. We decline to do so. Less than a year after *Wade* and *Gilbert* were decided, the Court explained the rule of those decisions as follows: "The rationale of those cases was that an accused is entitled to counsel at any 'critical stage of the *prosecution*,' and that a post-indictment lineup is such a 'critical stage.'" (Emphasis supplied.) Simmons v. United States, 390 U.S. 377, 382–383. We decline to depart from that rationale today by imposing a per se exclusionary rule upon testimony concerning an identification that took place long before the commencement of any prosecution whatever.

II

What has been said is not to suggest that there may not be occasions during the course of a criminal investigation when the police do abuse identification procedures. Such abuses are not beyond the reach of the Constitution. As the Court pointed out in *Wade* itself, it is always necessary to "scrutinize *any* pretrial confrontation...." 388 U.S., at 227. The Due Process Clause of the Fifth and Fourteenth Amendments forbids a lineup that is unnecessarily suggestive and conducive to irreparable mistaken identification....[9] When a person has not been formally charged with a criminal offense, *Stovall* strikes the appropriate constitutional balance between the right of a suspect to be protected from prejudicial procedures and the interest of society in the prompt and purposeful investigation of an unsolved crime.

The judgment is affirmed.[10]

---

214. The question left open in *Kirby*, whether there had been a denial of due process in the particular circumstances, was answered in the negative, in United States ex rel. Kirby v. Sturges, 510 F.2d 397 (7th Cir.1975). The court concluded that although the identification procedure used was unnecessarily suggestive, nothing more than "sloppy" police work had been involved and that the identification was sufficiently reliable. See also United States v. Oreto, 37 F.3d 739 (1st Cir.1994) (in-court witnesses were told where defendants were sitting prior to identification; identification procedure, although improper, did not require reversal).

215. The Due Process Clause does not invariably require a hearing outside the presence of the jury on the admissibility of identification evidence that the defendant claims was obtained improperly. While such a

9. In view of our limited grant of certiorari, we do not consider whether there might have been a deprivation of due process in the particularized circumstances of this case. That question remains open for inquiry in a federal habeas corpus proceeding.

[10] Chief Justice Burger wrote a brief concurring opinion. Justice Powell concurred in the result. Justice Brennan wrote a dissenting opinion which Justice Douglas and Justice Marshall joined. Justice White also wrote a dissenting opinion.

hearing may often be advisable and sometimes constitutionally required, there is no rule requiring such a hearing in every case. The Due Process Clause does not require "the abandonment of the time-honored process of cross-examination as the device best suited to determine the trustworthiness of testimonial evidence." Watkins v. Sowders, 449 U.S. 341, 349 (1981) (7–2).

216. The problem of identification of the defendant in court, when there is typically no lineup and the defendant is seated next to defense counsel, is discussed in United States v. Archibald, 734 F.2d 938, modified, 756 F.2d 223 (2d Cir.1984). The court held that despite the traditional use of in-court identifications, the circumstances may be unduly suggestive and that upon a proper request by the defendant the trial court should take steps to ensure a fair identification.

217. *Wade*, p. 369 above, rather than *Kirby*, was applied to an identification of the defendant by the victim of a rape, at a preliminary hearing at which the defendant was not represented by counsel. At that point, "adversary judicial criminal proceedings" against the defendant having begun, *Wade* required the exclusion at trial of evidence of the earlier identification. Moore v. Illinois, 434 U.S. 220 (1977).

Cf. McGee v. Estelle, 625 F.2d 1206 (5th Cir.1980), holding that the adversary process is *not* begun by an appearance before a magistrate, following a warrantless arrest, for the sole purpose of advising the defendant of his rights. At the time of the appearance, prosecuting authorities were still unaware of the arrest. The court held that *Kirby*, not *Wade*, was applicable to a lineup following the appearance.

Reiterating that "the right to counsel does not attach until the initiation of adversary judicial proceedings," the Court held that prisoners were not entitled to the appointment of counsel while they were in administrative detention following a prison proceeding at which it was determined that they were involved in crimes committed in the prison. Assuming that the detention was analogous to an arrest, the Court observed that the right to counsel does not attach at the time of arrest. The right to a speedy trial and the guarantee of due process, the Court noted, concern different protections from the right to counsel. United States v. Gouveia, 467 U.S. 180 (1984) (8–1).

218.

> The present case . . . involves an immediate on-the-scene confrontation at 5 o'clock in the morning when there would necessarily be a long delay in summoning appellant's counsel, or a substitute counsel, to observe a formal lineup. Such delay may not only cause the detention of an innocent suspect; it may also diminish the reliability of any identification obtained, thus defeating a principal purpose of the counsel requirement.
>
> Unquestionably, confrontations in which a single suspect is viewed in the custody of the police are highly suggestive. Whatever the police

actually say to the viewer, it must be apparent to him that they think they have caught the villain. Doubtless a man seen in handcuffs or through the grill of a police wagon looks more like a crook than the same man standing at ease and at liberty. There may also be unconscious or overt pressures on the witness to cooperate with the police by confirming their suspicions. And the viewer may have been emotionally unsettled by the experience of the fresh offense.

Yet, on the other hand, recognition of a person or face would seem to be as much the product of a subjective mental image as of articulable, consciously remembered characteristics. A man may see clearly in his "mind's eye" a face or a figure which he is hard put to describe adequately in words. Though the image of an "unforgettable face" may occasionally linger without any translation into words, photographic recall is most often ephemeral. Vivid in the flash of direct observation, it fades rapidly with time. And the conscious attempt to separate the ensemble impression into particular verbalized features, in order to preserve some recollection, may well distort the original accurate image so that it is the verbalized characteristics which are remembered and not the face or the man.

Balancing all the doubts left by the mysteries of human perception and recognition, it appears that prompt confrontations in circumstances like those of this case will "if anything promote fairness, by assuring reliability. . . ."[11]

Russell v. United States, 408 F.2d 1280, 1283–84 (D.C.Cir.1969). See Frank v. Blackburn, 605 F.2d 910 (5th Cir.1979), upholding an on-scene, one-on-one confrontation between a witness and a robber, following his arrest within a half hour of the crime.

Dissenting in *Kirby*, p. 378 above, Justice Brennan observed: "In the setting of a police station squad room where all present except petitioner and Bean were police officers, the danger was quite real that Shard's understandable resentment might lead him too readily to agree with the police that the pair under arrest, and the only persons exhibited to him, were indeed the robbers. . . . The State had no case without Shard's identification testimony, and safeguards against that consequence were therefore of critical importance. Shard's testimony itself demonstrates the necessity for such safeguards. On direct examination, Shard identified petitioner and Bean not as the alleged robbers on trial in the courtroom, but as the pair he saw at the police station." 406 U.S. at 700.

219. Photograph identifications. In Simmons v. United States, 390 U.S. 377 (1968), another aspect of which is considered in note 150 p. 278 above, one day after a bank robbery FBI agents showed photographs of two suspects to eyewitnesses. One of the suspects was identified in the photographs, which were mostly group photographs of the two suspects and others. At trial the eyewitnesses identified the defendant whose photograph they had identified earlier as one of the robbers. The Court rejected his

11. Wise v. United States, 383 F.2d at 209 [D.C.Cir.1967].

claim that the photograph identification procedure "was so unduly prejudiced as fatally to taint his conviction."

> It must be recognized that improper employment of photographs by police may sometimes cause witnesses to err in identifying criminals. A witness may have obtained only a brief glimpse of a criminal, or may have seen him under poor conditions. Even if the police subsequently follow the most correct photographic identification procedures and show him the pictures of a number of individuals without indicating whom they suspect, there is some danger that the witness may make an incorrect identification. This danger will be increased if the police display to the witness only the picture of a single individual who generally resembles the person he saw, or if they show him the pictures of several persons among which the photograph of a single such individual recurs or is in some way emphasized. The chance of misidentification is also heightened if the police indicate to the witness that they have other evidence that one of the persons pictured committed the crime. Regardless of how the initial misidentification comes about, the witness thereafter is apt to retain in his memory the image of the photograph rather than of the person actually seen, reducing the trustworthiness of subsequent lineup or courtroom identification.
>
> Despite the hazards of initial identification by photograph, this procedure has been used widely and effectively in criminal law enforcement, from the standpoint both of apprehending offenders and of sparing innocent suspects the ignominy of arrest by allowing eyewitnesses to exonerate them through scrutiny of photographs. The danger that use of the technique may result in convictions based on misidentification may be substantially lessened by a course of cross-examination at trial which exposes to the jury the method's potential for error. We are unwilling to prohibit its employment, either in the exercise of our supervisory power or, still less, as a matter of constitutional requirement. Instead, we hold that each case must be considered on its own facts, and that convictions based on eyewitness identification at trial following a pretrial identification by photograph will be set aside on that ground only if the photographic identification procedure was so impermissibly suggestive as to give rise to a very substantial likelihood of irreparable misidentification.

Id. at 383–84.

Among the factors on which the Court relied for its conclusion that the identification was not unduly prejudicial were: the need for prompt police action, the good opportunity for the witnesses to observe the defendant during the robbery, the freshness of their memory one day after the robbery, the lack of improper suggestion in the procedure (at least six photographs used, mostly group photographs, witnesses alone when shown photographs), and subsequent confirmation of the identifications. Id. at 385–86.

The defendant in *Simmons* had not been arrested when the photograph identifications were made. Relying on the historical construction of the right to counsel, the Court concluded in United States v. Ash, 413 U.S. 300 (1973) (6–3), that *Wade* did not apply to post-indictment photograph identifications. The Court said that photographic display was one of the variety of activities within the adversary system for which "the ethical responsibility of the prosecutor" was the "primary safeguard against abuses" and which were governed by the general rules and procedures of the system, including confrontation at trial. In *Ash*, almost three years after the crime and shortly before the trial was to begin, the prosecutor showed photographs including the photograph of the defendant to trial witnesses, as part of his preparation for trial. The Court did not consider whether the display violated the due process standard of *Simmons*.

The government's practice of not preserving photographic spreads shown to undercover agents for identification of suspects was sharply criticized in United States v. Sanchez, 603 F.2d 381 (2d Cir.1979).

220. Is it a denial of equal protection of the laws or otherwise constitutionally impermissible for an accused who cannot obtain his release on bail following indictment to be placed in a lineup, although other accused persons who are free on bail are not placed in a lineup? Does it matter whether the lineup concerns the crime for which the accused has been indicted or some other crime(s) of which he is suspected? See United States v. Jones, 403 F.2d 498 (7th Cir.1968); Rigney v. Hendrick, 355 F.2d 710 (3d Cir.1965). In United States v. Scarpellino, 296 F.Supp. 269, 272 (D.Minn.1969), the court observed that "one released on bail or personal recognizance can by court order, if a request from the United States Attorney is not honored, be required to return to jail or to the police department or elsewhere within reason and for a limited time to appear in a lineup." What limitations are there on such a practice? Compare Beightol v. Kunowski, 486 F.2d 293 (3d Cir.1973).

In United States v. Hammond, 419 F.2d 166 (4th Cir.1969), the district court ordered the defendant, who had been indicted for bank robbery and was detained in jail, to participate in reasonably scheduled lineups and "to wear any clothing or items, such as a false goatee; to speak any words; to walk in any manner; or to take any physical stance that may be required." The defendant refused. His conviction for criminal contempt was upheld. In Higgins v. Wainwright, 424 F.2d 177 (5th Cir.1970) (voice lineup), and United States v. Parhms, 424 F.2d 152 (9th Cir.1970), the prosecutor was allowed to bring before the jury the defendant's refusal to participate in a lineup.

How much force can be used to make an arrested person participate in a lineup? See Appeal of Maguire, 571 F.2d 675 (1st Cir.1978), upholding an order authorizing the use of "such reasonable force as is reasonably necessary" to compel a witness, then serving a long prison sentence, to appear in a lineup and submit to fingerprinting before a grand jury. See generally note 197, p. 361 above.

United States v. Dionisio

410 U.S. 1, 93 S.Ct. 764, 35 L.Ed.2d 67 (1973)

■ MR. JUSTICE STEWART delivered the opinion of the Court.

A special grand jury was convened in the Northern District of Illinois in February 1971, to investigate possible violations of federal criminal statutes relating to gambling. In the course of its investigation, the grand jury received in evidence certain voice recordings that had been obtained pursuant to court orders.

The grand jury subpoenaed approximately 20 persons, including the respondent Dionisio, seeking to obtain from them voice exemplars for comparison with the recorded conversations that had been received in evidence. Each witness was advised that he was a potential defendant in a criminal prosecution. Each was asked to examine a transcript of an intercepted conversation, and to go to a nearby office of the United States Attorney to read the transcript into a recording device. The witnesses were advised that they would be allowed to have their attorneys present when they read the transcripts. Dionisio and other witnesses refused to furnish the voice exemplars, asserting that these disclosures would violate their rights under the Fourth and Fifth Amendments.

The Government then filed separate petitions in the United States District Court to compel Dionisio and the other witnesses to furnish the voice exemplars to the grand jury. The petitions stated that the exemplars were "essential and necessary" to the grand jury investigation, and that they would "be used solely as a standard of comparison in order to determine whether or not the witness is the person whose voice was intercepted. . . ."

Following a hearing, the District Judge rejected the witnesses' constitutional arguments and ordered them to comply with the grand jury's request. He reasoned that voice exemplars, like handwriting exemplars or fingerprints, were not testimonial or communicative evidence, and that consequently the order to produce them would not compel any witness to testify against himself. The District Judge also found that there would be no Fourth Amendment violation, because the grand jury subpoena did not itself violate the Fourth Amendment, and the order to produce the voice exemplars would involve no unreasonable search and seizure within the proscription of that Amendment. . . . When Dionisio persisted in his refusal to respond to the grand jury's directive, the District Court adjudged him in civil contempt and ordered him committed to custody until he obeyed the court order, or until the expiration of 18 months.

The Court of Appeals for the Seventh Circuit reversed. 442 F.2d 276. It agreed with the District Court in rejecting the Fifth Amendment claims, but concluded that to compel the voice recordings would violate the Fourth Amendment. In the court's view, the grand jury was "seeking to obtain the voice exemplars of the witnesses by the use of its subpoena powers because probable cause did not exist for their arrest or for some other, less unusual, method of compelling the production of the exemplars." Id., at 280. The court found that the Fourth Amendment applied to grand jury process, and that "under the fourth amendment law enforcement officials may not compel the production of physical evidence absent a showing of the reasonableness of the seizure. Davis v. Mississippi, 394 U.S. 721. . . ." Ibid.

In *Davis* this Court held that it was error to admit the petitioner's fingerprints into evidence at his trial for rape, because they had been obtained during a police detention following a lawless wholesale roundup of the petitioner and more than 20 other youths. Equating the procedures followed by the grand jury in the present case to the fingerprint detentions in *Davis*, the Court of Appeals reasoned that "[t]he dragnet effect here, where approximately twenty persons were subpoenaed for purposes of identification, has the same invidious effect on fourth amendment rights as the practice condemned in *Davis*." Id., at 281.

[W]e granted the Government's petition for certiorari. . . .

I

The Court of Appeals correctly rejected the contention that the compelled production of the voice exemplars would violate the Fifth Amendment. It has long been held that the compelled display of identifiable physical characteristics infringes no interest protected by the privilege against compulsory self-incrimination. . . .

. . .

. . . The voice recordings were to be used solely to measure the physical properties of the witnesses' voices, not for the testimonial or communicative content of what was to be said.

II

The Court of Appeals held that the Fourth Amendment required a preliminary showing of reasonableness before a grand jury witness could be compelled to furnish a voice exemplar, and that in this case the proposed "seizures" of the voice exemplars would be unreasonable because of the large number of witnesses summoned by the grand jury and directed to produce such exemplars. We disagree.

. . .

As the Court made clear in *Schmerber* [v. California, 384 U.S. 757 (1966)], the obtaining of physical evidence from a person involves a potential Fourth Amendment violation at two different levels—the "seizure" of the "person" necessary to bring him into contact with government agents . . . and the subsequent search for and seizure of the evidence. . . . The constitutionality of the compulsory production of exemplars from a grand jury witness necessarily turns on the same dual inquiry—whether either the initial compulsion of the person to appear before the grand jury, or the subsequent directive to make a voice recording is an unreasonable "seizure" within the meaning of the Fourth Amendment.

It is clear that a subpoena to appear before a grand jury is not a "seizure" in the Fourth Amendment sense, even though that summons may be inconvenient or burdensome. Last Term we again acknowledged what has long been recognized, that "[c]itizens generally are not constitutionally immune from grand jury subpoenas. . . ." Branzburg v. Hayes, 408 U.S. 665, 682. . . .

These are recent reaffirmations of the historically grounded obligation of every person to appear and give his evidence before the grand jury. . . .

The compulsion exerted by a grand jury subpoena differs from the seizure effected by an arrest or even an investigative "stop" in more than civic obligation. For, as Judge Friendly wrote for the Court of Appeals for the Second Circuit:

> The latter is abrupt, is effected with force or the threat of it and often in demeaning circumstances, and, in the case of arrest, results in a record involving social stigma. A subpoena is served in the same manner as other legal process; it involves no stigma whatever; if the time for appearance is inconvenient, this can generally be altered; and it remains at all times under the control and supervision of a court.

United States v. Doe (Schwartz) 457 F.2d [895 (2d Cir.1972)], at 898. Thus, the Court of Appeals for the Seventh Circuit correctly recognized in a case subsequent to the one now before us, that a "grand jury subpoena to testify is not that kind of governmental intrusion on privacy against which the Fourth Amendment affords protection, once the Fifth Amendment is satisfied." Fraser v. United States, 452 F.2d 616, 620. . . .

This case is thus quite different from Davis v. Mississippi, supra. . . . For in *Davis* it was the initial seizure—the lawless dragnet detention—that violated the Fourth and Fourteenth Amendments, not the taking of the fingerprints. . . . *Davis* is plainly inapposite to a case where the initial restraint does not itself infringe the Fourth Amendment.

This is not to say that a grand jury subpoena is some talisman that dissolves all constitutional protections. . . . Grand juries are subject to judicial control and subpoenas to motions to quash. . . .

But we are here faced with no such constitutional infirmities in the subpoena to appear before the grand jury or in the order to make the voice recordings. There is, as we have said, no valid Fifth Amendment claim. There was no order to produce private books and papers, and no sweeping subpoena *duces tecum*. . . .

The Court of Appeals found critical significance in the fact that the grand jury had summoned approximately 20 witnesses to furnish voice exemplars. We think that fact is basically irrelevant to the constitutional issues here. The grand jury may have been attempting to identify a number of voices on the tapes in evidence, or it might have summoned the 20 witnesses in an effort to identify one voice. But whatever the case, "[a] grand jury's investigation is not fully carried out until every available clue has been run down and all witnesses examined in every proper way to find if a crime has been committed. . . ." United States v. Stone, 429 F.2d 138, 140. . . . The grand jury may well find it desirable to call numerous witnesses in the course of an investigation. It does not follow that each witness may resist a subpoena on the ground that too many witnesses have been called. Neither the order to Dionisio to appear, nor the order to make a voice recording, was rendered unreasonable by the fact that many others were subjected to the same compulsion.

But the conclusion that Dionisio's compulsory appearance before the grand jury was not an unreasonable "seizure" is the answer to only the first part of the Fourth Amendment inquiry here. Dionisio argues that the grand jury's subsequent directive to make the voice recording was itself an infringement of his rights under the Fourth Amendment. We cannot accept that argument.

In Katz v. United States, [389 U.S. 347 (1967)], we said that the Fourth Amendment provides no protection for what "a person knowingly exposes to the public, even in his own home or office. . . ." 389 U.S., at 351. The physical characteristics of a person's voice, its tone and manner, as opposed to the content of a specific conversation, are constantly exposed to the public. Like a man's facial characteristics, or handwriting, his voice is repeatedly produced for others to hear. No person can have a reasonable expectation that others will not know the sound of his voice, any more than he can reasonably expect that his face will be a mystery to the world. . . .

The required disclosure of a person's voice is thus immeasurably further removed from the Fourth Amendment protection than was the intrusion into the body effected by the blood extraction in *Schmerber*. . . . Similarly, a seizure of voice exemplars does not involve the "severe, though brief, intrusion upon cherished personal security," effected by the "pat-down" in *Terry* [v. Ohio, 392 U.S. 1 (1968)]—"surely . . . an annoying, frightening, and perhaps humiliating experience." Terry v. Ohio, 392 U.S., at 24–25. Rather, this is like the fingerprinting in *Davis*, where, though the initial dragnet detentions were constitutionally impermissible, we noted that the fingerprinting itself "involves none of the probing into an individual's private life and thoughts that marks an interrogation or search." Davis v. Mississippi, 394 U.S., at 727. . . .

Since neither the summons to appear before the grand jury nor its directive to make a voice recording infringed upon any interest protected by the Fourth Amendment, there was no justification for requiring the grand jury to satisfy even the minimal requirement of "reasonableness" imposed by the Court of Appeals. . . . A grand jury has broad investigative powers to determine whether a crime has been committed and who had committed it. The jurors may act on tips, rumors, evidence offered by the prosecutor, or their own personal knowledge. . . . No grand jury witness is "entitled to set limits to the investigation that the grand jury may conduct." Blair v. United States, 250 U.S., at 282. And a sufficient basis for an indictment may only emerge at the end of the investigation when all the evidence has been received. . . . Since Dionisio raised no valid Fourth Amendment claim, there is no more reason to require a preliminary showing of reasonableness here than there would be in the case of any witness who, despite the lack of any constitutional or statutory privilege, declined to answer a question or comply with a grand jury request. Neither the

Constitution nor our prior cases justify any such interference with grand jury proceedings.

The Fifth Amendment guarantees that no civilian may be brought to trial for an infamous crime "unless on a presentment or indictment of a Grand Jury." This constitutional guarantee presupposes an investigative body "acting independently of either prosecuting attorney or judge," Stirone v. United States, 361 U.S. 212, 218, whose mission is to clear the innocent, no less than to bring to trial those who may be guilty. Any holding that would saddle a grand jury with minitrials and preliminary showings would assuredly impede its investigation and frustrate the public's interest in the fair and expeditious administration of the criminal laws. . . . The grand jury may not always serve its historic role as a protective bulwark standing solidly between the ordinary citizen and an overzealous prosecutor, but if it is even to approach the proper performance of its constitutional mission, it must be free to pursue its investigations unhindered by external influence or supervision so long as it does not trench upon the legitimate rights of any witness called before it.

Since the Court of Appeals found an unreasonable search and seizure where none existed, and imposed a preliminary showing of reasonableness where none was required, its judgment is reversed and this case is remanded to that court for further proceedings consistent with this opinion. . . .[12]

---

221. In a companion case, United States v. Mara, 410 U.S. 19 (1973) (6–3), the Court extended the same reasoning used in *Dionisio* to a subpoena to furnish handwriting exemplars to a grand jury.

222. The appellant was a suspect in a bank robbery. The grand jury investigating the robbery subpoenaed him to appear in a lineup. When he failed to appear, he was found in contempt, and he appealed. The court of appeals, rejecting the appellant's effort to distinguish *Dionisio* and *Mara*, above, affirmed.

> Appellant argues . . . that there is a crucial difference between a lineup and the identification procedures at issue in *Dionisio* and *Mara*: a lineup is inherently a less reliable identification procedure than the providing of voice and handwriting exemplars. . . . But as neither the inconvenience of responding to the grand jury's directive nor the forced display of physical characteristics such as one's voice or face make the challenged order a "seizure" within the meaning of the fourth amendment, considerations such as the reliability of the identification procedure are largely irrelevant to whether the grand jury directive to appear violates the fourth amendment. It is simply immaterial to the constitutional analysis whether a lineup is less "scientific" than finger-

[12] Justice Brennan wrote an opinion concurring in part and dissenting in part. Justice Douglas and Justice Marshall wrote dissenting opinions.

> printing, voice and handwriting comparison, or other identification procedures. As the Court recognized in *Dionisio*, a grand jury's investigatory powers include the right to "act on tips, rumors, evidence offered by the prosecutor, or their own personal knowledge." 410 U.S. at 15. . . . And a lineup is a well-accepted investigatory method, far preferable to individual confrontations. Indeed, it is by now well established that, whenever possible, witnesses should view suspects in lineups rather than individually to avoid the misidentification that can result from a lone confrontation. . . . To deny the grand jury the power to require a suspect's participation in a lineup is therefore to place the Government in a dilemma: if it is to let the witness view the suspect at all, it must do so under circumstances which courts have repeatedly criticized as unduly suggestive. A lineup does not pose the same potential for unfairness, particularly where the suspect's counsel is present. . . . We note that the Government wisely intends to allow appellant's counsel to be present, and hence we are not confronted with whether it is required to do so by the sixth amendment. . . . We expressly refrain from deciding that forcing a suspect to appear in a lineup without tendering the right to counsel would be constitutional.
>
> The power to compel appearance at a lineup is, it is true, subject to possible oppressive misuse. A fingerprint or handwriting or voice exemplar need only be obtained once. There is no occasion, as with a lineup, to require the witness to return and give his evidence in other investigations. . . . One can imagine the temptation to call certain individuals with known criminal proclivities to appear repeatedly in lineups, and the absence of a standard of probable cause or reasonable suspicion adds to the potential for abuse. . . . But many investigatory powers of the grand jury are subject to abuse, and the remedy for this problem, if it should occur, is pointed out in *Dionisio*. . . . The oppressive use of orders to appear in lineups can and should be dealt with by refusal of a court to enforce the order. Here there is no suggestion of oppressive use and no need to interfere with the grand jury's power to issue the order. We conclude, therefore, that subject to the district court's continuing power and duty to prevent misuse, the grand jury is empowered to require a suspect to appear at a lineup.

In re Melvin, 550 F.2d 674, 676–77 (1st Cir.1977).

See United States v. Ferri, 778 F.2d 985 (3d Cir.1985) (grand jury subpoena to appear for ink printing of feet and shoes upheld); In re Grand Jury Proceedings (Mills), 686 F.2d 135 (3d Cir.1982) (grand jury order to furnish samples of facial and scalp hair upheld); In re Pantojas, 639 F.2d 822 (1st Cir.1980) (grand jury order to appear in lineup upheld). See also United States v. Smith, 687 F.2d 147 (6th Cir.1982) ("voluntary" production of handwriting exemplar in lieu of grand jury appearance upheld).

223. Davis v. Mississippi, 394 U.S. 721 (1969). Over a period of about ten days, the police took the defendant and at least 23 other youths to police headquarters and fingerprinted them in connection with investigation of a rape that had just occurred. The defendant did not voluntarily submit to the fingerprinting nor did the police have probable cause for his arrest at that time. Later, still without the defendant's consent and without probable cause for his arrest, the police fingerprinted him again and used the fingerprints against him at his trial for rape. Holding that none of the fingerprints had been validly obtained, the Court reversed the defendant's conviction.

The Court said:

> Detentions for the sole purpose of obtaining fingerprints are no less subject to the constraints of the Fourth Amendment. It is arguable, however, that because of the unique nature of the fingerprinting process, such detentions might, under narrowly defined circumstances, be found to comply with the Fourth Amendment even though there is no probable cause in the traditional sense. . . . Detention for fingerprinting may constitute a much less serious intrusion upon personal security than other types of police searches and detentions. Fingerprinting involves none of the probing into an individual's private life and thoughts which marks an interrogation or search. Nor can fingerprint detention be employed repeatedly to harass any individual, since the police need only one set of each person's prints. Furthermore, fingerprinting is an inherently more reliable and effective crime-solving tool than eyewitness identifications or confessions and is not subject to such abuses as the improper line-up and the "third degree." Finally, because there is no danger of destruction of fingerprints, the limited detention need not come unexpectedly or at an inconvenient time. For this same reason, the general requirement that the authorization of a judicial officer be obtained in advance of detention would seem not to admit of any exception in the fingerprinting context.
>
> We have no occasion in this case, however, to determine whether the requirements of the Fourth Amendment could be met by narrowly circumscribed procedures for obtaining, during the course of a criminal investigation, the fingerprints of individuals for whom there is no probable cause to arrest. For it is clear that no attempt was made here to employ procedures which might comply with the requirements of the Fourth Amendment. . . .

Id. at 727–28.

Hayes v. Florida

470 U.S. 811, 105 S.Ct. 1643, 84 L.Ed.2d 705 (1985)

■ JUSTICE WHITE delivered the opinion of the Court.

The issue before us in this case is whether the Fourth Amendment to the Constitution of the United States, applicable to the States by virtue of the Fourteenth Amendment, was properly applied by the District Court of Appeal of Florida, Second District, to allow police to transport a suspect to the station house for fingerprinting, without his consent and without probable cause or prior judicial authorization.

A series of burglary-rapes occurred in Punta Gorda, Florida, in 1980. Police found latent fingerprints on the doorknob of the bedroom of one of the victims, fingerprints they believed belonged to the assailant. The police also found a herringbone pattern tennis shoe print near the victim's front porch. Although they had little specific information to tie petitioner Hayes to the crime, after police interviewed him along with 30 to 40 other men who generally fit the description of the assailant, the investigators came to consider petitioner a principal suspect. They decided to visit petitioner's home to obtain his fingerprints or, if he was uncooperative, to arrest him. They did not seek a warrant authorizing this procedure.

Arriving at petitioner's house, the officers spoke to petitioner on his front porch. When he expressed reluctance voluntarily to accompany them to the station for fingerprinting, one of the investigators explained that they would therefore arrest him. Petitioner, in the words of the investigator, then "blurted out" that he would rather go with the officers to the station than be arrested. App. 20. While the officers were on the front porch, they also seized a pair of herringbone pattern tennis shoes in plain view.

Petitioner was then taken to the station house, where he was fingerprinted. When police determined that his prints matched those left at the scene of the crime, petitioner was placed under formal arrest. Before trial, petitioner moved to suppress the fingerprint evidence, claiming it was the fruit of an illegal detention. The trial court denied the motion and admitted the evidence without expressing a reason. Petitioner was convicted of the burglary and sexual battery committed at the scene where the latent fingerprints were found.

. . .

We agree with petitioner that Davis v. Mississippi, 394 U.S. 721 (1969), requires reversal of the judgment below. . . .

Here, as in *Davis*, there was no probable cause to arrest, no consent to the journey to the police station and no judicial authorization for such a detention for fingerprinting purposes. Unless later cases have undermined *Davis* or we now disavow that decision, the judgment below must be reversed.

None of our later cases have undercut the holding in *Davis* that transportation to and investigative detention at the station house without probable cause or judicial authorization together violate the Fourth Amendment. . . .

Nor are we inclined to forswear *Davis*. There is no doubt that at some point in the investigative process, police procedures can qualitatively and quantitatively be so intrusive with respect to a suspect's freedom of movement and privacy interests as to trigger the full protection of the Fourth and Fourteenth Amendments. . . . And our view continues to be that the line is crossed when the police, without probable cause or a warrant, forcibly remove a person from his home or other place in which he is entitled to be and transport him to the police station, where he is detained, although briefly, for investigative purposes. We adhere to the view that such seizures, at least where not under judicial supervision, are sufficiently like arrests to invoke the traditional rule that arrests may constitutionally be made only on probable cause.

None of the foregoing implies that a brief detention in the field for the purpose of fingerprinting, where there is only reasonable suspicion not amounting to probable cause, is necessarily impermissible under the Fourth Amendment. . . . There is . . . support in our cases for the view that the Fourth Amendment would permit seizures for the purpose of fingerprinting, if there is reasonable suspicion that the suspect has committed a criminal act, if there is a reasonable basis for believing that fingerprinting will establish or negate the suspect's connection with that crime, and if the procedure is carried out with dispatch. . . . Of course, neither reasonable suspicion nor probable cause would suffice to permit the officers to make a warrantless entry into a person's house for the purpose of obtaining fingerprint identification. . . .

We also do not abandon the suggestion in *Davis* . . . that under circumscribed procedures, the Fourth Amendment might permit the judiciary to authorize the seizure of a person on less than probable cause and his removal to the police station for the purpose of fingerprinting. We do not, of course, have such a case before us. We do note, however, that some States, in reliance on the suggestion in *Davis*, have enacted procedures for judicially authorized seizures for the purpose of fingerprinting. The state courts are not in accord on the validity of these efforts to insulate investigative seizures from Fourth Amendment invalidation. . . .

As we have said, absent probable cause and a warrant, Davis v. Mississippi, 394 U.S. 721 (1969), requires the reversal of the judgment of the Florida District Court of Appeal.

. . .[13]

---

224. If the police believe that they have fingerprints of an unidentified person who committed a crime, should they be allowed to summon a group of persons who are suspects to headquarters for fingerprinting (or require them to submit to fingerprinting at their homes)? What problems does that raise different from the problems raised by a requirement that all persons, say in their eighth year of school, be fingerprinted for a permanent record? If the police should have such authority, what "narrowly circumscribed procedures" should they have to follow? Could comparable procedures be developed for the application of lineups or other identification techniques to groups of suspects? Or personal searches? Or searches of

[13] Justice Brennan wrote an opinion concurring in the judgment, which Justice Marshall joined. Justice Blackmun concurred in the judgment.

premises in a defined area? If not, why not? If so, what procedures would you require? See generally Beightol v. Kunowski, 486 F.2d 293 (3d Cir. 1973) (police have no authority to arrest person for purpose of obtaining fingerprints and photograph).

In Thom v. New York Stock Exchange, 306 F.Supp. 1002 (S.D.N.Y. 1969), aff'd sub nom. Miller v. New York Stock Exchange, 425 F.2d 1074 (2d Cir.1970), the court upheld the constitutionality of a New York statute requiring employees of member firms of national security exchanges and others to be fingerprinted as a condition of employment. The statute was an effort to prevent thefts of securities. And in Biehunik v. Felicetta, 441 F.2d 228 (2d Cir.1971), the court of appeals held that a police commissioner could constitutionally order 62 policemen, on pain of discharge, to appear in a lineup for possible identification by civilians who claimed that they had been assaulted by policemen.

225. In State v. Hall, 461 A.2d 1155 (N.J.1983), the court upheld the authority of the state trial court of general jurisdiction to issue an order compelling a person suspected of participating in a robbery, but not arrested or charged, to appear in a lineup. The court said:

> We accordingly conclude that an evidential finding of probable cause to believe that a particular individual has committed a crime is not an absolute prerequisite for judicial authorization of an investigatory detention. We are satisfied that a court has jurisdiction to authorize an investigatory detention under the following limited circumstances. The court's authorization of an investigatory detention must, first, be based upon sufficient evidence to demonstrate that a particular crime has occurred, that the crime is unsolved and that it is under active investigation. Second, the police must demonstrate a reasonable and well-grounded basis to believe that the individual sought as the subject of the investigative detention may have committed the crime under investigation. Additionally, it must be shown that the results of the detention will significantly advance the criminal investigation and will serve to determine whether or not the suspect probably committed the crime. Further, it must also appear that these investigative results cannot otherwise practicably be obtained.
>
> In addition to these evidential standards that serve to limit the circumstances under which investigatory detentions may be judicially authorized without probable cause, we recognize that appropriate procedures must be fashioned to assure that the intrusiveness of the detention is properly circumscribed. Investigatory detentions can involve different kinds of evidence-gathering procedures with differing degrees of intrusiveness. The Supreme Court in *Davis* [v. Mississippi, 394 U.S. 721 (1969)] emphasized that a detention to permit fingerprinting constituted a limited intrusion into a person's liberty and privacy because fingerprinting did not "prob[e] into an individual's private life and thoughts." A detention for fingerprinting was also regarded as essentially a reliable, simple and expeditious proceeding that could be conducted fairly and without palpable abuse. *Davis* at

727. . . . Accordingly, we conclude that those identification procedures that are comparable to fingerprinting will be sustainable upon a showing of less than traditional probable cause.

In this case, we think that a lineup for the purpose of securing an identification of the criminal suspect can be conducted in conformity with such standards and likened to the fingerprinting process. The lineup involves no creative or unusual act on the part of the suspect; it involves only a display of evidence that is otherwise publicly visible. In this regard the lineup does not "prob[e] into an individual's private life and thoughts." *Davis*, supra, 394 U.S. at 727. . . . Furthermore, the lineup, when properly conducted, can protect against abuse and insure fairness. . . . When conducted properly and fairly the procedure can furnish reliable evidence and can often be an effective crime-solving tool. . . . Finally, the lineup procedure can be accomplished at a convenient time and need not entail a restraint upon the suspect for an unduly long period of time.

In order to safeguard constitutional interests and secure the overall reasonableness of such nontestimonial identification procedures, the conduct of investigatory detentions must be carefully circumscribed by other procedural protections. . . . Indeed, the Supreme Court in *Davis* observed that "abuses" can occur in an investigatory detention, mentioning specifically an "improper line-up." Davis v. Mississippi, supra, 394 U.S. at 727. . . . As a result, in order to guarantee that the detention and accompanying intrusion is not improper or abusive, it must be accomplished in a fashion designed to produce the least amount of harassment of, interference with, or prejudice to the suspect. . . . Further, in most cases, the suspect must be given sufficient notice of the proposed detention. . . . The suspect should also be given the opportunity to arrange a convenient time for the detention . . . and the opportunity to have counsel present during the detention. . . . In addition, unusual or untoward consequences to the suspect resulting from the detention should be avoided or minimized.

We think that these procedural safeguards protect citizens' constitutional rights. We are also satisfied that the evidential standard that we adopt . . . allows police to investigate serious offenses without unduly interfering with the liberty or privacy of a person who has not been charged with any crime. In our view, these procedural requirements, in conjunction with the evidential standard, represent a proper balancing of the public interest in effective law enforcement and the liberty and privacy interests of the individual under the federal and State constitutions.

. . .

Applying these judicially formulated guidelines to this case, we believe that the circumstances surrounding defendant's detention and lineup clearly and adequately satisfied his constitutional right to be free from unreasonable searches and seizures. Defendant was linked to the commission of serious offenses for which he was ultimately convicted. According to the affidavit in support of the motion to compel the lineup, defendant was identified by an informant as the robber depicted in the composite sketch that was prepared by the police with the assistance of the victims of the crime. Also, one eyewitness of the crime had already made an equivocal identification of defendant's photograph. Based on this substantial information, the prosecutor moved for a detention order. Defendant, accompanied by counsel, was permitted to contest the motion. The trial judge found that Detective Booket's affidavit established an articulable, well-founded belief that defendant was involved in the commission of the particular offenses. Thus, upon notice to the defendant and with provisions for him to be heard, the detention order was authorized by a neutral and detached judge.

Further, in this case, the degree of intrusion into the individual's interests was certainly reasonable when measured against the degree of proof presented and the government interest involved. The detention was brief. It was conducted upon ample notice and at a convenient time. Defendant was not required to perform any creative act or give evidence not otherwise readily visible. Significantly, no interrogation occurred. Unquestionably, defendant's lineup detention, safeguarded by adequate restrictions, was beyond legal reproach.

461 A.2d at 1160–63.

See In re Fingerprinting of M.B., 309 A.2d 3 (N.J.Super.Ct.1973) (order for taking of fingerprints of boys in eighth grade class, as part of homicide investigation, upheld).

CHAPTER 6

QUESTIONING

Spano v. New York

360 U.S. 315, 79 S.Ct. 1202, 3 L.Ed.2d 1265 (1959)

■ MR. CHIEF JUSTICE WARREN delivered the opinion of the Court.

This is another in the long line of cases presenting the question whether a confession was properly admitted into evidence under the Fourteenth Amendment. As in all such cases, we are forced to resolve a conflict between two fundamental interests of society; its interest in prompt and efficient law enforcement, and its interest in preventing the rights of its individual members from being abridged by unconstitutional methods of law enforcement. . . .

The State's evidence reveals the following: Petitioner Vincent Joseph Spano is a derivative citizen of this country, having been born in Messina, Italy. He was 25 years old at the time of the shooting in question and had graduated from junior high school. He had a record of regular employment. The shooting took place on January 22, 1957.

On that day, petitioner was drinking in a bar. The decedent, a former professional boxer weighing almost 200 pounds who had fought in Madison Square Garden, took some of petitioner's money from the bar. Petitioner followed him out of the bar to recover it. A fight ensued, with the decedent knocking petitioner down and then kicking him in the head three or four times. Shock from the force of these blows caused petitioner to vomit. After the bartender applied some ice to his head, petitioner left the bar, walked to his apartment, secured a gun, and walked eight or nine blocks to a candy store where the decedent was frequently to be found. He entered the store in which decedent, three friends of decedent, at least two of whom were ex-convicts, and a boy who was supervising the store were present. He fired five shots, two of which entered the decedent's body, causing his death. The boy was the only eyewitness; the three friends of decedent did not see the person who fired the shot. Petitioner then disappeared for the next week or so.

On February 1, 1957, the Bronx County Grand Jury returned an indictment for first-degree murder against petitioner. Accordingly, a bench warrant was issued for his arrest, commanding that he be forthwith brought before the court to answer the indictment, or, if the court had adjourned for the term, that he be delivered into the custody of the Sheriff of Bronx County. . . .

On February 3, 1957, petitioner called one Gaspar Bruno, a close friend of 8 or 10 years' standing who had attended school with him. Bruno was a fledgling police officer, having at that time not yet finished attending police academy. According to Bruno's testimony, petitioner told him "that he took a terrific beating, that the deceased hurt him real bad and he dropped him a couple of times and he was dazed; he didn't know what he was doing and that he went and shot at him." Petitioner told Bruno that he intended to get a lawyer and give himself up. Bruno relayed this information to his superiors.

The following day, February 4, at 7:10 p.m., petitioner, accompanied by counsel, surrendered himself to the authorities in front of the Bronx County Building, where both the office of the Assistant District Attorney who ultimately prosecuted his case and the courtroom in which he was ultimately tried were located. His attorney had cautioned him to answer no questions, and left him in the custody of the officers. He was promptly taken to the office of the Assistant District Attorney and at 7:15 p.m. the questioning began, being conducted by Assistant District Attorney Goldsmith, Lt. Gannon, Detectives Farrell, Lehrer and Motta, and Sgt. Clarke. The record reveals that the questioning was both persistent and continuous. Petitioner, in accordance with his attorney's instructions, steadfastly refused to answer. Detective Motta testified: "He refused to talk to me." "He just looked up to the ceiling and refused to talk to me." Detective Farrell testified:

> Q. And you started to interrogate him?
>
> A. That is right.
>
> . . .
>
> Q. What did he say?
>
> A. He said "you would have to see my attorney. I tell you nothing but my name."
>
> . . .
>
> Q. Did you continue to examine him?
>
> A. Verbally, yes, sir.

He asked one officer, Detective Ciccone, if he could speak to his attorney, but that request was denied. Detective Ciccone testified that he could not find the attorney's name in the telephone book. He was given two sandwiches, coffee and cake at 11 p.m.

At 12:15 a.m. on the morning of February 5, after five hours of questioning in which it became evident that petitioner was following his attorney's instructions, on the Assistant District Attorney's orders petitioner was transferred to the 46th Squad, Ryer Avenue Police Station. The Assistant District Attorney also went to the police station and to some extent continued to participate in the interrogation. Petitioner arrived at 12:30 and questioning was resumed at 12:40. The character of the questioning is revealed by the testimony of Detective Farrell:

Q. Who did you leave him in the room with?

A. With Detective Lehrer and Sergeant Clarke came in and Mr. Goldsmith came in or Inspector Halk came in. It was back and forth. People just came in, spoke a few words to the defendant or they listened a few minutes and they left.

But petitioner persisted in his refusal to answer, and again requested permission to see his attorney, this time from Detective Lehrer. His request was again denied.

It was then that those in charge of the investigation decided that petitioner's close friend, Bruno, could be of use. He had been called out on the case around 10 or 11 p.m., although he was not connected with the 46th Squad or Precinct in any way. Although, in fact, his job was in no way threatened, Bruno was told to tell petitioner that petitioner's telephone call had gotten him "in a lot of trouble," and that he should seek to extract sympathy from petitioner for Bruno's pregnant wife and three children. Bruno developed this theme with petitioner without success, and petitioner, also without success, again sought to see his attorney, a request which Bruno relayed unavailingly to his superiors. After this first session with petitioner, Bruno was again directed by Lt. Gannon to play on petitioner's sympathies, but again no confession was forthcoming. But the Lieutenant a third time ordered Bruno falsely to importune his friend to confess, but again petitioner clung to his attorney's advice. Inevitably, in the fourth such session directed by the Lieutenant, lasting a full hour, petitioner succumbed to his friend's prevarications and agreed to make a statement. Accordingly at 3:25 a.m. the Assistant District Attorney, a stenographer, and several other law enforcement officials entered the room where petitioner was being questioned, and took his statement in question and answer form with the Assistant District Attorney asking the questions. The statement was completed at 4:05 a.m.

But this was not the end. At 4:30 a.m. three detectives took petitioner to Police Headquarters in Manhattan. On the way they attempted to find the bridge from which petitioner said he had thrown the murder weapon. They crossed the Triborough Bridge into Manhattan, arriving at Police Headquarters at 5 a.m., and left Manhattan for the Bronx at 5:40 a.m. via the Willis Avenue Bridge. When petitioner recognized neither bridge as the one from which he had thrown the weapon, they reentered Manhattan via the Third Avenue Bridge, which petitioner stated was the right one, and then returned to the Bronx well after 6 a.m. During that trip the officers also elicited a statement from petitioner that the deceased was always "on [his] back," "always pushing" him and that he was "not sorry" he had shot the deceased. All three detectives testified to that statement at the trial.

Court opened at 10 a.m. that morning, and petitioner was arraigned at 10:15.

At the trial, the confession was introduced in evidence over appropriate objections. The jury was instructed that it could rely on it only if it was found to be voluntary. The jury returned a guilty verdict and petitioner was sentenced to death. The New York Court of Appeals affirmed the conviction over three dissents . . . and we granted certiorari to resolve the serious problem presented under the Fourteenth Amendment. . . .

Petitioner's first contention is that his absolute right to counsel in a capital case . . . became operative on the return of an indictment against him, for at that time he was in every sense a defendant in a criminal case, the grand jury having found sufficient cause to believe that he had committed the crime. He argues accordingly that following indictment no confession obtained in the absence of counsel can be used without violating the Fourteenth Amendment. . . . We find it unnecessary to reach that contention, for we find use of the confession obtained here inconsistent with the Fourteenth Amendment under traditional principles.

The abhorrence of society to the use of involuntary confessions does not turn alone on their inherent untrustworthiness. It also turns on the deep-rooted feeling that the police must obey the law while enforcing the law; that in the end life and liberty can be as much endangered from illegal methods used to convict those thought to be criminals as from the actual criminals themselves. Accordingly, the actions of police in obtaining confessions have come under scrutiny in a long series of cases. Those cases suggest that in recent years law enforcement officials have become increasingly aware of the burden which they share, along with our courts, in protecting fundamental rights of our citizenry, including that portion of our citizenry suspected of crime. The facts of no case recently in this Court have quite approached the brutal beatings in Brown v. Mississippi, 297 U.S. 278 (1936) or the 36 consecutive hours of questioning present in Ashcraft v. Tennessee, 322 U.S. 143 (1944). But as law enforcement officers become more responsible, and the methods used to extract confessions more sophisticated, our duty to enforce federal constitutional protections does not cease. It only becomes more difficult because of the more delicate judgments to be made. Our judgment here is that, on all the facts, this conviction cannot stand.

Petitioner was a foreign-born young man of 25 with no past history of law violation or of subjection to official interrogation, at least insofar as the record shows. He had progressed only one-half year into high school and the record indicates that he had a history of emotional instability. He did not make a narrative statement, but was subject to the leading questions of a skillful prosecutor in a question and answer confession. He was subjected to questioning not by a few men, but by many. They included Assistant District Attorney Goldsmith, one Hyland of the District Attorney's Office, Deputy Inspector Halks, Lieutenant Gannon, Detective Ciccone, Detective Motta, Detective Lehrer, Detective Marshal, Detective Farrell, Detective Leira, Detective Murphy, Detective Murtha, Sergeant Clarke, Patrolman Bruno and Stenographer Baldwin. All played some part, and the effect of such massive official interrogation must have been felt. Petitioner was questioned for virtually eight straight hours before he confessed, with his only respite being a transfer to an arena presumably considered more appropriate by the police for the task at hand. Nor was the questioning conducted during normal business hours, but began in early evening, continued into the night, and did not bear fruition until the not-too-early morning. The drama was not played out, with the final admissions obtained, until almost sunrise. In such circumstances slowly mounting fatigue does, and is calculated to, play its part. The questioners persisted in the face of his repeated refusals to answer on the advice of his attorney, and they ignored his reasonable requests to contact the local attorney whom he had already retained and who had personally delivered him into the custody of these officers in obedience to the bench warrant.

The use of Bruno, characterized in this Court by counsel for the State as a "childhood friend" of petitioner's, is another factor which deserves mention in the totality of the situation. Bruno's was the one face visible to petitioner in which he could put some trust. There was a bond of friendship between them going back a decade into adolescence. It was with this material that the officers felt that they could overcome petitioner's will. They instructed Bruno falsely to state that petitioner's telephone call had gotten him into trouble, that his job was in jeopardy, and that loss of his job would be disastrous to his three children, his wife and his unborn child. And Bruno played this part of a worried father, harried by his superiors, in not one but four different acts, the final one lasting an hour. . . . Petitioner was apparently unaware of John Gay's famous couplet:

An open foe may prove a curse,
But a pretended friend is worse,

and he yielded to his false friend's entreaties.

We conclude that petitioner's will was overborne by official pressure, fatigue and sympathy falsely aroused, after considering all the facts in their post-indictment setting. Here a grand jury had already found sufficient cause to require petitioner to face trial on a charge of first-degree murder, and the police had an eyewitness to the shooting. The police were not therefore merely trying to solve a crime, or even to absolve a suspect. . . . They were rather concerned primarily with securing a statement from defendant on which they could convict him. The undeviating intent of the officers to extract a confession from petitioner is therefore patent. When such an intent is shown, this Court has held that the confession obtained must be examined with the most careful scrutiny, and has reversed a conviction on facts less compelling than these. . . . Accordingly, we hold that petitioner's conviction cannot stand under the Fourteenth Amendment.

. . .[1]

---

[1] Justice Douglas wrote a concurring opinion which Justice Black and Justice Brennan joined. Justice Stewart wrote a concurring opinion which Justice Douglas and Justice Brennan joined. Both opinions indicated that the concurring Justices believed that the right to counsel had attached after Spano was indicted.

226. Declaring that a defendant's disturbed psychiatric condition at the time a confession is made is not by itself a basis for exclusion of the confession on constitutional grounds, the Court held in Colorado v. Connelly, 479 U.S. 157, 167 (1986) (7–2), that "coercive police activity is a necessary predicate to the finding that a confession is not 'voluntary' within the meaning of the Due Process Clause of the Fourteenth Amendment."

Connelly was rejected in State v. Bowe, 881 P.2d 538 (Haw.1994). Relying on the state constitution's due process clause and privilege against self-incrimination, the court said: "[A]n individual's capacity to make a rational and free choice between confessing and remaining silent may be overborne as much by the coercive conduct of a private individual as by the coercive conduct of the police. Accordingly, we hold that admitting coerced confessions, regardless of the source of the coercion, is fundamentally unfair." Id. at 546.

In Mincey v. Arizona, 437 U.S. 385 (1978) (8–1), the Court concluded that a defendant's will was overborne by questioning while he was seriously wounded and in the intensive care unit of a hospital, and that his statements were therefore involuntary and inadmissible. See also Woods v. Clusen, 794 F.2d 293 (7th Cir.1986) (totality of circumstances, including defendant's youth and lack of previous contact with the criminal justice system, the intimidating circumstances of his arrest and questioning, and deliberate deception by the police to suggest that they already had incriminating evidence violated defendant's privilege against compulsory self-incrimination); United States v. Murphy, 763 F.2d 202 (6th Cir.1985) (confession made while defendant was being attacked by police dog was involuntary, but admission of the confession was harmless error).

In United States v. Braxton, 112 F.3d 777 (4th Cir.1997), the defendant, an adult, was interviewed at his mother's house by police officers who suspected him of illegally purchasing firearms. He was not in custody. In the course of the interview, an officer told the defendant that they "needed" to talk to him and that he could face five years in prison because he was not "coming clean"; they did not inform him of the consequences of a confession, in particular that he would subject himself to prosecution. Rejecting the defendant's contention that in the circumstances, the confession was involuntary, the court observed that "the mere existence of threats, violence, implied promises, improper influence, or other coercive police activity . . . does not automatically render a confession involuntary." Id. at 780. To hold the confession involuntary on the basis of the officers' statements, the court said, would impose on officers an obligation to give something like *Miranda* warnings even in the absence of custodial interrogation.

Whether or not a confession is voluntary is ultimately a question of law and requires an independent determination by the federal court on federal collateral attack of a state conviction. Miller v. Fenton, 474 U.S. 104 (1985) (8–1).

227. In State v. Patton, 826 A.2d 783 (N.J.Super.2003), the police arrested the defendant for murder. While he was detained at headquarters, the police fabricated an audiotape that purported to be an interview with an eyewitness to the murder, who identified the defendant. Having given the defendant *Miranda* warnings, the police played the audiotape for him, after which he confessed. At trial, the prosecutor introduced the fabricated audiotape to show that the defendant's confession was voluntary. Observing that the interview on the audiotape contained a scenario that conformed to the prosecution's theory of the case, the court declared a "bright-line" rule that "the use of police-fabricated evidence to induce a confession that is then used at trial to support the voluntariness of a confession is per se a violation of due process." Id. at 805.

Massiah v. United States

377 U.S. 201, 84 S.Ct. 1199, 12 L.Ed.2d 246 (1964)

■ MR. JUSTICE STEWART delivered the opinion of the Court.

The petitioner was indicted for violating the federal narcotics laws. He retained a lawyer, pleaded not guilty, and was released on bail. While he was free on bail a federal agent succeeded by surreptitious means in listening to incriminating statements made by him. Evidence of these statements was introduced against the petitioner at his trial over his objection. He was convicted, and the Court of Appeals affirmed. We granted certiorari to consider whether, under the circumstances here presented, the prosecution's use at the trial of evidence of the petitioner's own incriminating statements deprived him of any right secured to him under the Federal Constitution. . . .

The petitioner, a merchant seaman, was in 1958 a member of the crew of the S.S. *Santa Maria*. In April of that year federal customs officials in New York received information that he was going to transport a quantity of narcotics aboard that ship from South America to the United States. As a result of this and other information, the agents searched the *Santa Maria* upon its arrival in New York and found in the afterpeak of the vessel five packages containing about three and a half pounds of cocaine. They also learned of circumstances, not here relevant, tending to connect the petitioner with the cocaine. He was arrested, promptly arraigned, and subsequently indicted for possession of narcotics aboard a United States vessel. In July a superseding indictment was returned, charging the petitioner and a man named Colson with the same substantive offense, and in separate counts charging the petitioner, Colson, and others with having conspired to possess narcotics aboard a United States vessel, and to import, conceal, and facilitate the sale of narcotics. The petitioner, who had retained a lawyer, pleaded not guilty and was released on bail, along with Colson.

A few days later, and quite without the petitioner's knowledge, Colson decided to cooperate with the government agents in their continuing investigation of the narcotics activities in which the petitioner, Colson, and others had allegedly been engaged. Colson permitted an agent named Murphy to install a Schmidt radio transmitter under the front seat of Colson's automobile, by means of which Murphy, equipped with an appropriate receiving device, could overhear from some distance away conversations carried on in Colson's car.

On the evening of November 19, 1959, Colson and the petitioner held a lengthy conversation while sitting in Colson's automobile, parked on a New York street. By prearrangement with Colson, and totally unbeknown to the petitioner, the agent Murphy sat in a car parked out of sight down the street and listened over the radio to the entire conversation. The petitioner made several incriminating statements during the course of this conversation. At the petitioner's trial these incriminating statements were brought before the jury through Murphy's testimony, despite the insistent objection of defense counsel. The jury convicted the petitioner of several related narcotics offenses, and the convictions were affirmed by the Court of Appeals.

The petitioner argues that it was an error of constitutional dimensions to permit the agent Murphy at the trial to testify to the petitioner's incriminating statements which Murphy had overheard under the circumstances disclosed by this record. This argument is based upon two distinct and independent grounds. First, we are told that Murphy's use of the radio equipment violated the petitioner's rights under the Fourth Amendment, and, consequently, that all evidence which Murphy thereby obtained was . . . inadmissible against the petitioner at the trial. Secondly, it is said that the petitioner's Fifth and Sixth Amendment rights were violated by the use in evidence against him of incriminating statements which government agents had deliberately elicited from him after he had been indicted and in the absence of his retained counsel. Because of the way we dispose of the case, we do not reach the Fourth Amendment issue.

In Spano v. New York, 360 U.S. 315, the Court reversed a state criminal conviction because a confession had been wrongly admitted into evidence against the defendant at his trial. In that case the defendant had already been indicted for first-degree murder at the time he confessed. The Court held that the defendant's conviction could not stand under the Fourteenth Amendment. While the Court's opinion relied upon the totality of the circumstances under which the confession had been obtained, four concurring Justices pointed out that the Constitution required reversal of the conviction upon the sole and specific ground that the confession had been deliberately elicited by the police after the defendant had been indicted, and therefore at a time when he was clearly entitled to a lawyer's help. It was pointed out that under our system of justice the most elemental concepts of due process of law contemplate that an indictment be followed by a trial, "in an orderly courtroom, presided over by a judge, open to the public, and protected by all the procedural safeguards of the law."

360 U.S., at 327 (Stewart, J., concurring). It was said that a Constitution which guarantees a defendant the aid of counsel at such a trial could surely vouchsafe no less to an indicted defendant under interrogation by the police in a completely extrajudicial proceeding. Anything less, it was said, might deny a defendant "effective representation by counsel at the only stage when legal aid and advice would help him." 360 U.S., at 326 (Douglas, J., concurring).

. . .

This view no more than reflects a constitutional principle established as long ago as Powell v. Alabama, 287 U.S. 45, where the Court noted that ". . . during perhaps the most critical period of the proceedings . . . that is to say, from the time of their arraignment until the beginning of their trial, when consultation, thoroughgoing investigation and preparation [are] vitally important, the defendants . . . [are] as much entitled to such aid [of counsel] during that period as at the trial itself." Id., at 57. And since the *Spano* decision the same basic constitutional principle has been broadly reaffirmed by this Court. . . .

Here we deal not with a state court conviction, but with a federal case, where the specific guarantee of the Sixth Amendment directly applies. . . . We hold that the petitioner was denied the basic protections of that guarantee when there was used against him at his trial evidence of his own incriminating words, which federal agents had deliberately elicited from him after he had been indicted and in the absence of his counsel. It is true that in the *Spano* case the defendant was interrogated in a police station, while here the damaging testimony was elicited from the defendant without his knowledge while he was free on bail. But, as Judge Hays pointed out in his dissent in the Court of Appeals, "if such a rule is to have any efficacy it must apply to indirect and surreptitious interrogations as well as those conducted in the jailhouse. In this case, Massiah was more seriously imposed upon . . . because he did not even know that he was under interrogation by a government agent." 307 F.2d, at 72–73.

The Solicitor General, in his brief and oral argument, has strenuously contended that the federal law enforcement agents had the right, if not indeed the duty, to continue their investigation of the petitioner and his alleged criminal associates even though the petitioner had been indicted. He points out that the Government was continuing its investigation in order to uncover not only the source of narcotics found on the S.S. *Santa Maria*, but also their intended buyer. He says that the quantity of narcotics involved was such as to suggest that the petitioner was part of a large and well-organized ring, and indeed that the continuing investigation confirmed this suspicion, since it resulted in criminal charges against many defendants. Under these circumstances the Solicitor General concludes that the government agents were completely "justified in making use of Colson's cooperation by having Colson continue his normal associations and by surveilling them."

We may accept and, at least for present purposes, completely approve all that this argument implies, Fourth Amendment problems to one side.

We do not question that in this case, as in many cases, it was entirely proper to continue an investigation of the suspected criminal activities of the defendant and his alleged confederates, even though the defendant had already been indicted. All that we hold is that the defendant's own incriminating statements, obtained by federal agents under the circumstances here disclosed, could not constitutionally be used by the prosecution as evidence against *him* at his trial.

. . .[2]

---

228. The reach of the principle announced in *Massiah* was discussed in United States v. Henry, 447 U.S. 264 (1980) (6–3). There, the defendant had been indicted for armed robbery and was detained in jail pending trial. While in jail, he made incriminating statements to another inmate, who testified about the statements at the defendant's trial. The inmate had for some time previously been an informant for the government. Federal agents had instructed him to be alert for statements by the defendant but not to question him or initiate conversations.

The Court affirmed the ruling below that under *Massiah* the statements should not have been admitted. It said that the test is whether a government agent had "deliberately elicited" the incriminating statements within the meaning of *Massiah*. The Court said that three factors were important to its decision: (1) the inmate had been acting under instructions as a paid informant, (2) the inmate was, so far as the defendant knew, only another inmate and not a government agent, and (3) the defendant was under indictment and in custody when the conversation occurred. "By intentionally creating a situation likely to induce Henry to make incriminating statements without the assistance of counsel, the government violated Henry's Sixth Amendment right to counsel." Id. at 274.

Massiah and *Henry* were applied in Maine v. Moulton, 474 U.S. 159 (1985) (5–4). The Court said that the rule of those cases applied even though the defendant had initiated the conversations with the government informer (a codefendant). "[K]nowing exploitation by the State of an opportunity to confront the accused without counsel being present is as much a breach of the State's obligation not to circumvent the right to the assistance of counsel as is the intentional creation of such an opportunity. Accordingly, the Sixth Amendment is violated when the State obtains incriminating statements by knowingly circumventing the accused's right to have counsel present in a confrontation between the accused and a state agent." Id. at 176. The Court said also, reaffirming its conclusion in *Massiah*, that evidence obtained by circumventing the defendant's right to counsel is not admissible even though the police are also investigating other crimes for which no charges are pending. Evidence would be admissible at a

[2] Justice White wrote a dissenting opinion which Justice Clark and Justice Harlan joined.

trial for the latter crimes if the defendant were subsequently prosecuted but not at the trial for charges as to which the right to counsel was violated.

Massiah was applied in United States v. Anderson, 523 F.2d 1192 (5th Cir.1975), in which several months after the defendant, a doctor, had been indicted in connection with illegal distribution of drugs and one week before trial, a government informer visited him in his office and represented herself as a patient. The court held that her testimony about the meeting with the defendant should not have been admitted. The court said that it did not question "the propriety of continuing governmental investigation of an indicted defendant's suspected criminal activities," but that here there was no such investigation. "Rather, it appears that a special single-shot confrontation was arranged . . . to obtain from the defendant evidence of specific intent to shore up the government's case, and that it was arranged at a time, place and under circumstances that defendant's attorney would not be present." Id. at 1196.

Henry was distinguished in Kuhlmann v. Wilson, 477 U.S. 436 (1986) (6–3). An informer was placed in the defendant's cell while he was awaiting trial. The informer was there for the express purpose of listening to and reporting to the police any statements bearing on the crimes with which the defendant was charged. The particular interest of the police was to identify the defendant's confederates. Without questioning the defendant or prompting him in any way, the informant heard and reported his incriminating statements. In those circumstances, the Court said, the principle of *Massiah* and *Henry* was not violated. "[T]he primary concern of the *Massiah* line of decisions is secret interrogation by investigatory techniques that are the equivalent of direct police interrogation. . . . [A] defendant does not make out a violation of . . . [the right to counsel] simply by showing that an informant, either through prior arrangement or voluntarily, reported his incriminating statements to the police. Rather, the defendant must demonstrate that the police and their informant took some action, beyond merely listening, that was designed deliberately to elicit incriminating remarks." Id. at 459.

Henry was distinguished also in United States v. Malik, 680 F.2d 1162 (7th Cir.1982), in which an inmate deliberately elicited incriminating statements from the defendant on his own initiative, in hope of gaining some advantage with respect to his own prosecution. See also United States v. Moore, 917 F.2d 215 (6th Cir.1990), in which the defendant, while incarcerated, made incriminating statements to his girlfriend in a telephone conversation, which the police overheard and taped with her permission.

See generally Illinois v. Perkins, 496 U.S. 292 (1990), p. 469 below.

229. The *Miranda* rules provide that before a person is subjected to custodial interrogation, he must be given advice designed to protect the privilege against compulsory self-incrimination. See Miranda v. Arizona, p. 417 below. In Brewer v. Williams, 430 U.S. 387 (1977) (5–4), without deciding whether the *Miranda* rules had been violated, the court held that statements that the defendant made to a police detective had been obtained in violation of his right to counsel. The defendant had surrendered to the police on a warrant for his arrest on a charge of abduction. He was suspected of murder. He was brought before a judge who advised him of his rights and was committed to jail. At several points, he consulted with a lawyer and was advised not to make any statements. Before police transported him from the city where he was arrested to the city where the crime occurred, his lawyer stated explicitly that there was to be no questioning during the trip. During the trip, without asking questions, a detective made comments intended to elicit incriminating statements from the defendant. The Court said that the right to counsel means "at least that a person is entitled to the help of a lawyer at or after the time that judicial proceedings have been initiated against him—'whether by way of formal charge, preliminary hearing, indictment, information or arraignment' " (citing, inter alia, Kirby v. Illinois, 406 U.S. 682, 689 (1972), p. 378 above). 430 U.S. at 398. It was unquestioned that judicial proceedings had been initiated against the defendant and that the purpose of the detective in the car was "to elicit information . . . just as surely as . . . if he had formally interrogated" the defendant. The facts were, therefore, "constitutionally indistinguishable" from those of *Massiah*. Id. at 399, 400. For the subsequent history of Brewer v. Williams, see Nix v. Williams, 467 U.S. 431 (1984), p. 147 note 77 above.

In Patterson v. Illinois, 487 U.S. 285, 300 (1988) (5–4), after the defendant had been indicted, he was questioned by police officers and made incriminating statements. The questioning was preceded by *Miranda* warnings. Over the objection that *Miranda* warnings are insufficient to sustain a waiver of the right to counsel (as contrasted with the privilege against compulsory self-incrimination) the Court held that the incriminating statements were admissible. The *Miranda* warnings, properly given, advise the defendant sufficiently to make his waiver of the right to counsel "knowing and intelligent." Id. at 300.

"[W]hatever warnings suffice for *Miranda*'s purposes will also be sufficient in the context of postindictment questioning. The State's decision to take an additional step and commence formal adversarial proceedings against the accused does not substantially increase the value of counsel to the accused at questioning, or expand the limited purpose that an attorney serves when the accused is questioned by authorities. With respect to this inquiry, we do not discern a substantial difference between the usefulness of a lawyer to a suspect during custodial interrogation, and his value to an accused at post-indictment questioning." Id. at 298–99.

In Fellers v. United States, 540 U.S. ___ (2004), after the defendant had been indicted, police officers went to his home and, in a discussion with him about his involvement in the crime, elicited incriminating statements. They then took him to a jail, where he was given *Miranda* warnings. He waived his rights under *Miranda* and repeated the incriminating statements. Finding that the discussion at his house violated his Sixth Amendment rights under *Massiah*, the Court remanded the case for consideration whether the violation of the Sixth Amendment required suppression of the statements at the jail, as its fruits. See Oregon v. Elstad, p. 431 below.

On the relationship between *Massiah* and *Miranda* generally, see Rhode Island v. Innis, 446 U.S. 291, 300 n.4 (1980), p. 432 below. See also Michigan v. Jackson, 475 U.S. 625 (1986), p. 443 below.

230. Brewer v. Williams, p. 408 note 229 above, indicates that *Massiah* is not limited to the period after the defendant has been formally accused but applies after the initiation of *judicial* proceedings. See Kirby v. Illinois, p. 378 above. *Massiah* is not applicable, however, following an arrest, even though the arrest is pursuant to a complaint and warrant. United States v. Pace, 833 F.2d 1307 (9th Cir.1987); United States v. Duvall, 537 F.2d 15 (2d Cir.1976).

In United States v. Brown, 551 F.2d 639 (5th Cir.1977), rev'd on other grounds, 569 F.2d 236 (1978), the defendant was arrested by state officials on charges involving an interstate theft. Five days later, while she was waiting (in state custody) in a corridor of the county courthouse for the public defender, she was approached by two agents of the FBI. The public defender had already been appointed to represent her; she was in the courthouse for a preliminary hearing, which was scheduled to start about a half hour after the time of her meeting with the FBI agents. They gave her *Miranda* warnings and one of them questioned her. She was not indicted for a federal crime for more than six months thereafter. At her trial, she claimed that her responses to the questions should be suppressed under *Massiah*. What result?

231. In Hoffa v. United States, 385 U.S. 293, 310 (1966), the Court observed that "there is no constitutional right to be arrested." Does *Massiah* have any application before a defendant is arrested? Once the police have a clear basis for an arrest and have decided eventually to arrest a person, are they required under *Massiah* not to try to elicit incriminating statements from him in the absence of counsel? See United States ex rel. Molinas v. Mancusi, 370 F.2d 601 (2d Cir.1967); cf. Garcia v. United States, 364 F.2d 306 (10th Cir.1966); Gascar v. United States, 356 F.2d 101 (9th Cir.1965). If not, can they delay arrest in order to utilize investigative techniques that would be barred by *Massiah* after arrest (or indictment)?

232. The right to counsel is "offense-specific." McNeil v. Wisconsin, 501 U.S. 171 (1991) (6–3). It attaches only to the offense with which the defendant is charged and other offenses not formally charged that would be considered the same offense under the *Blockberger* test for double jeopardy (see note 635, p. 1216 below). Texas v. Cobb, 532 U.S. 162 (2001) (5–4). It does not apply to distinct offenses, however closely related factually. Id. In United States v. Coker, 298 F.Supp.2d 184 (D.Mass.2003), the court relied on the theory of separate sovereignties, see note 638 p. 1218 below, to conclude that the right to counsel, which had attached to the defendant with respect to state arson charges, did not bar questioning by federal agents with respect to federal crimes involving the same incident.

Suppose that after the defendant has been indicted for one crime, the police, investigating his involvement in another crime, obtain evidence against him pertaining to the crime for which he has already been indicted. Is the evidence admissible at the trial for that crime? Compare United States v. Terzado-Madruga, 897 F.2d 1099 (11th Cir.1990), and Mealer v. Jones, 741 F.2d 1451 (2d Cir.1984), with United States v. Darwin, 757 F.2d 1193 (11th Cir.1985).

Massiah does not prohibit surreptitious investigation of defendant's efforts to obstruct justice after entry of a plea of guilty and before sentence. The results of such investigation can be revealed to the judge at sentencing. United States v. Pineda, 692 F.2d 284 (2d Cir.1982).

Why should police efforts to obtain information from an individual be more circumscribed after the police or the prosecutor have taken official steps to institute proceedings against him? Suppose the following situation: After making a general investigation of a homicide which included questioning *A* and *B* among others, the detectives of the homicide squad conclude that *A* is guilty of the crime. Having probable cause to believe that he is guilty, they arrest him. They believe that *B* is innocent of the crime but has information which will help to convict *A*. *A* (who has been brought before a magistrate and released on bail) is ignored by the police. *B* is subjected to polite but insistent questioning; in entire good faith, the police urge him to tell what he knows about the crime. *B* gives the police information which leads to *B*'s subsequent arrest and conviction for the crime. *A* is released.

Assuming that the guilt *as such* of the defendant is not the significant factor—he is after all equally guilty (or innocent) before and after he is arrested—what "happened" when *A* was arrested and brought before a magistrate that should deny the police access to him as a source of information? Does *Massiah* provide an answer? Is it sufficient to say that an indictment should be "followed by a trial" or that a defendant has the right to counsel after he has been indicted because that is a " 'critical period of the proceedings,' " pp. 405, 406 above?

Escobedo v. Illinois

378 U.S. 478, 84 S.Ct. 1758, 12 L.Ed.2d 977 (1964)

■ MR. JUSTICE GOLDBERG delivered the opinion of the Court.

The critical question in this case is whether, under the circumstances, the refusal by the police to honor petitioner's request to consult with his lawyer during the course of an interrogation constitutes a denial of "the Assistance of Counsel" in violation of the Sixth Amendment to the Constitution as "made obligatory upon the States by the Fourteenth Amendment," Gideon v. Wainwright, 372 U.S. 335, 342, and thereby renders inadmissible in a state criminal trial any incriminating statement elicited by the police during the interrogation.

On the night of January 19, 1960, petitioner's brother-in-law was fatally shot. In the early hours of the next morning, at 2:30 a.m., petitioner was arrested without a warrant and interrogated. Petitioner made no statement to the police and was released at 5 that afternoon pursuant to a state court writ of habeas corpus obtained by Mr. Warren Wolfson, a lawyer who had been retained by petitioner.

On January 30, Benedict DiGerlando, who was then in police custody and who was later indicted for the murder along with petitioner, told the police that petitioner had fired the fatal shots. Between 8 and 9 that evening, petitioner and his sister, the widow of the deceased, were arrested and taken to police headquarters. En route to the police station, the police "had handcuffed the defendant behind his back," and "one of the arresting officers told defendant that DiGerlando had named him as the one who shot" the deceased. Petitioner testified, without contradiction, that the "detectives said they had us pretty well, up pretty tight, and we might as well admit to this crime," and that he replied, "I am sorry but I would like to have advice from my lawyer." A police officer testified that although petitioner was not formally charged "he was in custody" and "couldn't walk out the door."

Shortly after petitioner reached police headquarters, his retained lawyer arrived. The lawyer described the ensuing events in the following terms:

> On that day I received a phone call [from "the mother of another defendant"] and pursuant to that phone call I went to the Detective Bureau at 11th and State. The first person I talked to was the Sergeant on duty at the Bureau Desk, Sergeant Pidgeon. I asked Sergeant Pidgeon for permission to speak to my client, Danny Escobedo. . . . Sergeant Pidgeon made a call to the Bureau lockup and informed me that the boy had been taken from the lockup to the Homicide Bureau. This was between 9:30 and 10:00 in the evening. Before I went anywhere, he called the Homicide Bureau and told them there was an attorney waiting to see Escobedo. He told me I could not see him. Then I went upstairs to the Homicide Bureau. There were several Homicide Detectives around and I talked to them. I identified myself as Escobedo's attorney and asked permission to see him. They said I could not. . . . The police officer told me to see Chief Flynn who was on duty. I identified myself to Chief Flynn and asked permission to see my client. He said I could not. . . . I think it was approximately 11:00 o'clock. He said I couldn't see him because they hadn't completed questioning. . . . [F]or a second or two I spotted him in an office in the Homicide Bureau. The door was open and I could see through the office. . . . I waved to him and he waved back and then the door was

closed, by one of the officers at Homicide.[3] There were four or five officers milling around the Homicide Detail that night. As to whether I talked to Captain Flynn any later that day, I waited around for another hour or two and went back again and renewed by [sic] request to see my client. He again told me I could not. . . . I filed an official complaint with Commissioner Phelan of the Chicago Police Department. I had a conversation with every police officer I could find. I was told at Homicide that I couldn't see him and I would have to get a writ of habeas corpus. I left the Homicide Bureau and from the Detective Bureau at 11th and State at approximately 1:00 A.M. [Sunday morning]. I had no opportunity to talk to my client that night. I quoted to Captain Flynn the Section of the Criminal Code which allows an attorney the right to see his client.

Petitioner testified that during the course of the interrogation he repeatedly asked to speak to his lawyer and that the police said that his lawyer "didn't want to see" him. The testimony of the police officers confirmed these accounts in substantial detail.

Notwithstanding repeated requests by each, petitioner and his retained lawyer were afforded no opportunity to consult during the course of the entire interrogation. At one point, as previously noted, petitioner and his attorney came into each other's view for a few moments but the attorney was quickly ushered away. Petitioner testified "that he heard a detective telling the attorney the latter would not be allowed to talk to [him] 'until they were done' " and that he heard the attorney being refused permission to remain in the adjoining room. A police officer testified that he had told the lawyer that he could not see petitioner until "we were through interrogating" him.

There is testimony by the police that during the interrogation, petitioner, a 22-year-old of Mexican extraction with no record of previous experience with the police, "was handcuffed" in a standing position and that he "was nervous, he had circles under his eyes and he was upset" and was "agitated" because "he had not slept well in over a week."

It is undisputed that during the course of the interrogation Officer Montejano, who "grew up" in petitioner's neighborhood, who knew his family, and who uses "Spanish language in [his] police work," conferred alone with petitioner "for about a quarter of an hour...." Petitioner testified that the officer said to him "in Spanish that my sister and I could go home if I pinned it on Benedict DiGerlando," that "he would see to it that we would go home and be held only as witnesses, if anything, if we had made a statement against DiGerlando . . . that we would be able to go home that night." Petitioner testified that he made the statement in issue because of this assurance. Officer Montejano denied offering any such assurance.

3. Petitioner testified that this ambiguous gesture "could have meant most anything," but that he "took it upon [his] own to think that [the lawyer was telling him] not to say anything," and that the lawyer "wanted to talk" to him.

A police officer testified that during the interrogation the following occurred:

> I informed him of what DiGerlando told me and when I did, he told me that DiGerlando was [lying] and I said, "Would you care to tell DiGerlando that?" and he said, "Yes, I will." So, I brought . . . Escobedo in and he confronted DiGerlando and he told him that he was lying and said, "I didn't shoot Manuel, you did it."

In this way, petitioner, for the first time, admitted to some knowledge of the crime. After that he made additional statements further implicating himself in the murder plot. At this point an Assistant State's Attorney, Theodore J. Cooper, was summoned "to take" a statement. Mr. Cooper, an experienced lawyer who was assigned to the Homicide Division to take "statements from some defendants and some prisoners that they had in custody," "took" petitioner's statement by asking carefully framed questions apparently designed to assure the admissibility into evidence of the resulting answers. Mr. Cooper testified that he did not advise petitioner of his constitutional rights, and it is undisputed that no one during the course of the interrogation so advised him.

Petitioner moved both before and during trial to suppress the incriminating statement, but the motions were denied. Petitioner was convicted of murder. . . .

. . .

In Massiah v. United States, 377 U.S. 201, this Court observed that "a Constitution which guarantees a defendant the aid of counsel at . . . trial could surely vouchsafe no less to an indicted defendant under interrogation by the police in a completely extrajudicial proceeding. Anything less . . . might deny a defendant 'effective representation by counsel at the only stage when legal aid and advice would help him.'" Id. at 204, quoting Douglas, J., concurring in Spano v. New York, 360 U.S. 315, 326.

The interrogation here was conducted before petitioner was formally indicted. But in the context of this case, that fact should make no difference. When petitioner requested, and was denied, an opportunity to consult with his lawyer, the investigation had ceased to be a general investigation of "an unsolved crime." Spano v. New York, 360 U.S. 315, 327 (Stewart, J., concurring). Petitioner had become the accused, and the purpose of the interrogation was to "get him" to confess his guilt despite his constitutional right not to do so. At the time of his arrest and throughout the course of the interrogation, the police told petitioner that they had convincing evidence that he had fired the fatal shots. Without informing him of his absolute right to remain silent in the face of this accusation, the police urged him to make a statement. As this Court observed many years ago:

> It cannot be doubted that, placed in the position in which the accused was when the statement was made to him that the other suspected person had charged him with crime, the result was to produce upon his mind the fear that if he remained silent it would be considered an admission of guilt, and therefore render certain his being

> committed for trial as the guilty person, and it cannot be conceived that the converse impression would not also have naturally arisen, that by denying there was hope of removing the suspicion from himself.

Bram v. United States, 168 U.S. 532, 562. Petitioner, a layman, was undoubtedly unaware that under Illinois law an admission of "mere" complicity in the murder plot was legally as damaging as an admission of firing of the fatal shots. . . . The "guiding hand of counsel" was essential to advise petitioner of his rights in this delicate situation. Powell v. Alabama, 287 U.S. 45, 69. This was the "stage when legal aid and advice" were most critical to petitioner. Massiah v. United States, supra, at 204. It was a stage surely as critical as was the arraignment in Hamilton v. Alabama, 368 U.S. 52, and the preliminary hearing in White v. Maryland, 373 U.S. 59. What happened at this interrogation could certainly "affect the whole trial," Hamilton v. Alabama, supra, at 54, since rights "may be as irretrievably lost, if not then and there asserted, as they are when an accused represented by counsel waives a right for strategic purposes." Ibid. It would exalt form over substance to make the right to counsel, under these circumstances, depend on whether at the time of the interrogation, the authorities had secured a formal indictment. Petitioner had, for all practical purposes, already been charged with murder.

. . .

In Gideon v. Wainwright, 372 U.S. 335, we held that every person accused of a crime, whether state or federal, is entitled to a lawyer at trial. The rule sought by the State here, however, would make the trial no more than an appeal from the interrogation; and the "right to use counsel at the formal trial [would be] a very hollow thing [if], for all practical purposes, the conviction is already assured by pretrial examination." In re Groban, 352 U.S. 330, 344 (Black, J., dissenting). "One can imagine a cynical prosecutor saying: 'Let them have the most illustrious counsel, now. They can't escape the noose. There is nothing that counsel can do for them at the trial.' " Ex parte Sullivan, 107 F.Supp. 514, 517–18.

It is argued that if the right to counsel is afforded prior to indictment, the number of confessions obtained by the police will diminish significantly, because most confessions are obtained during the period between arrest and indictment, and "any lawyer worth his salt will tell the suspect in no uncertain terms to make no statement to police under any circumstances." Watts v. Indiana, 338 U.S. 49, 59 (Jackson, J., concurring in part and dissenting in part). This argument, of course, cuts two ways. The fact that many confessions are obtained during this period points up its critical nature as a "stage when legal aid and advice" are surely needed. Massiah v. United States, supra, at 204. . . . The right to counsel would indeed be hollow if it began at a period when few confessions were obtained. There is necessarily a direct relationship between the importance of a stage to the police in their quest for a confession and the criticalness of that stage to the accused in his need for legal advice. Our Constitution, unlike some others, strikes the balance in favor of the right of the accused to be advised by his lawyer of his privilege against self-incrimination. . . .

We have learned the lesson of history, ancient and modern, that a system of criminal law enforcement which comes to depend on the "confession" will, in the long run, be less reliable and more subject to abuses than a system which depends on extrinsic evidence independently secured through skillful investigation. As Dean Wigmore so wisely said:

> [A]*ny system of administration which permits the prosecution to trust habitually to compulsory self-disclosure as a source of proof must itself suffer morally thereby.* The inclination develops to rely mainly upon such evidence, and to be satisfied with an incomplete investigation of the other sources. The exercise of the power to extract answers begets a forgetfulness of the just limitations of that power. The simple and peaceful process of questioning breeds a readiness to resort to bullying and to physical force and torture. If there is a right to an answer, there soon seems to be a right to the expected answer,—that is, to a confession of guilt. Thus the legitimate use grows into the unjust abuse; ultimately, the innocent are jeopardized by the encroachments of a bad system. Such seems to have been the course of experience in those legal systems where the privilege was not recognized.

8 Wigmore, Evidence (3d ed. 1940), 309. (Emphasis in original.) This Court also has recognized that "history amply shows that confessions have often been extorted to save law enforcement officials the trouble and effort of obtaining valid and independent evidence. . . ." Haynes v. Washington, 373 U.S. 503, 519.

We have also learned the companion lesson of history that no system of criminal justice can, or should, survive if it comes to depend for its continued effectiveness on the citizens' abdication through unawareness of their constitutional rights. No system worth preserving should have to *fear* that if an accused is permitted to consult with a lawyer, he will become aware of, and exercise, these rights. If the exercise of constitutional rights will thwart the effectiveness of a system of law enforcement, then there is something very wrong with that system.

We hold, therefore, that where, as here, the investigation is no longer a general inquiry into an unsolved crime but has begun to focus on a particular suspect, the suspect has been taken into police custody, the police carry out a process of interrogations that lends itself to eliciting incriminating statements, the suspect has requested and been denied an opportunity to consult with his lawyer, and the police have not effectively warned him of his absolute constitutional right to remain silent, the accused has been denied "the Assistance of Counsel" . . . and that no statement elicited by the police during the interrogation may be used against him at a criminal trial.

. . .

Nothing we have said today affects the powers of the police to investigate "an unsolved crime," Spano v. New York, 360 U.S. 315, 327 (Stewart, J., concurring), by gathering information from witnesses and by other "proper investigative efforts." Haynes v. Washington, 373 U.S. 503, 519. We hold only that when the process shifts from investigatory to accusatory—when its focus is on the accused and its purpose is to elicit a confession—our adversary system begins to operate, and, under the circumstances here, the accused must be permitted to consult with his lawyer. . . .[4]

---

233. The Court has said that the holding of *Escobedo* is "limited . . . to its own facts," Kirby v. Illinois, 406 U.S. 682, 689 (1972), p. 378 above. See Moran v. Burbine, 475 U.S. 412 (1986) (6–3), p. 444 below.

Miranda v. Arizona

384 U.S. 436, 86 S.Ct. 1602, 16 L.Ed.2d 694 (1966)

■ MR. CHIEF JUSTICE WARREN delivered the opinion of the Court.

The cases before us raise questions which go to the roots of our concepts of American criminal jurisprudence: the restraints society must observe consistent with the Federal Constitution in prosecuting individuals for crime. More specifically, we deal with the admissibility of statements obtained from an individual who is subjected to custodial police interrogation and the necessity for procedures which assure that the individual is accorded his privilege under the Fifth Amendment to the Constitution not to be compelled to incriminate himself.

. . .

Our holding will be spelled out with some specificity in the pages which follow but briefly stated it is this: the prosecution may not use statements, whether exculpatory or inculpatory, stemming from custodial interrogation of the defendant unless it demonstrates the use of procedural safeguards effective to secure the privilege against self-incrimination. By custodial interrogation, we mean questioning initiated by law enforcement officers after a person has been taken into custody or otherwise deprived of his freedom of action in any significant way. As for the procedural safeguards to be employed, unless other fully effective means are devised to inform accused persons of their right of silence and to assure a continuous opportunity to exercise it, the following measures are required. Prior to any questioning, the person must be warned that he has a right to remain silent, that any statement he does make may be used as evidence against him, and that he has a right to the presence of an attorney, either retained or appointed. The defendant may waive effectuation of these rights, provid-

[4] Justice Harlan and Justice Stewart wrote dissenting opinions. Justice White also wrote a dissenting opinion, which Justice Clark and Justice Stewart joined.

ed the waiver is made voluntarily, knowingly and intelligently. If, however, he indicates in any manner and at any stage of the process that he wishes to consult with an attorney before speaking there can be no questioning. Likewise, if the individual is alone and indicates in any manner that he does not wish to be interrogated, the police may not question him. The mere fact that he may have answered some questions or volunteered some statements on his own does not deprive him of the right to refrain from answering any further inquiries until he has consulted with an attorney and thereafter consents to be questioned.

I.

The constitutional issue we decide in each of these cases is the admissibility of statements obtained from a defendant questioned while in custody or otherwise deprived of his freedom of action in any significant way. In each, the defendant was questioned by police officers, detectives, or a prosecuting attorney in a room in which he was cut off from the outside world. In none of these cases was the defendant given a full and effective warning of his rights at the outset of the interrogation process. In all the cases, the questioning elicited oral admissions, and in three of them, signed statements as well which were admitted at their trials. They all thus share salient features—incommunicado interrogation of individuals in a police-dominated atmosphere, resulting in self-incriminating statements without full warnings of constitutional rights.

An understanding of the nature and setting of this in-custody interrogation is essential to our decisions today. The difficulty in depicting what transpires at such interrogations stems from the fact that in this country they have largely taken place incommunicado. From extensive factual studies undertaken in the early 1930s, including the famous Wickersham Report to Congress by a Presidential Commission, it is clear that police violence and the "third degree" flourished at that time. In a series of cases decided by this Court long after these studies, the police resorted to physical brutality—beating, hanging, whipping—and to sustained and protracted questioning incommunicado in order to extort confessions. The Commission on Civil Rights in 1961 found much evidence to indicate that "some policemen still resort to physical force to obtain confessions," 1961 Comm'n on Civil Rights Rep., Justice, pt. 5, 17. The use of physical brutality and violence is not, unfortunately, relegated to the past or to any part of the country. . . .

The examples given above are undoubtedly the exception now, but they are sufficiently widespread to be the object of concern. Unless a proper limitation upon custodial interrogation is achieved—such as these decisions will advance—there can be no assurance that practices of this nature will be eradicated in the foreseeable future. . . .

Again we stress that the modern practice of in-custody interrogation is psychologically rather than physically oriented. . . . Interrogation still takes place in privacy. Privacy results in secrecy and this in turn results in a gap in our knowledge as to what in fact goes on in the interrogation rooms. A valuable source of information about present police practices, however, may be found in various police manuals and texts which document procedures employed with success in the past, and which recommend various other effective tactics. These texts are used by law enforcement agencies themselves as guides. It should be noted that these texts professedly present the most enlightened and effective means presently used to obtain statements through custodial interrogation. By considering these texts and other data, it is possible to describe procedures observed and noted around the country.

. . .

[T]he setting prescribed by the manuals and observed in practice becomes clear. In essence, it is this: To be alone with the subject is essential to prevent distraction and to deprive him of any outside support. The aura of confidence in his guilt undermines his will to resist. He merely confirms the preconceived story the police seek to have him describe. Patience and persistence, at times relentless questioning, are employed. To obtain a confession, the interrogator must "patiently maneuver himself or his quarry into a position from which the desired objective may be attained."[5] When normal procedures fail to produce the needed result, the police may resort to deceptive stratagems such as giving false legal advice. It is important to keep the subject off balance, for example, by trading on his insecurity about himself or his surroundings. The police then persuade, trick, or cajole him out of exercising his constitutional rights.

Even without employing brutality, the "third degree" or the specific stratagems described above, the very fact of custodial interrogation exacts a heavy toll on individual liberty and trades on the weakness of individuals. . . .

In the cases before us today, given this background, we concern ourselves primarily with this interrogation atmosphere and the evils it can bring. . . .

In these cases, we might not find the defendants' statements to have been involuntary in traditional terms. Our concern for adequate safeguards to protect precious Fifth Amendment rights is, of course, not lessened in the slightest. In each of the cases, the defendant was thrust into an unfamiliar atmosphere and run through menacing police interrogation procedures. . . . To be sure, the records do not evince overt physical coercion or patent psychological ploys. The fact remains that in none of these cases did the officers undertake to afford appropriate safeguards at the outset of the interrogation to insure that the statements were truly the product of free choice.

It is obvious that such an interrogation environment is created for no purpose other than to subjugate the individual to the will of his examiner. This atmosphere carries its own badge of intimidation. To be sure, this is not physical intimidation, but it is equally destructive of human dignity.

5. Inbau & Reid, Lie Detection and Criminal Interrogation 185 (3rd ed. 1953).

The current practice of incommunicado interrogation is at odds with one of our Nation's most cherished principles—that the individual may not be compelled to incriminate himself. Unless adequate protective devices are employed to dispel the compulsion inherent in custodial surroundings, no statement obtained from the defendant can truly be the product of his free choice.

From the foregoing, we can readily perceive an intimate connection between the privilege against self-incrimination and police custodial questioning. It is fitting to turn to history and precedent underlying the Self-Incrimination Clause to determine its applicability in this situation.

II.

We sometimes forget how long it has taken to establish the privilege against self-incrimination, the sources from which it came and the fervor with which it was defended. Its roots go back into ancient times. . . .

. . .

[W]e may view the historical development of the privilege as one which groped for the proper scope of governmental power over the citizen. As a "noble principle often transcends its origins," the privilege has come rightfully to be recognized in part as an individual's substantive right, a "right to a private enclave where he may lead a private life. That right is the hallmark of our democracy." United States v. Grunewald, 233 F.2d 556, 579, 581–82 (Frank, J., dissenting), rev'd, 353 U.S. 391 (1957). . . . [T]he privilege against self-incrimination—the essential mainstay of our adversary system—is founded on a complex of values. . . . All these policies point to one overriding thought: the constitutional foundation underlying the privilege is the respect a government—state or federal—must accord to the dignity and integrity of its citizens. To maintain a "fair state-individual balance," to require the government "to shoulder the entire load," 8 Wigmore, Evidence 317 (McNaughton rev.1961), to respect the inviolability of the human personality, our accusatory system of criminal justice demands that the government seeking to punish an individual produce the evidence against him by its own independent labors, rather than by the cruel, simple expedient of compelling it from his own mouth. . . . In sum, the privilege is fulfilled only when the person is guaranteed the right "to remain silent unless he chooses to speak in the unfettered exercise of his own will." Malloy v. Hogan, 378 U.S. 1, 8 (1964).

The question in these cases is whether the privilege is fully applicable during a period of custodial interrogation. In this Court, the privilege has consistently been accorded a liberal construction. . . . We are satisfied that all the principles embodied in the privilege apply to informal compulsion exerted by law-enforcement officers during in-custody questioning. An individual swept from familiar surroundings into police custody, surrounded by antagonistic forces, and subjected to the techniques of persuasion described above cannot be otherwise than under compulsion to speak. As a practical matter, the compulsion to speak in the isolated setting of the police station may well be greater than in courts or other official investigations, where there are often impartial observers to guard against intimidation or trickery.

. . .

Our holding [in Escobedo v. Illinois, 378 U.S. 478 (1964),] stressed the fact that the police had not advised the defendant of his constitutional privilege to remain silent at the outset of the interrogation, and we drew attention to that fact at several points in the decision. . . . This was no isolated factor, but an essential ingredient in our decision. The entire thrust of police interrogation there, as in all the cases today, was to put the defendant in such an emotional state as to impair his capacity for rational judgment. The abdication of the constitutional privilege—the choice on his part to speak to the police—was not made knowingly or competently because of the failure to apprise him of his rights; the compelling atmosphere of the in-custody interrogation, and not an independent decision on his part, caused the defendant to speak.

A different phase of the *Escobedo* decision was significant in its attention to the absence of counsel during the questioning. There, as in the cases today, we sought a protective device to dispel the compelling atmosphere of the interrogation. In *Escobedo*, however, the police did not relieve the defendant of the anxieties which they had created in the interrogation rooms. Rather, they denied his request for the assistance of counsel. . . . This heightened his dilemma, and made his later statements the product of this compulsion. . . . The denial of the defendant's request for his attorney thus undermined his ability to exercise the privilege—to remain silent if he chose or to speak without any intimidation, blatant or subtle. The presence of counsel, in all the cases before us today, would be the adequate protective device necessary to make the process of police interrogation conform to the dictates of the privilege. His presence would insure that statements made in the government-established atmosphere are not the product of compulsion.

It was in this manner that *Escobedo* explicated another facet of the pre-trial privilege, noted in many of the Court's prior decisions: the protection of rights at trial. That counsel is present when statements are taken from an individual during interrogation obviously enhances the integrity of the fact-finding processes in court. The presence of an attorney, and the warnings delivered to the individual, enable the defendant under otherwise compelling circumstances to tell his story without fear, effectively, and in a way that eliminates the evils in the interrogation process. Without the protections flowing from adequate warnings and the rights of counsel, "all the careful safeguards erected around the giving of testimony, whether by an accused or any other witness, would become empty formalities in a procedure where the most compelling possible evidence of guilt, a confession, would have already been obtained at the unsupervised pleasure of the police." Mapp v. Ohio, 367 U.S. 643, 685 (1961) (Harlan, J., dissenting). . . .

III.

Today, then, there can be no doubt that the Fifth Amendment privilege is available outside of criminal court proceedings and serves to protect persons in all settings in which their freedom of action is curtailed in any significant way from being compelled to incriminate themselves. We have concluded that without proper safeguards the process of in-custody interrogation of persons suspected or accused of crime contains inherently compelling pressures which work to undermine the individual's will to resist and to compel him to speak where he would not otherwise do so freely. In order to combat these pressures and to permit a full opportunity to exercise the privilege against self-incrimination, the accused must be adequately and effectively apprised of his rights and the exercise of those rights must be fully honored.

It is impossible for us to foresee the potential alternatives for protecting the privilege which might be devised by Congress or the States in the exercise of their creative rule-making capacities. Therefore we cannot say that the Constitution necessarily requires adherence to any particular solution for the inherent compulsions of the interrogation process as it is presently conducted. Our decision in no way creates a constitutional straightjacket which will handicap sound efforts at reform, nor is it intended to have this effect. We encourage Congress and the States to continue their laudable search for increasingly effective ways of protecting the rights of the individual while promoting efficient enforcement of our criminal laws. However, unless we are shown other procedures which are at least as effective in apprising accused persons of their right of silence and in assuring a continuous opportunity to exercise it, the following safeguards must be observed.

At the outset, if a person in custody is to be subjected to interrogation, he must first be informed in clear and unequivocal terms that he has the right to remain silent. For those unaware of the privilege, the warning is needed simply to make them aware of it—the threshold requirement for an intelligent decision as to its exercise. More important, such a warning is an absolute prerequisite in overcoming the inherent pressures of the interrogation atmosphere. It is not just the subnormal or woefully ignorant who succumb to an interrogator's imprecations, whether implied or expressly stated, that the interrogation will continue until a confession is obtained or that silence in the face of accusation is itself damning and will bode ill when presented to a jury. Further, the warning will show the individual that his interrogators are prepared to recognize his privilege should he choose to exercise it.

The Fifth Amendment privilege is so fundamental to our system of constitutional rule and the expedient of giving an adequate warning as to the availability of the privilege so simple, we will not pause to inquire in individual cases whether the defendant was aware of his rights without a warning being given. Assessments of the knowledge the defendant possessed, based on information as to his age, education, intelligence, or prior contact with authorities, can never be more than speculation; a warning is a clearcut fact. More important, whatever the background of the person interrogated, a warning at the time of the interrogation is indispensable to overcome its pressures and to insure that the individual knows he is free to exercise the privilege at that point in time.

The warning of the right to remain silent must be accompanied by the explanation that anything said can and will be used against the individual in court. This warning is needed in order to make him aware not only of the privilege, but also of the consequences of forgoing it. It is only through an awareness of these consequences that there can be any assurance of real understanding and intelligent exercise of the privilege. Moreover, this warning may serve to make the individual more acutely aware that he is faced with a phase of the adversary system—that he is not in the presence of persons acting solely in his interest.

The circumstances surrounding in-custody interrogation can operate very quickly to overbear the will of one merely made aware of his privilege by his interrogators. Therefore, the right to have counsel present at the interrogation is indispensable to the protection of the Fifth Amendment privilege under the system we delineate today. Our aim is to assure that the individual's right to choose between silence and speech remains unfettered throughout the interrogation process. A once-stated warning, delivered by those who will conduct the interrogation, cannot itself suffice to that end among those who most require knowledge of their rights. A mere warning given by the interrogators is not alone sufficient to accomplish that end. . . . Even preliminary advice given to the accused by his own attorney can be swiftly overcome by the secret interrogation process. . . . Thus, the need for counsel to protect the Fifth Amendment privilege comprehends not merely a right to consult with counsel prior to questioning, but also to have counsel present during any questioning if the defendant so desires.

The presence of counsel at the interrogation may serve several significant subsidiary functions as well. If the accused decides to talk to his interrogators, the assistance of counsel can mitigate the dangers of untrustworthiness. With a lawyer present the likelihood that the police will practice coercion is reduced, and if coercion is nevertheless exercised the lawyer can testify to it in court. The presence of a lawyer can also help to guarantee that the accused gives a fully accurate statement to the police and that the statement is rightly reported by the prosecution at trial. . . .

An individual need not make a pre-interrogation request for a lawyer. While such request affirmatively secures his right to have one, his failure to ask for a lawyer does not constitute a waiver. No effective waiver of the right to counsel during interrogation can be recognized unless specifically made after the warnings we here delineate have been given. The accused who does not know his rights and therefore does not make a request may be the person who most needs counsel. . . .

Accordingly we hold that an individual held for interrogation must be clearly informed that he has the right to consult with a lawyer and to have the lawyer with him during interrogation under the system for protecting the privilege we delineate today. As with the warnings of the right to remain silent and that anything stated can be used in evidence against him, this warning is an absolute prerequisite to interrogation. No amount of circumstantial evidence that the person may have been aware of this right will suffice to stand in its stead. Only through such a warning is there ascertainable assurance that the accused was aware of this right.

If an individual indicates that he wishes the assistance of counsel before any interrogation occurs, the authorities cannot rationally ignore or deny his request on the basis that the individual does not have or cannot afford a retained attorney. The financial ability of the individual has no relationship to the scope of the rights involved here. The privilege against self-incrimination secured by the Constitution applies to all individuals. The need for counsel in order to protect the privilege exists for the indigent as well as the affluent. In fact, were we to limit these constitutional rights to those who can retain an attorney, our decisions today would be of little significance. The cases before us as well as the vast majority of confession cases with which we have dealt in the past involve those unable to retain counsel. While authorities are not required to relieve the accused of his poverty, they have the obligation not to take advantage of indigence in the administration of justice. Denial of counsel to the indigent at the time of interrogation while allowing an attorney to those who can afford one would be no more supportable by reason or logic than the similar situation at trial and on appeal struck down in Gideon v. Wainwright, 372 U.S. 335 (1963), and Douglas v. California, 372 U.S. 353 (1963).

In order fully to apprise a person interrogated of the extent of his rights under this system then, it is necessary to warn him not only that he has the right to consult with an attorney, but also that if he is indigent a lawyer will be appointed to represent him. Without this additional warning, the admonition of the right to consult with counsel would often be understood as meaning only that he can consult with a lawyer if he has one or has the funds to obtain one. The warning of a right to counsel would be hollow if not couched in terms that would convey to the indigent—the person most often subjected to interrogation—the knowledge that he too has a right to have counsel present. As with the warnings of the right to remain silent and of the general right to counsel, only by effective and express explanation to the indigent of this right can there be assurance that he was truly in a position to exercise it.

Once warnings have been given, the subsequent procedure is clear. If the individual indicates in any manner, at any time prior to or during questioning, that he wishes to remain silent, the interrogation must cease. At this point he has shown that he intends to exercise his Fifth Amendment privilege; any statement taken after the person invokes his privilege cannot be other than the product of compulsion, subtle or otherwise. Without the right to cut off questioning the setting of in-custody interrogation operates on the individual to overcome free choice in producing a statement after the privilege has been once invoked. If the individual states that he wants an attorney, the interrogation must cease until an attorney is present. At that time, the individual must have an opportunity to confer with the attorney and to have him present during any subsequent questioning. If the individual cannot obtain an attorney and he indicates that he wants one before speaking to police, they must respect his decision to remain silent.

This does not mean, as some have suggested, that each police station must have a "station house lawyer" present at all times to advise prisoners. It does mean, however, that if police propose to interrogate a person they must make known to him that he is entitled to a lawyer and that if he cannot afford one, a lawyer will be provided for him prior to any interrogation. If authorities conclude that they will not provide counsel during a reasonable period of time in which investigation in the field is carried out, they may refrain from doing so without violating the person's Fifth Amendment privilege so long as they do not question him during that time.

If the interrogation continues without the presence of an attorney and a statement is taken, a heavy burden rests on the government to demonstrate that the defendant knowingly and intelligently waived his privilege against self-incrimination and his right to retained or appointed counsel. Escobedo v. Illinois, 378 U.S. 478, 490, n.14. This Court has always set high standards of proof for the waiver of constitutional rights . . . and we reassert these standards as applied to in-custody interrogation. Since the State is responsible for establishing the isolated circumstances under which the interrogation takes place and has the only means of making available corroborated evidence of warnings given during incommunicado interrogation, the burden is rightly on its shoulders.

An express statement that the individual is willing to make a statement and does not want an attorney followed closely by a statement could constitute a waiver. But a valid waiver will not be presumed simply from the silence of the accused after warnings are given or simply from the fact that a confession was in fact eventually obtained. . . . Moreover, where in-custody interrogation is involved, there is no room for the contention that the privilege is waived if the individual answers some questions or gives some information on his own prior to invoking his right to remain silent when interrogated.

Whatever the testimony of the authorities as to waiver of rights by an accused, the fact of lengthy interrogation or incommunicado incarceration before a statement is made is strong evidence that the accused did not validly waive his rights. In these circumstances the fact that the individual eventually made a statement is consistent with the conclusion that the compelling influence of the interrogation finally forced him to do so. It is inconsistent with any notion of a voluntary relinquishment of the privilege. Moreover, any evidence that the accused was threatened, tricked, or cajoled into a waiver will, of course, show that the defendant did not voluntarily waive his privilege. The requirement of warnings and waiver of rights is a fundamental with respect to the Fifth Amendment privilege and not simply a preliminary ritual to existing methods of interrogation.

The warnings required and the waiver necessary in accordance with our opinion today are, in the absence of a fully effective equivalent, prerequisites to the admissibility of any statement made by a defendant. No distinction can be drawn between statements which are direct confessions and statements which amount to "admissions" of part or all of an offense. The privilege against self-incrimination protects the individual from being compelled to incriminate himself in any manner; it does not distinguish degrees of incrimination. Similarly, for precisely the same reason, no distinction may be drawn between inculpatory statements and statements alleged to be merely "exculpatory." If a statement made were in fact truly exculpatory it would, of course, never be used by the prosecution. In fact, statements merely intended to be exculpatory by the defendant are often used to impeach his testimony at trial or to demonstrate untruths in the statement given under interrogation and thus to prove guilt by implication. These statements are incriminating in any meaningful sense of the word and may not be used without the full warnings and effective waiver required for any other statement. In *Escobedo* itself, the defendant fully intended his accusation of another as the slayer to be exculpatory as to himself.

The principles announced today deal with the protection which must be given to the privilege against self-incrimination when the individual is first subjected to police interrogation while in custody at the station or otherwise deprived of his freedom of action in any significant way. It is at this point that our adversary system of criminal proceedings commences, distinguishing itself at the outset from the inquisitorial system recognized in some countries. Under the system of warnings we delineate today or under any other system which may be devised and found effective, the safeguards to be erected about the privilege must come into play at this point.

Our decision is not intended to hamper the traditional function of police officers in investigating crime. . . . When an individual is in custody on probable cause, the police may, of course, seek out evidence in the field to be used at trial against him. Such investigation may include inquiry of persons not under restraint. General on-the-scene questioning as to facts surrounding a crime or other general questioning of citizens in the fact-finding process is not affected by our holding. It is an act of responsible citizenship for individuals to give whatever information they may have to aid in law enforcement. In such situations the compelling atmosphere inherent in the process of in-custody interrogation is not necessarily present.

In dealing with statements obtained through interrogation, we do not purport to find all confessions inadmissible. Confessions remain a proper element in law enforcement. Any statement given freely and voluntarily without any compelling influences is, of course, admissible in evidence. The fundamental import of the privilege while an individual is in custody is not whether he is allowed to talk to the police without the benefit of warnings and counsel, but whether he can be interrogated. There is no requirement that police stop a person who enters a police station and states that he wishes to confess to a crime, or a person who calls the police to offer a confession or any other statement he desires to make. Volunteered statements of any kind are not barred by the Fifth Amendment and their admissibility is not affected by our holding today.

To summarize, we hold that when an individual is taken into custody or otherwise deprived of his freedom by the authorities in any significant way and is subjected to questioning, the privilege against self-incrimination is jeopardized. Procedural safeguards must be employed to protect the privilege, and unless other fully effective means are adopted to notify the person of his right of silence and to assure that the exercise of the right will be scrupulously honored, the following measures are required. He must be warned prior to any questioning that he has the right to remain silent, that anything he says can be used against him in a court of law, that he has the right to the presence of an attorney, and that if he cannot afford an attorney one will be appointed for him prior to any questioning if he so desires. Opportunity to exercise these rights must be afforded to him throughout the interrogation. After such warnings have been given, and such opportunity afforded, the individual may knowingly and intelligently waive these rights and agree to answer questions or make a statement. But unless and until such warnings and waiver are demonstrated by the prosecution at trial, no evidence obtained as a result of interrogation can be used against him.

IV.

A recurrent argument made in these cases is that society's need for interrogation outweighs the privilege. This argument is not unfamiliar to this Court. . . . The whole thrust of our foregoing discussion demonstrates that the Constitution has prescribed the rights of the individual when confronted with the power of government when it provided in the Fifth Amendment that an individual cannot be compelled to be a witness against himself. That right cannot be abridged. . . .

If the individual desires to exercise his privilege, he has the right to do so. This is not for the authorities to decide. An attorney may advise his client not to talk to police until he has had an opportunity to investigate the case, or he may wish to be present with his client during any police questioning. In doing so an attorney is merely exercising the good professional judgment he has been taught. This is not cause for considering the attorney a menace to law enforcement. He is merely carrying out what he is sworn to do under his oath—to protect to the extent of his ability the rights of his client. In fulfilling this responsibility the attorney plays a vital role in the administration of criminal justice under our Constitution.

In announcing these principles, we are not unmindful of the burdens which law enforcement officials must bear, often under trying circumstances. We also fully recognize the obligation of all citizens to aid in enforcing the criminal laws. This Court, while protecting individual rights, has always given ample latitude to law enforcement agencies in the legitimate exercise of their duties. The limits we have placed on the interrogation process should not constitute an undue interference with a proper system of law enforcement. As we have noted, our decision does not in any way preclude police from carrying out their traditional investigatory functions. Although confessions may play an important role in some convictions, the cases before us present graphic examples of the overstatement of the "need" for confessions. In each case authorities conducted interrogations ranging up to five days in duration despite the presence, through standard investigating practices, of considerable evidence against each defendant. Further examples are chronicled in our prior cases. . . .

It is also urged that an unfettered right to detention for interrogation should be allowed because it will often redound to the benefit of the person questioned. When police inquiry determines that there is no reason to believe that the person has committed any crime, it is said, he will be released without need for further formal procedures. The person who has committed no offense, however, will be better able to clear himself after warnings with counsel present than without. It can be assumed that in such circumstances a lawyer would advise his client to talk freely to police in order to clear himself.

. . .

Custodial interrogation, by contrast, does not necessarily afford the innocent an opportunity to clear themselves. A serious consequence of the present practice of the interrogation alleged to be beneficial for the innocent is that many arrests "for investigation" subject large numbers of innocent persons to detention and interrogation. . . .

. . .

V.

Because of the nature of the problem and because of its recurrent significance in numerous cases, we have to this point discussed the relationship of the Fifth Amendment privilege to police interrogation without specific concentration on the facts of the cases before us. We turn now to these facts to consider the application to these cases of the constitutional principles discussed above. In each instance, we have concluded that statements were obtained from the defendant under circumstances that did not meet constitutional standards for protection of the privilege.

. . .[6]

---

[6] Justice Clark wrote an opinion dissenting in three of the cases before the Court and concurring in the result in one. Justice Harlan wrote a dissenting opinion which Justice Stewart and Justice White joined. Justice White also wrote a dissenting opinion which Justice Harlan and Justice Stewart joined.

234. In a dissenting opinion, Justice Harlan described and discussed the facts of Miranda v. Arizona:[7]

> On March 3, 1963, an 18-year-old girl was kidnapped and forcibly raped near Phoenix, Arizona. Ten days later, on the morning of March 13, petitioner Miranda was arrested and taken to the police station. At this time Miranda was 23 years old, indigent, and educated to the extent of completing half the ninth grade. He had "an emotional illness" of the schizophrenic type, according to the doctor who eventually examined him; the doctor's report also stated that Miranda was "alert and oriented as to time, place, and person," intelligent within normal limits, competent to stand trial, and sane within the legal definition. At the police station, the victim picked Miranda out of a lineup, and two officers then took him into a separate room to interrogate him, starting about 11:30 a.m. Though at first denying his guilt, within a short time Miranda gave a detailed oral confession and then wrote out in his own hand and signed a brief statement admitting and describing the crime. All this was accomplished in two hours or less without any force, threats or promises and—I will assume this though the record is uncertain . . . —without any effective warnings at all.
>
> Miranda's oral and written confessions are now held inadmissible under the Court's new rules. One is entitled to feel astonished that the Constitution can be read to produce this result. These confessions were obtained during brief, daytime questioning conducted by two officers and unmarked by any of the traditional indicia of coercion. They assured a conviction for a brutal and unsettling crime, for which the police had and quite possibly could obtain little evidence other than the victim's identifications, evidence which is frequently unreliable. There was, in sum, a legitimate purpose, no perceptible unfairness, and certainly little risk of injustice in the interrogation. Yet the resulting confessions, and the responsible course of police practice they represent, are to be sacrificed to the Court's own finespun conception of fairness which I seriously doubt is shared by many thinking citizens in this country.

384 U.S. at 518–19.

235. In 1968, Congress enacted 18 U.S.C. § 3501, which provides that in any federal prosecution, a confession is admissible "if it is voluntarily given." 18 U.S.C. § 3501(a). The test of voluntariness is the pre-*Miranda* totality-of-the-circumstances test, including but not limited to whether or not the person had been advised of his rights. Notwithstanding the statute, the courts continued to apply *Miranda*. Finally, in Dickerson v. United States, 530 U.S. 428, 444 (2000) (7–2), the Court declared that "*Miranda* announced a constitutional rule that Congress may not supersede legisla-

7. *Miranda* was one of four cases which the Supreme Court considered in its opinion and to which it applied the new requirements. Miranda himself was again convicted of kidnapping and rape at a subsequent trial, in which the confession which the Supreme Court had concluded was unconstitutionally obtained was not admitted. State v. Miranda, 450 P.2d 364 (Ariz.1969).

tively." Observing that the *Miranda* warnings "have become part of our national culture," id. at 430, the Court added that it would not overrule *Miranda*.

236. The *Miranda* warnings do not have to be given in the exact form stated in that opinion. California v. Prysock, 453 U.S. 355 (1981) (6–3). In particular, advising a defendant that if he is indigent, a lawyer will be appointed for him "if and when you go to court" is not defective because of the inclusion of that phrase. Duckworth v. Eagan, 492 U.S. 195 (1989) (5–4).

In United States v. Caba, 955 F.2d 182 (2d Cir.1992), the court generally disapproved the practice of having an informant or codefendant give a translation of the *Miranda* warnings to a person who does not understand English, but said that there is no per se rule to that effect.

237. At about 3:00 a.m., Hill, a 17-year-old boy, was arrested at his home and brought to the police station "for questioning" in connection with a street gang killing earlier that night. He was fully warned of his constitutional rights. In response to questioning, he denied any knowledge of the killing. Over the next three hours, on three or four separate occasions lasting about ten or 15 minutes each, the same detective questioned him again. On each occasion, he was alone with the detective in an interview room. At about 6:00 a.m., after the detective had called for a car to transport Hill to the police lockup, he called the detective back into the room and made a statement denying his guilt but implicating himself. No warnings were given after the initial warnings. "[C]onsidering the fact that the adequacy of the *Miranda* warnings is not disputed here, that the questioning was not for an inordinate period of time, that the period of interrogation had concluded as far as the police were concerned before the statement was made, that the defendant never sought to terminate the questioning, and that Hill's admission was a self protective attempt to shift the blame onto another and thereby relieve himself of all fault," the court held that the statement was admissible. People v. Hill, 233 N.E.2d 367, 372 (Ill.1968). The court declined to adopt "an automatic second-warning system," which, it said, would "add a perfunctory ritual to police procedures." Id. at 371.

In Michigan v. Mosley, 423 U.S. 96 (1975) (7–2), detectives gave the defendant the *Miranda* warnings and then questioned him about the robbery charges for which he had been arrested. When he said he did not want to answer questions, the questioning stopped. A few hours later, after repeating the warnings, other detectives questioned the defendant about a homicide for which he had not been arrested. His answers incriminated him and he was subsequently prosecuted for murder. The Court held that the resumption of questioning in those circumstances, each session being independent of the other and accompanied by warnings, did not violate *Miranda*. That case, the Court said, did not "create a per se proscription of indefinite duration upon any further questioning by any police officer on any subject, once the person in custody has indicated a desire to remain silent." So long as a person's "right to cut off questioning" is "scrupulously honored," as the court concluded it had been, a resumption of questioning is permissible. Id. at 102–103, 104.

238. An initial failure to give *Miranda* warnings does not render inadmissible statements made after the warnings are given, even though the person made incriminating admissions before they were given. Oregon v. Elstad, 470 U.S. 298 (1985) (6–3). Police arrested the defendant, who was eighteen years old, at his home. An officer questioned him briefly in the living room while another officer talked with his mother. He made brief damaging admissions. He was then taken to the police station and, about an hour later, was given *Miranda* warnings. He gave the police a full statement about the burglary for which he had been arrested.

Observing that the *Miranda* exclusionary rule may exclude a person's statements even though they are not coerced and that there has been no violation of the Fifth Amendment privilege, the Court said that the rule does not require that the statements and their fruits be regarded as "inherently tainted," Id. at 307. Provided that statements are voluntary, subsequent statements made after compliance with *Miranda* are admissible. The psychological impact of having "let the cat out of the bag" by the first statements does not, without more, render the later statements involuntary. Nor is it essential that a person have been told that his prior statements are not admissible. The Court said:

> Far from establishing a rigid rule, we direct courts to avoid one; there is no warrant for presuming coercive effect where the suspect's initial inculpatory statement, though technically in violation of *Miranda*, was voluntary. The relevant inquiry is whether, in fact, the second statement was also voluntarily made. As in any such inquiry, the finder of fact must examine the surrounding circumstances and the entire course of police conduct with respect to the suspect in evaluating the voluntariness of his statements. The fact that a suspect chooses to speak after being informed of his rights is, of course, highly probative. We find that the dictates of *Miranda* and the goals of the Fifth Amendment proscription against use of compelled testimony are fully satisfied in the circumstances of this case by barring use of the unwarned statement in the case in chief. No further purpose is served by imputing "taint" to subsequent statements obtained pursuant to a voluntary and knowing waiver. We hold today that a suspect who has once responded to unwarned yet uncoercive questioning is not thereby disabled from waiving his rights and confessing after he has been given the requisite *Miranda* warnings.

Id. at 318.

In State v. Seibert, 93 S.W.3d 700 (Mo.2002), cert. granted, 538 U.S. 1031 (2003), a police officer deliberately questioned the defendant without giving her *Miranda* warnings. After he obtained incriminating statements, he interrupted the questioning for twenty minutes and then, giving the defendant *Miranda* warnings, resumed. The officer's evident purpose was to elicit statements in the first session that the defendant would repeat after the warnings were given. The court held that the intentional violation of *Miranda* distinguished the case from *Elstad* and that in those circumstances, exclusion of the second statement was required. Contra, United States v. Orso, 234 F.3d 436 (9th Cir.2000) (en banc). See People v. Neal, 72 P.3d 280 (Cal.2003), generally in agreement with *Seibert*, in which the court concluded that in all the circumstances—the deliberate violation of *Miranda* in the first interrogation, as well as the defendant's youth, inexperience, low intelligence, and minimal education, and the deprivations and isolation of his confinement during the interrogations—the post-*Miranda* statements were involuntary.

See note 271 (Michigan v. Tucker), p. 482 below.

239. Compulsory questioning by itself does not violate the privilege against compulsory self-incrimination, if the answers are never used in any criminal proceeding. "[A] violation of the constitutional *right* against self-incrimination occurs only if one has been compelled to be a witness against himself in a criminal case." Chavez v. Martinez, 538 U.S. 760, 770 (2003) (6–3). The plaintiff, who was never charged with a crime, had brought an action against the officer who questioned him, under 42 U.S.C. § 1983.

Rhode Island v. Innis

446 U.S. 291, 100 S.Ct. 1682, 64 L.Ed.2d 297 (1980)

■ MR. JUSTICE STEWART delivered the opinion of the Court.

In Miranda v. Arizona, 384 U.S. 436, 474, the Court held that, once a defendant in custody asks to speak with a lawyer, all interrogation must cease until a lawyer is present. The issue in this case is whether the respondent was "interrogated" in violation of the standards promulgated in the *Miranda* opinion.

I

On the night of January 12, 1975, John Mulvaney, a Providence, R.I., taxicab driver, disappeared after being dispatched to pick up a customer. His body was discovered four days later buried in a shallow grave in Coventry, R.I. He had died from a shotgun blast aimed at the back of his head.

On January 17, 1975, shortly after midnight, the Providence police received a telephone call from Gerald Aubin, also a taxicab driver, who reported that he had just been robbed by a man wielding a sawed-off shotgun. Aubin further reported that he had dropped off his assailant near Rhode Island College in a section of Providence known as Mount Pleasant. While at the Providence police station waiting to give a statement, Aubin noticed a picture of his assailant on a bulletin board. Aubin so informed one of the police officers present. The officer prepared a photo array, and again Aubin identified a picture of the same person. That person was the respondent. Shortly thereafter, the Providence police began a search of the Mount Pleasant area.

At approximately 4:30 a.m. on the same date, Patrolman Lovell, while cruising the streets of Mount Pleasant in a patrol car, spotted the respondent standing in the street facing him. When Patrolman Lovell stopped his car, the respondent walked towards it. Patrolman Lovell then arrested the respondent, who was unarmed, and advised him of his so-called *Miranda* rights. While the two men waited in the patrol car for other police officers to arrive, Patrolman Lovell did not converse with the respondent other than to respond to the latter's request for a cigarette.

Within minutes, Sergeant Sears arrived at the scene of the arrest, and he also gave the respondent the *Miranda* warnings. Immediately thereafter, Captain Leyden and other police officers arrived. Captain Leyden advised the respondent of his *Miranda* rights. The respondent stated that he understood those rights and wanted to speak with a lawyer. Captain Leyden then directed that the respondent be placed in a "caged wagon," a four-door police car with a wire screen mesh between the front and rear seats, and be driven to the central police station. Three officers, Patrolmen Gleckman, Williams, and McKenna, were assigned to accompany the respondent to the central station. They placed the respondent in the vehicle and shut the doors. Captain Leyden then instructed the officers not to question the respondent or intimidate or coerce him in any way. The three officers then entered the vehicle, and it departed.

While en route to the central station, Patrolman Gleckman initiated a conversation with Patrolman McKenna concerning the missing shotgun. As Patrolman Gleckman later testified:

> A. At this point, I was talking back and forth with Patrolman McKenna stating that I frequent this area while on patrol and [that because a school for handicapped children is located nearby,] there's a lot of handicapped children running around in this area, and God forbid one of them might find a weapon with shells and they might hurt themselves.

App. 43–44. Patrolman McKenna apparently shared his fellow officer's concern:

> A. I more or less concurred with him [Gleckman] that it was a safety factor and that we should, you know, continue to search for the weapon and try to find it.

Id., at 53. While Patrolman Williams said nothing, he overheard the conversation between the two officers:

> A. He [Gleckman] said it would be too bad if the little—I believe he said a girl—would pick up the gun, maybe kill herself.

Id., at 59. The respondent then interrupted the conversation, stating that the officers should turn the car around so he could show them where the gun was located. At this point, Patrolman McKenna radioed back to Captain Leyden that they were returning to the scene of the arrest, and that the respondent would inform them of the location of the gun. At the time the respondent indicated that the officers should turn back, they had traveled no more than a mile, a trip encompassing only a few minutes.

The police vehicle then returned to the scene of the arrest where a search for the shotgun was in progress. There, Captain Leyden again advised the respondent of his *Miranda* rights. The respondent replied that he understood those rights but that he "wanted to get the gun out of the way because of the kids in the area in the school." The respondent then led the police to a nearby field, where he pointed out the shotgun under some rocks by the side of the road.

On March 20, 1975, a grand jury returned an indictment charging the respondent with the kidnapping, robbery, and murder of John Mulvaney. Before trial, the respondent moved to suppress the shotgun and the statements he had made to the police regarding it. After an evidentiary hearing at which the respondent elected not to testify, the trial judge found that the respondent had been "repeatedly and completely advised of his *Miranda* rights." He further found that it was "entirely understandable that [the officers in the police vehicle] would voice their concern [for the safety of the handicapped children] to each other." The judge then concluded that the respondent's decision to inform the police of the location of the shotgun was "a waiver, clearly, and on the basis of the evidence that I have heard, and [*sic*] intelligent waiver, of his [*Miranda*] right to remain silent." Thus, without passing on whether the police officers had in fact "interrogated" the respondent, the trial court sustained the admissibility of the shotgun and testimony related to its discovery. That evidence was later introduced at the respondent's trial, and the jury returned a verdict of guilty on all counts.

On appeal, the Rhode Island Supreme Court, in a 3–2 decision, set aside the respondent's conviction. . . . [T]he court concluded that the respondent had invoked his *Miranda* right to counsel and that, contrary to *Miranda*'s mandate that, in the absence of counsel, all custodial interrogation then cease, the police officers in the vehicle had "interrogated" the respondent without a valid waiver of his right to counsel. . . .

We granted certiorari to address for the first time the meaning of "interrogation" under Miranda v. Arizona. . . .

II

. . .

In the present case, the parties are in agreement that the respondent was fully informed of his *Miranda* rights and that he invoked his *Miranda* right to counsel when he told Captain Leyden that he wished to consult with a lawyer. It is also uncontested that the respondent was "in custody" while being transported to the police station.

The issue, therefore, is whether the respondent was "interrogated" by the police officers in violation of the respondent's undisputed right under *Miranda* to remain silent until he had consulted with a lawyer. In resolving this issue, we first define the term "interrogation" under *Miranda* before turning to a consideration of the facts of this case.

A

The starting point for defining "interrogation" in this context is, of course, the Court's *Miranda* opinion. There the Court observed that "[b]y custodial interrogation, we mean *questioning* initiated by law enforcement officers after a person has been taken into custody or otherwise deprived of his freedom of action in any significant way." Id., at 444 (emphasis added). This passage and other references throughout the opinion to "questioning" might suggest that the *Miranda* rules were to apply only to those police interrogation practices that involve express questioning of a defendant while in custody.

We do not, however, construe the *Miranda* opinion so narrowly. The concern of the Court in *Miranda* was that the "interrogation environment" created by the interplay of interrogation and custody would "subjugate the individual to the will of his examiner" and thereby undermine the privilege against compulsory self-incrimination. Id., at 457–58. The police practices that evoked this concern included several that did not involve express questioning. For example, one of the practices discussed in *Miranda* was the use of lineups in which a coached witness would pick the defendant as the perpetrator. This was designed to establish that the defendant was in fact guilty as a predicate for further interrogation. . . . A variation on this theme discussed in *Miranda* was the so-called "reverse line-up" in which a defendant would be identified by coached witnesses as the perpetrator of a fictitious crime, with the object of inducing him to confess to the actual crime of which he was suspected in order to escape the false prosecution. . . . The Court in *Miranda* also included in its survey of interrogation practices the use of psychological ploys, such as to "posi[t]" "the guilt of the subject," to "minimize the moral seriousness of the offense," and "to cast blame on the victim or on society." Id., at 450. It is clear that these techniques of persuasion, no less than express questioning, were thought, in a custodial setting, to amount to interrogation.

This is not to say, however, that all statements obtained by the police after a person has been taken into custody are to be considered the product of interrogation. . . . It is clear . . . that the special procedural safeguards outlined in *Miranda* are required not where a suspect is simply taken into custody, but rather where a suspect in custody is subjected to interrogation. "Interrogation," as conceptualized in the *Miranda* opinion, must reflect a measure of compulsion above and beyond that inherent in custody itself.[8]

8. There is language in the opinion of the Rhode Island Supreme Court in this case suggesting that the definition of "interrogation" under *Miranda* is informed by this Court's decision in Brewer v. Williams, 430 U.S. 387. . . . This suggestion is erroneous. Our decision in *Brewer* rested solely on the Sixth and Fourteenth Amendment right to counsel. . . . That right, as we held in Massiah v. United States, 377 U.S. 201, 206, prohibits law enforcement officers from "deliberately elicit[ing]" incriminating information from a defendant in the absence of counsel after a formal charge against the defendant

We conclude that the *Miranda* safeguards come into play whenever a person in custody is subjected to either express questioning or its functional equivalent. That is to say, the term "interrogation" under *Miranda* refers not only to express questioning, but also to any words or actions on the part of the police (other than those normally attendant to arrest and custody) that the police should know are reasonably likely to elicit an incriminating response from the suspect. The latter portion of this definition focuses primarily upon the perceptions of the suspect, rather than the intent of the police. This focus reflects the fact that the *Miranda* safeguards were designed to vest a suspect in custody with an added measure of protection against coercive police practices, without regard to objective proof of the underlying intent of the police. A practice that the police should know is reasonably likely to evoke an incriminating response from a suspect thus amounts to interrogation.[9] But, since the police surely cannot be held accountable for the unforeseeable results of their words or actions, the definition of interrogation can extend only to words or actions on the part of police officers that they *should have known* were reasonably likely to elicit an incriminating response.

B

Turning to the facts of the present case, we conclude that the respondent was not "interrogated" within the meaning of *Miranda*. It is undisputed that the first prong of the definition of "interrogation" was not satisfied, for the conversation between Patrolmen Gleckman and McKenna included no express questioning of the respondent. Rather, that conversation was, at least in form, nothing more than a dialogue between the two officers to which no response from the respondent was invited.

Moreover, it cannot be fairly concluded that the respondent was subjected to the "functional equivalent" of questioning. It cannot be said, in short, that Patrolmen Gleckman and McKenna should have known that their conversation was reasonably likely to elicit an incriminating response from the respondent. There is nothing in the record to suggest that the officers were aware that the respondent was peculiarly susceptible to an appeal to his conscience concerning the safety of handicapped children. Nor

has been filed. Custody in such a case is not controlling; indeed, the petitioner in *Massiah* was not in custody. By contrast, the right to counsel at issue in the present case is based not on the Sixth and Fourteenth Amendments, but rather on the Fifth and Fourteenth Amendments as interpreted in the *Miranda* opinion. The definitions of "interrogation" under the Fifth and Sixth Amendments, if indeed the term "interrogation" is even apt in the Sixth Amendment context, are not necessarily interchangeable, since the policies underlying the two constitutional protections are quite distinct. . . .

9. This is not to say that the intent of the police is irrelevant, for it may well have a bearing on whether the police should have known that their words or actions were reasonably likely to evoke an incriminating response. In particular, where a police practice is designed to elicit an incriminating response from the accused, it is unlikely that the practice will not also be one which the police should have known was reasonably likely to have that effect.

is there anything in the record to suggest that the police knew that the respondent was unusually disoriented or upset at the time of his arrest.

The case thus boils down to whether, in the context of a brief conversation, the officers should have known that the respondent would suddenly be moved to make a self-incriminating response. Given the fact that the entire conversation appears to have consisted of no more than a few offhand remarks, we cannot say that the officers should have known that it was reasonably likely that Innis would so respond. This is not a case where the police carried on a lengthy harangue in the presence of the suspect. Nor does the record support the respondent's contention that, under the circumstances, the officers' comments were particularly "evocative." It is our view, therefore, that the respondent was not subjected by the police to words or actions that the police should have known were reasonably likely to elicit an incriminating response from him.

The Rhode Island Supreme Court erred, in short, in equating "subtle compulsion" with interrogation. That the officers' comments struck a responsive chord is readily apparent. Thus, it may be said, as the Rhode Island Supreme Court did say, that the respondent was subjected to "subtle compulsion." But that is not the end of the inquiry. It must also be established that a suspect's incriminating response was the product of words or actions on the part of the police that they should have known were reasonably likely to elicit an incriminating response. This was not established in the present case.

For the reasons stated, the judgment of the Supreme Court of Rhode Island is vacated, and the case is remanded to that court for further proceedings not inconsistent with this opinion.

. . .[10]

---

240. *Miranda* is not applicable to "routine booking questions" or to "carefully scripted instructions" and "limited and carefully worded inquiries" related to a legitimate police procedure. Pennsylvania v. Muniz, 496 U.S. 582 (1990) (8–1).

241. After the defendant, having been arrested and advised of his rights, said that he did not want to make any statements unless his lawyer was present, police allowed his wife, at her urging, to speak with him in the presence of an officer. The officer openly taped the defendant's conversation with his wife. The Court concluded that the police action was not the "functional equivalent" of interrogation and was permissible. The Court noted that the police had not encouraged the defendant or his wife to speak to one another, but had yielded to her insistence, and that there were legitimate reasons, such as the wife's safety and security generally, to have an officer present. Arizona v. Mauro, 481 U.S. 520 (1987) (5–4).

---

[10] Justice White wrote a brief note, indicating his concurrence. Chief Justice Burger wrote an opinion concurring in the judgment. Justice Marshall wrote a dissenting opinion, which Justice Brennan joined. Justice Stevens also wrote a dissenting opinion.

Waiver

---

242. In *Miranda*, the Court said that the defendant can waive "effectuation" of his rights, "provided the waiver is made voluntarily, knowingly and intelligently," pp. 417–418 above. In a dissenting opinion, Justice White asked how a defendant could be permitted to waive his rights without first consulting an attorney, if he could not (but for the waiver) be permitted voluntarily to answer questions without the advice of counsel. 384 U.S. at 536. When is a waiver "made voluntarily, knowingly and intelligently"?

> [I]f a prisoner is told that he has a right to say nothing and that what he says may be used against him, and that he has a right to an attorney and to his presence during any interrogation, at public expense if he is indigent, the objective of *Miranda* is fully met. It is irrelevant that the prisoner, so advised, chooses to speak without counsel because he misconceives his need for aid or the utility of a lawyer. . . .
>
> . . .
>
> There is no right to escape detection. There is no right to commit a perfect crime or to an equal opportunity to that end. The Constitution is not at all offended when a guilty man stubs his toe. On the contrary, it is decent to hope that he will. Nor is it dirty business to use evidence a defendant himself may furnish in the detectional stage. Voluntary confessions accord with high moral values, and as to the culprit who reveals his guilt unwittingly with no intent to shed his inner burden, it is no more unfair to use the evidence he thereby reveals than it is to turn against him clues at the scene of the crime which a brighter, better informed, or more gifted criminal would not have left. Thus the Fifth Amendment does not say that a man shall not be permitted to incriminate himself, or that he shall not be persuaded to do so. It says no more than that a man shall not be "compelled" to give evidence against himself.
>
> Hence while we are solicitous of the right to counsel at the trial stage to the end that a defendant shall not suffer injustice because he is not equipped to protect himself, it would be thoughtless to transfer the same right to counsel to the detectional scene. If it be granted that a man may seek legal advice as to how to avoid detection, it is not because the Constitution guarantees him that right. Surely *Miranda* does not say that a man's deed or word may not be used against him merely because he was unaware of its incriminating thrust . . . or unless he first rejected an opportunity for advice by counsel. . . . A

man could not escape his confession to a friend or relative because he thought that what he said did not constitute proof of a crime or that the friend or relative could not testify against him. It is consonant with good morals, and the Constitution, to exploit a criminal's ignorance or stupidity in the detectional process. This must be so if Government is to succeed in its primary mission to protect the first right of the individual to live free from criminal attack.

. . .

. . . Nowhere does *Miranda* suggest that the waiver of counsel at the detectional stage would not be "knowing" or "intelligent" if the suspect did not understand the law relating to the crime, the possible defenses, and the hazards of talking without the aid of counsel, or if the suspect was not able to protect his interests without such aid, or . . . if it was not "wise" of the prisoner to forego counsel or the right to silence. . . . However relevant to "waiver" of the right to counsel at trial or in connection with a plea of guilty, those factors are foreign to the investigational scene where the detection of the guilty is the legitimate aim.

Hence if a defendant was given the *Miranda* warnings, if the coercion of custodial interrogation was thus dissipated, his "waiver" was no less "voluntary" and "knowing" and "intelligent" because he misconceived the inculpatory thrust of the facts he admitted, or because he thought that what he said could not be used because it was only oral or because he had his fingers crossed, or because he could well have used a lawyer. A man need not have the understanding of a lawyer to waive one. Such matters, irrelevant when the defendant volunteers his confession to a friend or to a policeman passing on his beat, are equally irrelevant when the confession is made in custody after the coercion of custodial interrogation has been dispelled by the *Miranda* warnings. With such warnings, the essential fact remains that defendant understood he had the right to remain silent and thereby to avoid the risk of self-incrimination. That is what the Fifth Amendment privilege is about.

State v. McKnight, 243 A.2d 240 (N.J.1968).

243. 18 U.S.C. § 5033 provides that when a juvenile is taken in custody, the juvenile's parents must immediately be notified and must also be notified of his rights and the nature of the alleged offense. In United States v. Wendy G., 255 F.3d 761 (9th Cir.2001), the court held that the parents must be informed that they will have an opportunity "to advise and counsel" the juvenile before interrogation.

In Fare v. Michael C., 442 U.S. 707 (1979) (5–4), the Court held that the request of a juvenile who was in custody in connection with a murder to speak to his probation officer was not the equivalent of a request to speak to an attorney and did not, therefore, per se require that questioning stop, as would have a request to speak to an attorney, see note 246, p. 439 below. The juvenile had been given his *Miranda* warnings and had asked to see his probation officer when he was advised of his right to see an attorney. The Court declared that the question of waiver in this case should be decided on the basis of all the circumstances, and concluded that the juvenile court's finding of waiver was correct.

See United States ex rel. Riley v. Franzen, 653 F.2d 1153 (7th Cir. 1981) (*Michael C.* applied; juvenile's request to see parent invoked neither right to counsel nor right to remain silent). *Miranda* aside, state law may require police to give a juvenile an opportunity to speak to his parent or another adult before questioning him. See, e.g., Commonwealth v. Henderson, 437 A.2d 387 (Pa.1981).

244.

Three days after the commission of a homicide in the course of a robbery, the police of Newport News, Virginia, arrested Harris and took him to the police station at about 9:15 p.m. Captain Weaver of the Detective Bureau told Harris that he was charged with armed robbery and murder and correctly read him his *Miranda* rights. Harris said he understood them. Some 20 minutes later Lt. Austin repeated the *Miranda* warnings and again advised Harris of the charges against him, requesting that Harris sign a waiver-of-rights form. Harris refused to sign, but expressed his willingness to talk and reaffirmed that he understood the explanation to him of his *Miranda* rights.

Lt. Austin knew Harris' parents and telephoned the boy's mother and requested she come to the station right away. Lt. Austin also permitted Harris to telephone his girlfriend and later his sister. While all this was going on, Harris talked freely, insisting that, although present at the place of robbery and homicide, and although carrying a pistol, he did not fire it.

About an hour after beginning their conversation, Harris and Lt. Austin were joined by Harris' uncle, who had come in response to the telephone call to Harris' mother. In the uncle's presence, Harris was advised of his *Miranda* rights for the third time. He told his uncle he had not been mistreated in any way. Harris and his uncle were offered the opportunity to talk privately but declined. Harris was then asked by Lt. Austin to relate the facts of the robbery to his uncle, and Harris substantially repeated his earlier oral statement. It was this statement before his uncle that was later admitted into evidence against him.

During the course of making his confession, according to Lt. Austin's testimony, Harris explained to Austin that he was willing to talk about it but would not sign anything. The Lieutenant's testimony is susceptible to three interpretations, and for decisional purposes we read it (favorably to Harris) to mean that Harris talked freely but would not sign anything because (1) Harris thought that if he simply told about it, it would be Lt. Austin's word against his and, if he later decided to deny the conversation, the judge would believe him rather than Austin; (2) Harris thought an oral confession inadmissible in court; and (3) Harris misunderstood the elements of felony murder and thought that proof that he personally fired the gun was essential to convicting him of the graver offense.

Harris was 17 years old. His I.Q. was 67, which is within the "dull-normal" range of intelligence at about the sixth-grade level. His poorly developed language skills were at about the third-grade level. At trial the defense psychiatrist conceded, however, that Harris understood both his right to remain silent and that anything he said could and would be used against him, though, as to the latter, he might not understand "to what degree and to what extent it would be used or what charges [it would support]." The psychiatrist further testified that Harris' limited understanding of the consequences of talking would be shared by "many people even with a superior I.Q.," and that the primary source of Harris' confusion was his ignorance of the felony-murder doctrine.

Harris' confession was admitted over objection that it was not the product of a knowing and intelligent waiver of his right to keep silent within the meaning of *Miranda*.

Harris v. Riddle, 551 F.2d 936, 937 (4th Cir.1977).

Assuming that Lt. Austin perceived that Harris's willingness to answer questions was based on a misunderstanding of the law and that he would not answer questions if he understood the consequences, was Austin under any (constitutional) obligation to explain the situation?

245. In North Carolina v. Butler, 441 U.S. 369 (1979) (5–3), the Supreme Court said that *Miranda* does not require that a waiver of the right to the presence of a lawyer during custodial interrogation be made expressly orally or in writing. While the prosecution has a heavy burden of proof to establish such a waiver, "in at least some cases waiver can be clearly inferred from the actions and words of the person interrogated." Id. at 373. In Colorado v. Connelly, 479 U.S. 157 (1986) (5–4), the Court specified that the prosecution is required to prove that a defendant has waived his right to the assistance of counsel during custodial interrogation by a preponderance of the evidence. See Tague v. Louisiana, 444 U.S. 469 (1980) (7–2) (no waiver).

246. Edwards v. Arizona, 451 U.S. 477 (1981). "[W]hen an accused has invoked his right to have counsel present during custodial interrogation, a valid waiver of that right cannot be established by showing only that he responded to further police-initiated custodial interrogation even if he has been advised of his rights. . . . [A]n accused . . . having expressed his desire to deal with the police only through counsel, is not subject to further interrogation by the authorities until counsel has been made available to him, unless the accused himself initiates further communication, exchanges, or conversations with the police." Id. at 484–85.

The Court applied *Edwards* in Oregon v. Bradshaw, 462 U.S. 1039 (1983) (5–4). It was agreed by all the Justices that, under *Edwards*, questioning of a defendant who has requested counsel may not be resumed unless (1) the defendant initiates further conversation with the police, and

(2) he in fact waives his right to counsel. Beyond that, the Court indicated considerable disagreement about the stringency of the test of a waiver. See Smith v. Illinois, 469 U.S. 91 (1984) (6–3), holding that no subsequent responses of the defendant to further questions can be used to cast doubt on the original request for counsel, which bars questioning. See also Solem v. Stumes, 465 U.S. 638, 646 (1984) (6–3) (*Edwards* not applied retroactively), emphasizing the "bright line" rule laid down by *Edwards*.

The *Edwards* rule, cutting off questioning, comes into play only if a suspect "unambiguously request[s] counsel." Davis v. United States, 512 U.S. 452, 459 (1994). The Court said that it would not "extend *Edwards* and require law enforcement officers to cease questioning immediately upon the making of an ambiguous or equivocal reference to an attorney." Id. "The rationale underlying *Edwards* is that the police must respect a suspect's wishes regarding his right to have an attorney present during custodial interrogation. But when the officers conducting the questioning reasonably do not know whether or not the suspect wants a lawyer, a rule requiring the immediate cessation of questioning . . . would needlessly prevent the police from questioning a suspect in the absence of counsel even if the suspect did not wish to have a lawyer present." Id. at 460. The Court acknowledged "that requiring a clear assertion of the right to counsel might disadvantage some suspects who—because of fear, intimidation, lack of linguistic skills, or a variety of other reasons—will not clearly articulate their right to counsel although they actually want to have a lawyer present." Id. But, the Court said, "the primary protection afforded suspects subject to custodial interrogation is the *Miranda* warnings themselves." Id.

In a concurring opinion, four Justices expressed the view that the rule should be that "when a suspect under custodial interrogation makes an ambiguous statement that might reasonably be understood as expressing a wish that a lawyer be summoned (and questioning cease), interrogators' questions should be confined to verifying whether the individual meant to ask for a lawyer." Id. at 476. The majority observed that asking such clarifying questions would "often be good police practice," but made clear that it was not required. Id. at 461.

Davis was applied in Clark v. Murphy, 331 F.3d 1062 (9th Cir.2003) ("I think I would like to talk to a lawyer" not unambiguous and unequivocal). See Coleman v. Singletary, 30 F.3d 1420 (11th Cir.1994) (equivocal statement that the defendant did not want to answer further questions); Midkiff v. Commonwealth, 462 S.E.2d 112 (Va.1995) ("I'll be honest with you, I'm scared to say anything without talking to a lawyer" not "clear and unambiguous").

In Connecticut v. Barrett, 479 U.S. 523 (1987) (7–2), the defendant was given *Miranda* warnings and thereafter agreed to talk with the police but said that he would not give a written statement unless his attorney were present. At trial, the defendant testified that he understood the *Miranda* warnings. Reversing a decision of the state supreme court, the Court held that *Edwards* did not require suppression of the defendant's oral statements. Even though a request for counsel should be broadly construed, the defendant's statements to the police were not ambiguous and should be understood as he evidently intended them.

Hawaii has adopted the view of the concurring opinion in *Davis*. State v. Hoey, 881 P.2d 504 (Haw.1994) (other cases cited).

Edwards prohibits the police from reinitiating an interrogation of a suspect without counsel present, whether or not the suspect has had an opportunity to consult with counsel. "A single consultation with an attorney does not remove the suspect from persistent attempts by officials to persuade him to waive his rights, or from the coercive pressures that accompany custody and that may increase as custody is prolonged." Minnick v. Mississippi, 498 U.S. 146, 487 (1990) (6–2). *Edwards* applies, furthermore, to questioning about an unrelated crime, whether such questioning is by the same officers who elicited the request or by others. Arizona v. Roberson, 486 U.S. 675 (1988) (6–2).

In United States v. Kelsey, 951 F.2d 1196 (10th Cir.1991), after the defendant was arrested but before he was given *Miranda* warnings, he asked to speak with his lawyer. Later, he was given *Miranda* warnings and then questioned. The government contended that *Edwards* was inapplicable, because the defendant's request to speak with his lawyer preceded any questioning and the giving of the warnings. The court held that *Edwards* was applicable and that the questioning was improper.

Edwards was applied to a confession obtained by police questioning following the defendant's request for appointed counsel at an initial appearance ("arraignment") before a magistrate, in Michigan v. Jackson, 475 U.S. 625 (1986) (6–3). The Court said that application of the strict *Edwards* rule was even more appropriate for the right to counsel than for the privilege against compulsory self-incrimination and that the factual differences in the circumstances in which the request for counsel is made do not warrant a departure from the rule. Accordingly, "if police initiate interrogation after a defendant's assertion, at an arraignment or similar proceeding, of his right to counsel, any waiver of the defendant's right to counsel for that police-initiated interrogation is invalid." Id. at 636.

In McNeil v. Wisconsin, 501 U.S. 171 (1991) (6–3), the defendant was arrested on a charge of armed robbery. Formal proceedings began and his right to counsel attached. Then, police officers initiated questioning about other crimes, and the defendant waived his rights under *Miranda*. The Court held that the right to counsel that had attached for one crime did not prevent police from initiating questioning about other crimes. It said that the right to counsel as such (i.e., not in the context of custodial interrogation) being offense-specific, "[i]t cannot be invoked once for all future prosecutions, for it does not attach until a prosecution is commenced." Id. at 175.

Edwards was distinguished in Wyrick v. Fields, 459 U.S. 42 (1982) (8–1), which involved questioning following voluntary submission to a polygraph examination. After having been arrested on a charge of rape and having retained counsel, the defendant requested the polygraph examination, before which he waived the right to have counsel present. The Court said that the waiver applied to the post-examination questioning as well and that no additional *Miranda* warnings had to be given.

Moran v. Burbine

475 U.S. 412, 106 S.Ct. 1135, 89 L.Ed.2d 410 (1986)

■ JUSTICE O'CONNOR delivered the opinion of the Court.

After being informed of his rights pursuant to Miranda v. Arizona, 384 U.S. 436 (1966), and after executing a series of written waivers, respondent confessed to the murder of a young woman. At no point during the course of interrogation, which occurred prior to arraignment, did he request an attorney. While he was in police custody, his sister attempted to retain a lawyer to represent him. The attorney telephoned the police station and received assurances that respondent would not be questioned further until the next day. In fact, the interrogation session that yielded the inculpatory statements began later that evening. The question presented is whether either the conduct of the police or respondent's ignorance of the attorney's efforts to reach him taints the validity of the waivers and therefore requires exclusion of the confessions.

I

On the morning of March 3, 1977, Mary Jo Hickey was found unconscious in a factory parking lot in Providence, Rhode Island. Suffering from injuries to her skull apparently inflicted by a metal pipe found at the scene, she was rushed to a nearby hospital. Three weeks later she died from her wounds.

Several months after her death, the Cranston, Rhode Island police arrested respondent and two others in connection with a local burglary. Shortly before the arrest, Detective Ferranti of the Cranston police force had learned from a confidential informant that the man responsible for Ms. Hickey's death lived at a certain address and went by the name of "Butch." Upon discovering that respondent lived at that address and was known by that name, Detective Ferranti informed respondent of his *Miranda* rights. When respondent refused to execute a written waiver, Detective Ferranti spoke separately with the two other suspects arrested on the breaking and entering charge and obtained statements further implicating respondent in Ms. Hickey's murder. At approximately 6 p.m., Detective Ferranti telephoned the police in Providence to convey the information he had uncovered. An hour later, three officers from that department arrived at the Cranston headquarters for the purpose of questioning respondent about the murder.

That same evening, at about 7:45 p.m., respondent's sister telephoned the Public Defender's Office to obtain legal assistance for her brother. Her sole concern was the breaking and entering charge, as she was unaware that respondent was then under suspicion for murder. She asked for Richard Casparian who had been scheduled to meet with respondent earlier that afternoon to discuss another charge unrelated to either the break-in or the murder. As soon as the conversation ended, the attorney who took the call attempted to reach Mr. Casparian. When those efforts were unsuccessful, she telephoned Allegra Munson, another Assistant Public Defender, and told her about respondent's arrest and his sister's subsequent request that the office represent him.

At 8:15 p.m., Ms. Munson telephoned the Cranston police station and asked that her call be transferred to the detective division. In the words of the Supreme Court of Rhode Island . . . the conversation proceeded as follows:

> A male voice responded with the word "Detectives." Ms. Munson identified herself and asked if Brian Burbine was being held; the person responded affirmatively. Ms. Munson explained to the person that Burbine was represented by attorney Casparian who was not available; she further stated that she would act as Burbine's legal counsel in the event that the police intended to place him in a lineup or question him. The unidentified person told Ms. Munson that the police would not be questioning Burbine or putting him in a lineup and that they were through with him for the night. Ms. Munson was not informed that the Providence Police were at the Cranston police station or that Burbine was a suspect in Mary's murder.

State v. Burbine, 451 A.2d 22, 23–24 (1982). At all relevant times, respondent was unaware of his sister's efforts to retain counsel and of the fact and contents of Ms. Munson's telephone conversation.

Less than an hour later, the police brought respondent to an interrogation room and conducted the first of a series of interviews concerning the murder. Prior to each session, respondent was informed of his *Miranda* rights, and on three separate occasions he signed a written form acknowledging that he understood his right to the presence of an attorney and explicitly indicating that he "[did] not want an attorney called or appointed for [him]" before he gave a statement. App. to Pet. for Cert. 94, 103, 107. Uncontradicted evidence at the suppression hearing indicated that at least twice during the course of the evening, respondent was left in a room where he had access to a telephone, which he apparently declined to use. . . . Eventually, respondent signed three written statements fully admitting to the murder.

Prior to trial, respondent moved to suppress the statements. The court denied the motion, finding that respondent had received the *Miranda* warnings and had "knowingly, intelligently, and voluntarily waived his privilege against self-incrimination [and] his right to counsel." App. to Pet. for Cert. 116. Rejecting the contrary testimony of the police, the court found that Ms. Munson did telephone the detective bureau on the evening in question, but concluded that "there was no . . . conspiracy or collusion on the part of the Cranston Police Department to secrete this defendant from his attorney." Id., at 114. In any event, the court held, the constitutional right to request the presence of an attorney belongs solely to the defendant and may not be asserted by his lawyer. Because the evidence was clear that respondent never asked for the services of an attorney, the telephone call had no relevance to the validity of the waiver or the admissibility of the statements.

The jury found respondent guilty of murder in the first degree, and he appealed to the Supreme Court of Rhode Island. A divided court rejected his contention that the Fifth and Fourteenth Amendments to the Constitution required the suppression of the inculpatory statements and affirmed the conviction. . . . [T]he court noted that because two different police departments were operating in the Cranston station house on the evening in question, the record supported the trial court's finding that there was no "conspiracy or collusion" to prevent Ms. Munson from seeing respondent. 451 A.2d, at 30, n.5. In any case, the court held, the right to the presence of counsel belongs solely to the accused and may not be asserted by "benign third parties, whether or not they happen to be attorneys." Id., at 28.

After unsuccessfully petitioning the United States District Court for the District of Rhode Island for a writ of habeas corpus . . . respondent appealed to the Court of Appeals for the First Circuit. That court reversed. 753 F.2d 178 (1985). Finding it unnecessary to reach any arguments under the Sixth and Fourteenth Amendments, the court held that the police's conduct had fatally tainted respondent's "otherwise valid" waiver of his Fifth Amendment privilege against self-incrimination and right to counsel. Id., at 184. The court reasoned that by failing to inform respondent that an attorney had called and that she had been assured that no questioning would take place until the next day, the police had deprived respondent of information crucial to his ability to waive his rights knowingly and intelligently. The court also found that the record would support "no other explanation for the refusal to tell Burbine of Attorney Munson's call than . . . deliberate or reckless irresponsibility." Id., at 185. This kind of "blameworthy action by the police," the court concluded, together with respondent's ignorance of the telephone call, "vitiate[d] any claim that [the] waiver of counsel was knowing and voluntary." Id., at 185, 187.

We granted certiorari to decide whether a prearraignment confession preceded by an otherwise valid waiver must be suppressed either because the police misinformed an inquiring attorney about their plans concerning the suspect or because they failed to inform the suspect of the attorney's efforts to reach him. . . . We now reverse.

II

In Miranda v. Arizona, the Court recognized that custodial interrogations, by their very nature, generate "compelling pressures which work to undermine the individual's will to resist and to compel him to speak where he would not otherwise do so freely." 384 U.S., at 467. To combat this inherent compulsion, and thereby protect the Fifth Amendment privilege against self-incrimination, *Miranda* imposed on the police an obligation to follow certain procedures in their dealings with the accused. In particular, prior to the initiation of questioning, they must fully apprise the suspect of the State's intention to use his statements to secure a conviction, and must inform him of his rights to remain silent and to "have counsel present . . . if [he] so desires." Id., at 468–70. Beyond this duty to inform, *Miranda* requires that the police respect the accused's decision to exercise the rights outlined in the warnings. "If the individual indicates in any manner, at any time prior to or during questioning, that he wishes to remain silent, [or if he] states that he wants an attorney, the interrogation must cease." *Miranda*, 384 U.S., at 473–74. . . .

Respondent does not dispute that the Providence police followed these procedures with precision. The record amply supports the state-court findings that the police administered the required warnings, sought to assure that respondent understood his rights, and obtained an express written waiver prior to eliciting each of the three statements. Nor does respondent contest the Rhode Island courts' determination that he at no point requested the presence of a lawyer. He contends instead that the confessions must be suppressed because the police's failure to inform him of the attorney's telephone call deprived him of information essential to his ability to knowingly waive his Fifth Amendment rights. In the alternative, he suggests that to fully protect the Fifth Amendment values served by *Miranda*, we should extend that decision to condemn the conduct of the Providence police. We address each contention in turn.

A

Echoing the standard first articulated in Johnson v. Zerbst, 304 U.S. 458, 464 (1938), *Miranda* holds that "[t]he defendant may waive effectuation" of the rights conveyed in the warnings "provided the waiver is made voluntarily, knowingly and intelligently." 384 U.S., at 444, 475. The inquiry has two distinct dimensions. . . . First the relinquishment of the right must have been voluntary in the sense that it was the product of a free and deliberate choice rather than intimidation, coercion or deception. Second, the waiver must have been made with a full awareness both of the nature of the right being abandoned and the consequences of the decision to abandon it. Only if the "totality of the circumstances surrounding the interrogation" reveals both an uncoerced choice and the requisite level of comprehension may a court properly conclude that the *Miranda* rights have been waived. Fare v. Michael C., 442 U.S. 707, 725 (1979). . . .

Under this standard, we have no doubt that respondent validly waived his right to remain silent and to the presence of counsel. The voluntariness of the waiver is not at issue. As the Court of Appeals correctly acknowledged, the record is devoid of any suggestion that police resorted to physical or psychological pressure to elicit the statements. . . . Indeed it appears that it was respondent, and not the police, who spontaneously initiated the conversation that led to the first and most damaging confession. . . . Nor is there any question about respondent's comprehension of the full panoply of rights set out in the *Miranda* warnings and of the potential consequences of a decision to relinquish them. Nonetheless, the Court of Appeals believed that the "[d]eliberate or reckless" conduct of the police, in particular their failure to inform respondent of the telephone call, fatally undermined the validity of the otherwise proper waiver. We find this conclusion untenable as a matter of both logic and precedent.

Events occurring outside of the presence of the suspect and entirely unknown to him surely can have no bearing on the capacity to comprehend and knowingly relinquish a constitutional right. Under the analysis of the Court of Appeals, the same defendant, armed with the same information and confronted with precisely the same police conduct, would have knowingly waived his *Miranda* rights had a lawyer not telephoned the police station to inquire about his status. Nothing in any of our waiver decisions or in our understanding of the essential components of a valid waiver requires so incongruous a result. No doubt the additional information would have been useful to respondent; perhaps even it might have affected his decision to confess. But we have never read the Constitution to require that the police supply a suspect with a flow of information to help him calibrate his self-interest in deciding whether to speak or stand by his rights. . . . Once it is determined that a suspect's decision not to rely on his rights was uncoerced, that he at all times knew he could stand mute and request a lawyer, and that he was aware of the State's intention to use his statements to secure a conviction, the analysis is complete and the waiver is valid as a matter of law. The Court of Appeals' conclusion to the contrary was in error.

Nor do we believe that the level of the police's culpability in failing to inform respondent of the telephone call has any bearing on the validity of the waivers. In light of the state-court findings that there was no "conspiracy or collusion" on the part of the police, 451 A.2d, at 30, n.5, we have serious doubts about whether the Court of Appeals was free to conclude that their conduct constituted "deliberate or reckless irresponsibility." 753 F.2d, at 185; see 28 U.S.C. § 2254(d). But whether intentional or inadvertent, the state of mind of the police is irrelevant to the question of the intelligence and voluntariness of respondent's election to abandon his rights. Although highly inappropriate, even deliberate deception of an attorney could not possibly affect a suspect's decision to waive his *Miranda* rights unless he were at least aware of the incident. . . . Nor was the failure to inform respondent of the telephone call the kind of "trick[ery]" that can vitiate the validity of a waiver. *Miranda*, 384 U.S., at 476. Granting that the "deliberate or reckless" withholding of information is objectionable as a matter of ethics, such conduct is only relevant to the constitutional validity of a waiver if it deprives a defendant of knowledge essential to his ability to understand the nature of his rights and the consequences of abandoning them. Because respondent's voluntary decision to speak was made with full awareness and comprehension of all the information *Miranda* requires the police to convey, the waivers were valid.

B

At oral argument respondent acknowledged that a constitutional rule requiring the police to inform a suspect of an attorney's efforts to reach him would represent a significant extension of our precedents. . . . He contends, however, that the conduct of the Providence police was so inimical to the Fifth Amendment values *Miranda* seeks to protect that we should read that decision to condemn their behavior. Regardless of any issue of waiver, he urges, the Fifth Amendment requires the reversal of a conviction if the police are less than forthright in their dealings with an attorney or if they fail to tell a suspect of a lawyer's unilateral efforts to contact him. Because the proposed modification ignores the underlying purposes of the *Miranda* rules and because we think that the decision as written strikes the proper balance between society's legitimate law enforcement interests and the protection of the defendant's Fifth Amendment rights, we decline the invitation to further extend *Miranda*'s reach.

At the outset, while we share respondent's distaste for the deliberate misleading of an officer of the court, reading *Miranda* to forbid police deception of an *attorney* "would cut [the decision] completely loose from its own explicitly stated rationale." Beckwith v. United States, 425 U.S. 341, 345 (1976). As is now well established, "[t]he . . . *Miranda* warnings are 'not themselves rights protected by the Constitution but [are] instead measures to insure that the [suspect's] right against compulsory self-incrimination [is] protected.'" New York v. Quarles, 467 U.S. 649, 654 (1984), quoting Michigan v. Tucker, 417 U.S. 433, 444 (1974). Their objective is not to mold police conduct for its own sake. Nothing in the Constitution vests in us the authority to mandate a code of behavior for state officials wholly unconnected to any federal right or privilege. The purpose of the *Miranda* warnings instead is to dissipate the compulsion inherent in custodial interrogation and, in so doing, guard against abridgment of the suspect's Fifth Amendment rights. Clearly, a rule that focuses on how the police treat an attorney—conduct that has no relevance at all to the degree of compulsion experienced by the defendant during interrogation—would ignore both *Miranda*'s mission and its only source of legitimacy.

Nor are we prepared to adopt a rule requiring that the police inform a suspect of an attorney's efforts to reach him. While such a rule might add marginally to *Miranda*'s goal of dispelling the compulsion inherent in custodial interrogation, overriding practical considerations counsel against its adoption. As we have stressed on numerous occasions, "[o]ne of the principal advantages" of *Miranda* is the ease and clarity of its application. Berkemer v. McCarty, 468 U.S. 420, 430 (1984). . . . We have little doubt that the approach urged by respondent and endorsed by the Court of Appeals would have the inevitable consequence of muddying *Miranda*'s otherwise relatively clear waters. The legal questions it would spawn are legion: To what extent should the police be held accountable for knowing that the accused has counsel? Is it enough that someone in the station house knows, or must the interrogating officer himself know of counsel's efforts to contact the suspect? Do counsel's efforts to talk to the suspect concerning one criminal investigation trigger the obligation to inform the defendant before interrogation may proceed on a wholly separate matter? We are unwilling to modify *Miranda* in a manner that would so clearly undermine the decision's central "virtue of informing police and prosecutors with specificity . . . what they may do in conducting [a] custodial interrogation, and of informing courts under what circumstances statements obtained during such interrogation are not admissible." Fare v. Michael C., supra, at 718.

Moreover, problems of clarity to one side, reading *Miranda* to require the police in each instance to inform a suspect of an attorney's efforts to reach him would work a substantial and, we think, inappropriate shift in the subtle balance struck in that decision. Custodial interrogations implicate two competing concerns. On the one hand, "the need for police questioning as a tool for effective enforcement of criminal laws" cannot be doubted. Schneckloth v. Bustamonte, 412 U.S. 218, 225 (1973). Admissions of guilt are more than merely "desirable," United States v. Washington, 431 U.S. [181 (1977)], at 186; they are essential to society's compelling interest in finding, convicting and punishing those who violate the law. On the other hand, the Court has recognized that the interrogation process is "inherently coercive" and that, as a consequence, there exists a substantial risk that the police will inadvertently traverse the fine line between legitimate efforts to elicit admissions and constitutionally impermissible compulsion. New York v. Quarles, 467 U.S., at 656. *Miranda* attempted to reconcile these opposing concerns by giving the *defendant* the power to exert some control over the course of the interrogation. Declining to adopt the more extreme position that the actual presence of a lawyer was necessary to dispel the coercion inherent in custodial interrogation . . . the Court found that the suspect's Fifth Amendment rights could be adequately protected by less intrusive means. Police questioning, often an essential part of the investigatory process, could continue in its traditional form, the Court held, but only if the suspect clearly understood that, at any time, he could bring the proceeding to a halt or, short of that, call in an attorney to give advice and monitor the conduct of his interrogators.

The position urged by respondent would upset this carefully drawn approach in a manner that is both unnecessary for the protection of the Fifth Amendment privilege and injurious to legitimate law enforcement. Because, as *Miranda* holds, full comprehension of the rights to remain silent and request an attorney are sufficient to dispel whatever coercion is inherent in the interrogation process, a rule requiring the police to inform the suspect of an attorney's efforts to contact him would contribute to the protection of the Fifth Amendment privilege only incidentally, if at all. This minimal benefit, however, would come at a substantial cost to society's legitimate and substantial interest in securing admissions of guilt. Indeed, the very premise of the Court of Appeals was not that awareness of Ms. Munson's phone call would have dissipated the coercion of the interrogation room, but that it might have convinced respondent not to speak at all. . . . Because neither the letter nor purposes of *Miranda* require this additional handicap on otherwise permissible investigatory efforts, we are unwilling to expand the *Miranda* rules to require the police to keep the suspect abreast of the status of his legal representation.

We acknowledge that a number of state courts have reached a contrary conclusion. . . . We recognize also that our interpretation of the Federal Constitution, if given the dissent's expansive gloss, is at odds with the policy recommendations embodied in the American Bar Association Standards of Criminal Justice. . . . Notwithstanding the dissent's protestations, however, our interpretive duties go well beyond deferring to the numerical preponderance of lower court decisions or to the subconstitutional recommendations of even so esteemed a body as the American Bar Association. . . . Nothing we say today disables the States from adopting different requirements for the conduct of its employees and officials as a matter of state law. We hold only that the Court of Appeals erred in construing the Fifth Amendment to the Federal Constitution to require the exclusion of respondent's three confessions.

III

Respondent also contends that the Sixth Amendment requires exclusion of his three confessions. It is clear, of course, that, absent a valid waiver, the defendant has the right to the presence of an attorney during any interrogation occurring after the first formal charging proceeding, the point at which the Sixth Amendment right to counsel initially attaches. . . . And we readily agree that once the right *has* attached, it follows that the police may not interfere with the efforts of a defendant's attorney to act as a " 'medium' between [the suspect] and the State" during the interrogation. Maine v. Moulton, 474 U.S. 159, 176 (1985). . . . The difficulty for respondent is that the interrogation sessions that yielded the inculpatory statements took place *before* the initiation of "adversary judicial proceedings." United States v. Gouveia, [467 U.S. 180 (1984)], at 192. He contends, however, that this circumstance is not fatal to his Sixth Amendment claim. At least in some situations, he argues, the Sixth Amendment protects the integrity of the attorney-client relationship regardless of whether the prosecution has in fact commenced "by way of formal charge, preliminary hearing, indictment, information or arraignment." 467 U.S., at 188. Placing principal reliance on a footnote in *Miranda*, 384 U.S., at 465, n.35, and on Escobedo v. Illinois, 378 U.S. 478 (1964), he maintains that *Gouveia*, *Kirby* [v. Illinois, 406 U.S. 682 (1972)] and our other "critical stage" cases, concern only the narrow question of when the right *to* counsel—that is, to the appointment or presence of counsel—attaches. The right to non-interference with an attorney's dealings with a criminal suspect, he asserts, arises the moment that the relationship is formed, or, at the very least, once the defendant is placed in custodial interrogation.

We are not persuaded. At the outset, subsequent decisions foreclose any reliance on *Escobedo* and *Miranda* for the proposition that the Sixth Amendment right, in any of its manifestations, applies prior to the initiation of adversary judicial proceedings. Although *Escobedo* was originally decided as a Sixth Amendment case, "the Court in retrospect perceived that the 'prime purpose' of *Escobedo* was not to vindicate the constitutional right to counsel as such, but, like *Miranda*, 'to guarantee full effectuation of the privilege against self-incrimination. . . .' " Kirby v. Illinois, supra, at 689, quoting Johnson v. New Jersey, 384 U.S. 719, 729 (1966). Clearly then, *Escobedo* provides no support for respondent's argument. Nor, of course, does *Miranda*, the holding of which rested exclusively on the Fifth Amendment. Thus, the decision's brief observation about the reach of *Escobedo*'s Sixth Amendment analysis is not only dictum, but reflects an understanding of the case that the Court has expressly disavowed. . . .

Questions of precedent to one side, we find respondent's understanding of the Sixth Amendment both practically and theoretically unsound. As a practical matter, it makes little sense to say that the Sixth Amendment right to counsel attaches at different times depending on the fortuity of whether the suspect or his family happens to have retained counsel prior to interrogation. . . . More importantly, the suggestion that the existence of an attorney-client relationship itself triggers the protections of the Sixth Amendment misconceives the underlying purposes of the right to counsel. The Sixth Amendment's intended function is not to wrap a protective cloak around the attorney-client relationship for its own sake any more than it is to protect a suspect from the consequences of his own candor. Its purpose, rather, is to assure that in any "criminal prosecutio[n]," U.S. Const., Amdt. 6, the accused shall not be left to his own devices in facing the " 'prosecutorial forces of organized society.' " Maine v. Moulton, supra, at 170 (quoting Kirby v. Illinois, 406 U.S., at 689). By its very terms, it becomes applicable only when the government's role shifts from investigation to accusation. For it is only then that the assistance of one versed in the "intricacies . . . of law," ibid., is needed to assure that the prosecution's case encounters "the crucible of meaningful adversarial testing." United States v. Cronic, 466 U.S. 648, 656 (1984).

. . .

Respondent contends, however, that custodial interrogations require a different rule. Because confessions elicited during the course of police questioning often seal a suspect's fate, he argues, the need for an advocate—and the concomitant right to noninterference with the attorney-client relationship—is at its zenith, regardless of whether the state has initiated the first adversary judicial proceeding. We do not doubt that a lawyer's presence could be of value to the suspect; and we readily agree that if a suspect confesses, his attorney's case at trial will be that much more difficult. But these concerns are no more decisive in this context than they were for the equally damaging preindictment lineup at issue in *Kirby*. . . . For an interrogation, no more or less than for any other "critical" pretrial event, the possibility that the encounter may have important consequences at trial, standing alone, is insufficient to trigger the Sixth Amendment right to counsel. As *Gouveia* made clear, until such time as the " 'government has committed itself to prosecute, and . . . the adverse positions of government and defendant have solidified' " the Sixth Amendment right to counsel does not attach. 467 U.S., at 189 (quoting Kirby v. Illinois, 406 U.S., at 689).

Because, as respondent acknowledges, the events that led to the inculpatory statements preceded the formal initiation of adversary judicial proceedings, we reject the contention that the conduct of the police violated his rights under the Sixth Amendment.

IV

Finally, respondent contends that the conduct of the police was so offensive as to deprive him of the fundamental fairness guaranteed by the Due Process Clause of the Fourteenth Amendment. Focusing primarily on the impropriety of conveying false information to an attorney, he invites us to declare that such behavior should be condemned as violative of canons fundamental to the " 'traditions and conscience of our people.' " Rochin v. California, 342 U.S. 165, 169 (1952), quoting Snyder v. Massachusetts, 291 U.S. 97, 105 (1934). We do not question that on facts more egregious than those presented here police deception might rise to a level of a due process violation. . . . We hold only that, on these facts, the challenged conduct falls short of the kind of misbehavior that so shocks the sensibilities of civilized society as to warrant a federal intrusion into the criminal processes of the States.

We hold therefore that the Court of Appeals erred in finding that the Federal Constitution required the exclusion of the three inculpatory statements. Accordingly, we reverse and remand for proceedings consistent with this opinion.

. . .[11]

---

247. The defendant was arrested for illegal sale of firearms, while he was making a sale to an undercover agent. He was given *Miranda* warnings and signed a statement that he was willing to answer questions. He was questioned about the firearms transactions that led to his arrest. Thereafter, on the basis of information that the agents had received before the arrest, they questioned him about a homicide. The Court held that the failure to advise the defendant that he would be questioned about the homicide did not make his waiver of the right not to be questioned invalid. A valid waiver does not require that a defendant be told all information that might affect his decision to confess. Failure to tell the defendant that he would be questioned about the homicide was not "trickery" of a kind that would invalidate the waiver. Colorado v. Spring, 479 U.S. 564 (1987) (7–2).

[11] Justice Stevens wrote a dissenting opinion, which Justice Brennan and Justice Marshall joined.

248. A number of states have rejected the Court's holding in Moran v. Burbine and imposed a different rule under state law. In State v. Stoddard, 537 A.2d 446, 452 (Conn.1988), for example, the Supreme Court of Connecticut said: "In light of both the historical record and our due process tradition, we conclude that a suspect must be informed promptly of timely efforts by counsel to render pertinent legal assistance. Armed with that information, the suspect must be permitted to choose whether he wishes to speak with counsel, in which event interrogation must cease, or whether he will forego assistance of counsel, in which event counsel need not be afforded access to the suspect. The police may not preclude the suspect from exercising the choice to which he is constitutionally entitled by responding in less than forthright fashion to the efforts by counsel to contact the suspect. The police, because they are responsible for the suspect's isolation, have a duty to act reasonably, diligently and promptly to provide counsel with accurate information and to apprise the subject of the efforts by counsel." The court said that a failure to inform the arrested person does not necessarily require exclusion of his statements during detention. Rather, the trial court must consider the failure to inform in the context of all the circumstances and decide whether, had the person been informed, he would nevertheless have waived his right to the presence of counsel before making the statements. If so, exclusion is not required.

The Supreme Court of California rejected Moran v. Burbine in People v. Houston, 724 P.2d 1166 (Cal.1986), but its ruling was subsequently overturned by a state constitutional amendment providing that relevant evidence is to be excluded from criminal proceedings only if exclusion is required by the federal Constitution. See People v. Ledesma, 251 Cal.Rptr. 417 (Ct.App.1988). Other states that have rejected Moran v. Burbine include Delaware, Bryan v. State, 571 A.2d 170 (Del.1990); Florida, Haliburton v. State, 514 So.2d 1088 (Fla.1987); Illinois, People v. McCauley, 645 N.E.2d 923 (Ill.1994); People v. Chipman, 743 N.E.2d 48 (Ill.2000) (*McCauley* applicable only if attorney is present at police station); Massachusetts v. Mavredakis, 725 N.E.2d 169 (2000); Michigan, People v. Bender, 551 N.W.2d 71 (Mich.1996); and New Jersey, State v. Reed, 627 A.2d 630 (N.J.1993).

If police officers arrest a person who they believe has committed a serious crime, can they be expected to warn and advise him *effectively* about his rights? The plain import of the *Miranda* opinion is that perfunctory, ritualistic compliance with its requirements is inadequate. Can the police be expected to do more? Is it possible *effectively* to convey the information contained in the *Miranda* warnings without at least intimating that the arrested person would be well advised not to answer questions until he speaks to a lawyer? Put the matter differently: Is it likely that the arrested person will take the *Miranda* warnings very seriously if they are given by a policeman who obviously would like to ask questions and intends to do so unless the person objects? (Consider the "bright line" rule of Edwards v.

Arizona, p. 441 note 246 above, in this connection.) If not, are the *Miranda* warnings likely too often to be ineffective? Or have they some function to perform other than simply to inform arrested persons of their rights?

Orozco v. Texas

394 U.S. 324, 89 S.Ct. 1095, 22 L.Ed.2d 311 (1969)

■ MR. JUSTICE BLACK delivered the opinion of the Court.

The petitioner, Reyes Arias Orozco, was convicted in the Criminal District Court of Dallas County, Texas, of murder without malice and was sentenced to serve in the state prison not less than two nor more than 10 years. The Court of Criminal Appeals of Texas affirmed the conviction, rejecting petitioner's contention that a material part of the evidence against him was obtained in violation of the provision of the Fifth Amendment to the United States Constitution, made applicable to the States by the Fourteenth Amendment, that "No person . . . shall be compelled in any criminal case to be a witness against himself."

The evidence introduced at trial showed that petitioner and the deceased had quarreled outside the El Farleto Cafe in Dallas shortly before midnight. The deceased had apparently spoken to petitioner's female companion inside the restaurant. In the heat of the quarrel outside, the deceased is said to have beaten petitioner about the face and called him "Mexican Grease." A shot was fired killing the deceased. Petitioner left the scene and returned to his boarding house to sleep. At about 4 a.m. four police officers arrived at petitioner's boarding house, were admitted by an unidentified woman, and were told that petitioner was asleep in the bedroom. All four officers entered the bedroom and began to question petitioner. From the moment he gave his name, according to the testimony of one of the officers, petitioner was not free to go where he pleased but was "under arrest." The officers asked him if he had been to the El Farleto restaurant that night and when he answered "yes" he was asked if he owned a pistol. Petitioner admitted owning one. After being asked a second time where the pistol was located, he admitted that it was in the washing machine in a backroom of the boarding house. Ballistics tests indicated that the gun found in the washing machine was the gun that fired the fatal shot. At petitioner's trial, held after the effective date of this Court's decision in Miranda v. Arizona, 384 U.S. 436 (1966), the trial court allowed one of the officers, over the objection of petitioner's lawyer, to relate the statements made by petitioner concerning the gun and petitioner's presence at the scene of the shooting. The trial testimony clearly shows that the officers questioned petitioner about incriminating facts without first informing him of his right to remain silent, his right to have the advice of a lawyer before making any statement, and his right to have a lawyer appointed to assist him if he could not afford to hire one. The Texas Court of Criminal Appeals held, with one judge dissenting, that the admission of testimony concerning the statements petitioner had made without the above warnings was not precluded by *Miranda*. We disagree and hold that the use of these admissions obtained in the absence of the required warnings was a flat violation of the Self-Incrimination Clause of the Fifth Amendment as construed in *Miranda*.

The State has argued here that since petitioner was interrogated on his own bed, in familiar surroundings, our *Miranda* holding should not apply. It is true that the Court did say in *Miranda* that "compulsion to speak in the isolated setting of the police station may be greater than in courts or other official investigations where there are often impartial observers to guard against intimidation or trickery." 384 U.S. 436, 461. But the opinion iterated and reiterated the absolute necessity for officers interrogating people "in custody" to give the described warnings. . . . According to the officer's testimony, petitioner was under arrest and not free to leave when he was questioned in his bedroom in the early hours of the morning. The *Miranda* opinion declared that the warnings were required when the person being interrogated was "in custody at the station *or otherwise deprived of his freedom of action in any significant way*." 384 U.S. 436, 477. (Emphasis supplied.) The decision of this Court in *Miranda* was reached after careful consideration and was announced in lengthy opinions by both the majority and dissenting Justices. There is no need to recanvass those arguments again. We do not, as the dissent implies, expand or extend to the slightest extent our *Miranda* decision. We do adhere to our well-considered holding in that case and therefore reverse the conviction below.

. . .

■ MR. JUSTICE WHITE, with whom MR. JUSTICE STEWART joins, dissenting.

. . . The rule [that "once arrest occurs, the application of *Miranda* is automatic"] is simple but it ignores the purpose of *Miranda* to guard against what was thought to be the corrosive influence of practices which station house interrogation makes feasible. The Court wholly ignores the question whether similar hazards exist or even are possible when police arrest and interrogate on the spot, whether it be on the street corner or in the home, as in this case. No predicate is laid for believing that practices outside the station house are normally prolonged, carried out in isolation, or often productive of the physical or psychological coercion made so much of in *Miranda*. It is difficult to imagine the police duplicating in a person's home or on the street those conditions and practices which the Court found prevalent in the station house and which were thought so threatening to the right to silence. Without such a demonstration, *Miranda* hardly reaches this case or any cases similar to it.

. . .

I cannot accept the dilution of the custody requirements of *Miranda* to this level, where the hazards to the right to silence are so equivocal and unsupported by experience in a recurring number of cases. . . . Even if there were reason to encourage suspects to consult lawyers to tell them to be silent before quizzing at the station house, there is no reason why police in the field should have to preface every casual question of a suspect with the full panoply of *Miranda* warnings. The same danger of coercion is simply not present in such circumstances, and the answers to the questions may as often clear a suspect as help convict him. . . .

. . .[12]

---

249. Whether or not a person is in custody for purposes of the *Miranda* requirements depends on the objective circumstances of the interrogation. It does not depend on the subjective view of either the person interrogated or the officers who conduct the interrogation. Stansbury v. California, 511 U.S. 318 (1994) (per curiam). In *Stansbury*, the Court concluded that the California court had mistakenly given independent significance to the fact that the investigation had not yet focused on the defendant rather than considering it only insofar as it had a bearing on the objective circumstances. Following *Stansbury* and again emphasizing that whether a person is in custody depends on the objective circumstances, the Court has suggested, without quite holding, that a person's individual characteristics, including his age and experience with the law, have little, if any, relevance. Yarborough v. Alvarado, 541 U.S. ___ (2004) (5–4). The Court said that the objective test was intended to give the police clear guidance. It equivocated somewhat about whether obvious characteristics (perhaps including age) or characteristics known to the police who conduct an interrogation might properly be considered, as part of the objective circumstances.

250. Suspecting that Duffy was involved in a robbery during the course of which one of the victims had been stabbed, Nevin, a police officer, went to the house where the defendant was staying and was admitted and taken to the bedroom where the defendant was asleep. "Officer Nevin testified that upon entering the room he noticed a knife sticking out from under the mattress of Duffy's bed and, before arousing the latter, he withdrew it. He then woke Duffy and greeted him with the query, 'is this the knife you used in the fight?' According to Officer Nevin, Duffy's response was, 'no, I had it with me and I dropped it during the fight. Joe Louis picked it up. Then I got it back. I don't know who stabbed the guy.' Appellant was then arrested. . . ." Duffy v. State, 221 A.2d 653, 655 (Md.1966). Is Duffy's statement admissible in evidence against him? Does it make any difference that Duffy was not arrested until after he made the statement? Suppose Officer Nevin testified that he did not believe that he had probable cause to arrest Duffy and did not intend to arrest him until after he heard Duffy's statement.

[12] Justice Harlan wrote a brief concurring opinion. Justice Stewart wrote a brief memorandum.

251. Detectives arrested Daniel W. for car theft and were told by him that Rodney P. was his accomplice. They went to Rodney P.'s home at about 8:00 p.m. and found him standing with two friends on the side steps of the house. One of the detectives asked the two friends to leave and then questioned Rodney P. for about four minutes. Rodney P. admitted that he had taken the car. He was 16 years old. People v. Rodney P. (Anon.), 233 N.E.2d 255 (N.Y.1967). Can Rodney P.'s admission be used against him?

252.

> Shortly after . . . ["the fatal stabbing of one Marie Huggins on a public street in Valley Township, Chester County"] as a result of a phone call from headquarters, Police Officer Edward Hollingsworth, who was on patrol, proceeded to the hospital to investigate. In the hospital accident ward, he found several persons, including the defendant, Jefferson, who had a towel over her forehead and left eye. . . .
>
> Upon entering the hospital accident ward, Hollingsworth asked: "What happened?" Jefferson replied: "There was a fight." . . . "They jumped me and I stabbed them." Hollingsworth immediately phoned [Chief of Police] Zevtchin at his home, who responded by coming to the hospital within minutes.
>
> Upon his arrival Zevtchin received a short briefing from Hollingsworth in the hallway of the hospital and then entered the accident ward. He asked, "Who did the stabbing?" Jefferson raised her hand and said, "I did. I think I got the wrong one." Then in response to further questions by Zevtchin, Jefferson detailed the occurrence and its background.

Commonwealth v. Jefferson, 226 A.2d 765, 766 (Pa.1967). Is Jefferson's reply to Officer Hollingsworth admissible against her? Her reply to Officer Zevtchin's first question? Her further statements?

253. "At approximately 9:15 p.m. on the evening of March 11, 1966, nine Houston police officers, carrying a valid search warrant and firearms, entered a downtown drugstore of which Kenneth Jordan Brown was the manager. The warrant authorized a search for narcotics, and the affidavit upon which it was issued named Brown as the possessor of the suspected contraband. The doors of the store were closed, and Brown was summoned from a back room, where he had been lying down, to witness the officers as they searched the premises. After the store had been carefully searched for a period of 30 to 45 minutes, one of the officers discovered a brown paper sack under a display counter which contained two plastic bags filled with a substance later determined to be heroin. As the officer raised the sack from its place of concealment, he exhibited it to Brown and asked him 'What is this?' Brown replied: 'It's heroin. You've got me this time.'" Brown v. Beto, 468 F.2d 1284, 1285 (5th Cir.1972). Is Brown's statement admissible against him?

254. "As a result of thorough police investigation [of a holdup killing], the defendant was discovered to be staying in a certain hotel and detectives went there to apprehend him. The defendant having gone out, the detectives awaited his return; two of them were let into the room by the hotel clerk, while a third remained in the lobby. The defendant arrived at about one o'clock in the morning, carrying a package under his left arm. Spotted by the officer in the lobby, he was followed upstairs and accosted in front of the door to his room. The door opened and one of the detectives inside the room, observing the defendant 'reaching for the package' under his arm, dashed from the room and grabbed him. During the ensuing struggle, in which considerable force was required to subdue the defendant, the package was torn open to reveal a loaded gun. One of the officers yelled, 'I have the gun. I have the murder weapon.' The defendant reacted to this by blurting out, 'No, no, I was only driving the car. I didn't do it. I didn't do it. The kid did it.' " People v. Hill, 216 N.E.2d 588, 590 (N.Y.1966). Is the defendant's statement admissible against him? See also United States v. Miles, 440 F.2d 1175 (5th Cir.1971); Hill v. State, 420 S.W.2d 408 (Tex.Crim.App.1967) (*Miranda* inapplicable to "res gestae statements" by defendant arrested during commission of crime).

255.

Appellant and White lived in a second-floor room of a rooming house. At about 5:00 a.m. on Saturday, March 20, 1965, the police responded to a report initiated by Appellant that there was an unconscious man in her room. They were met by Appellant, who told them she could not rouse White. She told the police that White had arrived home from work Friday evening bleeding from a wound in his chest which he said he had received at the hands of some "jitterbugs" who had jumped, robbed, and stabbed him. The police found White dead in bed with wounds in his chest and jaw. There was a small amount of blood on the undershirt and shorts he was wearing, on the sheet and blanket, and on the floor between the bed and the wall. There was no sign of disorder in the room. The police found White's jacket, which had a hole corresponding with his chest wound, and his overcoat, which had blood on it but no hole.

The police questioned Appellant about White's habits, the route he would have taken home from work, his friends, associates, and debtors and about her own activities that evening. At 6:15 a.m. Detective Cannon sent other officers to verify the place of White's employment, which Appellant had described as a hotel near a stated intersection, and to trace his route homeward.

Cannon told Appellant he intended to take her to the Homicide Squad Office at Police Headquarters to prepare a written report of what she had told them; she was also told she would be taken home when this was finished. Detective Cannon testified that while he generally considers everyone found on the scene of a homicide as a "suspect in a way," he did not consider Appellant a suspect; in short her statements were considered plausible.

On the way to Headquarters with Appellant, the police attempted to locate White's sister and made another stop to buy a package of cigarettes which Appellant requested. They arrived at Headquarters at 6:40 a.m. and went to a private room in the rear of the Homicide Squad Office. Appellant was interviewed and her statement was typed in about two hours, 45 minutes being consumed by interruptions for Cannon to attend to other police business.

Cannon asked Appellant to read and sign the statement if she found it to be accurate. As she started to read it, she said she was "in trouble." Cannon asked what she meant by that and she responded, "Well, it just looks like I am in trouble." He offered her a phone to call a lawyer, assuring her that the lawyer "will tell you that you are a witness and what you are saying is what you know about the man's death." Shortly thereafter she signed. Cannon then offered to provide a ride home as soon as a driver was available. While they were waiting, they talked about a church where Appellant had been the previous evening and with which Cannon was acquainted. In the midst of this conversation, Appellant repeated her fear about being "in trouble," and at 9:05 a.m., she leaned forward and said "Well, I might as well tell you, I stabbed him." Cannon testified that at once he said "stop right there. I want to tell you right now you are under arrest. You are charged with homicide. You are entitled to the services of a lawyer and a bondsman. You don't have to say anything. If you do, I am going to take it down and it can possibly be used against you. If you can't get your own lawyer, the Court will appoint one."

Hicks v. United States, 382 F.2d 158, 160 (D.C.Cir.1967). Is the appellant's admission that she stabbed White admissible against her? See also United States v. Roark, 753 F.2d 991 (11th Cir.1985) (defendant initially posed as victim of crime); United States v. Cobb, 449 F.2d 1145 (D.C.Cir.1971) (same).

256. Whether a person convicted in a state court is "in custody" for the purpose of the *Miranda* requirements at the time he makes incriminating statements is a "mixed question of law and fact," which is reviewed independently by a federal court in habeas corpus proceedings, rather than a question of fact about which the state court's findings are entitled to a presumption of correctness, under 28 U.S.C. § 2254(d). Thompson v. Keohane, 516 U.S. 99 (1995) (7–2).

257. Oregon v. Mathiason, 429 U.S. 492 (1977) (6–2). Having some reason to believe that the defendant was involved in a burglary, a police officer left a note at the defendant's home, in which he asked the defendant to call the police station. The defendant was a parolee. He called and arranged to meet the officer at the station house. At the meeting, the defendant was told that he was not under arrest and was then questioned briefly about the burglary; the officer told the defendant that he believed the defendant was involved in it. Within five minutes the defendant admitted his guilt. After the questioning ended, the defendant was allowed to leave. In these circumstances, the Court said, the *Miranda* warnings

were not required. "Any interview of one suspected of a crime by a police officer will have coercive aspects to it, simply by virtue of the fact that the police officer is part of a law enforcement system which may ultimately cause the suspect to be charged with a crime. But police officers are not required to administer *Miranda* warnings to everyone whom they question. Nor is the requirement of warnings to be imposed simply because the questioning takes place in the station house, or because the questioned person is one whom the police suspect. *Miranda* warnings are required only where there has been such a restriction on a person's freedom as to render him 'in custody.' It was *that* sort of coercive environment to which *Miranda* by its terms was made applicable, and to which it is limited." Id. at 495. *Mathiason* was followed in California v. Beheler, 463 U.S. 1121 (1983) (6–3). See Minnesota v. Murphy, 465 U.S. 420 (1984) (6–3), in which the defendant, as required by the terms of his probation, met with his probation officer and submitted to questioning by her. The Court concluded that *Miranda* was not applicable and that the admission of his statements did not violate his Fifth Amendment privilege.

A patient of a state psychiatric hospital was in custody for purposes of the *Miranda* requirements when he was interviewed intensively as a definite criminal suspect, in a secluded area reserved for police activities, in isolation from other patients, notwithstanding that he was told that he was free to leave the interrogation area. State v. Stott, 794 A.2d 120 (N.J.2002).

Mathiason was applied in Barfield v. Alabama, 552 F.2d 1114 (5th Cir.1977). The defendant was a suspect in a murder case. Four days after the killing, a police officer interviewed her about the murder in a conversation on the street. He asked her to come to his office for another interview on the following day, and she agreed. At the second interview, after some questions he left to get her a soda. When he returned, she was on the floor "in a fetal type position" and was talking. The officer stood at the door and listened without saying anything. She confessed to the killing. Afterwards, the officer helped her to calm herself and gave her the *Miranda* warnings. After further cooperation with the police, she was put in jail. The court observed that the defendant "was not informed that she was not under arrest, but neither was she informed that she was," and that if she was indeed told not to leave the room, as she alleged, inasmuch as she was left alone and her departure was unimpeded, the statement was "more in the nature of a precatory request than a command." Id. at 1118. See also United States v. Charles, 738 F.2d 686 (5th Cir.1984) (interview of defendants, who were police officers, in district attorney's office, not custodial interrogation).

258. Mathis v. United States, 391 U.S. 1 (1968). The defendant was a prisoner in a state penitentiary. At the prison, an agent of the Internal Revenue Service interviewed him in the course of a "routine tax investigation." The Service subsequently initiated a criminal investigation of possible tax offenses committed by the defendant and prosecuted him for tax fraud. Part of the evidence used against the defendant was obtained from him during the interview in prison. The Supreme Court reversed his conviction; it held that failure to give the *Miranda* warnings before interviewing the defendant made the evidence obtained from him inadmissible. The Court said that it was irrelevant that no prosecution was contemplated when the interview took place, because "tax investigations frequently lead to criminal prosecutions," and "there was always the possibility" that there would be a prosecution in this case. Nor was it significant that the defendant's custody was unrelated to the tax offenses; there was "nothing in the *Miranda* opinion which calls for a curtailment of the warnings to be given persons under interrogation by officers based on the reason why the person is in custody." Id. at 4–5. See United States v. Chamberlain, 163 F.3d 499 (8th Cir.1998) (interview of prisoner in prison office, in all the circumstances, was custodial interrogation).

When an agent of the Internal Revenue Service interviews a taxpayer who is *not* in custody, *Miranda* warnings are not required, even if the interview is in connection with an investigation that may lead to a criminal prosecution. Such an interview "simply does not present the elements which the *Miranda* Court found so inherently coercive as to require its holding." Beckwith v. United States, 425 U.S. 341, 347 (1976) (7–1). See United States v. Hall, 421 F.2d 540 (2d Cir.1969) (federal agents' interview with suspect in bank robbery, at his home). But see United States v. Carter, 884 F.2d 368 (8th Cir.1989) (postal investigators' questioning of bank employee in office of bank president was custodial interrogation).

In United States v. Leahey, 434 F.2d 7 (1st Cir.1970), the court held that when the IRS failed to follow its own policy (announced following the decision in *Mathis*, above) of giving such warnings when a criminal prosecution was contemplated, whether or not required by *Miranda*, information obtained from the taxpayer would be suppressed.

259. Four members of the Court concluded that *Miranda* warnings are not required when a person testifies before a grand jury, even if he is a target of the grand jury's investigation. United States v. Mandujano, 425 U.S. 564 (1976). "[T]he *Miranda* Court simply did not perceive judicial inquiries and custodial interrogation as equivalents"; to extend its holding "to questioning before a grand jury inquiring into criminal activity under the guidance of a judge is an extravagant expansion never remotely contemplated by this Court in *Miranda*." Id. at 579, 580. Despite the lack of a majority for this view in *Mandujano*, it is understood to be the law. See United States v. Washington, 431 U.S. 181, 182 n.1 (1977) (7–2). Compare United States v. Doss, 563 F.2d 265 (6th Cir.1977) (due process violated when person already indicted is summoned before grand jury and questioned about crimes charged without disclosure of indictment).

Section 9–11.151 of the United States Attorneys' Manual, which includes policy and directives promulgated by the Department of Justice for all United States Attorneys' offices, states that "notwithstanding the lack of a clear constitutional imperative," it is the Department's policy to advise a grand jury witness of the general subject matter of the inquiry, of his right to refuse to answer a question the answer to which would tend to incriminate him, that anything he says may be used against him, and that he will be permitted to consult with counsel outside the grand jury room if he wishes. In addition, "targets" of an investigation are told that their conduct is being investigated.

260. The defendant was convicted of being an accessory to a homicide. Part of the evidence against him was a statement that he made to a detective investigating the homicide during an interview in a prosecutor's office, where the defendant was being held on another charge. The defendant made the incriminating statement after the detective told him that he was wanted only as a witness and that there was no intention to prosecute him in connection with the homicide. The detective gave this assurance in good faith; the decision to prosecute the defendant was made later. People v. Caserino, 212 N.E.2d 884 (N.Y.1965). Was the defendant's statement admissible?

261.

In the early morning hours of March 16, 1965 defendant George McKie reported to a neighborhood patrolman that he had discovered the body of Manella Morris in the second floor apartment of a two-family house located at 65 Walter Avenue, Inwood, Nassau County. The defendant had spent the night of March 15 in the first floor apartment which had been rented by his friend. He allegedly discovered the body when he went to the Morris apartment to use the toilet, since the toilet in the first floor apartment was not working.

Detective Matthew Bonora and other members of the homicide squad soon arrived at the scene of the crime and went upstairs to view the body. The face and head of the deceased were completely obscured; the head was covered with a blanket and rope was tied securely around the neck. In the course of questioning McKie outside the house, Detective Bonora asked him what he thought the police might do with respect to this serious situation. According to the detective, the defendant replied that: "We are going to have to stop whoever is going around hitting these people in the head."

At this point no one had seen the victim's head, and they all thought that death had been caused by strangulation. Detective Bonora and Dr. Lukash, the medical examiner, immediately went upstairs and cut the ropes around the neck of the deceased. Upon removing the blanket, it was revealed that it was not a strangulation but that the deceased had died from a fractured skull. The defendant naturally became the prime suspect. Concededly, defendant was taken to police headquarters and interrogated extensively about his connection with the homicide. The interrogation proved fruitless, for he neither confessed nor made a single damaging admission.

Shortly thereafter, however, as a result of evidence obtained during the over-all investigation, the defendant was arrested and charged with several unrelated misdemeanors (gambling and sale of alcoholic beverages without a license). The District Court Judge assigned Patrick Adams, Esq., to represent defendant on the misdemeanor charges. Defendant pleaded guilty to one of the charges in satisfaction of all and received a jail sentence of six months which he served.

During all this time Detective Bonora and others continued the investigation of the Morris homicide but were unable to uncover any evidence to link McKie with the crime. Following McKie's release from jail on the misdemeanor charges, Detective Bonora approached him on many occasions to question him about the homicide. This caused McKie to get in touch with Adams, the attorney who had represented him earlier. Adams told Detective Bonora not to examine or talk to McKie. . . . Adams continued to represent McKie for all purposes including the investigation of the homicide. As late as April 21, 1966, when Detective Bonora visited McKie's apartment, Adams told him over the telephone: "I told you once, I told you twice, I told you many times not to examine or not to talk to McKie."

About one month later, on May 18, 1966, Detective Bonora, Detective Oliva and Patrolman Monroe, who never ceased in their efforts to unravel the truth and build their case against their prime suspect, set out to find McKie and again question him. Detective Bonora testified that they spotted McKie on the street and followed him in their car. McKie entered a small building and the officers parked at the curb. Patrolman Monroe got out of the car and went into an apartment house near the building that McKie entered, in order to investigate a report of a prowler. When McKie came out he approached the car, leaned in the window and said to Detective Bonora, "It's not going to work, Matt. When are you guys going to stop bugging me?" At that point Patrolman Monroe came out of the building and McKie began an altercation with him shouting and yelling. As the argument became heated McKie said to Monroe, "You can be killed too," and Monroe replied, "You're not dealing with any little old lady now." Observing the intensity of this verbal duel, Bonora and Oliva got out of the car and Bonora said to McKie, "You seem to be so brave now; you weren't so brave when you killed that little old lady" to which McKie replied, "Sure I did it, but you guys can't prove it."

As a result of this statement, McKie was arrested and charged with the murder of Mrs. Morris.

People v. McKie, 250 N.E.2d 36, 36–37 (N.Y.1969).

Is McKie's statement to Bonora admissible against him?

Dunaway v. New York

442 U.S. 200, 99 S.Ct. 2248, 60 L.Ed.2d 824 (1979)

■ MR. JUSTICE BRENNAN delivered the opinion of the Court.

We decide in this case the question reserved 10 years ago in Morales v. New York, 396 U.S. 102 (1969), namely, "the question of the legality of custodial questioning on less than probable cause for a full-fledged arrest." Id., at 106.

I

On March 26, 1971, the proprietor of a pizza parlor in Rochester, N.Y., was killed during an attempted robbery. On August 10, 1971, Detective Anthony Fantigrossi of the Rochester Police was told by another officer that an informant had supplied a possible lead implicating petitioner in the crime. Fantigrossi questioned the supposed source of the lead—a jail inmate awaiting trial for burglary—but learned nothing that supplied "enough information to get a warrant" for petitioner's arrest. App., at 60. Nevertheless, Fantigrossi ordered other detectives to "pick up" petitioner and "bring him in." Id., at 54. Three detectives located petitioner at a neighbor's house on the morning of August 11. Petitioner was taken into custody; although he was not told he was under arrest, he would have been physically restrained if he had attempted to leave. . . . He was driven to police headquarters in a police car and placed in an interrogation room, where he was questioned by officers after being given the warnings required by Miranda v. Arizona, 384 U.S. 436 (1966). Petitioner waived counsel and eventually made statements and drew sketches that incriminated him in the crime.

At petitioner's jury trial for attempted robbery and felony murder, his motions to suppress the statements and sketches were denied, and he was convicted. . . . [T]his Court . . . vacated the judgment, and remanded the case for further consideration in light of the Court's supervening decision in Brown v. Illinois, 422 U.S. 590 (1975). . . . The petitioner in *Brown*, like petitioner Dunaway, made inculpatory statements after receiving *Miranda* warnings during custodial interrogation following his seizure—in that case a formal arrest—on less than probable cause. Brown's motion to suppress the statements was also denied and the statements were used to convict him. Although the Illinois Supreme Court recognized that Brown's arrest was unlawful, it affirmed the admission of the statements on the ground that the giving of *Miranda* warnings served to break the causal connection between the illegal arrest and the giving of the statements. This Court reversed, holding that the Illinois courts erred in adopting a per se rule that *Miranda* warnings in and of themselves sufficed to cure the Fourth Amendment violation; rather the Court held that in order to use such statements, the prosecution must show not only that the statements meet the Fifth Amendment voluntariness standard, but also that the causal connection between the statements and the illegal arrest is broken sufficiently to purge the primary taint of the illegal arrest in light of the distinct policies and interests of the Fourth Amendment.

. . .

The County Court determined after a supplementary suppression hearing that Dunaway's motion to suppress should have been granted.

Although reaffirming that there had been "full compliance with the mandate of Miranda v. Arizona," the County Court found that "this case does not involve a situation where the defendant voluntarily appeared at police headquarters in response to a request of the police. . . ." App., at 117. . . . The County Court further held that "the factual predicate in this case did not amount to probable cause sufficient to support the arrest of defendant," that "the *Miranda* warnings by themselves did not purge the taint of the defendant's illegal seizure[,] Brown v. Illinois, supra . . . and [that] there was no claim or showing by the People of any attenuation of the defendant's illegal detention," App., at 121. Accordingly petitioner's motion to suppress was granted. . . .

A divided Appellate Division reversed. . . .

We granted certiorari . . . to clarify the Fourth Amendment's requirements as to the permissible grounds for custodial interrogation and to review the New York court's application of Brown v. Illinois. We reverse.

II

We first consider whether the Rochester police violated the Fourth and Fourteenth Amendments when, without probable cause to arrest, they took petitioner into custody, transported him to the police station, and detained him there for interrogation.

. . . There can be little doubt that petitioner was "seized" in the Fourth Amendment sense when he was taken involuntarily to the police station. And respondent State concedes that the police lacked probable cause to arrest petitioner before his incriminating statement during interrogation. Nevertheless respondent contends that the seizure of petitioner did not amount to an arrest and was therefore permissible under the Fourth Amendment because the police had a "reasonable suspicion" that petitioner possessed "intimate knowledge about a serious and unsolved crime." Brief for Respondent, at 10. We disagree.

. . .

Terry [v. Ohio, 392 U.S. 1 (1968)] for the first time recognized an exception to the requirement that Fourth Amendment seizures of persons must be based on probable cause. . . . *Terry* departed from traditional Fourth Amendment analysis in two respects. First, it defined a special category of Fourth Amendment "seizures" so substantially less intrusive than arrests that the general rule requiring probable cause to make Fourth Amendment "seizures" reasonable could be replaced by a balancing test. Second, the application of this balancing test led the Court to approve this narrowly defined less intrusive seizure on grounds less rigorous than probable cause, but only for the purpose of a pat-down for weapons.

Because *Terry* involved an exception to the general rule requiring probable cause, this Court has been careful to maintain its narrow scope.

. . .

Respondent State now urges the Court to apply a balancing test, rather than the general rule, to custodial interrogations, and to hold that "seizures" such as that in this case may be justified by mere "reasonable suspicion." *Terry* and its progeny clearly do not support such a result. The narrow intrusions involved in those cases were judged by a balancing test rather than by the general principle that Fourth Amendment seizures must be supported by the "long prevailing standards" of probable cause, Brinegar v. United States, supra, 338 U.S., at 176, only because these intrusions fell far short of the kind of intrusion associated with an arrest. . . .

In contrast to the brief and narrowly circumscribed intrusions involved in those cases, the detention of petitioner was in important respects indistinguishable from a traditional arrest. Petitioner was not questioned briefly where he was found. Instead, he was taken from a neighbor's home to a police car, transported to a police station, and placed in an interrogation room. He was never informed that he was "free to go"; indeed, he would have been physically restrained if he had refused to accompany the officers or had tried to escape their custody. The application of the Fourth Amendment's requirement of probable cause does not depend on whether an intrusion of this magnitude is termed an "arrest" under state law. The mere facts that petitioner was not told he was under arrest, was not "booked," and would not have had an arrest record if the interrogation had proved fruitless, while not insignificant for all purposes . . . obviously do not make petitioner's seizure even roughly analogous to the narrowly defined intrusions involved in *Terry* and its progeny. Indeed, any "exception" that could cover a seizure as intrusive as that in this case would threaten to swallow the general rule that Fourth Amendment seizures are "reasonable" only if based on probable cause.

The central importance of the probable cause requirement to the protection of a citizen's privacy afforded by the Fourth Amendment's guarantees cannot be compromised in this fashion. . . . The familiar threshold standard of probable cause for Fourth Amendment seizures reflects the benefit of extensive experience accommodating the factors relevant to the "reasonableness" requirement of the Fourth Amendment, and provides the relative simplicity and clarity necessary to the implementation of a workable rule. . . .

In effect, respondents urge us to adopt a multifactor balancing test of "reasonable police conduct under the circumstances" to cover all seizures that do not amount to technical arrests. But the protections intended by the Framers could all too easily disappear in the consideration and balancing of the multifarious circumstances presented by different cases, especially when that balancing may be done in the first instance by police officers engaged in the "often competitive enterprise of ferreting out crime." Johnson v. United States, 333 U.S. 10, 14 (1948). A single, familiar standard is essential to guide police officers, who have only limited time and expertise to reflect on and balance the social and individual interests involved in the specific circumstances they confront. Indeed, our recognition of these dangers, and our consequent reluctance to depart from the proven protections afforded by the general rule, is reflected in the narrow limitations emphasized in the cases employing the balancing test. For all but those narrowly defined intrusions, the requisite "balancing" has been performed in centuries of precedent and is embodied in the principle that seizures are "reasonable" only if supported by probable cause.

. . .

[D]etention for custodial interrogation—regardless of its label—intrudes so severely on interests protected by the Fourth Amendment as necessarily to trigger the traditional safeguards against illegal arrest. We accordingly hold that the Rochester police violated the Fourth and Fourteenth Amendments when, without probable cause, they seized petitioner and transported him to the police station for interrogation.

III

There remains the question whether the connection between this unconstitutional police conduct and the incriminating statements and sketches obtained during petitioner's illegal detention was nevertheless sufficiently attenuated to permit the use at trial of the statements and sketches. . . .

The New York courts have consistently held, and petitioner does not contest, that proper *Miranda* warnings were given and that his statements were "voluntary" for purposes of the Fifth Amendment. But Brown v. Illinois, supra, settled that "[t]he exclusionary rule . . . when utilized to effectuate the Fourth Amendment, serves interests and policies that are distinct from those it serves under the Fifth," 422 U.S., at 601, and held therefore that "*Miranda* warnings, and the exclusion of a confession made without them, do not alone sufficiently deter a Fourth Amendment violation." Ibid.

. . .

Consequently, although a confession after proper *Miranda* warnings may be found "voluntary" for purposes of the Fifth Amendment, this type of "voluntariness" is merely a "threshold requirement" for Fourth Amendment analysis, 422 U.S., at 604. Indeed, if the Fifth Amendment has been violated, the Fourth Amendment issue would not have to be reached.

Beyond this threshold requirement, *Brown* articulated a test designed to vindicate the "distinct policies and interests of the Fourth Amendment." Id., at 602. Following *Wong Sun*, the Court eschewed any per se or "but for" rule, and identified the relevant inquiry as "whether Brown's statements were obtained by exploitation of the illegality of his arrest," id., at 600; see Wong Sun v. United States, 372 U.S. 471, 488 (1963). *Brown*'s focus on "the causal connection between the illegality and the confession," 422 U.S., at 603, reflected the two policies behind the use of the exclusionary rule to effectuate the Fourth Amendment. When there is a close causal connection between the illegal seizure and the confession, not only is exclusion of the evidence more likely to deter similar police misconduct in the future, but use of the evidence is more likely to compromise the integrity of the courts.

Brown identified several factors to be considered "in determining whether the confession is obtained by exploitation of an illegal arrest[: t]he temporal proximity of the arrest and the confession, the presence of intervening circumstances . . . and, particularly the purpose and flagrancy of the official misconduct. . . . And the burden of showing admissibility rests, of course, on the prosecution." Id., at 603–604. Examining the case before it, the Court readily concluded that the State had failed to sustain its burden of showing the confession was admissible. In the "less than two hours" that elapsed between the arrest and the confession "there was no intervening event of significance whatsoever." Ibid. Furthermore, the arrest without probable cause had a "quality of purposefulness" in that it was an "expedition for evidence" admittedly undertaken "in the hope that something might turn up." Id., at 605.

The situation in this case is virtually a replica of the situation in *Brown*. Petitioner was also admittedly seized without probable cause in the hope that something might turn up, and confessed without any intervening event of significance. . . . No intervening events broke the connection between petitioner's illegal detention and his confession. To admit petitioner's confession in such a case would allow "law enforcement officers to violate the Fourth Amendment with impunity, safe in the knowledge that they could wash their hands in the 'procedural safeguards' of the Fifth."[13] [14]

---

262. In Kaupp v. Texas, 538 U.S. 626 (2003) (per curiam), police went to the home of the defendant, who was seventeen years old, late at night. They woke him and said, "[W]e need to go and talk." The defendant said "Okay." He was handcuffed and taken to the police station in his underwear, and, after being given *Miranda* warnings, he was questioned. The state court held that he was not arrested until after he confessed. Citing *Dunaway*, the Supreme Court summarily reversed.

Dunaway and *Brown*, p. 122 above, were applied in Taylor v. Alabama, 457 U.S. 687 (1982) (5–4).

Illinois v. Perkins

496 U.S. 292, 110 S.Ct. 2394, 110 L.Ed.2d 243 (1990)

■ JUSTICE KENNEDY delivered the opinion of the Court.

An undercover government agent was placed in the cell of respondent Perkins, who was incarcerated on charges unrelated to the subject of the

13. Comment, 25 Emory L.J. 227, 238 (1976).

[14] Justice White and Justice Stevens wrote concurring opinions. Justice Rehnquist wrote a dissenting opinion, which Chief Justice Burger joined.

agent's investigation. Respondent made statements that implicated him in the crime that the agent sought to solve. Respondent claims that the statements should be inadmissible because he had not been given *Miranda* warnings by the agent. We hold that the statements are admissible. *Miranda* warnings are not required when the suspect is unaware that he is speaking to a law enforcement officer and gives a voluntary statement.

I

In November 1984, Richard Stephenson was murdered in a suburb of East St. Louis, Illinois. The murder remained unsolved until March 1986, when one Donald Charlton told police that he had learned about a homicide from a fellow inmate at the Graham Correctional Facility, where Charlton had been serving a sentence for burglary. The fellow inmate was Lloyd Perkins, who is the respondent here. Charlton told police that, while at Graham, he had befriended respondent, who told him in detail about a murder that respondent had committed in East St. Louis. On hearing Charlton's account, the police recognized details of the Stephenson murder that were not well known, and so they treated Charlton's story as a credible one.

By the time the police heard Charlton's account, respondent had been released from Graham, but police traced him to a jail in Montgomery County, Illinois, where he was being held pending trial on a charge of aggravated battery, unrelated to the Stephenson murder. The police wanted to investigate further respondent's connection to the Stephenson murder, but feared that the use of an eavesdropping device would prove impracticable and unsafe. They decided instead to place an undercover agent in the cellblock with respondent and Charlton. The plan was for Charlton and undercover agent John Parisi to pose as escapees from a work release program who had been arrested in the course of a burglary. Parisi and Charlton were instructed to engage respondent in casual conversation and report anything he said about the Stephenson murder.

Parisi, using the alias "Vito Bianco," and Charlton, both clothed in jail garb, were placed in the cellblock with respondent at the Montgomery County jail. The cellblock consisted of 12 separate cells that opened onto a common room. Respondent greeted Charlton who, after a brief conversation with respondent, introduced Parisi by his alias. Parisi told respondent that he "wasn't going to do any more time," and suggested that the three of them escape. Respondent replied that the Montgomery County jail was "rinky-dink" and that they could "break out." The trio met in respondent's cell later that evening, after the other inmates were asleep, to refine their plan. Respondent said that his girlfriend could smuggle in a pistol. Charlton said: "Hey, I'm not a murderer, I'm a burglar. That's your guys' profession." After telling Charlton that he would be responsible for any murder that occurred, Parisi asked respondent if he had ever "done" anybody. Respondent said that he had and proceeded to describe at length the events of the Stephenson murder. Parisi and respondent then engaged in some casual conversation before respondent went to sleep. Parisi did not give respondent *Miranda* warnings before the conversations.

Respondent was charged with the Stephenson murder. Before trial, he moved to suppress the statements made to Parisi in the jail. The trial court granted the motion to suppress, and the State appealed. The Appellate Court of Illinois affirmed . . . holding that Miranda v. Arizona, 384 U.S. 436 (1966), prohibits all undercover contacts with incarcerated suspects that are reasonably likely to elicit an incriminating response.

We granted certiorari . . . to decide whether an undercover law enforcement officer must give *Miranda* warnings to an incarcerated suspect before asking him questions that may elicit an incriminating response. We now reverse.

II

. . .

Conversations between suspects and undercover agents do not implicate the concerns underlying *Miranda*. The essential ingredients of a "police-dominated atmosphere" and compulsion are not present when an incarcerated person speaks freely to someone whom he believes to be a fellow inmate. Coercion is determined from the perspective of the suspect. . . . When a suspect considers himself in the company of cellmates and not officers, the coercive atmosphere is lacking. . . . There is no empirical basis for the assumption that a suspect speaking to those whom he assumes are not officers will feel compelled to speak by the fear of reprisal for remaining silent or in the hope of more lenient treatment should he confess.

It is the premise of *Miranda* that the danger of coercion results from the interaction of custody and official interrogation. We reject the argument that *Miranda* warnings are required whenever a suspect is in custody in a technical sense and converses with someone who happens to be a government agent. Questioning by captors, who appear to control the suspect's fate, may create mutually reinforcing pressures that the Court has assumed will weaken the suspect's will, but where a suspect does not know that he is conversing with a government agent, these pressures do not exist. The state court here mistakenly assumed that because the suspect was in custody, no undercover questioning could take place. When the suspect has no reason to think that the listeners have official power over him, it should not be assumed that his words are motivated by the reaction he expects from his listeners. . . .

Miranda forbids coercion, not mere strategic deception by taking advantage of a suspect's misplaced trust in one he supposes to be a fellow prisoner. As we recognized in *Miranda*, "[c]onfessions remain a proper element in law enforcement. Any statement given freely and voluntarily without any compelling influences is, of course, admissible in evidence." 384 U.S., at 478. Ploys to mislead a suspect or lull him into a false sense of security that do not rise to the level of compulsion or coercion to speak are not within *Miranda*'s concerns. . . .

Miranda was not meant to protect suspects from boasting about their criminal activities in front of persons whom they believe to be their cellmates. This case is illustrative. Respondent had no reason to feel that undercover agent Parisi had any legal authority to force him to answer questions or that Parisi could affect respondent's future treatment. Respondent viewed the cellmate-agent as an equal and showed no hint of being intimidated by the atmosphere of the jail. In recounting the details of the Stephenson murder, respondent was motivated solely by the desire to impress his fellow inmates. He spoke at his own peril.

The tactic employed here to elicit a voluntary confession from a suspect does not violate the Self-Incrimination Clause. We held in Hoffa v. United States, 385 U.S. 293 (1966), that placing an undercover agent near a suspect in order to gather incriminating information was permissible under the Fifth Amendment. . . . The only difference between this case and *Hoffa* is that the suspect here was incarcerated, but detention, whether or not for the crime in question, does not warrant a presumption that the use of an undercover agent to speak with an incarcerated suspect makes any confession thus obtained involuntary.

. . .

This Court's Sixth Amendment decisions in Massiah v. United States, 377 U.S. 201 (1964) . . . [and other cases] do not avail respondent. We held in those cases that the government may not use an undercover agent to circumvent the Sixth Amendment right to counsel once a suspect has been charged with the crime. . . . In the instant case no charges had been filed on the subject of the interrogation, and our Sixth Amendment precedents are not applicable.

Respondent can seek no help from his argument that a bright-line rule for the application of *Miranda* is desirable. Law enforcement officers will have little difficulty putting into practice our holding that undercover agents need not give *Miranda* warnings to incarcerated suspects. The use of undercover agents is a recognized law enforcement technique, often employed in the prison context to detect violence against correctional officials or inmates, as well as for the purposes served here. The interests protected by *Miranda* are not implicated in these cases, and the warnings are not required to safeguard the constitutional rights of inmates who make voluntary statements to undercover agents.

We hold that an undercover law enforcement officer posing as a fellow inmate need not give *Miranda* warnings to an incarcerated suspect before asking questions that may elicit an incriminating response. The statements at issue in this case were voluntary, and there is no federal obstacle to their admissibility at trial. We now reverse and remand for proceedings not inconsistent with our opinion.

. . . [15]

Perkins follows the general approach to the *Miranda* requirements that was taken in Moran v. Burbine, p. 444 above: What a defendant does not know has no bearing on his state of mind and, therefore, does not implicate any issue of compulsion to speak. In both cases, the situation in which the defendant found himself, a jail cell in *Perkins* and a police station in *Burbine*, was entirely within the control of the police and not one that the defendant himself chose voluntarily. Can that fact be made the basis for an argument that *Miranda* does—or should—apply?

---

263. Following a remand to the state trial court, Perkins claimed that he had asserted his right to counsel after his arrest on the aggravated battery charge and that the subsequent questioning by undercover agents violated his privilege against compulsory self-incrimination. People v. Perkins, 618 N.E.2d 1275 (Ill.App.1993). The court said that the government's procedure was calculated to deceive the defendant so that he was not "given an opportunity to knowingly and intelligently waive his previously asserted right to have counsel present during questioning." Id. at 1280. In those circumstances, the court concluded, Arizona v. Roberson, p. 443 above, applied.

In United States v. Ingle, 157 F.3d 1147 (8th Cir.1998), the defendant, who was being detained on an unrelated charge, agreed to be transported to a jail elsewhere, in order to talk with federal agents and appear before a grand jury in connection with the investigation of a murder which he was suspected of having committed. The public defender was appointed to represent him "in all further proceedings." After talking with counsel, he refused to talk with the investigators or to testify before a grand jury. Two inmates at the jail, one of whom wore a recording device, talked with the defendant in a jail cell. The court held that the recorded conversation was admissible in evidence. Following *Perkins*, it held that there was no *Miranda* violation. And following *Massiah* and Moran v. Burbine, there was no Sixth Amendment violation, notwithstanding the appointment of counsel, because formal proceedings had not begun.

264. Berkemer v. McCarty, 468 U.S. 420 (1984). A highway patrol officer stopped the defendant, who was driving in an erratic manner. After the defendant was out of the car, the officer decided to arrest him for drunk driving. He did not tell the defendant that he was under arrest. He asked the defendant whether he had been using intoxicants. The defendant replied that he had drunk beer and smoked marijuana shortly before. He

[15] Justice Brennan wrote an opinion concurring in the judgment. Justice Marshall wrote a dissenting opinion.

was then arrested and taken to the jail, where the officer asked him further questions about his having been drinking. The defendant's answers were incriminating. No *Miranda* warnings were given.

Rejecting the contention that *Miranda*'s requirements should not apply to minor offenses—misdemeanors, or traffic offenses—the Court held that "a person subjected to custodial interrogation is entitled to the benefit of the procedural safeguards enunciated in *Miranda* regardless of the nature or severity of the offense of which he is suspected or for which he was arrested." Id. at 434. The Court said that any other rule would undermine the clarity of the *Miranda* requirements, which was a "crucial advantage." Id. at 430.

Secondly, however, the Court concluded that roadside questioning of a motorist during a routine traffic stop is not "custodial interrogation" within the meaning of *Miranda*, even though the motorist is not free to leave. Such a stop, the Court observed, is usually brief, and the motorist does not feel "completely at the mercy of the police." Id. at 438. In these respects, a traffic stop resembles a *Terry* stop, to which the *Miranda* requirements do not apply, more than an arrest. If a traffic stop is prolonged and the person is treated as " 'in custody' for practical purposes," id. at 440, the *Miranda* requirements are applicable. On that basis, the Court concluded that the defendant's statements on the highway were admissible and his statements at the jail were not admissible.

See United States v. Dortch, 199 F.3d 193 (5th Cir.1999) (continued detention of defendant after justification for traffic stop was eliminated was an unreasonable seizure).

New York v. Quarles

467 U.S. 649, 104 S.Ct. 2626, 81 L.Ed.2d 550 (1984)

■ JUSTICE REHNQUIST delivered the opinion of the Court.

Respondent Benjamin Quarles was charged in the New York trial court with criminal possession of a weapon. The trial court suppressed the gun in question, and a statement made by respondent, because the statement was obtained by police before they read respondent his "*Miranda* rights." . . . We granted certiorari . . . and we now reverse. We conclude that under the circumstances involved in this case, overriding considerations of public safety justify the officer's failure to provide *Miranda* warnings before he asked questions devoted to locating the abandoned weapon.

On September 11, 1980, at approximately 12:30 a.m., Officer Frank Kraft and Officer Sal Scarring were on road patrol in Queens, N.Y., when a young woman approached their car. She told them that she had just been raped by a black male, approximately six feet tall, who was wearing a black jacket with the name "Big Ben" printed in yellow letters on the back. She told the officers that the man had just entered an A & P supermarket located nearby and that the man was carrying a gun.

The officers drove the woman to the supermarket, and Officer Kraft entered the store while Officer Scarring radioed for assistance. Officer Kraft quickly spotted respondent, who matched the description given by the woman, approaching a check-out counter. Apparently upon seeing the officer, respondent turned and ran toward the rear of the store, and Officer Kraft pursued him with a drawn gun. When respondent turned the corner at the end of an aisle, Officer Kraft lost sight of him for several seconds, and upon regaining sight of respondent, ordered him to stop and put his hands over his head.

Although more than three other officers had arrived on the scene by that time, Officer Kraft was the first to reach respondent. He frisked him and discovered that he was wearing a shoulder holster which was then empty. After handcuffing him, Officer Kraft asked him where the gun was. Respondent nodded in the direction of some empty cartons and responded, "the gun is over there." Officer Kraft thereafter retrieved a loaded .38-caliber revolver from one of the cartons, formally placed respondent under arrest, and read him his *Miranda* rights from a printed card. Respondent indicated that he would be willing to answer questions without an attorney present. Officer Kraft then asked respondent if he owned the gun and where he had purchased it. Respondent answered that he did own it and that he had purchased it in Miami, Fla.

In the subsequent prosecution of respondent for criminal possession of a weapon, the judge excluded the statement, "the gun is over there," and the gun because the officer had not given respondent the warnings required by our decision in Miranda v. Arizona, 384 U.S. 436 (1966), before asking him where the gun was located. The judge excluded the other statements about respondent's ownership of the gun and the place of purchase, as evidence tainted by the prior *Miranda* violation. . . .

. . . For the reasons which follow, we believe that this case presents a situation where concern for public safety must be paramount to adherence to the literal language of the prophylactic rules enunciated in *Miranda*.

. . .

In this case we have before us no claim that respondent's statements were actually compelled by police conduct which overcame his will to resist. . . . Thus the only issue before us is whether Officer Kraft was justified in failing to make available to respondent the procedural safeguards associated with the privilege against compulsory self-incrimination since *Miranda*.

. . .

We hold that on these facts there is a "public safety" exception to the requirement that *Miranda* warnings be given before a suspect's answers may be admitted into evidence, and that the availability of that exception does not depend upon the motivation of the individual officers involved. In a kaleidoscopic situation such as the one confronting these officers, where spontaneity rather than adherence to a police manual is necessarily the order of the day, the application of the exception which we recognize today should not be made to depend on post hoc findings at a suppression hearing concerning the subjective motivation of the arresting officer. Undoubtedly most police officers, if placed in Officer Kraft's position, would act out of a host of different, instinctive, and largely unverifiable motives—their own safety, the safety of others, and perhaps as well the desire to obtain incriminating evidence from the suspect.

Whatever the motivation of individual officers in such a situation, we do not believe that the doctrinal underpinnings of *Miranda* require that it be applied in all its rigor to a situation in which police officers ask questions reasonably prompted by a concern for the public safety. . . .

The police in this case, in the very act of apprehending a suspect, were confronted with the immediate necessity of ascertaining the whereabouts of a gun which they had every reason to believe the suspect had just removed from his empty holster and discarded in the supermarket. So long as the gun was concealed somewhere in the supermarket, with its actual whereabouts unknown, it obviously posed more than one danger to the public safety: an accomplice might make use of it, a customer or employee might later come upon it.

In such a situation, if the police are required to recite the familiar *Miranda* warnings before asking the whereabouts of the gun, suspects in Quarles' position might well be deterred from responding. Procedural safeguards which deter a suspect from responding were deemed acceptable in *Miranda* in order to protect the Fifth Amendment privilege; when the primary social cost of those added protections is the possibility of fewer convictions, the *Miranda* majority was willing to bear that cost. Here, had *Miranda* warnings deterred Quarles from responding to Officer Kraft's question about the whereabouts of the gun, the cost would have been something more than merely the failure to obtain evidence useful in convicting Quarles. Officer Kraft needed an answer to his question not simply to make his case against Quarles but to insure that further danger to the public did not result from the concealment of the gun in a public area.

We conclude that the need for answers to questions in a situation posing a threat to the public safety outweighs the need for the prophylactic rule protecting the Fifth Amendment's privilege against self-incrimination. We decline to place officers such as Officer Kraft in the untenable position of having to consider, often in a matter of seconds, whether it best serves society for them to ask the necessary questions without the *Miranda* warnings and render whatever probative evidence they uncover inadmissible, or for them to give the warnings in order to preserve the admissibility of evidence they might uncover but possibly damage or destroy their ability to obtain that evidence and neutralize the volatile situation confronting them.

In recognizing a narrow exception to the *Miranda* rule in this case, we acknowledge that to some degree we lessen the desirable clarity of that rule. At least in part in order to preserve its clarity, we have over the years refused to sanction attempts to expand our *Miranda* holding. . . . As we have in other contexts, we recognize here the importance of a workable rule "to guide police officers, who have only limited time and expertise to reflect on and balance the social and individual interests involved in the specific circumstances they confront." Dunaway v. New York, 442 U.S. 200, 213–14 (1979). But as we have pointed out, we believe that the exception which we recognize today lessens the necessity of that on-the-scene balancing process. The exception will not be difficult for police officers to apply because in each case it will be circumscribed by the exigency which justifies it. We think police officers can and will distinguish almost instinctively between questions necessary to secure their own safety or the safety of the public and questions designed solely to elicit testimonial evidence from a suspect.

The facts of this case clearly demonstrate that distinction and an officer's ability to recognize it. Officer Kraft asked only the question necessary to locate the missing gun before advising respondent of his rights. It was only after securing the loaded revolver and giving the warnings that he continued with investigatory questions about the ownership and place of purchase of the gun. The exception which we recognize today, far from complicating the thought processes and the on-the-scene judgments of police officers, will simply free them to follow their legitimate instincts when confronting situations presenting a danger to the public safety.[16]

We hold that the Court of Appeals in this case erred in excluding the statement, "the gun is over there," and the gun because of the officer's failure to read respondent his *Miranda* rights before attempting to locate the weapon. Accordingly we hold that it also erred in excluding the subsequent statements as illegal fruits of a *Miranda* violation. We therefore reverse and remand for further proceedings not inconsistent with this opinion.

. . .[17]

---

265. In United States v. DeSantis, 870 F.2d 536 (9th Cir.1989), the court held that the *Quarles* public safety exception warranted relaxation of the *Edwards* requirement (p. 441 note 246 above) that all questioning stop once an arrested person makes a request to talk to counsel. See United

16. Although it involves police questions in part relating to the whereabouts of a gun, Orozco v. Texas, 394 U.S. 324 (1969), is in no sense inconsistent with our disposition of this case. . . . In *Orozco* . . . the questions about the gun were clearly investigatory; they did not in any way relate to an objectively reasonable need to protect the police or the public from any immediate danger associated with the weapon. In short there was no exigency requiring immediate action by the officers beyond the normal need expeditiously to solve a serious crime. . . .

[17] Justice O'Connor wrote an opinion concurring in part in the judgment and dissenting in part. Justice Marshall wrote a dissenting opinion, which Justice Brennan and Justice Stevens joined.

States v. Mobley, 40 F.3d 688 (4th Cir.1994), in which the court agreed with *DeSantis* that *Quarles* might justify an exception to the *Edwards* requirement but concluded that the circumstances did not justify an exception in that case.

In United States v. Lackey, 334 F.3d 1224 (10th Cir.2003), the defendant was arrested on a warrant for offenses including the illegal discharge of a firearm. After he was handcuffed but before he was given *Miranda* warnings, an arresting officer asked if he had any guns or sharp objects on his person. The defendant responded that there was a gun in his car. The court held that his response was within the public safety exception to *Miranda*. Accord, United States v. Reyes, 353 F.3d 148 (2d Cir.2003).

266. *Miranda* warnings are "not essential to the validity of a confession which has been given in a foreign country." United States v. Mundt, 508 F.2d 904, 906 (10th Cir.1974). Accord United States v. Martindale, 790 F.2d 1129 (4th Cir.1986); United States v. Chavarria, 443 F.2d 904 (9th Cir.1971).

267. Do the *Miranda* requirements apply only to the police and other government officials engaged in criminal investigations? Or to all government officials? Does it have any application to persons who are not government officials?

"Schaumberg was a slot machine repairman employed at Harrah's. Cox, his brother-in-law, was visiting at Schaumberg's home. Shortly after 6:00 A.M. on September 21, 1964, Schaumberg was observed working on a dollar slot machine by a pit boss of Harrah's, Ovlan Fritz. After performing some mechanics within the machine, he adjusted it so that it was turned partially on the base plate and then left the area. Immediately thereafter, Cox went to the machine, moved it squarely onto the base plate, whereupon it registered a $5,000.00 jackpot. Fritz reported what he saw to two other supervisors. Together with a security guard employed by Harrah's they asked Cox to accompany them to the security office. Leaving him in the office, they proceeded to locate Schaumberg whom they found in a washroom. Schaumberg accompanied them to the manager's office. The security guard remained outside the office while two of the supervisors, Howland and Curry, questioned Schaumberg. In all, four supervisors testified Schaumberg admitted that he had rigged the slot machine because Cox needed money." Schaumberg v. State, 432 P.2d 500, 501 (Nev.1967).

The supervisors who questioned Schaumberg did not advise him of his rights. Can his admissions be used against him in a prosecution for conspiracy to cheat and defraud Harrah's? See also In the Matter of Victor F., 169 Cal.Rptr. 455 (Ct.App.1980) (school principal); People v. Raitano, 401 N.E.2d 278 (Ill.1980) (store security guard).

See generally Colorado v. Connelly, 479 U.S. 157 (1986), p. 403 note 226 above.

Harris v. New York

401 U.S. 222, 91 S.Ct. 643, 28 L.Ed.2d 1 (1971)

■ MR. CHIEF JUSTICE BURGER delivered the opinion of the Court.

We granted the writ in this case to consider petitioner's claim that a statement made by him to police under circumstances rendering it inadmissible to establish the prosecution's case in chief under Miranda v. Arizona, 384 U.S. 436 (1966), may not be used to impeach his credibility.

The State of New York charged petitioner in a two-count indictment with twice selling heroin to an undercover police officer. At a subsequent jury trial the officer was the State's chief witness, and he testified as to details of the two sales. A second officer verified collateral details of the sales, and a third offered testimony about the chemical analysis of the heroin.

Petitioner took the stand in his own defense. He admitted knowing the undercover police officer but denied a sale on January 4, 1966. He admitted making a sale of contents of a glassine bag to the officer on January 6 but claimed it was baking powder and part of a scheme to defraud the purchaser.

On cross-examination petitioner was asked seriatim whether he had made specified statements to the police immediately following his arrest on January 7—statements that partially contradicted petitioner's direct testimony at trial. In response to the cross-examination, petitioner testified that he could not remember virtually any of the questions or answers recited by the prosecutor. At the request of petitioner's counsel the written statement from which the prosecutor had read questions and answers in his impeaching process was placed in the record for possible use on appeal; the statement was not shown to the jury.

The trial judge instructed the jury that the statements attributed to petitioner by the prosecution could be considered only in passing on petitioner's credibility and not as evidence of guilt. In closing summations both counsel argued the substance of the impeaching statements. The jury then found petitioner guilty on the second count of the indictment. . . .

At trial the prosecution made no effort in its case in chief to use the statements allegedly made by petitioner, conceding that they were inadmissible under Miranda v. Arizona. . . . The transcript of the interrogation used in the impeachment, but not given to the jury, shows that no warning of a right to appointed counsel was given before questions were put to petitioner when he was taken into custody. Petitioner makes no claim that the statements made to the police were coerced or involuntary.

Some comments in the *Miranda* opinion can indeed be read as indicating a bar to use of an uncounseled statement for any purpose, but discussion of that issue was not at all necessary to the Court's holding and cannot be regarded as controlling. *Miranda* barred the prosecution from making its case with statements of an accused made while in custody prior to having or effectively waiving counsel. It does not follow from *Miranda* that evidence inadmissible against an accused in the prosecution's case in chief is barred for all purposes, provided of course that the trustworthiness of the evidence satisfies legal standards.

In Walder v. United States, 347 U.S. 62 (1954), the Court permitted physical evidence, inadmissible in the case in chief, to be used for impeachment purposes.

> It is one thing to say that the Government cannot make an affirmative use of evidence unlawfully obtained. It is quite another to say that the defendant can turn the illegal method by which evidence in the Government's possession was obtained to his own advantage, and provide himself with a shield against contradiction of his untruths. [. . .]
>
> [T]here is hardly justification for letting the defendant affirmatively resort to perjurious testimony in reliance on the Government's disability to challenge his credibility.

347 U.S., at 65.

It is true that Walder was impeached as to collateral matters included in his direct examination, whereas petitioner here was impeached as to testimony bearing more directly on the crimes charged. We are not persuaded that there is a difference in principle that warrants a result different from that reached by the Court in *Walder*. Petitioner's testimony in his own behalf concerning the events of January 7 contrasted sharply with what he told the police shortly after his arrest. The impeachment process here undoubtedly provided valuable aid to the jury in assessing petitioner's credibility, and the benefits of this process should not be lost, in our view, because of the speculative possibility that impermissible police conduct will be encouraged thereby. Assuming that the exclusionary rule has a deterrent effect on proscribed police conduct, sufficient deterrence flows when the evidence in question is made unavailable to the prosecution in its case in chief.

Every criminal defendant is privileged to testify in his own defense, or to refuse to do so. But that privilege cannot be construed to include the right to commit perjury. Having voluntarily taken the stand, petitioner was under an obligation to speak truthfully and accurately, and the prosecution here did no more than utilize the traditional truth-testing devices of the adversary process. Had inconsistent statements been made by the accused to some third person, it could hardly be contended that the conflict could not be laid before the jury by way of cross-examination and impeachment.

The shield provided by *Miranda* cannot be perverted into a license to use perjury by way of a defense, free from the risk of confrontation with prior inconsistent utterances. We hold, therefore, that petitioner's credibility was appropriately impeached by use of his earlier conflicting statements.

Affirmed.[18]

---

[18] Justice Brennan wrote a dissenting opinion which Justice Douglas and Justice Marshall joined. Justice Black noted his dissent.

268. Doyle v. Ohio, 426 U.S. 610 (1976) (6–3). Notwithstanding *Harris*, above, the use for impeachment purposes of a defendant's *silence* following his arrest and after receiving *Miranda* warnings is a violation of due process. The defendants were prosecuted for a narcotics offense. At trial, they testified and gave an exculpatory account that they had not mentioned earlier. Over objection, the prosecutor cross-examined them about their failure to give the arresting officer their account. Reversing the convictions, the Court said: "Silence in the wake of these warnings may be nothing more than the arrestee's exercise of these *Miranda* rights. Thus, every post-arrest silence is insolubly ambiguous because of what the State is required to advise the person arrested. . . . Moreover, while it is true that the *Miranda* warnings contain no express assurance that silence will carry no penalty, such assurance is implicit to any person who receives the warnings. In such circumstances, it would be fundamentally unfair and a deprivation of due process to allow the arrested person's silence to be used to impeach an explanation subsequently offered at trial." Id. at 617–18. See United States v. Hale, 422 U.S. 171 (1975).

Doyle was applied in Wainwright v. Greenfield, 474 U.S. 284 (1986). The defendant pleaded not guilty by reason of insanity. The Court held that his silence after being given a *Miranda* warning following his arrest could not be used at trial as evidence of his sanity. Compare Greer v. Miller, 483 U.S. 756 (1987) (6–3) (prosecutor's question in violation of *Doyle*, objection to which was sustained, did not require reversal of conviction); United States v. Stubbs, 944 F.2d 828 (11th Cir.1991) (witness's brief comment about defendant's post-arrest silence not a *Doyle* violation).

In Jenkins v. Anderson, 447 U.S. 231 (1980) (7–2), the Court held that it was permissible for the prosecutor to cross-examine the defendant about his failure to give an exculpatory account of the alleged crime to the police before his arrest. The "use of prearrest silence to impeach a defendant's credibility," id. at 238, violates neither the privilege against compulsory self-incrimination nor the fundamental fairness required by the Due Process Clause. *Doyle* was distinguished on the ground that here "no governmental action induced petitioner to remain silent before arrest." Id. at 240. The Court observed that the states were free to adopt evidentiary rules admitting or excluding such evidence as they thought appropriate.

Jenkins was applied in Fletcher v. Weir, 455 U.S. 603 (1982) (7–1–1). There, the defendant was cross-examined about his failure to give an exculpatory version (self-defense) of a homicide to police officers after his arrest. There was no indication in the record that he had been given *Miranda* warnings. The Court said: "In the absence of the sort of affirmative assurances embodied in the *Miranda* warnings, we do not believe that it violates due process of law for a State to permit cross-examination as to postarrest silence when a defendant chooses to take the stand. A State is entitled, in such situations, to leave to the judge and jury under its own rules of evidence the resolution of the extent to which postarrest silence may be deemed to impeach a criminal defendant's own testimony." Id. at 607.

Doyle "does not apply to cross-examination that merely inquires into prior inconsistent statements. Such questioning makes no unfair use of silence because a defendant who voluntarily speaks after receiving *Miranda* warnings has not been induced to remain silent. As to the subject matter of his statements, the defendant has not remained silent at all." Anderson v. Charles, 447 U.S. 404, 408 (1980) (7–2).

269. *Harris* was applied in Oregon v. Hass, 420 U.S. 714 (1975) (6–2), in which a state police officer gave the defendant full *Miranda* warnings at the time of his arrest. In the patrol car, the defendant said that he would like to talk to an attorney, which the officer said he could do when they got to the police station. Before they got to the station, the defendant made incriminating statements. The officer was allowed to testify about those statements for the limited purpose of impeaching the credibility of the defendant as a witness on the stand. The Court said that it saw no valid distinction between this case and *Harris*. Here, as there, "the shield provided by *Miranda* is not to be perverted to a license to testify inconsistently, or even perjuriously, free from the risk of confrontation with prior inconsistent utterances." 420 U.S. at 722.

270. Relying on the privilege against self-incrimination in the state constitution, the Supreme Court of California rejected the holding of *Harris* in People v. Disbrow, 545 P.2d 272 (Cal.1976). Its principal objection to *Harris*, the court said, was "the considerable potential that a jury, even with the benefit of a limiting instruction, will view prior inculpatory statements as substantive evidence of guilt rather than as merely reflecting on the declarant's veracity." 545 P.2d at 279. The Supreme Court of Hawaii made a similar determination. State v. Santiago, 492 P.2d 657 (Haw.1971). *Disbrow* was presumably overturned by a state constitutional amendment, see note 248, p. 454 above.

271. Michigan v. Tucker, 417 U.S. 433 (1974) (8–1). The defendant was arrested on a charge of rape and taken to the police station. Before he was questioned, the police asked him whether he knew the crime for which he had been arrested, whether he wanted a lawyer, and whether he understood his constitutional rights. He responded that he knew why he was arrested and knew his rights, and did not want a lawyer. The police advised him that his statements could be used against him. They did not advise him, as required by *Miranda*, that he could have free legal advice if he could not afford to pay for it. During the questioning, the defendant made exculpatory statements that led the police to one Henderson. Henderson gave the police information that incriminated the defendant. The questioning of the defendant occurred before *Miranda* was decided, but his trial followed that decision. At trial, the defendant's own incriminating statements were excluded. A motion to exclude Henderson's testimony was denied, and Henderson testified against the defendant.

Declining to decide the extent to which *Miranda* requires exclusion of evidence other than responses to questions derived from violations of the *Miranda* rules, the Court held that Henderson's statements were properly admitted.

The *Miranda* rules, the Court said, established a set of "procedural safeguards" that "were not themselves rights protected by the Constitution but were instead measures to insure that the right against compulsory self-incrimination was protected." In this case, the questioning did not deprive the defendant of his constitutional right "but rather failed to make available to him the full measure of procedural safeguards associated with that right since *Miranda*." Id. at 444. The Court noted the timetable of the case in relation to *Miranda* and the fact that the police were in compliance with existing law when they questioned the defendant. It observed that exclusion of Henderson's testimony in addition to the defendant's testimony would not augment *Miranda*'s purpose to deter illegal police conduct; furthermore, failure to give the defendant the full *Miranda* warnings did not cast doubt on the reliability of Henderson's testimony.

Before the decision in Dickerson v. United States, 530 U.S. 428 (2000) (7–2), note 235 p. 429 above, courts generally concluded that *Tucker* and Oregon v. Elstad, 470 U.S. 298 (1985), note 238 p. 431 above, dictated the conclusion that physical evidence that is the fruit of a *Miranda* violation need not be excluded. E.g., United States v. Elie, 111 F.3d 1135 (4th Cir.1997). The question has been considered anew after the decision in *Dickerson*, with varying results. Several circuits have concluded that the prior rule remains valid. E.g., United States v. Villalba-Alvarado, 345 F.3d 1007 (8th Cir.2003). In United States v. Patane, 304 F.3d 1013 (10th Cir.2002), however, the court held that such evidence is not admissible. And in United States v. Faulkingham, 295 F.3d 85 (1st Cir.2002), the court held that whether physical evidence should be excluded depended on the need for deterrence of police misconduct in the circumstances of the case and that the evidence should not be excluded if the *Miranda* violation was not intentional but merely negligent. The Supreme Court has granted certiorari in *Patane*, 538 U.S. 976 (2003). A decision is expected in 2004.

In United States v. Morales, 788 F.2d 883 (2d Cir.1986), the court held that a voluntary statement that was obtained by police officers acting in good faith but in violation of the *Miranda* rules could be considered as part of the probable cause for an arrest. The defendant made the statement in response to a police officer's question while he was lawfully detained but before he was arrested. Referring to cases including *Tucker* and *Elstad*, the court said: "[W]e can find no 'valid and useful purpose' to be served by disregarding . . . [the defendant's] pre-warning statement to the officers who were acting in good faith. Where, as here, there is no indication of trickery or coercion, there is no justification for requiring a police officer to ignore incriminating admissions in arriving at a conclusion that there is probable cause for an arrest. Suppression of the uncounseled statements at the trial is sufficient to further the purposes of *Miranda*." 788 F.2d at 886.

272. Does anyone other than the person questioned have standing to object to the admission of evidence obtained in violation of the *Miranda* requirements? In People v. Varnum, 427 P.2d 772, 775 (Cal.1967), the court said no.

> Non-coercive questioning is not in itself unlawful . . . and the Fifth and Sixth Amendment rights protected by *Escobedo, Dorado,*[19] and *Miranda* are violated only when evidence obtained without the required warnings and waiver is introduced against the person whose questioning produced the evidence. The basis for the warnings required by *Miranda* is the privilege against self-incrimination . . . and that privilege is not violated when the information elicited from an unwarned suspect is not used against him. . . . Similarly the right to counsel protected by *Escobedo* and *Dorado* is not infringed when the exclusion of any evidence obtained through the violation of the rules of those cases precludes any interference with the suspect's right to effective representation. . . . Unlike unreasonable searches and seizures, which always violate the Constitution, there is nothing unlawful in questioning an unwarned suspect so long as the police refrain from physically and psychologically coercive tactics condemned by due process and do not use against the suspect any evidence obtained. Accordingly, in the absence of such coercive tactics, there is no basis for excluding physical or other non-hearsay evidence acquired as a result of questioning a suspect in disregard of his Fifth and Sixth Amendment rights when such evidence is offered at the trial of another person.

Accord People v. Denham, 241 N.E.2d 415 (Ill.1968). See also Bradford v. Michigan, 394 U.S. 1022 (1969) (testimony coerced from witness); People v. Portelli, 205 N.E.2d 857 (N.Y.1965) (same).

Further Aspects of the Privilege Against Compulsory Self-Incrimination

---

Fisher v. United States

425 U.S. 391, 96 S.Ct. 1569, 48 L.Ed.2d 39 (1976)

■ MR. JUSTICE WHITE delivered the opinion of the Court.

In these two cases we are called upon to decide whether a summons directing an attorney to produce documents delivered to him by his client in connection with the attorney-client relationship is enforceable over

[19] People v. Dorado, 398 P.2d 361 (Cal. 1965), in which the Supreme Court of California applied the rationale of *Escobedo*.

claims that the documents were constitutionally immune from summons in the hands of the client and retained that immunity in the hands of the attorney.

I

In each case, an Internal Revenue agent visited the taxpayer or taxpayers and interviewed them in connection with an investigation of possible civil or criminal liability under the federal income tax laws. Shortly after the interviews—one day later in No. 74–611 and a week or two later in No. 74–18—the taxpayers obtained from their respective accountants certain documents relating to the preparation by the accountants of their tax returns. Shortly after obtaining the documents—later the same day in No. 74–611 and a few weeks later in No. 74–18—the taxpayers transferred the documents to their lawyer—respondent Kasmir and petitioner Fisher, respectively—each of whom was retained to assist the taxpayer in connection with the investigation. Upon learning of the whereabouts of the documents, the Internal Revenue Service served summonses on the attorneys directing them to produce documents listed therein. In No. 74–611, the documents were described as "the following records of Tannebaum Bindler & Lewis [the accounting firm]."

> 1. Accountant's work papers pertaining to Dr. E.J. Mason's books and records of 1969, 1970 and 1971.
>
> 2. Retained copies of E.J. Mason's income tax returns for 1969, 1970 and 1971.
>
> 3. Retained copies of reports and other correspondence between Tannebaum Bindler & Lewis and Dr. E.J. Mason during 1969, 1970 and 1971.

In No. 74–18, the documents demanded were analyses by the accountant of the taxpayers' income and expenses which had been copied by the accountant from the taxpayers' canceled checks and deposit receipts. In No. 74–611, a summons was also served on the accountant directing him to appear and testify concerning the documents to be produced by the lawyer. In each case, the lawyer declined to comply with the summons directing production of the documents, and enforcement actions were commenced by the Government under 26 U.S.C. §§ 7402(b) and 7604(a). In No. 74–611, the attorney raised in defense of the enforcement action the taxpayer's accountant-client privilege, his attorney-client privilege, and his Fourth and Fifth Amendment rights. In No. 74–18, the attorney claimed that enforcement would involve compulsory self-incrimination of the taxpayers in violation of their Fifth Amendment privilege, would involve a seizure of the papers without necessary compliance with the Fourth Amendment, and would violate the taxpayers' right to communicate in confidence with their attorney. In No. 74–18 the taxpayers intervened and made similar claims.

In each case the summons was ordered enforced by the District Court and its order was stayed pending appeal. In No. 74–18, 500 F.2d 683 (CA3 1974), petitioners' appeal raised, in terms, only their Fifth Amendment claim, but they argued in connection with that claim that enforcement of the summons would involve a violation of the taxpayers' reasonable expectation of privacy and particularly so in light of the confidential relationship of attorney to client. The Court of Appeals for the Third Circuit after reargument en banc affirmed the enforcement order, holding that the taxpayers had never acquired a possessory interest in the documents and that the papers were not immune in the hands of the attorney. In No. 74–611, a divided panel of the Court of Appeals for the Fifth Circuit reversed the enforcement order, 499 F.2d 444 (1974). The court reasoned that by virtue of the Fifth Amendment the documents would have been privileged from production pursuant to summons directed to the taxpayer had he retained possession and, in light of the confidential nature of the attorney-client relationship, the taxpayer retained, after the transfer to his attorney, "a legitimate expectation of privacy with regard to the materials he placed in his attorney's custody, that he retained constructive possession of the evidence, and thus . . . retained Fifth Amendment protection." Id., at 453. We granted certiorari to resolve the conflict created. . . . Because in our view the documents were not privileged either in the hands of the lawyers or of their clients, we affirm the judgment of the Third Circuit in No. 74–18 and reverse the judgment of the Fifth Circuit in No. 74–611.

II

All of the parties in these cases and the Court of Appeals for the Fifth Circuit have concurred in the proposition that if the Fifth Amendment would have excused a *taxpayer* from turning over the accountant's papers had he possessed them, the *attorney* to whom they are delivered for the purpose of obtaining legal advice should also be immune from subpoena. Although we agree with this proposition for the reasons set forth in Part III, infra, we are convinced that, under our decision in Couch v. United States, 409 U.S. 322 (1973), it is not the taxpayer's Fifth Amendment privilege that would excuse the *attorney* from production.

. . . The taxpayer's privilege under this Amendment is not violated by enforcement of the summonses involved in these cases because enforcement against a taxpayer's lawyer would not "compel" the taxpayer to do anything—and certainly would not compel him to be a "witness" against himself. The Court has held repeatedly that the Fifth Amendment is limited to prohibiting the use of "physical or moral compulsion" exerted on the person asserting the privilege, Perlman v. United States, 247 U.S. 7, 15 (1918). . . . In Couch v. United States, supra, we recently ruled that the Fifth Amendment rights of a taxpayer were not violated by the enforcement of a documentary summons directed to her accountant and requiring production of the taxpayer's own records in the possession of the accountant. We did so on the ground that in such a case "the ingredient of personal compulsion against an accused is lacking." 409 U.S., at 329.

Here, the taxpayers are compelled to do no more than was the taxpayer in *Couch*. The taxpayers' Fifth Amendment privilege is therefore not violated by enforcement of the summonses directed toward their attorneys.

This is true whether or not the Amendment would have barred a subpoena directing the taxpayer to produce the documents while they were in his hands.

The fact that the attorneys are agents of the taxpayers does not change this result. *Couch* held as much, since the accountant there was also the taxpayer's agent, and in this respect reflected a long-standing view. In Hale v. Henkel, 201 U.S. 43, 69–70 (1906), the Court said that the privilege "was never intended to permit [a person] to plead the fact that some third person might be incriminated by his testimony, even though he were the agent of such person. . . . [T]he Amendment is limited to a person who shall be compelled in any criminal case to be a witness against *himself*." (Emphasis in original.) "It is extortion of information from the accused himself that offends our sense of justice." Couch v. United States, supra, at 328. Agent or no, the lawyer is not the taxpayer. The taxpayer is the "accused," and nothing is being extorted from him.

Nor is this one of those situations, which *Couch* suggested might exist, where constructive possession is so clear or relinquishment of possession so temporary and insignificant as to leave the personal compulsion upon the taxpayer substantially intact. . . .

Respondents in No. 74–611 and petitioners in No. 74–18 argue, and the Court of Appeals for the Fifth Circuit apparently agreed, that if the summons was enforced, the taxpayers' Fifth Amendment privilege would be, but should not be, lost solely because they gave their documents to their lawyers in order to obtain legal advice. But this misconceives the nature of the constitutional privilege. The Amendment protects a person from being compelled to be a witness against himself. Here, the taxpayers retained any privilege they ever had not to be compelled to testify against themselves and not to be compelled themselves to produce private papers in their possession. *This* personal privilege was in no way decreased by the transfer. It is simply that by reason of the transfer of the documents to the attorneys, those papers may be subpoenaed without compulsion on the taxpayer. The protection of the Fifth Amendment is therefore not available. "A party is privileged from producing evidence but not from its production." Johnson v. United States, [228 U.S. 457 (1913)], at 458.

The Court of Appeals for the Fifth Circuit suggested that because legally and ethically the attorney was required to respect the confidences of his client, the latter had a reasonable expectation of privacy for the records in the hands of the attorney and therefore did not forfeit his Fifth Amendment privilege with respect to the records by transferring them in order to obtain legal advice. It is true that the Court has often stated that one of the several purposes served by the constitutional privilege against compelled testimonial self-incrimination is that of protecting personal privacy. . . . But the Court has never suggested that every invasion of privacy violates the privilege. Within the limits imposed by the language of the Fifth Amendment, which we necessarily observe, the privilege truly serves privacy interests; but the Court has never on any ground, personal privacy included, applied the Fifth Amendment to prevent the otherwise proper acquisition or use of evidence which, in the Court's view, did not involve compelled testimonial self-incrimination of some sort.

The proposition that the Fifth Amendment protects private information obtained without compelling self-incriminating testimony is contrary to the clear statements of this Court that under appropriate safeguards private incriminating statements of an accused may be overheard and used in evidence, if they are not compelled at the time they were uttered . . . and that disclosure of private information may be compelled if immunity removes the risk of incrimination. If the Fifth Amendment protected generally against the obtaining of private information from a man's mouth or pen or house, its protections would presumably not be lifted by probable cause and a warrant or by immunity. The privacy invasion is not mitigated by immunity; and the Fifth Amendment's strictures, unlike the Fourth's, are not removed by showing reasonableness. The Framers addressed the subject of personal privacy directly in the Fourth Amendment. They struck a balance so that when the State's reason to believe incriminating evidence will be found becomes sufficiently great, the invasion of privacy becomes justified and a warrant to search and seize will issue. They did not seek in still another Amendment—the Fifth—to achieve a general protection of privacy but to deal with the more specific issue of compelled self-incrimination.

. . .

Insofar as private information not obtained through compelled self-incriminating testimony is legally protected, its protection stems from other sources—the Fourth Amendment's protection against seizures without warrant or probable cause and against subpoenas which suffer from "too much indefiniteness or breadth in the things required to be 'particularly described,'" Oklahoma Press Pub. Co. v. Walling, 327 U.S. 186, 208 (1946) . . . the First Amendment . . . or evidentiary privileges such as the attorney-client privilege.

III

Our above holding is that compelled production of documents from an attorney does not implicate whatever Fifth Amendment privilege the taxpayer might have enjoyed from being compelled to produce them himself. The taxpayers in these cases, however, have from the outset consistently urged that they should not be forced to expose otherwise protected documents to summons simply because they have sought legal advice and turned the papers over to their attorneys. . . . In this posture of the case, we feel obliged to inquire whether the attorney-client privilege applies to documents in the hands of an attorney which would have been privileged in the hands of the client by reason of the Fifth Amendment.

Confidential disclosures by a client to an attorney made in order to obtain legal assistance are privileged. . . . The purpose of the privilege is to encourage clients to make full disclosure to their attorneys. . . . As a practical matter, if the client knows that damaging information could more readily be obtained from the attorney following disclosure than from himself in the absence of disclosure, the client would be reluctant to confide in his lawyer and it would be difficult to obtain fully informed legal advice. However, since the privilege has the effect of withholding relevant information from the factfinder, it applies only where necessary to achieve its purpose. Accordingly it protects only those disclosures—necessary to obtain informed legal advice—which might not have been made absent the privilege. . . . This Court and the lower courts have thus uniformly held that pre-existing documents which could have been obtained by court process from the client when he was in possession may also be obtained from the attorney by similar process following transfer by the client in order to obtain more informed legal advice. . . . The purpose of the privilege requires no broader rule. Pre-existing documents obtainable from the client are not appreciably easier to obtain from the attorney after transfer to him. Thus, even absent the attorney-client privilege, clients will not be discouraged from disclosing the documents to the attorney, and their ability to obtain informed legal advice will remain unfettered. It is otherwise if the documents are not obtainable by subpoena *duces tecum* or summons while in the exclusive possession of the client, for the client will then be reluctant to transfer possession to the lawyer unless the documents are also privileged in the latter's hands. Where the transfer is made for the purpose of obtaining legal advice, the purposes of the attorney-client privilege would be defeated unless the privilege is applicable. "It follows, then, that *when the client himself would be privileged* from production of the document, either as a party at common law . . . or as exempt from self-incrimination, the attorney having possession of the document is not bound to produce." 8 Wigmore § 2307, p. 592. Lower courts have so held. . . . This proposition was accepted by the Court of Appeals for the Fifth Circuit below, is asserted by petitioners in No. 74–18 and respondents in No. 74–611, and was conceded by the Government in its brief and at oral argument. Where the transfer to the attorney is for the purpose of obtaining legal advice, we agree with it.

Since each taxpayer transferred possession of the documents in question from himself to his attorney, in order to obtain legal assistance in the tax investigations in question, the papers, if unobtainable by summons from the client, are unobtainable by summons directed to the attorney by reason of the attorney-client privilege. We accordingly proceed to the question whether the documents could have been obtained by summons addressed to the taxpayer while the documents were in his possession. The only bar to enforcement of such summons asserted by the parties or the courts below is the Fifth Amendment's privilege against self-incrimination. . . .

IV

The proposition that the Fifth Amendment prevents compelled production of documents over objection that such production might incriminate stems from Boyd v. United States, 116 U.S. 616 (1886). *Boyd* involved a civil forfeiture proceeding brought by the Government against two partners for fraudulently attempting to import 35 cases of glass without paying the prescribed duty. . . . At trial, the Government obtained a court order directing the partners to produce an invoice the partnership had received. . . . The invoice was disclosed, offered in evidence, and used, over the Fifth Amendment objection of the partners, to establish that the partners were fraudulently claiming a greater exemption from duty than they were entitled to. . . . This Court held that the invoice was inadmissible and reversed the judgment in favor of the Government. The Court ruled that the Fourth Amendment applied to court orders in the nature of subpoenas *duces tecum* in the same manner in which it applies to search warrants . . . ; and that the Government may not, consistent with the Fourth Amendment, seize a person's documents or other property as evidence unless it can claim a proprietary interest in the property superior to that of the person from whom the property is obtained. . . . The invoice in question was thus held to have been obtained in violation of the Fourth Amendment. The Court went on to hold that the accused in a criminal case or the defendant in a forfeiture action could not be forced to produce evidentiary items without violating the Fifth Amendment as well as the Fourth. More specifically, the Court declared, "a compulsory production of the private books and papers of the owner of goods sought to be forfeited . . . is compelling him to be a witness against himself, within the meaning of the Fifth Amendment to the Constitution." Id., at 634–35. Admitting the partnership invoice into evidence had violated both the Fifth and Fourth Amendments.

Among its several pronouncements, *Boyd* was understood to declare that the seizure, under warrant or otherwise, of any purely evidentiary materials violated the Fourth Amendment and that the Fifth Amendment rendered these seized materials inadmissible. Gouled v. United States, 255 U.S. 298 (1921). . . . That rule applied to documents as well as to other evidentiary items. . . . Private papers taken from the taxpayer, like other "mere evidence," could not be used against the accused over his Fourth and Fifth Amendment objections.

Several of *Boyd*'s express or implicit declarations have not stood the test of time. The application of the Fourth Amendment to subpoenas was limited by Hale v. Henkel, 201 U.S. 43 (1906), and more recent cases. . . . Purely evidentiary (but "nontestimonial") materials, as well as contraband and fruits and instrumentalities of crime, may now be searched for and seized under proper circumstances. . . . Also, any notion that "testimonial" evidence may never be seized and used in evidence is inconsistent with Katz v. United States, 389 U.S. 347 (1967) . . . approving the seizure under appropriate circumstances of conversations of a person suspected of crime. . . .

It is also clear that the Fifth Amendment does not independently proscribe the compelled production of every sort of incriminating evidence but applies only when the accused is compelled to make a *testimonial* communication that is incriminating. We have, accordingly, declined to extend the protection of the privilege to the giving of blood samples . . . to the giving of handwriting exemplars . . . voice exemplars . . . or the donning of a blouse worn by the perpetrator. . . . Furthermore, despite *Boyd*, neither a partnership nor the individual partners are shielded from compelled production of partnership records on self-incrimination grounds. . . . It would appear that under that case the precise claim sustained in *Boyd* would now be rejected for reasons not there considered.

The pronouncement in *Boyd* that a person may not be forced to produce his private papers has nonetheless often appeared as dictum in later opinions of this Court. . . . To the extent, however, that the rule against compelling production of private papers rested on the proposition that seizures of or subpoenas for "mere evidence," including documents, violated the Fourth Amendment and therefore also transgressed the Fifth . . . the foundations for the rule have been washed away. In consequence, the prohibition against forcing the production of private papers has long been a rule searching for a rationale consistent with the proscriptions of the Fifth Amendment against compelling a person to give "testimony" that incriminates him. Accordingly, we turn to the question of what, if any, incriminating testimony within the Fifth Amendment's protection, is compelled by a documentary summons.

A subpoena served on a taxpayer requiring him to produce an accountant's workpapers in his possession without doubt involves substantial compulsion. But it does not compel oral testimony; nor would it ordinarily compel the taxpayer to restate, repeat, or affirm the truth of the contents of the documents sought. Therefore, the Fifth Amendment would not be violated by the fact alone that the papers on their face might incriminate the taxpayer, for the privilege protects a person only against being incriminated by his own compelled testimonial communications. . . . The accountant's workpapers are not the taxpayer's. They were not prepared by the taxpayer, and they contain no testimonial declarations by him. Furthermore, as far as this record demonstrates, the preparation of all of the papers sought in these cases was wholly voluntary, and they cannot be said to contain compelled testimonial evidence, either of the taxpayers or of anyone else. The taxpayer cannot avoid compliance with the subpoena merely by asserting that the item of evidence which he is required to produce contains incriminating writing, whether his own or that of someone else.

The act of producing evidence in response to a subpoena nevertheless has communicative aspects of its own, wholly aside from the contents of the papers produced. Compliance with the subpoena tacitly concedes the existence of the papers demanded and their possession or control by the taxpayer. It also would indicate the taxpayer's belief that the papers are those described in the subpoena. . . . The elements of compulsion are clearly present, but the more difficult issues are whether the tacit averments of the taxpayer are both "testimonial" and "incriminating" for purposes of applying the Fifth Amendment. These questions perhaps do not lend themselves to categorical answers; their resolution may instead depend on the facts and circumstances of particular cases or classes thereof. In light of the records now before us, we are confident that however incriminating the contents of the accountant's workpapers might be, the act of producing them—the only thing which the taxpayer is compelled to do—would not itself involve testimonial self-incrimination.

It is doubtful that implicitly admitting the existence and possession of the papers rises to the level of testimony within the protection of the Fifth Amendment. The papers belong to the accountant, were prepared by him, and are the kind usually prepared by an accountant working on the tax returns of his client. Surely the Government is in no way relying on the "truthtelling" of the taxpayer to prove the existence of or his access to the documents. . . . The existence and location of the papers are a foregone conclusion and the taxpayer adds little or nothing to the sum total of the Government's information by conceding that he in fact has the papers. Under these circumstances by enforcement of the summons "no constitutional rights are touched. The question is not of testimony but of surrender." In re Harris, 221 U.S. 274, 279 (1911).

When an accused is required to submit a handwriting exemplar he admits his ability to write and impliedly asserts that the exemplar is his writing. But in common experience, the first would be a near truism and the latter self-evident. In any event, although the exemplar may be incriminating to the accused and although he is compelled to furnish it, his Fifth Amendment privilege is not violated because nothing he has said or done is deemed to be sufficiently testimonial for purposes of the privilege. This Court has also time and again allowed subpoenas against the custodian of corporate documents or those belonging to other collective entities such as unions and partnerships and those of bankrupt businesses over claims that the documents will incriminate the custodian despite the fact that producing the documents tacitly admits their existence and their location in the hands of their possessor. . . . The existence and possession or control of the subpoenaed documents being no more in issue here than in the above cases, the summons is equally enforceable.

Moreover, assuming that these aspects of producing the accountant's papers have some minimal testimonial significance, surely it is not illegal to seek accounting help in connection with one's tax returns or for the accountant to prepare workpapers and deliver them to the taxpayer. At this juncture, we are quite unprepared to hold that either the fact of existence of the papers or of their possession by the taxpayer poses any realistic threat of incrimination to the taxpayer.

As for the possibility that responding to the subpoena would authenticate the workpapers, production would express nothing more than the taxpayer's belief that the papers are those described in the subpoena. The taxpayer would be no more competent to authenticate the accountant's workpapers or reports by producing them than he would be to authenticate them if testifying orally. The taxpayer did not prepare the papers and could not vouch for their accuracy. The documents would not be admissible in evidence against the taxpayer without authenticating testimony. Without more, responding to the subpoena in the circumstances before us would not appear to represent a substantial threat of self-incrimination. . . .

Whether the Fifth Amendment would shield the taxpayer from producing his own tax records in his possession is a question not involved here; for the papers demanded here are not his "private papers," see Boyd v. United States, 116 U.S., at 634–35. We do hold that compliance with a summons directing the taxpayer to produce the accountant's documents involved in these cases would involve no incriminating testimony within the protection of the Fifth Amendment.

. . .[20]

---

273. The Court relied on its holding in *Fisher*, above, for its holding in Andresen v. Maryland, 427 U.S. 463 (1976), p. 251 note 140 above, that a defendant's privilege against self-incrimination was not violated when business records were seized during a search of his office pursuant to a warrant.

274. The Court has indicated, but not quite held, that its unanswered question in *Fisher*—whether the Fifth Amendment shields a taxpayer "from producing his own tax records in his possession," above—should be answered in the negative. In United States v. Doe, 465 U.S. 605 (1984) (6–3), a grand jury ordered a witness to produce business records of companies owned by him. The Court held that the records, which were prepared voluntarily, were not covered by the privilege, whether they were in the witness's possession or not. Although papers are not protected, their production is protected if it is an independently incriminating testimonial act.

The "act of production" privilege is discussed in United States v. Hubbell, 530 U.S. 27 (2000), in which the Court held that the defendant could not be compelled to produce a broad range of incriminating documents that the government was unable to specify with particularity. For additional cases in which an "act of production" privilege was upheld, see United States v. Grable, 98 F.3d 251 (6th Cir.1996); United States v. Fox, 721 F.2d 32 (2d Cir.1983); In re Grand Jury Proceedings United States, 626 F.2d 1051 (1st Cir.1980).

The sole shareholder of a corporation, acting in his capacity as custodian of corporate records, may not resist a subpoena to produce the records on the ground that the act of production would violate his privilege against compulsory self-incrimination. So, generally, the custodian of corporate records may not resist their production on the ground that the content of the records would incriminate him. However, since the act of production is made by the individual in his capacity as a corporate agent, no evidentiary use can be made of it as an act of the individual; it must be regarded as the act of the corporation. Braswell v. United States, 487 U.S. 99 (1988) (5–4).

[20] Justice Brennan and Justice Marshall wrote opinions concurring in the judgment.

The Fifth Amendment does not prohibit a court from issuing an order directing a defendant to sign a consent directive that would enable the government to obtain records from a foreign bank. Signing the directive does not involve a testimonial communication and can therefore be compelled. Doe v. United States, 487 U.S. 201 (1988) (8–1). The consent form that petitioner was ordered to sign pursuant to a grand jury investigation was worded to avoid any representation that the records in question existed or that any records that the bank might turn over were authentic.

The privilege against compulsory self-incrimination does not prevent the state from ordering a mother, subject to conditions imposed by the juvenile court concerning her care for her child, to produce the child, even though production of the child might be incriminating. Baltimore City Department of Social Services v. Bouknight, 493 U.S. 549 (1990) (7–2). The woman subject to the order was suspected of having abused or possibly killed her child. The Court said that the privilege did not protect her from having to produce the child in compliance with the order because "she has assumed custodial duties related to production and because production is required as part of a noncriminal regulatory regime." Id. at 555–56. The Court noted that her privilege could still be protected by appropriate limitations on the state's use of incriminating information obtained as a result of the order.

275. The defendant was classified by his draft board as a conscientious objector available for civilian work, and was mailed an order to report for work. He did not do so. When the case was considered for prosecution, counsel for the Selective Service System found that there was no indication in the file that the defendant had been mailed a notice of classification and that he had a right to appeal; without such mailing, he could not be prosecuted. The draft board wrote to the defendant, asking him to appear and to bring with him the notice of classification. He did so, and the notice showed the date on which it had been mailed. Later, the defendant was prosecuted and convicted. United States v. Casias, 306 F.Supp. 166 (D.Colo. 1969).

Was the defendant entitled to be told by the draft board why it wanted him to produce the notice of classification?

Immunity From Prosecution

Garrity v. New Jersey

385 U.S. 493, 87 S.Ct. 616, 17 L.Ed.2d 562 (1967)

■ MR. JUSTICE DOUGLAS delivered the opinion of the Court.

Appellants were police officers in certain New Jersey boroughs. The Supreme Court of New Jersey ordered that alleged irregularities in handling cases in the municipal courts of those boroughs be investigated by the Attorney General, invested him with broad powers of inquiry and investigation, and directed him to make a report to the court. The matters investigated concerned alleged fixing of traffic tickets.

Before being questioned, each appellant was warned (1) that anything he said might be used against him in any state criminal proceeding; (2) that he had the privilege to refuse to answer if the disclosure would tend to incriminate him; but (3) that if he refused to answer he would be subject to removal from office.

Appellants answered the questions. No immunity was granted, as there is no immunity statute applicable in these circumstances. Over their objections, some of the answers given were used in subsequent prosecutions for conspiracy to obstruct the administration of the traffic laws. Appellants were convicted and their convictions were sustained over their protests that their statements were coerced, by reason of the fact that, if they refused to answer, they could lose their positions with the police department. . . .

. . .

The choice given petitioners was either to forfeit their jobs or to incriminate themselves. The option to lose their means of livelihood or to pay the penalty of self-incrimination is the antithesis of free choice to speak out or to remain silent. That practice, like interrogation practices we reviewed in Miranda v. Arizona, 384 U.S. 436, 464–65, is "likely to exert such pressure upon an individual as to disable him from making a free and rational choice." We think the statements were infected by the coercion inherent in this scheme of questioning and cannot be sustained as voluntary under our prior decisions.

It is said that there was a "waiver." . . .

Where the choice is "between the rock and the whirlpool," duress is inherent in deciding to "waive" one or the other. . . .

[T]hough petitioners succumbed to compulsion, they preserved their objections, raising them at the earliest possible point. . . . The cases are therefore quite different from the situation where one who is anxious to make a clean breast of the whole affair volunteers the information.

Mr. Justice Holmes in McAuliffe v. New Bedford, 29 N.E. 517, stated a dictum on which New Jersey heavily relies:

> The petitioner may have a constitutional right to talk politics, but he has no constitutional right to be a policeman. There are few employments for hire in which the servant does not agree to suspend his constitutional right of free speech, as well as of idleness, by the implied terms of his contract. The servant cannot complain, as he takes the

> employment on the terms which are offered him. On the same principle, the city may impose any reasonable condition upon holding offices within its control.

29 N.E., at 517–18.

The question in this case, however, is not cognizable in those terms. Our question is whether a State, contrary to the requirement of the Fourteenth Amendment, can use the threat of discharge to secure incriminatory evidence against an employee.

We held in Slochower v. Board of Education, 350 U.S. 551, that a public school teacher could not be discharged merely because he had invoked the Fifth Amendment privilege against self-incrimination when questioned by a congressional committee:

> The privilege against self-incrimination would be reduced to a hollow mockery if its exercise could be taken as equivalent either to a confession of guilt or a conclusive presumption of perjury. . . . The privilege serves to protect the innocent who otherwise might be ensnared by ambiguous circumstances.

Id., at 557–58.

We conclude that policemen, like teachers and lawyers, are not relegated to a watered-down version of constitutional rights.

There are rights of constitutional statute whose exercise a State may not condition by the exaction of a price. . . . We now hold the protection of the individual under the Fourteenth Amendment against coerced statements prohibits use in subsequent criminal proceedings of statements obtained under threat of removal from office, and that it extends to all, whether they are policemen or other members of our body politic.

■ MR. JUSTICE HARLAN, whom MR. JUSTICE CLARK and MR. JUSTICE STEWART join, dissenting.

. . .

I.

. . .

It would be difficult to imagine interrogations to which these criteria of duress were more completely inapplicable or in which the requirements which have subsequently been imposed by this Court on police questioning were more thoroughly satisfied. Each of the petitioners received a complete and explicit reminder of his constitutional privilege. Three of the petitioners had counsel present; at least a fourth had consulted counsel but freely determined that his presence was unnecessary. These petitioners were not in any fashion "swept from familiar surroundings into police custody, surrounded by antagonistic forces, and subjected to the techniques of persuasion. . . ." Miranda v. Arizona, 384 U.S. 436, 461. I think it manifest that, under the standards developed by this Court to assess voluntariness, there is no basis for saying that any of these statements were made involuntarily.

II.

The issue remaining is whether the statements were inadmissible because they were "involuntary as a matter of law," in that they were given after a warning that New Jersey policemen may be discharged for failure to provide information pertinent to their public responsibilities. . . . The central issues here are therefore identical to those presented in Spevack v. Klein, [385 U.S. 511 (1967)]: whether consequences may properly be permitted to result to a claimant after his invocation of the constitutional privilege, and if so, whether the consequence in question is permissible. For reasons which I have stated in Spevack v. Klein,[21] in my view nothing in the logic or purposes of the privilege demands that all consequences which may result from a witness' silence be forbidden merely because that silence is privileged. The validity of a consequence depends both upon the hazards, if any, it presents to the integrity of the privilege and upon the urgency of the public interests it is designed to protect.

It can hardly be denied that New Jersey is permitted by the Constitution to establish reasonable qualifications and standards of conduct for its public employees. Nor can it be said that it is arbitrary or unreasonable for New Jersey to insist that its employees furnish the appropriate authorities with information pertinent to their employment. . . . Finally, it is surely plain that New Jersey may in particular require its employees to assist in the prevention and detection of unlawful activities by officers of the state government. The urgency of these requirements is the more obvious here, where the conduct in question is that of officials directly entrusted with the administration of justice. . . . It must be concluded, therefore, that the sanction at issue here is reasonably calculated to serve the most basic interests of the citizens of New Jersey.

The final question is the hazard, if any, which this sanction presents to the constitutional privilege. The purposes for which, and the circumstances in which, an officer's discharge might be ordered under New Jersey law plainly may vary. It is of course possible that discharge might in a given case be predicated on an imputation of guilt drawn from the use of the privilege, as was thought by this Court to have occurred in Slochower v. Board of Education [350 U.S. 551 (1956)]. But from our vantage point, it would be quite improper to assume that New Jersey will employ these procedures for purposes other than to assess in good faith an employee's continued fitness for public employment. . . . We are not entitled to assume that discharges will be used either to vindicate impermissible inferences of guilt or to penalize privileged silence, but must instead presume that this procedure is only intended and will only be used to establish and enforce standards of conduct for public employees. As such, it does not minimize or endanger the petitioners' constitutional privilege against self-incrimination.

. . .[22]

---

[21] P. 498 below.

[22] Justice White wrote a dissenting opinion, applicable also to Spevack v. Klein, below.

No QB

Spevack v. Klein

385 U.S. 511, 87 S.Ct. 625, 17 L.Ed.2d 574 (1967)

■ MR. JUSTICE DOUGLAS announced the judgment of the Court and delivered an opinion in which THE CHIEF JUSTICE, MR. JUSTICE BLACK and MR. JUSTICE BRENNAN concur.

This is a proceeding to discipline petitioner, a member of the New York Bar, for professional misconduct. Of the various charges made, only one survived, *viz.*, the refusal of petitioner to honor a subpoena *duces tecum* served on him in that he refused to produce the demanded financial records and refused to testify at the judicial inquiry. Petitioner's sole defense was that the production of the records and his testimony would tend to incriminate him. The Appellate Division of the New York Supreme Court ordered petitioner disbarred, holding that the constitutional privilege against self-incrimination was not available to him in light of our decision in Cohen v. Hurley, 366 U.S. 117. . . . The Court of Appeals affirmed. . . .

. . .

. . . We conclude that . . . the Self-Incrimination Clause of the Fifth Amendment has been absorbed in the Fourteenth, that it extends its protection to lawyers as well as to other individuals, and that it should not be watered down by imposing the dishonor of disbarment and the deprivation of a livelihood as a price for asserting it. . . .

We said in Malloy v. Hogan [378 U.S. 1 (1964)]:

> The Fourteenth Amendment secures against state invasion the same privilege that the Fifth Amendment guarantees against federal infringement—the right of a person to remain silent unless he chooses to speak in the unfettered exercise of his own will, and to suffer no penalty . . . for such silence.

378 U.S., at 8.

In this context "penalty" is not restricted to fine or imprisonment. It means, as we said in Griffin v. California, 380 U.S. 609, the imposition of any sanction which makes assertion of the Fifth Amendment privilege "costly." Id., at 614. . . .

The threat of disbarment and the loss of professional standing, professional reputation, and of livelihood are powerful forms of compulsion to make a lawyer relinquish the privilege. That threat is indeed as powerful an instrument of compulsion as "the use of legal process to force from the lips of the accused individual the evidence necessary to convict him. . . ." United States v. White, 322 U.S. 694, 698. As we recently stated in Miranda v. Arizona, 384 U.S. 436, 461, "In this Court, the privilege has consistently been accorded a liberal construction." . . . We find no room in the privilege against self-incrimination for classifications of people so as to deny it to some and extend it to others. Lawyers are not excepted from the words "No person . . . shall be compelled in any criminal case to be a witness against himself"; and we can imply no exception. Like the school teacher in

Slochower v. Board of Education, 350 U.S. 551, and the policemen in Garrity v. New Jersey,[23] ante, lawyers also enjoy first-class citizenship.

. . .

■ MR. JUSTICE HARLAN, whom MR. JUSTICE CLARK and MR. JUSTICE STEWART join, dissenting.

. . .

It cannot be claimed that the purposes served by the New York rules [requiring disclosure of the information which the petitioner refused to disclose] at issue here, compendiously aimed at "ambulance chasing" and its attendant evils, are unimportant or unrelated to the protection of legitimate state interests. . . .

. . .

Without denying the urgency or significance of the public purposes served by these rules, the plurality opinion has seemingly concluded that they may not be enforced because any consequence of a claim of the privilege against self-incrimination which renders that claim "costly" is an "instrument of compulsion" which impermissibly infringes on the protection offered by the privilege. . . . The Court has not before held that the Federal Government and the States are forbidden to permit any consequences to result from a claim of the privilege; it has instead recognized that such consequences may vary widely in kind and intensity and that these differences warrant individual examination both of the hazard, if any, offered to the essential purposes of the privilege, and of the public interests protected by the consequence. This process is far better calculated than the broad prohibition embraced by the plurality to serve both the purposes of the privilege and the other important public values which are often at stake in such cases. It would assure the integrity of the privilege, and yet guarantee the most generous opportunities for the pursuit of other public values, by selecting the rule or standard most appropriate for the hazards and characteristics of each consequence.

One such rule has already been plainly approved by this Court. It seems clear to me that this rule is applicable to the situation now before us. The Court has repeatedly recognized that it is permissible to deny a status or authority to a claimant of the privilege against self-incrimination if his claim has prevented full assessment of his qualifications for the status or authority. Under this rule, the applicant may not both decline to disclose information necessary to demonstrate his fitness, and yet demand that he receive the benefits of the status. He may not by his interjection of the privilege either diminish his obligation to establish his qualifications, or escape the consequences exacted by the State for a failure to satisfy that obligation.

. . .

23. Whether a policeman, who invokes the privilege when his conduct as a police officer is questioned in disciplinary proceedings, may be discharged for refusing to testify is a question we did not reach.

. . . The petitioner was not denied his privilege against self-incrimination, nor was he penalized for its use; he was denied his authority to practice law within the State of New York by reason of his failure to satisfy valid obligations imposed by the State as a condition of that authority. The only hazard in this process to the integrity of the privilege is the possibility that it might induce involuntary disclosures of incriminating materials; the sanction precisely calculated to eliminate that hazard is to exclude the use by prosecuting authorities of such materials and of their fruits. . . . It is true that this Court has on occasion gone a step further, and forbidden the practices likely to produce involuntary disclosures, but those cases are readily distinguishable. They have uniformly involved either situations in which the entire process was thought both to present excessive risks of coercion and to be foreign to our accusatorial system . . . or situations in which the only possible purpose of the practice was thought to be to penalize the accused for his use of the constitutional privilege. . . . Both situations are plainly remote from that in issue here. None of the reasons thought to require the prohibitions established in those cases have any relevance in the situation now before us; nothing in New York's efforts in good faith to assure the integrity of its judicial system destroys, inhibits, or even minimizes the petitioner's constitutional privilege. There is therefore no need to speculate whether lawyers, or those in any other profession or occupation, have waived in some unspecified fashion a measure of the protection afforded by the constitutional privilege; it suffices that the State is earnestly concerned with an urgent public interest, and that it has selected methods for the pursuit of that interest which do not prevent attainment of the privilege's purposes.

. . .[24]

---

276. In Gardner v. Broderick, 392 U.S. 273 (1968), the Court held that a New York City patrolman who was called before a grand jury to testify concerning the performance of his official duties could not be discharged for refusing to waive immunity from prosecution before testifying. It observed, however, that the position of the patrolman was different from that of a lawyer; "unlike the lawyer who is directly responsible to his client, the policeman is either responsible to the State or to no one." Id. at 278. Therefore, the Court said, "if appellant, a policeman, had refused to answer questions specifically, directly, and narrowly relating to the performance of his official duties, without being required to waive his immunity with respect to the use of his answers or the fruits thereof in a criminal prosecution of himself . . . the privilege against self-incrimination would not have been a bar to his dismissal." Id. Since, however, "he was discharged from office, not for failure to answer relevant questions about

[24] Justice Fortas wrote an opinion concurring in the judgment. Justice White wrote a dissenting opinion.

his official duties, but for refusal to waive a constitutional right . . . for failure to relinquish the protections of the privilege against self-incrimination," the discharge was invalid. Id.

In a companion case, Uniformed Sanitation Men Association, Inc. v. Commissioner of Sanitation of the City of New York, 392 U.S. 280 (1968), the Court reached the same conclusion respecting the dismissal of employees of the Department of Sanitation who refused on the ground of self-incrimination to testify in an investigation into their official conduct or, in some cases, to sign waivers of immunity after being called before the grand jury. Again the Court said that the men involved, "being public employees, subject themselves to dismissal if they refuse to account for their performance of their public trust, after proper proceedings, which do not involve an attempt to coerce them to relinquish their constitutional rights." Id. at 285.

Concurring in the result in both cases, Justice Harlan observed that he found in the two opinions "a procedural formula whereby, for example, public officials may now be discharged and lawyers disciplined for refusing to divulge to appropriate authority information pertinent to the faithful performance of their offices." Id. at 285.

See Lefkowitz v. Cunningham, 431 U.S. 801 (1977) (7–1) (statute removing political party officer from office and barring him from holding public or private office for five years because of assertion of privilege was invalid); Lefkowitz v. Turley, 414 U.S. 70 (1973) (disqualification of architects from public contracts following refusal to waive privilege against self-incrimination was invalid); Benjamin v. City of Montgomery, 785 F.2d 959 (11th Cir.1986) (police officers; discharge invalid); Gulden v. McCorkle, 680 F.2d 1070 (5th Cir.1982) (discharge of public employees for refusal to submit to polygraph test, without waiver of privilege, upheld); Confederation of Police v. Conlisk, 489 F.2d 891 (7th Cir.1973) (police officers; discharge invalid). See also United States v. Friedrick, 842 F.2d 382 (D.C.Cir.1988) (*Garrity* applied to FBI agent's statements in interviews with Justice Department lawyers).

277. In McKune v. Lile, 536 U.S. 24 (2002) (5–4), the defendant was imprisoned for rape. Several years before he was to be released, prison officials ordered him to participate in a Sex Abuse Treatment Program, which was designed to reduce the likelihood of recidivism. Part of the program required him to accept responsibility for the crime for which he was convicted and to give a history of his sexual activities, including criminal activities for which he had not been prosecuted. There was no immunity from use of the information in a subsequent criminal prosecution. The defendant refused to participate, on the ground that the requirements violated his privilege against compulsory self-incrimination. As a consequence of his refusal, he was moved to a less desirable prison unit and lost certain prison privileges. Noting the valid purpose of the SATP program and the limited nature of the penalties imposed, the Court held that the defendant's Fifth Amendment privilege had not been violated.

278. Immunity statutes. The use of immunity statutes to overcome the privilege against self-incrimination and obtain testimony is common. The first federal immunity statute, which gave immunity to persons testifying in a congressional inquiry, was enacted in 1857. 11 Stat. 155. The statute was modified in 1862 to prevent a witness from getting an "immunity bath" protecting him altogether from prosecution for "any fact or act touching which he shall be required to testify," 11 Stat. at 156. See 12 Stat. 333. The modified statute, however, in terms gave immunity only from the use of the witness's testimony in evidence against him. That formula, which might allow the government to use the immunized testimony as a lead to other evidence, was held insufficient to overcome the constitutional privilege against self-incrimination, in Counselman v. Hitchcock, 142 U.S. 547 (1892). After 1893, federal immunity statutes again gave full immunity from prosecution "for or on account of any transaction, matter or thing, concerning which . . . [a witness] may testify, or produce evidence." 49 U.S.C. § 46 (testimony before Interstate Commerce Commission). Federal legislation regularly authorized administrative agencies to compel testimony by giving a witness immunity. In 1968 Congress gave the Department of Justice power to compel testimony in court by granting immunity in proceedings involving any of a very broad range of federal crimes. 82 Stat. 216, since repealed, 84 Stat. 930.

Language in Counselman v. Hitchcock created doubt whether a statute that gave a witness full "use" immunity—immunity from the use of his testimony and its fruits—would be sufficient to overcome the constitutional privilege. In 1970, Congress enacted a general immunity statute covering proceedings, among others, in a court or before a grand jury. The statute grants immunity only from the use of compelled "testimony or other information" or "any information directly or indirectly derived from such testimony or other information." 18 U.S.C. § 6002. Doubt whether the statute was constitutional was resolved by Kastigar v. United States, below.

Kastigar v. United States

406 U.S. 441, 92 S.Ct. 1653, 32 L.Ed.2d 212 (1972)

■ MR. JUSTICE POWELL delivered the opinion of the Court.

This case presents the question whether the United States Government may compel testimony from an unwilling witness, who invokes the Fifth Amendment privilege against compulsory self-incrimination, by conferring on the witness immunity from use of the compelled testimony in subsequent criminal proceedings, as well as immunity from use of evidence derived from the testimony.

Petitioners were subpoenaed to appear before a United States grand jury in the Central District of California on February 4, 1971. The Government believed that petitioners were likely to assert their Fifth Amendment privilege. Prior to the scheduled appearances, the Government applied to the District Court for an order directing petitioners to answer questions and produce evidence before the grand jury under a grant of immunity conferred pursuant to 18 U.S.C. §§ 6002–6003. Petitioners opposed issuance of the order, contending primarily that the scope of the immunity provided by the statute was not coextensive with the scope of the privilege against self-incrimination, and therefore was not sufficient to supplant the privilege and compel their testimony. The District Court rejected this contention, and ordered petitioners to appear before the grand jury and answer its questions under the grant of immunity.

Petitioners appeared but refused to answer questions, asserting their privilege against compulsory self-incrimination. They were brought before the District Court, and each persisted in his refusal to answer the grand jury's questions, notwithstanding the grant of immunity. The court found both in contempt, and committed them to the custody of the Attorney General until either they answered the grand jury's questions or the term of the grand jury expired. The Court of Appeals for the Ninth Circuit affirmed. . . . This Court granted certiorari to resolve the important question whether testimony may be compelled by granting immunity from the use of compelled testimony and evidence derived therefrom ("use and derivative use" immunity), or whether it is necessary to grant immunity from prosecution for offenses to which compelled testimony relates ("transactional" immunity). . . .

I

The power of government to compel persons to testify in court or before grand juries and other governmental agencies is firmly established in Anglo–American jurisprudence. . . . The power to compel testimony, and the corresponding duty to testify, are recognized in the Sixth Amendment requirements that an accused be confronted with the witnesses against him, and have compulsory process for obtaining witnesses in his favor. . . .

But the power to compel testimony is not absolute. There are a number of exemptions from the testimonial duty, the most important of which is the Fifth Amendment privilege against compulsory self-incrimination. The privilege reflects a complex of our fundamental values and aspirations, and marks an important advance in the development of our liberty. It can be asserted in any proceeding, civil or criminal, administrative or judicial, investigatory or adjudicatory; and it protects against any disclosures that the witness reasonably believes could be used in a criminal prosecution or could lead to other evidence that might be so used. This Court has been zealous to safeguard the values that underlie the privilege.

Immunity statutes, which have historical roots deep in Anglo–American jurisprudence, are not incompatible with these values. Rather, they seek a rational accommodation between the imperatives of the privilege and the legitimate demands of government to compel citizens to testify. The existence of these statutes reflects the importance of testimony, and the fact that many offenses are of such a character that the only persons capable of giving useful testimony are those implicated in the crime. Indeed, their origins were in the context of such offenses, and their primary use has been to investigate such offenses. Congress included immunity statutes in many of the regulatory measures adopted in the first half of this century. Indeed, prior to the enactment of the statute under consideration in this case, there were in force over 50 federal immunity statutes. In addition, every State in the Union, as well as the District of Columbia and Puerto Rico, has one or more such statutes. The commentators, and this Court on several occasions, have characterized immunity statutes as essential to the effective enforcement of various criminal statutes. As Mr. Justice Frankfurter observed, speaking for the Court in Ullmann v. United States, 350 U.S. 422 (1956), such statutes have "become part of our constitutional fabric." Id., at 438.

II

Petitioners contend, first, that the Fifth Amendment's privilege against compulsory self-incrimination, which is that "[n]o person . . . shall be compelled in any criminal case to be a witness against himself," deprives Congress of power to enact laws that compel self-incrimination, even if complete immunity from prosecution is granted prior to the compulsion of the incriminatory testimony. In other words, petitioners assert that no immunity statute, however drawn, can afford a lawful basis for compelling incriminatory testimony. They ask us to reconsider and overrule Brown v. Walker, 161 U.S. 591 (1896), and Ullmann v. United States, supra, decisions that uphold the constitutionality of immunity statutes. We find no merit to this contention and reaffirm the decisions in *Brown* and *Ullmann*.

III

Petitioners' second contention is that the scope of immunity provided by the federal witness immunity statute, 18 U.S.C. § 6002, is not coextensive with the scope of the Fifth Amendment privilege against compulsory self-incrimination, and therefore is not sufficient to supplant the privilege and compel testimony over a claim of the privilege. The statute provides that when a witness is compelled by district court order to testify over a claim of the privilege:

> the witness may not refuse to comply with the order on the basis of his privilege against self-incrimination; but no testimony or other information compelled under the order (or any information directly or indirectly derived from such testimony or other information) may be used against the witness in any criminal case, except a prosecution for perjury, giving a false statement, or otherwise failing to comply with the order.

18 U.S.C. § 6002.

The constitutional inquiry, rooted in logic and history, as well as in the decisions of this Court, is whether the immunity granted under this statute is coextensive with the scope of the privilege. If so, petitioners' refusals to answer based on the privilege were unjustified, and the judgments of contempt were proper, for the grant of immunity has removed the dangers against which the privilege protects. . . . If, on the other hand, the immunity granted is not as comprehensive as the protection afforded by the privilege, petitioners were justified in refusing to answer, and the judgments of contempt must be vacated. . . .

Petitioners draw a distinction between statutes that provide transactional immunity and those that provide, as does the statute before us, immunity from use and derivative use. They contend that a statute must at a minimum grant full transactional immunity in order to be coextensive with the scope of the privilege. In support of this contention, they rely on Counselman v. Hitchcock, 142 U.S. 547 (1892), the first case in which this Court considered a constitutional challenge to an immunity statute. The statute, a re-enactment of the Immunity Act of 1868, provided that no "evidence obtained from a party or witness by means of a judicial proceeding . . . shall be given in evidence, or in any manner used against him . . . in any court of the United States. . . ." Notwithstanding a grant of immunity and order to testify under the revised 1868 Act, the witness, asserting his privilege against compulsory self-incrimination, refused to testify before a federal grand jury. He was consequently adjudged in contempt of court. On appeal, this Court construed the statute as affording a witness protection only against the use of the specific testimony compelled from him under the grant of immunity. This construction meant that the statute "could not, and would not, prevent the use of his testimony to search out other testimony to be used in evidence against him."[25] Since the revised 1868 Act, as construed by the Court, would permit the use against the immunized witness of evidence derived from his compelled testimony, it did not protect the witness to the same extent that a claim of the privilege would protect him. Accordingly, under the principle that a grant of immunity cannot supplant the privilege, and is not sufficient to compel testimony over a claim of the privilege, unless the scope of the grant of immunity is coextensive with the scope of the privilege, the witness' refusal to testify was held proper. In the course of its opinion, the Court made the following statement, on which petitioners heavily rely:

> We are clearly of opinion that no statute which leaves the party or witness subject to prosecution after he answers the criminating question put to him, can have the effect of supplanting the privilege conferred by the Constitution of the United States. [The immunity statute under consideration] does not supply a complete protection from all the perils against which the constitutional prohibition was designed to guard, and is not a full substitute for that prohibition. In view of the constitutional provision, a statutory enactment, to be valid, must afford absolute immunity against future prosecution for the offence to which the question relates.

142 U.S., at 585–86.

25. Counselman v. Hitchcock, supra, at 564.

Sixteen days after the *Counselman* decision, a new immunity bill was introduced by Senator Cullom, who urged that enforcement of the Interstate Commerce Act would be impossible in the absence of an effective immunity statute. The bill, which became the Compulsory Testimony Act of 1893, was drafted specifically to meet the broad language in *Counselman* set forth above. The new Act removed the privilege against self-incrimination in hearings before the Interstate Commerce Commission and provided that:

> no person shall be prosecuted or subjected to any penalty or forfeiture for or on account of any transaction, matter or thing, concerning which he may testify, or produce evidence, documentary or otherwise. . . .

Act of Feb. 11, 1893, 27 Stat. 444. This transactional immunity statute became the basic form for the numerous federal immunity statutes until 1970, when, after re-examining applicable constitutional principles and the adequacy of existing law, Congress enacted the statute here under consideration. The new statute, which does not "afford [the] absolute immunity against future prosecution" referred to in *Counselman*, was drafted to meet what Congress judged to be the conceptual basis of *Counselman*, as elaborated in subsequent decisions of the Court, namely, that immunity from the use of compelled testimony and evidence derived therefrom is coextensive with the scope of the privilege.

The statute's explicit proscription of the use in any criminal case of "testimony or other information compelled under the order (or any information directly or indirectly derived from such testimony or other information)" is consonant with Fifth Amendment standards. We hold that such immunity from use and derivative use is coextensive with the scope of the privilege against self-incrimination, and therefore is sufficient to compel testimony over a claim of the privilege. While a grant of immunity must afford protection commensurate with that afforded by the privilege, it need not be broader. Transactional immunity, which accords full immunity from prosecution for the offense to which the compelled testimony relates, affords the witness considerably broader protection than does the Fifth Amendment privilege. The privilege has never been construed to mean that one who invokes it cannot subsequently be prosecuted. Its sole concern is to afford protection against being "forced to give testimony leading to the infliction of 'penalties affixed to . . . criminal acts.' "[26] Immunity from the use of compelled testimony, as well as evidence derived directly and indirectly therefrom, affords this protection. It prohibits the prosecutorial authorities from using the compelled testimony in *any* respect, and it therefore insures that the testimony cannot lead to the infliction of criminal penalties on the witness.

Our holding is consistent with the conceptual basis of *Counselman*. The *Counselman* statute, as construed by the Court, was plainly deficient

26. Ullmann v. United States, 350 U.S., at 438–39, quoting Boyd v. United States, 116 U.S. [616 (1886)], at 634. . . .

in its failure to prohibit the use against the immunized witness of evidence derived from his compelled testimony. The Court repeatedly emphasized this deficiency. . . . The broad language in *Counselman* relied upon by petitioners was unnecessary to the Court's decision, and cannot be considered binding authority.

. . .

IV

Although an analysis of prior decisions and the purpose of the Fifth Amendment privilege indicates that use and derivative-use immunity is coextensive with the privilege, we must consider additional arguments advanced by petitioners against the sufficiency of such immunity. We start from the premise, repeatedly affirmed by this Court, that an appropriately broad immunity grant is compatible with the Constitution.

Petitioners argue that use and derivative-use immunity will not adequately protect a witness from various possible incriminating uses of the compelled testimony: for example, the prosecutor or other law enforcement officials may obtain leads, names of witnesses, or other information not otherwise available that might result in a prosecution. It will be difficult and perhaps impossible, the argument goes, to identify, by testimony or cross-examination, the subtle ways in which the compelled testimony may disadvantage a witness, especially in the jurisdiction granting the immunity.

This argument presupposes that the statute's prohibition will prove impossible to enforce. The statute provides a sweeping proscription of any use, direct or indirect, of the compelled testimony and any information derived therefrom. . . . This total prohibition on use provides a comprehensive safeguard, barring the use of compelled testimony as an "investigatory lead," and also barring the use of any evidence obtained by focusing investigation on a witness as a result of his compelled disclosures.

A person accorded this immunity under 18 U.S.C. § 6002, and subsequently prosecuted, is not dependent for the preservation of his rights upon the integrity and good faith of the prosecuting authorities. As stated in *Murphy* [v. Waterfront Commission, 378 U.S. 52 (1964)]:

> Once a defendant demonstrates that he has testified, under a state grant of immunity, to matters related to the federal prosecution, the federal authorities have the burden of showing that their evidence is not tainted by establishing that they had an independent, legitimate source for the disputed evidence.

378 U.S., at 79 n.18. This burden of proof, which we reaffirm as appropriate, is not limited to a negation of taint; rather, it imposes on the prosecution the affirmative duty to prove that the evidence it proposes to use is derived from a legitimate source wholly independent of the compelled testimony.

This is very substantial protection, commensurate with that resulting from invoking the privilege itself. The privilege assures that a citizen is not compelled to incriminate himself by his own testimony. It usually operates to allow a citizen to remain silent when asked a question requiring an incriminatory answer. This statute, which operates after a witness has given incriminatory testimony, affords the same protection by assuring that the compelled testimony can in no way lead to the infliction of criminal penalties. The statute, like the Fifth Amendment, grants neither pardon nor amnesty. Both the statute and the Fifth Amendment allow the government to prosecute using evidence from legitimate independent sources.

The statutory proscription is analogous to the Fifth Amendment requirement in cases of coerced confessions. A coerced confession, as revealing of leads as testimony given in exchange for immunity, is inadmissible in a criminal trial, but it does not bar prosecution. Moreover, a defendant against whom incriminating evidence has been obtained through a grant of immunity may be in a stronger position at trial than a defendant who asserts a Fifth Amendment coerced-confession claim. One raising a claim under this statute need only show that he testified under a grant of immunity in order to shift to the government the heavy burden of proving that all of the evidence it proposes to use was derived from legitimate independent sources. On the other hand, a defendant raising a coerced-confession claim under the Fifth Amendment must first prevail in a voluntariness hearing before his confession and evidence derived from it become inadmissible.

There can be no justification in reason or policy for holding that the Constitution requires an amnesty grant where, acting pursuant to statute and accompanying safeguards, testimony is compelled in exchange for immunity from use and derivative use when no such amnesty is required where the government, acting without colorable right, coerces a defendant into incriminating himself.

We conclude that the immunity provided by 18 U.S.C. § 6002 leaves the witness and the prosecutorial authorities in substantially the same position as if the witness had claimed the Fifth Amendment privilege. The immunity therefore is coextensive with the privilege and suffices to supplant it. The judgment of the Court of Appeals for the Ninth Circuit accordingly is

Affirmed.[27]

---

279. The meaning of "derivative use" in connection with use immunity is discussed in Pillsbury Co. v. Conboy, 459 U.S. 248 (1983) (7–2), in which the Court held that "a deponent's civil deposition testimony, closely tracking his prior immunized testimony, is not, without duly authorized assurance of immunity at the time, immunized testimony within the meaning of § 6002, and therefore may not be compelled over a valid assertion of his Fifth Amendment privilege." Id. at 263.

[27] Justice Douglas and Justice Marshall wrote dissenting opinions.

Testimony that a person gives before a grand jury pursuant to a grant of immunity cannot constitutionally be used to impeach his credibility if he is subsequently prosecuted and testifies as a witness at trial. New Jersey v. Portash, 440 U.S. 450 (1979) (7–2). Compare Harris v. New York and Oregon v. Hass, pp. 479, 482 above.

280. Cases exploring the problem of establishing an independent source of evidence against a defendant who has testified under a grant of immunity include United States v. Overmyer, 899 F.2d 457 (6th Cir.1990); United States v. Hampton, 775 F.2d 1479 (11th Cir.1985); United States v. Pantone, 634 F.2d 716 (3d Cir.1980); United States v. Romano, 583 F.2d 1 (1st Cir.1978); United States v. Nemes, 555 F.2d 51 (2d Cir.1977); and United States v. De Diego, 511 F.2d 818 (D.C.Cir.1975).

In *Nemes*, above, the court held that the government's burden of establishing an independent source could not be met simply by the prosecutor's denial that he had had access to the immunized testimony. "The inference that the prosecutor's lack of access to compelled testimony assures the existence of independent sources cannot be relied upon to afford the witness the full protection the Constitution guarantees. The prosecutor may have never seen the witness's testimony and may believe in good faith that no one associated with the federal prosecution has seen it, but such a disclaimer does not preclude the possibility that someone who has seen the compelled testimony was thereby led to evidence that was furnished to federal investigators. Only by affirmatively proving that his evidence comes from sources independent of the immunized testimony can the prosecutor assure that the witness is in the same position he would have enjoyed had his self-incrimination privilege not been displaced by use immunity." 555 F.2d at 55. See United States v. Harris, 973 F.2d 333 (4th Cir. 1992) (assistant United States attorney who heard immunized testimony later obtained indictment; indictment dismissed).

In *Hinton*, above, the court concluded that "as a matter of fundamental fairness, a Government practice of using the same grand jury that heard the immunized testimony of a witness to indict him after he testifies, charging him with criminal participation in the matters being studied by the grand jury" should not be allowed. 543 F.2d at 1010. Relying on its supervisory authority, the court prohibited the practice. Other courts of appeals have declined to adopt the per se prohibition of *Hinton* and have held only that the defendant is entitled to a hearing at which to challenge the government's claim that the indictment was based on information from independent sources. E.g., United States v. Bartel, 19 F.3d 1105 (6th Cir.1994).

The question whether a prosecutor who has had access to a witness's testimony pursuant to a grant of immunity may participate in a subsequent decision to indict the witness is explored in United States v. Byrd, 765 F.2d 1524 (11th Cir.1985). Observing that *Kastigar* does not require that the position of an immunized witness before and after testifying "remain absolutely identical in every conceivable and theoretical respect," the court concluded: "So long as none of the evidence presented to the grand jury is derived, directly or indirectly, from the immunized testimony, it can fairly be said that the defendant's immunized testimony has not been used to incriminate him." Id. at 1530.

While awaiting trial, the appellant was summoned as a witness against a codefendant being tried on the same charges. The appellant's case was scheduled for trial subsequently before the same judge and was to be tried by the same prosecutor. The appellant was granted immunity. He refused to testify on the basis that despite the grant of immunity, in the circumstances his testimony would inevitably be used against him. The court held that he could be compelled to testify, since he would have an opportunity in pretrial proceedings in his own case to object to any use of his testimony. Graves v. United States, 472 A.2d 395 (D.C.App.1984). See generally In re Sealed Case, 791 F.2d 179 (D.C.Cir.1986).

281. Observing that "in theory, strict application of use and derivative use immunity would remove the hazard of incrimination," but that "in our imperfect world . . . we doubt that workaday measures can, *in practice*, protect adequately against use and derivative use," the Supreme Court of Alaska held that the state constitutional provision against compulsory self-incrimination required transactional immunity as a condition of compelled incriminating testimony. State v. Gonzalez, 853 P.2d 526 (Alaska 1993). The court cites cases in Hawaii, Massachusetts, and Oregon reaching the same result.

282. "Dual sovereignties." Murphy v. Waterfront Commission, 378 U.S. 52 (1964), denies to the states or to the federal government use for prosecutorial purposes of testimony obtained by the other sovereignty by a grant of immunity. *Murphy* is discussed at length and much of its reasoning is rejected in *Balsys*, note 283 below.

283. A fear of prosecution by a foreign government does not invoke the privilege against compulsory self-incrimination. United States v. Balsys, 524 U.S. 666 (1998) (7–2). Balsys had been summoned to testify before the Office of Special Investigations of the Department of Justice about activities during World War II which might make him subject to deportation. He claimed that his responses might subject him to criminal prosecution in Lithuania, Israel, and Germany. The district court found that the danger of prosecution in the first two countries was "real and substantial," id. at 671.

284. The federal statutes before 1970 gave immunity not only from prosecution but also from "penalty or forfeiture" in connection with compelled testimony. Does the Constitution require that immunity extend beyond criminal proceedings? If so, how far? What kinds of "penalty or forfeiture" are barred? See Boyd v. United States, 116 U.S. 616 (1886); Lee v. Civil Aeronautics Board, 225 F.2d 950 (D.C.Cir.1955). Does *Spevack*, p. 498 above, have a bearing on this question? If the Constitution does not require immunity beyond criminal prosecution, should it nevertheless be granted?

285. The courts have rejected a variety of grounds for refusing to testify that do not involve subsequent governmental action. In Branzburg v. Hayes, 408 U.S. 665 (1972), the Court rejected the claim that a newspaper reporter is generally privileged under the First Amendment not to reveal the names of confidential sources of news in response to questions of the grand jury. A First Amendment "scholar's privilege" was rejected in United States v. Doe, 460 F.2d 328 (1st Cir.1972). In Bursey v. United States, 466 F.2d 1059 (9th Cir.1972), however, the court upheld witnesses' refusal to answer questions on the ground that First Amendment rights were involved; the court concluded that the government had not shown a sufficiently compelling interest to overcome those rights.

In LaTona v. United States, 449 F.2d 121 (8th Cir.1971), the court refused to accept a witness's claim to be excused from testifying before the grand jury because he would be subject to "underworld reprisals" and might be killed if he testified. To the same effect, see In re Grand Jury Proceedings (Taylor v. United States), 509 F.2d 1349 (5th Cir.1975). But see United States v. Banks, 942 F.2d 1576, 1578 (11th Cir.1991), holding that a person who refuses to testify before the grand jury because of a "legitimate and well-founded fear" for his own and his family's safety cannot be convicted of corruptly endeavoring to obstruct justice.

In general, claims of a privilege not to testify against a member of one's family have been rejected. In a lengthy opinion reviewing and confirming the rule in other jurisdictions, the court held that there is no parent-child or child-parent privilege not to testify, in In re Grand Jury, 103 F.3d 1140 (3d Cir.1997).

In In re Grand Jury, 111 F.3d 1083 (3d Cir.1997), the court held that a grant of use and derivative use immunity to a witness summoned before a grand jury, by which she was promised that her testimony and any fruits thereof would not be used against her husband, who was the subject of the grand jury's investigation, and that an indictment against her husband would not be sought before the same grand jury, was sufficient to defeat her privilege against giving adverse spousal testimony.

286. A witness's assertion that the answer to a question would tend to incriminate him usually is not contested. The government may, however, challenge the assertion and oppose the witness's claim under the privilege against compulsory self-incrimination on that basis. See, e.g., United States v. Castro, 129 F.3d 226 (1st Cir.1997) (claim upheld); In re Brogna, 589 F.2d 24 (1st Cir.1978) (same).

On the issue of waiver of the privilege with respect to subsequent questions by answering previous incriminating questions, see Klein v. Harris, 667 F.2d 274, 287–89 (2d Cir.1981); United States v. Seifert, 648 F.2d 557, 561 (9th Cir.1980).

Neither a defendant's guilty plea nor her statements during the colloquy with the judge when the plea is entered constitute a waiver of her privilege against compulsory self-incrimination at sentencing. Mitchell v. United States, 526 U.S. 314 (1999).

287. If a witness refuses to testify before the grand jury, he can be committed to jail for civil contempt until he obeys the order of court directing him to testify. In a federal proceeding, the maximum period of confinement is 18 months. 28 U.S.C. § 1826. It has been held that confinement for civil contempt should not be continued once it becomes clear that the witness's detention has no coercive impact and will not induce him to testify. See Simkin v. United States, 715 F.2d 34 (2d Cir.1983). "As long as the judge is satisfied that the coercive sanction might yet produce its intended result, the confinement may continue. But if the judge is persuaded, after a conscientious consideration of the circumstances pertinent to the individual contemnor, that the contempt power has ceased to have a coercive effect, the civil contempt remedy should be ended. The contemnor will not have avoided all sanction by his irrevocable opposition to the court's order. Once it is determined that the civil contempt remedy is unavailing, the criminal contempt sanction is available." Id. at 37.

288. Reporting requirements. Federal law imposes excise and occupational taxes on the business of accepting wagers. 26 U.S.C. §§ 4401, 4411. Persons who are subject to the occupational tax are required to register with the Internal Revenue Service. 26 U.S.C. § 4412. The Service is directed to make a list of those who pay the tax available for public inspection. In Marchetti v. United States, 390 U.S. 39 (1968), noting that "wagering and its ancillary activities are very widely prohibited under both federal and state law," id. at 44, the Supreme Court concluded that the requirements of payment of the occupational tax and registration created a substantial possibility of self-incrimination and, therefore, that a person who asserted the constitutional privilege could not be criminally punished for failing to perform those acts.

In Grosso v. United States, 390 U.S. 62 (1968), the Court applied the same reasoning to the excise tax, payment of which was required to be accompanied by submission of a special tax return applicable only to those in the wagering business. On the same basis, in Haynes v. United States, 390 U.S. 85 (1968), the Court reversed a conviction for possession of a firearm that had not been registered as required by law, 26 U.S.C. §§ 5841, 5851; and in Leary v. United States, 395 U.S. 6 (1969), the Court reversed a conviction for violation of the Marijuana Tax Act, 26 U.S.C. §§ 4741, 4744.

In each of the cases, the Court declined to uphold the challenged provisions and impose a restriction on use of the information obtained thereby, because it thought that such a resolution of the competing interests was not contemplated by the statutory scheme and should be reached, if at all, by Congress rather than the Court. The Gun Control Act of 1968, 82 Stat. 1214, retained the firearm registration requirement and enacted a use restriction providing that except for a prosecution for furnishing false information, no information obtained thereby shall "be used, directly or indirectly, as evidence against that person in a criminal proceeding with respect to a violation of law occurring prior to or concurrently with the filing of the application or registration, or the compiling of the records containing the information or evidence." 26 U.S.C. § 5848(a). The amended statute was upheld in United States v. Freed, 401 U.S. 601 (1971).

In Garner v. United States, 424 U.S. 648 (1976), the Court held that since the defendant could have asserted the privilege against self-incrimination as a basis for refusing to give information on his income-tax returns, having given the information, he had no basis on which to object to the introduction of the information against him in a criminal trial. Unlike the disclosure requirements involved in *Marchetti* and *Grosso*, above, federal income tax returns are not directed peculiarly at persons engaged in illegal activities. Nor was the reasoning in Garrity v. New Jersey, 385 U.S. 493 (1967), p. 494 above, applicable, since a person who validly exercised the privilege when filing his return could not be prosecuted for failure to file a return; the possibility that the validity of a claim of the privilege would be tested in a criminal prosecution was not the kind of compulsion with which *Garrity* was concerned.

The Court held in California v. Byers, 402 U.S. 424 (1971) (5–4), that a "hit and run" statute which requires the driver of a motor vehicle involved in an accident to stop at the scene and give his name and address does not violate the privilege against self-incrimination.

An arrest is commonly described as taking a person into custody so that he can be held to answer a charge against him. E.g., ALI, Code of Criminal Procedure § 18 (1930). Often, however, an arrest may be more an aspect of the investigation of crime than of prosecution. While police actions are in some respects restricted after they have taken a person into custody, at least as significant are actions that may be taken as incidents of an arrest. Police have no general authority to demand information for their records from the community at large, or to fingerprint persons or examine their bodies, or to place them in lineups for observation by others. It is assumed generally that a person who has been arrested should not be held in custody until his trial but should be released as soon as possible after his arrest. In most cases the conditions of his release, if any are imposed, give little assurance of his appearance for trial; more dependable are the habits and relationships that tie him to the community and the threat of penalty if he does not appear. See Chapter Eight, below.

Each of the investigative techniques that are now incidents of arrest might be authorized without a precedent arrest. The questioning of witnesses, for example, is a major aspect of ordinary criminal investigation which does not depend on the power to arrest; rather an arrest has the effect of limiting questioning of the person arrested. With respect to both what it authorizes and what it precludes, the significance of an arrest is that it gives the arrested person the status of an "accused." Because he has been accused, a person who is arrested is required to submit to the actions described above, but, also because he has been accused, he cannot be questioned except in a carefully controlled atmosphere.

What is the quality of an accusation of crime? What, aside from its functional consequences, is its significance? Should the process of criminal investigation make so much depend on the existence of an accusation? Would it be desirable to lessen dependence on this fact, so far as constitutional doctrine permits?

In a number of contexts something of this sort has happened or has been urged. Central to the stop-and-frisk issue is the question whether police ought to have general authority to stop (and question, or frisk) persons whom they cannot validly accuse of a crime. In Davis v. Mississippi, 394 U.S. 721 (1969), p. 391 note 223 above, the Court speculated whether police might not be authorized to fingerprint persons who are not accused of a crime. It is now assumed in many jurisdictions that persons who have been arrested and released can be required to appear for inclusion in a lineup, see note 220, p. 385 above; given the factual premises of United States v. Wade, 388 U.S. 218 (1967), p. 369 above, it is plausible to suppose that police may sometimes request persons who are suspected but not accused of crime to participate in a lineup rather than be observed in less neutral circumstances.

Are official interferences in our lives, diminutions of the right to be let alone by the government, more or less to be feared if they are tied closely to the criminal process? Is the loss in human dignity greater when police engage in "aggressive patrolling" which harasses large groups in a community who are not suspected of any crime or when police stop and frisk an individual who is singled out from the community because he has behaved not criminally, but suspiciously? Does each of us lose more actually and potentially if privacy is lost to the community generally, as by a general requirement of disclosure to an official body of some hitherto private information or, if some practice like eavesdropping is authorized but limited to the investigation of (serious) crime?

PART TWO

PROSECUTION

When the investigation of a crime is completed and the investigating officials have concluded firmly that an identified person is guilty, what should happen next? The person may or may not have participated in the investigation; if he was arrested, once the investigative functions of the arrest have been accomplished, what should be done to terminate the arrest? If the investigation does not point firmly to his guilt, so far as criminal process is concerned, he should, of course, be released.

One answer to the question of what to do next is that, the government's agencies having concluded in good faith after thorough investigation that Smith is guilty, nothing remains to be done but decide whether and, if so, how much to punish Smith; then, to punish him. Constitutional requirements aside, how would such a process be lacking? What more needs to be done to complete satisfactorily the process leading to the imposition of punishment for crime? How should it be done? According to what schedule?

FEDERAL RULES OF CRIMINAL PROCEDURE

Rule 58

PETTY OFFENSES AND OTHER MISDEMEANORS

(a) Scope.

(1) *In General.* These rules apply in petty offense and other misdemeanor cases and on appeal to a district judge in a case tried by a magistrate judge, unless this rule provides otherwise.

(2) *Petty Offense Case Without Imprisonment.* In a case involving a petty offense for which no sentence of imprisonment will be imposed, the court may follow any provision of these rules that is not inconsistent with this rule and that the court considers appropriate.

(3) *Definition.* As used in this rule, the term "petty offense for which no sentence of imprisonment will be imposed" means a petty offense for which the court determines that, in the event of conviction, no sentence of imprisonment will be imposed.

(b) Pretrial Procedure.

(1) *Charging Document.* The trial of a misdemeanor may proceed on an indictment, information, or complaint. The trial of a petty offense may also proceed on a citation or violation notice.

(2) *Initial Appearance.* At the defendant's initial appearance on a petty offense or other misdemeanor charge, the magistrate judge must inform the defendant of the following:

(A) the charge, and the minimum and maximum possible penalties, including imprisonment, fines, any special assessment under 18 U.S.C. § 3013, and restitution under 18 U.S.C. § 3556;

(B) the right to retain counsel;

(C) the right to request the appointment of counsel if the defendant is unable to retain counsel—unless the charge is a petty offense for which the appointment of counsel is not required;

(D) the defendant's right not to make a statement, and that any statement made may be used against the defendant;

(E) the right to trial, judgment, and sentencing before a district judge—unless:

(i) the charge is a petty offense; or

(ii) the defendant consents to trial, judgment, and sentencing before a magistrate judge;

(F) the right to a jury trial before either a magistrate judge or a district judge—unless the charge is a petty offense; and

(G) if the defendant is held in custody and charged with a misdemeanor other than a petty offense, the right to a preliminary hearing under Rule 5.1, and the general circumstances, if any, under which the defendant may secure pretrial release.

(3) *Arraignment.*

(A) *Plea Before a Magistrate Judge.* A magistrate judge may take the defendant's plea in a petty offense case. In every other misdemeanor case, a magistrate judge may take the plea only if the defendant consents either in writing or on the record to be tried before a magistrate judge and specifically waives trial before a district judge. The defendant may plead not guilty, guilty, or (with the consent of the magistrate judge) nolo contendere.

(B) *Failure to Consent.* Except in a petty offense case, the magistrate judge must order a defendant who does not consent to trial before a magistrate judge to appear before a district judge for further proceedings.

(c) Additional Procedures in Certain Petty Offense Cases. The following procedures also apply in a case involving a petty offense for which no sentence of imprisonment will be imposed:

(1) *Guilty or Nolo Contendere Plea.* The court must not accept a guilty or nolo contendere plea unless satisfied that the defendant understands the nature of the charge and the maximum possible penalty.

(2) *Waiving Venue.*

(A) *Conditions of Waiving Venue.* If a defendant is arrested, held, or present in a district different from the one where the indictment, information, complaint, citation, or violation notice is pending, the defendant may state in writing a desire to plead guilty or nolo contendere; to waive venue and trial in the district where the proceeding is pending; and to consent to the court's disposing of the case in the district where the defendant was arrested, is held, or is present.

(B) *Effect of Waiving Venue.* Unless the defendant later pleads not guilty, the prosecution will proceed in the district where the defendant was arrested, is held, or is present. The district clerk must notify the clerk in the original district of the defendant's waiver of venue. The defendant's statement of a desire to plead guilty or nolo contendere is not admissible against the defendant.

(3) *Sentencing.* The court must give the defendant an opportunity to be heard in mitigation and then proceed immediately to sentencing. The court may, however, postpone sentencing to allow the probation service to investigate or to permit either party to submit additional information.

(4) *Notice of a Right to Appeal.* After imposing sentence in a case tried on a not-guilty plea, the court must advise the defendant of a right to appeal the conviction and of any right to appeal the sentence. If the defendant was convicted on a plea of guilty or nolo contendere, the court must advise the defendant of any right to appeal the sentence.

(d) Paying a Fixed Sum in Lieu of Appearance.

(1) *In General.* If the court has a local rule governing forfeiture of collateral, the court may accept a fixed-sum payment in lieu of the defendant's appearance and end the case, but the fixed sum may not exceed the maximum fine allowed by law.

(2) *Notice to Appear.* If the defendant fails to pay a fixed sum, request a hearing, or appear in response to a citation or violation notice, the district clerk or a magistrate judge may issue a notice for the defendant to appear before the court on a date certain. The notice may give the defendant an additional opportunity to pay a fixed sum in lieu of appearance. The district clerk must serve the notice on the defendant by mailing a copy to the defendant's last known address.

(3) *Summons or Warrant.* Upon an indictment or upon a showing by one of the other charging documents specified in Rule 58(b)(1) of probable cause to believe that an offense has been committed and that the defendant has committed it, the court may issue an arrest warrant or, if no warrant is requested by an attorney for the government, a summons. The showing of probable cause must be made under oath or under penalty of perjury, but the affiant need not appear before the court. If the defendant fails to appear before the court in response to a summons, the court may summarily issue a warrant for the defendant's arrest.

(e) Recording the Proceedings. The court must record any proceedings under this rule by using a court reporter or a suitable recording device.

(f) New Trial. Rule 33 applies to a motion for a new trial.

(g) Appeal.

(1) *From a District Judge's Order or Judgment.* The Federal Rules of Appellate Procedure govern an appeal from a district judge's order or a judgment of conviction or sentence.

(2) *From a Magistrate Judge's Order or Judgment.*

(A) *Interlocutory Appeal.* Either party may appeal an order of a magistrate judge to a district judge within 10 days of its entry if a district judge's order could similarly be appealed. The party appealing must file a notice with the clerk specifying the order being appealed and must serve a copy on the adverse party.

(B) *Appeal From a Conviction or Sentence.* A defendant may appeal a magistrate judge's judgment of conviction or sentence to a district judge within 10 days of its entry. To appeal, the defendant must file a notice with the clerk specifying the judgment being appealed and must serve a copy on an attorney for the government.

(C) *Record.* The record consists of the original papers and exhibits in the case; any transcript, tape, or other recording of the proceedings; and a certified copy of the docket entries. For purposes of the appeal, a copy of the record of the proceedings must be made available to a defendant who establishes by affidavit an inability to pay or give security for the record. The Director of the Administrative Office of the United States Courts must pay for those copies.

(D) *Scope of Appeal.* The defendant is not entitled to a trial de novo by a district judge. The scope of the appeal is the same as in an appeal to the court of appeals from a judgment entered by a district judge.

(3) *Stay of Execution and Release Pending Appeal.* Rule 38 applies to a stay of a judgment of conviction or sentence. The court may release the defendant pending appeal under the law relating to release pending appeal from a district court to a court of appeals.

AO86A (Rev. 4/91) Consent to Proceed—Misdemeanor

UNITED STATES DISTRICT COURT

_______________ DISTRICT OF _______________

UNITED STATES OF AMERICA
V.

CONSENT TO PROCEED BEFORE UNITED STATES MAGISTRATE JUDGE IN A MISDEMEANOR CASE

Case Number:

The United States magistrate judge has explained to me the nature of the offense(s) with which I am charged and the maximum possible penalties which might be imposed if I am found guilty. The magistrate judge has informed me of my right to the assistance of legal counsel. The magistrate judge has informed me of my right to trial, judgment, and sentencing before a United States district judge or a United States magistrate judge.

I HEREBY: Waive (give up) my right to trial, judgment, and sentencing before a United States district judge, and I consent to trial, judgment and sentencing before a United States magistrate judge.

X _______________________________ ,
Defendant

WAIVER OF RIGHT TO TRIAL BY JURY

The magistrate judge has advised me of my right to trial by jury.

I HEREBY: Waive (give up) my right to trial by jury. _______________________________
Defendant

Consented to by United States _______________________________
Signature

____
Name and Title

WAIVER OF RIGHT TO HAVE THIRTY DAYS TO PREPARE FOR TRIAL

The magistrate judge has also advised me of my right to have at least thirty days to prepare for trial before the magistrate judge.

I HEREBY: Waive (give up) my right to have at least thirty days to prepare for trial.

X _______________________________ ,
Defendant

____
Defendant's Attorney (if any)

Approved By: _______________________________
U.S. Magistrate Judge

____
Date

AO 245I (Rev. 12/03) Judgment in a Criminal Case for a Petty Offense
Sheet 1

UNITED STATES DISTRICT COURT

_______________ District of _______________

UNITED STATES OF AMERICA
V.

JUDGMENT IN A CRIMINAL CASE
(For a Petty Offense)

CASE NUMBER:

USM NUMBER:

____
Defendant's Attorney

THE DEFENDANT:

☐ **THE DEFENDANT** pleaded ☐ guilty ☐ nolo contendere to count(s) _______________

☐ **THE DEFENDANT** was found guilty on count(s) _______________

The defendant is adjudicated guilty of these offenses:

Title & Section	Nature of Offense	Offense Ended	Count

The defendant is sentenced as provided in pages 2 through ______ of this judgment.

☐ **THE DEFENDANT** was found not guilty on count(s) _______________

☐ Count(s) _______________ ☐ is ☐ are dismissed on the motion of the United States.

It is ordered that the defendant must notify the United States attorney for this district within 30 days of any change of name, residence, or mailing address until all fines, restitution, costs, and special assessments imposed by this judgment are fully paid. If ordered to pay restitution, the defendant must notify the court and United States attorney of material changes in economic circumstances.

Defendant's Soc. Sec. No.: _______________

Defendant's Date of Birth: _______________

Defendant's Residence Address:

____

____

____

____

Defendant's Mailing Address:

____

____

____

____

____
Date of Imposition of Judgment

____
Signature of Judge

____
Name and Title of Judge

____
Date

CHAPTER 7

PRELIMINARY HEARING

Gerstein v. Pugh

420 U.S. 103, 95 S.Ct. 854, 43 L.Ed.2d 54 (1975)

■ MR. JUSTICE POWELL delivered the opinion of the Court.

The issue in this case is whether a person arrested and held for trial under a prosecutor's information is constitutionally entitled to a judicial determination of probable cause for pretrial restraint of liberty.

I

In March 1971 respondents Pugh and Henderson were arrested in Dade County, Fla. Each was charged with several offenses under a prosecutor's information. Pugh was denied bail because one of the charges against him carried a potential life sentence, and Henderson remained in custody because he was unable to post a $4,500 bond.

In Florida, indictments are required only for prosecution of capital offenses. Prosecutors may charge all other crimes by information, without a prior preliminary hearing and without obtaining leave of court. . . . At the time respondents were arrested, a Florida rule seemed to authorize adversary preliminary hearings to test probable cause for detention in all cases. . . . But the Florida courts had held that the filing of an information foreclosed the suspect's right to a preliminary hearing. . . . They had also held that habeas corpus could not be used, except perhaps in exceptional circumstances, to test the probable cause for detention under an information. . . . The only possible methods for obtaining a judicial determination of probable cause were a special statute allowing a preliminary hearing after 30 days . . . and arraignment, which the District Court found was often delayed a month or more after arrest. . . . As a result, a person charged by information could be detained for a substantial period solely on the decision of a prosecutor.

Respondents Pugh and Henderson filed a class action against Dade County officials in the Federal District Court, claiming a constitutional right to a judicial hearing on the issue of probable cause and requesting declaratory and injunctive relief. Respondents Turner and Faulk, also in custody under informations, subsequently intervened. Petitioner Gerstein, the State Attorney for Dade County, was one of several defendants.

[T]he District Court granted the relief sought. . . . The court . . . held that the Fourth and Fourteenth Amendments give all arrested persons charged by information a right to a judicial hearing on the question of probable cause. The District Court ordered the Dade County defendants to give the named plaintiffs an immediate preliminary hearing to determine probable cause for further detention. It also ordered them to submit a plan providing preliminary hearings in all cases instituted by information. . . .

II

As framed by the proceedings below, this case presents two issues: whether a person arrested and held for trial on an information is entitled to a judicial determination of probable cause for detention, and if so, whether the adversary hearing ordered by the District Court and approved by the Court of Appeals is required by the Constitution.

A

Both the standards and procedures for arrest and detention have been derived from the Fourth Amendment and its common-law antecedents. . . . The standard for arrest is probable cause, defined in terms of facts and circumstances "sufficient to warrant a prudent man in believing that the [suspect] had committed or was committing an offense." Beck v. Ohio, 379 U.S. 89, 91 (1964). . . . This standard, like those for searches and seizures, represents a necessary accommodation between the individual's right to liberty and the State's duty to control crime. . . .

To implement the Fourth Amendment's protection against unfounded invasions of liberty and privacy, the Court has required that the existence of probable cause be decided by a neutral and detached magistrate whenever possible. . . .

Maximum protection of individual rights could be assured by requiring a magistrate's review of the factual justification prior to any arrest, but such a requirement would constitute an intolerable handicap for legitimate law enforcement. Thus, while the Court has expressed a preference for the use of arrest warrants when feasible . . . it has never invalidated an arrest supported by probable cause solely because the officers failed to secure a warrant. . . .

Under this practical compromise, a policeman's on-the-scene assessment of probable cause provides legal justification for arresting a person suspected of crime, and for a brief period of detention to take the administrative steps incident to arrest. Once the suspect is in custody, however, the reasons that justify dispensing with the magistrate's neutral judgment evaporate. There no longer is any danger that the suspect will escape or commit further crimes while the police submit their evidence to a magistrate. And, while the State's reasons for taking summary action subside, the suspect's need for a neutral determination of probable cause increases significantly. The consequences of prolonged detention may be more serious than the interference occasioned by arrest. Pretrial confinement may imperil the suspect's job, interrupt his source of income, and impair his family relationships. . . . Even pretrial release may be accompanied by burdensome conditions that effect a significant restraint of liberty. . . .

When the stakes are this high, the detached judgment of a neutral magistrate is essential if the Fourth Amendment is to furnish meaningful protection from unfounded interference with liberty. Accordingly, we hold that the Fourth Amendment requires a judicial determination of probable cause as a prerequisite to extended restraint of liberty following arrest.

This result has historical support in the common law that has guided interpretation of the Fourth Amendment. . . . At common law it was customary, if not obligatory, for an arrested person to be brought before a justice of the peace shortly after arrest. . . . The justice of the peace would "examine" the prisoner and the witnesses to determine whether there was reason to believe the prisoner had committed a crime. If there was, the suspect would be committed to jail or bailed pending trial. If not, he would be discharged from custody. . . . The initial determination of probable cause also could be reviewed by higher courts on a writ of habeas corpus. . . . This practice furnished the model for criminal procedure in America immediately following the adoption of the Fourth Amendment . . . and there are indications that the Framers of the Bill of Rights regarded it as a model for a "reasonable" seizure. . . .

B

Under the Florida procedures challenged here, a person arrested without a warrant and charged by information may be jailed or subjected to other restraints pending trial without any opportunity for a probable cause determination. Petitioner defends this practice on the ground that the prosecutor's decision to file an information is itself a determination of probable cause that furnishes sufficient reason to detain a defendant pending trial. Although a conscientious decision that the evidence warrants prosecution affords a measure of protection against unfounded detention, we do not think prosecutorial judgment standing alone meets the requirements of the Fourth Amendment. Indeed, we think the Court's previous decisions compel disapproval of the Florida procedure. In Albrecht v. United States, 273 U.S. 1, 5 (1927), the Court held that an arrest warrant issued solely upon a United States Attorney's information was invalid because the accompanying affidavits were defective. Although the Court's opinion did not explicitly state that the prosecutor's official oath could not furnish probable cause, that conclusion was implicit in the judgment that the arrest was illegal under the Fourth Amendment. More recently, in Coolidge v. New Hampshire, 403 U.S. 443, 449–53 (1971), the Court held that a prosecutor's responsibility to law enforcement is inconsistent with the constitutional role of a neutral and detached magistrate. We reaffirmed that principle in Shadwick v. City of Tampa, 407 U.S. 345 (1972), and held that probable cause for the issuance of an arrest warrant must be determined by someone independent of police and prosecution. . . . The reason for this separation of functions was expressed by Mr. Justice Frankfurter in a similar context:

> A democratic society, in which respect for the dignity of all men is central, naturally guards against the misuse of the law enforcement

> process. Zeal in tracking down crime is not in itself an assurance of soberness of judgment. Disinterestedness in law enforcement does not alone prevent disregard of cherished liberties. Experience has therefore counseled that safeguards must be provided against the dangers of the overzealous as well as the despotic. The awful instruments of the criminal law cannot be entrusted to a single functionary. The complicated process of criminal justice is therefore divided into different parts, responsibility for which is separately vested in the various participants upon whom the criminal law relies for its vindication.

McNabb v. United States, 318 U.S. 332, 343 (1943).

In holding that the prosecutor's assessment of probable cause is not sufficient alone to justify restraint of liberty pending trial, we do not imply that the accused is entitled to judicial oversight or review of the decision to prosecute. Instead, we adhere to the Court's prior holding that a judicial hearing is not prerequisite to prosecution by information. . . . Nor do we retreat from the established rule that illegal arrest or detention does not void a subsequent conviction. . . . Thus, as the Court of Appeals noted below, although a suspect who is presently detained may challenge the probable cause for that confinement, a conviction will not be vacated on the ground that the defendant was detained pending trial without a determination of probable cause. . . .

III

Both the District Court and the Court of Appeals held that the determination of probable cause must be accompanied by the full panoply of adversary safeguards—counsel, confrontation, cross-examination, and compulsory process for witnesses. A full preliminary hearing of this sort is modeled after the procedure used in many States to determine whether the evidence justifies going to trial under an information or presenting the case to a grand jury. . . . The standard of proof required of the prosecution is usually referred to as "probable cause," but in some jurisdictions it may approach a prima facie case of guilt. . . . When the hearing takes this form, adversary procedures are customarily employed. The importance of the issue to both the State and the accused justifies the presentation of witnesses and full exploration of their testimony on cross-examination. This kind of hearing also requires appointment of counsel for indigent defendants. . . . And, as the hearing assumes increased importance and the procedures become more complex, the likelihood that it can be held promptly after arrest diminishes. . . .

These adversary safeguards are not essential for the probable cause determination required by the Fourth Amendment. The sole issue is whether there is probable cause for detaining the arrested person pending further proceedings. This issue can be determined reliably without an adversary hearing. The standard is the same as that for arrest. That standard—probable cause to believe the suspect has committed a crime—traditionally has been decided by a magistrate in a nonadversary proceeding on hearsay and written testimony, and the Court has approved these informal modes of proof. . . .

The use of an informal procedure is justified not only by the lesser consequences of a probable cause determination but also by the nature of the determination itself. It does not require the fine resolution of conflicting evidence that a reasonable-doubt or even a preponderance standard demands, and credibility determinations are seldom crucial in deciding whether the evidence supports a reasonable belief in guilt. . . . This is not to say that confrontation and cross-examination might not enhance the reliability of probable cause determinations in some cases. In most cases, however, their value would be too slight to justify holding, as a matter of constitutional principle, that these formalities and safeguards designed for trial must also be employed in making the Fourth Amendment determination of probable cause.

Because of its limited function and its nonadversary character, the probable cause determination is not a "critical stage" in the prosecution that would require appointed counsel. The Court has identified as "critical stages" those pretrial procedures that would impair defense on the merits if the accused is required to proceed without counsel. Coleman v. Alabama, 399 U.S. 1 (1970); United States v. Wade, 388 U.S. 218, 226–27 (1967). In Coleman v. Alabama, where the Court held that a preliminary hearing was a critical stage of an Alabama prosecution, the majority and concurring opinions identified two critical factors that distinguish the Alabama preliminary hearing from the probable cause determination required by the Fourth Amendment. First, under Alabama law the function of the preliminary hearing was to determine whether the evidence justified charging the suspect with an offense. A finding of no probable cause could mean that he would not be tried at all. The Fourth Amendment probable cause determination is addressed only to pretrial custody. To be sure, pretrial custody may affect to some extent the defendant's ability to assist in preparation of his defense, but this does not present the high probability of substantial harm identified as controlling in *Wade* and *Coleman*. Second, Alabama allowed the suspect to confront and cross-examine prosecution witnesses at the preliminary hearing. The Court noted that the suspect's defense on the merits could be compromised if he had no legal assistance for exploring or preserving the witnesses' testimony. This consideration does not apply when the prosecution is not required to produce witnesses for cross-examination.

Although we conclude that the Constitution does not require an adversary determination of probable cause, we recognize that state systems of criminal procedure vary widely. There is no single preferred pretrial procedure, and the nature of the probable cause determination usually will be shaped to accord with a State's pretrial procedure viewed as a whole. While we limit our holding to the precise requirement of the Fourth Amendment, we recognize the desirability of flexibility and experimentation by the States. It may be found desirable, for example, to make the probable cause determination at the suspect's first appearance before a judicial officer . . . or the determination may be incorporated into the procedure for setting bail or fixing other conditions of pretrial release. In some States, existing procedures may satisfy the requirement of the Fourth Amendment. Others may require only minor adjustment, such as acceleration of existing preliminary hearings. Current proposals for criminal procedure reform suggest other ways of testing probable cause for detention. Whatever procedure a State may adopt, it must provide a fair and reliable determination of probable cause as a condition for any significant pretrial restraint of liberty,[1] and this determination must be made by a judicial officer either before or promptly after arrest.

IV

We agree with the Court of Appeals that the Fourth Amendment requires a timely judicial determination of probable cause as a prerequisite to detention, and we accordingly affirm that much of the judgment. As we do not agree that the Fourth Amendment requires the adversary hearing outlined in the District Court's decree, we reverse in part and remand to the Court of Appeals for further proceedings consistent with this opinion.

. . .[2]

County of Riverside v. McLaughlin

500 U.S. 44, 111 S.Ct. 1661, 114 L.Ed.2d 49 (1991)

■ Justice O'Connor delivered the opinion of the Court.

In Gerstein v. Pugh, 420 U.S. 103 (1975), this Court held that the Fourth Amendment requires a prompt judicial determination of probable cause as a prerequisite to an extended pretrial detention following a warrantless arrest. This case requires us to define what is "prompt" under *Gerstein*.

I

This is a class action brought under 42 U.S.C. § 1983 challenging the manner in which the county of Riverside, California (County), provides probable cause determinations to persons arrested without a warrant. At issue is the County's policy of combining probable cause determinations with its arraignment procedures. Under County policy . . . arraignments must be conducted without unnecessary delay and, in any event, within two

1. Because the probable cause determination is not a constitutional prerequisite to the charging decision, it is required only for those suspects who suffer restraints on liberty other than the condition that they appear for trial. There are many kinds of pretrial release and many degrees of conditional liberty. . . . We cannot define specifically those that would require a prior probable cause determination, but the key factor is significant restraint on liberty.

[2] Justice Stewart wrote a concurring opinion, which Justice Douglas, Justice Brennan, and Justice Marshall joined.

days of arrest. This two-day requirement excludes from computation weekends and holidays. Thus, an individual arrested without a warrant late in the week may in some cases be held for as long as five days before receiving a probable cause determination. Over the Thanksgiving holiday, a 7-day delay is possible.

. . .

In August 1987, Donald Lee McLaughlin filed a complaint in the United States District Court for the Central District of California, seeking injunctive and declaratory relief on behalf of himself and " 'all others similarly situated.' " The complaint alleged that McLaughlin was then currently incarcerated in the Riverside County Jail and had not received a probable cause determination. He requested " 'an order and judgment requiring that the defendants and the County of Riverside provide in-custody arrestees, arrested without warrants, prompt probable cause, bail and arraignment hearings.' " Pet. for Cert. 6. . . .

. . .

The second amended complaint named three additional plaintiffs—Johnny E. James, Diana Ray Simon, and Michael Scott Hyde—individually and as class representatives. The amended complaint alleged that each of the named plaintiffs had been arrested without a warrant, had received neither prompt probable cause nor bail hearings, and was still in custody. . . . In November 1988, the District Court certified a class comprising "all present and future prisoners in the Riverside County Jail including those pretrial detainees arrested without warrants and held in the Riverside County Jail from August 1, 1987 to the present, and all such future detainees who have been or may be denied prompt probable cause, bail or arraignment hearings." 1 App. 7.

In March 1989, plaintiffs asked the District Court to issue a preliminary injunction requiring the County to provide all persons arrested without a warrant a judicial determination of probable cause within 36 hours of arrest. . . . The District Court issued the injunction, holding that the County's existing practice violated this Court's decision in *Gerstein*. Without discussion, the District Court adopted a rule that the County provide probable cause determinations within 36 hours of arrest, except in exigent circumstances. The court "retained jurisdiction indefinitely" to ensure that the County established new procedures that complied with the injunction. 2 App. 333–34.

. . .

On November 8, 1989, the Court of Appeals affirmed the order granting the preliminary injunction against Riverside County. . . .

The Court of Appeals . . . determined that the County's policy of providing probable cause determinations at arraignment within 48 hours was "not in accord with *Gerstein*'s requirement of a determination 'promptly after arrest' " because no more than 36 hours were needed "to complete the administrative steps incident to arrest." [888 F.2d], at 1278.

The Ninth Circuit thus joined the Fourth and Seventh Circuits in interpreting *Gerstein* as requiring a probable cause determination immediately following completion of the administrative procedures incident to arrest. . . . By contrast, the Second Circuit understands *Gerstein* to "stres[s] the need for flexibility" and to permit States to combine probable cause determinations with other pretrial proceedings. . . . We granted certiorari to resolve this conflict among the Circuits as to what constitutes a "prompt" probable cause determination under *Gerstein*.

. . .

III

A

. . .

. . . Our purpose in *Gerstein* was to make clear that the Fourth Amendment requires every State to provide prompt determinations of probable cause, but that the Constitution does not impose on the States a rigid procedural framework. Rather, individual States may choose to comply in different ways.

Inherent in *Gerstein*'s invitation to the States to experiment and adapt was the recognition that the Fourth Amendment does not compel an immediate determination of probable cause upon completing the administrative steps incident to arrest. Plainly, if a probable cause hearing is constitutionally compelled the moment a suspect is finished being "booked," there is no room whatsoever for "flexibility and experimentation by the States." [420 U.S., at 123.] Incorporating probable cause determinations "into the procedure for setting bail or fixing other conditions of pretrial release"—which *Gerstein* explicitly contemplated, id., at 124—would be impossible. Waiting even a few hours so that a bail hearing or arraignment could take place at the same time as the probable cause determination would amount to a constitutional violation. Clearly, *Gerstein* is not that inflexible.

. . . As we have explained, *Gerstein* struck a balance between competing interests; a proper understanding of the decision is possible only if one takes into account both sides of the equation.

. . .

B

Given that *Gerstein* permits jurisdictions to incorporate probable cause determinations into other pretrial procedures, some delays are inevitable. For example, where, as in Riverside County, the probable cause determination is combined with arraignment, there will be delays caused by paperwork and logistical problems. Records will have to be reviewed, charging documents drafted, appearance of counsel arranged, and appropriate bail determined. On weekends, when the number of arrests is often higher and available resources tend to be limited, arraignments may get pushed back even further. In our view, the Fourth Amendment permits a reasonable postponement of a probable cause determination while the police cope with the everyday problems of processing suspects through an overly burdened criminal justice system.

But flexibility has its limits; *Gerstein* is not a blank check. A State has no legitimate interest in detaining for extended periods individuals who have been arrested without probable cause. The Court recognized in *Gerstein* that a person arrested without a warrant is entitled to a fair and reliable determination of probable cause and that this determination must be made promptly.

Unfortunately, as lower court decisions applying *Gerstein* have demonstrated, it is not enough to say that probable cause determinations must be "prompt." This vague standard simply has not provided sufficient guidance. Instead, it has led to a flurry of systemic challenges to city and county practices, putting federal judges in the role of making legislative judgments and overseeing local jailhouse operations. . . .

Our task in this case is to articulate more clearly the boundaries of what is permissible under the Fourth Amendment. Although we hesitate to announce that the Constitution compels a specific time limit, it is important to provide some degree of certainty so that States and counties may establish procedures with confidence that they fall within constitutional bounds. Taking into account the competing interests articulated in *Gerstein*, we believe that a jurisdiction that provides judicial determinations of probable cause within 48 hours of arrest will, as a general matter, comply with the promptness requirement of *Gerstein*. For this reason, such jurisdictions will be immune from systemic challenges.

This is not to say that the probable cause determination in a particular case passes constitutional muster simply because it is provided within 48 hours. Such a hearing may nonetheless violate *Gerstein* if the arrested individual can prove that his or her probable cause determination was delayed unreasonably. Examples of unreasonable delay are delays for the purpose of gathering additional evidence to justify the arrest, a delay motivated by ill will against the arrested individual, or delay for delay's sake. In evaluating whether the delay in a particular case is unreasonable, however, courts must allow a substantial degree of flexibility. Courts cannot ignore the often unavoidable delays in transporting arrested persons from one facility to another, handling late-night bookings where no magistrate is readily available, obtaining the presence of an arresting officer who may be busy processing other suspects or securing the premises of an arrest, and other practical realities.

Where an arrested individual does not receive a probable cause determination within 48 hours, the calculus changes. In such a case, the arrested individual does not bear the burden of proving an unreasonable delay. Rather, the burden shifts to the government to demonstrate the existence of a bona fide emergency or other extraordinary circumstance. The fact that in a particular case it may take longer than 48 hours to consolidate pretrial proceedings does not qualify as an extraordinary circumstance. Nor, for that matter, do intervening weekends. A jurisdiction that chooses to offer combined proceedings must do so as soon as is reasonably feasible, but in no event later than 48 hours after arrest.

. . .

Everyone agrees that the police should make every attempt to minimize the time a presumptively innocent individual spends in jail. One way to do so is to provide a judicial determination of probable cause immediately upon completing the administrative steps incident to arrest—i.e., as soon as the suspect has been booked, photographed, and fingerprinted. . . . [S]everal States, laudably, have adopted this approach. The Constitution does not compel so rigid a schedule, however. Under *Gerstein*, jurisdictions may choose to combine probable cause determinations with other pretrial proceedings, so long as they do so promptly. This necessarily means that only certain proceedings are candidates for combination. Only those proceedings that arise very early in the pretrial process—such as bail hearings and arraignments—may be chosen. Even then, every effort must be made to expedite the combined proceedings. . . .

IV

For the reasons we have articulated, we conclude that Riverside County is entitled to combine probable cause determinations with arraignments. The record indicates, however, that the County's current policy and practice do not comport fully with the principles we have outlined. The County's current policy is to offer combined proceedings within two days, exclusive of Saturdays, Sundays, or holidays. As a result, persons arrested on Thursdays may have to wait until the following Monday before they receive a probable cause determination. The delay is even longer if there is an intervening holiday. Thus, the County's regular practice exceeds the 48-hour period we deem constitutionally permissible, meaning that the County is not immune from systemic challenges, such as this class action.

As to arrests that occur early in the week, the County's practice is that "arraignment[s] usually tak[e] place on the last day" possible. 1 App. 82. There may well be legitimate reasons for this practice; alternatively, this may constitute delay for delay's sake. We leave it to the Court of Appeals and the District Court, on remand, to make this determination.

The judgment of the Court of Appeals is vacated and the case is remanded for further proceedings consistent with this opinion.

. . .[3]

---

289. Before the adoption of the federal rules, leave of court had to be obtained in order to initiate a prosecution by information; the court, moreover, was required to make a determination that there was probable

[3] Justice Marshall wrote a dissenting opinion which Justice Blackmun and Justice Stevens joined. Justice Scalia also wrote a dissenting opinion.

cause for the prosecution.[4] Albrecht v. United States, 273 U.S. 1, 5 (1927). See Gerstein v. Pugh, p. 522 above. The requirement of leave of court is omitted from Rule 7(c). Rule 9(a), however, which provides for the issuance of a warrant or summons based on an indictment or information, allows a warrant to issue on an information only "if one or more affidavits accompanying the information establish probable cause."

290. A two-hour detention, during which the defendant made incriminating statements and after which she was released from custody, is an unreasonable delay in the probable cause determination, because it was solely for investigative purposes. United States v. Davis, 174 F.3d 941 (8th Cir.1999).

FEDERAL RULES OF CRIMINAL PROCEDURE

Rule 5

INITIAL APPEARANCE

(a) In General.

(1) *Appearance Upon an Arrest.*

(A) A person making an arrest within the United States must take the defendant without unnecessary delay before a magistrate judge, or before a state or local judicial officer as Rule 5(c) provides, unless a statute provides otherwise.

(B) A person making an arrest outside the United States must take the defendant without unnecessary delay before a magistrate judge, unless a statute provides otherwise.

(2) *Exceptions.*

(A) An officer making an arrest under a warrant issued upon a complaint charging solely a violation of 18 U.S.C. § 1073 need not comply with this rule if:

(i) the person arrested is transferred without unnecessary delay to the custody of appropriate state or local authorities in the district of arrest; and

(ii) an attorney for the government moves promptly, in the district where the warrant was issued, to dismiss the complaint.

(B) If a defendant is arrested for violating probation or supervised release, Rule 32.1 applies.

(C) If a defendant is arrested for failing to appear in another district, Rule 40 applies.

4. An information is a formal charge against the defendant. It is like an indictment in content but is filed by the prosecutor independently, without action by the grand jury. See Fed.R.Crim.P. 7, p. 666 below.

(3) *Appearance Upon a Summons.* When a defendant appears in response to a summons under Rule 4, a magistrate judge must proceed under Rule 5(d) or (e), as applicable.

(b) Arrest Without a Warrant. If a defendant is arrested without a warrant, a complaint meeting Rule 4(a)'s requirement of probable cause must be promptly filed in the district where the offense was allegedly committed.

(c) Place of Initial Appearance; Transfer to Another District.

(1) *Arrest in the District Where the Offense Was Allegedly Committed.* If the defendant is arrested in the district where the offense was allegedly committed:

(A) the initial appearance must be in that district; and

(B) if a magistrate judge is not reasonably available, the initial appearance may be before a state or local judicial officer.

(2) *Arrest in a District Other Than Where the Offense Was Allegedly Committed.* If the defendant was arrested in a district other than where the offense was allegedly committed, the initial appearance must be:

(A) in the district of arrest; or

(B) in an adjacent district if:

(i) the appearance can occur more promptly there; or

(ii) the offense was allegedly committed there and the initial appearance will occur on the day of arrest.

(3) *Procedures in a District Other Than Where the Offense Was Allegedly Committed.* If the initial appearance occurs in a district other than where the offense was allegedly committed, the following procedures apply:

(A) the magistrate judge must inform the defendant about the provisions of Rule 20;

(B) if the defendant was arrested without a warrant, the district court where the offense was allegedly committed must first issue a warrant before the magistrate judge transfers the defendant to that district;

(C) the magistrate judge must conduct a preliminary hearing if required by Rule 5.1 or Rule 58(b)(2)(G);

(D) the magistrate judge must transfer the defendant to the district where the offense was allegedly committed if:

(i) the government produces the warrant, a certified copy of the warrant, a facsimile of either, or other appropriate form of either; and

(ii) the judge finds that the defendant is the same person named in the indictment, information, or warrant; and

(E) when a defendant is transferred and discharged, the clerk must promptly transmit the papers and any bail to the clerk in the district where the offense was allegedly committed.

(d) Procedure in a Felony Case.

(1) *Advice.* If the defendant is charged with a felony, the judge must inform the defendant of the following:

(A) the complaint against the defendant, and any affidavit filed with it;

(B) the defendant's right to retain counsel or to request that counsel be appointed if the defendant cannot obtain counsel;

(C) the circumstances, if any, under which the defendant may secure pretrial release;

(D) any right to a preliminary hearing; and

(E) the defendant's right not to make a statement, and that any statement made may be used against the defendant.

(2) *Consulting with Counsel.* The judge must allow the defendant reasonable opportunity to consult with counsel.

(3) *Detention or Release.* The judge must detain or release the defendant as provided by statute or these rules.

(4) *Plea.* A defendant may be asked to plead only under Rule 10.

(e) Procedure in a Misdemeanor Case. If the defendant is charged with a misdemeanor only, the judge must inform the defendant in accordance with Rule 58(b)(2).

(f) Video Teleconferencing. Video teleconferencing may be used to conduct an appearance under this rule if the defendant consents.

Rule 5.1

PRELIMINARY HEARING

(a) In General. If a defendant is charged with an offense other than a petty offense, a magistrate judge must conduct a preliminary hearing unless:

(1) the defendant waives the hearing;

(2) the defendant is indicted;

(3) the government files an information under Rule 7(b) charging the defendant with a felony;

(4) the government files an information charging the defendant with a misdemeanor; or

(5) the defendant is charged with a misdemeanor and consents to trial before a magistrate judge.

(b) Selecting a District. A defendant arrested in a district other than where the offense was allegedly committed may elect to have the preliminary hearing conducted in the district where the prosecution is pending.

(c) Scheduling. The magistrate judge must hold the preliminary hearing within a reasonable time, but no later than 10 days after the initial appearance if the defendant is in custody and no later than 20 days if not in custody.

(d) Extending the Time. With the defendant's consent and upon a showing of good cause—taking into account the public interest in the prompt disposition of criminal cases—a magistrate judge may extend the time limits in Rule 5.1(c) one or more times. If the defendant does not consent, the magistrate judge may extend the time limits only on a showing that extraordinary circumstances exist and justice requires the delay.

(e) Hearing and Finding. At the preliminary hearing, the defendant may cross-examine adverse witnesses and may introduce evidence but may not object to evidence on the ground that it was unlawfully acquired. If the magistrate judge finds probable cause to believe an offense has been committed and the defendant committed it, the magistrate judge must promptly require the defendant to appear for further proceedings.

(f) Discharging the Defendant. If the magistrate judge finds no probable cause to believe an offense has been committed or the defendant committed it, the magistrate judge must dismiss the complaint and discharge the defendant. A discharge does not preclude the government from later prosecuting the defendant for the same offense.

(g) Recording the Proceedings. The preliminary hearing must be recorded by a court reporter or by a suitable recording device. A recording of the proceeding may be made available to any party upon request. A copy of the recording and a transcript may be provided to any party upon request and upon any payment required by applicable Judicial Conference regulations.

(h) Producing a Statement.

(1) *In General.* Rule 26.2(a)–(d) and (f) applies at any hearing under this rule, unless the magistrate judge for good cause rules otherwise in a particular case.

(2) *Sanctions for Not Producing a Statement.* If a party disobeys a Rule 26.2 order to deliver a statement to the moving party, the magistrate judge must not consider the testimony of a witness whose statement is withheld.

---

291. With respect to the requirement of Rule 5(b) that a complaint filed after an arrest show probable cause, see United States v. Fernandez-Guzman, 577 F.2d 1093, 1099 (7th Cir.1978): "[W]hen the facts known to the officers at the time of arrest are such as to make the arrest constitutional when it occurred, the omission of some of those facts from later-filed 5(b) complaints cannot make the arrest retroactively unconstitutional."

292. The provision of Rule 5.1(a)(2)–(4) that there shall be no preliminary hearing if the defendant has been indicted or an information has been filed reflects settled law. "A post-indictment preliminary examination would be an empty ritual, as the government's burden of showing probable cause would be met merely by offering the indictment. Even if the commissioner disagreed with the grand jury, he could not undermine the authority of its finding." Sciortino v. Zampano, 385 F.2d 132, 133 (2d Cir.1967). "Should the judicial officer determine that for the purpose of the detention hearing no probable cause exists that the defendant committed the crime for which he was indicted, presumably the defendant would still be brought to trial upon the same indictment." United States v. Contreras, 776 F.2d 51, 55 (2d Cir.1985).

"It reasonably cannot be doubted that, in the court to which the indictment is returned, the finding of an indictment, fair upon its face, by a properly constituted grand jury, conclusively determines the existence of probable cause for the purpose of holding the accused to answer." Ex parte United States, 287 U.S. 241, 250 (1932). See People v. Glass, 627 N.W.2d 261 (Mich.2001), overruling a prior decision, People v. Duncan, 201 N.W.2d 629 (Mich.1972), that had given already indicted defendants the right to a preliminary examination. See generally Costello v. United States, 350 U.S. 359, 363 (1956), p. 679 below.

The Court has said repeatedly that there is no constitutional objection to a prosecution by information without any prior judicial determination of probable cause (provided that the defendant's liberty is not restrained). E.g., Beck v. Washington, 369 U.S. 541, 545 (1962). In Gerstein v. Pugh, p. 522 above, the Court said that it did not depart from its "prior holding that a judicial hearing is not prerequisite to prosecution by information." Is that holding consistent with the Court's holdings involving the requirement of a judicial determination of probable cause when a person's rights under the Fourth Amendment are involved, e.g., in Gerstein v. Pugh itself? If so, on what basis?

In State v. Mitchell, 512 A.2d 140 (Conn.1986), the court discussed a recently enacted provision of the state constitution that a person shall not be prosecuted for a crime punishable by death or life imprisonment "unless upon probable cause shown at a hearing in accordance with procedures prescribed by law." The court said that the provision "guarantees that no one will be forced to stand trial for a serious crime unless a court has first made a finding of probable cause at an open hearing in which the accused is provided with a full panoply of adversarial rights." Id. at 144–45. In order to give effect to the provision, the court said, an opportunity for appellate review of the determination of probable cause was required.

United States Ex Rel. Wheeler v. Flood

269 F.Supp. 194 (E.D.N.Y.1967)

■ WEINSTEIN, DISTRICT JUDGE.

Petitioners—as yet unindicted though in federal custody—seek a writ of habeas corpus in order to compel a United States Commissioner to hold a preliminary examination pursuant to subdivision (c) of Rule 5 of the Rules of Criminal Procedure. For the reasons set out below, if such a hearing is not granted forthwith, petitioners are entitled to be released.

Petitioner Susan Wheeler has been in custody since her arrest on May 12, 1967, pursuant to a warrant issued upon a detailed sworn complaint. She was charged with conspiring to illegally import narcotic drugs. 21 U.S.C. § 174 (illegal importation of narcotic drug into United States); 26 U.S.C. § 4704(a) (sale of untaxed narcotic). She was brought before a Commissioner that day. Represented by counsel she demanded an immediate preliminary examination. Charged with the same conspiracy, petitioner Robert Wyler has been in custody since May 17, 1967; he appeared before a Commissioner on May 18, 1967, when his counsel also sought such an examination.

At the request of the United States, the Commissioner set June 5, 1967, in both cases for preliminary examination—some three and one-half weeks after Wheeler's arrest and two and one-half weeks from Wyler's arrest. The adjournment was sought, in the words of the Assistant United States Attorney prosecuting the two cases, "to allow me sufficient time to gather up my evidence in a presentable form." Bail was set for $25,000 for each petitioner but they have remained in custody.

On May 22, 1967, petitioners obtained an order to show cause, returnable May 24th, why a writ of habeas corpus should not issue in view of the failure to provide a preliminary examination. The next day, May 23rd, the United States Attorney began presenting evidence in the matter to the Grand Jury.

Defendants' position is that subdivision (c) of Rule 5 requires a preliminary examination "within a reasonable time" after an accused is brought before the Commissioner; and that, having been in jail for more than a week unable to raise bail, more than a "reasonable time" has elapsed. . . .

The Assistant United States Attorney argues that in good faith he sought an adjournment of the preliminary examination until June 5 and that subsequent events permitted him to proceed earlier before the Grand Jury. He declares that inasmuch as the "hearing date had been fixed by the United States Commissioners," he had "not the right to advance the date" nor did he have an obligation to let the defendant know that the United States was in fact prepared to present evidence to the Commissioner. He also points out that he "freely" offered the defendant the right to appear before the Grand Jury and that an immediate hearing before the Commissioner would place "a burden upon me which is unfair." In his view the evidence already presented to the Grand Jury "would be more than sufficient to warrant the return of an indictment even as of this moment" and it was sufficient to require the Commissioner to find probable cause. In addition, he states, "if these people are released, I fear for the safety of several people."

While the argument was not made on behalf of the United States, it might have been added that in this case the government was following a widespread practice "of delaying preliminary hearing until an indictment can be obtained." 8 Moore's Federal Practice, ¶ 5.04[3]. . . . Most courts have felt compelled to deny relief on the ground that the issue of delay was mooted by indictment. . . .

Part of the prosecution's attitude undoubtedly stems from its view that both preliminary examinations and Grand Jury indictments serve equally to assure that an accused is being held on probable cause—a main purpose of our criminal pretrial machinery. But from the defendant's vantage point—looking forward to a possible trial at which he will have to defend himself—these devices operate quite differently.

Rule 5 preliminary hearings require the government to produce evidence—although it is not clear whether it must be admissible at a trial . . .—before a Commissioner, who in this district is an experienced lawyer. The defendant is entitled to have counsel present even if he cannot afford to pay an attorney; the government's witnesses are subject to cross-examination; the defendant has the right to present evidence and to subpoena witnesses. . . . He may obtain a transcript whether or not he has funds to pay for it. . . .

At least since the opinion in United States v. Costello, 350 U.S. 359, 363 (1956), evidence introduced before the Grand Jury need not be admissible at a trial. The defendant cannot be present while evidence against him is received. If he appears, he is not permitted to have counsel with him. He has no opportunity to cross-examine witnesses and the Grand Jury minutes are generally not available to him.

Although the primary purpose served by the federal preliminary examination is to insure that there is "probable cause to believe that an offense has been committed" (Crump v. Anderson, 352 F.2d 649, 652 (1965) . . .), in practice this hearing may provide the defense with the most valuable discovery technique available to him. . . . Nevertheless, many defense counsel prefer to waive preliminary hearings since they may harden and preserve the government's case. . . .

Under the Federal Rules the choice of waiver is the defendant's, not the government's. Upon a defendant's demand, a hearing is required within a "reasonable time." While some delay is envisaged . . . the hearing cannot, as in this case, be put off for weeks. It is significant that the Task Force on Administration of Justice of the President's Commission on Law Enforcement and Administration of Justice recently declared: "If the defendant is jailed, the preliminary hearing should be held within 72 hours." p. 85 (1967). The Task Force suggested a maximum of seven days delay where the defendant is not in custody. Ibid. The New York system—which, in many respects seems more protective of defendant's rights prior to trial than does the federal system—limits adjournments of the preliminary examination to 48 hours. N.Y. Code of Criminal Procedure, § 191.

It was unreasonable in this case to delay a preliminary hearing for incarcerated accuseds beyond the time the United States was prepared to present the matter to the Grand Jury. Should the United States Attorney ask for an adjournment of the preliminary examination on the ground that he is not prepared to proceed with the hearing, he should assume the obligation to inform defense counsel when he is ready. He should then cooperate in arranging for the examination as promptly as possible.

At the insistence of the defendant, the preliminary hearing of a defendant brought before a Commissioner prior to indictment should take place before, or simultaneously with, presentment to the Grand Jury unless, of course, the Grand Jury is operating independently of the United States Attorney—a circumstance most rare. . . . Inconvenience to the prosecutor is never an excuse for denying the preliminary examination. Inconvenience to witnesses can be minimized. "Where the preliminary hearing serves as a discovery device, presentment of the case to the grand jury on the same day as the preliminary hearing would avoid bringing the witnesses to the courthouse twice." Task Force on Administration of Justice, The President's Commission on Law Enforcement and Administration of Justice, 85 (1967).

Accordingly, Susan Wheeler and Robert Wyler are ordered released from custody unless a hearing is held today, May 24, 1967, pursuant to subdivision (c) of Rule 5 of the Rules of Criminal Procedure for the United States District Court.

. . .

---

293. The rule that a preliminary hearing need not be held once the defendant has been indicted is applied even if the hearing has been continued at the request of the government, so long as no prejudice to the defendant is shown. E.g., United States v. Mulligan, 520 F.2d 1327 (6th Cir.1975).

In United States v. Gurary, 793 F.2d 468 (2d Cir.1986), however, the court questioned an order of the district court extending the time for return of an indictment by sixty days (under 18 U.S.C. § 3161(h)(8)(A), see p. 820 below) and simultaneously extending the time for a preliminary hearing to the same later date. The court observed that although there might be special circumstances in which extensions of both the indictment and the preliminary hearing would coincide, in this case the apparent purpose of the extension of the hearing was to enable the government to avoid it by the return of an indictment.

> Rule 5 [now 5.1] contemplates that a preliminary hearing will be held promptly after arrest so that the existence of probable cause may be tested by the defendant before a neutral magistrate. Only in the event that the Government initiates a prosecution by an indictment or obtains the return of an indictment prior to the scheduled date of the

preliminary hearing may the hearing be obviated. The grand jury's decision to indict is thought to be an adequate determination of the existence of probable cause. . . . However, the provision of Rule 5 that dispenses with a preliminary hearing when an indictment is returned before the hearing date is not a license to the Government or to the District Court to postpone a preliminary hearing for whatever length of time may be justified to secure the return of an indictment. Indeed, the time limits in Rule 5(c) and the strict "extraordinary circumstances" standard for granting continuances were added to the Rule in 1972 to prohibit the practice in some districts of routinely granting a continuance to allow the Government to satisfy the probable cause requirement by filing an indictment. . . . Rule 5 recognizes the Government's opportunity to accelerate the grand jury investigation so that an indictment is returned prior to the scheduled date for the preliminary injunction; it does not allow the hearing date to be retarded to accommodate the pace of the grand jury investigation.

The scheme of the Speedy Trial Act and the Rules of Criminal Procedure also make it evident that preliminary hearings are not to be routinely continued for the period necessary for return of an indictment. Initially, the time period for a preliminary hearing, ten days for an incarcerated defendant and twenty days for a defendant on pretrial release, is shorter than the time period for return of an indictment, thirty days where a grand jury is in session and sixty days where one is not in session. Furthermore, continuance of the time to indict is governed by the somewhat flexible "ends of justice" standard of section 3161(h)(8)(A), whereas continuance of the time for a preliminary hearing, over a defendant's objection, is subject to the far more rigorous criteria of Rule 5(c) that "extraordinary circumstances" exist and that delay is "indispensable" to the interests of justice. Not only are the standards different, but, of greater significance, the purposes of the continuances differ. Extension of the time to indict permits the grand jury to complete its investigation of the defendant and to determine the appropriate charges on which trial should be held; extension of the time for a preliminary hearing is justified only to permit the prosecution to ready its presentation of probable cause to support the arrest on charges already made in the complaint.

Id. at 472–73.

294. The government can properly prosecute by indictment following dismissal of a complaint for lack of probable cause at a preliminary hearing. United States v. Kysar, 459 F.2d 422 (10th Cir.1972); United States v. Coley, 441 F.2d 1299 (5th Cir.1971). To the same effect, see People v. Noline, 917 P.2d 1256 (1996). In similar circumstances, if it were otherwise permissible, could the government prosecute by information?

AO 468 (Rev. 1/86) Waiver of Preliminary Examination or Hearing

UNITED STATES DISTRICT COURT

_______________ DISTRICT OF _______________

UNITED STATES OF AMERICA
V.

WAIVER OF PRELIMINARY EXAMINATION OR HEARING (Rule 5 or 32.1, Fed. R. Crim. P.)

CASE NUMBER:

I, _______________, charged in a ☐ complaint ☐ petition

pending in this District with _______________

in violation of Title _______________, U.S.C., _______________,

and having appeared before this Court and been advised of my rights as required by Rule 5 or Rule 32.1, Fed. R. Crim. P., including my right to have a preliminary ☐ examination ☐ hearing , do hereby waive (give up) my right to a preliminary ☐ examination ☐ hearing.

____
Defendant

_______________ *Date*

____
Counsel for Defendant

United States v. Quinn

357 F.Supp. 1348 (N.D.Ga.1973)

■ EDENFIELD, DISTRICT JUDGE.

Defendant seeks to quash the indictment returned against him on January 24, 1973, charging a violation of the Hobbs Act, 18 U.S.C. § 1951. In the alternative defendant moves that the preliminary examination which was begun before a United States Magistrate as provided in Rule 5(c), Fed.R.Crim.P., and which was cancelled subsequent to the return of an indictment, be reopened, presumably for the purpose of allowing defendant's counsel to complete cross-examination of a government witness. The facts alleged are as follows.

Defendant was arrested on January 6, 1973, and brought before a federal magistrate who set January 12, 1973 as the date for the preliminary examination. At the examination, an FBI agent testified for the government on the only issue to be determined in that proceeding, viz., whether or not there was probable cause to bind defendant over to the grand jury. During the course of his testimony the agent referred to written "field notes" which on cross-examination defendant's counsel demanded to inspect. The government objected to revealing the contents of the agent's notes, and the magistrate continued the examination until January 26, 1973, apparently for the purpose of allowing the agent to remove from his notes any material which was unrelated to the subject matter of defense counsel's cross-examination. Before the proceedings could be recommended, a federal grand jury returned an indictment on January 24, 1973, and the preliminary examination was cancelled.

Defendant claims that the indictment should be quashed because "[o]nce the preliminary examination has begun, the United States Magistrate has jurisdiction over the matter and the action of the grand jury must defer to that jurisdiction." In support of his position, defendant cites 18 U.S.C. § 3060, which in relevant part states: "(e) No preliminary examination in compliance with subsection (a) of this section shall be required to be accorded an arrested person . . . if at any time subsequent to the initial appearance of such persons before a judge or magistrate and *prior to the date fixed for the preliminary examination pursuant to subsections (b) and (c) an indictment is returned. . . .*" (Emphasis added.) Defendant argues that since the indictment was returned after the preliminary hearing had begun, by the terms of the statute, and under the substantially similar language of Rule 5(c), defendant was entitled to have the preliminary examination proceed.

In addition, defendant cites three cases from the District of Columbia Circuit which hold generally that the denial of a timely requested preliminary examination, or defects in a preliminary examination, are not excused by an intervening grand jury indictment. . . . Particularly noted is United States v. Pollard [335 F.Supp. 868 (D.D.C.1971)], where as a condition to the government's conduct of a lineup, the examining magistrate required the government to provide defense counsel with any prior descriptions given to the police or to the government by each witness who would be present at the lineup. Not wishing to comply with a ruling which it considered an undesirable precedent, the government immediately entered a *nolle prosequi* and obtained a grand jury indictment of defendant some two months later. The court found in the face of allegations that the government deliberately misled defense counsel into believing that the case was not being presented to the grand jury, that an "already scheduled preliminary hearing should not be barred where, as here, the indictment does not intervene in the normal course of events, but rather is the result of unilateral action of the Government, solely for its own benefit, and accompanied by indicia of vexatiousness." 335 F.Supp. at 870.

Without passing on whether the government's conduct in the present case was "vexatious," the court is in sympathy with the notion that the government ought not to be allowed to freely abandon its prosecution in a preliminary examination the moment that an unfavorable ruling is made or an adverse result seems imminent. Such a practice does nothing to encourage respect for law, creating as it does a feeling that the search for probable cause in a preliminary examination amounts to no more than a game in which the government can never lose, regardless of what the evidence reveals. Nevertheless, while this court may object to how the game is played, in the present case no substantive rights of the defendant have been lost, and consistent with the strong weight of authority, contrary to the cited cases in the District of Columbia Circuit, defendant's motions must be denied.

In United States v. Coley, 441 F.2d 1299 (5th Cir.1971), defendant Coley cited as error the district court's denial of his motion to quash the indictment. The reviewing court found that at Coley's preliminary examination, prior to indictment, a government witness refused to answer questions propounded by defendant's counsel. "Though advised by the United States Commissioner [precursor to the present position of United States Magistrate] that he must reply or risk dismissal of the case, the witness continued to refuse. The commissioner then dismissed the charges against Coley. Subsequently, however, a grand jury indicted Coley for the same offense." Similar to the present defendant, Coley maintained that "he had a substantial right to cross-examine witnesses at the preliminary hearing and that the commissioner's failure to enforce this right denied him due process." 441 F.2d at 1300. The Court of Appeals, in affirming the district court, replied to this argument that "the primary function of a preliminary hearing is not to expedite discovery. The purpose of such a hearing is to ascertain whether or not there is probable cause to warrant detention of the accused pending a grand jury hearing." There is no constitutional right to a preliminary hearing, and "[i]n the instant case, the distinction between an aborted preliminary hearing and no hearing is one without a difference." 441 F.2d at 1301.

In *Coley* the court had before it the relevant provisions of 18 U.S.C. § 3060(e). In *Coley*, not only was the defendant denied the right to cross-examine the government witness at the preliminary examination, but after the magistrate had dismissed the charges against him, he was subsequently and lawfully indicted by a grand jury. From this decision it seems clear that the magistrate in the present case had no power to compel the FBI agent to disclose his notes to defendant's counsel, as long as the government was willing to accept a dismissal of the charges against defendant. The magistrate had no power to compel disclosure on January 26th and he has no such power now. A finding of probable cause in this case was returned by the grand jury indictment on January 24th. Therefore, under the court's decision in *Coley*, which controls the case at bar, both defendant's motions to quash the indictment and to reopen the preliminary examination must be denied. . . .

Before concluding, two things should perhaps be noted to dispel at least somewhat the atmosphere of unfairness left when an intervening indictment cuts short a preliminary examination. First, a defendant's opportunity for discovery is not denied, by the abridgement of a preliminary examination, it is merely delayed. Rule 16, Fed.R.Crim.P., and the disclosure requirements of Brady v. Maryland, 373 U.S. 83 (1963), as applied in Giglio v. United States, 405 U.S. 150 (1972), and in Williams v. Dutton, 400 F.2d 797 (5th Cir.1968), afford ample opportunity for discovery after an indictment has been returned. If it is argued to the contrary that additional discovery is necessary then, as stated by Professor Wright, it should be provided by "carefully considered amendment of the rules, rather than by a novel construction of the existing rule." 1 C. Wright, Federal Practice and Procedure, Criminal: § 80 at 139–40 (1969 ed.).

Second, the preliminary examination does serve an important, substantive purpose, although at times the proceedings must appear to the defendant as little more than a legal charade. Even though the grand jury indictment, not the preliminary examination, is dispositive of determining probable cause, the magistrate's examination stands as a safeguard to ensure that the defendant will not be held in custody without probable cause while the government waits to present its evidence to the grand jury. A cogent statement of the preliminary hearing's place in our system of justice is provided by Professor A. Kenneth Pye's testimony in support of the predecessor "commissioner's hearing," before the Subcommittee on Improvements in Judicial Machinery of the Senate Judiciary Committee: "One of the most important purposes is to provide protection against arrests for investigation. It is not only a determination of probable cause but a determination of probable cause shortly after the arrest which is significant. The requirement that the defendant be brought before the Commissioner without unnecessary delay and the right of the defendant to have a hearing to determine whether there is probable cause combine to discourage law enforcement officers from arresting on suspicion and then investigating the case at their leisure to determine whether there is probable cause. The elimination of the Commissioner's hearing is an open invitation to arrests for investigation. If a subsequent investigation develops no probable cause, or establishes the defendant's innocence, the grand jury can be requested to return an ignoramus. During the interval, the defendant will have been deprived of his liberty in violation of the Constitution, but will be without redress. The present hearing provision is one of the best devices which we have found to implement the Fourth Amendment's requirement of arrest on probable cause." Hearings on the United States Commissioner System, before the Subcommittee on Improvements in Judicial Machinery of the Senate Committee on the Judiciary, 89th Cong., 1st Sess., pt. 2, at 270 (1965).

In certain cases the government's ability to opt out of an unfavorable proceeding may undermine belief in and respect for the fair administration of justice. Such conduct is not to be applauded. Nevertheless, in those cases where the government abandons prosecution rather than suffer the consequences, the principal overriding value of the preliminary examination is vindicated and remains undisturbed. In the present case no substantive rights of defendant have been lost and for the reasons stated above, defendant's motions are denied.

---

295. In some parts of the discussion in *Quinn*, above, the court evidently did not distinguish between the purpose of the initial appearance, as explained in Gerstein v. Pugh, p. 522 above, and the preliminary hearing, discussed in Coleman v. Alabama, below. If there was found to be probable cause at the initial appearance and subsequently, at the preliminary hearing, it was found that there was not probable cause, presumably the magistrate judge would order that the defendant be released pending an indictment. Once an indictment was returned, however, the defendant would again be subject to custody. In practice, once a magistrate judge has determined at the initial appearance that there is probable cause, it is highly unlikely that the same magistrate judge or a different magistrate judge would thereafter conclude otherwise, even though the defendant would have a greater opportunity to challenge the government's evidence of probable cause at the preliminary hearing. For practical purposes, the issue of probable cause is ordinarily resolved at the initial appearance (or by the issuance of an arrest warrant). The function of the preliminary hearing, aside from its collateral benefits to the defense, is questionable. Often enough, the defense waives a preliminary hearing despite the potential benefits of discovery or fixing prosecution witnesses' testimony. One reason for such waiver is simply that defense counsel has not yet received payment of an agreed fee "up front." See p. 553 note 300 below.

Coleman v. Alabama

399 U.S. 1, 90 S.Ct. 1999, 26 L.Ed.2d 387 (1970)

■ MR. JUSTICE BRENNAN announced the judgment of the Court and delivered the following opinion.

Petitioners were convicted in an Alabama Circuit Court of assault with intent to murder in the shooting of one Reynolds after he and his wife parked their car on an Alabama highway to change a flat tire. The Alabama Court of Appeals affirmed . . . and the Alabama Supreme Court denied review. . . . We granted certiorari. . . . We vacate and remand.

Petitioners . . . argue that the preliminary hearing prior to their indictment was a "critical stage" of the prosecution and that Alabama's failure to provide them with appointed counsel at the hearing therefore unconstitutionally denied them the assistance of counsel.

. . .

II

This Court has held that a person accused of crime "requires the guiding hand of counsel at every step in the proceedings against him," Powell v. Alabama, 287 U.S. 45, 69 (1932), and that that constitutional principle is not limited to the presence of counsel at trial. "It is central to that principle that in addition to counsel's presence at trial, the accused is guaranteed that he need not stand alone against the State at any stage of the prosecution, formal or informal, in court or out, where counsel's absence might derogate from the accused's right to a fair trial." United States v. Wade, [388 U.S. 218 (1967)] at 226. Accordingly, "the principle of Powell v. Alabama and succeeding cases requires that we scrutinize *any* pretrial confrontation of the accused to determine whether the presence of his counsel is necessary to preserve the defendant's basic right to a fair trial as affected by his right meaningfully to cross-examination the witnesses against him and to have effective assistance of counsel at the trial itself. It calls upon us to analyze whether potential substantial prejudice to defendant's rights inheres in the particular confrontation and the ability of counsel to help avoid that prejudice." Id., at 227. . . .

The preliminary hearing is not a required step in an Alabama prosecution. The prosecutor may seek an indictment directly from the grand jury without a preliminary hearing. . . . The opinion of the Alabama Court of Appeals in this case instructs us that under Alabama law the sole purposes of a preliminary hearing are to determine whether there is sufficient evidence against the accused to warrant presenting his case to the grand jury, and if so to fix bail if the offense is bailable. . . . The court continued:

> At the preliminary hearing . . . the accused is not required to advance any defenses, and failure to do so does not preclude him from availing himself of every defense he may have upon the trial of the case. Also Pointer v. State of Texas [380 U.S. 400 (1965)] bars the admission of testimony given at a pretrial proceeding where the accused did not have the benefit of cross-examination by and through counsel. Thus, nothing occurring at the preliminary hearing in absence of counsel can substantially prejudice the rights of the accused on trial.

211 So.2d, at 921.

This Court is of course bound by this construction of the governing Alabama law. . . . However, from the fact that in cases where the accused has no lawyer at the hearing the Alabama courts prohibit the State's use at trial of anything that occurred at the hearing, it does not follow that the Alabama preliminary hearing is not a "critical stage" of the State's criminal process. The determination whether the hearing is a "critical stage" requiring the provision of counsel depends, as noted, upon an analysis "whether potential substantial prejudice to defendant's rights inheres in the . . . confrontation and the ability of counsel to help avoid that prejudice." United States v. Wade, supra, at 227. Plainly the guiding hand of counsel at the preliminary hearing is essential to protect the indigent accused against an erroneous or improper prosecution. First, the lawyer's skilled examination and cross-examination of witnesses may expose fatal weaknesses in the State's case that may lead the magistrate to refuse to bind the accused over. Second, in any event, the skilled interrogation of witnesses by an experienced lawyer can fashion a vital impeachment tool for use in cross-examination of the State's witnesses at the trial, or preserve testimony favorable to the accused of a witness who does not appear at the trial. Third, trained counsel can more effectively discover the case the State has against his client and make possible the preparation of a proper defense to meet that case at the trial. Fourth, counsel can also be influential at the preliminary hearing in making effective arguments for the accused on such matters as the necessity for an early psychiatric examination or bail.

The inability of the indigent accused on his own to realize these advantages of a lawyer's assistance compels the conclusion that the Alabama preliminary hearing is a "critical stage" of the State's criminal process at which the accused is "as much entitled to such aid [of counsel] . . . as at the trial itself." Powell v. Alabama, supra, at 57.

. . .

[The Court remanded the case for a determination whether the failure to provide counsel at the preliminary hearing was harmless error.][5]

FEDERAL RULES OF CRIMINAL PROCEDURE

Rule 44

RIGHT TO AND APPOINTMENT OF COUNSEL

(a) Right to Appointed Counsel. A defendant who is unable to obtain counsel is entitled to have counsel appointed to represent the defendant at every stage of the proceeding from initial appearance through appeal, unless the defendant waives this right.

(b) Appointment Procedure. Federal law and local court rules govern the procedure for implementing the right to counsel.

(c) Inquiry Into Joint Representation.

(1) *Joint Representation.* Joint representation occurs when:

(A) two or more defendants have been charged jointly under Rule 8(b) or have been joined for trial under Rule 13; and

(B) the defendants are represented by the same counsel, or counsel who are associated in law practice.

(2) *Court's Responsibilities in Cases of Joint Representation.* The court must promptly inquire about the propriety of joint representation and must personally advise each defendant of the right to the effective assistance of counsel, including separate representation. Unless there is good cause to believe that no conflict of interest is likely to arise, the court must take appropriate measures to protect each defendant's right to counsel.

[5] Justice Black and Justice White wrote concurring opinions. Justice Douglas, who joined Justice Brennan's opinion, also wrote a separate opinion. Justice Harlan wrote an opinion concurring in part and dissenting in part. Chief Justice Burger wrote a dissenting opinion. Justice Stewart wrote a dissenting opinion, which Chief Justice Burger joined.

---

296. In Gideon v. Wainwright, 372 U.S. 335 (1963), the Court held that the Sixth Amendment right to the assistance of counsel requires the appointment of counsel for indigent defendants in state courts as it had previously been required in federal courts. Gideon was accused of a felony. Nine years later, *Gideon* was extended to a defendant accused of a misdemeanor for which a sentence of imprisonment was authorized, in Argersinger v. Hamlin, 407 U.S. 25 (1972). The Court held that "absent a knowing and intelligent waiver, no person may be imprisoned for any offense, whether classified as petty, misdemeanor, or felony, unless he was represented by counsel at his trial." Id. at 37. In Scott v. Illinois, 440 U.S. 367 (1979) (5–4), the Court held that an indigent defendant who is charged with a crime for which a sentence of imprisonment is authorized but who, if he is convicted, is sentenced only to pay a fine is not constitutionally entitled to appointed counsel. "[T]he Sixth and Fourteenth Amendments to the United States Constitution require only that no indigent criminal defendant be sentenced to a term of imprisonment unless the State has afforded him the right to assistance of appointed counsel in his defense." Id. at 373–74. The Court said that such a line had been drawn in *Argersinger*, but that even if it had not, "the central premise of *Argersinger*—that actual imprisonment is a penalty different in kind from fines or the mere threat of imprisonment—is eminently sound and warrants adoption of actual imprisonment as the line defining the constitutional right to appointment of counsel." Id. at 373. *Scott* is applied in Alabama v. Shelton, 535 U.S. 654 (2002) (5–4). The defendant was tried without appointment of counsel and was convicted of assault and sentenced to a jail term of 30 days. The trial court suspended execution of the sentence and placed the defendant on probation for two years. The Court held that, the defendant not having been appointed counsel, the suspended sentence was invalid, even though no actual jail time had been imposed. Since it might eventuate in an actual deprivation of liberty, the suspended sentence constituted a "term of imprisonment" for purposes of *Scott*.

In a dissenting opinion in *Scott*, Justice Brennan urged that the proper constitutional standard "would require the appointment of counsel for indigents accused of any offense for which imprisonment for any time is authorized." Id. at 382. He pointed out that the defendant, who was convicted of theft, the authorized penalty for which was up to a year in prison, would have been entitled to appointed counsel under the law of at least 33 states.

The right of an indigent to be assigned counsel does not require a court to honor a request for the assignment of a particular lawyer, even if that lawyer is willing to accept the appointment. United States v. Davis, 604 F.2d 474 (7th Cir.1979). But see People v. Perez, 594 P.2d 1 (Cal.1979), in which the court upheld the representation of indigent defendants, with their consent, by "certified" law students acting under the supervision of a regular attorney.

In Fuller v. Oregon, 417 U.S. 40 (1974), the Supreme Court upheld a state scheme which provided counsel for indigent defendants but required that a defendant who was convicted repay the cost of his defense if he later became financially able to do so.

AO 458 (Rev. 10/95) Appearance

UNITED STATES DISTRICT COURT

____________________ DISTRICT OF ____________________

APPEARANCE

Case Number:

To the Clerk of this court and all parties of record:

Enter my appearance as counsel in this case for

I certify that I am admitted to practice in this court.

Date	Signature
	Print Name — Bar Number
	Address
	City — State — Zip Code
	Phone Number — Fax Number

297. Title 18 U.S.C. § 3006A(a) provides for the appointment of counsel "for any person financially unable to obtain adequate representation." In Wood v. United States, 389 U.S. 20, 21 (1967), the Supreme Court vacated the defendant's conviction and remanded the case for consideration of the question whether the defendant's request for appointment of counsel pursuant to § 3006A was improperly denied in light of "the relevant criteria" of the act. The statute itself contains no criteria for determining whether a defendant is entitled to appointment of counsel other than the phrase "financially unable" (or "financially able"). The legislative history indicates that appointment was not to be limited to "destitute" persons. H.R.Rep. No. 864, 88th Cong., 2d Sess. 7 (1964) (letter of the Attorney General).

Section 3006A(e)(1) provides that "counsel for a person who is financially unable to obtain investigative, expert, or other services necessary for adequate representation may request them in an ex parte application." Holding that the defendant was entitled to appointment of a fingerprint expert, the court in United States v. Patterson, 724 F.2d 1128, 1130 (5th Cir.1984), said, "[W]here the government's case rests heavily on a theory most completely addressed to expert testimony, an indigent defendant must be afforded the opportunity to prepare and present his defense to such a theory with the assistance of his own expert pursuant to section 3006A(e)." See Ake v. Oklahoma, 470 U.S. 68, 74 (1985) (8–1), holding that "when a defendant has made a preliminary showing that his sanity at the time of the offense is likely to be a significant factor at trial, the Constitution requires that a State provide access to a psychiatrist's assistance on this issue, if the defendant cannot otherwise afford one."

298. Federal statutory provisions authorizing forfeiture to the government of the proceeds of illegal drug activities and collateral provisions authorizing pretrial restraint against transfer of assets potentially forfeitable under the statute, 21 U.S.C. § 853, contain no exemption for assets that the defendant intends to use to pay attorney's fees in the criminal case. Application of the provisions to prevent a defendant from transferring assets to an attorney for his defense does not violate the Sixth Amendment right to counsel or the Due Process Clause. United States v. Monsanto, 491 U.S. 600 (1989) (5–4); Caplin & Drysdale v. United States, 491 U.S. 617 (1989) (5–4).

On the nature of the hearing required to authorize pretrial restraint of a transfer of assets needed to retain counsel of choice, see United States v. Monsanto, 924 F.2d 1186 (2d Cir.1991).

299. Title 18 U.S.C. § 3006A provides for compensation to be paid to appointed counsel. The maximum hourly rate of compensation is determined by the Judicial Conference "for each circuit . . . with variations by district, where appropriate, taking into account such factors as the minimum range of the prevailing hourly rates for qualified attorneys in the district in which the representation is provided and the recommendations of the judicial councils of the circuits." § 3006(A)(d)(1). Although the Judicial Conference has approved an hourly rate of $75 for in-court and out-of-court work in all districts (except the District of Rhode Island, where the rates are $65 and $45), the actual rates in most districts in early 1998 were $65 and $45, due to the unavailability of funds. The maximum

CJA 20 APPOINTMENT OF AND AUTHORITY TO PAY COURT APPOINTED COUNSEL (Rev. 5/99)

1. CIR./DIST./ DIV. CODE	2. PERSON REPRESENTED	VOUCHER NUMBER	
3. MAG. DKT./DEF. NUMBER	4. DIST. DKT./DEF. NUMBER	5. APPEALS DKT./DEF. NUMBER	6. OTHER DKT. NUMBER
7. IN CASE/MATTER OF *(Case Name)*	8. PAYMENT CATEGORY ☐ Felony ☐ Petty Offense ☐ Misdemeanor ☐ Other ☐ Appeal	9. TYPE PERSON REPRESENTED ☐ Adult Defendant ☐ Appellant ☐ Juvenile Defendant ☐ Appellee ☐ Other	10. REPRESENTATION TYPE *(See Instructions)*

11. OFFENSE(S) CHARGED (Cite U.S. Code, Title & Section) *If more than one offense, list (up to five) major offenses charged, according to severity of offense.*

12. ATTORNEY'S NAME *(First Name, M.I., Last Name, including any suffix)*, AND MAILING ADDRESS

Telephone Number : ____

14. NAME AND MAILING ADDRESS OF LAW FIRM *(Only provide per instructions)*

13. COURT ORDER
☐ O Appointing Counsel ☐ C Co-Counsel
☐ F Subs For Federal Defender ☐ R Subs For Retained Attorney
☐ P Subs For Panel Attorney ☐ Y Standby Counsel

Prior Attorney's
Appointment Dates: ____

☐ Because the above-named person represented has testified under oath or has otherwise satisfied this Court that he or she (1) is financially unable to employ counsel and (2) does not wish to waive counsel, and because the interests of justice so require, the attorney whose name appears in Item 12 is appointed to represent this person in this case, OR
☐ Other *(See Instructions)*

Signature of Presiding Judicial Officer or By Order of the Court

Date of Order Nunc Pro Tunc Date

Repayment or partial repayment ordered from the person represented for this service at time appointment. ☐ YES ☐ NO

CLAIM FOR SERVICES AND EXPENSES | **FOR COURT USE ONLY**

	CATEGORIES *(Attach itemization of services with dates)*	HOURS CLAIMED	TOTAL AMOUNT CLAIMED	MATH/TECH. ADJUSTED HOURS	MATH/TECH. ADJUSTED AMOUNT	ADDITIONAL REVIEW
15.	a. Arraignment and/or Plea					
	b. Bail and Detention Hearings					
	c. Motion Hearings					
In	d. Trial					
Court	e. Sentencing Hearings					
	f. Revocation Hearings					
	g. Appeals Court					
	h. Other *(Specify on additional sheets)*					
	(RATE PER HOUR = $) TOTALS:					
16.	a. Interviews and Conferences					
Out of	b. Obtaining and reviewing records					
Court	c. Legal research and brief writing					
	d. Travel time					
	e. Investigative and other work *(Specify on additional sheets)*					
	(RATE PER HOUR = $) TOTALS:					
17.	Travel Expenses *(lodging, parking, meals, mileage, etc.)*					
18.	Other Expenses *(other than expert, transcripts, etc.)*					
	GRAND TOTALS (CLAIMED AND ADJUSTED):					

19. CERTIFICATION OF ATTORNEY/PAYEE FOR THE PERIOD OF SERVICE FROM ____ TO: ____	20. APPOINTMENT TERMINATION DATE IF OTHER THAN CASE COMPLETION	21. CASE DISPOSITION

22. CLAIM STATUS ☐ Final Payment ☐ Interim Payment Number ____ ☐ Supplemental Payment

Have you previously applied to the court for compensation and/or reimbursement for this ☐ YES ☐ NO If yes, were you paid? ☐ YES ☐ NO
Other than from the Court, have you, or to your knowledge has anyone else, received payment *(compensation or anything of value)* from any other source in connection with this representation? ☐ YES ☐ NO If yes, give details on additional sheets.
I swear or affirm the truth or correctness of the above statements.

Signature of Attorney ____ Date ____

APPROVED FOR PAYMENT — COURT USE ONLY

23. IN COURT COMP.	24. OUT OF COURT COMP.	25. TRAVEL EXPENSES	26. OTHER EXPENSES	27. TOTAL AMT. APPR./CERT.
28. SIGNATURE OF THE PRESIDING JUDICIAL OFFICER			DATE	28a. JUDGE/MAG. JUDGE CODE
29. IN COURT COMP.	30. OUT OF COURT COMP.	31. TRAVEL EXPENSES	32. OTHER EXPENSES	33. TOTAL AMT. APPROVED
34. SIGNATURE OF CHIEF JUDGE, COURT OF APPEALS (OR DELEGATE) *Payment approved in excess of the statutory threshold amount.*			DATE	34a. JUDGE CODE

amount payable for representation of a defendant charged with a felony before the magistrate judge or in the district court is $5,200, and for a defendant charged with a misdemeanor, $1,500. § 3006(A)(d)(2). The maximums may be exceeded if "necessary to provide fair compensation." § 3006(A)(d)(3).

United States v. Gipson

517 F.Supp. 230 (W.D.Mich.1981)

■ ENSLEN, DISTRICT JUDGE.

This matter is before the Court on Defendant, Thomas P. Gipson's (hereinafter Defendant) Motion for Court Appointed Counsel. Presently, Defendant is represented by retained counsel, who in the Court's estimation has heretofore provided Defendant with exemplary services.[6] The Court notes that on May 26, 1981 the Defendant pled guilty to one count of the Indictment and inquiry discloses that, nevertheless, counsel for the Defendant desires to proceed with the Motion. The sole issue is whether that representation should continue through the appointment of counsel. For the reasons discussed below, the Court is of the opinion that such appointment is inappropriate.

The Criminal Justice Act of 1964 provides that the court, "if satisfied after appropriate inquiry that the defendant is financially unable to obtain counsel, shall appoint counsel to represent him." 18 U.S.C. § 3006A(b). Financial inability as considered for the purposes of the Act does not mean indigency. The Defendant does not have to be destitute to be eligible for an appointment of counsel. The Court need only be satisfied that the representation essential to an adequate defense is beyond the means of the Defendant. . . .

In the case at bar, the Defendant has submitted as indicia of indigency a financial affidavit, which after careful consideration by this Court, does not reveal a Defendant without adequate means of obtaining legal representation. The Affidavit discloses that Defendant has approximately $42,850 of assets and a monthly income of $600, being the salary of his wife. Defendant is currently on indefinite lay-off from the Niles Township Police force. In addition, the Affidavit reflects a total indebtedness of $27,785, and total monthly bills of approximately $530.40. Thus far, according to Defendant's allegation in his brief in support, he has expended approximately $2,500 in the furtherance of his defense. Since the Defendant has already pled guilty to one count of the Indictment filed against him in return for the dismissal of the other counts in the Indictment and his cooperation at the trial of co-defendants in this matter, and because that trial is expected to be expeditiously resolved, the Court is of the opinion that the Defendant has sufficient resources to marshall his remaining defenses. I cannot say, based upon his Affidavit as submitted, that the Defendant cannot afford legal counsel of his own choosing.

6. The Motion in no way implies that the Defendant is dissatisfied with the legal services rendered by his counsel of record to date. Indeed, the Defendant desires that in the event his Motion is granted that his current counsel be appointed by the Court to continue his defense.

Moreover, even if the Defendant in the case sub judice were unable to afford counsel at this juncture, his present attorney of record is under a continuing duty to represent him in a punctilious and zealous manner. Lawyers, as guardians of the law, play a vital role in the preservation of our society. As such, it is not only the right but the duty of the legal profession as a whole to utilize such methods as may be developed to bring the services of its members to those who need them, so long as this can be done ethically and with dignity. ABA Opinion 250 (1965). . . .

As President Theodore Roosevelt aptly put it, "Every man owes some of his time to the upbuilding of the profession to which he belongs." The soundness and the necessity of President Roosevelt's admonition insofar as it relates to the legal profession cannot be doubted. . . . These enlightening principles are embodied in the Code of Professional Responsibility. There, it is stated:

> The legal profession cannot remain a viable force in fulfilling its role in our society unless its members receive adequate compensation for services rendered, and reasonable fees should be charged in appropriate cases to clients able to pay them. Nevertheless, persons unable to pay all or a portion of a reasonable fee should be able to obtain necessary legal services, and lawyers should support and participate in ethical activities designed to achieve that objective.

EC 2–16.

In the instant case, counsel for the Defendant should be guided by the exhortations of the aforementioned ethical consideration. See also EC 2–17 and 2–18. Additionally, the Court directs counsel for the Defendant to EC 6–4 where it is stated in part: "Having undertaken representation, a lawyer should use proper care to safeguard the interest of his client." See for example, DR 2–110, which provides that a lawyer must take reasonable steps to avoid foreseeable prejudice to the rights of his client if the lawyer moves to withdraw his or her services from the case. It appears to the Court that if the spirit and letter of the Code of Professional Responsibility are to be followed in this case, then the Defendant, who has already employed legal counsel is entitled to that particular counsel's best representation regardless of intervening financial difficulties. Counsel's obligation to represent a criminal Defendant is not so slight or so transitory as to obviate the need for undaunted protection from the impending onslaught of the prosecution in the criminal justice system.

Defendant's Motion is therefore denied.

300.

(i)

The defendant is charged with a felony. He earns $800 per week as a truck driver. He has no dependents, and no property. He asks that counsel be appointed to defend him.

Should the magistrate appoint counsel? See Samuel v. United States, 420 F.2d 371 (5th Cir.1969).

Assume that the magistrate declines to appoint counsel on the ground that the defendant is not "financially unable to obtain an adequate

CJA 23
Rev. 5/98

FINANCIAL AFFIDAVIT

IN SUPPORT OF REQUEST FOR ATTORNEY, EXPERT OR OTHER COURT SERVICES WITHOUT PAYMENT OF FEE

IN UNITED STATES ☐ MAGISTRATE ☐ DISTRICT ☐ APPEALS COURT or ☐ OTHER PANEL (Specify below)

IN THE CASE OF ______ V.S. ______

FOR ______

AT ______

LOCATION NUMBER

PERSON REPRESENTED (Show your full name)

CHARGE/OFFENSE (describe if applicable & check box →) ☐ Felony ☐ Misdemeanor

1 ☐ Defendant—Adult
2 ☐ Defendant - Juvenile
3 ☐ Appellant
4 ☐ Probation Violator
5 ☐ Parole Violator
6 ☐ Habeas Petitioner
7 ☐ 2255 Petitioner
8 ☐ Material Witness
9 ☐ Other ______

DOCKET NUMBERS
Magistrate
District Court
Court of Appeals

ANSWERS TO QUESTIONS REGARDING ABILITY TO PAY

ASSETS

EMPLOYMENT

Are you now employed? ☐ Yes ☐ No ☐ Am Self-Employed

Name and address of employer: ______

IF YES, how much do you earn per month? $ ______

IF NO, give month and year of last employment
How much did you earn per month? $ ______

If married is your Spouse employed? ☐ Yes ☐ No

IF YES, how much does your Spouse earn per month? $ ______

If a minor under age 21, what is your Parents or Guardian's approximate monthly income? $ ______

OTHER INCOME

Have you received within the past 12 months any income from a business, profession or other form of self-employment, or in the form the form of rent payments, interest, dividends, retirement or annuity payments, or other sources? ☐ Yes ☐ No

IF YES, GIVE THE AMOUNT RECEIVED & IDENTIFY THE SOURCES

RECEIVED	SOURCES
$	
$	

CASH

Have you any cash on hand or money in savings or checking accounts? ☐ Yes ☐ No **IF YES,** state total amount $ ______

PROPERTY

Do you own any real estate, stocks, bonds, notes, automobiles, or other valuable property (excluding ordinary household furnishings and clothing)? ☐ Yes ☐ No

IF YES, GIVE THE VALUE AND DESCRIBE IT

VALUE	DESCRIPTION
$	

OBLIGATIONS & DEBTS

DEPENDENTS

MARITAL STATUS
____ SINGLE
____ MARRIED
____ WIDOWED
____ SEPARATED OR DIVORCED

Total No. of Dependents ______

List persons you actually support and your relationship to them ______

DEBTS & MONTHLY BILLS (LIST ALL CREDITORS, INCLUDING BANKS, LOAN COMPANIES, CHARGE ACCOUNTS, ETC.)

APARTMENT OR HOME: Creditors	Total Debt	Monthly Paymt.
	$	$
	$	$
	$	$
	$	$

I certify under penalty of perjury that the foregoing is true and correct. Executed on (date) ______

SIGNATURE OF DEFENDANT (OR PERSON REPRESENTED) ______

defense." The defendant then states that the charges against him are unfounded, that in his own judgment he cannot afford to retain counsel, and that he does not intend to do so. What should the magistrate do?

(ii)

The defendant is charged with a serious narcotics offense. He is a graduate student at a large private university. He receives a tuition scholarship from the university and occasionally does odd jobs from which he earns about $400 per week; he has no other income. He is not physically or otherwise unable to maintain regular employment but does not choose to do so. He has completed all coursework for his graduate program and has no present obligation other than to write a dissertation. He asks that counsel be appointed to defend him.

Should the magistrate appoint counsel? See March v. Municipal Court, 498 P.2d 437, 442 (Cal.1972), in which, applying the indigency standard to students, the court said: "The relevant consideration in determining indigency is whether the petitioner's *current financial status* affords him equal access to the legal process. Such a determination cannot include an evaluation of the appellant's future earning potential or even his present potential had he chosen to employ himself in a more financially rewarding manner."

Coleman v. Burnett

477 F.2d 1187 (D.C.Cir.1973)

■ SPOTTSWOOD W. ROBINSON, III, CIRCUIT JUDGE.

This appeal tenders for resolution questions as to the examinatorial entitlements of the criminally accused at federal preliminary hearings. Appellants, Lawrence D. Coleman, Jorge D. Dancis and Ronald Shepard, were arrested and charged with the commission of unrelated crimes within the District of Columbia. Following arrest, each was brought before a judicial officer for the proceedings prescribed by then Rule 5 of the Federal Rules of Criminal Procedure. Coleman and Dancis each sought, and each was denied, a subpoena requiring the attendance at his preliminary hearing of the only apparent eyewitness to his alleged offenses. Shepard, during his preliminary hearing, was restricted in cross-examination of the complainant and a corroborating Government witness, and in the presentation of evidence of his own.

Subsequent to the preliminary hearings, the three appellants joined in a class-action complaint in the District Court. They sought declaratory judgments that the preliminary hearings were defective, writs of mandamus reopening them, and an injunction restraining, pendente lite, presentation of their cases for grand jury consideration. The District Court denied a preliminary injunction and dismissed the action, and this appeal ensued. For reasons which follow, we reverse the District Court's judgment to the extent that it denied a declaration that Dancis' preliminary hearing was faulty and remand the case in order that the declaration may be made. In all other respects we affirm, but without prejudice to rectification in the criminal proceeding pending against Dancis of the error committed at his preliminary hearing.

Some of the questions advanced on appeal are common to the cases of two or more of the three appellants. Each appeal, however, also tenders an issue not present in either of the others. We therefore treat the three cases separately.

I. COLEMAN'S APPEAL

After joining in this appeal, Coleman was indicted in two bills for multiple violations of the federal narcotic laws. Two days before oral argument on the appeal, he entered a plea of guilty to two counts, one in each of the two indictments. He insists that his preliminary hearing, at which the charges laid in one of the indictments were aired, was fatally infirm and that we should now direct that it be reopened. He further argues, as he must, that the plea does not stand in the way of the appeal brought here for that purpose. We do not agree.

. . .

[The court held that Coleman's appeal was barred by the plea of guilty.]

II. SHEPARD'S APPEAL

Appellant Shepard was charged with assaulting a Deputy United States Marshal while a prisoner in the cellblock of the District of Columbia Court of General Sessions. A judge of that court, sitting as a committing magistrate, presided over his preliminary hearing. The complaining witness, Deputy Marshal John H. Lonien, testified that while he was on duty in the cellblock, Shepard committed an unprovoked attack upon him, striking him above the right eye with a fist. Another Government witness, Herbert Rutherford, employed as a guard in the cellblock, corroborated Marshal Lonien's testimony.

Shepard's counsel was permitted considerable latitude in cross-examination of these witnesses as to matters they had testified to on direct examination. The judge, however, sustained the Government's objections to a number of inquiries directed to them on other topics. The specific complaint Shepard refers to us runs to the judge's rulings on eleven questions propounded to Marshal Lonien and four to Guard Rutherford. Those questions, in the main, solicited testimony as to disparaging remarks assertedly directed to cellblock personnel by prisoners other than Shepard, and to the nature and extent of any injuries inflicted by Shepard on Marshal Lonien and of injuries allegedly sustained by Shepard himself. The judge also ruled out Shepard's proffer of photographs purporting to show his post-altercation physical condition, and inquiry of a defense witness as to whether cellblock personnel had tried to confiscate the photographs.

The more common basis of the Government's objections to defense counsel's cross-examinatorial approach was that he was venturing beyond the boundaries of a hearing designed to explore probable cause and embarking on a quest for discovery of elements of the Government's case. After some amount of prior ambivalence on the subject, Shepard now disclaims any attempt at discovery, as distinguished from refutation of probable cause. He further argues that the questions addressed to Marshal Lonien and Guard Rutherford bore a substantial relationship to the existence or nonexistence of probable cause.

. . .

A. *Discovery at Preliminary Hearings*

Former Rule 5(c) granted the accused, and its present counterpart continues to confer, the right to "cross-examine witnesses against him" at a preliminary hearing. The true dimension of that right is bound to depend in considerable measure upon the degree to which discovery by the defense may be a purpose the preliminary hearing is designed to serve. That, in turn, is a topic upon which the judges of this court have expressed views which, to say the least, have not been entirely harmonious. One view has been that the sole objective of a preliminary hearing is to determine whether there is probable cause to believe that the accused has committed an offense, and that the accused may lay claim to the benefit of only so much discovery as may become incidental to a properly conducted inquiry into probable cause. That view has now been incorporated into federal jurisprudence by the Federal Magistrates Act.

This Act provides mandatorily, with exceptions later to be considered, for "a preliminary [hearing] . . . to determine whether there is probable cause to believe that an offense has been committed and that the arrested person has committed it." The reason the Act indulges the preliminary hearing no independent discovery role is evident from its legislative history. During hearings before the Senate Committee on the Judiciary, witnesses urged "that preliminary examination afforded a necessary and useful medium for defense counsel to obtain discovery of the prosecution's evidence."[7] The Committee, however, was "of the opinion that the problem of discovery should be treated separately from that of the preliminary hearing."[8] Although the need for expanded pretrial discovery procedures was recognized, the Committee felt that

> The preliminary hearing does not present an ideal opportunity for discovery. It is designed for another purpose; namely, that of determining whether there is probable cause to justify further proceedings against an arrested person. Thus, the degree of discovery obtained in a preliminary hearing will vary depending upon how much evidence the presiding judicial officer thinks is necessary to establish probable cause in a particular case. This may be quite a bit, or it may be very little, but in either event it need not be all the evidence within the possession of the Government that should be subject to discovery.[9]

The Committee accordingly concluded "that discovery procedure should remain separate and distinct from the preliminary examination. . . ."[10]

That settles the matter, of course, for Shepard and others whose hearings took place after the effective date of the Act. The mission of the hearing is an investigation into probable cause for further proceedings against the accused. It does not include discovery for the sake of discovery. To be sure, the evidence the Government offers to establish probable cause is by nature also discovery for the accused. So also is information adduced

7. S.Rep. No. 371, 90th Cong., 1st Sess. 34 (1967).

8. Id.

9. Id.

10. Id. at 35.

on cross-examination of Government witnesses on the aspects of direct-examination testimony tending to build up probable cause. In those senses, some discovery becomes a by-product of the process of demonstrating probable cause. But in no sense is discovery a legitimate end unto itself.

B. *Cross-Examination at Preliminary Hearings*

To say merely that discovery is not a primary function of federal preliminary hearings is to respond only incompletely to the issue Shepard poses. As we have said, former Rule 5(c) conferred upon the accused the right to "cross-examine witnesses against him," and that right he continues to enjoy. Moreover, in Coleman v. Alabama,[11] the Supreme Court, in holding that a preliminary hearing to ascertain probable cause to bind an accused for additional proceedings is a critical stage of the criminal process at which the Sixth Amendment right to counsel obtains, pointed out as one of the considerations supporting its holding that "the lawyer's skilled examination and cross-examination of witnesses may expose fatal weaknesses in the [prosecution's] case that may lead the magistrate to refuse to bind the accused over."[12] Since the right to counsel is the right to effective assistance of counsel, *Coleman* requires us to evaluate Shepard's challenge with the increased solicitude appropriate when constitutional rights are at stake. This we have done, and we are led to the conclusion that the District Court's disposition of Shepard's grievance should not be disturbed.

According to Shepard's brief on appeal, the purpose of his counsel's questions on cross-examination of the two Government witnesses was to show that "(a) there were no physical injuries to the Marshals; (b) there were severe injuries to Mr. Shepard rendering him unconscious; (c) the assault charge was brought as a subterfuge for the Marshals' own conduct; (d) the Marshals were provoked by disparaging remarks by prisoners other than Mr. Shepard; (e) there was mass confusion in the cellblock seriously impeding the perception of the Marshals; and (f) there was evidence that Mr. Shepard acted in self-defense, if he acted at all." The first difficulty we have encountered is that the handling of the cross-examination made this understanding all too difficult to come by. Cross-examination at a preliminary hearing, like the hearing itself, is confined by the principle that a probe into probable cause is the end and aim of the proceeding, and the line between refutation of probable cause and discovery into the prosecution's case ofttimes is thin. Here counsel's purpose in propounding the questions which the presiding judge excluded was unquestionably blurred by the fact that counsel frequently appeared to be off on an impermissible quest for discovery. At no time prior to the rulings complained of did counsel delineate for the judge's edification the factual thesis he was seeking to promote. Only as the hearing neared its close, and after the rulings had been made, did counsel broach anything remotely similar to the defensive theory now explained on appeal. Our reading of the hearing record leaves us with the conviction that the presiding judge, when ruling on counsel's

11. 399 U.S. 1 (1970).

12. . . . 399 U.S. at 9.

questions, could hardly divine what counsel had in mind. Therefore, we cannot say that he committed error in barring responses to inquiries that seemed unrelated to the task of evaluating probable cause.

Moreover, cross-examination is properly to be limited at preliminary hearing, as at trial, to the scope of the witness' direct examination. To the extent that it is not—and here it was not—cross-examination ostensibly, even if undesignedly, becomes an effort at some sort of discovery. We do not suggest that magistrates may not indulge variations from the usual order of offering evidence, and during presentation of the Government's case permit the defense to get in elements of its own. But when cross-examination exceeds the range of direct examination unaccompanied by an elucidation of its connection with probable cause, it is small wonder that discovery is taken to be the examiner's goal.

An even more important consideration stems from the difference between the objective of the preliminary hearing and that of the trial. While, of course, conviction necessitates proof at trial of all elements of a crime beyond a reasonable doubt, it suffices for purposes of a binding over for trial that the evidence show "probable cause to believe that an offense has been committed and that the defendant has committed it." The preliminary hearing is not a minitrial of the issue of guilt, but is rather an investigation into the reasonableness of the bases for the charge, and examination of witnesses thereat does not enjoy the breadth it commands at trial. "A preliminary hearing," the Supreme Court has said, "is ordinarily a much less searching exploration into the merits of a case than a trial, simply because its function is the more limited one of determining whether probable cause exists to hold the accused for trial."[13]

It is the contrast of probable cause and proof beyond a reasonable doubt that inevitably makes for examinatorial differences between the preliminary hearing and the trial. Probable cause signifies evidence sufficient to cause a person of ordinary prudence and caution to conscientiously entertain a reasonable belief of the accused's guilt. Proof beyond a reasonable doubt, on the other hand, connotes evidence strong enough to create an abiding conviction of guilt to a moral certainty. The gap between these two concepts is broad. A magistrate may become satisfied about probable cause on much less than he would need to be convinced. Since he does not sit to pass on guilt or innocence, he could legitimately find probable cause while personally entertaining some reservations. By the same token, a showing of probable cause may stop considerably short of proof beyond a reasonable doubt, and evidence that leaves some doubt may yet demonstrate probable cause. In the instance before us, the testimony of two witnesses on direct examination furnished more than an ample foundation for a finding of probable cause which the cross-examination allowed did not impair. By our appraisal the convoluted defensive theory Shepard now says he wanted to develop was not likely to change the result. Whatever its potency as a basis for a reasonable doubt at trial, its capability to dissolve

13. Barber v. Page, 390 U.S. 719, 725 (1968).

enough of the Government's showing to negate probable cause strikes us as highly improbable. We speak not only of the cross-examination which was banned but also of the items of similar purport which on Shepard's presentation were excluded. In any event, the situation is far too cloudy to warrant a grant of the extraordinary relief which Shepard seeks.

Magistrates presiding over preliminary hearings, no less than judges presiding over trials, are endowed with broad powers to supervise examination of witnesses. Beyond that, they should be indulged some leeway in their resolution of probable cause issues. Courts should not upset these judgmatic exercises unless a supervisory excess or a decisional error is clearly shown, and we do not perceive either here. Shepard's counsel was permitted to cross-examine each Government witness closely as to the elements of his direct testimony and, for the reasons stated, we cannot say that disallowance of the questions ruled out was improper. For similar reasons, we are unable to say that the photographs and the questions as to the defense witness possessed such a tendency to dissolve probable cause that their exclusion was erroneous. A writ of mandamus lies only to enforce a plain, positive duty; it is not available to exact a response to a dubious claim. At best, any obligation to reverse the rulings on the excluded evidence is entirely too unclear. We accordingly affirm as to Shepard.

III. DANCIS' APPEAL

Dancis, our third appellant, was charged with two violations of the Marijuana Tax Act. The charges came on for ventilation at a preliminary hearing over which a United States Magistrate presided. The magistrate denied his counsel's request for a subpoena requiring the attendance of an unnamed undercover agent, who apparently was the sole available eyewitness to the two marijuana transactions attributed to Dancis. The Government's only witness at the hearing was the agent's supervisor, whose testimony as to the alleged transactions was necessarily hearsay, and as to the transactor's identity was simply that the agent had identified Dancis from a six-year old photograph. The magistrate, on a finding of probable cause, held Dancis for grand jury action, and the District Court, in the case under review, held that the hearing was legally sufficient.

Dancis argues that each of two flaws vitiated his preliminary hearing. One is that the magistrate's refusal to allow him access to the undercover agent's testimony was prejudicial error. The other is that the Confrontation Clause outlaws the magistrate's finding of probable cause solely upon the hearsay testimony of the agent's supervisor. We deem it unnecessary to reach the constitutional issue posed by Dancis' second contention because we agree that he is on sound ground in advancing the first.

A. *Defensive Evidence at Preliminary Hearings*

Former Rule 5(c) confirmed the right of an accused to "introduce evidence in his own behalf" at his preliminary hearing. It also imposed the requirement that an affirmative decision on probable cause be reached "on the evidence." The specifications of present Rule 5.1(a) are identical. Thus a federal preliminary hearing is not only the occasion upon which the Government must justify continued detention by a showing of probable cause, but also an opportunity for the accused to rebut that showing. Rule 5(c) made it clear that it is as much the arrestee's prerogative to endeavor to minimize probable cause as it is the Government's to undertake to maximize it, and that both sides must be indulged reasonably in their respective efforts. And the Government's demonstration on probable cause must surmount not only difficulties of its own but also any attack the accused may be able to mount against it.[14]

In sum, "the evidence" which alone must guide resolution of the probable cause issue is the whole evidence—for the defense as well as the prosecution. The magistrate must "listen to . . . [the] versions [of all witnesses] and observe their demeanor and provide an opportunity to defense counsel to explore their account on cross-examination."[15] The magistrate "sits as a judicial officer to sift all the evidence before resolving the probable cause issue. . . ."[16] He "cannot decline to issue subpoenas on the ground that only the Government's evidence is probative."[17]

These provisions of the Rules and our interpretations of them are now reinforced by the holding in Coleman v. Alabama that the Sixth Amendment secures for the accused the assistance of counsel at a preliminary hearing having for its purpose a determination on probable cause to hold him for further proceedings. Among counsel's potential contributions, the Court stated, is "skilled examination . . . of witnesses [which] may expose fatal weaknesses in the [prosecution's] case that may lead the magistrate to refuse to bind the accused over." It cannot be gainsaid that what the Sixth Amendment mandated for Alabama's preliminary hearing it exacts equally for the federal preliminary hearing which, we repeat, is exclusively an exploration into probable cause to hold the accused to answer the prosecution further. Nor can it be doubted that *Coleman* demands more than the mere presence of counsel at the hearing. The right to counsel which *Coleman* declared would amount to no more than a pious overture unless it is a right to counsel able to function efficaciously in his client's behalf. The Sixth Amendment's guaranty of counsel is a pledge of effective assistance

14. While the standard of probable cause which the Government must meet at preliminary hearings is roughly equivalent to the standard required for issuance of an arrest warrant or for an arrest without a warrant . . . the procedure at preliminary hearings differs from that upon the issuance of a warrant or a warrantless arrest in at least one very important respect. That difference is the presence of the accused at the preliminary hearing and his right to cross-examine prosecution witnesses and introduce evidence in his own behalf. Arrest warrants, on the other hand, are issued upon the Government's ex parte presentation to a magistrate, and warrantless arrests are made on information communicated ex parte to arresting officers. The traditional function of the preliminary hearing is a second determination on probable cause, this time after according the accused a reasonable opportunity to rebut it. Unless the accused is indulged in that respect, the preliminary hearing is little more than a duplication of the probable cause decisions that foreran his arrest.

15. Ross v. Sirica, 380 F.2d [557] at 565 (statement of Judges McGowan and Leventhal).

16. 380 F.2d at 559.

17. Id.

by counsel, and *Coleman* makes it clear that federal preliminary hearings, as critical stages of criminal prosecutions, require no less. If the accused's counsel is reduced to a state of impotence in the discharge of this responsibility, it is evident that the accused is deprived of the very benefit which the Sixth Amendment's boon of counsel was designed to confer.

So, an accused is normally entitled to subpoenas compelling the attendance at his preliminary hearing of witnesses whose testimony promises appreciable assistance on the issue of probable cause. The test, our past utterances on the subject have indicated, couples the witness's materiality with an absence of good cause for not requiring his presence, and its operation does not depend upon which side might have been expected to call the witness. Certainly an accused will not in every instance qualify for a subpoena for the production of a Government witness at his preliminary hearing, but where he succeeds in a plausible showing that that witness could contribute significantly to the accuracy of the probable cause determination, the request for the subpoena should be granted. "This," we have said, "is consistent with the principal purpose of the preliminary hearing as a mechanism to determine whether the evidence is adequate to establish probable cause."[18]

We think the testimony of the undercover agent Dancis desired at his preliminary hearing met the standard of materiality. From aught that appears, he was the only available person who could testify to the two charged marijuana transfers from personal observation, and by the same token the only one who could directly identify the party responsible for them. Since probable cause to bind Dancis over for further prosecution depended on the caliber of the Government's showing that he was that party and that what he did on the two occasions under scrutiny was illegal, it seems clear that the witness he requested could have given testimony bearing critically upon those matters. In Washington v. Clemmer[19] it was the complainant in a rape case who was sought, and in Ross v. Sirica the only three eyewitnesses to a murder. In both cases we held that denial of the accused's access to them was error, and it appears to us that the sole eyewitness to the transgressions laid to Dancis was equally material.

As we admonished in *Ross*, "[w]hatever the full reach of the accused's subpoena rights at a preliminary hearing . . . he is entitled to compel the attendance of eyewitnesses unless, of course, 'because of physical or psychological disability in a particular case' such witnesses cannot attend."[20] That seems the more so when the nature of the Government's presentation at Dancis' preliminary hearing is taken fully into account. The Government offered but one witness, and he could testify on the vital issues of offenses and identity only from hearsay, and it is evident that that weakened the showing. To the extent that hearsay is employed, the effort to establish probable cause becomes more prone to attack since the reliability of the

18. Ross v. Sirica, supra note 15, 380 F.2d at 560.

19. . . . [339 F.2d 715, 725 (D.C.Cir. 1964)].

20. Ross v. Sirica, supra n.15, 380 F.2d at 560, quoting Washington v. Clemmer [330 F.2d 715 (D.C.Cir.1964)] at 718 n.11.

absent hearsay declarant always becomes an added factor to be reckoned with. In *Ross*, where, similarly to Dancis' case the Government's one witness at a preliminary hearing on a murder charge was a police officer who could merely relay what three eyewitnesses had told him about the crime, two judges of this court aptly observed, without dispute from the rest, that

> A judicial officer engaged in a judicial determination of probable cause can hardly rest easy solely with the hearsay account of the policeman of what these eyewitnesses told him if the eyewitnesses can be available, so that he can listen to their versions and observe their demeanor, and provide an opportunity to defense counsel to explore their account on cross-examination. The presence of those witnesses impresses us as falling within the orbit of the rights conferred upon the accused by the fourth sentence of Rule 5(c). . . .[21]

Indeed, the problem addressed in *Ross* is compounded in the situation before us now. The Government's evidence at Dancis' preliminary hearing was not only hearsay but also hearsay without any apparent means of refutation whatever. The undercover agent was not only absent from the hearing but at the time was also totally unidentified. He did not sign the complaint against Dancis, nor was he named in it, and the testimony at the hearing referred to him simply by his code name "John P." Defense counsel's inquiries on cross-examination as to his real name, and even as to generic characteristics, drew objections from the Government which the magistrate sustained. There was little or nothing in the Government's presentation to lend credit to the reliability of either the agent or the observations purportedly incriminating and identifying Dancis. It is difficult to imagine a case wherein the accused was more helpless to defend against a hearsay attribution of probable cause.

To say, as we do, that the testimony of the absent witness was material does not mean necessarily that the refusal of the subpoena was error vitiating the preliminary hearing. A refusal may be justified, and if it is a finding of probable cause climaxing the hearing must stand. The record before us, however, is singularly devoid of any such justification. There is no hint that the undercover officer was physically unamenable to a subpoena or in any way disabled from responding to it. There is no suggestion that his information about the episodes under exploration was to any extent privileged from compulsory disclosure. Nor is there a basis for attributing the denial of the subpoena to the exigencies of any undercover operation. The magistrate did not predicate the denial upon any of these grounds, nor did the Government even urge any of them. And to the extent that the record may furnish indications that the magistrate was satisfied on probable cause without hearing from the undercover agent, it suffices to repeat that the issue thereon cannot properly be resolved without accom-

21. Ross v. Sirica, supra n.15, 380 F.2d at 565 (statement of Judges McGowan and Leventhal) (footnote omitted). See also Washington v. Clemmer [330 F.2d 715 (D.C.Cir. 1964)] at 728.

modating reasonable demands of the prosecution and the defense for the production of evidence capable of shaping the outcome.

. . .[22]

---

301. See United States v. King, 482 F.2d 768 (D.C.Cir.1973), in which, relying on *Coleman*, above, the court held that in the absence of reasons why the complainant was unavailable, a defendant charged with rape was entitled to a subpoena for her attendance as a witness. "It was, of course, possible—perhaps probable—that her testimony would have been unhelpful or even damaging to appellant, but it cannot be gainsaid that it also could have weakened or destroyed probable cause. With that capability, it was for appellant, not the judge, to say whether the try was to be made." Id. at 775.

302. Review. In what circumstances, by what procedure, can a magistrate's determination that there is probable cause to believe that a person has committed a crime be challenged? See DiCesare v. Chernenko, 303 F.2d 423 (4th Cir.1962); United States v. Vassallo, 282 F.Supp. 928 (E.D.Pa.1968); United States v. Florida, 165 F.Supp. 328 (E.D.Ark.1958); United States v. Zerbst, 111 F.Supp. 807 (E.D.S.C.1953).

The preliminary hearing in federal procedure is evidently something of a hybrid. Ostensibly intended to determine whether there is a basis for holding the defendant for trial, it rarely serves that function explicitly because the matter of bail is resolved before the hearing takes place. A determination that there is not probable cause is rare and, in any case, would affect the defendant's situation only if the prosecutor did not obtain an indictment and proceeded by information. On the other hand, although the preliminary hearing is not intended to be a pretrial proceeding, it may serve a number of pretrial functions for the defense, as the courts recognized in Coleman v. Alabama and Coleman v. Burnett, pp. 545, 555 above. In view of these conflicting considerations, how should the magistrate proceed? Would it be desirable to assign to the preliminary hearing functions expressly related not only to the defendant's present detention or binding over but also to the subsequent prosecution? If so, how could that be accomplished without converting the preliminary hearing into a mini-trial? If it were intended expressly to serve pretrial functions like discovery and fixing testimony, how ought its procedures be modified?

---

[22] The court remanded the case to the district court for an appropriate remedy consistent with the fact that Dancis had already been indicted; among the possible remedies, the court said, were disclosure of the agent's testimony before the grand jury, a deposition of the agent by written interrogatories, and so forth.

CHAPTER 8

BAIL

"[The] tendency to rely on only polar alternatives is at its worst in our law of conditional release pending trial. American practice almost universally utilizes only two extremes: release upon purchase of a bond without any formal police or other supervision during what may be a prolonged pretrial period, or total imprisonment under the most deplorable conditions to be found in American penological practice today. The one extreme subjects society to unjustifiable risks, the other severely penalizes the unconvicted detainee." Foote, "Introduction: The Comparative Study of Conditional Release," 108 U. Pa. L. Rev. 290, 299–300 (1960).

303. U.S. Constitution amend. VIII: "Excessive bail shall not be required. . . ."

"We take for granted that, contrary to earlier cases . . . the prohibition in the Eighth Amendment against requiring excessive bail must now be regarded as applying to the States, under the Fourteenth Amendment." Pilkinton v. Circuit Court of Howell County, 324 F.2d 45, 46 (8th Cir.1963).

"The right to release before trial is conditioned upon the accused's giving adequate assurance that he will stand trial and submit to sentence if found guilty. . . . Like the ancient practice of securing the oaths of responsible persons to stand as sureties for the accused, the modern practice of requiring a bail bond or the deposit of a sum of money subject to forfeiture serves as additional assurance of the presence of an accused. Bail set at a figure higher than an amount reasonably calculated to fulfill this purpose is 'excessive' under the Eighth Amendment." Stack v. Boyle, 342 U.S. 1, 4–5 (1951).

Upholding the denial of bail to certain aliens taken into custody pending a determination of deportability, the Court said in Carlson v. Landon, 342 U.S. 524, 545–46 (1952): "The bail clause was lifted with slight changes from the English Bill of Rights Act. In England that clause has never been thought to accord a right to bail in all cases, but merely to provide that bail shall not be excessive in those cases where it is proper to grant bail. When this clause was carried over into our Bill of Rights, nothing was said that indicated any different concept. The Eighth Amendment has not prevented Congress from defining the classes of cases in which bail shall be allowed in this country. Thus in criminal cases bail is not compulsory where the punishment may be death. Indeed, the very language of the Amendment fails to say all arrests must be bailable."

Dissenting, Justice Black observed that "when scrutinized with a hostile eye" the "literal language of the framers" of the Eighth Amendment might lend itself to the Court's interpretation, but it was nonetheless a "weird, devitalizing interpretation." Id. at 556.

See Hunt v. Roth, 648 F.2d 1148 (8th Cir.1981), vacated as moot sub nom. Murphy v. Hunt, 455 U.S. 478 (1982), holding that a provision of the Nebraska Constitution denying bail to persons accused of specified noncapital sexual offenses is a violation of the Eighth Amendment. The subject of bail in capital cases is discussed at length in State v. Menillo, 268 A.2d 667 (Conn.1970). See White v. United States, 412 F.2d 145 (D.C.Cir.1968) (defendant in capital case released on personal recognizance with conditions).

A court has inherent power to order that a defendant be detained before trial, in order to protect witnesses. United States v. Payden, 768 F.2d 487 (2d Cir.1985) (defendant attempted to contract for murder of witness; detention order upheld).

In United States v. Dohm, 618 F.2d 1169 (5th Cir.1980), the court rejected the defendant's claim that incriminating statements at the initial appearance, made in order to secure reasonable bail, should not be admitted at trial, lest a defendant be forced to choose between his constitutional right to bail and the privilege against compulsory self-incrimination; provided proper warnings are given, the statements are admissible. But see United States v. Perry, 788 F.2d 100 (3d Cir.1986), holding that the presumption of dangerousness under the federal bail statute, see p. 713 below, requires that the defendant's testimony have use immunity to avoid unconstitutionality.

304. It is well-established that bail is not excessive in the constitutional sense merely because the defendant is unable to pay it. E.g., Hodgdon v. United States, 365 F.2d 679 (8th Cir.1966). In United States v. McConnell, 842 F.2d 105 (5th Cir.1988), the court held that that rule is not contradicted by the provision of 18 U.S.C. § 3142(c)(2) that bail may not include "a financial condition that results in the pretrial detention of the person." The court said that although that provision precludes the automatic setting of high bail in order to detain, bail can be set as high as necessary to assure the person's appearance, even if such amount is more than the person can pay and results in his detention.

The problem of money bail for indigents is discussed extensively in Pugh v. Rainwater, 572 F.2d 1053 (5th Cir.1978). The court concluded that it is not a denial of equal protection to permit the setting of money bail for an indigent defendant without a presumption that other forms of bail are to be used when practicable. See also Schilb v. Kuebel, 404 U.S. 357 (1971), in which the Court upheld, against the argument that it violated the Equal Protection Clause, the Illinois 10%-deposit practice, pursuant to which 10% of the deposit (1% of the amount of bail) is retained by the clerk of court as "costs"; the amount retained is used to meet the cost of administering the bail system.

"We are faced with the familiar argument that appellant claims to be an indigent and cannot put up a bond of this size and consequently he should be released on his personal recognizance and upon compliance with non-financial conditions. When this argument is carried to its logical

AO 470 (Rev. 8/85) Order of Temporary Detention

UNITED STATES DISTRICT COURT

_______________ District of _______________

UNITED STATES OF AMERICA

V.

ORDER OF TEMPORARY DETENTION PENDING HEARING PURSUANT TO BAIL REFORM ACT

____
Defendant

Case Number:

Upon motion of the _______________, it is ORDERED that a detention hearing is set for _______________ * at _______________
Date *Time*

before _______________
Name of Judicial Officer

____
Location of Judicial Officer

Pending this hearing, the defendant shall be held in custody by (the United States marshal)

(_______________) and produced for the hearing.
Other Custodial Official

Date: _______________ _______________
Judicial Officer

*If not held immediately upon defendant's first appearance, the hearing may be continued for up to three days upon motion of the Government, or up to five days upon motion of the defendant. 18 U.S.C. § 3142(f)(2).

A hearing is required whenever the conditions set forth in 18 U.S.C. § 3142(f) are present. Subsection (1) sets forth the grounds that may be asserted only by the attorney for the Government; subsection (2) states that a hearing is mandated upon the motion of the attorney for the Government or upon the judicial officer's own motion if there is a serious risk that the defendant (a) will flee or (b) will obstruct or attempt to obstruct justice, or threaten, injure, or intimidate, or attempt to threaten, injure, or intimidate a prospective witness or juror.

conclusion, every indigent person would always be released on non-financial conditions and the requirement for reasonable bail would be meaningless as it would be turned into a requirement for release of all indigents without bail and solely on non-financial conditions in every instance. In our opinion, the requirement for reasonable bail is a direction that bail be imposed that is reasonable when consideration is given to all circumstances of the case: the nature of the crime, its enormity, the character of the defendant, his ties to the community and similar items." United States v. Cook, 442 F.2d 723, 724 (D.C.Cir.1970).

Section 3142(c)(2) of the federal bail statute, above, explicitly rejects the practice familiar in the past (and the present practice in many state courts) of setting bail high enough to ensure the defendant's detention rather than as a condition of release. The practice was a way of avoiding doubts, addressed in the federal statute, about pretrial detention of someone on the ground that his release was dangerous to the community.

Bail of $1,000,000 cash was upheld pursuant to § 3142(c), in United States v. Szott, 768 F.2d 159 (7th Cir.1985). The court said: "The statute does not require that a defendant be able to post the bail 'readily.' The purpose of bail is not served unless losing the sum would be a deeply-felt hurt to the defendant and his family; the hurt must be so severe that defendant will return for trial rather than flee. This implies that a court must be able to induce a defendant to go to great lengths to raise the funds without violating the condition in § 3142(c) that bail may not be used to deny release altogether." Id. at 160.

The court went further in United States v. McConnell, 842 F.2d 105 (5th Cir.1988). It said that if no other condition will assure the defendant's appearance at trial, bail may be set at an amount higher than what the defendant is able to meet, without violating § 3142(c). The court relied on the legislative history of the Bail Reform Act, which indicated that a court may fix bail in an amount high enough to assure the defendant's appearance, without regard to the defendant's ability to meet the amount.

BAIL REFORM ACT OF 1984

18 U.S.C. §§ 3141–3150

§ 3141. Release and detention authority generally

(a) Pending trial. A judicial officer authorized to order the arrest of a person under section 3041 of this title before whom an arrested person is brought shall order that such person be released or detained, pending judicial proceedings, under this chapter.

(b) Pending sentence or appeal. A judicial officer of a court of original jurisdiction over an offense, or a judicial officer of a Federal appellate court, shall order that, pending imposition or execution of sentence, or pending appeal of conviction or sentence, a person be released or detained under this chapter.

§ 3142. Release or detention of a defendant pending trial

(a) In general. Upon the appearance before a judicial officer of a person charged with an offense, the judicial officer shall issue an order that, pending trial, the person be—

(1) released on personal recognizance or upon execution of an unsecured appearance bond, under subsection (b) of this section;

(2) released on a condition or combination of conditions under subsection (c) of this section;

(3) temporarily detained to permit revocation of conditional release, deportation, or exclusion under subsection (d) of this section; or

(4) detained under subsection (e) of this section.

(b) Release on personal recognizance or unsecured appearance bond. The judicial officer shall order the pretrial release of the person on personal recognizance, or upon execution of an unsecured appearance bond in an amount specified by the court, subject to the condition that the person not commit a Federal, State, or local crime during the period of release, unless the judicial officer determines that such release will not reasonably assure the appearance of the person as required or will endanger the safety of any other person or the community.

(c) Release on conditions.

(1) If the judicial officer determines that the release described in subsection (b) of this section will not reasonably assure the appearance of the person as required or will endanger the safety of any other person or the community, such judicial officer shall order the pretrial release of the person—

(A) subject to the condition that the person not commit a Federal, State, or local crime during the period of release; and

(B) subject to the least restrictive further condition, or combination of conditions, that such judicial officer determines will reasonably assure the appearance of the person as required and the safety of any other person and the community, which may include the condition that the person—

(i) remain in the custody of a designated person, who agrees to assume supervision and to report any violation of a release condition to the court, if the designated person is able reasonably to assure the judicial officer that the person will appear as required and will not pose a danger to the safety of any other person or the community;

(ii) maintain employment, or, if unemployed, actively seek employment;

(iii) maintain or commence an educational program;

(iv) abide by specified restrictions on personal associations, place of abode, or travel;

(v) avoid all contact with an alleged victim of the crime and with a potential witness who may testify concerning the offense;

(vi) report on a regular basis to a designated law enforcement agency, pretrial services agency, or other agency;

(vii) comply with a specified curfew;

(viii) refrain from possessing a firearm, destructive device, or other dangerous weapon;

(ix) refrain from excessive use of alcohol, or any use of a narcotic drug or other controlled substance, as defined in section 102 of the Controlled Substances Act (21 U.S.C. 802), without a prescription by a licensed medical practitioner;

(x) undergo available medical, psychological, or psychiatric treatment, including treatment for drug or alcohol dependency, and remain in a specified institution if required for that purpose;

(xi) execute an agreement to forfeit upon failing to appear as required, property of a sufficient unencumbered value, including money, as is reasonably necessary to assure the appearance of the person as required, and shall provide the court with proof of ownership and the value of the property along with information regarding existing encumbrances as the judicial office may require;

(xii) execute a bail bond with solvent sureties; who will execute an agreement to forfeit in such amount as is reasonably necessary to assure appearance of the person as required and shall provide the court with information regarding the value of the assets and liabilities of the surety if other than an approved surety and the nature and extent of encumbrances against the surety's property; such surety shall have a net worth which shall have sufficient unencumbered value to pay the amount of the bail bond;

(xiii) return to custody for specified hours following release for employment, schooling, or other limited purposes; and

(xiv) satisfy any other condition that is reasonably necessary to assure the appearance of the person as required and to assure the safety of any other person and the community.

(2) The judicial officer may not impose a financial condition that results in the pretrial detention of the person.

(3) The judicial officer may at any time amend the order to impose additional or different conditions of release.

(d) Temporary detention to permit revocation of conditional release, deportation, or exclusion. If the judicial officer determines that—

(1) such person—

(A) is, and was at the time the offense was committed, on—

(i) release pending trial for a felony under Federal, State, or local law;

(ii) release pending imposition or execution of sentence, appeal of sentence or conviction, or completion of sentence, for any offense under Federal, State or local law; or

(iii) probation or parole for any offense under Federal, State, or local law; or

(B) is not a citizen of the United States or lawfully admitted for permanent residence, as defined in section 101(a)(20) of the Immigration and Nationality Act (8 U.S.C. 1101(a)(20)); and

(2) the person may flee or pose a danger to any other person or the community;

such judicial officer shall order the detention of such person, for a period of not more than ten days, excluding Saturdays, Sundays, and holidays, and direct the attorney for the Government to notify the appropriate court, probation or parole official, or State or local law enforcement official, or the appropriate official of the Immigration and Naturalization Service. If the official fails or declines to take the person into custody during that period, the person shall be treated in accordance with the other provisions of this section, notwithstanding the applicability of other provisions of law governing release pending trial or deportation or exclusion proceedings. If temporary detention is sought under paragraph (1)(B) of this subsection, the person has the burden of proving to the court such person's United States citizenship or lawful admission for permanent residence.

(e) Detention. If, after a hearing pursuant to the provisions of subsection (f) of this section, the judicial officer finds that no condition or combination of conditions will reasonably assure the appearance of the person as required and the safety of any other person and the community, such judicial officer shall order the detention of the person before trial. In a case described in subsection (f)(1) of this section, a rebuttable presumption arises that no condition or combination of conditions will reasonably assure the safety of any other person and the community if such judicial officer finds that—

(1) the person has been convicted of a Federal offense that is described in subsection (f)(1) of this section, or of a State or local offense that would have been an offense described in subsection (f)(1) of this section if a circumstance giving rise to Federal jurisdiction had existed;

(2) the offense described in paragraph (1) of this subsection was committed while the person was on release pending trial for a Federal, State, or local offense; and

(3) a period of not more than five years has elapsed since the date of conviction, or the release of the person from imprisonment, for the

offense described in paragraph (1) of this subsection, whichever is later.

Subject to rebuttal by the person, it shall be presumed that no condition or combination of conditions will reasonably assure the appearance of the person as required and the safety of the community if the judicial officer finds that there is probable cause to believe that the person committed an offense for which a maximum term of imprisonment of ten years or more is prescribed in the Controlled Substances Act (21 U.S.C. 801 et seq.), the Controlled Substances Import and Export Act (21 U.S.C. 951 et seq.), the Maritime Drug Law Enforcement Act (46 U.S.C.App. 1901 et seq.), or an offense under section 924(c), 956(a), or 2332b of this title, or an offense involving a minor victim under section 1201, 1591, 2241, 2242, 2244(a)(1), 2245, 2251, 2251A, 2252(a)(1), 2252(a)(2), 2252(a)(3), 2252A(a)(1), 2252A(a)(2), 2252A(a)(3), 2252A(a)(4), 2260, 2421, 2422, 2423, or 2425 of this title.

(f) Detention hearing. The judicial officer shall hold a hearing to determine whether any condition or combination of conditions set forth in subsection (c) of this section will reasonably assure the appearance of such person as required and the safety of any other person and the community—

(1) upon motion of the attorney for the Government, in a case that involves—

(A) a crime of violence;

(B) an offense for which the maximum sentence is life imprisonment or death;

(C) an offense for which a maximum term of imprisonment of ten years or more is prescribed in the Controlled Substances Act (21 U.S.C. 801 et seq.), the Controlled Substances Import and Export Act (21 U.S.C. 951 et seq.), or the Maritime Drug Law Enforcement Act (46 U.S.C.App. 1901 et seq.); or

(D) any felony if the person has been convicted of two or more offenses described in subparagraphs (A) through (C) of this paragraph, or two or more State or local offenses that would have been offenses described in subparagraphs (A) through (C) of this paragraph if a circumstance giving rise to Federal jurisdiction had existed, or a combination of such offenses; or

(2) upon motion of the attorney for the Government or upon the judicial officer's own motion, in a case that involves—

(A) a serious risk that such person will flee; or

(B) a serious risk that the person will obstruct or attempt to obstruct justice, or threaten, injure, or intimidate, or attempt to threaten, injure, or intimidate, a prospective witness or juror.

The hearing shall be held immediately upon the person's first appearance before the judicial officer unless that person, or the attorney for the Government, seeks a continuance. Except for good cause, a continuance on motion of the person may not exceed five days (not including any intermediate Saturday, Sunday, or legal holiday), and a continuance on motion of the attorney for the Government may not exceed three days (not including any intermediate Saturday, Sunday, or legal holiday). During a continuance, such person shall be detained, and the judicial officer, on motion of the attorney for the Government or sua sponte, may order that, while in custody, a person who appears to be a narcotics addict receive a medical examination to determine whether such person is an addict. At the hearing, such person has the right to be represented by counsel, and, if financially unable to obtain adequate representation, to have counsel appointed. The person shall be afforded an opportunity to testify, to present witnesses, to cross-examine witnesses who appear at the hearing, and to present information by proffer or otherwise. The rules concerning admissibility of evidence in criminal trials do not apply to the presentation and consideration of information at the hearing. The facts the judicial officer uses to support a finding pursuant to subsection (e) that no condition or combination of conditions will reasonably assure the safety of any other person and the community shall be supported by clear and convincing evidence. The person may be detained pending completion of the hearing. The hearing may be reopened, before or after a determination by the judicial officer, at any time before trial if the judicial officer finds that information exists that was not known to the movant at the time of the hearing and that has a material bearing on the issue whether there are conditions of release that will reasonably assure the appearance of the person as required and the safety of any other person and the community.

(g) Factors to be considered. The judicial officer shall, in determining whether there are conditions of release that will reasonably assure the appearance of the person as required and the safety of any other person and the community, take into account the available information concerning—

(1) the nature and circumstances of the offense charged, including whether the offense is a crime of violence or involves a narcotic drug;

(2) the weight of the evidence against the person;

(3) the history and characteristics of the person, including—

(A) the person's character, physical and mental condition, family ties, employment, financial resources, length of residence in the community, community ties, past conduct, history relating to drug or alcohol abuse, criminal history, and record concerning appearance at court proceedings; and

(B) whether, at the time of the current offense or arrest, the person was on probation, on parole, or on other release pending trial, sentencing, appeal, or completion of sentence for an offense under Federal, State, or local law; and

(4) the nature and seriousness of the danger to any person or the community that would be posed by the person's release. In considering the conditions of release described in subsection (c)(1)(B)(xi) or (c)(1)(B)(xii) of this section, the judicial officer may upon his own motion, or shall upon the motion of the Government, conduct an inquiry into the source of the property to be designated for potential forfeiture or offered as collateral to secure a bond, and shall decline to accept the designation, or the use as collateral, of property that,

because of its source, will not reasonably assure the appearance of the person as required.

(h) Contents of release order. In a release order issued under subsection (b) or (c) of this section, the judicial officer shall—

(1) include a written statement that sets forth all the conditions to which the release is subject, in a manner sufficiently clear and specific to serve as a guide for the person's conduct; and

(2) advise the person of—

(A) the penalties for violating a condition of release, including the penalties for committing an offense while on pretrial release;

(B) the consequences of violating a condition of release, including the immediate issuance of a warrant for the person's arrest; and

(C) sections 1503 of this title (relating to intimidation of witnesses, jurors, and officers of the court), 1510 (relating to obstruction of criminal investigations), 1512 (tampering with a witness, victim, or an informant), and 1513 (retaliating against a witness, victim, or an informant).

(i) Contents of detention order. In a detention order issued under subsection (e) of this section, the judicial officer shall—

(1) include written findings of fact and a written statement of the reasons for the detention;

(2) direct that the person be committed to the custody of the Attorney General for confinement in a corrections facility separate, to the extent practicable, from persons awaiting or serving sentences or being held in custody pending appeal;

(3) direct that the person be afforded reasonable opportunity for private consultation with counsel; and

(4) direct that, on order of a court of the United States or on request of an attorney for the Government, the person in charge of the corrections facility in which the person is confined deliver the person to a United States marshal for the purpose of an appearance in connection with a court proceeding.

The judicial officer may, by subsequent order, permit the temporary release of the person, in the custody of a United States marshal or another appropriate person, to the extent that the judicial officer determines such release to be necessary for preparation of the person's defense or for another compelling reason.

(j) Presumption of innocence. Nothing in this section shall be construed as modifying or limiting the presumption of innocence.

§ 3143. Release or detention of a defendant pending sentence or appeal

(a) Release or detention pending sentence.

(1) Except as provided in paragraph (2), the judicial officer shall order that a person who has been found guilty of an offense and who is awaiting imposition or execution of sentence, other than a person for whom the applicable guideline promulgated pursuant to 28 U.S.C. 994 does not recommend a term of imprisonment, be detained, unless the judicial officer finds by clear and convincing evidence that the person is not likely to flee or pose a danger to the safety of any other person or the community if released under section 3142(b) or (c). If the judicial officer makes such a finding, such judicial officer shall order the release of the person in accordance with section 3142(b) or (c).

(2) The judicial officer shall order that a person who has been found guilty of an offense in a case described in subparagraph (A), (B), or (C) of subsection (f)(1) of section 3142 and is awaiting imposition or execution of sentence be detained unless—

(A)(i) the judicial officer finds there is a substantial likelihood that a motion for acquittal or new trial will be granted; or

(ii) an attorney for the Government has recommended that no sentence of imprisonment be imposed on the person; and

(B) the judicial officer finds by clear and convincing evidence that the person is not likely to flee or pose a danger to any other person or the community.

(b) Release or detention pending appeal by the defendant.

(1) Except as provided in paragraph (2), the judicial officer shall order that a person who has been found guilty of an offense and sentenced to a term of imprisonment, and who has filed an appeal or a petition for a writ of certiorari, be detained, unless the judicial officer finds—

(A) by clear and convincing evidence that the person is not likely to flee or pose a danger to the safety of any other person or the community if released under section 3142(b) or (c) of this title; and

(B) that the appeal is not for the purpose of delay and raises a substantial question of law or fact likely to result in—

(i) reversal,

(ii) an order for a new trial,

(iii) a sentence that does not include a term of imprisonment, or

(iv) a reduced sentence to a term of imprisonment less than the total of the time already served plus the expected duration of the appeal process.

If the judicial officer makes such findings, such judicial officer shall order the release of the person in accordance with section 3142(b) or (c) of this title, except that in the circumstance described in subparagraph (B)(iv) of this paragraph, the judicial officer shall order the detention terminated at the expiration of the likely reduced sentence.

(2) The judicial officer shall order that a person who has been found guilty of an offense in a case described in subparagraph (A), (B), or (C) of subsection (f)(1) of section 3142 and sentenced to a term of imprisonment,

and who has filed an appeal or a petition for a writ of certiorari, be detained.

(c) Release or detention pending appeal by the government. The judicial officer shall treat a defendant in a case in which an appeal has been taken by the United States under section 3731 of this title, in accordance with section 3142 of this title, unless the defendant is otherwise subject to a release or detention order. Except as provided in subsection (b) of this section, the judicial officer, in a case in which an appeal has been taken by the United States under section 3742, shall—

(1) if the person has been sentenced to a term of imprisonment, order that person detained; and

(2) in any other circumstance, release or detain the person under section 3142.

§ 3144. Release or detention of a material witness

. . . [p. 965 note 494 below]

§ 3145. Review and appeal of a release or detention order

(a) Review of a release order. If a person is ordered released by a magistrate, or by a person other than a judge of a court having original jurisdiction over the offense and other than a Federal appellate court—

(1) the attorney for the Government may file, with the court having original jurisdiction over the offense, a motion for revocation of the order or amendment of the conditions of release; and

(2) the person may file, with the court having original jurisdiction over the offense, a motion for amendment of the conditions of release.

The motion shall be determined promptly.

(b) Review of a detention order. If a person is ordered detained by a magistrate judge, or by a person other than a judge of a court having original jurisdiction over the offense and other than a Federal appellate court, the person may file, with the court having original jurisdiction over the offense, a motion for revocation or amendment of the order. The motion shall be determined promptly.

(c) Appeal from a release or detention order. An appeal from a release or detention order, or from a decision denying revocation or amendment of such an order, is governed by the provisions of section 1291 of title 28 and section 3731 of this title.[1] The appeal shall be determined promptly. A person subject to detention pursuant to section 3143(a)(2) or (b)(2), and who meets the conditions of release set forth in section 3143(a)(1) or (b)(1), may be ordered released, under appropriate conditions, by the judicial officer, if it is clearly shown that there are exceptional reasons why such person's detention would not be appropriate.

1. Section 1291 of title 28 provides the general statutory basis for appeals from judgments of the federal district courts. Section 3731 of title 18, so far as pertinent to bail, provides: "An appeal by the United States shall lie to a court of appeals from a decision or order, entered by a district court of the United States, granting the release of a person charged with or convicted of an offense, or denying a motion for revocation of, or modification of the conditions of, a decision or order granting release."

§ 3146. Penalty for failure to appear

(a) Offense. Whoever, having been released under this chapter knowingly—

(1) fails to appear before a court as required by the conditions of release; or

(2) fails to surrender for service of sentence pursuant to a court order;

shall be punished as provided in subsection (b) of this section.

(b) Punishment.

(1) The punishment for an offense under this section is—

(A) if the person was released in connection with a charge of, or while awaiting sentence, surrender for service of sentence, or appeal or certiorari after conviction for—

(i) an offense punishable by death, life imprisonment, or imprisonment for a term of 15 years or more, a fine under this title or imprisonment for not more than ten years, or both;

(ii) an offense punishable by imprisonment for a term of five years or more, a fine under this title or imprisonment for not more than five years, or both;

(iii) any other felony, a fine under this title or imprisonment for not more than two years, or both; or

(iv) a misdemeanor, a fine under this chapter or imprisonment for not more than one year, or both; and

(B) if the person was released for appearance as a material witness, a fine under this chapter or imprisonment for not more than one year, or both.

(2) A term of imprisonment imposed under this section shall be consecutive to the sentence of imprisonment for any other offense.

(c) Affirmative defense. It is an affirmative defense to a prosecution under this section that uncontrollable circumstances prevented the person from appearing or surrendering, and that the person did not contribute to the creation of such circumstances in reckless disregard of the requirement to appear or surrender, and that the person appeared or surrendered as soon as such circumstances ceased to exist.

(d) Declaration of forfeiture. If a person fails to appear before a court as required, and the person executed an appearance bond pursuant to section 3142(b) of this title or is subject to the release condition set forth in clause (xi) or (xii) of section 3142(c)(1)(B) of this title, the judicial officer may, regardless of whether the person has been charged with an offense under this section, declare any property designated pursuant to that section to be forfeited to the United States.

AO 199A (Rev. 6/97) Order Setting Conditions of Release Page 1 of ______ Pages

UNITED STATES DISTRICT COURT

______________________ **District of** ______________________

United States of America

V.

ORDER SETTING CONDITIONS OF RELEASE

____
Defendant

Case Number:

IT IS ORDERED that the release of the defendant is subject to the following conditions:

(1) The defendant shall not commit any offense in violation of federal, state or local law while on release in this case.

(2) The defendant shall immediately advise the court, defense counsel and the U.S. attorney in writing before any change in address and telephone number.

(3) The defendant shall appear at all proceedings as required and shall surrender for service of any sentence imposed as directed. The defendant shall appear at (if blank, to be notified) ______________________
Place

______________________ on ______________________
Date and Time

Release on Personal Recognizance or Unsecured Bond

IT IS FURTHER ORDERED that the defendant be released provided that:

(✔) (4) The defendant promises to appear at all proceedings as required and to surrender for service of any sentence imposed.

( ) (5) The defendant executes an unsecured bond binding the defendant to pay the United States the sum of ______________________ dollars ($ __________) in the event of a failure to appear as required or to surrender as directed for service of any sentence imposed.

DISTRIBUTION: COURT DEFENDANT PRETRIAL SERVICES U.S. ATTORNEY U.S. MARSHAL

AO 472 (Rev. 3/86) Order of Detention Pending Trial

UNITED STATES DISTRICT COURT

____________________ District of ____________________

UNITED STATES OF AMERICA
V.

ORDER OF DETENTION PENDING TRIAL

____________________ Case Number:
Defendant

In accordance with the Bail Reform Act, 18 U.S.C. § 3142(f), a detention hearing has been held. I conclude that the following facts require the detention of the defendant pending trial in this case.

Part I—Findings of Fact

☐ (1) The defendant is charged with an offense described in 18 U.S.C. § 3142(f)(1) and has been convicted of a ☐ federal offense ☐ state or local offense that would have been a federal offense if a circumstance giving rise to federal jurisdiction had existed - that is
- ☐ a crime of violence as defined in 18 U.S.C. § 3156(a)(4).
- ☐ an offense for which the maximum sentence is life imprisonment or death.
- ☐ an offense for which a maximum term of imprisonment of ten years or more is prescribed in ____________________.*
- ☐ a felony that was committed after the defendant had been convicted of two or more prior federal offenses described in 18 U.S.C. § 3142(f)(1)(A)-(C), or comparable state or local offenses.

☐ (2) The offense described in finding (1) was committed while the defendant was on release pending trial for a federal, state or local offense.
☐ (3) A period of not more than five years has elapsed since the ☐ date of conviction ☐ release of the defendant from imprisonment for the offense described in finding (1).
☐ (4) Findings Nos. (1), (2) and (3) establish a rebuttable presumption that no condition or combination of conditions will reasonably assure the safety of (an) other person(s) and the community. I further find that the defendant has not rebutted this presumption.

Alternative Findings (A)

☐ (1) There is probable cause to believe that the defendant has committed an offense
- ☐ for which a maximum term of imprisonment of ten years or more is prescribed in ____________________.
- ☐ under 18 U.S.C. § 924(c).

☐ (2) The defendant has not rebutted the presumption established by finding 1 that no condition or combination of conditions will reasonably assure the appearance of the defendant as required and the safety of the community.

Alternative Findings (B)

☐ (1) There is a serious risk that the defendant will not appear.
☐ (2) There is a serious risk that the defendant will endanger the safety of another person or the community.

Part II—Written Statement of Reasons for Detention

I find that the credible testimony and information submitted at the hearing establishes by ☐ clear and convincing evidence ☐ a preponderance of the evidence that

Part III—Directions Regarding Detention

The defendant is committed to the custody of the Attorney General or his designated representative for confinement in a corrections facility separate, to the extent practicable, from persons awaiting or serving sentences or being held in custody pending appeal. The defendant shall be afforded a reasonable opportunity for private consultation with defense counsel. On order of a court of the United States or on request of an attorney for the Government, the person in charge of the corrections facility shall deliver the defendant to the United States marshal for the purpose of an appearance in connection with a court proceeding.

____________________ ____________________
Date *Signature of Judicial Officer*

____
Name of Judicial Officer *Title of Judicial Officer*

*Insert as applicable: (a) Controlled Substances Act (21 U.S.C. § 801 *et seq.*); (b) Controlled Substances Import and Export Act (21 U.S.C. § 951 *et seq.*); or (c) Section 1 of Act of Sept. 15, 1980 (21 U.S.C. § 955a).

§ 3147. Penalty for an offense committed while on release

A person convicted of an offense committed while released under this chapter shall be sentenced, in addition to the sentence prescribed for the offense to—

(1) a term of imprisonment of not more than ten years if the offense is a felony; or

(2) a term of imprisonment of not more than one year if the offense is a misdemeanor.

A term of imprisonment imposed under this section shall be consecutive to any other sentence of imprisonment.

§ 3148. Sanctions for violation of a release condition

(a) Available sanctions. A person who has been released under section 3142 of this title, and who has violated a condition of his release, is subject to a revocation of release, an order of detention, and a prosecution of contempt of court.

(b) Revocation of release. The attorney for the Government may initiate a proceeding for revocation of an order of release by filing a motion with the district court. A judicial officer may issue a warrant for the arrest of a person charged with violating a condition of release, and the person shall be brought before a judicial officer in the district in which such person's arrest was ordered for a proceeding in accordance with this section. To the extent practicable, a person charged with violating the condition of release that such person not commit a Federal, State, or local crime during the period of release, shall be brought before the judicial officer who ordered the release and whose order is alleged to have been violated. The judicial officer shall enter an order of revocation and detention if, after a hearing, the judicial officer—

(1) finds that there is—

(A) probable cause to believe that the person has committed a Federal, State, or local crime while on release; or

(B) clear and convincing evidence that the person has violated any other condition of release; and

(2) finds that—

(A) based on the factors set forth in section 3142(g) of this title, there is no condition or combination of conditions of release that will assure that the person will not flee or pose a danger to the safety of any other person or the community; or

(B) the person is unlikely to abide by any condition or combination of conditions of release.

If there is probable cause to believe that, while on release, the person committed a Federal, State, or local felony, a rebuttable presumption arises that no condition or combination of conditions will assure that the person will not pose a danger to the safety of any other person or the community. If the judicial officer finds that there are conditions of release that will assure that the person will not flee or pose a danger to the safety of any other person or the community, and that the person will abide by such conditions, the judicial officer shall treat the person in accordance with the provisions of section 3142 of this title and may amend the conditions of release accordingly.

(c) Prosecution for contempt. The judicial officer may commence a prosecution for contempt, under section 401 of this title, if the person has violated a condition of release.

§ 3149. Surrender of an offender by a surety

A person charged with an offense, who is released upon the execution of an appearance bond with a surety, may be arrested by the surety, and if so arrested, shall be delivered promptly to a United States marshal and brought before a judicial officer. The judicial officer shall determine in accordance with the provisions of section 3148(b) whether to revoke the release of the person, and may absolve the surety of responsibility to pay all or part of the bond in accordance with the provisions of Rule 46 of the Federal Rules of Criminal Procedure. The person so committed shall be held in official detention until released pursuant to this chapter or another provision of law.

§ 3150. Applicability to a case removed from a State court

The provisions of this chapter apply to a criminal case removed to a Federal court from a State court.

---

305. In United States v. Salerno, 481 U.S. 739 (1987) (6–3), the Court upheld the Bail Reform Act against the challenge that its provision for the detention of a defendant before trial on the ground of dangerousness violated due process and the Eighth Amendment's bail clause.

With respect to due process, the Court said:

> Respondents first argue that the Act violates substantive due process because the pretrial detention it authorizes constitutes impermissible punishment before trial. . . . The Government, however, has never argued that pretrial detention could be upheld if it were "punishment." The Court of Appeals assumed that pretrial detention under the Bail Reform Act is regulatory, not penal, and we agree that it is.
>
> As an initial matter, the mere fact that a person is detained does not inexorably lead to the conclusion that the government has imposed punishment. . . . To determine whether a restriction on liberty constitutes impermissible punishment or permissible regulation, we first look to legislative intent. . . . Unless Congress expressly intended to impose punitive restrictions, the punitive-regulatory distinction turns on " 'whether an alternative purpose to which [the restriction] may rationally be connected is assignable for it, and whether it appears excessive in relation to the alternative purpose assigned [to it].' " [Schall v. Martin, 467 U.S. 253 (1984)], quoting Kennedy v. Mendoza-Martinez, 372 U.S. 144, 168–69 (1963).
>
> We conclude that the detention imposed by the Act falls on the regulatory side of the dichotomy. The legislative history of the Bail Reform Act clearly indicates that Congress did not formulate the

> pretrial detention provisions as punishment for dangerous individuals. . . . Congress instead perceived pretrial detention as a potential solution to a pressing societal problem. . . . There is no doubt that preventing danger to the community is a legitimate regulatory goal. . . .
>
> Nor are the incidents of pretrial detention excessive in relation to the regulatory goal Congress sought to achieve. The Bail Reform Act carefully limits the circumstances under which detention may be sought to the most serious of crimes. . . . The arrestee is entitled to a prompt detention hearing . . . and the maximum length of pretrial detention is limited by the stringent time limitations of the Speedy Trial Act. . . . Moreover, as in Schall v. Martin, the conditions of confinement envisioned by the Act "appear to reflect the regulatory purposes relied upon by the" Government. 467 U.S., at 270. As in *Schall*, the statute at issue here requires that detainees be housed in a "facility separate, to the extent practicable, from persons awaiting or serving sentences or being held in custody pending appeal." 18 U.S.C. § 3142(i)(2). We conclude, therefore, that the pretrial detention contemplated by the Bail Reform Act is regulatory in nature, and does not constitute punishment before trial in violation of the Due Process Clause.

Id. at 746–48.

Also under the Due Process Clause, the respondents argued that even as a regulatory measure, pretrial detention because of dangerousness is impermissible, without regard to the duration of detention. The Court said:

> We do not think the Clause lays down any such categorical imperative. We have repeatedly held that the Government's regulatory interest in community safety can, in appropriate circumstances, outweigh an individual's liberty interest. For example, in times of war or insurrection, when society's interest is at its peak, the Government may detain individuals whom the Government believes to be dangerous. . . . Even outside the exigencies of war, we have found that sufficiently compelling governmental interests can justify detention of dangerous persons. Thus, we have found no absolute constitutional barrier to detention of potentially dangerous resident aliens pending deportation proceedings. . . . We have also held that the government may detain mentally unstable individuals who present a danger to the public . . . and dangerous defendants who become incompetent to stand trial. . . . We have approved of postarrest regulatory detention of juveniles when they present a continuing danger to the community. . . . Even competent adults may face substantial liberty restrictions as a result of the operation of our criminal justice system. If the police suspect an individual of a crime, they may arrest and hold him until a neutral magistrate determines whether probable cause exists. . . . Finally, respondents concede and the Court of Appeals noted that an arrestee may be incarcerated until trial if he presents a risk of flight . . . or a danger to witnesses.
>
> Respondents characterize all of these cases as exceptions to the "general rule" of substantive due process that the government may not detain a person prior to a judgment of guilt in a criminal trial. Such a "general rule" may freely be conceded, but we think that these

cases show a sufficient number of exceptions to the rule that the congressional action challenged here can hardly be characterized as totally novel. Given the well-established authority of the government, in special circumstances, to restrain individuals' liberty prior to or even without criminal trial and conviction, we think that the present statute providing for pretrial detention on the basis of dangerousness must be evaluated in precisely the same manner that we evaluated the laws in the cases discussed above.

. . .

On the other side of the scale, of course, is the individual's strong interest in liberty. We do not minimize the importance and fundamental nature of this right. But, as our cases hold, this right may, in circumstances where the government's interest is sufficiently weighty, be subordinated to the greater needs of society. We think that Congress' careful delineation of the circumstances under which detention will be permitted satisfies this standard. When the Government proves by clear and convincing evidence that an arrestee presents an identified and articulable threat to an individual or the community, we believe that, consistent with the Due Process Clause, a court may disable the arrestee from executing that threat. Under these circumstances, we cannot categorically state that pretrial detention "offends some principle of justice so rooted in the traditions and conscience of our people as to be ranked as fundamental." Snyder v. Massachusetts, 291 U.S. 97, 105 (1934).

Id. at 748–51.

With respect to the Eighth Amendment claim, the Court said:

Respondents . . . contend that this Clause grants them a right to bail calculated solely upon considerations of flight. They rely on Stack v. Boyle, 342 U.S. 1, 5 (1951), in which the Court stated that "[b]ail set at a figure higher than an amount reasonably calculated [to ensure the defendant's presence at trial] is 'excessive' under the Eighth Amendment." . . . Respondents concede that the right to bail they have discovered in the Eighth Amendment is not absolute. A court may, for example, refuse bail in capital cases. And . . . a court may refuse bail when the defendant presents a threat to the judicial process by intimidating witnesses. . . . Respondents characterize these exceptions as consistent with what they claim to be the sole purpose of bail—to ensure integrity of the judicial process.

While we agree that a primary function of bail is to safeguard the courts' role in adjudicating the guilt or innocence of defendants, we reject the proposition that the Eighth Amendment categorically prohibits the government from pursuing other admittedly compelling interests through regulation of pretrial release. The above-quoted *dictum* in Stack v. Boyle is far too slender a reed on which to rest this argument. The Court in *Stack* had no occasion to consider whether the Excessive Bail Clause requires courts to admit all defendants to bail, because the statute before the Court in that case in fact allowed the defendants to be bailed. Thus, the Court had to determine only whether bail, admittedly available in that case, was excessive if set at a sum greater than that necessary to ensure the arrestees' presence at trial.

> The holding of *Stack* is illuminated by the Court's holding just four months later in Carlson v. Landon, 342 U.S. 524 (1952). In that case, remarkably similar to the present action, the detainees had been arrested and held without bail pending a determination of deportability. The Attorney General refused to release the individuals, "on the ground that there was reasonable cause to believe that [their] release would be prejudicial to the public interest and *would endanger the welfare and safety of the United States*." Id., at 529 (emphasis added). The detainees brought the same challenge that respondents bring to us today: the Eighth Amendment required them to be admitted to bail. The Court squarely rejected this proposition. . . .
>
> Carlson v. Landon was a civil case, and we need not decide today whether the Excessive Bail Clause speaks at all to Congress' power to define the classes of criminal arrestees who shall be admitted to bail. For even if we were to conclude that the Eighth Amendment imposes some substantive limitations on the National Legislature's powers in this area, we would still hold that the Bail Reform Act is valid. Nothing in the text of the Bail Clause limits permissible government considerations solely to questions of flight. The only arguable substantive limitation of the Bail Clause is that the government's proposed conditions of release or detention not be "excessive" in light of the perceived evil. Of course, to determine whether the government's response is excessive, we must compare that response against the interest the government seeks to protect by means of that response. Thus, when the government has admitted that its only interest is in preventing flight, bail must be set by a court at a sum designed to ensure that goal, and no more. . . . We believe that when Congress has mandated detention on the basis of a compelling interest other than prevention of flight, as it has here, the Eighth Amendment does not require release on bail.

Id. at 752–55.

The most substantial arguments against the constitutionality of the Bail Reform Act are found in Justice Marshall's dissenting opinion in *Salerno*, id. at 755, and Judge Newman's opinion for the court of appeals in United States v. Melendez-Carrion, 790 F.2d 984 (2d Cir.1986).

In a footnote in *Salerno*, the Court suggested that there was a "point at which detention in a particular case might become excessively prolonged, and therefore punitive, in relation to Congress' regulatory goal." 481 U.S. at 747 n.4. In United States v. Hare, 873 F.2d 796 (5th Cir.1989), the court said that a hearing was required to determine whether that point had been reached. The defendant had been detained for over ten months, and trial was not scheduled to begin for another five months. See United States v. Millan, 4 F.3d 1038 (2d Cir.1993) (30 months detention not violative of due process); United States v. Gelfuso, 838 F.2d 358 (9th Cir.1988) (ten months detention not violative of due process).

United States v. Ramey

602 F.Supp. 821 (E.D.N.C.1985)

ORDER

■ BRITT, CHIEF JUDGE.

Defendant stands indicted in two indictments for (1) two counts of conspiracy to violate the drug laws of the United States, (2) two counts of possession of controlled substances with intent to distribute, and (3) two counts of interstate travel with the intent to carry on an unlawful activity related to controlled substances.

After defendant's arrest, and upon motion of the government pursuant to Section 3142(f) of the Bail Reform Act of 1984, a detention hearing was held before Magistrate Charles K. McCotter, Jr., on 12 February 1985. 18 U.S.C. § 3142(f) (Supp.1984). Finding that ". . . no conditions of release will reasonably assure the appearance of defendant as required and the safety of the community" Magistrate McCotter ordered the defendant to be detained. See id.

Defendant moved the court for a review of the Detention Order of Magistrate McCotter. . . . Consistent with the requirement of 18 U.S.C. § 3145(b) that the motion be determined promptly, a hearing was held before the undersigned district judge at 2 p.m. on 15 February 1985.

Upon motion of a detainee to a district judge for review of a Detention Order of a magistrate it is the duty of the district court to conduct a de novo hearing. . . . As the hearing before Magistrate McCotter was tape recorded, the court advised the parties at the beginning of the review hearing that it would rely on the tapes for a review of the evidence presented before Magistrate McCotter and would entertain such additional evidence and argument of counsel as they might desire.

. . .

From the evidence presented at the hearing before Magistrate McCotter and reviewed by the undersigned, the record in the case and the stipulations of the parties, the court makes the following

FINDINGS OF FACT

1. In late 1984, indictment No. 84–49–02–CR–5 was returned against the defendant by the grand jury for the Eastern District of North Carolina. That indictment charged him with (a) conspiracy to violate the drug laws of the United States, an offense punishable by imprisonment up to fifteen years; (b) possession with intent to distribute marijuana, an offense punishable by imprisonment up to fifteen years; and (c) two counts of unlawful travel in interstate commerce with intent to promote an unlawful business activity involving narcotics and controlled substances, offenses punishable by imprisonment up to five years on each count.

2. In January 1985, indictment No. 85–10–02–CR–5 was returned against the defendant by the grand jury for the Eastern District of North Carolina which charged him with (a) conspiracy to violate the drug laws of the United States, an offense punishable by imprisonment up to fifteen years; and (b) possession with intent to distribute cocaine, an offense punishable by imprisonment up to fifteen years.

3. Defendant was aware that he was a target of an investigation by the grand jury. He employed counsel, Herman Gaskins, Esq., who advised the office of the United States Attorney of his representation sometime during calendar year 1984.

4. The indictments in both of these cases were sealed by a United States magistrate upon motion of the government.

5. Warrants for the arrest of defendant were issued on 30 January 1985. A check by law enforcement officers at his residence and other places normally frequented by him proved to be fruitless as defendant could not be located. Members of his family professed to be unaware of his whereabouts.

6. Defendant voluntarily surrendered to the United States Marshal on 8 February 1985.

7. Defendant is a lifelong resident of Franklin County, North Carolina, and has lived in the same home for the past 23 years. He is married and the father of two adult children, both of whom live in fairly close proximity to defendant. For approximately 24 years defendant operated a Gulf service station in Franklinton, North Carolina.

8. Defendant is the owner of, or financially interested in, two western wear stores in Durham and Raleigh, North Carolina, Big Dukes Western Wear, one of which is operated by his daughter.

9. Defendant's son operates a tire business in Youngsville, North Carolina, a short distance from Franklinton.

10. Defendant has two sisters living in Franklinton, North Carolina.

11. Defendant is a veteran of the United States Army, having served in Korea during the hostilities there. He was honorably discharged upon completion of his tour of duty.

12. Defendant has no criminal record and has no prior arrests.

13. Defendant is in good physical condition except for having high blood pressure, a condition for which he takes medication.

14. Defendant's financial condition is not apparent to the court. Although he has several deeds of trust on his residence he is financially interested in the two western wear stores. His sisters are the owners of some real estate which they are willing to pledge as security for his release on bail.

15. The co-defendant, Douglas Freeman Ross, who has not yet been apprehended, is the reputed leader of an organization which has been dealing in controlled substances for many years, at least as far back as 1978. Since that time defendant has been a close associate of Ross. He is reputed to be second in command. During a period of time when co-defendant Ross was in prison in Florida the defendant was in charge of the local drug organization.

16. Defendant has been observed by at least three witnesses dealing in large quantities of controlled substances, including up to 2 kilos of cocaine, hundreds of pounds of marijuana and hundreds of thousands of quaalude tablets. He has a reputation in the drug community as the man to see if you are interested in transferring drugs.

17. Defendant is, himself, a drug user.

18. The investigation of defendant Ross and others was well known in Franklin County, North Carolina, and surrounding areas. On at least one occasion a witness who had been subpoenaed to testify before the grand jury was confronted by defendant who inquired of the witness what he was going to testify to. The witness was further advised by defendant that he would check back with the witness after his testimony. That witness was not again contacted by defendant. He was, however, contacted by telephone by the co-defendant Ross who threatened to kill the witness.

19. Co-defendant Ross employed a private investigator to interview grand jury witnesses, some of whom were interviewed on the premises of Big Dukes Western Wear.

20. Threats to the safety of one witness who testified before the grand jury were sufficiently serious that the United States Marshal's service approved the witness for the witness protection program.

21. During the process of the investigation some witnesses have been told that if they cooperated with the government they, or members of their families, would be harmed.

Based on the foregoing findings of fact and in accordance with the legal principles discussed above, the court makes the following

CONCLUSIONS OF LAW

A. There is probable cause to believe that defendant has committed offenses under the Controlled Substances Act for which a maximum term of imprisonment of ten years or more is prescribed.

B. A rebuttable presumption has arisen that no condition or combination of conditions will reasonably assure defendant's appearance as required and the safety of the community.

C. Defendant has failed to offer sufficient evidence to rebut the presumption.

D. There is clear and convincing evidence that no condition or combination of conditions will reasonably assure the appearance of defendant as required and the safety of other persons and the community. Although defendant has never been arrested or convicted of any other offense, the statutory presumption is bolstered by evidence from the government, from which the findings of fact were made, that defendant has longstanding ties with the leader of the drug organization, is himself a user of controlled substances and has participated in harassment and intimidation of grand jury witnesses.

E. The detention of defendant prior to trial is required.

IT IS, THEREUPON, ORDERED that defendant remain committed to the custody of the Attorney General, subject to the following provisions:

a. he shall be confined in a corrections facility separate, to the extent practicable, from persons awaiting or serving sentences or being held in custody pending appeal;

AO 98 (Rev. 8/85) Appearance Bond

UNITED STATES DISTRICT COURT

_______________ District of _______________

UNITED STATES OF AMERICA
V.

APPEARANCE BOND

____
Defendant

Case Number:

☐ Non-surety: I, the undersigned defendant acknowledge that I and my . . .
☐ Surety: We, the undersigned, jointly and severally acknowledge that we and our . . .
personal representatives, jointly and severally, are bound to pay to the United States of America the sum of
$ _______________ , and there has been deposited in the Registry of the Court the sum of
$ _______________ in cash or _______________ (describe other security.)

The conditions of this bond are that the _______________ (Name)
is to appear before this court and at such other places as the defendant may be required to appear, in accordance with any and all orders and directions relating to the defendant's appearance in this case, including appearance for violation of a condition of defendant's release as may be ordered or notified by this court or any other United States District Court to which the defendant may be held to answer or the cause transferred. The defendant is to abide by any judgment entered in such matter by surrendering to serve any sentence imposed and obeying any order or direction in connection with such judgment.

It is agreed and understood that this is a continuing bond (including any proceeding on appeal or review) which shall continue until such time as the undersigned are exonerated.

If the defendant appears as ordered or notified and otherwise obeys and performs the foregoing conditions of this bond, then this bond is to be void, but if the defendant fails to obey or perform any of these conditions, payment of the amount of this bond shall be due forthwith. Forfeiture of this bond for any breach of its conditions may be declared by any United States District Court having cognizance of the above entitled matter at the time of such breach and if the bond is forfeited and if the forfeiture is not set aside or remitted, judgment, may be entered upon motion in such United States District Court against each debtor jointly and severally for the amount above stated, together with interest and costs, and execution may be issued and payment secured as provided by the Federal Rules of Criminal Procedure and any other laws of the United States.

This bond is signed on _______________ (Date) at _______________ (Place)

Defendant _______________ Address _______________

Surety _______________ Address _______________

Surety _______________ Address _______________

Signed and acknowledged before me _______________ (Date)

____
Judicial Officer/Clerk

Approved _______________

JUSTIFICATION OF SURETIES

I, the undersigned surety, say that I reside at ______________________________

______________________________ ; and that my net worth is the sum of

______________________________ dollars ($ ______________).

I further state that

____
Surety

Sworn to before me and subscribed in my presence ______________________________
Date

at ______________________________ .
Place

______________________________ ______________________________
Name and Title Signature of Judicial Officer/Clerk

I, the undersigned surety, state that I reside ______________________________

______________________________ ; and that my net worth is the sum of

______________________________ dollars ($ ______________).

I further state that

____
Surety

Sworn to before me and subscribed in my presence ______________________________
Date

at ______________________________ .
Place

______________________________ ______________________________
Name and Title Signature of Judicial Officer/Clerk

Justification Approved: ______________________________
Judicial Officer

b. he shall be afforded reasonable opportunity for private consultation with his counsel; and,

c. on order of a court of the United States or on request of an attorney for the government the person in charge of the corrections facility in which he is confined shall deliver him to a United States Marshal for the purpose of an appearance in connection with a court proceeding.

---

306. Section 3142(f) of the Bail Reform Act provides for a detention hearing at the defendant's first appearance unless the defendant or the attorney for the government seeks a continuance, which, "except for good cause," may not be for more than five days if requested by the defendant or three days if requested by the government.

Failure to comply with the prompt hearing provision does not require that the person be released. In United States v. Montalvo-Murillo, 495 U.S. 711 (1990) (6–3), the detention hearing was held 13 days after the defendant's arrest; there had been no request for a waiver of the time limit, no finding of good cause for a continuance, and no objection to the continuance. The Court said that even assuming that the government was responsible for the delay, it was not barred from seeking a detention order. "It is inevitable that, despite the most diligent efforts of the Government and the courts, some errors in the application of the time requirements of § 3142(f) will occur. Detention proceedings take place during the disordered period following arrest. . . . [C]ircumstances such as the involvement of more than one district, doubts about whether the defendant was subject to temporary detention under § 3142(d), and ambiguity in requests for continuances may contribute to a missed deadline for which no real blame can be fixed. In these situations, there is no reason to bestow upon the defendant a windfall and to visit upon the Government and the citizens a severe penalty by mandating release of possibly dangerous defendants every time some deviation from the strictures of § 3142(f)." Id. at 720. "Whatever other remedies may exist for detention without a timely hearing or for conduct that is aggravated or intentional . . . we hold that once the Government discovers that the time limits have expired, it may ask for a prompt detention hearing and make its case to detain based upon the requirements set forth in the statute." Id. at 721.

In United States v. Dominguez, 783 F.2d 702 (7th Cir.1986) the court held that "first appearance" means first appearance in the charging district rather than in the district where the defendant is arrested. It observed: "In some cases, of course, circumstances may make it appropriate to request detention in the arresting district. Nevertheless, we believe that the most informed decisions will almost always be made in the charging district by prosecutors that have supervised the investigations and by courts that will supervise the remaining proceedings. Those officials should always have the option of seeking detention within the statute's limits and according to its procedures." Id. at 705. Were the rule otherwise, the court said, prosecutors in the district where the defendant is arrested would be obliged routinely to request continuances of the detention hearing until information could be obtained from the prosecutor in the charging district.

Section 3142(f) provides that a finding that a person's release would be dangerous to another person or the community "shall be supported by clear and convincing evidence." See, e.g., United States v. Portes, 786 F.2d 758 (7th Cir.1985) (narcotics offenses, threats of reprisals, and possession of dangerous weapons sufficient to support finding); United States v. Delker, 757 F.2d 1390 (3d Cir.1985) (racketeering and extortion offenses, prior convictions for assault, and threats of witnesses sufficient to support finding). Pretrial detention was upheld in United States v. Tortora, 922 F.2d 880 (1st Cir.1990), over the "mind-boggling" argument that the defendant, a reputed member of an organized crime ring, could pursue his criminal activities from jail and was, therefore, no *more* dangerous if he were released than if he were detained. Id. at 889. Section 3142(e) prescribes certain presumptions of dangerousness, which shift "the burden of production, but not the burden of persuasion to the defendants." United States v. Portes, above, 786 F.2d at 764. The presumptions are "of the so-called 'middle ground' variety; that is, they do not disappear when rebutted, like a 'bursting bubble' presumption, nor do they actually shift the burden of persuasion to the defendant. They are 'rebutted' when the defendant meets a 'burden of production' by coming forward with some evidence that he will not flee or endanger the community if released. Once this burden of production is met, the presumption is 'rebutted'. . . . [T]he rebutted presumption is not erased. Instead it remains in the case as an evidentiary finding militating against release, to be weighed along with other evidence relevant to factors listed in § 3142(g). . . . The burden of persuasion remains with the government once the burden of production is met." *Dominguez*, above, 783 F.2d at 707. See United States v. Perry, 788 F.2d 100 (3d Cir.1986).

In United States v. Carbone, 793 F.2d 559 (3d Cir.1986), construing § 3142(g), the court said that the fact that friends of the defendant had posted a million dollars in property as surety for his appearance was significant evidence to rebut the presumption that he posed a danger to the community. "Although posting a property bond normally goes to the question of defendant's appearance at trial, where the surety takes the form of residential property posted by community members the act of placing the surety is a strong indication that the private sureties are also vouching for defendant's character." Id. at 561. Judge Garth, dissenting, observed that the friends' action indicated their loyalty to the defendant and confidence that he would appear but had no bearing on the question whether there was a danger that he would continue to engage in large-scale drug sales.

The statute does not specify the standard of proof for a finding that a person may not appear as required. The courts have concluded that the standard should be a preponderance of the evidence, as under the prior law. E.g., United States v. Portes, above; United States v. Fortna, 769 F.2d 243 (5th Cir.1985) (sophisticated international narcotics enterprise and vast sums of money sufficient to support finding); United States v. Motamedi, 767 F.2d 1403 (9th Cir.1985)(finding not supported; bond of $750,000 and other conditions of release imposed).

On various procedural aspects of the detention hearing, see United States v. Perry, United States v. Fortna and United States v. Delker, all above.

When a district court reviews a magistrate's order for release or for detention under § 3145, the court may refer to and rely on evidence presented at the detention hearing. It may, however, conduct a further hearing. The determination of the district court is de novo. United States v. Delker, above; see United States v. Portes, above; United States v. Fortna, above. In United States v. Maull, 773 F.2d 1479 (8th Cir.1985), the court held that upon a request by the defendant for review of conditions of release under 18 U.S.C. § 3145(a)(2), the reviewing court may initiate a pretrial detention proceeding in the manner of § 3142(f), on its own motion.

On appeal from a release or detention order under § 3145(c), the courts of appeals have applied different standards of review. The largest number have concluded that the court should accept the factual findings of the court below if they are not plainly erroneous, but should make an "independent determination" of ultimate facts. E.g., United States v. Perry, above; United States v. Portes, above. Other courts have concluded that the determination below should be accepted if not "clearly erroneous," or if "supported by the proceedings below." Cases are collected in *Portes*, above, 786 F.2d at 762.

307. Section 3149 provides that "a person charged with an offense . . . may be arrested by the surety." The only express qualification on the authority to arrest is that the person "shall be delivered promptly to a United States marshal." On the surety's authority to arrest generally, see Kear v. Hilton, 699 F.2d 181 (4th Cir.1983). Kear, a professional bondsman, arrested a bail jumper in Canada and brought him back to the United States to face trial in Florida. The surety for whom Kear worked had given a bond in the amount of $137,500 to assure the person's appearance. Canada sought Kear's extradition to Canada on a charge of kidnapping. The court observed: "Professional bondsmen in the United States enjoy extraordinary powers to capture and use force to compel peremptory return of a bail jumper. They may do so not only in the state where the bail was granted, but in other states as well, without resort to public authorities, either the police to effect the arrest or the appropriate state officials to bring about extradition." Id. at 182. Concluding that these powers extend only within the United States, the court held that Kear should be extradited to Canada. See also United States v. Trunko, 189 F.Supp. 559 (E.D.Ark. 1960).

AO 471 (Rev. 8/85) Order of Temporary Detention

UNITED STATES DISTRICT COURT

_______________ District of _______________

UNITED STATES OF AMERICA

V.

____
Defendant

ORDER OF TEMPORARY DETENTION TO PERMIT REVOCATION OF CONDITIONAL RELEASE, DEPORTATION OR EXCLUSION

Case Number:

I find that the defendant

☐ is, and was at the time the alleged offense was committed:

☐ on release pending trial for a felony under federal, state, or local law.

☐ on release pending imposition or execution of sentence, appeal of sentence or conviction, or completion of sentence, for an offense under federal, state, or local law.

☐ on probation or parole for an offense under federal, state, or local law; or

☐ is not a citizen of the United States or lawfully admitted for permanent residence as defined at (8 U.S.C. §1101(a)(20)).

and I further find that the defendant may

☐ flee, or ☐ pose a danger to another person or the community.

I accordingly ORDER the detention of the defendant without bail to and including _______________, which is not more than ten days from the date of this Order, excluding Saturdays, Sundays, and holidays.

I further direct the attorney for the Government to notify the appropriate court, probation or parole official, or state or local law enforcement official, or the appropriate official of the Immigration and Naturalization Service so that the custody of the defendant can be transferred and a detainer placed in connection with this case.

If custody is not transferred by the above date, I direct the production of the defendant before me on that date so that further proceedings may be considered in accordance with the provisions of 18 U.S.C. § 3142.

Date: _______________

____
Judicial Officer

United States v. Penn

Crim.No. 1434–67 (D.C.Ct.Gen.Sess., Jan. 30, 1968)

■ HALLECK, J.

The Court has before it an application for review of conditions of release pursuant to 18 U.S.C. § 3146(d).[2] The defendant has been indicted for robbery in the United States District Court. However, the application has been filed in this Court because the defendant has been committed to jail in default of $5,000 bond first set by this Court on October 23, 1967. When the defendant was arrested, bond was set and the case was continued for two days. On the continued date, another Judge held the preliminary hearing, found probable cause, and held Penn for the action of the Grand Jury.

Thereafter, Penn was indicted on November 15, 1967, and from that point the case has been in the U.S. District Court. The Daily Washington Law Reporter, Vol. 96, No. 15, at p. 121, indicates that the case is now on the ready calendar. . . .

The defendant's three month delay in seeking review of conditions of release is unexplained. Nevertheless, this Court must consider it now. . . .

The Metropolitan Police Department Statement of Facts (P.D. Form 163) initially was considered by the Court in setting bond. Therein, it appears that this defendant, and another, were observed by two policemen in the act of committing a yoke robbery, and were promptly apprehended. Property of the victim was recovered from the defendant. The victim identified this defendant at the scene of the offense. Although this defendant is presumed to be innocent of this charge, it is clear that the case against him is very strong, indeed.

At the time bail was set the Court was presented with the usual completed form prepared by the District of Columbia Bail Agency. That Agency was created by an Act of Congress in 1966. See D.C.Code § 23–901 et seq. It is assigned, by statute, a very limited function. It

> shall secure pertinent data and provide for any judicial officer in the District of Columbia reports containing verified information concerning any individual with respect to whom a bail determination is to be made.

D.C.Code § 23–901. The Agency is required by § 23–903 to interview any person charged with an offense in the District of Columbia, and thereafter, it

> shall seek independent verification of information obtained during the interview, shall secure any such person's prior criminal record which shall be made available by the Metropolitan Police Department, and shall prepare a written report of such information for submission to the appropriate judicial officer.

In addition, the Agency is to provide a copy of such report to the prosecutor and to counsel for the person concerning whom the report is made. At this

2. The statutory provisions discussed in the opinion preceded enactment of the Bail Reform Act of 1984.

point the Agency's task is completed, and by law it has no further obligation or responsibility in the matter.

The Report of the President's Commission on Law Enforcement and Administration of Justice, published in February, 1967, examines the problem of pre-trial release in Chapter Five, and concludes that money bail should be imposed only when reasonable alternatives are not available. The report goes on to say such a release procedure presupposes an information-gathering technique that can promptly provide a magistrate with an array of facts about a defendant's history, circumstances, problems and way of life.

The Bail Bond Reform Act of 1966 deals with pre-trial release criteria in Section 3146(b). The judge

> shall, on the basis of available information, take into account the nature and circumstances of the offense charged, the weight of the evidence against the accused, the accused's family ties, employment, financial resources, character and mental condition, the length of his residence in the community, his record of convictions, and his record of appearance at court proceedings or of flight to avoid prosecution or failure to appear at court proceedings.

Initially, it should be observed that the District of Columbia Bail Agency is primarily staffed by bright, young, law students who have little or no practical experience. In preparing reports containing verified information for the Court, these young men do very little more than call the home address given by the defendant and speak to someone there in order to determine if the defendant lives there; and thereafter call his employer to determine if the defendant is employed. Verification is, in the vast majority of cases, made either by placing a telephone call or speaking with some person in Court who identifies himself or herself as a relative or a friend of the defendant. For the most part, the reports prepared by the District of Columbia Bail Agency reflect little more than a defendant's current address, the length of time he has lived in the District of Columbia and a brief notation of the name of his employer and the length of time he has been employed. The extent to which the information is, or is not, verified is frequently never disclosed. The information itself is usually of the sketchiest sort. In fact, it has been this Court's experience that in several cases information put in the supposedly verified reports subsequently turns out to be in error. The shortage of personnel, the lack of experience, and the press of time makes the so-called verified report a mere shadow of the report apparently envisaged by the Crime Commission Report. The judge sitting in the Assignment Branch of the Court of General Sessions frequently has over one hundred cases to deal with each day. He must, of necessity, rely upon the Bail Agency, the prosecutor, and defense counsel for information. By and large, very little is forthcoming from those sources. Yet,

> A determination by the judicial officer is to be made on the basis of "available information." The Act does not indicate how the information is to be gathered, but the report suggests that in most instances the information will be supplied by the accused or his attorney. It is imperative that no coercion be brought to bear on the accused when he is requested to supply information.

[Analysis of The Bail Reform Act of 1966, Criminal Division, Department of Justice, at p. 15.] It would seem that the Act contemplates lengthy and extensive investigation of a defendant, possibly coupled with a full hearing where testimony may be elicited. Such investigation takes time—often several days.

> Since it is the duty of the judicial officer to make a determination concerning the appropriate release condition to be applied to an accused, it would seem that some affirmative effort on the part of such officers is required to insure that necessary information is available at the bail hearing. Therefore, the judicial officer probably has a duty to question the defendant, if there is no available information, in order to obtain the necessary facts. The duty to make a determination should also include an attempt to collect information from the appropriate Government officials concerning the past criminal history of the defendant. If such request has been made and the information is not immediately available or the defendant is unwilling to give any information, the officer should proceed with his determination on the basis of the available facts. [Id. p. 16]
>
> The emphasis of the Bail Reform Act is on the careful study of the individual in order to tailor properly release conditions to him. In the first instance a factual inquiry must be made to develop a profile of the accused. [Id. p. 19]

The Bail Agency report in the present case is typically sparse, but better than most. The opening sentence states

> The following VERIFIED INFORMATION is submitted pursuant to PL–519 for use in determining conditions of release under the Bail Reform Act of 1966 (PL 89–456).

However, the final sentence in the report discloses that the Bail Agency is unable to recommend personal recognizance or other nonfinancial condition of release *because they are unable to verify any of the information*. The report is, therefore, a non-sequitur. The "unverified" verified information discloses an address for the defendant where he supposedly lives with his brother, who is listed as the only family tie in the area. The report states that the defendant has resided in the District of Columbia area for five years, and with his brother for two years. The defendant is listed as unemployed. His method of support is listed as unascertained. Under a heading "prior convictions" there is listed a 1967 charge of assault and 1967 charges of robbery and carrying a dangerous weapon which are "pending in Va." Also listed is a 1967 assault on a police officer and carrying a gun charge. The Metropolitan Police Department criminal record of this defendant does not appear anywhere in the Court papers. Of course, the local police department would have no record of any convictions of a defendant in any other jurisdiction; nor information regarding his status on parole or probation; nor any other pertinent information from other jurisdictions which could be furnished by the F.B.I. but not by the Metropolitan Police Department. The Bail Agency's "unverified" verified report concludes by pointing out the interview was difficult and that the defendant became belligerent during the interview. Although the Report Form provides a place for the signature of the person submitting the report, it is typically unsigned.

The Bail Bond Reform Act of 1966 creates a presumption in favor of release on personal recognizance. It appears that Congress intended that every accused shall be released when at all possible. In the Report submitted by the Committee on the Judiciary of the United States Senate, accompanying the Act, the release provision was summarized.

> In summary, section 3146(a) is intended to require that every person accused of a noncapital offense, as defined in section 3152(2), is presumed entitled to be released pending trial on his own recognizance or upon the execution of an unsecured appearance bond. Only if factors appear which reasonably suggest that such a procedure will not adequately assure the appearance of the accused may the judicial officer impose one or more of the additional conditions of release enumerated in the bill or utilize "any other condition deemed reasonably necessary to assure appearance as required." [Senate Report 750, 89th Congress, 1st session, page 11]

In most cases the Court is placed in an untenable situation. On the one hand the defendant is now presumed to be entitled to release on personal bond, unless factors appear which reasonably suggest that such a procedure would not assure the appearance of the accused at trial. On the other hand, the burden is placed on the Court to justify any condition other than personal bond. In order to do this, the Court must point to reasons why it acts, but because of the totally inadequate information-gathering technique provided for by the statutory scheme the Court is usually without sufficient information to make any informed decision, or to point to reasons for denying personal bond. The less the Judge knows about a defendant, the higher the risk in placing him on personal bond. Yet, the less the Judge knows, the more difficult it is to justify any condition other than personal bond.

The Bail Bond Reform Act also requires that, in the event the Court does not release a defendant on personal bond, it must then consider the alternative conditions seriatim, and find adequate reasons to reject each one, before money bond may be set. The first alternative is to place a prisoner in the custody of an individual or an organization agreeing to supervise him. It is the Court's experience that very few capable persons or qualified organizations are available to supervise defendants. Supervising a defendant requires the exercise of some degree of active control over him, and a regulating of his comings or goings. As soon as the Court explains to a friend, lawyer, family member, minister, or some organization or group that a definite responsibility is involved, more often than not it develops that such persons or groups are unwilling to assume those responsibilities. The typical example is the mother who is willing to sign for custody of her defendant son, but frequently states that she has no control over him. This is usually obvious by reference to his record and indicated work habits, as well as his proclivity for late hours and bad company.

Rejecting third party custody or supervision, the Court must next consider placing restrictions on travel, association, or place of abode of the defendant during his period of release. The greatest difficulty with these provisions is that no practical way exists to assure that the conditions are being complied with. The Bail Agency is charged solely with the duty of interviewing arrested defendants, verifying information and presenting it to the Court to assist in setting bond. The Bail Agency is not required to supervise anybody when they are out on personal bond awaiting trial. In fact, even mailing post cards to defendants reminding them of trial dates is beyond their authority and represents an unauthorized gratuitous act. The probation department is so overworked now it cannot properly supervise its probationers. The police certainly cannot be expected to be baby-sitters in blue for the defendants they have apprehended.

More importantly, there are no penalties provided for failure to comply with conditions of release, nor are there any sanctions that may be applied to any person assuming the task of supervising a defendant if that task is not performed. The Court is, at most, limited to imposing a penalty of thirty days for contempt of court. Contempt power must be used sparingly, and only against deliberate or wilful contemptuous conduct toward the Court. Third party custodians under The Bail Reform Act hardly fit into such a category.

Section 3146(c) requires that upon releasing a defendant pursuant to the Act the judicial officer who authorizes the release "shall inform such person of the penalties applicable to violations of the conditions of his release and shall advise him that a warrant for his arrest will be issued immediately upon any such violation." As a practical matter, the warnings are hollow threats. Penalties are limited or non-existent, and General Sessions rarely issues warrants, and when they are issued practically no one is assigned to serve them. In order for the Judge to advise a defendant of the penalties, reference must be made to § 3150, "Penalties for Failure to Appear." The penalties provided for in that Section apply only to a defendant who "wilfully fails to appear before any court or judicial officer as required." *There is no penalty for anything other than failure to appear before a Court or Judicial Officer*. Therefore, the Court cannot advise a defendant of penalties for violating "conditions of release" since there are no penalties for such violations. Violations of any conditions of release, which may be established by the Court, cannot be punished except by the Court's contempt powers, which are minimal in terms of the problem. Several examples will illustrate the problem. A frequent condition of release is that a defendant be home by a certain hour every evening. Aside from the fact that no one ever reports to the Court when the defendant is late coming home, the Act provides no penalties for such failure. Another frequently used condition is that a defendant report to a police precinct at stated intervals. Police precincts maintain a notebook on the counter for such defendants to sign, indicating the date and time. Persons signing these books are rarely, if ever, required to identify themselves, so that it is possible for any person to sign on behalf of the defendant. Furthermore, the police department does not supervise the persons who are required to sign in, nor indeed do the police ascertain if these persons actually did sign in as frequently as required. Finally, no penalties exist if the defendant does not report regularly. In short, while the act contemplates that Judges will go to great lengths to establish a variety of conditions of release other than money bail, the act provides no method of enforcement and no penalty for violation of such conditions of release. The only penalties provided for are the penalties for wilful failure to appear before any Court or Judicial Officer *as required.*

Added to the above difficulties are the high rate of failures to appear by persons on personal bond, coupled with the number of offenses committed by persons out on personal bond. No one has accurate figures on these two groups, although some estimates run into the thousands. All of these things must necessarily be considered by this Court when it is called upon to review a money bond previously set and to consider release of the defendant on personal bond. Of course, danger to the community cannot be considered at all. If a professional criminal of demonstrated dangerousness has family ties, a job, and a good record of appearing for trial, he must be let out on personal bond to continue to prey upon innocent citizens while the courts take longer than a year to bring him to trial. When the Bail Reform Act was being considered, Congress recognized this serious problem. . . .

This defendant was caught in the act of a yoke robbery. The "presumption of innocence" cannot wipe out this simple fact when the Court comes to considering the problem of bail. This Court knows full well that if a professional bondsman stands to lose $5,000 in the event this defendant disappears, the likelihood of his disappearing for any period of time is remote. The bondsman will do a better job of keeping track of his investment than will all of the other overworked and understaffed agencies operating under The Bail Reform Act who have no personal or financial interest in the outcome of the matter.

The Court set a money bond initially because the defendant does not appear to have adequate family ties in the community, nor a stable work record. His reported criminal record makes him appear to be untrustworthy, or to put it another way, his "character" appears to be poor. Most importantly, anything short of money bond would be at best impractical and nonenforceable. No reliable person or organization has indicated a willingness to supervise him. The delay in seeking a review of conditions of release has rendered obsolete the little unverified information which was originally presented by the Bail Agency. None of the information presented in his application for review of conditions of release bespeaks a modification of the terms of bond. The defendant has presented nothing new or of value in seeking release on personal bond. Although the drafters of The Bail Reform Act would seem to want everyone out on personal bond, the decision is still one addressed to judicial discretion. A court owes an obligation to society, to its own processes, and to the practical integrity of the judicial system, as well as to defendants.

For the foregoing reasons the Court declines to alter the conditions of release previously imposed.[3]

---

308. "A trial judge indisputably has broad powers to ensure the orderly and expeditious progress of a trial. For this purpose, he has the

[3] It was subsequently ordered that Penn be permitted to deposit 10% of the amount of bail instead of posting bond with sureties. The deposit was not made. On May 28, 1968, Penn pleaded guilty and was sentenced to imprisonment for one to three years.

power to revoke bail and to remit the defendant to custody. But this power must be exercised with circumspection. It may be invoked only when and to the extent justified by danger which the defendant's conduct presents or by danger of significant interference with the progress or order of the trial." Bitter v. United States, 389 U.S. 15, 16 (1967). The Court concluded that an order committing the defendant because of "a single, brief incident of tardiness" was unjustified. Id. at 17. In United States v. LaFontaine, 210 F.3d 125 (2d Cir.2000), at a bail revocation hearing under the federal bail act, a finding of danger to the community was upheld on the basis of nonviolent witness tampering. See United States v. Bentvena, 288 F.2d 442 (2d Cir.1961), in which the court of appeals upheld an order of the district court revoking the defendants' bail and remanding them to custody until the termination of their trial. The court observed that "the dangers of releasing a defendant on bail during the course of a trial are substantially greater than those existing before trial," and said that "under all the circumstances of the case, especially a succession of misadventures which have already caused numerous delays and adjournments in the presentation of the evidence, the order of the trial judge was a proper exercise of discretion for the purpose of ensuring the orderly completion of the trial." Id. at 444, 445. The defendants' subsequent application for bail to Justice Harlan was similarly denied. Fernandez v. United States, 81 S.Ct. 642 (1961).

For cases in which the defendant contended unsuccessfully that his detention before trial interfered with the preparation of his defense, see Hodgdon v. United States, 365 F.2d 679, 686–87 (8th Cir.1966); United States ex rel. Hyde v. McMann, 263 F.2d 940 (2d Cir.1959).

Even though a defendant may not be able to show special prejudice from detention before or during trial, there is considerable evidence that in general defendants who are released on bail fare better at trial (and, if convicted, at sentencing) than those who are detained. Among the explanations are the detained defendant's inability to contribute money and labor to investigations for his defense; his inability to locate witnesses and evidence peculiarly accessible to him; difficulties of contact with counsel, who must visit him in inadequate jail facilities during specified hours; and the impact on judge and jury of "prison pallor" and the demeanor that a period of detention in jail may produce. See, e.g., D. Freed & P. Wald, Bail in the United States: 1964, pp. 45–48; Foote, "The Coming Constitutional Crisis in Bail: II," 113 U. Pa. L. Rev. 1125, 1137–51 (1965); Wald, "Pretrial Detention and Ultimate Freedom: A Statistical Study, Foreword," 39 N.Y.U. L. Rev. 631 (1964).

Bell v. Wolfish

441 U.S. 520, 99 S.Ct. 1861, 60 L.Ed.2d 447 (1979)

■ MR. JUSTICE REHNQUIST delivered the opinion of the Court.

Over the past five Terms, this Court has in several decisions considered constitutional challenges to prison conditions or practices by convicted prisoners. This case requires us to examine the constitutional rights of pretrial detainees—those persons who have been charged with a crime but who have not yet been tried on the charge. The parties concede that to ensure their presence at trial, these persons legitimately may be incarcerated by the Government prior to a determination of their guilt or innocence . . . and it is the scope of their rights during this period of confinement prior to trial that is the primary focus of this case.

This lawsuit was brought as a class action in the United States District Court for the Southern District of New York to challenge numerous conditions of confinement and practices at the Metropolitan Correctional Center (MCC), a federally operated short-term custodial facility in New York City designed primarily to house pretrial detainees. The District Court, in the words of the Court of Appeals for the Second Circuit, "intervened broadly into almost every facet of the institution" and enjoined no fewer than 20 MCC practices on constitutional and statutory grounds. The Court of Appeals largely affirmed the District Court's constitutional rulings and in the process held that under the Due Process Clause of the Fifth Amendment, pretrial detainees may "be subjected to only those 'restrictions and privations' which 'inhere in their confinement itself or which are justified by compelling necessities of jail administration.'" Wolfish v. Levi, 573 F.2d 118, 124 (1978), quoting Rhem v. Malcolm, 507 F.2d 333, 336 (CA2 1974). We granted certiorari to consider the important constitutional questions raised by these decisions and to resolve an apparent conflict among the Circuits. . . . We now reverse.

I

The MCC was constructed in 1975 to replace the converted waterfront garage on West Street that had served as New York City's federal jail since 1928. It is located adjacent to the Foley Square federal courthouse and has as its primary objective the housing of persons who are being detained in custody prior to trial for federal criminal offenses in the United States District Courts for the Southern and Eastern Districts of New York and for the District of New Jersey. Under the Bail Reform Act, 18 U.S.C. § 3146, a person in the federal system is committed to a detention facility only because no other less drastic means can reasonably ensure his presence at trial. In addition to pretrial detainees, the MCC also houses some convicted inmates who are awaiting sentencing or transportation to federal prison or who are serving generally relatively short sentences in a service capacity at the MCC, convicted prisoners who have been lodged at the facility under writs of habeas corpus *ad prosequendum* or *ad testificandum* issued to ensure their presence at upcoming trials, witnesses in protective custody, and persons incarcerated for contempt.[4]

4. This group of nondetainees may comprise, on a daily basis, between 40% and 60% of the MCC population. . . . Prior to the District Court's order, 50% of all MCC inmates spent less than 30 days at the facility and 73% less than 60 days. . . . However, of

The MCC differs markedly from the familiar image of a jail; there are no barred cells, dank, colorless corridors, or clanging steel gates. It was intended to include the most advanced and innovative features of modern design of detention facilities. As the Court of Appeals stated: "[I]t represented the architectural embodiment of the best and most progressive penological planning." 573 F.2d, at 121. The key design element of the 12-story structure is the "modular" or "unit" concept, whereby each floor designed to house inmates has one or two largely self-contained residential units that replace the traditional cellblock jail construction. Each unit in turn has several clusters or corridors of private rooms or dormitories radiating from a central 2-story "multipurpose" or common room, to which each inmate has free access approximately 16 hours a day. Because our analysis does not turn on the particulars of the MCC concept or design, we need not discuss them further.

When the MCC opened in August 1975, the planned capacity was 449 inmates, an increase of 50% over the former West Street facility. . . . Despite some dormitory accommodations, the MCC was designed primarily to house these inmates in 389 rooms, which originally were intended for single occupancy. While the MCC was under construction, however, the number of persons committed to pretrial detention began to rise at an "unprecedented" rate. . . . The Bureau of Prisons took several steps to accommodate this unexpected flow of persons assigned to the facility, but despite these efforts, the inmate population at the MCC rose above its planned capacity within a short time after its opening. To provide sleeping space for this increased population, the MCC replaced the single bunks in many of the individual rooms and dormitories with double bunks. Also, each week some newly arrived inmates had to sleep on cots in the common areas until they could be transferred to residential rooms as space became available. . . .

On November 28, 1975, less than four months after the MCC had opened, the named respondents initiated this action by filing in the District Court a petition for a writ of habeas corpus. The District Court certified the case as a class action on behalf of all persons confined at the MCC, pretrial detainees and sentenced prisoners alike. The petition served up a veritable potpourri of complaints that implicated virtually every facet of the institution's conditions and practices. Respondents charged, inter alia, that they had been deprived of their statutory and constitutional rights because of overcrowded conditions, undue length of confinement, improper searches, inadequate recreational, educational, and employment opportunities, insufficient staff, and objectionable restrictions on the purchase and receipt of personal items and books.

In two opinions and a series of orders, the District Court enjoined numerous MCC practices and conditions. With respect to pretrial detainees, the court held that because they are "presumed to be innocent and held only to ensure their presence at trial, 'any deprivation or restriction of . . .

the unsentenced detainees, over half spent less than 10 days at the MCC, three-quarters were released within a month and more than 85% were released within 60 days. . . .

rights beyond those which are necessary for confinement alone, must be justified by a compelling necessity.' " United States ex rel. Wolfish v. Levi, 439 F.Supp. 114, 124 (1977), quoting Detainees of Brooklyn House of Detention v. Malcolm, 520 F.2d 392, 397 (CA2 1975). And while acknowledging that the rights of sentenced inmates are to be measured by the different standard of the Eighth Amendment, the court declared that to house "an inferior minority of persons . . . in ways found unconstitutional for the rest" would amount to cruel and unusual punishment. United States ex rel. Wolfish v. United States, 428 F.Supp. 333, 339 (1977).

Applying these standards on cross-motions for partial summary judgment, the District Court enjoined the practice of housing two inmates in the individual rooms and prohibited enforcement of the so-called "publisher-only" rule, which at the time of the court's ruling prohibited the receipt of all books and magazines mailed from outside the MCC except those sent directly from a publisher or a book club. After a trial on the remaining issues, the District Court enjoined, inter alia, the doubling of capacity in the dormitory areas, the use of the common rooms to provide temporary sleeping accommodations, the prohibition against inmates' receipt of packages containing food and items of personal property, and the practice of requiring inmates to expose their body cavities for visual inspection following contact visits. The court also granted relief in favor of pretrial detainees, but not convicted inmates, with respect to the requirement that detainees remain outside their rooms during routine inspections by MCC officials.

The Court of Appeals largely affirmed the District Court's rulings, although it rejected that court's Eighth Amendment analysis of conditions of confinement for convicted prisoners because the "parameters of judicial intervention into . . . conditions . . . for sentenced prisoners are more restrictive than in the case of pretrial detainees." 573 F.2d, at 125. Accordingly, the court remanded the matter to the District Court for it to determine whether the housing for sentenced inmates at the MCC was constitutionally "adequate." But the Court of Appeals approved the due process standard employed by the District Court in enjoining the conditions of pretrial confinement. It therefore held that the MCC had failed to make a showing of "compelling necessity" sufficient to justify housing two pretrial detainees in the individual rooms. Id., at 126–27. And for purposes of our review (since petitioners challenge only some of the Court of Appeals' rulings), the court affirmed the District Court's granting of relief against the "publisher-only" rule, the practice of conducting body-cavity searches after contact visits, the prohibition against receipt of packages of food and personal items from outside the institution, and the requirement that detainees remain outside their rooms during routine searches of the rooms by MCC officials. . . .

II

As a first step in our decision, we shall address "double-bunking" as it is referred to by the parties, since it is a condition of confinement that is alleged only to deprive pretrial detainees of their liberty without due process of law in contravention of the Fifth Amendment. We will treat in order the Court of Appeals' standard of review, the analysis which we believe the Court of Appeals should have employed, and the conclusions to which our analysis leads us in the case of "double-bunking."

A

The Court of Appeals did not dispute that the Government may permissibly incarcerate a person charged with a crime but not yet convicted to ensure his presence at trial. However, reasoning from the "premise that an individual is to be treated as innocent until proven guilty," the court concluded that pretrial detainees retain the "rights afforded unincarcerated individuals," and that therefore it is not sufficient that the conditions of confinement for pretrial detainees "merely comport with contemporary standards of decency prescribed by the cruel and unusual punishment clause of the eighth amendment." 573 F.2d, at 124. Rather, the court held, the Due Process Clause requires that pretrial detainees "be subjected to only those 'restrictions and privations' which 'inhere in their confinement itself or which are justified by compelling necessities of jail administration.' " Ibid., quoting Rhem v. Malcolm, 507 F.2d, at 336. Under the Court of Appeals' "compelling necessity" standard, "deprivation of the rights of detainees cannot be justified by the cries of fiscal necessity . . . administrative convenience . . . or by the cold comfort that conditions in other jails are worse." 573 F.2d, at 124. The court acknowledged, however, that it could not "ignore" our admonition in Procunier v. Martinez, 416 U.S. 396, 405 (1974), that "courts are ill equipped to deal with the increasingly urgent problems of prison administration," and concluded that it would "not [be] wise for [it] to second-guess the expert administrators on matters on which they are better informed." 573 F.2d, at 124.

Our fundamental disagreement with the Court of Appeals is that we fail to find a source in the Constitution for its compelling-necessity standard. Both the Court of Appeals and the District Court seem to have relied on the "presumption of innocence" as the source of the detainee's substantive right to be free from conditions of confinement that are not justified by compelling necessity. . . . But the presumption of innocence provides no support for such a rule.

The presumption of innocence is a doctrine that allocates the burden of proof in criminal trials; it also may serve as an admonishment to the jury to judge an accused's guilt or innocence solely on the evidence adduced at trial and not on the basis of suspicions that may arise from the fact of his arrest, indictment, or custody, or from other matters not introduced as proof at trial. It is "an inaccurate, shorthand description of the right of the accused to 'remain inactive and secure, until the prosecution has taken up its burden and produced evidence and effected persuasion . . .' an 'assumption' that is indulged in the absence of contrary evidence." Taylor v. Kentucky, [436 U.S. 478 (1978)], at 484 n.12. Without question, the presumption of innocence plays an important role in our criminal justice system. . . . But it has no application to a determination of the rights of a pretrial detainee during confinement before his trial has even begun.

The Court of Appeals also relied on what it termed the "indisputable rudiments of due process" in fashioning its compelling-necessity test. We do not doubt that the Due Process Clause protects a detainee from certain conditions and restrictions of pretrial detainment. . . . Nonetheless, that Clause provides no basis for application of a compelling-necessity standard to conditions of pretrial confinement that are not alleged to infringe any other, more specific guarantee of the Constitution.

It is important to focus on what is at issue here. We are not concerned with the initial decision to detain an accused and the curtailment of liberty that such a decision necessarily entails. . . . Neither respondents nor the courts below question that the Government may permissibly detain a person suspected of committing a crime prior to a formal adjudication of guilt. . . . Nor do they doubt that the Government has a substantial interest in ensuring that persons accused of crimes are available for trials and, ultimately, for service of their sentences, or that confinement of such persons pending trial is a legitimate means of furthering that interest. . . . Instead, what is at issue when an aspect of pretrial detention that is not alleged to violate any express guarantee of the Constitution is challenged, is the detainee's right to be free from punishment . . . and his understandable desire to be as comfortable as possible during his confinement, both of which may conceivably coalesce at some point. It seems clear that the Court of Appeals did not rely on the detainee's right to be free from punishment, but even if it had that right does not warrant adoption of that court's compelling-necessity test. . . . And to the extent the court relied on the detainee's desire to be free from discomfort, it suffices to say that this desire simply does not rise to the level of those fundamental liberty interests delineated in [other] cases. . . .

B

In evaluating the constitutionality of conditions or restrictions of pretrial detention that implicate only the protection against deprivation of liberty without due process of law, we think that the proper inquiry is whether those conditions amount to punishment of the detainee. For under the Due Process Clause, a detainee may not be punished prior to an adjudication of guilt in accordance with due process of law. . . .

Not every disability imposed during pretrial detention amounts to "punishment" in the constitutional sense, however. Once the Government has exercised its conceded authority to detain a person pending trial, it obviously is entitled to employ devices that are calculated to effectuate this detention. Traditionally, this has meant confinement in a facility which, no matter how modern or how antiquated, results in restricting the movement of a detainee in a manner in which he would not be restricted if he simply were free to walk the streets pending trial. Whether it be called a jail, a prison, or a custodial center, the purpose of the facility is to detain. Loss of freedom of choice and privacy are inherent incidents of confinement in such a facility. And the fact that such detention interferes with the detainee's understandable desire to live as comfortably as possible and with as little restraint as possible during confinement does not convert the conditions or restrictions of detention into "punishment."

This Court has recognized a distinction between punitive measures that may not constitutionally be imposed prior to a determination of guilt and regulatory restraints that may. . . . In Kennedy v. Mendoza-Martinez, [372 U.S. 144 (1963)], the Court examined the automatic forfeiture-of-citizenship provisions of the immigration laws to determine whether that sanction amounted to punishment or a mere regulatory restraint. While it is all but impossible to compress the distinction into a sentence or a paragraph, the Court there described the tests traditionally applied to determine whether a governmental act is punitive in nature:

> Whether the sanction involves an affirmative disability or restraint, whether it has historically been regarded as a punishment, whether it comes into play only on a finding of scienter, whether its operation will promote the traditional aims of punishment—retribution and deterrence, whether the behavior to which it applies is already a crime, whether an alternative purpose to which it may rationally be connected is assignable for it, and whether it appears excessive in relation to the alternative purpose assigned are all relevant to the inquiry, and may often point in differing directions.

372 U.S., at 168–69 (footnotes omitted). Because forfeiture of citizenship traditionally had been considered punishment and the legislative history of the forfeiture provisions "conclusively" showed that the measure was intended to be punitive, the Court held that forfeiture of citizenship in such circumstances constituted punishment that could not constitutionally be imposed without due process of law. Id., at 167–70, 186.

The factors identified in *Mendoza-Martinez* provide useful guideposts in determining whether particular restrictions and conditions accompanying pretrial detention amount to punishment in the constitutional sense of that word. A court must decide whether the disability is imposed for the purpose of punishment or whether it is but an incident of some other legitimate governmental purpose. . . . Absent a showing of an expressed intent to punish on the part of detention facility officials, that determination generally will turn on "whether an alternative purpose to which [the restriction] may rationally be connected is assignable for it, and whether it appears excessive in relation to the alternative purpose assigned [to it]." Kennedy v. Mendoza-Martinez, supra, at 168–69. . . . Thus, if a particular condition or restriction of pretrial detention is reasonably related to a legitimate governmental objective, it does not, without more, amount to "punishment."[5] Conversely, if a restriction or condition is not reasonably related to a legitimate goal—if it is arbitrary or purposeless—a court

5. This is not to say that the officials of a detention facility can justify punishment. They cannot. It is simply to say that in the absence of a showing of intent to punish, a court must look to see if a particular restriction or condition, which may on its face appear to be punishment, is instead but an incident of a legitimate nonpunitive govern-

permissibly may infer that the purpose of the governmental action is punishment that may not constitutionally be inflicted upon detainees *qua* detainees. . . . Courts must be mindful that these inquiries spring from constitutional requirements and that judicial answers to them must reflect that fact rather than a court's idea of how best to operate a detention facility. . . .

One further point requires discussion. The petitioners assert, and respondents concede, that the "essential objective of pretrial confinement is to insure the detainees' presence at trial." Brief for Petitioners 43; see Brief for Respondents 33. While this interest undoubtedly justifies the original decision to confine an individual in some manner, we do not accept respondents' argument that the Government's interest in ensuring a detainee's presence at trial is the *only* objective that may justify restraints and conditions once the decision is lawfully made to confine a person. . . . The Government also has legitimate interests that stem from its need to manage the facility in which the individual is detained. These legitimate operational concerns may require administrative measures that go beyond those that are, strictly speaking, necessary to ensure that the detainee shows up at trial. For example, the Government must be able to take steps to maintain security and order at the institution and make certain no weapons or illicit drugs reach detainees. Restraints that are reasonably related to the institution's interest in maintaining jail security do not, without more, constitute unconstitutional punishment, even if they are discomforting and are restrictions that the detainee would not have experienced had he been released while awaiting trial. We need not here attempt to detail the precise extent of the legitimate governmental interests that may justify conditions or restrictions of pretrial detention. It is enough simply to recognize that in addition to ensuring the detainees' presence at trial, the effective management of the detention facility once the individual is confined is a valid objective that may justify imposition of conditions and restrictions of pretrial detention and dispel any inference that such restrictions are intended as punishment.[6]

C

Judged by this analysis, respondents' claim that "double-bunking" violated their due process rights fails. Neither the District Court nor the

mental objective. . . . Retribution and deterrence are not legitimate nonpunitive governmental objectives. . . . Conversely, loading a detainee with chains and shackles and throwing him in a dungeon may ensure his presence at trial and preserve the security of the institution. But it would be difficult to conceive of a situation where conditions so harsh, employed to achieve objectives that could be accomplished in so many alternative and less harsh methods, would not support a conclusion that the purpose for which they were imposed was to punish.

6. In determining whether restrictions or conditions are reasonably related to the Government's interest in maintaining security and order and operating the institution in a manageable fashion, courts must heed our warning that "[s]uch considerations are peculiarly within the province and professional expertise of corrections officials, and, in the absence of substantial evidence in the record to indicate that the officials have exaggerated their response to these considerations, courts should ordinarily defer to their expert judgment in such matters." Pell v. Procunier, 417 U.S. [817 (1974)], at 827.

Court of Appeals intimated that it considered "double-bunking" to constitute punishment; instead, they found that it contravened the compelling-necessity test, which today we reject. On this record, we are convinced as a matter of law that "double-bunking" as practiced at the MCC did not amount to punishment and did not, therefore, violate respondents' rights under the Due Process Clause of the Fifth Amendment.

Each of the rooms at the MCC that house pretrial detainees has a total floor space of approximately 75 square feet. Each of them designated for "double-bunking" . . . contains a double bunkbed, certain other items of furniture, a wash basin, and an uncovered toilet. Inmates generally are locked into their rooms from 11 p.m. to 6:30 a.m. and for brief periods during the afternoon and evening head counts. During the rest of the day, they may move about freely between their rooms and the common areas.

Based on affidavits and a personal visit to the facility, the District Court concluded that the practice of "double-bunking" was unconstitutional. The court relied on two factors for its conclusion: (1) the fact that the rooms were designed to house only one inmate . . .; and (2) its judgment that confining two persons in one room or cell of this size constituted a "fundamental denia[l] of decency, privacy, personal security, and, simply, civilized humanity. . . ." Id., at 339. The Court of Appeals agreed with the District Court. In response to petitioners' arguments that the rooms at the MCC were larger and more pleasant than the cells involved in the cases relied on by the District Court, the Court of Appeals stated:

> [W]e find the lack of privacy inherent in double-celling in rooms intended for one individual a far more compelling consideration than a comparison of square footage or the substitution of doors for bars, carpet for concrete, or windows for walls. The government has simply failed to show any substantial justification for double-celling.

573 F.2d, at 127.

We disagree with both the District Court and the Court of Appeals that there is some sort of "one man, one cell" principle lurking in the Due Process Clause of the Fifth Amendment. While confining a given number of people in a given amount of space in such a manner as to cause them to endure genuine privations and hardship over an extended period of time might raise serious questions under the Due Process Clause as to whether those conditions amounted to punishment, nothing even approaching such hardship is shown by this record.[7]

7. Respondents seem to argue that "double-bunking" was unreasonable because petitioners were able to comply with the District Court's order forbidding "double-bunking" and still accommodate the increased numbers of detainees simply by transferring all but a handful of sentenced inmates who had been assigned to the MCC for the purpose of performing certain services and by committing those tasks to detainees. . . . That petitioners were able to comply with the District Court's order in this fashion does not mean that petitioners' chosen method of coping with the increased inmate population—"double-bunking"—was unreasonable. Governmental action does not have to be the only alternative or even the best alternative for it to be reasonable, to say nothing of constitutional. . . .

Detainees are required to spend only seven or eight hours each day in their rooms, during most or all of which they presumably are sleeping. The rooms provide more than adequate space for sleeping. During the remainder of the time, the detainees are free to move between their rooms and the common area. While "double-bunking" may have taxed some of the equipment or particular facilities in certain of the common areas . . . this does not mean that the conditions at the MCC failed to meet the standards required by the Constitution. Our conclusion in this regard is further buttressed by the detainees' length of stay at the MCC. . . . Nearly all of the detainees are released within 60 days. . . . We simply do not believe that requiring a detainee to share toilet facilities and this admittedly rather small sleeping place with another person for generally a maximum period of 60 days violates the Constitution.

III

Respondents also challenged certain MCC restrictions and practices that were designed to promote security and order at the facility on the ground that these restrictions violated the Due Process Clause of the Fifth Amendment, and certain other constitutional guarantees, such as the First and Fourth Amendments. The Court of Appeals seemed to approach the challenges to security restrictions in a fashion different from the other contested conditions and restrictions. It stated that "once it has been determined that the mere fact of confinement of the detainee justifies the restrictions, the institution must be permitted to use reasonable means to insure that its legitimate interests in security are safeguarded." 573 F.2d, at 124. The court might disagree with the choice of means to effectuate those interests, but it should not "second-guess the expert administrators on matters on which they are better informed. . . . Concern with minutiae of prison administration can only distract the court from detached consideration of the one overriding question presented to it: does the practice or condition violate the Constitution?" Id., at 124–25. Nonetheless, the court affirmed the District Court's injunction against several security restrictions. The court rejected the arguments of petitioners that these practices served the MCC's interest in security and order and held that the practices were unjustified interferences with the retained constitutional rights of *both* detainees and convicted inmates. . . . In our view, the Court of Appeals failed to heed its own admonition not to "second-guess" prison administrators.

Our cases have established several general principles that inform our evaluation of the constitutionality of the restrictions at issue. First, we have held that convicted prisoners do not forfeit all constitutional protections by reason of their conviction and confinement in prison. . . . *A fortiori*, pretrial detainees, who have not been convicted of any crimes, retain at least those constitutional rights that we have held are enjoyed by convicted prisoners.

But our cases also have insisted on a second proposition: simply because prison inmates retain certain constitutional rights does not mean that these rights are not subject to restrictions and limitations. . . . This principle applies equally to pretrial detainees and convicted prisoners. A detainee simply does not possess the full range of freedoms of an unincarcerated individual.

Third, maintaining institutional security and preserving internal order and discipline are essential goals that may require limitation or retraction of the retained constitutional rights of both convicted prisoners and pretrial detainees. . . . Prison officials must be free to take appropriate action to ensure the safety of inmates and corrections personnel and to prevent escape or unauthorized entry. Accordingly, we have held that even when an institutional restriction infringes a specific constitutional guarantee, such as the First Amendment, the practice must be evaluated in the light of the central objective of prison administration, safeguarding institutional security. . . .

Finally, as the Court of Appeals correctly acknowledged, the problems that arise in the day-to-day operation of a corrections facility are not susceptible of easy solutions. Prison administrators therefore should be accorded wide-ranging deference in the adoption and execution of policies and practices that in their judgment are needed to preserve internal order and discipline and to maintain institutional security. . . . "Such considerations are peculiarly within the province and professional expertise of corrections officials, and, in the absence of substantial evidence in the record to indicate that the officials have exaggerated their response to these considerations, courts should ordinarily defer to their expert judgment in such matters." Pell v. Procunier, 417 U.S., at 827. We further observe that, on occasion, prison administrators may be "experts" only by Act of Congress or of a state legislature. But judicial deference is accorded not merely because the administrator ordinarily will, as a matter of fact in a particular case, have a better grasp of his domain than the reviewing judge, but also because the operation of our correctional facilities is peculiarly the province of the Legislative and Executive Branches of our Government, not the Judicial. . . . With these teachings of our cases in mind, we turn to an examination of the MCC security practices that are alleged to violate the Constitution.

A

At the time of the lower courts' decisions, the Bureau of Prisons' "publisher-only" rule, which applies to all Bureau facilities, permitted inmates to receive books and magazines from outside the institution only if the materials were mailed directly from the publisher or a book club. . . . The warden of the MCC stated in an affidavit that "serious" security and administrative problems were caused when bound items were received by inmates from unidentified sources outside the facility. App. 24. He noted that in order to make a "proper and thorough" inspection of such items, prison officials would have to remove the covers of hardback books and to leaf through every page of all books and magazines to ensure that drugs, money, weapons, or other contraband were not secreted in the material.

"This search process would take a substantial and inordinate amount of available staff time." Ibid. However, "there is relatively little risk that material received directly from a publisher or book club would contain contraband, and therefore, the security problems are significantly reduced without a drastic drain on staff resources." Ibid.

The Court of Appeals rejected these security and administrative justifications and affirmed the District Court's order enjoining enforcement of the "publisher-only" rule at the MCC. The Court of Appeals held that the rule "severely and impermissibly restricts the reading material available to inmates" and therefore violates their First Amendment and due process rights. 573 F.2d, at 130.

It is desirable at this point to place in focus the precise question that now is before this Court. Subsequent to the decision of the Court of Appeals, the Bureau of Prisons amended its "publisher-only" rule to permit the receipt of books and magazines from bookstores as well as publishers and book clubs. . . . In addition, petitioners have informed the Court that the Bureau proposes to amend the rule further to allow receipt of paperback books, magazines, and other soft-covered materials from any source. . . . The Bureau regards hardback books as the "more dangerous source of risk to institutional security," however, and intends to retain the prohibition against receipt of hardback books unless they are mailed directly from publishers, book clubs, or bookstores. . . . Accordingly, petitioners request this Court to review the District Court's injunction only to the extent it enjoins petitioners from prohibiting receipt of hard-cover books that are not mailed directly from publishers, book clubs, or bookstores. . . .

We conclude that a prohibition against receipt of hardback books unless mailed directly from publishers, book clubs, or bookstores does not violate the First Amendment rights of MCC inmates. That limited restriction is a rational response by prison officials to an obvious security problem. It hardly needs to be emphasized that hardback books are especially serviceable for smuggling contraband into an institution; money, drugs, and weapons easily may be secreted in the bindings. . . . They also are difficult to search effectively. There is simply no evidence in the record to indicate that MCC officials have exaggerated their response to this security problem and to the administrative difficulties posed by the necessity of carefully inspecting each book mailed from unidentified sources. Therefore, the considered judgment of these experts must control in the absence of prohibitions far more sweeping than those involved here. . . .

Our conclusion that this limited restriction on receipt of hardback books does not infringe the First Amendment rights of MCC inmates is influenced by several other factors. The rule operates in a neutral fashion, without regard to the content of the expression. . . . And there are alternative means of obtaining reading material that have not been shown to be burdensome or insufficient. . . . The restriction, as it is now before us, allows soft-bound books and magazines to be received from any source and hardback books to be received from publishers, bookstores, and book clubs. In addition, the MCC has a "relatively large" library for use by inmates. . . . To the limited extent the rule might possibly increase the cost of obtaining published materials, this Court has held that where "other avenues" remain available for the receipt of materials by inmates, the loss of "cost advantages does not fundamentally implicate *free speech* values." See Jones v. North Carolina Prisoners' Labor Union, [433 U.S. 119 (1977)] at 130–31. We are also influenced in our decision by the fact that the rule's impact on pretrial detainees is limited to a maximum period of approximately 60 days. . . . In sum, considering all the circumstances, we view the rule, as we now find it, to be a "reasonable 'time, place and manner' regulatio[n that is] necessary to further significant governmental interests. . . ." Grayned v. City of Rockford, 408 U.S. 104, 115 (1972). . . .

B

Inmates at the MCC were not permitted to receive packages from outside the facility containing items of food or personal property, except for one package of food at Christmas. This rule was justified by MCC officials on three grounds. First, officials testified to "serious" security problems that arise from the introduction of such packages into the institution, the "traditional file in the cake kind of situation" as well as the concealment of drugs "in heels of shoes [and] seams of clothing." App. 80; see id., at 24, 84–85. As in the case of the "publisher-only" rule, the warden testified that if such packages were allowed, the inspection process necessary to ensure the security of the institution would require a "substantial and inordinate amount of available staff time." Id., at 24. Second, officials were concerned that the introduction of personal property into the facility would increase the risk of thefts, gambling, and inmate conflicts, the "age-old problem of you have it and I don't." Id., at 80; see id., at 85. Finally, they noted storage and sanitary problems that would result from inmates' receipt of food packages. . . . Inmates are permitted, however, to purchase certain items of food and personal property from the MCC commissary.

The District Court dismissed these justifications as "dire predictions." It was unconvinced by the asserted security problems because other institutions allow greater ownership of personal property and receipt of packages than does the MCC. And because the MCC permitted inmates to purchase items in the commissary, the court could not accept official fears of increased theft, gambling, or conflicts if packages were allowed. Finally, it believed that sanitation could be assured by proper housekeeping regulations. Accordingly, it ordered the MCC to promulgate regulations to permit receipt of at least items of the kind that are available in the commissary. . . . The Court of Appeals accepted the District Court's analysis and affirmed, although it noted that the MCC could place a ceiling on the permissible dollar value of goods received and restrict the number of packages.

Neither the District Court nor the Court of Appeals identified which provision of the Constitution was violated by this MCC restriction. We assume, for present purposes, that their decisions were based on the Due Process Clause of the Fifth Amendment, which provides protection for convicted prisoners and pretrial detainees alike against the deprivation of their property without due process of law. . . . But as we have stated, these due process rights of prisoners and pretrial detainees are not absolute; they are subject to reasonable limitation or retraction in light of the legitimate security concerns of the institution.

We think that the District Court and the Court of Appeals have trenched too cavalierly into areas that are properly the concern of MCC officials. It is plain from their opinions that the lower courts simply disagreed with the judgment of MCC officials about the extent of the security interests affected and the means required to further those interests. But our decisions have time and again emphasized that this sort of unguided substitution of judicial judgment for that of the expert prison administrators on matters such as this is inappropriate. . . . We do not doubt that the rule devised by the District Court and modified by the Court of Appeals may be a reasonable way of coping with the problems of security, order, and sanitation. It simply is not, however, the only constitutionally permissible approach to these problems. Certainly, the Due Process Clause does not mandate a "lowest common denominator" security standard, whereby a practice permitted at one penal institution must be permitted at all institutions.

Corrections officials concluded that permitting the introduction of packages of personal property and food would increase the risks of gambling, theft, and inmate fights over that which the institution already experienced by permitting certain items to be purchased from its commissary. "It is enough to say that they have not been conclusively shown to be wrong in this view." Jones v. North Carolina Prisoners' Labor Union, 433 U.S., at 132. It is also all too obvious that such packages are handy devices for the smuggling of contraband. There simply is no basis in this record for concluding that MCC officials have exaggerated their response to these serious problems or that this restriction is irrational. It does not therefore deprive the convicted inmates or pretrial detainees of the MCC of their property without due process of law in contravention of the Fifth Amendment.

C

The MCC staff conducts unannounced searches of inmate living areas at irregular intervals. These searches generally are formal unit "shakedowns" during which all inmates are cleared of the residential units, and a team of guards searches each room. Prior to the District Court's order, inmates were not permitted to watch the searches. Officials testified that permitting inmates to observe room inspections would lead to friction between the inmates and security guards and would allow the inmates to attempt to frustrate the search by distracting personnel and moving contraband from one room to another ahead of the search team.

The District Court held that this procedure could not stand as applied to pretrial detainees because MCC officials had not shown that the restriction was justified by "compelling necessity." The court stated that "[a]t least until or unless [petitioners] can show a pattern of violence or other disruptions taxing the powers of control—a kind of showing not remotely approached by the Warden's expressions—the security argument for banishing inmates while their rooms are searched must be rejected." 439 F.Supp., at 149. It also noted that in many instances inmates suspected guards of thievery. . . . The Court of Appeals agreed with the District Court. It saw "no reason whatsoever not to permit a detainee to observe the search of his room and belongings from a reasonable distance," although the court permitted the removal of any detainee who became "obstructive." 573 F.2d, at 132.

The Court of Appeals did not identify the constitutional provision on which it relied in invalidating the room-search rule. The District Court stated that the rule infringed the detainee's interest in privacy and indicated that this interest in privacy was founded on the Fourth Amendment. . . . It may well be argued that a person confined in a detention facility has no reasonable expectation of privacy with respect to his room or cell and that therefore the Fourth Amendment provides no protection for such a person. . . . In any case, given the realities of institutional confinement, any reasonable expectation of privacy that a detainee retained necessarily would be of a diminished scope. . . . Assuming, *arguendo*, that a pretrial detainee retains such a diminished expectation of privacy after commitment to a custodial facility, we nonetheless find that the room-search rule does not violate the Fourth Amendment.

It is difficult to see how the detainee's interest in privacy is infringed by the room-search rule. No one can rationally doubt that room searches represent an appropriate security measure and neither the District Court nor the Court of Appeals prohibited such searches. And even the most zealous advocate of prisoners' rights would not suggest that a warrant is required to conduct such a search. Detainees' drawers, beds, and personal items may be searched, even after the lower courts' rulings. Permitting detainees to observe the searches does not lessen the invasion of their privacy; its only conceivable beneficial effect would be to prevent theft or misuse by those conducting the search. The room-search rule simply facilitates the safe and effective performance of the search which all concede may be conducted. The rule itself, then, does not render the searches "unreasonable" within the meaning of the Fourth Amendment.

D

Inmates at all Bureau of Prisons facilities, including the MCC, are required to expose their body cavities for visual inspection as a part of a strip search conducted after every contact visit with a person from outside the institution. Corrections officials testified that visual cavity searches were necessary not only to discover but also to deter the smuggling of weapons, drugs, and other contraband into the institution. . . . The District Court upheld the strip-search procedure but prohibited the body-cavity searches, absent probable cause to believe that the inmate is concealing contraband. . . . Because petitioners proved only one instance in the MCC's short history where contraband was found during a body-cavity search, the Court of Appeals affirmed. In its view, the "gross violation of personal privacy inherent in such a search cannot be outweighed by the government's security interest in maintaining a practice of so little actual utility." 573 F.2d, at 131.

Admittedly, this practice instinctively gives us the most pause. However, assuming for present purposes that inmates, both convicted prisoners and pretrial detainees, retain some Fourth Amendment rights upon commitment to a corrections facility . . . we nonetheless conclude that these searches do not violate that Amendment. The Fourth Amendment prohibits only unreasonable searches . . . and under the circumstances, we do not believe that these searches are unreasonable.

The test of reasonableness under the Fourth Amendment is not capable of precise definition or mechanical application. In each case it requires a balancing of the need for the particular search against the invasion of personal rights that the search entails. Courts must consider the scope of the particular intrusion, the manner in which it is conducted, the justification for initiating it, and the place in which it is conducted. . . . A detention facility is a unique place fraught with serious security dangers. Smuggling of money, drugs, weapons, and other contraband is all too common an occurrence. And inmate attempts to secrete these items into the facility by concealing them in body cavities are documented in this record . . . and in other cases. . . . That there has been only one instance where an MCC inmate was discovered attempting to smuggle contraband into the institution on his person may be more a testament to the effectiveness of this search technique as a deterrent than to any lack of interest on the part of the inmates to secrete and import such items when the opportunity arises.

We do not underestimate the degree to which these searches may invade the personal privacy of inmates. Nor do we doubt, as the District Court noted, that on occasion a security guard may conduct the search in an abusive fashion. . . . Such abuse cannot be condoned. The searches must be conducted in a reasonable manner. . . . But we deal here with the question whether visual body-cavity inspections as contemplated by the MCC rules can *ever* be conducted on less than probable cause. Balancing the significant and legitimate security interests of the institution against the privacy interests of the inmates, we conclude that they can.

IV

Nor do we think that the four MCC security restrictions and practices described in Part III, supra, constitute "punishment" in violation of the rights of pretrial detainees under the Due Process Clause of the Fifth Amendment. Neither the District Court nor the Court of Appeals suggested that these restrictions and practices were employed by MCC officials with an intent to punish the pretrial detainees housed there. Respondents do not even make such a suggestion; they simply argue that the restrictions were greater than necessary to satisfy petitioners' legitimate interest in maintaining security. . . . Therefore, the determination whether these restrictions and practices constitute punishment in the constitutional sense depends on whether they are rationally related to a legitimate nonpunitive governmental purpose and whether they appear excessive in relation to that purpose. . . . Ensuring security and order at the institution is a permissible nonpunitive objective, whether the facility houses pretrial detainees, convicted inmates, or both. . . . For the reasons set forth in Part III, supra, we think that these particular restrictions and practices were reasonable responses by MCC officials to legitimate security concerns. Respondents simply have not met their heavy burden of showing that these officials have exaggerated their response to the genuine security considerations that actuated these restrictions and practices. . . . And as might be expected of restrictions applicable to pretrial detainees, these restrictions were of only limited duration so far as the MCC pretrial detainees were concerned. . . .

V

There was a time not too long ago when the federal judiciary took a completely "hands-off" approach to the problem of prison administration. In recent years, however, these courts largely have discarded this "hands-off" attitude and have waded into this complex arena. The deplorable conditions and Draconian restrictions of some of our Nation's prisons are too well known to require recounting here, and the federal courts rightly have condemned these sordid aspects of our prison systems. But many of these same courts have, in the name of the Constitution, become increasingly enmeshed in the minutiae of prison operations. Judges, after all, are human. They, no less than others in our society, have a natural tendency to believe that their individual solutions to often intractable problems are better and more workable than those of the persons who are actually charged with and trained in the running of the particular institution under examination. But under the Constitution, the first question to be answered is not whose plan is best, but in what branch of the Government is lodged the authority to initially devise the plan. This does not mean that constitutional rights are not to be scrupulously observed. It does mean, however, that the inquiry of federal courts into prison management must be limited to the issue of whether a particular system violates any prohibition of the Constitution or, in the case of a federal prison, a statute. The wide range of "judgment calls" that meet constitutional and statutory requirements are confided to officials outside of the Judicial Branch of Government.

The judgment of the Court of Appeals is, accordingly, reversed, and the case is remanded for proceedings consistent with this opinion.

. . .[8]

---

309. Relying on Bell v. Wolfish, in Block v. Rutherford, 468 U.S. 576 (1984), the Court held that pretrial detainees do not have a constitutional

[8] Justice Powell wrote a brief opinion concurring in part and dissenting in part. Justice Marshall wrote a dissenting opinion. Justice Stevens wrote a dissenting opinion, which Justice Brennan joined.

right to contact visits with members of their families or others. "[T]he Constitution does not require that detainees be allowed contact visits when responsible, experienced administrators have determined, in their sound discretion, that such visits will jeopardize the security of the facility." Id. at 589. In the same case, the Court reaffirmed its holding in *Bell* that detainees do not have a constitutional right to watch "shakedown" searches of their cells. On the general question of detainees' right to privacy under the Fourth Amendment, to which the Court adverts in *Bell*, see Hudson v. Palmer, 468 U.S. 517 (1984), p. 292 note 163 above, holding that "the Fourth Amendment has no applicability to a prison cell," id. at 536.

A much more protective attitude toward pretrial detainees' rights was evident in a Second Circuit case decided before *Bell*. Marcera v. Chinlund, 595 F.2d 1231 (2d Cir.), vacated and remanded, 442 U.S. 915 (1979). The majority opinion and opinion dissenting in part in Campbell v. McGruder, 580 F.2d 521 (D.C.Cir.1978), also contain lengthy discussions of the problem of pretrial detention and jail conditions in the District of Columbia.

310. Bail pending appeal. In McKane v. Durston, 153 U.S. 684 (1894), the Court held that there is no constitutional right to bail pending appeal from a conviction:

> A review by an appellate court of the final judgment in a criminal case, however grave the offence of which the accused is convicted, was not at common law and is not now a necessary element of due process of law. It is wholly within the discretion of the state to allow or not to allow such a review. . . .
>
> It is, therefore, clear that the right of appeal may be accorded by the state to the accused upon such terms as in its wisdom may be deemed proper.

Id. at 687–88. See the provisions of 18 U.S.C. § 3143(b), p. 575 above.

Section 3143(b)(2) was construed in United States v. Powell, 761 F.2d 1227 (8th Cir.1985). The court concluded: "We hold that a defendant who wishes to be released on bail after the imposition of a sentence including a term of imprisonment must first show that the question presented by the appeal is substantial, in the sense that it is a close question or one that could go either way. It is not sufficient to show simply that reasonable judges could differ (presumably every judge who writes a dissenting opinion is still 'reasonable') or that the issue is fairly debatable or not frivolous. On the other hand, the defendant does not have to show that it is likely or probable that he or she will prevail on the issue on appeal. If this part of the test is satisfied, the defendant must then show that the substantial question he or she seeks to present is so integral to the merits of the conviction that it is more probable than not that reversal or a new trial will occur if the question is decided on the defendant's favor. In deciding whether this part of the burden has been satisfied, the court or judge to whom application for bail is made must assume that the substantial question presented will go the other way on appeal and then assess the impact of such assumed error on the conviction. This standard will, we think, carry out the manifest purpose of Congress to reduce substantially the numbers of convicted persons released on bail pending appeal, without eliminating such release entirely or limiting it to a negligible number of appellants." Id. at 1233–34.

In some other circuits, a somewhat less restrictive standard of what counts as a substantial question has been adopted. See, generally in accord with *Powell*, United States v. Perholtz, 836 F.2d 554 (D.C.Cir.1987); United States v. Bayko, 774 F.2d 516 (1st Cir.1985) (reviewing cases in other courts of appeals). See also United States v. Smith, 793 F.2d 85 (3d Cir.1986). Finetti v. Harris, 609 F.2d 594 (2d Cir.1979), discusses federal review on habeas corpus of a state court's denial of bail pending appeal. Sections 3143(b)(2) and § 3145(c) (appeal from a detention order) are construed in United States v. Koon, 6 F.3d 561 (9th Cir.1993).

In United States v. Garcia, 340 F.3d 1013 (9th Cir.2003), the court construed § 3145(c), p. 576 above, which provides that a person who has been convicted of an especially serious offense and is detained pursuant to § 3143(b)(2) may be released on bail pending appeal only if there are "exceptional reasons" why detention would not be appropriate. The court said that a district court has "broad discretion . . . to consider all the particular circumstances of the case" and "should examine the totality of the circumstances and, on the basis of that examination, determine whether, due to any truly unusual factors or combination of factors (bearing in mind the congressional policy that offenders who have committed crimes of violence should not, except in exceptional cases, be released pending appeal) it would be unreasonable to incarcerate the defendant prior to the appellate court's resolution of his appeal." 340 F.3d at 1018–1019. Among the factors that might be considered, the court said, are the nature of the criminal act, the length of the sentence, the likelihood of unusual hardships or risks in prison, and the strength of the defendant's arguments on appeal, provided that the circumstances were exceptional.

A district court determining whether a state prisoner whose conviction has been overturned on habeas corpus should be released or detained while the latter decision is under review, or a court of appeals reviewing such determination, see Fed.R.App.P. 23(c)–(d), is not restricted to considering the risk that the prisoner will flee. It may also consider the risk that the prisoner, if released, will pose a danger to the community and the state's interest in continuing custody and rehabilitation pending a final determination of the habeas corpus proceeding. The likelihood that the state will succeed on appeal and the strength of the state's case on the merits are also relevant factors. Hilton v. Braunskill, 481 U.S. 770 (1987) (6–3).

311. Forfeiture. Fed.R.Crim.P. 46(f)–(g):

(f) Bail Forfeiture.

(1) *Declaration.* The court must declare the bail forfeited if a condition of the bond is breached.

(2) *Setting Aside.* The court may set aside in whole or in part a bail forfeiture upon any condition the court may impose if:

(A) the surety later surrenders into custody the person released on the surety's appearance bond; or

(B) it appears that justice does not require bail forfeiture.

(3) *Enforcement.*

(A) *Default Judgment and Execution.* If it does not set aside a bail forfeiture, the court must, upon the government's motion, enter a default judgment.

(B) *Jurisdiction and Service.* By entering into a bond, each surety submits to the district court's jurisdiction and irrevocably appoints the district clerk as its agent to receive service of any filings affecting its liability.

(C) *Motion to Enforce.* The court may, upon the government's motion, enforce the surety's liability without an independent action. The government must serve any motion, and notice as the court prescribes, on the district clerk. If so served, the clerk must promptly mail a copy to the surety at its last known address.

(4) *Remission.* After entering a judgment under Rule 46(f)(3), the court may remit in whole or in part the judgment under the same conditions specified in Rule 46(f)(2).

(g) Exoneration. The court must exonerate the surety and release any bail when a bond condition has been satisfied or when the court has set aside or remitted the forfeiture. The court must exonerate a surety who deposits cash in the amount of the bond or timely surrenders the defendant into custody.

Observing that remission of a forfeited bond is not granted while the defendant remains at large, the court of appeals said that, in order to show that "justice necessitates remission," one must show that "the bond forfeiture bears no reasonable relation to several factors: 1) the cost and inconvenience to the government in regaining custody of the defendant, 2) the amount of delay caused by the defendant's default and the stage of the proceedings at the time of his disappearance, 3) the willfulness of the defendant's breach of conditions and the prejudice suffered by the government, and 4) the public interest and necessity of effectuating the appearance of the defendant." United States v. Diaz, 811 F.2d 1412, 1415 (11th Cir.1987) (forfeiture upheld). See United States v. Nguyen, 279 F.3d 1112 (9th Cir.2002) (forfeiture upheld); United States v. Bass, 573 F.2d 258 (5th Cir.1978) (remission of partial forfeiture indicated); United States v. Kirkman, 426 F.2d 747 (4th Cir.1970) (remissions ordered); United States v. Foster, 417 F.2d 1254 (7th Cir.1969) (remanded for consideration of remission).

CHAPTER 9

THE DECISION TO PROSECUTE

312.

Few subjects are less adapted to judicial review than the exercise by the Executive of his discretion in deciding when and whether to institute criminal proceedings, or what precise charge shall be made, or whether to dismiss a proceeding once brought.

The United States Attorney, under the direction and control of the Attorney General, is the attorney for the Executive, charged with faithful execution of the laws, protection of the interests of the United States, and prosecution of offenses against the United States. As such he must have broad discretion. . . .

. . .

An attorney for the United States, as any other attorney, however, appears in a dual role. He is at once an officer of the court and the agent and attorney for a client; in the first capacity he is responsible to the Court for the manner of his conduct of a case, i.e., his demeanor, deportment and ethical conduct; but in his second capacity, as agent and attorney for the Executive, he is responsible to his principal and the courts have no power over the exercise of his discretion or his motives as they relate to the execution of his duty within the framework of his professional employment. . . .

To say that the United States Attorney must literally treat every offense and every offender alike is to delegate him an impossible task; of course this concept would negate discretion. Myriad factors can enter into the prosecutor's decision. Two persons may have committed what is precisely the same legal offense but the prosecutor is not compelled by law, duty or tradition to treat them the same as to charges. On the contrary, he is expected to exercise discretion and common sense to the end that if, for example, one is a young first offender and the other older, with a criminal record, or one played a lesser and the other a dominant role, one the instigator and the other a follower, the prosecutor can and should take such factors into account; no court has any jurisdiction to inquire into or review his decision.

It is assumed that the United States Attorney will perform his duties and exercise his powers consistent with his oaths; and while this discretion is subject to abuse or misuse just as is judicial discretion, deviations from his duty as an agent of the Executive are to be dealt with by his superiors.

> The remedy lies ultimately within the establishment where power and discretion reside. The President has abundant supervisory and disciplinary powers—including summary dismissal—to deal with misconduct of his subordinates; it is not the function of the judiciary to review the exercise of executive discretion whether it be that of the President himself or those to whom he has delegated certain of his powers.

Newman v. United States, 382 F.2d 479, 480–82 (D.C.Cir.1967).

See also United States v. Gainey, 440 F.2d 290 (D.C.Cir.1971) (district judge may not dismiss charges to reduce court congestion, over prosecutor's objection); United States v. Cox, 342 F.2d 167 (5th Cir.1965), p. 689 note 346 below.

Yick Wo v. Hopkins

118 U.S. 356, 6 S.Ct. 1064, 30 L.Ed. 220 (1886)

■ MR. JUSTICE MATTHEWS delivered the opinion of the court.

. . .

[The appellants were found guilty of violating ordinances of the board of supervisors of San Francisco County which prohibited anyone from operating a laundry without the consent of the board except in a building of brick or stone.]

We are . . . constrained, at the outset, to differ from the Supreme Court of California upon the real meaning of the ordinances in question. That court considered these ordinances as vesting in the board of supervisors a not unusual discretion in granting or withholding their assent to the use of wooden buildings as laundries, to be exercised in reference to the circumstances of each case, with a view to the protection of the public against the dangers of fire. We are not able to concur in that interpretation of the power conferred upon the supervisors. There is nothing in the ordinances which points to such a regulation of the business of keeping and conducting laundries. They seem intended to confer, and actually do confer, not a discretion to be exercised upon a consideration of the circumstances of each case, but a naked and arbitrary power to give or withhold consent, not only as to places, but as to persons. So that, if an applicant for such consent, being in every way a competent and qualified person, and having complied with every reasonable condition demanded by any public interest, should, failing to obtain the requisite consent of the supervisors to the prosecution of his business, apply for redress by the judicial process of *mandamus*, to require the supervisors to consider and act upon his case, it would be a sufficient answer for them to say that the law had conferred upon them authority to withhold their assent, without reason and without responsibility. The power given to them is not confided to their discretion in the legal sense of that term, but is granted to their mere will. It is purely arbitrary, and acknowledges neither guidance nor restraint.

. . .

It is contended on the part of the petitioners that the ordinances for violations of which they are severally sentenced to imprisonment, are void on their face, as being within the prohibitions of the Fourteenth Amendment; and, in the alternative, if not so, that they are void by reason of their administration, operating unequally, so as to punish in the present petitioners what is permitted to others as lawful, without any distinction of circumstances—an unjust and illegal discrimination, it is claimed, which, though not made expressly by the ordinances is made possible by them.

When we consider the nature and the theory of our institutions of government, the principles upon which they are supposed to rest, and review the history of their development, we are constrained to conclude that they do not mean to leave room for the play and action of purely personal and arbitrary power. Sovereignty itself is, of course, not subject to law, for it is the author and source of law; but in our system, while sovereign powers are delegated to the agencies of government, sovereignty itself remains with the people, by whom and for whom all government exists and acts. And the law is the definition and limitation of power. It is, indeed, quite true, that there must always be lodged somewhere, and in some person or body, the authority of final decision; and in many cases of mere administration the responsibility is purely political, no appeal lying except to the ultimate tribunal of the public judgment, exercised either in the pressure of opinion or by means of the suffrage. But the fundamental rights to life, liberty, and the pursuit of happiness, considered as individual possessions, are secured by those maxims of constitutional law which are the monuments showing the victorious progress of the race in securing to men the blessings of civilization under the reign of just and equal laws, so that, in the famous language of the Massachusetts Bill of Rights, the government of the commonwealth "may be a government of laws and not of men." For, the very idea that one man may be compelled to hold his life, or the means of living, or any material right essential to the enjoyment of life, at the mere will of another, seems to be intolerable in any country where freedom prevails, as being the essence of slavery itself.

. . .

. . . In the present cases we are not obliged to reason from the probable to the actual, and pass upon the validity of the ordinances complained of, as tried merely by the opportunities which their terms afford, of unequal and unjust discrimination in their administration. For the cases present the ordinances in actual operation, and the facts shown establish an administration directed so exclusively against a particular class of persons as to warrant and require the conclusion, that, whatever may have been the intent of the ordinances as adopted, they are applied by the public authorities charged with their administration, and thus representing the State itself, with a mind so unequal and oppressive as to amount to a practical denial by the State of that equal protection of the laws, which is secured to the petitioners, as to all other persons, by the broad and benign provisions of the Fourteenth Amendment to the Constitution of the United States. Though the law itself be fair on its face and impartial in appearance, yet, if it is applied and administered by public authority with an evil eye and an unequal hand, so as practically to make unjust and illegal discriminations between persons in similar circumstances, material to their rights, the denial of equal justice is still within the prohibition of the Constitution. . . .

The present cases, as shown by the facts disclosed in the record, are within this class. It appears that both petitioners have complied with every requisite, deemed by the law or by the public officers charged with its administration, necessary for the protection of neighboring property from fire, or as a precaution against injury to the public health. No reason whatever, except the will of the supervisors, is assigned why they should not be permitted to carry on, in the accustomed manner, their harmless and useful occupation, on which they depend for a livelihood. And while this consent of the supervisors is withheld from them and from two hundred others who have also petitioned, all of whom happen to be Chinese subjects, eighty others, not Chinese subjects, are permitted to carry on the same business under similar conditions. The fact of this discrimination is admitted. No reason for it is shown, and the conclusion cannot be resisted, that no reason for it exists except hostility to the race and nationality to which the petitioners belong, and which in the eye of the law is not justified. The discrimination is, therefore, illegal, and the public administration which enforces it is a denial of the equal protection of the laws and a violation of the Fourteenth Amendment of the Constitution. The imprisonment of the petitioners is, therefore, illegal, and they must be discharged. . . .

Wayte v. United States

470 U.S. 598, 105 S.Ct. 1524, 84 L.Ed.2d 547 (1985)

■ JUSTICE POWELL delivered the opinion of the Court.

The question presented is whether a passive enforcement policy under which the Government prosecutes only those who report themselves as having violated the law, or who are reported by others, violates the First and Fifth Amendments.

I

On July 2, 1980, pursuant to his authority under § 3 of the Military Selective Service Act, 62 Stat. 605, as amended, 50 U.S.C.App. § 453, the President issued Presidential Proclamation No. 4771, 3 CFR 82 (1981). This proclamation directed male citizens and certain male residents born during 1960 to register with the Selective Service System during the week of July 21, 1980. Petitioner fell within that class but did not register.

Instead, he wrote several letters to Government officials, including the President, stating that he had not registered and did not intend to do so.

Petitioner's letters were added to a Selective Service file of young men who advised that they had failed to register or who were reported by others as having failed to register. For reasons we discuss, infra . . . Selective Service adopted a policy of passive enforcement under which it would investigate and prosecute only the cases of nonregistration contained in this file. In furtherance of this policy, Selective Service sent a letter on June 17, 1981, to each reported violator who had not registered and for whom it had an address. The letter explained the duty to register, stated that Selective Service had information that the person was required to register but had not done so, requested that he either comply with the law by filling out an enclosed registration card or explain why he was not subject to registration, and warned that a violation could result in criminal prosecution and specified penalties. Petitioner received a copy of this letter but did not respond.

On July 20, 1981, Selective Service transmitted to the Department of Justice, for investigation and potential prosecution, the names of petitioner and 133 other young men identified under its passive enforcement system—all of whom had not registered in response to the Service's June letter. At two later dates, it referred the names of 152 more young men similarly identified. After screening out the names of those who appeared not to be in the class required to register, the Department of Justice referred the remaining names to the Federal Bureau of Investigation for additional inquiry and to the United States Attorneys for the districts in which the nonregistrants resided. Petitioner's name was one of those referred.

Pursuant to Department of Justice policy, those referred were not immediately prosecuted. Instead, the appropriate United States Attorney was required to notify identified nonregistrants by registered mail that, unless they registered within a specified time, prosecution would be considered. In addition, an FBI agent was usually sent to interview the nonregistrant before prosecution was instituted. This effort to persuade nonregistrants to change their minds became known as the "beg" policy. Under it, young men who registered late were not prosecuted, while those who never registered were investigated further by the Government. Pursuant to the "beg" policy, the United States Attorney for the Central District of California sent petitioner a letter on October 15, 1981, urging him to register or face possible prosecution. Again petitioner failed to respond.

On December 9, 1981, the Department of Justice instructed all United States Attorneys not to begin seeking indictments against nonregistrants until further notice. On January 7, 1982, the President announced a grace period to afford nonregistrants a further opportunity to register without penalty. This grace period extended until February 28, 1982. Petitioner still did not register.

Over the next few months, the Department decided to begin prosecuting those young men who, despite the grace period and "beg" policy, continued to refuse to register. It recognized that under the passive enforcement system those prosecuted were "liable to be vocal proponents of nonregistration" or persons "with religious or moral objections." Memorandum of March 17, 1982 from Lawrence Lippe, Chief General Litigation and Legal Advice Section, Criminal Division, Department of Justice, to D. Lowell Jensen, Assistant Attorney General, Criminal Division, App. 301. It also recognized that prosecutions would "undoubtedly result in allegations that the [case was] brought in retribution for the nonregistrant's exercise of his first amendment rights." Ibid. The Department was advised, however, that Selective Service could not develop a more "active" enforcement system for quite some time. . . . Because of this, the Department decided to begin seeking indictments under the passive system without further delay. On May 21, 1982, United States Attorneys were notified to begin prosecution of nonregistrants. On June 28, 1982, FBI agents interviewed petitioner and he continued to refuse to register. Accordingly, on July 22, 1982, an indictment was returned against him for knowingly and willfully failing to register with the Selective Service in violation of sections 3 and 12(a) of the Military Selective Service Act. . . . This was the first indictment returned against any individual under the passive policy.

II

Petitioner moved to dismiss the indictment on the ground of selective prosecution. He contended that he and the other indicted nonregistrants were "vocal" opponents of the registration program who had been impermissibly targeted (out of an estimated 674,000 nonregistrants) for prosecution on the basis of their exercise of First Amendment rights. . . .

[T]he District Court dismissed the indictment on the ground that the Government had failed to rebut petitioner's prima facie case of selective prosecution. . . .

The Court of Appeals reversed. . . .

Recognizing both the importance of the question presented and a division in the Circuits, we granted certiorari on the question of selective prosecution. . . . We now affirm.

III

In our criminal justice system, the Government retains "broad discretion" as to whom to prosecute. . . . "[S]o long as the prosecutor has probable cause to believe that the accused committed an offense defined by statute, the decision whether or not to prosecute, and what charge to file or bring before a grand jury, generally rests entirely in his discretion." Bordenkircher v. Hayes, 434 U.S. 357, 364 (1978). This broad discretion rests largely on the recognition that the decision to prosecute is particularly ill-suited to judicial review. Such factors as the strength of the case, the prosecution's general deterrence value, the Government's enforcement priorities, and the case's relationship to the Government's overall enforcement plan are not readily susceptible to the kind of analysis the courts are competent to undertake. Judicial supervision in this area, moreover, entails systemic costs of particular concern. Examining the basis of a prosecution delays the criminal proceeding, threatens to chill law enforcement by subjecting the prosecutor's motives and decisionmaking to outside inquiry, and may undermine prosecutorial effectiveness by revealing the Government's enforcement policy. All these are substantial concerns that make the courts properly hesitant to examine the decision whether to prosecute.

As we have noted in a slightly different context, however, although prosecutorial discretion is broad, it is not " 'unfettered.' Selectivity in the enforcement of criminal laws is . . . subject to constitutional constraints." United States v. Batchelder, 442 U.S. 114, 125 (1979) (footnote omitted). In particular, the decision to prosecute may not be " 'deliberately based upon an unjustifiable standard such as race, religion, or other arbitrary classification,' " Bordenkircher v. Hayes, supra, at 364, quoting Oyler v. Boles, 368 U.S. 448, 456 (1962), including the exercise of protected statutory and constitutional rights. . . .

It is appropriate to judge selective prosecution claims according to ordinary equal protection standards. . . . Under our prior cases, these standards require petitioner to show both that the passive enforcement system had a discriminatory effect and that it was motivated by a discriminatory purpose. . . . All petitioner has shown here is that those eventually prosecuted, along with many not prosecuted, reported themselves as having violated the law. He has not shown that the enforcement policy selected nonregistrants for prosecution on the basis of their speech. Indeed, he could not have done so given the way the "beg" policy was carried out. The Government did not prosecute those who reported themselves but later registered. Nor did it prosecute those who protested registration but did not report themselves or were not reported by others. In fact, the Government did not even investigate those who wrote letters to Selective Service criticizing registration unless their letters stated affirmatively that they had refused to comply with the law. . . . The Government, on the other hand, did prosecute people who reported themselves or were reported by others but who did not publicly protest. These facts demonstrate that the Government treated all reported nonregistrants similarly. It did not subject vocal nonregistrants to any special burden. Indeed, those prosecuted in effect selected themselves for prosecution by refusing to register after being reported and warned by the Government.

Even if the passive policy had a discriminatory effect, petitioner has not shown that the Government intended such a result. The evidence he presented demonstrated only that the Government was aware that the passive enforcement policy would result in prosecution of vocal objectors and that they would probably make selective prosecution claims. As we have noted, however, " '[d]iscriminatory purpose' . . . implies more than . . . intent as awareness of consequences. It implies that the decisionmaker . . . selected or reaffirmed a particular course of action at least in part 'because of,' not merely 'in spite of,' its adverse effects upon an identifiable group." Personnel Administrator of Mass. v. Feeney, [442 U.S. 256 (1979)], at 279 (footnotes and citations omitted). In the present case, petitioner has not shown that the Government prosecuted him because of his protest activities. Absent such a showing, his claim of selective prosecution fails.

IV

Petitioner also challenges the passive enforcement policy directly on First Amendment grounds. . . .

. . .

We conclude that the Government's passive enforcement system together with its "beg" policy violated neither the First nor Fifth Amendments. Accordingly, we affirm the judgment of the Court of Appeals.

It is so ordered.[1]

---

313. "To support a defense of selective or discriminatory prosecution, a defendant bears the heavy burden of establishing, at least *prima facie*, (1) that, while others similarly situated have not generally been proceeded against because of conduct of the type forming the basis of the charge against him, he had been singled out for prosecution, and (2) that the government's discriminatory selection of him for prosecution has been invidious or in bad faith, i.e., based upon such impermissible considerations as race, religion, or the desire to prevent his exercise of constitutional rights." United States v. Berrios, 501 F.2d 1207, 1211 (2d Cir.1974). See United States v. Ross, 719 F.2d 615 (2d Cir.1983) (allegation of selective prosecution because defendant refused to act as informer or agent for investigators; prosecution held not improper); United States v. Bourque, 541 F.2d 290 (1st Cir.1976) (allegation that personal vindictiveness motivated tax prosecution was insufficient without further allegation that prosecutions were not normally instituted for offenses charged).

People v. Utica Daw's Drug Co.

16 A.D.2d 12, 225 N.Y.S.2d 128 (1962)

■ HALPERN, JUSTICE.

This case presents the question of the proper way in which to deal with a claim by a defendant in a criminal case that the law has been enforced in a discriminatory manner against him in violation of the equal protection clauses of the State and Federal Constitutions.

The defendant maintains a drug store in the City of Utica, New York, which operates under a policy of selling at reduced prices, generally characteristic of stores known as "cut-rate" stores or discount houses. The

[1] Justice Marshall wrote a dissenting opinion, which Justice Brennan joined.

drug store is open on Sunday as all drug stores are permitted to be under the Sunday statute (Penal Law, § 2147). However, the items which drug stores are permitted to sell on Sunday are limited by the statute. The defendant was indicted for violation of the Sunday statute, it being charged that defendant on Sunday, December 18, 1960, "unlawfully did publicly sell and expose for sale certain property, to wit, a pair of gloves, a doll, a brown belt and a drinking cup" in violation of section 2147 of the Penal Law.

The defendant did not contest the charge that the enumerated items had been sold and offered for sale in its store but contended that similar items had been sold and offered for sale on Sunday throughout the City of Utica and County of Oneida by all other drug stores and that other items, the sale of which on Sunday was prohibited by section 2147 of the Penal Law, had been regularly offered for sale and sold in other types of stores, without any attempt on the part of the public authorities to interfere with the sale or to prosecute the vendors. Only the defendant and one other company (not a drug store) also engaged in a discount operation were prosecuted. The defendant maintained that the prosecution was part of a discriminatory design aimed at the defendant and others engaged in the same type of "cut-rate" operation. It maintained that the public authorities intentionally discriminated against that class and allowed others outside the class to continue to sell the forbidden items in violation of the Sunday law without molestation.

The trial court, with the acquiescence of the District Attorney, held that the defendant's contention, if established, would constitute a good defense to the criminal charge and it submitted the case to the jury accordingly. It left it to the jury to decide as a question of fact whether the defendant's proof established "a clear and intentional discrimination against this defendant and against those in the same class." At the request of the defendant, the court charged in language taken from Yick Wo v. Hopkins, 118 U.S. 356, 373–74: "Though the law itself be fair on its face, and impartial in appearance, yet, if it is applied and administered by public authority with an evil eye and an unequal hand, so as practically to make unjust and illegal discriminations between persons in similar circumstances, material to their rights, the denial of equal justice is still within the prohibition of the Constitution." The jury found the defendant guilty and this appeal followed.

Under the theory upon which the case was tried and submitted, the judgment of conviction cannot be permitted to stand. While the court accurately stated the principle of Yick Wo v. Hopkins and the cases which have followed it, it did not consistently apply the principle during the course of the trial. The defendant attempted to prove that 21 other drug stores in the City of Utica had engaged in offering for sale and in selling forbidden items on Sunday, December 18, 1960, and on other Sundays but the court sustained objections to most of the questions designed to elicit this proof. While the court allowed the defendant to prove that the stores had been open on Sunday, it sustained objections to questions as to the items which they had offered for sale on Sunday. The court also sustained objection to a question designed to show that a witness who was in the business of selling flags and decorations, advertised that his business was open on Sunday and that in fact he had sold flags and decorations on Sunday. Similar objections were sustained with regard to proof of sales on Sunday by various other types of stores.

It also appeared upon the trial that, after the defendant's arrest on December 18, the defendant engaged a private detective, formerly a member of the police department, to make an investigation on its behalf. On the following Sunday, December 25, he found that throughout the City of Utica in various drug stores which he listed by name and address, he was able to purchase and did purchase items forbidden for sale on Sunday under the statute. He also made purchases of forbidden items at smoke shops, news stores and grocery stores. The private detective then, at the request of the defendant's counsel, went to the Clerk of the City Court and offered to sign and swear to depositions with respect to each of the purchases made by him but the secretary of the City Court Judge who handled the matter declined to accept the depositions. Proof of these facts was admitted upon the trial. However, the court refused to allow the defendant's counsel to prove that he had subsequently written a letter to the Chief of Police of the city, a copy of which was marked for identification, advising of the purchases made by the investigator and offering to have the investigator sign and swear to depositions with respect thereto and requesting the Chief of Police to have officers in his department execute the necessary informations and obtain warrants of arrest. Objection to the admission of the letter into evidence was sustained and the Chief of Police was not allowed to testify with respect to its receipt and his failure to take action thereon.

It is thus apparent that while the court recognized the validity of the defense put forward by the defendant, it prevented the defendant from introducing material evidence which would have tended to support the defense. The court held that the evidence was irrelevant, upon the authority of . . . cases holding that nonenforcement of itself is not sufficient to establish discrimination. In so ruling, the court misconstrued the cases upon which it relied. While it is true that they held that mere nonenforcement is insufficient of itself to establish discrimination, they did not hold that proof of nonenforcement is not admissible in evidence, in a case in which the defendant asserts that there had been intentional discrimination. It is true that in order to find a violation of the constitutional guarantee, the trier of the facts must be satisfied that there was intentional discrimination, and not mere laxity in enforcement, but in the effort to persuade the trier of the facts of the truth of its ultimate contention, the defendant is entitled to introduce evidence of nonenforcement as relevant evidence bearing upon that contention. . . .

We have therefore concluded that, upon the basis upon which the case was tried and submitted, the judgment of conviction must be reversed because of errors in the exclusion of evidence.

However, we believe that the entire approach to the problem, adopted by the trial court with the approval or acquiescence of the counsel on both sides, was erroneous and that a different approach should be followed, upon the remand of the case. The claim of discriminatory enforcement should not be treated as a defense to the criminal charge, to be tried before the jury and submitted to it for decision, but should be treated as an application to the court for a dismissal or quashing of the prosecution upon constitutional grounds. Insofar as a question of fact may be involved, the court should take the evidence in the absence of the jury and should decide the question itself. If the court finds that there was an intentional and purposeful discrimination, the court should quash the prosecution, not because the defendant is not guilty of the crime charged, but because the court, as an agency of government, should not lend itself to a prosecution the maintenance of which would violate the constitutional rights of the defendant.

. . .

. . . The claim of discriminatory enforcement does not go to the question of the guilt or innocence of the defendant, which is within the province of the jury. The question is rather whether in a community in which there is general disregard of a particular law with the acquiescence of the public authorities, the authorities should be allowed sporadically to select a single defendant or a single class of defendants for prosecution because of personal animosity or some other illegitimate reason. The wrong sought to be prevented is a wrong by the public authorities. To allow such arbitrary and discriminatory enforcement of a generally disregarded law is to place in the hands of the police and the prosecutor a power of the type frequently invoked in countries ruled by a dictator but wholly out of harmony with the principle of equal justice under law prevailing in democratic societies. The court is asked to stop the prosecution at the threshold, not because the defendant is innocent but because the public authorities are guilty of a wrong in engaging in a course of conduct designed to discriminate unconstitutionally against the defendant. Clearly, a contention of this kind is addressed to the court and should be passed upon by the court and not left to the jury.

. . .

Of course, we express no opinion as to whether the prosecution in the present case should be held to be a discriminatory one or not. That is for the trial court to decide after hearing all the evidence, including the evidence which was erroneously excluded upon the first trial and including any countervailing evidence which may be offered by the District Attorney. A heavy burden rests on the defendant to establish conscious, intentional discrimination, but if it succeeds in sustaining that burden, the defendant will be entitled to a dismissal of the prosecution as a matter of law. We believe this to be the necessary consequence of the principle of equal protection of the laws proclaimed in both the Federal and State Constitutions. . . .

. . .

The courts in some States have indicated a reluctance to enjoin a criminal prosecution on the ground of unconstitutional discrimination, for fear that guilty persons would thereby escape prosecution and the flouting of the law would be encouraged. . . . This fear, in our opinion, is an unfounded one. As has been pointed out, the burden resting upon the defendant is a heavy one and, even if the defendant succeeds in sustaining it, he will not be immune from a new prosecution, when and if the public authorities undertake a generalized enforcement of the law. Furthermore, even if the enforcement of a particular law is selective, it does not necessarily follow that it is unconstitutionally discriminatory. Selective enforcement may be justified when the meaning or constitutionality of the law is in doubt and a test case is needed to clarify the law or to establish its validity. Selective enforcement may also be justified when a striking example or a few examples are sought in order to deter other violators, as part of a bona fide rational pattern of general enforcement, in the expectation that general compliance will follow and that further prosecutions will be unnecessary. It is only when the selective enforcement is designed to discriminate against the persons prosecuted, without any intention to follow it up by general enforcement against others, that a constitutional violation may be found. . . .

. . .

---

314. The courts have agreed that it is not an unconstitutional discrimination to prosecute, as part of a general pattern of prosecution, persons who will furnish a "striking example" because of their public prominence. In United States v. Peskin, 527 F.2d 71, 86 (7th Cir.1975), for example, the court said: "It makes good sense to prosecute those who will receive the media's attention. Publication of the proceedings may enhance the deterrent effect of the prosecution and maintain public faith in the precept that public officials are not above the law." In United States v. Ojala, 544 F.2d 940 (8th Cir.1976), the defendant claimed that he was selected for prosecution for a violation of the tax laws because of his public refusal to pay his taxes as a protest against the government's policies. The court concluded that even if his claim were correct, there had been no violation of his rights. "The government lacks the means to investigate and prosecute every suspected violation of the tax laws. Selection based in part upon the potential deterrent effect on others serves a legitimate interest in promoting more general compliance with the tax laws, which depend substantially upon a system of voluntary disclosure and reporting. It is difficult to conceive of a more legitimate object of prosecution than one who exploits his own public office and reputation to urge a political position by announcing publicly that he had gone on strike against the tax laws of the nation." Id. at 945. See, to the same effect, United States v. Amon, 669 F.2d 1351 (10th Cir.1981); United States v. Catlett, 584 F.2d 864 (8th Cir.1978).

People v. Walker

14 N.Y.2d 901, 200 N.E.2d 779 (1964)

[The defendant was convicted of violations of the Multiple Dwelling Law and the Administrative Code of the City of New York, in that, as president and controlling stockholder of the corporate owner of a house in the City of New York, she failed to obtain a rooming house permit, made unlawful alterations to said premises and failed to repair or replace a broken wheel on the sprinkler valve on said premises.]

MEMORANDUM. The judgment of conviction should be reversed and a new trial ordered. The prosecution of defendant for violations of the Multiple Dwelling Law, Consol.Laws, c. 61–A, came closely in sequence upon the exposure by her of corrupt practices in the Department of Buildings. She contends that the prosecution was the result of an intentional discrimination which deprived her of the constitutional right to equal protection of the laws. She was unduly restricted on the trial in her attempts to prove this contention. Latitude should be allowed in this complex area of proof. We do not hold that defendant has demonstrated intentional discrimination in her prosecution. We rule, merely, that she should have a fair opportunity to establish it on her trial.

■ DESMOND, CHIEF JUDGE (dissenting). I protest what appears to be the introduction into our criminal law of a novel and mischievous defense. Is a person guilty of crimes to go free because local officials were actuated by corrupt or vengeful motives in prosecuting? There is no precedent for such a holding. It will certainly worsen the current crisis in criminal law enforcement if we let the culprit go free because the police officer or inspector has not proceeded against every other guilty person. The gambler and the narcotics peddler (even the speeder) will have a new kind of license to violate the law. None of the earlier decisions go so far. From Yick Wo v. Hopkins, 118 U.S. 356 . . . to People v. Utica Daw's Drug Co., 16 A.D.2d 12, the cited cases all refer to a "pattern of discrimination" (see People v. Friedman, 302 N.Y. 75, 81) meaning a situation where the statute itself contemplates or leads to discrimination or where a generally unenforced law is dug up to harass a particular defendant or group. What has all this to do with the State Multiple Dwelling Law and the New York City Administrative Code sections which, as our own records show, are enforced against building owners in thousands of cases?

. . .

■ BURKE, JUDGE (dissenting). If the constitutional defense of unequal protection of the laws were maintainable solely upon a showing of bad motive on the part of those responsible for the placing of the violations of which appellant is admittedly guilty, then I would concur for reversal. This, however, is not the law; nor does the court say it is. Since the legislation under which appellant has been convicted is itself valid, and since appellant is admittedly guilty of the violations, the defense of unequal protection is established only upon a showing of both bad motive in the subject case and nonenforcement as to others similarly situated. . . . The element of uneven enforcement is of the very essence and substance of the constitutional claim. The violations are not hypertechnical nor have they fallen into a sort of desuetude. The violations, among which are the creation of an additional room by a partition, an additional class B room out of a vestibule, and the maintenance of a defective sprinkler valve, are, in my experience, commonly enforced in New York City. In any event they should not be assumed to be dead letters in the total absence of evidence to that effect.

The fact that the trial court was apparently prepared to exclude any evidence other than that bearing directly on guilt or innocence does not excuse appellant from offering to prove all of the elements of her defense. Concededly, all her offers of proof went solely to the point of bad motive in her individual case. Sympathetic as we may be toward appellant's unfortunate position as the result of what she alleges were numerous bribe solicitations by Building Department officials, we have no license to play fast and lose with the elements of so volatile a doctrine as equal protection of the laws. If the statutory requirements to which appellant was held were generally enforced, then there was no infringement of her constitutional right when she was prosecuted for their violation—no matter how contemptible may have been the motives of those who enforced the law. Were the law otherwise all enforcement proceedings could be turned into subjective expeditions into motive without the stabilizing, objectively verifiable, element of an unequal pattern of enforcement. No one has a constitutional right to random enforcement of the law. No one has a constitutional right to sincere enforcement of the law. The right is to equal enforcement of the law. All of the cases dealing with this question have required such a showing. . . . Appellant, after all, has the burden of proof of all the elements of this defense and if in fact the violation of which she is guilty were not enforced against others similarly situated it would not be difficult to so prove. Building Department records are amenable to subpoena and the Building Department officials who testified could have been questioned as to the pattern of enforcement of the relevant regulations. None of this was done. According to the respondent, this omission was calculated because it would have shown that the rigorous inspection to which appellant's building was subjected was the result of an established policy of reinspecting all buildings previously inspected by an official under suspicion of misconduct—as was the case with appellant's building. Whether this is true or not is a question essential to appellant's defense and one which she ought to have pursued at the trial in order to now make her constitutional argument. Not having done so, she is without remedy in this court. . . .

On remand, the defendant was convicted of a violation of the Administrative Code of the City of New York, and appealed. The appellate court reversed the conviction and directed that the complaint be dismissed. It said:

> The defendant demonstrated, by a clear preponderance of evidence, that she was singled out for criminal prosecution by an intentional, purposeful and unusual selection process. The manner of prosecution was not the same as that used in the case of other property owners similarly situated and was in sharp contrast to the then existing pattern of enforcement of housing laws in New York City. The time allowed to defendant for correction of alleged housing violations was so unreasonably short as to make correction an impossibility and criminal conviction a certainty. The evidence leads irresistibly to the conclusion that this intentional discrimination and prosecution was in retaliation for defendant's public exposure of corruption in the Department of Buildings and was in no wise aimed at securing compliance with the housing laws.

People v. Walker, 271 N.Y.S.2d 447, 448 (Sup.Ct.1966).

---

315. In United States v. Armstrong, 517 U.S. 456 (1996) (8–1), the Court considered what threshold showing a defendant was required to make in order to obtain discovery of prosecutorial records pertinent to a claim of discriminatory prosecution. The defendants were prosecuted for conspiracy to possess and to distribute crack cocaine. In their motion for discovery, they alleged that they were selected for prosecution because they were black. Accompanying the motion was an affidavit of a person in the public defender's office, which stated that all of the 24 persons prosecuted for those offenses during the preceding year were black. The district court issued an order directing the United States Attorney's office to provide information from its files, with which the office refused to comply. The court dismissed the indictment.

The Court held that the affidavit supporting the motion for discovery was insufficient. It said: "If discovery is ordered, the Government must assemble from its own files documents which might corroborate or refute the defendant's claim. Discovery thus imposes many of the costs present when the Government must respond to a prima facie case of selective prosecution. It will divert prosecutors' resources and may disclose the Government's prosecutorial strategy. The justifications for a rigorous standard for the elements of a selective-prosecution claim thus require a correspondingly rigorous standard for discovery in aid of such a claim." Id. at 468. In order to make the necessary threshold showing of racially discriminatory prosecution, the Court said the defendant was required to "produce some evidence that similarly situated defendants of other races could have been prosecuted, but were not." Id. at 469. The fact that all those who were prosecuted were black was an insufficient basis for an inference of discriminatory prosecution without "a credible showing of different treatment of similarly situated persons." Id. at 470.

"Certainly, the prospect of government prosecutors being called to the stand by every criminal defendant for cross-examination as to their motives in seeking an indictment is to be avoided. That does not mean that a criminal defendant is never to be afforded an opportunity to prove that the prosecution stems from an improper prosecutorial design or that he may never question a prosecutor under oath. The presumption is always that a prosecution for violation of a criminal law is undertaken in good faith and in nondiscriminatory fashion for the purpose of fulfilling a duty to bring violators to justice. However, when a defendant alleges intentional purposeful discrimination and presents facts sufficient to raise a reasonable doubt about the prosecutor's purpose, we think a different question is raised." United States v. Falk, 479 F.2d 616, 620–21 (7th Cir.1973). The court concluded that the defendant had made a prima facie case of discriminatory enforcement of the draft laws and that the government had the burden of going forward with proof to the contrary. In a dissenting opinion, Judge Cummings observed: "I have been unable to find a single case where a United States Attorney or his superiors in the Department of Justice were required to explain their motives for seeking an indictment at a defendant's behest and as a part of his case under any circumstances, and the majority has cited none." Id. at 631.

See United States v. Bass, 536 U.S. 862 (2002) (per curiam) (*Armstrong* applied; insufficient showing to justify discovery relating to government's charging practice with regard to capital offenses).

MacDonald v. Musick

425 F.2d 373 (9th Cir.1970)

■ Duniway, Circuit Judge.

Habeas corpus. The District Court denied the writ. We reverse. MacDonald has exhausted his state remedies.

On January 9, 1965, MacDonald was driving his car in Newport Beach, California. He was stopped by the local police and ultimately arrested and taken to the police station. There he was booked as violating section 23102(a) of the Vehicle Code of California, which makes it a misdemeanor for "any person who is under the influence of intoxicating liquor . . . to drive a vehicle upon any highway." On January 11, 1965, a complaint was filed in the Municipal Court of the Newport Beach Judicial District charging him with that offense. On January 14, 1965, MacDonald pled not guilty and demanded a jury trial, which was set for January 26.

On January 26, the prosecutor moved to dismiss the charge. The court asked if MacDonald would stipulate that there was probable cause for his arrest. MacDonald declined, and the prosecutor withdrew the motion. In California, only the court may dismiss a criminal action. . . . Had the action been dismissed, the dismissal would have been a bar to further prosecution for the offense charged. . . . Trial was set for February 2.

On February 2, the prosecutor moved . . . for leave to file an amended complaint, adding a second count charging MacDonald with resisting arrest . . . also a misdemeanor. The motion was opposed, and was fully argued on February 3. The court granted the motion. MacDonald was then rearraigned and pled not guilty to both charges. Trial before a jury was had, beginning February 9, and on February 11, the jury acquitted MacDonald on the drunk driving charge and found him guilty of resisting arrest.

There was considerable conflict in the evidence as to the events leading to MacDonald's arrest, and particularly as to whether there was probable cause for the arrest, as well as about what happened thereafter. We need not analyze the evidence, however, because of the ground upon which we decide the case. Nor need we consider MacDonald's claim that he was convicted under a statute that makes it illegal to resist an unlawful arrest . . . and that such a conviction violates his federal constitutional rights.

The reason for the prosecutor's withdrawing his motion to dismiss the drunk driving charge and for then seeking to file an amendment to add the resisting arrest charge, is made clear by the record in the state case. At the hearing on the motion for leave to file an amended complaint, on February 3, there were a number of stipulations. MacDonald proposed to call as witnesses six deputies in the District Attorney's office. The prosecutor stipulated:

> It is so stipulated that all these Deputies indicated either displeasure with the case or that it was a weak case or that they would not care to prosecute it.

It was further stipulated that one deputy said:

> "It appears that the police department has a hard on against this defendant and are out to get him," or words to that effect, close quote.

It was also stipulated that a police lieutenant said:

> that he would stipulate that they did in fact delete the second charge of resisting arrest from their record, did in fact reduce the bail, and would stipulate that a police official, I think it was a policewoman, did state to the defendant's witness, "You will be happy to know that the resisting arrest charge has been dropped."

In support of the motion for leave to amend, the prosecutor said:

> Normally a defendant will stipulate to probable cause, and there is only one reason, let's face it, for that stipulation, so that the defendant cannot sue the police department. This particular defendant would not stipulate to probable cause, which made it obvious, at least, there was an inference drawn, that perhaps here is a defendant that does have in mind suing the police department.
>
> . . .
>
> It seems to me that it is the duty of the Deputy District Attorney, in addition to prosecuting criminals, to protect the police officers, and in

so protecting the police officers, it seems to me, after evaluating the facts, any Deputy District Attorney worth his salt would have at that point included any offense, obviously, in the report on which the defendant could have been convicted.

We strongly disagree. It is no part of the proper duty of a prosecutor to use a criminal prosecution to forestall a civil proceeding by the defendant against policemen, even where the civil case arises from the events that are also the basis for the criminal charge. We do not mean that the prosecutor cannot present such a criminal charge. What he cannot do is condition a voluntary dismissal of a charge upon a stipulation by the defendant that is designed to forestall the latter's civil case. The situation is made no better by the fact that here the record indicates that it was the court that asked MacDonald whether he would stipulate. Rather, it makes it worse. It brings the court to the aid of the prosecutor in coercing the defendant into agreeing to what amounts to a forfeiture of his civil rights. Nor can the prosecutor, because of failure to obtain the demanded stipulation, then introduce another charge in the hope of defeating the possible civil action of the defendant.

The impropriety of the prosecutor's conduct requires little exposition. In California, extortion is defined as "the obtaining of property from another . . . induced by a wrongful use of . . . fear, or under color of official right." (Cal.Pen.C. § 518.) There is no doubt that a cause of action for personal injuries is property. . . . Section 519 of the same code defines "fear" as "induced by a threat . . . 2. To accuse the individual threatened . . . of any crime. . . ." . . .

The Canons of Ethics have long prohibited misuse of the criminal process by an attorney to gain advantage for his client in a civil case. . . . In this respect, we can see no difference between public prosecutors and other lawyers. . . .

. . .

In this case, MacDonald asserts that his arrest was unlawful, that he had a right to resist, and that as a result of his doing so he was badly beaten by the police. We express no views as to the merits of these claims. But MacDonald, in addition to whatever rights he had under the law of California, had a claim to a federal right under the Civil Rights Act, 42 U.S.C. § 1983. . . . Thus in this case, the attempt, by imposing the stipulation as a condition to the dismissal of the drunk driving charge, was to hamper MacDonald in asserting, by civil action, both state and federal civil rights. And the revival of the resisting arrest charge was the bludgeon behind the attempt.

The order appealed from is reversed and the matter is remanded with directions to grant the writ of habeas corpus.

■ Kilkenny, Circuit Judge (dissenting):

I believe the approach of the majority is wholly unrealistic. On many occasions, in the criminal field, the prosecutor must make a decision on whether he will go forward with the prosecution on the original charge or add another count. On some occasions, he may feel that the overall evidence is somewhat weak, even though he believes there is probable cause for the arrest. If, under these circumstances, the charge is dismissed, some person, including the arresting officer, might well be faced with a civil action, even though there was probable cause for the arrest. Of course, this was true long before the passage of the Civil Rights Act. The latter merely gives to the plaintiff, in some instances, a choice of forums.

The civil rights actions, under state law, include among others, those for false arrest and false imprisonment. It is my firm belief that those in charge of prosecution of criminal actions have a duty to protect, if probable cause exists, arresting officers from both state or federal civil actions. We are not here concerned with a coerced plea of guilty. Appellant had his day in court and was found guilty of resisting arrest. The fact that he was acquitted on the original charge does not signify that there was no probable cause for the arrest. It merely means that the state failed to prove guilt beyond a reasonable doubt.

My thinking processes do not shudder at the portrait of the state judge asking appellant if he would agree to probable cause for the arrest. Many, many exceptionally able trial judges use this procedure to determine the appropriate action to take on the motion to dismiss. If appellant had so stipulated, the judge might well have denied the motion to dismiss. Beyond question, he would have inquired, in depth, of the prosecutor as to the appropriateness of a dismissal under these circumstances. The prosecutor, when appellant refused to agree to probable cause, was well within his rights in asking for a withdrawal of the motion to dismiss. In my view, there is nothing constitutionally objectionable in the district attorney's statement that it was his duty to include in the complaint any offense of which the appellant might be convicted. I am persuaded that the majority has erroneously raised a simple procedural act of the prosecutor to the dignity of constitutional dimensions.

. . .

---

316. Rumery was arrested for "tampering with a witness" in violation of state law. The charges grew out of telephone calls that he made to a woman who was the alleged victim and principal witness in a prosecution for aggravated sexual assault against his former hunting companion. The woman was a social and business acquaintance of Rumery. According to the police chief, Rumery made statements suggesting that the woman might be hurt if she testified. Rumery said that he made no threats. The county attorney learned that the woman did not want to testify against Rumery; there was no corroborating evidence of the telephone conversations. He discussed with Rumery's lawyer the possibility of dropping the charges against Rumery if he signed a covenant not to sue the persons connected with his arrest. The lawyer drafted the covenant, which Rumery signed, before a probable cause hearing was to take place. The charges against him were dropped. A little less than a year later, Rumery filed a complaint under 42 U.S.C. § 1983 alleging a violation of his civil rights arising out of the arrest. Town officials pleaded the covenant as an affirmative defense. Rumery was an experienced businessman. The town was a small New England town. Rumery v. Town of Newton, 778 F.2d 66 (1st Cir.1985).

The court of appeals held that the covenant not to sue was void as against public policy. It said: "The need closely to scrutinize contracts or agreements in the criminal law context is particularly important because of the special relationship between a criminal prosecution and the public interest. . . . Since the object of a criminal prosecution is to vindicate the public, not a private individual, an agreement not to prosecute should be upheld only where the *public* interest is served. It is difficult to envision how release agreements, negotiated in exchange for a decision not to prosecute, serve the public interest. Enforcement of such covenants would tempt prosecutors to trump up charges in reaction to a defendant's civil rights claim, suppress evidence of police misconduct, and leave unremedied deprivations of constitutional rights. We agree with those courts which have found that such releases have the effect of injuring the public interest." Id. at 69.

The Court reversed. Town of Newton v. Rumery, 480 U.S. 386 (1987) (5–4). The Court said that although a defendant's promise not to sue in return for dismissal of the charges against him might be unenforceable, because it was not informed and voluntary or because it was contrary to the public interest, there should not be a per se rule against the validity of such agreements. It compared such agreements with plea bargains, in which the defendant may give up constitutional rights; and it noted that prosecutors often have legitimate reasons for an agreement, such as avoiding the burden of defending against an insubstantial lawsuit. Examining the facts of this case, the Court concluded that the agreement was enforceable.

317. With MacDonald v. Musick, p. 635 above, and Rumery v. Town of Newton, note 316 above, compare cases in which a defendant moves for dismissal on the ground that the prosecution is due to prosecutorial vindictiveness. In United States v. Andrews, 633 F.2d 449 (6th Cir.1980), for example, the defendants were indicted for narcotics and firearms offenses. The government opposed their release on bail. The magistrate denied bail, and the defendants appealed. The district judge overturned the magistrate's decision, and the defendants were released on bail. Two days later, the Assistant United States Attorney obtained a superseding indictment adding a count of conspiracy. In those circumstances, the court of appeals discussed the issue of prosecutorial vindictiveness. A majority of the court concluded that the test of prosecutorial vindictiveness, which if found would bar the added charge, is "whether, in the particular factual situation presented, there existed a 'realistic likelihood of vindictiveness' for the prosecutor's augmentation of the charges." Id. at 453. See United States v. Groves, 571 F.2d 450 (9th Cir.1978) (indictment for related charge, returned after defendant moved for dismissal of another charge under Speedy Trial Act, dismissed as vindictive). Cf. United States v. Adams, 870 F.2d 1140 (6th Cir.1989) (defendants, allegedly prosecuted for tax offense in retaliation for lawsuit against EEOC, entitled to discovery of basis for prosecution). See generally Bordenkircher v. Hayes, 434 U.S. 357 (1978), p. 724 note 367 below, and North Carolina v. Pearce, 395 U.S. 711 (1969), p. 1141 note 596 below.

Denial of a pretrial motion to dismiss an indictment on the ground of prosecutorial vindictiveness is not a final decision immediately appealable under 28 U.S.C. § 1291. United States v. Hollywood Motor Car Co., 458 U.S. 263 (1982) (6–3).

318.

> On June 6, appellant was stopped by two police officers for alleged traffic violations [failing to obey the instructions of a police officer, and stopping a vehicle in a manner that obstructed the orderly flow of traffic]. He was neither charged nor ticketed at that time. Two days later, appellant delivered a written complaint to the police department concerning the conduct of the officers who had stopped him. At this point appellant and the Corporation Counsel's office apparently entered into a tacit agreement: appellant would not proceed further with his complaint and the Government would not prosecute the traffic charges.
>
> On September 1, 1965, however, appellant filed a formal complaint with the District of Columbia Commission's Council on Human Relations. After some "hearings" at the Corporation Counsel's office, appellant refused to withdraw the complaint. As a result he was charged with the two traffic offenses. As the then Chief of the Law Enforcement Division of the Corporation Counsel explained: We had discussed it back when it originally occurred and, at the time, everybody was happy to forget the whole thing. . . . But three months later he comes in and makes a formal complaint. So we said "If you are going to play ball like that why shouldn't we proceed with our case?" . . . I had no reason to file until he changed back on his understanding of what we had all agreed on. This is done in many cases.

Dixon v. District of Columbia, 394 F.2d 966, 968 (D.C.Cir.1968). Should the prosecution be dismissed?

319. Unenforced statutes. Is it proper for a prosecutor to prosecute under a statute which has been disregarded for many years? Or to refuse to enforce such a statute? Does anything depend on the reasons why the statute has been disregarded by the public, or the police, or the prosecutor? Does anything depend on the reasons why the statute has not been repealed by the legislature? Should any of such questions of fact be subject to proof at trial? Can a judge take judicial notice of facts bearing on any of these questions?

In Poe v. Ullman, 367 U.S. 497 (1961), the Court declined to hear appeals from judgments dismissing actions for a declaratory judgment that the Connecticut statute outlawing the use of contraceptives was unconstitutional. Speaking also for three other Justices, Justice Frankfurter said: "The undeviating policy of nullification by Connecticut of its anti-contraceptive laws throughout all the long years that they have been on the statute books bespeaks more than prosecutorial paralysis. What was said in another context is relevant here. 'Deeply embedded traditional ways of carrying out state policy . . .'—or not carrying it out—'are often tougher and truer law than the dead words of the written text.' Nashville, C. & St. L.R. Co. v. Browning, 310 U.S. 362, 369." 367 U.S. at 502.[2]

With Poe v. Ullman, compare District of Columbia v. John R. Thompson Co., 346 U.S. 100 (1953), in which the Court upheld the validity of a criminal prosecution under acts of the Legislative Assembly of the District of Columbia enacted in 1872 and 1873. The information charged the defendant with refusing to serve persons at a restaurant within the District of Columbia solely on account of race and color, in violation of the acts. The Legislative Assembly was established in 1871 as part of a scheme of local government for the District of Columbia. It ceased to exist in 1874, by act of Congress. The opinion of the Court mentions no prior prosecutions under the acts, and notes that licenses had for 75 years been issued to restaurants in the District without regard to the requirements of the acts. The Court said, "The repeal of laws is as much a legislative function as their enactment." Id. at 114. "Cases of hardship are put where criminal laws so long in disuse as to be no longer known to exist are enforced against innocent parties. But that condition does not bear on the continuing validity of the law; it is only an ameliorating factor in enforcement." Id. at 117.

Should the government be estopped from prosecuting for a violation of the antitrust laws on the ground that over a period of ten years it knew about and acquiesced in the bidding system that was the basis of the alleged violation? See United States v. New Orleans Chapter, Associated General Contractors of America, 238 F.Supp. 273, 279–83 (E.D.La.1964), rev'd per curiam, 382 U.S. 17 (1965).

United States v. Bufalino

285 F.2d 408 (2d Cir.1960)

■ LUMBARD, CHIEF JUDGE.

Russell Bufalino and nineteen co-defendants appeal from judgments of conviction in the Southern District of New York for conspiring to obstruct justice and commit perjury (18 U.S.C. §§ 371, 1503, 1621) by giving, before federal grand juries, false and evasive testimony regarding a gathering attended by them and at least 39 others at the home of Joseph Barbara,

2. Four years later, the Court did consider and determine the constitutionality of the Connecticut statute, in Griswold v. Connecticut, 381 U.S. 479 (1965).

Sr., in Apalachin, New York, on November 14, 1957. Named as members of the conspiracy were seven other co-defendants and 36 co-conspirators. The appellants were all sentenced to prison terms running from three to five years, and in addition thirteen of them were each fined $10,000.

The indictment . . . alleged a conspiracy from November 14, 1957, the date of the Apalachin gathering, to the filing of the indictment on May 13, 1959. The 29 overt acts of the indictment which the court submitted to the jury charged that pursuant to the conspiracy various conspirators made statements and gave testimony under oath at different stated places and times from November 14, 1957 to May 11, 1959, including testimony on eleven occasions before federal grand juries in the Southern District of New York.

The indictment did not allege what the November 14, 1957 gathering at Apalachin was about, and the government stated at the beginning of the trial that it could present no evidence of its purpose. There is nothing in the record of the trial to show that any violation of federal or state law took place or was planned at the gathering, although federal grand juries in the Southern and Western Districts of New York on twenty occasions over the following year and one-half, and a variety of other federal and state officials on numerous other occasions, questioned many of those present about the Apalachin gathering and the surrounding circumstances.

. . .

[The court found that the evidence was insufficient to prove the crime charged.]

The administration of our system of criminal justice and our basic concepts of fair dealing are centered on the requirement that in each case we reach a result based solely on the charges made in the particular indictment and on the evidence which appears on the record with regard to those charges. Doubtless many of Barbara's visitors are bad people, and it is surely a matter of public concern that more is not known of their activities. But bad as many of these alleged conspirators may be, their conviction for a crime which the government could not prove, on inferences no more valid than others equally supported by reason and experience, and on evidence which a jury could not properly assess, cannot be permitted to stand.

Reversed and remanded with directions to dismiss the conspiracy count of the indictment.

■ CLARK, CIRCUIT JUDGE (concurring).

I agree with the decision and opinion herein, but believe it desirable to point out what seems to me an even more basic failure of proof than the two so fully delineated by Chief Judge Lumbard. Perhaps the most curious feature of this strange case is the fact that after all these years there is not a shred of legal evidence that the Apalachin gathering was illegal or even improper in either purpose or fact. For thirteen years prior to the meeting as a modern Inspector Javert State Trooper Croswell pursued Barbara, Sr., in all ways possible (including tapping of his telephone) and got no evidence of illegality, although he did get wind of the meeting if not of its purpose. After it occurred on November 14, 1957, there were no less than 133 examinations of those present (as the government reports in its brief) by various state and federal officials, including 27 instances before federal grand juries and 29 by the FBI. The results were fruitless, as is highlighted by the government's frank admission at the outset of the trial that it would not be able to show what was going on at the meeting. The only suggestion, outside of an innuendo not here provable that the defendants were evil, is the bizarre nature of the gathering itself. But that gets us nowhere; common experience does not suggest that plotting to commit crime is done in convention assembled, or even the converse, also suggested here, namely, plotting to desist from crime. It must be taken, therefore, that for aught we can know the gathering was innocent.

. . .

From its inception this case was given unusual and disturbing publicity in newspapers, journals, and magazines; and this unfortunate feature has persisted up to this date, with even the prosecutors indulging in highly colored accounts while the case has been pending on appeal. Much of this has been in terms of a crisis in law administration seemingly demonstrated by an unexplained gathering of arch criminals and of a general satisfaction that somehow they have now met their just deserts of long imprisonment. This is vastly unfortunate; not only does it go beyond the judicial record necessary for its support, but it suggests that the administration of the criminal law is in such dire straits that crash methods have become a necessity. But it seems we should have known better, and a prosecution framed on such a doubtful basis should never have been initiated or allowed to proceed so far. For in America we still respect the dignity of the individual, and even an unsavory character is not to be imprisoned except on definite proof of specific crime. And nothing in present criminal law administration suggests or justifies sharp relaxation of traditional standards.

. . .

---

320. Is it proper for the government to select for intensive tax investigations those whom it believes, on the basis of evidence that is reliable but inadmissible or otherwise unavailable for use at a trial, to be leaders of organized crime or otherwise dangerous criminals? The *Boston Globe* reported on June 1, 1966, at 3, that "at the height of the gangland murders," the Attorney General of Massachusetts had requested a "massive check" on the tax status of 287 persons, including "a number of Boston's big names in organized and even freelance crime"; the Internal Revenue Service apparently granted the request, "in a concerted state-Federal drive against Boston's hoodlum element." The *New York Times* reported on July 30, 1971, at 1, that: "Pornography pushers, pimps, prostitutes and others allied with these businesses will be hit with charges of everything from tax evasion to littering under plans discussed yesterday by Mayor Lindsay's cabinet-level task force established to drive prostitution and pornography out of mid-Manhattan." See United States v. Accardo, 298 F.2d 133 (7th Cir.1962), involving the tax prosecution of a defendant who was characterized by one newspaper as "Chicago's jet-age Capone."

The defendants, certified public accountants, were prosecuted for tax offenses. They offered evidence to show that their prosecutions were part of "Project ACE," an Internal Revenue Service program that gave "special priorities" to the prosecution of attorneys, certified public accountants, and enrolled practitioners because of their "special obligation and responsibility to the tax laws." United States v. Swanson, 509 F.2d 1205, 1208 (8th Cir.1975). Is Project ACE proper?

321. Suppose a state's attorney general concludes that the greatest threat to the public order in his state is a vast network of intertwined criminal and lawful activities, over which a small syndicate presides. The criminal activities are "business" enterprises: gambling operations, narcotics distribution, prostitution, extortion, etc. The lawful activities are such things as laundry and motel ownership. Because of the great resources available to the syndicate and the apparent willingness of its members to carry out threats of extreme violence, no investigation or prosecution against any participants in the organization except those at its lowest level has been successful.

Is it proper or desirable for the attorney general to seek the assignment of a special corps of investigators to the investigation of the activities of the syndicate and the assignment of a special group of prosecutors to the preparation of cases against its members? Compare the measures taken by the FBI detailed in Giancana v. Johnson, 335 F.2d 366 (7th Cir.1964), p. 350 note 193 above, apparently not only for investigative purposes but also for harassment.

322. A college student who is employed as a temporary mail carrier during the Christmas holidays is found to have stolen about $100 from several letters given to him for delivery. He is contrite and anxious to make restitution. He is not in great need of money and has no explanation for the thefts. The post office, which has a continuing problem of theft by mail carriers, expends substantial resources to uncover such cases. There are presently pending several other cases of theft, some involving temporary workers including students and some involving regular employees. The postal authorities propose that the student be prosecuted for theft from the mails, a felony which carries a maximum sentence of imprisonment for five years and a fine, 18 U.S.C. § 1709. The court has authority to suspend the imposition of sentence. Should the student be prosecuted? If not, what disposition should the United States attorney's office make of the case?

323. On the same morning, three shoplifters are apprehended by a store detective for a large department store and brought to the office of the district attorney for the filing of a complaint:

(i) A college sophomore, who was observed slipping a sweater worth $60 into her purse. She is well-dressed and comes from a comfortable home. She is embarrassed and contrite. She explains that on the previous night she had a quarrel with her boyfriend and was unable to sleep. She had gone to the department store rather than go to classes in order to forget about the quarrel. The sweater is not of a kind that she would ordinarily wear. She states that she has not previously been in trouble with the law. Final examinations will be held at the college during the following week. She is accompanied by a lawyer.

(ii) A woman of 19, who was observed slipping a pocketbook worth $40 into a shopping bag. She is married and has a child. She works part time behind the counter in a luncheonette and receives welfare payments. Her husband does not live with her and contributes little to her or her child's support. She did not complete high school education. She offers no explanation for her act. So far as anyone knows, she has not previously been in trouble with the law.

(iii) A woman of 60, who was observed taking a bead necklace worth $40 into the ladies' washroom; the necklace was found in her pocketbook by the store detective as the woman was about to walk out of the store. The detective states that she had seen the woman do the same thing with other items of small value on many previous occasions and, despite the store's general policy of ignoring occasional acts of this kind by well-to-do patrons, had decided to arrest the woman if she did it again. The woman is wealthy and is an established member of the community. She indignantly denies any intention to steal; she states that she had gone into the washroom to look at the necklace in a mirror and had absent-mindedly put it in her pocketbook. She threatens to sue the store for false arrest. She states that she has not previously been in trouble with the law. She is accompanied by a lawyer.

How should the assistant district attorney who is in charge of the complaint desk respond to the three cases?

United States Attorneys' Manual

9.27. Principles of Federal Prosecution

. . .

9–27.220 *Grounds for Commencing or Declining Prosecution*

A. The attorney for the government should commence or recommend Federal prosecution if he/she believes that the person's conduct constitutes a Federal offense and that the admissible evidence will probably be sufficient to obtain and sustain a conviction, unless, in his/her judgment, prosecution should be declined because:

1. No substantial Federal interest would be served by prosecution;

2. The person is subject to effective prosecution in another jurisdiction; or

3. There exists an adequate non-criminal alternative to prosecution.

B. Comment

. . .

The potential that—despite the law and the facts that create a sound, prosecutable case—the factfinder is likely to acquit the defendant because of the unpopularity of some factor involved in the prosecution or because of the overwhelming popularity of the defendant or his/her cause, is not a factor prohibiting prosecution. For example, in a civil rights case or a case involving an extremely popular political figure, it might be clear that the evidence of guilt—viewed objectively by an unbiased factfinder—would be sufficient to obtain and sustain a conviction, yet the prosecutor might reasonably doubt whether the jury would convict. In such a case, despite his/her negative assessment of the likelihood of a guilty verdict (based on factors extraneous to an objective view of the law and the facts), the prosecutor may properly conclude that it is necessary and desirable to commence or recommend prosecution and allow the criminal process to operate in accordance with its principles.

Merely because the attorney for the government believes that a person's conduct constitutes a Federal offense and that the admissible evidence will be sufficient to obtain and sustain a conviction, does not mean that he/she necessarily should initiate or recommend prosecution: USAM 9–27.220 notes three situations in which the prosecutor may properly decline to take action nonetheless: when no substantial Federal interest would be served by prosecution; when the person is subject to effective prosecution in another jurisdiction; and when there exists an adequate non-criminal alternative to prosecution. It is left to the judgment of the attorney for the government whether such a situation exists. In exercising that judgment, the attorney for the government should consult USAM 9–27.230, 9–27.240, or 9–27.250, infra, as appropriate.

9–27.230 *Substantial Federal Interest*

A. In determining whether prosecution should be declined because no substantial Federal interest would be served by prosecution, the attorney for the government should weigh all relevant considerations, including:

1. Federal law enforcement priorities;

2. The nature and seriousness of the offense;

3. The deterrent effect of prosecution;

4. The person's culpability in connection with the offense;

5. The person's history with respect to criminal activity;

6. The person's willingness to cooperate in the investigation or prosecution of others; and

7. The probable sentence or other consequences if the person is convicted.

B. Comment

. . .

1. Federal Law Enforcement Priorities

Federal law enforcement resources and Federal judicial resources are not sufficient to permit prosecution of every alleged offense over which Federal jurisdiction exists. Accordingly, in the interest of allocating its limited resources as to achieve an effective nationwide law enforcement program, from time to time the Department establishes national investigative and prosecutorial priorities. These priorities are designed to focus Federal law enforcement efforts on those matters within the Federal jurisdiction that are most deserving of Federal attention and are most likely to be handled effectively at the Federal level. In addition, individual United States Attorneys may establish their own priorities, within the national priorities, in order to concentrate their resources on problems of particular local or regional significance. In weighing the Federal interest in a particular prosecution, the attorney for the government should give careful consideration to the extent to which prosecution would accord with established priorities.

2. Nature and Seriousness of Offense

It is important that limited Federal resources not be wasted in prosecuting inconsequential cases or cases in which the violation is only technical. Thus, in determining whether a substantial Federal interest exists that requires prosecution, the attorney for the government should consider the nature and seriousness of the offense involved. A number of factors may be relevant. One factor that is obviously of primary importance is the actual or potential impact of the offense on the community and on the victim.

The impact of an offense on the community in which it is committed can be measured in several ways: in terms of economic harm done to community interests; in terms of physical danger to the citizens or damage to public property; and in terms of erosion of the inhabitants' peace of mind and sense of security. In assessing the seriousness of the offense in these terms, the prosecutor may properly weigh such questions as whether the violation is technical or relatively inconsequential in nature, and what the public attitude is toward prosecution under the circumstances of the case. The public may be indifferent, or even opposed, to enforcement of the controlling statute, whether on substantive grounds, or because of a history of non-enforcement, or because the offense involves essentially a minor matter of private concern and the victim is not interested in having it pursued. On the other hand, the nature and circumstances of the offense, the identity of the offender or the victim, or the attendant publicity, may be such as to create strong public sentiment in favor of prosecution. While public interest, or lack thereof, deserves the prosecutor's careful attention, it should not be used to justify a decision to prosecute, or to take other action, that cannot be supported on other grounds. Public and professional responsibility sometimes will require the choosing of a particularly unpopular course.

Economic, physical, and psychological considerations are also important in assessing the impact of the offense on the victim. In this connection, it is appropriate for the prosecutor to take into account such matters as the victim's age or health, and whether full or partial restitution has been made. Care should be taken in weighing the matter of restitution, however, to ensure against contributing to an impression that an offender can escape prosecution merely by returning the spoils of his/her crime.

3. Deterrent Effect of Prosecution

Deterrence of criminal conduct, whether it be criminal activity generally or a specific type of criminal conduct, is one of the primary goals of the criminal law. This purpose should be kept in mind, particularly when deciding whether a prosecution is warranted for an offense that appears to be relatively minor; some offenses, although seemingly not of great importance by themselves, if commonly committed would have a substantial cumulative impact on the community.

4. The Person's Culpability

Although the prosecutor has sufficient evidence of guilt, it is nevertheless appropriate for him/her to give consideration to the degree of the person's culpability in connection with the offenses, both in the abstract and in comparison with any others involved in the offense. If, for example, the person was a relatively minor participant in a criminal enterprise conducted by others, or his/her motive was worthy, and no other circumstances require prosecution, the prosecutor might reasonably conclude that some course other than prosecution would be appropriate.

5. The Person's Criminal History

If a person is known to have a prior conviction or is reasonably believed to have engaged in criminal activity at an earlier time, this should be considered in determining whether to initiate or recommend Federal prosecution. In this connection, particular attention should be given to the nature of the person's prior criminal involvement, when it occurred, its relationship if any to the present offense, and whether he/she previously avoided prosecution as a result of an agreement not to prosecute in return for cooperation or as a result of an order compelling his/her testimony. By the same token, a person's lack of prior criminal involvement or his/her previous cooperation with the law enforcement officials should be given due consideration in appropriate cases.

6. The Person's Willingness to Cooperate

A person's willingness to cooperate in the investigation or prosecution of others is another appropriate consideration in the determination whether a Federal prosecution should be undertaken. Generally speaking, a willingness to cooperate should not by itself relieve a person of criminal liability. There may be some cases, however, in which the value of a person's cooperation clearly outweighs the Federal interest in prosecuting him/her. These matters are discussed more fully . . . in connection with plea agreements and non-prosecution agreements in return for cooperation.

7. The Person's Personal Circumstances

In some cases, the personal circumstances of an accused may be relevant in determining whether to prosecute or to take other action. Some circumstances peculiar to the accused, such as extreme youth, advanced age, or mental or physical impairment, may suggest that prosecution is not the most appropriate response to his/her offense; other circumstances, such as the fact that the accused occupied a position of trust or responsibility which he/she violated in committing the offense, might weigh in favor of prosecution.

8. The Probable Sentence

In assessing the strength of the Federal interest in prosecution, the attorney for the government should consider the sentence, or other consequence, that is likely to be imposed if prosecution is successful, and whether such a sentence or other consequence would justify the time and effort of prosecution. If the offender is already subject to a substantial sentence, or is already incarcerated, as a result of a conviction for another offense, the prosecutor should weigh the likelihood that another conviction will result in a meaningful addition to his/her sentence, might otherwise have a deterrent effect, or is necessary to ensure that the offender's record accurately reflects the extent of his/her criminal conduct. For example, it might be desirable to commence a bail-jumping prosecution against a person who already has been convicted of another offense so that law enforcement personnel and judicial officers who encounter him/her in the future will be aware of the risk of releasing him/her on bail. On the other hand, if the person is on probation or parole as a result of an earlier conviction, the prosecutor should consider whether the public interest might better be served by instituting a proceeding for violation of probation or revocation of parole, than by commencing a new prosecution. The prosecutor should also be alert to the desirability of instituting prosecution to prevent the running of the statute of limitations and to preserve the availability of a basis for an adequate sentence if there appears to be a chance that an offender's prior conviction may be reversed on appeal or collateral attack. Finally, if a person previously has been prosecuted in another jurisdiction for the same offense or a closely related offense, the attorney for the government should consult existing departmental policy statements on the subject of "successive prosecution" or "dual prosecution," depending on whether the earlier prosecution was federal or nonfederal. . . .

Just as there are factors that it is appropriate to consider in determining whether a substantial Federal interest would be served by prosecution in a particular case, there are considerations that deserve no weight and should not influence the decision. These include the time and resources expended in Federal investigation of the case. No amount of investigative effort warrants commencing a Federal prosecution that is not fully justified on other grounds.

. . .

9–27.250 *Non-Criminal Alternatives to Prosecution*

A. In determining whether prosecution should be declined because there exists an adequate non-criminal alternative to prosecution, the attorney for the government should consider all relevant factors, including:

1. The sanctions available under the alternative means of disposition;

2. The likelihood that an appropriate sanction will be imposed; and

3. The effect of non-criminal disposition on Federal law enforcement interests.

B. Comment

When a person has committed a Federal offense, it is important that the law respond promptly, fairly, and effectively. This does not mean, however, that a criminal prosecution must be initiated. In recognition of the fact that resort to the criminal process is not necessarily the only appropriate response to serious forms of antisocial activity, Congress and state legislatures have provided civil and administrative remedies for many types of conduct that may also be subject to criminal sanction. Examples of such non-criminal approaches include civil tax proceedings; civil actions under the securities, customs, antitrust, or other regulatory laws; and reference of complaints to licensing authorities or to professional organizations such as bar associations. Another potentially useful alternative to prosecution in some cases is pre-trial diversion. . . .

. . .

9–27.260 *Impermissible Considerations*

A. In determining whether to commence or recommend prosecution or take other action against a person, the attorney for the government should not be influenced by:

1. The person's race, religion, sex, national origin, or political association, activities or beliefs;

2. The attorney's own personal feelings concerning the person, the person's associates, or the victim; or

3. The possible effect of the decision on the attorney's own professional or personal circumstances.

. . .

9–27.300 *Charging Most Serious Offenses*

A. Except as provided in USAM 9–27.300 (precharge plea agreement), once the decision to prosecute has been made, the attorney for the government should charge, or should recommend that the grand jury charge, the most serious offense that is consistent with the nature of the defendant's conduct, and that is likely to result in a sustainable conviction. If mandatory minimum sentences are also involved, their effect must be considered, keeping in mind the fact that a mandatory minimum is statutory and generally overrules a guideline. The "most serious" offense is generally that which yields the highest range under the sentencing guidelines.

However, a faithful and honest application of the Sentencing Guidelines is not incompatible with selecting charges or entering into plea agreements on the basis of an individualized assessment of the extent to which particular charges fit the specific circumstances of the case, are consistent with the purposes of the Federal criminal code, and maximize the impact of Federal resources on crime. Thus, for example, in determining "the most serious offense that is consistent with the nature of the defendant's conduct that is likely to result in a sustainable conviction," it is appropriate that the attorney for the government consider, inter alia, such factors as the Sentencing Guideline range yielded by the charge, whether the penalty yielded by such sentencing range (or potential mandatory minimum charge, if applicable) is proportional to the seriousness of the defendant's conduct, and whether the charge achieves such purposes of the criminal law as punishment, protection of the public, specific and general deterrence, and rehabilitation. Note that these factors may also be considered by the attorney for the government when entering into plea agreements. USAM 9–27.400.

To ensure consistency and accountability, charging and plea agreement decisions must be made at an appropriate level of responsibility and documented with an appropriate record of the factors applied.

B. Comment

Once it has been determined to initiate prosecution, either by filing a complaint or an information, or by seeking an indictment from the grand jury, the attorney for the government must determine what charges to file or recommend. When the conduct in question consists of a single criminal act, or when there is only one applicable statute, this is not a difficult task. Typically, however, a defendant will have committed more than one criminal act and his/her conduct may be prosecuted under more than one statute. Moreover, selection of charges may be complicated further by the fact that different statutes have different proof requirements and provide substantially different penalties. In such cases, considerable care is required to ensure selection of the proper charge or charges. In addition to reviewing the concerns that prompted the decision to prosecute in the first instance, particular attention should be given to the need to ensure that the prosecution will be both fair and effective.

At the outset, the attorney for the government should bear in mind that at trial he/she will have to produce admissible evidence sufficient to obtain and sustain a conviction or else the government will suffer a dismissal. For this reason, he/she should not include in an information or recommend in an indictment charges that he/she cannot reasonably expect to prove beyond a reasonable doubt by legally sufficient evidence at trial.

. . .

As stated, a Federal prosecutor should initially charge the most serious, readily provable offense or offenses consistent with the defendant's conduct. Charges should not be filed simply to exert leverage to induce a plea, nor should charges be abandoned in an effort to arrive at a bargain that fails to reflect the seriousness of the defendant's conduct.

USAM 9–27.300 expresses the principle that the defendant should be charged with the most serious offense that is encompassed by his/her conduct and that is readily provable. Ordinarily . . . this will be the offense for which the most severe penalty is provided by law and the guidelines. Where two crimes have the same statutory maximum and the same guideline range, but only one contains a mandatory minimum penalty, the one with the mandatory minimum is more serious. This principle provides the framework for ensuring equal justice in the prosecution of Federal criminal offenders. It guarantees that every defendant will start from the same position, charged with the most serious criminal act he/she commits. . . .

. . .

9–27.320 *Additional Charges*

A. Except as hereafter provided, the attorney for the government should also charge, or recommend that the grand jury charge, other offenses only when, in his/her judgment, additional charges:

1. Are necessary to ensure that the information or indictment:

a. Adequately reflects the nature and extent of the criminal conduct involved; and

b. Provides the basis for an appropriate sentence under all the circumstances of the case; or

2. Will significantly enhance the strength of the government's case against the defendant or a codefendant.

. . .

---

324. In Berra v. United States, 351 U.S. 131 (1956) (7–2), the defendant was prosecuted for wilfully attempting to evade federal income taxes, a felony punishable by imprisonment for not more than five years and a fine. A different section of the code made it a misdemeanor punishable by imprisonment for not more than one year and a fine to deliver to the Collector a false statement with intent to avoid a tax. The Court held that since in the context of the case the two statutes "covered precisely the same ground" and the facts necessary to prove guilt of the two crimes were "identical," id. at 134, the defendant was not entitled to a jury instruction on the lesser offense.[3] The jury's role, the Court said, was to determine the issues of fact. "When the jury resolved those issues against petitioner, its function was exhausted, since there is here no statutory provision giving to the jury the right to determine the punishment to be imposed after the determination of guilt." Id. at 135.

Justice Black dissented:

> The Government admits here and the Court assumes that filing a false and fraudulent income tax return is both a misdemeanor . . . and a felony.
>
> . . . The Government argues that the action of the trial judge must be upheld because "the government may choose to invoke either applicable law," and "the prosecution may be for a felony even though the Government could have elected to prosecute for a misdemeanor." Election by the Government of course means election by a prosecuting attorney or the Attorney General. I object to any such interpretation of . . . [the statute]. I think we should construe these sections so as not to place control over the liberty of citizens in the unreviewable discretion of one individual—a result which seems to me to be wholly incompatible with our system of justice. Since Congress has specifically made the conduct charged in the indictment a misdemeanor, I would not permit prosecution for a felony. . . . Criminal statutes, which forfeit life, liberty or property, should be construed narrowly, not broadly.
>
> . . .
>
> A basic principle of our criminal law is that the Government only prosecutes people for crimes under statutes passed by Congress which fairly and clearly define the conduct made criminal and the punishment which can be administered. This basic principle is flouted if either of these statutes can be selected as the controlling law at the whim of the prosecuting attorney or the Attorney General. . . .
>
> A congressional delegation of such vast power to the prosecuting department would raise serious constitutional questions. Of course it is true that under our system Congress may vest the judge and jury with broad power to say how much punishment shall be imposed for a particular offense. But it is quite different to vest such powers in a prosecuting attorney. A judge and jury act under procedural rules carefully prescribed to protect the liberty of the individual. Their judgments and verdicts are reached after a public trial in which a defendant has the right to be represented by an attorney. No such protections are thrown around decisions by a prosecuting attorney. Substitution of the prosecutor's caprice for the adjudicatory process is an action I am not willing to attribute to Congress in the absence of clear command. Our system of justice rests on the conception of

3. See note 559, p. 1085 below.

> impersonality in the criminal law. This great protection to freedom is lost if the Government is right in its contention here. . . .
>
> The Government's contention here also challenges our concept that all people must be treated alike under the law. This principle means that no different or higher punishment should be imposed upon one than upon another if the offense and the circumstances are the same. It is true that there may be differences due to different appraisals given the circumstances of different cases by different judges and juries. But in these cases the discretion in regard to conviction and punishment for crime is exercised by the judge and jury in their constitutional capacities in the administration of justice.
>
> I would reverse this case or at least remand for resentencing under the misdemeanor statute. . . .

Id. at 138–40.

See the opinion of Judge Bazelon, dissenting from denial of a petition for rehearing by the whole court in Lloyd v. United States, 343 F.2d 242, 243 (D.C.Cir.1964). Compare Hutcherson v. United States, 345 F.2d 964 (D.C.Cir.1965) (same offenses under federal and D.C. statutes).

The Decision Not To Prosecute

---

325. The plaintiff, a spectator at a baseball game at Fenway Park, was struck in the head by a baseball thrown from the visiting team's bullpen. He obtained a complaint from the Municipal Court charging the pitcher who had thrown the ball with assault and battery with a dangerous weapon. At a probable cause hearing, the court dismissed the charge. The district attorney's office declined to pursue the complaint further. Upholding the decisions below, the Supreme Judicial Court said: "The victim of an alleged crime has no right to challenge a judicial determination which forecloses further prosecution of that alleged crime. Although a victim may seek a complaint against the alleged criminal . . . the prosecution of any complaint, once issued, is conducted in the interests of the Commonwealth and not on behalf of the alleged victim." Manning v. Municipal Court, 361 N.E.2d 1274, 1276 (Mass.1977). See generally Linda R.S. v. Richard D., 410 U.S. 614, 619 (1973): "The Court's prior decisions consistently hold that a citizen lacks standing to contest the policies of the prosecuting authority when he himself is neither prosecuted nor threatened with prosecution. . . . [I]n American jurisprudence at least, a private citizen lacks a judicially cognizable interest in the prosecution or nonprosecution of another."

A robbery of the First Federal Savings and Loan Association in Evansville, Indiana, occurred on October 8, 1962. A witness identified Del Monico as a suspect when his photograph appeared in a local newspaper on May 3, 1963. Thereafter, a group of eyewitnesses to the robbery picked Del Monico's photograph from a group of nine photographs and identified him in person. Every witness, without dissent, identified Del Monico's photograph and Del Monico.

The bank robbery aroused great interest in Evansville. Del Monico's identification as the robber and his subsequent indictment were well-known facts in the community.

UNITED STATES DISTRICT COURT
SOUTHERN DISTRICT OF INDIANA
EVANSVILLE DIVISION

UNITED STATES OF AMERICA)
v.) NO. EV 64–CR-17
CHARLES DEL MONICO)

MOTION FOR LEAVE TO DISMISS THE INDICTMENT

Richard P. Stein, United States Attorney for the Southern District of Indiana, by direction of Nicholas Katzenbach, Attorney General of the United States, moves for leave of this Court, under and pursuant to the provisions of Rule 48(a), Federal Rules of Criminal Procedure, to dismiss without prejudice the indictment heretofore returned in the captioned cause on June 15, 1964.

In support of this motion, the United States respectfully shows to the Court as follows:

On May 4, 1964, the defendant's counsel submitted to the United States a copy of a report setting forth the results of a polygraph examination which the defendant had undergone on April 27–28, 1964. The examiner, an established expert in his field, concluded that the defendant was truthful in his denial of involvement in the subject bank robbery.

On June 15, 1964, the United States received from the defendant's counsel the names of witnesses who would testify that the defendant was in Miami Beach, Florida on October 8, 1962, the date of the alleged bank robbery. These witnesses were subsequently made available for interview by agents of the Federal Bureau of Investigation and by the attorneys for the United States. No substantial basis for discrediting the crucial portions of their testimony has yet been uncovered.

On January 22–24, 1965, the defendant submitted to narcoanalysis at Sibley Hospital in Washington, D.C., by Dr. Leon Salzman, Professor of Clinical Psychiatry at the Washington School of Psychiatry. Based upon his examinations, Dr. Salzman concluded that the defendant had no knowledge of the alleged bank robbery.

On January 25–26, 1965, the defendant submitted to a second polygraph examination by John Reid and Associates, Chicago, Illinois, the foremost experts in this field. The examiners again concluded that the defendant was truthful in his denial of knowledge or implication in the subject bank robbery.

On January 29, 1965, the defendant submitted to narcoanalysis a second time by an expert chosen by the United States. The results of this examination, which were made available to the Attorney General and the attorneys for the United States on January 30, 1965, again reflect no findings justifying the conclusion that the defendant was involved in the subject bank robbery.

While the great weight of judicial authority holds that the results of these tests would not be admissible in evidence in the trial of this case, nevertheless, in the light of all the circumstances, they must be accorded some weight in determining whether or not prosecution should be continued at this time.

The evidence of the United States consists entirely of the testimony of eyewitnesses to the robbery, who first identified the defendant as the robber on or about May 3, 1963, seven months after the robbery. Despite intensive investigation by the Federal Bureau of Investigation for many months, no evidence of any kind has been uncovered that would corroborate the testimony of the eyewitnesses or even establish that the defendant was ever in Evansville.

Because of the inherent danger of a miscarriage of justice grounded upon the possibility of honest but mistaken eyewitness identification, the Attorney General has concluded that the proper administration of justice requires that the present indictment be dismissed without prejudice pending further investigation.

WHEREFORE, the United States respectfully prays that the Court grant leave to dismiss the indictment.

Richard P. Stein
United States

Do you agree that the indictment should be dismissed? How much weight should a prosecutor give to the fact that a grand jury has returned an indictment? How much weight should a prosecutor give to the fact that evidence of a defendant's innocence which is presented to him will be inadmissible at trial? How much weight should he give to inadmissible evidence of the defendant's guilt?

326. Should the judge before whom a motion to dismiss an indictment is made exercise independent discretion in deciding whether or not to grant the motion? Fed.R.Crim.P. 48(a) requires "leave of court" for the dismissal of an indictment, information or complaint, and the consent of the defendant for dismissal during trial. In United States v. Cowan, 524

F.2d 504, 512–13 (5th Cir.1975), the court said that the rule "should and can be construed to preserve the essential judicial function of protecting the public interest in the evenhanded administration of criminal justice without encroaching on the primary duty of the Executive to take care that the laws are faithfully executed." Accordingly, the prosecutor was "the first and presumptively the best judge of whether a pending prosecution should be terminated," and his judgment "should not be judicially disturbed unless clearly contrary to manifest public interest." Other cases are cited id. at 511. See generally United States v. Ammidown, 497 F.2d 615 (D.C.Cir.1973), p. 741 note 379 below.

See Rinaldi v. United States, 434 U.S. 22 (1977) (6–3), in which the government moved to dismiss the indictment under Rule 48(a) following the defendant's trial and conviction. The government made the motion because the conviction violated the "Petite" policy against federal and state prosecutions for the same act, see note 638, p. 1218 below. The district court denied the motion because it was not made until the trial was completed and because the prosecutor had acted in bad faith earlier when he advised the court that the prosecution was proper notwithstanding the defendant's state prosecution for the same offense. (The government had pursued the federal prosecution because it had feared a reversal of the state conviction.) The Court held that the motion to dismiss not being "clearly contrary to manifest public interest" (citing *Cowan*, above), it was an abuse of discretion to deny the motion. Id. at 30. It noted also that the "principal object" of requiring leave of court in Rule 48(a) "is apparently to protect a defendant against prosecutorial harassment, e.g., charging, dismissing and recharging, when the Government moves to dismiss an indictment over the defendant's objection." Id. at 29 n.15. See In re United States, 345 F.3d 450 (7th Cir.2003) (refusal to grant government's motion to dismiss was abuse of discretion); United States v. Jacobo-Zavala, 241 F.3d 1009 (8th Cir.2001) (same).

In United States v. Moller-Butcher, 723 F.2d 189, 190 (1st Cir.1983), the court observed that "absent extraordinary circumstances, a defendant has no standing to appeal the dismissal of an indictment." See United States v. Palomares, 119 F.3d 556 (7th Cir.1997) (dismissal upheld); United States v. Salinas, 693 F.2d 348 (5th Cir.1982) (order granting government's motion to dismiss was improper, because motion was not made in good faith); United States v. Hamm, 659 F.2d 624 (5th Cir.1981) (order denying government's motion to dismiss following plea of guilty reversed); United States v. Hastings, 447 F.Supp. 534 (E.D.Ark.1977) (government's motion to dismiss because of improper conduct of investigation granted).

CHAPTER 10

INDICTMENT

327. "No person shall be held to answer for a capital, or otherwise infamous crime, unless on a presentment or indictment of a grand jury, except in cases arising in the land or naval forces, or in the militia, when in actual service in time of war or public danger. . . ." U.S. Constitution amend. V.[1]

The states are not required by the Due Process Clause of the Fourteenth Amendment to prosecute by indictment in any case. Hurtado v. California, 110 U.S. 516 (1884). Many states now prosecute entirely by information. The grand jury has been abolished in England, where it originated. Administration of Justice Act, 1933, 23 & 24 Geo. 5, ch. 36.

In Rose v. Mitchell, 443 U.S. 545 (1979) (7–2), the defendants, who were black, appealed from a state conviction of murder on the ground that their pretrial motion to dismiss the indictment was wrongly denied; their motion alleged that the grand jury array and the foreman of the grand jury had been selected in a racially discriminatory fashion. The convictions were affirmed. The defendants then filed a petition for habeas corpus in the federal district court. In the Supreme Court, only the selection of the foreman was in issue. The Court concluded that the defendants had not established that there was racial discrimination. It reaffirmed, however, that discrimination in the selection of the grand jury is ground for setting aside a conviction. "Because discrimination on the basis of race in the selection of members of a grand jury . . . strikes at the fundamental values of our judicial system and our society as a whole, the Court has recognized that a criminal defendant's right to equal protection of the laws has been denied when he is indicted by a grand jury from which members of a racial group purposefully have been excluded. . . . For this same reason, the Court also has reversed the conviction and ordered the indictment quashed in such cases without inquiry into whether the defendant was prejudiced in fact by the discrimination at the grand jury stage." Id. at 556.

In an opinion concurring only in the judgment, Justice Stewart argued that a grand jury proceeding is "merely one to decide whether there is a

1. "The question is whether the crime is one for which the statutes authorize the court to award an infamous punishment, not whether the punishment ultimately awarded is an infamous one. When the accused is in danger of being subjected to an infamous punishment if convicted, he has the right to insist that he shall not be put upon his trial, except on the accusation of a grand jury. . . .

"What punishments shall be considered as infamous may be affected by the changes of public opinion from one age to another." Ex parte Wilson, 114 U.S. 417, 426–27 (1885). See Duke v. United States, 301 U.S. 492 (1937).

prima-facie case" against the defendant. "Any possible prejudice to the defendant resulting from an indictment returned by an invalid grand jury thus disappears when a constitutionally valid trial jury later finds him guilty beyond a reasonable doubt. In short, a convicted defendant who alleges that he was indicted by a discriminatorily selected grand jury is complaining of an antecedent constitutional violation that could have had no conceivable impact on the fairness of the trial that resulted in his conviction." Id. at 575–76. Justice Stewart observed that other means were available to vindicate the "compelling constitutional interest" in eliminating racial discrimination. Id. at 578. Rose v. Mitchell was followed in Vasquez v. Hillery, 474 U.S. 254 (1986) (6–3).

Discrimination in the selection of the foreman of a federal grand jury, which caused black persons and women not to be selected but did not cause them to be under-represented on the grand jury, does not require dismissal of an indictment against a defendant who is a white male. Hobby v. United States, 468 U.S. 339 (1984) (6–3). The Court observed that the position of foreman is ministerial; and the responsibilities attached to the office are essentially clerical. Accordingly, "the role of the foreman of a federal grand jury is not so significant to the administration of justice that discrimination in the appointment of that office impugns the fundamental fairness of the process itself so as to undermine the integrity of the indictment." Nor does discrimination invade the defendant's distinct interests under the Due Process Clause. 468 U.S. at 345. In Rose v. Mitchell, the Court had assumed that discrimination in the selection of the foreman of a state grand jury would require dismissal of an indictment. In *Hobby*, the court distinguished Rose v. Mitchell on the grounds that the defendants in the latter case, as members of the disfavored race, had a claim under the Equal Protection Clause and further, that in the state system in question, the foreman was an additional grand juror, whose selection affected the composition of the jury as a whole and who played a much more significant role than is played by a federal foreman.

Hobby was distinguished in Campbell v. Louisiana, 523 U.S. 392 (1998), in which the Court held that the defendant, who was white, had standing to challenge an indictment (by motion to quash) on the ground that the selection of the foreman of the grand jury was racially discriminatory, systematically excluding black persons. Referring to Rose v. Mitchell, the Court noted that, unlike *Hobby*, selection as foreman in *Campbell* was also the basis for inclusion of the person selected as a member of the grand jury, and, therefore, the selection process affected the composition of the grand jury itself. The court relied on Peters v. Kiff, 407 U.S. 493 (1972), p. 901 note 446 below, and Powers v. Ohio, 499 U.S. 400 (1991) (7–2), p. 912 note 453 below, for its conclusion that the defendant had standing to raise the issue.

328.

Prosecution of infamous crimes solely by indictment or presentment by a grand jury was provided for almost universally in American constitutions in our formative period. Informations ex officio by the attorney general were the basis of political prosecutions in England in the seventeenth and eighteenth centuries and the odium which attached to those prosecutions was attributed to the mode by which they were instituted. It was supposed that the requirement of indictment was a guarantee against oppressive prosecutions. But the grand jury had its real justification in the system of private prosecutions which never obtained in the United States. Although in historical origin it had another function, it came to be a check on private prosecutions, insuring that privately instituted proceedings should not go forward unless a representative body of men of the neighborhood found there was probable cause therefor. There was no need of such a check in a régime of public prosecutions. Under such a régime the grand jury merely adds one more to the long series of mitigating devices and opportunities for escape in which our prosecuting system abounds. In effect, as things are today, there are usually three preliminary examinations: One extralegal, conducted by the prosecuting attorney, one before a magistrate to bind accused over to the grand jury, and one before the grand jury.

. . . [T]here has been ample experience of the workings of a system of prosecution by information. . . . [I]t appears abundantly that prosecution by information has uniformly proved most satisfactory in practice and that none of the bad results feared by those who would retain the old system have been realized.

It is important, in view of the continually increasing demands upon the public purse, that the expense of administering justice be not augmented unnecessarily by inherited institutions which serve no useful purpose. That the grand-jury system is expensive is obvious. But it involves more than expenditure of money. In large cities grand juries must often sit continuously, or almost continuously, throughout the year. If there are to be good juries, excessive drain is made on the time of busy men who can ill afford to devote to public service the time which such a system, appropriate to the rural communities of the past, demands of them. There is economic waste also in requiring witnesses to attend two preliminary hearings, one before a magistrate and one before the grand jury. Moreover, this requirement of repeated attendance of witnesses, under conditions which obtain in large and busy cities, discourages witnesses and not infrequently leads to no prosecution where one ought to go forward. Again the extra step of indictment by a grand jury contributes to slowing up the already overburdened machinery of prosecution. It offers an additional opportunity of escape where there are now too many, and allows responsibility for failure to prosecute to fall down between the prosecutor and the grand jury. Thus the system wastes money, time, and energy, and diffuses responsibility in a field where responsibility ought to be concentrated.

Protection of the citizen against hasty and unfounded prosecutions, the advantage claimed for the requirement of an indictment in case of all infamous crimes, is more theoretical than real in the urban community of today. With the enormous lists of arrests in our large cities there is no guaranty against hasty or oppressive prosecutions in a body which can give but little time to the general run of cases and must depend on the prosecuting attorney for its information as to facts. Under such circumstances it must be a very weak case which can not be presented so as to procure an indictment. Where the number of prosecutions is large, it is hard for the grand jury in any ordinary case to get at other facts than those presented to them, or even to know that it is authorized to get at them. It is unusual for grand juries to go into a thorough, independent investigation of any ordinary case unless the prosecutor is willing. If the work of sifting were done as it should be by proper criminal investigation at the outset and by the prosecuting attorney, the grand jury could be given a basis for doing its work thoroughly and well. But the loose methods of investigation and sifting, which prevail generally in large cities, cause that work to be mechanical and perfunctory, except in a small number of sensational or unusual cases.

It should be added that the requirement of indictment by a grand jury in all prosecutions for infamous crimes involves a number of needless procedural difficulties which do not obtain in a régime of prosecution by information. Thus an indictment can not be amended, while an information may be. There are statutory requirements as to the drawing and composition of grand juries which frequently give rise to dilatory objections to the indictment. There are necessary rules as to the procedure of grand juries, and in particular as to who may be present during their inquiries and deliberations, which likewise offer opportunities for dilatory objections. To-day the grand jury is useful only as a general investigating body for inquiring into the conduct of public officers and in case of large conspiracies. It should be retained as an occasional instrument for such purposes, and the requirement of it as a necessary basis of all prosecutions for infamous crimes should be done away with.

National Commission on Law Observance and Enforcement (Wickersham Commission), Report on Prosecution 34–37 (1931).

329. The authority of the grand jury to issue "reports" without indicting anyone or to name persons as "unindicted coconspirators" or otherwise accuse them of crimes without formally indicting them is discussed extensively in United States v. Briggs, 514 F.2d 794 (5th Cir.1975). The court concluded that the grand jury lacks authority to accuse named persons of crimes without indicting them and that for it to do so is a denial of due process. See United States v. International Harvester Co., 720 F.2d 418 (5th Cir.1983) (person named but not charged in indictment not entitled to expungement, because he was indicted in related case in which government would be put to proof).

See generally Ealy v. Littlejohn, 569 F.2d 219 (5th Cir.1978), in which the court held that a grand jury inquiry into the organization and activities of a private association, as a result of public statements made in the name of the association and without any showing of a legitimate investigative purpose, was a violation of First Amendment rights.

FEDERAL RULES OF CRIMINAL PROCEDURE

Rule 6

THE GRAND JURY

(a) Summoning a Grand Jury.

(1) *In General.* When the public interest so requires, the court must order that one or more grand juries be summoned. A grand jury must have 16 to 23 members, and the court must order that enough legally qualified persons be summoned to meet this requirement.

(2) *Alternate Jurors.* When a grand jury is selected, the court may also select alternate jurors. Alternate jurors must have the same qualifications and be selected in the same manner as any other juror. Alternate jurors replace jurors in the same sequence in which the alternates were selected. An alternate juror who replaces a juror is subject to the same challenges, takes the same oath, and has the same authority as the other jurors.

(b) Objection to the Grand Jury or to a Grand Juror.

(1) *Challenges.* Either the government or a defendant may challenge the grand jury on the ground that it was not lawfully drawn, summoned, or selected, and may challenge an individual juror on the ground that the juror is not legally qualified.

(2) *Motion to Dismiss an Indictment.* A party may move to dismiss the indictment based on an objection to the grand jury or on an individual juror's lack of legal qualification, unless the court has previously ruled on the same objection under Rule 6(b)(1). The motion to dismiss is governed by 28 U.S.C. § 1867(e).[2] The court must not dismiss the indictment on the ground that a grand juror was not legally qualified if the record shows that at least 12 qualified jurors concurred in the indictment.

(c) Foreperson and Deputy Foreperson. The court will appoint one juror as the foreperson and another as the deputy foreperson. In the foreperson's absence, the deputy foreperson will act as the foreperson. The foreperson may administer oaths and affirmations and will sign all indictments. The foreperson—or another juror designated by the foreperson—will record the number of jurors concurring in every indictment and will file the record with the clerk, but the record may not be made public unless the court so orders.

[2] Enacted as part of the Jury Selection and Service Act of 1968 and containing provisions for challenging the method of selection of grand or petit jurors.

(d) Who May Be Present.

(1) *While the Grand Jury is in Session.* The following persons may be present while the grand jury is in session: attorneys for the government, the witness being questioned, interpreters when needed, and a court reporter or an operator of a recording device.

(2) *During Deliberations and Voting.* No person other than the jurors, and any interpreter needed to assist a hearing-impaired or speech-impaired juror, may be present while the grand jury is deliberating or voting.

(e) Recording and Disclosing the Proceedings.

(1) *Recording the Proceedings.* Except while the grand jury is deliberating or voting, all proceedings must be recorded by a court reporter or by a suitable recording device. But the validity of a prosecution is not affected by the unintentional failure to make a recording. Unless the court orders otherwise, an attorney for the government will retain control of the recording, the reporter's notes, and any transcript prepared from those notes.

(2) *Secrecy.*

(A) No obligation of secrecy may be imposed on any person except in accordance with Rule 6(e)(2)(B).

(B) Unless these rules provide otherwise, the following persons must not disclose a matter occurring before the grand jury:

(i) a grand juror;

(ii) an interpreter;

(iii) a court reporter;

(iv) an operator of a recording device;

(v) a person who transcribes recorded testimony;

(vi) an attorney for the government; or

(vii) a person to whom disclosure is made under Rule 6(e)(3)(A)(ii) or (iii).

(3) *Exceptions.*

(A) Disclosure of a grand-jury matter—other than the grand jury's deliberations or any grand juror's vote—may be made to:

(i) an attorney for the government for use in performing that attorney's duty;

(ii) any government personnel—including those of a state or state subdivision or of an Indian tribe—that an attorney for the government considers necessary to assist in performing that attorney's duty to enforce federal criminal law; or

(iii) a person authorized by 18 U.S.C. § 3322.

(B) A person to whom information is disclosed under Rule 6(e)(3)(A)(ii) may use that information only to assist an attorney for the government in performing that attorney's duty to enforce federal criminal law. An attorney for the government must promptly provide the court that impaneled the grand jury with the names of all persons to whom a disclosure has been made, and must certify that the attorney has advised those persons of their obligation of secrecy under this rule.

(C) An attorney for the government may disclose any grand-jury matter to another federal grand jury.

(D) An attorney for the government may disclose any grand-jury matter involving foreign intelligence, counter-intelligence (as defined in 50 U.S.C. § 401a), or foreign intelligence information (as defined in Rule 6(e)(3)(D)(iii)) to any federal law enforcement, intelligence, protective, immigration, national defense, or national security official to assist the official receiving the information in the performance of that official's duties.

(i) Any federal official who receives information under Rule 6(e)(3)(D) may use the information only as necessary in the conduct of that person's official duties subject to any limitations on the unauthorized disclosure of such information.

(ii) Within a reasonable time after disclosure is made under Rule 6(e)(3)(D), an attorney for the government must file, under seal, a notice with the court in the district where the grand jury convened stating that such information was disclosed and the departments, agencies, or entities to which the disclosure was made.

(iii) As used in Rule 6(e)(3)(D), the term "foreign intelligence information" means:

(a) information, whether or not it concerns a United States person, that relates to the ability of the United States to protect against—

- actual or potential attack or other grave hostile acts of a foreign power or its agent;
- sabotage or international terrorism by a foreign power or its agent; or
- clandestine intelligence activities by an intelligence service or network of a foreign power or by its agent; or

(b) information, whether or not it concerns a United States person, with respect to a foreign power or foreign territory that relates to—

- the national defense or the security of the United States; or
- the conduct of the foreign affairs of the United States.

(E) The court may authorize disclosure—at a time, in a manner, and subject to any other conditions that it directs—of a grand-jury matter:

(i) preliminarily to or in connection with a judicial proceeding;

(ii) at the request of a defendant who shows that a ground may exist to dismiss the indictment because of a matter that occurred before the grand jury;

(iii) at the request of the government if it shows that the matter may disclose a violation of state or Indian tribal criminal law, as long as the disclosure is to an appropriate state, state-subdivision, or Indian tribal official for the purpose of enforcing that law; or

(iv) at the request of the government if it shows that the matter may disclose a violation of military criminal law under the Uniform Code of Military Justice, as long as the disclosure is to an appropriate military official for the purpose of enforcing that law.

(F) A petition to disclose a grand-jury matter under Rule 6(e)(3)(E)(i) must be filed in the district where the grand jury convened. Unless the hearing is ex parte—as it may be when the government is the petitioner—the petitioner must serve the petition on, and the court must afford a reasonable opportunity to appear and be heard to:

(i) an attorney for the government;

(ii) the parties to the judicial proceeding; and

(iii) any other person whom the court may designate.

(G) If the petition to disclose arises out of a judicial proceeding in another district, the petitioned court must transfer the petition to the other court unless the petitioned court can reasonably determine whether disclosure is proper. If the petitioned court decides to transfer, it must send to the transferee court the material sought to be disclosed, if feasible, and a written evaluation of the need for continued grand-jury secrecy. The transferee court must afford those persons identified in Rule 6(e)(3)(F) a reasonable opportunity to appear and be heard.

(4) *Sealed Indictment*. The magistrate judge to whom an indictment is returned may direct that the indictment be kept secret until the defendant is in custody or has been released pending trial. The clerk must then seal the indictment, and no person may disclose the indictment's existence except as necessary to issue or execute a warrant or summons.

(5) *Closed Hearing*. Subject to any right to an open hearing in a contempt proceeding, the court must close any hearing to the extent necessary to prevent disclosure of a matter occurring before a grand jury.

(6) *Sealed Records*. Records, orders, and subpoenas relating to grand-jury proceedings must be kept under seal to the extent and as

long as necessary to prevent the unauthorized disclosure of a matter occurring before a grand jury.

(7) *Contempt*. A knowing violation of Rule 6 may be punished as a contempt of court.

(f) Indictment and Return. A grand jury may indict only if at least 12 jurors concur. The grand jury—or its foreperson or deputy foreperson—must return the indictment to a magistrate judge in open court. If a complaint or information is pending against the defendant and 12 jurors do not concur in the indictment, the foreperson must promptly and in writing report the lack of concurrence to the magistrate judge.

(g) Discharging the Grand Jury. A grand jury must serve until the court discharges it, but it may serve more than 18 months only if the court, having determined that an extension is in the public interest, extends the grand jury's service. An extension may be granted for no more than 6 months, except as otherwise provided by statute.

(h) Excusing a Juror. At any time, for good cause, the court may excuse a juror either temporarily or permanently, and if permanently, the court may impanel an alternate juror in place of the excused juror.

(i) "Indian Tribe" Defined. "Indian tribe" means an Indian tribe recognized by the Secretary of the Interior on a list published in the Federal Register under 25 U.S.C. § 479a–1.

Rule 7

THE INDICTMENT AND THE INFORMATION

(a) When Used.

(1) *Felony*. An offense (other than criminal contempt) must be prosecuted by an indictment if it is punishable:

(A) by death; or

(B) by imprisonment for more than one year.

(2) *Misdemeanor*. An offense punishable by imprisonment for one year or less may be prosecuted in accordance with Rule 58(b)(1).

(b) Waiving Indictment. An offense punishable by imprisonment for more than one year may be prosecuted by information if the defendant—in open court and after being advised of the nature of the charge and of the defendant's rights—waives prosecution by indictment.

(c) Nature and Contents.

(1) *In General*. The indictment or information must be a plain, concise, and definite written statement of the essential facts constituting the offense charged and must be signed by an attorney for the government. It need not contain a formal introduction or conclusion. A count may incorporate by reference an allegation made in another count. A count may allege that the means by which the defendant committed the offense are unknown or that the defendant committed it by one or more specified means. For each count, the indictment or

information must give the official or customary citation of the statute, rule, regulation, or other provision of law that the defendant is alleged to have violated.

(2) *Criminal Forfeiture*. No judgment of forfeiture may be entered in a criminal proceeding unless the indictment or the information provides notice that the defendant has an interest in property that is subject to forfeiture in accordance with the applicable statute.

(3) *Citation Error*. Unless the defendant was misled and thereby prejudiced, neither an error in a citation nor a citation's omission is a ground to dismiss the indictment or information or to reverse a conviction.

(d) Surplusage. Upon the defendant's motion, the court may strike surplusage from the indictment or information.

(e) Amending an Information. Unless an additional or different offense is charged or a substantial right of the defendant is prejudiced, the court may permit an information to be amended at any time before the verdict or finding.

(f) Bill of Particulars. The court may direct the government to file a bill of particulars. The defendant may move for a bill of particulars before or within 10 days after arraignment or at a later time if the court permits. The government may amend a bill of particulars subject to such conditions as justice requires.

Rule 48
DISMISSAL

(a) By the Government. The government may, with leave of court, dismiss an indictment, information, or complaint. The government may not dismiss the prosecution during trial without the defendant's consent.

(b) By the Court. The court may dismiss an indictment, information, or complaint if unnecessary delay occurs in:

(1) presenting a charge to a grand jury;

(2) filing an information against a defendant; or

(3) bringing a defendant to trial.

---

330. Rule 6(e)(4). An indictment is "found" for purposes of the statute of limitations when the grand jury votes to indict and the foreman signs the indictment. The fact that the indictment is then sealed is not relevant to the statute of limitations. United States v. Thompson, 287 F.3d 1244 (10th Cir.2002). The court noted that other courts have a different rule, to the effect that if an indictment is sealed *improperly*, the statute of limitations is not tolled until the indictment is unsealed. In this case, however, the court found that the indictment was not sealed in conformity with Rule 6(e)(4) and that the error was not harmless, and it ordered that the indictment be dismissed for that reason.

AO 455 (Rev. 5/85) Waiver of Indictment

UNITED STATES DISTRICT COURT

_______________ DISTRICT OF _______________

UNITED STATES OF AMERICA
V.

WAIVER OF INDICTMENT

CASE NUMBER:

I, _______________, the above named defendant, who is accused of

being advised of the nature of the charge(s), the proposed information, and of my rights, hereby waive in open court on _______________ prosecution by indictment and consent that the pro-
Date
ceeding may be by information rather than by indictment.

____
Defendant

____
Counsel for Defendant

Before _______________
Judicial Officer

331. Waiver. Rule 7(b) does not permit waiver of indictment in capital cases. See generally Smith v. United States, 360 U.S. 1 (1959). On withdrawal of a waiver of indictment, see Bartlett v. United States, 354 F.2d 745 (8th Cir.1966), in which the court upheld a ruling that the defendant could withdraw his plea of guilty but not a waiver of indictment.

332. Rule 6(e)(2) provides that the proceedings of the grand jury shall generally remain secret. In Butterworth v. Smith, 494 U.S. 624 (1990), however, the Court held that a state statute that prohibited *witnesses* before a grand jury from disclosing their testimony is unconstitutional, insofar as it prohibits a witness from disclosing his own testimony after the term of the grand jury has ended. Such a prohibition, the Court said, violates the First Amendment.

United States v. Mechanik

475 U.S. 66, 106 S.Ct. 938, 89 L.Ed.2d 50 (1986)

■ JUSTICE REHNQUIST delivered the opinion of the Court.

Federal Rule of Criminal Procedure 6(d) states that only specified persons including "the witness under examination" may be present at a grand jury proceeding. In this case, two Government witnesses testified in tandem before the grand jury, which indicted respondents and cross-petitioners (hereafter defendants) Mechanik and Lill for various drug-related offenses and conspiracy to commit such offenses. The Court of Appeals for the Fourth Circuit held that the simultaneous presence of these two witnesses violated Rule 6(d), and that even though the petit jury subsequently returned a verdict of guilty against defendants, the verdict must be set aside on any count that corresponds to a "tainted" portion of the indictment. We believe that the petit jury's verdict of guilty beyond a reasonable doubt demonstrates *a fortiori* that there was probable cause to charge the defendants with the offenses for which they were convicted. Therefore, the convictions must stand despite the rule violation.

A fairly detailed summary of the District Court proceedings will help to illustrate the nature and extent of our holding. A grand jury returned an indictment charging defendants with drug-related offenses and conspiracy. This indictment was concededly free from any claim of error. The grand jury then returned a superseding indictment in which the conspiracy charge was expanded. In support of this superseding indictment, the United States Attorney presented the testimony of two law enforcement agents who were sworn together and questioned in tandem before the grand jury.

The defendants did not learn about this joint testimony until after trial began. Before trial, they filed an omnibus motion requesting, inter alia, the names of all the people who appeared before the grand jury. The Government responded that there were no unauthorized persons appearing before the grand jury, and the District Court denied the motion. Trial began in February 1980, and concluded in early July of the same year. During the second week of trial, one Jerry Rinehart, an agent of the Drug Enforcement Administration, testified as a Government witness. At the time of his testimony, the Government furnished the defendants with a portion of the transcript of his grand jury testimony as required by the Jencks Act, 18 U.S.C. § 3500. The transcript disclosed that Rinehart and his fellow agent, Randolph James, had testified in tandem before the grand jury.

The defendants moved for dismissal of the indictment on the ground that the simultaneous presence of the two agents had violated Federal Rule of Criminal Procedure 6(d). . . . Judge Copenhaver took the motion under advisement until the conclusion of trial.

In August 1980, after the jury had returned its guilty verdict, Judge Copenhaver ruled upon and denied the defendants' motion for dismissal of the indictment. 511 F.Supp. 50 (S.D.W.Va.1980). He first decided . . . that the joint testimony of Agents Rinehart and James *did* constitute a violation of Rule 6(d). . . . But he declined to set aside the defendants' indictment and convictions because, on the basis of a comparison between the two indictments and the evidence on which the indictments rested, the violation of Rule 6(d) had not harmed the defendants. . . . He justified this conclusion with respect to the substantive counts on the ground that they were materially unchanged from the valid initial indictment to the superseding indictment. . . . With respect to the conspiracy count, which had been expanded by the superseding indictment, he justified his conclusion on the ground that the grand jury "had before it ample independent evidence [apart from the joint testimony] to support a probable cause finding of the charges." Id., at 61. In light of these conclusions, Judge Copenhaver determined that a post-trial dismissal of the indictment would simply confer a windfall benefit on the defendants "who stand convicted after a three-month trial conducted at enormous expense to the United States and the defendants." Ibid. The judge nevertheless undertook to ensure future compliance with the one-witness rule by directing the Government to keep the court advised concerning compliance with Rule 6(d) in future criminal cases. . . .

A divided Court of Appeals reversed the conspiracy convictions, affirmed the others, and dismissed the conspiracy portion of the indictment. 735 F.2d 136 (1984). It reasoned that the language of Rule 6(d) is so "plain and unequivocal in limiting who may appear before a grand jury," id., at 139, that its transgression requires automatic reversal of any subsequent conviction regardless of the lack of prejudice. . . . But the court reversed only the conspiracy convictions because it found that the violation of Rule 6(d) tainted only the portion of the superseding indictment that related to them. . . . A divided en banc decision agreed. . . .

We assume for the sake of argument that the simultaneous presence and testimony of the two Government witnesses before the grand jury violated Rule 6(d), and that the District Court would have been justified in dismissing portions of the indictment on that basis had there been actual prejudice and had the matter been called to its attention before the commencement of the trial. But although the defendants appear to have been reasonably diligent in attempting to discover any error at the grand jury proceeding, they did not acquire the transcript showing that the two agents had appeared jointly in the grand jury proceeding until the second week of trial. Nor is there any suggestion that the Government designedly withheld the information. . . . Although we do not believe that the defendants can be faulted for any lack of diligence, we nonetheless hold that the supervening jury verdict made reversal of the conviction and dismissal of the indictment inappropriate.

Both the District Court and the Court of Appeals observed that Rule 6(d) was designed, in part, "to ensure that grand jurors, sitting without the direct supervision of a judge, are not subject to undue influence that may come with the presence of an unauthorized person." 735 F.2d, at 139. The Rule protects against the danger that a defendant will be required to defend against a charge for which there is no probable cause to believe him guilty. The error involving Rule 6(d) in these cases had the theoretical potential to affect the grand jury's determination whether to indict these particular defendants for the offenses with which they were charged. But the petit jury's subsequent guilty verdict not only means that there was probable cause to believe that the defendants were guilty as charged, but that they are in fact guilty as charged beyond a reasonable doubt. Measured by the petit jury's verdict, then, any error in the grand jury proceeding connected with the charging decision was harmless beyond a reasonable doubt.

It might be argued in some literal sense that because the Rule was designed to protect against an erroneous charging decision by the *grand jury*, the indictment should not be compared to the evidence produced by the Government at *trial*, but to the evidence produced before the *grand jury*. But even if this argument were accepted, there is no simple way after the verdict to restore the defendant to the position in which he would have been had the indictment been dismissed before trial. He will already have suffered whatever inconvenience, expense, and opprobrium that a proper indictment may have spared him. In courtroom proceedings as elsewhere, "the moving finger writes, and having writ moves on." Thus reversal of a conviction after a trial free from reversible error cannot restore to the defendant whatever benefit might have accrued to him from a trial on an indictment returned in conformity with Rule 6(d).

We cannot accept the Court of Appeals' view that a violation of Rule 6(d) requires automatic reversal of a subsequent conviction regardless of the lack of prejudice. Federal Rule of Criminal Procedure 52(a) provides that errors not affecting substantial rights shall be disregarded. We see no reason not to apply this provision to "errors, defects, irregularities or variances" occurring before a grand jury just as we have applied it to such error occurring in the criminal trial itself. . . .

The reversal of a conviction entails substantial social costs: it forces jurors, witnesses, courts, the prosecution, and the defendants to expend further time, energy, and other resources to repeat a trial that has already once taken place; victims may be asked to relive their disturbing experiences. . . . The "[p]assage of time, erosion of memory, and dispersion of witnesses may render retrial difficult, even impossible." Engle v. Isaac, 456 U.S. 107, 127–28 (1982). Thus, while reversal "may, in theory, entitle the defendant only to retrial, in practice it may reward the accused with complete freedom from prosecution," id., at 128, and thereby "cost society the right to punish admitted offenders." Id., at 127. Even if a defendant is convicted in a second trial, the intervening delay may compromise society's "interest in the prompt administration of justice," United States v. Hasting [461 U.S. 499 (1983)], at 509, and impede accomplishment of the objectives of deterrence and rehabilitation. These societal costs of reversal and retrial are an acceptable and often necessary consequence when an error in the first proceeding has deprived a defendant of a fair determination of the issue of guilt or innocence. But the balance of interest tips decidedly the other way when an error has had no effect on the outcome of the trial.

We express no opinion as to what remedy may be appropriate for a violation of Rule 6(d) that has affected the grand jury's charging decision and is brought to the attention of the trial court before the commencement of trial. We hold only that however diligent the defendants may have been in seeking to discover the basis for the claimed violation of Rule 6(d), the petit jury's verdict rendered harmless any conceivable error in the charging decision that might have flowed from the violation. In such a case, the societal costs of retrial after a jury verdict of guilty are far too substantial to justify setting aside the verdict simply because of an error in the earlier grand jury proceedings. The judgment of the Court of Appeals is therefore reversed to the extent it set aside the conspiracy convictions and dismissed the indictment, but is otherwise affirmed.

It is so ordered.[3]

---

333. Declaring that "a federal court may not invoke supervisory power to circumvent the harmless-error inquiry prescribed by Federal Rule of Criminal Procedure 52(a)," the Court held that a district court may not dismiss an indictment for errors in grand jury proceedings unless the errors caused prejudice to the defendants. "[A]t least where dismissal is sought for nonconstitutional error," such prejudice is not shown unless it is established that the error "substantially influenced" the grand jury's decision to indict or there is "grave doubt" that the decision to indict was free from such influence. Bank of Nova Scotia v. United States, 487 U.S. 250, 254, 256 (1988) (8–1). The Court concluded that the errors in question, multiple violations of the requirements of Rule 6(d) and (e), were harmless.

Mechanik notwithstanding, an order denying the defendant's motion to dismiss an indictment for an alleged violation of Rule 6(e)(2), prohibiting

[3] Justice O'Connor argued in an opinion concurring in the judgment, which Justice Brennan and Justice Blackmun joined, that the Court's analysis rendered the rules governing grand jury proceedings "a dead letter," because it shifted the focus of harmless error from the effect of a violation on the indictment to its effect on the verdict. Even though a verdict has been returned, she argued, "the focus of the court's inquiry should remain on the grand jury's charging decision." 475 U.S. at 73, 76. In a dissenting opinion, Justice Marshall agreed and added that a clear violation of Rule 6 should require dismissal of the indictment even after verdict without a case-by-case analysis to see whether the error was harmless.

public disclosure of matters occurring before the grand jury, is not appealable as an interlocutory appeal before final judgment. Midland Asphalt Corp. v. United States, 489 U.S. 794 (1989). The Court declined to decide whether *Mechanik* applies to violations of Rule 6(e). It said that if such violations can be a basis for reversal of a conviction on appeal, then there was no reason to allow an interlocutory appeal. And if a violation cannot be the basis for reversal, it would be because the alleged violation did not involve a fundamental issue completely separable from the merits of the action, again making an interlocutory appeal unavailable.

United States v. Miller

471 U.S. 130, 105 S.Ct. 1811, 85 L.Ed.2d 99 (1985)

■ JUSTICE MARSHALL delivered the opinion of the Court.

The issue presented is whether the Fifth Amendment's grand jury guarantee is violated when a defendant is tried under an indictment that alleges a certain fraudulent scheme but is convicted based on trial proof that supports only a significantly narrower and more limited, though included, fraudulent scheme.

A grand jury in the Northern District of California returned an indictment charging respondent Miller with three counts of mail fraud in violation of 18 U.S.C. § 1341. After the Government moved to dismiss the third count, Miller was tried before a jury and convicted of the remaining two. He appealed asserting that there had been a fatal variance between the "scheme and artifice" to defraud charged in the indictment and that which the Government proved at trial. The Court of Appeals for the Ninth Circuit agreed and vacated the judgment of conviction. . . . We granted certiorari . . . and reverse.

I

A

The indictment had charged Miller with various fraudulent acts in connection with a burglary at his business. Miller allegedly had defrauded his insurer both by consenting to the burglary in advance and by lying to the insurer about the value of his loss. The trial proof, however, concerned only the latter allegation, focusing on whether, prior to the burglary, Miller actually had possessed all the property that he later claimed was taken. This proof was clearly sufficient to support a jury finding that Miller's claim to his insurer had grossly inflated the value of any actual loss.

The Government moved to strike the part of the indictment that alleged prior knowledge of the burglary, and it correctly argued that even without that allegation the indictment still made out a violation of § 1341. Respondent's counsel opposed the change, and at his urging the entire indictment was sent to the jury. The jury found Miller guilty, and respondent appealed on the basis that the trial proof had fatally varied from the scheme alleged in the indictment.

Agreeing that Miller's Fifth Amendment right to be tried only on a grand jury indictment had been violated, the Court of Appeals vacated the conviction. . . .

B

Miller's indictment properly alleged violations of 18 U.S.C. § 1341, and it fully and clearly set forth a number of ways in which the acts alleged constituted violations. The facts proved at trial clearly conformed to one of the theories of the offense contained within that indictment, for the indictment gave Miller clear notice that he would have to defend against an allegation that he "well knew that the amount of copper claimed to have been taken during the alleged burglary was grossly inflated for the purpose of fraudulently obtaining $150,000 from Aetna Insurance Company." 715 F.2d, at 1361–62 (quoting indictment). Competent defense counsel certainly should have been on notice that that offense was charged and would need to be defended against. Accordingly, there can be no showing here that Miller was prejudicially surprised at trial by the absence of proof concerning his alleged complicity in the burglary; nor can there be a showing that the variance prejudiced the fairness of respondent's trial in any other way. . . . The indictment was also sufficient to allow Miller to plead it in the future as a bar to subsequent prosecutions. Therefore, none of these "notice" related concerns—which of course are among the important concerns underlying the requirement that criminal charges be set out in an indictment—would support the result of the Court of Appeals. . . .

The Court of Appeals did not disagree, but instead argued that Miller had been prejudiced in his right to be free from a trial for any offense other than that alleged in the grand jury's indictment. . . . It reasoned that a grand jury's willingness to indict an individual for participation in a broad criminal plan does not establish that the same grand jury would have indicted the individual for participating in a substantially narrower, even if wholly included, criminal plan. . . . Relying on the Fifth Amendment's grand jury guarantee, the Court of Appeals concluded that a conviction could not stand where the trial proof corresponded to a fraudulent scheme much narrower than, though included within, the scheme that the grand jury had alleged. . . .

II

. . . The Court has long recognized that an indictment may charge numerous offenses or the commission of any one offense in several ways. As long as the crime and the elements of the offense that sustain the conviction are fully and clearly set out in the indictment, the right to a grand jury is not normally violated by the fact that the indictment alleges more crimes or other means of committing the same crime. . . . Indeed, a number of longstanding doctrines of criminal procedure are premised on the notion that each offense whose elements are fully set out in an indictment can independently sustain a conviction. . . .

A review of prior cases allowing convictions to stand in the face of variances between the indictment and proof makes the Court of Appeals' error clear. Convictions generally have been sustained as long as the proof upon which they are based corresponds to an offense that was clearly set out in the indictment. A part of the indictment unnecessary to and independent from the allegations of the offense proved may normally be treated as "a useless averment" that "may be ignored." Ford v. United States, 273 U.S. 593, 602 (1927). . . .

This treatment of allegations independent of and unnecessary to the offense on which a conviction ultimately rests has not been confined to allegations that, like those in *Ford*, would have had no legal relevance if proved. In Salinger v. United States, [272 U.S. 542 (1926)], for example, the Court was presented with facts quite similar to the instant case. A grand jury charged Salinger with mail fraud in an indictment containing several counts, "[a]ll relat[ing] to the same scheme to defraud, but each charg[ing] a distinct use of the mail for the purpose of executing the scheme." 272 U.S., at 546. As was the case with Miller, Salinger's "scheme to defraud as set forth in the indictment . . . comprehended several relatively distinct plans for fleecing intended victims." Id., at 548. Because the evidence only sustained the charge as to one of the plans, the trial judge withdrew from the jury those portions of the indictment that related to all other plans. Salinger argued then, just as Miller argues now, that the variance between the broad allegations in the indictment and the narrower proof at trial violated his right to have had a grand jury screen any alleged offenses upon which he might be convicted at trial.

This Court unanimously rejected Salinger's argument on the ground that the offense proved was fully contained within the indictment. Nothing had been added to the indictment which, in the Court's view, "remained just as it was returned by the grand jury." Ibid. "[T]he trial was on the charge preferred in it and not on a modified charge," ibid., and there was thus "not even remotely an infraction of the constitutional provision that 'no person shall be held to answer for a capital or otherwise infamous crime unless on a presentment or indictment of a grand jury.' " Id., at 549. . . .

The result reached by the Court of Appeals thus conflicts with the results reached by this court in such cases as *Salinger* and *Ford*. . . .

III

The Court of Appeals principally relied on this Court's decision in Stirone v. United States, 361 U.S. 212 (1960), to support its conclusion that the Fifth Amendment's grand jury right is violated by a conviction for a criminal plan narrower than, but fully included within, the plan set forth in the indictment. *Stirone*, however, stands for a very different proposition. In *Stirone* the offense proved at trial was *not* fully contained in the indictment, for trial evidence had "amended" the indictment by *broadening* the possible bases for conviction from that which appeared in the indictment.

Stirone was thus wholly unlike the cases discussed in Part II, supra, and unlike respondent's case, all of which involve trial evidence that narrowed the indictment's charges without adding any new offenses. As the *Stirone* Court said, the issue was "whether [Stirone] was convicted of an offense *not charged in the indictment.*" 361 U.S., at 213 (emphasis added).

. . .

Miller has shown no deprivation of his "substantial right to be tried only on charges presented in an indictment returned by a grand jury." 361 U.S., at 217. In contrast to Stirone, Miller was tried on an indictment that clearly set out the offense for which he was ultimately convicted. His complaint is not that the indictment failed to charge the offense for which he was convicted, but that the indictment charged more than was necessary.

. . .

V

In light of the foregoing, the proper disposition of this case is clear. The variance complained of added nothing new to the grand jury's indictment and constituted no broadening. As in *Salinger* and *Ford*, what was removed from the case was in no way essential to the offense on which the jury convicted. We therefore disagree with the Court of Appeals on the issue of whether Miller has shown any compromise of his right to be tried only on offenses for which a grand jury has returned an indictment. No such compromise has been shown. The judgment of the Court of Appeals is accordingly reversed.

. . .

---

334. For cases discussing the problem of variance between the indictment and proof, see, e.g., United States v. Tsinhnahijinnie, 112 F.3d 988 (9th Cir.1997) (variance between date of crime alleged in indictment and proof; conviction reversed); United States v. Leichtnam, 948 F.2d 370 (7th Cir.1991) (variance between indictment and theory of case according to evidence and instructions; conviction reversed); United States v. Weissman, 899 F.2d 1111 (11th Cir.1990) (jury instruction constructively amended indictment and created variance between actual indictment and proof; conviction reversed). See generally Russell v. United States, 369 U.S. 749 (1962).

335. Overruling the holding in an old case, Ex parte Bain, 121 U.S. 1 (1887), which had held that if an indictment omits an element of the offense charged, the defect deprives the court of jurisdiction, the Court held that such a defect is not "jurisdictional"; it does not deprive the court of jurisdiction to try the case and render judgment. United States v. Cotton, 535 U.S. 625 (2002). The Court held also that the defect in question (failure to include in the indictment facts required by Apprendi v. New Jersey, p. 1082 below) was not plain error requiring vacation of the sentence imposed.

In United States v. Goldstein, 502 F.2d 526 (3d Cir.1974), the court held that a material variance between an indictment for a misdemeanor

AO110 (Rev. 12/89) Subpoena to Testify Before Grand Jury

UNITED STATES DISTRICT COURT

_______________ DISTRICT OF _______________

TO:

SUBPOENA TO TESTIFY
BEFORE GRAND JURY

SUBPOENA FOR:
☐ PERSON ☐ DOCUMENT(S) OR OBJECT(S)

YOU ARE HEREBY COMMANDED to appear and testify before the Grand Jury of the United States District Court at the place, date, and time specified below.

PLACE	COURTROOM
	DATE AND TIME

YOU ARE ALSO COMMANDED to bring with you the following document(s) or object(s):*

☐ *Please see additional information on reverse.*

This subpoena shall remain in effect until you are granted leave to depart by the court or by an officer acting on behalf of the court.

CLERK	DATE
(By) Deputy Clerk	

This subpoena is issued on application of the United States of America	NAME, ADDRESS AND PHONE NUMBER OF ASSISTANT U.S. ATTORNEY

* If not applicable, enter "none".

and the proof was fatal to the conviction, even though the government could have proceeded by information. While amendment to an information is permitted, having elected to proceed by indictment, the government was bound by the rules applicable to an indictment. See Watson v. Jago, 558 F.2d 330, 339 (6th Cir.1977), in which the court of appeals concluded that, while the grand jury provision of the Fifth Amendment does not apply to the States, "to allow the prosecution to amend the indictment at trial so as to enable the prosecution to seek a conviction on a charge not brought by the grand jury unquestionably constituted a denial of due process by not giving appellant fair notice of criminal charges to be brought against him." To the same effect, see Koontz v. Glossa, 731 F.2d 365 (6th Cir.1984) (indictment charging arson by defendant failed to give notice of accusation that defendant hired another person to commit arson).

336. Counsel. "A witness before a grand jury cannot insist, as a matter of constitutional right, on being represented by his counsel. . . ." In re Groban, 352 U.S. 330, 333 (1957). Federal Rule 6(d)(1), p. 663 above, preserves the practice that a witness summoned before a grand jury may not be accompanied by counsel. In United States v. Capaldo, 402 F.2d 821, 824 (2d Cir.1968), the court observed that a rule that excluded counsel but allowed a witness "to leave the grand jury room at any time to consult with counsel is a reasonable and workable accommodation of the traditional investigatory role of the grand jury, preserved in the Fifth Amendment, and the self-incrimination and right to counsel provisions of the Fifth and Sixth Amendments." But see In re Grand Jury Proceedings (Matter of Lowry), 713 F.2d 616, 617–18 (11th Cir.1983), in which the court observed: "Grand jury witnesses have no right to the presence of counsel in the jury room during questioning. . . . Nor does a witness have a constitutional right to disrupt the grand jury's proceedings by leaving the room to consult with his attorney after every question." See generally Anonymous Nos. 6 and 7 v. Baker, 360 U.S. 287 (1959) (5–4).

The practice of allowing a witness before the grand jury to leave the room at any time to consult with an attorney has been restricted in cases of a witness who has been granted immunity from prosecution. See, e.g., United States v. Soto, 574 F.Supp. 986 (D.Conn.1983), in which the witness sought to write down each question as it was asked and to consult with her attorney after each question. The court ruled: "The Court finds that a practical accommodation for all parties concerned shall be as follows: (1) The Grand Jury shall question the witness Soto continuously for twenty (20) minutes and then allow her ten (10) minutes in which to consult privately with her attorney; and (2) Miss Soto shall not delay the proceedings by writing down the questions during the interrogation, nor her answers. The transcribing process impedes the investigation, virtually brings the attorney into the Grand Jury room, and allows for the possibility that the testimony given will be more that of the witness' counsel than that of the witness. This procedure will expedite the Grand Jury investigation while allowing the witness any necessary legal advice." Id. at 993.

In In re Investigation Before Feb., 1977, Lynchburg Grand Jury (United States v. Barker), 563 F.2d 652 (4th Cir.1977), the court upheld an order disqualifying certain lawyers from representing their clients as witnesses before the grand jury, on the ground that their presence would interfere with the grand jury's function. In one case the lawyer himself and in another other clients of the lawyer were targets of the grand jury's investigation. In that circumstance, the court concluded, the right to be represented by counsel of one's choice had to give way. (The court noted that there was doubt about the witnesses' right to representation before the grand jury, but assumed that there was.)

337. A subpoena duces tecum issued by a grand jury is not required to meet the standards of relevance, admissibility, and specificity that apply to a subpoena issued for trial (see note 491, p. 962 below). Since the purpose of a grand jury investigation is to determine whether a crime may have been committed, it necessarily is permitted to investigate more broadly than the inquiry at trial. A grand jury's subpoena is presumed to be reasonable and, if it is challenged on the ground of irrelevance, must be upheld unless "there is no reasonable possibility that the category of materials the Government seeks will produce information relevant to the general subject of the grand jury's investigation." United States v. R. Enterprises, Inc., 498 U.S. 292, 301 (1991). See generally United States v. Dionisio, 410 U.S. 1 (1973) (7–2).

Costello v. United States

350 U.S. 359, 76 S.Ct. 406, 100 L.Ed. 397 (1956)

■ MR. JUSTICE BLACK delivered the opinion of the Court.

We granted certiorari in this case to consider a single question: "May a defendant be required to stand trial and a conviction be sustained where only hearsay evidence was presented to the grand jury which indicted him?" 350 U.S. 819.

Petitioner, Frank Costello, was indicted for wilfully attempting to evade payment of income taxes due the United States for the years 1947, 1948 and 1949. The charge was that petitioner falsely and fraudulently reported less income than he and his wife actually received during the taxable years in question. Petitioner promptly filed a motion for inspection of the minutes of the grand jury and for a dismissal of the indictment. His motion was based on an affidavit stating that he was firmly convinced there could have been no legal or competent evidence before the grand jury which indicted him since he had reported all his income and paid all taxes due. The motion was denied. At the trial which followed the Government offered evidence designed to show increases in Costello's net worth in an attempt to prove that he had received more income during the years in question than he had reported. To establish its case the Government called and examined 144 witnesses and introduced 368 exhibits. All of the testimony and documents related to business transactions and expenditures by petitioner and his wife. The prosecution concluded its case by calling three government agents. Their investigations had produced the evidence used against petitioner at the trial. They were allowed to summarize the vast amount of evidence already heard and to introduce computations showing, if correct, that petitioner and his wife had received far greater income than they had reported. We have held such summarizations admissible in a "net worth" case like this. . . .

Counsel for petitioner asked each government witness at the trial whether he had appeared before the grand jury which returned the indictment. This cross-examination developed the fact that the three investigating officers had been the only witnesses before the grand jury. After the Government concluded its case, petitioner again moved to dismiss the indictment on the ground that the only evidence before the grand jury was "hearsay," since the three officers had no firsthand knowledge of the transactions upon which their computations were based. Nevertheless the trial court again refused to dismiss the indictment, and petitioner was convicted. The Court of Appeals affirmed, holding that the indictment was valid even though the sole evidence before the grand jury was hearsay. Petitioner here urges: (1) that an indictment based solely on hearsay evidence violates that part of the Fifth Amendment providing that "No person shall be held to answer for a capital, or otherwise infamous crime, unless on a presentment or indictment of a Grand Jury . . ." and (2) that if the Fifth Amendment does not invalidate an indictment based solely on hearsay we should now lay down such a rule for the guidance of federal courts.

. . .

The Fifth Amendment provides that federal prosecutions for capital or otherwise infamous crimes must be instituted by presentments or indictments of grand juries. But neither the Fifth Amendment nor any other constitutional provision prescribes the kind of evidence upon which grand juries must act. . . .

In Holt v. United States, 218 U.S. 245, this Court had to decide whether an indictment should be quashed because supported in part by incompetent evidence. Aside from the incompetent evidence "there was very little evidence against the accused." The Court refused to hold that such an indictment should be quashed, pointing out that "The abuses of criminal practice would be enhanced if indictments could be upset on such a ground." 218 U.S., at 248. The same thing is true where as here all the evidence before the grand jury was in the nature of "hearsay." If indictments were to be held open to challenge on the ground that there was inadequate or incompetent evidence before the grand jury, the resulting delay would be great indeed. The result of such a rule would be that before trial on the merits a defendant could always insist on a kind of preliminary trial to determine the competency and adequacy of the evidence before the grand jury. This is not required by the Fifth Amendment. An indictment returned by a legally constituted and unbiased grand jury, like an information drawn by the prosecutor, if valid on its face, is enough to call for trial of the charge on the merits. The Fifth Amendment requires nothing more.

Petitioner urges that this Court should exercise its power to supervise the administration of justice in federal courts and establish a rule permitting defendants to challenge indictments on the ground that they are not supported by adequate or competent evidence. No persuasive reasons are advanced for establishing such a rule. It would run counter to the whole history of the grand jury institution, in which laymen conduct their inquiries unfettered by technical rules. Neither justice nor the concept of a fair trial requires such a change. In a trial on the merits, defendants are entitled to a strict observance of all the rules designed to bring about a fair verdict. Defendants are not entitled, however, to a rule which would result in interminable delay but add nothing to the assurance of a fair trial.[4]

---

338. The reasoning of the Court in United States v. Calandra, 414 U.S. 338 (1974), in which the Court held that the exclusionary rule is inapplicable to grand jury proceedings, effectively extends *Costello* to evidence obtained unconstitutionally.

The United States Attorneys' Manual 9–11.231 states: "A prosecutor should not present to the grand jury for use against a person whose constitutional rights clearly have been violated evidence which the prosecutor personally knows was obtained as a direct result of the constitutional violation."

339. In United States v. Basurto, 497 F.2d 781 (9th Cir.1974), the prosecutor learned before trial that a main witness had lied before the grand jury. He told counsel but neither the judge nor the grand jury. In his opening statement at trial, he acknowledged the witness's lie. The court reversed the conviction:

> We hold that the Due Process Clause of the Fifth Amendment is violated when a defendant has to stand trial on an indictment which the government knows is based partially on perjured testimony, when the perjured testimony is material, and when jeopardy has not attached. Whenever the prosecutor learns of any perjury committed before the grand jury, he is under a duty to immediately inform the court and opposing counsel—and, if the perjury may be material, also the grand jury—in order that appropriate action may be taken.
>
> We base our decision on a long line of cases which recognize the existence of a duty of good faith on the part of the prosecutor with respect to the court, the grand jury, and the defendant. While the facts of these cases may not exactly parallel those of the instant case, we hold that their rulings regarding the consequences of a violation or abuse of this prosecutorial duty must be applied where the prosecutor has knowledge that testimony before the grand jury was perjured.

Id. at 785–86.

Basurto was not followed in United States v. Udziela, 671 F.2d 995 (7th Cir.1982), in which the prosecutor learned just before trial that a witness before the grand jury had committed perjury. He disclosed the

[4] Justice Burton wrote a concurring opinion.

perjury to defense counsel. During the trial, defense counsel moved to dismiss the indictment. The court of appeals held that the motion was properly denied. It said: "[W]here perjured testimony supporting an indictment is discovered before trial the government has the option of either voluntarily withdrawing the tainted indictment and seeking a new one before the grand jury when it reconvenes, unless it is already sitting, or of appearing with defense counsel before the district court for an *in camera* inspection of the grand jury transcripts for a determination whether other, sufficient evidence exists to support the indictment. If other, sufficient evidence is present so that the grand jury may have indicted without giving any weight to the perjured testimony, the indictment cannot be challenged on the basis of the perjury. . . . Our rationale for these rules is simple enough: errors before the grand jury, such as perjured testimony, normally can be corrected at trial, where evidentiary and procedural rules safeguard the accused's constitutional rights. . . . Put differently, grand jury proceedings need not be perfect." Id. at 1001. See United States v. Adamo, 742 F.2d 927 (6th Cir.1984), agreeing with *Basurto*'s "basic ethical philosophy," but affirming the prosecutor's independent responsibility to assess the significance of perjured testimony before the grand jury and take appropriate action.

340. "[The grand jury's] power is only to accuse, not to convict. Its indictment does not even create a presumption of guilt; all that it charges must later be proved before the trial jury, and then beyond a reasonable doubt. The grand jury need not be unanimous. It does not hear both sides but only the prosecution's evidence, and does not face the problem of a choice between two adversaries. Its duty is to indict if the prosecution's evidence, unexplained, uncontradicted and unsupplemented, would warrant a conviction. If so, its indictment merely puts the accused to trial. The difference between the function of the trial jury and the function of the grand jury is all the difference between deciding a case and merely deciding that a case should be tried." Cassell v. Texas, 339 U.S. 282, 302 (1950) (Jackson, J., dissenting).

United States v. Williams

504 U.S. 36, 112 S.Ct. 1735, 118 L.Ed.2d 352 (1992)

■ JUSTICE SCALIA delivered the opinion of the Court.

The question presented in this case is whether a district court may dismiss an otherwise valid indictment because the Government failed to disclose to the grand jury "substantial exculpatory evidence" in its possession.

I

On May 4, 1988, respondent John H. Williams, Jr., a Tulsa, Oklahoma investor, was indicted by a federal grand jury on seven counts of "knowingly mak[ing] [a] false statement or report . . . for the purpose of influencing . . . the action [of a federally insured financial institution]," in violation of 18 U.S.C. § 1014 (1988 ed., Supp. II). According to the indictment, between September 1984 and November 1985 Williams supplied four Oklahoma banks with "materially false" statements that variously overstated the value of his current assets and interest income in order to influence the banks' actions on his loan requests.

Williams' misrepresentation was allegedly effected through two financial statements provided to the banks, a "Market Value Balance Sheet" and a "Statement of Projected Income and Expense." The former included as "current assets" approximately $6 million in notes receivable from three venture capital companies. Though it contained a disclaimer that these assets were carried at cost rather than at market value, the Government asserted that listing them as "current assets"—i.e., assets quickly reducible to cash—was misleading, since Williams knew that none of the venture capital companies could afford to satisfy the notes in the short term. The second document—the Statement of Projected Income and Expense—allegedly misrepresented Williams' interest income, since it failed to reflect that the interest payments received on the notes of the venture capital companies were funded entirely by Williams' own loans to those companies. The Statement thus falsely implied, according to the Government, that Williams was deriving interest income from "an independent outside source." Brief for United States 3.

Shortly after arraignment, the District Court granted Williams' motion for disclosure of all exculpatory portions of the grand jury transcripts. . . . Upon reviewing this material, Williams demanded that the District Court dismiss the indictment, alleging that the Government had failed to fulfill its obligation under the Tenth Circuit's prior decision in United States v. Page, 808 F.2d 723, 728 (1987), to present "substantial exculpatory evidence" to the grand jury (emphasis omitted). His contention was that evidence which the Government had chosen not to present to the grand jury—in particular, Williams' general ledgers and tax returns, and Williams' testimony in his contemporaneous Chapter 11 bankruptcy proceeding—disclosed that, for tax purposes and otherwise, he had regularly accounted for the "notes receivable" (and the interest on them) in a manner consistent with the Balance Sheet and the Income Statement. This, he contended, belied an intent to mislead the banks, and thus directly negated an essential element of the charged offense.

The District Court initially denied Williams' motion, but upon reconsideration ordered the indictment dismissed without prejudice. . . . Upon the Government's appeal, the Court of Appeals affirmed the District Court's order. . . . We granted certiorari. . . .

. . .

III

Respondent does not contend that the Fifth Amendment itself obliges the prosecutor to disclose substantial exculpatory evidence in his possession to the grand jury. Instead, building on our statement that the federal courts "may within limits, formulate procedural rules not specifically required by the Constitution or the Congress," United States v. Hasting, 461 U.S. 499, 505 (1983), he argues that imposition of the Tenth Circuit's disclosure rule is supported by the courts' "supervisory power." We think not. *Hasting*, and the cases that rely upon the principle it expresses, deal strictly with the courts' power to control their *own* procedures. That power has been applied not only to improve the truth-finding process of the trial . . . but also to prevent parties from reaping benefit or incurring harm from violations of substantive or procedural rules (imposed by the Constitution or laws) governing matters apart from the trial itself. . . . Thus, Bank of Nova Scotia v. United States, 487 U.S. 250 (1988), makes clear that the supervisory power can be used to dismiss an indictment because of misconduct before the grand jury, at least where that misconduct amounts to a violation of one of those "few, clear rules which were carefully drafted and approved by this Court and by Congress to ensure the integrity of the grand jury's functions," United States v. Mechanik, 475 U.S. 66, 74 (1986) (O'Connor, J., concurring in judgment).

We did not hold in *Bank of Nova Scotia*, however, that the courts' supervisory power could be used, not merely as a means of enforcing or vindicating legally compelled standards of prosecutorial conduct before the grand jury, but as a means of *prescribing* those standards of prosecutorial conduct in the first instance—just as it may be used as a means of establishing standards of prosecutorial conduct before the courts themselves. It is this latter exercise that respondent demands. Because the grand jury is an institution separate from the courts, over whose functioning the courts do not preside, we think it clear that, as a general matter at least, no such "supervisory" judicial authority exists, and that the disclosure rule applied here exceeded the Tenth Circuit's authority.

A

[T]he grand jury is mentioned in the Bill of Rights, but not in the body of the Constitution. It has not been textually assigned, therefore, to any of the branches described in the first three Articles. . . . In fact the whole theory of its function is that it belongs to no branch of the institutional Government, serving as a kind of buffer or referee between the Government and the people. . . . Although the grand jury normally operates, of course, in the courthouse and under judicial auspices, its institutional relationship with the Judicial Branch has traditionally been, so to speak, at arm's length. Judges' direct involvement in the functioning of the grand jury has generally been confined to the constitutive one of calling the grand jurors together and administering their oaths of office. . . .

. . .

Given the grand jury's operational separateness from its constituting court, it should come as no surprise that we have been reluctant to invoke the judicial supervisory power as a basis for prescribing modes of grand jury procedure. . . .

[A]ny power federal courts may have to fashion, on their own initiative, rules of grand jury procedure is a very limited one, not remotely comparable to the power they maintain over their own proceedings. . . . It certainly would not permit judicial reshaping of the grand jury institution, substantially altering the traditional relationships between the prosecutor, the constituting court, and the grand jury itself. . . . As we proceed to discuss, that would be the consequence of the proposed rule here.

B

Respondent argues that the Court of Appeals' rule can be justified as a sort of Fifth Amendment "common law," a necessary means of assuring the constitutional right to the judgment "of an independent and informed grand jury," Wood v. Georgia, 370 U.S. 375, 390 (1962). Brief for Respondent 27. Respondent makes a generalized appeal to functional notions: Judicial supervision of the quantity and quality of the evidence relied upon by the grand jury plainly facilitates, he says, the grand jury's performance of its twin historical responsibilities, i.e., bringing to trial those who may be justly accused and shielding the innocent from unfounded accusation and prosecution. . . . We do not agree. The rule would neither preserve nor enhance the traditional functioning of the institution that the Fifth Amendment demands. To the contrary, requiring the prosecutor to present exculpatory as well as inculpatory evidence would alter the grand jury's historical role, transforming it from an accusatory to an adjudicatory body.

It is axiomatic that the grand jury sits not to determine guilt or innocence, but to assess whether there is adequate basis for bringing a criminal charge. . . . That has always been so; and to make the assessment it has always been thought sufficient to hear only the prosecutor's side. . . . As a consequence, neither in this country nor in England has the suspect under investigation by the grand jury ever been thought to have a right to testify, or to have exculpatory evidence presented. . . .

Imposing upon the prosecutor a legal obligation to present exculpatory evidence in his possession would be incompatible with this system. If a "balanced" assessment of the entire matter is the objective, surely the first thing to be done—rather than requiring the prosecutor to say what he knows in defense of the target of the investigation—is to entitle the target to tender his own defense. To require the former while denying (as we do) the latter would be quite absurd. It would also be quite pointless, since it would merely invite the target to circumnavigate the system by delivering his exculpatory evidence to the prosecutor, whereupon it would *have* to be passed on to the grand jury—unless the prosecutor is willing to take the chance that a court will not deem the evidence important enough to qualify for mandatory disclosure. . . .

Respondent acknowledges (as he must) that the "common law" of the grand jury is not violated if the *grand jury itself* chooses to hear no more evidence than that which suffices to convince it an indictment is proper. . . . Thus, had the Government offered to familiarize the grand jury in this case with the five boxes of financial statements and deposition testimony alleged to contain exculpatory information, and had the grand jury rejected the offer as pointless, respondent would presumably agree that the resulting indictment would have been valid. Respondent insists, however, that courts must require the modern prosecutor to alert the grand jury to the nature and extent of the available exculpatory evidence, because otherwise the grand jury "merely functions as an arm of the prosecution." Brief for Respondent 27. We reject the attempt to convert a nonexistent duty of the grand jury itself into an obligation of the prosecutor. The authority of the prosecutor to seek an indictment has long been understood to be "coterminous with the authority of the grand jury to entertain [the prosecutor's] charges." United States v. Thompson, 251 U.S., at 414. If the grand jury has no obligation to consider all "substantial exculpatory" evidence, we do not understand how the prosecutor can be said to have a binding obligation to present it.

There is yet another respect in which respondent's proposal not only fails to comport with, but positively contradicts, the "common law" of the Fifth Amendment grand jury. Motions to quash indictments based upon the sufficiency of the evidence relied upon by the grand jury were unheard of at common law in England. . . . And the traditional American practice was described by Justice Nelson, riding circuit in 1852, as follows:

> No case has been cited, nor have we been able to find any, furnishing an authority for looking into and revising the judgment of the grand jury upon the evidence for the purpose of determining whether or not the finding was founded upon sufficient proof, or whether there was a deficiency in respect to any part of the complaint. . . .

United States v. Reed, 27 Fed.Cas. 727, 738 (No. 16,134) (CCNDNY 1852). We accepted Justice Nelson's description in Costello v. United States, where we held that "it would run counter to the whole history of the grand jury institution" to permit an indictment to be challenged "on the ground that there was incompetent evidence before the grand jury." 350 U.S., at 363–64. And we reaffirmed this principle recently in *Bank of Nova Scotia*, where we held that "the mere fact that evidence itself is unreliable is not sufficient to require a dismissal of the indictment," and that "a challenge to the reliability or competence of the evidence presented to the grand jury" will not be heard. 487 U.S., at 261. It would make little sense, we think, to abstain from reviewing the evidentiary support for the grand jury's judgment while scrutinizing the sufficiency of the prosecutor's presentation. A complaint about the quality or adequacy of the evidence can always be recast as a complaint that the prosecutor's presentation was "incomplete" or "misleading." Our words in *Costello* bear repeating: Review of facially valid indictments on such grounds "would run counter to the whole history of the grand jury institution[,] [and] [n]either justice nor the concept of a fair trial requires [it]." 350 U.S., at 364.

. . .

[R]espondent argues that a rule requiring the prosecutor to disclose exculpatory evidence to the grand jury would, by removing from the docket unjustified prosecutions, save valuable judicial time. That depends, we suppose, upon what the ratio would turn out to be between unjustified prosecutions eliminated and grand jury indictments challenged—for the latter as well as the former consume "valuable judicial time." We need not pursue the matter; if there is an advantage to the proposal, Congress is free to prescribe it. For the reasons set forth above, however, we conclude that courts have no authority to prescribe such a duty pursuant to their inherent supervisory authority over their own proceedings. The judgment of the Court of Appeals is accordingly reversed and the cause remanded for further proceedings consistent with this opinion.

. . .[5]

---

341. On the question whether there is a constitutional right not to be prosecuted unless there is probable cause, see generally Albright v. Oliver, 510 U.S. 266 (1994) (7–2).

342. Before the decision in *Williams*, above, the Court of Appeals for the Second Circuit had taken the lead in requiring the prosecutor to make a reasonably full and objective presentation of the evidence to the grand jury. In United States v. Ciambrone, 601 F.2d 616, 623 (2d Cir.1979) (conviction affirmed), for example, it said that "where a prosecutor is aware of any substantial evidence negating guilt he should, in the interest of justice, make it known to the grand jury, at least where it might reasonably be expected to lead the jury not to indict." And in United States v. Estepa, 471 F.2d 1132 (2d Cir.1972) (convictions reversed and indictment dismissed), it strongly disapproved the needless use of hearsay evidence before the grand jury. See also United States v. Hogan, 712 F.2d 757 (2d Cir.1983) (convictions reversed and indictment dismissed for prosecutorial misconduct before grand jury). Other federal courts had been more cautious about their exercise of supervisory power over the prosecutor. E.g., United States v. McKenzie, 678 F.2d 629, 631 (5th Cir.1982) (even in case of "the most 'egregious prosecutorial misconduct,' " indictment should be dismissed only if defendant's case has been unfairly prejudiced); United States v. Welch, 572 F.2d 1359, 1360 (9th Cir.1978) (indictment dismissed only if prosecutorial discretion is "abused to such an extent as to be arbitrary and capricious and violative of due process"). The Ninth Circuit upheld dismissal of an indictment in United States v. Samango, 607 F.2d 877, 884 (9th Cir.1979), saying that "the manner in which the prosecution obtained the indictment represented a serious threat to the integrity of the judicial process."

Ciambrone is overruled by *Williams*, as, evidently, is *Estepa*. How much of *Basurto*, p. 681 note 339 above, remains is unclear.

[5] Justice Stevens wrote a dissenting opinion, which Justice Blackmun and Justice O'Connor joined and part of which Justice Thomas joined.

343. Noting the Supreme Court's holding in *Williams* that the federal courts lack authority to declare a rule requiring dismissal of an indictment if the prosecutor does not present substantial exculpatory evidence to the grand jury, the United States Attorney's Manual § 9–11.233 says that "[i]t is the policy of the Department of Justice . . . that when a prosecutor conducting a grand jury inquiry is personally aware of substantial evidence that directly negates the guilt of a subject of the investigation, the prosecutor must present or otherwise disclose such evidence to the grand jury before seeking an indictment against such a person."

Observing that "the adversary system does not extend to grand jury proceedings," the Supreme Court of California has held that when a district attorney is aware of evidence "reasonably tending to negate guilt" he is required to tell the grand jury about it, so that it can exercise its power to have the evidence produced. Johnson v. Superior Court, 539 P.2d 792, 796 (Cal.1975). The reasoning of *Johnson* was disapproved in Buzbee v. Donnelly, 634 P.2d 1244, 1253 (N.M.1981). See State v. Bell, 589 P.2d 517 (Haw.1978), in which the court said that "where evidence of a clearly exculpatory nature is known to the prosecution, such evidence must be presented to the grand jury." Id. at 520. An example of such evidence, the court said, is "a witness whose testimony is not directly contradicted by any other witness and who maintains that the accused was nowhere near the scene of the crime when it occurred." Id. To the same effect, see State v. Hogan, 676 A.2d 533, 543 (N.J.1996) (prosecutor has duty to disclose only evidence that directly negates guilt and is clearly exculpatory; additional cases cited).

On the duty of the prosecutor to instruct the grand jury about possible defenses to the crimes in issue, see State v. Hogan, 764 A.2d 1012 (N.J.Super.2001). The court said that such a duty is related to the duty to present exculpatory evidence and is limited to defenses that would provide a complete defense to the charges. Further, the duty to instruct arises only when facts known to the prosecutor clearly indicate the appropriateness of such instructions.

344. Should a potential defendant be given an opportunity to appear before the grand jury before it decides whether or not to indict him? Why (not)? The United States Attorneys' Manual 9–11.152 states:

> It is not altogether uncommon for subjects or targets of the grand jury's investigation, particularly in white-collar cases, to request or demand the opportunity to tell the grand jury their side of the story. While the prosecutor has no legal obligation to permit such witnesses to testify . . . a refusal to do so can create the appearance of unfairness. Accordingly, under normal circumstances, where no burden upon the grand jury or delay of its proceedings is involved, reasonable requests by a "subject" or "target" of an investigation . . . to testify personally before the grand jury ordinarily should be given favorable consideration, provided that such witness explicitly waives his or her privilege against self-incrimination, on the record before the grand

> jury, and is represented by counsel or voluntarily and knowingly appears without counsel and consents to full examination under oath.
>
> Such witnesses may wish to supplement their testimony with the testimony of others. The decision whether to accommodate such requests or to reject them after listening to the testimony of the target or the subject, or to seek statements from the suggested witnesses, is a matter left to the sound discretion of the grand jury. When passing on such requests, it must be kept in mind that the grand jury was never intended to be and is not properly either an adversary proceeding or the arbiter of guilt or innocence.

Section 9–11.153 states: "When a target is not called to testify . . . and does not request to testify on his or her own motion . . . the prosecutor, in appropriate cases, is encouraged to notify such person a reasonable time before seeking an indictment in order to afford him or her an opportunity to testify before the grand jury subject to the conditions set forth in USAM 9–11.152. Notification would not be appropriate in routine clear cases or where such action might jeopardize the investigation or prosecution because of the likelihood of flight, destruction or fabrication or evidence, endangerment of other witnesses, undue delay or otherwise would be inconsistent with the ends of justice."

345. In United States v. Klubock, 832 F.2d 649, aff'd by an equally divided court, 832 F.2d 664 (1st Cir.1987), the court upheld the authority of the district court to issue a local rule as follows: "It is unprofessional conduct for a prosecutor to subpoena an attorney to a grand jury without prior judicial approval in circumstances where the prosecutor seeks to compel the attorney-witness to provide evidence concerning a person who is represented by the attorney-witness." A similar rule had been promulgated by the state supreme court (Massachusetts), at the urging of the state bar association. Is the rule consistent with *Williams*, above?

346. On the relationship between the prosecutor and the grand jury, see United States v. Cox, 342 F.2d 167, 170–72 (5th Cir.1965):

> The constitutional requirement of an indictment or presentment as a predicate to a prosecution for capital or infamous crimes has for its primary purpose the protection of the individual from jeopardy except on a finding of probable cause by a group of his fellow citizens, and is designed to afford a safeguard against oppressive actions of the prosecutor or a court. The constitutional provision is not to be read as conferring on or preserving to the grand jury, as such, any rights or prerogatives. The constitutional provision is, as has been said, for the benefit of the accused. . . .
>
> . . .
>
> The judicial power of the United States is vested in the federal courts, and extends to prosecutions for violations of the criminal laws of the United States. The executive power is vested in the President of the United States, who is required to take care that the laws be faithfully executed. The Attorney General is the hand of the President

in taking care that the laws of the United States in legal proceedings and in the prosecution of offenses, be faithfully executed. The role of the grand jury is restricted to a finding as to whether or not there is probable cause to believe that an offense has been committed. The discretionary power of the attorney for the United States in determining whether a prosecution shall be commenced or maintained may well depend upon matters of policy wholly apart from any question of probable cause. Although as a member of the bar, the attorney for the United States is an officer of the court, he is nevertheless an executive official of the Government, and it is as an officer of the executive department that he exercises a discretion as to whether or not there shall be a prosecution in a particular case. It follows, as an incident of the constitutional separation of powers, that the courts are not to interfere with the free exercise of the discretionary powers of the attorneys of the United States in their control over criminal prosecutions. The provision of Rule 7, requiring the signing of the indictment by the attorney for the Government, is a recognition of the power of Government counsel to permit or not to permit the bringing of an indictment. If the attorney refuses to sign, as he has the discretionary power of doing, we conclude that there is no valid indictment. . . . [T]he requirement of the signature is for the purpose of evidencing the joinder of the attorney for the United States with the grand jury in instituting a criminal proceeding in the Court. . . .

Dennis v. United States

384 U.S. 855, 86 S.Ct. 1840, 16 L.Ed.2d 973 (1966)

[The defendants were convicted of a violation of the general conspiracy statute, 18 U.S.C. § 371, the conspiracy having to do with the filing of false affidavits under the National Labor Relations Act.]

■ MR. JUSTICE FORTAS delivered the opinion of the Court.

. . .

We turn now to petitioners' contention that the trial court committed reversible error by denying their motion to require production for petitioners' examination of the grand jury testimony of four government witnesses. Alternatively, petitioners sought *in camera* inspection by the trial judge to be followed by production to petitioners in the event the judge found inconsistencies between trial testimony and that before the grand jury.

The trial judge denied the motions, made at the conclusion of the direct examination of each of the witnesses, on the ground that no "particularized need" had been shown. See Pittsburgh Plate Glass Co. v. United States, 360 U.S. 395, 400. On appeal the Court of Appeals held that the denial of the motions was not reversible error. . . .

[W]e disagree, and we reverse.

This Court has recognized the "long-established policy that maintains the secrecy of the grand jury proceedings in the federal courts." United States v. Procter & Gamble Co., 356 U.S. 677, 681. And it has ruled that, when disclosure is permitted, it is to be done "discreetly and limitedly." Id., at 683. Accordingly, the Court has refused in a civil case to permit pretrial disclosure of an entire grand jury transcript where the sole basis for discovery was that the transcript had been available to the Government in preparation of its case. *Procter & Gamble*, supra. And, in Pittsburgh Plate Glass Co. v. United States, supra, the Court sustained a trial court's refusal to order disclosure of a witness' grand jury testimony where the defense made no showing of need, but insisted upon production of the minutes as a matter of right, and where there was "overwhelming" proof of the offense charged without reference to the witness' trial testimony.

In general, however, the Court has confirmed the trial court's power under Rule 6(e) of the Federal Rules of Criminal Procedure to direct disclosure of grand jury testimony "preliminarily to or in connection with a judicial proceeding." In United States v. Socony–Vacuum Oil Co., 310 U.S. 150, 234, the Court acknowledged that "after the grand jury's functions are ended, disclosure is wholly proper where the ends of justice require it." In *Procter & Gamble*, supra, the Court stated that "problems concerning the use of the grand jury transcript at the trial to impeach a witness, to refresh his recollection, to test his credibility . . ." are "cases of particularized need where the secrecy of the proceedings is lifted discretely and limitedly." 356 U.S., at 683. And in *Pittsburgh Plate Glass*, supra, where four members of the Court concluded that even on the special facts of that case the witness' grand jury testimony should have been supplied to the defense, the entire Court was agreed that upon a showing of "particularized need" defense counsel might have access to relevant portions of the grand jury testimony of a trial witness, 360 U.S., at 400, 405. In a variety of circumstances, the lower federal courts, too, have made grand jury testimony available to defendants.

These developments are entirely consonant with the growing realization that disclosure, rather than suppression, of relevant materials ordinarily promotes the proper administration of criminal justice. . . .

Certainly in the context of the present case, where the Government concedes that the importance of preserving the secrecy of the grand jury minutes is minimal and also admits the persuasiveness of the arguments advanced in favor of disclosure, it cannot fairly be said that the defense has failed to make out a "particularized need." The showing made by petitioners, both in the trial court and here, goes substantially beyond the minimum required by Rule 6(e) and the prior decisions of his Court. The record shows the following circumstances:

1. The events as to which the testimony in question related occurred between 1948 and 1955. The grand jury testimony was taken in 1956, while these events were relatively fresh. The trial testimony which petitioners seek to compare with the 1956 grand jury testimony was not taken until 1963. Certainly, there was reason to assay the latter testimony, some of

which is 15 years after the event, against the much fresher testimony before the grand jury.

2. The motions in question involved the testimony of four of the eight government witnesses. They were key witnesses. The charge could not be proved on the basis of evidence exclusive of that here involved.

3. The testimony of the four witnesses concerned conversations and oral statements made in meetings. It was largely uncorroborated. Where the question of guilt or innocence may turn on exactly what was said, the defense is clearly entitled to all relevant aid which is reasonably available to ascertain the precise substance of the statements.

4. Two of the witnesses were accomplices, one of these being also a paid informer. A third had separated from the union and had reasons for hostility toward petitioners.

5. One witness admitted on cross-examination that he had in earlier statements been mistaken about significant dates.

A conspiracy case carries with it the inevitable risk of wrongful attribution of responsibility to one or more of the multiple defendants. . . . Under these circumstances, it is especially important that the defense, the judge and the jury should have the assurance that the doors that may lead to truth have been unlocked. In our adversary system for determining guilt or innocence, it is rarely justifiable for the prosecution to have exclusive access to a storehouse of relevant fact. Exceptions to this are justifiable only by the clearest and most compelling considerations. For this reason, we cannot accept the view of the Court of Appeals that it is "safe to assume" no inconsistencies would have come to light if the grand jury testimony had been examined. There is no justification for relying upon "assumption."

In *Pittsburgh Plate Glass*, supra, the Court reserved decision on the question whether *in camera* inspection by the trial judge is an appropriate or satisfactory measure when there is a showing of a "particularized need" for disclosure. 360 U.S., at 401. This procedure, followed by production to defense counsel in the event the trial judge finds inconsistencies, has been adopted in some of the Courts of Appeals. In the Second Circuit it is available as a matter of right. While this practice may be useful in enabling the trial court to rule on a defense motion for production to it of grand jury testimony—and we do not disapprove it for that purpose—it by no means disposes of the matter. Trial judges ought not be burdened with the task or the responsibility of examining sometimes voluminous grand jury testimony in order to ascertain inconsistencies with trial testimony. In any event, "it will be extremely difficult for even the most able and experienced trial judge under the pressures of conducting a trial to pick out all of the grand jury testimony that would be useful in impeaching a witness." Pittsburgh Plate Glass, 360 U.S., at 410 (dissenting opinion). Nor is it realistic to assume that the trial court's judgment as to the utility of material for impeachment or other legitimate purposes, however conscientiously made, would exhaust the possibilities. In our adversary system, it is enough for judges to judge. The determination of what may be useful to the defense can properly and effectively be made only by an advocate. The trial judge's function in this respect is limited to deciding whether a case has been made for production, and to supervise the process: for example, to cause the elimination of extraneous matter and to rule upon applications by the Government for protective orders in unusual situations, such as those involving the Nation's security or clearcut dangers to individuals who are identified by the testimony produced. . . .

Because petitioners were entitled to examine the grand jury minutes relating to trial testimony of the four government witnesses, and to do so while those witnesses were available for cross-examination, we reverse the judgment below and remand for a new trial.

It is so ordered.[6]

---

347. The Court in *Dennis* referred to "the reasons traditionally advanced to justify nondisclosure of grand jury minutes," 384 U.S. at 872 n.18, as set forth by Justice Brennan in Pittsburgh Plate Glass Co. v. United States, 360 U.S. 395, 405 (1959) (dissenting opinion): "Essentially four reasons have been advanced as justification for grand jury secrecy. (1) To prevent the accused from escaping before he is indicted and arrested or from tampering with the witnesses against him. (2) To prevent disclosure of derogatory information presented to the grand jury against an accused who has not been indicted. (3) To encourage complainants and witnesses to come before the grand jury and speak freely without fear that their testimony will be made public thereby subjecting them to possible discomfort or retaliation. (4) To encourage the grand jurors to engage in uninhibited investigation and deliberation by barring disclosure of their votes and comments during the proceedings."

In Douglas Oil Co. v. Petrol Stops Northwest, 441 U.S. 211 (1979) (6–3), the Supreme Court reaffirmed that "the proper functioning of our grand jury system depends upon the secrecy of grand jury proceedings." It said that parties seeking disclosure of grand jury transcripts under Federal Rule 6(e) "must show that the material they seek is needed to avoid a possible injustice in another judicial proceeding, that the need for disclosure is greater than the need for continued secrecy, and that their request is structured to cover only material so needed." Id. at 222. The Court added that the need for secrecy is not gone when the grand jury has completed its work; the effects of disclosure on future grand juries have to be considered.

The Court said further that when disclosure is sought under Rule 6(e), the request should be made to the court of the jurisdiction in which the grand jury sat, which should evaluate the need for continued secrecy; but

[6] Justice Black wrote an opinion concurring in part and dissenting in part, which Justice Douglas joined.

that if the request is for use in a case pending elsewhere, the question whether there is a need for disclosure should, when appropriate, be referred to the court where the case is pending.

See In re Grand Jury Testimony, 832 F.2d 60 (5th Cir.1987) (*Douglas Oil Co.* applied).

348. The Jencks Act, 18 U.S.C. § 3500, as amended in 1970, gives effect to the Court's holding in *Dennis*. The statute (and Fed.R.Crim.P. 26.2(f)(3)) explicitly include among the pretrial statements of government witnesses that shall be disclosed to the defense after the witness has testified on direct examination at trial "the witness's statement to a grand jury, however taken or recorded, or a transcription of such a statement." See p. 1001.

In United States v. Head, 586 F.2d 508 (5th Cir.1978), the prosecutor deliberately avoided recording certain grand jury witnesses' testimony, to avoid the creation of Jencks Act statements. The court held that the prosecutor's action was improper but that in the absence of some showing of prejudice to the defendant it was not required that the witnesses be barred from testifying at trial. The issue is eliminated by amended Rule 6(e)(1), which provides that proceedings of the grand jury shall be recorded.

Rule 16(a)(1)(B)(iii) provides that upon request of a defendant, the government must disclose and make available "the defendant's recorded testimony before a grand jury relating to the charged offense." Rule 16(a)(3) states that except as otherwise provided, the rule (having to do generally with discovery) "does not apply to the discovery or inspection of a grand jury's recorded proceedings."

349. Rule 6(e)(3)(A) permits disclosure of grand jury proceedings to "an attorney for the government for use in performing that attorney's duty" as well as "any government personnel . . . that an attorney for the government considers necessary to assist in performing that attorney's duty to enforce federal criminal law." Rule 51(b)(1) defines "attorney for the government" to include the Attorney General or an authorized assistant, a United States Attorney or an authorized assistant, and "any other attorney authorized by law to conduct proceedings under these rules as a prosecutor."

In United States v. Sells Engineering, Inc., 463 U.S. 418 (1983) (5–4), attorneys in the Justice Department sought disclosure of grand jury materials for use in a civil suit. The Court held that automatic disclosure under Rule 6(e)(3)(A) is limited "to use by those attorneys who conduct the criminal matters to which the materials pertain." Id. at 427. That conclusion, the Court said, was required "by the general purposes and policies of grand jury secrecy, by the limited policy reasons why Government attorneys are granted access to grand jury materials for criminal use, and by the legislative history of Rule 6(e)." Id. Rule 6(e)(3)(E) provides for a court to authorize disclosure in other circumstances. See *Douglas Oil Co.*, p. 693 note 347 above.

In United States v. John Doe, Inc. I, 481 U.S. 102 (1987) (5–3), however, the Court held that a government attorney who is involved in a grand jury proceeding may use information obtained during that proceeding in a subsequent civil proceeding in which he is involved, without a disclosure order under Rule 6(e). It said that the rule prohibits disclosure of information about the grand jury proceeding to persons who are not authorized to have access to it, but not "the continued use of information by attorneys who legitimately obtained access to the information through the grand jury investigation." Id. at 108. The Court also upheld a disclosure order issued for attorneys who had not been involved in the grand jury proceeding. It said that "the question that must be asked is whether the public benefits of the disclosure . . . outweigh the dangers created by the limited disclosure requested." Id. at 113.

Construing Rule 6(e) further, in United States v. Baggot, 463 U.S. 476 (1983) (8–1), the Court held that an order for disclosure "preliminarily to or in connection with a judicial proceeding," under subdivision (E)(i), could not be issued for use by the IRS to determine a taxpayer's civil tax liability. The primary function of such use, the Court said, was to assess taxes and not to prepare for or conduct litigation.

Neither the preliminary examination nor the grand jury proceeding provides effective supervision of the prosecutor's exercise of discretion (although they may have an effect on how he exercises his discretion). Each of them suggests a kind of supervision that might be available. Would it be desirable to require a prosecutor to obtain leave of court before filing formal charges (perhaps only of serious crimes) against a person? If so, what should be the procedure for obtaining leave to prosecute, and what showing should the prosecutor have to make? Alternatively, would it be desirable to make grand jury proceedings an effective exercise of community control over prosecutorial discretion? Would it be desirable to encourage the grand jury—some changing body of private citizens—to reject prosecution when, whatever the law, the "sentiment of the community" is against it?

CHAPTER 11

PLEAS AND PLEA BARGAINING

---

350. Criminal defendants disposed of in United States District Courts, July 1, 2001–June 30, 2002:[1]

Total Defendants	Not Convicted				Convicted and Sentenced				
	Total	Dis-missed	Acquitted by		Total	Plea of Guilty	Nolo Con-tendere	Convicted by	
			Court	Jury				Court	Jury
76,827	7,873	7,150	327	396	68,954	65,811	292	592	2,259

FEDERAL RULES OF CRIMINAL PROCEDURE

Rule 10

ARRAIGNMENT

(a) In General. An arraignment must be conducted in open court and must consist of:

(1) ensuring that the defendant has a copy of the indictment or information;

(2) reading the indictment or information to the defendant or stating to the defendant the substance of the charge; and then

(3) asking the defendant to plead to the indictment or information.

(b) Waiving Appearance. A defendant need not be present for the arraignment if:

(1) the defendant has been charged by indictment or misdemeanor information;

(2) the defendant, in a written waiver signed by both the defendant and defense counsel, has waived appearance and has affirmed that the defendant received a copy of the indictment or information and that the plea is not guilty; and

(3) the court accepts the waiver.

(c) Video Teleconferencing. Video teleconferencing may be used to arraign a defendant if the defendant consents.

1. From Table D–4, Annual Report of the Director of the Administrative Office of the United States Courts, 2002.

Rule 11

PLEAS

(a) Entering a Plea.

(1) *In General.* A defendant may plead not guilty, guilty, or (with the court's consent) nolo contendere.

(2) *Conditional Plea.* With the consent of the court and the government, a defendant may enter a conditional plea of guilty or nolo contendere, reserving in writing the right to have an appellate court review an adverse determination of a specified pretrial motion. A defendant who prevails on appeal may then withdraw the plea.

(3) *Nolo Contendere Plea.* Before accepting a plea of nolo contendere, the court must consider the parties' views and the public interest in the effective administration of justice.

(4) *Failure to Enter a Plea.* If a defendant refuses to enter a plea or if a defendant organization fails to appear, the court must enter a plea of not guilty.

(b) Considering and Accepting a Guilty or Nolo Contendere Plea.

(1) *Advising and Questioning the Defendant.* Before the court accepts a plea of guilty or nolo contendere, the defendant may be placed under oath, and the court must address the defendant personally in open court. During this address, the court must inform the defendant of, and determine that the defendant understands, the following:

(A) the government's right, in a prosecution for perjury or false statement, to use against the defendant any statement that the defendant gives under oath;

(B) the right to plead not guilty, or having already so pleaded, to persist in that plea;

(C) the right to a jury trial;

(D) the right to be represented by counsel—and if necessary have the court appoint counsel—at trial and at every other stage of the proceeding;

(E) the right at trial to confront and cross-examine adverse witnesses, to be protected from compelled self-incrimination, to testify and present evidence, and to compel the attendance of witnesses;

(F) the defendant's waiver of these trial rights if the court accepts a plea of guilty or nolo contendere;

(G) the nature of each charge to which the defendant is pleading;

(H) any maximum possible penalty, including imprisonment, fine, and term of supervised release;

(I) any mandatory minimum penalty;

(J) any applicable forfeiture;

(K) the court's authority to order restitution;

(L) the court's obligation to impose a special assessment;

(M) the court's obligation to apply the Sentencing Guidelines, and the court's discretion to depart from those guidelines under some circumstances; and

(N) the terms of any plea-agreement provision waiving the right to appeal or to collaterally attack the sentence.

(2) *Ensuring That a Plea Is Voluntary.* Before accepting a plea of guilty or nolo contendere, the court must address the defendant personally in open court and determine that the plea is voluntary and did not result from force, threats, or promises (other than promises in a plea agreement).

(3) *Determining the Factual Basis for a Plea.* Before entering judgment on a guilty plea, the court must determine that there is a factual basis for the plea.

(c) Plea Agreement Procedure.

(1) *In General.* An attorney for the government and the defendant's attorney, or the defendant when proceeding pro se, may discuss and reach a plea agreement. The court must not participate in these discussions. If the defendant pleads guilty or nolo contendere to either a charged offense or a lesser or related offense, the plea agreement may specify that an attorney for the government will:

(A) not bring, or will move to dismiss, other charges;

(B) recommend, or agree not to oppose the defendant's request, that a particular sentence or sentencing range is appropriate or that a particular provision of the Sentencing Guidelines, or policy statement, or sentencing factor does or does not apply (such a recommendation or request does not bind the court); or

(C) agree that a specific sentence or sentencing range is the appropriate disposition of the case, or that a particular provision of the Sentencing Guidelines, or policy statement, or sentencing factor does or does not apply (such a recommendation or request binds the court once the court accepts the plea agreement).

(2) *Disclosing a Plea Agreement.* The parties must disclose the plea agreement in open court when the plea is offered, unless the court for good cause allows the parties to disclose the plea agreement in camera.

(3) *Judicial Consideration of a Plea Agreement.*

(A) To the extent the plea agreement is of the type specified in Rule 11(c)(1)(A) or (C), the court may accept the agreement, reject it, or defer a decision until the court has reviewed the presentence report.

(B) To the extent the plea agreement is of the type specified in Rule 11(c)(1)(B), the court must advise the defendant that the defendant has no right to withdraw the plea if the court does not follow the recommendation or request.

(4) *Accepting a Plea Agreement.* If the court accepts the plea agreement, it must inform the defendant that to the extent the plea agreement is of the type specified in Rule 11(c)(1)(A) or (C), the agreed disposition will be included in the judgment.

(5) *Rejecting a Plea Agreement.* If the court rejects a plea agreement containing provisions of the type specified in Rule 11(c)(1)(A) or (C), the court must do the following on the record and in open court (or, for good cause, in camera):

(A) inform the parties that the court rejects the plea agreement;

(B) advise the defendant personally that the court is not required to follow the plea agreement and give the defendant an opportunity to withdraw the plea; and

(C) advise the defendant personally that if the plea is not withdrawn, the court may dispose of the case less favorably toward the defendant than the plea agreement contemplated.

(d) Withdrawing a Guilty or Nolo Contendere Plea. A defendant may withdraw a plea of guilty or nolo contendere:

(1) before the court accepts the plea, for any reason or no reason; or

(2) after the court accepts the plea, but before it imposes sentence if:

(A) the court rejects a plea agreement under Rule 11(c)(5); or

(B) the defendant can show a fair and just reason for requesting the withdrawal.

(e) Finality of a Guilty or Nolo Contendere Plea. After the court imposes sentence, the defendant may not withdraw a plea of guilty or nolo contendere, and the plea may be set aside only on direct appeal or collateral attack.

(f) Admissibility or Inadmissibility of a Plea, Plea Discussions, and Related Statements. The admissibility or inadmissibility of a plea, a plea discussion, and any related statement is governed by Federal Rule of Evidence 410.

(g) Recording the Proceedings. The proceedings during which the defendant enters a plea must be recorded by a court reporter or by a suitable recording device. If there is a guilty plea or a nolo contendere plea, the record must include the inquiries and advice to the defendant required under Rule 11(b) and (c).

(h) Harmless Error. A variance from the requirements of this rule is harmless error if it does not affect substantial rights.

---

351. Rule 32.2(b)(4) provides that if the government seeks a forfeiture of property, in a case in which a jury returns a verdict of guilty, upon request of the defendant the jury must determine whether "the government has established the requisite nexus between the property and the offense committed by the defendant." In Libretti v. United States, 516 U.S. 29 (1995) (8–1), declaring that the right to a jury determination regarding forfeitability was not part of the Sixth Amendment right to a jury trial, the Court held that a judge accepting a plea of guilty need not, under Rule 11(b)(1), specifically advise a defendant that by pleading guilty he waives that right.

352. Rule 11(f) provides that the admissibility of a plea, plea discussion, or any related statement is governed by Federal Rule of Evidence 410. Rule 410 provides generally that a plea of guilty that is later withdrawn or a plea of nolo contendere, as well as any statements regarding such pleas made during plea proceedings or during discussions with an attorney for the government that do not result in a plea are not admissible in any civil or criminal proceeding against the defendant who made the plea or participated in discussions about the plea. Rule 410 provides, however, that such a statement is admissible if another statement made in the same plea proceeding or discussions has been introduced and the statement "ought in fairness be considered contemporaneously with it" and is admissible also in a prosecution for perjury if it was made under oath in the presence of counsel.

In United States v. Mezzanatto, 513 U.S. 196 (1995) (7–2), the Court held that the provision can be waived. The dissent noted that many prosecutors now routinely require such a waiver before entering into plea discussions. In *Mezzanatto*, the defendant's statements were admitted on cross-examination to impeach his testimony on direct examination. The dissent observed that if a requirement of waiver were extended to the government's case in chief, it would effectively preclude a defendant from going to trial after having engaged in plea discussions. Three Justices, who concurred in the judgment, noted that allowing a waiver with respect to the government's case in chief was not before the Court and was not decided.

McCarthy v. United States

394 U.S. 459, 89 S.Ct. 1166, 22 L.Ed.2d 418 (1969)

■ MR. CHIEF JUSTICE WARREN delivered the opinion of the Court.

This case involves the procedure that must be followed under Rule 11 of the Federal Rules of Criminal Procedure before a United States District

Court may accept a guilty plea and the remedy for a failure to follow that procedure.

On April 1, 1966, petitioner was indicted on three counts in the United States District Court for the Northern District of Illinois for violating § 7201 of the Internal Revenue Code. He was charged with "willfully and knowingly" attempting to evade tax payments of $928.74 for 1959 (count 1), $5,143.70 for 1960 (count 2), and $1,207.12 for 1961 (count 3). At his arraignment two weeks later, petitioner, who was represented by retained counsel, pleaded not guilty to each count. The court scheduled his trial for June 30; but on June 29, it granted the Government's motion to postpone the trial because of petitioner's illness. The trial was rescheduled for July 15.

On that day, after informing the court that he had "advised . . . [petitioner] of the consequences of a plea," defense counsel moved to withdraw petitioner's plea of not guilty to count 2 and to enter a plea of guilty to that count. The district judge asked petitioner if he desired to plead guilty and if he understood that such a plea waived his right to a jury trial and subjected him to imprisonment for as long as five years and to a fine as high as $10,000. Petitioner stated that he understood these consequences and wanted to plead guilty. The Government consented to this plea change and informed the court that if petitioner's plea of guilty to count 2 were accepted, the Government would dismiss counts 1 and 3. Before the plea was accepted, however, the prosecutor asked the judge to inquire whether it had been induced by any threats or promises. In response to the judge's inquiry, petitioner replied that his plea was not the product of either. He stated that it was entered of his "own volition." The court ordered a presentence investigation and continued the case to September 14, 1966.

At the commencement of the sentencing hearing on September 14, petitioner asserted that his failure to pay taxes was "not deliberate" and that they would have been paid if he had not been in poor health. The prosecutor stated that the "prime consideration" for the Government's agreement to dismiss counts 1 and 3 was petitioner's promise to pay all taxes, penalties, and interest. The prosecutor then requested the court to refer expressly to this agreement. After noting that petitioner possessed sufficient attachable assets to meet these obligations, the court imposed a sentence of one year and a fine of $2,500. Petitioner's counsel immediately moved to suspend the sentence. He emphasized that petitioner, who was then 65 years of age, was in poor health and contended that his failure to pay his taxes had resulted from his "neglectful" and "inadvertent" method of bookkeeping during a period when he had been suffering from a very serious drinking problem. Consequently, asserted petitioner's counsel, "there was never any disposition to deprive the United States of its due." The judge, however, after indicating he had examined the presentence report, stated his opinion that "the manner in which [petitioner's] books were kept was not inadvertent." He declined, therefore, to suspend petitioner's sentence.

On appeal to the United States Court of Appeals for the Seventh Circuit, petitioner argued that his plea should be set aside because it had been accepted in violation of Rule 11 of the Federal Rules of Criminal Procedure. Specifically, petitioner contended that the District Court had accepted his plea (1) "without first addressing [him] . . . personally and determining that the plea [was] . . . made voluntarily with understanding of the nature of the charge . . ." and (2) that the court had entered judgment without determining "that there [was] . . . a factual basis for the plea." In affirming petitioner's conviction, the Court of Appeals held that the District Judge had complied with Rule 11. . . .

[W]e granted certiorari. . . . We agree with petitioner that the District Judge did not comply with Rule 11 in this case; and in reversing the Court of Appeals, we hold that a defendant is entitled to plead anew if a United States district court accepts his guilty plea without fully adhering to the procedure provided for in Rule 11. This decision is based solely upon our construction of Rule 11 and is made pursuant to our supervisory power over the lower federal courts; we do not reach any of the constitutional arguments petitioner urges as additional grounds for reversal.

I.

Rule 11 expressly directs the district judge to inquire whether a defendant who pleads guilty understands the nature of the charge against him and whether he is aware of the consequences of his plea. At oral argument, however, counsel for the Government repeatedly conceded that the judge did not personally inquire whether petitioner understood the nature of the charge. At one point, counsel stated quite explicitly: "The subject on which he [the District Judge] did not directly address the defendant, which is raised here, is the question of the defendant's understanding of the charge." Nevertheless, the Government argues that since petitioner stated his desire to plead guilty, and since he was informed of the consequences of his plea, the District Court "could properly *assume* that petitioner was entering that plea with a complete understanding of the charge against him." (Emphasis added.)

We cannot accept this argument, which completely ignores the two purposes of Rule 11 and the reasons for its recent amendment. First, although the procedure embodied in Rule 11 has not been held to be constitutionally mandated, it is designed to assist the district judge in making the constitutionally required determination that a defendant's guilty plea is truly voluntary. Second, the Rule is intended to produce a complete record at the time the plea is entered of the factors relevant to this voluntariness determination. Thus, the more meticulously the Rule is adhered to, the more it tends to discourage, or at least to enable more expeditious disposition of, the numerous and often frivolous post-conviction attacks on the constitutional validity of guilty pleas.

Prior to the 1966 amendment, however, not all district judges personally interrogated defendants before accepting their guilty pleas. With an awareness of the confusion over the Rule's requirements in this respect, the draftsmen amended it to add a provision "expressly requiring the court to address the defendant personally."[2] This clarification of the judge's responsibilities quite obviously furthers both of the Rule's purposes. By personally interrogating the defendant, not only will the judge be better able to ascertain the plea's voluntariness, but he also will develop a more complete record to support his determination in a subsequent post-conviction attack.

These two purposes have their genesis in the nature of a guilty plea. A defendant who enters such a plea simultaneously waives several constitutional rights, including his privilege against compulsory self-incrimination, his right to trial by jury, and his right to confront his accusers. For this waiver to be valid under the Due Process Clause, it must be "an intentional relinquishment or abandonment of a known right or privilege." Johnson v. Zerbst, 304 U.S. 458, 464 (1938). Consequently, if a defendant's guilty plea is not equally voluntary and knowing, it has been obtained in violation of due process and is therefore void. Moreover, because a guilty plea is an admission of all the elements of a formal criminal charge, it cannot be truly voluntary unless the defendant possesses an understanding of the law in relation to the facts.

Thus, in addition to directing the judge to inquire into the defendant's understanding of the nature of the charge and the consequences of his plea, Rule 11 also requires the judge to satisfy himself that there is a factual basis for the plea. The judge must determine "that the conduct which the defendant admits constitutes the offense charged in the indictment or information or an offense included therein to which the defendant has pleaded guilty."[3] Requiring this examination of the relation between the law and the acts the defendant admits having committed is designed to "protect a defendant who is in the position of pleading voluntarily with an understanding of the nature of the charge but without realizing that his conduct does not actually fall within the charge."[4]

To the extent that the district judge thus exposes the defendant's state of mind on the record through personal interrogation, he not only facilitates his own determination of a guilty plea's voluntariness, but he also facilitates that determination in any subsequent post-conviction proceeding based upon a claim that the plea was involuntary. Both of these goals are undermined in proportion to the degree the district judge resorts to "assumptions" not based upon recorded responses to his inquiries. For this reason, we reject the Government's contention that Rule 11 can be com-

2. [Notes of Advisory Committee, U.S.C.A., following Fed.R.Crim.P. 11.]

3. Fed. Rule Crim.Proc. 11, Notes of Advisory Committee on Criminal Rules.

4. Ibid.

plied with although the district judge does not personally inquire whether the defendant understood the nature of the charge.[5]

II.

Having decided that the Rule has not been complied with, we must also determine the effect of that non-compliance, an issue that has engendered a sharp difference of opinion among the courts of appeals. In Heiden v. United States, 353 F.2d 53 (1965), the Court of Appeals for the Ninth Circuit held that when the district court does not comply fully with Rule 11 the defendant's guilty plea must be set aside and his case remanded for another hearing at which he may plead anew. Other courts of appeals, however, have consistently rejected this holding, either expressly or tacitly. Instead, they have adopted the approach urged by the Government, which is to place upon the Government the burden of demonstrating from the record of the Rule 11 hearing that the guilty plea was voluntarily entered with an understanding of the charge. . . . In these circuits, if voluntariness cannot be determined from the record, the case is remanded for an evidentiary hearing on that issue. . . .

We are persuaded that the Court of Appeals for the Ninth Circuit has adopted the better rule. From the defendant's perspective, the efficacy of shifting the burden of proof to the Government at a later voluntariness hearing is questionable. In meeting its burden, the Government will undoubtedly rely upon the defendant's statement that he desired to plead guilty and frequently a statement that the plea was not induced by any threats or promises. This prima facie case for voluntariness is likely to be treated as irrebuttable in cases such as this one, where the defendant's reply is limited to his own plaintive allegations that he did not understand the nature of the charge and therefore failed to assert a valid defense or to limit his guilty plea only to a lesser included offense. No matter how true these allegations may be, rarely, if ever, can a defendant corroborate them in a post-plea voluntariness hearing.

Rule 11 is designed to eliminate any need to resort to a later fact-finding proceeding "in this highly subjective area." Heiden v. United States, supra, at 55. The Rule "contemplates that disputes as to the understanding of the defendant and the voluntariness of his action are to be eliminated at the outset. . . ." Ibid. As the Court of Appeals for the Sixth Circuit explained in discussing what it termed the "persuasive rationale" of *Heiden*: "When the ascertainment is subsequently made, greater uncertainty is bound to exist since in the resolution of disputed contentions problems of credibility and of reliability of memory cannot be

5. The nature of the inquiry required by Rule 11 must necessarily vary from case to case, and therefore, we do not establish any general guidelines other than those expressed in the Rule itself. As our discussion of the facts in this particular case suggests, however, where the charge encompasses lesser included offenses, personally addressing the defendant as to his understanding of the essential elements of the charge to which he pleads guilty would seem a necessary prerequisite to a determination that he understands the meaning of the charge. In all such inquiries, "[m]atters of reality, and not mere ritual, should be controlling." Kennedy v. United States, 397 F.2d 16, 17 (C.A.6th Cir.1968).

avoided. . . ." Waddy v. Herr, 383 F.2d 789, 794 (1967). There is no adequate substitute for demonstrating *in the record at the time the plea is entered* the defendant's understanding of the nature of the charge against him.

The wisdom of Rule 11's requirements and the difficulty of achieving its purposes through a post-conviction voluntariness hearing are particularly apparent in this case. Petitioner, who was 65 years old and in poor health at the time he entered his plea, had been suffering from a serious drinking problem during the time he allegedly evaded his taxes. He pleaded guilty to a crime that requires a "knowing and willful" attempt to defraud the Government of its tax money; yet, throughout his sentencing hearing, he and his counsel insisted that his acts were merely "neglectful," "inadvertent," and committed without "any disposition of depriving the United States of its due." Remarks of this nature cast considerable doubt on the Government's assertion that petitioner pleaded guilty with "full awareness of the nature of the charge." Nevertheless, confronted with petitioner's statement that he entered his plea of his "own volition," his counsel's statement that he explained the nature of the charges, and evidence that petitioner did owe the Government back taxes, both the District Court and the Court of Appeals concluded that petitioner's guilty plea was voluntary.

Despite petitioner's inability to convince the courts below that he did not fully understand the charge against him, it is certainly conceivable that he may have intended to acknowledge only that he in fact owed the Government the money it claimed without necessarily admitting that he committed the crime charged; for that crime requires the very type of specific intent that he repeatedly disavowed. . . . Moreover, since the elements of the offense were not explained to petitioner, and since the specific acts of tax evasion do not appear of record, it is also possible that if petitioner had been adequately informed he would have concluded that he was actually guilty of one of two closely related lesser included offenses, which are mere misdemeanors.

On the other hand, had the District Court scrupulously complied with Rule 11, there would be no need for such speculation. At the time the plea was entered, petitioner's own replies to the court's inquiries might well have attested to his understanding of the essential elements of the crime charged, including the requirement of specific intent, and to his knowledge of the acts which formed the basis for the charge. Otherwise, it would be apparent to the court that the plea could not be accepted. Similarly, it follows that, if the record had been developed properly, and if it demonstrated that petitioner entered his plea freely and intelligently, his subsequent references to neglect and inadvertence could have been summarily dismissed as nothing more than overzealous supplications for leniency.

We thus conclude that prejudice inheres in a failure to comply with Rule 11, for noncompliance deprives the defendant of the Rule's procedural safeguards, which are designed to facilitate a more accurate determination of the voluntariness of his plea. Our holding that a defendant whose plea has been accepted in violation of Rule 11 should be afforded the opportunity to plead anew not only will insure that every accused is afforded those procedural safeguards, but also will help reduce the great waste of judicial resources required to process the frivolous attacks on guilty plea convictions that are encouraged, and are more difficult to dispose of, when the original record is inadequate. It is, therefore, not too much to require that, before sentencing defendants to years of imprisonment, district judges take the few minutes necessary to inform them of their rights and to determine whether they understand the action they are taking.

We therefore reverse the judgment of the Court of Appeals for the Seventh Circuit and remand the case for proceedings consistent with this opinion.[6]

---

353. In Boykin v. Alabama, 395 U.S. 238, 242 (1969), the Court held that in a state proceeding it was constitutional error for the trial judge to accept a plea of guilty "without an affirmative showing that it was intelligent and voluntary," and that such a showing must appear in the record. "What is at stake for an accused facing death or imprisonment demands the utmost solicitude of which courts are capable in canvassing the matter with the accused to make sure he has a full understanding of what the plea connotes and of its consequence." Id. at 243–44.

Before acceptance of a guilty plea, the court is required to advise a defendant who is not represented by counsel that he has a right to be represented at entry of the plea and that counsel will be appointed if necessary. Rule 11(b)(1)(D). So long as a defendant is so informed and is otherwise advised as Rule11(b) requires, the court is not required to advise the defendant also that if he waives the assistance of counsel he may overlook a viable defense or that he will lose the opportunity to have an independent opinion about the advisability of pleading guilty. In all cases, the requirement is that a waiver of counsel be knowing, voluntary, and intelligent. Iowa v. Tovar, 541 U.S. ___ (2004).

354. The standard of competence to plead guilty or to waive the right to counsel is the same as the standard of competence to stand trial. Godinez v. Moran, 509 U.S. 389 (1993) (7–2). The defendant in *Godinez* pleaded guilty to three counts of first-degree murder, for which he was sentenced to death. Subsequently he filed a petition for post-conviction relief, on the ground that he was mentally incompetent to represent himself. The Court noted that before accepting a plea of guilty, in addition to finding that the defendant is competent to plead guilty, a court must find that the plea is knowing and voluntary.

The defendant, who was mentally retarded, was indicted for first-degree murder. He pleaded guilty to second-degree murder. On collateral attack, he claimed that the plea was involuntary because he was not informed by his lawyers or the court, and did not know, that intent to

[6] Justice Black wrote a brief concurring opinion.

cause death was an element of the offense. Finding that there was nothing in the record that could "substitute for either a finding after trial, or a voluntary admission" that the defendant had the necessary intent, the Court upheld his claim. It said: "Normally the record contains either an explanation of the charge by the trial judge, or at least a representation by defense counsel that the nature of the offense has been explained to the accused. Moreover, even without such an express representation, it may be appropriate to presume that in most cases defense counsel routinely explain the nature of the offense in sufficient detail to give the accused notice of what he is being asked to admit. This case is unique because the trial judge found as a fact that the element of intent was not explained to respondent. Moreover, respondent's unusually low mental capacity provides a reasonable explanation for counsel's oversight; it also forecloses the conclusion that the error was harmless beyond a reasonable doubt, for it lends at least a modicum of credibility to defense counsel's appraisal of the homicide as a manslaughter rather than a murder." Henderson v. Morgan, 426 U.S. 637, 646, 647 (1976) (7–2).

No person shall be . . . deprived . . . without due process of law . . .

See DeVille v. Whitley, 21 F.3d 654 (5th Cir.1994) (*Henderson* distinguished); Gaddy v. Linahan, 780 F.2d 935 (11th Cir.1986) ("malice murder," defendant illiterate and possessing "minimal mental capacity"; remanded for evidentiary hearing to determine what defendant understood prior to plea); Gregory v. Solem, 774 F.2d 309 (8th Cir.1985) (*Henderson* distinguished); Ames v. New York State Division of Parole, 772 F.2d 13 (2d Cir.1985) (distinguishing elements of the offense and affirmative defenses).

In Allard v. Helgemoe, 572 F.2d 1 (1st Cir.1978), the court observed that "there is no indication in . . . [*Henderson*] that the Court ever considered the problem of a fully informed defendant who lacked the capacity to understand some part of the charges against him." Id. at 5. *Henderson*, it said, was concerned with "a constitutional failure that could be easily determined and prevented," id., and was not establishing a test for guilty pleas that required an inquiry into the defendant's actual understanding of the nature of the offense. Provided that a defendant is fully informed and is competent to plead guilty, "the objective requirements of due process" ordinarily are satisfied. Id. at 6. See Nelson v. Callahan, 721 F.2d 397 (1st Cir.1983) (*Allard* applied).

355. Rule 11(b) sets forth the information and advice that a judge must give the defendant before accepting a plea of guilty.

"The court must not rely on a routine boilerplate question to the defendant designed to elicit an acknowledgement of understanding. . . . Nor should the court rely solely upon statements that it makes to the defendant. In adhering to the rule's mandate that it address the defendant personally, the court should engage in [as] extensive an interchange as necessary to assure itself and any subsequent reader of the transcript that the defendant does indeed fully understand the charges. With respect to some points the court may choose to have the defendant recount his or her understanding of the charges in narrative form and in his or her own language. We do not suggest an arcane definition of the legal concepts, nor a law review exegesis, but enough simple language that a person unlearned, untutored and unschooled could understand the charges." United States v. Coronado, 554 F.2d 166, 173 (5th Cir.1977).

Concluding that not every failure to comply precisely with the requirements of Rule 11 (which, it noted, are now much more complex than they were when *McCarthy* was decided) requires vacation of a plea of guilty, the court observed, in United States v. Dayton, 604 F.2d 931, 937–38, 943 (5th Cir.1979):

> [W]e are unable to state a simple or mechanical rule but offer some general observations that we hope will be helpful. For simple charges . . . a reading of the indictment, followed by an opportunity given the defendant to ask questions about it, will usually suffice. Charges of a more complex nature, incorporating esoteric terms or concepts unfamiliar to the lay mind, may require more explication. In the case of charges of extreme complexity, an explanation of the elements of the offense like that given the jury in its instructions may be required; this, of course, is the outer limit, for if an instruction informs a jury of the nature of the charge sufficiently for it to convict

the defendant of it, surely it informs the defendant sufficiently for him to convict himself. We can do no more than commit these matters to the good judgment of the court, to its calculation of the relative difficulty of comprehension of the charges and of the defendant's sophistication and intelligence.

. . .

. . . What is necessary is that the trial court, given the nature of the charges and the character and capacities of the defendant, personally participate in the colloquy mandated by Rule 11 and satisfy himself fully that, within those limits, the defendant understands what he is admitting and what the consequences of that admission may be, as well as that what he is admitting constitutes the crime charged, and that his admission is voluntarily made. If the court does those things, and if the record of that hearing shows a common-sense basis for agreeing that he did so, we will not disturb its actions.

The colloquy between the judge and the defendant required by Rule 11(b) is subject to harmless error analysis under Rule 11(h). See United States v. Lujano-Perez, 274 F.3d 219 (5th Cir.2001) (failure to explain nature of charge not harmless error); United States v. Goldberg, 862 F.2d 101 (6th Cir.1988) (failure to ascertain factual basis for plea not harmless error).

The plain error standard (see Rule 52(b), p. 1169 below) applies to errors in proceedings for the entry of a guilty plea to which the defendant made no objection; a reviewing court can look at the entire record to determine whether that standard is met. United States v. Vonn, 535 U.S. 55 (2002).

356.

[I]t is highly doubtful that a uniform mandatory catechism of pleading defendants should be required. . . . The circumstances are too various. There are knowledgeable and criminally experienced defendants and there are those who are lacking in intellect or experience, or both. There are cases where the seriousness of the crime, the competency and experience of counsel, the actual intensive participation by counsel, the nature of the crime as clearly understood by laymen, the rationality of the "plea bargain," and the speed or slowness of procedure in the particular criminal court provide ample data as to how far the court should go in questioning defendants before taking a guilty plea. These are all matters best left to the discretion of the court. In some instances even the most rigorous standards thus far suggested, either in the American Bar Association project[7] or by the Federal rule, are hardly adequate; in others the standards become an unnecessary formalism. . . .

The competency of counsel and the degree of actual participation by counsel as well as his opportunity for and the fact of consultation with the pleading defendant, are particularly important. Indeed, if

7. ABA Standards, Pleas of Guilty (1968).

independent and good advice in the interest of the defendant is the goal, it is more important that he consult with competent counsel than that a harried, calendar-conscious Judge be the one to perform the function in displacement of the lawyer. Moreover, there are many reasons why a defendant may not wish to be subjected to an inquisition by officials; it may affect him on his prison or parole status; it may be an added pillory for him to experience that he would eschew. . . .

Nevertheless, the standards promulgated by the Bar Association committee, albeit tentatively, and those included in the Federal rule, implement principles that may not be ignored. It is not tolerable for the State to punish its members over protestations of innocence if there be doubt as to their guilt, or if they be unaware of their rights, or if they have not had opportunity to make a voluntary and rational decision with proper advice in pleading guilty. . . .

It is also quite clear that where initial inquiry exposes difficulties or subsequent interpositions by defendant on sentencing raise questions, the court should be quick to offer the defendant an opportunity to withdraw his plea and at the very least conduct a hearing. Such opportunities offered will squelch the faker and protect the truly misguided ones; and, prompt hearings will be better than later ones after direct appeal or collateral postconviction attack. . . .

The promptness or staleness of complaint with respect to propriety of a guilty plea has already been noted as a significant factor to be considered.

In cases involving defendants without lawyers, or those ignorant of the language of the court, particular pains must be taken. Of course these days, it is not likely that there will be many uncounselled defendants, but there will still be . . . defendants who say they do not want a lawyer. In such cases inquiry, well beyond the standards thus far propounded, is indicated.

But overall, it would seem that a sound discretion exercised in cases on an individual basis is best rather than to mandate a uniform procedure which, like as not, would become a purely ritualistic device. Indeed, today, there is reason to suspect that many pleading defendants are prepared to give the categorical answers only because they know that this is the route to eligibility for the lesser plea. A ritualistic form just because it may save the trouble of thinking is likely to eliminate thinking. . . . An oral questionnaire can become just as mechanical as one printed. The taking of the guilty plea should not be made that easy for the defendant or the court or his lawyer. Moreover, there is a weakness in the catechism system, one which some may think can be avoided if legislation were devised to cover the area in question. It should never be enough to undo a plea because of some omission in inquiry at the time of plea without a showing of prejudice. . . . While the essence of justice may be procedure there can be a point at which the administration of justice becomes only procedure and the essence of justice is lost.

People v. Nixon, 234 N.E.2d 687, 695–97 (N.Y.1967).

357. See Fontaine v. United States, 411 U.S. 213, 215 (1973), in which the Court observed that while the purpose of Rule 11 is to avoid later invalidation of a guilty plea, "like any procedural mechanism, its exercise is neither always perfect nor uniformly invulnerable to subsequent challenge calling for an opportunity to prove the allegations." In Blackledge v. Allison, 431 U.S. 63 (1977), the Court discussed generally what procedure should be followed on a request for post-conviction collateral relief from a guilty plea that is proper on the record. The Court said that "the federal courts cannot fairly adopt a per se rule excluding all possibility that a defendant's representations at the time his guilty plea was accepted were so much the product of such factors as misunderstanding, duress, or misrepresentation by others as to make the guilty plea a constitutionally inadequate basis for imprisonment." Id. at 75. The Court made it clear on the other hand that a full evidentiary hearing was not always warranted; the usual procedures, such as a motion for summary judgment, were available to avoid an unnecessary hearing.

Collateral attack on a conviction is not available when all that is alleged is a failure to comply with the formal requirements of Rule 11. A formal violation of the rule "is neither constitutional nor jurisdictional." United States v. Timmreck, 441 U.S. 780, 783 (1979). The Court observed that it was not deciding whether collateral relief would be available for a violation of the rule if there were "other aggravating circumstances." Id. at 785. See United States v. Bernal, 861 F.2d 434 (5th Cir.1988) (violation of "core concerns" of Rule 11 requires reversal of conviction).

358. A plea of guilty "is also a waiver of trial—and unless the applicable law otherwise provides, a waiver of the right to contest the admissibility of any evidence the state might have offered against the defendant." McMann v. Richardson, 397 U.S. 759, 766 (1970). In *McMann*, the defendant sought by collateral attack to vacate his plea of guilty on the ground that his plea was prompted by an unlawfully coerced confession. The Court rejected his claim. "In our view a defendant's plea of guilty based on reasonably competent advice is an intelligent plea not open to attack on the grounds that counsel may have misjudged the admissibility of the defendant's confession. Whether a plea of guilty is unintelligent and therefore vulnerable when motivated by a confession erroneously thought admissible in evidence depends as an initial matter not on whether a court would retrospectively consider counsel's advice to be right or wrong, but on whether that advice was within the range of competence demanded of attorneys in criminal cases." Id. at 770–71.

The reasoning of *McMann* was applied to foreclose collateral attack on a conviction following a plea of guilty in Tollett v. Henderson, 411 U.S. 258 (1973). The defendant claimed that the grand jury that indicted him was unconstitutionally composed. The Court indicated that *McMann* may apply even though the defendant's counsel did not discuss with him the constitutional claim that was foregone by the guilty plea.

> A guilty plea, voluntarily and intelligently entered, may not be vacated because the defendant was not advised of every conceivable constitutional plea in abatement he might have to the charge, no matter how peripheral such a plea might be to the normal focus of counsel's inquiry. And just as it is not sufficient for the criminal defendant seeking to set aside such a plea to show that his counsel in retrospect may not have correctly appraised the constitutional significance of certain historical facts . . . it is likewise not sufficient that he show that if counsel had pursued a certain factual inquiry such a pursuit would have uncovered a possible constitutional infirmity in the proceedings.
>
> The principal value of counsel to the accused in a criminal prosecution often lies not in counsel's ability to abstract, nor in his ability, if time permitted, to amass a large quantum of factual data and inform the defendant of it. Counsel's concern is the faithful representation of the interest of his client and such representation frequently involves highly practical considerations as well as specialized knowledge of the law. Often the interests of the accused are not advanced by challenges that would only delay the inevitable date of prosecution . . . or by contesting all guilt. . . . A prospect of plea bargaining, the expectation or hope of a lesser sentence, or the convincing nature of the evidence against the accused are considerations that might well suggest the advisability of a guilty plea without elaborate consideration of whether pleas in abatement, such as unconstitutional grand jury selection procedures, might be factually supported.

Id. at 267–68.

A knowing and voluntary waiver of the right to appeal as part of a plea agreement is valid, but a court of appeals may grant relief from the waiver in appropriate circumstances. United States v. Teeter, 257 F.3d 14 (1st Cir.2001).

The two-part standard for testing a claim of incompetence of counsel announced in Strickland v. Washington, 466 U.S. 668 (1984), p. 1036 below, applies to claims arising out of the entry of a plea of guilty. In particular, a defendant must not only show that his lawyer's representation fell below the standard of competence; he must also show that the lawyer's ineffective performance was prejudicial, meaning "that there is a reasonable probability that, but for counsel's errors, he would not have pleaded guilty and would have insisted on going to trial." Hill v. Lockhart, 474 U.S. 52 (1985). In *Hill*, the defendant's lawyer told him that he would be eligible for parole after serving one-third of his term of imprisonment. The defendant was not eligible until he had served half his term. The Court held that in the circumstances of the case, prejudice was not shown.

See Downs-Morgan v. United States, 765 F.2d 1534 (11th Cir.1985), in which the defendant alleged that he pleaded guilty on the erroneous advice of his counsel that he would not be subject to deportation if convicted. The court said that in view of the especially harsh alleged consequences of deportation (long-term imprisonment and possibly execution) and the defendant's "at least colorable claim of innocence," an evidentiary hearing on the claim of ineffective assistance of counsel was necessary. See also Iaea v. Sunn, 800 F.2d 861 (9th Cir.1986) (ineffective assistance; remand for determination of prejudice); Dufresne v. Moran, 729 F.2d 18 (1st Cir.1984) (ineffective assistance; prejudice not shown).

359. Does a defendant have a constitutional right to be informed of the prosecution's offer of a plea bargain and to make the final decision whether or not to accept it? In Johnson v. Duckworth, 793 F.2d 898, 902 (7th Cir.1986), the court said: "[I]n the ordinary case criminal defense attorneys have a duty to inform their clients of plea agreements proffered by the prosecution, and . . . failure to do so constitutes ineffective assistance of counsel under the sixth and fourteenth amendments. Apart from merely being informed about the proffered agreement . . . a defendant must be involved in the decision-making process regarding the agreement's ultimate acceptance or rejection." However, in the circumstances of the case, which involved a juvenile defendant, the court concluded that defense counsel's decision to reject the bargain, with the concurrence of the defendant's parents, was not ineffective assistance of counsel.

360. A guilty plea does not foreclose collateral attack based on a constitutional claim that bars prosecution altogether. Blackledge v. Perry, 417 U.S. 21 (1974). See Menna v. New York, 423 U.S. 61 (1975), in which the Court held that a claim of double jeopardy was not waived by the defendant's plea of guilty. For a general discussion of which constitutional claims are foreclosed by a guilty plea and which are not, see United States v. Curcio, 712 F.2d 1532 (2d Cir.1983).

In United States v. Broce, 488 U.S. 563 (1989) (6–3), the defendants pleaded guilty to two separate indictments for conspiracy. Later, they filed a motion to vacate the convictions under the second indictment, on the ground that the facts showed only one conspiracy and their conviction on the second violated the Double Jeopardy Clause. The Supreme Court held that their claim of double jeopardy was waived by the plea of guilty. *Blackledge* and *Menna* were distinguishable, the Court said, because in those cases the constitutional barrier to prosecution was apparent on the face of the record and did not require an evidentiary hearing, which would be required here.

In Lefkowitz v. Newsome, 420 U.S. 283 (1975) (5–4), the Court held that a claim (based on denial of a motion to suppress evidence) that would have been waived by a guilty plea in federal court but was not waived according to state law could be raised by a petition for habeas corpus in federal court. The state law, the Court said, guaranteed that review of the defendant's constitutional claims would continue to be available despite his plea of guilty.

The provision for entry of a conditional plea of guilty in Rule 11(a)(2) was added in 1983. The Note of the Advisory Committee on Rules states: "It must be emphasized that the only avenue of review of the specified pretrial ruling permitted under a rule 11(a)(2) conditional plea is an appeal, which must be brought in compliance with Fed.R.App.P. 4(b). Relief via 28 U.S.C. § 2255 is not available for this purpose." The Note states further that the rule "should not be interpreted as either broadening or narrowing the *Menna-Blackledge* doctrine or as establishing procedures for its application." 18 U.S.C.A., following Fed.R.Crim.P. 11.

361. A district court may not without the consent of the government accept a plea of guilty to a lesser offense necessarily included in the offense charged in the indictment. "[T]he plea contemplated by Rules 10 and 11 is a plea to the offense charged in the indictment or information, and . . . a plea to a lesser included offense may not be tendered, and cannot be accepted by the court, unless the government consents." United States v. Gray, 448 F.2d 164, 168 (9th Cir.1971).

Factual Basis for the Plea

---

362. What constitutes a "factual basis" for a plea of guilty, as required by Rule 11(b)(3)? The Note of the Advisory Committee on Rules that accompanied the 1966 amendment adding the predecessor provision of Rule 11(b)(3) states: "The court should satisfy itself, by inquiry of the defendant or the attorney for the government, or by examining the presentence report, or otherwise, that the conduct which the defendant admits constitutes the offense charged in the indictment or information or an offense included therein to which the defendant has pleaded guilty. Such inquiry should, e.g., protect a defendant who is in the position of pleading voluntarily with an understanding of the nature of the charge but without realizing that his conduct does not actually fall within the charge." 18 U.S.C.A., following Fed.R.Crim.P. 11.

In North Carolina v. Alford, 400 U.S. 25 (1970), the defendant was indicted for first-degree murder, a capital offense. He pleaded guilty to second-degree murder. Before accepting the plea, the trial court heard testimony of several witnesses for the state. The defendant told the court that he was innocent and that he was pleading guilty on the advice of counsel to limit his penalty to that provided for second-degree murder. The Supreme Court held that it was not constitutionally improper to accept the plea.

> [W]hile most pleas of guilty consist of both a waiver of trial and an express admission of guilt, the latter element is not a constitutional requisite to the imposition of criminal penalty. An individual accused of crime may voluntarily, knowingly, and understandably consent to the imposition of a prison sentence even if he is unwilling or unable to admit his participation in the acts constituting the crime.

> Nor can we perceive any material difference between a plea which refuses to admit commission of the criminal act and a plea containing a protestation of innocence when, as in the instant case, a defendant intelligently concludes that his interests require entry of a guilty plea and the record before the judge contains strong evidence of actual guilt. . . .
>
> . . . The prohibitions against involuntary or unintelligent pleas should not be relaxed, but neither should an exercise in arid logic render those constitutional guarantees counterproductive and put in jeopardy the very human values they were meant to preserve.

Id. at 37, 39. The Court emphasized that it was dealing only with constitutional requirements and that states might prohibit the result reached in this case. Nor does *Alford* require that a guilty plea in comparable circumstances be accepted in the federal courts.

The Court's statement of facts recites that Alford pleaded guilty to the reduced charge eight days after he was indicted. The unusually short period of time is not otherwise mentioned in the opinion.

See United States v. Tunning, 69 F.3d 107 (6th Cir.1995) (factual basis for plea not shown, where defendant failed to admit facts constituting offense); United States v. Cox, 923 F.2d 519 (7th Cir.1991) (*Alford* situation; trial court had discretion to reject plea); United States v. Keiswetter, 860 F.2d 992 (10th Cir.1988), modified, 866 F.2d 1301 (1989) (en banc) (*Alford* situation, factual basis for plea not evident from record; plea vacated).

The requirement of a factual basis for a plea does not apply to part of a plea agreement that stipulates a forfeiture of assets pursuant to 21 U.S.C. § 853. Libretti v. United States, 516 U.S. 29 (1995) (8–1).

363. In People v. Foster, 225 N.E.2d 200 (N.Y.1967), the court held that the defendant was properly convicted and sentenced on his plea of guilty to the "logically and legally impossible" crime of attempted manslaughter. (Manslaughter was defined as an unintentional crime; a specific intent to commit the crime attempted was an element of the crime of attempt.) "While there may be question whether a plea to attempted manslaughter is technically and logically consistent, such a plea should be sustained on the ground that it was sought by a defendant and freely taken as part of a bargain which was struck for the defendant's benefit." Id. at 202. *Foster* was distinguished in People v. Hassin, 368 N.Y.S.2d 253 (App.Div.1975), in which the defendant pleaded guilty to two counts of " 'attempted' felony murder." The court said that there is no such crime and dismissed those counts of the indictment. In *Foster*, the court said, the defendant pleaded guilty to a lesser offense included in the crime charged in the indictment; here the impossible crime, to which the defendant pleaded guilty, was actually charged in the indictment.

364.

It has been raised as a problem of ethics whether an attorney may advise the defendant first that the evidence implicating him is so overwhelming that a guilty plea is his best salvation, and second that this plea will not be accepted unless defendant, departing from truth if need be, states facts that show he is guilty. Freedman, "Professional Responsibility of the Criminal Defense Lawyer: The Three Hardest Questions," 64 Mich. L. Rev. 1469 (1966).

We have no hesitation in saying that an attorney, an officer of the court, may not counsel or practice such a deliberate deception.

Bruce v. United States, 379 F.2d 113, 119 n.17 (D.C.Cir.1967).

[T]o this Court it appears utterly unreasonable for counsel to recommend a guilty plea to a defendant without first cautioning him that, no matter what, he should not plead guilty unless he believed himself guilty. Most certainly such a recommendation should not be made when the defendant in the past has maintained his innocence and has stated that he has two witnesses whom counsel has not attempted to interview. It may well have been trial counsel's opinion that even if defendant were innocent he would still be convicted. Such a view is not only cynical but unwarranted. Innocent men in the past have been convicted; but such instances have been so rare and our judicial system has so many safeguards that no lawyer worthy of his profession justifiably may assume that an innocent person will be convicted.

Guilty pleas play a necessary and valid role in the criminal process. Plea bargaining, despite understandable criticism, also is proper. But guilty pleas and plea bargaining place a heavy responsibility on defense counsel to insure that neither the rights or interests of defendants nor the integrity of the judicial system are thereby jeopardized. This means that defense attorneys, in their roles as counsel and as officers of the Court, must exercise scrupulous care to see to it that an innocent man does not plead guilty.

United States v. Rogers, 289 F.Supp. 726, 729–30 (D.Conn.1968).

365. ABA Standards for Criminal Justice, The Prosecution Function (1971) (since deleted): "4.2 Plea disposition when accused maintains innocence. A prosecutor may not properly participate in a disposition by plea of guilty if he is aware that the accused persists in denying guilt or the factual basis for the plea, without disclosure to the court."

ABA Standards for Criminal Justice, The Defense Function (1971) (since deleted): "5.3 Guilty plea when accused denies guilt. If the accused discloses to the lawyer facts which negate guilt and the lawyer's investigation does not reveal a conflict with the facts disclosed but the accused persists in entering a plea of guilty, the lawyer may not properly participate in presenting a guilty plea, without disclosure to the court."

How should the defense lawyer advise his client if he believes that the judge to whom the case is assigned will accept a plea of guilty only if, at the time the plea is entered, the defendant describes the crime in sufficient detail to establish his guilt?

Plea Bargaining

Brady v. United States

397 U.S. 742, 90 S.Ct. 1463, 25 L.Ed.2d 747 (1970)

■ MR. JUSTICE WHITE delivered the opinion of the Court.

In 1959, petitioner was charged with kidnaping in violation of 18 U.S.C. § 1201(a). Since the indictment charged that the victim of the kidnaping was not liberated unharmed, petitioner faced a maximum penalty of death if the verdict of the jury should so recommend. Petitioner, represented by competent counsel throughout, first elected to plead not guilty. Apparently because the trial judge was unwilling to try the case without a jury, petitioner made no serious attempt to reduce the possibility of a death penalty by waiving a jury trial. Upon learning that his codefendant, who had confessed to the authorities, would plead guilty and be available to testify against him, petitioner changed his plea to guilty. His plea was accepted after the trial judge twice questioned him as to the voluntariness of his plea. Petitioner was sentenced to 50 years' imprisonment, later reduced to 30.

In 1967, petitioner sought relief under 28 U.S.C. § 2255, claiming that his plea of guilty was not voluntarily given because § 1201(a) operated to coerce his plea, because his counsel exerted impermissible pressure upon him, and because his plea was induced by representations with respect to reduction of sentence and clemency. It was also alleged that the trial judge had not fully complied with Rule 11 of the Federal Rules of Criminal Procedure.

After a hearing, the District Court for the District of New Mexico denied relief. According to the District Court's findings, petitioner's counsel did not put impermissible pressure on petitioner to plead guilty and no representations were made with respect to a reduced sentence or clemency. The court held that § 1201(a) was constitutional and found that petitioner decided to plead guilty when he learned that his codefendant was going to plead guilty; petitioner pleaded guilty "by reason of other matters and not by reason of the statute" or because of any acts of the trial judge. The court concluded that "the plea was voluntarily and knowingly made."

The Court of Appeals for the Tenth Circuit affirmed, determining that the District Court's findings were supported by substantial evidence and specifically approving the finding that petitioner's plea of guilty was voluntary. . . . We granted certiorari . . . to consider the claim that the Court of

Appeals was in error in not reaching a contrary result on the authority of this Court's decision in United States v. Jackson, 390 U.S. 570 (1968). We affirm.

I

In United States v. Jackson, supra, the defendants were indicted under § 1201(a). The District Court dismissed the § 1201(a) count of the indictment, holding the statute unconstitutional because it permitted imposition of the death sentence only upon a jury's recommendation and thereby made the risk of death the price of a jury trial. This Court held the statute valid, except for the death penalty provision; with respect to the latter, the Court agreed with the trial court "that the death penalty provision . . . imposes an impermissible burden upon the exercise of a constitutional right. . . ." 390 U.S., at 572. The problem was to determine "whether the Constitution permits the establishment of such a death penalty, applicable only to those defendants who assert the right to contest their guilt before a jury." 390 U.S., at 581. The inevitable effect of the provision was said to be to discourage assertion of the Fifth Amendment right not to plead guilty and to deter exercise of the Sixth Amendment right to demand a jury trial. Because the legitimate goal of limiting the death penalty to cases in which a jury recommends it could be achieved without penalizing those defendants who plead not guilty and elect a jury trial, the death penalty provision "needlessly penalize[d] the assertion of a constitutional right," 390 U.S., at 583, and was therefore unconstitutional.

Since the "inevitable effect" of the death penalty provision of § 1201(a) was said by the Court to be the needless encouragement of pleas of guilty and waivers of jury trial, Brady contends that *Jackson* requires the invalidation of every plea of guilty entered under that section, at least when the fear of death is shown to have been a factor in the plea. Petitioner, however, has read far too much into the *Jackson* opinion.

The Court made it clear in *Jackson* that it was not holding § 1201(a) inherently coercive of guilty pleas: "the fact that the Federal Kidnaping Act tends to discourage defendants from insisting upon their innocence and demanding trial by jury hardly implies that every defendant who enters a guilty plea to a charge under the Act does so involuntarily." 390 U.S., at 583. . . .

Moreover, the Court in *Jackson* rejected a suggestion that the death penalty provision of § 1201(a) be saved by prohibiting in capital kidnaping cases all guilty pleas and jury waivers, "however clear [the defendants'] guilt and however strong their desire to acknowledge it in order to spare themselves and their families the spectacle and expense of protracted courtroom proceedings." "[T]hat jury waivers and guilty pleas may occasionally be rejected" was no ground for automatically rejecting all guilty pleas under the statute, for such a rule "would rob the criminal process of much of its flexibility." 390 U.S., at 584.

Plainly, it seems to us, *Jackson* ruled neither that all pleas of guilty encouraged by the fear of a possible death sentence are involuntary pleas nor that such encouraged pleas are invalid whether involuntary or not. *Jackson* prohibits the imposition of the death penalty under § 1201(a), but that decision neither fashioned a new standard for judging the validity of guilty pleas nor mandated a new application of the test theretofore fashioned by courts and since reiterated that guilty pleas are valid if both "voluntary" and "intelligent." . . .

That a guilty plea is a grave and solemn act to be accepted only with care and discernment has long been recognized. Central to the plea and the foundation for entering judgment against the defendant is the defendant's admission in open court that he committed the acts charged in the indictment. He thus stands as a witness against himself and he is shielded by the Fifth Amendment from being compelled to do so—hence the minimum requirement that his plea be the voluntary expression of his own choice. But the plea is more than an admission of past conduct; it is the defendant's consent that judgment of conviction may be entered without a trial—a waiver of his right to trial before a jury or a judge. Waivers of constitutional rights not only must be voluntary but must be knowing, intelligent acts done with sufficient awareness of the relevant circumstances and likely consequences. On neither score was Brady's plea of guilty invalid.

II

The trial judge in 1959 found the plea voluntary before accepting it; the District Court in 1968, after an evidentiary hearing, found that the plea was voluntarily made; the Court of Appeals specifically approved the finding of voluntariness. We see no reason on this record to disturb the judgment of those courts. Petitioner, advised by competent counsel, tendered his plea after his codefendant, who had already given a confession, determined to plead guilty and became available to testify against petitioner. It was this development that the District Court found to have triggered Brady's guilty plea.

The voluntariness of Brady's plea can be determined only by considering all of the relevant circumstances surrounding it. . . . One of these circumstances was the possibility of a heavier sentence following a guilty verdict after a trial. It may be that Brady, faced with a strong case against him and recognizing that his chances for acquittal were slight, preferred to plead guilty and thus limit the penalty to life imprisonment rather than to elect a jury trial which could result in a death penalty. But even if we assume that Brady would not have pleaded guilty except for the death penalty provision of § 1201(a), this assumption merely identifies the penalty provision as a "but for" cause of his plea. That the statute caused the plea in this sense does not necessarily prove that the plea was coerced and invalid as an involuntary act.

The State to some degree encourages pleas of guilty at every important step in the criminal process. For some people, their breach of a State's law is alone sufficient reason for surrendering themselves and accepting punishment. For others, apprehension and charge, both threatening acts by the

Government, jar them into admitting their guilt. In still other cases, the post-indictment accumulation of evidence may convince the defendant and his counsel that a trial is not worth the agony and expense to the defendant and his family. All these pleas of guilty are valid in spite of the State's responsibility for some of the factors motivating the pleas; the pleas are no more improperly compelled than is the decision by a defendant at the close of the State's evidence at trial that he must take the stand or face certain conviction.

Of course, the agents of the State may not produce a plea by actual or threatened physical harm or by mental coercion overbearing the will of the defendant. But nothing of the sort is claimed in this case; nor is there evidence that Brady was so gripped by fear of the death penalty or hope of leniency that he did not or could not, with the help of counsel, rationally weigh the advantages of going to trial against the advantages of pleading guilty. Brady's claim is of a different sort: that it violates the Fifth Amendment to influence or encourage a guilty plea by opportunity or promise of leniency and that a guilty plea is coerced and invalid if influenced by the fear of a possibly higher penalty for the crime charged if a conviction is obtained after the State is put to its proof.

Insofar as the voluntariness of his plea is concerned, there is little to differentiate Brady from (1) the defendant, in a jurisdiction where the judge and jury have the same range of sentencing power, who pleads guilty because his lawyer advises him that the judge will very probably be more lenient than the jury; (2) the defendant, in a jurisdiction where the judge alone has sentencing power, who is advised by counsel that the judge is normally more lenient with defendants who plead guilty than with those who go to trial; (3) the defendant who is permitted by prosecutor and judge to plead guilty to a lesser offense included in the offense charged; and (4) the defendant who pleads guilty to certain counts with the understanding that other charges will be dropped. In each of these situations,[8] as in Brady's case, the defendant might never plead guilty absent the possibility or certainty that the plea will result in a lesser penalty than the sentence that could be imposed after a trial and a verdict of guilty. We decline to hold, however, that a guilty plea is compelled and invalid under the Fifth Amendment whenever motivated by the defendant's desire to accept the certainty or probability of a lesser penalty rather than face a wider range of possibilities extending from acquittal to conviction and a higher penalty authorized by law for the crime charged.

The issue we deal with is inherent in the criminal law and its administration because guilty pleas are not constitutionally forbidden, because the criminal law characteristically extends to judge or jury a range

8. We here make no reference to the situation where the prosecutor or judge, or both, deliberately employ their charging and sentencing powers to induce a particular defendant to tender a plea of guilty. In Brady's case there is no claim that the prosecutor threatened prosecution on a charge not justified by the evidence or that the trial judge threatened Brady with a harsher sentence if convicted after trial in order to induce him to plead guilty.

of choice in setting the sentence in individual cases, and because both the State and the defendant often find it advantageous to preclude the possibility of the maximum penalty authorized by law. For a defendant who sees slight possibility of acquittal, the advantages of pleading guilty and limiting the probable penalty are obvious—his exposure is reduced, the correctional processes can begin immediately, and the practical burdens of a trial are eliminated. For the State there are also advantages—the more promptly imposed punishment after an admission of guilt may more effectively attain the objectives of punishment; and with the avoidance of trial, scarce judicial and prosecutorial resources are conserved for those cases in which there is a substantial issue of the defendant's guilt or in which there is substantial doubt that the State can sustain its burden of proof. It is this mutuality of advantage that perhaps explains the fact that at present well over three-fourths of the criminal convictions in this country rest on pleas of guilty, a great many of them no doubt motivated at least in part by the hope or assurance of a lesser penalty than might be imposed if there were a guilty verdict after a trial to judge or jury.

Of course, that the prevalence of guilty pleas is explainable does not necessarily validate those pleas or the system which produces them. But we cannot hold that it is unconstitutional for the State to extend a benefit to a defendant who in turn extends a substantial benefit to the State and who demonstrates by his plea that he is ready and willing to admit his crime and to enter the correctional system in a frame of mind that affords hope for success in rehabilitation over a shorter period of time than might otherwise be necessary.

A contrary holding would require the States and Federal Government to forbid guilty pleas altogether, to provide a single invariable penalty for each crime defined by the statutes, or to place the sentencing function in a separate authority having no knowledge of the manner in which the conviction in each case was obtained. In any event, it would be necessary to forbid prosecutors and judges to accept guilty pleas to selected counts, to lesser included offenses, or to reduced charges. The Fifth Amendment does not reach so far.

. . .

The standard as to the voluntariness of guilty pleas must be essentially that defined by Judge Tuttle of the Court of Appeals for the Fifth Circuit:

> [A] plea of guilty entered by one fully aware of the direct consequences, including the actual value of any commitments made to him by the court, prosecutor, or his own counsel, must stand unless induced by threats (or promises to discontinue improper harassment), misrepresentation (including unfulfilled or unfulfillable promises), or perhaps by promises that are by their nature improper as having no proper relationship to the prosecutor's business (e.g. bribes). 242 F.2d at page 115.[9]

9. Shelton v. United States, 246 F.2d 271, 572 n.2 (C.A. 5th Cir.1957). . . .

Under this standard, a plea of guilty is not invalid merely because entered to avoid the possibility of a death penalty.

III

The record before us also supports the conclusion that Brady's plea was intelligently made. He was advised by competent counsel, he was made aware of the nature of the charge against him, and there was nothing to indicate that he was incompetent or otherwise not in control of his mental faculties; once his confederate had pleaded guilty and became available to testify, he chose to plead guilty, perhaps to ensure that he would face no more than life imprisonment or a term of years. Brady was aware of precisely what he was doing when he admitted that he had kidnaped the victim and had not released her unharmed.

It is true that Brady's counsel advised him that § 1201(a) empowered the jury to impose the death penalty and that nine years later in United States v. Jackson, supra, the Court held that the jury had no such power as long as the judge could impose only a lesser penalty if trial was to the court or there was a plea of guilty. But these facts do not require us to set aside Brady's conviction.

Often the decision to plead guilty is heavily influenced by the defendant's appraisal of the prosecution's case against him and by the apparent likelihood of securing leniency should a guilty plea be offered and accepted. Considerations like these frequently present imponderable questions for which there are no certain answers; judgments may be made that in the light of later events seem improvident, although they were perfectly sensible at the time. The rule that a plea must be intelligently made to be valid does not require that a plea be vulnerable to later attack if the defendant did not correctly assess every relevant factor entering into his decision. A defendant is not entitled to withdraw his plea merely because he discovers long after the plea has been accepted that his calculus misapprehended the quality of the State's case or the likely penalties attached to alternative courses of action. More particularly, absent misrepresentation or other impermissible conduct by state agents . . . a voluntary plea of guilty intelligently made in the light of the then applicable law does not become vulnerable because later judicial decisions indicate that the plea rested on a faulty premise. A plea of guilty triggered by the expectations of a competently counseled defendant that the State will have a strong case against him is not subject to later attack because the defendant's lawyer correctly advised him with respect to the then existing law as to possible penalties but later pronouncements of the courts, as in this case, hold that the maximum penalty for the crime in question was less than was reasonably assumed at the time the plea was entered.

The fact that Brady did not anticipate United States v. Jackson, supra, does not impugn the truth or reliability of his plea. We find no requirement in the Constitution that a defendant must be permitted to disown his solemn admissions in open court that he committed the act with which he is charged simply because it later develops that the State would have had a weaker case than the defendant had thought or that the maximum penalty then assumed applicable has been held inapplicable in subsequent judicial decisions.

This is not to say that guilty plea convictions hold no hazards for the innocent or that the methods of taking guilty pleas presently employed in this country are necessarily valid in all respects. This mode of conviction is no more foolproof than full trials to the court or to the jury. Accordingly, we take great precautions against unsound results, and we should continue to do so, whether conviction is by plea or by trial. We would have serious doubts about this case if the encouragement of guilty pleas by offers of leniency substantially increased the likelihood that defendants, advised by competent counsel, would falsely condemn themselves. But our view is to the contrary and is based on our expectations that courts will satisfy themselves that pleas of guilty are voluntarily and intelligently made by competent defendants with adequate advice of counsel and that there is nothing to question the accuracy and reliability of the defendants' admissions that they committed the crimes with which they are charged. In the case before us, nothing in the record impeaches Brady's plea or suggests that his admissions in open court were anything but the truth.

Although Brady's plea of guilty may well have been motivated in part by a desire to avoid a possible death penalty, we are convinced that his plea was voluntarily and intelligently made and we have no reason to doubt that his solemn admission of guilt was truthful.

. . .[10]

366.

The disposition of criminal charges by agreement between the prosecutor and the accused, sometimes loosely called "plea bargaining," is an essential component of the administration of justice. Properly administered, it is to be encouraged. If every criminal charge were subjected to a full-scale trial, the States and the Federal Government would need to multiply by many times the number of judges and court facilities.

Disposition of charges after plea discussions is not only an essential part of the process but a highly desirable part for many reasons. It leads to prompt and largely final disposition of most criminal cases; it avoids much of the corrosive impact of enforced idleness during pre-trial confinement for those who are denied release pending trial; it protects the public from those accused persons who are prone to continue criminal conduct even while on pre-trial release; and by shortening the time between charges and disposition, it enhances

[10] Justice Black noted his concurrence in the judgment and "substantially all" of the Court's opinion. Justice Brennan wrote an opinion concurring in the result, which Justice Douglas and Justice Marshall joined.

> whatever may be the rehabilitative prospects of the guilty when they are ultimately imprisoned.

Santobello v. New York, 404 U.S. 257, 261 (1971). See also Blackledge v. Allison, 431 U.S. 63, 76 (1977).

367. Bordenkircher v. Hayes, 434 U.S. 357 (1978) (5–4). The defendant was indicted on a charge of uttering a forged instrument for $88.30, an offense punishable by imprisonment for two to ten years. After he was arraigned, he and defense counsel met with the prosecutor to discuss a guilty plea. The prosecutor offered to recommend a sentence of five years' imprisonment if the defendant pleaded guilty. If the defendant did not accept the offer, the prosecutor said, he would seek to indict the defendant as a habitual criminal, which would subject him to a mandatory sentence of life imprisonment. The defendant did not plead guilty, was indicted and convicted as a habitual criminal and sentenced. On habeas corpus, the Court upheld the conviction. "As a practical matter," it said, "this case would be no different if the grand jury had indicted Hayes as a recidivist from the outset, and the prosecutor had offered to drop that charge as part of the plea bargain." Id. at 360–61. "[T]he course of conduct engaged in by the prosecutor in this case, which no more than openly presented the defendant with the unpleasant alternatives of foregoing trial or facing charges on which he was plainly subject to prosecution, did not violate the Due Process Clause of the Fourteenth Amendment." Id. at 363–65.

In Corbitt v. New Jersey, 439 U.S. 212 (1978) (6–3), the Court upheld a state statute against the claim that it was invalid for the same reasons that were applied to the federal statute in United States v. Jackson, 390 U.S. 570 (1968), discussed in the *Brady* opinion, pp. 718–19 above. The New Jersey statute provided that the mandatory sentence for a defendant convicted at a jury trial (non-jury trials not being permitted in murder cases) of first-degree murder is life imprisonment. A defendant who pleaded *non vult* or *nolo contendere* (a simple guilty plea not being permitted) in a murder case could be sentenced to life imprisonment or a term of up to 30 years. The Court distinguished *Jackson* on the grounds that (1) here the death penalty was not involved, and (2) here, unlike *Jackson*, a defendant could not wholly avoid the possibility of the more serious sentence (life imprisonment) by a plea. It observed that "not every burden on the exercise of a constitutional right, and not every pressure or encouragement to waive such a right, is invalid." 439 U.S. at 218. The Court said that the case of the defendant in *Corbitt*, who went to trial and was convicted, could not be distinguished constitutionally from that of the defendant in Bordenkircher v. Hayes. "The States and the Federal Government are free to abolish guilty pleas and plea bargaining; but absent such action, as the Constitution has been construed in our cases, it is not forbidden to extend a proper degree of leniency in return for guilty pleas." Id. at 223.

Bordenkircher v. Hayes was followed in United States v. Goodwin, 457 U.S. 368 (1982) (7–2). The Court rejected the defendant's claim that his indictment on a felony charge following his rejection of a guilty plea and demand for a jury trial on misdemeanor charges was invalid on the ground of prosecutorial vindictiveness. The Court distinguished pretrial situations of this kind from cases in which the prosecutor's allegedly vindictive action occurs after trial. See note 596, p. 1141 below.

In Re Ibarra

34 Cal.3d 277, 666 P.2d 980 (1983)

■ BROUSSARD, JUSTICE.

Petitioner seeks a writ of habeas corpus after conviction upon a plea of guilty of robbery (Pen.Code, § 211) while armed (Pen.Code, § 12022, subd. (a)), and assault with a deadly weapon (Pen.Code, § 245, subd. (a)). Petitioner's plea was entered pursuant to a "package-deal" plea bargain in which his two codefendants also pled guilty. He was sentenced in accordance with the bargain to a three-year term for the robbery, a one-year armed enhancement and a consecutive term of one year for assault with a deadly weapon.

Petitioner raises three basic contentions. First, he claims that he was denied effective assistance of counsel because his attorney urged him to accept a coercive plea bargain. Second, he argues that his plea was involuntary because he had not been properly advised of his rights. Finally, he maintains that his plea bargain was per se invalid because a "package-deal" arrangement is inherently coercive.

We have rejected the ineffective assistance of counsel claim because counsel's decision was a tactical one which might be made by competent counsel. We have also decided that, under normal circumstances, the trial court may properly rely on a validly executed waiver form in determining the voluntariness of a guilty plea. Nevertheless, when a defendant pleads guilty pursuant to a "package-deal" arrangement, the trial court has a duty to conduct further inquiry into the voluntariness of the plea: although such a bargain is not per se coercive, it may be so under a totality of the circumstances. Because petitioner has not alleged sufficient facts to support a showing of coercion, however, we are required to deny the petition for writ of habeas corpus without prejudice to his filing a new petition alleging sufficient facts in accordance with this opinion.

Two armed gunmen robbed a store in Downey. Police obtained a description of the getaway car, and began pursuit. The front-seat passenger of the car leaned out of the window and began shooting at the police. An officer observed the petitioner grabbing the assailant's belt buckle. Eventually, the car pulled over. Petitioner's two codefendants, the driver and frontseat passenger, were later identified by witnesses as the armed robbers.

Petitioner claims that, contrary to his plea, he is not guilty of any offense. He instead alleges that he had been intoxicated and asleep in the back seat of the car. To support his allegation, he cites the testimony of an investigative officer at the preliminary hearing that petitioner had been intoxicated and smelled of alcohol at the time of arrest. The officer also testified that an empty rum bottle was found in the back seat of the car. The sole set of fingerprints found on the bottle belonged to petitioner.

In explaining his guilty plea, petitioner sets out the following sequence of occurrences: He met with his appointed counsel about 15 minutes before his court appearance. Counsel advised him of a proffered plea bargain for a five-year term; however, the bargain was only available if all three defendants were to plead guilty. Counsel informed petitioner that he had filed motions to set aside the information, for severance and for discovery, but urged petitioner to accept the plea bargain, as a jury might nevertheless find him guilty. Counsel also warned petitioner that if the bargain was refused, it would be withdrawn as to his codefendants, who would likely be found guilty and face severe sentences. Counsel then asked petitioner to initial a printed waiver form, which enunciated certain constitutional rights, in order to save the court time in taking his plea. Petitioner complied.

The record of the plea proceeding does not reflect any of these allegations; however, it does show that the judge questioned petitioner as to whether he had read the form, understood his rights and discussed them with counsel. Petitioner replied affirmatively. He now claims that he had not read the form, nor discussed its contents with his attorney, but had responded affirmatively because he felt it was required and expected of him.

At sentencing, petitioner was not advised of his limited appeal rights. He alleges that he did not become aware of these rights until after time for appeal had expired. He nevertheless sent a "Notice of Appeal" to the Los Angeles County Superior Court, which was received but not filed. Petitioner then filed a petition for writ of habeas corpus with the Court of Appeal.

The Court of Appeal sent the Attorney General an ex parte communication requesting a response to the petition for habeas corpus. After receiving the response, but before petitioner could file a traverse, the Court of Appeal denied the petition. Petitioner then petitioned this court for a hearing, which we granted, and issued an order to show cause.

. . .

[The Court's discussion of the defendant's first two contentions, (1) that counsel's urging him to accept a "package-deal" plea bargain was per se ineffective assistance of counsel and (2) that he was not properly advised of his rights, is omitted.]

III. *A "package-deal" plea bargain is not coercive per se; nevertheless, the court must be persuaded that the plea is given voluntarily under the totality of the circumstances before accepting a guilty plea pursuant to such a bargain.*

Petitioner urges us to adopt a rule invalidating the so-called "package-deal" plea bargain in which the prosecutor offers a defendant the opportunity to plead guilty to a lesser charge, and receive a lesser sentence, contingent upon a guilty plea by *all* codefendants. We decline to do so, but instead hold that such bargains, while not per se coercive, may nevertheless be so upon an examination of the totality of the circumstances. Therefore . . . the trial court must determine whether the plea is being entered into pursuant to a package deal bargain, and, if so, conduct an inquiry into possible coercive forces prior to accepting the guilty plea.

. . .

Single plea bargains, as opposed to "package-deal" ones, although containing some elements of coercion, have nevertheless been upheld as proper. . . . In the normal bargain, a defendant must choose between pleading guilty and receiving a lesser sentence, or taking his chances at a trial (in which he may be convicted and receive a greater sentence). The prosecutor seeks to avoid the time and expense of trial. These are proper considerations by both parties that do not amount to such coercion as to unduly force a defendant to plead guilty. . . .

"Package-deal" plea bargains, however, may approach the line of unreasonableness. Extraneous factors not related to the case or the prosecutor's business may be brought into play. For example, a defendant may fear that his wife will be prosecuted and convicted if he does not plead guilty; or, a defendant may fear, as alleged in this case, that his codefendant will attack him if he does not plead guilty. Because such considerations do not bear any direct relation to whether the defendant himself is guilty, special scrutiny must be employed to ensure a voluntary plea. . . .

As we point out below, certain factors may appear to render a plea pursuant to a "package-deal" bargain coercive, or not coercive, upon close examination. Because we believe that it is possible for such a plea to be entered without undue force, we choose not to invalidate all "package-deal" bargains as coercive per se. Rather, the trial court assumes a duty to conduct an inquiry into the *totality of the circumstances* to determine whether, in fact, a plea has been unduly coerced, or is instead freely and voluntarily given.

The totality of the circumstances test in examining the voluntariness of a guilty plea pursuant to a "package-deal" bargain appears to be the prevailing view. . . . In those jurisdictions, special care is taken to determine the voluntariness of the plea. . . . We go one step further, however, by *requiring* an inquiry into the totality of the circumstances whenever a plea is taken pursuant to a "package-deal" bargain. We are satisfied that this requirement will suffice to discover any unduly coercive forces which might render such a plea involuntary.

Various factors must be considered at the inquiry. First, the court must determine whether the inducement for the plea is proper. The court should be satisfied that the prosecution has not misrepresented facts to the defendant, and that the substance of the inducement is within the proper scope of the prosecutor's business.[11] . . . The prosecutor must also have a reasonable and good faith case against the third parties to whom leniency is promised. . . .

Second, the factual basis for the guilty plea must be considered. If the guilty plea is not supported by the evidence, it is less likely that the plea was the product of the accused's free will. The same would be true if the "bargained-for" sentence were disproportionate to the accused's culpability.

Third, the nature and degree of coerciveness should be carefully examined. Psychological pressures sufficient to indicate an involuntary plea might be present if the third party promised leniency is a close friend or family member whom the defendant feels compelled to help. . . . If the defendant bears no special relationship to the third party promised leniency, he may nevertheless feel compelled to plead guilty due to physical threat. For example, if the third party had made a specific threat against defendant if he refused to plead guilty, the plea is likely to be involuntary. On the other hand, if the defendant merely thought, as in the case at bar, that his codefendant would attack him if he did not plead guilty, sufficient coercive factors may not be at play.

Fourth, a plea is not coerced if the promise of leniency to a third party was an insignificant consideration by a defendant in his choice to plead guilty. For example, if the motivating factor to plead guilty was the realization of the likelihood of conviction at trial, the defendant cannot be said to have been "forced" into pleading guilty, unless the coercive factors present had nevertheless remained a *substantial factor* in his decision. . . .

Our list is by no means exhaustive. Other factors which may be relevant can and should be taken into account at the inquiry. For example, the age of the defendant . . . whether defendant or the prosecutor had initiated the plea negotiations . . . and whether charges have already been pressed against a third party . . . might be important considerations.

. . .

The petition for habeas corpus is denied without prejudice to petitioner filing a new petition in the superior court alleging sufficient facts to establish that his plea to the charges of robbery and assault with a deadly weapon was involuntary.

. . .

---

11. We recognize that the "package-deal" may be a *valuable tool* to the prosecutor, who has a need for *all* defendants, or none, to plead guilty. The prosecutor may be properly interested in avoiding the time, delay and expense of trial of all the defendants. He is also placed in a difficult position should one defendant plead and another go to trial, because the defendant who pleads may become an adverse witness on behalf of his codefendant, free of jeopardy. Thus, the prosecutor's motivation for proposing a "package-deal" bargain may be strictly legitimate and free of extrinsic forces.

368. *Ibarra* was approved in State v. Solano, 724 P.2d 17 (Ariz.1986). See also United States v. Carr, 80 F.3d 413 (10th Cir.1996) (package plea bargain upheld); United States v. Gonzalez, 918 F.2d 1129 (3d Cir.1990) (prosecutor's insistence on package-deal and refusal to accept individual defendant's plea not improper). Compare United States v. Washington, 969 F.2d 1073 (D.C.Cir.1992), holding that it was an abuse of discretion for the trial judge to refuse to accept a guilty plea because the defendant refused to incriminate his codefendant.

In Cortez v. United States, 337 F.2d 699 (9th Cir.1964), the defendant and his wife were indicted on narcotics charges, the penalty for which was a minimum sentence of five years with no probation and a maximum sentence of 20 years. He pleaded guilty. His wife, who was seven months pregnant, pleaded guilty to a lesser charge and was sentenced to the minimum term of two years' imprisonment. On a motion to vacate the conviction under 28 U.S.C. § 2255, the defendant claimed that he pleaded guilty in exchange for his wife's being allowed to plead to the lesser charge, as part of a deal between the prosecutor and his lawyer. Upholding the conviction, the court observed that other factors might have led the defendant to plead guilty, including the strength of the government's case and the possibility of having a more lenient judge for sentencing. The court said:

> No competent lawyer, discussing a possible guilty plea with a client, could fail to canvass these possible alternatives with him. Nor would he fail to ascertain the willingness of the prosecutor to "go along." Moreover, if a co-defendant is involved, and if the client is anxious to help that co-defendant, a competent lawyer would be derelict in his duty if he did not assist in that regard. At the same time, the lawyer is bound to advise his client fully as to his rights, as to the alternatives available to him, and of the fact that neither the lawyer nor the prosecutor nor anyone else can bargain for the court. There is nothing wrong, however, with a lawyer's giving his client the benefit of his judgment as to what the court is likely to do, always making it clear that he is giving advice, not making a promise.

Id. at 701.

369. The Fifth Amendment's Due Process Clause and the Sixth Amendment's right to a jury trial do not require a prosecutor to disclose impeachment evidence regarding its witnesses or evidence relating to a potential affirmative defense before entering a binding plea agreement with the defendant. United States v. Ruiz, 536 U.S. 622 (2002).

370. The defendant was indicted for robbery and other crimes committed against Rodriguez. After the prosecutor had announced the case ready for trial, Rodriguez died. Four days after the prosecutor learned of Rodriguez's death, plea negotiations were completed and the defendant entered a plea of guilty. The prosecutor did not tell the defendant or his counsel that Rodriguez, the principal prosecution witness, had died. The Court of Appeals held that, at least in the absence of an assertion of innocence by the defendant, due process did not require disclosure before the plea of guilty was entered. People v. Jones, 375 N.E.2d 41 (N.Y.1978).

Would you, as prosecutor, have disclosed the death of the witness?

See also Fambo v. Smith, 433 F.Supp. 590 (W.D.N.Y.), aff'd, 565 F.2d 233 (2d Cir.1977), in which the district attorney did not disclose conclusive evidence that the defendant was not guilty of the crime charged in the second of two counts of the indictment. He was, however, guilty of the same crime, on another date, as charged in the first count. (The two counts charged possession of dynamite on different dates. Before the later date, police officers had discovered the tube containing the dynamite, replaced the dynamite with sawdust, and put the tube back where it had been found. The defendant recovered the tube filled with sawdust, possession of which was the subject of the second count.) The defendant pleaded guilty to a lesser included offense on the second count and the first count was dismissed. Should the plea be vacated?

How much difference does it make that evidence undisclosed before a plea bargain bears directly on the defendant's actual guilt, as in *Fambo*, rather than the likelihood of his being convicted, as in *Jones*?

371.

On June 3, 1978, appellant William L. Campbell, III, used his key to enter the apartment of his former wife, Sheila Campbell. Campbell had been living in the apartment with Sheila and their children until about two weeks earlier. In his statement to the police, Campbell said that he went to the apartment to remove some of his personal property, including a .22 caliber automatic pistol and approximately 300 rounds of ammunition. He alleges that he was drunk and fell asleep at the kitchen table after placing the gun and ammunition on a divider between the table and the apartment's front door. Sometime after midnight Sheila Campbell, their children, and a male companion entered the apartment. Campbell told the police that he asked the man who he was, and the man replied, "Franket." Campbell further stated that several months earlier a friend had warned him that Ronald Franket had a gun and was "looking for him." Campbell claimed that although he saw no gun, he saw Franket reach into his pocket, and Campbell, therefore, shot Ronald Franket five times. He also shot Sheila Campbell three times. Both died.

Campbell turned himself in the following day and was subsequently indicted by a Columbiana County, Ohio grand jury on two counts of aggravated murder with specifications and one count of aggravated burglary. The specifications alleged that Campbell committed each murder as a part of the killing of two or more persons and that each was committed during the course of an aggravated burglary. Under Ohio law, Campbell could have received the death penalty if convicted of aggravated murder and at least one of the specifications. . . . If convicted of aggravated murder but neither of the specifications, Campbell's maximum possible sentence was life imprisonment for each count. . . . The aggravated burglary count carried a possible sentence of 4 to 25 years. . . .

As a part of Campbell's plea bargain, the prosecutor moved both to strike the specifications from the aggravated murder portion of the indictment and to enter a nolle prosequi as to the aggravated burglary charge. In return, Campbell entered a plea of guilty to the two aggravated murder counts.

Before his plea hearing, Campbell was given a document entitled "Judicial Advice to Defendant." That document contained a discussion of each of the constitutional rights Campbell would waive by pleading guilty, the elements of the crime to which he intended to plead, and the maximum penalties he could receive. Campbell completed a written "Defendant's Response to Court" indicating that he had read and understood the information in the "Judicial Advice to Defendant." In his "Response" he also answered specific questions to establish that his guilty plea was knowing, intelligent, and voluntary. At the plea hearing the state court judge determined that Campbell had read and understood these documents. He also questioned Campbell as to his knowledge of the consequences of his guilty plea and discussed some of the rights Campbell was waiving. The court did not specifically inform Campbell in court that the plea would waive his right to be free from self-incrimination, his right of confrontation, and his right to compulsory process, although a discussion of the waiver of each of these rights was included in the "Judicial Advice to Defendant." When asked by the court why he shot Ronald Franket and Sheila Campbell, Campbell replied, "Because he was with my wife," and "Because she was with him." The court accepted Campbell's guilty plea and sentenced him to two consecutive life sentences.

Before Campbell decided to plead guilty, his counsel made a specific written request for discovery from the prosecution. He requested any evidence material to Campbell's guilt or punishment as well as a list of the tangible objects which the prosecution intended to use at trial. Campbell subsequently learned that the police had found a .25 caliber semi-automatic pistol on Franket's body and had taken that gun into their possession. The palm-sized weapon was found in the left, rear, hip pocket of Franket's pants. Although they were aware of the gun's existence and had the gun in their possession, the prosecution did not disclose the gun to Campbell or his counsel.

Campbell v. Marshall, 769 F.2d 314, 315–16 (6th Cir.1985).

Campbell subsequently claimed "that he pleaded guilty only because he had no believable self-defense claim and that he would have gone to a jury with that defense had he known of the gun." Id. at 317. If Campbell's lawyer had not made the discovery request, should the prosecutor have disclosed that the gun had been found on Franket's body before Campbell pleaded guilty? Was the prosecutor obligated to do so? In view of Campbell's statements to the court at the plea hearing, should his conviction on the plea of guilty be vacated because the request for discovery was not met?

(Ordinarily, failure to disclose exculpatory material at trial may be a denial of due process. See pp. 943–52 below.)

See White v. United States, 858 F.2d 416 (8th Cir.1988).

372. Defendants Smith and Jones have been indicted jointly in a three-count indictment, as follows:

FIRST COUNT: On or about December 10, 2003, within the State of Ames, Sam Smith and John Jones feloniously did take, use, operate and remove, one certain automobile, property of Theodore Todd, and in the custody of Adam Angle, from a certain street, and did operate and drive said automobile, for their own profit, use, and purpose, without the consent of Theodore Todd, the owner of said automobile, and without the consent of Adam Angle.

SECOND COUNT: On or about December 10, 2003, within the State of Ames, Sam Smith and John Jones entered the yard of L & L, Inc., a body corporate, with intent to steal property of another.

THIRD COUNT: On or about December 10, 2003, within the State of Ames, Sam Smith and John Jones stole property of L & L, Inc., a body corporate, of the value of about $100.00, consisting of one battery of the value of $100.00.

As the prosecuting attorney assigned to the case, you have investigated it, with the following results:

Theodore Todd will testify that he left his car at Queen's Garage for repairs on the afternoon of December 10. He was notified at 10:30 p.m. that night that his car had been stolen and was recovered by the police. He does not know defendants Smith and Jones. There was no damage to his car.

Adam Angle will testify that he is employed as a mechanic at Queen's Garage. He was there when Todd brought his car in for repairs on December 10. The car was parked in the street beside the garage when Angle left work at 9:00 p.m. He learned that it had been stolen the next morning. He does not know the defendants Smith and Jones.

Mack Matthews, the manager of L & L, Inc., will testify that L & L is an automobile sales agency. He was notified by the police at about 10:00 p.m. on December 10 that the defendants Smith and Jones had been arrested on L & L's used car lot. He was told that they had stolen a battery which was recovered and which he later valued at $100.00. He does not know the defendants.

Private Earl Ernest, a member of the municipal police force, will testify that he and a companion officer were staked out at the L & L used car lot on the night of December 10, 1993, because there had been reports of thefts. The lot is open and separated from the sidewalk only by a low chain. At about 9:50 p.m., he and his companion observed a car, subsequently identified as belonging to Todd, pull into the lot. A man, who proved to be Jones, got out and went to a car parked in the lot. Ernest saw him remove a battery from under the hood of the parked car and return with it to Todd's car which Jones had been driving. As Jones was passing the battery to someone seated on the passenger side of the front seat, Ernest emerged from his cover and arrested Jones. A man, later identified as Smith, came out of the car and Ernest arrested him. Before he was arrested, Jones threw a wrench under the car he was driving. Ernest's companion officer will testify to the same effect if needed.

Jones has a lengthy criminal record, including many detentions for investigation and arrests for "drunks" and "disorderlies." He has been arrested but not prosecuted for robbery and grand larceny. He has six convictions for petit larceny, one for assault, one for soliciting prostitution, and one for a narcotics offense. He is 51 years old.

Smith is 29. When he was 21, he was detained for investigation and released without charge. When he was 22, he was arrested for disorderly conduct and elected to forfeit $25.

Smith's lawyer has discussed the case with you. She has informed you that Smith's defense will be that he and Jones were near Queen's Garage on December 10, and Smith decided to visit his wife, from whom he was estranged. Since he was a friend of Angle, he and Jones went to Queen's Garage, and Smith asked Angle to let them use Todd's car, which was parked on the street. Angle agreed. Smith could not drive and asked Jones to drive. En route to Smith's wife's apartment, Jones said he had to pick up a battery to give a friend a "hot shot" for a stalled car. Smith had been drinking a bit and didn't question Jones; he thought Jones worked at L & L. He wasn't suspicious at the time and could give no explanation for not telling the police this story at the time of his arrest.

Jones is a tough-looking man who has not been released on bail and will not make a good impression on the witness stand. Smith has been released, holds a steady job, and will make a good impression; he and his wife have been reunited since his indictment.

Petit larceny (third count) carries a maximum sentence of imprisonment for one year.

Unauthorized use of a vehicle (first count) carries a maximum sentence of imprisonment for five years.

Housebreaking (second count) carries a maximum sentence of imprisonment for 15 years.

One hour before the trial is to begin, Jones's lawyer comes to your office and offers to have his client plead guilty to the third count of the indictment if you will dismiss the others. Your witnesses have been summoned to court and are waiting in the witness room.

What should you do?

Assume that you reject the offer. Jones's lawyer then offers to have his client plead guilty to the first count of the indictment if you will dismiss the others.

What should you do?

Assume that you have reason to believe that Angle was lying when he talked to you and that Smith's account of how he and Jones got the car is true.

Assume that Angle will (will not) support Smith's story on the witness stand.

373. United States ex rel. Elksnis v. Gilligan, 256 F.Supp. 244 (S.D.N.Y.1966). The defendant was indicted for second-degree murder, punishable by an indeterminate sentence of imprisonment for not less than 20 years to life. He pleaded guilty to first-degree manslaughter, the maximum penalty for which was imprisonment for 20 years, on the sentencing judge's promise to him and his counsel that the sentence would be not more than ten years' imprisonment. He was sentenced and imprisoned. He subsequently sought his release on habeas corpus on the ground that his conviction on the plea of guilty denied him due process of law.

> A crucial question here is the impact, if any, of the judge's promise upon the defendant. The fact that the promise may not have been deliberately designed or intended to influence or to induce the defendant to plead guilty is not material—the question is did it have that impact.
>
> . . .
>
> The unequal positions of the judge and the accused, one with the power to commit to prison and the other deeply concerned to avoid prison, at once raise a question of fundamental fairness. When a judge becomes a participant in plea bargaining he brings to bear the full force and majesty of his office. His awesome power to impose a substantially longer or even maximum sentence in excess of that proposed is present whether referred to or not. A defendant needs no reminder that if he rejects the proposal, stands upon his right to trial and is convicted, he faces a significantly longer sentence. One facing a prison term, whether of longer or shorter duration, is easily influenced to accept what appears the more preferable choice. Intentionally or otherwise, and no matter how well motivated the judge may be, the accused is subjected to a subtle but powerful influence. A guilty plea predicated upon a judge's promise of a definite sentence by its very nature does not qualify as a free and voluntary act. The plea is so interlaced with the promise that the one cannot be separated from the other; remove the promise and the basis for the plea falls.
>
> A judge's prime responsibility is to maintain the integrity of the judicial system; to see that due process of law, equal protection of the laws and the basic safeguards of a fair trial are upheld. The judge stands as the symbol of evenhanded justice, and none can seriously question that if this central figure in the administration of justice promises an accused that upon a plea of guilty a fixed sentence will follow, his commitment has an all-pervasive and compelling influence in inducing the accused to yield his right to trial. A plea entered upon a

> bargain agreement between a judge and an accused cannot be squared with due process requirements of the Fourteenth Amendment.
>
> . . .
>
> Finally, a bargain agreement between a judge and a defendant, however free from any calculated purpose to induce a plea, has no place in a system of justice. It impairs the judge's objectivity in passing upon the voluntariness of the plea when offered. As a party to the arrangement upon which the plea is based, he is hardly in a position to discharge his function of deciding the validity of the plea—a function not satisfied by routine inquiry, but only, as the Supreme Court has stressed, by "a penetrating and comprehensive examination of all the circumstances under which such a plea is tendered."[12]

Id. at 253–55.

"The line may well be a fine one between a trial judge 'participating' in the plea bargaining process and a judge merely 'ratifying' an agreement already reached between the accused and the prosecutor. But the likelihood that the judge will overawe the defendant or surrender his impartiality is at least sharply reduced if he does not play a role in the negotiations leading to the formation of a bargain." Scott v. United States, 419 F.2d 264, 275 (D.C.Cir.1969).

In United States v. Werker, 535 F.2d 198, 201 (2d Cir.1976), the court said that the provision of Rule 11(e)(1) that a judge shall not participate in plea negotiations means that "the sentencing judge should take no part whatever in any discussion or communication regarding the sentence to be imposed prior to the entry of a plea of guilty or conviction, or submission to him of a plea agreement." That prohibition applies to the disclosure by a judge of the sentence that he would impose were a plea of guilty entered. The court said:

> It is immaterial whether we consider pre-plea disclosure of sentence to be per se coercive . . . or only one factor to be considered in determining voluntariness. . . . Rule 11 is obviously intended totally to eliminate pressures emanating from judicial involvement in the plea bargaining process, and this necessarily includes any involvement of the court in divulging pre-plea sentence proposals which are equally likely to generate such pressures.
>
> Rule 11 implicitly recognizes that participation in the plea bargaining process depreciates the image of the trial judge that is necessary to public confidence in the impartial and objective administration of criminal justice. As a result of his participation, the judge is no longer a judicial officer or a neutral arbiter. Rather, he becomes or seems to become an advocate for the resolution he has suggested to the defendant.
>
> It would be naive to believe that disclosure of a sentence prior to entry of the plea merely supplies the parties with additional informa-

12. Von Moltke v. Gillies, 332 U.S. 708, 724 . . . (1948).

> tion and therefore does not alter the status of the trial judge. The judge's promise to indicate a specific sentence soon becomes the focal point of further discussions. His assurances to the defendant are the ultimate inducement to the plea. . . . The judge's determination is not simply one more fact to be considered by the defendant in deciding upon a course of action. The defendant, as in this case, is unlikely to approach the judge until the parties have exhausted their own abilities to compromise. Thus, the judge's response to the inquiry becomes the essential element in the ensuing discussions. Consequently, the judge's indication of sentence necessarily constitutes "participat(ion) in such discussions."
>
> Furthermore, the indication of sentence inevitably invites alterations and clarifications of the proposed sentence through direct negotiations with the judge. A defense counsel who obtains assurance, initially based solely on the presentence report, of a maximum sentence on charges similar to those involved in this case would probably next inquire if the judge would modify the sentence still further should the defendant cooperate with government, or if the judge would accept a plea to a lesser offense. Once the judge enters the plea process by announcing a proposed sentence, it becomes impossible not to indicate a response to additional relevant inquiries. Rule 11(e)(1) was designed to avert this very situation. The Rule is based on the sound principle that the interests of justice are best served if the judge remains aloof from all discussions preliminary to the determination of guilt or innocence so that his impartiality and objectivity shall not be open to any question or suspicion when it becomes his duty to impose sentence.

Id. at 203. See United States v. Casallas, 59 F.3d 1173 (11th Cir.1995) (judge's effort to be sure that defendant's decision not to plead guilty was well informed crossed line into participation in plea negotiations and invalidated plea); Frank v. Blackburn, note 375 below.

374. If a defendant pleads guilty in reliance on an explicit statement of the court that he cannot or will not be given more than a specific sentence and the defendant is subsequently given a more severe sentence, the plea of guilty is subject to attack. Smith v. United States, 321 F.2d 954 (9th Cir.1963). "Quite apart from any question of inducement, if a court informs a defendant prior to accepting his plea that five years is the maximum sentence, we think this must in fact be the maximum." Workman v. United States, 337 F.2d 226, 227 (1st Cir.1964). See United States v. Amaya, 111 F.3d 386 (5th Cir.1997) (plea in reliance on judge's commitment to ensure that prosecutor moved for downward sentencing departure, which judge was unable to do; conviction vacated).

375. "[I]t has always been the rule in both the federal and state systems that leniency is always extended on pleas of guilty that is not extended when defendants go to trial. . . ." United States ex rel. Starner v. Russell, 378 F.2d 808, 811–12 (3d Cir.1967).

If it is proper for a trial judge to let it be known that he gives consideration to the fact that a defendant pleads guilty, is it proper for him also to let it be known that he is less likely to be lenient toward a defendant who does not plead guilty? Is there a difference between the two propositions?

Consider Frank v. Blackburn, 646 F.2d 873 (5th Cir.1980), modified, 646 F.2d 902 (1981):

> We agree wholeheartedly . . . that a defendant cannot be punished *simply* for exercising his constitutional right to stand trial. . . . We do not agree, however, that the mere imposition of a longer sentence than the defendant would have received had he pleaded guilty automatically constitutes such punishment. The Supreme Court's plea bargaining decisions make it clear that a state is free to encourage guilty pleas by offering substantial benefits to a defendant, or by threatening an accused with more severe punishment should a negotiated plea be refused. . . . It is equally clear that a defendant is free to accept or reject the "bargain" offered by the state. Once the bargain—whether it be reduced charges, a recommended sentence, or some other concession—is rejected, however, the defendant cannot complain that the denial of the rejected offer constitutes a punishment or is evidence of judicial vindictiveness. To accept such an argument is to ignore completely the underlying philosophy and purposes of the plea bargaining system. If a defendant can successfully demand the same leniency after standing trial that was offered to him prior to trial in exchange for a guilty plea, all the incentives to plea bargain disappear; the defendant has nothing to lose by going to trial.

Id. at 882–83. "Once the defendant elects to go to trial," the court said, "all bets are off." Id. at 887.

In United States v. Derrick, 519 F.2d 1 (6th Cir.1975), the court held that it was improper to increase a defendant's sentence because he had pleaded not guilty and gone to trial.

> In holding that it is improper for a trial judge to impose a heavier penalty because a defendant in a given case has availed himself of his constitutional right to a fair trial by jury, we simply reaffirm its availability to all citizens and, therefore, necessarily to the guilty as well as the innocent. . . .
>
> We do not doubt that in a given case, sentences for the same offense and otherwise same circumstances may differ where one follows a plea and another is after jury conviction. Realistically many factors come into play in the sentencing process. The most obvious factor is that in pleading guilty, a defendant owns up to what he has done. If it is true that confession is good for the soul, it must be acknowledged that a free and honest admission of guilt is perhaps the first and largest step toward ultimate rehabilitation. It is this concept, we suspect, which prompts most pleas of guilty in the first place. Certainly a trial judge is likely to take into account the difference in

> mental attitude between the defendant who admits his guilt and seeks to reform and the defendant who, although proved guilty beyond a reasonable doubt, gives no indication of his willingness to be rehabilitated.
>
> Another factor which we see as almost inevitably influencing the decision of a trial judge is that in a plea of guilty, the crime pleaded is understood only as related in somewhat sterile fashion through the plea taking process or through a printed narration in the presentence report. The sentencing following a trial upon the merits, on the other hand, sees the trial judge in possession not only of more of the detailed facts of the offense itself, but of the flavor of the event and the impact upon any victims. It is for that reason a more real and accurate appraisal of the circumstances which brought the defendant to the bar of justice, and almost inevitably this added knowledge will affect the judge's consideration of what penalty appears most appropriate. This can, of course, work to the benefit or the detriment of the defendant according to the degree of culpability shown by the proofs.
>
> We do not intend to imply such factors as those mentioned do not or should not influence the trial judge's decisions in sentencing. We simply hold that it is improper for a trial judge to impose a heavier sentence as a penalty for the exercise of the right of jury trial, or as an example to deter others from exercising the right. Such motives are objectionable because they are coercive and because they have little if any relevance to the proper objectives of sentencing.

Id. at 4–5.

If the practice of plea bargaining depends on the assumption that defendants have something to gain by bargaining—i.e., that defendants who plead guilty generally receive lighter sentences than defendants who are convicted after trial—would it be preferable to make this assumption explicit? If not, why not? If so, what form should the explicit statement take?

In view of the general assumption that a defendant who pleads guilty has a good chance to receive a lighter sentence than he would have received had he gone to trial, how realistic is it to assert, as in *Derrick*, above, that "in pleading guilty, a defendant owns up to what he has done"? Is making the best deal you can "perhaps the first and largest step toward ultimate rehabilitation," a view generally suggested in *Brady*, p. 717 above, as well? In *Derrick*, the court notes the difference between the "somewhat sterile" account of the defendant's crime if he pleads guilty, on one hand, and the more vivid presentation of the facts at a trial, on the other. Might one conclude that if there is any likelihood of "owning up" either way, it is *greater* if there is a trial?

376. "[W]hen a plea rests in any significant degree on a promise or agreement of the prosecutor, so that it can be said to be part of the inducement or consideration, such promise must be fulfilled." Santobello v. New York, 404 U.S. 257, 262 (1971). If such a promise is not fulfilled, it is immaterial whether the failure is deliberate or inadvertent. Id. See United States v. Benchimol, 471 U.S. 453 (1985) (prosecutor's "less-than-enthusiastic" recommendation to sentencing judge did not violate plea agreement), with which compare United States v. Grandinetti, 564 F.2d 723 (5th Cir.1977) (prosecutor's ineffective recommendation was not fulfillment of bargain).

In United States v. Randolph, 230 F.3d 243 (6th Cir.2000), the defendant entered a plea agreement with the United States attorney's office that he would not be subject to further prosecution. The court said that fundamental fairness required that prosecution by another United States attorney's office, on the basis of information that the defendant supplied pursuant to the plea agreement, be barred.

The defendant pleaded guilty pursuant to a plea agreement that his sentence would be 10–40 years' imprisonment, and was sentenced accordingly. Four days later, the prosecutor and trial judge sent a letter to the state parole board, as provided in state law, in which the prosecutor described the circumstances of the crime and the prosecutor and judge jointly recommended that the defendant serve the maximum time possible under the sentence. During the plea negotiations, the subject of parole had not been mentioned. The court of appeals held that the letter did not violate the plea agreement and that the plea of guilty and sentence were valid. United States ex rel. Robinson v. Israel, 603 F.2d 635 (7th Cir.1979).

A New York state policy of recognizing only plea agreements that are on the record of the plea proceeding is valid and an off-the-record undertaking of the prosecutor is not enforceable. Siegel v. New York, 691 F.2d 620 (2d Cir.1982). The court observed that the state policy increased the likelihood that pleas of guilty are accurate, "enhanced the integrity of the plea bargain process," and assured the finality of convictions.

A defendant is not entitled to enforcement of a prosecutor's offer of a proposed plea bargain, which the defendant accepted before it was withdrawn by the prosecutor. The defendant later pleaded guilty pursuant to a subsequent offer of the prosecutor that was harsher than the original offer. Since the defendant was fully informed of the nature of the bargain before he pleaded guilty, the plea was valid. Mabry v. Johnson, 467 U.S. 504 (1984).

377. "Mere prediction by counsel of the court's likely attitude on sentence, short of some implication of an agreement or understanding, is not ground for attacking a plea. . . . Nor, generally, is other advice, simply because it turns out poorly." Domenica v. United States, 292 F.2d 483, 485 (1st Cir.1961). See Knight v. United States, 611 F.2d 918 (1st Cir.1979) (*Domenica* followed). "[A] mere disappointed expectation of leniency, as opposed to an understanding with the trial judge, is not sufficient cause to vitiate a plea." United States ex rel. McGrath v. LaVallee, 319 F.2d 308, 314 (2d Cir.1963). To the same effect, see Harris v. United States, 434 F.2d 23 (9th Cir.1970).

Suppose the defendant's expectation is based on his *mis*understanding of the judge's statements to him, see Pilkington v. United States, 315 F.2d 204 (4th Cir.1963), or to his counsel, see United States v. Lias, 173 F.2d 685 (4th Cir.1949). Suppose his expectation is based on a *mis*understanding created by statements of the prosecutor, see United States v. Lester, 247 F.2d 496 (2d Cir.1957), or other government officials, see Aiken v. United States, 282 F.2d 215 (4th Cir.1960) (postal inspectors). Suppose it is based on the incorrect advice of counsel, see United States v. Unger, 665 F.2d 251 (8th Cir.1981) (plea induced by counsel's incorrect representation of fact about what sentence would be is involuntary). For an alternative argument in such cases, based on a claim of ineffective assistance of counsel, see, e.g., Downs-Morgan v. United States, 765 F.2d 1534 (11th Cir.1985). Suppose counsel's incorrect advice did not concern the sentence but some collateral consequence of conviction. See Michel v. United States, 507 F.2d 461 (2d Cir.1974) (counsel incorrectly advised defendant that he would not be subject to deportation; additional cases cited). In a case in which the defendant claims that he was unfairly surprised by his sentence, how much weight should be given to the fact that a defendant does not move to withdraw his plea of guilty promptly after sentence is imposed? See Georges v. United States, 262 F.2d 426, 431 (5th Cir.1959). In cases of this kind, how can the government avoid letting the defendant treat his plea of guilty as "a mere trial balloon to test the attitude of the trial judge," United States v. Weese, 145 F.2d 135, 136 (2d Cir.1944)?

378. The defendant was indicted for first-degree robbery. If convicted, he would have been sentenced as a multiple offender within a sentencing range of 15 to 60 years' imprisonment. At a pretrial conference in which the trial judge participated, the defendant agreed to plead guilty to second degree robbery, the sentencing range for which was 7½ to 30 years' imprisonment. At the conference the trial judge did not indicate what sentence he would impose, but observed that the defendant would be able to avoid the very heavy sentence on a conviction of first-degree robbery if he pleaded guilty to the lesser offense. The judge sentenced the defendant to 29 to 30 years' imprisonment. "Before imposing this punishment, the judge indicated he was influenced by the accused's unsavory criminal record . . . specifically detailed in a probation report very recently made available to him, but not completed and transmitted to him before he accepted the guilty plea. Indeed, the judge expressed regret, at the time of sentencing, that he had accepted the plea to the lesser offense and indicated that appellant's exceptionally bad record called for a prison term not materially below the statutory maximum." United States ex rel. McGrath v. LaVallee, 348 F.2d 373, 375 (2d Cir.1965).

Years after being sentenced, the defendant claimed that, having determined to impose the maximum sentence the judge should have allowed the defendant to reinstate his plea of not guilty. "Fundamental fairness is somehow lacking, we are told, when a trial judge discusses with a defendant and his counsel the acceptance of a proffered plea on the basis of certain necessarily incomplete information and then, in sentencing, takes into account new, allegedly erroneous information which becomes routinely available in assessing the punishment to be imposed." Id. at 378. What result? Why?

379. The prosecutor and defense counsel negotiated a bargain that the defendant would plead guilty to second-degree murder and testify against an accomplice in his trial for murder, and the charge of first-degree murder against the defendant would be dismissed. The trial judge refused to accept the plea because he believed that the defendant should be convicted of first-degree murder. The defendant pleaded guilty and was convicted of first-degree murder. On appeal the court reversed and remanded with directions that the plea of guilty to second-degree murder be accepted.

The court said that a trial judge was not required to accept a defendant's plea of guilty to an offense less than that charged but that his discretion was not unconstrained.

> First, the trial judge must provide a reasoned exercise of discretion in order to justify a departure from the course agreed on by the prosecution and defense. This is not a matter of absolute judicial prerogative. The authority has been granted to the judge to assure protection of the public interest, and this in turn involves one or more of the following components: (a) fairness to the defense, such as protection against harassment; (b) fairness to the prosecution interest, as in avoiding a disposition that does not serve due and legitimate prosecutorial interests; (c) protection of the sentencing authority reserved to the judge. The judge's statement or opinion must identify the particular interest that leads him to require an unwilling defendant and prosecution to go to trial.
>
> We now turn to the content of these components, and begin by passing any discussion of fairness to the defense, since it is not directly involved in the case at bar. . . . As to fairness to the prosecution interest, here we have a matter in which the primary responsibility, obviously, is that of the prosecuting attorney. The District Court cannot disapprove of his action on the ground of incompatibility with prosecutive responsibility unless the judge is in effect ruling that the prosecutor has abused his discretion. The requirement of judicial approval entitles the judge to obtain and evaluate the prosecutor's reasons. . . . The judge may withhold approval if he finds that the prosecutor has failed to give consideration to factors that must be given consideration in the public interest, factors such as the deterrent aspects of the criminal law. However, trial judges are not free to withhold approval of guilty pleas on this basis merely because their conception of the public interest differs from that of the prosecuting attorney. The question is not what the judge would do if he were the prosecuting attorney, but whether he can say that the action of the prosecuting attorney is such a departure from sound prosecutorial principle as to mark it an abuse of prosecutorial discretion.

> In like vein, we note that a judge is free to condemn the prosecutor's agreement as a trespass on judicial authority only in a blatant and extreme case. In ordinary circumstances, the change in grading of an offense presents no question of the kind of action that is reserved for the judiciary.

United States v. Ammidown, 497 F.2d 615, 622 (D.C. Cir.1973). See United States v. Torres-Echavarria, 129 F.3d 692 (2d Cir.1997) (refusal to accept plea upheld); United States v. Severino, 800 F.2d 42 (2d Cir.1986). But see United States v. Shepherd, 102 F.3d 558 (D.C. Cir.1996) (refusal to allow one codefendant to plead guilty to the indictment during trial was abuse of discretion).

380. "We think that plea bargaining serves a useful purpose both for society and the prisoner and is a permanent part of the criminal courtroom scene, but we think that it ought to be brought out into the open. We do not suggest that defense counsel and the prosecutor actually conduct their negotiations in open court, but we do urge that in this circuit a full and complete disclosure of such negotiations be announced to the court and made a part of the record. The matter is, after all, public business, and we deplore the hypocrisy of silent pretense that it has not occurred. Here it seems rather obvious that in return for pleading guilty to one count permitting the court ample latitude for adequate punishment (ten years), the prosecutor agreed, quite properly we think, to dismiss the other counts. Why not say so? Such disclosure would enable the trial judge to exercise a proper controlling influence and to reject any such arrangement he deemed unfair either to the defendant or to the public." United States v. Williams, 407 F.2d 940, 948–49 (4th Cir.1969). To the same effect, see The President's Commission on Law Enforcement and Administration of Justice, The Challenge of Crime in a Free Society 135–36 (1967).

Does Rule 11(c)(2), p. 698 above, fully accomplish the objective suggested in *Williams*, above?

The U.S. National Advisory Commission on Criminal Justice Standards and Goals recommended that plea bargaining be prohibited "as soon as possible." Courts 46 (1973). Among the arguments of the commission are the following:

> Not only does the Commission believe that plea negotiation serves no legitimate function in the processing of criminal cases, it also has concluded that it exacts unacceptable costs from all concerned. Perhaps the major cost is that of reduced rationality in the processing of criminal defendants. Whether a defendant is convicted should depend upon the evidence available to convict him, and what disposition is made of a convicted offender should depend upon what action best serves rehabilitative and deterrent needs. The likelihood that these factors will control conviction and disposition is minimized in the inevitable "horsetrading" atmosphere of plea negotiation. Some defendants suffer from the resulting irrationality.

> But the public's interest in disposition of cases to serve its interest in protection also suffers. The Commission is convinced that rationality cannot be brought into the system by raising the visibility of the plea negotiation process and structuring the making of the administrative decisions in it. Inherent in plea negotiations is the consideration of factors that should be irrelevant to the disposition of the case. This cannot be prevented by any means short of abolishing the process.
>
> Another major cost involved in plea negotiation is the burden it inevitably places upon the exercise of the rights involved in trial—the rights to jury trial, to confront and cross-examine witnesses, to have the judge or jury convinced of guilt beyond a reasonable doubt, and similar matters. It is inherent in plea negotiation that leniency will be given in return for nonassertion of these rights.
>
> . . .
>
> It is inevitable that exercising these rights often will involve financial costs to defendants, time commitments, and the emotionally unpleasant experience of litigation. But it is wholly unacceptable to add to this the necessity of forfeiting a discount that could otherwise have been obtained. Probably the major individual victim of today's plea bargaining system is the defendant who exercises his right to trial and suffers a substantially more severe sentence than he would have received had he pleaded guilty.
>
> By imposing a penalty upon the exercise of procedural rights in those cases in which there is a reasonable likelihood that the rights will be vindicated, the plea negotiation system creates a significant danger to the innocent. Many of the rights it discourages are rights designed to prevent the conviction of innocent defendants. To the extent these rights are rendered nonoperative by the plea negotiation system, innocent defendants are endangered. Plea negotiation not only serves no legitimate function in the processing of criminal defendants, but it also encourages irrationality in the court process, burdens the exercise of individual rights, and endangers the right of innocent defendants to be acquitted.

Id. at 48.

In United States v. Griffin, 462 F.Supp. 928 (E.D.Ark.1978), Judge Eisele explained his refusal to consider a plea agreement as provided in Rule 11(e). He said:

> The Court wishes to make clear some of its reasons for refusing to hear plea bargains. It is the Court's opinion, probably a minority opinion, that the process of negotiating pleas has a tendency to demean all participants: the attorneys, the defendant, and even the court.[13]

13. Judges should not shut their eyes to the dynamics of the process, or its effects, upon them personally—consciously or unconsciously. Some judges, like many lawyers, fear, or do not like trials. They would like to avoid them. All judges welcome the settlement of civil cases. Few are unhappy when a defendant, charged with a crime, decides to

There are "back-room," sinister implications (albeit unjustified) which simply cannot be removed. The result: public cynicism and lack of faith in the integrity of the judicial process. In emphasizing expediency, allegedly based on dollar costs, plea bargaining derogates from the attempt of the Court to deal justice and substitutes therefor a concern for a cost efficient method of disposing of cases. Even if one accepts the validity of the cost argument, which this Court does not (in the federal system), it surely constitutes a poor justification for the process.

Inasmuch as plea bargaining provides leeway for a strong prosecutor to overwhelm a poorly prepared or timid defense counsel, or a strong defense counsel to take advantage of an inept or overworked prosecutor, there is a tendency to emphasize the disparity of counsel, which has less impact when a case is heard in open court, with all the attendant safeguards of a trial. Perhaps only trial judges fully understand the pervasiveness of the "fear of trial" experienced by even excellent attorneys. Although good lawyers will not permit this fear to rise to the level of a conscious factor in plea negotiations, it must often remain subconsciously at work in the process, encouraging acceptance of a negotiated plea on some basis other than the merits.

Another point: when the convicted defendant goes to prison, the opportunity to compare bargains with other inmates and to speculate on what factors may have influenced the various outcomes lends itself to the creation of cynical disdain for a system that proclaims justice as its goal but, arguably, dispenses deals instead. And this Court is of the opinion that it is very important, overall, how the defendants within the system perceive the operation and effect of that system.

And what about the rights of the public? Assume that a United States Attorney chooses to present cases against a person to the grand jury, and the grand jury chooses to indict that person on the basis of the evidence. Now, assuming the integrity of the prosecutorial decision and the evidentiary basis therefor (and why should this not be assumed?), the rights of the public are immediately implicated. Either

plead guilty. There certainly is nothing wrong with such feelings or attitudes. Where negotiated pleas are not accepted, these natural attitudes have no effect on the dispensation of justice. But now introduce plea bargaining. Suddenly the decision of the judge to accept or reject a plea bargain may make the difference between a hard six-weeks trial or, possibly, a chance to clean up his motion calendar. This could conceivably influence his decision—even if only on a subconscious level. Additionally, the reputation of the judge becomes a significant factor in the ability of the prosecutor, or the defense counsel, to prevail upon the defendant to agree to a plea bargain. If it can be demonstrated from the record that those who go to trial and lose get the "book thrown" at them, or that it "will cost you to see the hole card" (i.e., if one pleads not guilty and goes to trial), chances are that the defendant will seek an agreement. If, on the other hand, the judge has a reputation for being lenient or even fair, defendants and defense attorneys would be less likely to feel the compulsion to agree. So, nationwide, the process would tend to disparity rather than uniformity. And many argue cogently that reasonable uniformity should be a goal of the federal criminal justice system. So, consciously or unconsciously, a judge may act in a way which has an effect one way or the other on the entire plea bargaining process, perhaps entirely unknown to him.

the man is guilty or he is not. The unimpeded process will produce the proper (just) result. But, one says, the prosecutor may *know* the defendant is guilty but simply cannot get the necessary evidence, so why not prosecute, get a deal and at least put him away for a while? Prosecutorial integrity? Sound public policy? Query.

Revealing the existence of plea bargains and their content is, of course, superior to the silent acceptance of *sub rosa* plea agreements. It is obviously preferable to require that the process be spread on the record to maximize protection for the accused and the public. . . . In the opinion of this Court, even plea agreements acknowledged in the record do not serve the cause of justice. It would be better to insist that there be none (except *possibly* in cases involving great national interests, perhaps certified to, as such, by the Attorney General or the President himself.) Rule 11(e) at least allows the Court the option to refuse to hear bargained pleas. This Court exercises its discretion by so refusing, thereby giving no sanction to the practice.

It has been said that without plea bargaining the wheels of justice would grind to a halt and that efficient administration of the courts requires the use of plea agreements. This Court doubts the factual basis for this argument in the federal court context. It has been able to handle its criminal docket expeditiously, and has not found clear-cut evidence that there is any great disparity in the percentage of its criminal cases which proceed to trial, when compared to courts in other districts which do accept plea agreements. Even if the refusal to accept plea bargains clearly results, overall, in a greater number of trials, what difference should this make? That is what the courts are for. They should not be considered agencies created to preside over settlement negotiations. But what about delay? The simple answer is that there can be no significant delay in the disposition of criminal cases in the federal system based on clogged dockets. If the Constitution were not enough, we have the Speedy Trial Act.

Further, there must be more than a lingering concern, when a negotiated plea is heard, that an innocent defendant has been prevailed upon, or has chosen to "play the odds," rather than to staunchly maintain his innocence. In fact, must it not be accepted by the proponents of plea bargaining that, statistically, a certain number of innocent people will suffer judicial penalties *because of that system*? The potential risk of consequences of much greater penalties may drag from the mouth of an innocent man a guilty plea if it is coupled with the guarantee of a significantly lesser penalty. One can say that, in such situations, the defendant is simply exercising rational choices affecting his self-interest. That is true, and it may not be unreasonable for him to make such a choice. But should the federal criminal justice system give an innocent man that choice? This Court says, "No."

We always get back to it: when is a plea voluntarily made? The plea "taken to avoid the risk of being convicted of a more serious

> crime . . . is truly no more voluntary than is the choice of the rock to avoid the whirlpool."[14]

462 F.Supp. at 930–33.

Judge Eisele's practice of refusing to consider a plea bargain was upheld as within his authority in In re Yielding, 599 F.2d 251 (8th Cir.1979).

381. ABA Standards for Criminal Justice, Pleas of Guilty, Standard 14–1.8 (3d ed. 1999)[15]:

> Consideration of plea in final disposition.
>
> (a) The fact that a defendant has entered a plea of guilty or nolo contendere should not, by itself alone, be considered by the court as a mitigating factor in imposing sentence. It is proper for the court to approve or grant charge and sentence concessions to a defendant who enters a plea of guilty or nolo contendere when consistent with governing law and when there is substantial evidence to establish, for example, that:
>
> (i) the defendant is genuinely contrite and has shown a willingness to assume responsibility for his or her conduct;
>
> (ii) the concessions will make possible alternative correctional measures which are better adapted to achieving protective, deterrent, or other purposes of correctional treatment, or will prevent undue harm to the defendant from the form of conviction;
>
> (iii) the defendant, by making public trial unnecessary, has demonstrated genuine remorse or consideration for the victims of his or her criminal activity; or

14. Kuh, Book Review, 82 Harv. L. Rev. 497, 500 (1968).

15. Compare The President's Commission on Law Enforcement and Administration of Justice, The Challenge of Crime in a Free Society 135 (1967):

"The negotiated guilty plea serves important functions. As a practical matter, many courts could not sustain the burden of having to try all cases coming before them. The quality of justice in all cases would suffer if overloaded courts were faced with a great increase in the number of trials. Tremendous investments of time, talent, and money, all of which are in short supply and can be better used elsewhere, would be necessary if all cases were tried. It would be a serious mistake, however, to assume that the guilty plea is no more than a means of disposing of criminal cases at minimal cost. It relieves both the defendant and the prosecution of the inevitable risks and uncertainties of trial. It imports a degree of certainty and flexibility into a rigid, yet frequently erratic system. The guilty plea is used to mitigate the harshness of mandatory sentencing provisions and to fix a punishment that more accurately reflects the specific circumstances of the case than otherwise would be possible under inadequate penal codes. It is frequently called upon to serve important law enforcement needs by agreements through which leniency is exchanged for information, assistance, and testimony about other serious offenders.

"At the same time the negotiated plea of guilty can be subject to serious abuses. In hard-pressed courts, where judges and prosecutors are unable to deal effectively with all cases presented to them, dangerous offenders may be able to manipulate the system to obtain unjustifiably lenient treatment. There are also real dangers that excessive rewards will be offered to induce pleas or that prosecutors will threaten to seek a harsh sentence if the defendant does not plead guilty. Such practices place unacceptable burdens on the defendant who legitimately insists upon his right to trial."

(iv) that the defendant has given or agreed to give cooperation.

(b) The court should not impose upon a defendant any sentence in excess of that which would be justified by any of the protective, deterrent, or other purposes of the criminal law because the defendant has chosen to require the prosecution to prove guilt at trial rather than to enter a plea of guilty or nolo contendere.

Is paragraph (a) consistent with paragraph (b)? If the reference in paragraph (b) to "the rehabilitative, protective, deterrent or other purposes of the criminal law" relates to the imposition of punishment on a particular defendant who has chosen to plead not guilty and not to all defendants generally, can the two paragraphs be made consistent?

382. On September 22, 2003, Attorney General John Ashcroft issued a directive to all federal prosecutors about "Department Policy Concerning Charging Criminal Offenses, Disposition of Charges, and Sentencing." Affirming the principles of consistency in sentencing and effective deterrence, the directive announced a departmental policy "that in all federal criminal cases, federal prosecutors must charge and pursue the most serious, readily provable offense or offenses that are supported by the facts of the case," subject to limited exceptions in special cases. With respect to plea agreements, the directive declares that federal prosecutors may not "be party to any plea agreement that results in the sentencing court having less than a full understanding of all readily provable facts relevant to sentencing." If a plea agreement is negotiated, "the court must be informed that a more serious, readily provable offense was not charged or that an applicable statutory enhancement was not filed." Prosecutors may enter a plea agreement regarding sentence only if the agreed sentence is within the range specified by the Sentencing Guidelines for that offense. Other departures from the Guidelines are authorized only in exceptional circumstances. "Prosecutors must affirmatively oppose downward departures that are not supported by the facts and the law, and must not agree to 'stand silent' with respect to such departures." (On the Sentencing Guidelines, see p. 1109 below.)

The directive is understood severely to limit plea bargaining in federal prosecutions. The reaction among persons in the field was generally dismay and a prediction that the announced policy was unworkable and could not be fully implemented. See, e.g., George Fisher, "A Practice as Old as Justice Itself," The New York Times, September 28, 2003, at D11.

Suppose a defendant obtains the prosecutor's agreement to a sentence concession and then, in good faith and before any action is taken, changes his mind and decides to stand trial. If he is tried and convicted, on what basis can the prosecutor or the court impose a sentence in excess of that which would have been imposed had he pleaded guilty? If the lesser sentence would have been sufficient had he pleaded guilty, on what basis consistent with paragraph (b) of the standards set out in note 381, p. 746 above can a greater sentence be imposed?[16] Is the same question applicable to a person who from the beginning declines to plead guilty? Is the troubling figure in the plea-bargaining process always the person who bargains successfully or may it sometimes be the person who does not bargain, as the President's Commission suggested, p. 746 n.15 above?

Withdrawal of Guilty Plea

FEDERAL RULES OF CRIMINAL PROCEDURE

Rule 11

PLEAS

. . .

(d) Withdrawing a Guilty or Nolo Contendere Plea. A defendant may withdraw a plea of guilty or nolo contendere:

(1) before the court accepts the plea, for any reason or no reason; or

(2) after the court accepts the plea, but before it imposes sentence if:

(A) the court rejects a plea agreement under Rule 11(c)(5); or

(B) the defendant can show a fair and just reason for requesting the withdrawal.

Everett v. United States

336 F.2d 979 (D.C.Cir.1964)

■ BURGER, CIRCUIT JUDGE.

Appellant entered a guilty plea to Counts 3 and 4 of a six-count indictment; prior to sentence he sought leave to withdraw these pleas and

16. A defendant who is tried and convicted and who successfully appeals from the conviction may not be sentenced more severely following conviction at a second trial, unless reasons based on events subsequent to the first trial affirmatively appear on the record. There is no comparable bar to a more severe sentence if the first conviction was pursuant to a guilty plea. Alabama v. Smith, 490 U.S. 794 (1989) (8–1). Among the reasons that the Court gave for this distinction are that if the first conviction was based on a guilty plea, "in the course of the proof at trial the judge may gather a fuller appreciation of the nature and extent of the crime charged," that "the defendant's conduct during trial may give the judge insights into his moral character and suitability for rehabilitation," and that "after trial, the factors that may have indicated leniency as consideration for the guilty plea are no longer present." Id. at 801. See note 596, p. 1141 below.

go to trial on these two counts. After an extended colloquy with appellant in the course of the hearing, the District Court permitted withdrawal of the guilty plea as to Count 3 but declined it as to Count 4 because no valid reason or basis for withdrawal had been claimed or shown. On the remaining guilty plea to Count 4 he sentenced appellant to nine years imprisonment under the Youth Corrections Act, 18 U.S.C. § 5010(c) (1958).

The six-count indictment charged three offenses arising out of unrelated robberies and one attempted robbery on a fourth occasion, spanning a period from April 1962 to January 1963.

At arraignment under FED.R.CRIM.P. 10 on February 25, 1963, appellant entered a plea of not guilty as to all six counts and was released on bail. Two months later, with retained counsel, he withdrew the pleas of not guilty to Count 3 (robbery) and Count 4 (assault with intent to commit robbery) and entered pleas of guilty as to both of these counts.[17] Before accepting these guilty pleas, the District Judge, pursuant to FED.R.CRIM.P. 11 and Resolution of the Judges of the U.S. District Court for the District of Columbia promulgated June 24, 1959 thereunder, conducted an extensive interrogation of appellant as to the facts of the alleged crimes and his reasons for pleading guilty thereto. Appellant freely admitted the charges: as to Count 3 he said, "I went in and robbed the place . . . by myself . . . [and took] about $200.00, sir"; as to Count 4 he said, "Well I entered the liquor store and I demanded money, sir; and well I just remember being shot; that's about all." He stated further that he had brandished a gun both times but did not shoot it; that on the later occasion one of the liquor store employees had shot him; and that he had been apprehended the following day when he had gone to the hospital for treatment of the gunshot wound. The District Judge interrogated appellant carefully as to his awareness of the possible sentence; appellant reiterated his guilt and said he was pleading guilty because he was guilty and not because the Government had moved to dismiss four other counts should he plead guilty to Counts 3 and 4.

Three weeks later, appellant, with his retained counsel, filed a motion under FED.R.CRIM.P. 32(d) to withdraw his guilty pleas to Counts 3 and 4.[18] On June 27, 1963, the District Court conducted a hearing on the motion and at this time appellant said he was innocent of the Count 3 robbery charge and had pleaded guilty to that count only because he "was so confused and worried . . . [and] wanted to try to get this over as soon as possible." As to Count 4, however, he stated to the Court: "Well, Your Honor, I am guilty of that charge. I did attempt to rob this place. That's all." The District Judge granted the motion to withdraw the plea as to Count 3 but denied the motion as to Count 4 on which guilt was admitted.

17. On the basis of these two guilty pleas, the United States Attorney's Office moved the dismissal of the remaining four counts. Ruling on this motion has been held in abeyance by the District Judge pending disposition of this appeal.

[18] Former Rule 32(d) was similar to current Rule 11(d).

Appellant is now represented by court-appointed counsel who urges that the District Court committed reversible error in refusing to permit withdrawal of the guilty plea to Count 4 in the circumstances shown here.

We disagree emphatically. We have held that withdrawal of a guilty plea, made by a defendant unrepresented by counsel, "should be freely allowed" when he seeks withdrawal *before* sentencing. . . . [I]n Gearhart v. United States, 272 F.2d 499, 502 (1959), Judge Washington, speaking for a unanimous court, noted that:

> [T]he Supreme Court in broad dictum already had said that "The court in exercise of its discretion will permit one accused to substitute a plea of not guilty and have a trial if for *any reason* the granting of the privilege seems *fair and just*." . . .
>
> This is not to say that the District Court lacks all discretion in dealing with a motion of the present sort. But discretion must be exercised on the basis of sound information, soundly viewed. Where the accused seeks to withdraw his plea of guilty before sentencing, on the ground that he has a defense to the charge, the District Court should not attempt to decide the merits of the proffered defense, thus determining the guilt or innocence of the defendant. In certain situations, where the issue raised by the motion to withdraw is one of tangential nature, resolvable apart from the merits of the case, the District Court may appropriately hold a factual hearing to determine whether the accused has a "fair and just" reason for asking to withdraw his plea of guilty.

Far from showing a " 'fair and just' reason" for a change of plea to Count 4, appellant demonstrated by his repeated statements that he had no reason other than wanting a trial on a charge of which he admitted his guilt. Unlike Gearhart, appellant offered no defense to the charge, nor did he allege involuntariness or any other factor which would militate against the correctness and truth of his guilty plea to Count 4 which was entered when he was represented by retained counsel. His contention is virtually a claim of an absolute right to withdraw a guilty plea prior to imposition of sentence. No court has ever so held; our use of the language "freely allowed" plainly implies the existence of some circumstances in which a defendant is not entitled to withdraw a plea of guilty before sentencing, and negates any absolute right to do so. Overwhelming authority holds, as has this court, that withdrawal of a guilty plea before sentencing is not an absolute right but a decision within the sound discretion of the trial court which will be reversed by an appellate court only for an abuse of that discretion.

A defendant who stands before a court freely admitting his attempted robbery does not remotely meet the standard of offering a "fair and just reason" for withdrawing his plea of guilty prior to sentence. He must give some reason other than a desire to have a trial the basic purpose of which is to determine the very facts the defendant has just volunteered to the court on the record and while attended by his own counsel.

The record reveals a guilty plea, intelligently and voluntarily made with assistance of retained counsel and candid admission of all essential elements of the crime in open court; this is hardly a predicate for an appellate holding that the District Judge abused his discretion in refusing to permit a withdrawal. We are not disposed to encourage accused persons to "play games" with the courts at the expense of already overburdened calendars and the rights of other accused persons awaiting trial, whose cases may lose both their position on the calendar and the Court's time and facilities which are thus diverted for no useful purpose.

---

383. Under Rule 11(d)(1), a plea of guilty or nolo contendere may be withdrawn "before the court accepts the plea, for any reason or no reason." After the plea is accepted and before the court imposes sentence, the plea may be withdrawn if the court rejects the plea agreement pursuant to which the plea was entered or if the defendant shows "a fair and just reason" for requesting the withdrawal. In United States v. Shaker, 279 F.3d 494 (7th Cir.2002), the judge indicated that the requirements for a valid plea were satisfied but deferred acceptance or rejection until he had read the presentence report. The government argued that the judge's finding that the requirements of a plea were satisfied was the "functional equivalent" of acceptance. The court held otherwise; the plea not having been accepted, the defendant was entitled to withdraw it without giving any reason. In United States v. Hyde, 520 U.S. 670 (1997), however, the judge accepted the plea but deferred a decision whether to accept the plea agreement. In that circumstance, the Court said, the requirement of a "fair and just reason" for withdrawal was applicable. Otherwise, the provision allowing withdrawal if the plea agreement were rejected would have no significance. Furthermore, allowing the defendant to withdraw his plea at will after it was accepted would debase the proceeding at which the plea is entered.

384. In United States v. Nagelberg, 323 F.2d 936 (2d Cir.1963), the defendant had pleaded guilty to three counts of an indictment charging narcotics violations. Four months later, before sentencing, he moved to withdraw the plea on the ground that "he had subsequently cooperated with and been of assistance to governmental authorities," id. The government acquiesced in the motion. The trial judge held that he had no power to grant the motion on such grounds, and sentenced the defendant to the statutory minimum of five years' imprisonment on each count, the sentences to run concurrently. The court of appeals affirmed, saying that the defendant's "willingness to be of assistance to the government is not a sufficient basis for permitting his plea of guilty to be withdrawn," and noting that the defendant had never denied his guilt or claimed that his plea was improperly induced. Id. In the Supreme Court, the government stated that it had acquiesced in the motion to withdraw the plea because it intended to dismiss the indictment and substitute lesser charges. In these circumstances, the Court said, the trial court had discretion to permit the plea to be withdrawn. Nagelberg v. United States, 377 U.S. 266 (1964).

385. The defendant and his wife were indicted for conspiracy to distribute counterfeit money. The defendant pleaded guilty. Sentencing was deferred until after the trial of his wife. Four months later her case was called for trial. After hearing all of the government's case, she pleaded guilty. Before sentence was imposed on him, the defendant made a motion to withdraw his guilty plea; he alleged that he had pleaded guilty in the expectation that other pending charges against him would be dropped or that he would otherwise be treated favorably. There was no indication that he had been misled in this respect by the prosecutor or by his lawyer. The government opposed withdrawal of the plea on the grounds that by waiting until after the trial of his wife the defendant had learned the government's case and that the government's witnesses were reluctant to come to court another time. Should the motion to withdraw the plea be allowed? See United States v. Stayton, 408 F.2d 559 (3d Cir.1969).

See United States v. Hickok, 907 F.2d 983 (10th Cir.1990) (withdrawal before sentence not allowed); United States v. Spencer, 836 F.2d 236 (6th Cir.1987) (same); United States v. Picone, 773 F.2d 224 (8th Cir.1985) (withdrawal before sentence, following acquittal of codefendant on same charge, not allowed); Nunez Cordero v. United States, 533 F.2d 723 (1st Cir.1976) (defendant unaware that if convicted he would be deported; withdrawal before sentence not allowed). In United States v. Blauner, 337 F.Supp. 1394 (S.D.N.Y.1971), after the defendant pleaded guilty the indictment against co-defendants was dismissed because of unnecessary delay by the government; the defendant's motion to withdraw the plea of guilty and for dismissal of the indictment was denied. See also United States v. Davis, 239 F.3d 283 (2d Cir.2001), p. 1034 below.

Nolo Contendere

UNITED STATES ATTORNEYS' MANUAL

9.27. Principles of Federal Prosecution

. . .

9–27.500 Offers to Plead Nolo Contendere—*Opposition Except in Unusual Circumstances*

A. The attorney for the government should oppose the acceptance of a plea of nolo contendere unless the Assistant Attorney General with supervisory responsibility over the subject matter concludes that the circumstances of the case are so unusual that acceptance of such a plea would be in the public interest. . . .

B. Comment

Rule 11(b) of the Federal Rules of Criminal Procedure requires the court to consider "the views of the parties and the interest of the public in the effective administration of justice" before it accepts a plea of nolo contendere. Thus, it is clear that a criminal defendant has no absolute right to enter a nolo contendere plea. The Department has long attempted to discourage the disposition of criminal cases by means of nolo pleas. The basic objections to nolo pleas were expressed by Attorney General Herbert Brownell, Jr., in a departmental directive in 1953:

> One of the factors which has tended to breed contempt for federal law enforcement in recent times has been the practice of permitting as a matter of course in many criminal indictments the plea of nolo contendere. While it may serve a legitimate purpose in a few extraordinary situations and where civil litigation is also pending, I can see no justification for it as an everyday practice, particularly where it is used to avoid certain indirect consequences of pleading guilty, such as loss of license or sentencing as a multiple offender. Uncontrolled use of the plea has led to shockingly low sentences and insignificant fines which are not deterrent to crime. As a practical matter it accomplished little that is useful even where the Government has civil litigation pending. Moreover, a person permitted to plead nolo contendere admits his guilt for the purpose of imposing punishment for his acts and yet, for all other purposes, and as far as the public is concerned, persists in his denial of wrongdoing. It is no wonder that the public regards consent to such a plea by the Government as an admission that it has only a technical case at most and that the whole proceeding was just a fiasco.

For these reasons, government attorneys have been instructed for many years not to consent to nolo pleas except in the most unusual circumstances, and to do so then only with departmental approval. Federal prosecutors should oppose the acceptance of a nolo plea, unless the responsible Assistant Attorney General concludes that the circumstances are so unusual that acceptance of the plea would be in the public interest. Such a determination might be made, for example, in an unusually complex antitrust case if the only alternative to a protracted trial is acceptance of a nolo plea.

9–27.520 *Offer of Proof*

A. In any case in which a defendant seeks to enter a plea of nolo contendere, the attorney for the government should make an offer of proof of the facts known to the government to support the conclusion that the defendant has in fact committed the offense charged. . . .

B. Comment

If a defendant seeks to avoid admitting guilt by offering to plead nolo contendere, the attorney for the government should make an offer of proof of the facts known to the government to support the conclusion that the defendant has in fact committed the offense charged. This should be done even in the rare case in which the government does not oppose the entry of a nolo plea. In addition, as is the case with respect to guilty pleas, the attorney for the government should urge the court to require the defendant to admit publicly the facts underlying the criminal charges. These precautions should minimize the effectiveness of any subsequent efforts by the defendant to portray himself/herself as technically liable perhaps, but not seriously culpable.

9–27.530 *Argument in Opposition of Nolo Contendere Plea*

A. If a plea of nolo contendere is offered over the government's objection, the attorney for the government should state for the record why acceptance of the plea would not be in the public interest; and should oppose the dismissal of any charges to which the defendant does not plead nolo contendere.

B. Comment

When a plea of nolo contendere is offered over the government's objection, the prosecutor should take full advantage of Rule 11(b), Federal Rules of Criminal Procedure, to state for the record why acceptance of the plea would not be in the public interest. In addition to reciting the facts that could be proved to show the defendant's guilt, the prosecutor should bring to the court's attention whatever arguments exist for rejecting the plea. At the very least, such a forceful presentation should make it clear to the public that the government is unwilling to condone the entry of a special plea that may help the defendant avoid legitimate consequences of his/her guilt. If the nolo plea is offered to fewer than all charges, the prosecutor should also oppose the dismissal of the remaining charges.

United States v. Hines

507 F.Supp. 139 (W.D.Mo.1981)

■ SACHS, DISTRICT JUDGE.

The question before the Court is whether I should accept a plea of *nolo contendere* offered by the defendant but opposed by the United States Attorney, pursuant to a departmental policy dating back to a 1953 directive, recently restated. . . . Although a guilty plea may be greatly preferred to a *nolo* plea, I . . . will generally accept a *nolo* plea if necessary to disposition of a criminal case without trial. Because . . . [this] position is said to be extraordinary . . . an explanation of my current thinking on the subject is desirable.

Prior to 1966 it could be said that the "only distinguishable feature between a plea of *nolo contendere* and that of guilty is that the former cannot be used against the defendant as an admission in any civil suit for the same act." Bell v. Commissioner of Internal Revenue, 320 F.2d 953, 956 (8th Cir.1963). By the 1966 amendment to Rule 11, Federal Rules of

Criminal Procedure, however, the *nolo* plea serves a new purpose in that, as distinguished from a guilty plea, a *nolo* plea may be accepted without the usual prerequisite of fully satisfying the Court that the defendant has in fact committed the crime charged. . . . The *nolo* plea has thus become quite useful, in the Federal system, for dealing with the defendant who denies guilt, or elects to stand mute, while agreeing to entry of an adverse judgment and the imposition of punishment. Compare North Carolina v. Alford, 400 U.S. 25 (1970), sustaining the constitutionality of accepting a state court guilty plea of a defendant who had in fact denied guilt. The Supreme Court observed in *Alford* (l.c. 36, note 8) that the revisers of Rule 11 thought it "desirable to permit defendants to plead *nolo* without making any inquiry into their actual guilt."

The Department of Justice now offers a stereotype that *nolo* pleas are reserved for "affluent white collar defendants," and may result in lenient treatment. Neither of these suppositions fits my experience, and greater use of *nolo* pleas may alter the generalizations.

A *nolo* plea does not affect my sentencing practices, except that I may take into account that a person offering a guilty plea may be more favorably considered because of apparent honesty and contrition. I would generally not consider protestations of innocence, as grounds for lenient sentencing, any more than I would consider such protestations after a jury verdict of guilty.

It has been my practice to accept a *nolo* plea on request, when a defendant resists admitting guilt in open court. It is generally very desirable for a defendant to make a full confession; that is, however, not always obtainable. Inquiry from the government as to the evidentiary basis for the plea is then useful to limit the possibility that the Court has before it an innocent person. The purpose of the distinction in Rule 11 would be defeated, however, by adamant insistence that the defendant in this case should herself provide a statement showing guilt.

The Court of Appeals for the District of Columbia has ruled that a district judge has a duty to accept a guilty plea tendered by a defendant who protests innocence, if there is a factual basis for the plea. . . . While the distinction may be one of word usage, I would treat such a tender as an offer of a *nolo* plea, rather than a "guilty" plea, and would generally accept it.

Trial in such an instance would usually be a wasteful ritual contrary to the effective administration of justice, and is therefore not required. Rule 11(b), Federal Rules of Criminal Procedure. It is not only "protracted litigation" . . . which should be avoided by accepting such pleas. Unnecessary trial of a short case is also wasteful. . . . [I]t may also be considered an unfair ordeal to impose on a defendant who does not wish to contest the government's case.

Based on the above reasons and the particular facts presented to the Court, defendant's plea of *nolo contendere* will be accepted, and a judgment of guilty based on that plea will be entered in the record. So ordered.

United States v. Chin Doong Art

193 F.Supp. 820 (E.D.N.Y.1961)

■ BARTELS, DISTRICT JUDGE.

This is an application by the defendant Chin Doong Art, a/k/a Arthur Lem, to enter a plea of *nolo contendere* to the first count of the indictment, alleging a conspiracy to violate the Criminal Code of the United States with respect to the entry, residence and citizenship of the defendant and others. The case against this defendant and others on the first and several other counts in the indictment was tried last year and the trial extended over a period of eight weeks, resulting in a deadlocked jury.

In support of his application defendant argues that a new trial would involve many additional witnesses on both sides; that the result would depend upon oral testimony mostly in a foreign language involving Chinese family genealogy; that even if an acquittal were obtained, it would not be conclusive because defendant would be subjected to further prosecution under two other counts which had been previously severed from the first count; that he was a prominent and useful citizen and named "Man of the Year" by the Town of Hempstead in 1958; that a plea of guilty would result in a loss of face not only to him but also to the Chinese community of which he has been a prominent figure; that such a plea would be prejudicial to him in a subsequent civil proceeding before the Immigration and Naturalization Service; and that no useful purpose would be served by a plea of guilty, whereas defendant would be spared harsh and unnecessary results by a plea of *nolo contendere*.

The Government opposes acceptance of this plea and argues that the co-defendant Chin Suie Tung has already entered a plea of guilty to count one and is available to the Government as a witness, and that four other alleged co-conspirators (not named as defendants herein) have entered pleas of guilty to charges of perjury before the Grand Jury; that today it is in a better position than ever to retry the case because it has many more witnesses; that since the defendant is an alien he would be subjected only to the administrative proceeding involving the cancellation of his citizenship certificate, with respect to which the proof and procedure would be the same whether or not he pleaded *nolo contendere*; that there are no extraordinary and exceptional circumstances present to justify the acceptance of a plea of *nolo contendere* and that to do so would be against the public interest and would breed contempt for Federal law enforcement.

There can be no question that this Court may, in its discretion, accept or reject the tendered plea. . . . Such principles as there are to guide it in the exercise of its discretion have been enunciated in many cases and need not be repeated here.

In this case a plea of *nolo contendere* would probably be beneficial to the defendant as far as his standing in the community is concerned and perhaps in other respects. This, however, is not the test. The Court must decide whether the circumstances of the case are so exceptional as to appeal to a favorable exercise of its discretion. Against such circumstances it must weigh the public interest which in the final analysis is paramount. As previously indicated, the policy of this Court has not been favorable to the acceptance of a plea of *nolo contendere*, unless the situation is an extraordinary one. Even then the interest of the public cannot be ignored. The presence of moral turpitude in the charge, as in this case, is often a factor in the determination. However, it has never been held that the nature of the proof to be advanced is relevant since such consideration by the Court might involve an investigation into the issues, the materiality of the proof and to some extent, the merits of the case, which are obviously beyond the scope of this application. Further, any difficulty in proof in this case imposes a greater burden upon the United States Attorney, who has the responsibility of deciding the Government's chance of success in determining the advantage to the Government of dispensing with the trial by consenting to the plea. Acting upon the recommendation of the Attorney General, the United States Attorney has most vigorously opposed the acceptance of this plea. Consequently, the defendant's statement that the previous trial resulted in a hung jury and that the case depends upon oral testimony, loses most of its appeal.

The fact that the case is a difficult and protracted one for the defendant does not per se present an exceptional circumstance for this plea, because again the burden is upon the Government to prove its case beyond a reasonable doubt. While the fact that the defendant had a good record in the past and is a prominent man who would lose face by a plea of guilty must be considered in his favor, it cannot override more important interests. Some question has been raised about the collateral effect of a plea of guilty as opposed to a plea of *nolo* in this case, but it is very doubtful whether a plea of *nolo* would offer the defendant any advantage in subsequent administrative proceedings involving his citizenship certificate. It is true that although one item alone may not be sufficient, all the circumstances related by a defendant when taken together may present a picture of exceptional hardship, justifying the acceptance of the plea. The Court, however, cannot reach a conclusion without at the same time considering the other factors militating against the acceptance of such a plea. After careful consideration of all the arguments and particulars, the Court is of the opinion that it cannot accept a plea of *nolo* in this case.

The primary purpose of accepting a plea of *nolo* is to promote the administration of justice. This means justice not only for the defendant but also for the public. The Court cannot permit its action with respect to a plea of this type to breed contempt for law enforcement. After acceptance of a plea of guilty from the co-conspirator (who is now available as a witness for the Government) and the pleas of guilty from the other defendants, it would not only be discriminatory and incongruous but would reflect upon law enforcement generally if the Court accepted a plea of *nolo contendere* from the most prominent of the two defendants. Therefore, the application is denied.

CHAPTER 12

PROCEEDINGS BEFORE TRIAL

FEDERAL RULES OF CRIMINAL PROCEDURE

Rule 12

PLEADINGS AND PRETRIAL MOTIONS

(a) Pleadings. The pleadings in a criminal proceeding are the indictment, the information, and the pleas of not guilty, guilty, and nolo contendere.

(b) Pretrial Motions.

(1) *In General.* Rule 47 applies to a pretrial motion.

(2) *Motions That May Be Made Before Trial.* A party may raise by pretrial motion any defense, objection, or request that the court can determine without a trial of the general issue.

(3) *Motions That Must Be Made Before Trial.* The following must be raised before trial:

(A) a motion alleging a defect in instituting the prosecution;

(B) a motion alleging a defect in the indictment or information—but at any time while the case is pending, the court may hear a claim that the indictment or information fails to invoke the court's jurisdiction or to state an offense;

(C) a motion to suppress evidence;

(D) a Rule 14 motion to sever charges or defendants; and

(E) a Rule 16 motion for discovery.

(4) *Notice of the Government's Intent to Use Evidence.*

(A) *At the Government's Discretion.* At the arraignment or as soon afterward as practicable, the government may notify the defendant of its intent to use specified evidence at trial in order to afford the defendant an opportunity to object before trial under Rule 12(b)(3)(C).

(B) *At the Defendant's Request.* At the arraignment or as soon afterward as practicable, the defendant may, in order to have an opportunity to move to suppress evidence under Rule 12(b)(3)(C), request notice of the government's intent to use (in its evidence-in-chief at trial) any evidence that the defendant may be entitled to discover under Rule 16.

(c) Motion Deadline. The court may, at the arraignment or as soon afterward as practicable, set a deadline for the parties to make pretrial motions and may also schedule a motion hearing.

(d) Ruling on a Motion. The court must decide every pretrial motion before trial unless it finds good cause to defer a ruling. The court must not defer ruling on a pretrial motion if the deferral will adversely affect a party's right to appeal. When factual issues are involved in deciding a motion, the court must state its essential findings on the record.

(e) Waiver of a Defense, Objection, or Request. A party waives any Rule 12(b)(3) defense, objection, or request not raised by the deadline the court sets under Rule 12(c) or by any extension the court provides. For good cause, the court may grant relief from the waiver.

(f) Recording the Proceedings. All proceedings at a motion hearing, including any findings of fact and conclusions of law made orally by the court, must be recorded by a court reporter or a suitable recording device.

(g) Defendant's Continued Custody or Release Status. If the court grants a motion to dismiss based on a defect in instituting the prosecution, in the indictment, or in the information, it may order the defendant to be released or detained under 18 U.S.C. § 3142 for a specified time until a new indictment or information is filed. This rule does not affect any federal statutory period of limitations.

(h) Producing Statements at a Suppression Hearing. Rule 26.2 applies at a suppression hearing under Rule 12(b)(3)(C). At a suppression hearing, a law enforcement officer is considered a government witness.

---

386. In United States v. Barletta, 644 F.2d 50 (1st Cir.1981), the government sought a pretrial ruling that certain evidence that had been excluded at a prior trial was admissible. The government sought the ruling to protect its opportunity to appeal an adverse ruling under 18 U.S.C. § 3731, p. 879 below. The court of appeals held that the trial court may not defer such a ruling to the prejudice of the government's right to appeal under § 3731, if the ruling is "capable of determination without the trial of the general issue" (Rule 12(b), substantially unchanged in current Rule 12(b)(2)) and the relevant proof is "almost entirely segregable from the evidence to be introduced at trial." Id. at 59.

Davis v. United States

411 U.S. 233, 93 S.Ct. 1577, 36 L.Ed.2d 216 (1973)

■ MR. JUSTICE REHNQUIST delivered the opinion of the Court.

We are called upon to determine the effect of Rule 12(b)(2) of the Federal Rules of Criminal Procedure on a post-conviction motion for relief which raises for the first time a claim of unconstitutional discrimination in the composition of a grand jury. An indictment was returned in the District Court charging petitioner Davis, a Negro, and two white men with entry into a federally insured bank with intent to commit larceny in violation of 18 U.S.C. §§ 2 and 2113(a). Represented by appointed counsel, petitioner entered a not-guilty plea at his arraignment and was given 30 days within which to file pretrial motions. He timely moved to quash his indictment on the ground that it was the result of an illegal arrest, but made no other pretrial motions relating to the indictment.

On the opening day of the trial, following voir dire of the jury, the District Judge ruled on petitioner's pretrial motions in chambers and ordered that the motion to quash on the illegal arrest ground be carried with the case. He then asked twice if there were anything else before commencing trial. Petitioner was convicted and sentenced to 14 years' imprisonment. His conviction was affirmed on appeal. . . .

Post-conviction motions were thereafter filed and denied, but none dealt with the issue presented in this case. Almost three years after his conviction, petitioner filed the instant motion to dismiss the indictment, pursuant to 28 U.S.C. § 2255, alleging that the District Court had acquiesced in the systematic exclusion of qualified Negro jurymen by reason of the use of a "key man" system of selection, an asserted violation of the "mandatory requirement of the statute laws set forth . . . in title 28, U.S.C.A. Section 1861, 1863, 1864, and the 5th amendment of the United States Constitution." His challenge only went to the composition of the grand jury and did not include the petit jury which found him guilty. The District Court . . . denied the motion. In its memorandum opinion it relied on Shotwell Mfg. Co. v. United States, 371 U.S. 341 (1963), and concluded that petitioner had waived his right to object to the composition of the grand jury because such a contention is waived under Rule 12(b)(2) unless raised by motion prior to trial. Also, since the "key man" method of selecting grand jurors had been openly followed for many years prior to petitioner's indictment; since the same grand jury that indicted petitioner indicted his two white accomplices; and since the case against petitioner was "a strong one," the court determined that there was nothing in the facts of the case or in the nature of the claim justifying the exercise of the power to grant relief under Rule 12(b)(2) for "cause shown."

The Court of Appeals affirmed on the basis of *Shotwell*, supra, and Rule 12(b)(2). . . . [W]e granted certiorari. . . .

Petitioner contends that because his § 2255 motion alleged deprivation of a fundamental constitutional right . . . his collateral attack on his conviction may be precluded only after a hearing in which it is established that he "deliberately bypassed" or "understandingly and knowingly" waived his claim of unconstitutional grand jury composition. . . .

I

Rule 12(b)(2) provides in pertinent part that "[d]efenses and objections based on defects in the institution of the prosecution or in the indictment . . . may be raised only by motion before trial" [substantially unchanged in current Rule 12(b)(3)(A)], and that failure to present such defenses or objections "constitutes a waiver thereof, but the court for cause shown may grant relief from the waiver" [substantially unchanged in current Rule 12(e)]. By its terms, it applies to both procedural and constitutional defects in the institution of prosecutions which do not affect the jurisdiction of the trial court. According to the Notes of the Advisory Committee on Rules, the waiver provision was designed to continue existing law, which . . . was, inter alia, that defendants who pleaded to an indictment and went to trial without making any nonjurisdictional objection to the grand jury, even one unconstitutionally composed, waived any right of subsequent complaint on account thereof. Not surprisingly, therefore, the Advisory Committee's Notes expressly indicate that claims such as petitioner's are meant to be within the Rule's purview. . . .

This Court had occasion to consider the Rule's application in Shotwell Mfg. Co. v. United States. . . .

Shotwell . . . confirms that Rule 12(b)(2) precludes untimely challenges to grand jury arrays, even when such challenges are on constitutional grounds. Despite the strong analogy between the effect of the Rule as construed in *Shotwell* and petitioner's § 2255 allegations, he nonetheless contends that . . . he is not precluded from raising his constitutional challenge in a federal habeas corpus proceeding. . . . We disagree.

. . .

Shotwell held that a claim of unconstitutional grand jury composition raised four years after conviction, but while the appeal proceedings were still alive, was governed by Rule 12(b)(2). Both the reasons for the Rule and the normal rules of statutory construction clearly indicate that no more lenient standard of waiver should apply to a claim raised three years after conviction simply because the claim is asserted by way of collateral attack rather than in the criminal proceeding itself.

The waiver provisions of Rule 12(b)(2) are operative only with respect to claims of defects in the institution of criminal proceedings. If its time limits are followed, inquiry into an alleged defect may be concluded and, if necessary, cured before the court, the witnesses, and the parties have gone to the burden and expense of a trial. If defendants were allowed to flout its time limitations, on the other hand, there would be little incentive to comply with its terms when a successful attack might simply result in a new indictment prior to trial. Strong tactical considerations would militate in favor of delaying the raising of the claim in hopes of an acquittal, with the thought that if those hopes did not materialize, the claim could be used to upset an otherwise valid conviction at a time when reprosecution might well be difficult.

. . .

We think it inconceivable that Congress, having in the criminal proceeding foreclosed the raising of a claim such as this after the commencement of trial in the absence of a showing of "cause" for relief from waiver, nonetheless intended to perversely negate the Rule's purpose by permitting an entirely different but much more liberal requirement of waiver in federal habeas proceedings. We believe that the necessary effect of the congressional adoption of Rule 12(b)(2) is to provide that a claim once waived pursuant to that Rule may not later be resurrected, either in the criminal proceedings or in federal habeas, in the absence of the showing of "cause" which that Rule requires. We therefore hold that the waiver standard expressed in Rule 12(b)(2) governs an untimely claim of grand jury discrimination, not only during the criminal proceeding, but also later on collateral review.

. . .

II

The principles of Rule 12(b)(2), as construed in *Shotwell*, are not difficult to apply to the facts of this case. Petitioner alleged the deprivation of a substantial constitutional right, recognized by this Court as applicable to state criminal proceedings. . . . But he failed to assert the claim until long after his trial, verdict, sentence, and appeal had run their course. In findings challenged only half-heartedly here, the District Court determined that no motion, oral or otherwise, raised the issue of discrimination in the selection of the grand jurors prior to trial. The Court of Appeals affirmed, and on petition for rehearing conducted its own search of the record in a vain effort to see whether the files or docket entries in the case supported petitioner's contention that he had made such a motion. We will not disturb the coordinate findings of these two courts on a question such as this.

The waiver provision of the Rule therefore coming into play, the District Court held that there had been no "cause shown" which would justify relief. It said:

> Petitioner offers no plausible explanation of his failure to timely make his objection to the composition of the grand jury. The method of selecting grand jurors then in use was the same system employed by this court for years. No reason has been suggested why petitioner or his attorney could not have ascertained all of the facts necessary to present the objection to the court prior to trial. The same grand jury that indicted petitioner also indicted his two white accomplices. The case had no racial overtones. The government's case against petitioner was, although largely circumstantial, a strong one. There was certainly sufficient evidence against petitioner to justify a grand jury in determining that he should stand trial for the offense with which he was charged. . . . Petitioner has shown no cause why the court should grant him relief from his waiver of the objection to the composition of the grand jury. . . .

In denying the relief, the court took into consideration the question of prejudice to petitioner. This approach was approved in *Shotwell* where the Court stated:

> [W]here, as here, objection to the jury selection has not been timely raised under Rule 12(b)(2), it is entirely proper to take absence of prejudice into account in determining whether a sufficient showing has been made to warrant relief from the effect of that Rule.

371 U.S., at 363.

. . .

We hold that the District Court did not abuse its discretion in denying petitioner relief from the application of the waiver provision of Rule 12(b)(2), and that having concluded he was not entitled to such relief, it properly dismissed his application for federal habeas corpus. Accordingly, the judgment of the Court of Appeals is Affirmed.[1]

---

387. The reasoning and result of *Davis* were applied in a comparable state case in which the defendant sought federal habeas corpus. "[C]onsiderations of comity and federalism," the Court said, required that the state policy, like the federal policy expressed in Rule 12, be given effect. Francis v. Henderson, 425 U.S. 536, 541 (1976).

Bill of Particulars

FEDERAL RULES OF CRIMINAL PROCEDURE

Rule 7

THE INDICTMENT AND THE INFORMATION

. . .

(f) Bill of Particulars. The court may direct the government to file a bill of particulars. The defendant may move for a bill of particulars before or within 10 days after arraignment or at a later time if the court permits. The government may amend a bill of particulars subject to such conditions as justice requires.

---

[1] Justice Marshall wrote a dissenting opinion, which Justice Douglas and Justice Brennan joined.

United States v. Moore

57 F.R.D. 640 (N.D.Ga.1972)

■ EDENFIELD, DISTRICT JUDGE.

Defendant is charged in an indictment whose complete text reads as follows: "That, on or about the 10th day of May, 1972, in the Northern District of Georgia, Andrea Moore knowingly and intentionally did unlawfully distribute about 1.07 grams of heroin hydrochloride, a Schedule I narcotic drug controlled substance in violation of Title 21, United States Code, Section 841(a)(1)." By her present motions defendant asks that the government file a bill of particulars and that she be allowed to inspect and copy certain enumerated items.

The requested bill of particulars asks the government to:

(1) State the location and address of the alleged distribution;

(2) State whether the alleged distribution occurred inside or outside a building, and if inside a building, state the type of building and the name of any residents or owners thereof;

(3) State the exact date and time of day that the alleged distribution occurred;

(4) State the names and addresses of all persons who directly or indirectly took part in the alleged distribution, either prior to, during, or immediately after the alleged occurrence;

(5) State whether any of the above-named persons were in the employ or were present at the insistence of the United States government, or in the employ of any State or local government;

(6) State the name and address of any informer acting in behalf of the United States government during the alleged distribution.

In its response, the government states that the alleged distribution took place "during the early evening hours" on May 10, 1972, at a residence located in an apartment building at 117 Davage Street, Atlanta, Fulton County, Georgia. The court finds that this information satisfies defendant's requests (1), (2) and (3), above, and as to these requests defendant's motion is denied.

The government has refused to disclose the information requested in paragraphs (4), (5) and (6), above, stating that, "It is sufficient for the purposes of Rule 7(c), Federal Rules of Criminal Procedure, that the indictment apprise the defendant of all the essential facts of the offense charged," and that "The indictment in this case closely follows the language contained in Title 21 U.S.C. § 841(a)(1)." The court disagrees with the notion that a statement of facts sufficient to sustain an indictment is a conclusive argument against granting a bill of particulars. As stated in United States v. Smith, 16 F.R.D. 372, 374 (W.D.Mo.1954), "[T]he fact that an indictment or information conforms to the simple form suggested in the rules is no answer or defense to a motion for a bill of particulars under Rule 7(f). Rule 7(f) necessarily presupposes an indictment or information good against a motion to quash or a demurrer." Rather, "[T]he court may exercise its discretion to order the filing of the bill for the purposes of: (1) informing defendant of the facts constituting the offense and the nature of the charge with sufficient particularity to enable the preparation of an adequate defense; (2) avoiding or minimizing the danger of surprise at trial; and (3) perfecting the record so as to bar a subsequent prosecution for the same offense. [Citations omitted.]" United States v. Davis, 330 F.Supp. 899, 901 (N.D.Ga.1971).

Because the motion for a bill of particulars is directed to the discretion of the court, and is addressed to dissimilar fact situations, it is unsurprising that the decided cases differ as to whether a defendant should be apprised of those who allegedly participated in the wrongful conduct charged, and whether or not their identity as government agents should be ordered disclosed. . . . While no definite rules in this area are possible, guidance is provided by the 1966 Amendment to Rule 7(f) and a number of decisions which have contributed to a desirable decline in the "sporting theory" of criminal justice. . . .

The 1966 Amendment to Rule 7(f) of the Federal Rules of Criminal Procedure, in the words of the Advisory Committee, was "designed to encourage a more liberal attitude by the courts toward bills of particulars without taking away the discretion which courts must have in dealing with such motions in individual cases." Especially recommended by the Committee as an illustration of "wise use of this discretion" was the opinion of Justice Whittaker in United States v. Smith, supra, written when he was a district judge for the Western District of Missouri. In *Smith* the information charged that on August 29, 1954, in Kansas City, Missouri, the defendant transferred several grains of heroin hydrochloride and one marijuana cigarette in violation of federal law. On motion of the defendant the court ordered the government to furnish a bill of particulars stating the date, time and location of the offense, along with the name of the person or persons to whom the defendant allegedly sold and transferred the controlled substances, and whether such person or persons were, at the time of the alleged transfer, employed by or acting at the instance of the government. Said the court: "Nor is it any answer to a motion for a bill of particulars for the government to say: 'The defendant knows what he did, and, therefore, has all the information necessary.' This argument could be valid only if the defendant be *presumed to be guilty*. For only if he is presumed guilty could he know the facts and details of the crime. Instead of being presumed guilty, he is presumed to be innocent. Being presumed to be innocent, it must be assumed 'that he is ignorant of the facts on which the pleader founds his charges.' (citations omitted) . . . Without definite specification of the time and place of commission of the overt acts complained of, *and of the identity of the person or persons dealt with* (emphasis supplied), there may well be difficulty in preparing to meet the general charges of the information, and some danger of surprise." At 375 of 16 F.R.D.

A decision which addresses the exact issue presented here, in the context of an almost identical fact situation, and is specifically cited by the Advisory Committee as an example of how Rule 7(f) should be applied, is strong authority for granting the requested relief.

In addition to *Smith* several cases both prior and subsequent to the 1966 Amendment have required the government to disclose the identity of persons either participants in, or victims of the crime allegedly committed.

. . .

The court recognizes that the present indictment makes no mention of the participants in the alleged unlawful distribution of heroin. Any distinction drawn between this case and those cited above, however, on the basis of the government having excluded reference to an easily supplied "John Doe" or to unnamed conspirators, the court finds to be insubstantial relative to the rights of the accused. In this case, as in *Smith* . . . the defendant has a right to know the names and addresses of those persons, known to the government, who directly took part in the alleged illegal act, and whether such persons were agents of the government. To hold otherwise, as stated in *Smith*, would be to charge the defendant with knowledge of an offense to which she is presumed innocent until proven guilty, and would be to deny information favorable to her case as either direct or impeaching evidence. . . . As a matter of technical pleading it may be questioned that the government should be required to disclose, pursuant to a motion for a bill of particulars, which if any participants in an alleged crime were agents of the government. A request for such disclosure, it might be argued, should be made in the form of a motion for discovery. . . . In the present action, however, such a two-step procedure would involve unnecessary delay where the government, required to disclose the identity of participants known to it, has only to indicate which of those participants were in its employ.

Defendant's motion for particulars is not granted as requested. Here . . . the court must rationalize the disclosure timetable of the Jencks Act, 18 U.S.C. § 3500 (1970), by which statements of witnesses to be called by the government need not be disclosed until trial, with that of Brady v. Maryland, 373 U.S. 83 (1963), and its progeny, requiring the production of information helpful to the defense "at the appropriate time requested." Williams v. Dutton, 400 F.2d [797 (5th Cir.1968)] at 800. There exist here competing considerations of the defendant's right to information which will allow preparation of an adequate defense, and "the prosecution's concern that the furnishing of its witness list to an accused might lead to intimidation of the witnesses and might provide an accused with the opportunity to learn the witnesses' testimony in advance of trial and fabricate appropriate alibis." United States v. Houston, 339 F.Supp. [762 (N.D.Ga.1972)] at 765–66. In allowing defendant's request for particulars, therefore, the court requires the government to disclose the identity of only those persons who participated in and were present at the alleged distribution, or distributions if there were more than one, and does not require the disclosure, at this time, of the names and addresses of non-participant witnesses. . . .

. . .

---

388. "When a bill of particulars has been furnished, the government is strictly limited to the particulars which it has specified, i.e., the bill limits the scope of the government's proof at the trial. . . . This is not to say that any variance in the proof from the information in the bill of particulars is grounds for reversal. It is well settled that a variance between the proof and the bill of particulars is not grounds for reversal unless the defendant was prejudiced by the variance." United States v. Haskins, 345 F.2d 111, 114 (6th Cir.1965).

389. "It is obviously a matter of degree how far an accused must be advised in advance of the details of the evidence that will be produced against him, and no definite rules are possible. All that can be said is that he must know enough to be able to produce in season whatever evidence he may have in answer, and that the charge must become clear enough at the trial to make the judgment available to him on a future plea of 'former jeopardy.' The general doctrine is that the extent of the particulars granted lies in the discretion of the trial court, and any abuse of that discretion can of course be reviewed upon appeal." United States v. Russo, 260 F.2d 849, 850 (2d Cir.1958). Accord United States v. Davidoff, 845 F.2d 1151 (2d Cir.1988) (RICO prosecution; bill of particulars detailing uncharged racketeering acts required).

390. The defendant was indicted for perjury before a grand jury. One count of the indictment charged that she had falsely given a negative answer to the question: "Did you ever collect dues for the Communist Party?" Before trial the government filed a bill of particulars stating that the dues in question had been collected from two named persons "[s]ometime during the day in the months of August, September and October of 1946. Sometime during the day in January, 1948." On the day after the trial started, the government filed a supplemental bill of particulars listing three additional persons from whom dues had been collected in "1945 and 1946." The prosecuting attorney indicated that although he had the information on which the second bill was based at the time the first bill was filed, it had slipped his mind when he filed the first bill due to "the busyness of his office" and he had recalled it to mind for the first time when he filed the supplemental bill; as soon as he recalled the information, he called defense counsel and advised him of it prior to filing the supplemental bill. Defense counsel moved that the supplemental bill be stricken or that the defense be given a ten-day continuance to prepare to meet the evidence included in the supplemental bill. United States v. Neff, 212 F.2d 297 (3d Cir.1954). Finding that "the burden of the defense was greatly increased by reason of the permitted filing of the second supplemental bill of particulars and that she was deprived of adequate opportunity to meet the charge therein contained," id. at 309–10, the court concluded that one or the other of the remedies sought by the defendant should have been granted, and it reversed the conviction on the related count.

Joinder

FEDERAL RULES OF CRIMINAL PROCEDURE

Rule 8

JOINDER OF OFFENSES OR DEFENDANTS

(a) Joinder of Offenses. The indictment or information may charge a defendant in separate counts with 2 or more offenses if the offenses charged—whether felonies or misdemeanors or both—are of the same or similar character, or are based on the same act or transaction, or are connected with or constitute parts of a common scheme or plan.

(b) Joinder of Defendants. The indictment or information may charge 2 or more defendants if they are alleged to have participated in the same act or transaction, or in the same series of acts or transactions, constituting an offense or offenses. The defendants may be charged in one or more counts together or separately. All defendants need not be charged in each count.

Rule 13

JOINT TRIAL OF SEPARATE CASES

The court may order that separate cases be tried together as though brought in a single indictment or information if all offenses and all defendants could have been joined in a single indictment or information.

Rule 14

RELIEF FROM PREJUDICIAL JOINDER

(a) Relief. If the joinder of offenses or defendants in an indictment, an information, or a consolidation for trial appears to prejudice a defendant or the government, the court may order separate trials of counts, sever the defendants' trials, or provide any other relief that justice requires.

(b) Defendant's Statements. Before ruling on a defendant's motion to sever, the court may order an attorney for the government to deliver to the court for in camera inspection any defendant's statement that the government intends to use as evidence.

---

391. "Joint trials play a vital role in the criminal justice system, accounting for almost one third of federal criminal trials in the past five years. . . . Many joint trials—for example, those involving large conspiracies to import and distribute illegal drugs—involve a dozen or more codefendants. Confessions by one or more of the defendants are commonplace—and indeed the probability of confession increases with the number of participants, since each has reduced assurance that he will be protected by his own silence. It would impair both the efficiency and the fairness of the criminal justice system to require, in all these cases of joint crimes where incriminating statements exist, that prosecutors bring separate proceedings, presenting the same evidence again and again, requiring victims and witnesses to repeat the inconvenience (and sometimes trauma) of testifying, and randomly favoring the last-tried defendants who have the advantage of knowing the prosecution's case beforehand. Joint trials generally serve the interests of justice by avoiding inconsistent verdicts and enabling more accurate assessment of relative culpability—advantages which sometimes operate to the defendant's benefit. Even apart from these tactical considerations, joint trials generally serve the interests of justice by avoiding the scandal and inequity of inconsistent verdicts." Richardson v. Marsh, 481 U.S. 200, 209–10 (1987) (6–3).

United States v. Satterfield

548 F.2d 1341 (9th Cir.1977)

■ ANTHONY M. KENNEDY, CIRCUIT JUDGE:

In this case we reverse a robbery conviction, for the appellant was improperly joined with a codefendant for trial.

On October 9, 1974 a ten-count indictment was returned against appellant Satterfield and one Harvey Willard Merriweather. The charges pertained to five Oregon bank robberies committed in the greater Portland area during the summer of 1974. Merriweather and Satterfield were joined in a single indictment charging that Merriweather alone had perpetrated the first, second, and fifth robberies, and that Merriweather and appellant Satterfield together had committed the third and the fourth.

It was never alleged that Satterfield was involved in the first, second, and fifth robberies, whether as a participant in a common plan or in any other manner. The Government conceded as much at trial. The indictment, moreover, did not charge the defendants with conspiracy. A jury found both defendants guilty as charged. We affirm Merriweather's conviction by separate unpublished memorandum. We reverse the judgment against Satterfield and remand for further proceedings.

At various stages of the proceedings below, Satterfield timely moved for a separate trial on the ground that under Fed.R.Crim.P. 8(b), he had been improperly joined in the indictment. He contends that the trial court erred in refusing to grant his motions. We agree.

. . . Rule 8(a) applies only to joinder of offenses against a single defendant. Where more than one defendant is named in an indictment, the provisions of rule 8(b) control. . . .

Nevertheless, in evaluating an allegation of misjoinder of persons under rule 8(b), the controlling standards for such joinder are best understood by contrasting them with the standards for joinder of offenses in a single defendant trial under rule 8(a). While rule 8(a) permits joinder against one defendant of offenses "of the same or similar character," even where those offenses arise out of wholly separate, unconnected transactions . . . rule 8(b) treats joinder of *multiple* defendants differently. In United States v. Roselli, [432 F.2d 879 (9th Cir.1970),] we described the operation of the rule as follows:

> Under Rule 8(b), the sole basis for joinder of charges against multiple defendants is that the defendants "are alleged to have participated in the same act or transaction or in the same series of acts or transactions constituting an offense or offenses." It is irrelevant that Rule 8(a) permits charges "of the same or similar character" to be joined against a single defendant, even though they do not arise out of the same or connected transactions. Charges against multiple defendants may not be joined merely because they are similar in character, and even dissimilar charges may be joined against multiple defendants if they arise out of the same series of transactions constituting an offense or offenses.

432 F.2d at 898 (citations omitted).

From the foregoing, it follows that Satterfield was properly joined in the indictment and for trial only if all of the offenses charged in the indictment arose out of the same series of transactions. Joinder under rule 8(b) cannot be based on a finding that the offenses charged were merely of the same or a similar character. In considering what constitutes a "series of transactions" we have stated that the term "transaction" is a word of flexible meaning. . . . Whether or not multiple offenses joined in an indictment constitute a "series of acts or transactions" turns on the degree to which they are related. In the cases under rule 8(b), that relation is most often established by showing that substantially the same facts must be adduced to prove each of the joined offenses. . . . We have thus stated that rule 8(b)'s " 'goal of maximum trial convenience consistent with minimum prejudice' is best served by permitting initial joinder of charges against multiple defendants whenever the common activity constitutes a substantial portion of the proof of the joint charges." United States v. Roselli, 432 F.2d at 899. Other logical relationships might also be sufficient to establish that a group of offenses constitutes a "series of acts or transactions," but a mere showing that the events occurred at about the same time, or that the acts violated the same statutes, is not enough. . . .

Notwithstanding our express policy that rule 8(b) should be construed broadly in favor of initial joinder . . . we are convinced that in the instant case Satterfield was improperly joined with the codefendant, Merriweather.

Most of the testimony at the trial related to the first, second, and fifth robberies, which were committed by Merriweather alone. The evidence against Merriweather was strong. Descriptions of a vehicle leaving the scene of the fifth robbery matched his car. A search of the car pursuant to a warrant revealed $5,000 in currency, and a mask and clothing similar to that worn at one or more of the robberies by a person later identified as Merriweather. Eye witness testimony and bank surveillance films from closed circuit television cameras were also introduced at trial to identify Merriweather as the perpetrator of the first, second, and fifth robberies. The evidence adduced at trial relative to the first, second, and fifth robberies pertained solely to acts undertaken by Merriweather alone. Furthermore, in a separate trial of Satterfield for the third and fourth robberies, evidence pertaining to the first, second, and fifth robberies would have been irrelevant. Thus, this is not a situation where substantially the same facts would have been adduced at separate trials. Since a nexus between each offense charged in the indictment was absent, we cannot say, on these facts, that the five robberies each arose out of the same series of acts or transactions. Joinder of Satterfield cannot be justified merely because the robberies which Merriweather perpetrated alone were somewhat similar in character to the robberies in which both defendants participated.

Relying on our holding in United States v. Patterson, 455 F.2d 264 (9th Cir.1972), the Government nevertheless argues that joinder was proper in this case because one of the defendants named in the indictment was mentioned in every count and because the modus operandi in each bank robbery was similar. It contends that this similarity provides the needed nexus between the joined offenses and establishes that the offenses charged constituted "a series of transactions." In *Patterson*, the indictment charged that the appellant and one Mortillaro had engaged in multiple counts of mail fraud; it was also alleged that Mortillaro and a third defendant, one Aquino, had engaged in offenses with substantially the same modus operandi. In holding that joinder under rule 8(b) was proper, we noted that Mortillaro was a common participant in each count and that the modus operandi in each count was "basically the same." Id. at 266. We concluded that appellant and the others were charged with "the same basic fraudulent scheme which they jointly and individually executed within a six month period." Id.

Patterson is distinguishable from this case on various grounds. First, a mere similarity in the manner in which several offenses are carried out—a similar "modus operandi"—is insufficient by itself to justify joinder under rule 8(b), absent some factual or logical relation among those offenses. In *Patterson*, the indictment charged that each incident of mail fraud had been carried out in an intricate and highly sophisticated manner that suggested a close connection among the offenses charged against the three defendants. Indeed, we found the existence of a "scheme" that had been jointly and individually executed. In this case, as noted above, the Government conceded at trial that the first, second, and fifth robberies were not part of any common scheme or plan in which Satterfield had participated.

As a practical matter, moreover, the five robberies in this case did not reflect a distinct pattern. They were certainly not virtually identical. Although the robbers were disguised during the robberies, the disguises were not the same every time. In any event, use of disguises is so common in bank robberies that resorting to the device on different occasions does not by itself constitute a common pattern. Any similarity between the disguises worn at the several robberies fails to reach the level of similarity present in *Patterson*, where each count charged that the defendants had engaged in complex criminal ventures that had been carried out in virtually the same manner. Given these factors, we reject the Government's claim that a similar modus operandi justified joining Satterfield in an indictment that charged Merriweather with the five robberies.

The Government makes a second argument, related to the "modus operandi" justification discussed above. It claims that evidence as to all the robberies would have been admissible to establish Merriweather's motive, intent, etc., even if he and Satterfield had been tried jointly in a prosecution limited to the third and fourth robberies. Citing our decision in *Roselli*, the Government concludes that because the evidence as to all robberies would have been admissible in a trial limited to the crimes in which both defendants allegedly participated, joinder was proper.

Although superficially appealing, the argument, on closer scrutiny, is unpersuasive. Even assuming that at a joint trial limited to the third and fourth robberies evidence of Merriweather's involvement in the other three offenses would have been admissible against him to show motive, etc., it does not follow that joinder under rule 8(b) was proper. The evidence put forth to prove an offense for which a defendant is tried will generally be more extensive, and thus more damaging, than that which would be adduced to establish a prior crime as proof of such matters as motive or intent. At a joint trial, where one defendant is charged with offenses in which the other defendants did not participate, the detailed evidence introduced to establish guilt of the separate offense may shift the focus of the trial to the crimes of the single defendant. In such cases, codefendants run a high risk of being found guilty merely by association. That risk was present here, where highly probative evidence was introduced to show that Merriweather had committed the first, second, and fifth robberies.

It is also significant that where evidence of prior criminal acts is proffered, the trial court has discretion to limit, or even to exclude, such evidence if its probative value is substantially outweighed by the danger of unfair prejudice, confusion of the issues, or misleading the jury, or by considerations of undue delay, waste of time, or needless presentation of cumulative evidence. . . . Where multiple offenses are charged in an indictment, however, a trial judge must permit the prosecution to establish each of those offenses beyond a reasonable doubt.

The Government's argument, moreover, is conceptually wrong. Where the prosecution introduces evidence of prior crimes to show motive or like matters, the test of admissibility is frequently whether the prior offenses are similar to those charged. As noted above, while such similarity permits joinder under rule 8(a), it is simply not sufficient for joinder under rule 8(b).

Finally, the Government argues that if joinder under rule 8(b) was improper the error was harmless and reversal is not required. The foregoing discussion, however, shows that Satterfield was substantially prejudiced by joinder with Merriweather. To reiterate: The jury first heard evidence on the fifth robbery, proof of which was exceptionally strong against Meriweather. Subsequently the jury heard evidence pertaining to the first and second robberies. This evidence, relating to Merriweather alone, could have had no other effect than to prejudice Satterfield in the precise manner against which rule 8(b) seeks to protect. Furthermore, the case against Merriweather for the three robberies committed by him alone was stronger than the case against Satterfield for the third and fourth robberies. Although the trial court instructed the jury that the evidence relating to the first, second, and fifth robberies concerned Merriweather alone, in our view the substantial proof of Merriweather's involvement in these robberies prejudiced Satterfield.

We recognize that even permissible joinder will often result in some prejudice to a defendant. The purpose of rule 8(b) is to limit joinder to those cases where considerations of trial efficiency clearly outweigh a defendant's interest in a separate trial. . . . In this case, serious prejudice to Satterfield has been demonstrated. Misjoinder under rule 8(b) therefore requires that his conviction be set aside.

. . .

392.

The justification for a liberal rule on joinder of offenses appears to be the economy of a single trial. The argument against joinder is that the defendant may be prejudiced for one or more of the following reasons: (1) he may become embarrassed or confounded in presenting separate defenses; (2) the jury may use the evidence of one of the crimes charged to infer a criminal disposition on the part of the defendant from which is found his guilt of the other crime or crimes charged; or (3) the jury may cumulate the evidence of the various crimes charged and find guilt when, if considered separately, it would not so find. A less tangible, but perhaps equally persuasive, element of prejudice may reside in a latent feeling of hostility engendered by the charging of several crimes as distinct from only one. Thus in any given case the court must weigh prejudice to the defendant caused by the joinder against the obviously important considerations of economy and expedition in judicial administration.

. . .

It is a principle of long standing in our law that evidence of one crime is inadmissible to prove *disposition* to commit crime, from which the jury may infer that the defendant committed the crime charged. Since the likelihood that juries will make such an improper inference is high, courts presume prejudice and exclude evidence of other crimes unless that evidence can be admitted for some substantial, legitimate purpose. The same dangers appear to exist when two crimes are joined for trial, and the same principles of prophylaxis are applicable.

Evidence of other crimes is admissible when relevant to (1) motive, (2) intent, (3) the absence of mistake or accident, (4) a common scheme or plan embracing the commission of two or more crimes so related to each other that proof of the one tends to establish the other, and (5) the identity of the person charged with the commission of the crime on trial. When the evidence is relevant and important to one of these five issues, it is generally conceded that the prejudicial effect may be outweighed by the probative value.

If, then, under the rules relating to other crimes, the evidence of each of the crimes on trial would be admissible in a separate trial for the other, the possibility of "criminal propensity" prejudice would be in no way enlarged by the fact of joinder. When, for example, the two crimes arose out of a continuing transaction or the same set of events, the evidence would be independently admissible in separate trials. Similarly, if the facts surrounding the two or more crimes on trial show that there is a reasonable probability that the same person committed both crimes due to the concurrence of unusual and distinctive facts relating to the manner in which the crimes were committed, the evidence of one would be admissible in the trial of the other to prove identity. In such cases the prejudice that might result from the jury's hearing the evidence of the other crime in a joint trial would be no different from that possible in separate trials.

The federal courts . . . have, however, found no prejudicial effect from joinder when the evidence of each crime is simple and distinct, even though such evidence might not have been admissible in separate trials under the rules just discussed. This rests upon the assumption that, with a proper charge, the jury can easily keep such evidence separate in their deliberations and, therefore, the danger of the jury's cumulating the evidence is substantially reduced. . . .

. . .

In summary, then, even where the evidence would not have been admissible in separate trials, if, from the nature of the crimes charged, it appears that the prosecutor might be able to present the evidence in such a manner that the accused is not confounded in his defense and the jury will be able to treat the evidence relevant to each charge separately and distinctly, the trial judge need not order severance or election at the commencement of the trial. If, however, it appears at any later stage in the trial that the defendant will be embarrassed in making his defense or that there is a possibility that the jury will become or has become confused, then, upon proper motion, the trial judge should order severance.

Drew v. United States, 331 F.2d 85, 88–92 (D.C.Cir.1964).

There is a helpful discussion of the matter of joinder generally and the relationship among the provisions of Rule 8(a) and (b) and Rule 14 in United States v. Velasquez, 772 F.2d 1348 (7th Cir.1985). With respect to the element of same or similar transactions, see United States v. Grey Bear, 863 F.2d 572 (8th Cir.1988).

393. "Prejudice may develop when an accused wishes to testify on one but not the other of two joined offenses which are clearly distinct in time, place and evidence. His decision whether to testify will reflect a balancing of several factors with respect to each count: the evidence against him, the availability of defense evidence other than his testimony, the plausibility and substantiality of his testimony, the possible effects of demeanor, impeachment, and cross-examination. But if the two charges are joined for trial, it is not possible for him to weigh these factors separately as to each count. If he testifies on one count, he runs the risk that any adverse effects will influence the jury's consideration of the other count. Thus he bears the risk on both counts, although he may benefit on only one. Moreover, a defendant's silence on one count would be damaging in the face of his express denial of the other. Thus he may be coerced into testifying on the count upon which he wished to remain silent." Cross v. United States, 335 F.2d 987, 989 (D.C.Cir.1964).

"[N]o need for a severance exists until the defendant makes a convincing showing that he has both important testimony to give concerning one count and strong need to refrain from testifying on the other. In making such a showing, it is essential that the defendant present enough information—regarding the nature of the testimony he wishes to give on one count and his reasons for not wishing to testify on the other—to satisfy the court that the claim of prejudice is genuine and to enable it intelligently to weigh the considerations of 'economy and expedition in judicial administration' against the defendant's interest in having a free choice with respect to testifying." Baker v. United States, 401 F.2d 958, 977 (D.C.Cir.1968).

See United States v. Jordan, 112 F.3d 14 (1st Cir.1997) (defendant prevented from testifying on one count lest he subject himself to cross-examination on another count; conviction reversed); United States v. Dockery, 955 F.2d 50 (D.C.Cir.1992) (evidence of prior felony conviction, inadmissible as to one count if tried separately, admitted; conviction reversed).

Courts have sometimes said that an acquittal on some counts of an indictment indicates that the jury based its verdict on the evidence material to each count and that the defendant was not prejudiced by the joinder with respect to the counts on which he was found guilty. E.g., Gornick v. United States, 320 F.2d 325, 326 (10th Cir.1963). But see *Cross*, note 393 above, 355 F.2d at 991.

394. The courts of appeals have usually declined to reverse a conviction because a motion under Rule 14 for separate trials of defendants was denied. So long as joinder was proper under Rule 8(b), the courts have relied on the rule that severance pursuant to Rule 14 is a matter within the discretion of the trial judge, whose ruling will not be reversed unless it is an abuse of discretion, and on the giving of instructions to the jury in order to prevent prejudice to the defendant.

Confirming this practice, in Zafiro v. United States, 506 U.S. 534 (1993), the Court held that there is no "bright-line rule" that requires severance when codefendants have conflicting defenses. It said that "[m]utually antagonistic defenses are not prejudicial *per se*," and that even if prejudice is shown, severance is not necessarily required; rather, the appropriate relief, including measures like limiting instructions, is a matter for the "district court's sound discretion." Id. at 538–39. Noting the preference for a joint trial of codefendants indicted together, the Court said: "[W]hen defendants properly have been joined under Rule 8(b), a district court should grant a severance under Rule 14 only if there is a serious risk that a joint trial would compromise a specific trial right of one of the defendants, or prevent the jury from making a reliable judgment about guilt or innocence." Such a situation might exist, it said, when evidence that a jury should not consider with regard to one defendant is admissible with regard to the other or if exculpatory evidence with respect to one defendant would not be admissible at a joint trial. Id. at 539.

On the other hand, if there has been an improper joinder of defendants under Rule 8(b), courts have not hesitated to reverse. Misjoinder of defendants is not reversible error per se, however, and is subject to harmless-error analysis. United States v. Lane, 474 U.S. 438 (1986) (7–2).

395. Bruton v. United States, 391 U.S. 123 (1968), casts doubt on courts' reliance on jury instructions to prevent prejudice in joint trials. Overruling Delli Paoli v. United States, 352 U.S. 232 (1957), the Court held that it was reversible error to admit a codefendant's confession inculpating the defendant even though the trial judge instructed the jury that the confession was inadmissible hearsay against the defendant and should not be considered in determining his guilt or innocence. Admission of the confession violated the defendant's "right of cross-examination secured by the Confrontation Clause of the Sixth Amendment," 391 U.S. at 126.[2] The Court said: "[In many cases] . . . the jury can and will follow the trial judge's instructions. . . . Nevertheless . . . there are some contexts in which the risk that the jury will not, or cannot, follow instructions is so great, and the consequences of failure so vital to the defendant, that the practical and human limitations of the jury system cannot be ignored. . . . Such a context is presented here, where the powerfully incriminating extrajudicial statements of a codefendant, who stands accused side-by-side with the defendant, are deliberately spread before the jury in a joint trial." Id. at 135–36.

2. The Court noted that the confession was clearly inadmissible against the defendant "under traditional rules of evidence," and that its conclusion was not an intimation that recognized exceptions to the hearsay rule "necessarily raise questions under the Confrontation Clause." 391 U.S. at 128 n.3.

"[W]here a nontestifying codefendant's confession incriminating the defendant is not directly admissible against the defendant . . . the Confrontation Clause bars its admission at their joint trial, even if the jury is instructed not to consider it against the defendant and even if the defendant's own confession is admitted against him. Of course, the defendant's confession may be considered at trial in assessing whether his codefendant's statements are supported by sufficient 'indicia of reliability' to be directly admissible against him (assuming the 'unavailability' of the codefendant) despite the lack of opportunity for cross-examination . . . and may be considered on appeal in assessing whether any Confrontation Clause violation was harmless. . . ." Cruz v. New York, 481 U.S. 186, 193–94 (1987) (5–4).

In Richardson v. Marsh, 481 U.S. 200 (1987) (6–3), the Court held that *Bruton* does not require exclusion of a codefendant's confession from which all references to the defendant have been eliminated and which incriminate her only when linked with other evidence introduced at the trial. "[T]he Confrontation Clause is not violated by admission of a nontestifying codefendant's confession with a proper limiting instruction when, as here, the confession is redacted to eliminate not only the defendant's name, but any reference to her existence." Id. at 211. Distinguishing inferential incrimination from direct incrimination in the codefendant's confession itself, the Court observed: "[W]hile it may not always be simple for the members of the jury to obey the instruction that they disregard an incriminating inference, there does not exist the overwhelming probability of their inability to do so that is the foundation of Bruton's exception to the general rule." Id. at 208. *Bruton* applies, however, if the defendant's name is redacted from the codefendant's confession and replaced by a blank or the word "deleted." Gray v. Maryland, 523 U.S. 185 (1998) (5–4). *Richardson* was distinguished on the basis that there the confession had been redacted to omit any indication that another person had been named. Exclusion of a codefendant's confession is not required if he takes the stand and denies having made the confession. "[W]here a codefendant takes the stand in his own defense, denies making an alleged out-of-court statement implicating the defendant, and proceeds to testify favorably to the defendant concerning the underlying facts, the defendant has been denied no rights protected by the Sixth and Fourteenth Amendments." Nelson v. O'Neil, 402 U.S. 622, 629–30 (1971) (6–3). Cf. Tennessee v. Street, 471 U.S. 409 (1985). In United States v. Hill, 901 F.2d 880 (10th Cir.1990), the court held that, the codefendant not having testified, *Bruton* was violated even though the codefendant's counsel had stated in the opening statement that the codefendant would testify. The court observed that the defendant should not be penalized for his codefendant's change of strategy.

396. For cases involving possible or actual prejudice from the joint trial of several defendants, see, e.g., United States v. Mayfield, 189 F.3d 895 (9th Cir.1999) (inconsistent defenses; conviction reversed); United States v. Breinig, 70 F.3d 850 (6th Cir.1995) (otherwise inadmissible prejudicial evidence admitted; conviction reversed); United States v. Romanello, 726

F.2d 173 (5th Cir.1984) (antagonistic defenses; conviction reversed); United States v. Provenzano, 688 F.2d 194 (3d Cir.1982) (inconsistent defenses, inability to call codefendant as witness; convictions affirmed); United States v. Crawford, 581 F.2d 489 (5th Cir.1978) (irreconcilable and antagonistic defenses; convictions reversed); United States v. Walton, 552 F.2d 1354 (10th Cir.1977) (codefendant's unexpected testimony incriminated defendant; conviction affirmed); United States v. Rosenwasser, 550 F.2d 806 (2d Cir.1977) (evidence admitted of similar crimes committed by codefendant, which implicated defendant; conviction affirmed).

United States v. Zafiro, 945 F.2d 881 (7th Cir.1991), aff'd, 506 U.S. 534 (1993), see p. 775 note 394 above, contains a good discussion of the circumstances in which a severance should be granted. The court observed that "mutual antagonism, finger-pointing, and other manifestations or characterizations of the effort of one defendant to shift the blame from himself to a codefendant neither control nor illuminate the question of severance." Id. at 886. See United States v. Novod, 927 F.2d 726, 728 (2d Cir.1991), in which the court said that the defendant must show "compelling prejudice" to invoke "retroactive misjoinder" of counts.

397. The defendants were indicted as follows:

Count One. The two Schaffers and the three Stracuzzas, for transporting stolen goods from New York to Pennsylvania, between May 15, 1953, and July 27, 1953;

Count Two. Marco and the Stracuzzas, for transporting stolen goods from New York to West Virginia, between June 11, 1953, and July 27, 1953;

Count Three. Karp and the Stracuzzas, for transporting stolen goods from New York to Massachusetts from May 21, 1953, to July 27, 1953;

Count Four. All defendants, for conspiracy to commit the substantive offenses charged in the first three counts.

It was conceded that the joinder of the charges in the indictment and the joint trial of the defendants were proper. At the close of the government's case, however, the conspiracy count was dismissed for failure of proof, the evidence having shown three separate operations all involving the Stracuzzas. On that showing, there was no basis for a joint trial of the Schaffers, Marco, and Karp. Schaffer v. United States, 362 U.S. 511 (1960).

Should the trial court grant a severance and a new trial to those defendants, the prosecution of the Stracuzzas having already been terminated by pleas? Suppose all counts had been submitted to the jury and its verdict was that the defendants were guilty respectively of all the offenses charged in the first three counts and they were all not guilty of conspiracy. See id. at 523–24 (Douglas, J., dissenting). See also United States v. Diaz-Munoz, 632 F.2d 1330 (5th Cir.1980) (*Schaffer* situation, in which trial court relied on government representation that proper joinder would be established; conviction reversed); United States v. Lane, 584 F.2d 60 (5th Cir.1978) (*Schaffer* situation; convictions reversed).

Consolidation

United States v. McDaniels

57 F.R.D. 171 (E.D.La.1972)

Alvin B. Rubin, District Judge. Twelve cases have been consolidated for the hearing of pre-trial motions. Some of the defendants moved to consolidate six of these cases for trial, into two groups of three each. The combinations sought are:

Criminal Action Nos.	Group I. Defendants
72–330	Deola R. Richardson, Clyde Jacquet, Carolyn S. McDaniels, Thelma L. Jones
72–331	Deola R. Richardson, Clyde Jacquet, Sharon Morgan, Doris Augustine, Gladys Fascio, Althea Oates
72–334	Deola R. Richardson
	Group II.
72–332	Deola R. Richardson, Theresa Robinson
72–333	Deola R. Richardson, Eartha Brown, Eartha St. Ann
72–335	Audrey Lee Delair, Eartha St. Ann, Samaria Justine Lambert, Valencia L. Smith, Brenda Cryer

Each Group would include eight defendants. The Group I trials would involve two conspiracies charged as 30 separate substantive offenses—a total of 24 counts—while the Group II trials would involve three conspiracies charged separately—32 separate substantive offenses totaling 24 counts.

Defendants urge consolidation on the following grounds: the prosecutions involve allegations of "identical related conduct," charged under the same federal statutes; the time span of the conspiracies and substantive acts charged in each case are virtually the same; it is likely that many of the witnesses in each case will be the same and that much of their testimony will be repetitious; the same defenses [as yet undisclosed] will be developed; the court will be called on to make the same rulings; and the instructions to the jury will be the same. Consolidation will enable counsel to concentrate their efforts and provide a more effective defense.

Further, the consolidation would:

A. Reduce the number of trials involving these two groups from six to two.

B. Only one instead of three defendants would face multiple trials.

C. Mrs. Richardson would face two trials instead of five.

Each argument requires separate examination.

Rule 13, F.R.Cr.P., permits the Court to order two or more indictments to be tried together "if the offenses, and the defendants if there is more than one, could have been joined in a single indictment. . . ." Rule 8(b) determines when two or more defendants may be charged in the same indictment: "if they are alleged to have participated in the *same* act or transaction or in the *same* series of acts or transactions constituting an offense or offenses." (Emphasis supplied.)

When, as here, more than one defendant is involved, the only applicable test for joinder is Rule 8(b). . . .

Rule 8(b) speaks of an allegation of joint participation in the acts or transactions constituting the offense or offenses, but it is not necessary to satisfy its terms that the allegation actually be made. it is enough if, on the facts, a single indictment covering all the defendants could properly have been drawn. . . . Separate indictments can be tried together under Rule 13, therefore, not only if they patently satisfy Rule 8(b) but if, given the facts, the charges could have been written in a way that would meet the requirements of Rule 8(b).

Rule 8(b) also permits a conspiracy count against all of the named defendants to be joined with substantive offenses, each against less than all the defendants, if the substantive offenses arose out of the conspiracy. . . .

Moreover, if defendants are charged jointly with a conspiracy and with substantive acts, the joinder is proper even if the jury acquits on the conspiracy count, the trial court dismisses the conspiracy count for lack of evidence, or the conspiracy count is reversed by an appellate court. . . . Thus, the permissibility of joinder depends not on the fact of joint participation in a conspiracy by all of the defendants but on whether such an allegation could reasonably have been made. . . .

Finally, the Court of Appeals for the Fifth Circuit has held that the Rule's joinder provisions "should not be interpreted in a technical or legalistic sense," but rather with a view toward its purpose of avoiding repetitious proof in separate trials. Tillman v. United States, 5 Cir.1969, 406 F.2d 930, 934.

Essentially, it is defendants' contention that the separate conspiracies charged in Nos. 72–330 and 72–331 could have been charged in one conspiracy in a single indictment, together with substantive offenses charged in Nos. 72–330, 72–331 and 72–334, and that the separate conspiracies charged in Nos. 72–332, 72–333 and 72–335 could have been charged in a single conspiracy, together with the substantive counts alleged in those three indictments.

But the defendants who are alleged to have conspired with Mrs. Richardson and Mrs. Jacquet in 72–330 and 72–331 are not alleged to have acted jointly with each other. While it is settled conspiracy law that all of the conspirators need not have contact with or even knowledge of the identity of all the other conspirators, so long as each conspired with common conspirators in a joint plan . . . it is necessary that there be some evidence that there was in fact a joint or common plan before joinder can be effected under 8(b).

The offenses must arise out of the same transaction or be connected. . . . The conduct upon which each of the counts is based must be part of a factually related transaction or series of events in which all the defendants participated, though not all of the defendants need participate in every act constituting the offense or offenses. . . . And even then, the common activity must constitute a substantial portion of the proof of the joined charges or joinder must fail. . . . The fact that the defendants in 72–330 and 72–331 are charged with the same or similar violations of the law based on conduct taking place during the same time span is not a basis in and of itself for a joint trial. . . .

The situation presented here is much the same as if A, B and C were charged with a conspiracy to rob Y Bank during the period September 1–15, 1972, and with the substantive crime of bank robbery on September 15, while, by separate indictment, A, B and D are charged with a conspiracy to rob Y Bank during the period September 1–15, 1972, and with the substantive crime of bank robbery on September 14. The offenses charged would be unconnected, not properly joinable. The government might fail in its burden of proof, and the defendants might be acquitted. Or it might develop at the trial that in fact there was one joint plan by A, B, C and D to commit two bank robberies. In that event, the charges of two separate conspiracies might fail. But the trial of the hypothetical charges would properly be separate and distinct.

The propriety of a joint trial must be determined on the facts presently available. These do not show that the defendants in the separate cases sought to be consolidated are charged with "identical related conduct" but only that they are charged with committing like crimes involving the names of other applicants during the same general span of time. Without additional factual data, the court can neither assume that there was a joint plan nor that the government will try to prove one.

In No. 72–330 and 72–334, Mrs. Richardson and Mrs. Jacquet are charged with conspiring with two other defendants in a scheme to use the United States mails to receive money fraudulently from the Louisiana Department of Welfare in the period October 7, 1970 to March 15, 1972. In No. 72–331, the same two defendants are charged with conspiracy with four other named defendants to accomplish the same crime in the period October 7, 1970 to February 15, 1972. The evidence adduced at the hearing on the motion to require handwriting exemplars tends to indicate that the offenses charged in these two indictments involve different applications for assistance in different names and different alleged forged endorsements.

In 72–334, where Mrs. Richardson is charged alone, there is no conspiracy allegation, but Mrs. Richardson is charged with substantive offenses that appear to have arisen out of the conspiracies separately alleged in 72–330 and 72–331. . . . It may well be that, by agreement, the counts against Mrs. Richardson that relate to one case could be severed from those relating to the other case, and those counts consolidated with the respective cases, but no motion to this effect has been urged, and the court doubts its authority to order such a division.

The defendants contend that the grand jury could easily have charged one conspiracy involving all of the defendants in 72–330 and 72–331, together with the substantive counts charged in the three indictments. Whether or not the evidence would support such a charge is unknown to the court. If a single conspiracy had been charged, it would have been necessary for the prosecution to prove that only one conspiracy existed, and proof of two separate conspiracies involving different parties would have required acquittal. . . . It is not for the court then to say, a priori, that there must have been evidence of one conspiracy.

Nor does this lodge absolute control over the form of trial in the government and the grand jury. The government and the grand jury have charged certain discrete crimes. The defendants may well urge that, whatever they have done, they have not committed the crimes charged.

Like considerations apply to the requested consolidation of Nos. 72–332, 72–333 and 72–335. In Count I of each of these indictments separate conspiracies are charged. The time periods of the conspiracies alleged in 72–332, 72–333 and 72–335 are September 30, 1970 to February 15, 1972; October 6, 1970 to February 15, 1972 and May 6, 1971 to February 15, 1972, respectively. Each alleges conspiracy to use the United States mail to obtain money fraudulently from the Louisiana Department of Welfare. In 72–333, Mrs. Richardson and Mrs. St. Ann are charged as co-conspirators with one other defendant. In 72–332, Mrs. Richardson is charged with conspiracy with another defendant. In 72–335, Mrs. St. Ann is charged with conspiracy with four others. These are each charges of separate conspiracies and separate crimes.

Finally, we deal with some of the arguments of administrative convenience. While the background testimony may be the same in each case, the details must necessarily be different. Each application must be separately considered. Each check must be separately introduced. It will not be necessary (or even permissible) for *all* of the applications and *all* of the checks to be introduced repeatedly. The handwriting experts will testify separately as to each individual and separately with respect to each application. No great time saving in these will result from consolidation.

Whether or not the defenses will be the same as to each defendant in each case, only the defendants' counsel knows and they perhaps cannot be certain at this time. Experienced defense counsel, like good quarterbacks, should, and do, reserve the power to call audibles even after the team is lined up for the play.

That rulings on the same legal issues may be required in various cases creates no problem. Presumably in connection with legal issues that arise at trial, like those considered in these pre-trial motions, the ruling in the first case on any issue will create a precedent in later cases. The same jury instructions may be required in each case, but, once framed, the court will be able to follow its charge in the initial case as a basic outline.

It must be conceded that consolidation would enable defense counsel to concentrate their efforts and perhaps to provide a more effective defense. But the fact that multiple defendants have chosen to employ one set of defense counsel should not alone be reason for consolidation.

The first of the separate trials will be shorter than a single consolidated trial. It is conceivable that the verdict in the first case might affect further proceedings. For example, if the defendants in the first case are acquitted, the United States might decide not to prosecute all or some of the remaining defendants. Or, if there is a conviction, some of the defendants might alter their strategy. Finally, consolidation would in any event result in multiple trials, since it is urged only that six of twelve pending cases be consolidated.

While, on the whole, administrative convenience would likely be better served by consolidation, the jury charges would be more complex because the jury would be considering three separate indictments, and the chances of jury confusion would be greater.

The requirements of 8(b) not having been met, the considerations relating to administrative efficiency are perhaps irrelevant. . . . But if the court has discretion, the efficiency and administrative desirability of consolidated trials do not appear to be so great as to justify consolidation, over the objection of either party. For these reasons, the motion to consolidate is denied.

Venue

"The trial of all crimes . . . shall be held in the state where the said crimes shall have been committed; but when not committed within any state, the trial shall be at such place or places as the Congress may by law have directed." U.S. Constitution art. III, § 2.

"In all criminal prosecutions, the accused shall enjoy the right to a speedy and public trial, by an impartial jury of the State and district wherein the crime shall have been committed, which district shall have been previously ascertained by law. . . ." U.S. Constitution amend. VI.

398.

Aware of the unfairness and hardship to which trial in an environment alien to the accused exposes him, the Framers wrote into the Constitution that "The Trial of all Crimes . . . shall be held in the State where the said Crimes shall have been committed . . ." Article III, § 2, cl. 3. As though to underscore the importance of this safeguard, it was reinforced by the provision of the Bill of Rights requiring trial "by an impartial jury of the State and district wherein the crime shall have been committed." Sixth Amendment. By utilizing the doctrine of a continuing offense, Congress may, to be sure, provide that the locality of a crime shall extend over the whole area through which force propelled by an offender operates. Thus, an illegal use of the mails or of other instruments of commerce may subject the user to prosecution in the district where he sent the goods, or in the district of their arrival, or in any intervening district. Plainly enough, such leeway not only opens the door to needless hardship to an accused by prosecution remote from home and from appropriate facilities for defense. It also leads to the appearance of abuses, if not to abuses, in the selection of what may be deemed a tribunal favorable to the prosecution.

These are matters that touch closely the fair administration of criminal justice and public confidence in it, on which it ultimately rests. These are important factors in any consideration of the effective enforcement of the criminal law. They have been adverted to, from time to time, by eminent judges; and Congress has not been unmindful of them. Questions of venue in criminal cases, therefore, are not merely matters of formal legal procedure. They raise deep issues of public policy in the light of which legislation must be construed. If an enactment of Congress equally permits the underlying spirit of the

> constitutional concern for trial in the vicinage to be respected rather than to be disrespected, construction should go in the direction of constitutional policy even though not commanded by it.

United States v. Johnson, 323 U.S. 273, 275–76 (1944).

Although proper venue is a constitutional right and is a fact to be proved, it does not have to be proved beyond a reasonable doubt like other elements of an offense. Proof by a preponderance of the evidence is sufficient. Furthermore, the test of waiver of a right to proper venue is more relaxed than the test for waiver of other constitutional rights. A failure to instruct on venue is not, like a failure to instruct on other essential elements of an offense, invariably plain error requiring reversal. United States v. Miller, 111 F.3d 747 (10th Cir.1997) (failure to instruct on venue was reversible error because not clear beyond a reasonable doubt that guilty verdict incorporated finding of proper venue).

In United States v. Perez, 280 F.3d 318 (3d Cir.2002), the court discusses when the matter of venue is an issue of material fact requiring an instruction and submission to the jury. Noting a conflict among the circuits and disagreeing with the Tenth Circuit in *Miller*, the court concluded that if there is no facial defect in the indictment, failure to instruct on venue is reviewable error only if the defendant objects to venue no later than the close of the prosecution's case in chief, there is a genuine issue of material fact regarding venue, and the defendant timely requests a jury instruction.

FEDERAL RULES OF CRIMINAL PROCEDURE

Rule 18

PLACE OF PROSECUTION AND TRIAL

Unless a statute or these rules permit otherwise, the government must prosecute an offense in a district where the offense was committed. The court must set the place of trial within the district with due regard to the convenience of the defendant and the witnesses, and the prompt administration of justice.

Rule 20

TRANSFER FOR PLEA AND SENTENCE

(a) Consent to Transfer. A prosecution may be transferred from the district where the indictment or information is pending, or from which a warrant on a complaint has been issued, to the district where the defendant is arrested, held, or present if:

(1) the defendant states in writing a wish to plead guilty or nolo contendere and to waive trial in the district where the indictment,

information, or complaint is pending, consents in writing to the court's disposing of the case in the transferee district, and files the statement in the transferee district; and

(2) the United States attorneys in both districts approve the transfer in writing.

(b) Clerk's Duties. After receiving the defendant's statement and the required approvals, the clerk where the indictment, information, or complaint is pending must send the file, or a certified copy, to the clerk in the transferee district.

(c) Effect of a Not Guilty Plea. If the defendant pleads not guilty after the case has been transferred under Rule 20(a), the clerk must return the papers to the court where the prosecution began, and that court must restore the proceeding to its docket. The defendant's statement that the defendant wished to plead guilty or nolo contendere is not, in any civil or criminal proceeding, admissible against the defendant.

(d) Juveniles.

(1) *Consent to Transfer.* A juvenile, as defined in 18 U.S.C. § 5031, may be proceeded against as a juvenile delinquent in the district where the juvenile is arrested, held, or present if:

(A) the alleged offense that occurred in the other district is not punishable by death or life imprisonment;

(B) an attorney has advised the juvenile;

(C) the court has informed the juvenile of the juvenile's rights—including the right to be returned to the district where the offense allegedly occurred—and the consequences of waiving those rights;

(D) the juvenile, after receiving the court's information about rights, consents in writing to be proceeded against in the transferee district, and files the consent in the transferee district;

(E) the United States attorneys for both districts approve the transfer in writing; and

(F) the transferee court approves the transfer.

(2) *Clerk's Duties.* After receiving the juvenile's written consent and the required approvals, the clerk where the indictment, information, or complaint is pending or where the alleged offense occurred must send the file, or a certified copy, to the clerk in the transferee district.

Rule 21

TRANSFER FOR TRIAL

(a) For Prejudice. Upon the defendant's motion, the court must transfer the proceeding against that defendant to another district if the court is satisfied that so great a prejudice against the defendant exists in the transferring district that the defendant cannot obtain a fair and impartial trial there.

(b) For Convenience. Upon the defendant's motion, the court may transfer the proceeding, or one or more counts, against that defendant to another district for the convenience of the parties and witnesses and in the interest of justice.

(c) Proceedings on Transfer. When the court orders a transfer, the clerk must send to the transferee district the file, or a certified copy, and any bail taken. The prosecution will then continue in the transferee district.

(d) Time to File a Motion to Transfer. A motion to transfer may be made at or before arraignment or at any other time the court or these rules prescribe.

---

399. "[T]he *locus delicti* must be determined from the nature of the crime alleged and the location of the act or acts constituting it." United States v. Anderson, 328 U.S. 699, 703 (1946). For example, if the crime consists of failure to perform an act which the defendant has a duty to perform, the place where the act should have been performed is the *locus delicti*. See, e.g., United States v. Rodriguez-Moreno, 526 U.S. 275 (1999); (7–2) (*locus delicti* of carrying firearm during a crime of violence is any United States v. DiJames, 731 F.2d 758 (11th Cir.1984) (prosecution for failure to file required report; venue only in place prescribed by statute for filing, even though agency would have accepted report elsewhere); United States v. Bagnell, 679 F.2d 826 (11th Cir.1982) (interstate obscenity prosecution). See generally Travis v. United States, 364 U.S. 631, 634–35 (1961).

400. "[V]enue is an essential element to be proved by the Government. However, venue need not be proved by direct evidence. It may be established, as any other facts, by the evidence as a whole or by circumstantial evidence." United States v. Budge, 359 F.2d 732, 734 (7th Cir. 1966). "The general rule governing proof of venue is that there need be no positive testimony that the violation occurred at a specific place, but that it is sufficient if it can be concluded from the evidence as a whole that the act was committed at the place alleged in the indictment." United States v. Karavias, 170 F.2d 968, 970 (7th Cir.1948). See United States v. Miller, 111 F.3d 747 (10th Cir.1997).

AO 94 (Rev. 8/97) Commitment to Another District

UNITED STATES DISTRICT COURT

District of

UNITED STATES OF AMERICA
V.

COMMITMENT TO ANOTHER DISTRICT

DOCKET NUMBER		MAGISTRATE JUDGE CASE NUMBER	
District of Arrest	District of Offense	District of Arrest	District of Offense

CHARGES AGAINST THE DEFENDANT ARE BASED UPON AN

☐ Indictment ☐ Information ☐ Complaint ☐ Other (specify)

charging a violation of **U.S.C. §**

DISTRICT OF OFFENSE

DESCRIPTION OF CHARGES:

CURRENT BOND STATUS:

☐ Bail fixed at $ and conditions were not met
☐ Government moved for detention and defendant detained after hearing in District of Arrest
☐ Government moved for detention and defendant detained pending detention hearing in District of Offense
☐ Other (specify)

Representation: ☐ Retained Own Counsel ☐ Federal Defender Organization ☐ CJA Attorney ☐ None

Interpreter Required? ☐ No ☐ Yes Language:

DISTRICT OF

TO: THE UNITED STATES MARSHAL

You are hereby commanded to take custody of the above named defendant and to transport that defendant with a certified copy of this commitment forthwith to the district of offense as specified above and there deliver the defendant to the United States Marshal for that District or to some other officer authorized to receive the defendant.

Date United States Judge or Magistrate Judge

RETURN

This commitment was received and executed as follows:

DATE COMMITMENT ORDER RECEIVED	PLACE OF COMMITMENT	DATE DEFENDANT COMMITTED

DATE	UNITED STATES MARSHAL	(BY) DEPUTY MARSHAL

401. 18 U.S.C. § 3237.

Offenses begun in one district and completed in another.

(a) Except as otherwise expressly provided by enactment of Congress, any offense against the United States begun in one district and completed in another, or committed in more than one district, may be inquired of and prosecuted in any district in which such offense was begun, continued, or completed.

Any offense involving the use of the mails, transportation in interstate or foreign commerce, or the importation of an object or person into the United States is a continuing offense and, except as otherwise expressly provided by enactment of Congress, may be inquired of and prosecuted in any district from, through, or into which such commerce, mail matter, or imported object or person moves.

. . .

United States v. Busic

549 F.2d 252 (2d Cir.1977)

■ Irving R. Kaufman, Chief Judge:

Prominent among the injuries inflicted upon the American colonists by King George III, according to the signers of the Declaration of Independence, was the despised practice of "transporting us beyond Seas to be tried for pretended offences."[3] This revulsion for adjudication of criminal charges in a remote region, before a jury drawn from a hostile or insouciant citizenry, was responsible for the codification of both Article III, section 2 and the Sixth Amendment to the Constitution. Today, when our vast country can be traversed in a matter of hours, these provisions stand as bulwarks against prosecutorial overreaching in forcing the defendant to answer accusations in a spatially distant and unfriendly environment. But two centuries have wrought changes in our society that have increased both the range of crimes that federal courts confront and the factors underlying the selection of the proper situs of trial. The instant case presents to us five alleged "skyjackers," a variety of malefactor of which the Founders never would have dreamed, and requires us to determine whether it is impermissible to try them in the Eastern District of New York, which embraces the busy airport at which they boarded the airplane they are charged with hijacking and is part of the major metropolitan area in which they reside and effected significant steps toward the ultimate commission of their crime. We believe that trial in that District is proper under the Air Piracy Act, and accords with the relevant constitutional policy. Accordingly, we reverse the order of the district court that dismissed on the basis of improper venue the substantive counts of the indictment, and remand the case for trial.

3. H. Commager, Documents of American History 101 (8 ed. 1968).

I. FACTS

. . .

Zvonko and Julienne Busic, Petar Matanic, Frane Pesut and Mark Vlasic were indicted for the September 10, 1976 hijacking of TWA Flight 355, which was scheduled to fly from LaGuardia Airport in New York City to Chicago. During the preceding several days, pursuant to a carefully devised plan, appellee Zvonko Busic had supplied false names when purchasing five tickets for the flight at various locations in New York City, including LaGuardia Airport. Prior to embarkation he placed a powerful explosive device in a Grand Central Station locker and discarded the key in the Hudson River. The appellees boarded the aircraft with a previously prepared typewritten hijack note and several cast iron pots, which escaped confiscation by security personnel because of an ingenious ruse. By wrapping them with gift paper and ribbons, the appellees convinced the operators of the airport's metal detection devices that the pots were presents for acquaintances. In addition, prior to boarding the appellees had prepared several imitation dynamite sticks by wrapping a quantity of putty in black tape commonly used by electricians. They also had filled their luggage with political pamphlets which they intended to scatter widely by throwing them out of the aircraft as it flew over several European cities.

These were the largely unknown background facts as they existed when the flight crew closed the doors of TWA Flight 355. Shortly thereafter, but before the airplane left the ground, a passenger attempted to use a lavatory in the rear of the cabin. Prior to reaching his destination, however, he confronted Vlasic, who was blocking the aisle. Drawing the passenger's attention to a large leather bag at his feet, Vlasic uttered the following command: "Stop, do not use the lavatory, there are three bombs in this bag. This is a hijack, return to your seat." The passenger complied.

The import of Vlasic's statement was clear and correct. Scant moments later, at an undetermined point beyond the boundaries of the Eastern District of New York, Zvonko Busic handed a note to a flight attendant for transmittal to the pilot. It read:

1. This airplane is hijacked.

2. We are in possession of five gelignite bombs, four of which are set up in cast iron pans, giving them the same kind of force as a giant grenade.

3. In addition, we have left the same kind of bomb in a locker across from the Commodore Hotel on 42nd Street. To find the locker, take the subway entrance by the Bowery Savings Bank. After passing through the token booth, there are three windows belonging to the bank. To the left of these windows are the lockers. The number of the locker is 5713.

4. Further instructions are contained in a letter inside this locker. The bomb can only be activated by pressing the switch to which it is attached, but caution is suggested.

5. The appropriate authorities should be notified from the plane immediately.

6. The plane will ultimately be heading in the direction of London, England.

Two to six minutes later, when the aircraft was in the vicinity of Buffalo, New York, the pilot received the message. By this time Busic, who had transformed the iron pots into imitation bombs in the lavatory, appeared in the cockpit and opened his jacket to reveal a "dynamite vest," which he threatened to detonate if his demands were not met. The pilot, pursuant to the hijacker's orders, flew the airplane first to Montreal and then to Gander, Newfoundland where 33 hostages were released prior to a transatlantic voyage. The hijackers eventually surrendered in Paris.

Authorities in New York, meanwhile, descended upon the locker in Grand Central Station referred to in the hijacking message and which contained the authentic explosive device planted by Busic as well as a list of demands. Following the instructions concerning publication set forth in the note, the New York Times, Washington Post, Chicago Tribune, Los Angeles Times and International Herald Tribune proceeded to afford prominent coverage in their morning editions to a Croatian "Appeal to the American People." Tragically, New York City police officer Brian Murray was killed while attempting to defuse the Grand Central bomb. Upon his return to New York, Zvonko Busic is alleged to have said: "We are proud of what we did. Don't be surprised if you hear about other attacks in the future. We are defending a just cause, yet we are with handcuffs on our wrists."

II. PROCEEDINGS BELOW

The grand jury charged the two Busics, Matanic, Pesut and Vlasic with two counts of air piracy, which are identical except that the first also alleges that the commission of the offense resulted in the death of officer Murray, 49 U.S.C. § 1472(i)(2), and conspiracy, 18 U.S.C. § 371. The appellees moved to dismiss the substantive counts of the indictment[4] because, they argued, venue was improper in the Eastern District. Judge Bartels granted the motion on November 22, 1976 and the Government appealed.

Judge Bartels was aware, as he stated in his opinion, that "none of the defendants and none of the witnesses will have anything more than a fortuitous connection with any district over which the plan flew other than the Eastern District of New York and its surrounding metropolitan area." Moreover, he realized that "the most logical place for air piracy cases to be tried would be in the district where defendants boarded the aircraft." He

4. It is conceded that venue for the conspiracy count is proper in the Eastern District of New York, where several overt acts occurred. . . .

stressed that the appellees "conspired, prepared to commit the offense, had the intent to commit the crime and boarded the plane in this district." Nevertheless, he said they had not seized and exercised actual control over the aircraft before it had entered the airspace of the Western District of New York. And he reasoned that although 49 U.S.C. § 1473(a) authorized the laying of venue in, inter alia, any district where the offense of air piracy had "begun," the acts here had not reached that stage "where the preparations have progressed to the first steps toward the commission of the crime, such as the first contact with the aircraft personnel notifying them of the intention to hijack" prior to the airplane's passing the boundaries of the Eastern District. Thus he concluded that under the relevant statutory provision venue clearly was improper in Brooklyn. We disagree and believe that the appellees plainly are triable in the place where the crime had "begun," the Eastern District of New York.

III. DISCUSSION

The Constitution and 49 U.S.C. § 1473(a) establish the parameters for our consideration of the instant appeal. Article III, section 2 provides that trials "shall be held in the State where the said Crimes shall have been committed; but when not committed within any State, the Trial shall be at such Place or Places as the Congress may by Law have directed." The Sixth Amendment, adopted after the Judiciary Act of 1789 divided the states into federal judicial districts, speaks similarly: "In all criminal prosecutions, the accused shall enjoy the right to a speedy and public trial, by an impartial jury of the State and district wherein the crime shall have been committed, which district shall have been previously ascertained by law. . . ." In cases of air piracy, Congress by special statute has determined that

> Whenever the offense is begun in one jurisdiction and completed in another, or committed in more than one jurisdiction, it may be dealt with, inquired of, tried, determined, and punished in any jurisdiction in which such offense was begun, continued, or completed, in the same manner as if the offense had been actually or wholly committed therein.

49 U.S.C. § 1473(a).

The appellees contend that the facts presented here make § 1473(a) susceptible to only one narrow constitutional reading, which would advance the moment of beginning so near the point of consummation of the crime that the words might as well be read as synonymous and without any significant statutory difference. They argue that the essence of the crime of air piracy, according to the language in the Act, is the intentional and forcible "seizure or exercise of control" of an aircraft. Thus the offense charged here cannot be committed until there is a transfer of control from pilot to hijacker. This, they say, did not occur until the airplane was flying over Buffalo. Moreover, they claim that the requisite transfer of control had not "begun" until Busic gave his threatening note to a member of the flight crew who then transmitted it to the captain. This event transpired, they argue, after the aircraft left the Eastern District and thus, the appellees are not triable there since all of their conduct prior to the precise moment when the hijack note was passed constituted "mere preparation" rather than a "beginning" of the crime.

We do not think that this tortured and hyperconstricted reading of the statute is warranted. Congress responded to a national epidemic of hijackings by making air piracy a federal crime. A major benefit of this action, according to the Report of the House Committee on Interstate and Foreign Commerce, was the expected alleviation of the insuperable difficulties that law enforcement officials encountered in determining the exact state and county in which the seizure of an aircraft occurred. Recent airborne crimes had dramatically underscored gaps in existing laws that provided suspects with a haven from prosecution. . . . Any rational construction of § 1473(a) must account for Congress's special concern to permit a just and convenient locus for prosecution of this most unique crime which can begin and continue to be committed over several states in this high speed jet travel age in a matter of minutes. Accordingly, it appears—and the appellees do not seriously dispute—that Congress intended the Government to enjoy the broadest possible choice of venue within constitutional bounds.

The facts of this case bear eloquent testimony to the fact that the crime of hijacking had begun in the Eastern District of New York. Essential to the success of the appellees' scheme was their ability to board the aircraft with the cast iron pots and imitation dynamite sticks. Their goal was accomplished through an ingeniously conceived stratagem designed to circumvent the suspicion of airport security personnel. Busic purchased tickets for the flight at LaGuardia and elsewhere through the use of fictitious names. He planted a bomb in a locker at Grand Central Terminal with a list of demands. The appellees also filled their luggage with Croatian freedom pamphlets for ultimate distribution in European cities. Once aboard the airplane, and before it left the ground, Vlasic obstructed access to the lavatory (into which Busic went to construct his imitation explosive devices) and announced, "This is a hijack." In short, every one of the appellees' acts prior to the actual transmittal of the typewritten note was unambiguously corroborative of their unequivocal intention to hijack Flight 355. Under these circumstances it is obvious to us that 49 U.S.C. § 1473(a) serves its purpose well and intelligently by permitting prosecution in the Eastern District of New York.

It is equally clear to us that this result does not violate any constitutional rights of the appellees. Although Article III, section 2 concerns venue (place of trial) and the Sixth Amendment vicinage (residence of petit jurors), both can be traced to the ancient historical fact that at one time jurors decided cases on the basis of personal knowledge . . . and were drawn from the vicinity of the crime. . . . An even more significant source of these constitutional standards, however, can be discerned in the vigorous reaction of the American colonists evoked by Parliament's provision that trials of individuals accused of treason in Massachusetts be conducted in England. The Virginia Resolves responded to that edict by declaring: "thereby the inestimable Privilege of being tried by a Jury from the Vicinage, as well as the Liberty of summoning and producing Witnesses on such Trial, will be taken away from the Party accused." Journals of the House of Burgesses of Virginia, 1766–69, at 214 (Kennedy ed. 1906).

The Framers' mandate for trial in the vicinity of the crime was meant to be a safeguard against the injustice and hardship involved when the accused was prosecuted in a place remote from his home and acquaintances. Indeed, the appellees in this case urge us to enforce this privilege, and cite to us Justice Frankfurter's oft-repeated language in United States v. Johnson . . . [p. 785 above].

Of course, the appellees would have us hold that the "vicinage" contemplated by the Founders and Justice Frankfurter forbade the Government, in this instance, from proceeding in the Eastern District and mandated that it prosecute in Buffalo, a city whose only contact with this case is the mere fortuity of being five miles below the speeding jet airplane that the appellees had just hijacked. We cannot perceive any justification in the Constitution for such a result.

We do not believe that the appellees' blind insistence that the dictionary meaning of the term "seizure" mechanically govern our interpretation of "begun" is warranted. Congress did not direct its statute to an abstract world of Platonic forms, but to the real world of action. We are compelled, therefore, to reject the appellees' attempt, by their crabbed construction of the term "begun," to fasten upon the federal Air Piracy Act the precise over-technicality that Congress explicitly wished to avoid. The many purposeful and unambiguous acts of the appellees in the Eastern District clearly support our determination that the crime of hijacking had begun there within the intent of Congress. It is incomprehensible to us that courts must conduct a potentially fruitless search to determine exactly where a crime is committed when the alleged perpetrators are traveling at 600 m.p.h. In the case before us the note was passed in New Jersey or Pennsylvania, but Busic first confronted the pilot in western New York State. If the steward had tripped, Busic may not have reached his destination until the aircraft passed over Ohio, or was speeding over the middle of Lake Erie. And since the appellees concede that the Government could indict and try them at any point over which the jet flew after leaving the Buffalo airspace, we are hard pressed to accept the validity of the argument that constitutional restrictions on prosecutorial discretion preclude trying this case in the Eastern District of New York, which Judge Bartels correctly recognized as the sensible one, but instead permit prosecution in other districts over which the aircraft chanced to fly after seizure, no matter how fortuitous the contact.

Finally, we believe that the extensive case law under 18 U.S.C. § 3237(a), the venue provision for so-called continuous crimes after which 49 U.S.C. § 1473(a) was modeled, supports, to the extent that it is relevant, the result we have reached. Generally applicable to mobile offenses other than air piracy, section 3237 requires an initial judicial inquiry into whether a particular crime involves a single act or movement. If the court determines, after considering the nature of the offense and the legislative and constitutional policies . . . that it requires only a single act, then the prosecution must proceed in the district where the crime was committed *in toto*; if the crime, however, involves a continuous course of conduct, the offense may be tried wherever it was "begun, continued or completed." Since the appellees concede, as they must, that hijacking is by its very nature a continuous crime, the many cases that limit prosecution to the solitary district in which the offense was "committed," and adjure conducting the trial where mere preparatory acts took place, are clearly distinguishable. . . .

The proper focus of our inquiry, rather, is upon cases such as United States v. Cashin, 281 F.2d 669 (2d Cir.1960), in which this court realized that the crime of use of the mails to facilitate a fraudulent scheme in violation of the Securities Act was begun in Alabama where "most of the acts necessary to [the] execution" of the crime occurred, although the alleged mailing took place in New York. Id. at 674. . . . The principle that is gleaned from these cases is that when the nature of the offense defies the notion that it was committed in a single district Congress may, within constitutional norms, fix venue wherever sufficient purposeful acts occurred. . . . In the case before us involving hijacking, a crime which Congress considered sufficiently unique to require its own special venue provision, we conclude that the appellees' alleged acts in the Eastern District of New York easily surpassed this behavioral threshold.

. . .

---

402. "[M]ere inconvenience, interference with one's routine occupational and personal activities, and other incidental burdens which normally follow when one is called upon to resist a serious charge do not ipso facto make the necessary showing that a transfer is required in the interest of justice. As a general rule a criminal prosecution should be retained in the original district. To warrant a transfer from the district where an indictment was properly returned it should appear that a trial there would be so unduly burdensome that fairness requires the transfer to another district of proper venue where a trial would be less burdensome; and, necessarily, any such determination must take into account any countervailing considerations which may militate against removal." United States v. United States Steel Corporation, 233 F.Supp. 154, 157 (S.D.N.Y.1964).

In United States v. Jessup, 38 F.R.D. 42 (M.D.Tenn.1965), a prosecution for mail fraud (18 U.S.C. §§ 1341–42), the court concluded on the basis of "such practical factors as the place of residence of the defendant, the expense and trouble to be caused by a trial in a far removed district, the expense involved in the transportation of witnesses, the volume of records and the difficulty of moving them, the economic loss to be suffered by an extended period away from one's place of work, [and] the advantage of being able to provide the jury with views of immovable exhibits, if permitted by the court,'' that the case should be transferred from Tennessee to Mississippi to avoid ''substantial hardship'' to the defendants. Id. at 45, 48. The court said that ''apparently the only factor on the Government's side disfavoring a transfer is the fact that the indictments were obtained in this district and the United States Attorney here is familiar with this complex case, and has doubtless engaged in some preliminary preparation''; this, the court said, ''is of little moment since all of the factors militating in favor of a transfer were, or should have been known to the Government when it chose to prosecute in this district rather than in Mississippi or in one of the many other districts wherein it alleges these charges could have been brought.'' Id. at 48. Compare United States v. Stratton, 649 F.2d 1066 (5th Cir.1981) (grant of motion to transfer by some defendants resulted in improper venue for nonconsenting codefendants). See generally Jones v. Gasch, 404 F.2d 1231 (D.C.Cir.1967).

403. A motion for transfer is ''addressed to the sound discretion of the trial court,'' whose decision ''should not be overturned where there is no clear showing of abuse.'' Estes v. United States, 335 F.2d 609, 613–14 (5th Cir.1964).

Speedy Trial

''In all criminal prosecutions, the accused shall enjoy the right to a speedy and public trial. . . .'' U.S. Constitution amend. VI.

''The right of a speedy trial is necessarily relative. It is consistent with delays and depends upon circumstances. It secures rights to a defendant. It does not preclude the rights of public justice.'' Beavers v. Haubert, 198 U.S. 77, 87 (1905). See Pollard v. United States, 352 U.S. 354 (1957). ''[T]he Sixth Amendment's guarantee of a speedy trial . . . is an important safeguard to prevent undue and oppressive incarceration prior to trial, to minimize anxiety and concern accompanying public accusation and to limit the possibilities that long delay will impair the ability of an accused to defend himself. However, in large measure because of the many procedural safeguards provided an accused, the ordinary procedures for criminal prosecution are designed to move at a deliberate pace. A requirement of unreasonable speed would have a deleterious effect both upon the rights of the accused and upon the ability of society to protect itself.'' United States v. Ewell, 383 U.S. 116, 120 (1966).

---

404. "The right to a speedy trial is not a theoretical or abstract right but one rooted in hard reality on the need to have charges promptly exposed. If the case for the prosecution calls on the accused to meet charges rather than rest on the infirmities of the prosecution's case, as is the defendant's right, the time to meet them is when the case is fresh. Stale claims have never been favored by the law, and far less so in criminal cases. Although a great many accused persons seek to put off the confrontation as long as possible, the right to a prompt inquiry into criminal charges is fundamental and the duty of the charging authority is to provide a prompt trial. This is brought sharply into focus when, as here, the accused presses for an early confrontation with his accusers and with the State. Crowded dockets, the lack of judges or lawyers, and other factors no doubt make some delays inevitable. Here, however, no valid reason for the delay existed; it was exclusively for the convenience of the State. On this record the delay with its consequent prejudice is intolerable as a matter of fact and impermissible as a matter of law." Dickey v. Florida, 398 U.S. 30, 37–38 (1970).

In Smith v. Hooey, 393 U.S. 374 (1969), the Court elaborated the reasons for affording a speedy trial and said that they were fully applicable to a person already in prison for another offense.

> At first blush it might appear that a man already in prison under a lawful sentence is hardly in a position to suffer from "undue and oppressive incarceration prior to trial." But the fact is that delay in bringing such a person to trial on a pending charge may ultimately result in as much oppression as is suffered by one who is jailed without bail upon an untried charge. First, the possibility that the defendant already in prison might receive a sentence at least partially concurrent with the one he is serving may be forever lost if trial of the pending charge is postponed. Secondly, under procedures now widely practiced, the duration of his present imprisonment may be increased, and the conditions under which he must serve his sentence greatly worsened, by the pendency of another criminal charge outstanding against him.
>
> And while it might be argued that a person already in prison would be less likely than others to be affected by "anxiety and concern accompanying public accusation," there is reason to believe that an outstanding untried charge (of which even a convict may, of course, be innocent) can have fully as depressive an effect upon a prisoner as upon a person who is at large. . . .
>
> Finally, it is self-evident that "the possibilities that long delay will impair the ability of an accused to defend himself" are markedly increased when the accused is incarcerated in another jurisdiction. Confined in a prison, perhaps far from the place where the offense covered by the outstanding charge allegedly took place, his ability to confer with potential defense witnesses, or even to keep track of their whereabouts, is obviously impaired. And, while "evidence and witnesses disappear, memories fade, and events lose their perspective" [Note, 77 Yale L.J. 767, 769 (1968)], a man isolated in prison is

> powerless to exert his own investigative efforts to mitigate these erosive effects of the passage of time.

Id. at 378–80. The Court held that a state could not disregard a defendant's right to a speedy trial on the sole ground that he was imprisoned in another jurisdiction.

405. In Klopfer v. North Carolina, 386 U.S. 213, 226 (1967), the Court declared that the right to a speedy trial was "one of the most basic rights preserved by our Constitution," and held that it was an element of due process constitutionally required of the states in state criminal proceedings.

Klopfer was a professor at Duke University who participated in a civil rights sit-in at a restaurant. He was indicted and prosecuted for criminal trespass, a misdemeanor. After one trial at which the jury failed to reach a verdict, the prosecutor obtained a "*nolle prosequi* with leave," over Klopfer's objection.

> Under North Carolina criminal procedure, when the prosecuting attorney of a county, denominated the solicitor, determines that he does not desire to proceed further with a prosecution, he may take a *nolle prosequi*, thereby declaring "that he will not, at that time, prosecute the suit further. Its effect is to put the defendant without day, that is, he is discharged and permitted to go whithersoever he will, without entering into a recognizance to appear at any other time." Wilkinson v. Wilkinson, 159 N.C. 265, 266–67 (1912). But the taking of the *nolle prosequi* does not permanently terminate proceedings on the indictment. On the contrary, "When a *nolle prosequi* is entered, the case may be restored to the trial docket when ordered by the judge upon the solicitor's application." State v. Klopfer, 266 N.C. 349, 350 (1966). And if the solicitor petitions the court to *nolle prosequi* the case "with leave," the consent required to reinstate the prosecution at a future date is implied in the order "and the solicitor (without further order) may have the case restored for trial." Ibid. Since the indictment is not discharged by either a *nolle prosequi* or a *nolle prosequi* with leave, the statute of limitations remains tolled. . . .
>
> . . .
>
> The consequence of this extraordinary criminal procedure is made apparent by the case before the Court. A defendant indicted for a misdemeanor may be denied an opportunity to exonerate himself in the discretion of the solicitor and held subject to trial, over his objection, throughout the unlimited period in which the solicitor may restore the case to the calendar. During that period, there is no means by which he can obtain a dismissal or have the case restored to the calendar for trial. In spite of this result, both the Supreme Court and the Attorney General state as a fact, and rely upon it for affirmance in this case, that this procedure as applied to the petitioner placed no limitations upon him, and was in no way violative of his rights. With this we cannot agree.
>
> . . .
>
> . . . The petitioner is not relieved of the limitations placed upon his liberty by this prosecution merely because its suspension permits

> him to go "whithersoever he will." The pendency of the indictment may subject him to public scorn and deprive him of employment, and almost certainly will force curtailment of his speech, associations and participation in unpopular causes. By indefinitely prolonging this oppression, as well as the "anxiety and concern accompanying public accusation,"[5] the criminal procedure condoned in this case by the Supreme Court of North Carolina clearly denies the petitioner the right to a speedy trial which we hold is guaranteed to him by the Sixth Amendment of the Constitution of the United States.

386 U.S. at 214, 216, 221–22.

406. Median time intervals from filing to disposition of criminal defendants disposed of by United States District Courts, Oct. 1, 2001–Sept. 30, 2002:[6]

	Total	Dismissed	Plea of Guilty	Court Trial	Jury Trial
Number	78,835	7,217	68,188	759	2,671
Median (months)	6.2	5.2	6.1	3.0	11.9

Barker v. Wingo

407 U.S. 514, 92 S.Ct. 2182, 33 L.Ed.2d 101 (1972)

■ MR. JUSTICE POWELL delivered the opinion of the Court.

. . .

I

On July 20, 1958, in Christian County, Kentucky, an elderly couple was beaten to death by intruders wielding an iron tire tool. Two suspects, Silas Manning and Willie Barker, the petitioner, were arrested shortly thereafter. The grand jury indicted them on September 15. Counsel was appointed on September 17, and Barker's trial was set for October 21. The Commonwealth had a stronger case against Manning, and it believed that Barker could not be convicted unless Manning testified against him. Manning was naturally unwilling to incriminate himself. Accordingly, on October 23, the day Silas Manning was brought to trial, the Commonwealth sought and obtained the first of what was to be a series of 16 continuances of Barker's trial.[7] Barker made no objection. By first convicting Manning,

5. United States v. Ewell, 383 U.S. 116, 120 (1966).

6. From Table D–6, Annual Report of the Director of the Administrative Office of the United States Courts, 2002. "Filing" means the return of an indictment or the filing of an information. "Disposition" means dismissal of the case, return of a verdict of not guilty, or the imposition of sentence following a guilty plea or verdict of guilty.

7. There is no explanation in the record why although Barker's initial trial was set for October 21, no continuance was sought until October 23, two days after the trial should have begun.

the Commonwealth would remove possible problems of self-incrimination and would be able to assure his testimony against Barker.

The Commonwealth encountered more than a few difficulties in its prosecution of Manning. The first trial ended in a hung jury. A second trial resulted in a conviction, but the Kentucky Court of Appeals reversed because of the admission of evidence obtained by an illegal search. . . . At his third trial, Manning was again convicted, and the Court of Appeals again reversed because the trial court had not granted a change of venue. . . . A fourth trial resulted in a hung jury. Finally, after five trials, Manning was convicted, in March 1962, of murdering one victim, and after a sixth trial, in December 1962, he was convicted of murdering the other.

The Christian County Circuit Court holds three terms each year—in February, June, and September. Barker's initial trial was to take place in the September term of 1958. The first continuance postponed it until the February 1959 term. The second continuance was granted for one month only. Every term thereafter for as long as the Manning prosecutions were in process, the Commonwealth routinely moved to continue Barker's case to the next term. When the case was continued from the June 1959 term until the following September, Barker, having spent 10 months in jail, obtained his release by posting a $5,000 bond. He thereafter remained free in the community until his trial. Barker made no objection, through his counsel, to the first 11 continuances.

When on February 12, 1962, the Commonwealth moved for the twelfth time to continue the case until the following term, Barker's counsel filed a motion to dismiss the indictment. The motion to dismiss was denied two weeks later, and the Commonwealth's motion for a continuance was granted. The Commonwealth was granted further continuances in June 1962 and September 1962, to which Barker did not object.

In February 1963, the first term of court following Manning's final conviction, the Commonwealth moved to set Barker's trial for March 19. But on the day scheduled for trial, it again moved for a continuance until the June term. It gave as its reason the illness of the ex-sheriff who was the chief investigating officer in the case. To this continuance, Barker objected unsuccessfully.

The witness was still unable to testify in June, and the trial, which had been set for June 19, was continued again until the September term over Barker's objection. This time the court announced that the case would be dismissed for lack of prosecution if it were not tried during the next term. The final trial date was set for October 9, 1963. On that date, Barker again moved to dismiss the indictment, and this time specified that his right to a speedy trial had been violated. The motion was denied; the trial commenced with Manning as the chief prosecution witness; Barker was convicted and given a life sentence.

Barker appealed his conviction to the Kentucky Court of Appeals, relying in part on his speedy trial claim. The court affirmed. . . .

II

The right to a speedy trial is generically different from any of the other rights enshrined in the Constitution for the protection of the accused. In addition to the general concern that all accused persons be treated according to decent and fair procedures, there is a societal interest in providing a speedy trial which exists separate from, and at times in opposition to, the interests of the accused. The inability of courts to provide a prompt trial has contributed to a large backlog of cases in urban courts which, among other things, enables defendants to negotiate more effectively for pleas of guilty to lesser offenses and otherwise manipulate the system. In addition, persons released on bond for lengthy periods awaiting trial have an opportunity to commit other crimes. It must be of little comfort to the residents of Christian County, Kentucky, to know that Barker was at large on bail for over four years while accused of a vicious and brutal murder of which he was ultimately convicted. Moreover, the longer an accused is free awaiting trial, the more tempting becomes his opportunity to jump bail and escape. Finally, delay between arrest and punishment may have a detrimental effect on rehabilitation.

If an accused cannot make bail, he is generally confined, as was Barker for 10 months, in a local jail. This contributes to the overcrowding and generally deplorable state of those institutions. Lengthy exposure to these conditions "has a destructive effect on human character and makes the rehabilitation of the individual offender much more difficult."[8] At times the result may even be violent rioting. Finally, lengthy pretrial detention is costly. The cost of maintaining a prisoner in jail varies from $3 to $9 per day, and this amounts to millions across the Nation. In addition, society loses wages which might have been earned, and it must often support families of incarcerated breadwinners.

A second difference between the right to speedy trial and the accused's other constitutional rights is that deprivation of the right may work to the accused's advantage. Delay is not an uncommon defense tactic. As the time between the commission of the crime and trial lengthens, witnesses may become unavailable or their memories may fade. If the witnesses support the prosecution, its case will be weakened, sometimes seriously so. And it is the prosecution which carries the burden of proof. Thus, unlike the right to counsel or the right to be free from compelled self-incrimination, deprivation of the right to speedy trial does not per se prejudice the accused's ability to defend himself.

Finally, and perhaps most importantly, the right to speedy trial is a more vague concept than other procedural rights. It is, for example, impossible to determine with precision when the right has been denied. We cannot definitely say how long is too long in a system where justice is supposed to be swift but deliberate. As a consequence, there is no fixed

8. Testimony of James V. Bennett, Director, Bureau of Prisons, Hearings on Federal Bail Procedures before the Subcommittee on Constitutional Rights and the Subcommittee on Improvements in Judicial Machinery of the Senate Committee on the Judiciary, 88th Cong., 2d Sess., 46 (1964).

point in the criminal process when the State can put the defendant to the choice of either exercising or waiving the right to a speedy trial. If, for example, the State moves for a 60-day continuance, granting that continuance is not a violation of the right to speedy trial unless the circumstances of the case are such that further delay would endanger the values the right protects. It is impossible to do more than generalize about when those circumstances exist. There is nothing comparable to the point in the process when a defendant exercises or waives his right to counsel or his right to a jury trial. Thus . . . any inquiry into a speedy trial claim necessitates a functional analysis of the right in the particular context of the case. . . .

The amorphous quality of the right also leads to the unsatisfactorily severe remedy of dismissal of the indictment when the right has been deprived. This is indeed a serious consequence because it means that a defendant who may be guilty of a serious crime will go free, without having been tried. Such a remedy is more serious than an exclusionary rule or a reversal for a new trial, but it is the only possible remedy.

III

Perhaps because the speedy trial right is so slippery, two rigid approaches are urged upon us as ways of eliminating some of the uncertainty which courts experience in protecting the right. The first suggestion is that we hold that the Constitution requires a criminal defendant to be offered a trial within a specified time period. The result of such a ruling would have the virtue of clarifying when the right is infringed and of simplifying courts' application of it. Recognizing this, some legislatures have enacted laws, and some courts have adopted procedural rules which more narrowly define the right. The United States Court of Appeals for the Second Circuit has promulgated rules for the district courts in that Circuit establishing that the government must be ready for trial within six months of the date of arrest, except in unusual circumstances, or the charge will be dismissed. This type of rule is also recommended by the American Bar Association.

But such a result would require this Court to engage in legislative or rulemaking activity, rather than in the adjudicative process to which we should confine our efforts. We do not establish procedural rules for the States, except when mandated by the Constitution. We find no constitutional basis for holding that the speedy trial right can be quantified into a specified number of days or months. The States, of course, are free to prescribe a reasonable period consistent with constitutional standards, but our approach must be less precise.

The second suggested alternative would restrict consideration of the right to those cases in which the accused has demanded a speedy trial. Most States have recognized what is loosely referred to as the "demand rule," although eight States reject it. It is not clear, however, precisely what is meant by that term. Although every federal court of appeals that has considered the question has endorsed some kind of demand rule, some have regarded the rule within the concept of waiver, whereas others have viewed it as a factor to be weighed in assessing whether there has been a deprivation of the speedy trial right. We shall refer to the former approach as the demand-waiver doctrine. The demand-waiver doctrine provides that a defendant waives any consideration of his right to speedy trial for any period prior to which he has not demanded a trial. Under this rigid approach, a prior demand is a necessary condition to the consideration of the speedy trial right. This essentially was the approach the Sixth Circuit took below.

Such an approach, by presuming waiver of a fundamental right from inaction, is inconsistent with this Court's pronouncements on waiver of constitutional rights. The Court has defined waiver as "an intentional relinquishment or abandonment of a known right or privilege." Johnson v. Zerbst, 304 U.S. 458, 464 (1938). Courts should "indulge every reasonable presumption against waiver," Aetna Ins. Co. v. Kennedy, 301 U.S. 389, 393 (1937), and they should "not presume acquiescence in the loss of fundamental rights," Ohio Bell Tel. Co. v. Public Utilities Comm'n, 301 U.S. 292, 307 (1937). . . . The Court has ruled similarly with respect to waiver of other rights designed to protect the accused. . . .

In excepting the right to speedy trial from the rule of waiver we have applied to other fundamental rights, courts that have applied the demand-waiver rule have relied on the assumption that delay usually works for the benefit of the accused and on the absence of any readily ascertainable time in the criminal process for a defendant to be given the choice of exercising or waiving his right. But it is not necessarily true that delay benefits the defendant. There are cases in which delay appreciably harms the defendant's ability to defend himself. Moreover, a defendant confined to jail prior to trial is obviously disadvantaged by delay as is a defendant released on bail but unable to lead a normal life because of community suspicion and his own anxiety.

The nature of the speedy trial right does make it impossible to pinpoint a precise time in the process when the right must be asserted or waived, but that fact does not argue for placing the burden of protecting the right solely on defendants. A defendant has no duty to bring himself to trial; the State has that duty as well as the duty of insuring that the trial is consistent with due process. Moreover, for the reasons earlier expressed, society has a particular interest in bringing swift prosecutions, and society's representatives are the ones who should protect that interest.

It is also noteworthy that such a rigid view of the demand-waiver rule places defense counsel in an awkward position. Unless he demands a trial early and often, he is in danger of frustrating his client's right. If counsel is willing to tolerate some delay because he finds it reasonable and helpful in preparing his own case, he may be unable to obtain a speedy trial for his client at the end of that time. Since under the demand-waiver rule no time runs until the demand is made, the government will have whatever time is otherwise reasonable to bring the defendant to trial after a demand has been made. Thus, if the first demand is made three months after arrest in a jurisdiction which prescribes a six-month rule, the prosecution will have a total of nine months—which may be wholly unreasonable under the circumstances. The result in practice is likely to be either an automatic, pro forma demand made immediately after appointment of counsel or delays which, but for the demand-waiver rule, would not be tolerated. Such a result is not consistent with the interests of defendants, society, or the Constitution.

We reject, therefore, the rule that a defendant who fails to demand a speedy trial forever waives his right. This does not mean, however, that the defendant has no responsibility to assert his right. We think the better rule is that the defendant's assertion of or failure to assert his right to a speedy trial is one of the factors to be considered in an inquiry into the deprivation of the right. Such a formulation avoids the rigidities of the demand-waiver rule and the resulting possible unfairness in its application. It allows the trial court to exercise a judicial discretion based on the circumstances, including due consideration of any applicable formal procedural rule. It would permit, for example, a court to attach a different weight to a situation in which the defendant knowingly fails to object from a situation in which his attorney acquiesces in long delay without adequately informing his client, or from a situation in which no counsel is appointed. It would also allow a court to weigh the frequency and force of the objections as opposed to attaching significant weight to a purely pro forma objection.

In ruling that a defendant has some responsibility to assert a speedy trial claim, we do not depart from our holdings in other cases concerning the waiver of fundamental rights, in which we have placed the entire responsibility on the prosecution to show that the claimed waiver was knowingly and voluntarily made. Such cases have involved rights which must be exercised or waived at a specific time or under clearly identifiable circumstances, such as the rights to plead not guilty, to demand a jury trial, to exercise the privilege against self incrimination, and to have the assistance of counsel. We have shown above that the right to a speedy trial is unique in its uncertainty as to when and under what circumstances it must be asserted or may be deemed waived. But the rule we announce today, which comports with constitutional principles, places the primary burden on the courts and the prosecutors to assure that cases are brought to trial. We hardly need add that if delay is attributable to the defendant, then his waiver may be given effect under standard waiver doctrine, the demand rule aside.

We, therefore, reject both of the inflexible approaches—the fixed-time period because it goes further than the Constitution requires; the demand-waiver rule because it is insensitive to a right which we have deemed fundamental. The approach we accept is a balancing test, in which the conduct of both the prosecution and the defendant are weighed.[9]

9. Nothing we have said should be interpreted as disapproving a presumptive rule adopted by a court in the exercise of its supervisory powers which establishes a fixed time period within which cases must normally be brought. . . .

IV

A balancing test necessarily compels courts to approach speedy trial cases on an ad hoc basis. We can do little more than identify some of the factors which courts should assess in determining whether a particular defendant has been deprived of his right. Though some might express them in different ways, we identify four such factors: Length of delay, the reason for the delay, the defendant's assertion of his right, and prejudice to the defendant.

The length of the delay is to some extent a triggering mechanism. Until there is some delay which is presumptively prejudicial, there is no necessity for inquiry into the other factors that go into the balance. Nevertheless, because of the imprecision of the right to speedy trial, the length of delay that will provoke such an inquiry is necessarily dependent upon the peculiar circumstances of the case. To take but one example, the delay that can be tolerated for an ordinary street crime is considerably less than for a serious, complex conspiracy charge.

Closely related to length of delay is the reason the government assigns to justify the delay. Here, too, different weights should be assigned to different reasons. A deliberate attempt to delay the trial in order to hamper the defense should be weighed heavily against the government. A more neutral reason such as negligence or overcrowded courts should be weighed less heavily but nevertheless should be considered since the ultimate responsibility for such circumstances must rest with the government rather than with the defendant. Finally, a valid reason, such as a missing witness, should serve to justify appropriate delay.

We have already discussed the third factor, the defendant's responsibility to assert his right. Whether and how a defendant asserts his right is closely related to the other factors we have mentioned. The strength of his efforts will be affected by the length of the delay, to some extent by the reason for the delay, and most particularly by the personal prejudice, which is not always readily identifiable, that he experiences. The more serious the deprivation, the more likely a defendant is to complain. The defendant's assertion of his speedy trial right, then, is entitled to strong evidentiary weight in determining whether the defendant is being deprived of the right. We emphasize that failure to assert the right will make it difficult for a defendant to prove that he was denied a speedy trial.

A fourth factor is prejudice to the defendant. Prejudice, of course, should be assessed in the light of the interests of defendants which the speedy trial right was designed to protect. This Court has identified three such interests: (i) to prevent oppressive pretrial incarceration; (ii) to minimize anxiety and concern of the accused; and (iii) to limit the possibility that the defense will be impaired. Of these, the most serious is the last, because the inability of a defendant adequately to prepare his case skews the fairness of the entire system. If witnesses die or disappear during a delay, the prejudice is obvious. There is also prejudice if defense witnesses are unable to recall accurately events of the distant past. Loss of memory, however, is not always reflected in the record because what has been forgotten can rarely be shown.

We have discussed previously the societal disadvantages of lengthy pretrial incarceration, but obviously the disadvantages for the accused who cannot obtain his release are even more serious. The time spent in jail awaiting trial has a detrimental impact on the individual. It often means loss of a job; it disrupts family life; and it enforces idleness. Most jails offer little or no recreational or rehabilitative programs. The time spent in jail is simply dead time. Moreover, if a defendant is locked up, he is hindered in his ability to gather evidence, contact witnesses, or otherwise prepare his defense. Imposing those consequences on anyone who has not yet been convicted is serious. It is especially unfortunate to impose them on those persons who are ultimately found to be innocent. Finally, even if an accused is not incarcerated prior to trial, he is still disadvantaged by restraints on his liberty and by living under a cloud of anxiety, suspicion, and often hostility. . . .

We regard none of the four factors identified above as either a necessary or sufficient condition to the finding of a deprivation of the right of speedy trial. Rather, they are related factors and must be considered together with such other circumstances as may be relevant. In sum, these factors have no talismanic qualities; courts must still engage in a difficult and sensitive balancing process. But, because we are dealing with a fundamental right of the accused, this process must be carried out with full recognition that the accused's interest in a speedy trial is specifically affirmed in the Constitution.

V

The difficulty of the task of balancing these factors is illustrated by this case, which we consider to be close. It is clear that the length of delay between arrest and trial—well over five years—was extraordinary. Only seven months of that period can be attributed to a strong excuse, the illness of the ex-sheriff who was in charge of the investigation. Perhaps some delay would have been permissible under ordinary circumstances, so that Manning could be utilized as a witness in Barker's trial, but more than four years was too long a period, particularly since a good part of that period was attributable to the Commonwealth's failure or inability to try Manning under circumstances that comported with due process.

Two counterbalancing factors, however, outweigh these deficiencies. The first is that prejudice was minimal. Of course, Barker was prejudiced to some extent by living for over four years under a cloud of suspicion and anxiety. Moreover, although he was released on bond for most of the period, he did spend 10 months in jail before trial. But there is no claim that any of Barker's witnesses died or otherwise became unavailable owing to the delay. The trial transcript indicates only two very minor lapses of memory—one on the part of a prosecution witness—which were in no way significant to the outcome.

More important than the absence of serious prejudice, is the fact that Barker did not want a speedy trial. Counsel was appointed for Barker immediately after his indictment and represented him throughout the period. No question is raised as to the competency of such counsel. Despite the fact that counsel had notice of the motions for continuances, the record shows no action whatever taken between October 21, 1958, and February 12, 1962, that could be construed as the assertion of the speedy trial right. On the latter date, in response to another motion for continuance, Barker moved to dismiss the indictment. The record does not show on what ground this motion was based, although it is clear that no alternative motion was made for an immediate trial. Instead the record strongly suggests that while he hoped to take advantage of the delay in which he had acquiesced, and thereby obtain a dismissal of the charges, he definitely did not want to be tried. . . . The probable reason for Barker's attitude was that he was gambling on Manning's acquittal. The evidence was not very strong against Manning, as the reversals and hung juries suggest, and Barker undoubtedly thought that if Manning were acquitted, he would never be tried. . . .

That Barker was gambling on Manning's acquittal is also suggested by his failure, following the pro forma motion to dismiss filed in February 1962, to object to the Commonwealth's next two motions for continuances. Indeed, it was not until March 1963, after Manning's convictions were final, that Barker, having lost his gamble, began to object to further continuances. At that time, the Commonwealth's excuse was the illness of the ex-sheriff, which Barker has conceded justified the further delay.

We do not hold that there may never be a situation in which an indictment may be dismissed on speedy trial grounds where the defendant has failed to object to continuances. There may be a situation in which the defendant was represented by incompetent counsel, was severely prejudiced, or even cases in which the continuances were granted ex parte. But barring extraordinary circumstances, we would be reluctant indeed to rule that a defendant was denied this constitutional right on a record that strongly indicates, as does this one, that the defendant did not want a speedy trial. We hold, therefore, that Barker was not deprived of his due process right to a speedy trial.

. . .[10]

---

407. In Dillingham v. United States, 423 U.S. 64 (1975), the Court emphasized that once the defendant is arrested, the constitutional right to a speedy trial comes into play, whether or not he has been formally charged by indictment or information.

Delay attributable to the government's interlocutory appeal while the defendant is under indictment or subject to restraint is governed by *Barker*. United States v. Loud Hawk, 474 U.S. 302 (1986) (5–4).

[10] Justice White wrote a concurring opinion, which Justice Brennan joined.

The right to a speedy trial applies to the period between conviction and sentence. See Pollard v. United States, 352 U.S. 354, 361 (1957) ("arguendo"); Perez v. Sullivan, 793 F.2d 249 (10th Cir.1986) (additional cases cited). In *Perez*, the court concluded that a 15-month delay between conviction pursuant to a guilty plea and sentence, during which period the defendant was in jail, did not violate the right to a speedy trial. See Burkett v. Cunningham, 826 F.2d 1208 (3d Cir.1987) (5½-year delay in sentencing; conviction vacated). See also United States v. Mohawk, 20 F.3d 1480 (9th Cir.1994) (10-year delay between defendant's conviction and decision of his timely appeal, although "appalling" and "unconscionable," does not prohibit retrial following reversal of his conviction).

In Moore v. Arizona, 414 U.S. 25, 26 (1973), the Court observed that in Barker v. Wingo, it had "expressly rejected the notion that an affirmative demonstration of prejudice was necessary to prove a denial of the constitutional right to a speedy trial. . . . In addition to possible prejudice, any court must thus carefully weigh the reasons for the delay in bringing an incarcerated defendant to trial." On the element of prejudice, see Cain v. Smith, 686 F.2d 374, 385 (6th Cir.1982), in which the court described a delay of 11½ months from arrest to trial as a "paradigm example" of the prejudice suffered by a defendant who is detained before trial. The court mentioned the disruption of the defendant's family life, isolation from his friends, and inability to work and "the harsh and often times violent atmosphere of jail," id. at 385. The case was remanded for a determination whether the defendant's right to a speedy trial had been denied. See also United States v. Calloway, 505 F.2d 311 (D.C.Cir.1974) (discussing the harmful personal effects of pretrial detention; indictment dismissed).

The Court held that an 8½-year delay between the defendant's indictment and trial violated his right to a speedy trial, in Doggett v. United States, 505 U.S. 647 (1992) (5–4). The Court observed that the right to a speedy trial protects a defendant's interest in fair adjudication, which excessive delay may affect in unidentifiable ways. In this case, the delay presumptively prejudiced the defendant, despite his failure to cite specific demonstrable prejudice. The other *Barker* factors also weighing in the defendant's favor, his right to a speedy trial was denied.

For a very restrictive application of the *Barker* test, see Flowers v. Warden, Connecticut Correctional Institution, Somers, 853 F.2d 131 (2d Cir.1988) (other cases cited), reversing 677 F.Supp. 1275 (D.Conn.1988).

Courts have held that the Due Process Clause confers a right to the decision of a criminal appeal without unreasonable delay; and, although *Barker* was based on the Sixth Amendment's right to a speedy trial, they have applied the *Barker* tests to determine whether the appeal right was violated. E.g., United States v. Smith, 94 F.3d 204 (6th Cir.1996).

408. The Court confirmed the statement in Barker v. Wingo that "the only possible remedy" for denial of the right to a speedy trial is dismissal of the charges, p. 802 above, in Strunk v. United States, 412 U.S. 434 (1973).

The denial of a pretrial motion to dismiss an indictment because of alleged denial of the right to a speedy trial is *not* an order that is subject to interlocutory appellate review. United States v. MacDonald, 435 U.S. 850 (1978). The Court contrasted denial of a pretrial motion to dismiss on the ground of double jeopardy, see Abney v. United States, 431 U.S. 651 (1977). The basis for the speedy trial claim, the Court said, is often not clear before the trial, because it may not be possible to measure prejudice from the delay. Furthermore, the right to a speedy trial is denied by the delay before trial, not by the trial itself—unlike the protection of the Double Jeopardy Clause, which is a right not to be tried a second time. Also, allowance of an interlocutory appeal would furnish an easy means of delaying trial. The Court observed that denial of a motion to dismiss before trial does not mean that another motion made after trial, when prejudice would be apparent, would also be denied.

United States v. Marion

404 U.S. 307, 92 S.Ct. 455, 30 L.Ed.2d 468 (1971)

■ MR. JUSTICE WHITE delivered the opinion of the Court.

This appeal requires us to decide whether dismissal of a federal indictment was constitutionally required by reason of a period of three years between the occurrence of the alleged criminal acts and the filing of the indictment.

On April 21, 1970, the two appellees were indicted and charged in 19 counts with operating a business known as Allied Enterprises, Inc., which was engaged in the business of selling and installing home improvements such as intercom sets, fire control devices, and burglary detection systems. Allegedly, the business was fraudulently conducted and involved misrepresentations, alterations of documents, and deliberate nonperformance of contracts. The period covered by the indictment was March 15, 1965, to February 6, 1967; the earliest specific act alleged occurred on September 3, 1965, the latest on January 19, 1966.

On May 5, 1970, appellees filed a motion to dismiss the indictment "for failure to commence prosecution of the alleged offenses charged therein within such time as to afford [them their] rights to due process of law and to a speedy trial under the Fifth and Sixth Amendments to the Constitution of the United States." No evidence was submitted, but from the motion itself and the arguments of counsel at the hearing on the motion, it appears that Allied Enterprises had been subject to a Federal Trade Commission cease-and-desist order on February 6, 1967, and that a series of articles appeared in the Washington Post in October 1967, reporting the results of that newspaper's investigation of practices employed by home improvement firms such as Allied. The articles also contained purported statements of the then United States Attorney for the District of Columbia describing his office's investigation of these firms and predicting that indictments would soon be forthcoming. Although the statements attributed to the United States Attorney did not mention Allied specifically, that company was mentioned in the course of the newspaper stories. In the summer of 1968, at the request of the United States Attorney's office, Allied delivered certain of its records to that office, and in an interview there appellee Marion discussed his conduct as an officer of Allied Enterprises. The grand jury that indicted appellees was not impaneled until September 1969, appellees were not informed of the grand jury's concern with them until March 1970, and the indictment was finally handed down in April.

Appellees moved to dismiss because the indictment was returned "an unreasonably oppressive and unjustifiable time after the alleged offenses." They argued that the indictment required memory of many specific acts and conversations occurring several years before, and they contended that the delay was due to the negligence or indifference of the United States Attorney in investigating the case and presenting it to a grand jury. No specific prejudice was claimed or demonstrated. The District Court judge dismissed the indictment for "lack of speedy prosecution" at the conclusion of the hearing and remarked that since the Government must have become aware of the relevant facts in 1967, the defense of the case "is bound to have been seriously prejudiced by the delay of at least some three years in bringing the prosecution that should have been brought in 1967, or at the very latest early 1968."

[W]e reverse the judgment of the District Court.

. . .

II

Appellees do not claim that the Sixth Amendment was violated by the two-month delay between the return of the indictment and its dismissal. Instead, they claim that their rights to a speedy trial were violated by the period of approximately three years between the end of the criminal scheme charged and the return of the indictment; it is argued that this delay is so substantial and inherently prejudicial that the Sixth Amendment required the dismissal of the indictment. In our view, however, the Sixth Amendment speedy trial provision has no application until the putative defendant in some way becomes an "accused," an event that occurred in this case only when the appellees were indicted on April 21, 1970.

. . . On its face, the protection of the Amendment is activated only when a criminal prosecution has begun and extends only to those persons who have been "accused" in the course of that prosecution. These provisions would seem to afford no protection to those not yet accused, nor would they seem to require the Government to discover, investigate, and accuse any person within any particular period of time. The Amendment would appear to guarantee to a criminal defendant that the Government will move with the dispatch that is appropriate to assure him an early and proper disposition of the charges against him. "[T]he essential ingredient is orderly expedition and not mere speed." Smith v. United States, 360 U.S. 1, 10 (1959).

Our attention is called to nothing in the circumstances surrounding the adoption of the Amendment indicating that it does not mean what it appears to say, nor is there more than marginal support for the proposition that, at the time of the adoption of the Amendment, the prevailing rule was that prosecutions would not be permitted if there had been long delay in presenting a charge. The framers could hardly have selected less appropriate language if they had intended the speedy trial provision to protect against pre-accusation delay. No opinions of this Court intimate support for appellees' thesis, and the courts of appeals that have considered the question in constitutional terms have never reversed a conviction or dismissed an indictment solely on the basis of the Sixth Amendment's speedy trial provision where only pre-indictment delay was involved.

Legislative efforts to implement federal and state speedy trial provisions also plainly reveal the view that these guarantees are applicable only after a person has been accused of a crime. . . .

. . .

Appellees' position is, therefore, at odds with long-standing legislative and judicial constructions of the speedy trial provisions in both national and state constitutions.

III

It is apparent also that very little support for appellees' position emerges from a consideration of the purposes of the Sixth Amendment's speedy trial provision, a guarantee that this Court has termed "an important safeguard to prevent undue and oppressive incarceration prior to trial, to minimize anxiety and concern accompanying public accusation and to limit the possibilities that long delay will impair the ability of an accused to defend himself." United States v. Ewell, 383 U.S. 116, 120 (1966). . . . Inordinate delay between arrest, indictment, and trial may impair a defendant's ability to present an effective defense. But the major evils protected against by the speedy trial guarantee exist quite apart from actual or possible prejudice to an accused's defense. To legally arrest and detain, the Government must assert probable cause to believe the arrestee has committed a crime. Arrest is a public act that may seriously interfere with the defendant's liberty, whether he is free on bail or not, and that may disrupt his employment, drain his financial resources, curtail his associations, subject him to public obloquy, and create anxiety in him, his family and his friends. . . . So viewed, it is readily understandable that it is either a formal indictment or information or else the actual restraints imposed by arrest and holding to answer a criminal charge that engage the particular protections of the speedy trial provision of the Sixth Amendment.

Invocation of the speedy trial provision thus need not await indictment, information, or other formal charge. But we decline to extend the reach of the amendment to the period prior to arrest. Until this event occurs, a citizen suffers no restraints on his liberty and is not the subject of public accusation; his situation does not compare with that of a defendant who has been arrested and held to answer. Passage of time, whether before or after arrest, may impair memories, cause evidence to be lost, deprive the defendant of witnesses, and otherwise interfere with his ability to defend himself. But this possibility of prejudice at trial is not itself sufficient reason to wrench the Sixth Amendment from its proper context. Possible prejudice is inherent in any delay, however short; it may also weaken the Government's case.

The law has provided other mechanisms to guard against possible as distinguished from actual prejudice resulting from the passage of time between crime and arrest or charge. As we said in United States v. Ewell, supra, at 122, "the applicable statute of limitations . . . is . . . the primary guarantee against bringing overly stale criminal charges." Such statutes represent legislative assessments of relative interests of the State and the defendant in administering and receiving justice; they "are made for the repose of society and the protection of those who may [during the limitation] . . . have lost their means of defence." Public Schools v. Walker, 9 Wall. 282, 288 (1870). These statutes provide predictability by specifying a limit beyond which there is an irrebuttable presumption that a defendant's right to a fair trial would be prejudiced. As this Court observed in Toussie v. United States, 397 U.S. 112, 114–15 (1970):

> The purpose of a statute of limitations is to limit exposure to criminal prosecution to a certain fixed period of time following the occurrence of those acts the legislature has decided to punish by criminal sanctions. Such a limitation is designed to protect individuals from having to defend themselves against charges when the basic facts may have become obscured by the passage of time and to minimize the danger of official punishment because of acts in the far-distant past. Such a time limit may also have the salutary effect of encouraging law enforcement officials promptly to investigate suspected criminal activity.

There is thus no need to press the Sixth Amendment into service to guard against the mere possibility that pre-accusation delays will prejudice the defense in a criminal case since statutes of limitation already perform that function.

Since appellees rely only on potential prejudice and the passage of time between the alleged crime and the indictment, see Part IV, infra, we perhaps need go no further to dispose of this case, for the indictment was the first official act designating appellees as accused individuals and that event occurred within the statute of limitations. Nevertheless, since a criminal trial is the likely consequence of our judgment and since appellees may claim actual prejudice to their defense, it is appropriate to note here that the statute of limitations does not fully define the appellees' rights with respect to the events occurring prior to indictment. Thus, the Government concedes that the Due Process Clause of the Fifth Amendment would require dismissal of the indictment if it were shown at trial that the pre-indictment delay in this case caused substantial prejudice to appellees' rights to a fair trial and that the delay was an intentional device to gain tactical advantage over the accused. . . . However, we need not, and could not now, determine when and in what circumstances actual prejudice resulting from preaccusation delays requires the dismissal of the prosecution. Actual prejudice to the defense of a criminal case may result from the shortest and most necessary delay; and no one suggests that every delay-caused detriment to a defendant's case should abort a criminal prosecution. To accommodate the sound administration of justice to the rights of the defendant to a fair trial will necessarily involve a delicate judgment based on the circumstances of each case. It would be unwise at this juncture to attempt to forecast our decision in such cases.

IV

In the case before us, neither appellee was arrested, charged, or otherwise subjected to formal restraint prior to indictment. It was this event, therefore, that transformed the appellees into "accused" defendants who are subject to the speedy trial protections of the Sixth Amendment.

The 38-month delay between the end of the scheme charged in the indictment and the date the defendants were indicted did not extend beyond the period of the applicable statute of limitations here. Appellees have not, of course, been able to claim undue delay pending trial, since the indictment was brought on April 21, 1970, and dismissed on June 8, 1970. Nor have appellees adequately demonstrated that the pre-indictment delay by the Government violated the Due Process Clause. No actual prejudice to the conduct of the defense is alleged or proved, and there is no showing that the Government intentionally delayed to gain some tactical advantage over appellees or to harass them. Appellees rely solely on the real possibility of prejudice inherent in any extended delay: that memories will dim, witnesses become inaccessible, and evidence be lost. In light of the applicable statute of limitations, however, these possibilities are not in themselves enough to demonstrate that appellees cannot receive a fair trial and to therefore justify the dismissal of the indictment. Events of the trial may demonstrate actual prejudice, but at the present time appellees' due process claims are speculative and premature.

. . .[11]

---

409. *Marion* was applied in United States v. MacDonald, 456 U.S. 1 (1982) (6–3). In that case, the defendant, an army officer, was charged with murder by the military authorities. The charges were subsequently dismissed. More than four years later, he was indicted for the murders by a

[11] Justice Douglas wrote an opinion concurring in the result, which Justice Brennan and Justice Marshall joined, in which he urged that the right to a speedy trial was applicable to the period before indictment but, unless actual prejudice could be shown, had not been violated in this case.

grand jury. The Court declared that during the interim period, the defendant was in the same position as a person under investigation but not charged with any crime. The Court indicated that its reasoning would apply in ordinary situations in which a defendant is charged, the charges are dismissed, and the defendant is subsequently charged a second time.

In United States v. Loud Hawk, 474 U.S. 302 (1986) (5–4), the indictment of the defendants was dismissed with prejudice under Rule 48(b), p. 667 above, and the government appealed under 18 U.S.C. § 3731 (p. 879 below). Almost four years later, the court of appeals reversed the dismissal. The defendants were not detained during the intervening period. They were subsequently indicted again. After further proceedings, the indictments were dismissed on the basis that the defendants' right to a speedy trial had been violated. The Court held that the period after dismissal of the first indictment, when the defendants were not subject to any restriction of their liberty, was covered by *MacDonald* and should not be considered in weighing a claim that the right to a speedy trial has been denied.

See United States v. Lai Ming Tanu, 589 F.2d 82 (2d Cir.1978), in which the defendant was arrested by state police and thereafter indicted by the state. Federal officials had cooperated in the investigation leading to the arrest. Later, the state court dismissed the prosecution on speedy trial grounds. Long afterwards, she was prosecuted by federal officials for the same offense. Without concluding that the right to a speedy trial or due process could never be invoked in such a case, the court held that dismissal of the federal indictment was not required. See also United States v. Ashford, 924 F.2d 1416 (7th Cir.1991) (5½-year delay between arrest and trial not violative of due process).

410. In United States v. Lovasco, 431 U.S. 783, 790–95 (1977) (8–1) the Court reaffirmed its conclusion in *Marion*, above,

> that proof of prejudice is generally a necessary but not sufficient element of a due process claim, and that the due process inquiry must consider the reasons for the delay as well as the prejudice to the accused. . . .
>
> It requires no extended argument to establish that prosecutors do not deviate from "fundamental conceptions of justice" when they defer seeking indictments until they have probable cause to believe an accused is guilty; indeed it is unprofessional conduct for a prosecutor to recommend an indictment on less than probable cause. It should be equally obvious that prosecutors are under no duty to file charges as soon as probable cause exists but before they are satisfied they will be able to establish the suspect's guilt beyond a reasonable doubt. To impose such a duty "would have a deleterious effect both upon the rights of the accused and upon the ability of society to protect itself," United States v. Ewell, 383 U.S. [116 (1966)] at 120. From the perspective of potential defendants, requiring prosecutions to commence when probable cause is established is undesirable because it

would increase the likelihood of unwarranted charges being filed, and would add to the time during which defendants stand accused but untried. These costs are by no means insubstantial since, as we recognized in *Marion*, a formal accusation may "interfere with the defendant's liberty . . . disrupt his employment, drain his financial resources, curtail his associations, subject him to public obloquy, and create anxiety in him, his family and his friends." 404 U.S., at 320. From the perspective of law enforcement officials, a requirement of immediate prosecution upon probable cause is equally unacceptable because it could make obtaining proof of guilt beyond a reasonable doubt impossible by causing potentially fruitful sources of information to evaporate before they are fully exploited. And from the standpoint of the courts, such a requirement is unwise because it would cause scarce resources to be consumed on cases that prove to be insubstantial, or that involve only some of the responsible parties or some of the criminal acts. Thus, no one's interests would be well served by compelling prosecutors to initiate prosecutions as soon as they are legally entitled to do so.

It might be argued that once the Government has assembled sufficient evidence to prove guilt beyond a reasonable doubt, it should be constitutionally required to file charges promptly, even if its investigation of the entire criminal transaction is not complete. Adopting such a rule, however, would have many of the same consequences as adopting a rule requiring immediate prosecution upon probable cause.

First, compelling a prosecutor to file public charges as soon as the requisite proof has been developed against one participant on one charge would cause numerous problems in those cases in which a criminal transaction involves more than one person or more than one illegal act. In some instances, an immediate arrest or indictment would impair the prosecutor's ability to continue his investigation, thereby preventing society from bringing lawbreakers to justice. In other cases, the prosecutor would be able to obtain additional indictments despite an early prosecution, but the necessary result would be multiple trials involving a single set of facts. Such trials place needless burdens on defendants, law enforcement officials, and courts.

Second, insisting on immediate prosecution once sufficient evidence is developed to obtain a conviction would pressure prosecutors into resolving doubtful cases in favor of early—and possibly unwarranted—prosecutions. The determination of when the evidence available to the prosecution is sufficient to obtain a conviction is seldom clear-cut, and reasonable persons often will reach conflicting conclusions. . . . The decision whether to prosecute, therefore, required a necessarily subjective evaluation of the strength of the circumstantial evidence available and the credibility of respondent's denial. Even if a prosecutor concluded that the case was weak and further investigation appropriate, he would have no assurance that a reviewing court would agree. To avoid the risk that a subsequent indictment would be dismissed for preindictment delay, the prosecutor might feel constrained to file premature charges, with all the disadvantages that entails.

Finally, requiring the Government to make charging decisions immediately upon assembling evidence sufficient to establish guilt would preclude the Government from giving full consideration to the desirability of not prosecuting in particular cases. The decision to file criminal charges, with the awesome consequences it entails, requires consideration of a wide range of factors in addition to the strength of the Government's case, in order to determine whether prosecution would be in the public interest. Prosecutors often need more information than proof of a suspect's guilt, therefore, before deciding whether to seek an indictment. . . . Requiring prosecution once the evidence of guilt is clear, however, could prevent a prosecutor from awaiting the information necessary for such a decision.

We would be most reluctant to adopt a rule which would have these consequences absent a clear constitutional command to do so. We can find no such command in the Due Process Clause of the Fifth Amendment.

In United States v. Crouch, 84 F.3d 1497, 1523 (5th Cir.1996) (en banc), the court held that a dismissal for pre-indictment delay requires a showing that the delay "was intentionally brought about by the government for the purpose of gaining some tactical advantage over the accused in the contemplated prosecution or for some other bad faith purpose" and that "the delay caused actual, substantial prejudice to his defense." The requisite delay may not be presumed, rebuttably or otherwise, merely from the length of the delay. See United States v. McMutuary, 217 F.3d 477 (7th Cir.2000) (five-year delay during which witness became unavailable); Bennett v. Lockhart, 39 F.3d 848 (8th Cir.1994) (nine-year delay); United States v. Bartlett, 794 F.2d 1285 (8th Cir.1986) (five-year delay); Stoner v. Graddick, 751 F.2d 1535 (11th Cir.1985) (19-year delay). In all the preceding cases, the court found that the delay did not deprive the defendant of due process.

On the problem of delay before an arrest in order to protect the "cover" of an undercover police officer who makes a large number of narcotics purchases before "surfacing," see United States v. Jones, 524 F.2d 834 (D.C.Cir.1975); Ross v. United States, 349 F.2d 210 (D.C.Cir. 1965).

FEDERAL RULES OF CRIMINAL PROCEDURE

Rule 48

DISMISSAL

. . .

(b) By the Court. The court may dismiss an indictment, information, or complaint if unnecessary delay occurs in:

(1) presenting a charge to a grand jury;

(2) filing an information against a defendant; or

(3) bringing a defendant to trial.

SPEEDY TRIAL ACT OF 1974

18 U.S.C. §§ 3161–3174

§ 3161. Time limits and exclusions

(a) In any case involving a defendant charged with an offense, the appropriate judicial officer, at the earliest practicable time, shall, after consultation with the counsel for the defendant and the attorney for the Government, set the case for trial on a day certain, or list it for trial on a weekly or other short-term trial calendar at a place within the judicial district, so as to assure a speedy trial.

(b) Any information or indictment charging an individual with the commission of an offense shall be filed within thirty days from the date on which such individual was arrested or served with a summons in connection with such charges. If an individual has been charged with a felony in a district in which no grand jury has been in session during such thirty-day period, the period of time for filing of the indictment shall be extended an additional thirty days.

(c)(1) In any case in which a plea of not guilty is entered, the trial of a defendant charged in an information or indictment with the commission of an offense shall commence within seventy days from the filing date (and making public) of the information or indictment, or from the date the defendant has appeared before a judicial officer of the court in which such charge is pending, whichever date last occurs. If a defendant consents in writing to be tried before a magistrate on a complaint, the trial shall commence within seventy days from the date of such consent.

(2) Unless the defendant consents in writing to the contrary, the trial shall not commence less than thirty days from the date on which the defendant first appears through counsel or expressly waives counsel and elects to proceed pro se.

(d)(1) If any indictment or information is dismissed upon motion of the defendant, or any charge contained in a complaint filed against an individual is dismissed or otherwise dropped, and thereafter a complaint is filed against such defendant or individual charging him with the same offense or an offense based on the same conduct or arising from the same criminal episode, or an information or indictment is filed charging such defendant with the same offense or an offense based on the same conduct or arising from the same criminal episode, the provisions of subsections (b) and (c) of this section shall be applicable with respect to such subsequent complaint, indictment, or information, as the case may be.

(2) If the defendant is to be tried upon an indictment or information dismissed by a trial court and reinstated following an appeal, the trial shall commence within seventy days from the date the action occasioning the trial becomes final, except that the court retrying the case may extend the period for trial not to exceed one hundred and eighty days from the date the action occasioning the trial becomes final if the unavailability of witnesses or other factors resulting from the passage of time shall make trial within seventy days impractical. The periods of delay enumerated in section 3161(h) are excluded in computing the time limitations specified in this section. The sanctions of section 3162 apply to this subsection.

(e) If the defendant is to be tried again following a declaration by the trial judge of a mistrial or following an order of such judge for a new trial, the trial shall commence within seventy days from the date the action occasioning the retrial becomes final. If the defendant is to be tried again following an appeal or a collateral attack, the trial shall commence within seventy days from the date the action occasioning the retrial becomes final, except that the court retrying the case may extend the period for retrial not to exceed one hundred and eighty days from the date the action occasioning the retrial becomes final if unavailability of witnesses or other factors resulting from passage of time shall make trial within seventy days impractical. The periods of delay enumerated in section 3161(h) are excluded in computing the time limitations specified in this section. The sanctions of section 3162 apply to this subsection.

. . .

(h) The following periods of delay shall be excluded in computing the time within which an information or an indictment must be filed, or in computing the time within which the trial of any such offense must commence:

(1) Any period of delay resulting from other proceedings concerning the defendant, including but not limited to—

(A) delay resulting from any proceeding, including any examinations, to determine the mental competency or physical capacity of the defendant;

(B) delay resulting from any proceeding, including any examination of the defendant, pursuant to section 2902 of title 28, United States Code;[12]

(C) delay resulting from deferral of prosecution pursuant to section 2902 of title 28, United States Code;

(D) delay resulting from trial with respect to other charges against the defendant;

12. 28 U.S.C. § 2902 provides for examination of persons charged with an offense to determine whether they are addicted to narcotics and "likely to be rehabilitated through treatment," and, if so, for their civil commitment for treatment.

(E) delay resulting from any interlocutory appeal;

(F) delay resulting from any pretrial motion, from the filing of the motion through the conclusion of the hearing on, or other prompt disposition of, such motion;

(G) delay resulting from any proceeding relating to the transfer of a case or the removal of any defendant from another district under the Federal Rules of Criminal Procedure;

(H) delay resulting from transportation of any defendant from another district, or to and from places of examination or hospitalization, except that any time consumed in excess of ten days from the date an order of removal or an order directing such transportation, and the defendant's arrival at the destination shall be presumed to be unreasonable;

(I) delay resulting from consideration by the court of a proposed plea agreement to be entered into by the defendant and the attorney for the Government; and

(J) delay reasonably attributable to any period, not to exceed thirty days, during which any proceeding concerning the defendant is actually under advisement by the court.

(2) Any period of delay during which prosecution is deferred by the attorney for the Government pursuant to written agreement with the defendant, with the approval of the court, for the purpose of allowing the defendant to demonstrate his good conduct.

(3)(A) Any period of delay resulting from the absence or unavailability of the defendant or an essential witness.

(B) For purposes of subparagraph (A) of this paragraph, a defendant or an essential witness shall be considered absent when his whereabouts are unknown and, in addition, he is attempting to avoid apprehension or prosecution or his whereabouts cannot be determined by due diligence. For purposes of such subparagraph, a defendant or an essential witness shall be considered unavailable whenever his whereabouts are known but his presence for trial cannot be obtained by due diligence or he resists appearing at or being returned for trial.

(4) Any period of delay resulting from the fact that the defendant is mentally incompetent or physically unable to stand trial.

(5) Any period of delay resulting from the treatment of the defendant pursuant to section 2902 of title 28, United States Code.

(6) If the information or indictment is dismissed upon motion of the attorney for the Government and thereafter a charge is filed against the defendant for the same offense, or any offense required to be joined with that offense, any period of delay from the date the charge was dismissed to the date the time limitation would commence to run as to the subsequent charge had there been no previous charge.

(7) A reasonable period of delay when the defendant is joined for trial with a codefendant as to whom the time for trial has not run and no motion for severance has been granted.

(8)(A) Any period of delay resulting from a continuance granted by any judge on his own motion or at the request of the defendant or his counsel or at the request of the attorney for the Government, if the judge granted such continuance on the basis of his findings that the ends of justice served by taking such action outweigh the best interest of the public and the defendant in a speedy trial. No such period of delay resulting from a continuance granted by the court in accordance with this paragraph shall be excludable under this subsection unless the court sets forth, in the record of the case, either orally or in writing, its reasons for finding that the ends of justice served by the granting of such continuance outweigh the best interests of the public and the defendant in a speedy trial.

(B) The factors, among others, which a judge shall consider in determining whether to grant a continuance under subparagraph (A) of this paragraph in any case are as follows:

(i) Whether the failure to grant such a continuance in the proceeding would be likely to make a continuation of such proceeding impossible, or result in a miscarriage of justice.

(ii) Whether the case is so unusual or so complex, due to the number of defendants, the nature of the prosecution, or the existence of novel questions of fact or law, that it is unreasonable to expect adequate preparation for pretrial proceedings or for the trial itself within the time limits established by this section.

(iii) Whether, in a case in which arrest precedes indictment, delay in the filing of the indictment is caused because the arrest occurs at a time such that it is unreasonable to expect return and filing of the indictment within the period specified in section 3161(b), or because the facts upon which the grand jury must base its determination are unusual or complex.

(iv) Whether the failure to grant such a continuance in a case which, taken as a whole, is not so unusual or so complex as to fall within clause (ii), would deny the defendant reasonable time to obtain counsel, would unreasonably deny the defendant or the Government continuity of counsel, or would deny counsel for the defendant or the attorney for the Government the reasonable time necessary for effective preparation, taking into account the exercise of due diligence.

(C) No continuance under subparagraph (A) of this paragraph shall be granted because of general congestion of the court's calendar, or lack of diligent preparation or failure to obtain available witnesses on the part of the attorney for the Government.

(9) Any period of delay, not to exceed one year, ordered by a district court upon an application of a party and a finding by a

preponderance of the evidence that an official request, as defined in section 3292 of this title, has been made for evidence of any such offense and that it reasonably appears, or reasonably appeared at the time the request was made, that such evidence is, or was, in such foreign country.

(i) If trial did not commence within the time limitation specified in section 3161 because the defendant had entered a plea of guilty or nolo contendere subsequently withdrawn to any or all charges in an indictment or information, the defendant shall be deemed indicted with respect to all charges therein contained within the meaning of section 3161, on the day the order permitting withdrawal of the plea becomes final.

(j)(1) If the attorney for the Government knows that a person charged with an offense is serving a term of imprisonment in any penal institution, he shall promptly—

(A) undertake to obtain the presence of the prisoner for trial; or

(B) cause a detainer to be filed with the person having custody of the prisoner and request him to so advise the prisoner and to advise the prisoner of his right to demand trial.

(2) If the person having custody of such prisoner receives a detainer, he shall promptly advise the prisoner of the charge and of the prisoner's right to demand trial. If at any time thereafter the prisoner informs the person having custody that he does demand trial, such person shall cause notice to that effect to be sent promptly to the attorney for the Government who caused the detainer to be filed.

(3) Upon receipt of such notice, the attorney for the Government shall promptly seek to obtain the presence of the prisoner for trial.

(4) When the person having custody of the prisoner receives from the attorney for the Government a properly supported request for temporary custody of such prisoner for trial, the prisoner shall be made available to that attorney for the Government (subject, in cases of interjurisdictional transfer, to any right of the prisoner to contest the legality of his delivery).

(k)(1) If the defendant is absent (as defined by subsection (h)(3)) on the day set for trial, and the defendant's subsequent appearance before the court on a bench warrant or other process or surrender to the court occurs more than 21 days after the day set for trial, the defendant shall be deemed to have first appeared before a judicial officer of the court in which the information or indictment is pending within the meaning of subsection (c) on the date of the defendant's subsequent appearance before the court.

(2) If the defendant is absent (as defined by subsection (h)(3)) on the day set for trial, and the defendant's subsequent appearance before the court on a bench warrant or other process or surrender to the court occurs not more than 21 days after the day set for trial, the time limit required by subsection (c), as extended by subsection (h), shall be further extended by 21 days.

§ 3162. Sanctions

(a)(1) If, in the case of any individual against whom a complaint is filed charging such individual with an offense, no indictment or information is filed within the time limit required by section 3161(b) as extended by section 3161(h) of this chapter, such charge against that individual contained in such complaint shall be dismissed or otherwise dropped. In determining whether to dismiss the case with or without prejudice, the court shall consider, among others, each of the following factors: the seriousness of the offense; the facts and circumstances of the case which led to the dismissal; and the impact of a reprosecution on the administration of this chapter and on the administration of justice.

(2) If a defendant is not brought to trial within the time limit required by section 3161(c) as extended by section 3161(h), the information or indictment shall be dismissed on motion of the defendant. The defendant shall have the burden of proof of supporting such motion but the Government shall have the burden of going forward with the evidence in connection with any exclusion of time under subparagraph 3161(h)(3). In determining whether to dismiss the case with or without prejudice, the court shall consider, among others, each of the following factors: the seriousness of the offense; the facts and circumstances of the case which led to the dismissal; and the impact of a reprosecution on the administration of this chapter and on the administration of justice. Failure of the defendant to move for dismissal prior to trial or entry of a plea of guilty or nolo contendere shall constitute a waiver of the right to dismissal under this section.

(b) In any case in which counsel for the defendant or the attorney for the Government

(1) knowingly allows the case to be set for trial without disclosing the fact that a necessary witness would be unavailable for trial;

(2) files a motion solely for the purpose of delay which he knows is totally frivolous and without merit;

(3) makes a statement for the purpose of obtaining a continuance which he knows to be false and which is material to the granting of a continuance; or

(4) otherwise willfully fails to proceed to trial without justification consistent with section 3161 of this chapter, the court may punish any such counsel or attorney, as follows:

(A) in the case of an appointed defense counsel, by reducing the amount of compensation that otherwise would have been paid to such counsel pursuant to section 3006A of this title in an amount not to exceed 25 per centum thereof;

(B) in the case of a counsel retained in connection with the defense of a defendant, by imposing on such counsel a fine of not to exceed 25 per centum of the compensation to which he is entitled in connection with his defense of such defendant;

(C) by imposing on any attorney for the Government a fine of not to exceed $250;

(D) by denying any such counsel or attorney for the Government the right to practice before the court considering such case for a period of not to exceed ninety days; or

(E) by filing a report with an appropriate disciplinary committee.

The authority to punish provided for by this subsection shall be in addition to any other authority or power available to such court.

(c) The court shall follow procedures established in the Federal Rules of Criminal Procedure in punishing any counsel or attorney for the Government pursuant to this section.

. . .

§ 3164. Persons detained or designated as being of high risk

(a) The trial or other disposition of cases involving—

(1) a detained person who is being held in detention solely because he is awaiting trial, and

(2) a released person who is awaiting trial and has been designated by the attorney for the Government as being of high risk,

shall be accorded priority.

(b) The trial of any person described in subsection (a)(1) or (a)(2) of this section shall commence not later than ninety days following the beginning of such continuous detention or designation of high risk by the attorney for the Government. The periods of delay enumerated in section 3161(h) are excluded in computing the time limitation specified in this section.

(c) Failure to commence trial of a detainee as specified in subsection (b), through no fault of the accused or his counsel, or failure to commence trial of a designated releasee as specified in subsection (b), through no fault of the attorney for the Government, shall result in the automatic review by the court of the conditions of release. No detainee, as defined in subsection (a), shall be held in custody pending trial after the expiration of such ninety-day period required for the commencement of his trial. A designated releasee, as defined in subsection (a), who is found by the court to have intentionally delayed the trial of his case shall be subject to an order of the court modifying his nonfinancial conditions of release under this title to insure that he shall appear at trial as required.

. . .

§ 3173. Sixth amendment rights

No provision of this chapter shall be interpreted as a bar to any claim of denial of speedy trial as required by amendment VI of the Constitution.

. . .[13]

---

411. Section 3161(c)(1) of the Speedy Trial Act provides that a trial must begin within 70 days of the filing of an indictment or information. A trial begins for purposes of the Act with the voir dire of the jury. In United States v. Fox, 788 F.2d 905 (2d Cir.1986), the voir dire was conducted and a jury was selected just before the statutory period would have expired. The trial was then adjourned by the court; the jury was not sworn and the trial did not begin until more than five months later. The trial judge gave no reason for the delay. The court of appeals said that "nothing in the Act justifies this kind of delay," id. at 909, and dismissed the indictment. It remanded for a determination whether the dismissal should be with or without prejudice. See United States v. Barnes, 159 F.3d 4 (1st Cir.1998) (four-month delay; dismissal without prejudice); United States v. Stayton, 791 F.2d 17 (2d Cir.1986) (23-month delay between voir dire and trial; dismissal with prejudice).

The provision in § 3161(c)(2) that a trial shall not commence "less than thirty days from the date on which the defendant first appears through counsel" does not require that a new 30-day period begin when a superseding indictment is filed. United States v. Rojas-Contreras, 474 U.S. 231 (1985).

On the provisions of § 3161(h) for exclusion of certain delays from the period within which the trial must begin, especially subsection (8) dealing with continuances, see United States v. Carrasquillo, 667 F.2d 382 (3d Cir.1981).

The excludable delay covered by § 3161(h)(1)(F) of the Speedy Trial Act for a hearing on a motion is not limited to delay that is "reasonably necessary." Excluded from the Act's 70-day limitation is "all time between the filing of a motion and the conclusion of the hearing on that motion, whether or not a delay in holding that hearing is 'reasonably necessary.' " Henderson v. United States, 476 U.S. 321, 330 (1986) (5–4). The Court held that delay after the conclusion of a hearing on a motion while a court is awaiting the submission of additional papers is also excluded. In United States v. Moran, 998 F.2d 1368 (6th Cir.1993), however, the court held that the period of a continuance for filing suppression motions and the period after all papers are submitted while the motion is pending, in excess of the 30 days allowed by the Rule, are not excludable; nor could a retroactive "ends of justice" ruling authorize the exclusion after the fact.

[13] Other provisions of the Speedy Trial Act, omitted here, provide for each district court to adopt a plan for implementation of the Act and for periodic reports to Congress.

UNITED STATES DISTRICT COURT
DISTRICT OF MASSACHUSETTS

UNITED STATES OF AMERICA MAG. JUDGE NO. ______________

V. CRIMINAL NO.________________

____

ORDER OF EXCLUDABLE DELAY

In accordance with the Speedy Trial Act of 1974, as amended, this Court hereby orders excludable delay from ______________ to ____________________ for the reason checked below.

____________________ ____________________
Date U.S. District Judge
U.S. Magistrate Judge

REFER TO DOCUMENT(S) # ______________________________

[ ]	XA	Proceedings including examinations to determine mental competency or physical capacity	18 U.S.C.§3161(h)(1)(A)
[ ]	XB	NARA examination pursuant to 28 U.S.C. 2902	18 U.S.C.§3161(h)(1)(B)
[ ]	XC	Trial on other charges against defendant	18 U.S.C.§3161(h)(1)(D)
[ ]	XD	Interlocutory Appeal	18 U.S.C.§3161(h)(1)(E)
[ ]	XE	Pretrial motions from filing date to hearing or disposition	18 U.S.C.§3161(h)(1)(F)
[ ]	XF	Transfer (Rule 20) or Removal (Rule 40) proceedings	18 U.S.C.§3161(h)(1)(G)
[ ]	XG	Proceedings under advisement	18 U.S.C.§3161(h)(1)(J)
[ ]	XH	Miscellaneous proceedings concerning defendant	18 U.S.C.§3161(h)(1)
[ ]	XI	Prosecution deferred	18 U.S.C.§3161(h)(2)
[ ]	XJ	Transportation from other district	18 U.S.C.§3161(h)(1)(H)
[ ]	XK	Consideration of proposed plea agreement	18 U.S.C.§3161(h)(1)(I)
[ ]	XM	Absence or unavailability of defendant or essential government witness	18 U.S.C.§3161(h)(3)
[ ]	XN	Period of mental or physical incompetency or physical inability to stand trial	18 U.S.C.§3161(h)(4)
[ ]	XO	Period of NARA commitment and treatment	18 U.S.C.§3161(h)(5)
[ ]	XP	Superseding indictment and/or new charges	18 U.S.C.§3161(h)(6)
[ ]	XR	Defendant joined with codefendant for whom time has not run	18 U.S.C.§3161(h)(7)
[ ]	XU	Time from first arraignment to withdrawal of guilty plea	18 U.S.C.§3161(i)
[ ]	XW	Grand Jury indictment time extended	18 U.S.C.§3161(b)
[ ]	XT	Continuance granted in the interest of justice	18 U.S.C.§3161(h)(8)

(Xdelay-all.wpd - 10/99) [koexcl.]

On the provision of § 3162(a)(1) for dismissal with or without prejudice, see United States v. Giambrone, 920 F.2d 176 (2d Cir.1990); (dismissal with prejudice justified by government's "extremely lax" attitude to speedy trial); United States v. Brown, 770 F.2d 241 (1st Cir.1985) (dismissal without prejudice upheld).

In United States v. Taylor, 487 U.S. 326, 343 (1988) (6–3), the Court concluded that, in light of all the circumstances, including the district court's failure to give sufficient explicit consideration to the factors set forth in § 3162(a)(2) of the Speedy Trial Act, the district court's decision to dismiss with, rather than without, prejudice, "in order to send a strong message to the Government that unexcused delays will not be tolerated," was an abuse of discretion.

Denial of a motion to dismiss under the Speedy Trial Act is not an order subject to interlocutory appellate review. United States v. Bilsky, 664 F.2d 613 (6th Cir.1981) (following *MacDonald*, p. 809 above).

Continuance

---

412. "The matter of continuance is traditionally within the discretion of the trial judge, and it is not every denial of a request for more time that violates due process even if the party fails to offer evidence or is compelled to defend without counsel. . . . Contrariwise, a myopic insistence upon expeditiousness in the face of a justifiable request for delay can render the right to defend with counsel an empty formality. . . . There are no mechanical tests for deciding when a denial of a continuance is so arbitrary as to violate due process. The answer must be found in the circumstances present in every case, particularly in the reasons presented to the trial judge at the time the request is denied." Ungar v. Sarafite, 376 U.S. 575, 589 (1964). See Morris v. Slappy, 461 U.S. 1 (1983).

> A motion for a continuance is addressed to the sound discretion of the trial court, and its ruling will not be disturbed on appeal unless there is a showing that there has been an abuse of that discretion. . . . This issue must be decided on a case by case basis in light of the circumstances presented, particularly the reasons for continuance presented to the trial court at the time the request is denied. . . .
>
> . . .
>
> [T]he cases are so numerous and involve such varying factual contexts and bases for decision that merely cataloging them is a task of significant proportion. We have deemed the following factors highly relevant in assessing claims of inadequate preparation time: the quantum of time available for preparation, the likelihood of prejudice from denial, the accused's role in shortening the effective preparation time, the degree of complexity of the case, and the availability of discovery from the prosecution. We have also explicitly considered the adequacy

of the defense actually provided at trial, the skill and experience of the attorney, any pre-appointment or pre-retention experience of the attorney with the accused or the alleged crime, and any representation of the defendant by other attorneys that accrues to his benefit.

Within this general category of cases, a particularly common claim is that a continuance was necessary to interview and subpoena potential witnesses. The panels of this court that have ruled on such claims have considered the diligence of the defense in interviewing witnesses and procuring their presence, the probability of procuring their testimony within a reasonable time, the specificity with which the defense is able to describe their expected knowledge or testimony, the degree to which such testimony is expected to be favorable to the accused, and the unique or cumulative nature of the testimony. A general rule recently has emerged: "A movant must show that due diligence has been exercised to obtain the attendance of the witness, that substantial favorable testimony would be tendered by the witness, that the witness is available and willing to testify, and that the denial of a continuance would materially prejudice the defendant." United States v. Miller, 513 F.2d 791, 793 (5 Cir.1975). . . .

. . .

Several lessons to defense lawyers should emerge. . . . The first is that, in cases where there is a substantial basis for a continuance, the attorney should present the claim as early as possible. Second, the attorney should exercise all reasonable diligence to prepare for trial despite the time constraints confronting him. Finally, such claims should be advanced with all the specificity and detail that is feasible under the circumstances. While some of these "lessons" are rules of law under *Miller* with respect to continuances to interview and subpoena witnesses, they are counsels of wisdom in any continuance situation. Only with detailed information as to counsel's efforts and the legitimate justifications for extra time can the court conclude that the motion is made for reasons other than delay. Only then can it be expected to subordinate the very legitimate needs of both the criminal justice system and the defendant for speedy and economical justice.

Finally . . . we must reiterate that a scheduled trial date should never become such an overarching end that it results in the erosion of the defendant's right to a fair trial. If forcing a defendant to an early trial date substantially impairs his ability to effectively present evidence to rebut the prosecution's case or to establish defenses, then pursuit of the goal of expeditiousness is far more detrimental to our common purposes in the criminal justice system than the delay of a few days or weeks that may be sought. The district courts to whom these difficult and inexact judgments are committed have, in the majority of cases, made them with a proper consideration of the rights of defendants to due process of law as well as the demands of judicial economy. Where . . . it is possible to see how a denial of continuance resulted from a reasonable resolution of the various factors confronting a court, we will uphold its action, even if it may seem somewhat harsh.

United States v. Uptain, 531 F.2d 1281, 1285–87, 1290–91 (5th Cir.1976).

———

United States ex rel. Carey v. Rundle

409 F.2d 1210 (3d Cir.1969)

■ ALDISERT, CIRCUIT JUDGE.

In this case we come to grips with a familiar phrase: "every defendant in a criminal proceeding is entitled to have counsel of his own choice." This is a lay expression, albeit often articulated by those trained in the law as a paraphrase of the Sixth Amendment: "In all criminal prosecutions, the accused shall . . . have the Assistance of Counsel for his defense."

We must decide whether the Sixth and Fourteenth Amendments command an absolute right to a particular counsel for a particular trial at a particular time.

The relator was arrested on June 2, 1966, and appeared at a preliminary hearing on June 4, at which time he was represented by private counsel. After he was indicted by the grand jury, his case came on for trial on August 29, at which time the Commonwealth appeared with its witnesses and was prepared to go to trial. The defendant, however, reported that he could not proceed because he did not have counsel.

Upon ascertaining that the defendant had been represented by Attorney A. Charles Peruto at the preliminary hearing, the court summoned Mr. Peruto to the courtroom. The attorney reported that although he had represented the defendant at the preliminary hearing, he had entered no appearance as counsel for the defendant in the court proceedings. He stated unequivocally that he did not represent the defendant and that he had no intention of doing so. Because of the defendant's insistence that he desired private counsel, the court postponed the trial until September 28 to afford him an additional thirty days to obtain counsel of his choice. At the same time the court ordered the Voluntary Defender to file an appearance for the defendant and to be ready to proceed on the September date in the event the defendant was not successful in his attempt to retain private counsel.

The appointed day came and the case was called for trial. The Commonwealth again was ready to proceed. Still without private counsel but represented by the Voluntary Defender, the defendant requested a continuance of one day to obtain notes of the testimony adduced at the preliminary hearing. Two days passed. On September 30, the case was again called, at which time the Commonwealth was ready to proceed for the third time. Speaking through the Voluntary Defender, the defendant again requested a continuance, stating that he did not desire representation by the Voluntary Defender and insisted upon retaining private counsel. The motion was denied; the court ordered the Voluntary Defender to sit with the defendant at counsel table and the trial began. Thereupon, the defendant elected to proceed nonjury.

At the noon recess, Attorney Milton Leidner appeared in the courtroom and informed the court: "The mother of Harry Carey was at my office and as a result of conversation I told her I would enter my appearance and represent him. I subsequently went on trial and in my absence she did bring a check into the office and it is a good check." He said that he had not filed his appearance, but he was prepared to do so: "If the case is continued, yes. I cannot try it now. I am already on trial." The court then announced that "this case is continued until Monday morning at 10 A.M." Mr. Leidner interjected that he had another case listed for the same day. The court refused to continue the trial any later than Monday. Mr. Leidner then said, "I will withdraw my appearance and refund the retainer which I didn't receive but only placed it in my drawer." The trial then proceeded to a conclusion; the defendant was found guilty.

After exhausting state remedies, Carey filed a petition for federal habeas corpus relief alleging a denial of due process. The writ was granted and the Commonwealth has appealed.

We begin with the premise that the right to counsel is a vital ingredient in the scheme of due process. . . .

. . .

Concurrently a doctrine has evolved which guarantees the defendant sufficient time and opportunity to obtain counsel of his own choice.

Desirable as it is that a defendant obtain private counsel of his own choice, that goal must be weighed and balanced against an equally desirable public need for the efficient and effective administration of criminal justice. The calendar control of modern criminal court dockets, especially in metropolitan communities, is a sophisticated operation constantly buffeted by conflicting forces. The accused's rights—such as those relating to a speedy trial, to an adequate opportunity to prepare the defense, and to confront witnesses—are constantly in potential or real conflict with the prosecution's legitimate demands for some stability in the scheduling of cases. The availability of prosecution witnesses is often critically dependent on the predictability of the trial list. That delays and postponements only increase the reluctance of witnesses to appear in court, especially in criminal matters, is a phenomenon which scarcely needs elucidation.

Moreover, it is not only the prosecution which may suffer from unscheduled changes in the calendar. To permit a continuance to accommodate one defendant may in itself prejudice the rights of another defendant whose trial is delayed because of the continuance. Played to an extreme conclusion, this indiscriminate game of judicial musical chairs could collapse any semblance of sound administration, and work to the ultimate prejudice of many defendants awaiting trial in criminal courts.

This is not to say that there should be an arbitrary and inelastic calendaring of cases without due regard, for example, to the existence of conflicting demands for the service of a particular counsel by different courts or by the schedules within a multi-judge court. In judicial administration, too, there should be no absolutes. It is the trial judge who must balance the conflicting demands of court administration with the rights of the accused, conscious, however, that when he considers the rights of those accused of crime, he must consider not only those involved in the case immediately before him but also those of other defendants awaiting trial whose rights may be affected by the consequences of trial delay.

. . .

Due process demands that the defendant be afforded a fair opportunity to obtain the assistance of counsel of his choice to prepare and conduct his defense. The constitutional mandate is satisfied so long as the accused is afforded a fair or reasonable opportunity to obtain particular counsel, and so long as there is no arbitrary action prohibiting the effective use of such counsel. The conclusion becomes inescapable, therefore, that although the right to counsel is absolute, there is no absolute right to a particular counsel.

In the case at bar the defendant was afforded due process. Putting aside the two and a half month period from June 4, when he was represented by private counsel at the preliminary hearing, until August 28, when he was advised in open court that this lawyer was not representing him at the trial, the defendant was specifically informed that the court was affording him one additional month to obtain private counsel to prepare his defense and that his trial was postponed for one month to a day certain. One month is not a constitutionally inadequate time period in which to obtain counsel and prepare a defense, where, as here, the lines of communication were at all times open and defendant can show no good reason why he could not have contacted and retained an attorney within this time period.

To offset any further delay or complications, counsel was appointed for him in the person of the Voluntary Defender, who, in the intervening month, made several attempts to prepare his defense. The defendant steadfastly refused this assistance. When the appointed day came, he was still without private counsel. Nevertheless, a second continuance of two days was granted to enable counsel to gather certain specific information. On the Friday when the trial began, he was given the opportunity of counsel which he rejected, preferring to go to trial in *propria persona*. The court ordered appointed counsel to sit at his side and to be available for expert advice and counsel. It was only when the trial was already in progress that private counsel did in fact appear in the courtroom.

When the trial judge expressed a willingness to adjourn the hearing and begin anew the following Monday, he was extending a courtesy not required, under these circumstances, by the constitutional demands of due process. On three different occasions, the case had been called for trial. On three different occasions the Commonwealth had assembled its witnesses and announced its readiness to proceed.

In accommodating the conflicting considerations of either extending additional time for the defendant to obtain counsel of his choice or moving forward with the orderly process of judicial administration, the trial judge was called upon to exercise his discretion. We cannot say that the discretion he exercised impinged upon the constitutional rights of the defendant before him.

Accordingly, we will reverse the judgment of the district court.

---

413. The difficulty of reconciling a reluctant defendant's right to counsel with the need for orderly, expeditious proceedings has troubled the courts. In Bostick v. United States, 400 F.2d 449 (5th Cir.1968), for example, the trial judge stated:

> This Court undertook for a period of seven months to bring this case to trial. During this interval the defendants Bostick and Lainhart, though incarcerated and unable to make bond, used every device and machination known to the law, and then perhaps invented a few of their own, to defeat the orderly disposition of the case. The transcript of these preliminary proceedings, which I have just re-read to refresh my recollection, is so fantastic as to be almost beyond belief. It presents the question as to whether ever, under any circumstances, a district court in the orderly administration of its functions can bring a criminal case to trial over the objection of the defendant.
>
> . . .
>
> I am convinced beyond the shadow of a doubt that the various artifices practiced by these two defendants prior to trial in continually gaining continuances, and in claiming that while entirely able financially to do so they were still unsuccessful in securing counsel of their own choice were deliberate, were not in good faith, and—with the knowledge that they had no hopes of success in the trial court—was for the express purpose of preserving this question for appeal and, thereafter habeas corpus.

Id. at 453–54. The court of appeals agreed: "The defendants used their right to counsel as a means of frustrating the orderly processes of justice." Id. at 451.

For other cases in which the denial of a continuance to obtain the services of counsel was upheld, see, e.g., United States v. Poston, 902 F.2d 90 (D.C.Cir.1990); Sampley v. Attorney General of North Carolina, 786 F.2d 610 (4th Cir.1986). But see United States v. Goldberg, 67 F.3d 1092 (3d Cir.1995) (defendant's dilatory tactics did not forfeit right to counsel).

The denial of a continuance was held to be an abuse of discretion in United States v. Nguyen, 262 F.3d 998 (9th Cir.2001) (continuance denied without hearing; breakdown of attorney-client relationship); United States v. Rankin, 779 F.2d 956 (3d Cir.1986) (counsel occupied in another trial); United States v. Gallo, 763 F.2d 1504 (6th Cir.1985) (complex case, counsel allowed only ten days following arraignment to prepare for trial); Gandy v. Alabama, 569 F.2d 1318 (5th Cir.1978) (counsel occupied in another trial). *Gandy* is distinguished in United States v. Barrentine, 591 F.2d 1069 (5th Cir.1979), in which defense counsel was engaged in another trial. Affirming the conviction, the court said that the defendants and their counsel "made a calculated attempt to force a continuance," id. at 1075.

414. When defense counsel is retained by an unknown defendant who is not obviously a "good risk" and who is reasonably likely to be convicted and sentenced to prison, it is common for defense counsel not to proceed with the case until he has received at least some part of his fee. If defense counsel appears before the magistrate and requests a continuance of the preliminary hearing or before the calendar judge and requests a continuance of the trial without good reason except that the defendant has not paid a fee as agreed, should the magistrate or judge grant the continuance (the defendant presumably having consented)? If not, should counsel be permitted to withdraw from the case (making a continuance inevitable)? See generally United States v. Uptain, 531 F.2d 1281, 1290 (5th Cir.1976).[14]

415. Consider the situation of a defendant in a "big" case, who is indicted only after the prosecutor has completed an intensive investigation of the facts of the alleged crime and the possibility of proving the crime in court. The prosecutor is generally limited only by the statute of limitations, which usually allows him all the time he needs to develop his case, track down leads, evaluate potential witnesses, and the like. He may, and in the case of the federal government at least, ordinarily will have available whatever resources are reasonably necessary for investigation and trial preparation. This will include not only the superior laboratory and other resources of the Federal Bureau of Investigation, such as experience in preparing charts and diagrams and other trial exhibits; it will include also the means for the prosecutor himself to travel and do what else is necessary for him to prepare for the trial. A prosecutor assigned to a big, complex case may have no other assignment to distract his attention. Within broad limits, he is not obliged to weigh the cost in time and his own or his client's money of an investigation or a particular piece of trial preparation. When he wishes to interview potential witnesses, he has the authority of the government behind him, and can take advantage of the ordinary citizen's habit of supporting the law. He can, for example, summon witnesses to his office or arrange to visit them in their places of work or at their homes, by using an "official" document or an "official" tone of voice, which has no more force behind it than a request.

The defendant may be aroused to action only after the prosecution has made its case. Witnesses may already have been lined up, and those who have not may be unwilling to discuss the matter further with anyone. Investigative leads may be cold or too uncertain to be pursued easily or, given limitations of resources, at all.

14. "Misunderstandings about fees are a vexatious and unnecessary irritant in the lawyer-client relationship. . . . Counsel is cautioned to advise the client that failure to pay the full fee before trial will result in counsel's withdrawal from the case: Experience indicates that criminal fees are hard to collect after trial, no matter what its outcome." 1 A. Amsterdam, Trial Manual 5 for the Defense of Criminal Cases 119 (5th ed. 1988). See Cross v. United States, 392 F.2d 360, 364–68 (8th Cir.1968) (trial counsel assertedly followed "principle he had learned in some twenty years of practice—that of not representing a criminal defendant unless paid in advance").

The questions posed by differences in resources are by no means answered by the judicious granting and withholding of continuances. Nevertheless, continuances are relevant to the disparity between prosecution and defense with respect to the resource of time, which exists because the prosecution is the initiator of a criminal case and, within very broad limits, can wait until he is ready. The significance of the disparity depends to a large extent on the availability of other resources for quick, effective action. See generally United States v. Cronic, 466 U.S. 648 (1984), p. 1028 below.

Most defense counsel will be quick to point out that so long as a defendant is not in prison, he is well off. The passage of time may make prosecution witnesses unavailable or uncertain or unconvincing. A big case developed by a prosecutor is to some extent "his" or "her" case—which cannot easily be prosecuted by someone else should the prosecutor become unavailable. On the other hand, justice delayed is to some extent justice denied, even if, as in criminal cases, criminal justice is not intended to and does not "right" a wrong. The relevance of punishment to a crime is diminished by too long delay; society's response loses some of its character as punishment and to that extent loses its justification.

How far should we honor the request for a continuance based on alleged difficulties and delays in investigation and trial preparation? A timely request for a continuance of a few days or weeks ordinarily would and certainly should be granted. What of cases in which the indictment follows a year or more of investigation and the defense requests a continuance of several months (and then perhaps a second continuance of several months more)?

Discovery

FEDERAL RULES OF CRIMINAL PROCEDURE

Rule 16

DISCOVERY AND INSPECTION

(a) Government's Disclosure.

(1) *Information Subject to Disclosure.*

(A) *Defendant's Oral Statement.* Upon a defendant's request, the government must disclose to the defendant the substance of any relevant oral statement made by the defendant, before or after arrest, in response to interrogation by a person the defendant knew was a government agent if the government intends to use the statement at trial.

(B) *Defendant's Written or Recorded Statement.* Upon a defendant's request, the government must disclose to the defendant, and make available for inspection, copying, or photographing all of the following:

(i) any relevant written or recorded statement by the defendant if:

- the statement is within the government's possession, custody, or control; and
- the attorney for the government knows—or through due diligence could know—that the statement exists;

(ii) the portion of any written record containing the substance of any relevant oral statement made before or after arrest if the defendant made the statement in response to interrogation by a person the defendant knew was a government agent; and

(iii) the defendant's recorded testimony before a grand jury relating to the charge offense.

(C) *Organizational Defendant.* Upon a defendant's request, if the defendant is an organization, the government must disclose to the defendant any statement described in Rule 16(a)(1)(A) and (B) if the government contends that the person making the statement:

(i) was legally able to bind the defendant regarding the subject of the statement because of that person's position as the defendant's director, officer, employee, or agent; or

(ii) was personally involved in the alleged conduct constituting the offense and was legally able to bind the defendant regarding that conduct because of that person's position as the defendant's director, officer, employee, or agent.

(D) *Defendant's Prior Record.* Upon a defendant's request, the government must furnish the defendant with a copy of the defendant's prior criminal record that is within the government's possession, custody, or control if the attorney for the government knows—or through due diligence could know—that the record exists.

(E) *Documents and Objects.* Upon a defendant's request, the government must permit the defendant to inspect and to copy or photograph books, papers, documents, data, photographs, tangible objects, buildings or places, or copies or portions of any of these items, if the item is within the government's possession, custody, or control and:

(i) the item is material to preparing the defense;

(ii) the government intends to use the item in its case-in-chief at trial; or

(iii) the item was obtained from or belongs to the defendant.

(F) *Reports of Examinations and Tests.* Upon a defendant's request, the government must permit a defendant to inspect and to copy or photograph the results or reports of any physical or mental examination and of any scientific test or experiment if:

(i) the item is within the government's possession, custody, or control;

(ii) the attorney for the government knows—or through due diligence could know—that the item exists; and

(iii) the item is material to preparing the defense or the government intends to use the item in its case-in-chief at trial.

(G) *Expert Witnesses.* At the defendant's request, the government must give to the defendant a written summary of any testimony that the government intends to use under Rules 702, 703, or 705 of the Federal Rules of Evidence during its case-in-chief at trial. If the government requests discovery under subdivision (b)(1)(C)(ii) and the defendant complies, the government must, at the defendant's request, give to the defendant a written summary of testimony that the government intends to use under rules 702, 703, or 705 of the Federal Rules of Evidence as evidence at trial on the issue of the defendant's mental condition. The summary provided under this subparagraph must describe the witness's opinions, the bases and reasons for those opinions, and the witness's qualifications.

(2) *Information Not Subject to Disclosure.* Except as Rule 16(a)(1) provides otherwise, this rule does not authorize the discovery or inspection of reports, memoranda, or other internal government documents made by an attorney for the government or other government agent in connection with investigating or prosecuting the case. Nor does this rule authorize the discovery or inspection of statements made by prospective government witnesses except as provided in 18 U.S.C. § 3500.

(3) *Grand Jury Transcripts.* This rule does not apply to the discovery or inspection of a grand jury's recorded proceedings, except as provided in Rules 6, 12(h), 16(a)(1), and 26.2.

(b) Defendant's Disclosure.

(1) *Information Subject to Disclosure.*

(A) *Documents and Objects.* If a defendant requests disclosure under Rule 16(a)(1)(E) and the government complies, then the defendant must permit the government, upon request, to inspect and to copy or photograph books, papers, documents, data, photographs, tangible objects, buildings or places, or copies or portions of any of these items if:

(i) the item is within the defendant's possession, custody, or control; and

(ii) the defendant intends to use the item in the defendant's case-in-chief at trial.

(B) *Reports of Examinations and Tests.* If a defendant requests disclosure under rule 16(a)(1)(F) and the government complies, the defendant must permit the government, upon request, to inspect and to copy or photograph the results or reports of any physical or mental examination and of any scientific test or experiment if:

(i) the item is within the defendant's possession, custody, or control; and

(ii) the defendant intends to use the item in the defendant's case-in-chief at trial, or intends to call the witness who prepared the report and the report relates to the witness's testimony.

(C) *Expert Witnesses.* The defendant must, at the government's request, give to the government a written summary of any testimony that the defendant intends to use under Rules 702, 703, or 705 of the Federal Rules of Evidence as evidence at trial, if—

(i) the defendant requests disclosure under subdivision (a)(1)(G) and the government complies; or

(ii) the defendant has given notice under Rule 12.2(b) of an intent to present expert testimony on the defendant's mental condition.

This summary must describe the witness's opinions, the bases and reasons for those opinions, and the witness's qualifications.

(2) *Information Not Subject to Disclosure.* Except for scientific or medical reports, Rule 16(b)(1) does not authorize discovery or inspection of:

(A) reports, memoranda, or other documents made by the defendant, or the defendant's attorney or agent, during the case's investigation or defense; or

(B) a statement made to the defendant, or the defendant's attorney or agent, by:

(i) the defendant;

(ii) a government or defense witness; or

(iii) a prospective government or defense witness.

(c) Continuing Duty to Disclose. A party who discovers additional evidence or material before or during trial must promptly disclose its existence to the other party or the court if:

(1) the evidence or material is subject to discovery or inspection under this rule; and

(2) the other party previously requested, or the court ordered, its production.

(d) Regulating Discovery.

(1) *Protective and Modifying Orders.* At any time the court may, for good cause, deny, restrict, or defer discovery or inspection, or grant other appropriate relief. The court may permit a party to show good cause by a written statement that the court will inspect ex parte. If relief is granted, the court must preserve the entire text of the party's statement under seal.

(2) *Failure to Comply.* If a party fails to comply with this rule, the court may:

(A) order that party to permit the discovery or inspection; specify its time, place, and manner; and prescribe other just terms and conditions;

(B) grant a continuance;

(C) prohibit that party from introducing the undisclosed evidence; or

(D) enter any other order that is just under the circumstances.

---

416. There is extensive authority for the proposition that the federal courts have "inherent" authority to order discovery in criminal cases independently of and beyond that for which provision is made in the federal rules. "Prior to the promulgation of the Rules, federal criminal procedure grew out of the inherent power of the courts to develop their own procedure. Sometimes this residual power was exercised by the enactment of local rules of court and sometimes by the process of adjudication. I doubt that the Rules, although a comprehensive regulation of federal criminal procedure, entirely supplant the residual power of the court. I doubt the advisability of reading an imaginative implication into Rule 16 that would deprive the court of its inherent power, shut off the development of discovery by adjudication and thus freeze its limits along the lines determined by cases which had been decided when the Rules were formulated. In my view, to the extent that Rule 16 does not express a policy prohibiting discovery not explicitly authorized by the Rules, the court is free, either by local rule or by adjudication, to permit discovery on the basis of its inherent power. The question as to when the court should permit this discovery is essentially one of policy, not of power." United States v. Taylor, 25 F.R.D. 225, 228 (E.D.N.Y.1960). See generally United States v. Nolte, 39 F.R.D. 359 (N.D.Cal.1965). Cf. United States v. Nobles, 422 U.S. 225, 231 (1975), referring to "the federal judiciary's inherent power to require the prosecution to produce the previously recorded statements of its witnesses so that the defense may get the full benefit of cross-examination and the truth-finding process may be enhanced."

Defendant's Statements

---

417. In Cicenia v. La Gay, 357 U.S. 504 (1958), the Court adhered to the view expressed in Leland v. Oregon, 343 U.S. 790, 801–802 (1952), that although it might be "better practice" to make a defendant's statements available to the defense before trial, "in the absence of a showing of prejudice to the defendant it was not a violation of due process for a State to deny counsel an opportunity before trial to inspect his client's confession," 357 U.S. at 511. Compare the statement in Clewis v. Texas, 386 U.S. 707, 712 n.8 (1967), that "in some circumstances it may be a denial of due process for a defendant to be refused any discovery of his statements to the police."

418. See United States v. Bailleaux, 685 F.2d 1105, 1114 (9th Cir. 1982), discussing Rule 16(a)(1)(A) (now 16(a)(1)(A)–(C)), in which the court said: "[T]he government should disclose any statement made by the defendant that may be relevant to any possible defense or contention that the defendant might assert. Ordinarily, a statement made by the defendant during the course of the investigation of the crime charged should be presumed to be subject to disclosure, unless it is clear that the statement cannot be relevant. Where the Government is in doubt, the written or recorded statement should be disclosed, if a proper request is made."

In United States v. McElroy, 697 F.2d 459, 464 (2d Cir.1982), the court observed: "Rule 16(a)(1)(A) requires the government to disclose the substance not only of the incriminating post-arrest oral statements which it intends to use at trial, but also the substance of the defendant's responses to any *Miranda* warnings which preceded the statements. Disclosure, to be meaningful, must be made of the defendant's responses both to the warnings which immediately preceded his admissions and to any other set(s) of warnings given the defendant from arrest onwards. Requiring the government to make such disclosure will bring to light *Miranda* violations that might otherwise remain hidden because the defendant misunderstands his rights, fails fully to inform defense counsel, or is unable to remember."

Rule 16(a)(1) does not cover written notes that record oral statements made to persons other than known government agents. In re United States, 834 F.2d 283 (2d Cir.1987). The court also reaffirmed that Rule 16(a)(1) does not apply to statements of coconspirators. The district court had ordered the government to disclose statements of coconspirators that the government intended to offer in evidence as containing an admission of the defendant.

United States v. Gladney, 563 F.2d 491 (1st Cir.1977), discusses the government's obligation to furnish items "the existence of which is known, or by the exercise of due diligence may become known, to the attorney for the government" (substantially unchanged in current Rule 16(a)(1)(B)).

419. "The government requests that if the motion [by defendant Ross for an order permitting him to inspect and copy his statement to government officials] be granted the order be so restricted as to bar counsel for Ross from permitting examination of the statement by counsel for his co-defendants. While the court is empowered . . . to so limit the order, I do not believe that the showing made by the government is sufficient to justify the requested restriction. The government argues that Rule 16(a)(1) is available only to the author of a statement or confession. This is true, but the purpose of Rule 16(a)(1) is not simply to permit a confessing defendant to refresh his recollection. A statement produced under the rule serves not only to inform a defendant of the contents of the statement, so that he may explain his admissions, but provides his counsel with information which might lead to the discovery of other evidence important to the defense. Persons mentioned in the statement as accomplices are certainly sources of information, and counsel should be permitted to interview them. Such interviews, even if ethically permissible, are not likely to be fruitful unless counsel for the co-defendants consent, and it is improbable that consent would be given without pre-knowledge of the contents of the statement. To grant the government's request would rob Rule 16(a)(1) of much of its vitality." United States v. Bailey, 262 F.Supp. 331, 332–33 (D.Kan.1967).

Documents, Tangible Objects, Reports of Examinations and Tests

---

United States v. Gatto

763 F.2d 1040 (9th Cir.1985)

■ WALLACE, CIRCUIT JUDGE:

The federal government appeals the district court's order excluding evidence seized by Utah state officials in a trash search operation about which the federal government failed to notify the defense until a few weeks before trial was to begin, even though the state had obtained the evidence two years earlier. It also appeals the district court's subsequent dismissal of the action with prejudice for failing to proceed to trial before the appeal of the exclusion order was resolved. . . . We reverse and remand.

I

Early in 1982, the Sacramento field office of the Federal Bureau of Investigation (FBI) began investigating operations at the Los Gatos, California, office of Sunburst Industries, a company with offices there and in Salt Lake City, Utah. On July 7, 1982, as a result of the Sacramento investigation, a grand jury returned an indictment charging the defendants with 47 counts of mail fraud, wire fraud, interstate transportation of forged or altered securities, and conspiracy. The district court ordered the federal government to provide discovery "in accordance with F.R.Crim.P. 16." Over the next eighteen months, there were numerous pretrial motions dealing with discovery and admissibility of evidence. Finally, a jury trial was set for April 24, 1984.

On March 28, 1984, however, the federal prosecutors notified defense counsel that they had just discovered, and intended to introduce into evidence during their case-in-chief, numerous documents obtained by the State of Utah's Organized Crime and Criminal Identification Bureau (Utah Bureau) in a trash search operation conducted at the Salt Lake City office of Sunburst Industries between November 30, 1981 and May 19, 1982. They claimed that a conversation between Sacramento-based FBI agents and a Utah state official on March 21, 1984 had made them aware of the documents for the first time. The district court granted a defense motion for an evidentiary hearing on why the existence of this evidence had not been disclosed earlier in the discovery process.

After holding a six-day evidentiary hearing, the district judge issued an order excluding any evidence the federal government obtained from the Utah authorities which the Utah authorities had seized pursuant to the trash search operation, as well as such evidence obtained as a result of the trash search. He also ordered the government to identify any evidence it possessed and intended to introduce during trial that could be directly traced to the trash search operation. The trial date was continued to May 1, 1984.

The district judge based his ruling on the authority of rule 16(d)(2), Fed.R.Crim.P., and his inherent supervisory powers. He explicitly did not base it on the fourth amendment. He observed that rule 16(a)(1)(C) required the government to make available to the defense any documents within the government's possession, custody, or control that are material to the defense or intended for use in the government's case-in-chief. He further stated that rule 16(d)(2) gives federal courts the discretionary authority to grant a continuance, exclude evidence, or enter any other order deemed just in the circumstances if any party fails to comply with a discovery order. The district judge also reasoned that he had inherent supervisory power to punish discovery misconduct. . . .

The district judge concluded that the facts of this case allowed him to exercise both his rule 16(d)(2) and his supervisory powers against the government because the federal prosecutors and the Sacramento FBI agents helping them were either negligent or reckless in not discovering and disclosing the existence of the trash search evidence in a more timely manner. The record shows that neither the Sacramento-based officials nor the Salt Lake City FBI agent who served as a liaison between the Sacramento investigators and the federal investigation of Sunburst's Utah activities actually possessed, had custody of, or controlled the trash search evidence before March 27, 1984. Moreover, the district judge never made any finding to the contrary. He merely found that the federal officials were negligent or reckless in not learning about, asserting control over, and disclosing the existence of the documents earlier. He found that a number of federal officials unconnected with the Sacramento investigation had at least heard about the trash search operation as early as December 1981. He also found that the Salt Lake City FBI agent had heard about the operation and had passed on one document which could be traced to the trash search operation long before the Sacramento-based officials alleged that they learned about the operation. The district judge said he found it inconceivable that the experienced Salt Lake City FBI agent would not have reported the existence of the trash search material to his fellow investigators in Sacramento. He made no finding, however, that the federal prosecutors had any advance knowledge of the trash search or that the Salt Lake City FBI agent realized the extent or importance of the documents in the state's possession. Moreover, he stopped short of finding that the Sacramento-based FBI agents were lying about their asserted ignorance. The district judge concluded, however, that the behavior of the Sacramento-based FBI agents amounted either to negligence or recklessness because not even bureaucratic difficulties could excuse their failure to learn about the trash search.

The district judge reasoned that these facts neither required him to dismiss the case nor allowed him merely to order a continuance, which he admitted was the normal remedy. He stated that dismissal was unacceptable because there was no proof that the government had intentionally or willfully concealed the evidence, the problem occurred before trial began, the evidence was not exculpatory, and any tainted evidence left over could be dealt with at trial on a piece-by-piece basis. He maintained that a continuance was insufficient, however, because it failed to satisfy either the demands of due process or notions of fair play and substantial justice, because the time, effort, and money that would be lost would be prejudicial, unfair, and unjust to the defendants. He observed that the indictment had been filed nearly two years before, and thus the sword had hung over the defendants long enough, that they had spent sufficient money on their defense, and that the court had expended sufficient judicial resources in managing the case. Moreover, the trial was set to begin in four days, and postponing it would inconvenience both the court and the defense attorneys in reclearing their calendars. Finally, a related state trial would be delayed if a continuance were ordered.

The government appealed this exclusionary order pursuant to 18 U.S.C. § 3731 before trial began. While its appeal was pending, the government unsuccessfully attempted either to stay the commencement of trial or to convince the district court that it had lost jurisdiction over the case while the appeal was pending. On the day trial was to begin, the government refused to proceed on the ground that it was entitled first to exercise its statutory right to appeal the exclusionary order under 18 U.S.C. § 3731. It argued that to proceed would take the meaning out of its right to appeal the exclusionary order because the evidence excluded was substantial proof of material facts. The district judge advised the government of his planned action and then dismissed the case pursuant to rule 48(b), Fed.R.Crim.P., with prejudice. He reasoned that the government was willing to proceed before discovering the trash search evidence, apparently concluding that it had sufficient evidence to convict the defendants. He cited several cases to build the proposition that rule 48(b) gave him the discretionary authority to dismiss a case for unnecessary delay either with or without prejudice, whether or not there are constitutional rights at stake. He justified his dismissal of the case with prejudice on grounds that the government's refusal to proceed was a "flagrant refusal to abide by this Court's previous orders," an "unnecessary delay," and the "rankest abuse of prosecutorial discretion." The government also appealed this dismissal, and we granted its motion to consolidate its two appeals.

II

. . .

The delay in disclosure in this case did not violate any constitutional provision, federal statute, specific discovery order, or any other recognized right except perhaps rule 16, Fed.R.Crim.P. . . . Moreover, the fact that rule 16 contains specific remedies for its violation eliminates any justification for an exercise of supervisory power to create any other remedy for it. We hold, therefore, that the separation-of-powers principle barred the district court from exercising any supervisory power to exclude the evidence in this case.

III

The government also argues that the district court erred in excluding the evidence pursuant to rule 16(d)(2), Fed.R.Crim.P., because rule 16 applies only to documents that are within the federal government's actual possession, custody, or control, because the prosecution's failure to learn about the trash search documents and to make its disclosure earlier was not negligent or reckless, because a continuance was the appropriate remedy if it did violate rule 16, and because the exclusionary order was overbroad. We agree with the government's first reason, and therefore need not reach the remaining issues.

Rule 16(d)(2) states that a district court has discretionary authority to "order [a] party to permit the discovery or inspection, grant a continuance, or prohibit the party from introducing evidence not disclosed, or it may enter such other order as it deems just under the circumstances" to remedy a failure by the government to permit inspection and copying of tangible evidence described by rule 16(a)(1)(C), which is evidence "within the possession, custody or control of the government, and which [is] material to the preparation of [the] defense or [is] intended for use by the government as evidence in chief at the trial." The government intended to use the trash search evidence in its case-in-chief. Thus, the only question is whether the evidence was "within the possession, custody or control" of the federal government.

The record shows that neither the Sacramento-based officials nor the Salt Lake City FBI agent actually possessed, had custody of, or controlled the trash search evidence before March 27, 1984. Moreover, the district judge never made any finding to the contrary. Thus, the precise issue we face is whether rule 16(a)(1)(C) ever requires the federal government to disclose and produce documents that are in the actual possession, custody or control of state officials, the relevance of which the federal government negligently or recklessly fails to appreciate. . . .

Our first question is whether, pursuant to rule 16(a)(1)(C), the "government" includes any persons other than the prosecutors. We have not faced this question before. The district court appears to have taken the position that the "government" included the Sacramento-based FBI agents assisting the federal prosecutor in this case as well as the FBI agent in Salt Lake City who was coordinating information.

. . . We need not resolve whether the district court correctly included the identified FBI agents for purposes of rule 16(a)(1)(C). Even if we assume the district judge was correct, the critical issue pertains to possession of the records.

The important question, therefore, is whether the documents must be in the actual possession or control of the FBI agents or whether constructive possession or control is sufficient. Under rule 16(a)(1)(A), which deals with statements of a defendant, we have recognized that the prosecutor's actual possession is not necessary in all cases. . . .

The cases discussing a prosecutor's due diligence obligation under rule 16(a)(1)(A) are not relevant to our case under rule 16(a)(1)(C). We have already assumed for purposes of this appeal that the government included the designated FBI agents. Rule 16(a)(1)(A) only requires the government to disclose any of the defendant's statements that are "within the possession, custody or control of the government, the existence of which is known, or by the exercise of due diligence may become known, to the attorney for the government." Thus, the due diligence requirement establishing constructive possession relates solely to the prosecutor and whether he should have been aware of a statement in the possession of another *federal* agency. As no such language is found in rule 16(a)(1)(C), a literal reading of the entire rule requires us to conclude that Congress intended no such constructive possession extension. Moreover, even if such language were found in rule 16(a)(1)(C), it would only create a due diligence requirement over documents in the possession, custody, or control of some federal agency. We would still be required to find some special reason to justify extending the requirement to documents in the possession, custody, or control of state authorities.

Because we find no due diligence language in rule 16(a)(1)(C) at all, nor any special reason to deviate from its plain language, we conclude that it triggers the government's disclosure obligation only with respect to documents within the federal government's actual possession, custody, or control. . . .

. . .

Therefore, we conclude that the triggering requirement under rule 16(a)(1)(C) is that the papers, documents, and tangible objects be in the actual possession, custody or control of the government. Here, they were not. The fashioning of a due diligence constructive possession or control addition to the rule by the district judge was erroneous and, therefore, his suppression of the trash cover evidence based upon rule 16 must be reversed.

The defendants may have been put into a difficult position because the government announced, four weeks before trial, that it had 382 tangible items it planned to introduce into evidence. Although the district court could not suppress the evidence pursuant to any supervisory powers or rule 16, and the parties have cited to us no other authority for such an order, the district judge could have considered more searchingly whether a continuance was appropriate under the circumstances simply as a matter of proper case management. The record is barren as to how much time longer than four weeks, if any, the defendants would have needed to prepare to meet this new evidence—indeed, the defendants did not even request a continuance. Thus, we cannot review whether a continuance would have been appropriate here.

. . .

■ SCHROEDER, CIRCUIT JUDGE, dissenting.

I respectfully dissent. Fed.R.Crim.P. 16(a)(1)(C) requires the prosecution to produce relevant documents anywhere within the government's "possession, custody or control." The rule is not limited to documents physically resting in federal agency file folders and should reach at least far enough to encompass these documents, which were at the prosecutors' fingertips.

The documents in question were the product of a joint investigation by Utah and Federal Authorities. The Utah trash search was linked to this Sacramento prosecution by an extensive network of state and federal authorities, including an FBI agent in Utah who acted as liaison between the Utah investigators and the Sacramento prosecutors. The trash search was also linked to this prosecution by a federally funded computer network designed to make evidence readily available to all participating state and federal agencies. No reasonable explanation appears in this record for the prosecutors' twin failures to obtain and disclose these documents long before the eve of trial. The district court found the prosecution negligent to the point of recklessness and came just short of finding an intentional withholding of documents.

In my view, these documents were within the government's "control" pursuant to the meaning of rule 16. The majority's contrary holding rewards prosecutors who wait until the last minute to examine available evidence. It encourages gamesmanship and delay rather than forthrightness and efficiency.

That these documents were material, indeed key, to the prosecution is demonstrated by the government's refusal to go forward with its case upon their suppression. Prejudice to the defendants, had the district court refused to order suppression, is similarly clear. As the district court observed, the government created a dilemma for defendants by forcing them to go to trial unprepared or to expend more time and money in further preparation of an already very costly case. Therefore, I would hold that in the circumstances of this case, the district court did not abuse its discretion when it dismissed the indictment with prejudice after the government refused to proceed. . . .

---

420. In United States v. Armstrong, 517 U.S. 456, 462 (1996) (8–1), another aspect of which is considered in note 315, p. 634 above, the Court held that the reference in Rule 16(a)(1)(C) to documents, tangible objects, and so forth that are "material to the preparation of the defendant's defense" (substantially unchanged in current Rule 16(a)(1)(E)(i)) includes only items that are material to "the defendant's response to the Government's case in chief." In particular, it did not cover items that might have a bearing on the defendant's claim of discriminatory prosecution.

421. The government's obligation of discovery under Rule 16(a)(1)(E) is not limited to documents within the judicial district, in the actual possession of the prosecutor. Its obligation turns on "the extent to which the prosecutor has knowledge of and access to the documents sought by the defendant in each case. . . . The prosecutor will be deemed to have knowledge of and access to anything in the possession, custody or control of any federal agency participating in the same investigation of the defendant." United States v. Bryan, 868 F.2d 1032, 1036 (9th Cir.1989). In United States v. Santiago, 46 F.3d 885 (9th Cir.1995), the court emphasized that a government agency's involvement in the investigation of the defendant is a sufficient, but not necessary, factor to show the prosecutor's knowledge of and access to documents.

422. The defendant, Barnard, was convicted of murder in the Louisiana courts and attacked the conviction by a federal petition for habeas corpus.

> Prior to the trial he moved for permission of the Court to allow inspection of the murder weapon and bullet by a ballistics expert of his own choosing. That this was not a frivolous request is evident since one of the most damaging pieces of evidence against Barnard was the identification of the murder bullet as having been fired by a .22 Luger pistol traced to his possession. Seventy-five percent of this slug was destroyed and the identification was made on the remaining 25%. This fact alone raises the possibility that had Barnard been assisted by a ballistics expert of his own he may have been able to shake the identification testimony of the State's experts. Barnard's motion was denied.
>
> Under Louisiana procedure pre-trial discovery of evidence in the hands of the prosecution is limited to the defendant's confessions and to narcotics. . . . In affirming Barnard's conviction the Supreme Court

> of Louisiana said that, although . . . production of evidence is required where the evidence is favorable to the accused, there had been no showing that an examination of the murder weapon and bullet would be favorable to Barnard. . . . [D]ue process cannot be sidestepped by such a facile distinction.
>
> The question is not one of discovery but rather the defendant's right to the means necessary to conduct his defense. . . . Fundamental fairness is violated when a criminal defendant on trial for his liberty is denied the opportunity to have an expert of his choosing, bound by appropriate safeguards imposed by the Court, examine a piece of critical evidence whose nature is subject to varying expert opinion.
>
> Neither are we persuaded by the State's contention that Barnard waived his right to complain of the denial of this request to examine the weapon by failing to move for a continuance when the pistol was placed into evidence.
>
> . . .
>
> . . . In view of the earlier unsuccessful effort to obtain inspection upon which to base countervailing expert opinion the asserted practice of allowing a continuance—more accurately, an interruption of a trial then in progress—has built-in hazards so prejudicial to the accused in the eyes of the jury that it does not under the circumstances of this case present a viable alternative to pretrial discovery going to the very heart of the case and fundamental due process fairness.

Barnard v. Henderson, 514 F.2d 744, 746–47 (5th Cir.1975) (conviction vacated).

Barnard was discussed and applied in White v. Maggio, 556 F.2d 1352 (5th Cir.1977) (failure to grant pretrial discovery of bullets used to show that fatal bullet came from defendant's gun). The court said that "under *Barnard* a writ of habeas corpus should issue only if the state prevented inspection by defense experts of tangible evidence that is both 'critical' to the conviction and subject to varying expert opinion." Id. at 1356.

423. Does the court have authority, on motion of the defendant or otherwise, to require the complaining witness or another witness for the prosecution to submit to a mental or physical examination? If so, on what basis? See, for example, United States v. Dildy, 39 F.R.D. 340 (D.D.C.1966), in which the defendant, who was charged with rape, moved that the court require the complainant to submit to a psychiatric examination and blood tests of herself and her infant child. See generally United States v. Benn, 476 F.2d 1127, 1130–31 (D.C.Cir.1972).

FEDERAL RULES OF CRIMINAL PROCEDURE

Rule 17

SUBPOENA

. . .

(c) Producing Documents and Objects.

(1) *In General.* A subpoena may order the witness to produce any books, papers, documents, data, or other objects the subpoena desig-

nates. The court may direct the witness to produce the designated items in court before trial or before they are to be offered in evidence. When the items arrive, the court may permit the parties and their attorneys to inspect all or part of them.

(2) *Quashing or Modifying the Subpoena.* On motion made promptly, the court may quash or modify the subpoena if compliance would be unreasonable or oppressive.

424.

It was intended by the rules to give some measure of discovery. Rule 16 was adopted for that purpose. It gave discovery as to documents and other materials otherwise beyond the reach of the defendant which . . . might be numerous and difficult to identify. The rule was to apply not only to documents and other materials belonging to the defendant, but also to those belonging to others which had been obtained by seizure or process. This was a departure from what had theretofore been allowed in criminal cases.

Rule 16 deals with documents and other materials that are in the possession of the Government and provides how they may be made available to the defendant for his information. In the interest of orderly procedure in the handling of books, papers, documents and objects in the custody of the Government accumulated in the course of an investigation and subpoenaed for use before the grand jury and on the trial, it was provided by Rule 16 that the court could order such materials made available to the defendant for inspection and copying or photographing. In that way, the control and possession of the Government is not disturbed. Rule 16 provides the only way the defendant can reach such materials so as to inform himself.

But if such materials or any part of them are not put in evidence by the Government, the defendant may subpoena them under Rule 17(c) and use them himself. It would be strange indeed if the defendant discovered some evidence by the use of Rule 16 which the Government was not going to introduce and yet could not require its production by Rule 17(c). There may be documents and other materials in the possession of the Government not subject to Rule 16. No good reason appears to us why they may not be reached by subpoena under Rule 17(c) as long as they are evidentiary. That is not to say that the materials thus subpoenaed must actually be used in evidence. It is only required that a good-faith effort be made to obtain evidence. The court may control the use of Rule 17(c) to that end by its power to rule on motions to quash or modify.

> It was not intended by Rule 16 to give a limited right of discovery, and then by Rule 17 to give a right of discovery in the broadest terms. Rule 17 provided for the usual subpoena *ad testificandum* and *duces tecum*, which may be issued by the clerk, with the provision that the court may direct the materials designated in the subpoena *duces tecum* to be produced at a specified time and place for inspection by the defendant. Rule 17(c) was not intended to provide an additional means of discovery. Its chief innovation was to expedite the trial by providing a time and place *before* trial for the inspection of the subpoenaed materials. . . . However, the plain words of the Rule are not to be ignored. They must be given their ordinary meaning to carry out the purpose of establishing a more liberal policy for the production, inspection and use of materials at the trial. There was no intention to exclude from the reach of process of the defendant any material that had been used before the grand jury or could be used at the trial. In short, any document or other materials, admissible as evidence, obtained by the Government by solicitation or voluntarily from third persons is subject to subpoena.

Bowman Dairy Co. v. United States, 341 U.S. 214, 218–21 (1951).

Witnesses

---

18 U.S.C. § 3432

Indictment and list of jurors and witnesses for prisoner in capital cases

A person charged with treason or other capital offense shall at least three entire days before commencement of trial be furnished with a copy of the indictment and a list of the veniremen, and of the witnesses to be produced on the trial for proving the indictment, stating the place of abode of each venireman and witness, except that such list of the veniremen and witnesses need not be furnished if the court finds by a preponderance of the evidence that providing the list may jeopardize the life or safety of any person.

The amendments to Rule 16 transmitted to Congress in 1974 included a subsection (a)(1)(E) as follows:

> Government witnesses. Upon request of the defendant the government shall furnish to the defendant a written list of the names and addresses of all government witnesses which the attorney for the government intends to call in the presentation of the case in chief together with any record of prior felony convictions of any such witness which is within the knowledge of the attorney for the government.

When a request for discovery of the names and addresses of witnesses has been made by a defendant, the government shall be allowed to perpetuate the testimony of such witnesses in accordance with the provisions of Rule 15.

The Advisory Committee's Note accompanying this provision observed that many states had provisions for pretrial disclosure of witnesses for the prosecution and that the ABA Standards also provided for such disclosure. Disclosure of the criminal record of prosecution witnesses, the Committee said, "places the defense in the same position as the government, which normally has knowledge of the defendant's record and the record of anticipated defense witnesses. In addition, the defendant often lacks means of procuring this information on his own." With respect to the danger that witnesses would be intimidated not to testify or to change their testimony, the Committee said that the government could move for a protective order or for an order to perpetuate a witness's testimony by deposition for use at trial if the witness became unavailable or changed his testimony.

After considerable debate, Congress deleted that provision from the amended rule. The Conference Report stated only: "A majority of the Conferees believe it is not in the interest of the effective administration of criminal justice to require that the government or the defendant be forced to reveal the names and addresses of its witnesses before trial. Discouragement of witnesses and improper contacts directed at influencing their testimony were deemed paramount concerns in the formulation of this policy." H.R.Rep. No. 94–414 (to accompany H.R. 6799), 94th Cong., 1st Sess. 12 (1975).

Rule 12.1, p. 856 below, however, provides for reciprocal discovery of witnesses whose testimony will be offered to sustain or contradict a defense of alibi.

Rule 16(a)(1)(G) provides for the government to give the defendant, on request, a summary of testimony of expert witnesses that it intends to use in its case-in-chief as provided in Federal Rules of Evidence 702, 703, and 705. Rule 16(b)(1)(C) contains a reciprocal provision for discovery by the government. The summary must "describe the witness's opinions, the bases and reasons for those opinions, and the witness's qualifications."

UNITED STATES ATTORNEYS' MANUAL

9–6.200 Pretrial Disclosure of Witness Identity

. . .

[I]t is the Department's position that pretrial disclosure of a witness' identity should not be made if there is, in the judgment of the prosecutor, any reason to believe that such disclosure would endanger the safety of the witness or any other person, or lead to efforts to obstruct justice. Factors relevant to the possibility of witness intimidation or obstruction of justice include, but are not limited to, the types of charges pending against the defendant, any record or information about the propensity of the defendant or the defendant's confederates to engage in witness intimidation or obstruction of justice, and any threats directed by the defendant or others against the witness. In addition, pretrial disclosure of a witness' identity should not ordinarily be made against the known wishes of any witness.

However, pretrial disclosure of the identity of a government witness may often promote the prompt and just resolution of the case. Such disclosure may enhance the prospects that the defendant will plead guilty or lead to the initiation of plea negotiations; in the event the defendant goes to trial, such disclosure may expedite the conduct of the trial by eliminating the need for a continuance.

Accordingly, with respect to prosecutions in federal court, a prosecutor should give careful consideration, as to each prospective witness, whether—absent any indication of potential adverse consequences of the kind mentioned above—reason exists to disclose such witness' identity prior to trial. It should be borne in mind that a decision by the prosecutor to disclose pretrial the identity of potential government witnesses may be conditioned upon the defendant's making reciprocal disclosure as to the identity of potential defense witnesses. Similarly, where appropriate in light of the facts and circumstances of the case, a prosecutor may determine to disclose only the identity, but not the current address or whereabouts, of a witness.

In sum, whether or not to disclose the identity of a witness prior to trial is committed to the discretion of the federal prosecutor, and that discretion should be exercised on a case-by-case, and witness-by-witness basis. Considerations of witness safety and willingness to cooperate, and the integrity of the judicial process, are paramount.

Gregory v. United States

369 F.2d 185 (D.C.Cir.1966)

[The defendant was convicted of murder, robbery, and assault.]

■ J. SKELLY WRIGHT, CIRCUIT JUDGE:

. . .

The prosecutor embarrassed and confounded the accused in the preparation of his defense by advising the witnesses to the robberies and murder not to speak to anyone unless he were present. Six days before the trial began, defense counsel and the prosecutor, Mr. Weitzel, appeared before a motions judge. Defense counsel asked for the judge's assistance because two eye witnesses to the murder and robbery had declined "to talk to me unless Mr. Weitzel is present or unless Mr. Weitzel authorizes him to talk to me." Defense counsel asked the judge to direct Mr. Weitzel to allow the witnesses to talk to him. The court ruled: "I can't direct the Government to permit you to talk to a Government witness."

On the day the trial opened, defense counsel asked for the assistance of the trial judge with respect to his difficulty in interviewing the witnesses to the events on trial. Defense counsel stated to the court that the witnesses had refused to talk to him because "the United States Attorney told them not to talk to us." At this point the prosecutor, Mr. Weitzel, stated: "I instructed all the witnesses that they were free to speak to anyone they like. However, it was my advice that they not speak to anyone about the case unless I was present." Mr. Weitzel further advised the trial court that defense counsel's motion had already been denied by a motions judge, whereupon the trial court stated: "Well, I think that disposes of the matter."

After the prosecutor had completed his opening statement, defense counsel called to the court's attention the fact that, according to the opening statement, several witnesses on the list of witnesses provided defense counsel as required by 18 U.S.C. § 3432 would not be called by the Government. Apparently thinking that if the Government had no use for these witnesses he might have, defense counsel again pointed out that he had not been able to interview these witnesses because "they have been told not to talk to us," and asked the court's assistance at least with reference to interviewing the witnesses on the list the Government would not use. The court stated: "There is nothing I can do about it."

The purpose of 18 U.S.C. § 3432 requiring that in capital cases the defendant be furnished a list of the names and addresses of the witnesses to be called by the Government is to assist defense counsel in preparing the defense by interviewing the witnesses. Witnesses, particularly eye witnesses, to a crime are the property of neither the prosecution nor the defense. Both sides have an equal right, and should have an equal opportunity, to interview them. Here the defendant was denied that opportunity which, not only the statute, but elemental fairness and due process required that he have. It is true that the prosecutor stated he did not instruct the witnesses not to talk to defense counsel. He did admit that he advised the witnesses not to talk to anyone unless he, the prosecutor, were present.

We accept the prosecutor's statement as to his advice to the witnesses as true. But we know of nothing in the law which gives the prosecutor the right to interfere with the preparation of the defense by effectively denying defense counsel access to the witnesses except in his presence. Presumably the prosecutor, in interviewing the witnesses, was unencumbered by the presence of defense counsel, and there seems to be no reason why defense counsel should not have an equal opportunity to determine, through interviews with the witnesses, what they know about the case and what they will testify to. In fact, Canon 39 of the Canons of Professional Ethics makes explicit the propriety of such conduct: "A lawyer may properly interview any witness or prospective witness for the opposing side in any civil or criminal action without the consent of opposing counsel or party." Canon 10 of the Code of Trial Conduct of the American College of Trial Lawyers is an almost verbatim provision.

We do not, of course, impugn the motives of the prosecutor in giving his advice to the witnesses. Tampering with witnesses and subornation of perjury are real dangers, especially in a capital case. But there are ways to avert this danger without denying defense counsel access to eye witnesses to the events in suit unless the prosecutor is present to monitor the interview. We cannot indulge the assumption that this tactic on the part of the prosecution is necessary. Defense counsel are officers of the court. And defense counsel are not exempted from prosecution under the statutes denouncing the crimes of obstruction of justice and subornation of perjury. In fact, the Government's motivation in disallowing defense counsel to interview witnesses apparently stems from factors other than fear of tampering. Recent records in this court reveal that the same policy followed in this case is followed even when the witness involved is a member of the police force. . . .

A criminal trial, like its civil counterpart, is a quest for truth. That quest will more often be successful if both sides have an equal opportunity to interview the persons who have the information from which the truth may be determined. The current tendency in the criminal law is in the direction of discovery of the facts before trial and elimination of surprise at trial. A related development in the criminal law is the requirement that the prosecution not frustrate the defense in the preparation of its case. Information favorable to the defense must be made available to the defense. . . . Reversals of convictions for suppression of such evidence, and even for mere failure to disclose, have become commonplace. It is not suggested here that there was any direct suppression of evidence. But there was unquestionably a suppression of the means by which the defense could obtain evidence. The defense could not know what the eye witnesses to the events in suit were to testify to or how firm they were in their testimony unless defense counsel was provided a fair opportunity for interview. In our judgment the prosecutor's advice to these eye witnesses frustrated that effort and denied appellant a fair trial.

. . .

---

425. "[W]e recognize that abuses can easily result when officials elect to inform potential witnesses of their right not to speak with defense counsel. An accused and his counsel have rights of access to potential witnesses that are no less than the accessibility to the potential prosecutors and their investigatory agents. It is imperative that prosecutors and other officials maintain a posture of strict neutrality when advising witnesses of their duties and rights. Their role as public servants and as protectors of the integrity of the judicial process permits nothing less." United States v. Rich, 580 F.2d 929, 934 (9th Cir.1978).

Gregory was distinguished in United States v. Black, 767 F.2d 1334 (9th Cir.1985). The prosecutor sent a letter to prospective witnesses that explained trial and pretrial procedures. The letter said: "At some point prior to trial you may be contacted by an attorney on behalf of the defendant. You may speak to this person if you choose, but have no obligation to do so." The court concluded that the letter stated the law correctly and was not improper. But see United States v. Rogers, 642 F.Supp. 934 (D.Colo.1986), finding that a similar letter was improper and directing that a follow-up letter recommending cooperation with defense counsel be sent. See also People v. Davis, 98 Cal.Rptr. 71 (Ct.App.1971) (disapproving prosecutor's letter to complaining witnesses in statutory rape cases advising them that they did not have to submit to court-ordered psychiatric examination).

When the government finds it necessary to place a prosecution witness in protective custody before trial, "it becomes the duty of the trial court to ensure that counsel for defense has access to the secluded witness under controlled arrangements." United States v. Walton, 602 F.2d 1176, 1180 (4th Cir.1979). The witness may, however, refuse to be interviewed.

426. ABA Standards for Criminal Justice, Prosecution Function and Defense Function (3d ed. 1993): Prosecution Function Standard 3–3.1(d): "A prosecutor should not discourage or obstruct communication between prospective witnesses and defense counsel. A prosecutor should not advise any person or cause any person to be advised to decline to give to the defense information which such person has the right to give."

FEDERAL RULES OF CRIMINAL PROCEDURE

Rule 15

DEPOSITIONS

(a) When Taken.

(1) *In General.* A party may move that a prospective witness be deposed in order to preserve testimony for trial. The court may grant the motion because of exceptional circumstances and in the interest of justice. If the court orders the deposition to be taken, it may also require the deponent to produce at the deposition any designated material that is not privileged, including any book, paper, document, record, recording, or data.

(2) *Detained Material Witness.* A witness who is detained under 18 U.S.C. § 3144 may request to be deposed by filing a written motion and giving notice to the parties. The court may then order that the deposition be taken and may discharge the witness after the witness has signed under oath the deposition transcript.

(b) Notice.

(1) *In General.* A party seeking to take a deposition must give every other party reasonable written notice of the deposition's date and location. The notice must state the name and address of each depo-

nent. If requested by a party receiving the notice, the court may, for good cause, change the deposition's date or location.

(2) *To the Custodial Officer.* A party seeking to take the deposition must also notify the officer who has custody of the defendant of the scheduled date and location.

(c) Defendant's Presence.

(1) *Defendant in Custody.* The officer who has custody of the defendant must produce the defendant at the deposition and keep the defendant in the witness's presence during the examination, unless the defendant:

(A) waives in writing the right to be present; or

(B) persists in disruptive conduct justifying exclusion after being warned by the court that disruptive conduct will result in the defendant's exclusion.

(2) *Defendant Not in Custody.* A defendant who is not in custody has the right upon request to be present at the deposition, subject to any conditions imposed by the court. If the government tenders the defendant's expenses as provided in Rule 15(d) but the defendant still fails to appear, the defendant—absent good cause—waives both the right to appear and any objection to the taking and use of the deposition based on that right.

(d) Expenses. If the deposition was requested by the government, the court may—or if the defendant is unable to bear the deposition expenses, the court must—order the government to pay:

(1) any reasonable travel and subsistence expenses of the defendant and the defendant's attorney to attend the deposition; and

(2) the costs of the deposition transcript.

(e) Manner of Taking. Unless these rules or a court order provides otherwise, a deposition must be taken and filed in the same manner as a deposition in a civil action, except that:

(1) A defendant may not be deposed without that defendant's consent.

(2) The scope and manner of the deposition examination and cross-examination must be the same as would be allowed during trial.

(3) The government must provide to the defendant or the defendant's attorney, for use at the deposition, any statement of the deponent in the government's possession to which the defendant would be entitled at trial.

(f) Use as Evidence. A party may use all or part of a deposition as provided by the Federal Rules of Evidence.

(g) Objections. A party objecting to deposition testimony or evidence must state the grounds for the objection during the deposition.

(h) Depositions by Agreement Permitted. The parties may by agreement take and use a deposition with the court's consent.

AO90 (Rev. 11/91) Deposition Subpoena in a Criminal Case

UNITED STATES DISTRICT COURT

_______________ DISTRICT OF _______________

UNITED STATES OF AMERICA
V.

**DEPOSITION SUBPOENA
IN A CRIMINAL CASE**

Case Number:

TO:

☐ YOU ARE COMMANDED to appear at the place, date, and time specified below to testify at the taking of a deposition in the above case.

PLACE	DATE AND TIME

☐ YOU ARE ALSO COMMANDED to bring with you the following document(s) or object(s):

Any organization not a party to this suit that is subpoenaed for the taking of a deposition shall designate one or more officers, directors, or managing agents, or other persons who consent to testify on its behalf, and may set forth, for each person designated, the matters on which the person will testify. Federal Rules of Civil Procedure, 30(b)(6).

U.S. MAGISTRATE JUDGE OR CLERK OF COURT	DATE
(By) Deputy Clerk	

ATTORNEY'S NAME, ADDRESS AND PHONE NUMBER:

427. In United States v. Mann, 590 F.2d 361 (1st Cir.1978), the government took a deposition of a witness for the prosecution, a 17-year-old Australian, who was then allowed to return to Australia without objection from the government. Over the defendant's objection, the deposition was admitted at trial. The court of appeals held that the government's motion to take a deposition should not have been granted, there not being the "exceptional circumstances" required by Rule 15(a), and that the deposition should not have been admitted at trial, because the government had not met its burden of showing that the witness was "unavailable." The court indicated that the government should not have acquiesced in the departure of the witness, whose testimony was critical, and that having done so, it should have made stronger efforts to obtain her appearance at trial.

428. The provision in Rule 15(d)(1) (now 15(e)(1)) that a defendant shall not be deposed without his consent applies to a codefendant who has pleaded guilty but has not yet been sentenced. United States v. Cassese, 622 F.2d 26 (2d Cir.1979).

Defendant's Disclosure

FEDERAL RULES OF CRIMINAL PROCEDURE

[See Rule 16(b), p. 835 above]

Rule 12.1

NOTICE OF AN ALIBI DEFENSE

(a) Government's Request for Notice and Defendant's Response.

(1) *Government's Request.* An attorney for the government may request in writing that the defendant notify an attorney for the government of any intended alibi defense. The request must state the time, date, and place of the alleged offense.

(2) *Defendant's Response.* Within 10 days after the request, or at some other time the court sets, the defendant must serve written notice on an attorney for the government of any intended alibi defense. The defendant's notice must state:

(A) each specific place where the defendant claims to have been at the time of the alleged offense; and

(B) the name, address, and telephone number of each alibi witness on whom the defendant intends to rely.

(b) Disclosing Government Witnesses.

(1) *Disclosure.* If the government serves a Rule 12.1(a)(2) notice, an attorney for the government must disclose in writing to the defendant or the defendant's attorney:

(A) the name, address, and telephone number of each witness the government intends to rely on to establish the defendant's presence at the scene of the alleged offense; and

(B) each government rebuttal witness to the defendant's alibi defense.

(2) *Time to Disclose.* Unless the court directs otherwise, an attorney for the government must give its Rule 12.1(b)(1) disclosure within 10 days after the defendant serves notice of an intended alibi defense under Rule 12.1(a)(2), but no later than 10 days before trial.

(c) Continuing Duty to Disclose. Both an attorney for the government and the defendant must promptly disclose in writing to the other party the name, address, and telephone number of each additional witness if:

(1) the disclosing party learns of the witness before or during trial; and

(2) the witness should have been disclosed under Rule 12.1(a) or (b) if the disclosing party had known of the witness earlier.

(d) Exceptions. For good cause, the court may grant an exception to any requirement of Rule 12.1(a)–(c).

(e) Failure to Comply. If a party fails to comply with this rule, the court may exclude the testimony of any undisclosed witness regarding the defendant's alibi. This rule does not limit the defendant's right to testify.

(f) Inadmissibility of Withdrawn Intention. Evidence of an intention to rely on an alibi defense, later withdrawn, or of a statement made in connection with that intention, is not, in any civil or criminal proceeding, admissible against the person who gave notice of the intention.

Rule 12.2

NOTICE OF AN INSANITY DEFENSE; MENTAL EXAMINATION

(a) Notice of an Insanity Defense. A defendant who intends to assert a defense of insanity at the time of the alleged offense must so notify an attorney for the government in writing within the time provided for filing a pretrial motion, or at any later time the court sets, and file a copy of the notice with the clerk. A defendant who fails to do so cannot rely on an insanity defense. The court may, for good cause, allow the defendant to file the notice late, grant additional trial-preparation time, or make other appropriate orders.

(b) Notice of Expert Evidence of a Mental Condition. If a defendant intends to introduce expert evidence relating to a mental disease or defect or any other mental condition of the defendant bearing on either (1) the issue of guilt or (2) the issue of punishment in a capital case, the defendant must—within the time provided for filing a pretrial motion or at any later time the court sets—notify an attorney for the government in writing of this intention and file a copy of the notice with the clerk. The court may, for good cause, allow the defendant to file the notice late, grant the parties additional trial-preparation time, or make other appropriate orders.

(c) Mental Examination.

(1) *Authority to Order an Examination; Procedures.*

(A) The court may order the defendant to submit to a competency examination under 18 U.S.C. § 4241.

(B) If the defendant provides notice under Rule 12.2(a), the court must, upon the government's motion, order the defendant to be examined under 18 U.S.C. § 4242. If the defendant provides notice under Rule 12.2(b) the court may, upon the government's motion, order the defendant to be examined under procedures ordered by the court.

(2) *Disclosing Results and Reports of Capital Sentencing Examination.* The results and reports of any examination conducted solely under Rule 12.2(c)(1) after notice under Rule 12.2(b)(2) must be sealed and must not be disclosed to any attorney for the government or the defendant unless the defendant is found guilty of one or more capital crimes and the defendant confirms an intent to offer during sentencing proceedings expert evidence on mental condition.

(3) *Disclosing Results and Reports of the Defendant's Expert Examination.* After disclosure under Rule 12.2(c)(2) of the results and reports of the government's examination, the defendant must disclose to the government the results and reports of any examination on mental condition conducted by the defendant's expert about which the defendant intends to introduce expert evidence.

(4) *Inadmissibility of a Defendant's Statements.* No statement made by a defendant in the course of any examination conducted under this rule (whether conducted with or without the defendant's consent), no testimony by the expert based on the statement, and no other fruits of the statement may be admitted into evidence against the defendant in any criminal proceeding except on an issue regarding mental condition on which the defendant:

(A) has introduced evidence of incompetency or evidence requiring notice under Rule12.2(a) or (b)(1), or

(B) has introduced expert evidence in a capital sentencing proceeding requiring notice under Rule 12.2(b)(2).

(d) Failure to Comply. If the defendant fails to give notice under Rule 12.2(b) or does not submit to an examination when ordered under Rule 12.2(c), the court may exclude any expert evidence from the defendant on the issue of the defendant's mental disease, mental defect, or any other mental condition bearing on the defendant's guilt or the issue of punishment in a capital case.

(e) Inadmissibility of Withdrawn Intention. Evidence of an intention as to which notice was given under Rule 12.2(a) or (b), later withdrawn, is not, in any civil or criminal proceeding, admissible against the person who gave notice of the intention.

Rule 12.3

NOTICE OF A PUBLIC-AUTHORITY DEFENSE

(a) Notice of the Defense and Disclosure of Witnesses.

(1) *Notice in General.* If a defendant intends to assert a defense of actual or believed exercise of public authority on behalf of a law enforcement agency or federal intelligence agency at the time of the alleged offense, the defendant must so notify an attorney for the government in writing and must file a copy of the notice with the clerk within the time provided for filing a pretrial motion, or at any later time the court sets. The notice filed with the clerk must be under seal if the notice identifies a federal intelligence agency as the source of public authority.

(2) *Contents of Notice.* The notice must contain the following information:

(A) the law enforcement agency or federal intelligence agency involved;

(B) the agency member on whose behalf the defendant claims to have acted; and

(C) the time during which the defendant claims to have acted with public authority.

(3) *Response to the Notice.* An attorney for the government must serve a written response on the defendant or the defendant's attorney within 10 days after receiving the defendant's notice, but no later than 20 days before trial. The response must admit or deny that the defendant exercised the public authority identified in the defendant's notice.

(4) *Disclosing Witnesses.*

(A) *Government's Request.* An attorney for the government may request in writing that the defendant disclose the name, address, and telephone number of each witness the defendant intends to rely on to establish a public-authority defense. An attorney for the government may serve the request when the government serves its response to the defendant's notice under Rule 12.3(a)(3), or later, but must serve the request no later than 20 days before trial.

(B) *Defendant's Response.* Within 7 days after receiving the government's request, the defendant must serve on an attorney for the government a written statement of the name, address, and telephone number of each witness.

(C) *Government's Reply.* Within 7 days after receiving the defendant's statement, an attorney for the government must serve on the defendant or the defendant's attorney a written statement of the name, address, and telephone number of each witness the government intends to rely on to oppose the defendant's public-authority defense.

(5) *Additional Time.* The court may, for good cause, allow a party additional time to comply with this rule.

(b) Continuing Duty to Disclose. Both an attorney for the government and the defendant must promptly disclose in writing to the other party the name, address, and telephone number of any additional witness if:

(1) the disclosing party learns of the witness before or during trial; and

(2) the witness should have been disclosed under Rule 12.3(a)(4) if the disclosing party had known of the witness earlier.

(c) Failure to Comply. If a party fails to comply with this rule, the court may exclude the testimony of any undisclosed witness regarding the public-authority defense. This rule does not limit the defendant's right to testify.

(d) Protective Procedures Unaffected. This rule does not limit the court's authority to issue appropriate protective orders or to order that any filings be under seal.

(e) Inadmissibility of Withdrawn Intention. Evidence of an intention as to which notice was given under Rule 12.3(a), later withdrawn, is not, in any civil or criminal proceeding, admissible against the person who gave notice of the intention.

Rule 12.4
DISCLOSURE STATEMENT

(a) Who Must File.

(1) *Nongovernmental Corporate Party*. Any nongovernmental corporate party to a proceeding in a district court must file a statement that identifies any parent corporation and any publicly held corporation that owns 10% or more of its stock or states that there is no such corporation.

(2) *Organizational Victim*. If an organization is a victim of the alleged criminal activity, the government must file a statement identifying the victim. If the organizational victim is a corporation, the statement must also disclose the information required by Rule 12.4(a)(1) to the extent it can be obtained through due diligence.

(b) Time for Filing; Supplemental Filing. A party must:

(1) file the Rule 12.4(a) statement upon the defendant's initial appearance; and

(2) promptly file a supplemental statement upon any change in the information that the statement requires.

Williams v. Florida

399 U.S. 78, 90 S.Ct. 1893, 26 L.Ed.2d 446 (1970)

■ MR. JUSTICE WHITE delivered the opinion of the Court.

Prior to his trial for robbery in the State of Florida, petitioner filed a "Motion for a Protective Order," seeking to be excused from the requirements of Rule 1.200 of the Florida Rules of Criminal Procedure. That rule requires a defendant, on written demand of the prosecuting attorney, to give notice in advance of trial if the defendant intends to claim an alibi, and to furnish the prosecuting attorney with information as to the place where he claims to have been and with the names and addresses of the alibi witnesses he intends to use. In his motion petitioner openly declared his intent to claim an alibi, but objected to the further disclosure requirements on the ground that the rule "compels the Defendant in a criminal case to be a witness against himself" in violation of his Fifth and Fourteenth Amendment rights. The motion was denied. . . . Petitioner was convicted as charged and was sentenced to life imprisonment. The District Court of Appeal affirmed, rejecting petitioner's claims that his Fifth . . . Amendment rights had been violated. We granted certiorari. . . .

I

Florida's notice-of-alibi rule is in essence a requirement that a defendant submit to a limited form of pretrial discovery by the State whenever he intends to rely at trial on the defense of alibi. In exchange for the defendant's disclosure of the witnesses he proposes to use to establish that defense, the State in turn is required to notify the defendant of any witnesses it proposes to offer in rebuttal to that defense. Both sides are under a continuing duty promptly to disclose the names and addresses of additional witnesses bearing on the alibi as they become available. The threatened sanction for failure to comply is the exclusion at trial of the defendant's alibi evidence—except for his own testimony—or, in the case of the State, the exclusion of the State's evidence offered in rebuttal of the alibi.

In this case, following the denial of his Motion for a Protective Order, petitioner complied with the alibi rule and gave the State the name and address of one Mary Scotty. Mrs. Scotty was summoned to the office of the State Attorney on the morning of the trial, where she gave pretrial testimony. At the trial itself, Mrs. Scotty, petitioner, and petitioner's wife all testified that the three of them had been in Mrs. Scotty's apartment during the time of the robbery. On two occasions during cross-examination of Mrs. Scotty, the prosecuting attorney confronted her with her earlier deposition in which she had given dates and times that in some respects did not correspond with the dates and times given at trial. Mrs. Scotty adhered to her trial story, insisting that she had been mistaken in her earlier testimony. The State also offered in rebuttal the testimony of one of the officers investigating the robbery who claimed that Mrs. Scotty had asked him for directions on the afternoon in question during the time when she claimed to have been in her apartment with petitioner and his wife.

We need not linger over the suggestion that the discovery permitted the State against petitioner in this case deprived him of "due process" or a "fair trial." Florida law provides for liberal discovery by the defendant against the State, and the notice-of-alibi rule is itself carefully hedged with reciprocal duties requiring state disclosure to the defendant. Given the ease with which an alibi can be fabricated, the State's interest in protecting itself against an eleventh-hour defense is both obvious and legitimate. Reflecting this interest, notice-of-alibi provisions, dating at least from 1927, are now in existence in a substantial number of States. The adversary system of trial is hardly an end in itself; it is not yet a poker game in which players enjoy an absolute right always to conceal their cards until played. We find ample room in that system, at least as far as "due process" is concerned, for the instant Florida rule, which is designed to enhance the search for truth in the criminal trial by insuring both the defendant and the State ample opportunity to investigate certain facts crucial to the determination of guilt or innocence.

Petitioner's major contention is that he was "compelled . . . to be a witness against himself" contrary to the commands of the Fifth and Fourteenth Amendments because the notice-of-alibi rule required him to give the State the name and address of Mrs. Scotty in advance of trial and thus to furnish the State with information useful in convicting him. No pretrial statement of petitioner was introduced at trial; but armed with Mrs. Scotty's name and address and the knowledge that she was to be petitioner's alibi witness, the State was able to take her deposition in advance of trial and to find rebuttal testimony. Also, requiring him to reveal the elements of his defense is claimed to have interfered with his right to wait until after the State had presented its case to decide how to defend against it. We conclude, however, as has apparently every other court that has considered the issue, that the privilege against self-incrimination is not violated by a requirement that the defendant give notice of an alibi defense and disclose his alibi witnesses.[15]

The defendant in a criminal trial is frequently forced to testify himself and to call other witnesses in an effort to reduce the risk of conviction. When he presents his witnesses, he must reveal their identity and submit them to cross-examination which in itself may prove incriminating or which may furnish the State with leads to incriminating rebuttal evidence. That the defendant faces such a dilemma demanding a choice between complete silence and presenting a defense has never been thought an invasion of the privilege against compelled self-incrimination. The pressures generated by the State's evidence may be severe but they do not vitiate the defendant's choice to present an alibi defense and witnesses to prove it, even though the attempted defense ends in catastrophe for the defendant. However "testimonial" or "incriminating" the alibi defense proves to be, it cannot be considered "compelled" within the meaning of the Fifth and Fourteenth Amendments.

15. We emphasize that this case does not involve the question of the validity of the threatened sanction, had petitioner chosen not to comply with the notice-of-alibi rule. Whether and to what extent a State can enforce discovery rules against a defendant who fails to comply, by excluding relevant, probative evidence is a question raising Sixth Amendment issues which we have no occasion to explore. . . . It is enough that no such penalty was exacted here.

Very similar constraints operate on the defendant when the State requires pretrial notice of alibi and the naming of alibi witnesses. Nothing in such a rule requires the defendant to rely on an alibi or prevents him from abandoning the defense; these matters are left to his unfettered choice. That choice must be made, but the pressures that bear on his pretrial decision are of the same nature as those that would induce him to call alibi witnesses at the trial: the force of historical fact beyond both his and the State's control and the strength of the State's case built on these facts. Response to that kind of pressure by offering evidence or testimony is not compelled self-incrimination transgressing the Fifth and Fourteenth Amendments.

In the case before us, the notice-of-alibi rule by itself in no way affected petitioner's crucial decision to call alibi witnesses or added to the legitimate pressures leading to that course of action. At most, the rule only compelled petitioner to accelerate the timing of his disclosure, forcing him to divulge at an earlier date information that the petitioner from the beginning planned to divulge at trial. Nothing in the Fifth Amendment privilege entitles a defendant as a matter of constitutional right to await the end of the State's case before announcing the nature of his defense, any more than it entitles him to await the jury's verdict on the State's case-in-chief before deciding whether or not to take the stand himself.

Petitioner concedes that absent the notice-of-alibi rule the Constitution would raise no bar to the court's granting the State a continuance at trial on the ground of surprise as soon as the alibi witness is called. Nor would there be self-incrimination problems if, during that continuance, the State was permitted to do precisely what it did here prior to trial: take the deposition of the witness and find rebuttal evidence. But if so utilizing a continuance is permissible under the Fifth and Fourteenth Amendments, then surely the same result may be accomplished through pretrial discovery, as it was here, avoiding the necessity of a disrupted trial. We decline to hold that the privilege against compulsory self-incrimination guarantees the defendant the right to surprise the State with an alibi defense. . . .[16]

---

429. In Wardius v. Oregon, 412 U.S. 470 (1973), the Court considered a notice-of-alibi rule that contained no provision for reciprocal discovery. The defendant had been barred from presenting evidence to support his alibi because he failed to comply with the rule. The court held that "the Due Process Clause of the Fourteenth Amendment forbids enforcement of alibi rules unless reciprocal discovery rights are given to criminal defendants." Id. at 472.

[16] Chief Justice Burger wrote a concurring opinion. Justice Black wrote an opinion, which Justice Douglas joined, in which he dissented from the Court's opinion on the notice-of-alibi issue. Justice Harlan, Justice Stewart, and Justice Marshall wrote opinions dealing with another aspect of the case.

> [A]lthough the Due Process Clause has little to say regarding the amount of discovery which the parties must be afforded . . . it does speak to the balance of forces between the accused and his accuser. . . . The *Williams* Court was therefore careful to note that "Florida law provides for liberal discovery by the defendant against the State, and the notice-of-alibi rule is itself carefully hedged with reciprocal duties requiring state disclosure to the defendant." 399 U.S., at 81 (footnote omitted). The same cannot be said of Oregon law. . . . Oregon grants no discovery rights to criminal defendants, and, indeed, does not even provide defendants with bills of particulars. More significantly, Oregon, unlike Florida, has no provision which requires the State to reveal the names and addresses of witnesses it plans to use to refute an alibi defense.
>
> We do not suggest that the Due Process Clause of its own force requires Oregon to adopt such provisions. . . . But we do hold that in the absence of a strong showing of state interests to the contrary, discovery must be a two-way street. The State may not insist that trials be run as a "search for truth" so far as defense witnesses are concerned, while maintaining "poker game" secrecy for its own witnesses. It is fundamentally unfair to require a defendant to divulge the details of his own case while at the same time subjecting him to the hazard of surprise concerning refutation of the very pieces of evidence which he disclosed to the State.

412 U.S. at 474–76.

See Mauricio v. Duckworth, 840 F.2d 454 (7th Cir.1988) (prosecution's failure to disclose alibi rebuttal witness, when defense disclosed all its witnesses, violated due process).

Taylor v. Illinois

484 U.S. 400, 108 S.Ct. 646, 98 L.Ed.2d 798 (1988)

■ JUSTICE STEVENS delivered the opinion of the Court.

As a sanction for failing to identify a defense witness in response to a pretrial discovery request, an Illinois trial judge refused to allow the undisclosed witness to testify. The question presented is whether that refusal violated the petitioner's constitutional right to obtain the testimony of favorable witnesses. We hold that such a sanction is not absolutely prohibited by the Compulsory Process Clause of the Sixth Amendment and find no constitutional error on the specific facts of this case.

I

A jury convicted petitioner in 1984 of attempting to murder Jack Bridges in a street fight on the south side of Chicago on August 6, 1981. The conviction was supported by the testimony of Bridges, his brother, and three other witnesses. They described a twenty-minute argument between Bridges and a young man named Derrick Travis, and a violent encounter that occurred over an hour later between several friends of Travis, including the petitioner, on the one hand, and Bridges, belatedly aided by his brother, on the other. The incident was witnessed by twenty or thirty bystanders. It is undisputed that at least three members of the group which included Travis and petitioner were carrying pipes and clubs that they used to beat Bridges. Prosecution witnesses also testified that petitioner had a gun, that he shot Bridges in the back as he attempted to flee, and that, after Bridges fell, petitioner pointed the gun at Bridges' head but the weapon misfired.

Two sisters, who are friends of petitioner, testified on his behalf. In many respects their version of the incident was consistent with the prosecution's case, but they testified that it was Bridges' brother, rather than petitioner, who possessed a firearm and that he had fired into the group hitting his brother by mistake. No other witnesses testified for the defense.

Well in advance of trial, the prosecutor filed a discovery motion requesting a list of defense witnesses. In his original response, petitioner's attorney identified the two sisters who later testified and two men who did not testify. On the first day of trial, defense counsel was allowed to amend his answer by adding the names of Derrick Travis and a Chicago Police Officer; neither of them actually testified.

On the second day of trial, after the prosecution's two principal witnesses had completed their testimony, defense counsel made an oral motion to amend his "Answer to Discovery" to include two more witnesses, Alfred Wormley and Pam Berkhalter. In support of the motion, counsel represented that he had just been informed about them and that they had probably seen the "entire incident."

In response to the court's inquiry about the defendant's failure to tell him about the two witnesses earlier, counsel acknowledged that defendant had done so, but then represented that he had been unable to locate Wormley. After noting that the witnesses' names could have been supplied even if their addresses were unknown, the trial judge directed counsel to bring them in the next day, at which time he would decide whether they could testify. The judge indicated that he was concerned about the possibility "that witnesses are being found that really weren't there."

The next morning Wormley appeared in court with defense counsel. After further colloquy about the consequences of a violation of discovery rules, counsel was permitted to make an offer of proof in the form of Wormley's testimony outside the presence of the jury. It developed that Wormley had not been a witness to the incident itself. He testified that prior to the incident he saw Jack Bridges and his brother with two guns in a blanket, that he heard them say "they were after Ray [petitioner] and the other people," and that on his way home he "happened to run into Ray and them" and warned them "to watch out because they got weapons." On cross-examination, Wormley acknowledged that he had first met the defendant "about four months ago" (i.e., over two years after the incident). He also acknowledged that defense counsel had visited him at his home on the Wednesday of the week before the trial began. Thus, his testimony rather dramatically contradicted defense counsel's representations to the trial court.

After hearing Wormley testify, the trial judge concluded that the appropriate sanction for the discovery violation was to exclude his testimony. The judge explained:

> THE COURT: All right, I am going to deny Wormley an opportunity to testify here. He is not going to testify. I find this a blatant violation of the discovery rules, willful violation of the rules. I also feel that defense attorneys have been violating discovery in this courtroom in the last three or four cases blatantly and I am going to put a stop to it and this is one way to do so.
>
> Further, for whatever value it is, because this is a jury trial, I have a great deal of doubt in my mind as to the veracity of this young man that testified as to whether he was an eyewitness on the scene, sees guns that are wrapped up. He doesn't know Ray but he stops Ray.
>
> At any rate, Mr. Wormley is not going to testify, be a witness in this courtroom.

App. 28.

. . .

In this Court petitioner makes two arguments. He first contends that the Sixth Amendment bars a court from ever ordering the preclusion of defense evidence as a sanction for violating a discovery rule. Alternatively, he contends that even if the right to present witnesses is not absolute, on the facts of this case the preclusion of Wormley's testimony was constitutional error. Before addressing these contentions, we consider the State's argument that the Compulsory Process Clause of the Sixth Amendment is merely a guarantee that the accused shall have the power to subpoena witnesses and simply does not apply to rulings on the admissibility of evidence.

II

In the State's view, no Compulsory Process Clause concerns are even raised by authorizing preclusion as a discovery sanction, or by the application of the Illinois rule in this case. . . .

As we noted just last Term, "[o]ur cases establish, at a minimum, that criminal defendants have the right to the government's assistance in compelling the attendance of favorable witnesses at trial and the right to put before a jury evidence that might influence the determination of guilt." Pennsylvania v. Ritchie, 480 U.S. 39, 56 (1987). Few rights are more fundamental than that of an accused to present witnesses in his own defense. . . . Indeed, this right is an essential attribute of the adversary system itself. . . . The right to compel a witness' presence in the courtroom could not protect the integrity of the adversary process if it did not embrace the right to have the witness' testimony heard by the trier of fact. The right to offer testimony is thus grounded in the Sixth Amendment even though it is not expressly described in so many words. . . . We cannot accept the State's argument that this constitutional right may never be offended by the imposition of a discovery sanction that entirely excludes the testimony of a material defense witness.

III

Petitioner's claim that the Sixth Amendment creates an absolute bar to the preclusion of the testimony of a surprise witness is just as extreme and just as unacceptable as the State's position that the Amendment is simply irrelevant. The accused does not have an unfettered right to offer testimony that is incompetent, privileged, or otherwise inadmissible under standard rules of evidence. The Compulsory Process Clause provides him with an effective weapon, but it is a weapon that cannot be used irresponsibly.

There is a significant difference between the Compulsory Process Clause weapon and other rights that are protected by the Sixth Amendment—its availability is dependent entirely on the defendant's initiative. Most other Sixth Amendment rights arise automatically on the initiation of the adversarial process and no action by the defendant is necessary to make them active in his or her case. While those rights shield the defendant from potential prosecutorial abuses, the right to compel the presence and present the testimony of witnesses provides the defendant with a sword that may be employed to rebut the prosecution's case. The decision whether to employ it in a particular case rests solely with the defendant. The very nature of the right requires that its effective use be preceded by deliberate planning and affirmative conduct.

The principle that undergirds the defendant's right to present exculpatory evidence is also the source of essential limitations on the right. The adversary process could not function effectively without adherence to rules of procedure that govern the orderly presentation of facts and arguments to provide each party with a fair opportunity to assemble and submit evidence to contradict or explain the opponent's case. The trial process would be a shambles if either party had an absolute right to control the time and content of his witnesses' testimony. Neither may insist on the right to interrupt the opposing party's case and obviously there is no absolute right to interrupt the deliberations of the jury to present newly discovered evidence. The State's interest in the orderly conduct of a criminal trial is sufficient to justify the imposition and enforcement of firm, though not always inflexible, rules relating to the identification and presentation of evidence.

The defendant's right to compulsory process is itself designed to vindicate the principle that the "ends of criminal justice would be defeated if judgments were to be founded on a partial or speculative presentation of the facts." United States v. Nixon, 418 U.S. [683 (1974)], at 709. Rules that provide for pretrial discovery of an opponent's witnesses serve the same high purpose. Discovery, like cross-examination, minimizes the risk that a judgment will be predicated on incomplete, misleading, or even deliberately fabricated testimony. The "State's interest in protecting itself against an eleventh-hour defense"[17] is merely one component of the broader public interest in a full and truthful disclosure of critical facts.

To vindicate that interest we have held that even the defendant may not testify without being subjected to cross-examination. . . . Moreover, in United States v. Nobles, 422 U.S. 225 (1975), we upheld an order excluding the testimony of an expert witness tendered by the defendant because he had refused to permit discovery of a "highly relevant" report. . . .

Petitioner does not question the legitimacy of a rule requiring pretrial disclosure of defense witnesses, but he argues that the sanction of preclusion of the testimony of a previously undisclosed witness is so drastic that it should never be imposed. He argues, correctly, that a less drastic sanction is always available. Prejudice to the prosecution could be minimized by granting a continuance or a mistrial to provide time for further investigation; moreover, further violations can be deterred by disciplinary sanctions against the defendant or defense counsel.

It may well be true that alternative sanctions are adequate and appropriate in most cases, but it is equally clear that they would be less effective than the preclusion sanction and that there are instances in which they would perpetuate rather than limit the prejudice to the State and the harm to the adversary process. One of the purposes of the discovery rule itself is to minimize the risk that fabricated testimony will be believed. Defendants who are willing to fabricate a defense may also be willing to fabricate excuses for failing to comply with a discovery requirement. The risk of a contempt violation may seem trivial to a defendant facing the threat of imprisonment for a term of years. A dishonest client can mislead an honest attorney, and there are occasions when an attorney assumes that the duty of loyalty to the client outweighs elementary obligations to the court.

We presume that evidence that is not discovered until after the trial is over would not have affected the outcome. It is equally reasonable to presume that there is something suspect about a defense witness who is not identified until after the eleventh hour has passed. If a pattern of discovery violations is explicable only on the assumption that the violations were designed to conceal a plan to present fabricated testimony, it would be entirely appropriate to exclude the tainted evidence regardless of whether other sanctions would also be merited.

In order to reject petitioner's argument that preclusion is never a permissible sanction for a discovery violation it is neither necessary nor appropriate for us to attempt to draft a comprehensive set of standards to guide the exercise of discretion in every possible case. It is elementary, of course, that a trial court may not ignore the fundamental character of the defendant's right to offer the testimony of witnesses in his favor. But the

17. . . . Williams v. Florida, 399 U.S. 78, 81–82 (1970). . . .

mere invocation of that right cannot automatically and invariably outweigh countervailing public interests. The integrity of the adversary process, which depends both on the presentation of reliable evidence and the rejection of unreliable evidence; the interest in the fair and efficient administration of justice; and the potential prejudice to the truth-determining function of the trial process must also weigh in the balance.

A trial judge may certainly insist on an explanation for a party's failure to comply with a request to identify his or her witnesses in advance of trial. If that explanation reveals that the omission was willful and motivated by a desire to obtain a tactical advantage that would minimize the effectiveness of cross-examination and the ability to adduce rebuttal evidence, it would be entirely consistent with the purposes of the Confrontation Clause simply to exclude the witness' testimony. . . .

The simplicity of compliance with the discovery rule is also relevant. As we have noted, the Compulsory Process Clause cannot be invoked without the prior planning and affirmative conduct of the defendant. Lawyers are accustomed to meeting deadlines. Routine preparation involves location and interrogation of potential witnesses and the serving of subpoenas on those whose testimony will be offered at trial. The burden of identifying them in advance of trial adds little to these routine demands of trial preparation.

It would demean the high purpose of the Compulsory Process Clause to construe it as encompassing an absolute right to an automatic continuance or mistrial to allow presumptively perjured testimony to be presented to a jury. We reject petitioner's argument that a preclusion sanction is never appropriate no matter how serious the defendant's discovery violation may be.

IV

Petitioner argues that the preclusion sanction was unnecessarily harsh in this case because the voir dire examination of Wormley adequately protected the prosecution from any possible prejudice resulting from surprise. Petitioner also contends that it is unfair to visit the sins of the lawyer upon his client. Neither argument has merit.

More is at stake than possible prejudice to the prosecution. We are also concerned with the impact of this kind of conduct on the integrity of the judicial process itself. The trial judge found that the discovery violation in this case was both willful and blatant. In view of the fact that petitioner's counsel had actually interviewed Wormley during the week before the trial began and the further fact that he amended his Answer to Discovery on the first day of trial without identifying Wormley while he did identify two actual eyewitnesses whom he did not place on the stand, the inference that he was deliberately seeking a tactical advantage is inescapable. Regardless of whether prejudice to the prosecution could have been avoided in this particular case, it is plain that the case fits into the category of willful misconduct in which the severest sanction is appropriate. After all, the court, as well as the prosecutor, has a vital interest in protecting the trial process from the pollution of perjured testimony. Evidentiary rules which apply to categories of inadmissible evidence—ranging from hearsay to the fruits of illegal searches—may properly be enforced even though the particular testimony being offered is not prejudicial. The pretrial conduct revealed by the record in this case gives rise to a sufficiently strong inference "that witnesses are being found that really weren't there," to justify the sanction of preclusion.

The argument that the client should not be held responsible for his lawyer's misconduct strikes at the heart of the attorney-client relationship. Although there are basic rights that the attorney cannot waive without the fully informed and publicly acknowledged consent of the client, the lawyer has—and must have—full authority to manage the conduct of the trial. The adversary process could not function effectively if every tactical decision required client approval. Moreover, given the protections afforded by the attorney-client privilege and the fact that extreme cases may involve unscrupulous conduct by both the client and the lawyer, it would be highly impracticable to require an investigation into their relative responsibilities before applying the sanction of preclusion. In responding to discovery, the client has a duty to be candid and forthcoming with the lawyer, and when the lawyer responds, he or she speaks for the client. Putting to one side the exceptional cases in which counsel is ineffective, the client must accept the consequences of the lawyer's decision to forgo cross-examination, to decide not to put certain witnesses on the stand, or to decide not to disclose the identity of certain witnesses in advance of trial. In this case, petitioner has no greater right to disavow his lawyer's decision to conceal Wormley's identity until after the trial had commenced than he has to disavow the decision to refrain from adducing testimony from the eyewitnesses who were identified in the Answer to Discovery. Whenever a lawyer makes use of the sword provided by the Compulsory Process Clause, there is some risk that he may wound his own client.

. . .[18]

---

430. In Michigan v. Lucas, 500 U.S. 145 (1991) (7–2), the Court held that the Sixth Amendment does not flatly prohibit a rule that precludes a defendant in a rape case from introducing evidence concerning the alleged rape victim's past sexual conduct as a sanction for failing to give the required notice of his intention to offer such evidence. The Court said that the notice provision "serves legitimate state interests in protecting against surprise, harassment, and undue delay," which "in some cases justify even the severe sanction" of exclusion of evidence. Id. at 153.

---

[18] Justice Brennan wrote a dissenting opinion, which Justice Marshall and Justice Blackmun joined. Justice Blackmun also wrote a brief dissenting opinion.

United States v. Myers

550 F.2d 1036 (5th Cir.1977)

■ CLARK, CIRCUIT JUDGE:

Larry Allen Myers challenges the validity of his federal bank robbery conviction. He contends that the district court committed reversible error when it (1) refused to strike the testimony of alibi rebuttal witnesses whose identities were not disclosed before the trial. . . . We agree, and therefore we reverse the decision of the district court.

On June 13, 1974, at approximately two o'clock in the afternoon, a branch of the First Federal Savings and Loan Association of Largo, located in Clearwater, Florida, was robbed by a lone gunman. He escaped with an estimated $1500. After changing cars at a nearby motel, the robber disappeared. There is no dispute about how the robbery was committed; the central issue in this case, despite two eye witnesses and hundreds of still photographs taken by an automatic camera, is by whom. The government has proceeded on the theory that it was Myers who entered the bank brandishing a revolver, ordered a teller to place the contents of her cash drawer in a flimsy brown paper bag, and fled. Myers has steadfastly maintained that it was not.

On September 13, 1975, a federal grand jury charged Myers with three counts of violating 18 U.S.C.A. § 2113(a), (b) & (d) (Supp.1976). The government's task in prosecuting Myers on these charges was complicated when a friend of Myers named Dennis Coffie, who bears a remarkable physical resemblance to Myers, pled guilty to having been the lone gunman in the Florida robbery. A superseding indictment consolidating the Florida charges into one count was returned against Myers on August 13, 1975. Since then Myers has been tried twice. The first trial ended with the declaration of a mistrial after the jury announced its inability to reach a verdict. A fortnight later, a second jury found Myers guilty as charged. The district court sentenced him to ten years' imprisonment on February 17, 1976.

Nondisclosure of Alibi Rebuttal Witnesses

Myers' primary argument on this appeal is that the district court committed reversible error when it refused to strike the testimony of the witnesses on whom the government relied to discredit his alibi defense. In order to properly assess the merit of this contention, it is necessary to examine in detail some of the circumstances surrounding the first and second trials.

Prior to the first trial, the government served Myers with a written demand for notice of his intent to assert an alibi defense, pursuant to Rule 12.1 of the Federal Rules of Criminal Procedure. Myers responded on December 23, 1975, indicating that he did intend to offer an alibi defense, and named Ronald Akers, Marlin Downey, and Coffie as his proposed alibi witnesses. The following day the government filed a document styled "Government's Response to Notice of Alibi Defense," in which it listed two tellers from the robbed bank and Janice Johns as the witnesses on whose testimony it planned to rely in attempting to establish Myers' presence at the scene of the robbery. It further stated:

> Names and addresses of other witnesses to be relied on to rebut testimony of defendant's alibi witnesses shall be made known to defendant as they are ascertained by the Government under its continuing duty pursuant to the Rule.

Neither Myers nor the government ever supplemented their witness lists.

At the first trial Myers used all three of his proposed witnesses in attempting to establish his alibi defense. Coffie testified that he committed the Florida robbery by himself, and Downey stated that on the afternoon of the robbery he had encountered Myers at Disneyworld, an amusement park located approximately 80 miles from Clearwater. Despite the importance of their testimony, the fate of Myers' alibi defense rested largely on the testimony of Ronald Akers. Akers testified that he and Myers had spent the entire afternoon of June 13, 1974—the day on which the robbery occurred—at Disneyworld, in the company of two girls whom Akers had met the previous evening. Akers explained that he was certain of the date because the girls had to catch a United Airlines flight to Detroit on Saturday, June 15, 1974. He said that he remembered their airline, destination, and date of departure, because he had seen their tickets and because he drove them to the Tampa airport on Saturday morning.

During the week following the first trial, the government investigated Akers' story. On the day before the defense began to present its evidence in the second trial, the United States Attorney prosecuting the case contacted Myers' counsel and suggested that he warn his witnesses against perjuring themselves. He did not mention the possibility that the government might call additional witnesses at the second trial.

The testimony of Coffie, Akers, and Downey at the second trial was substantially the same as it had been at the first. But in reply the government called four witnesses not listed in its response to Myers' notice of his intent to offer an alibi defense, whose statements were designed to discredit Akers' testimony. One of them was Robert Labrenz, an employee of United Airlines. He testified that United had no flight from Tampa to Detroit on June 15, 1974, but that other airlines had such flights. The other three witnesses, Patricia Coogle, Raymond LaBranch, and Roy Pruitt were all employees of a car dealership in Tampa, Florida. Their combined testimony indicated that Akers had been employed at the same car dealership as a mechanic, and had worked 48 hours during the week of June 10, 1974. This was inconsistent with Akers' testimony that he had been unemployed during June of 1974, and tended to conflict with his statement that he had not worked on Thursday and Friday of the week of June 10, 1974.

Before the case was given to the jury, defendant's counsel moved for a mistrial, and, in the alternative, for an order striking the testimony of the four new government witnesses, on the grounds that their names had not been disclosed prior to trial as required by Rule 12.1. The district court denied both motions. It held, first, that the government had not violated the rule, and second, that if it had, good cause existed to grant the government an exemption from the requirements of sections (b) and (c).

. . .

The language of section (b) appears to require disclosure of two types of witnesses: (1) those relied upon "to establish the defendant's presence at the scene of the alleged offense," and (2) "any other witnesses to be relied on to rebut testimony of any of the defendant's alibi witnesses." We think that all four of the undisclosed government witnesses fall within the class delineated by the second phrase. Rebuttal evidence is evidence introduced to refute, contradict, or disprove evidence adduced by an adverse party. Since the testimony of the undisclosed witnesses was concededly introduced for the purpose of showing that Akers' testimony concerning his activities during the week of June 10, 1974, was false, they are alibi rebuttal witnesses within the meaning of Rule 12.1(b). Accordingly, the government had a continuing duty under section (c) to notify the defendant of their existence.

The government's duty to disclose was not discharged by the oblique warning which counsel for the government gave Myers' attorney orally on the eve of the second trial. Section 12.1(b) expressly requires "a written notice stating the names and addresses of the witnesses upon whom the government intends to rely."

. . .

The district court found that in the event the government had violated sections (b) and (c), its noncompliance should be excused. Although the precatory language of section (e) gives the district court the discretionary power to grant exceptions "for good cause shown," there are two reasons why the court below abused its discretion by granting one in this case.

First, the district court failed to describe the circumstances that constituted good cause. Absent such an explanation, granting an exception is improper. We note in passing that none of the after the fact justifications proffered by the Government—that the undisclosed witnesses were merely rebuttal witnesses, that they were not discovered until immediately before trial, and that their testimony was not conclusive—would be sufficient to satisfy the good cause requirement. Second, the government did not apply for an exception to the disclosure requirements at the time the new witnesses were discovered, when compliance with sections (b) and (c) would have been possible if its request had been denied. Rule 12.1 was intended to prevent prejudicial surprise to the parties and to obviate the need for continuances which arise when one side introduces unexpected testimony at trial. . . . These purposes would be frustrated if applications for exceptions could be tendered after undisclosed witnesses had already testified. By then, the harm which the Rule seeks to prevent would have occurred, and the trial judge would be reduced to trying to mitigate the injury to the defendant's case by granting a continuance, retroactively excluding the improper testimony, or in extreme cases, declaring a mistrial.

The district court also abused the discretion conferred upon it by section (d) when he denied the defendant's motions to strike the testimony and documentary evidence furnished by the undisclosed witnesses. . . .

In determining how to exercise its discretionary power to exclude the testimony of undisclosed witnesses under section (d), a district court should consider (1) the amount of prejudice that resulted from the failure to disclose, (2) the reason for nondisclosure, (3) the extent to which the harm caused by nondisclosure was mitigated by subsequent events, (4) the weight of the properly admitted evidence supporting the defendant's guilt, and (5) other relevant factors arising out of the circumstances of the case. . . .

Here the prejudice to the defense was substantial and remained unabated. Myers' counsel was deprived of the opportunity to interview the four undisclosed witnesses, to recheck the stories of Myers, Akers, and Downey in light of the additional evidence, and, most importantly, to reconsider his decision to put Akers and Downey on the stand. The Rule entitles a defendant to evaluate the strategy of advancing an alibi defense in light of the named rebuttal witnesses. In addition, the government's reason for nondisclosure is feeble: it asserts that it did not believe that the witnesses were within the scope of the Rule. While this falls short of bad faith, it thwarts the central purposes of a provision designed to make criminal trials fairer because it tests coverage through confrontation at trial, rather than by submission to the district court in advance. Finally, as counsel for the government conceded at oral argument, the evidence against Myers is weak. Since all four of the factors present in this case weigh in favor of exclusion, the district court abused its discretion when it failed to exclude the testimony of the undisclosed alibi rebuttal witnesses.

. . .

---

431. Criminal discovery and civil discovery. The Food and Drug Administration instituted a civil *in rem* action against products of a corporation of which defendants were officers. The government served interrogatories on the corporation. After the interrogatories were filed, the FDA served notice on the corporation and the defendants that a criminal prosecution was being contemplated. The defendants moved to stay the civil proceedings or to extend the time for filing answers to the interrogatories until after the criminal proceedings were terminated. The motion was denied. The FDA decided to recommend prosecution before answers to the interrogatories were received. The Court affirmed the subsequent convictions.

> The respondents urge that . . . the Government's conduct . . . reflected such unfairness and want of consideration for justice as independently to require the reversal of their convictions. On the

record before us, we cannot agree that the respondents have made out either a violation of due process or a departure from proper standards in the administration of justice requiring the exercise of our supervisory power. The public interest in protecting consumers throughout the Nation from misbranded drugs requires prompt action by the agency charged with responsibility for administration of the federal food and drug laws. But a rational decision whether to proceed criminally against those responsible for the misbranding may have to await consideration of a fuller record than that before the agency at the time of the civil seizure of the offending products. It would stultify enforcement of federal law to require a governmental agency such as the FDA invariably to choose either to forgo recommendation of a criminal prosecution once it seeks civil relief, or to defer civil proceedings pending the ultimate outcome of a criminal trial.

We do not deal here with a case where the Government has brought a civil action solely to obtain evidence for its criminal prosecution or has failed to advise the defendant in its civil proceeding that it contemplates his criminal prosecution; nor with a case where the defendant is without counsel or reasonably fears prejudice from adverse pretrial publicity or other unfair injury; nor with any other special circumstances that might suggest the unconstitutionality or even the impropriety of this criminal prosecution.

Overturning these convictions would be tantamount to the adoption of a rule that the Government's use of interrogatories directed against a corporate defendant in the ordinary course of a civil proceeding would always immunize the corporation's officers from subsequent criminal prosecution. The Court of Appeals was correct in stating that "the Government may not use evidence against a defendant in a criminal case which has been coerced from him under penalty of either giving the evidence or suffering a forfeiture of his property."[19] But on this record there was no such violation of the Constitution, and no such departure from the proper administration of criminal justice.

United States v. Kordel, 397 U.S. 1, 11–13 (1970).

In In re Grand Jury, 286 F.3d 153 (3d Cir.2002), the grand jury issued a subpoena to the appellant, who was the target of the grand jury's investigation. The subpoena demanded production of documents that the appellant had produced in discovery in an ongoing civil litigation, which were covered by a protective order to preserve their confidentiality. The appellant filed a motion to quash the subpoena, which was denied. The court of appeals affirmed. Noting a conflict among the circuits, it held that "a grand jury subpoena supercedes a protective order unless the party seeking to quash the subpoena can demonstrate exceptional circumstances that clearly favor subordinating the subpoena to the protective order." Id at 165.

19. 407 F.2d at 575–76.

In United States v. Parrott, 248 F.Supp. 196, 202 (D.D.C.1965), the court said that "the Government may not bring a parallel civil proceeding and avail itself of civil discovery devises to obtain evidence for subsequent criminal prosecution." In Campbell v. Eastland, 307 F.2d 478 (5th Cir. 1962), the situations were reversed. Contemplating that they would be indicted for tax fraud, the plaintiffs instituted a civil suit for a tax refund and sought discovery pursuant to Fed.R.Civ.P. 34 of material in the government's files which could not be obtained pursuant to the provisions for criminal discovery. The court of appeals held that the government should not be required to disclose in those circumstances: "[T]axpayers under criminal investigation [should not be able] to subvert the civil rules into a device for obtaining pre-trial discovery against the Government in criminal proceedings," Id. at 488. Similarly, in Securities and Exchange Commission v. Doody, 186 F.Supp.2d 379 (S.D.N.Y.2002), discovery by the defendant in a civil case was stayed until completion of a related criminal case.

432. In Weatherford v. Bursey, 429 U.S. 545, 559 (1977), the Court observed that "there is no general constitutional right to discovery in a criminal case." Nevertheless, discovery in criminal cases is closely related to the prosecution's constitutional duty to disclose information if nondisclosure would deny the defendant a fair trial. The relation between Rule 16 and the prosecutor's constitutional obligation is discussed, in Giles v. Maryland, 386 U.S. 66 (1967), in the opinions of Justice Fortas, id. at 101–102, and Justice Harlan, id. at 117–18. See United States v. Presser, 844 F.2d 1275 (6th Cir.1988); United States v. Kaplan, 554 F.2d 577 (3d Cir.1977). See generally pp. 943–51 below.

Motions to Suppress Evidence

FEDERAL RULES OF CRIMINAL PROCEDURE

Rule 41

SEARCH AND SEIZURE

. . .

(h) Motion to Suppress. A defendant may move to suppress evidence in the court where the trial will occur, as Rule 12 provides.

---

433. What rules of evidence and standards of proof are applicable in hearings on a motion to suppress? In United States v. Matlock, 415 U.S. 164, 173 (1974), another aspect of which is discussed at p. 165 above, the Court observed that "the same rules of evidence governing criminal jury trials are not generally thought to govern hearings before a judge to determine evidentiary questions." In *Matlock*, the Court concluded that the trial judge had improperly refused to consider reliable hearsay evidence at a suppression hearing; it suggested further that "exclusionary rules, aside from rules of privilege, should not be applicable; and the judge should receive the evidence and give it such weight as his judgment and experience counsel." Id. at 175.

The burden of proof in suppression hearings is discussed in United States v. De La Fuente, 548 F.2d 528, 533–34 (5th Cir.1977): "It is well established that the burdens of production and persuasion generally rest upon the movant in a suppression hearing. . . . Concededly, in some well-defined situations the ultimate burden of persuasion may shift to the government upon an initial showing of certain facts by the defendant. For example, if a defendant produces evidence that he was arrested or subjected to a search without a warrant, the burden shifts to the government to justify the warrantless arrest or search. . . . Or if a defendant shows that a confession was obtained while he was under custodial interrogation, the government then has the burden of proving that the defendant voluntarily waived his privilege against self-incrimination. . . . Similarly, if a defendant seeks to suppress evidence as the fruit of an illegal wiretap and he proves that the tap was in fact unlawful, the burden shifts to the prosecution to prove that the evidence in question was obtained from another source and is not tainted by the illegal surveillance. . . . [E]ven in those situations, the defendant must first discharge his initial burden of producing some evidence on specific factual allegations sufficient to make a prima facie showing of illegality."

434. Rule 12(b)(3)(C) provides that a motion to suppress evidence "must be raised before trial." Rule 12(c) provides that the court may "at the arraignment or as soon afterward as practicable" set a deadline for pretrial motions and schedule a motion hearing. A motion to suppress evidence not raised by the deadline is waived, but the court "[f]or good cause" may grant relief from the waiver. Rule 12(e).

In Stone v. Powell, 428 U.S. 465, 469 (1976) (6–3), the Court held that federal habeas corpus is not available for consideration of a claim by a state prisoner "that evidence obtained by an unconstitutional search or seizure was introduced at his trial, when he has previously been afforded an opportunity for full and fair litigation of his claim in the state courts." The Court based its holding on the conclusion that "the nature and purpose of the Fourth Amendment exclusionary rule" did not require that it be implemented by a federal collateral hearing in those circumstances. Id. at 481.

"[T]he additional contribution, if any, of the consideration of search-and-seizure claims of state prisoners on collateral review is small in relation to the costs. To be sure, each case in which such claim is considered may add marginally to an awareness of the values protected by the Fourth Amendment. There is no reason to believe, however, that the overall educative effect of the exclusionary rule would be appreciably diminished if search-and-seizure claims could not be raised in federal habeas corpus review of state convictions. Nor is there reason to assume that any specific disincentive already created by the risk of exclusion of evidence at trial or the reversal of convictions on direct review would be enhanced if there were the further risk that a conviction obtained in state court and affirmed on direct review might be overturned in collateral proceedings often occurring years after the incarceration of the defendant. The view that the deterrence of Fourth Amendment violations would be furthered rests on the dubious assumption that law enforcement authorities would fear that federal habeas review might reveal flaws in a search or seizure that went undetected at trial and on appeal. Even if one rationally could assume that some additional incremental deterrent effect would be present in isolated cases, the resulting advance of the legitimate goal of furthering Fourth Amendment rights would be outweighed by the acknowledged costs to other values vital to a rational system of criminal justice." Id. at 493–94. The Court said that except insofar as its supervisory authority over the federal courts might indicate otherwise, a similar rule was applicable to collateral review of claims by a federal prisoner who had failed without cause to comply with Rule 12. See id. at 481 n.16.

In Willett v. Lockhart, 37 F.3d 1265 (8th Cir.1994) (en banc), the court of appeals considered what was meant in Stone v. Powell by "an opportunity for full and fair litigation" of a Fourth Amendment claim. Reviewing cases in other circuits, the court concluded that "a Fourth Amendment claim is *Stone*-barred, and thus unreviewable by a federal habeas court, unless either the state provided no procedure by which the prisoner could raise his Fourth Amendment claim, or the prisoner was foreclosed from using that procedure because of an unconscionable breakdown in the system." 37 F.3d at 1273. It explained: "As *Stone* makes clear, Fourth Amendment claims asserted by state prisoners in federal habeas petitions are to be treated differently from other constitutional claims because of the nature and purpose of the exclusionary rule and the incremental value gained from its implementation in the federal habeas situation compared with the costs it imposes upon the administration of justice. The federal courts on habeas review of such claims are not to consider whether full and fair litigation of the claims *in fact* occurred in the state courts, but only whether the state provided an opportunity for such litigation." Id.

The holding in Stone v. Powell reversed the direction of previous decisions increasing the availability of federal collateral review of state and federal convictions. The cases are reviewed in the Court's opinion and in the dissenting opinion of Justice Brennan. See generally Wainwright v. Sykes, 433 U.S. 72 (1977), p. 1228 below. Stone v. Powell is not applicable to a claim that a conviction was based on statements obtained in violation of Miranda v. Arizona, 384 U.S. 436 (1966), p. 417 above. Withrow v. Williams, 507 U.S. 680 (1993) (5–4). In *Withrow*, the Court observed that, unlike the exclusion of evidence on Fourth Amendment grounds, the *Miranda* rules safeguard a fundamental trial right and are related to the fairness of the trial itself and the accuracy of the result. Nor does Stone v. Powell bar consideration of a Sixth Amendment claim of ineffectiveness of counsel based on counsel's alleged failure to assert defendant's claims under the Fourth Amendment. Kimmelman v. Morrison, 477 U.S. 365 (1986). See note 646, p. 1244 below.

---

18 U.S.C. § 3731. Appeal by United States

. . .

An appeal by the United States shall lie to a court of appeals from a decision or order of a district court suppressing or excluding evidence or requiring the return of seized property in a criminal proceeding, not made after the defendant has been put in jeopardy and before the verdict or finding on an indictment or information, if the United States attorney certifies to the district court that the appeal is not taken for purpose of delay and that the evidence is a substantial proof of a fact material in the proceeding.

An appeal by the United States shall lie to a court of appeals from a decision or order, entered by a district court of the United States, granting the release of a person charged with or convicted of an offense, or denying a motion for revocation of, or modification of the conditions of, a decision or order granting release.

The appeal in all such cases shall be taken within thirty days after the decision, judgment or order has been rendered and shall be diligently prosecuted.

The provisions of this section shall be liberally construed to effectuate its purposes.

---

435. In some cases, an order of the district court that is not directly an order "suppressing or excluding evidence," but has the practical effect of exclusion—e.g., a discovery order with which the government has declared it will not comply, the penalty for noncompliance being exclusion of certain evidence—has been held to be within the terms of § 3731. See United States v. Kane, 646 F.2d 4 (1st Cir.1981) (citing cases).

During the pendency of an appeal under § 3731, the district court retains jurisdiction over the case and may in appropriate circumstances grant the defendant's motion to dismiss the indictment with or without prejudice under Rule 48(b). United States v. Gatto, 763 F.2d 1040, 1049–50 (9th Cir.1985).

FEDERAL RULES OF CRIMINAL PROCEDURE

Rule 17.1

PRETRIAL CONFERENCE

On its own, or on a party's motion, the court may hold one or more pretrial conferences to promote a fair and expeditious trial. When a conference ends, the court must prepare and file a memorandum of any matters agreed to during the conference. The government may not use any statement made during the conference by the defendant or the defendant's attorney unless it is in writing and is signed by the defendant and the defendant's attorney.

CHAPTER 13

TRIAL

---

436. The involuntary administration of antipsychotic drugs to a criminal defendant in order to render him competent to stand trial is permitted "only if the treatment is medically appropriate, is substantially unlikely to have side effects that may undermine the fairness of the trial, and, taking account of less intrusive alternatives, is necessary significantly to further important governmental trial-related interests." Sell v. United States, 539 U.S. 166 (2003) (6–3) (order for administration of drugs vacated and case remanded).

FEDERAL RULES OF CRIMINAL PROCEDURE

Rule 43

DEFENDANT'S PRESENCE

(a) When Required. Unless this rule, Rule 5, or Rule 10 provides otherwise, the defendant must be present at:

(1) the initial appearance, the initial arraignment, and the plea;

(2) every trial stage, including jury impanelment and the return of the verdict; and

(3) sentencing.

(b) When Not Required. A defendant need not be present under any of the following circumstances:

(1) *Organizational Defendant.* The defendant is an organization represented by counsel who is present.

(2) *Misdemeanor Offense.* The offense is punishable by fine or by imprisonment for not more than one year, or both, and with the defendant's written consent, the court permits arraignment, plea, trial, and sentencing to occur in the defendant's absence.

(3) *Conference or Hearing on a Legal Question.* The proceeding involves only a conference or hearing on a question of law.

(4) *Sentence Correction.* The proceeding involves the correction or reduction of sentence under Rule 35 or 18 U.S.C. § 3582(c).

(c) Waiving Continued Presence.

(1) *In General.* A defendant who was initially present at trial, or who had pleaded guilty or nolo contendere, waives the right to be present under the following circumstances:

(A) when the defendant is voluntarily absent after the trial has begun, regardless of whether the court informed the defendant of an obligation to remain during trial;

(B) in a noncapital case, when the defendant is voluntarily absent during sentencing; or

(C) when the court warns the defendant that it will remove the defendant from the courtroom for disruptive behavior, but the defendant persists in conduct that justifies removal from the courtroom.

(2) *Waiver's Effect.* If the defendant waives the right to be present, the trial may proceed to completion, including the verdict's return and sentencing, during the defendant's absence.

---

437. The absence of the defendant and his counsel when the judge received and responded to a request for information from the jury about an appropriate form of verdict was the basis for reversal of a conviction in Rogers v. United States, 422 U.S. 35 (1975). The Court said that under Rule 43, "the jury's message should have been answered in open court and . . . petitioner's counsel should have been given an opportunity to be heard before the trial judge responded." Id. at 39. It added that while a violation of Rule 43 might sometimes be harmless error, it was not in this case, since there was basis for objection by the defense to the judge's response to the jury.

See United States v. Gagnon, 470 U.S. 522 (1985) (6–2) (brief discussion between judge and juror in chambers, in presence of defendant's lawyer; defendant's absence harmless error); Rushen v. Spain, 464 U.S. 114 (1983) (ex parte communication between judge and juror; harmless error); Rice v. Wood, 77 F.3d 1138 (9th Cir.1996) (en banc) (defendant's absence at capital sentencing; harmless error); United States v. Fontanez, 878 F.2d 33 (2d Cir.1989) (supplementary instruction; defendant's absence not harmless error); United States v. Toliver, 541 F.2d 958 (2d Cir.1976) (continuation of government testimony during absence of one codefendant because of illness; harmless error).

Allowing the defendant to appear at imposition of sentence only by video teleconferencing does not satisfy Rule 43. United States v. Lawrence, 248 F.3d 300 (4th Cir.2001).

438. Rule 43 does not permit a defendant to be tried in absentia if he absconds before the trial and is absent at its beginning. Crosby v. United States, 506 U.S. 255 (1993). Distinguishing cases in which a trial under way continues after the defendant has absconded, the Court said: "As a general matter, the costs of suspending a proceeding already under way will be greater than the cost of postponing a trial not yet begun. If a clear line is to be drawn marking the point at which the costs of delay are likely to outweigh the interests of the defendant and society in having the defendant present, the commencement of trial is at least a plausible place at which to draw that line." Id. at 261. The Court observed that a defendant who departs during trial is likely to realize that the trial will continue, and that allowing the trial to continue in those circumstances prevents the defendant from aborting a trial if he thinks the verdict will go against him. The Court noted that it did not reach the claim that the Constitution does not permit a trial in absentia in the circumstances of this case. For cases considering a defendant's waiver of the right to be present by voluntarily absenting himself from the trial, see Taylor v. United States, 414 U.S. 17 (1973) (voluntary absence constituted waiver). In United States v. Benavides, 596 F.2d 137 (5th Cir.1979), however, the court held that it was error for the trial judge to proceed with a trial in the defendants' absence, when they voluntarily absented themselves after the jury was selected but before any witnesses were called. The court said that in order to preserve the defendants' right to be present, the trial judge should have considered whether a continuance to give the defendants an opportunity to appear was practicable. See United States v. Latham, 874 F.2d 852 (1st Cir.1989) (defendant's absence due to hospitalization for an overdose of cocaine was not voluntary and did not constitute a waiver).

For purposes of Rule 43(c)(1)(A), having to do with the defendant's voluntary absence, a trial begins when jury selection begins. United States v. Bradford, 237 F.3d 1306 (11th Cir.2001).

Illinois v. Allen

397 U.S. 337, 90 S.Ct. 1057, 25 L.Ed.2d 353 (1970)

■ MR. JUSTICE BLACK delivered the opinion of the Court.

The Confrontation Clause of the Sixth Amendment to the United States Constitution provides that: "In all criminal prosecutions, the accused shall enjoy the right . . . to be confronted with the witnesses against him. . . ." We have held that the Fourteenth Amendment makes the guarantees of this clause obligatory upon the States. . . . One of the most basic of the rights guaranteed by the Confrontation Clause is the accused's right to be present in the courtroom at every stage of his trial. . . . The question presented in this case is whether an accused can claim the benefit of this constitutional right to remain in the courtroom while at the same time he engages in speech and conduct which is so noisy, disorderly, and disruptive that it is exceedingly difficult or wholly impossible to carry on the trial.

The issue arose in the following way. The respondent, Allen, was convicted by an Illinois jury of armed robbery and was sentenced to serve 10 to 30 years in the Illinois State Penitentiary. The evidence against him showed that on August 12, 1956, he entered a tavern in Illinois and, after ordering a drink, took $200 from the bartender at gunpoint. The Supreme

Court of Illinois affirmed his conviction . . . and this Court denied certiorari. . . . Later Allen filed a petition for a writ of habeas corpus in federal court alleging that he had been wrongfully deprived by the Illinois trial judge of his constitutional right to remain present throughout his trial. . . .

The facts surrounding Allen's expulsion from the courtroom are set out in the Court of Appeals' opinion sustaining Allen's contention:

> After his indictment and during the pretrial stage, the petitioner [Allen] refused court-appointed counsel and indicated to the trial court on several occasions that he wished to conduct his own defense. After considerable argument by the petitioner, the trial judge told him, "I'll let you be your own lawyer, but I'll ask Mr. Kelly [court-appointed counsel] [to] sit in and protect the record for you, insofar as possible."
>
> The trial began on September 9, 1957. After the State's Attorney had accepted the first four jurors following their voir dire examination, the petitioner began examining the first juror and continued at great length. Finally, the trial judge interrupted the petitioner, requesting him to confine his questions solely to matters relating to the prospective juror's qualifications. At that point, the petitioner started to argue with the judge in a most abusive and disrespectful manner. At last, and seemingly in desperation, the judge asked appointed counsel to proceed with the examination of the jurors. The petitioner continued to talk, proclaiming that the appointed attorney was not going to act as his lawyer. He terminated his remarks by saying, "When I go out for lunchtime, you're [the judge] going to be a corpse here." At that point he tore the file which his attorney had and threw the papers on the floor. The trial judge thereupon stated to the petitioner, "One more outbreak of that sort and I'll remove you from the courtroom." This warning had no effect on the petitioner. He continued to talk back to the judge, saying, "There's not going to be no trial, either. I'm going to sit here and you're going to talk and you can bring your shackles out and straight jacket and put them on me and tape my mouth, but it will do no good because there's not going to be no trial." After more abusive remarks by the petitioner, the trial judge ordered the trial to proceed in the petitioner's absence. The petitioner was removed from the courtroom. The voir dire examination then continued and the jury was selected in the absence of the petitioner.
>
> After a noon recess and before the jury was brought into the courtroom, the petitioner, appearing before the judge, complained about the fairness of the trial and his appointed attorney. He also said he wanted to be present in the court during his trial. In reply, the judge said that the petitioner would be permitted to remain in the courtroom if he "behaved [himself] and [did] not interfere with the introduction of the case." The jury was brought in and seated. Counsel for the petitioner then moved to exclude the witnesses from the courtroom. The [petitioner] protested this effort on the part of his attorney, saying: "There is going to be no proceeding. I'm going to

> start talking and I'm going to keep on talking all through the trial. There's not going to be no trial like this. I want my sister and my friends here in court to testify for me." The trial judge thereupon ordered the petitioner removed from the courtroom.

413 F.2d, at 233–34. After this second removal, Allen remained out of the courtroom during the presentation of the State's case-in-chief, except that he was brought in on several occasions for purposes of identification. During one of these latter appearances, Allen responded to one of the judge's questions with vile and abusive language. After the prosecution's case had been presented, the trial judge reiterated his promise to Allen that he could return to the courtroom whenever he agreed to conduct himself properly. Allen gave some assurances of proper conduct and was permitted to be present through the remainder of the trial, principally his defense, which was conducted by his appointed counsel.

The Court of Appeals went on to hold that the Supreme Court of Illinois was wrong in ruling that Allen had by his conduct relinquished his constitutional right to be present. . . .

. . .

The Court of Appeals felt that the defendant's Sixth Amendment right to be present at his own trial was so "absolute" that, no matter how unruly or disruptive the defendant's conduct might be, he could never be held to have lost that right so long as he continued to insist upon it, as Allen clearly did. Therefore the Court of Appeals concluded that a trial judge could never expel a defendant from his own trial and that the judge's ultimate remedy when faced with an obstreperous defendant like Allen who determines to make his trial impossible is to bind and gag him. We cannot agree that the Sixth Amendment, the cases upon which the Court of Appeals relied, or any other cases of this Court so handicap a trial judge in conducting a criminal trial. . . . We accept instead the statement of Mr. Justice Cardozo who, speaking for the Court in Snyder v. Massachusetts, 291 U.S. 97, 106 (1934), said: "No doubt the privilege [of personally confronting witnesses] may be lost by consent or at times even by misconduct." Although mindful that courts must indulge every reasonable presumption against the loss of constitutional rights . . . we explicitly hold today that a defendant can lose his right to be present at trial if, after he has been warned by the judge that he will be removed if he continues his disruptive behavior, he nevertheless insists on conducting himself in a manner so disorderly, disruptive, and disrespectful of the court that his trial cannot be carried on with him in the courtroom. Once lost, the right to be present can, of course, be reclaimed as soon as the defendant is willing to conduct himself consistently with the decorum and respect inherent in the concept of courts and judicial proceedings.

It is essential to the proper administration of criminal justice that dignity, order, and decorum be the hallmarks of all court proceedings in our country. The flagrant disregard in the courtroom of elementary standards of proper conduct should not and cannot be tolerated. We believe trial judges confronted with disruptive contumacious, stubbornly defiant defendants must be given sufficient discretion to meet the circumstances of each case. No one formula for maintaining the appropriate courtroom atmosphere will be best in all situations. We think there are at least three constitutionally permissible ways for a trial judge to handle an obstreperous defendant like Allen: (1) bind and gag him, thereby keeping him present; (2) cite him for contempt; (3) take him out of the courtroom until he promises to conduct himself properly.

I

Trying a defendant for a crime while he sits bound and gagged before the judge and jury would to an extent comply with that part of the Sixth Amendment's purposes that accords the defendant an opportunity to confront the witnesses at the trial. But even to contemplate such a technique, much less see it, arouses a feeling that no person should be tried while shackled and gagged except as a last resort. Not only is it possible that the sight of shackles and gags might have a significant effect on the jury's feelings about the defendant, but the use of this technique is itself something of an affront to the very dignity and decorum of judicial proceedings that the judge is seeking to uphold. Moreover, one of the defendant's primary advantages of being present at the trial, his ability to communicate with his counsel, is greatly reduced when the defendant is in a condition of total physical restraint. It is in part because of these inherent disadvantages and limitations in this method of dealing with disorderly defendants that we decline to hold . . . that a defendant cannot under any possible circumstances be deprived of his right to be present at trial. However, in some situations which we need not attempt to foresee, binding and gagging might possibly be the fairest and most reasonable way to handle a defendant who acts as Allen did here.

II

In a footnote the Court of Appeals suggested the possible availability of contempt of court as a remedy to make Allen behave in his robbery trial, and it is true that citing or threatening to cite a contumacious defendant for criminal contempt might in itself be sufficient to make a defendant stop interrupting a trial. If so, the problem would be solved easily, and the defendant could remain in the courtroom. Of course, if the defendant is determined to prevent *any* trial, then a court in attempting to try the defendant for contempt is still confronted with the identical dilemma that the Illinois court faced in this case. And criminal contempt has obvious limitations as a sanction when the defendant is charged with a crime so serious that a very severe sentence such as death or life imprisonment is likely to be imposed. In such a case the defendant might not be affected by a mere contempt sentence when he ultimately faces a far more serious sanction. Nevertheless, the contempt remedy should be borne in mind by a judge in the circumstances of this case.

Another aspect of the contempt remedy is the judge's power, when exercised consistently with state and federal law, to imprison an unruly defendant such as Allen for civil contempt and discontinue the trial until such time as the defendant promises to behave himself. This procedure is consistent with the defendant's right to be present at trial, and yet it avoids the serious shortcomings of the use of shackles and gags. It must be recognized, however, that a defendant might conceivably, as a matter of calculated strategy, elect to spend a prolonged period in confinement for contempt in the hope that adverse witnesses might be unavailable after a lapse of time. A court must guard against allowing a defendant to profit from his own wrong in this way.

III

The trial court in this case decided under the circumstances to remove the defendant from the courtroom and to continue his trial in his absence until and unless he promised to conduct himself in a manner befitting an American courtroom. As we said earlier, we find nothing unconstitutional about this procedure. Allen's behavior was clearly of such an extreme and aggravated nature as to justify either his removal from the courtroom or his total physical restraint. Prior to his removal he was repeatedly warned by the trial judge that he would be removed from the courtroom if he persisted in his unruly conduct, and, as Judge Hastings observed in his dissenting opinion, the record demonstrates that Allen would not have been at all dissuaded by the trial judge's use of his criminal contempt powers. Allen was constantly informed that he could return to the trial when he would agree to conduct himself in an orderly manner. Under these circumstances we hold that Allen lost his right guaranteed by the Sixth and Fourteenth Amendments to be present throughout his trial.

IV

It is not pleasant to hold that the respondent Allen was properly banished from the court for a part of his own trial. But our courts, palladiums of liberty as they are, cannot be treated disrespectfully with impunity. Nor can the accused be permitted by his disruptive conduct indefinitely to avoid being tried on the charges brought against him. It would degrade our country and our judicial system to permit our courts to be bullied, insulted, and humiliated and their orderly progress thwarted and obstructed by defendants brought before them charged with crimes. As guardians of the public welfare, our state and federal judicial systems strive to administer equal justice to the rich and the poor, the good and the bad, the native and foreign born of every race, nationality, and religion. Being manned by humans, the courts are not perfect and are bound to make some errors. But, if our courts are to remain what the Founders intended, the citadels of justice, their proceedings cannot and must not be infected with the sort of scurrilous, abusive language and conduct paraded before the Illinois trial judge in this case. The record shows that the Illinois judge at all times conducted himself with that dignity, decorum, and patience that befit a judge. Even in holding that the trial judge had erred, the Court of Appeals praised his "commendable patience under severe provocation."

We do not hold that removing this defendant from his own trial was the only way the Illinois judge could have constitutionally solved the problem he had. We do hold, however, that there is nothing whatever in this record to show that the judge did not act completely within his discretion. Deplorable as it is to remove a man from his own trial, even for a short time, we hold that the judge did not commit legal error in doing what he did.

. . .[1]

---

439. "Because every criminal defendant is entitled under the fourteenth amendment's due process clause to a fair and impartial trial there are four sound reasons underlying the general rule that a defendant should never be shackled during his trial before a jury except in extraordinary circumstances. Without repeating all of them, we note the inherent prejudice to the accused when he is cast in the jury's eyes as a dangerous, untrustworthy and pernicious individual from the very start of the trial. Therefore, only upon a *clear showing* of necessity should shackles ever be employed. One element of such necessity is that less drastic security precautions to prevent escape, even at some additional cost to the state, will not provide the needed protection. In light of the identity of reasons underlying the principle against shackling a defendant during a jury trial, and the principles for dealing with an obstreperous defendant during the trial outlined by the Supreme Court in Illinois v. Allen, 397 U.S. 337 (1970), shackles should only be used as a last resort. Therefore, in our opinion, it is an abuse of discretion precipitously to employ shackles when less drastic security measures will adequately and reasonably suffice." Kennedy v. Cardwell, 487 F.2d 101, 111 (6th Cir.1973). The four reasons to which the court referred are that shackling prejudices the jury, limits the defendant's ability to defend himself by affecting his mental capacities and capacity to testify as a witness, limits his ability to consult with counsel, and detracts from the dignity and decorum of the judicial process.

The use of shackles has been upheld in a number of cases. E.g., United States v. Stewart, 20 F.3d 911 (8th Cir.1994) (defendant was accused of "vicious assault" on witness in a courtroom and was disruptive); Jones v. Meyer, 899 F.2d 883 (9th Cir.1990) (defendant on trial for murder had previous murder conviction and had made threats); United States v. Fountain, 768 F.2d 790 (7th Cir.1985) (defendants and witnesses were prison inmates previously convicted as murderers); Zygadlo v. Wainwright, 720 F.2d 1221 (11th Cir.1983) (defendant had previously tried to escape). See also Wilson v. McCarthy, 770 F.2d 1482 (9th Cir.1985) (shackling of defense witness upheld).

In Spain v. Rushen, 883 F.2d 712 (9th Cir.1989), however, the court held that the use of shackles denied the defendant due process. Referring to Estelle v. Williams, 425 U.S. 501 (1976), note 440 below, in Walker v. Butterworth, 599 F.2d 1074, 1076, 1080 (1st Cir.1979), the court held that the practice of requiring the defendant in certain cases to sit in the prisoner's dock, an enclosure "about four feet square and four feet high, open at the top so that the defendant's head and shoulders can be seen by the jury," was an anachronism and unconstitutional, because it might "dilute the presumption of innocence." The court applied *Walker* in Young

[1] Justice Brennan wrote a concurring opinion. Justice Douglas wrote an opinion stating that the court should not have reached the merits of the case on a stale record.

v. Callahan, 700 F.2d 32 (1st Cir.1983), but allowed the possibility that the dock might be used in cases where physical restraint of the defendant was necessary.

In Holbrook v. Flynn, 475 U.S. 560 (1986), the Court concluded that the presence in the courtroom of four uniformed, armed law enforcement officers for security reasons during the defendant's trial with five other defendants did not deny him a fair trial. The defendants were detained without bail. The officers were seated in the front row of the spectator section of the courtroom, not far behind the defendants' seats, throughout the trial, which lasted for more than two months. The Court observed that although the presence of security officers in a courtroom might be prejudicial in a particular case, there was no ground for a presumption of prejudice. Their presence, the Court said, is not "the sort of inherently prejudicial practice that, like shackling, should be permitted only where justified by an essential state interest specific to each trial." Id. at 568–69.

Applying Illinois v. Allen, the court upheld the expulsion of the defendant in Foster v. Wainwright, 686 F.2d 1382 (11th Cir.1982). Expulsion was held to have been improper in Badger v. Cardwell, 587 F.2d 968 (9th Cir.1978).

The involuntary administration of antipsychotic medication to a defendant during his trial, without findings by the trial court that such medication was both medically appropriate and, there being no less intrusive means, necessary to the conduct of the trial or to the safety of the defendant or others, violated his right to a fair trial under the Due Process Clause. Riggins v. Nevada, 504 U.S. 127 (1992) (7–2).

440. "[T]he State cannot, consistently with the Fourteenth Amendment, compel an accused to stand trial before a jury while dressed in identifiable prison clothes." Estelle v. Williams, 425 U.S. 501, 512 (1976). Referring to "the possible impairment of the presumption [of innocence] so basic to the adversary system," the Court said that the "constant reminder of the accused's condition implicit in such distinctive, identifiable attire may affect a juror's judgment." Id. at 504–505. The Court noted, however, that some defendants might prefer to be tried in jail clothes. If the defendant failed to make an objection to being tried in them, there was no compulsion and, therefore, no constitutional violation.

The courts have generally condemned a prosecutor's commenting in closing argument about a defendant's behavior in the courtroom and, in some cases, have reversed convictions. Such comment, it is reasoned, invites the jury to convict on a basis other than the evidence and, further, may indirectly call attention to a defendant's failure to testify. See United States v. Schuler, 813 F.2d 978 (9th Cir.1987).

United States v. Carrion

488 F.2d 12 (1st Cir.1973)

PER CURIAM.

Appellant, convicted of knowingly aiding and abetting the distribution of heroin in violation of 21 U.S.C. § 841(a)(1) and 18 U.S.C. § 2, contends that his Fifth and Sixth Amendment rights were abridged during trial because . . . the court refused to appoint an interpreter for him.

. . .

Appellant is a foreign-born national with a limited ability to speak and comprehend English. He claims that, although he admitted to the court some ability to communicate and understand, his counsel's assertion at the start of the trial of the possibility of a "problem of communication" should have prompted the court to hold a special hearing to determine the extent of the problem. As evidence of his difficulty with the language, appellant points to several instances during his own testimony where questions had to be repeated or where his responses were so unclear as to require that he rephrase them. On at least one occasion the court indicated that there was apparently a "language barrier."

The necessity for an interpreter to translate from a defendant's native language into English when the defendant is on the stand, and from English into the defendant's native language when others are testifying, has been elevated to a right when the defendant is indigent and has obvious difficulty with the language. . . . Clearly, the right to confront witnesses would be meaningless if the accused could not understand their testimony, and the effectiveness of cross-examination would be severely hampered. . . . If the defendant takes the stand in his own behalf, but has an imperfect command of English, there exists the additional danger that he will either misunderstand crucial questions or that the jury will misconstrue crucial responses. The right to an interpreter rests most fundamentally, however, on the notion that no defendant should face the Kafkaesque spectre of an incomprehensible ritual which may terminate in punishment.

Yet how high must the language barrier rise before a defendant has a right to an interpreter? It is well settled that there is no right to an interpreter if the foreign-born defendant speaks fluent English and is "completely aware of all the proceedings." Cervantes v. Cox, 350 F.2d 855 (10th Cir.1965). The status of the right becomes less certain, however, where, as in the present case, the defendant has some ability to understand and communicate, but clearly has difficulty.

Because the determination is likely to hinge upon various factors, including the complexity of the issues and testimony presented during trial and the language ability of the defendant's counsel, considerations of judicial economy would dictate that the trial court, coming into direct contact with the defendant, be granted wide discretion in determining whether an interpreter is necessary. . . . It would be a fruitless and frustrating exercise for the appellate court to have to infer language difficulty from every faltering, repetitious bit of testimony in the record. But precisely because the trial court is entrusted with discretion, it should make unmistakably clear to a defendant who may have a language difficulty that he has a right to a court-appointed interpreter if the court determines that one is needed, and, whenever put on notice that there may be some significant language difficulty, the court should make such a determination of need.

Although the trial court in the present case did not hold a formal hearing on the question whether the appellant required a translator, it was obviously sensitive to the appellant's plight in that it did grant pretrial motions made by the appellant's two co-defendants, each asking for an interpreter during the proceedings. Thus, a procedure was available for the appellant to allege and show a language difficulty before trial commenced. Moreover, the court specifically asked counsel whether the appellant was able to communicate and understand English, to which appellant's counsel responded in the affirmative. Finally, the court told the appellant that if, at any point in the proceedings, there was something he did not understand, he need only raise his hand and the testimony would be repeated. We are not prepared to hold that the appellant had a constitutional right to any more than this.

. . .

Voir Dire

FEDERAL RULES OF CRIMINAL PROCEDURE

Rule 23

JURY OR NONJURY TRIAL

(a) Jury Trial. If the defendant is entitled to a jury trial, the trial must be by jury unless:

(1) the defendant waives a jury trial in writing;

(2) the government consents; and

(3) the court approves.

(b) Jury Size.

(1) *In General.* A jury consists of 12 persons unless this rule provides otherwise.

(2) *Stipulation for a Smaller Jury.* At any time before the verdict, the parties may, with the court's approval, stipulate in writing that:

(A) the jury may consist of fewer than 12 persons; or

(B) a jury of fewer than 12 persons may return a verdict if the court finds it necessary to excuse a juror for good cause after the trial begins.

(3) *Court Order for a Jury of 11.* After the jury has retired to deliberate, the court may permit a jury of 11 persons to return a verdict, even without stipulation by the parties, if the court finds good cause to excuse a juror.

(c) Nonjury Trial. In a case tried without a jury, the court must find the defendant guilty or not guilty. If a party requests before the finding of guilty or not guilty, the court must state its specific findings of fact in open court or in a written decision or opinion.

---

441. "The trial of all crimes except in cases of impeachment shall be by jury. . . ." U.S. Constitution art. 3, § 2.

"In all criminal prosecutions, the accused shall enjoy the right to a speedy and public trial, by an impartial jury of the State and district wherein the crime shall have been committed, which district shall have been previously ascertained by law. . . ." U.S. Constitution amend. VI.

"Because we believe that trial by jury in criminal cases is fundamental to the American scheme of justice, we hold that the Fourteenth Amendment guarantees a right of jury trial in all criminal cases which—were they to be tried in a federal court—would come within the Sixth Amendment's guarantee." Duncan v. Louisiana, 391 U.S. 145, 149 (1968).[2]

In *Duncan*, the defendant was tried without a jury and convicted of simple battery, the maximum penalty for which was two years' imprisonment and a fine of $300; he was sentenced to 60 days' imprisonment and a fine of $150. The state contended that because his sentence was so light he was not entitled to a jury trial. The Court disagreed.

> It is doubtless true that there is a category of petty crimes or offenses which is not subject to the Sixth Amendment jury trial provision and should not be subject to the Fourteenth Amendment jury trial requirement here applied to the States. Crimes carrying possible penalties up to six months do not require a jury trial if they otherwise qualify as petty offenses. . . . But the penalty authorized for a particular crime is of major relevance in determining whether it is serious or not and may in itself, if severe enough, subject the trial to the mandates of the Sixth Amendment. District of Columbia v. Clawans, 300 U.S. 617 (1937). The penalty authorized by the law of the locality may be taken "as a gauge of its social and ethical judgments," 300 U.S., at 628, of the crime in question. In *Clawans* the defendant was jailed for 60 days, but it was the 90-day authorized punishment on which the Court focused in

2. "A criminal process which was fair and equitable but used no juries is easy to imagine. It would make use of alternative guarantees and protections which would serve the purposes that the jury serves in the English and American systems. Yet no American State has undertaken to construct such a system. Instead, every American State . . . uses the jury extensively, and imposes very serious punishments only after a trial at which the defendant has a right to a jury's verdict. In every State . . . the structure and style of the criminal process—the supporting framework and the subsidiary procedures—are of the sort that naturally complement jury trial, and have developed in connection with and in reliance upon jury trial." 391 U.S. at 150 n.14.

determining that the offense was not one for which the Constitution assured trial by jury. In the case before us the Legislature of Louisiana has made simple battery a criminal offense punishable by imprisonment for up to two years and a fine. The question, then, is whether a crime carrying such a penalty is an offense which Louisiana may insist on trying without a jury.

We think not. So-called petty offenses were tried without juries both in England and in the Colonies and have always been held to be exempt from the otherwise comprehensive language of the Sixth Amendment's jury trial provisions. There is no substantial evidence that the Framers intended to depart from this established common-law practice, and the possible consequences to defendants from convictions for petty offenses have been thought insufficient to outweigh the benefits to efficient law enforcement and simplified judicial administration resulting from the availability of speedy and inexpensive nonjury adjudications. These same considerations compel the same result under the Fourteenth Amendment. Of course the boundaries of the petty offense category have always been ill-defined, if not ambulatory. In the absence of an explicit constitutional provision, the definitional task necessarily falls on the courts, which must either pass upon the validity of legislative attempts to identify those petty offenses which are exempt from jury trial or, where the legislature has not addressed itself to the problem, themselves face the question in the first instance. In either case it is necessary to draw a line in the spectrum of crime, separating petty from serious infractions. This process, although essential, cannot be wholly satisfactory, for it requires attaching different consequences to events which, when they lie near the line, actually differ very little.

In determining whether the length of the authorized prison term or the seriousness of other punishment is enough in itself to require a jury trial, we are counseled by District of Columbia v. Clawans, supra, to refer to objective criteria, chiefly the existing laws and practices in the Nation. In the federal system, petty offenses are defined as those punishable by no more than six months in prison and a $500 fine. In 49 of the 50 States crimes subject to trial without a jury, which occasionally include simple battery, are punishable by no more than one year in jail. Moreover, in the late 18th century in America crimes triable without a jury were for the most part punishable by no more than a six-month prison term, although there appear to have been exceptions to this rule. We need not, however, settle in this case the exact location of the line between petty offenses and serious crimes. It is sufficient for our purposes to hold that a crime punishable by two years in prison is, based on past and contemporary standards in this country, a serious crime and not a petty offense. Consequently, appellant was entitled to a jury trial and it was error to deny it.

391 U.S. at 159–62.

UNITED STATES DISTRICT COURT
DISTRICT OF MASSACHUSETTS

UNITED STATES OF AMERICA

V. CRIMINAL NO. __________

____

WAIVER OF JURY TRIAL

Now comes the defendant, ____________________ and waives his right of trial by jury and elects to be tried before the court.

____
Defendant

____
Attorney for the Defendant

____
Assistant U.S. Attorney

APPROVED:

____
United States District Judge

____
Date

(Jury Trial Waiver.wpd - 12/98) [kwvjy.]

The Court drew the line between petty offenses and serious crimes in Baldwin v. New York, 399 U.S. 66 (1970). It held that "no offense can be deemed 'petty' for purposes of the right to trial by jury where imprisonment for more than six months is authorized." Id. at 69. The Court relied primarily on the nearly unanimous view that the possibility of imprisonment for six months warranted a right to jury trial:

> In the entire Nation, New York City alone denies an accused the right to interpose between himself and a possible prison term of over six months, the commonsense judgment of a jury of his peers.
>
> . . . This near-uniform judgment of the Nation furnishes us with the only objective criterion by which a line could ever be drawn—on the basis of the possible penalty alone—between offenses which are and which are not regarded as "serious" for purposes of trial by jury.

Id. at 71–73.

The category of petty offenses was elaborated further in Blanton v. City of North Las Vegas, 489 U.S. 538 (1989). The Court said that an offense carrying a maximum sentence of six months or less is presumptively, but not necessarily, a petty offense. "A defendant is entitled to jury trial in such circumstances only if he can demonstrate that any additional statutory penalties, viewed in conjunction with the maximum authorized period of incarceration, are so severe that they clearly reflect a legislative determination that the offense in question is a 'serious' one." Id. at 543. In *Blanton*, the crime was driving under the influence of alcohol. The maximum term of imprisonment was six months. The additional penalty of a fine of up to $1000 and the alternative penalty of 48 hours of community service "dressed in distinctive garb" that identifies the person as an offender was not enough to make the crime not a petty offense. *Blanton* was applied in United States v. Nachtigal, 507 U.S. 1 (1993), in which again the defendant was convicted of drunk driving, the maximum penalty for which was six months' imprisonment. The Court concluded that a maximum fine of $5000 and an alternative to imprisonment of five years' probation did not overcome the presumption of *Blanton* that the crime was a petty offense.

A defendant who is prosecuted in a single trial for multiple petty offenses the aggregate authorized penalties for which exceed six months' imprisonment does not have a constitutional right to a jury trial. Lewis v. United States, 518 U.S. 322 (1996) (7–2).

In a companion case to *Baldwin*, Williams v. Florida, 399 U.S. 78 (1970), the Court held that the constitutional right to a trial by jury did not require that the jury be composed of 12 members. "[T]hat particular feature of the jury system appears to have been a historical accident, unrelated to the great purposes which gave rise to the jury in the first place." And, "there is absolutely no indication in 'the intent of the Framers' of an explicit decision to equate the constitutional and common-law characteristics of the jury." Id. at 89–90, 99. Turning to the purpose of the jury trial "to prevent oppression by the Government," the court concluded:

> Given this purpose, the essential feature of a jury obviously lies in the interposition between the accused and his accuser of the commonsense judgment of a group of laymen, and in the community participation and shared responsibility that results from that group's determination of guilt or innocence. The performance of this role is not a function of the particular number of the body that makes up the jury. To be sure, the number should probably be large enough to promote group deliberation, free from outside attempts at intimidation, and to provide a fair possibility for obtaining a representative cross-section of the community. But we find little reason to think that these goals are in any meaningful sense less likely to be achieved when the jury numbers six, than when it numbers 12—particularly if the requirement of unanimity is retained. And, certainly the reliability of the jury as a factfinder hardly seems likely to be a function of its size.
>
> It might be suggested that the 12-man jury gives a defendant a greater advantage since he has more "chances" of finding a juror who will insist on acquittal and thus prevent conviction. But the advantage might just as easily belong to the State, which also needs only one juror out of twelve insisting on guilt to prevent acquittal. What few experiments have occurred—usually in the civil area—indicate that there is no discernible difference between the results reached by the two different-sized juries. In short, neither currently available evidence nor theory suggests that the 12-man jury is necessarily more advantageous to the defendant than a jury composed of fewer members.
>
> Similarly, while in theory the number of viewpoints represented on a randomly selected jury ought to increase as the size of the jury increases, in practice the difference between the 12-man and the six-man jury in terms of the cross-section of the community represented seems likely to be negligible. Even the 12-man jury cannot insure representation of every distinct voice in the community, particularly given the use of the peremptory challenge. As long as arbitrary exclusions of a particular class from the jury rolls are forbidden . . . the concern that the cross-section will be significantly diminished if the jury is decreased in size from 12 to six seems an unrealistic one.

Id. at 100–102.

A jury of six members, upheld in *Williams*, is, however, the smallest that is constitutionally permissible. Fearing that a jury of less than six would threaten the functions of the jury that made trial by jury a constitutional right, the Court held that a five-member jury was constitutionally inadequate, in Ballew v. Georgia, 435 U.S. 223 (1978). For "much the same reasons," the Court concluded, notwithstanding *Apodaca* and *Johnson*, below, that a person may not be convicted by the verdict of a six-person jury unless the verdict is unanimous. Burch v. Louisiana, 441 U.S. 130 (1979).

The Constitution does not require in *state* criminal prosecutions that the verdict be unanimous. Apodaca v. Oregon, 406 U.S. 404 (1972) (5–4); Johnson v. Louisiana, 406 U.S. 356 (1972) (5–4). In *Apodaca*, four Justices concluded that the Sixth Amendment's right to a jury did not require unanimity. In terms of the jury's function, as described in *Williams*, above, they saw "no difference between juries required to act unanimously and those permitted to convict or acquit by votes of 10 to two or 11 to one. Requiring unanimity would obviously produce hung juries in some situations where nonunanimous juries will convict or acquit. But in either case, the interest of the defendant in having the judgment of his peers interposed between himself and the officers of the State who prosecute and judge him is equally well served." 406 U.S. at 411. Justice Powell agreed that the Sixth Amendment did not require unanimity in state cases, but stated his conclusion that unanimity was required to convict in a *federal* criminal trial. Id. at 366, 371.

In *Johnson*, a majority of the Court concluded that a less than unanimous verdict does not violate the requirement of the Due Process Clause that guilt be proved beyond a reasonable doubt. The defendant was convicted of armed robbery by a 9–3 verdict. The Court said:

> [I]t is our view that the fact of three dissenting votes to acquit raises no question of constitutional substance about either the integrity or the accuracy of the majority verdict of guilt. Appellant's contrary argument breaks down into two parts, each of which we shall consider separately: first, that nine individual jurors will be unable to vote conscientiously in favor of guilt beyond a reasonable doubt when three of their colleagues are arguing for acquittal, and second, that guilt cannot be said to have been proved beyond a reasonable doubt when one or more of a jury's members at the conclusion of deliberation still possess such a doubt. Neither argument is persuasive.
>
> Numerous cases have defined a reasonable doubt as one "based on reason which arises from the evidence or lack of evidence." United States v. Johnson, 343 F.2d 5, 6 n.1 (CA2 1965). . . . In considering the first branch of appellant's argument, we can find no basis for holding that the nine jurors who voted for his conviction failed to follow their instructions concerning the need for proof beyond such a doubt or that the vote of any one of the nine failed to reflect an honest belief that guilt had been so proved. Appellant, in effect, asks us to assume that, when minority jurors express sincere doubts about guilt, their fellow jurors will nevertheless ignore them and vote to convict even if deliberation has not been exhausted and minority jurors have grounds for acquittal which, if pursued, might persuade members of the majority to acquit. But the mere fact that three jurors voted to acquit does not in itself demonstrate that, had the nine jurors of the majority attended further to reason and the evidence, all or one of them would have developed a reasonable doubt about guilt. We have no grounds for believing that majority jurors, aware of their responsibility and power over the liberty of the defendant, would simply refuse to listen to arguments presented to them in favor of acquittal, terminate discussion, and render a verdict. On the contrary it is far more likely that a juror presenting reasoned argument in favor of acquittal would either have his arguments answered or would carry enough other jurors with him to prevent conviction. A majority will cease discussion and outvote a minority only after reasoned discussion has ceased to

have persuasive effect or to serve any other purpose—when a minority, that is, continues to insist upon acquittal without having persuasive reasons in support of its position. At that juncture there is no basis for denigrating the vote of so large a majority of the jury or for refusing to accept their decision as being, at least in their minds, beyond a reasonable doubt. Indeed, at this point, a "dissenting juror should consider whether his doubt was a reasonable one . . . [when it made] no impression upon the minds of so many men, equally honest, equally intelligent with himself." Allen v. United States, 164 U.S. 492, 501 (1896). Appellant offers no evidence that majority jurors simply ignore the reasonable doubts of their colleagues or otherwise act irresponsibly in casting their votes in favor of conviction, and before we alter our own long-standing perceptions about jury behavior and overturn a considered legislative judgment that unanimity is not essential to reasoned jury verdicts, we must have some basis for doing so other than unsupported assumptions.

We conclude, therefore, that, as to the nine jurors who voted to convict, the State satisfied its burden of proving guilt beyond any reasonable doubt. The remaining question under the Due Process Clause is whether the vote of three jurors for acquittal can be said to impeach the verdict of the other nine and to demonstrate that guilt was not in fact proved beyond such doubt. We hold that it cannot.

Of course, the State's proof could perhaps be regarded as more certain if it had convinced all 12 jurors instead of only nine; it would have been even more compelling if it had been required to convince and had, in fact, convinced 24 or 36 jurors. But the fact remains that nine jurors—a substantial majority of the jury—were convinced by the evidence. In our view disagreement of three jurors does not alone establish reasonable doubt, particularly when such a heavy majority of the jury, after having considered the dissenters' views, remains convinced of guilt. That rational men disagree is not in itself equivalent to a failure of proof by the State, nor does it indicate infidelity to the reasonable-doubt standard. Jury verdicts finding guilt beyond a reasonable doubt are regularly sustained even though the evidence was such that the jury would have been justified in having a reasonable doubt . . . even though the trial judge might not have reached the same conclusion as the jury . . . and even though appellate judges are closely divided on the issue whether there was sufficient evidence to support a conviction. . . . That want of jury unanimity is not to be equated with the existence of a reasonable doubt emerges even more clearly from the fact that when a jury in a federal court, which operates under the unanimity rule and is instructed to acquit a defendant if it has a reasonable doubt about his guilt . . . cannot agree unanimously upon a verdict, the defendant is not acquitted, but is merely given a new trial. . . . If the doubt of a minority of jurors indicates the existence of a reasonable doubt, it would appear that a defendant should receive a directed verdict of acquittal rather than a retrial. We conclude, therefore, that verdicts rendered by nine out of 12

> jurors are not automatically invalidated by the disagreement of the dissenting three. Appellant was not deprived of due process of law.

406 U.S. at 360–63.

The Court rejected also the claim that the Equal Protection Clause did not allow a state to provide for unanimous verdicts in some cases and not others.

The Court has upheld, against the claim that it denied the right to a jury trial, a "two-tier" court system, by which a person accused of certain crimes is tried first in the lower court, where no jury is available, and then if he is convicted and appeals, is tried de novo in the upper court, where a jury is available. Ludwig v. Massachusetts, 427 U.S. 618 (1976) (5–4).

442. On the third day of what was a five-day trial, the judge excused a juror who had become ill. Over the defendant's objection, the judge continued the trial with eleven jurors. The defendant was convicted on some counts and acquitted on others. Without deciding whether the judge's ruling was a constitutional error, the court concluded that Rule 23(b) had been violated and that the violation required reversal without consideration whether the error might have been harmless. United States v. Curbelo, 343 F.3d 273 (4th Cir.2003).

443. In Singer v. United States, 380 U.S. 24, 26 (1965), the Court held that there is not a constitutional right to a nonjury trial and that Rule 23(a) of the Federal Rules of Criminal Procedure "sets forth a reasonable procedure governing attempted waivers of jury trials." "A defendant's only constitutional right concerning the method of trial is to an impartial trial by jury. We find no constitutional impediment to conditioning a waiver of this right on the consent of the prosecuting attorney and the trial judge when, if either refuses to consent, the result is simply that the defendant is subject to an impartial trial by jury—the very thing that the Constitution guarantees him. The Constitution recognizes an adversary system as the proper method of determining guilt, and the Government, as a litigant, has a legitimate interest in seeing that cases in which it believes a conviction is warranted are tried before the tribunal which the Constitution regards as most likely to produce a fair result." Id. at 36.

"Because of this confidence in the integrity of the federal prosecutor, Rule 23(a) does not require that the Government articulate its reasons for demanding a jury trial at the time it refuses to consent to a defendant's proffered waiver. Nor should we assume that federal prosecutors would demand a jury trial for an ignoble purpose." Id. at 37. The Court left open the possibility that there might be circumstances in which a refusal to consent to a nonjury trial would result in the denial of an impartial trial.

444. "An accused is entitled to have charges against him considered by a jury in the selection of which there has been neither inclusion nor exclusion because of race." Cassell v. Texas, 339 U.S. 282, 287 (1950); see Akins v. Texas, 325 U.S. 398 (1945). On the manner in which jury commissioners are required to perform their duty of preparing jury lists, in order to avoid racial discrimination, see *Cassell*. "The statements of the jury commissioners that they chose only whom they knew, and that they knew no eligible Negroes in an area where Negroes made up so large a proportion [15.5%] of the population, prove the intentional exclusion that is discrimination in violation of petitioner's constitutional rights." 339 U.S. at 290.

"[I]n order to show that an equal protection violation has occurred in the context of grand jury selection, the defendant must show that the procedure employed resulted in substantial under-representation of his race or of the identifiable group to which he belongs. The first step is to establish that the group is one that is a recognizable, distinct class, singled out for different treatment under the laws, as written or as applied. . . . Next, the degree of under-representation must be proved, by comparing the proportion of the group in the total population to the proportion called to serve as grand jurors, over a significant period of time. . . . This method of proof, sometimes called the 'rule of exclusion,' has been held to be available as a method of proving discrimination in jury selection against a delineated class. . . . Finally, as noted above, a selection procedure that is susceptible of abuse or is not racially neutral supports the presumption of discrimination raised by the statistical showing. . . . Once the defendant has shown substantial under-representation of his group, he has made out a prima facie case of discriminatory purpose, and the burden then shifts to the State to rebut that case." Castaneda v. Partida, 430 U.S. 482, 494–95 (1977) (5–4). The Court found that where the population of a county was 79.1% Mexican-American and over an 11-year period only 39% of the persons summoned for jury service were Mexican-American, there was substantial under-representation, and a prima facie case of discrimination was made out. The fact that a majority of the elected officials in the county were members of the under-represented group was not enough to rebut the showing of discrimination. See also, e.g., Rose v. Mitchell, 443 U.S. 545 (1979) (7–2) (racial discrimination in selection of foreman of grand jury not shown); Alexander v. Louisiana, 405 U.S. 625 (1972) (racial discrimination in selection of grand jury shown); Alston v. Manson, 791 F.2d 255 (2d Cir.1986) (racial discrimination in selection of petit jury shown); Bowen v. Kemp, 769 F.2d 672 (11th Cir.1985) (sexual discrimination in selection of sentencing jury shown).

Is it proper in any circumstances for the commissioners deliberately to include persons of a particular racial or religious group on the list from which jurors will be selected, or deliberately to seek sources of names of potential jurors that are likely to provide names of those in such groups? Or are the commissioners required, in their effort to avoid discrimination, to develop and pursue a means of preparing jury lists that is blind to race and religion? See Brooks v. Beto, 366 F.2d 1 (5th Cir.1966).

445. A defendant's right to a jury selected from a fair cross-section of the community, as part of the Sixth Amendment right to a jury trial, is violated by a provision excluding or automatically exempting women from jury duty that has the effect that women rarely serve on juries. Taylor v.

Louisiana, 419 U.S. 522 (1975). In *Taylor*, the Court rejected its earlier reasoning, in Hoyt v. Florida, 368 U.S. 57 (1961), that a state could give women an automatic exemption from jury service, if they wished, because of the special role of women in society:

> The States are free to grant exemptions from jury service to individuals in case of special hardship or incapacity and to those engaged in particular occupations the uninterrupted performance of which is critical to the community's welfare. . . . It would not appear that such exemptions would pose substantial threats that the remaining pool of jurors would not be representative of the community. A system excluding all women, however, is a wholly different matter. It is untenable to suggest these days that it would be a special hardship for each and every woman to perform jury service or that society cannot spare any women from their present duties. This may be the case with many, and it may be burdensome to sort out those who should be exempted from those who should serve. But that task is performed in the case of men, and the administrative convenience in dealing with women as a class is insufficient justification for diluting the quality of community judgment represented by the jury in criminal trials.

419 U.S. at 534–35.

Following *Taylor*, the Court invalidated a statute that exempted women, but not men, from jury service on request. Duren v. Missouri, 439 U.S. 357 (1979) (8–1).

446. The defendant, a white person, challenged the selection of grand jurors and petit jurors on the ground that black persons were systematically excluded. The Supreme Court upheld his standing to make the challenge. Peters v. Kiff, 407 U.S. 493 (1972). Three Justices did so on the ground that such exclusion violated a defendant's right to due process of law. Three Justices concurred on the basis that systematic racial exclusion was a crime, 18 U.S.C. § 243. Three Justices dissented on the basis that no prejudice to the defendant had been shown.

447. Voter lists and voter registration lists have become a preferred method for obtaining names of persons for jury duty. In the federal courts, the use of such lists is prescribed by a provision of the Jury Selection and Service Act of 1968, 28 U.S.C. § 1863(b)(2). The statute prescribes that other sources of names in addition to voter lists shall be used "where necessary to foster the policy and protect the rights secured by" the statute: the right to a jury "selected at random from a fair cross section of the community in the district or division wherein the court convenes" and the policy that "all citizens shall have the opportunity to be considered for service on" juries. 28 U.S.C. § 1861. In several cases, the courts have rejected a claim that sole reliance on voter lists is impermissible because identifiable groups do not register to vote. In United States v. Lewis, 472 F.2d 252 (3d Cir.1973), for example, the defendant argued that blacks in the community did not register and suggested use of social security rolls, public assistance rolls, and the census. The court said: "[A] group of persons who choose not to vote do not constitute a 'cognizable group.' Further, their non-registration is a result of their own inaction; not a result of affirmative conduct by others to bar their registration. Therefore, while a fairer cross section of the community may have been produced by the use of 'other sources of names,' the Plan's sole reliance on voter registration lists was constitutionally permissible." Id. at 256. See generally United States v. Brady, 579 F.2d 1121 (9th Cir.1978).

"A benign and theoretically neutral principle loses its aura of sanctity when it fails to function neutrally." Labat v. Bennett, 365 F.2d 698, 724 (5th Cir.1966). Is an otherwise reasonable basis for excusing prospective jurors from jury duty, such as economic hardship, impermissible if its application will have the effect of eliminating from juries most members of an identifiable racial or religious group? Compare *Labat* with United States v. Bowe, 360 F.2d 1, 7 n.3 (2d Cir.1966). See also Thiel v. Southern Pacific Co., 328 U.S. 217 (1946). See generally Carmical v. Craven, 457 F.2d 582 (9th Cir.1971) (intelligence test).

448. In what circumstances does unrepresentativeness of the jury panel with respect to age invalidate a conviction? Does "young adults" constitute a separately cognizable group? The courts have generally said not. See Johnson v. McCaughtry, 92 F.3d 585 (7th Cir.1996) (additional cases cited).

FEDERAL RULES OF CRIMINAL PROCEDURE

Rule 24

TRIAL JURORS

(a) Examination.

(1) *In General.* The court may examine prospective jurors or may permit the attorneys for the parties to do so.

(2) *Court Examination.* If the court examines the jurors, it must permit the attorneys for the parties to:

(A) ask further questions that the court considers proper; or

(B) submit further questions that the court may ask if it considers them proper.

(b) Peremptory Challenges. Each side is entitled to the number of peremptory challenges to prospective jurors specified below. The court may allow additional peremptory challenges to multiple defendants, and may allow the defendants to exercise those challenges separately or jointly.

(1) *Capital Case.* Each side has 20 peremptory challenges when the government seeks the death penalty.

(2) *Other Felony Case.* The government has 6 peremptory challenges and the defendant or defendants jointly have 10 peremptory

challenges when the defendant is charged with a crime punishable by imprisonment of more than one year.

(3) *Misdemeanor Case.* Each side has 3 peremptory challenges when the defendant is charged with a crime punishable by fine, imprisonment of one year or less, or both.

(c) Alternate Jurors.

(1) *In General.* The court may impanel up to 6 alternate jurors to replace any jurors who are unable to perform or who are disqualified from performing their duties.

(2) *Procedure.*

(A) Alternate jurors must have the same qualifications and be selected and sworn in the same manner as any other juror.

(B) Alternate jurors replace jurors in the same sequence in which the alternates were selected. An alternate juror who replaces a juror has the same authority as the other jurors.

(3) *Retaining Alternate Jurors.* The court may retain alternate jurors after the jury retires to deliberate. The court must ensure that a retained alternate does not discuss the case with anyone until that alternate replaces a juror or is discharged. If an alternate replaces a juror after deliberations have begun, the court must instruct the jury to begin its deliberations anew.

(4) *Peremptory Challenges.* Each side is entitled to the number of additional peremptory challenges to prospective alternate jurors specified below. These additional challenges may be used only to remove alternate jurors.

(A) *One or Two Alternates.* One additional peremptory challenge is permitted when one or two alternates are impaneled.

(B) *Three or Four Alternates.* Two additional peremptory challenges are permitted when three or four alternates are impaneled.

(C) *Five or Six Alternates.* Three additional peremptory challenges are permitted when five or six alternates are impaneled.

---

449. Rule 24(a) provides that the judge shall decide how the voir dire is conducted. Is it preferable that the judge examine prospective jurors or that defense counsel and the prosecutor do so? Why?

Appellate courts will not interfere with the manner in which the trial court conducted the voir dire examination unless there has been a clear abuse of discretion. . . .

It is not an abuse of discretion for the trial judge to insist upon conducting a voir dire examination, but if he does so, he must exercise a sound "judicial" discretion in the acceptance or rejection of supplemental questions proposed by counsel, to be propounded by the judge, as contemplated by Rule 24(a) of the Fed.R.Crim.Procedure.

Silverthorne v. United States, 400 F.2d 627, 638, 640 (9th Cir.1968) (abuse of discretion because judge's examination was "too restrictive in both scope and substance to accord to appellant the right to explore for the impartially fair juror").

450. Rule 24(b) leaves it to the discretion of the trial judge whether joint defendants shall together have more peremptory challenges than each would have if tried alone, and whether their challenges shall be exercised "separately or jointly."

"There is nothing in the Constitution of the United States which requires the Congress to grant peremptory challenges to defendants in criminal cases; trial by an impartial jury is all that is secured. The number of challenges is left to be regulated by the common law or the enactments of Congress. That body has seen fit to treat several defendants, for this purpose, as one party. If the defendants would avail themselves of this privilege they must act accordingly. It may be . . . that all defendants may not wish to exercise the right of peremptory challenge as to the same person or persons, and that some may wish to challenge those who are unobjectionable to others. But this situation arises from the exercise of a privilege granted by the legislative authority and does not invalidate the law. The privilege must be taken with the limitations placed upon the manner of its exercise." Stilson v. United States, 250 U.S. 583, 586–87 (1919).

451. 4 W. Blackstone, Commentaries *353: "[I]n criminal cases, or at least in capital cases, there is, *in favorem vitae*, allowed to the prisoner an arbitrary and capricious species of challenge to a certain number of jurors, without showing any cause at all; which is called a *peremptory* challenge: a provision full of that tenderness and humanity to prisoners, for which our English laws are justly famous. This is grounded on two reasons. 1. As every one must be sensible what sudden impressions and unaccountable prejudices we are apt to conceive upon the bare looks and gestures of another; and how necessary it is, that a prisoner (when put to defend his life) should have a good opinion of his jury, the want of which might totally disconcert him; the law wills not that he should be tried by any one man against whom he has conceived a prejudice, even without being able to assign a reason for such his dislike. 2. Because, upon challenges for cause shown, if the reasons assigned prove insufficient to set aside the juror, perhaps the bare questioning his indifference may sometimes provoke a resentment; to prevent all ill consequences from which the prisoner is still at liberty, if he pleases, peremptorily to set him aside."

452. The defendant in a capital murder case was required to use a peremptory challenge, one of nine available to the defense, to remove a juror whom the judge erroneously failed to remove for cause. None of the jurors who finally composed the jury was subject to challenge. State law provided that a defendant use peremptory challenges to remove jurors who should have been but were not removed for cause. In these circumstances, the Court concluded, although the defendant had been erroneously deprived of one of his peremptory challenges, there was no violation of his right to an impartial jury or any other constitutional right. Peremptory challenges are within the disposition of the state and are not required by the Constitution. Ross v. Oklahoma, 487 U.S. 81 (1988) (5–4). *Ross* was followed in United States v. Martinez-Salazar, 528 U.S. 304 (2000).

Batson v. Kentucky

476 U.S. 79, 106 S.Ct. 1712, 90 L.Ed.2d 69 (1986)

■ JUSTICE POWELL delivered the opinion of the Court.

This case requires us to reexamine that portion of Swain v. Alabama, 380 U.S. 202 (1965), concerning the evidentiary burden placed on a criminal defendant who claims that he has been denied equal protection through the State's use of peremptory challenges to exclude members of his race from the petit jury.

I

Petitioner, a black man, was indicted in Kentucky on charges of second-degree burglary and receipt of stolen goods. On the first day of trial in Jefferson Circuit Court, the judge conducted voir dire examination of the venire, excused certain jurors for cause, and permitted the parties to exercise peremptory challenges. The prosecutor used his peremptory challenges to strike all four black persons on the venire, and a jury composed only of white persons was selected. Defense counsel moved to discharge the jury before it was sworn on the ground that the prosecutor's removal of the black veniremen violated petitioner's rights under the Sixth and Fourteenth Amendments to a jury drawn from a cross-section of the community, and under the Fourteenth Amendment to equal protection of the laws. Counsel requested a hearing on his motion. Without expressly ruling on the request for a hearing, the trial judge observed that the parties were entitled to use their peremptory challenges to "strike anybody they want to." The judge then denied petitioner's motion, reasoning that the cross-section requirement applies only to selection of the venire and not to selection of the petit jury itself.

The jury convicted petitioner on both counts. On appeal to the Supreme Court of Kentucky, petitioner pressed, among other claims, the argument concerning the prosecutor's use of peremptory challenges. Conceding that Swain v. Alabama, supra, apparently foreclosed an equal protection claim based solely on the prosecutor's conduct in this case, petitioner urged the court to follow decisions of other states . . . and to hold that such conduct violated his rights under the Sixth Amendment and Section 11 of the Kentucky Constitution to a jury drawn from a cross-section of the community. Petitioner also contended that the facts showed that the prosecutor had engaged in a "pattern" of discriminatory challenges in this case and established an equal protection violation under *Swain*.

The Supreme Court of Kentucky affirmed. In a single paragraph, the court declined petitioner's invitation to adopt the reasoning of [the other state courts]. The court observed that it recently had reaffirmed its reliance on *Swain*, and had held that a defendant alleging lack of a fair cross-section must demonstrate systematic exclusion of a group of jurors from the venire. . . . We granted certiorari . . . and now reverse.

II

In Swain v. Alabama, this Court recognized that a "State's purposeful or deliberate denial to Negroes on account of race of participation as jurors in the administration of justice violates the Equal Protection Clause." 380 U.S., at 203–204. This principle has been "consistently and repeatedly" reaffirmed, id., at 204, in numerous decisions of this Court both preceding and following *Swain*. We reaffirm the principle today.

A

More than a century ago, the Court decided that the State denies a black defendant equal protection of the laws when it puts him on trial before a jury from which members of his race have been purposefully excluded. Strauder v. West Virginia, 100 U.S. 303 (1880). That decision laid the foundation for the Court's unceasing efforts to eradicate racial discrimination in the procedures used to select the venire from which individual jurors are drawn. In *Strauder*, the Court explained that the central concern of the recently ratified Fourteenth Amendment was to put an end to governmental discrimination on account of race. . . . Exclusion of black citizens from service as jurors constitutes a primary example of the evil the Fourteenth Amendment was designed to cure.

In holding that racial discrimination in jury selection offends the Equal Protection Clause, the Court in *Strauder* recognized, however, that a defendant has no right to a "petit jury composed in whole or in part of persons of his own race." Id., at 305. "The number of our races and nationalities stands in the way of evolution of such a conception" of the demand of equal protection. Akins v. Texas, 325 U.S. 398, 403 (1945). But the defendant does have the right to be tried by a jury whose members are selected pursuant to nondiscriminatory criteria. . . . The Equal Protection Clause guarantees the defendant that the State will not exclude members of his race from the jury venire on account of race . . . or on the false assumption that members of his race as a group are not qualified to serve as jurors. . . .

Purposeful racial discrimination in selection of the venire violates a defendant's right to equal protection because it denies him the protection that a trial by jury is intended to secure. "The very idea of a jury is a body . . . composed of the peers or equals of the person whose rights it is selected or summoned to determine; that is, of his neighbors, fellows, associates, persons having the same legal status in society as that which he holds." *Strauder*, supra, at 308. . . . The petit jury has occupied a central position in our system of justice by safeguarding a person accused of crime against the arbitrary exercise of power by prosecutor or judge. . . . Those on the venire must be "indifferently chosen,"[3] to secure the defendant's right under the Fourteenth Amendment to "protection of life and liberty against race or color prejudice." *Strauder*, supra, at 309.

Racial discrimination in selection of jurors harms not only the accused whose life or liberty they are summoned to try. Competence to serve as a juror ultimately depends on an assessment of individual qualifications and ability impartially to consider evidence presented at a trial. . . . A person's race simply "is unrelated to his fitness as a juror." [Thiel v. Southern Pacific Co., 328 U.S. 217 (1946)], at 227 (Frankfurter, J., dissenting). As long ago as *Strauder*, therefore, the Court recognized that by denying a person participation in jury service on account of his race, the State unconstitutionally discriminated against the excluded juror. . . .

The harm from discriminatory jury selection extends beyond that inflicted on the defendant and the excluded juror to touch the entire community. Selection procedures that purposefully exclude black persons from juries undermine public confidence in the fairness of our system of justice. . . . Discrimination within the judicial system is most pernicious because it is "a stimulant to that race prejudice which is an impediment to securing to [black citizens] that equal justice which the law aims to secure to all others." *Strauder*, supra, at 308.

B

In *Strauder*, the Court invalidated a state statute that provided that only white men could serve as jurors. . . . We can be confident that no state now has such a law. The Constitution requires, however, that we look beyond the fact of the statute defining juror qualifications and also consider challenged selections practices to afford "protection against action of the State through its administrative officers in effecting the prohibited discrimination." Norris v. Alabama, 294 U.S. [587 (1935)], at 589. . . . Thus, the Court has found a denial of equal protection whether the procedures implementing a neutral statute operated to exclude persons from the venire on racial grounds, and has made clear that the Constitution prohibits all forms of purposeful racial discrimination in selection of jurors. While decisions of this Court have been concerned largely with discrimination during selection of the venire, the principles announced there also forbid discrimination on account of race in selection of the petit jury. Since the Fourteenth Amendment protects an accused throughout the proceedings bringing him to justice . . . the State may not draw up its jury lists pursuant to neutral procedures but then resort to discrimination at "other stages in the selection process," Avery v. Georgia, 345 U.S. 559, 562 (1953). . . .

3. 4 W. Blackstone, Commentaries 350 (Cooley ed. 1899). . . .

Accordingly, the component of the jury selection process at issue here, the State's privilege to strike individual jurors through peremptory challenges, is subject to the commands of the Equal Protection Clause. Although a prosecutor ordinarily is entitled to exercise permitted peremptory challenges "for any reason at all, as long as that reason is related to his view concerning the outcome" of the case to be tried, United States v. Robinson, 421 F.Supp. 467, 473 (Conn.1976), mandamus granted sub nom. United States v. Newman, 549 F.2d 240 (CA2 1977), the Equal Protection Clause forbids the prosecutor to challenge potential jurors solely on account of their race or on the assumption that black jurors as a group will be unable impartially to consider the State's case against a black defendant.

III

The principles announced in *Strauder* never have been questioned in any subsequent decision of this Court. Rather, the Court has been called upon repeatedly to review the application of those principles to particular facts. A recurring question in these cases, as in any case alleging a violation of the Equal Protection Clause, was whether the defendant had met his burden of proving purposeful discrimination on the part of the State. . . . That question also was at the heart of the portion of Swain v. Alabama we reexamine today.

A

Swain required the Court to decide, among other issues, whether a black defendant was denied equal protection by the State's exercise of peremptory challenges to exclude members of his race from the petit jury. . . . The record in *Swain* showed that the prosecutor had used the State's peremptory challenges to strike the six black persons included on the petit jury venire. . . . While rejecting the defendant's claim for failure to prove purposeful discrimination, the Court nonetheless indicated that the Equal Protection Clause placed some limits on the State's exercise of peremptory challenges. . . .

The Court sought to accommodate the prosecutor's historical privilege of peremptory challenge free of judicial control . . . and the constitutional prohibition on exclusion of persons from jury service on account of race. . . . While the Constitution does not confer a right to peremptory challenges . . . those challenges traditionally have been viewed as one means of assuring the selection of a qualified and unbiased jury. . . . To preserve the peremptory nature of the prosecutor's challenge, the Court in *Swain* declined to scrutinize his actions in a particular case by relying on a presumption that he properly exercised the State's challenges. . . .

The Court went on to observe, however, that a State may not exercise its challenges in contravention of the Equal Protection Clause. It was impermissible for a prosecutor to use his challenges to exclude blacks from the jury "for reasons wholly unrelated to the outcome of the particular case on trial" or to deny to blacks "the same right and opportunity to participate in the administration of justice enjoyed by the white population." [380

U.S.], at 224. Accordingly, a black defendant could make out a prima facie case of purposeful discrimination on proof that the peremptory challenge system was "being perverted" in that manner. Ibid. For example, an inference of purposeful discrimination would be raised on evidence that a prosecutor, "in case after case, whatever the circumstances, whatever the crime and whoever the defendant or the victim may be, is responsible for the removal of Negroes who have been selected as qualified jurors by the jury commissioners and who have survived challenges for cause, with the result that no Negroes ever serve on petit juries." Id., at 223. Evidence offered by the defendant in *Swain* did not meet that standard. While the defendant showed that prosecutors in the jurisdiction had exercised their strikes to exclude blacks from the jury, he offered no proof of the circumstances under which prosecutors were responsible for striking black jurors beyond the facts of his own case. . . .

A number of lower courts following the teaching of *Swain* reasoned that proof of repeated striking of blacks over a number of cases was necessary to establish a violation of the Equal Protection Clause. Since this interpretation of *Swain* has placed on defendants a crippling burden of proof, prosecutors' peremptory challenges are now largely immune from constitutional scrutiny. For reasons that follow, we reject this evidentiary formulation as inconsistent with standards that have been developed since *Swain* for assessing a prima facie case under the Equal Protection Clause.

. . .

C

The standards for assessing a prima facie case in the context of discriminatory selection of the venire have been fully articulated since *Swain*. . . . These principles support our conclusion that a defendant may establish a prima facie case of purposeful discrimination in selection of the petit jury solely on evidence concerning the prosecutor's exercise of peremptory challenges at the defendant's trial. To establish such a case, the defendant first must show that he is a member of a cognizable racial group . . . and that the prosecutor has exercised peremptory challenges to remove from the venire members of the defendant's race. Second, the defendant is entitled to rely on the fact, as to which there can be no dispute, that peremptory challenges constitute a jury selection practice that permits "those to discriminate who are of a mind to discriminate." Avery v. Georgia, supra, at 562. Finally, the defendant must show that these facts and any other relevant circumstances raise an inference that the prosecutor used that practice to exclude the veniremen from the petit jury on account of their race. This combination of factors in the empanelling of the petit jury, as in the selection of the venire, raises the necessary inference of purposeful discrimination.

In deciding whether the defendant has made the requisite showing, the trial court should consider all relevant circumstances. For example, a "pattern" of strikes against black jurors included in the particular venire might give rise to an inference of discrimination. Similarly, the prosecutor's questions and statements during voir dire examination and in exercising his challenges may support or refute an inference of discriminatory purpose. These examples are merely illustrative. We have confidence that trial judges, experienced in supervising voir dire, will be able to decide if the circumstances concerning the prosecutor's use of peremptory challenges creates a prima facie case of discrimination against black jurors.

Once the defendant makes a prima facie showing, the burden shifts to the State to come forward with a neutral explanation for challenging black jurors. Though this requirement imposes a limitation in some cases on the full peremptory character of the historic challenge, we emphasize that the prosecutor's explanation need not rise to the level justifying exercise of a challenge for cause. . . . But the prosecutor may not rebut the defendant's prima facie case of discrimination by stating merely that he challenged jurors of the defendant's race on the assumption—or his intuitive judgment—that they would be partial to the defendant because of their shared race. . . . Just as the Equal Protection Clause forbids the States to exclude black persons from the venire on the assumption that blacks as a group are unqualified to serve as jurors . . . so it forbids the States to strike black veniremen on the assumption that they will be biased in a particular case simply because the defendant is black. The core guarantee of equal protection, ensuring citizens that their State will not discriminate on account of race, would be meaningless were we to approve the exclusion of jurors on the basis of such assumptions, which arise solely from the jurors' race. Nor may the prosecutor rebut the defendant's case merely by denying that he had a discriminatory motive or "affirm[ing his] good faith in individual selections." Alexander v. Louisiana, 405 U.S., at 632. If these general assertions were accepted as rebutting a defendant's prima facie case, the Equal Protection Clause "would be but a vain and illusory requirement." Norris v. Alabama, supra, at 598. The prosecutor therefore must articulate a neutral explanation related to the particular case to be tried. The trial court then will have the duty to determine if the defendant has established purposeful discrimination.

IV

The State contends that our holding will eviscerate the fair trial values served by the peremptory challenge. Conceding that the Constitution does not guarantee a right to peremptory challenges and that *Swain* did state that their use ultimately is subject to the strictures of equal protection, the State argues that the privilege of unfettered exercise of the challenge is of vital importance to the criminal justice system.

While we recognize, of course, that the peremptory challenge occupies an important position in our trial procedures, we do not agree that our decision today will undermine the contribution the challenge generally makes to the administration of justice. The reality of practice, amply reflected in many state and federal court opinions, shows that the challenge may be, and unfortunately at times has been, used to discriminate against black jurors. By requiring trial courts to be sensitive to the racially discriminatory use of peremptory challenges, our decision enforces the mandate of equal protection and furthers the ends of justice. In view of the heterogeneous population of our Nation, public respect for our criminal justice system and the rule of law will be strengthened if we ensure that no citizen is disqualified from jury service because of his race.

Nor are we persuaded by the State's suggestion that our holding will create serious administrative difficulties. In those states applying a version of the evidentiary standard we recognize today, courts have not experienced serious administrative burdens, and the peremptory challenge system has survived. We decline, however, to formulate particular procedures to be followed upon a defendant's timely objection to a prosecutor's challenges.

V

In this case, petitioner made a timely objection to the prosecutor's removal of all black persons on the venire. Because the trial court flatly rejected the objection without requiring the prosecutor to give an explanation for his action, we remand this case for further proceedings. If the trial court decides that the facts establish, prima facie, purposeful discrimination and the prosecutor does not come forward with a neutral explanation for his action, our precedents require that petitioner's conviction be reversed. . . . [4]

. . . [5]

---

453. A *Batson* claim is discussed at length in Miller-El v. Cockrell, 537 U.S. 322 (2003) (8–1).

Does *Batson* apply to separately identifiable groups other than African-Americans? Cf. Hernandez v. New York, below. See generally United States v. Di Pasquale, 864 F.2d 271 (3d Cir.1988) (Italian-Americans; question not answered). Cases holding that *Batson* does extend to other groups are cited in *Di Pasquale*.

In Murchu v. United States, 926 F.2d 50 (1st Cir.1991), the defendant was prosecuted for offenses involving the illegal exportation of firearms for use by the Irish Republican Army. The prosecutor used peremptory challenges to exclude several jurors with Irish surnames. The defendant also challenged several jurors with Irish surnames, and several persons who served on the jury had "arguably Irish surnames." The defendant argued that the prosecutor's peremptory challenges were invalid on *Batson* grounds. The argument was rejected on the ground that the defendant had

4. To the extent that anything in Swain v. Alabama, 380 U.S. 202 (1965), is contrary to the principles we articulate today, that decision is overruled.

[5] Justice White, Justice Marshall, and Justice O'Connor wrote concurring opinions. Justice Stevens wrote a concurring opinion, which Justice Brennan joined. Chief Justice Burger wrote a dissenting opinion, which Justice Rehnquist joined. Justice Rehnquist wrote a dissenting opinion, which Chief Justice Burger joined.

not established that persons of Irish ancestry are a cognizable group for *Batson* purposes.

In Holland v. Illinois, 493 U.S. 474 (1990) (5–4), the Court held that a white defendant's right under the Sixth Amendment to be tried by an impartial jury was not violated by a prosecutor's exercise of peremptory challenges to exclude the two black persons on the jury panel, even if the challenges were based on race. The Sixth Amendment requires that the panel be composed of a fair cross section of the community, but not that the jury itself be so composed.

The Equal Protection Clause is, however, applicable in such a case. Powers v. Ohio, 499 U.S. 400 (1991) (7–2). "[T]he Equal Protection Clause prohibits a prosecutor from using the State's peremptory challenges to exclude otherwise qualified and unbiased persons from the petit jury solely by reason of their race, a practice that forecloses a significant opportunity to participate in civic life. An individual juror does not have a right to sit on any particular petit jury, but he or she does possess the right not to be excluded from one on account of race." Id. at 409. "[A] criminal defendant may object to race-based exclusions of jurors effected through peremptory challenges whether or not the defendant and the excluded juror share the same race." Id. at 402. See Trevino v. Texas, 503 U.S. 562 (1992).

In Hernandez v. New York, 500 U.S. 352 (1991) (6–3), the Court upheld a state trial court's rejection of a *Batson* claim, saying that a trial court's conclusion that the prosecutor's peremptory challenges were not racially based should not be overturned on review unless it is clearly erroneous. The Court said also that "disparate impact should be given appropriate weight in determining whether the prosecutor acted with a forbidden intent," but it was not conclusive on the question whether a peremptory challenge is prima facie racially based. Id. at 362. In *Hernandez*, the defendant was Hispanic. The prosecutor challenged two bilingual Hispanic jurors, on the ground that he questioned their ability to accept the official translator's rendition of testimony in Spanish. The Court said that although in some contexts language proficiency might be a surrogate for race, whether that was so or not depended on the circumstances of the case.

See, e.g., United States v. Uwaezhoke, 995 F.2d 388 (3d Cir.1993) (peremptory challenge of black juror because she was a postal employee and might be involved in a "drug situation" was not facially invalid; finding that there was no discriminatory intent was not clearly erroneous); United States v. Bishop, 959 F.2d 820 (9th Cir.1992) (peremptory challenge of black juror, based in part on fact that juror lived in predominantly low income, black neighborhood and, the prosecutor thought, was therefore likely to believe that police "pick on black people," was not racially neutral); United States v. Dawn, 897 F.2d 1444 (8th Cir.1990) (use of six of seven peremptory challenges to exclude black jurors did not by itself establish prima facie case of discrimination); United States v. Horsley, 864 F.2d 1543 (11th Cir.1989) (peremptory challenge of single black juror made prima facie case of discrimination).

454. J.E.B. v. Alabama ex rel. T.B. The Equal Protection Clause prohibits peremptory challenges based solely on gender. 511 U.S. 127 (1994) (6–3). *J.E.B.* was a civil case, in which the State, acting on behalf of the mother of a minor child, brought a paternity action and a claim for child support against the petitioner. The State used its peremptory challenges to remove male jurors and the petitioner used his to strike female jurors. The jury was composed entirely of women. Reviewing the history of discrimination against women with respect to jury service, the Court said: "Intentional discrimination on the basis of gender by state actors violates the Equal Protection Clause, particularly where, as here, the discrimination serves to ratify and perpetuate invidious, archaic, and overbroad stereotypes about the relative abilities of men and women." Id. at 130–31. Responding to the State's contention that its challenges to male jurors were reasonably based on the perception that men would be more sympathetic to the petitioner than women, the Court said: "The Equal Protection Clause . . . acknowledges that a shred of truth may be contained in some stereotypes, but requires that state actors look beyond the surface before making judgments about people that are likely to stigmatize as well as to perpetuate historical patterns of discrimination." Id. at 139 n.11.

455. In Georgia v. McCollum, 505 U.S. 42 (1992) (7–2), the Court answered a question left open in *Batson*, 476 U.S. at 89 n.12, and barred racially-based peremptory challenges by the defense. "We hold that the Constitution prohibits a criminal defendant from engaging in purposeful discrimination on the ground of race in the exercise of peremptory challenges. Accordingly, if the State demonstrates a prima facie case of racial discrimination by the defendants, the defendants must articulate a racially neutral explanation for peremptory challenges." 505 U.S. at 59. The case involved charges of assault and battery by white defendants against black victims. The Court said: " '[B]e it at the hands of the State or the defense,' if a court allows jurors to be excluded because of group bias, '[it] is a willing participant in a scheme that could only undermine the very foundation of our system of justice—our citizens' confidence in it.' State v. Alvarado, 534 A.2d 440, 442 (1987). Just as public confidence in criminal justice is undermined by a conviction in a trial where racial discrimination has occurred in jury selection, so is public confidence undermined where a defendant, assisted by racially discriminatory peremptory strikes, obtains an acquittal." 505 U.S. at 49–50.

The Court found that peremptory challenges by the defense involved state action that implicated the Equal Protection Clause. "In exercising a peremptory challenge, a criminal defendant is wielding the power to choose a quintessential governmental body—indeed, the institution of government on which our judicial system depends." Id. at 54. Also, the State had standing to oppose discriminatory peremptory challenges. "As the representative of all its citizens, the State is the logical and proper party to assert the invasion of the constitutional rights of the excluded jurors in a criminal trial." Id. at 56.

456. "The well-settled rule is that, given a lawfully selected panel, free from any taint of invalid exclusions or procedures in selection and from which all disqualified for cause have been excused, no cause for complaint arises merely from the fact that the jury finally chosen happens itself not to be representative of the panel or indeed of the community." Frazier v. United States, 335 U.S. 497, 507–508 (1948).

457. In Witherspoon v. Illinois, 391 U.S. 510 (1968), the Court held that in a capital case in which the jury had responsibility for fixing the penalty and imposed a sentence of death, a jury from which were excluded "all who expressed conscientious or religious scruples against capital punishment and all who opposed it in principle," id. at 520, "fell woefully short of that impartiality to which the petitioner was entitled under the Sixth and Fourteenth Amendments," id. at 518.

"A man who opposes the death penalty, no less than one who favors it, can make the discretionary judgment entrusted to him by the State and can thus obey the oath he takes as a juror. But a jury from which all such men have been excluded cannot perform the task demanded of it. Guided by neither rule nor standard, 'free to select or reject as it [sees] fit,'[6] a jury that must choose between life imprisonment and capital punishment can do little more—and must do nothing less—than express the conscience of the community on the ultimate question of life or death. Yet, in a nation less than half of whose people believe in the death penalty, a jury composed exclusively of such people cannot speak for the community. Culled of all who harbor doubts about the wisdom of capital punishment—of all who would be reluctant to pronounce the extreme penalty—such a jury can speak only for a distinct and dwindling minority." Id. at 519–20.

The Court said that it would be permissible to exclude persons who stated that their opposition to capital punishment would prevent them from even considering imposition of the death penalty. And with respect to the verdict of guilt, the jury was acceptable; the evidence was "too tentative and fragmentary to establish that jurors not opposed to the death penalty tend to favor the prosecution in the determination of guilt." Id. at 517.

Witherspoon was applied in Adams v. Texas, 448 U.S. 38 (1980) (8–1). There the Court held that the exclusion of jurors "whose only fault was to take their responsibilities with special seriousness or to acknowledge honestly that they might or might not be affected" by the fact that capital punishment was involved went beyond the inquiry allowed by *Witherspoon* and was constitutionally impermissible. Id. at 50–51. The Constitution does not "permit the exclusion of jurors . . . if they aver that they will honestly find the facts and answer the questions in the affirmative if they are convinced beyond reasonable doubt, but not otherwise, yet who frankly concede that the prospects of the death penalty may affect what their honest judgment of the facts will be or what they may deem to be a reasonable doubt. Such assessments and judgments by jurors are inherent in the jury system, and to exclude all jurors who would be in the slightest

6. People v. Bernette, 197 N.E.2d 436, 443 (Ill.1964).

way affected by the prospect of the death penalty or by their views about such a penalty would be to deprive the defendant of the impartial jury to which he or she is entitled under the law." Id. at 50. See also Lockett v. Ohio, 438 U.S. 586 (1978), and Davis v. Georgia, 429 U.S. 122 (1976) (6–3).

Adams was reaffirmed in Wainwright v. Witt, 469 U.S. 412 (1985) (7–2). The proper standard for excluding a juror for cause because of the juror's views on capital punishment is "whether the juror's views would 'prevent or substantially impair the performance of his duties as a juror in accordance with his instructions and his oath' " (quoting from *Adams*, 448 U.S. at 45). Qualifying *Witherspoon*, the Court emphasized that, to be excludable, a juror need not assert that he would "automatically" vote against capital punishment; nor need a juror's inability to apply the law because of objections to capital punishment be shown with "unmistakable clarity." See Darden v. Wainwright, 477 U.S. 168 (1986) (5–4).

Extending a point made in *Witherspoon*, in Lockhart v. McCree, 476 U.S. 162, 165 (1986) (6–3), the Court held that the Constitution does not prohibit "the removal for cause, prior to the guilt phase of a bifurcated capital trial, of prospective jurors whose opposition to the death penalty is so strong that it would prevent or substantially impair the performance of their duties as jurors at the sentencing phase of the trial." In *Lockhart*, the Court assumed that a "death-qualified" jury was somewhat more likely to convict than one not so qualified. The requirement of a "fair cross-section" of the community, it said, applied to the process of selecting a jury, not its actual composition. And in any case, "groups defined solely in terms of shared attitudes that would prevent or substantially impair members of the group from performing one of their duties as jurors" are not distinctive groups for that purpose. Id. at 174. The Court noted that a state might properly want to have a single jury decide both the guilt and sentencing phases of a capital case. Id. at 175–76. Relying on Lockhart v. McCree, the Court held that the "death qualification" of jurors for the guilt phase of a joint trial at which the codefendant but not the defendant was subject to capital punishment did not violate the defendant's right to an impartial jury. Buchanan v. Kentucky, 483 U.S. 402 (1987) (6–3).

The erroneous exclusion for cause of a juror in a capital case, who is eligible under *Witherspoon*, is reversible constitutional error and may not be treated as harmless error. Gray v. Mississippi, 481 U.S. 648 (1987) (5–4).

In a capital case, in which the jury determines on the basis of aggravating and mitigating factors whether the death penalty should be imposed, the trial court may not refuse to ask potential jurors whether they would automatically impose the death penalty if the defendant were found guilty. Morgan v. Illinois, 504 U.S. 719 (1992) (6–3). "A juror who will automatically vote for the death penalty in every case will fail in good faith to consider the evidence of aggravating and mitigating circumstances as the instructions require him to do. . . . Therefore, based on the requirement of impartiality embodied in the Due Process Clause of the Fourteenth Amendment, a capital defendant may challenge for cause any prospective juror who maintains such views. If even one such juror is empaneled and the death sentence is imposed, the State is disentitled to execute the sentence." Id. at 729.

458. Does a defendant who is prosecuted in the District of Columbia for violation of the federal narcotics laws have the right to challenge for cause prospective jurors who are employees of the federal government? If not, does he have the right to challenge for cause employees of the Department of the Treasury whose work is not connected with the Bureau of Narcotics (administratively within the department)? Assuming that the answer to the first question is "No," is there a valid objection to a jury composed entirely of government employees as a consequence of the exercise of peremptory challenges by prosecution and defense, without any intention to obtain that result on the part of the prosecution? See Frazier v. United States, 335 U.S. 497 (1948). If the defendant were being tried for willfully failing to comply with a subpoena to appear before the Committee on Un-American Activities of the House of Representatives, would he have the right to challenge federal employees for cause? See Dennis v. United States, 339 U.S. 162 (1950). See generally United States v. Segal, 534 F.2d 578 (3d Cir.1976).

459. The defendant was prosecuted for narcotics violations. Shortly before the defendant's trial, some of the persons on the jury panel had been jurors in another case in which a government agent scheduled to testify in the defendant's trial had also testified. The defendant in the prior case had been convicted. Should the defendant's challenges for cause of the persons who had been jurors in the prior case be allowed? See United States v. Garcia, 936 F.2d 648 (2d Cir.1991). If a prospective juror previously sat on a case in which the same prosecutor appeared, should the defendant's challenge of the juror for cause be allowed? See generally United States v. Jefferson, 569 F.2d 260 (5th Cir.1978); United States v. Jones, 486 F.2d 476 (8th Cir.1973).

Less than a week before the defendant's trial for murder, several of the jurors had sat on a jury in a criminal case before another judge; the defendant in that case was tried for embezzlement and was acquitted. After the jury had returned its verdict, the judge criticized it for not convicting the defendant and said that he would have found the defendant guilty in "about two minutes." During the voir dire at the defendant's trial, defense counsel sought to ask prospective jurors who had participated in the earlier case whether the judge's comments would make them more likely to convict the defendant. The judge did not allow the questions. Treating the issue as one involving pretrial publicity (surrounding the verdict in the prior case), see note 460 below, the court of appeals held that the defendant had not been denied a fair trial. Wells v. Murray, 831 F.2d 468 (4th Cir.1987) (additional cases discussed).

460. Pretrial publicity. In Irvin v. Dowd, 366 U.S. 717 (1961), the petitioner was convicted of murder in the Indiana courts and sentenced to death. He sought a writ of habeas corpus based on the claim that he did not receive a fair trial. The Court upheld the claim and vacated the conviction.

It is not required . . . that the jurors be totally ignorant of the facts and issues involved. In these days of swift, widespread and diverse methods of communication, an important case can be expected to arouse the interest of the public in the vicinity, and scarcely any of those best qualified to serve as jurors will not have formed some impression or opinion as to the merits of the case. This is particularly true in criminal cases. To hold that the mere existence of any preconceived notion as to the guilt or innocence of an accused, without more, is sufficient to rebut the presumption of a prospective juror's impartiality would be to establish an impossible standard. It is sufficient if the juror can lay aside his impression or opinion and render a verdict based on the evidence presented in court. . . .

The adoption of such a rule, however, "cannot foreclose inquiry as to whether, in a given case, the application of that rule works a deprivation of the prisoner's life or liberty without due process of law." Lisenba v. California, 314 U.S. 219, 236. As stated in Reynolds [v. United States, 98 U.S. 145 (1878)], the test is "whether the nature and strength of the opinion formed are such as in law necessarily . . . raise the presumption of partiality. The question thus presented is one of mixed law and fact. . . ." At p. 156. "The affirmative of the issue is upon the challenger. Unless he shows the actual existence of such an opinion in the mind of the juror as will raise the presumption of partiality, the juror need not necessarily be set aside. . . . If a positive and decided opinion had been formed, he would have been incompetent even though it had not been expressed." At p. 157. . . .

. . .

Here the build-up of prejudice is clear and convincing. An examination of the then current community pattern of thought as indicated by the popular news media is singularly revealing. For example, petitioner's first motion for a change of venue from Gibson County alleged that the awaited trial of petitioner had become the *cause célèbre* of this small community—so much so that curbstone opinions, not only as to petitioner's guilt but even as to what punishment he should receive, were solicited and recorded on the public streets by a roving reporter, and later were broadcast over the local stations. A reading of the 46 exhibits which petitioner attached to his motion indicates that a barrage of newspaper headlines, articles, cartoons and pictures was unleashed against him during the six or seven months preceding his trial. The motion further alleged that the newspapers in which the stories appeared were delivered regularly to approximately 95% of the dwellings in Gibson County and that, in addition, the Evansville radio and TV stations, which likewise blanketed that county, also carried extensive newscasts covering the same incidents. These stories revealed the details of his background, including a reference to crimes committed when a juvenile, his convictions for arson almost 20 years previously, for burglary and by a court-martial on AWOL charges during the war. He was accused of being a parole violator. The headlines announced his police line-up identification, that he faced a lie detector test, had been placed at the scene of the crime and that the six murders were solved but petitioner refused to confess. Finally, they announced his confession to the six murders and the fact of his indictment for four of them in Indiana. They reported petitioner's offer to plead guilty if promised a 99-year sentence, but also the determination, on the other hand, of the prosecutor to secure the death penalty, and that petitioner had confessed to 24 burglaries (the *modus operandi* of these robberies was compared to that of the murders and the similarity noted). One story dramatically relayed the promise of a sheriff to devote his life to securing petitioner's execution by the State of Kentucky, where petitioner is alleged to have committed one of the six murders, if Indiana failed to do so. Another characterized petitioner as remorseless and without conscience but also as having been found sane by a court-appointed panel of doctors. In many of the stories petitioner was described as the "confessed slayer of six," a parole violator and fraudulent-check artist. Petitioner's court-appointed counsel was quoted as having received "much criticism over being Irvin's counsel" and it was pointed out, by way of excusing the attorney, that he would be subject to disbarment should he refuse to represent Irvin. On the day before the trial the newspapers carried the story that Irvin had orally admitted the murder of Kerr (the victim in this case) as well as "the robbery-murder of Mrs. Mary Holland; the murder of Mrs. Wilhelmina Sailer in Posey County, and the slaughter of three members of the Duncan family in Henderson County, Ky."

It cannot be gainsaid that the force of this continued adverse publicity caused a sustained excitement and fostered a strong prejudice among the people of Gibson County. In fact, on the second day devoted to the selection of the jury, the newspapers reported that "strong feelings, often bitter and angry, rumbled to the surface," and that "the extent to which the multiple murders—three in one family—have aroused feelings throughout the area was emphasized Friday when 27 of the 35 prospective jurors questioned were excused for holding biased pretrial opinions. . . ." A few days later the feeling was described as "a pattern of deep and bitter prejudice against the former pipe-fitter." Spectator comments, as printed by the newspapers, were "my mind is made up"; "I think he is guilty"; and "he should be hanged."

Finally, and with remarkable understatement, the headlines reported that "impartial jurors are hard to find." The panel consisted of 430 persons. The court itself excused 268 of those on challenges for cause as having fixed opinions as to the guilt of petitioner; 103 were excused because of conscientious objection to the imposition of the death penalty; 20, the maximum allowed, were peremptorily challenged by petitioner and 10 by the State; 12 persons and two alternates were selected as jurors and the rest were excused on personal grounds, e.g., deafness, doctor's orders, etc. An examination of the 2,783-page voir dire record shows that 370 prospective jurors or almost 90% of those examined on the point (10 members of the panel were never asked whether or not they had any opinion) entertained some opinion as to guilt—ranging in intensity from mere suspicion to absolute certainty. A number admitted that, if they were in the accused's place in the dock and he in theirs on the jury with their opinions, they would not want him on a jury.

Here the "pattern of deep and bitter prejudice" shown to be present throughout the community . . . was clearly reflected in the sum total of the voir dire examination of a majority of the jurors finally placed in the jury box. Eight out of the 12 thought petitioner was guilty. With such an opinion permeating their minds, it would be difficult to say that each could exclude this preconception of guilt from his deliberations. The influence that lurks in an opinion once formed is so persistent that it unconsciously fights detachment from the mental processes of the average man. . . . Where one's life is at stake—and accounting for the frailties of human nature—we can only say that in the light of the circumstances here the finding of impartiality does not meet constitutional standards. Two-thirds of the jurors had an opinion that petitioner was guilty and were familiar with the material facts and circumstances involved, including the fact that other murders were attributed to him, some going so far as to say that it would take evidence to overcome their belief. One said that he "could not . . . give the defendant the benefit of the doubt that he is innocent." Another stated that he had a "somewhat" certain fixed opinion as to petitioner's guilt. No doubt each juror was sincere when he said that he would be fair and impartial to petitioner, but the psychological impact requiring such a declaration before one's fellows is often its father. Where so many, so many times, admitted prejudice, such a statement of impartiality can be given little weight. As one of the jurors put it, "You can't forget what you hear and see." With his life at stake, it is not requiring too much that petitioner be tried in an atmosphere undisturbed by so huge a wave of public passion and by a jury other than one in which two-thirds of the members admit, before hearing any testimony, to possessing a belief in his guilt.

366 U.S. at 722–28.

See Patton v. Yount, 467 U.S. 1025 (1984) (6–2) (conviction sustained); Beck v. Washington, 369 U.S. 541 (1962) (same). See also Sheppard v. Maxwell, 384 U.S. 333, 335 (1966) (8–1), in which the Court concluded that "the massive, pervasive and prejudicial publicity that attended his prosecution" deprived the defendant of a fair trial. The Court emphasized both the pretrial publicity and the "carnival atmosphere at trial," id. at 358. The defendant, who was charged with murder, was subsequently retried and acquitted. The New York Times, Nov. 17, 1966, at 1.

In Mu'Min v. Virginia, 500 U.S. 415 (1991) (5–4), the Court considered the nature and extent of the voir dire required to test the defendant's claim of prejudicial pretrial publicity. The Court held that there was not an absolute requirement that the judge inquire into the specific content of what had been read by a juror who said that he had been exposed to news reports. It said that the trial judge has "wide discretion . . . in conducting voir dire in the area of pretrial publicity. . . . [T]his primary reliance on the judgment of the trial court makes good sense. The judge of that court sits in the locale where the publicity is said to have had its effect, and brings to his evaluation of any such claim his own perception of the depth and extent of news stories that might influence a juror. The trial court, of course, does not impute his own perceptions to the jurors who are being examined, but these perceptions should be of assistance to it in deciding how detailed an inquiry to make of the members of the jury venire." Id. at 427.

A state law that categorically denies a change of venue in a trial by jury for a misdemeanor regardless of the extent of local prejudice against the defendant violates the constitutional right to an impartial jury. Groppi v. Wisconsin, 400 U.S. 505 (1971). See Coleman v. Kemp, 778 F.2d 1487, 1538 (11th Cir.1985), in which the court, after discussing at length the pretrial publicity in a capital murder case, said, "If there were no constitutional right to a change in venue in the instant case, then one can conceive of virtually no case in which a change of venue would be a constitutional necessity."

461. Official witnesses. In a case in which the evidence against the defendant consists largely of the testimony of police officers, should defense counsel be permitted to ask prospective jurors whether they would give greater credence to the testimony of a police officer merely because he is an officer than they would give to the testimony of any other witness? See, e.g., United States v. Lancaster, 96 F.3d 734 (4th Cir.1996) (whether to ask question is within sound discretion of trial judge; no abuse of discretion); United States v. Baldwin, 607 F.2d 1295 (9th Cir.1979) (failure to ask question was error); United States v. Gassaway, 456 F.2d 624 (5th Cir. 1972) (failure to ask question was not abuse of discretion).

Ham v. South Carolina

409 U.S. 524, 93 S.Ct. 848, 35 L.Ed.2d 46 (1973)

■ MR. JUSTICE REHNQUIST delivered the opinion of the Court.

Petitioner was convicted in the South Carolina trial court of the possession of marihuana in violation of state law. He was sentenced to 18 months' confinement, and on appeal his conviction was affirmed by a divided South Carolina Supreme Court. . . . We granted certiorari limited to the question of whether the trial judge's refusal to examine jurors on voir dire as to possible prejudice against petitioner violated the latter's federal constitutional rights. . . .

Petitioner is a young, bearded Negro who has lived most of his life in Florence County, South Carolina. He appears to have been well known locally for his work in such civil rights activities as the Southern Christian

Leadership Conference and the Bi-Racial Committee of the City of Florence. He has never previously been convicted of a crime. His basic defense at the trial was that law enforcement officers were "out to get him" because of his civil rights activities, and that he had been framed on the drug charge.

Prior to the trial judge's voir dire examination of prospective jurors, petitioner's counsel requested the judge to ask jurors four questions relating to possible prejudice against petitioner.[7] The first two questions sought to elicit any possible racial prejudice against Negroes; the third question related to possible prejudice against beards; and the fourth dealt with pretrial publicity relating to the drug problem. The trial judge, while putting to the prospective jurors three general questions as to bias, prejudice, or partiality that are specified in the South Carolina statutes,[8] declined to ask any of the four questions posed by petitioner.

The dissenting justices in the Supreme Court of South Carolina thought that this Court's decision in Aldridge v. United States, 283 U.S. 308 (1931), was binding on the State. There a Negro who was being tried for the murder of a white policeman requested that prospective jurors be asked whether they entertained any racial prejudice. This Court reversed the judgment of conviction because of the trial judge's refusal to make such an inquiry. Mr. Chief Justice Hughes, writing for the Court, stated that the "essential demands of fairness" required the trial judge under the circumstances of that case to interrogate the veniremen with respect to racial prejudice upon the request of counsel for a Negro criminal defendant. Id., at 310.

The Court's opinion relied upon a number of state court holdings throughout the country to the same effect, but it was not expressly grounded upon any constitutional requirement. Since one of the purposes of the Due Process Clause of the Fourteenth Amendment is to insure these "essential demands of fairness," e.g., Lisenba v. California, 314 U.S. 219, 236 (1941), and since a principal purpose of the adoption of the Fourteenth

7. The four questions sought to be asked are the following:

"1. Would you fairly try this case on the basis of the evidence and disregarding the defendant's race?

"2. You have no prejudice against negroes? Against black people? You would not be influenced by the use of the term 'black'?

"3. Would you disregard the fact that this defendant wears a beard in deciding this case?

"4. Did you watch the television show about the local drug problem a few days ago when a local policeman appeared for a long time? Have you heard about that show? Have you read or heard about recent newspaper articles to the effect that the local drug problem is bad? Would you try this case solely on the basis of the evidence presented in this courtroom? Would you be influenced by the circumstances that the prosecution's witness, a police officer, has publicly spoken on TV about drugs?"

8. S.C.Code § 38–202 (1962). The three questions asked of all prospective jurors in this case were, in substance, the following:

"1. Have you formed or expressed any opinion as to the guilt or innocence of the defendant, Gene Ham?

"2. Are you conscious of any bias or prejudice for or against him?

"3. Can you give the State and the defendant a fair and impartial trial?"

Amendment was to prohibit the States from invidiously discriminating on the basis of race . . . we think that the Fourteenth Amendment required the judge in this case to interrogate the jurors upon the subject of racial prejudice. South Carolina law permits challenges for cause, and authorizes the trial judge to conduct voir dire examination of potential jurors. The State having created this statutory framework for the selection of juries, the essential fairness required by the Due Process Clause of the Fourteenth Amendment requires that under the facts shown by this record the petitioner be permitted to have the jurors interrogated on the issue of racial bias. . . .

We agree with the dissenting justices of the Supreme Court of South Carolina that the trial judge was not required to put the question in any particular form, or to ask any particular number of questions on the subject, simply because requested to do so by petitioner. The Court in *Aldridge* was at pains to point out, in a context where its authority within the federal system of courts allows a good deal closer supervision than does the Fourteenth Amendment, that the trial court "had a broad discretion as to the questions to be asked," 283 U.S., at 310. The discretion as to form and number of questions permitted by the Due Process Clause of the Fourteenth Amendment is at least as broad. In this context, either of the brief, general questions urged by the petitioner would appear sufficient to focus the attention of prospective jurors on any racial prejudice they might entertain.

The third of petitioner's proposed questions was addressed to the fact that he wore a beard. While we cannot say that prejudice against people with beards might not have been harbored by one or more of the potential jurors in this case, this is the beginning and not the end of the inquiry as to whether the Fourteenth Amendment required the trial judge to interrogate the prospective jurors about such possible prejudice. Given the traditionally broad discretion accorded to the trial judge in conducting voir dire, Aldridge v. United States, supra, and our inability to constitutionally distinguish possible prejudice against beards from a host of other possible similar prejudices, we do not believe the petitioner's constitutional rights were violated when the trial judge refused to put this question. The inquiry as to racial prejudice derives its constitutional stature from the firmly established precedent of *Aldridge* and the numerous state cases upon which it relied, and from a principal purpose as well as from the language of those who adopted the Fourteenth Amendment. The trial judge's refusal to inquire as to particular bias against beards, after his inquiries as to bias in general, does not reach the level of a constitutional violation.

Petitioner's final question related to allegedly prejudicial pretrial publicity. But the record before us contains neither the newspaper articles nor any description of the television program in question. Because of this lack of material in the record substantiating any pretrial publicity prejudicial to this petitioner, we have no occasion to determine the merits of his request to have this question posed on voir dire.

Because of the trial court's refusal to make any inquiry as to racial bias of the prospective jurors after petitioner's timely request therefor, the judgment of the Supreme Court of South Carolina is reversed.[9]

---

462. *Ham* was discussed and the circumstances of that case distinguished in Ristaino v. Ross, 424 U.S. 589 (1976) (6–2), involving a black defendant's prosecution for armed robbery and assault on a white security officer. The Court said: "The Constitution does not always entitle a defendant to have questions posed during voir dire specifically directed to matters that conceivably might prejudice veniremen against him. . . . [T]he State's obligation to the defendant to impanel an impartial jury generally can be satisfied by less than an inquiry into a specific prejudice feared by the defendant." Id. at 594–95. Unlike the special factors in *Ham*, the mere fact "that the victim of the crimes alleged was a white man and the defendants were Negroes" was not so likely "to distort the trial" that special inquiry was required. Id. at 597.

Ristaino v. Ross was distinguished in Turner v. Murray, 476 U.S. 28 (1986) (7–2), a capital case in which the defendant was black and the victim white. The Court held that "a capital defendant accused of an interracial crime is entitled to have prospective jurors informed of the race of the victim and questioned on the issue of racial bias." Id. at 36–37. That was necessary, the Court said, because there is otherwise "an unacceptable risk of racial prejudice infecting the capital sentence proceeding, in view of the fact that the crime involved interracial violence, the jury's broad discretion in capital sentencing, and the special seriousness of an improper sentence in a capital case." The Court held also (two different Justices dissenting from this portion of the Court's opinion), however, that *Ristaino* controlled with respect to the guilt phase of the trial, since the jury had no special discretion as to that.

Is it proper for the prosecutor or defense counsel to inquire into the religious beliefs of prospective jurors? If so, is it reversible error if the court does not allow defense counsel to ask prospective jurors whether they are affiliated with a church and, if so, what church? See Pope v. United States, 372 F.2d 710, 725–27 (8th Cir.1967), vacated, 392 U.S. 651 (1968). See United States v. Barnes, 604 F.2d 121, 133–43 (2d Cir.1979), for a full discussion of questioning prospective jurors about ethnic background and religion. The trial judge's refusal to ask such questions was upheld.

In United States v. Greer, 968 F.2d 433 (5th Cir.1992) (en banc), the defendants, members of a white supremacist group, were indicted for conspiring to deprive black, Hispanic, and Jewish persons of their constitutional rights. Defense counsel asked the trial judge to strike for cause all prospective jurors in those groups. The judge refused. Defense counsel also

[9] Justice Douglas and Justice Marshall wrote opinions concurring in part and dissenting in part.

asked the judge to ask prospective jurors whether they were Jewish, which request was also refused. The court of appeals held that the examination of prospective jurors for bias was adequate without that question and, sustaining both the trial judge's rulings, affirmed the convictions by an equally divided court. The dissenting judges concluded that the jurors should have been asked whether they were Jewish.

463. Should defense counsel be allowed to examine a list of the names and addresses (and occupations) of the jury panel before the voir dire? 18 U.S.C. § 3432, p. 848 above, provides that a person charged with a capital offense shall be given a list of the names and addresses of prospective jurors at least three days before trial.

In United States v. Gibbons, 602 F.2d 1044 (2d Cir.1979), counsel was given the names of prospective jurors but not their addresses. The trial judge denied defense counsel's request to ask potential jurors about their residence in New York beyond identifying the borough. On appeal, the defendant claimed that he was denied his right to exercise peremptory challenges. Affirming, the court said: "[T]he right of the peremptory challenge does not command a right to the peremptory question. Whatever the attorney's power to strike a number of venire-persons at will may be, to recognize a correlative right to question at will—without in any way identifying the motivating concern—would strip the judge of his control over the proceedings. Any question could be labelled necessary for some unspoken element in the decision to challenge peremptorily." Id. at 1051. See United States v. Edwards, 303 F.3d 606 (5th Cir.2002) (not an abuse of discretion to withhold information about potential jurors' names, addresses, and employment); United States v. Mansoori, 304 F.3d 635 (7th Cir. 2002) (error, but harmless, to withhold information about potential and actual jurors' names, addresses, and employment).

If the prosecuting attorney has a report of the FBI summarizing its investigation of the jury panel, for use at the voir dire, should the court direct him to furnish a copy of the report to defense counsel? See Best v. United States, 184 F.2d 131 (1st Cir.1950). See generally United States v. Falange, 426 F.2d 930 (2d Cir.1970).

464. Suppose that during the voir dire a prospective juror inadvertently fails to reveal facts that would have been the basis for a challenge for cause or which defense counsel would probably have regarded as warranting exercise of a peremptory challenge. If the person serves as a juror, the defendant is found guilty, and the undisclosed facts become known thereafter, what should be the result? See, e.g., Rushen v. Spain, 464 U.S. 114 (1983) (juror's knowledge of facts tangentially related to case; conviction sustained); United States v. Perkins, 748 F.2d 1519, 1529–34 (11th Cir. 1984) (juror's prior acquaintance with defendant, inter alia; conviction reversed); United States v. Vargas, 606 F.2d 341 (1st Cir.1979) (juror's history of mental illness and arrest record; conviction sustained). See also Dyer v. Calderon, 151 F.3d 970 (9th Cir.1998) (juror's false answers to questions warranted inference of bias; conviction reversed); Burton v. Johnson, 948 F.2d 1150 (10th Cir.1991) (juror's dishonest response to material question, correct answer to which would have provided basis for challenge for cause, denied defendant a fair trial).

465.

> We have long viewed with disfavor the practice prevailing in certain jurisdictions under which a party, ostensibly engaged in exploring the jury's qualifications, is in fact exercising hopefully sophisticated advocacy upon jurors whom it has no real intention of challenging. . . . This not only corrupts the purpose of the voir dire, but places undue emphasis upon those points the party so chooses to make.
>
> [I]n our opinion the purpose of the voir dire is to ascertain disqualifications, not to afford individual analysis in depth to permit a party to choose a jury that fits into some mold that he believes appropriate for his case.

Schlinsky v. United States, 379 F.2d 735, 738 (1st Cir.1967). Compare United States v. Dellinger, 472 F.2d 340, 366–70 (7th Cir.1972) (approving broad questioning).

466. The defendants were prosecuted for violation of the National Motor Vehicle Theft (Dyer) Act, 18 U.S.C. § 2312. Their defense was that they had the consent of the owner, a school principal, to their taking the automobile in question. They claimed that he had invited them to his home and performed a homosexual act on one of them; afterwards he gave them the automobile in return for their agreement not to expose him. If you were defense counsel, would you want to ask prospective jurors whether they would be prejudiced against the defendants if they asserted that the owner of the car had committed a homosexual act? If you were the trial judge, would you allow defense counsel to ask the question? If the trial judge did not allow the question and the defendants were convicted after presenting their defense, would you reverse on appeal? See Maguire v. United States, 358 F.2d 442 (10th Cir.1966).

467. Consider the following defense checklist for selection of jurors in a case involving the insanity defense:

> (1) *Religion.* Least desirable are Roman Catholics, with their "emphasis upon free will, moral responsibility and payment for sins." All "fundamentalist faiths," such as Mormon, Methodist, and Southern Baptist, are "generally non-receptive to the defense." Unitarians, Jews, Congregationalists, and Presbyterians are "most likely to understand the defense."
>
> (2) *Political Affiliation.* Party lines are not so important as "orientation toward liberalism." The "progressive, flexible viewpoint" is to be preferred to the conservative viewpoint. Members of extreme right-wing political groups should be avoided.
>
> (3) *Geographical Region.* The urban north is better than the rural south or the farming midwest. Self-reliant farmers and southern traditionalists should be avoided.

(4) *Nationality.* "For once the sentimental Irish and sympathetic Italian are to be avoided because of their affinity for Catholicism." Scandinavians are more desirable.

(5) *Occupation and Economic Status.* Inadequate education and "limitation of perspective" make members of the lower economic class undesirable. Among the wealthy, however, conservatism is to be feared. Occupations which may indicate a receptive attitude are public relations, teaching, writing, advertising, non-technical research, art, music, show business, and communications. To be avoided are banking, commerce, manufacturing, common labor, clerical, skilled trades, and career military men.

(6) *Race.* Black persons are "generally ill equipped to evaluate psychiatric testimony" because of economic and educational deprivations.

(7) *Intelligence and Education.* A high I.Q. and broad liberal arts education are "an ideal combination" for the defense.

(8) *Age and Sex.* Young persons generally better than extremely old jurors; "women may be slightly more receptive than men."

Law and Tactics in Federal Criminal Cases 265–66 (G. Shadoan ed. 1964).

468. The defendant is charged with murder in the first degree and assault with intent to have carnal knowledge. Insanity is the sole defense. The victim is a nine-year-old girl. The defendant is a somewhat retarded boy of 16. It is alleged that after assaulting his victim he drowned her in a bathtub. The penalty for first degree murder, if the jury returns a verdict of guilty without further recommendation, is death.

What questions would you as prosecutor seek to ask or have the judge ask of prospective jurors?

What questions would you as defense counsel seek to ask or have the judge ask of prospective jurors?

Would you as defense counsel ask any additional questions or omit any questions if, so far as you knew, the government's case rested almost entirely on a confession by the defendant the admission of which you expect to challenge on the ground that it was given involuntarily?

What questions which as prosecutor or defense counsel you would want to ask would you, as the trial judge, not allow?

Does the prosecutor have any (nonconstitutional) obligation not to ask questions designed to elicit facts such as age, membership in groups, religion, and occupation, which are irrelevant to the issues which the jury will decide but which, statistically, have a bearing on the way in which a juror will decide the issues? Does it make a difference whether defense counsel opens up such inquiries by asking such questions? Would an appropriate compromise be to forego asking the questions but to use answers to them, if they are asked by defense counsel, as the basis for peremptory challenges?

Opening Statement

Leonard v. United States

277 F.2d 834 (9th Cir.1960)

[The defendant was convicted before a jury of transporting a forged instrument in interstate commerce, 18 U.S.C. § 2314. In his opening statement, the prosecutor told the jury that the government's case would include proof of 83 crimes committed by the defendant in addition to the crime charged; this could be done, the prosecutor said, because such proof of other crimes would be admitted under traditional rules of evidence to show intent and to establish the defendant's identity. The other crimes, which the prosecutor catalogued on a blackboard and orally in his statement, involved a series of forged check transactions and attempts; the total number of crimes was reached by adding together each technical "crime" (e.g., each forged check passed gave rise to the distinct crimes of forging and uttering, each of which was counted separately in the total). He said in part: "Thus it is that the Government brings to you, not alone the one crime charged in the indictment, but a great number of other crimes, all of which will be shown to you as having been confessed to by this defendant, although they have not as yet been the subject of indictment or prosecution, conviction, or penalty. These crimes number 84. They are all felonies. Yes, you heard me correctly. I said 84. Incredible, but true. I should say, to be absolutely accurate, 83 other crimes other than the indictment crime." The prosecutor described briefly the method of committing the other crimes and mentioned in passing certain additional crimes (burglary, larceny, breaking and entering) allegedly involved in the series of transactions.

Following the opening statement, which lasted for about 40 minutes, defense counsel moved for a mistrial. The trial judge indicated that he thought the prosecutor had gone "too far afield," but since no objection had been made during the course of the statement, denied the motion for a mistrial. He instructed the jury that it was not to consider the prosecutor's remarks concerning crimes other than the one with which the defendant was charged and that the opening statement was not "evidence" but was "like an argument to the jury."

During the trial, the court ruled that evidence of other crimes was inadmissible. At the request of the prosecutor, the trial judge advised the jury that he had so ruled and that that was the reason why such evidence had not been presented. The blackboard cataloging the crimes remained visible throughout the trial.]

■ JERTBERG, CIRCUIT JUDGE.

. . .

In our view the record hereinbefore set out is more eloquent and convincing than any words of ours in demonstrating that the appellant was denied his constitutional right to a fair trial. For 40 minutes the trial judge sat silently by while the over-zealous prosecutor recounted crimes alleged to have been committed by the appellant, many of which by no stretch of the imagination were admissible to prove intent or identity. The record is clear that the trial judge was aware of the fact that the fair boundaries of an opening statement to the jury were being flagrantly breached, but expected appointed counsel for appellant to object. The court then denied appellant's motion for a mistrial on the ground that appellant had failed to make timely objection. "Plain errors or defects affecting substantial rights may be noticed although they were not brought to the attention of the court." Rule 52(b), Federal Rules of Criminal Procedure, 18 U.S.C.A. In large measure the statement made by government counsel was an opening statement in name only. An opening statement should be limited to a statement of facts which the government intends or in good faith expects to prove. It should not be argumentative in character, nor should it be designed to destroy the character of the defendant before the introduction of any evidence on the crime charged in the indictment. In our view the prejudice against the appellant which must have been created in the minds of the jurors by government counsel's diatribe was extremely grave. Such prejudice was not removed by subsequent proceedings.

The admonition given by the court to the jury following the motion of appellant for a mistrial was ineffectual. The court simply advised the jury that counsel had the right to make opening statements but that opening statements and arguments of counsel were not to be considered as evidence. The statement clearly implied that the court regarded the opening statement as proper. If at that time the court was of the opinion that the only offense upon which he would admit proof was the one charged in the indictment, he should have admonished the members of the jury to completely erase and put out of their minds all statements made by government counsel concerning other crimes and misconduct attributed to the appellant. . . . If the trial judge was of the view at that time that proof of some of the other alleged crimes would be relevant on the issues of intent and identity he should have so advised the jury, and at the same time should have instructed the jury to completely put out of their minds and disregard all statements by government counsel concerning other alleged crimes and misconduct of the appellant, and that it was their duty to do so. By the admonition to the jury the minds of the jurors were conditioned to expect and look forward to proof of all of the crimes and misconduct mentioned in the opening statement.

By the admonition of the trial court given to the jury at the close of testimony the jury was expressly told that the only reason for the failure of the government to introduce proof of the crimes described in the opening statement was occasioned by "an adverse ruling the government suffered in its efforts to introduce such material." Here again was presented an opportunity to the trial judge to instruct the jury that while opening statements of counsel should not be considered as evidence, the members of the jury must absolutely and completely disregard and put out of their minds all statements of other crimes and misconduct contained in the opening statement.

The prejudice occasioned to the appellant by the opening statement was heightened by the fact that the cataloging of such crimes on the blackboard remained as a constant reminder to the members of the jury throughout the trial.

The record in this case demonstrates that government counsel "overstepped the bounds of that propriety and fairness which should characterize the conduct of such an officer in the prosecution of a criminal offense." Berger v. United States, 295 U.S. 78. . . .

. . .

The judgment is reversed and the cause remanded with instructions to grant appellant a new trial.

---

469. "The only purpose of opening statements is to inform the jury what the case is about and to outline the proof that will be used—on the one hand to establish the commission of the crime and on the other to outline the defense—so that the jurors may more intelligently follow the testimony as it is related by the witnesses." Foster v. United States, 308 F.2d 751, 753 (8th Cir.1962).

470. Reversals on appeal because of improper remarks in the prosecutor's opening statement are rare. Appellate courts are reluctant to require a new trial on the basis of errors committed before the prior trial was well under way; they take the view that the harm of such errors, which in theory amount only to excessive rhetoric, may be removed by the trial judge's instructions and the jury's good sense. In Frazier v. Cupp, 394 U.S. 731 (1969), for example, the prosecutor referred in the opening statement to testimony of a person who later was called to the stand and refused to testify, asserting his privilege against self-incrimination. Before trial, defense counsel had warned the prosecutor that the witness would refuse to testify and that he should not refer to the expected testimony in the opening statement. The prosecutor had other indications that the witness might testify. The Court observed: "Many things might happen in the course of the trial which would prevent the presentation of all the evidence described in advance. Certainly not every variance between the advance description and the actual presentation constitutes reversible error, when a proper limiting instruction has been given." Id. at 736.

In Cook v. United States, 354 F.2d 529, 532 (9th Cir.1965), the court said it was "difficult to understand" why the prosecutor "chose the dangerous path" of referring in his opening statement to evidence later ruled inadmissible, but concluded that "under all the circumstances" the error was harmless. See also United States v. DeRosa, 548 F.2d 464 (3d Cir.1977) (wiretap evidence ruled inadmissible); United States v. West, 486 F.2d 468 (6th Cir.1973) (expected prosecution witness refused to testify); United States v. Wallace, 453 F.2d 420 (8th Cir.1972). What should defense counsel do to keep references to possibly or probably inadmissible evidence out of the prosecutor's opening statement?

471. "Alluding to the fact that the jury eventually acquitted him on the conspiracy counts, appellant Somers charged that references in the opening statement to his complicity in the conspiracies deprived him of a fair trial. We disagree. We know of no rule of law that requires a mistrial merely because the jury does not believe that a prosecutor's outline (presented in an opening statement) is true beyond a reasonable doubt. Provided that the outline is an objective summary of evidence which the Government reasonably expects to produce, a subsequent failure in proof will not lead to an automatic finding of misconduct. . . . Inasmuch as there is no indication in the record herein that the prosecutor outlined facts concerning Somers that he did not believe he could substantiate, we find no impropriety in the remarks suggesting that Somers played a role in the conspiracies." United States v. Somers, 496 F.2d 723, 738–39 (3d Cir.1974).

472. When does defense counsel make his opening statement? See Karikas v. United States, 296 F.2d 434, 438 (D.C.Cir.1961), in which the court of appeals observed that defense counsel "was within his rights in obtaining permission to withhold his opening statement until the United States had presented its case," and that to do so was "probably a good trial tactic" which enabled him "legitimately [to] frame his defense to meet the evidence adduced by the Government."

See generally United States v. Salovitz, 701 F.2d 17 (2d Cir.1983), holding that there is not a constitutional right to make an opening statement to the jury and that "the making and timing of opening statements" is within the discretion of the trial judge.

473. In United States v. McKeon, 738 F.2d 26 (2d Cir.1984), the court held that an inconsistent opening statement of defense counsel at a prior trial of the defendant on the same charges was admissible against the defendant. In limited circumstances, when there is no other explanation for the inconsistency, the opening statement can be regarded as one by the defendant and can be used to contradict the defendant's case. Since the statement was admissible, the trial judge ruled correctly that the defense counsel who made the statement was disqualified from appearing as counsel in the subsequent trial.

Prosecution and Defense

Moore v. Illinois

408 U.S. 786, 92 S.Ct. 2562, 33 L.Ed.2d 706 (1972)

■ MR. JUSTICE BLACKMUN delivered the opinion of the Court.

This state murder case, with the death penalty imposed by a jury, comes here from the Supreme Court of Illinois. . . .

I

Petitioner Lyman A. Moore was convicted in 1964 of the first-degree murder of Bernard Zitek. . . .

II

The homicide was committed on April 25, 1962. The facts are important:

A. The victim, Zitek, operated a bar-restaurant in the village of Lansing, southeast of Chicago. Patricia Hill was a waitress there. Donald O'Brien, Charles A. Mayer, and Henley Powell were customers.

Another bar called the Ponderosa Tap was located in Dolton, also southeast of Chicago. It was owned by Robert Fair. William Joyce was the bartender. One of Fair's customers was Virgle Sanders.

A third bar known as Wanda and Del's was in Chicago. Delbert Jones was the operator. William Leon Thompson was a patron.

The Westmoreland Country Club was in Wilmette, about 50 miles north of Lansing. The manager there was Herbert Anderson.

B. On the evening of April 25 Zitek was tending bar at his place in Lansing. Shortly before 10 p.m. two men, one with a moustache, entered and ordered beer. Zitek admonished the pair several times for using profane language. They continued in their profanity and, shortly, Zitek ejected them. About an hour later a man carrying a shotgun entered. He laid the weapon on the bar and shot and killed Zitek. The gunman ran out, pursued by patrons, and escaped in an automobile.

C. At the trial waitress Hill positively identified Moore as one of the two men ejected from the bar and as the one who returned and killed Zitek. She testified that she had a clear and close view from her working area at the bar and that she observed Zitek's ejection of the two men and the shotgun killing an hour later.

D. A second in-court identification of Moore as the man who killed Zitek was made by the customer Powell. Powell, who at the time was playing pinochle with others, testified that he observed Moore enter the bar with a shotgun and shoot Zitek; that after the shooting he pursued Moore; and that outside the bar Moore stopped momentarily, turned, and shouted, "Don't come any further or I'll shoot you, too."

E. Sanders testified that on April 27, two days after the murder, he was in the Ponderosa Tap and that a customer there, whom Sanders identified as "Slick," remarked to Sanders that it was "open season on bartenders'' and that he had shot one in Lansing. At the trial Sanders identified Moore as the man who was in the Ponderosa Tap on April 27. Moore was with another man who had a moustache. The two asked for a ride to Harvey, Illinois. The owner, Fair, agreed to give them the ride.

F. Fair testified that Moore was one of the two men who requested and were given the ride; that during the journey one of them was referred to as "Barbee"; and that one said "something like, 'Well, if we hadn't had that trouble with the bartender in Lansing, we'd have been all right.' "

G. The Ponderosa bartender, Joyce, testified that Sanders and Fair were in that tavern on April 27; that Moore was there at the same time; and that he arranged with Fair for Fair to give Moore and his companion a ride.

It is thus apparent that there were positive in-court identifications of Moore as the slayer by the waitress Hill and by the customer Powell, and that there were in-court identifications of Moore as having been present in the bar in Dolton two days later by Sanders, by Fair, and by Joyce.

H. Six months after the slaying, in the early morning hours of October 31, 1962, a Chicago police officer was shot at from a 1957 Ford automobile. Two men fled the scene. The police "staked out" the car, and several hours later Moore and a moustached man, later identified as Jerry Barbee, were arrested when they approached and entered the vehicle. The automobile proved to be owned by Barbee. A fully loaded sawed-off 16-gauge shotgun was in the car. The shotgun was introduced in evidence at Moore's trial. The State conceded that the gun so introduced was not the murder weapon, and that the State's ballistics technician, if called, would testify that the waddings taken from Zitek's body came, in his opinion, from a 12-gauge shotgun shell.

I. The defense called manager Anderson of the Westmoreland Country Club as a witness. He testified that Moore had been hired as a waiter there on April 24 (the day before the murder); that the club records indicated there was a special party at the club on the evening of April 25; and that Moore was paid for working until sometime between 10 p.m. and midnight. The club's bartender testified to the same effect. Each of these witnesses nevertheless admitted that he could not remember seeing Moore at the club that night, but said that he would have known if he had been absent for any substantial period of time. The club records also indicated that Moore worked at the club the afternoon of April 27, when, according to the testimony of Sanders, Fair, and Joyce, Moore was at the Ponderosa Tap in Dolton.

J. O'Brien, the customer at Zitek's testified for the defense that he observed Zitek eject two men the evening of the 25th, and that Moore was not one of them. Although he was in the restaurant at the time of the homicide, he did not see the person who shot Zitek. A police officer testified that in his opinion O'Brien was drunk at the time.

III

Prior to the trial, the defense moved for disclosure of all written statements taken by the police from any witness. The State agreed to furnish existing statements of prosecution witnesses. At the post-conviction hearing, Moore argued, and the claim is presented here, that he was denied a fair trial because six items of evidence, unknown to him at the time of the trial, were not produced and, in fact, were suppressed by the State:

A. On April 30, 1962, Sanders gave a statement to the police that he had met the man "Slick" for the first time "about six months ago" in Wanda and Del's tavern. Testimony at the post-conviction hearing by Lieutenant Turbin of the Lansing Police Department revealed that at the time of trial the police possessed an FBI report that Moore was in Leavenworth Penitentiary from 1957 to March 4, 1962. That report thus proved that Sanders could not have met Moore at Wanda and Del's in November 1961. The defense was not given a copy of the statement made by Sanders. The prosecuting attorney asserted at the post-conviction hearing that he did not recall having seen the statement before or during the trial.

B. On the day Sanders gave his statement, that is, on April 30, the police raided Wanda and Del's looking for "Slick." "Slick" was not there, but Jones, the tavern's operator, said that he could identify "Slick." After Moore was arrested, Jones was not asked by the police whether Moore was "Slick." The defense was not advised of the raid until after the trial. At the post-conviction hearing Jones testified that Moore was not "Slick." His testimony, however, was stricken on the ground that it pertained to innocence or guilt and was not admissible upon collateral review.

C. After the raid on Wanda and Del's, the police secured from their files a picture of James E. "Slick" Watts and assigned Lieutenant Turbin the task of finding Watts. His search was unsuccessful. Moore asserts that the attempt to find Watts was not made known to the defense until cross-examination of the Lansing police chief at the post-conviction hearing.

D. After Moore was arrested on October 31, he was photographed by the police. The photograph was shown to William Leon Thompson, the patron of Wanda and Del's. Thompson testified at the post-conviction hearing that he told Lieutenant Turbin that the picture "didn't, to the best of my knowledge, resemble the man that I knew" as "Slick." He identified a picture of Watts as "the Slick I know." Defense counsel testified that through the course of the trial neither the police nor the prosecutor advised them about Thompson and his disclaimer.

E. At the start of the trial Sanders observed Moore for the first time since the alleged bragging incident at the Ponderosa Tap. Sanders remarked to the prosecuting attorney and to police officers who accompanied him into the courtroom that the person he knew as "Slick" was about 30–40 pounds heavier than Moore and did not wear glasses. One of the officers responded, "Well, you know how the jailhouse beans are." Moore contends that he and defense counsel were not advised of this remark of Sanders until after the trial had concluded.

F. Mayer, one of the card players at Zitek's at the time of the murder, gave the police a written statement. On the back of the statement Officer Koppitz drew a sketch of the seating arrangement at the card table. The diagram shows that the corners of the table pointed north, south, east, and west. Cardplayer Powell was placed on the southwest side. The bar was about 10 feet north of the table. The door was to the southwest. Moore argues that the diagram is exculpatory and contradicts Powell's testimony that he observed the shooting. Defense counsel testified that they were not shown the diagram during the trial.

Moore argues, as to the first five items, that the State did not comply with the general request by the defense for all written statements given by prosecution witnesses; that the State failed to produce the pretrial statement of Sanders and the other evidence contradicting Sanders' identification of Moore as "Slick"; and that the evidence not produced was material and would have been helpful to his defense.

The Illinois court held that the State had not suppressed material evidence favorable to Moore, that the record shows that the prosecution presented its entire file to defense counsel, and that no further request for disclosure was made. . . . Moore submits here the alternative claim that a specific request is not an "indispensable prerequisite" for the disclosure of exonerating evidence by the State and that the defense could not be expected to make a request for specific evidence that it did not know was in existence.

In Brady v. Maryland, 373 U.S. 83 (1963), the petitioner and a companion were found guilty by a jury of first-degree murder and were sentenced to death. In his summation to the jury, Brady's counsel conceded that Brady was guilty, but argued that the jury should return its verdict "without capital punishment." Prior to the trial, counsel had requested that the prosecution allow him to examine the codefendant's extra-judicial statements. Some of these were produced, but another, in which the codefendant admitted the actual homicide, was withheld and did not come to Brady's notice until after his conviction. In a post-conviction proceeding, the Maryland Court of Appeals held that this denied Brady due process of law, and remanded the case for retrial on the issue of punishment. This Court affirmed. It held "that the suppression by the prosecution of evidence favorable to an accused upon request violates due process where the evidence is material either to guilt or to punishment, irrespective of the good faith or bad faith of the prosecution." 373 U.S., at 87.

The heart of the holding in *Brady* is the prosecution's suppression of evidence, in the face of a defense production request, where the evidence is favorable to the accused and is material either to guilt or to punishment. Important, then, are (a) suppression by the prosecution after a request by the defense, (b) the evidence's favorable character for the defense, and (c) the materiality of the evidence. These are the standards by which the prosecution's conduct in Moore's case is to be measured.

Moore's counsel asked several prosecution witnesses if they had given statements to the police. Each witness (Hill, Powell, Fair) who had given a statement admitted doing so and the statement was immediately tendered. The same inquiry was not made of witness Sanders. He was the only state witness who was not asked the question. At the post-conviction hearing the inquiry was made. Sanders admitted making a statement to the police and the statement was tendered.

The record discloses . . . that the prosecutor at the trial submitted his entire file to the defense. The prosecutor, however, has no recollection that Sanders' statement was in the file. The statement, therefore, either was in that file and not noted by the defense or it was not in the possession of the prosecution at the trial.

We know of no constitutional requirement that the prosecution make a complete and detailed accounting to the defense of all police investigatory work on a case. Here, the elusive "Slick" was an early lead the police abandoned when eyewitnesses to the killing and witnesses to Moore's presence at the Ponderosa were found. Unquestionably, as the State now concedes, Sanders was in error when he indicated to the police that he met Moore at Wanda and Del's about six months prior to April 30, 1962. Moore's incarceration at Leavenworth until March shows that conclusion to have been an instance of mistaken identity. But the mistake was as to the identification of Moore as "Slick," not as to the presence of Moore at the Ponderosa Tap on April 27.[10] "Sanders' testimony to the effect that it was Moore he spoke with at the Ponderosa Tap in itself is not significantly, if at all, impeached. Indeed, it is buttressed by the testimony of bartender Joyce and operator Fair, both of whom elaborated the incident by their description of the man, and by Moore's request for a ride to Harvey, Illinois, Fair's providing that ride, and Fair's hearing, on that trip, the reference to one of the men as 'Barbee,' and a second reference to trouble with a bartender in Lansing."

The other four of the first five items—that Jones told police he could identify "Slick" and subsequently testified that Moore was not "Slick"; that the police had a picture of Watts and assigned the lieutenant, unsuccessfully, to find Watts; that Thompson had been shown a picture of Moore and told the police that Moore was not "Slick"; and that on the day of the trial Sanders remarked that the man he knew as "Slick" looked heavier than Moore—are in exactly the same category. They all relate to "Slick,"

10. The dissent observes . . . "When confronted with this fact [Moore's imprisonment at Leavenworth], Sanders indicated that it was impossible that petitioner [Moore] was the man with whom he had spoken in the Ponderosa Tavern." This is a misreading of Sanders' testimony. The question and Sanders' answer were:

"Q. And did you tell me and also later on, did you tell the policeman from the State's Attorney's Office that if you had known that this fellow, Lyman Moore, was in the Federal Penitentiary until March 4, 1962, you would definitely not have identified him as being Slick that you knew?

"A. If he's in jail, it would have been impossible to be the same man." Abstract of Record 296.

not Moore, and quite naturally go off on Sanders' initial misidentification of "Slick" with Moore.

None of the five items serves to impeach in any way the positive identification by Hill and by Powell of Moore as Zitek's killer, or the testimony of Fair and Joyce that Moore was at the Ponderosa Tap on April 27, or the testimony of Fair that the moustached Barbee was accompanying Moore at that time, and that one of the two men made the additional and undisputed admission on the ride to Harvey. We conclude, in the light of all the evidence, that Sanders' misidentification of Moore as Slick was not material to the issue of guilt.

The remaining claim of suppression relates to the diagram on the back of Mayer's statement to the police.[11] Moore contends that the diagram shows that Powell was seated with his back to the entrance to Zitek's and, thus, necessarily contradicts his testimony that he was looking toward the entrance as he sat at the card table, and that the State knowingly permitted false testimony to remain uncorrected, in violation of Napue v. Illinois, 360 U.S. 264 (1959).

In *Napue* the principal prosecution witness at Napue's murder trial was an accomplice then serving a sentence for the crime. He testified, in response to an inquiry by the prosecutor, that he had received no promise of consideration in return for his testimony. In fact, the prosecutor had promised him consideration, but he did nothing to correct the witness' false testimony. This Court held that the failure of the prosecutor to correct the testimony, which he knew to be false, denied Napue due process of law, and that this was so even though the false testimony went only to the credibility of the witness. . . .

We are not persuaded that the diagram shows that Powell's testimony was false. The officer who drew the diagram testified at the post-conviction hearing that it did not indicate the direction in which Powell was facing or looking at the time of the shooting. Powell testified that his position at the table gave him a view of the bartender; that at the moment he could not bid in the pinochle game and had laid his hand down and was looking toward the door when Moore walked in. There is nothing in the diagram to indicate that Powell was looking in another direction or that it was impossible for him to see the nearby door from his seat at the card table. Furthermore, after the shooting he pursued Moore but stopped when the man warned him that he, too, might be shot.

In summary, the background presence of the elusive "Slick," while somewhat confusing, is at most an insignificant factor. The attempt to identify Moore as "Slick" encountered difficulty, but nothing served to destroy the two-witness identification of Moore as Zitek's assailant, the

11. Contrary to the assertion by the dissent that the Mayer statement, with its accompanying diagram, was never made available to the defense, post, at 803 and 809, the trial transcript indicates that during the cross-examination of Officer Koppitz a request was made by the defense for all written statements taken by the officer from persons in Zitek's restaurant at the time of the shooting. The court granted the request and the record recites that statements of Mayer and others were furnished to defense counsel.

three-witness identification of Moore as present at the Ponderosa Tap, and two-witness identification of Moore as one of the men who requested and obtained a ride from the Ponderosa in Dolton to Harvey, Illinois, and Fair's testimony as to the admission made on that ride.

We adhere to the principles of *Brady* and *Napue*, but hold that the present record embraces no violation of those principles.

IV

The 16-gauge shotgun was admitted into evidence at the trial over the objection of the defense that it was not the murder weapon, that it had no connection with the crime charged, and that it was inadmissible under Illinois law. During his closing argument to the jury, the prosecuting attorney stated that the 16-gauge shotgun was not used to kill Zitek, but that Moore and his companion, Barbee, were "the kind of people that use shotguns."[12]

The Supreme Court of Illinois held that the shotgun was properly admitted into evidence as a weapon in Moore's possession at the time of his arrest, and was a weapon "suitable for the commission of the crime charged . . . even though there is no showing that it was the actual weapon used." 246 N.E.2d, at 303. Moore claims that the gun's introduction denied him due process.

. . .

[W]e are unable to conclude that the shotgun's introduction deprived Moore of the due process of law guaranteed him by the Fourteenth Amendment. The 16-gauge shotgun, found in the car, was in the constructive possession of both Moore and Barbee when they were arrested after the shooting incident on October 31. There is substantial other evidence in the record that a shotgun was used to kill Zitek, and that he suffered the wounds one would expect from a shotgun fired at close range. The testimony as to the murder itself, with all the details as to the shotgun wounds, is such that we cannot say that the presentation of the shotgun was so irrelevant or so inflammatory that Moore was denied a fair trial. The case is not federally reversible on this ground.

V

[T]he Court today has ruled that the imposition of the death penalty under statutes such as those of Illinois is violative of the Eighth and Fourteenth Amendments, Furman v. Georgia [408 U.S. 238 (1972)]. . . .

The judgment, insofar as it imposes the death sentence, is reversed . . . and the case is remanded for further proceedings.

12. Later in his closing argument the prosecuting attorney referred to the 16-gauge shotgun and stated again that a 12-gauge shotgun killed Zitek. He argued that a shotgun is not "the most humane type weapon" and that the death penalty is appropriate in a case in which a shotgun is used to murder a person.

■ MR. JUSTICE MARSHALL, with whom MR. JUSTICE DOUGLAS, MR. JUSTICE STEWART, and MR. JUSTICE POWELL join, concurring in part and dissenting in part.

. . . I . . . agree that the introduction of the shotgun into evidence at petitioner's trial did not violate the Fourteenth Amendment.[13]

But, I believe that in failing to disclose to petitioner certain evidence that might well have been of substantial assistance to the defense, the State denied him a fair trial.

. . .

Two interrelated defenses were raised against the charge of murder—alibi and misidentification. Petitioner's theory of the case was that he was not at the scene when the murder was committed and that those witnesses who testified that they saw him there were confusing him with someone else.

Only two witnesses affirmatively asserted at trial that they saw the murder and that they could identify petitioner as the assailant. They were Patricia Hill, a waitress in the victim's bar, and Henley Powell, a customer. Aside from their testimony, the only other evidence introduced against petitioner related to statements that he allegedly made two days after the murder.

There is a problem with the eyewitness testimony of Powell that did not become apparent until the post-conviction hearing in the trial court. At trial he testified as follows:

> The defendant (indicating) came into the tavern while I was at the table. I first saw him when he walked in the door with a shotgun. I was sitting at the table along the wall. I was facing where the bartender

13. I find the constitutional question presented by the introduction of this evidence to be much harder than the majority seems to. It was uncontradicted at trial that the weapon introduced against petitioner had no bearing on the crime with which he was charged. It was, in fact, clear that the shotgun admitted into evidence was a 16-gauge gun, whereas the murder weapon was a 12-gauge gun. Despite the fact that the prosecution conceded this in a pretrial bill of particulars, it did everything possible to obfuscate the fact that the weapon admitted into evidence was not the murder weapon. This was highly improper. The record also indicates that the trial judge was confused as to why he thought the weapon should be admitted. At one point he said, "There was testimony here that this was a shotgun killing. And I can see nothing wrong if they say that this defendant, who will be identified by other people, was apprehended with this gun." Abstract of Record (Abs.), 65. If the trial judge meant to imply that because the crime was committed with a shotgun, it was sufficient to prove that the petitioner possessed *any* shotgun, whether or not it was the murder weapon, he surely erred. But it is impossible to tell from the record in this case precisely what was intended, or whether the judge confused the jury when he admitted the weapon. Although this highly prejudicial and irrelevant evidence was introduced, and although the prosecution did its best to lead the jury to believe that there was a relationship between the murder weapon and the shotgun in evidence, the fact that petitioner's counsel explained to the jury that the two weapons were not identical is, on the very closest balance, enough to warrant our finding that the jury was not improperly misled as to the nature of the evidence before it.

was standing and I also had a view of the man that walked in the door. I was looking to the west.

Abs. 32. But at the post-conviction hearing it was discovered that police officers who had investigated the murder possessed a statement by one Charles Mayer, who had been sitting with Powell at a table in the bar, which contained a diagram indicating that Powell was seated in a direction opposite that indicated in his trial testimony. This diagram was never made available to defense counsel.

Donald O'Brien, who had also been seated at Powell and Mayer's table, testified at trial and contradicted the testimony of both Powell and Patricia Hill. Although O'Brien admitted that he did not actually see the shooting because his back was to the bar, he was certain that petitioner was not the man who had been ejected from the victim's bar only an hour before the killing. O'Brien's testimony greatly undercut the apparent retaliatory motive that the prosecution attributed to petitioner.[14]

Because of the contradictory testimony of those persons who were present at the scene of the murder, the statements allegedly made by the petitioner after the crime were crucial to the prosecution's case. The key prosecution witness in this regard was Virgle Sanders. He testified that two days after the murder he was in the Ponderosa Tavern, that petitioner (whom he knew as "Slick") was there also, and that petitioner said "[s]omething about it's season or open season on bartenders or something like that." Abs. 44. The bartender also testified that he recognized petitioner as being present at the same time as Sanders. And the owner of the tavern stated that he gave petitioner and petitioner's friend a short ride in his automobile, at the end of which the friend mentioned something about "trouble with the bartender." Abs. 52.

After his trial and conviction petitioner learned that five days after the murder, Sanders gave a statement to the police in which he said that he had met "Slick" for the first time about six months before he spoke to him in the Ponderosa Tavern. As the Court notes, it would have been impossible for Sanders to have met the petitioner at the time specified, because petitioner was in federal prison at that time. At the post-conviction hearing, Sanders said that he was not positive when he first met the man known as "Slick," but that he definitely knew it was before Christmas 1961. Petitioner was not released from federal custody until March 1962. When confronted with this fact, Sanders indicated that it was impossible that petitioner was the man with whom he had spoken in the Ponderosa Tavern. Abs. 296. Sanders' trial identification was further impeached at the post-trial hearing by testimony that on the day of trial he told police officers that petitioner was approximately 30 or 40 pounds lighter than he remembered "Slick" being. Abs. 294.

14. The Court asserts that O'Brien may have been drunk. His testimony at trial made it clear beyond doubt that when the victim ejected the man alleged to be the petitioner from the bar, this witness was perfectly sober. Later, especially after the killing, the witness drank heavily and became intoxicated. No one contradicted this at trial.

Sanders' testimony that petitioner and "Slick" were not one and the same was corroborated at the hearing. The reason that Sanders could remember the first time that he had met "Slick" was that "Slick" had been involved in a scuffle with one William Thompson. Thompson testified at the hearing that he remembered the altercation, that he knew "Slick," that prior to the trial he had told police officers that petitioner was not "Slick," and that he remained certain that petitioner and "Slick" were different people. Finally, Sanders' testimony was corroborated by Delbert Jones, the owner of the tavern where "Slick" and Thompson scuffled. Jones testified that he was certain that petitioner was not the man known as "Slick."

The fact is that Thompson and Jones were both familiar with one James E. Watts, who they knew as "Slick," and who looked very much like the petitioner. The record makes clear that the police suspected Watts as the murderer and assigned a lieutenant to search for him. A raid of Jones' bar was even made in the hope of finding this suspect.

Sanders' testimony at the post-conviction hearing indicates that it was Watts who bragged about the murder, not petitioner. It is true that the bartender and the owner of the Ponderosa Tavern testified at trial that it was petitioner who was in the bar with Sanders, but the bartender had never seen "Slick" before, and the owner was drinking the entire afternoon. Furthermore, the fact remains that petitioner and Watts look very much alike.

Petitioner urges that when the State did not reveal to him Sanders' statement about meeting "Slick" at an earlier time and the corroborative statements of Thompson and Jones, it denied him due process. The Court answers this by saying that the statements were not material. It is evident from the foregoing that the statements were not merely material to the defense, they were absolutely critical. I find myself in complete agreement with Justice Schaeffer's dissent in the Illinois Supreme Court:

> The defendant's conviction rests entirely upon identification testimony. The facts developed at the post-conviction hearing seriously impeached, if indeed they did not destroy, Sanders's trial testimony. Had those facts, and the identifications of "Slick" Watts by Thompson and Jones, been available at the trial, the jury may well have been unwilling to act upon the identifications of Patricia Hill and Henley Powell. Far more is involved in this case, in my opinion, than "the following up of useless leads and discussions with immaterial witnesses." Certainly if Sanders's identification was material, the . . . testimony of the other witnesses which destroyed that identification [was] also material. Consequently, I believe that the State's nondisclosure denied the defendant the fundamental fairness guaranteed by the constitution. . . .

246 N.E.2d, at 308.

Petitioner also urges that the failure of the prosecution to disclose the information concerning where the eyewitness Powell was sitting when he allegedly saw petitioner is another instance of suppression of evidence in violation of the Fourteenth Amendment. Had this been the prosecution's only error, I would join the Court in finding the evidence to be immaterial. But if this evidence is considered together with other evidence that was suppressed, it must be apparent that the failure of the prosecution to disclose it contributed to the denial of due process.

Even if material exculpatory evidence was not made available to petitioner, the State argues that because petitioner did not demand to see the evidence, he cannot now complain about nondisclosure. This argument is disingenuous at best.

Prior to trial, petitioner moved for discovery of all statements given to the prosecutor or the police by any witness possessing information relevant to the case. Abs. 5. In explaining why such a broad motion was made, petitioner's counsel stated that, "We want to circumvent the possibility that a witness gets on the stand and says, 'Yes, I made a written statement,' and then the State's Attorney says, 'But no, we don't have it in our possession,' or they say, 'It's in the possession of Orlando Wilson [Superintendent of Police, Chicago, Ill.],' or 'The Chief of Police of Lansing.' " Abs. 8. In response to the motion, the prosecutor guaranteed defense counsel and the court that he would supply defense counsel with statements made either to the police or to the State's Attorney by witnesses who were called to testify at trial. Ibid. Based on this representation, the motion for discovery was denied. Never was there any implication by the prosecutor that his guarantee was in any way dependent upon petitioner's making repeated and specific requests for such statements after each witness testified at trial. The prosecutor's guarantee certainly covered Sanders' statement. As for the statements of the bartender and owner of the Ponderosa Tavern and the statement and diagram of Charles Mayer, petitioner clearly demanded to see these things before trial. The prosecution took the position that it was bound to reveal only the statements of witnesses who testified. Hence, it is hard to imagine what sort of further demand petitioner might have made. Moreover, the very fact that petitioner made his motion for extensive discovery placed the prosecution on notice that the defense wished to see all statements by any witness that might be exculpatory. The motion served "the valuable office of flagging the importance of the evidence for the defense and thus impos[ing] on the prosecutor a duty to make a careful check of his files." United States v. Keogh, 391 F.2d 138, 147 (CA2 1968).

In my view, both Brady v. Maryland, 373 U.S. 83 (1963), and Napue v. Illinois, 360 U.S. 264 (1959), require that the conviction in this case be reversed. *Napue* establishes that the Fourteenth Amendment is violated "when the State, although not soliciting false evidence, allows it to go uncorrected." Id., at 269. And *Brady* holds that suppression of material evidence requires a new trial "irrespective of the good faith or bad faith of the prosecution." Supra, at 87. There can be no doubt that there was suppression of evidence by the State and that the evidence that the State relied on was "false" in the sense that it was incomplete and misleading.

Both before and during the trial the prosecutor met with Sanders and went over the statement that he had given the police five days after the murder. Abs. 301, 315. Thus, it is apparent that the prosecutor not only knew of the statement, but was actively using it to prepare his case. There was also testimony at the post-conviction hearing from the prosecution that it had discussed the location where Powell was sitting when he allegedly saw the murder. While the prosecutor could not remember whether or not he actually had Mayer's statement and diagram in his possession, he had some recollection that before trial he was informed of exactly where everyone at Powell's table was sitting. Abs. 323. No attempt was ever made at trial to communicate this information to the defense.

Moreover, seated at the prosecutor's table throughout the trial was Police Lieutenant Turbin, who had investigated the case and who was assisting the prosecution. At the post-conviction hearing, he testified that throughout the trial he was not only aware of Sanders' statement and Mayer's diagram, but also that he had them in his file. He made no attempt to communicate his information to the prosecutor or to remind him about the evidence.

When the State possesses information that might well exonerate a defendant in a criminal case, it has an affirmative duty to disclose that information. While frivolous information and useless leads can be ignored, if evidence is clearly relevant and helpful to the defense, it must be disclosed.

Obviously some burden is placed on the shoulders of the prosecutor when he is required to be responsible for those persons who are directly assisting him in bringing an accused to justice. But this burden is the essence of due process of law. It is the State that tries a man, and it is the State that must insure that the trial is fair. "A citizen has the right to expect fair dealing from his government, see Vitarelli v. Seaton, 359 U.S. 535, and this entails . . . treating the government as a unit rather than as an amalgam of separate entities." S & E Contractors, Inc. v. United States, 406 U.S. 1, 10 (1972). "The prosecutor's office is an entity and as such it is the spokesman for the Government." Giglio v. United States, 405 U.S. 150, 154 (1972). . . .

My reading of the case leads me to conclude that the prosecutor knew that evidence existed that might help the defense, that the defense had asked to see it, and that it was never disclosed. It makes no difference whatever whether the evidence that was suppressed was found in the file of a police officer who directly aided the prosecution or in the file of the prosecutor himself. When the prosecutor consciously uses police officers as part of the prosecutorial team, those officers may not conceal evidence that the prosecutor himself would have a duty to disclose. It would be unconscionable to permit a prosecutor to adduce evidence demonstrating guilt without also requiring that he bear the responsibility of producing all known and relevant evidence tending to show innocence.

---

474. After the Court handed down its opinion in *Moore*, defense counsel obtained from Virgle Sanders a statement that the majority's construction of his testimony about "Slick" was wrong, and that the man in the Ponderosa Tap was "Slick," not the defendant. At an evidentiary hearing in March 1974, Sanders affirmed that statement and said also that Moore was too short to be "Slick."

On that basis, Moore argued that the Court's conclusion that the information about "Slick" that was withheld from the defense was not material was incorrect, that it clearly was material, and that Sanders' repudiation of his identification of Moore at trial required reversal of his conviction. After considering all the evidence in the case, the Supreme Court of Illinois concluded that Sanders' post-trial statements lacked "that quantum of credibility" that would warrant granting relief. Further, it found that there was enough other evidence to prove Moore's guilt beyond a reasonable doubt. People v. Moore, 327 N.E.2d 324 (Ill.1975). The Court denied certiorari, 423 U.S. 938 (1975). In a separate statement, Justice Stewart noted that the questions raised by Moore would be "fully amenable to reassessment in a federal habeas corpus proceeding." 423 U.S. at 939.

With respect to the non-disclosure of the lead to "Slick" Watts, see Bowen v. Maynard, 799 F.2d 593 (10th Cir.1986); Scurr v. Niccum, 620 F.2d 186 (8th Cir.1980); Grant v. Alldredge, 498 F.2d 376 (2d Cir.1974). In all three cases, the court held that disclosure of the lead to another suspect was required.

United States v. Agurs

427 U.S. 97, 96 S.Ct. 2392, 49 L.Ed.2d 342 (1976)

■ MR. JUSTICE STEVENS delivered the opinion of the Court.

After a brief interlude in an inexpensive motel room, respondent repeatedly stabbed James Sewell, causing his death. She was convicted of second-degree murder. The question before us is whether the prosecutor's failure to provide defense counsel with certain background information about Sewell, which would have tended to support the argument that respondent acted in self-defense, deprived her of a fair trial under the rule of Brady v. Maryland, 373 U.S. 83.

The answer to the question depends on (1) a review of the facts, (2) the significance of the failure of defense counsel to request the material, and (3) the standard by which the prosecution's failure to volunteer exculpatory material should be judged.

I

At about 4:30 p.m. on September 24, 1971, respondent, who had been there before, and Sewell, registered in a motel as man and wife. They were assigned a room without a bath. Sewell was wearing a bowie knife in a sheath, and carried another knife in his pocket. Less than two hours earlier, according to the testimony of his estranged wife, he had had $360 in cash on his person.

About 15 minutes later three motel employees heard respondent screaming for help. A forced entry into their room disclosed Sewell on top of respondent struggling for possession of the bowie knife. She was holding the knife; his bleeding hand grasped the blade; according to one witness he was trying to jam the blade into her chest. The employees separated the two and summoned the authorities. Respondent departed without comment before they arrived. Sewell was dead on arrival at the hospital.

Circumstantial evidence indicated that the parties had completed an act of intercourse, that Sewell had then gone to the bathroom down the hall, and that the struggle occurred upon his return. The contents of his pockets were in disarray on the dresser and no money was found; the jury may have inferred that respondent took Sewell's money and that the fight started when Sewell re-entered the room and saw what she was doing.

On the following morning respondent surrendered to the police. She was given a physical examination which revealed no cuts or bruises of any kind, except needle marks on her upper arm. An autopsy of Sewell disclosed that he had several deep stab wounds in his chest and abdomen, and a number of slashes on his arms and hands, characterized by the pathologist as "defensive wounds."

Respondent offered no evidence. Her sole defense was the argument made by her attorney that Sewell had initially attacked her with the knife, and that her actions had all been directed toward saving her own life. The support for this self-defense theory was based on the fact that she had screamed for help. Sewell was on top of her when help arrived, and his possession of two knives indicated that he was a violence-prone person. It took the jury about 25 minutes to elect a foreman and return a verdict.

Three months later defense counsel filed a motion for a new trial asserting that he had discovered (1) that Sewell had a prior criminal record that would have further evidenced his violent character; (2) that the prosecutor had failed to disclose this information to the defense; and (3) that a recent opinion of the United States Court of Appeals for the District of Columbia Circuit made it clear that such evidence was admissible even if not known to the defendant. Sewell's prior record included a plea of guilty to a charge of assault and carrying a deadly weapon in 1963, and another guilty plea to a charge of carrying a deadly weapon in 1971. Apparently both weapons were knives.

The Government opposed the motion, arguing that there was no duty to tender Sewell's prior record to the defense in the absence of an appropriate request; that the evidence was readily discoverable in advance of trial and hence was not the kind of "newly discovered" evidence justifying a new trial; and that, in all events, it was not material.

The District Court denied the motion. It rejected the Government's argument that there was no duty to disclose material evidence unless requested to do so, assumed that the evidence was admissible, but held that it was not sufficiently material. The District Court expressed the opinion that the prior conviction shed no light on Sewell's character that was not already apparent from the uncontradicted evidence, particularly the fact that he carried two knives; the court stressed the inconsistency between the claim of self-defense and the fact that Sewell had been stabbed repeatedly while respondent was unscathed.

The Court of Appeals reversed. The court found no lack of diligence on the part of the defense and no misconduct by the prosecutor in this case. It held, however, that the evidence was material, and that its nondisclosure required a new trial because the jury might have returned a different verdict if the evidence had been received.

The decision of the Court of Appeals represents a significant departure from this Court's prior holding; because we believe that that court has incorrectly interpreted the constitutional requirement of due process, we reverse.

II

The rule of Brady v. Maryland, 373 U.S. 83, arguably applies in three quite different situations. Each involves the discovery, after trial, of information which had been known to the prosecution but unknown to the defense.

In the first situation, typified by Mooney v. Holohan, 294 U.S. 103, the undisclosed evidence demonstrates that the prosecution's case includes perjured testimony and that the prosecution knew, or should have known, of the perjury. In a series of subsequent cases, the Court has consistently held that a conviction obtained by the knowing use of perjured testimony is fundamentally unfair, and must be set aside if there is any reasonable likelihood that the false testimony could have affected the judgment of the jury. It is this line of cases on which the Court of Appeals placed primary reliance. In those cases the Court has applied a strict standard of materiality, not just because they involve prosecutorial misconduct, but more importantly because they involve a corruption of the truth-seeking function of the trial process. Since this case involves no misconduct, and since there is no reason to question the veracity of any of the prosecution witnesses, the test of materiality followed in the *Mooney* line of cases is not necessarily applicable to this case.

The second situation, illustrated by the *Brady* case itself, is characterized by a pretrial request for specific evidence. In that case defense counsel had requested the extrajudicial statements made by Brady's accomplice, one Boblit. This Court held that the suppression of one of Boblit's statements deprived Brady of due process, noting specifically that the statement had been requested and that it was "material." A fair analysis of the holding in *Brady* indicates that implicit in the requirement of materiality is a concern that the suppressed evidence might have affected the outcome of the trial.

Brady was found guilty of murder in the first degree. Since the jury did not add the words "without capital punishment" to the verdict, he was sentenced to death. At his trial Brady did not deny his involvement in the deliberate killing, but testified that it was his accomplice, Boblit, rather than he, who had actually strangled the decedent. This version of the event was corroborated by one of several confessions made by Boblit but not given to Brady's counsel despite an admittedly adequate request.

After his conviction and sentence had been affirmed on appeal, Brady filed a motion to set aside the judgment, and later a post-conviction proceeding, in which he alleged that the State had violated his constitutional rights by suppressing the Boblit confession. The trial judge denied relief largely because he felt that Boblit's confession would have been inadmissible at Brady's trial. The Maryland Court of Appeals disagreed; it ordered a new trial on the issue of punishment. It held that the withholding of material evidence, even "without guile," was a denial of due process and that there were valid theories on which the confession might have been admissible in Brady's defense.

This Court granted certiorari to consider Brady's contention that the violation of his constitutional right to a fair trial vitiated the entire proceeding. The holding that the suppression of exculpatory evidence violated Brady's right to due process was affirmed, as was the separate holding that he should receive a new trial on the issue of punishment but not on the issue of guilt or innocence. The Court interpreted the Maryland Court of Appeals opinion as ruling that the confession was inadmissible on that issue. For that reason, the confession could not have affected the outcome on the issue of guilt but could have affected Brady's punishment. It was material on the latter issue but not the former. And since it was not material on the issue of guilt, the entire trial was not lacking in due process.

The test of materiality in a case like *Brady* in which specific information has been requested by the defense is not necessarily the same as in a case in which no such request has been made. Indeed, this Court has not yet decided whether the prosecutor has any obligation to provide defense counsel with exculpatory information when no request has been made. Before addressing that question, a brief comment on the function of the request is appropriate.

In *Brady* the request was specific. It gave the prosecutor notice of exactly what the defense desired. Although there is, of course, no duty to provide defense counsel with unlimited discovery of everything known by the prosecutor, if the subject matter of such a request is material, or indeed if a substantial basis for claiming materiality exists, it is reasonable to require the prosecutor to respond either by furnishing the information or by submitting the problem to the trial judge. When the prosecutor receives a specific and relevant request, the failure to make any response is seldom, if ever, excusable.

In many cases, however, exculpatory information in the possession of the prosecutor may be unknown to defense counsel. In such a situation he may make no request at all, or possibly ask for "all *Brady* material" or for "anything exculpatory." Such a request really gives the prosecutor no better notice than if no request is made. If there is a duty to respond to a general request of that kind, it must derive from the obviously exculpatory character of certain evidence in the hands of the prosecutor. But if the evidence is so clearly supportive of a claim of innocence that it gives the prosecution notice of a duty to produce, that duty should equally arise even if no request is made. Whether we focus on the desirability of a precise definition of the prosecutor's duty or on the potential harm to the defendant, we conclude that there is no significant difference between cases in which there has been merely a general request for exculpatory matter and cases, like the one we must now decide, in which there has been no request at all. The third situation in which the *Brady* rule arguably applies, typified by this case, therefore embraces the case in which only a general request for "*Brady* material" has been made.

We now consider whether the prosecutor has any constitutional duty to volunteer exculpatory matter to the defense, and if so, what standard of materiality gives rise to that duty.

III

We are not considering the scope of discovery authorized by the Federal Rules of Criminal Procedure, or the wisdom of amending those Rules to enlarge the defendant's discovery rights. We are dealing with the defendant's right to a fair trial mandated by the Due Process Clause of the Fifth Amendment to the Constitution. Our construction of that Clause will apply equally to the comparable clause in the Fourteenth Amendment applicable to trials in state courts.

The problem arises in two principal contexts. First, in advance of trial, and perhaps during the course of a trial as well, the prosecutor must decide what, if anything, he should voluntarily submit to defense counsel. Second, after trial a judge may be required to decide whether a nondisclosure deprived the defendant of his right to due process. Logically the same standard must apply at both times. For unless the omission deprived the defendant of a fair trial, there was no constitutional violation requiring that the verdict be set aside; and absent a constitutional violation, there was no breach of the prosecutor's constitutional duty to disclose.

Nevertheless, there is a significant practical difference between the pretrial decision of the prosecutor and the post-trial decision of the judge. Because we are dealing with an inevitably imprecise standard, and because the significance of an item of evidence can seldom be predicted accurately until the entire record is complete, the prudent prosecutor will resolve doubtful questions in favor of disclosure. But to reiterate a critical point, the prosecutor will not have violated his constitutional duty of disclosure unless his omission is of sufficient significance to result in the denial of the defendant's right to a fair trial.

The Court of Appeals appears to have assumed that the prosecutor has a constitutional obligation to disclose any information that might affect the jury's verdict. That statement of a constitutional standard of materiality approaches the "sporting theory of justice" which the Court expressly rejected in *Brady*. For a jury's appraisal of a case "might" be affected by an improper or trivial consideration as well as by evidence giving rise to a legitimate doubt on the issue of guilt. If everything that might influence a jury must be disclosed, the only way a prosecutor could discharge his constitutional duty would be to allow complete discovery of his files as a matter of routine practice.

Whether or not procedural rules authorizing such broad discovery might be desirable, the Constitution surely does not demand that much. While expressing the opinion that representatives of the State may not "suppress substantial material evidence," former Chief Justice Traynor of the California Supreme Court has pointed out that "they are under no duty to report sua sponte to the defendant all that they learn about the case and about their witnesses." In re Imbler, 387 P.2d 6, 14 (1963). And this Court recently noted that there is "no constitutional requirement that the prosecution to make a complete and detailed accounting to the defense of all police investigatory work on a case." Moore v. Illinois, 408 U.S. 786, 795. The mere possibility that an item of undisclosed information might have helped the defense, or might have affected the outcome of the trial, does not establish "materiality" in the constitutional sense.

Nor do we believe the constitutional obligation is measured by the moral culpability, or the willfulness, of the prosecutor. If evidence highly probative of innocence is in his file, he should be presumed to recognize its significance even if he has actually overlooked it. . . . Conversely, if evidence actually has no probative significance at all, no purpose would be served by requiring a new trial simply because an inept prosecutor incorrectly believed he was suppressing a fact that would be vital to the defense. If the suppression of evidence results in constitutional error, it is because of the character of the evidence, not the character of the prosecutor.

As the District Court recognized in this case, there are situations in which evidence is obviously of such substantial value to the defense that elementary fairness requires it to be disclosed even without a specific request. For though the attorney for the sovereign must prosecute the accused with earnestness and vigor, he must always be faithful to his client's overriding interest that "justice shall be done." He is the "servant of the law, the twofold aim of which is that guilt shall not escape or innocence suffer." Berger v. United States, 295 U.S. 78, 88. This description of the prosecutor's duty illuminates the standard of materiality that governs his obligation to disclose exculpatory evidence.

On the one hand, the fact that such evidence was available to the prosecutor and not submitted to the defense places it in a different category than if it had simply been discovered from a neutral source after trial. For that reason the defendant should not have to satisfy the severe burden of demonstrating that newly discovered evidence probably would have resulted in acquittal. If the standard applied to the usual motion for a new trial based on newly discovered evidence were the same when the evidence was in the State's possession as when it was found in a neutral source, there would be no special significance to the prosecutor's obligation to serve the cause of justice.

On the other hand, since we have rejected the suggestion that the prosecutor has a constitutional duty routinely to deliver his entire file to defense counsel, we cannot consistently treat every nondisclosure as though it were error. It necessarily follows that the judge should not order a new trial every time he is unable to characterize a nondisclosure as harmless under the customary harmless-error standard. Under that standard when error is present in the record, the reviewing judge must set aside the verdict and judgment unless his "conviction is sure that the error did not influence the jury, or had but very slight effect." Kotteakos v. United States, 328 U.S. 750, 764. Unless every nondisclosure is regarded as automatic error, the constitutional standard of materiality must impose a higher burden on the defendant.

The proper standard of materiality must reflect our overriding concern with the justice of the finding of guilt. Such a finding is permissible only if supported by evidence establishing guilt beyond a reasonable doubt. It necessarily follows that if the omitted evidence creates a reasonable doubt that did not otherwise exist, constitutional error has been committed. This means that the omission must be evaluated in the context of the entire record. If there is no reasonable doubt about guilt whether or not the additional evidence is considered, there is no justification for a new trial. On the other hand, if the verdict is already of questionable validity, additional evidence of relatively minor importance might be sufficient to create a reasonable doubt.

This statement of the standard of materiality describes the test which courts appear to have applied in actual cases although the standard has been phrased in different language. It is also the standard which the trial judge applied in this case. He evaluated the significance of Sewell's prior criminal record in the context of the full trial which he recalled in detail. Stressing in particular the incongruity of a claim that Sewell was the aggressor with the evidence of his multiple wounds and respondent's unscathed condition, the trial judge indicated his unqualified opinion that respondent was guilty. He noted that Sewell's prior record did not contradict any evidence offered by the prosecutor, and was largely cumulative of the evidence that Sewell was wearing a bowie knife in a sheath and carrying a second knife in his pocket when he registered at the motel.

Since the arrest record was not requested and did not even arguably give rise to any inference of perjury, since after considering it in the context of the entire record the trial judge remained convinced of respondent's guilt beyond a reasonable doubt, and since we are satisfied that his firsthand appraisal of the record was thorough and entirely reasonable, we hold that the prosecutor's failure to tender Sewell's record to the defense did not deprive respondent of a fair trial as guaranteed by the Due Process Clause of the Fifth Amendment. Accordingly, the judgment of the Court of Appeals is

Reversed.[15]

---

[15] Justice Marshall wrote a dissenting opinion, which Justice Brennan joined.

475. In United States v. Bagley, 473 U.S. 667 (1985) (5–3), five members of the Court agreed that the same general test of materiality is applicable whether there is a specific request, a general request, or no request for the evidence. Evidence is material "only if there is a reasonable probability that, had the evidence been disclosed to the defense, the result of the proceeding would have been different. A 'reasonable probability' is a probability sufficient to undermine confidence in the outcome." Id. at 682. See id. at 683 (opinion of White, J.). Writing only for himself and Justice O'Connor among the majority, Justice Blackmun observed that, when a specific request is made, a reviewing court should take into account the possibility that the prosecutor's implied representation that the evidence does not exist affected the preparation or presentation of the defense.

Also in *Bagley*, the Court said that there is no distinction with respect to the requirement of disclosure between impeachment evidence and exculpatory evidence generally. On remand, the court of appeals held that the facts of the case met the test enunciated by the Court and reversed the conviction. Bagley v. Lumpkin, 798 F.2d 1297 (9th Cir.1986).

The *Bagley* test of materiality was applied to *Brady* material in the context of a capital case, in Kyles v. Whitley, 514 U.S. 419 (1995) (5–4). The Court said that "once a reviewing court applying *Bagley* has found constitutional error there is no need for further harmless-error review." Id. at 435. See also Crivens v. Roth, 172 F.3d 991 (7th Cir.1999) (failure to disclose criminal record of prosecution witness; conviction reversed); Bowen v. Maynard, 799 F.2d 593 (10th Cir.1986) (failure to disclose material information concerning early suspect; conviction vacated); United States ex rel. Smith v. Fairman, 769 F.2d 386 (7th Cir.1985) (failure to disclose police report that gun allegedly used by defendant was inoperable; conviction vacated).

The *Brady* rule was discussed in Strickler v. Greene, 527 U.S. 263 (1999) (7–2), a capital case in which the Court found that the rule was violated by the prosecutor's failure to disclose documents that could have been used to impeach a witness. The Court nevertheless affirmed the conviction because the defendant did not establish that the undisclosed evidence was "material," i.e., that there was a "reasonable probability" that the result of the trial would have been different had the evidence not been withheld. In Banks v. Dretke, 540 U.S. ___ (2004) (7–2), another capital case, the Court also upheld a *Brady* claim. It found that the *Brady* rule was violated when, after telling defense counsel that the prosecution would provide full discovery, the prosecutor failed to disclose that a witness was a paid informant and did not correct the witness's false testimony that he had not discussed the case with the police until a few days before trial. The Court held that the defendant's claim for habeas corpus relief with respect to his capital sentence should have been allowed.

476. When must the disclosure required by cases like *Brady* and *Agurs* be made? In United States v. Kaplan, 554 F.2d 577, 579–80 (3d Cir.1977), the court said: "Where documentary evidence is exculpatory, it may be within both *Brady* and Rule 16. . . . Thus, on occasion there will be an overlap between the two means a federal defendant uses to obtain information in the possession of the prosecution." When *Brady* applies, the court said, "delayed disclosure by the prosecution is not per se reversible error. . . . If exculpatory evidence can be effectively presented at trial and the defendant is not prevented by lack of time to make needed investigation, there is no reversible prosecutorial conduct in ill-timed presentation." Id. at 580. Accord, United States v. Coppa, 267 F.3d 132 (2d Cir.2001).

Brady–Agurs material for use to challenge government witnesses' credibility on cross-examination need not be turned over before the day on which the witness testifies. "Disclosure at that time will fully allow appellees to effectively use that information to challenge the veracity of the government's witness." United States v. Higgs, 713 F.2d 39 (3d Cir.1983).

477. "More than 30 years ago this Court held that the Fourteenth Amendment cannot tolerate a state criminal conviction obtained by the knowing use of false evidence. Mooney v. Holohan, 294 U.S. 103. There has been no deviation from that established principle." Miller v. Pate, 386 U.S. 1, 7 (1967). In Napue v. Illinois, 360 U.S. 264, 269 (1959), the facts of which are outlined in *Moore*, p. 936 above, the Court said: "The principle that a State may not knowingly use false evidence, including false testimony, to obtain a tainted conviction, implicit in any concept of ordered liberty, does not cease to apply merely because the false testimony goes only to the credibility of the witness. The jury's estimate of the truthfulness and reliability of a given witness may well be determinative of guilt or innocence, and it is upon such subtle factors as the possible interest of the witness in testifying falsely that a defendant's life or liberty may depend." See Giglio v. United States, 405 U.S. 150 (1972), note 479 below; Brown v. Wainwright, 785 F.2d 1457 (11th Cir.1986) (*Giglio* applied).

"We do not believe . . . that the prosecution's duty to disclose false testimony by one of its witnesses is to be narrowly and technically limited to those situations where the prosecutor knows that the witness is guilty of the crime of perjury. Regardless of the lack of intent to lie on the part of the witness, *Giglio* and *Napue* require that the prosecutor apprise the court when he knows that his witness is giving testimony that is substantially misleading. This is not to say that the prosecutor must play the role of defense counsel, and ferret out ambiguities in his witness' responses on cross-examination. However, when it should be obvious to the Government that the witness' answer, although made in good faith, is untrue, the Government's obligation to correct that statement is as compelling as it is in a situation where the Government knows that the witness is intentionally committing perjury." United States v. Harris, 498 F.2d 1164, 1169 (3d Cir.1974).

Prosecutorial (Mis)Conduct

---

478. "Formulation of the duty [to disclose evidence to the defense] in terms of wilful or wrongful conduct would seem only to confuse here, and is not necessary under the governing law as we understand it." United States ex rel. Meers v. Wilkins, 326 F.2d 135, 139 (2d Cir.1964). "Where disclosable evidentiary material which came into the possession of the Government has been lost or destroyed, and is unavailable to the defense for that reason, the standards for determining whether sanctions should be imposed on the Government . . . depend on the extent of the Government's culpability for the loss or destruction and the amount of the prejudice to the defense which resulted." United States v. Miranda, 526 F.2d 1319, 1325–26 (2d Cir.1975). Sanctions have not been imposed "where the loss was inadvertent and not deliberate or in bad faith, and there was not such prejudice to the defendant as to deny him a fair trial." Id. at 1327. See, e.g., United States v. Rojas, 502 F.2d 1042 (5th Cir.1974) (accidental damage to tape of conversation); United States v. Sewar, 468 F.2d 236 (9th Cir.1972) (negligent failure to preserve blood sample); United States v. Shafer, 445 F.2d 579 (7th Cir.1971) (evidence taken from defendant destroyed because of dangerousness); Ingram v. Peyton, 367 F.2d 933 (4th Cir.1966) (prosecutor's error in naming principal prosecution witness prevented defense from discovering that witness had been convicted of perjury).

The Due Process Clause does not require law enforcement officials to preserve a sample of the breath of a suspected drunk driver in order to use the results of a breath-analysis test in a criminal prosecution. California v. Trombetta, 467 U.S. 479 (1984). The court noted that the officials had acted in good faith, that the likelihood that the samples would be exculpatory was extremely low, and that there were alternative ways to challenge the accuracy of the results.

479. In Giglio v. United States, 405 U.S. 150 (1972), an assistant United States attorney promised the principal government witness that he would not be prosecuted if he cooperated. The assistant who tried the case was unaware that the promise was made. At trial, the witness denied the existence of a promise. The Court held that *Napue*, note 477 above, was applicable. "[W]hether the nondisclosure was a result of negligence or design, it is the responsibility of the prosecutor. The prosecutor's office is an entity and as such it is the spokesman for the Government. A promise made by one attorney must be attributed, for these purposes, to the Government. . . . To the extent this places a burden on the large prosecution offices, procedures and regulations can be established to carry that burden and to insure communication of all relevant information on each case to every lawyer who deals with it." 405 U.S. at 154.

480. The defendant was convicted of assault with intent to murder and unauthorized use of a motor vehicle. The police had in their possession the results of ballistics and fingerprint tests which indicated that the defendant was not involved in the crimes charged. It was not shown that the prosecutor knew of the existence of the reports or that the tests had been made. The court of appeals held that the conviction was invalid.

> [T]he effect of the nondisclosure [is not] neutralized because the prosecuting attorney was not shown to have had knowledge of the exculpatory evidence. Failure of the police to reveal such material evidence in their possession is equally harmful to a defendant whether the information is purposely, or negligently, withheld. And it makes no difference if the withholding is by officials other than the prosecutor. The police are also part of the prosecution, and the taint on the trial is no less if they, rather than the State's Attorney, were guilty of the nondisclosure. If the police allow the State's Attorney to produce evidence pointing to guilt without informing him of other evidence in their possession which contradicts this inference, state officers are practicing deception not only on the State's Attorney but on the court and the defendant. "The cruelest lies are often told in silence." If the police silence as to the existence of the reports resulted from negligence rather than guile, the deception is no less damaging.
>
> The duty to disclose is that of the state, which ordinarily acts through the prosecuting attorney; but if he too is the victim of police suppression of the material information, the state's failure is not on that account excused. We cannot condone the attempt to connect the defendant with the crime by questionable inferences which might be refuted by undisclosed and unproduced documents then in the hands of the police. To borrow a phrase from Chief Judge Biggs, this procedure passes "beyond the line of tolerable imperfection and falls into the field of fundamental unfairness."[16]

Barbee v. Warden, Maryland Penitentiary, 331 F.2d 842, 846 (4th Cir. 1964). To the same effect, see Smith v. New Mexico Department of Corrections, 50 F.3d 801 (10th Cir.1995) (failure to disclose reports in possession of police but not known to prosecution was *Brady* violation, notwithstanding prosecutor's "open file" policy); United States ex rel. Smith v. Fairman, 769 F.2d 386 (7th Cir.1985) (police witness's failure to disclose exculpatory firearms report).

Citing cases in other circuits, in United States v. Brooks, 966 F.2d 1500 (D.C.Cir.1992), the court held that in responding to a *Brady* request, the government has a duty to search reasonably available files for exculpatory evidence of which it is unaware, if there is a "non-trivial" prospect that the search will yield such evidence. As the difficulty of the search increases, the

16. Curran v. State of Del., 259 F.2d 707, 713 (3d Cir.1958). . . .

existence of such a duty depends on the likelihood that evidence will be found increasing accordingly.

In Luna v. Beto, 395 F.2d 35 (5th Cir.1968), the principal witness for the state testified falsely (perhaps unintentionally) that there were no cases pending against him. In fact, the police had promised to help him with a case pending against him in return for his help in other cases. The prosecutor did not know of the police promise. While the witness was testifying, the police who knew of the promise were excluded from the courtroom as prospective witnesses and did not hear his testimony. Following the defendant's conviction, the defense learned of the promise. Should the conviction be reversed? If so, is reversal constitutionally required?

481. "The prosecutor in a criminal case shall . . . make timely disclosure to the defense of all evidence or information known to the prosecutor that tends to negate the guilt of the accused or mitigates the offense, and, in connection with sentencing, disclose to the defense and to the tribunal all unprivileged mitigating information known to the prosecutor, except when the prosecutor is relieved of this responsibility by a protective order of the tribunal. . . ." Rule 3.8(d), ABA Model Rules of Professional Conduct (2004).

Arizona v. Youngblood

488 U.S. 51, 109 S.Ct. 333, 102 L.Ed.2d 281 (1988)

■ CHIEF JUSTICE REHNQUIST delivered the opinion of the Court.

Respondent Larry Youngblood was convicted by a Pima County, Arizona, jury of child molestation, sexual assault, and kidnaping. The Arizona Court of Appeals reversed his conviction on the ground that the State had failed to preserve semen samples from the victim's body and clothing. 734 P.2d 592 (1986). We granted certiorari to consider the extent to which the Due Process Clause of the Federal Constitution requires the State to preserve evidentiary material that might be useful to a criminal defendant.

On October 29, 1983, David L., a 10-year-old boy, attended a church service with his mother. After he left the service at about 9:30 p.m., the boy went to a carnival behind the church, where he was abducted by a middle-aged man of medium height and weight. The assailant drove the boy to a secluded area near a ravine and molested him. He then took the boy to an unidentified, sparsely furnished house where he sodomized the boy four times. Afterwards, the assailant tied the boy up while he went outside to start his car. Once the assailant started the car, albeit with some difficulty, he returned to the house and again sodomized the boy. The assailant then sent the boy to the bathroom to wash up before he returned him to the carnival. He threatened to kill the boy if he told anyone about the attack. The entire ordeal lasted about 1½ hours.

After the boy made his way home, his mother took him to Kino Hospital. At the hospital, a physician treated the boy for rectal injuries. The physician also used a "sexual assault kit" to collect evidence of the attack. The Tucson Police Department provided such kits to all hospitals in Pima County for use in sexual assault cases. Under standard procedure, the victim of a sexual assault was taken to a hospital, where a physician used the kit to collect evidence. The kit included paper to collect saliva samples, a tube for obtaining a blood sample, microscopic slides for making smears, a set of Q-tip like swabs, and a medical examination report. Here, the physician used the swab to collect samples from the boy's rectum and mouth. He then made a microscopic slide of the samples. The doctor also obtained samples of the boy's saliva, blood, and hair. The physician did not examine the samples at any time. The police placed the kit in a secure refrigerator at the police station. At the hospital, the police also collected the boy's underwear and T-shirt. This clothing was not refrigerated or frozen.

Nine days after the attack, on November 7, 1983, the police asked the boy to pick out his assailant from a photographic lineup. The boy identified respondent as the assailant. Respondent was not located by the police until four weeks later; he was arrested on December 9, 1983.

On November 8, 1983, Edward Heller, a police criminologist, examined the sexual assault kit. He testified that he followed standard department procedure, which was to examine the slides and determine whether sexual contact had occurred. After he determined that such contact had occurred, the criminologist did not perform any other tests, although he placed the assault kit back in the refrigerator. He testified that tests to identify blood group substances were not routinely conducted during the initial examination of an assault kit and in only about half of all cases in any event. He did not test the clothing at this time.

Respondent was indicted on charges of child molestation, sexual assault, and kidnaping. The State moved to compel respondent to provide blood and saliva samples for comparison with the material gathered through the use of the sexual assault kit, but the trial court denied the motion on the ground that the State had not obtained a sufficiently large semen sample to make a valid comparison. The prosecutor then asked the State's criminologist to perform an ABO blood group test on the rectal swab sample in an attempt to ascertain the blood type of the boy's assailant. This test failed to detect any blood group substances in the sample.

In January 1985, the police criminologist examined the boy's clothing for the first time. He found one semen stain on the boy's underwear and another on the rear of his T-shirt. The criminologist tried to obtain blood group substances from both stains using the ABO technique, but was unsuccessful. He also performed a P–30 protein molecule test on the stains, which indicated that only a small quantity of semen was present on the clothing; it was inconclusive as to the assailant's identity. The Tucson

Police Department had just begun using this test, which was then used in slightly more than half of the crime laboratories in the country.

Respondent's principal defense at trial was that the boy had erred in identifying him as the perpetrator of the crime. In this connection, both a criminologist for the State and an expert witness for respondent testified as to what might have been shown by tests performed on the samples shortly after they were gathered, or by later tests performed on the samples from the boy's clothing had the clothing been properly refrigerated. The court instructed the jury that if they found the State had destroyed or lost evidence, they might "infer that the true fact is against the State's interest." 10 Tr. 90.

The jury found respondent guilty as charged, but the Arizona Court of Appeals reversed the judgment of conviction. It stated that " 'when identity is an issue at trial and the police permit the destruction of evidence that could eliminate the defendant as the perpetrator, such loss is material to the defense and is a denial of due process.' " 153 Ariz., at 54, quoting State v. Escalante, 153 Ariz. 55, 61 (App.1986). The Court of Appeals concluded on the basis of the expert testimony at trial that timely performance of tests with properly preserved semen samples could have produced results that might have completely exonerated respondent. The Court of Appeals reached this conclusion even though it did "not imply any bad faith on the part of the State." 153 Ariz., at 54. . . . We now reverse.

Decision of this case requires us to again consider "what might loosely be called the area of constitutionally guaranteed access to evidence." United States v. Valenzuela-Bernal, 458 U.S. 858, 867 (1982). In Brady v. Maryland, 373 U.S. 83 (1963), we held "that the suppression by the prosecution of evidence favorable to the accused upon request violates due process where the evidence is material either to guilt or to punishment, irrespective of the good faith or bad faith of the prosecution." Id., at 87. In United States v. Agurs, 427 U.S. 97 (1976), we held that the prosecution had a duty to disclose some evidence of this description even though no requests were made for it, but at the same time we rejected the notion that a "prosecutor has a constitutional duty routinely to deliver his entire file to defense counsel." Id., at 111. . . .

There is no question but that the State complied with *Brady* and *Agurs* here. The State disclosed relevant police reports to respondent, which contained information about the existence of the swab and the clothing, and the boy's examination at the hospital. The State provided respondent's expert with the laboratory reports and notes prepared by the police criminologist, and respondent's expert had access to the swab and to the clothing.

If respondent is to prevail on federal constitutional grounds, then, it must be because of some constitutional duty over and above that imposed by cases such as *Brady* and *Agurs*. Our most recent decision in this area of the law, California v. Trombetta, 467 U.S. 479 (1984), arose out of a drunk driving prosecution in which the State had introduced test results indicating the concentration of alcohol in the blood of two motorists. The defendants sought to suppress the test results on the ground that the State had failed to preserve the breath samples used in the test. We rejected this argument for several reasons: first, "the officers here were acting in 'good faith and in accord with their normal practice,' " id., at 488, quoting Killian v. United States, 368 U.S. 231, 242 (1961); second, in the light of the procedures actually used the chances that preserved samples would have exculpated the defendants were slim . . .; and, third, even if the samples might have shown inaccuracy in the tests, the defendants had "alternative means of demonstrating their innocence." Id., at 490. In the present case, the likelihood that the preserved materials would have enabled the defendant to exonerate himself appears to be greater than it was in *Trombetta*, but here, unlike in *Trombetta*, the State did not attempt to make any use of the materials in its own case in chief.

Our decisions in related areas have stressed the importance for constitutional purposes of good or bad faith on the part of the Government when the claim is based on loss of evidence attributable to the Government. . . .

The Due Process Clause of the Fourteenth Amendment, as interpreted in *Brady*, makes the good or bad faith of the State irrelevant when the State fails to disclose to the defendant material exculpatory evidence. But we think the Due Process Clause requires a different result when we deal with the failure of the State to preserve evidentiary material of which no more can be said than that it could have been subjected to tests, the results of which might have exonerated the defendant. Part of the reason for the difference in treatment is found in the observation made by the Court in *Trombetta*, supra, at 486, that "[w]henever potentially exculpatory evidence is permanently lost, courts face the treacherous task of divining the import of materials whose contents are unknown and, very often, disputed." Part of it stems from our unwillingness to read the "fundamental fairness" requirement of the Due Process Clause, see Lisenba v. California, 314 U.S. 219, 236 (1941), as imposing on the police an undifferentiated and absolute duty to retain and to preserve all material that might be of conceivable evidentiary significance in a particular prosecution. We think that requiring a defendant to show bad faith on the part of the police both limits the extent of the police's obligation to preserve evidence to reasonable bounds and confines it to that class of cases where the interests of justice most clearly require it, i.e., those cases in which the police themselves by their conduct indicate that the evidence could form a basis for exonerating the defendant. We therefore hold that unless a criminal defendant can show bad faith on the part of the police, failure to preserve potentially useful evidence does not constitute a denial of due process of law.

In this case, the police collected the rectal swab and clothing on the night of the crime; respondent was not taken into custody until six weeks later. The failure of the police to refrigerate the clothing and to perform tests on the semen samples can at worst be described as negligent. None of this information was concealed from respondent at trial, and the evidence—such as it was—was made available to respondent's expert who declined to perform any tests on the samples. The Arizona Court of Appeals noted in its opinion—and we agree—that there was no suggestion of bad faith on the part of the police. It follows, therefore, from what we have said, that there was no violation of the Due Process Clause.

The Arizona Court of Appeals also referred somewhat obliquely to the State's "inability to quantitatively test" certain semen samples with the newer P–30 test. 153 Ariz., at 54. If the court meant by this statement that the Due Process Clause is violated when the police fail to use a particular investigatory tool, we strongly disagree. The situation here is no different than a prosecution for drunk driving that rests on police observation alone; the defendant is free to argue to the finder of fact that a breathalizer test might have been exculpatory, but the police do not have a constitutional duty to perform any particular tests.

The judgment of the Arizona Court of Appeals is reversed. . . .

. . .[17]

---

482. The *New York Times* reported on August 11, 2000, at 12, that DNA tests unavailable at the time of his trial had cleared Youngblood of the crime for which he was convicted. Following the Supreme Court's decision in 1988, Youngblood's conviction was set aside by the state appellate court on state constitutional grounds; the conviction was later reinstated by the state supreme court. He served his sentence concurrently with a sentence for an unrelated crime. He was released in 1998 but was returned to prison for failing to report a change of address as required by a sex offender law.

483. *Youngblood* is applied in United States v. Cooper, 983 F.2d 928 (9th Cir.1993), in which federal drug agents permitted the destruction before trial of seized laboratory equipment, despite the defendant's claim that it was not adapted to the production of unlawful drugs. The equipment was destroyed because of concern that it might be contaminated.

In United States v. Brimage, 115 F.3d 73 (1st Cir.1997), the defendants were convicted of firearms offenses, in which they were implicated by a "sting" operation. Part of the sting involved the use of a wired informer, whose conversations with the defendants were overheard by federal agents. The conversations were not recorded. The defendants claimed that the failure to record the conversations was a deliberate effort to avoid the creation or preservation of exculpatory evidence and was, therefore, in bad faith, and they moved for dismissal of the charges. The court upheld the convictions. *Youngblood*, it said, had to do with a failure to preserve evidence already in existence and did not go so far as to require that investigators create evidence for use at trial. It concluded that in some circumstances investigators might have an obligation to record conversations but that there was no evidence of bad faith in this case.

[17] Justice Stevens wrote an opinion concurring in the judgment. Justice Blackmun wrote a dissenting opinion, which Justice Brennan and Justice Marshall joined.

484. Relying on the state constitution, the Supreme Court of Connecticut has held that bad faith is not essential to a finding that the failure of police to preserve potentially exculpatory evidence is a denial of due process. Rather, "a trial court must decide each case depending on its own facts, assess the materiality of the unpreserved evidence and the degree of prejudice to the accused, and formulate a remedy that vindicates his or her rights. . . . The ultimate question for the trial court in such a case is: What remedy best serves the interests of justice?" State v. Morales, 657 A.2d 585 (Conn.1995).

485. How far must the prosecutor go in advising defense counsel of the existence of eyewitnesses to an event whom the prosecutor intends not to call as witnesses? Assuming that he has an obligation to disclose the existence of witnesses who would testify affirmatively that the defendant was not the person who committed the crime in question, see, e.g., Jackson v. Wainwright, 390 F.2d 288 (5th Cir.1968), must the prosecutor, in order fairly to call witnesses who will identify the defendant, disclose the existence of witnesses who are unable to testify either way or who would testify that conditions were unsuitable for accurate observation? Can he constitutionally stop short of full disclosure of the names of all eyewitnesses known to him? If so, should he do so as a matter of professional ethics? As a matter of good tactics? Who decides who is an eyewitness? Does it make any difference whether the prosecutor intends to use any eyewitnesses himself? Suppose he concludes that no one—neither those who will nor those who will not identify the defendant—was in a position to observe the event accurately and that he will prove his case entirely by circumstantial evidence. See generally Clarke v. Burke, 440 F.2d 853 (7th Cir.1971); Lee v. United States, 388 F.2d 737 (9th Cir.1968).

486. The practice of a prosecutor communicating with a defendant in the absence of his counsel is discussed at length and sharply criticized, in United States v. Lopez, 765 F.Supp. 1433 (N.D.Cal.1991), vacated, 4 F.3d 1455 (9th Cir.1993) (confirming criticism made by district court). See also United States v. Hammad, 858 F.2d 834 (2d Cir.1988).

Responsibility of the Defense

---

487. "In the end, any allegation of suppression boils down to an assessment of what the State knows at trial in comparison to the knowledge held by the defense." Giles v. Maryland, 386 U.S. 66, 96 (1967) (White, J., concurring in judgment).

In determining whether the prosecutor's failure to disclose information to the defense requires reversal of a conviction, what is the significance of defense counsel's failure to pursue leads that would have led independently to the information?

The defendant was indicted for a violation of the Lindbergh Kidnapping Law, 18 U.S.C. § 1201. The government's case was that the defendant forcibly abducted a girl, drove with her across state lines, and thereafter raped her; he was not charged with rape, which was relevant only to the question whether the girl was returned unharmed (as bearing on the issue of "aggravation" of the kidnapping). The main effort of the defense was to show that the girl was not abducted but went willingly with the defendant. At a preliminary hearing, the girl testified that soon after the defendant's arrest she had been examined by a "Dr. Green." In fact, as federal agents and presumably the prosecutor knew, she had been examined by Dr. Stotlar. The prosecutor did not correct the girl's error or give any information to the defense about the examination. He did not call the doctor to testify or list him on the list of witnesses given to defense counsel, as required by 18 U.S.C. § 3432, p. 848 above. Defense counsel did not locate "Dr. Green" and did not pursue the matter. At trial, he objected to testimony of the girl about the physical examination on the ground of hearsay; he argued to the jury that the government should have produced the doctor to prove that there had been an act of intercourse. After the return of a verdict of guilty, defense counsel learned that the doctor's report indicated that there was no evidence of sexual intercourse. Should the conviction be reversed on appeal? If so, is reversal constitutionally required? See United States v. Poole, 379 F.2d 645 (7th Cir.1967). See Boss v. Pierce, 263 F.3d 734 (7th Cir.2001).

488. The defendant was prosecuted for rape. A laboratory test for evidence on the defendant's clothing was negative. A police officer told the defendant that the result of the test was negative. There was no other disclosure of the result, and defense counsel did not learn about the test until after the defendant was convicted. Should the conviction be reversed? The Supreme Court of Illinois said no. People v. Raymond, 248 N.E.2d 663 (Ill.1969). The federal court of appeals said yes. United States ex rel. Raymond v. Illinois, 455 F.2d 62 (7th Cir.1971).

489. Expert testimony. Suppose there is doubt about a defendant's sanity at the time of the commission of a crime, and both the prosecutor and defense counsel employ psychiatrists to examine the defendant. If the prosecutor's examining psychiatrist advises him that, in his opinion, the defendant was not sane at the time the crime was committed or that he has substantial doubt about the defendant's sanity, must the prosecutor advise defense counsel of the psychiatrist's opinion far enough in advance of trial for him to consider and prepare for use of the insanity defense? Suppose several other psychiatrists have examined the defendant for the prosecutor and have concluded that the defendant was clearly sane (and the prosecutor has so advised defense counsel). Does it make a difference whether the insanity defense was raised at the trial? See Ashley v. Texas, 319 F.2d 80 (5th Cir.1963); cf. United States v. Spagnoulo, 960 F.2d 990 (11th Cir. 1992).

How far should the prosecutor's duty to disclose *opinion* evidence be extended? Is there any reciprocal obligation of the defense to disclose opinion evidence? Does defense counsel have a professional obligation *not* to disclose opinion evidence?

Witnesses

---

490. "[T]he Fifth Amendment, in its direct application to the Federal Government, and in its bearing on the States by reason of the Fourteenth Amendment, forbids either comment by the prosecution on the accused's silence or instructions by the court that such silence is evidence of guilt." Griffin v. California, 380 U.S. 609, 615 (1965). *Griffin* was distinguished in United States v. Robinson, 485 U.S. 25 (1988) (5–3). There the Court held that the prosecutor's reference in his closing argument to the defendant's failure to testify, which was in response to defense counsel's statement that the government had not "allowed" the defendant to explain, was not impermissible.

If the defendant so requests, a trial judge is required to instruct the jury not to give evidentiary weight to the defendant's failure to testify. Carter v. Kentucky, 450 U.S. 288 (1981) (8–1). It does not violate the privilege against self-incrimination for the trial judge to give such an instruction over the defendant's objection. Lakeside v. Oregon, 435 U.S. 333 (1978).

FEDERAL RULES OF CRIMINAL PROCEDURE

Rule 17

SUBPOENA

(a) Content. A subpoena must state the court's name and the title of the proceeding, include the seal of the court, and command the witness to attend and testify at the time and place the subpoena specifies. The clerk must issue a blank subpoena—signed and sealed—to the party requesting it, and that party must fill in the blanks before the subpoena is served.

(b) Defendant Unable to Pay. Upon a defendant's ex parte application, the court must order that a subpoena be issued for a named witness if the defendant shows an inability to pay the witness's fees and the necessity of the witness's presence for an adequate defense. If the court orders a subpoena to be issued, the process costs and witness fees will be paid in the same manner as those paid for witnesses the government subpoenas.

(c) Producing Documents and Objects.

(1) *In General.* A subpoena may order the witness to produce any books, papers, documents, data or other objects the subpoena desig-

nates. The court may direct the witness to produce the designated items in court before trial or before they are to be offered in evidence. When the items arrive, the court may permit the parties and their attorneys to inspect all or part of them.

(2) *Quashing or Modifying the Subpoena.* On motion made promptly, the court may quash or modify the subpoena if compliance would be unreasonable or oppressive.

(d) Service. A marshal, a deputy marshal or any nonparty and who is at least 18 years of age may serve a subpoena. The server must deliver a copy of the subpoena to the witness and must tender to the witness one day's witness-attendance fee and the legal mileage allowance. The server need not tender the attendance fee or mileage allowance when the United States, a federal officer, or a federal agency has requested the subpoena.

(e) Place of Service.

(1) *In the United States.* A subpoena requiring a witness to attend a hearing or trial may be served at any place within the United States.

(2) *In a Foreign Country.* If the witness is in a foreign country, 28 U.S.C. § 1783 governs the subpoena's service.

(f) Issuing a Deposition Subpoena.

(1) *Issuance.* A court order to take a deposition authorizes the clerk in the district where the deposition is to be taken to issue a subpoena for any witness named or described in the order.

(2) *Place.* After considering the convenience of the witness and the parties, the court may order—and the subpoena may require—the witness to appear anywhere the court designates.

(g) Contempt. The court (other than a magistrate judge) may hold in contempt a witness who, without adequate excuse, disobeys a subpoena issued by a federal court in that district. A magistrate judge may hold in contempt a witness who, without adequate excuse, disobeys a subpoena issued by that magistrate judge as provided in 28 U.S.C. § 636(e).

(h) Information Not Subject to a Subpoena. No party may subpoena a statement of a witness or of a prospective witness under this rule. Rule 26.2 governs the production of the statement.

---

491. In United States v. Hathcock, 441 F.2d 197 (5th Cir.1971), the defendant sought a subpoena under Rule 17(b) for the production of a witness then in a federal prison in Kansas to testify at a trial in Texas. The cost of transporting the witness was estimated at about $800. The trial judge talked to the witness by telephone, and the witness indicated that he would give material testimony favorable to the defendant. The judge told defense counsel that he would have the witness produced if counsel would assure the court that he would use the witness. Counsel refused to give That assurance because he had not yet been able to interview the witness in private. The witness was not produced. On appeal, the court held that the trial judge had abused his discretion under Rule 17(b).

AO89 (Rev. 7/95) Subpoena in a Criminal Case

UNITED STATES DISTRICT COURT

DISTRICT OF

V.

SUBPOENA IN A CRIMINAL CASE

Case Number:

TO:

☐ YOU ARE COMMANDED to appear in the United States District Court at the place, date, and time specified below, or any subsequent place, date and time set by the court, to testify in the above referenced case. This subpoena shall remain in effect until you are granted leave to depart by the court or by an officer acting on behalf of the court.

PLACE	COURTROOM
	DATE AND TIME

☐ YOU ARE ALSO COMMANDED to bring with you the following document(s) or object(s):

U.S. MAGISTRATE JUDGE OR CLERK OF COURT	DATE
(By) Deputy Clerk	

ATTORNEY'S NAME, ADDRESS AND PHONE NUMBER:

"Our holding is merely that the appellant in this instance met the burden cast upon him by Rule 17(b) and that the district court abused its discretion in denying the production of the witness. The requirement that defense counsel bind himself in advance to put [the witness] on the stand, regardless of trial developments and the necessity counsel recognized to preserve options as to tactical trial decisions, was doubtless motivated by a desire to save money for the government. It was nonetheless, in our judgment, the imposition of unreasonable conditions upon the right to compulsory process and an almost classic example of abuse of judicial discretion. In stating this we emphasize that our decision in no wise impinges upon the trial judge's necessary discretion in the initial determination of the need for the testimony of the witness, arrived at by weighing numerous factors including materiality, relevancy and competency. Certainly there are frivolous requests for production of witnesses and just as certainly defendants may seek to abuse the right to compulsory process at government expense. In close cases the district court must exercise its sound discretion, bearing in mind that the burden of showing frivolousness or abuse of process is on the government." Id. at 200. See United States v. Greschner, 802 F.2d 373 (10th Cir.1986) (ruling on request for subpoena within discretion of trial judge); United States v. Hegwood, 562 F.2d 946 (5th Cir.1977) (subpoena properly refused); Welsh v. United States, 404 F.2d 414 (5th Cir.1968) (refusal to issue subpoena was error).

The purpose of allowing defense counsel to obtain subpoenas ex parte under Rule 17(b) is to protect an indigent defendant against advance disclosure of his defense. See *Greschner*, above; United States v. Meriwether, 486 F.2d 498 (5th Cir.1973).

United States v. Messercola, 701 F.Supp. 482 (D.N.J.1988), upholds issuance of a subpoena under Rule 17(c) that directs a person to submit to being photographed by the FBI, so the photograph can be used in a photo array to be shown to prosecution witnesses.

492. After failing to respond to a subpoena, Mrs. Carradine was brought into court pursuant to a bench warrant to testify for the state in a prosecution for homicide. After answering preliminary questions, she refused to testify because she feared for her own life and the lives of her six children. The homicide involved members of a slum "youth gang" in Chicago. The state offered to relocate her elsewhere in the city or in the United States, and offered to provide protection for her and her family. She indicated that she did not believe that they could protect her against members of the gang, and said that when she originally gave information about the homicide to a state prosecutor she did so only because he had promised her that she would not have to appear and testify. When she continued to refuse to testify, she was committed to jail. After two weeks in jail, she still refused to testify. She was held in contempt and sentenced to imprisonment for six months. Observing that the circumstances of the case were "particularly distressing," the Supreme Court of Illinois affirmed the sentence. It quoted remarks of the trial court: " '[O]ne of the problems that the court has is that unless we receive the cooperation of the citizens who see certain alleged events take place these events are not going to be rooted out, nor are perpetrators of these acts going to be brought before the bar of justice unless citizens stand up to be counted, and I think this [fear] is not a valid reason for not testifying. If it's a valid reason then we might as well close the doors.'" People v. Carradine, 287 N.E.2d 670, 672 (Ill.1972).

493. After a panel of the court had held that it was a violation of a federal statute prohibiting promises of favors in return for testimony, 18 U.S.C. § 201(c)(2), for a prosecutor to promise leniency to a defendant in return for testimony against his codefendant, United States v. Singleton, 144 F.3d 1343 (10th Cir.1998), the full court of appeals reheard the case en banc and reversed the panel's decision. The court observed the practice of granting leniency in return for testimony is a practice of long standing. 165 F.3d 1297 (1999). Accord, United States v. Lowery, 166 F.3d 1119 (11th Cir.1999) (cases in other circuits cited).

Reliance at trial on the testimony of a paid informer does not violate 18 U.S.C. § 201(c)(2). United States v. Anty, 203 F.3d 305 (4th Cir.2000).

494. 18 U.S.C. § 3144. Release or detention of a material witness.

> If it appears from an affidavit filed by a party that the testimony of a person is material in a criminal proceeding, and if it is shown that it may become impracticable to secure the presence of the person by subpoena, a judicial officer may order the arrest of the person and treat the person in accordance with the provisions of section 3142 of this title. No material witness may be detained because of inability to comply with any condition of release if the testimony of such witness can adequately be secured by deposition, and if further detention is not necessary to prevent a failure of justice. Release of a material witness may be delayed for a reasonable period of time until the deposition of the witness can be taken pursuant to the Federal Rules of Criminal Procedure.

See Bacon v. United States, 449 F.2d 933 (9th Cir.1971) (in absence of probable cause to believe that witness would not comply with subpoena, order for detention of witness in grand jury proceedings was invalid).

495. The defendant was prosecuted for murder. At trial, defense counsel offered to stipulate to the identity of the victim and to the fact of death. Over objection, the trial judge allowed the victim's mother to testify to those facts. During her testimony, she broke down and wept. The court upheld the prosecutor's refusal to accept the stipulation. "The weeping of the deceased's mother, a natural reaction to her testimony concerning her son, did not result in reversible prejudice to defendant." People v. Hairston, 294 N.E.2d 748, 753–54 (Ill.1973). "[D]espite a defendant's unequivocal offer to stipulate to an element of an offense, Rule 404(b) does not preclude the government from introducing evidence of other bad acts to prove that element." United States v. Crowder, 141 F.3d 1202, 1203 (D.C.Cir.1998). See United States v. O'Shea, 724 F.2d 1514 (11th Cir.1984) (offer to stipulate prior conviction of murder).

In Old Chief v. United States, 519 U.S. 172 (1997) (5–4), the Court held that the district court abused its discretion when it refused to accept the defendant's offer to stipulate a prior conviction to establish that element of the offense (possession of a firearm by someone with a prior felony conviction, 18 U.S.C. § 922(g)(1)) and instead allowed the prosecutor to present evidence of the prior conviction. The evidence indicated the nature of the offense and raised the possibility that the jury would rely on the prior conviction as evidence of the crime charged. In that circumstance, the Court said, the district court should have accepted the stipulation because the danger of prejudice to the defendant substantially outweighed the scant probative value of the evidence introduced in place of the stipulation.

The Court affirmed "the accepted rule that the prosecution is entitled to prove its case free from any defendant's option to stipulate the evidence away," id. at 189, but said that it did not apply when all that was at stake was whether or not the defendant had a prior conviction. See United States v. Becht, 267 F.3d 767 (8th Cir.2001) (*Old Chief* applied; conviction affirmed).

496.

> The exclusion of witnesses from the courtroom during trial is a time-honored practice designed to prevent the shaping of testimony by hearing what other witnesses say. . . . The decision to sequester or not is within the court's discretionary power and is reviewable only for abuse. . . .
>
> This court has held that permitting a witness to testify notwithstanding his disregard of the court's order of sequestration is not error, but is within the court's discretion. . . . Such is the general rule following Holder v. United States, 150 U.S. 91, 92 (1893), where it is stated: "If a witness disobeys the order of withdrawal, while he may be proceeded against for contempt and his testimony is open to comment to the jury by reason of his conduct, he is not thereby disqualified, and the weight of authority is that he cannot be excluded on that ground merely, although the right to exclude under particular circumstances may be supported as within the sound discretion of the trial court."
>
> The Supreme Court there upheld the trial court's admission of testimony from a disobedient witness and had no occasion to spell out the "particular circumstances" which would support a refusal to permit the witness to testify, nor has it done so in any subsequent case.
>
> Since the purpose of the order is to gain assurance of credibility and its violation is a legitimate subject of comment in this respect, it seems proper that unless the violation has somehow so discredited the witness as to render his testimony incredible as a matter of law he should not be disqualified from testifying. Since a refusal to permit him to testify penalizes the litigant rather than the disobedient witness himself, it would seem that the "special circumstances" justifying such refusal should be such as tend to make the litigant a party to and justly subject to sanction for the witness's disobedience.

Taylor v. United States, 388 F.2d 786, 788 (9th Cir.1967).

See Barnard v. Henderson, 514 F.2d 744 (5th Cir.1975) (exclusion of witness who inadvertently violated order was error). The trial court's refusal to allow a witness to testify was upheld in United States v. Kiliyan, 456 F.2d 555 (8th Cir.1972) (witness, defendant's wife, remained in court after need for her testimony appeared).

In Geders v. United States, 425 U.S. 80, 87 (1976), the Court affirmed that the trial judge has "broad power to sequester witnesses before, during, and after their testimony," but said that an order directing the defendant not to consult with defense counsel during an overnight recess between the defendant's direct testimony and cross-examination violated his right to counsel under the Sixth Amendment. The Court observed that there were other methods to avoid the danger of improper coaching of the defendant in such circumstances, including arrangement of the trial schedule to avoid prolonged interruptions of testimony.

Geders does not apply to a short recess while the defendant is testifying as a witness. Perry v. Leeke, 488 U.S. 272 (1989) (6–3). The recess in this case was for 15 minutes, between direct and cross examination. The Court reasoned that although a defendant might discuss general trial matters with his counsel overnight, during a short recess of the kind involved here, a defendant was unlikely to discuss anything other than the testimony he was then giving; and a defendant has no right to interrupt his testimony and discuss it with counsel while he is appearing as a witness. See Mudd v. United States, 798 F.2d 1509 (D.C.Cir.1986) (order that counsel not discuss testimony with defendant, then on the witness stand, over weekend was violation of right to counsel that requires reversal without showing of prejudice).

During the defendant's trial for murder, the prosecutor informed the court that a witness who had apparently been threatened by the defendant and had previously refused to testify against him was willing to do so but that she was concerned for her safety. The judge directed defense counsel not to discuss with the defendant the likelihood that the witness would testify. The court of appeals held that in view of the important countervailing interest, the direction of the judge did not infringe the defendant's right to consult with his attorney. Morgan v. Bennett, 204 F.3d 360 (2d Cir. 2000).

Lee Won Sing v. United States

215 F.2d 680 (D.C.Cir.1954)

■ PER CURIAM.

Appellant was indicted in one count for the illegal purchase and in another for the illegal concealment of narcotics. . . . Lee Poo was jointly charged with appellant in these counts, and separately in three others in the same indictment. He pleaded guilty and testified as the sole witness for appellant, who was convicted as charged. Had the jury believed Lee Poo's testimony the verdict might have been otherwise. His credibility, therefore, was an important factor in the case.

In cross-examining Lee Poo Government counsel asked if it were not a fact that appellant was giving him $20,000 to plead guilty—"to take the plea in this case." No objection was made to the question. Lee Poo answered in the negative and the Government did not offer evidence on the subject. After the judge's charge and before the jury retired defense counsel, pointing out the impact the question must have had on the jury, with its implication that Lee Poo was being paid to perjure himself, requested the court to instruct the jury that the Government, not having brought in evidence to the contrary, was bound by the negative answer given by Lee Poo. The court refused to charge in this manner but did instruct the jury that their verdict must rest upon the testimony of witnesses and other evidence, that questions are not evidence, and that the only thing the jury could properly regard as evidence were answers to questions propounded.

The subject matter of the question of course was highly relevant, having to do with the guilt of appellant and with bribery and perhaps perjury affecting Lee Poo's testimony. But it could not properly be asked unless the prosecution had evidence of or reasonable ground to believe the truth of its implication. . . . Since no effort was made to prove its truth, after Lee Poo's denial, the propriety of the question had to depend upon the existence of reasonable ground. All we have on this is that after the jury retired Government counsel at a bench conference advised the court of an anonymous letter in the hands of the police "from some Chinaman to somebody" to the effect that appellant gave Lee Poo $20,000 to take the blame, and also said there were like rumors. This, without at least some showing of an investigation and its result, is not enough, particularly in view of the highly prejudicial character of the question.

The general instruction given by the court did not remedy the particular problem. The damaging character of the question, considered with the inconclusiveness of the evidence of appellant's guilt, called for a more direct and positive elimination of its influence upon the jury, when request for some instruction to that end was made. For this reason the judgment will be reversed and a new trial awarded.

. . .

---

497. Criminal record. Whether or not the court gives cautionary instructions, the jury will often regard a defendant's failure to testify as an indication of his guilt. Cf. Griffin v. California, 380 U.S. 609, 617 (1965) (Stewart, J., dissenting). Consequently, there is great pressure on the defendant to testify. The rules of evidence generally permit the record of a witness, including the defendant, to be brought out on cross-examination to show that he is not a person of good character; the more precise inference that the jury is invited to make is that since he is a person who has been convicted of a crime he is likely to lie. It is commonly believed, however, that a jury is unable or unwilling to confine its regard of the defendant's criminal record to its consideration of his veracity as a witness and that it will make the impermissible leap from prior convictions to present guilt.

Rule 609(a) of the Rules of Evidence for United States Courts and Magistrates provides: "General rule. For the purpose of attacking the credibility of a witness, (1) evidence that a witness other than an accused has been convicted of a crime shall be admitted, subject to Rule 403, if the crime was punishable by death or imprisonment in excess of one year under the law under which the witness was convicted, and evidence that an accused has been convicted of such a crime shall be admitted if the court determines that the probative value of admitting this evidence outweighs its prejudicial effect to the accused; and (2) evidence that any witness has been convicted of a crime shall be admitted if it involved dishonesty or false statement, regardless of the punishment." Additional provisions of the rule limit or prohibit the use of such evidence if the conviction is more than ten years old and the person has not been confined pursuant to the conviction for more than ten years, if the conviction has been pardoned or annulled, etc., and if the conviction is a juvenile adjudication. The history of the adoption of the rule and its interpretation are discussed at length in United States v. Smith, 551 F.2d 348, 356–69 (D.C.Cir.1976). For a review of state cases and federal cases before the adoption of Rule 609, see People v. Jackson, 217 N.W.2d 22 (Mich.1974). On the use of prior convictions to impeach the defendant, see generally People v. Barrick, 654 P.2d 1243 (Cal.1982).

In United States v. Toney, 615 F.2d 277 (5th Cir.1980), the court held that under Rule 609(a)(2) of the Federal Rules of Evidence, a trial judge has no authority to prevent a prosecutor from using evidence of a past crime involving "dishonesty or false statement" to impeach the defendant as a witness, despite the possibility that the prejudicial effect of the evidence would outweigh its probative value. See also United States v. Washington, 746 F.2d 104 (2d Cir.1984), upholding a ruling that if the defendant testified, a prior conviction for the same kind of crime for which he was being prosecuted would be admissible on cross-examination.

In order to appeal from a trial judge's ruling *in limine* that a defendant's testimony may be impeached by a prior conviction, the defendant must testify. In the context of the actual testimony, the judge might change the previous ruling, or the prosecutor might conclude not to use the prior conviction for impeachment. Luce v. United States, 469 U.S. 38 (1984).

Luce was distinguished in Biller v. Lopes, 834 F.2d 41 (2d Cir.1987). There, the defendant requested a ruling *in limine* that a previous conviction, then on appeal in the state courts on the ground that it had been obtained in violation of the defendant's privilege against compulsory self-incrimination, would not be admissible on cross-examination, if he took the stand. The trial court declined to make such a ruling, and the defendant did not testify. The previous conviction was later overturned. The court of appeals held that, in those circumstances, failure to make the requested ruling had the effect of extending the constitutional error at the first trial and thereby denying the defendant's privilege against compulsory self-incrimination at the second trial.

Finding *Luce* "neither compelling nor applicable," the Colorado court held that a defendant has a right to a ruling on the admissibility of a prior conviction for impeachment before deciding whether to testify. Apodaca v. People, 712 P.2d 467 (Colo.1985). "A timely judicial ruling on a defendant's motion to suppress prior conviction evidence for the purpose of impeachment serves the vital function of providing the defendant with the meaningful opportunity to make the type of informed decision contemplated by the fundamental nature of the right to testify in one's own defense. The trial court deprived the defendant of that opportunity when it refused to rule on the defendant's motion to prohibit prosecutorial use of prior conviction evidence until such time as the prosecution actually sought to impeach the defendant with such evidence. In effect, the defendant could have testified in this case only by foregoing any opportunity to obtain in advance of actually taking the witness stand a judicial ruling on the most critical factor bearing on his decision whether to testify—that is, the constitutional admissibility of his prior conviction for the purpose of impeachment. We conclude that the trial court's refusal to timely rule on the defendant's motion impermissibly burdened the defendant's exercise of his constitutional right to testify in his own behalf. . . ." Id. at 473.

If, after a judge has ruled that evidence of a prior conviction will be admissible, the defendant himself preemptively introduces such evidence on direct examination, he cannot challenge the admission of the evidence on appeal. Ohler v. United States, 529 U.S. 753 (2000) (5–4).

Similar problems may arise when a defendant's character is put in issue generally and witnesses are asked about their knowledge of specific incidents in the defendant's life. Michelson v. United States, 335 U.S. 469 (1948), discusses at length the evidentiary rules governing character evidence. Concurring in the "general opinion . . . that much of this law is archaic, paradoxical and full of compromises and compensations by which an irrational advantage to one side is offset by a poorly reasoned counter-privilege to the other," id. at 486, the Court nevertheless declined an invitation to adopt new rules. Justice Rutledge, dissenting, argued that to allow a prosecutor to cross-examine character witnesses concerning their knowledge of specific incidents in the defendant's life that have little bearing on his present reputation but "give room for play of the jury's unguarded conjecture and prejudice" was "neither fair play nor *due* process," id. at 495. See Spencer v. Texas, 385 U.S. 554 (1967) (jury may be informed of prior convictions before determination of guilt for sole purpose of sentencing pursuant to habitual criminal statute). See also, discussing *Spencer*, Marshall v. Lonberger, 459 U.S. 422 (1983) (5–4), especially Justice Stevens's dissenting opinion, id. at 447.

In situations of this kind does the prosecutor have an obligation to weigh the probative value of evidence on the issue with respect to which it is admissible against the probable or possible prejudice to the defendant on an issue with respect to which the evidence is not admissible? Can he conscientiously rely on the rules of evidence as having made the relevant decisions for him? Can he rely on the judge's broad authority to control the conduct of a trial (and the judge's willingness to exercise his authority)? Does he have an *obligation* so to rely?

If a prosecutor determines not to use certain rebuttal evidence, such as a defendant's criminal record, because he thinks that it would be improper for him to do so, should he so advise defense counsel in time for him to take advantage of the prosecutor's decision? See United States v. Henderson, 489 F.2d 802, 806 (5th Cir.1973): "[I]t is settled in this circuit that a defendant is not entitled to a prospective ruling on the admissibility of impeachment evidence before he takes the stand. . . . It is the defense counsel's responsibility to evaluate the law and plan his strategy based upon his evaluation; the defendant must take the stand before he is entitled to a ruling on the admissibility of impeachment evidence." Accord United States v. Kennedy, 714 F.2d 968 (9th Cir.1983). What justification can there be for such a rule? Compare United States v. Oakes, 565 F.2d 170 (1st Cir.1977), encouraging the trial court to make an advance ruling.

Does defense counsel have any reciprocal obligations? Suppose the prosecutrix in a rape case was convicted ten years earlier of soliciting prostitution. Suppose further that defense counsel is convinced on the basis of reasonably certain evidence that the conviction was questionable substantively and procedurally defective (say, because obtained without the aid of counsel). Suppose also that defense counsel is convinced on the basis of reasonably certain evidence that the prosecutrix has lived an exemplary life for the past ten years and that he is aware that her husband and two young children, who know nothing about her conviction, will be in the courtroom during the trial. Should defense counsel cross-examine the prosecutrix about her conviction? Cf. Alford v. United States, 282 U.S. 687 (1931).

Suppose the positions are reversed. The woman in question is a witness for the defense. Her testimony will be that she knows the defendant and knows that he has a reputation for good character. Defense counsel, over objection by the prosecutor, has been allowed to show the witness's "credentials," outlined above. Should the prosecutor seek to cross-examine the witness about her conviction?

498. The use of mug shots at trial to help a witness make an identification is discussed and additional cases are cited in United States v. Harrington, 490 F.2d 487 (2d Cir.1973). The danger of such use is that it may reveal that a defendant who does not take the stand and whose criminal record would not otherwise be before the jury does in fact have a record. The court concluded that there were three prerequisites for introduction of mug shots: "1. The government must have a demonstrable need to introduce the photographs; and 2. The photographs themselves, if shown to the jury, must not imply that the defendant has a prior criminal record; and 3. The manner of introduction at trial must be such that it does not draw particular attention to the source or implications of the photographs." Id. at 494. See United States v. Fosher, 568 F.2d 207 (1st Cir.1978) (photographs improperly admitted); with which compare United States v. Cannon, 903 F.2d 849 (1st Cir.1990) (admission of photographs upheld).

499. What obligation does the government have to help a defendant to obtain the testimony of a witness?

In United States v. Domenech, 476 F.2d 1229 (2d Cir.1973), the defendant summoned his brother-in-law, Pereira, to testify. Pereira refused to testify, claiming the privilege against self-incrimination. It appeared that he had pleaded guilty to one count of an indictment and that the remaining count was to be dismissed after he had been sentenced. His claim of privilege was based on the still outstanding count. Should the prosecutor have been required to dismiss that count in order to make Pereira's testimony available to the defendant? The court of appeals said: "Appellant urges that the Government deliberately left count 2 open against Pereira in order to insure that he would not testify for appellant. There is no adequate proof of this charge; leaving the remaining counts open until sentence on the counts to which an accused had pled is the common practice—a reasonable procedure which avoids complexities where the defendant moves before sentence to set aside his guilty plea. In this instance the possible consequence of following the normal usage was to give Pereira a good excuse for refusing to take the stand, and thus of avoiding the dilemma, on the one hand, of a possible perjury charge or a feared impact on his sentence if he testified favorably to Domenech, or, on the other, of giving evidence against his close relative. But we see no escape from holding that Pereira had a constitutional right to act as he did, and, in the absence of any proof of deliberate manipulation or pre-arrangement by the United States Attorney, there is no penalty we can or should impose on the Government because the witness's exercise of his right, for his own purposes, may have redounded to the prosecutor's advantage." Id. at 1231.

The practice of deporting illegal aliens who are material witnesses to an offense for which the defendant is later prosecuted is discussed in United States v. Valenzuela-Bernal, 458 U.S. 858 (1982) (7–2). Relying on Roviaro v. United States, 353 U.S. 53 (1957), p. 995 below, the Court said that deportation of such persons before the defense counsel has had an opportunity to interview them is not always a violation of the defendant's constitutional rights. Such deportation furthers the federal immigration law and avoids the financial and physical burdens of prolonged detention. In order to establish a violation of his rights under either the Compulsory Process Clause of the Sixth Amendment or the Due Process Clause, the defendant must make a plausible showing that the lost testimony of the deported witnesses would have been material and favorable to the defense, in ways not merely cumulative to the testimony of available witnesses. The Court observed that the lack of an opportunity to interview the witnesses before they were deported would justify relaxing the requirement of specificity of the showing of materiality; but it did not justify dispensing with such a showing altogether.

The United States Attorney has broad authority to seek immunity for a potential witness whose "testimony or other information . . . may be necessary to the public interest" and who has invoked or is likely to invoke the privilege against self-incrimination. 18 U.S.C. § 6003(b). Should she ever be required to do so (subject to dismissal of the prosecution if she refuses) in order to obtain testimony favorable to the defendant? The courts have generally said not. In United States v. Turkish, 623 F.2d 769, 777 (2d Cir.1980), for example, the court said that there is not "in the Due Process Clause a general requirement that defense witness immunity must be ordered whenever it seems fair to grant it." Cf. United States v. Chitty, 760 F.2d 425 (2d Cir.1985). In *Chitty*, observing that "not every unfairness is a violation of due process," the court said: "To raise a constitutional claim, the witness' testimony must have been material, exculpatory, and neither cumulative nor available from any other source." Most courts have rejected the argument that the trial court has inherent authority to grant immunity despite the opposition of the prosecution. E.g., United States v. Thevis, 665 F.2d 616, 639 (5th Cir.1982): "[D]istrict courts may not grant immunity to defense witnesses simply because that witness has essential exculpatory information unavailable from other sources. . . . [T]he two major arguments against granting such judicial use immunity are that the immunity decision would carry the courts into policy assessments which are the traditional domain of the executive branch, and that the immunity would be subject to abuse." See also United States v. Capozzi, 883 F.2d 608 (8th Cir.1989); United States v. Paris, 827 F.2d 395 (9th Cir.1987). But see Government of the Virgin Islands v. Smith, 615 F.2d 964 (3d Cir.1980), holding that the government should be required to seek immunity where necessary to the fact-finding process and that, alternatively, the court has inherent authority to grant use immunity where a fair trial so requires.

Even if the prosecutor is not required to seek immunity for a defense witness, should she sometimes do so? If defense counsel asks her to do so and she declines, should the court at the request of defense counsel give a missing witness instruction?

In Bowles v. United States, 439 F.2d 536 (D.C.Cir.1970), the defendant was prosecuted for murder. Part of his defense was that Raymond Smith was in fact guilty of the crime. Smith indicated out of the hearing of the jury that he would invoke the privilege against self-incrimination. The court declined to give a missing witness instruction or to let the jury know why Smith was not called as a witness. He instructed counsel not to mention Smith's invocation of the privilege. On appeal, the conviction was affirmed.

> We find no error in these rulings. It is well settled that the jury is not entitled to draw any inferences from the decision of a witness to exercise his constitutional privilege whether those inferences be favorable to the prosecution or the defense. . . . The rule is grounded not only in the constitutional notion that guilt may not be inferred from the exercise of the Fifth Amendment privilege but also in the danger that a witness's invoking the Fifth Amendment in the presence of the jury will have a disproportionate impact on their deliberations. The jury may think it high courtroom drama of probative significance when a witness "takes the Fifth." In reality the probative value of the event is almost entirely undercut by the absence of any requirement that the

> witness justify his fear of incrimination and by the fact that it is a form of evidence not subject to cross-examination. . . .
>
> An obvious corollary to these precepts is the rule that a witness should not be put on the stand for the purpose of having him exercise his privilege before the jury. . . . This would only invite the jury to make an improper inference. For the same reason no valid purpose can be served by informing the jury that a witness has chosen to exercise his constitutional privilege. That fact is not one the jury is entitled to rely on in reaching its verdict.
>
> The other side of the coin, however, is the rule that the jury is not entitled to draw any inference from a failure to testify that is ascribable to the witness's reliance on his Fifth Amendment privilege. . . . Indeed, this court has held it inappropriate to spark a missing witness inference against the party who would have been called on to produce a witness to incriminate himself. . . .
>
> In the instant case the District Court properly admonished counsel to make no mention in their closing argument of the lack of testimony from a witness counsel knew would have invoked the Fifth Amendment. Certainly the judge was correct in refusing to charge the jury that an inference could be drawn from the absence of such a witness. . . .
>
> However, the trial judge could properly have given a neutralizing instruction, one calculated to reduce the danger that the jury will in fact draw an inference from the absence of such a witness. Had either counsel requested the court to instruct the jury that they should draw no inference from Smith's absence because he was not available to either side, it would have been error to refuse this instruction. Appellant's trial counsel did not request such an instruction. There are meaningful tactical reasons why a defense trial counsel might elect not to seek such an instruction. Had such an instruction been sought in this case, the District Court, which noted in colloquy with counsel that Smith "was not available to either side," would undoubtedly have granted the request. As it is we see no error in the court's handling of the issues presented when Smith decided to invoke his Fifth Amendment privilege.

Id. at 541–42.

Bowles states the general rule. In Namet v. United States, 373 U.S. 179 (1963), the prosecutor called witnesses who invoked the privilege against self-incrimination; the Court found that there was no error.

500. The defendant was prosecuted for murder. During the voir dire, defense counsel had identified Frank Twitty as a prospective defense witness. After the first day of trial, the prosecutor told Twitty that if the facts were as they appeared, Twitty might himself be liable for several crimes, such as obstruction of justice and being an accessory after the fact of the murder. He advised Twitty to consult an independent lawyer about his own constitutional rights and not to rely on the defendant's lawyer. Was the prosecutor's conduct proper?

After the court was informed of the above, it asked a public defender to advise Twitty. Later, Twitty concluded that he would not testify. The defendant was convicted. Should the conviction be reversed? See United States v. Smith, 478 F.2d 976 (D.C.Cir.1973). See also United States v. Vavages, 151 F.3d 1185 (9th Cir.1998) (prosecutor's admonitions to defense counsel induced defense witness not to testify; conviction reversed); United States v. Touw, 769 F.2d 571 (9th Cir.1985); (prosecutor's statement to judge that defense witness should be advised by counsel before testifying was not improper). Compare Peeler v. Wyrick, 734 F.2d 378 (8th Cir.1984) (police officer did not testify as character witness for defendants because police chief threatened him with loss of job; conviction affirmed).

In Webb v. Texas, 409 U.S. 95 (1972), the Court found that the trial judge's threats to prosecute the defendant's only witness for perjury if he lied on the stand "effectively drove that witness off the stand" and denied the defendant due process of law. *Webb* is applied in United States v. Arthur, 949 F.2d 211 (6th Cir.1991), in which the court held that it was an abuse of discretion to induce a defense witness to assert the privilege against self-incrimination. *Webb* is distinguished in United States v. Williams, 205 F.3d 23 (2d Cir.2000), in which government agents warned a defense witness about the consequences of perjury. Upholding the conviction, the court nevertheless criticized the government's failure to advise counsel of the agents' intention to interview the witness and their failure to advise the witness of his privilege against compulsory self-incrimination and of the need for him to consult counsel. *Webb* is distinguished also in United States v. Blackwell, 694 F.2d 1325 (D.C.Cir.1982) (prosecutor's and judge's warnings about perjury to defense witness not improper).

501. In Jaffee v. Redmond, 518 U.S. 1, (1996) (8–1), the Court held that under Rule 501 of the Federal Rules of Evidence (providing generally that testimonial privilege shall be governed "by the principles of the common law as they may be interpreted by the courts of the United States in the light of reason and experience") "confidential communications between a licensed psychotherapist and her patients in the course of diagnosis or treatment are protected from compelled disclosure." Id. at 15. The Court held also (7–2) that the privilege extends to confidential communications "made to licensed social workers in the course of psychotherapy." Id. The Court noted that all 50 states and the District of Columbia have enacted some form of psychotherapist privilege.

502. "[W]hen a defendant demonstrates to the trial judge that his sanity at the time of the offense is to be a significant factor at trial, the State must, at a minimum, assure the defendant access to a competent psychiatrist who will conduct an appropriate examination and assist in evaluation, preparation, and presentation of the defense. This is not to say, of course, that the indigent defendant has a constitutional right to choose a psychiatrist of his personal liking or to receive funds to hire his own. Our concern is that the indigent defendant have access to a competent psychiatrist for the purpose we have discussed, and as in the case of the provision of counsel we leave to the States the decision on how to implement this right." Ake v. Oklahoma, 470 U.S. 68, 83 (1985) (8–1).

California v. Green

399 U.S. 149, 90 S.Ct. 1930, 26 L.Ed.2d 489 (1970)

■ MR. JUSTICE WHITE delivered the opinion of the Court.

Section 1235 of the California Evidence Code, effective as of January 1, 1967, provides that "[e]vidence of a statement made by a witness is not made inadmissible by the hearsay rule if the statement is inconsistent with his testimony at the hearing and is offered in compliance with Section 770."[18] In People v. Johnson, 68 Cal.2d 646 (1968) . . . the California Supreme Court held that prior statements of a witness which were not subject to cross-examination when originally made could not be introduced under this section to prove the charges against a defendant without violating the defendant's right of confrontation guaranteed by the Sixth Amendment and made applicable to the States by the Fourteenth Amendment. In the case now before us the California Supreme Court applied the same ban to a prior statement of a witness made at a preliminary hearing, under oath and subject to full cross-examination by an adequately counseled defendant. We cannot agree with the California court for two reasons, one of which involves rejection of the holding in People v. Johnson.

I

In January 1967, one Melvin Porter, a 16-year-old minor, was arrested for selling marihuana to an undercover police officer. Four days after his arrest, while in the custody of juvenile authorities, Porter named respondent Green as his supplier. As recounted later by one Officer Wade, Porter claimed that Green had called him earlier that month, had asked him to sell some "stuff" or "grass," and had that same afternoon personally delivered a shopping bag containing 29 "baggies" of marihuana. It was from this supply that Porter had made his sale to the undercover officer. A week later, Porter testified at respondent's preliminary hearing. He again named respondent as his supplier, although he now claimed that instead of personally delivering the marihuana, Green had showed him where to pick up the shopping bag, hidden in the bushes at Green's parents' house. Porter's story at the preliminary hearing was subjected to extensive cross-examination by respondent's counsel—the same counsel who represented respondent at his subsequent trial. At the conclusion of the hearing,

18. Cal.Evid.Code § 1235 (1966). Section 770 merely requires that the witness be given an opportunity to explain or deny the prior statement at some point in the trial. See Cal.Evid.Code § 770 (1966). . . .

respondent was charged with furnishing marihuana to a minor in violation of California law.

Respondent's trial took place some two months later before a court sitting without a jury. The State's chief witness was again young Porter. But this time Porter, in the words of the California Supreme Court, proved to be "markedly evasive and uncooperative on the stand." People v. Green, 70 Cal.2d 654, 657 (1969). He testified that respondent had called him in January 1967, and asked him to sell some unidentified "stuff." He admitted obtaining shortly thereafter 29 plastic "baggies" of marihuana, some of which he sold. But when pressed as to whether respondent had been his supplier, Porter claimed that he was uncertain how he obtained the marihuana, primarily because he was at the time on "acid" (LSD), which he had taken 20 minutes before respondent phoned. Porter claimed that he was unable to remember the events which followed the phone call, and that the drugs he had taken prevented his distinguishing fact from fantasy. . . .

At various points during Porter's direct examination, the prosecutor read excerpts from Porter's preliminary hearing testimony. This evidence was admitted under § 1235 for the truth of the matter contained therein. With his memory "refreshed" by his preliminary hearing testimony, Porter "guessed" that he had indeed obtained the marihuana from the backyard of respondent's parents' home, and had given the money from its sale to respondent. On cross-examination, however, Porter indicated that it was his memory of the preliminary testimony which was "mostly" refreshed, rather than his memory of the events themselves, and he was still unsure of the actual episode. . . . Later in the trial, Officer Wade testified, relating Porter's earlier statement that respondent had personally delivered the marihuana. This statement was also admitted as substantive evidence. Porter admitted making the statement . . . and insisted that he had been telling the truth as he then believed it both to Officer Wade and at the preliminary hearing; but he insisted that he was also telling the truth now in claiming inability to remember the actual events.

Respondent was convicted. The District Court of Appeal reversed, holding that the use of Porter's prior statements for the truth of the matter asserted therein denied respondent his right of confrontation under the California Supreme Court's recent decision in People v. Johnson, supra. The California Supreme Court affirmed, finding itself "impelled" by recent decisions of this Court to hold § 1235 unconstitutional insofar as it permitted the substantive use of prior inconsistent statements of a witness, even though the statements were subject to cross-examination at a prior hearing. We granted the State's petition for certiorari. . . .

II

. . .

. . . The orthodox view, adopted in most jurisdictions, has been that the out-of-court statements are inadmissible for the usual reasons that have led to the exclusion of hearsay statements: the statement may not have been made under oath; the declarant may not have been subjected to cross-examination when he made the statement; and the jury cannot observe the declarant's demeanor at the time he made the statement. Accordingly, under this view, the statement may not be offered to show the truth of the matters asserted therein, but can be introduced under appropriate limiting instructions to impeach the credibility of the witness who has changed his story at trial.

In contrast, the minority view adopted in some jurisdictions and supported by most legal commentators and by recent proposals to codify the law of evidence would permit the substantive use of prior inconsistent statements on the theory that the usual dangers of hearsay are largely nonexistent where the witness testifies at trial. . . .

Our task in this case is not to decide which of these positions, purely as a matter of the law of evidence, is the sounder. The issue before us is the considerably narrower one of whether a defendant's constitutional right "to be confronted with the witnesses against him" is necessarily inconsistent with a State's decision to change its hearsay rules to reflect the minority view described above. While it may readily be conceded that hearsay rules and the Confrontation Clause are generally designed to protect similar values, it is quite a different thing to suggest that the overlap is complete and that the Confrontation Clause is nothing more or less than a codification of the rules of hearsay and their exceptions as they existed historically at common law. Our decisions have never established such a congruence. . . .

Given the similarity of the values protected, however, the modification of a State's hearsay rules to create new exceptions for the admission of evidence against a defendant, will often raise questions of compatibility with the defendant's constitutional right to confrontation. Such questions require attention to the reasons for, and the basic scope of, the protections offered by the Confrontation Clause.

. . .

Our own decisions seem to have recognized at an early date that it is this literal right to "confront" the witness at the time of trial that forms the core of the values furthered by the Confrontation Clause. . . . Viewed historically, then, there is good reason to conclude that the Confrontation Clause is not violated by admitting a declarant's out-of-court statements, as long as the declarant is testifying as a witness and subject to full and effective cross-examination.

This conclusion is supported by comparing the purposes of confrontation with the alleged dangers in admitting an out-of-court statement. Confrontation: (1) insures that the witness will give his statements under oath—thus impressing him with the seriousness of the matter and guarding against the lie by the possibility of a penalty for perjury; (2) forces the witness to submit to cross-examination, the "greatest legal engine ever invented for the discovery of truth";[19] (3) permits the jury that is to decide the defendant's fate to observe the demeanor of the witness in making his statement, thus aiding the jury in assessing his credibility.

It is, of course, true that the out-of-court statement may have been made under circumstances subject to none of these protections. But if the declarant is present and testifying at trial, the out-of-court statement for all practical purposes regains most of the lost protections. If the witness admits the prior statement is his, or if there is other evidence to show the statement is his, the danger of faulty reproduction is negligible and the jury can be confident that it has before it two conflicting statements by the same witness. Thus, as far as the oath is concerned, the witness must now affirm, deny, or qualify the truth of the prior statement under the penalty of perjury; indeed, the very fact that the prior statement was not given under a similar circumstance may become the witness' explanation for its inaccuracy—an explanation a jury may be expected to understand and take into account in deciding which, if either, of the statements represents the truth.

Second, the inability to cross-examine the witness at the time he made his prior statement cannot easily be shown to be of crucial significance as long as the defendant is assured of full and effective cross-examination at the time of trial. . . . The main danger in substituting subsequent for timely cross-examination seems to lie in the possibility that the witness' "[f]alse testimony is apt to harden and become unyielding to the blows of truth in proportion as the witness has opportunity for reconsideration and influence by the suggestions of others, whose interest may be, and often is, to maintain falsehood rather than truth." State v. Saporen, 285 N.W. 898, 901 (1939). That danger, however, disappears when the witness has changed his testimony so that, far from "hardening," his prior statement has softened to the point where he now repudiates it.

The defendant's task in cross-examination is, of course, no longer identical to the task that he would have faced if the witness had not changed his story and hence had to be examined as a "hostile" witness giving evidence for the prosecution. This difference, however, far from lessening, may actually enhance the defendant's ability to attack the prior statement. For the witness, favorable to the defendant, should be more than willing to give the usual suggested explanations for the inaccuracy of his prior statement, such as faulty perception or undue haste in recounting the event. Under such circumstances, the defendant is not likely to be hampered in effectively attacking the prior statement, solely because his attack comes later in time.

Similar reasons lead us to discount as a constitutional matter the fact that the jury at trial is foreclosed from viewing the declarant's demeanor when he first made his out-of-court statement. The witness who now relates a different story about the events in question must necessarily assume a position as to the truth value of his prior statement, thus giving

19. 5 Wigmore § 1367.

the jury a chance to observe and evaluate his demeanor as he either disavows or qualifies his earlier statement. The jury is alerted by the inconsistency in the stories, and its attention is sharply focused on determining either that one of the stories reflects the truth or that the witness who has apparently lied once is simply too lacking in credibility to warrant believing either story. The defendant's confrontation rights are not violated, even though some demeanor evidence that would have been relevant in resolving this credibility issue is forever lost.

It may be true that a jury would be in a better position to evaluate the truth of the prior statement if it could somehow be whisked magically back in time to witness a gruelling cross-examination of the declarant as he first gives his statement. But the question as we see it must be not whether one can somehow imagine the jury in "a better position," but whether subsequent cross-examination at the defendant's trial will still afford the trier of fact a satisfactory basis for evaluating the truth of the prior statement. On that issue, neither evidence nor reason convinces us that contemporaneous cross-examination before the ultimate trier of fact is so much more effective than subsequent examination that it must be made the touchstone of the Confrontation Clause.

Finally, we note that none of our decisions interpreting the Confrontation Clause requires excluding the out-of-court statements of a witness who is available and testifying at trial. The concern of most of our cases has been focused on precisely the opposite situation—situations where statements have been admitted in the absence of the declarant and without any chance to cross-examine him at trial. These situations have arisen through application of a number of traditional "exceptions" to the hearsay rule. . . .

We have no occasion in the present case to map out a theory of the Confrontation Clause that would determine the validity of all such hearsay "exceptions" permitting the introduction of an absent declarant's statements. For where the declarant is not absent, but is present to testify and to submit to cross-examination, our cases, if anything, support the conclusion that the admission of his out-of-court statements does not create a confrontation problem. . . .

. . .

We find nothing, then, in either the history or the purposes of the Confrontation Clause, or in the prior decisions of this Court, that compels the conclusion reached by the California Supreme Court concerning the validity of California's § 1235. Contrary to the judgment of that court, the Confrontation Clause does not require excluding from evidence the prior statements of a witness who concedes making the statements, and who may be asked to defend or otherwise explain the inconsistency between his prior and his present version of the events in question, thus opening himself to full cross-examination at trial as to both stories.

III

We also think that Porter's preliminary hearing testimony was admissible as far as the Constitution is concerned wholly apart from the question of whether respondent had an effective opportunity for confrontation at the subsequent trial. For Porter's statement at the preliminary hearing had already been given under circumstances closely approximating those that surround the typical trial. Porter was under oath; respondent was represented by counsel—the same counsel in fact who later represented him at the trial; respondent had every opportunity to cross-examine Porter as to his statement; and the proceedings were conducted before a judicial tribunal, equipped to provide a judicial record of the hearings. Under these circumstances, Porter's statement would, we think, have been admissible at trial even in Porter's absence if Porter had been actually unavailable, despite good-faith efforts of the State to produce him. That being the case, we do not think a different result should follow where the witness is actually produced.

This Court long ago held that admitting the prior testimony of an unavailable witness does not violate the Confrontation Clause. . . . In the present case respondent's counsel does not appear to have been significantly limited in any way in the scope or nature of his cross-examination of the witness Porter at the preliminary hearing. If Porter had died or was otherwise unavailable, the Confrontation Clause would not have been violated by admitting his testimony given at the preliminary hearing—the right of cross-examination then afforded provides substantial compliance with the purposes behind the confrontation requirement, as long as the declarant's inability to give live testimony is in no way the fault of the State. . . .

. . . It may be that the rules of evidence applicable in state or federal courts would restrict resort to prior sworn testimony where the declarant is present at the trial. But as a constitutional matter, it is untenable to construe the Confrontation Clause to permit the use of prior testimony to prove the State's case where the declarant never appears, but to bar that testimony where the declarant is present at the trial, exposed to the defendant and the trier of fact, and subject to cross-examination. As in the case where the witness is physically unproducible, the State here has made every effort to introduce its evidence through the live testimony of the witness; it produced Porter at trial, swore him as a witness, and tendered him for cross-examination. Whether Porter then testified in a manner consistent or inconsistent with his preliminary hearing testimony, claimed a loss of memory, claimed his privilege against compulsory self-incrimination, or simply refused to answer, nothing in the Confrontation Clause prohibited the State from also relying on his prior testimony to prove its case against Green.

IV

There is a narrow question lurking in this case concerning the admissibility of Porter's statements to Officer Wade. In the typical case to which the California court addressed itself, the witness at trial gives a version of the ultimate events different from that given on a prior occasion. In such a case, as our holding in Part II makes clear, we find little reason to distinguish among prior inconsistent statements on the basis of the circumstances under which the prior statements were given. The subsequent opportunity for cross-examination at trial with respect to both present and past versions of the event, is adequate to make equally admissible, as far as the Confrontation Clause is concerned, both the casual, off-hand remark to a stranger, and the carefully recorded testimony at a prior hearing. Here, however, Porter claimed at trial that he could not remember the events which occurred after respondent telephoned him and hence failed to give any current version of the more important events described in his earlier statement.

Whether Porter's apparent lapse of memory so affected Green's right to cross-examine as to make a critical difference in the application of the Confrontation Clause in this case is an issue which is not ripe for decision at this juncture. . . .

We therefore vacate the judgment of the California Supreme Court and remand the case to that court for further proceedings not inconsistent with this opinion.

. . .[20]

---

503. The Court considered the relationship between the Confrontation Clause and exceptions to the hearsay rule again in Dutton v. Evans, 400 U.S. 74 (1970). There, a prosecution witness was allowed to testify about an out-of-court statement made by one Williams, as a co-conspirator with the defendant. Williams's statement, as reported by the witness, incriminated the defendant. Williams himself was not called as a witness and did not testify. The court concluded, four Justices dissenting, that the witness's testimony was admissible.

In Crawford v. Washington, 541 U.S. ___ (2004), the Court overturned a rule it had previously announced that hearsay testimony of the statement of a person who is not present at trial is admissible if it has "adequate 'indicia of reliability,' " which is demonstrated either if the statement falls within "a firmly rooted hearsay exception" or if there is a "showing of particularized guarantees of 'trustworthiness,' " Ohio v. Roberts, 448 U.S. 56, 66 (1980) (6–3). In *Crawford*, the out-of-court statement was admitted on the latter basis. Reviewing the history of the Confrontation Clause, the Court said that the primary objective of the Clause was to bar the use against a defendant of ex parte examinations of witnesses. Accordingly, its focus is out-of-court "testimonial" statements, ones made for prosecutorial

[20] Chief Justice Burger and Justice Harlan wrote concurring opinions. Justice Brennan wrote a dissenting opinion.

use, rather than casual out-of-court remarks. Therefore, the Confrontation Clause requires that, whatever other indicia of reliability there may be, an out-of-court testimonial statement should not be admitted, unless it was subject to cross-examination at the time it was made. Nontestimonial hearsay evidence, the Court said, is not subject to the same rule and may be admitted or not according to a state's usual hearsay rule.

In Bourjaily v. United States, 483 U.S. 171 (1987) (6–3), the Court said that an out-of-court statement can be admitted under the co-conspirator exception to the hearsay rule. Similarly, statements can be admitted under the "spontaneous declaration" and "medical examination" exceptions to the hearsay rule. White v. Illinois, 502 U.S. 346 (1992). Those rulings, which preceded Crawford v. Washington, presumably remain valid. Cf. also Tennessee v. Street, 471 U.S. 409 (1985) (codefendants' confession admitted for limited nonhearsay purpose of rebutting defendant's claim that his confession was coerced and derived from codefendant's confession).

In United States v. Faison, 679 F.2d 292 (3d Cir.1982), the court of appeals held that it was an abuse of discretion for the trial judge to deny a request for an adjournment so that an important prosecution witness, who was ill, could testify before the jury; instead of the adjournment, the judge allowed the witness's testimony at a prior trial to be introduced.

Chambers v. Mississippi

410 U.S. 284, 93 S.Ct. 1038, 35 L.Ed.2d 297 (1973)

■ MR. JUSTICE POWELL delivered the opinion of the Court.

Petitioner, Leon Chambers, was tried by a jury in a Mississippi trial court and convicted of murdering a policeman. The jury assessed punishment at life imprisonment. . . . [T]he petition for certiorari was granted . . . to consider whether petitioner's trial was conducted in accord with principles of due process under the Fourteenth Amendment. We conclude that it was not.

I

The events that led to petitioner's prosecution for murder occurred in the small town of Woodville in southern Mississippi. On Saturday evening, June 14, 1969, two Woodville policemen, James Forman and Aaron "Sonny" Liberty, entered a local bar and pool hall to execute a warrant for the arrest of a youth named C.C. Jackson. Jackson resisted and a hostile crowd of some 50 or 60 persons gathered. The officers' first attempt to handcuff Jackson was frustrated when 20 or 25 men in the crowd intervened and wrestled him free. Forman then radioed for assistance and Liberty removed his riot gun, a 12-gauge sawed-off shotgun, from the car. Three deputy sheriffs arrived shortly thereafter and the officers again attempted to make their arrest. Once more, the officers were attacked by the onlookers and during the commotion five or six pistol shots were fired. Forman was looking in a different direction when the shooting began, but immediately saw that Liberty had been shot several times in the back. Before Liberty died, he turned around and fired both barrels of his riot gun into an alley in the area from which the shots appeared to have come. The first shot was wild and high and scattered the crowd standing at the face of the alley. Liberty appeared, however, to take more deliberate aim before the second shot and hit one of the men in the crowd in the back of the head and neck as he ran down the alley. That man was Leon Chambers.

Officer Forman could not see from his vantage point who shot Liberty or whether Liberty's shots hit anyone. One of the deputy sheriffs testified at trial that he was standing several feet from Liberty and that he saw Chambers shoot him. Another deputy sheriff stated that although he could not see whether Chambers had a gun in his hand, he did see Chambers "break his arm down" shortly before the shots were fired. The officers who saw Chambers fall testified that they thought he was dead but they made no effort at that time either to examine him or to search for the murder weapon. Instead, they attended to Liberty, who was placed in the police car and taken to a hospital where he was declared dead on arrival. A subsequent autopsy showed that he had been hit with four bullets from a .22-caliber revolver.

Shortly after the shooting, three of Chambers' friends discovered that he was not yet dead. James Williams, Berkley Turner, and Gable McDonald loaded him into a car and transported him to the same hospital. Later that night, when the county sheriff discovered that Chambers was still alive, a guard was placed outside his room. Chambers was subsequently charged with Liberty's murder. He pleaded not guilty and has asserted his innocence throughout.

The story of Leon Chambers is intertwined with the story of another man, Gable McDonald. McDonald, a lifelong resident of Woodville, was in the crowd on the evening of Liberty's death. Sometime shortly after that day, he left his wife in Woodville and moved to Louisiana and found a job at a sugar mill. In November of that same year, he returned to Woodville when his wife informed him that an acquaintance of his, known as Reverend Stokes, wanted to see him. Stokes owned a gas station in Natchez, Mississippi, several miles north of Woodville, and upon his return McDonald went to see him. After talking to Stokes, McDonald agreed to make a statement to Chambers' attorneys, who maintained offices in Natchez. Two days later, he appeared at the attorneys' offices and gave a sworn confession that he shot Officer Liberty. He also stated that he had already told a friend of his, James Williams, that he shot Liberty. He said that he used his own pistol, a nine-shot .22-caliber revolver, which he had discarded shortly after the shooting. In response to questions from Chambers' attorneys, McDonald affirmed that his confession was voluntary and that no one had compelled him to come to them. Once the confession had been transcribed, signed, and witnessed, McDonald was turned over to the local police authorities and was placed in jail.

One month later, at a preliminary hearing, McDonald repudiated his prior sworn confession. He testified that Stokes had persuaded him to confess that he shot Liberty. He claimed that Stokes had promised that he would not go to jail and that he would share in the proceeds of a lawsuit that Chambers would bring against the town of Woodville. On examination by his own attorney and on cross-examination by the State, McDonald swore that he had not been at the scene when Liberty was shot but had been down the street drinking beer in a cafe with a friend, Berkley Turner. When he and Turner heard the shooting, he testified, they walked up the street and found Chambers lying in the alley. He, Turner, and Williams took Chambers to the hospital. McDonald further testified at the preliminary hearing that he did not know what had happened, that there was no discussion about the shooting either going to or coming back from the hospital, and that it was not until the next day that he learned that Chambers had been felled by a blast from Liberty's riot gun. In addition, McDonald stated that while he once owned a .22-caliber pistol he had lost it many months before the shooting and did not own or possess a weapon at that time. The local justice of the peace accepted McDonald's repudiation and released him from custody. The local authorities undertook no further investigation of his possible involvement.

Chambers' case came on for trial in October of the next year. At trial, he endeavored to develop two grounds of defense. He first attempted to show that he did not shoot Liberty. Only one officer testified that he actually saw Chambers fire the shots. Although three officers saw Liberty shoot Chambers and testified that they assumed he was shooting his attacker, none of them examined Chambers to see whether he was still alive or whether he possessed a gun. Indeed, no weapon was ever recovered from the scene and there was no proof that Chambers had ever owned a .22-caliber pistol. One witness testified that he was standing in the street near where Liberty was shot, that he was looking at Chambers when the shooting began, and that he was sure that Chambers did not fire the shots.

Petitioner's second defense was that Gable McDonald had shot Officer Liberty. He was only partially successful, however, in his efforts to bring before the jury the testimony supporting this defense. Sam Hardin, a lifelong friend of McDonald's, testified that he saw McDonald shoot Liberty. A second witness, one of Liberty's cousins, testified that he saw McDonald immediately after the shooting with a pistol in his hand. In addition to the testimony of these two witnesses, Chambers endeavored to show the jury that McDonald had repeatedly confessed to the crime. Chambers attempted to prove that McDonald had admitted responsibility for the murder on four separate occasions, once when he gave the sworn statement to Chambers' counsel and three other times prior to that occasion in private conversations with friends.

In large measure, he was thwarted in his attempt to present this portion of his defense by the strict application of certain Mississippi rules of evidence. Chambers asserts in this Court, as he did unsuccessfully in his motion for new trial and on appeal to the State Supreme Court, that the application of these evidentiary rules rendered his trial fundamentally unfair and deprived him of due process of law. It is necessary, therefore, to examine carefully the rulings made during the trial.

II

Chambers filed a pretrial motion requesting the court to order McDonald to appear. Chambers also sought a ruling at that time that, if the State itself chose not to call McDonald, he be allowed to call him as an adverse witness. Attached to the motion were copies of McDonald's sworn confession and of the transcript of his preliminary hearing at which he repudiated that confession. The trial court granted the motion requiring McDonald to appear but reserved ruling on the adverse-witness motion. At trial, after the State failed to put McDonald on the stand, Chambers called McDonald, laid a predicate for the introduction of his sworn out-of-court confession, had it admitted into evidence, and read it to the jury. The State, upon cross-examination, elicited from McDonald the fact that he had rejected his prior confession. McDonald further testified, as he had at the preliminary hearing, that he did not shoot Liberty and that he confessed to the crime only on the promise of Reverend Stokes that he would not go to jail and would share in a sizable tort recovery from the town. He also retold his own story of his actions on the evening of the shooting, including his visit to the cafe down the street, his absence from the scene during the critical period, and his subsequent trip to the hospital with Chambers.

At the conclusion of the State's cross-examination, Chambers renewed his motion to examine McDonald as an adverse witness. The trial court denied the motion, stating: "He may be hostile, but he is not adverse in the sense of the word, so your request will be overruled." On appeal, the State Supreme Court upheld the trial court's ruling, finding that "McDonald's testimony was not adverse to appellant" because "[n]owhere did he point the finger at Chambers." 252 So.2d at 220.

Defeated in his attempt to challenge directly McDonald's renunciation of his prior confession, Chambers sought to introduce the testimony of the three witnesses to whom McDonald had admitted that he shot the officer. The first of these, Sam Hardin, would have testified that, on the night of the shooting, he spent the late evening hours with McDonald at a friend's house after their return from the hospital and that, while driving McDonald home later that night, McDonald stated that he shot Liberty. The State objected to the admission of this testimony on the ground that it was hearsay. The trial court sustained the objection.

Berkley Turner, the friend with whom McDonald said he was drinking beer when the shooting occurred, was then called to testify. In the jury's presence, and without objection, he testified that he had not been in the cafe that Saturday and had not had any beers with McDonald. The jury was then excused. In the absence of the jury, Turner recounted his conversations with McDonald while they were riding with James Williams to take Chambers to the hospital. When asked whether McDonald said anything regarding the shooting of Liberty, Turner testified that McDonald told him that he "shot him." Turner further stated that one week later, when he met McDonald at a friend's house, McDonald reminded him of their prior conversation and urged Turner not to "mess him up." Petitioner argued to the court that, especially where there was other proof in the case that was corroborative of these out-of-court statements, Turner's testimony as to McDonald's self-incriminating remarks should have been admitted as an exception to the hearsay rule. Again, the trial court sustained the State's objection.

The third witness, Albert Carter, was McDonald's neighbor. They had been friends for about 25 years. Although Carter had not been in Woodville on the evening of the shooting, he stated that he learned about it the next morning from McDonald. That same day, he and McDonald walked out to a well near McDonald's house and there McDonald told him that he was the one who shot Officer Liberty. Carter testified that McDonald also told him that he had disposed of the .22-caliber revolver later that night. He further testified that several weeks after the shooting, he accompanied McDonald to Natchez where McDonald purchased another .22 pistol to replace the one he had discarded. The jury was not allowed to hear Carter's testimony. Chambers urged that these statements were admissible, the State objected, and the court sustained the objection. On appeal, the State Supreme Court approved the lower court's exclusion of these witnesses' testimony on hearsay grounds. . . .

In sum, then, this was Chambers' predicament. As a consequence of the combination of Mississippi's "party-witness" or "voucher" rule and its hearsay rule, he was unable either to cross-examine McDonald or to present witnesses in his own behalf who would have discredited McDonald's repudiation and demonstrated his complicity. Chambers had, however, chipped away at the fringes of McDonald's story by introducing admissible testimony from other sources indicating that he had not been seen in the cafe where he said he was when the shooting started, that he had not been having beer with Turner, and that he possessed a .22 pistol at the time of the crime. But all that remained from McDonald's own testimony was a single written confession countered by an arguably acceptable renunciation. Chambers' defense was far less persuasive than it might have been had he been given an opportunity to subject McDonald's statements to cross-examination or had the other confessions been admitted.

III

The right of an accused in a criminal trial to due process is, in essence, the right to a fair opportunity to defend against the State's accusations. The rights to confront and cross-examine witnesses and to call witnesses in one's own behalf have long been recognized as essential to due process. Mr. Justice Black, writing for the Court in In re Oliver, 333 U.S. 257, 273 (1948), identified these rights as among the minimum essentials of a fair trial. . . . Both of these elements of a fair trial are implicated in the present case.

A

Chambers was denied an opportunity to subject McDonald's damning repudiation and alibi to cross-examination. He was not allowed to test the witness' recollection, to probe into the details of his alibi, or to "sift" his conscience so that the jury might judge for itself whether McDonald's testimony was worthy of belief. . . . The right of cross-examination is more than a desirable rule of trial procedure. It is implicit in the constitutional right of confrontation, and helps assure the "accuracy of the truth-determining process." Dutton v. Evans, 400 U.S. 74, 89 (1970). . . . It is, indeed, "an essential and fundamental requirement for the kind of fair trial which is this country's constitutional goal." Pointer v. Texas, 380 U.S. 400, 405 (1965). Of course, the right to confront and to cross-examine is not absolute and may, in appropriate cases, bow to accommodate other legitimate interests in the criminal trial process. . . . But its denial or significant diminution calls into question the ultimate " 'integrity of the fact-finding process' " and requires that the competing interest be closely examined. . . .

In this case, petitioner's request to cross-examine McDonald was denied on the basis of a Mississippi common-law rule that a party may not impeach his own witness. The rule rests on the presumption—without regard to the circumstances of the particular case—that a party who calls a witness "vouches for his credibility." Clark v. Lansford, 191 So.2d 123, 125 (Miss.1966). Although the historical origins of the "voucher" rule are uncertain, it appears to be a remnant of primitive English trial practice in which "oath-takers" or "compurgators" were called to stand behind a particular party's position in any controversy. Their assertions were strictly partisan and, quite unlike witnesses in criminal trials today, their role bore little relation to the impartial ascertainment of the facts.

Whatever validity the "voucher" rule may have once enjoyed, and apart from whatever usefulness it retains today in the civil trial process, it bears little present relationship to the realities of the criminal process. It might have been logical for the early common law to require a party to vouch for the credibility of witnesses he brought before the jury to affirm his veracity. Having selected them especially for that purpose, the party might reasonably be expected to stand firmly behind their testimony. But in modern criminal trials, defendants are rarely able to select their witnesses: they must take them where they find them. Moreover, as applied in this case, the "voucher" rule's impact was doubly harmful to Chambers' efforts to develop his defense. Not only was he precluded from cross-examining McDonald, but, as the State conceded at oral argument, he was also restricted in the scope of his direct examination by the rule's corollary requirement that the party calling the witness is bound by anything he might say. He was, therefore, effectively prevented from exploring the circumstances of McDonald's three prior oral confessions and from challenging the renunciation of the written confession.

In this Court, Mississippi has not sought to defend the rule or explain its underlying rationale. Nor has it contended that its rule should override the accused's right of confrontation. Instead, it argues that there is no incompatibility between the rule and Chambers' rights because no right of confrontation exists unless the testifying witness is "adverse" to the accused. The State's brief asserts that the "right of confrontation applies to witnesses '*against*' an accused." Relying on the trial court's determination that McDonald was not "adverse," and on the State Supreme Court's holding that McDonald did not "point the finger at Chambers,"[21] the State contends that Chambers' constitutional right was not involved.

The argument that McDonald's testimony was not "adverse" to, or "against," Chambers is not convincing. The State's proof at trial excluded the theory that more than one person participated in the shooting of Liberty. To the extent that McDonald's sworn confession tended to incriminate him, it tended also to exculpate Chambers. And, in the circumstances of this case, McDonald's retraction inculpated Chambers to the same extent that it exculpated McDonald. It can hardly be disputed that McDonald's testimony was in fact seriously adverse to Chambers. The availability of the right to confront and to cross-examine those who give damaging testimony against the accused has never been held to depend on whether the witness was initially put on the stand by the accused or by the State. We reject the notion that a right of such substance in the criminal process may be governed by that technicality or by any narrow and unrealistic definition of the word "against." The "voucher" rule, as applied in this case, plainly interfered with Chambers' right to defend against the State's charges.

B

We need not decide, however, whether this error alone would occasion reversal since Chambers' claimed denial of due process rests on the ultimate impact of that error when viewed in conjunction with the trial court's refusal to permit him to call other witnesses. The trial court refused to allow him to introduce the testimony of Hardin, Turner, and Carter. Each would have testified to the statements purportedly made by McDonald, on three separate occasions shortly after the crime, naming himself as the murderer. The State Supreme Court approved the exclusion of this evidence on the ground that it was hearsay.

The hearsay rule, which has long been recognized and respected by virtually every State, is based on experience and grounded in the notion that untrustworthy evidence should not be presented to the triers of fact. Out-of-court statements are traditionally excluded because they lacked the conventional indicia of reliability: they are usually not made under oath or other circumstances that impress the speaker with the solemnity of his statements; the declarant's word is not subject to cross-examination; and he is not available in order that his demeanor and credibility may be assessed by the jury. . . . A number of exceptions have developed over the years to allow admission of hearsay statements made under circumstances that tend to assure reliability and thereby compensate for the absence of the oath and opportunity for cross-examination. Among the most prevalent

21. 252 So.2d, at 220.

of these exceptions is the one applicable to declarations against interest—an exception founded on the assumption that a person is unlikely to fabricate a statement against his own interest at the time it is made. Mississippi recognizes this exception but applies it only to declarations against pecuniary interest. It recognizes no such exception for declarations, like McDonald's in this case, that are against the penal interest of the declarant. . . .

This materialistic limitation on the declaration-against-interest hearsay exception appears to be accepted by most States in their criminal trial processes, although a number of States have discarded it. Declarations against penal interest have also been excluded in federal courts under the authority of Donnelly v. United States, 228 U.S. 243, 272–73 (1913), although exclusion would not be required under the newly proposed Federal Rules of Evidence. Exclusion, where the limitation prevails, is usually premised on the view that admission would lead to the frequent presentation of perjured testimony to the jury. It is believed that confessions of criminal activity are often motivated by extraneous considerations and, therefore, are not as inherently reliable as statements against pecuniary or proprietary interest. While that rationale has been the subject of considerable scholarly criticism, we need not decide in this case whether, under other circumstances, it might serve some valid state purpose by excluding untrustworthy testimony.

The hearsay statements involved in this case were originally made and subsequently offered at trial under circumstances that provided considerable assurance of their reliability. First, each of McDonald's confessions was made spontaneously to a close acquaintance shortly after the murder had occurred. Second, each one was corroborated by some other evidence in the case—McDonald's sworn confession, the testimony of an eyewitness to the shooting, the testimony that McDonald was seen with a gun immediately after the shooting, and proof of his prior ownership of a .22-caliber revolver and subsequent purchase of a new weapon. The sheer number of independent confessions provided additional corroboration for each. Third, whatever may be the parameters of the penal-interest rationale, each confession here was in a very real sense self-incriminatory and unquestionably against interest. . . . McDonald stood to benefit nothing by disclosing his role in the shooting to any of his three friends and he must have been aware of the possibility that disclosure would lead to criminal prosecution. Indeed, after telling Turner of his involvement, he subsequently urged Turner not to "mess him up." Finally, if there was any question about the truthfulness of the extrajudicial statements, McDonald was present in the courtroom and had been under oath. He could have been cross-examined by the State, and his demeanor and responses weighed by the jury. . . . The availability of McDonald significantly distinguishes this case from the prior Mississippi precedent . . . and from the *Donnelly*-type situation, since in both cases the declarant was unavailable at the time of trial.

Few rights are more fundamental than that of an accused to present witnesses in his own defense. . . . In the exercise of this right, the accused, as is required of the State, must comply with established rules of procedure and evidence designed to assure both fairness and reliability in the ascertainment of guilt and innocence. Although perhaps no rule of evidence has been more respected or more frequently applied in jury trials than that applicable to the exclusion of hearsay, exceptions tailored to allow the introduction of evidence which in fact is likely to be trustworthy have long existed. The testimony rejected by the trial court here bore persuasive assurances of trustworthiness and thus was well within the basic rationale of the exception for declarations against interest. That testimony also was critical to Chambers' defense. In these circumstances, where constitutional rights directly affecting the ascertainment of guilt are implicated, the hearsay rule may not be applied mechanistically to defeat the ends of justice.

We conclude that the exclusion of this critical evidence, coupled with the State's refusal to permit Chambers to cross-examine McDonald, denied him a trial in accord with traditional and fundamental standards of due process. In reaching this judgment, we establish no new principles of constitutional law. Nor does our holding signal any diminution in the respect traditionally accorded to the States in the establishment and implementation of their own criminal trial rules and procedures. Rather, we hold quite simply that under the facts and circumstances of this case the rulings of the trial court deprived Chambers of a fair trial.

. . .[22]

---

504. See Green v. Georgia, 442 U.S. 95 (1979) (8–1), a capital case in which, relying on Chambers v. Mississippi, the Court held that the hearsay rule could not be allowed to bar testimony "highly relevant to a critical issue in the punishment phase of the trial," which the state had itself used in the trial of a codefendant.

Cf. Montana v. Egelhoff, 518 U.S. 37 (1996) (5–4), distinguishing *Chambers* and upholding a state statute providing that voluntary intoxication may not be taken into account in the determination of the existence of a mental state that is an element of a crime. See also United States v. Scheffer, 523 U.S. 303 (1998) (8–1), also distinguishing *Chambers*. In *Scheffer*, the Court held that a rule of the Military Rules of Evidence that makes polygraph evidence inadmissible in court-martial proceedings does not unconstitutionally restrict the right of an accused to present a defense.

505. The "voucher" rule at issue in Chambers v. Mississippi, above, is discussed in Lipinski v. New York, 557 F.2d 289, 293–94 (2d Cir.1977), in which the court observed: "The traditional justifications of the rule against impeaching one's own witness are plainly bankrupt. No thoughtful jurist or

[22] Justice White wrote a concurring opinion.
opinion. Justice Rehnquist wrote a dissenting

scholar will today defend the proposition that a party is morally bound by the testimony of his witnesses. And, since it is universally accepted that a party must take his witnesses where he finds them, it is completely unrealistic to imagine him as the guarantor of his witness's veracity in every respect." But, the court added, the rule "appears to be one of those atavisms that no quantity of reasoned criticism seems able to destroy," id. at 293. The rule has been eliminated in federal courts by Rule 607 of the Rules of Evidence for United States Courts and Magistrates, which provides: "The credibility of a witness may be attacked by any party, including the party calling the witness."

In Welcome v. Vincent, 549 F.2d 853 (2d Cir.1977), the court, relying on *Chambers*, held that the trial court should not have restricted defense counsel's effort to question a defense witness about a confession to the same crimes for which the defendants were on trial. On cross-examination by the prosecutor, the witness had denied his involvement in the crime; the defense counsel sought on redirect examination to question him about the confession as a prior inconsistent statement, to impeach his credibility. The trial court refused to permit such questioning on the ground that the witness, having been called by the defense and not having inculpated the defendants, was not a hostile witness. The court held that it is a denial of a fair trial "where another person, present on the witness stand, has previously confessed that he, rather than the defendant on trial, has perpetrated the crime . . . to restrict examination of such a witness, so that his prior confession may not be proven . . . at least when the confession, though retracted, has some semblance of reliability." Id. at 858–59.

Chambers is distinguished and an application of a state voucher rule upheld, in Maness v. Wainwright, 512 F.2d 88 (5th Cir.1975).

506. At separate successive trials of two defendants for the same murders, the prosecutor, who was the same at both trials, introduced inherently contradictory evidence, that pointed to the guilt of the defendant then on trial. Both defendants were convicted. Reversing the conviction of the first defendant to have been convicted, the court held that it was a violation of due process for the prosecutor to use "inconsistent, irreconcilable theories to secure convictions for the same offenses arising out of the same event." Smith v. Groose, 205 F.3d 1045, 1049 (8th Cir.2000).

507. In Davis v. Alaska, 415 U.S. 308 (1974), a main witness for the prosecution in a burglary and larceny case was a juvenile delinquent, who was on probation by order of a juvenile court. Before he testified, the prosecutor moved that there be no reference to the witness's juvenile record during cross-examination. The motion was in accordance with state law, the purpose of which was to protect a juvenile's anonymity and to further his rehabilitation. Defense counsel agreed not to use the juvenile record to impeach the witness's character but wanted to use the fact that he was on probation to show that he had a motive for cooperating with the police that suggested bias. The motion was granted. In response to defense counsel's questions, the witness testified in a way that intimated that he had not been in trouble with the police; because of the court's order, defense counsel was unable to inquire further.

The Court reversed the defendant's conviction. "The State's policy interest in protecting the confidentiality of a juvenile offender's record cannot require yielding of so vital a constitutional right as the effective cross-examination for bias of an adverse witness. The State could have protected [the witness] from exposure of his juvenile adjudication in these circumstances by refraining from using him to make out its case; the State cannot, consistent with the right of confrontation, require the petitioner to bear the full burden of vindicating the State's interest in the secrecy of juvenile criminal records." Id. at 320.

"[A] criminal defendant states a violation of the Confrontation Clause by showing that he was prohibited from engaging in otherwise appropriate cross-examination designed to show a prototypical form of bias on the part of the witness. . . ." Delaware v. Van Arsdall, 475 U.S. 673, 680 (1986) (7–2). Such a violation may, however, be harmless error. "The correct inquiry is whether, assuming that the damaging potential of the cross-examination were fully realized, a reviewing court might nonetheless say that the error was harmless beyond a reasonable doubt." Id. at 684.

In Crane v. Kentucky, 476 U.S. 683 (1986), having ruled that the defendant's confession to police was voluntary and admissible, the trial judge excluded evidence of the circumstances in which the confession was made, which the defense offered to cast doubt on its credibility. The Court held that the exclusion of potentially exculpatory evidence, without rational justification, denied the defendant a meaningful opportunity to present a defense, protected either by the Due Process Clause or by the Sixth Amendment's Compulsory Process and Confrontation Clauses. See United States v. Lindstrom, 698 F.2d 1154 (11th Cir.1983) (restriction of cross-examination of principal prosecution witness about her history of psychiatric illness and treatment denied right to confront witnesses).

The Confrontation Clause is not violated if an expert witness for the prosecution testifies to a fact and then states on cross-examination that he has forgotten the basis on which he reached his conclusion. Delaware v. Fensterer, 474 U.S. 15 (1985) (per curiam) (7–2). The witness, an FBI agent, testified that hair had been removed from the murder victim's head forcibly; on cross-examination he said that he could not recall which of three possible bases for such a conclusion was the one on which he had relied.

Relying on *Fensterer*, the Court held that neither the Confrontation Clause nor the federal hearsay rule bars admission of a witness's out-of-court identification statement if the witness is available at trial but unable, because of loss of memory, to testify about the basis for his statement. The witness testified at the trial that he remembered making the statement and that he was certain at that time that his identification was accurate. United States v. Owens, 484 U.S. 554 (1988) (6–2).

In Pennsylvania v. Ritchie, 480 U.S. 39 (1987) (5–4), a prosecution for child abuse, the Court held that the Confrontation Clause did not require the state to grant pretrial discovery of records of a social service agency containing information pertinent to the case. Under state law, the records were confidential. A plurality of the Court said that the right under the Confrontation Clause is a trial right, and that since defense counsel was permitted to cross-examine all trial witnesses fully, the defendant's right was not denied by nondisclosure of the records. (The Court noted, however, that under *Agurs*, p. 943 above, and *Bagley*, p. 950 note 475 above, the defendant had a right to disclosure of information if there was a reasonable probability that such disclosure would change the outcome of the trial. Id. at 57.) Similarly, in Kentucky v. Stincer, 482 U.S. 730 (1987) (6–3), the Court held that the exclusion of the defendant from a hearing to determine the competency to testify of two child witnesses for the prosecution did not violate his rights under the Confrontation Clause or his right under the Due Process Clause to be present at all stages of a criminal proceeding. The exclusion did not affect the defendant's opportunity for full, effective cross-examination of the witnesses, nor would his presence have helped to ensure a more reliable determination of their competence to testify.

The Confrontation Clause guarantees the right to confront witnesses face to face. The defendant in a child sexual abuse case was denied his right when the complaining witnesses were permitted to testify behind a screen, which allowed the defendant dimly to see them and to hear their testimony but prevented them from seeing him at all. The case was returned to the state court for consideration whether the violation was harmless error. Coy v. Iowa, 487 U.S. 1012 (1988) (6–2). Returning to the same issue in Maryland v. Craig, 497 U.S. 836 (1990) (5–4), the Court said: "[T]hough we reaffirm the importance of face-to-face confrontation with witnesses appearing at trial, we cannot say that such confrontation is an indispensable element of the Sixth Amendment's guarantee of the right to confront one's accusers." Id. at 849–50. "[W]here necessary to protect a child witness from trauma that would be caused by testifying in the physical presence of the defendant, at least where such trauma would impair the child's ability to communicate, the Confrontation Clause does not prohibit use of a procedure that, despite the absence of face-to-face confrontation, ensures the reliability of the evidence by subjecting it to rigorous adversarial testing and thereby preserves the essence of effective confrontation." Id. at 857. The Court upheld a procedure by which a child witness testifies out of the presence of the defendant, on closed-circuit, one-way television, if the judge finds that testimony in front of the defendant will cause serious emotional distress such that the child cannot reasonably communicate; the defendant is able to watch the testimony on television and to communicate with defense counsel electronically.

508. The exclusion of defendant's hypnotically refreshed testimony because of a flat rule excluding all such testimony violated her right to testify in her own behalf. The trial court's ruling excluding such testimony effectively prevented the defendant from testifying about most of the circumstances of the crime. Although a court might exclude evidence in a particular case if it were not reliable, the wholesale exclusion of the defendant's testimony on the basis of a per se rule was not permissible. Rock v. Arkansas, 483 U.S. 44 (1987) (5–4).

509. "[A] defendant is not entitled to an unlimited number of witnesses to testify in his behalf, lest our criminal justice system grind to a complete halt. He is entitled to have compulsory process served only on as many witnesses as will assist him in receiving a fair trial under the circumstances of his case." Ross v. Estelle, 694 F.2d 1008, 1111 (5th Cir.1983). The court held that the defendant was not denied due process by the trial judge's refusal to subpoena more than six out of 14 potential witnesses, whose testimony was "largely cumulative."

Roviaro v. United States

353 U.S. 53, 77 S.Ct. 623, 1 L.Ed.2d 639 (1957)

■ MR. JUSTICE BURTON delivered the opinion of the Court.

This case concerns a conviction for violation of the Narcotic Drugs Import and Export Act, as amended. The principal issue is whether the United States District Court committed reversible error when it allowed the Government to refuse to disclose the identity of an undercover employee who had taken a material part in bringing about the possession of certain drugs by the accused, had been present with the accused at the occurrence of the alleged crime, and might be a material witness as to whether the accused knowingly transported the drugs as charged. For the reasons hereafter stated, we hold that, under the circumstances here present, this was reversible error.

In 1955, in the Northern District of Illinois, petitioner, Albert Roviaro, was indicted on two counts by a federal grand jury. The first count charged that on August 12, 1954, at Chicago, Illinois, he sold heroin to one "John Doe" in violation of 26 U.S.C. § 2554(a). The second charged that on the same date and in the same city he "did then and there fraudulently and knowingly receive, conceal, buy and facilitate the transportation and concealment after importation of . . . heroin, knowing the same to be imported into the United States contrary to law; in violation of Section 174, Title 21, United States Code."

Before trial, petitioner moved for a bill of particulars requesting, among other things, the name, address and occupation of "John Doe." The Government objected on the ground that John Doe was an informer and that his identity was privileged. The motion was denied.

Petitioner, who was represented by counsel, waived a jury and was tried by the District Court. During the trial John Doe's part in the charged transaction was described by government witnesses, and counsel for petitioner, in cross-examining them, sought repeatedly to learn John Doe's identity. The court declined to permit this cross-examination and John Doe was not produced, identified, or otherwise made available. Petitioner was found guilty on both counts. . . . We granted certiorari . . . in order to pass upon the propriety of the nondisclosure of the informer's identity. . . .

At the trial, the Government relied on the testimony of two federal narcotics agents, Durham and Fields, and two Chicago police officers, Bryson and Sims, each of whom knew petitioner by sight. On the night of August 12, 1954, these four officers met at 75th Street and Prairie Avenue in Chicago with an informer described only as John Doe. Doe and his Cadillac car were searched and no narcotics were found. Bryson secreted himself in the trunk of Doe's Cadillac taking with him a device with which to raise the trunk lid from the inside. Doe then drove the Cadillac to 70th Place and St. Lawrence Avenue, followed by Durham in one government car and Field and Sims in another. After an hour's wait, at about 11 o'clock, petitioner arrived in a Pontiac, accompanied by an unidentified man. Petitioner immediately entered Doe's Cadillac, taking a front seat beside Doe. They then proceeded by a circuitous route to 74th Street near Champlain Avenue. Both government cars trailed the Cadillac but only the one driven by Durham managed to follow it to 74th Street. When the Cadillac came to a stop on 74th Street, Durham stepped out of his car onto the sidewalk and saw petitioner alight from the Cadillac about 100 feet away. Durham saw petitioner walk a few feet to a nearby tree, pick up a small package, return to the open right front door of the Cadillac, make a motion as if depositing the package in the car, and then wave to Doe and walk away. Durham went immediately to the Cadillac and recovered a package from the floor. He signaled to Bryson to come out of the trunk and then walked down the street in time to see petitioner re-enter the Pontiac, parked nearby, and ride away.

Meanwhile, Bryson, concealed in the trunk of the Cadillac, had heard a conversation between John Doe and petitioner after the latter had entered the car. He heard petitioner greet John Doe and direct him where to drive. At one point, petitioner admonished him to pull over to the curb, cut the motor, and turn out the lights so as to lose a "tail." He then told him to continue "further down." Petitioner asked about money Doe owed him. He advised Doe that he had brought him "three pieces this time." When Bryson heard Doe being ordered to stop the car, he raised the lid of the trunk slightly. After the car stopped, he saw petitioner walk to a tree, pick up a package, and return toward the car. He heard petitioner say, "Here it is," and "I'll call you in a couple of days." Shortly thereafter he heard Durham's signal to come out and emerged from the trunk to find Durham holding a small package found to contain three glassine envelopes containing a white powder.

A field test of the powder having indicated that it contained an opium derivative, the officers, at about 12:30 a.m., arrested petitioner at his home and took him, along with Doe, to Chicago police headquarters. There petitioner was confronted with Doe, who denied that he knew or had ever seen petitioner. Subsequent chemical analysis revealed that the powder contained heroin.

I

Petitioner contends that the trial court erred in upholding the right of the Government to withhold the identity of John Doe. He argues that Doe was an active participant in the illegal activity charged and that, therefore, the Government could not withhold his identity, his whereabouts, and whether he was alive or dead at the time of trial. The Government does not defend the nondisclosure of Doe's identity with respect to Count 1, which charged a sale of heroin to John Doe, but it attempts to sustain the judgment on the basis of the conviction on Count 2, charging illegal transportation of narcotics. It argues that the conviction on Count 2 may properly be upheld since the identity of the informer, in the circumstances of this case, has no real bearing on that charge and is therefore privileged.

What is usually referred to as the informer's privilege is in reality the Government's privilege to withhold from disclosure the identity of persons who furnish information of violations of law to officers charged with enforcement of that law. . . . The purpose of the privilege is the furtherance and protection of the public interest in effective law enforcement. The privilege recognizes the obligation of citizens to communicate their knowledge of the commission of crimes to law-enforcement officials and, by preserving their anonymity, encourages them to perform that obligation.

The scope of the privilege is limited by its underlying purpose. Thus, where the disclosure of the contents of a communication will not tend to reveal the identity of an informer, the contents are not privileged. Likewise, once the identity of the informer has been disclosed to those who would have cause to resent the communication, the privilege is no longer applicable.

A further limitation on the applicability of the privilege arises from the fundamental requirements of fairness. Where the disclosure of an informer's identity, or of the contents of his communication, is relevant and helpful to the defense of an accused, or is essential to a fair determination of a cause, the privilege must give way. In these situations the trial court may require disclosure and, if the Government withholds the information, dismiss the action. Most of the federal cases involving this limitation on the scope of the informer's privilege have arisen where the legality of a search without a warrant is in issue and the communications of an informer are claimed to establish probable cause. In these cases the Government has been required to disclose the identity of the informant unless there was sufficient evidence apart from his confidential communication.

. . .

We believe that no fixed rule with respect to disclosure is justifiable. The problem is one that calls for balancing the public interest in protecting the flow of information against the individual's right to prepare his defense. Whether a proper balance renders nondisclosure erroneous must depend on the particular circumstances of each case, taking into consideration the crime charged, the possible defenses, the possible significance of the informer's testimony, and other relevant factors.

II

The materiality of John Doe's possible testimony must be determined by reference to the offense charged in Count 2 and the evidence relating to that count. The charge is in the language of the statute. It does not charge mere possession; it charges that petitioner did "fraudulently and knowingly receive, conceal, buy and facilitate the transportation and concealment after importation of . . . heroin, knowing the same to be imported into the United States contrary to law. . . ." While John Doe is not expressly mentioned, this charge, when viewed in connection with the evidence introduced at the trial, is so closely related to John Doe as to make his identity and testimony highly material.

It is true that the last sentence of subdivision (c) of § 2 authorizes a conviction when the Government has proved that the accused possessed narcotics, unless the accused explains or justifies such possession. But this statutory presumption does not reduce the offense to one of mere possession or shift the burden of proof; it merely places on the accused, at a certain point, the burden of going forward with his defense. The fact that petitioner here was faced with the burden of explaining or justifying his alleged possession of the heroin emphasizes his vital need for access to any material witness. Otherwise, the burden of going forward might become unduly heavy.

The circumstances of this case demonstrate that John Doe's possible testimony was highly relevant and might have been helpful to the defense. So far as petitioner knew, he and John Doe were alone and unobserved during the crucial occurrence for which he was indicted. Unless petitioner waived his constitutional right not to take the stand in his own defense, John Doe was his one material witness. Petitioner's opportunity to cross-examine Police Officer Bryson and Federal Narcotics Agent Durham was hardly a substitute for an opportunity to examine the man who had been nearest to him and took part in the transaction. Doe had helped to set up the criminal occurrence and had played a prominent part in it. His testimony might have disclosed an entrapment. He might have thrown doubt upon petitioner's identity or on the identity of the package. He was the only witness who might have testified to petitioner's possible lack of knowledge of the contents of the package that he "transported" from the tree to John Doe's car. The desirability of calling John Doe as a witness, or at least interviewing him in preparation for trial, was a matter for the accused rather than the Government to decide.

Finally, the Government's use against petitioner of his conversation with John Doe while riding in Doe's car particularly emphasizes the unfairness of the nondisclosure in this case. The only person, other than petitioner himself, who could controvert, explain or amplify Bryson's report of this important conversation was John Doe. Contradiction or amplification might have borne upon petitioner's knowledge of the contents of the package or might have tended to show an entrapment.

This is a case where the Government's informer was the sole participant, other than the accused, in the transaction charged. The informer was the only witness in a position to amplify or contradict the testimony of government witnesses. Moreover, a government witness testified that Doe denied knowing petitioner or ever having seen him before. We conclude that, under these circumstances, the trial court committed prejudicial error in permitting the Government to withhold the identity of its undercover employee in the face of repeated demands by the accused for his disclosure. . . .[23]

---

510. "What *Roviaro* . . . makes clear is that this Court was unwilling to impose any absolute rule requiring disclosure of an informer's identity even in formulating evidentiary rules for federal criminal trials." McCray v. Illinois, 386 U.S. 300, 311 (1967).

The courts have generally held that *Roviaro* requires disclosure if the informant was a participant in or witness to the crime charged, but not if he was a mere "tipster" who informed the government about the offense. E.g., United States v. Price, 783 F.2d 1132 (4th Cir.1986); Gaines v. Hess, 662 F.2d 1364 (10th Cir.1981); United States v. Silva, 580 F.2d 144 (5th Cir.1978).

511. "[W]here the informant is shown to be a material witness and the government does not plan to use the informant as a witness it owes a duty to make every reasonable effort to have the informant made available to the defendant to interview or use as a witness, if desired." United States v. Barnes, 486 F.2d 776, 779–80 (8th Cir.1973). See, e.g., Renzi v. Virginia, 794 F.2d 155 (4th Cir.1986) (misleading information supplied to defense by prosecution deprived defense of opportunity to find and produce informer); United States v. Tornabene, 687 F.2d 312 (9th Cir.1982) (government failed to make reasonable efforts to produce informant; new trial ordered); United States v. Tuck, 380 F.2d 857 (2d Cir.1967) (government is not a "guarantor" of informant's appearance but must "accord reasonable cooperation" in securing his appearance).

512. It is a denial of the defendant's constitutional right to confront the witnesses against him to prevent defense counsel from eliciting a witness's true name and address on cross-examination. "[W]hen the credibility of a witness is in issue, the very starting point in 'exposing falsehood and bringing out the truth'[24] through cross-examination must necessarily be to ask the witness who he is and where he lives. The witness' name and address open countless avenues of in-court examination and out-of-court investigation. To forbid this most rudimentary inquiry at the threshold is effectively to emasculate the right of cross-examination itself." Smith v. Illinois, 390 U.S. 129, 131 (1968).

[23] Justice Clark wrote a dissenting opinion.

24. See Pointer v. Texas, 380 U.S., at 404.

513. In Brooks v. Tennessee, 406 U.S. 605 (1972) (6–3), the Court held that a state statute requiring a defendant to testify, if at all, before other defense witnesses testified was unconstitutional. It said that the statute restricted the defendant's privilege against self-incrimination, because it limited his ability to choose on the basis of the rest of the evidence whether to speak, and denied him due process, because it restricted his ability to prepare his case.

On the defendant's right to testify, see United States v. Panza, 612 F.2d 432 (9th Cir.1979) (defendant's direct testimony stricken after he refused to answer relevant questions on cross-examination).

514. On the practice of allowing jurors to participate in the examination of witnesses by presenting written questions to the judge who then asks the questions of the witnesses, see United States v. George, 986 F.2d 1176 (8th Cir.1993) (practice discussed and upheld); United States v. Sutton, 970 F.2d 1001 (1st Cir.1992) (practice is "fraught with perils" and should rarely be used, but is within trial judge's discretion). In United States v. Bush, 47 F.3d 511 (2d Cir.1995), the court said that it was within the trial judge's discretion to allow the practice, but discouraged it. *Bush* was followed in United States v. Ajmal, 67 F.3d 12 (2d Cir.1995). The court said that questioning by jurors should be reserved for exceptional circumstances and should not be allowed as "a matter of course." See also United States v. Feinberg, 89 F.3d 333 (7th Cir.1996) (practice is within district judge's discretion); United States v. Thompson, 76 F.3d 442 (2d Cir.1996) (jury improperly allowed to ask questions of witnesses; harmless error).

FEDERAL RULES OF CRIMINAL PROCEDURE

Rule 26.2

PRODUCING A WITNESS'S STATEMENT

(a) Motion to Produce. After a witness other than the defendant has testified on direct examination, the court, on motion of a party who did not call the witness, must order an attorney for the government or the defendant and the defendant's attorney to produce, for the examination and use of the moving party, any statement of the witness that is in their possession and that relates to the subject matter of the witness's testimony.

(b) Producing the Entire Statement. If the entire statement relates to the subject matter of the witness's testimony, the court must order that the statement be delivered to the moving party.

(c) Producing a Redacted Statement. If the party who called the witness claims that the statement contains information that is privileged or does not relate to the subject matter of the witness's testimony, the court must inspect the statement in camera. After excising any privileged or unrelated portions, the court must order delivery of the redacted statement to the moving party. If the defendant objects to an excision, the court must preserve the entire statement with the excised portion indicated, under seal, as part of the record.

(d) Recess to Examine a Statement. The court may recess the proceedings to allow time for a party to examine the statement and prepare for its use.

(e) Sanction for Failure to Produce or Deliver a Statement. If the party who called the witness disobeys an order to produce or deliver a statement, the court must strike the witness's testimony from the record. If an attorney for the government disobeys the order, the court must declare a mistrial if justice so requires.

(f) "Statement" Defined. As used in this rule, a witness's "statement" means:

(1) a written statement that the witness makes and signs, or otherwise adopts or approves;

(2) a substantially verbatim, contemporaneously recorded recital of the witness's oral statement that is contained in any recording or any transcription of a recording; or

(3) the witness's statement to a grand jury, however taken or recorded, or a transcription of such a statement.

(g) Scope. This rule applies at trial, at a suppression hearing under Rule 12, and to the extent specified in the following rules:

(1) Rule 5.1(h) (preliminary hearing);

(2) Rule 32(i)(2) (sentencing);

(3) Rule 32.1(e) (hearing to revoke or modify probation or supervised release);

(4) Rule 46(j) (detention hearing); and

(5) Rule 8 of the Rules Governing Proceedings under 28 U.S.C. § 2255.

---

515. In Jencks v. United States, 353 U.S. 657 (1957), the petitioner was convicted of swearing falsely that he was not a member of or affiliated with the communist party (see 18 U.S.C. § 1001). The government's principal witnesses were party members whom the F.B.I. paid to make contemporaneous reports of party activities. They testified at the trial concerning activities in which the petitioner had allegedly participated, and on cross-examination referred to their reports to the F.B.I. Motions for production of the reports for inspection and use in cross-examination were denied. The Court reversed the conviction. It held that the petitioner was entitled to inspect the reports even though a preliminary foundation of inconsistency between them and the witnesses' testimony was not established; "a sufficient foundation was established by the testimony of [the witnesses] that their reports were of the events and activities related in their testimony," id. at 666. "[T]he petitioner was entitled to an order directing the Government to produce for inspection all reports of . . . [the witnesses] in its possession, written and, when orally made, as recorded by the F.B.I., touching the events and activities as to which they testified at the trial. . . . [F]urther . . . the petitioner is entitled to inspect the reports to decide whether to use them in his defense. Because only the defense is adequately equipped to determine the effective use for purpose of discrediting the Government's witness and thereby furthering the accused's defense, the defense must initially be entitled to see them to determine what use may be made of them. Justice requires no less." Id. at 668–69. The Court held finally that if the government elected not to comply with an order to produce on the ground of privilege, the criminal action must be dismissed.

The "Jencks Act," 18 U.S.C. § 3500, was a congressional response to the Court's holding. It provided for the disclosure of statements of prosecution witnesses, in the manner set forth in Rule 26.2 above. It is clear from the legislative history of the act that it was intended to preserve the core of the Court's holding—that a defendant is entitled to inspect at trial statements of prosecution witnesses which might provide a basis for impeachment—but to eliminate the possibility of general disclosure of the government's files. House Report No. 700, 85th Cong., 1st Sess. 2, for example, stated that the proposed bill "sets standards of interpretation (1) for safeguarding the needless disclosure of confidential information in Government files and at the same time (2) assuring defendants access to the materials in those files which is pertinent to the testimony of Government witnesses."

Although it has generally been assumed that the requirements of the Jencks Act are not constitutionally based, see United States v. Augenblick, 393 U.S. 348, 356 (1969), the substance of the act has been accepted by state courts. E.g., State v. Hunt, 138 A.2d 1 (N.J.1958); State v. Foster, 407 P.2d 901 (Or.1965).

Rule 26.2 extends the provisions of the Jencks Act to disclosure of statements of defense witnesses as well. The Court evidently countenanced such an extension in United States v. Nobles, 422 U.S. 225 (1975). In *Nobles*, the trial judge ruled that if the defense called a defense investigator as a witness primarily to impeach the testimony of prosecution witnesses by prior statements made to the investigator, defense counsel would have to turn over to the prosecutor relevant portions of the investigator's report after he had finished testifying. Counsel refused, and the investigator was not allowed to testify about his interviews with the witnesses. The Court held that the ruling at trial was proper.

Judicial construction of the Jencks Act presumably is applicable to construction of Rule 26.2. For construction of the Act, see Simmons v. United States, 390 U.S. 377, 386–89 (1968) (photographs incorporated in statement); Campbell v. United States, 373 U.S. 487 (1963) (agent's report of witness interview was producible); Palermo v. United States, 360 U.S. 343 (1959) (memorandum summarizing witness interview not producible).

There is no exception from the category of "statements" producible under the Jencks Act for a lawyer's work product; a government lawyer's notes of his interview with a witness are producible if the requirements of the act are otherwise met. Goldberg v. United States, 425 U.S. 94 (1976).

The provisions of Rule 26.2 are not limited to witnesses at the trial itself. Rule 12(h), p. 759 above, provides expressly that Rule 26.2 applies to a hearing on a motion to suppress evidence under Rule 12(b)(3)(C). It provides further that in such a hearing, a law enforcement officer "is considered a government witness." See United States v. Rosa, 891 F.2d 1074 (3d Cir.1989) (Jencks Act material producible by government at sentencing hearing).

What should be the consequence if the government inadvertently loses or destroys statements of a witness? In Killian v. United States, 368 U.S. 231, 242 (1961), the Court said that the destruction of notes "in good faith and in accord with . . . normal practice" would not deprive the defendant of any right. In United States v. Beasley, 576 F.2d 626 (5th Cir.1978), however, the court concluded that a failure in good faith to produce a material statement required reversal of the conviction. Compare United States v. Perry, 471 F.2d 1057 (D.C.Cir.1972). Increasing experience with the requirements of the Act and Rule 26.2 makes it less likely that a court will find good faith if statements that are required to be produced are unavailable. In United States v. Harris, 543 F.2d 1247 (9th Cir.1976), for example, the court declared that the FBI could not consistently with the provisions of the Jencks Act continue its practice of routinely disposing of rough notes of interviews with prospective government witnesses. Preservation of such notes, the court said, "is necessary in order to permit courts to play their proper role in determining what evidence must be produced pursuant to the Jencks Act or other applicable law." Id. at 1253.

The remedy for an untimely production of Jencks Act material is not limited to those in 18 U.S.C. § 3500(d) or, presumably, Rule 26.2(e), if the delay in production was in good faith. In that circumstance, it is not construed as an election "not to comply" for purposes of that provision. Therefore, if the failure to produce is curable, the court can exercise its discretion to provide a remedy other than striking the testimony or declaring a mistrial. United States v. Wables, 731 F.2d 440 (7th Cir.1984).

"[T]he Jencks Act contemplates not only the furnishing of the statement of a witness but a reasonable opportunity to examine it and prepare for its use in the trial." United States v. Holmes, 722 F.2d 37, 40 (4th Cir.1983) (failure to grant continuance; conviction reversed).

FEDERAL RULES OF CRIMINAL PROCEDURE

Rule 26.3

MISTRIAL

Before ordering a mistrial, the court must give each defendant and the government an opportunity to comment on the propriety of the order, to state whether that party consents or objects, and to suggest alternatives.

Defense

ABA Standards for Criminal Justice, Prosecution Function and Defense Function (3d ed., 1993).

Defense Function Standards

4–1.2 The Function of Defense Counsel.

(a) Counsel for the accused is an essential component of the administration of criminal justice. A court properly constituted to hear a criminal case must be viewed as a tripartite entity consisting of the judge (and jury, where appropriate), counsel for the prosecution, and counsel for the accused.

(b) The basic duty defense counsel owes to the administration of justice and as an officer of the court is to serve as the accused's counselor and advocate with courage and devotion and to render effective, quality representation.

. . .

4–1.6 Trial Lawyer's Duty to Administration of Justice.

(a) The bar should encourage through every available means the widest possible participation in the defense of criminal cases by lawyers. Lawyers should be encouraged to qualify themselves for participation in criminal cases both by formal training and through experience as associate counsel.

(b) All such qualified lawyers should stand ready to undertake the defense of an accused regardless of public hostility toward the accused or personal distaste for the offense charged or the person of the defendant.

(c) Such qualified lawyers should not assert or announce a general unwillingness to appear in criminal cases. Law firms should encourage partners and associates to become qualified and to appear in criminal cases.

(d) Such qualified lawyers should not seek to avoid appointment by a tribunal to represent an accused except for good cause, such as: representing the accused is likely to result in violation of applicable ethical codes or other law, representing the accused is likely to result in an unreasonable financial burden on the lawyer, or the client or crime is so repugnant to the lawyer as to be likely to impair the client-lawyer relationship or the lawyer's ability to represent the client.

What limits are there on the obligation of a lawyer who is regularly engaged in the defense of criminal cases to accept as a client anyone who is prepared to pay for his services? On what is the obligation based?

ABA Model Rules of Professional Conduct (2004)

Rule 1.2: Scope of Representation and Allocation of Authority Between Client and Lawyer

. . .

(d) A lawyer shall not counsel a client to engage, or assist a client, in conduct that the lawyer knows is criminal or fraudulent, but a lawyer may discuss the legal consequences of any proposed course of conduct with a client and may counsel or assist a client to make a good faith effort to determine the validity, scope, meaning or application of the law.

Comment

. . .

Criminal, Fraudulent and Prohibited Transactions

[9] Paragraph (d) prohibits a lawyer from knowingly counseling or assisting a client to commit a crime or fraud. This prohibition, however, does not preclude the lawyer from giving an honest opinion about the actual consequences that appear likely to result from a client's conduct. Nor does the fact that a client uses advice in a course of action that is criminal or fraudulent of itself make a lawyer a party to the course of action. There is a critical distinction between presenting an analysis of legal aspects of questionable conduct and recommending the means by which a crime or fraud might be committed with impunity.

[10] When the client's course of action has already begun and is continuing, the lawyer's responsibility is especially delicate. The lawyer is required to avoid assisting the client, for example, by drafting or delivering documents that the lawyer knows are fraudulent or by suggesting how the wrongdoing might be concealed. A lawyer may not continue assisting a client in conduct that the lawyer originally supposed was legally proper but then discovers is criminal or fraudulent. The lawyer must, therefore, withdraw from the representation of the client in the matter. . . . In some cases, withdrawal alone might be insufficient. It may be necessary for the lawyer to give notice of the fact of withdrawal and to disaffirm any opinion, document, affirmation or the like. . . .

Rule 8.4: Misconduct

It is professional misconduct for a lawyer to:

. . .

(c) engage in conduct involving dishonesty, fraud, deceit or misrepresentation;

(d) engage in conduct that is prejudicial to the administration of justice. . . .

Hitch v. Pima County Superior Court

146 Ariz. 588, 708 P.2d 72 (1985)

■ CAMERON, JUSTICE.

This is a special action brought by defendant from an order of the trial court compelling defendant's attorney to deliver potentially inculpatory, physical evidence to the state and requiring that the attorney withdraw from representation. We have jurisdiction pursuant to Ariz. Const. Art. 6, § 5(3) and Rule 7, R.P.Sp.Act., 17A A.R.S.

We must decide three questions:

1. Does a defense attorney have an obligation to turn over to the state potentially inculpatory, physical evidence obtained from a third party?

2. If so, in what manner may this be done?

3. Must he then withdraw as attorney for the defendant?

The essential facts are not in dispute. Defendant was indicted for first degree murder and is currently awaiting trial on that charge. In the course of their investigation, the police interviewed defendant's girlfriend, Diane Heaton, who told them that the victim was in possession of a certain wristwatch shortly before his death. Subsequently, an investigator for the Pima County Public Defender's Office contacted Ms. Heaton and she informed him that she had found a wristwatch in defendant's suit jacket. She also stated that she did not want to turn the evidence over to the police. The investigator contacted defendant's attorney who told him to take possession of the watch and bring it to the attorney's office. The attorney indicated that he did this for two reasons. First, he wanted to examine the watch to determine whether it was the same one that Ms. Heaton had described to the police. Second, he was afraid that she might destroy or conceal the evidence. Shortly thereafter, defendant informed the police that he had taken a watch from the victim. The police were, however, unaware of the location of that watch.

On 11 June 1984, defendant's attorney filed a petition with the Ethics Committee of the Arizona State Bar, requesting an opinion concerning his duties with respect to the wristwatch. The Ethics Committee informed the attorney that he had a legal obligation to turn over the watch to the state and that he also might be compelled to testify as to the original location and source of the evidence. . . .

Defendant's attorney informed the Respondent Judge of the Committee's decision. Judge Veliz ordered that the watch be turned over to the state and that the attorney withdraw from the case. He also stayed the order to allow the filing of this petition for special action. We accepted jurisdiction because this case presents an issue of statewide importance in an area of the law that is unsettled.

I

Must Defendant's Attorney Turn the Evidence Over to the State?

We have previously held that an attorney need not turn over physical evidence obtained from his client if the evidence was such that it could not be obtained from the client against the client's will. . . . We have not, however, ruled as to physical evidence obtained from a third party. As to this question, cases from other jurisdictions are few in number. We do note, however, two cases that have dealt with the issue before us and have found that a defense attorney, as an officer of the court, has an obligation to turn over to the state material evidence obtained from third parties.

The Alaska Supreme Court was confronted with a case in which the defendant's attorney in a kidnapping case had received from a third party written plans for the kidnapping drawn by the client. In reviewing whether counsel violated defendant's right to adequate representation by making the existence of the plans known to the state, the court stated:

> As Morrell notes, authority in this area is surprisingly sparse. The existing authority seems to indicate, however, that a criminal defense attorney has an obligation to turn over to the prosecution physical evidence which comes into his possession, especially where the evidence comes into the attorney's possession through acts of a third party who is neither a client of the attorney nor an agent of a client. After turning over such evidence, an attorney may have either a right or a duty to remain silent as to the circumstances under which he obtained such evidence, but Morrell presents no authority which establishes that a criminal defendant whose attorney chooses to testify regarding to these matters is denied effective assistance of counsel.

Morrell v. State, 575 P.2d 1200, 1207 (Alaska 1978).

The California Court of Appeals, in a case in which the defendant's wife had given his attorney a pair of shoes, linked to the murder, which the state seized from defendant's attorney, stated:

> In any event, in the final analysis the controlling question is whether the State's seizure of the evidence violated defendant's rights. It did not. Neither the public defender nor substituted counsel for defendant had the right to withhold the evidence from the State by asserting an attorney-client privilege.

People v. Lee, 3 Cal.App.3d 514 (1970).

Both cases relied on dictum from State v. Olwell, P.2d 681 (1964), in finding that counsel had acted properly. In Olwell, defense counsel was served with a subpoena duces tecum in which he was asked to produce, at a coroner's inquest, all knives in his possession and control relating to the defendant. The attorney refused to indicate whether or not he was in possession of these knives, arguing that to do so would violate the confidential relationship of attorney and client. The Washington Supreme Court found that the subpoena was defective on its face because it required the attorney to reveal information given to him in the course of discussions with his client. The court stated, however:

> The attorney should not be a depository for criminal evidence . . . which in itself has little, if any, material value for the purposes of aiding counsel in the preparation of the defense of his client's case. Such evidence given the attorney during legal consultation for information purposes and used by the attorney in preparing the defense of his client's case, whether or not the case ever goes to trial, could clearly be withheld for a reasonable period of time. It follows that the attorney, after a reasonable period, should, as an officer of the court, on his own motion turn the same over to the prosecution.

Id. 394 P.2d at 684–85.

Of course, if the physical evidence is contraband, the attorney may be required to turn over the property even if he obtained that evidence from his client. For example, in a case where the attorney obtained from his client the money taken in a bank robbery and a sawed-off shotgun used in the crime, the attorney was required to turn the property over to the state. In Re Ryder, 381 F.2d 713 (4th Cir.1967). . . .

At issue is the conflict between a defense attorney's obligation to his client and to the court. As the Preamble to the Rules of Professional Conduct notes, a lawyer is both "a representative of [his] clients, an officer of the legal system and a public citizen having special responsibility for the quality of justice." As a representative of his client, a lawyer must act as a zealous advocate, demonstrating loyalty to his client and giving him the best legal advice possible within the bounds of the law. As part of this zealous representation, the lawyer is admonished not to reveal information relating to representation of his client. ER 1.6.

The Comment to ER 1.6 states:

> The principle of confidentiality is given effect in two related bodies of law, the attorney-client privilege (which includes the work product doctrine) in the law of evidence and the rule of confidentiality established in professional ethics. The attorney-client privilege applies in judicial and other proceedings in which a lawyer may be called as a witness or otherwise required to produce evidence concerning a client. The rule of client-lawyer confidentiality applies in situations other than those where evidence is sought from the lawyer through compulsion of law. The confidentiality rule applies not merely to matters communicated in confidence by the client but also to all information relating to the representation, whatever its source. A lawyer may not disclose such information except as authorized or required by the Rules of Professional Conduct or other law.

Because clients are aware that their lawyers will not repeat their communications, they feel that they may make both full and honest disclosure. Trial counsel is thus better able to evaluate the situation and prepare a proper defense. Thus, it has been said that "it is in the interest of public justice that the client be able to make full disclosure." Clark v. State, 159 Tex.Crim.App. 187, 199 (1953).

We note also that the lawyer's role as a zealous advocate is an important one, not only for the client but for the administration of justice. We have chosen an adversary system of justice in which, in theory, the state and the defendant meet as equals—"strength against strength, resource against resource, argument against argument." United States v. Bagley, 473 U.S. 667, 694 n.2 . . . (1985) (Marshall, J. dissenting). In order to close the gap between theory and practice and thereby ensure that the system is working properly, a defendant must have an attorney who will fight against the powerful resources of the state. It is only when this occurs that we can be assured that the system is functioning properly and only the guilty are convicted.

Balanced against the attorney's obligation to his client is the attorney's obligation as an officer of the court, which requires him "[to aid] in determining truth whenever possible." Note, "Ethics, Law and Loyalty: The Attorney's Duty to Turn Over Incriminating Evidence," 32 Stan. L. Rev. 977, 992 (1980). Both sides must have equal access to the relevant information. As the American Bar Association had noted: "[w]here the necessary evaluation and preparation are foreclosed by lack of information, the trial becomes a pursuit of truth and justice only by chance rather than by design, and generates a diminished respect for the criminal justice system, the judiciary and the attorney participants." II ABA Standards for Criminal Justice, comment to Standard 11–1.1(a) (2nd ed.1982) (footnote omitted). . . . Thus, in order to aid the truth determining process an attorney must refrain from impeding the flow of information to the state. The defendant's attorney can neither assist nor obstruct the prosecution in its efforts to discover evidence.

Defendant asks us, in balancing these competing interests, to hold that there is "no affirmative duty on the part of defense counsel to disclose possible inculpatory evidence obtained by counsel during the course of his representation of the client." Defendant maintains that to hold otherwise would cause irreparable harm to the attorney-client relationship.

The National Legal Aid and Defender Association in its amicus brief agrees with defendant that there should be no "absolute affirmative duty rule" requiring defendant's attorney to routinely disclose all physical evidence discovered during investigation of a case. The National Legal Aid and Defender Association suggests that we adopt the "Ethical Standard to Guide [A Lawyer] Who Receives Physical Evidence Implicating His Client in Criminal Conduct," proposed by the Criminal Justice Section's Ethics Committee. This standard reads as follows:

> (a) A lawyer who receives a physical item under circumstances implicating a client in criminal conduct shall disclose the location of or shall deliver that item to law enforcement authorities only: (1) if such is required by law or court order, or (2) as provided in paragraph (d).

> (b) Unless required to disclose, the lawyer shall return the item to the source from whom the lawyer receives it, as provided in paragraphs (c) and (d). In returning the item to the source, the lawyer shall advise the source of the legal consequences pertaining to possession or destruction of the item.
>
> (c) A lawyer may receive the item for a period of time during which the lawyer: (1) intends to return it to the owner; (2) reasonably fears that return of the item to the source will result in destruction of the item; (3) reasonably fears that return of the item to the source will result in physical harm to anyone; (4) intends to test, examine, inspect or use the item in any way as part of the lawyer's representation of the client; or (5) cannot return it to the source. If the lawyer retains the item, the lawyer shall do so in a manner that does not impede the lawful ability of law enforcement to obtain the item.
>
> (d) If the item received is contraband, or if in the lawyer's judgment the lawyer cannot retain the item in a way that does not pose an unreasonable risk of physical harm to anyone, the lawyer shall disclose the location of or shall deliver the item to law enforcement authorities.
>
> (e) If the lawyer discloses the location of or delivers the item to law enforcement authorities under paragraphs (a) or (d), or to a third party under paragraph (c)(1), the lawyer shall do so in the way best designed to protect the client's interest.

29 Cr. L. Rep. 2465–66 (26 August 1981).

We agree with defendant that any requirement that the defendant's attorney turn over to the prosecutor physical evidence which may aid in the conviction of the defendant may harm the attorney-client relationship. We do not believe, however, that this reason, by itself, is sufficient to avoid disclosure. We have stated that "[t]he duty of an attorney to a client * * * is subordinate to his responsibility for the due and proper administration of justice. In case of conflict, the former must yield to the latter." State v. Kruchten, 417 P.2d 510, 515 (1966). Thus, although we respect the relationship as an important one, we believe it must sometimes be subordinate to the free flow of information, upon which our adversary system is based. Other courts have shared our attitude. As the Kentucky Court of Appeals explained:

> It has been said that the reason underlying the attorney-client privilege is to encourage a client to disclose fully the facts and circumstances of his case to his attorney without fear that he or his attorney will be compelled to testify to the communications between them. Since the privilege results in the exclusion of evidence it runs counter to the widely held view that the fullest disclosure of the facts will best lead to the truth and ultimately to the triumph of justice. In reconciling these conflicting principles the courts have pointed out that since the policy of full disclosure is the more fundamental one the privilege is not to be viewed as absolute and is to be strictly limited to the purpose for which it exists.

Hughes v. Meade, 453 S.W.2d 538, 540 (Ky.App.1970). . . . Consistent with this philosophy, we feel that the potential damage to the adversary system is greater, and in need of greater protection, than the attorney-client relationship. We do not wish to create a situation in which counsel is made a repository for physical evidence—a serious and inevitable problem once clients become aware that evidence given to their attorneys, even by friends, may never be turned over to the state.

We, therefore, adopt essentially the ethical standard proposed by the Ethics Committee of the Section on Criminal Justice of the American Bar Association with regards to inculpatory evidence delivered to the attorney by a third party. Our holding is as follows: first, if the attorney reasonably believes that evidence will not be destroyed, he may return it to the source, explaining the laws on concealment and destruction. Second, if the attorney has reasonable grounds to believe that the evidence might be destroyed, or if his client consents, he may turn the physical evidence over to the prosecution. Applying this test to the instant facts, the trial court was correct in ordering the wristwatch to be turned over to the state.

II

How Should the Evidence Be Returned?

Having decided that the evidence must be turned over to the prosecution, we must determine how this can best be done without further prejudice to the defendant. The Ethics Committee's proposed standards provide that when this is done "the lawyer shall do so in [a] way best designed to protect the client's interest." *Standards*, supra.

Amicus National Legal Aid and Defender Association suggests that if the lawyer decides to disclose the item he should do so by delivering the evidence to an agent who would then deliver it to the police without disclosing the source of the item or the case involved. Defendant, however, suggests that the procedure followed in the District of Columbia be considered. According to defendant, inculpatory evidence is delivered to the District of Columbia's bar counsel for subsequent delivery to law enforcement officials. Defendant urges that this Court adopt a system whereby an attorney could anonymously deliver evidence to State Bar counsel, or presidents of local county bar associations, in a sealed package which indicates that it is being delivered due to the affirmative disclosure requirement.

We disagree with both suggestions. Not all items have evidentiary significance in and of themselves. In this case, for instance, the watch is not inculpatory per se; rather, it is the fact that the watch was found in defendant's jacket that makes the watch material evidence. By returning the watch anonymously to the police, this significance is lost. Assuming investigating officials are even able to determine to what case the evidence belongs, they may never be able to reconstruct where it was originally discovered or under what circumstances. . . .

We believe it is simpler and more direct for defendant's attorney to turn the matter over to the state as long as it is understood that the prosecutor may not mention in front of the jury the fact that the evidence came from the defendant or his attorney. . . .

If a defendant is willing to enter a stipulation concerning the chain of possession, location or condition of the evidence, then the evidence may be admitted without the jury becoming aware of the source of the evidence. . . . Under these circumstances, the attorney need not be called as a witness.

III

Must the Attorney Withdraw as Counsel?

Under these procedures, the attorney need not withdraw as counsel. If the attorneys can stipulate as to the chain of possession and no reference is made to the fact that the defendant's attorney turned the matter over to the prosecution, then there is no need for the attorney to withdraw as counsel for the defendant. There may be some cases where the client will believe that his attorney no longer has his best interest in mind. In such a case, it may be wise for the attorney to ask to withdraw. Such request should be liberally granted by the court. Where, however, the client does not object, there is no need for the attorney to withdraw from the case.

DISPOSITION

As to the instant case, we find that defense counsel was forced to take possession of the evidence because of a reasonable fear that to do otherwise would result in its destruction. Because the source was a nonclient, and because he had reason to believe that the witness (source) would conceal or destroy the evidence, the attorney had an obligation to disclose the item and its source to the prosecution.

The order requiring disclosure is affirmed and the order requiring defendant's attorney to withdraw is reversed. The matter is remanded for further proceedings consistent with this opinion.

■ FELDMAN, JUSTICE, dissenting,

. . .

In my view . . . defense counsel should never be put in the position of helping the government prove its case. Of course, counsel may not mislead, tamper with evidence, lie or promote such acts. To do so would violate his duty as an officer of a court which seeks to ascertain the truth. On the other hand, because defense counsel is neither an assistant to nor an investigator for the prosecutor, his function is neither to gather nor preserve inculpatory evidence for the prosecution. If he engages in such conduct, how can he then put the government to its proof? How can he be a zealous advocate for the defendant when at the same time he is likely to make himself a star witness for the prosecution?

I am led to the inevitable conclusion that defense counsel has no obligation to take possession of inculpatory evidence from third parties.

Further, caution and common sense dictate that as a general rule he should never actively seek to obtain such evidence and should refuse possession even if it is offered to him. His guiding principle should be to leave things as they are found. If counsel has reasonable grounds to believe that evidence is in danger of being tampered with or destroyed by a third party, his obligations are satisfied by cautioning that person against such conduct. The majority opinion is ambiguous on this issue, but I believe that we should make it clear to the defense bar that the general rule to be followed in connection with inculpatory evidence is "hands off."

Of course, there are limited exceptions to that general rule. The defense lawyer is justified in obtaining possession of evidence where necessary to test, examine or inspect that evidence in order to determine whether it is exculpatory. Also, the lawyer may expect to use the evidence in the representation of the client. Such limited circumstances are recognized in the standard proposed by the Ethics Committee of the Criminal Justice Section of the American Bar Association. . . .

Although the court purports "essentially" to adopt the standard . . . I believe it misconstrues it. The standard permits defense counsel to give inculpatory evidence to the prosecution only if it is required by court order or rule, if the item received is contraband or if it poses "an unreasonable risk of physical harm to anyone." (See subsec. (a) and (d)). No provision is made for delivery of inculpatory evidence to the prosecution simply because defense counsel fears that it may be destroyed if given back to its source.

In fact, the standard does cover the situation posed by this case. One of the reasons which prompted defense counsel to take the watch from Ms. Heaton was the need to examine it to determine whether it was the watch involved in the burglary. . . . Subsection (c) of the Standard indicates that this is a legitimate purpose for obtaining the evidence. It also indicates that when lawyers have received evidence which proves to be inculpatory it shall be returned to the source "from whom the lawyer receives it" and enjoins the lawyer to "advise the source of the legal consequences pertaining to possession or destruction of the item."

In my view, therefore, the standard clearly contemplates that the defense lawyer shall not obtain or take possession of evidence without good reason; but if he does receive it, when finished with it he must return it to its source and restore everything to the *status quo ante*. It is only if he finds that he is in possession of contraband or an item which may cause serious physical injury to others that the standard permits counsel to deliver inculpatory evidence to the prosecution. Nor does the standard contemplate that the lawyer make himself a repository for the evidence. In fact, the standard indicates that the lawyer may retain evidence only: 1) if he fears that return to the source will result in its destruction; 2) if he believes that on return it may cause serious harm to others; 3) because he intends to test, examine or use the evidence in his representation; or, 4) because he cannot return it to the source. Only under these limited circumstances may the lawyer retain the item "in a manner that does not impede the lawful ability of law enforcement to obtain the item."

Properly interpreted, therefore, the standard would instruct us as follows in the present case: if defense counsel had a legitimate reason to obtain the evidence, such as examination or testing, then it was proper to receive it from the third person who had possession. When so received, it was proper for defense counsel to retain the item while he examined it or had it tested. When he had finished with it and had discovered that he would not need it for trial, it was his duty to return it to the source with instructions as to the consequences of tampering or destruction. If he had a good faith belief that return to the source would result in damage to or destruction of the evidence, then it was his duty to retain the evidence in his possession "in a manner that [did] not impede the lawful ability of law enforcement to obtain the item."

Thus, I believe the majority is incorrect in holding that defense counsel should turn the evidence over to the prosecution. This holding has not only made defense counsel an assistant to the prosecutor's investigator but also an important witness for the prosecution. The future consequences of such a confusion of roles is bound to damage a system which, despite what we are told during periods of hysteria, has survived the test of time.

ABA Standards for Criminal Justice, Prosecution Function and Defense Function (3d ed. 1993).

Defense Function Standards

Part III. Lawyer–Client Relationship

4–3.1 Establishment of Relationship.

(a) Defense counsel should seek to establish a relationship of trust and confidence with the accused and should discuss the objectives of the representation and whether defense counsel will continue to represent the accused if there is an appeal. Defense counsel should explain the necessity of full disclosure of all facts known to the client for an effective defense, and defense counsel should explain the extent to which counsel's obligation of confidentiality makes privileged the accused's disclosures.

. . .

4–3.2 Interviewing the Client.

(a) As soon as practicable, defense counsel should seek to determine all relevant facts known to the accused. In so doing, defense counsel should probe for all legally relevant information without seeking to influence the direction of the client's responses.

(b) Defense counsel should not instruct the client or intimate to the client in any way that the client should not be candid in revealing facts so as to afford defense counsel free rein to take action which would be precluded by counsel's knowing of such facts.

---

516. In United States v. Morrison, 602 F.2d 529 (3d Cir.1979), an agent of the federal Drug Enforcement Agency visited the defendant and discussed her case with her before the trial in the absence of counsel and without his knowledge. The agent was interested in obtaining her cooperation in an investigation, and suggested that she might be treated leniently if she did so; in that event, he urged, she should replace her lawyer with the public defender. He also questioned the quality of her lawyer's services. Finding that there was "a deliberate attempt to destroy the attorney-client relationship and to subvert the defendant's right to effective assistance of counsel and a fair trial," id. at 533, the court concluded that even without a showing of prejudice, the only remedy was a dismissal of the indictment with prejudice.

The court reversed. Assuming that the defendant's right to counsel had been violated, it concluded nevertheless that, in the absence of any prejudice to the defendant, dismissal of the indictment was inappropriate. 449 U.S. 361 (1981).

See United States v. Walker, 839 F.2d 1483 (11th Cir.1988) (*Morrison* applied).

517.

On the night of April 3, 1976, Wade (the victim) and Jacqueline Otis, a friend of the defendants, entered a club known as Rich Jimmy's. Defendant Scott remained outside by a shoeshine stand. A few minutes later codefendant Meredith arrived outside the club. He told Scott he planned to rob Wade, and asked Scott to go into the club, find Jacqueline Otis, and ask her to get Wade to go out to Wade's car parked outside the club.

In the meantime, Wade and Otis had left the club and walked to a liquor store to get some beer. Returning from the store, they left the beer in a bag by Wade's car and reentered the club. Scott then entered the club also and, according to the testimony of Laurie Ann Sam (a friend of Scott's who was already in the club), Scott asked Otis to get Wade to go back out to his car so Meredith could "knock him in the head."

When Wade and Otis did go out to the car, Meredith attacked Wade from behind. After a brief struggle, two shots were fired; Wade fell, and Meredith, witnessed by Scott and Sam, ran from the scene.

Scott went over to the body and, assuming Wade was dead, picked up the bag containing the beer and hid it behind a fence. Scott later returned, retrieved the bag, and took it home where Otis and Meredith joined him.

. . . James Schenk, Scott's first appointed attorney . . . visited Scott in jail more than a month after the crime occurred and solicited information about the murder, stressing that he had to be fully acquainted with the facts to avoid being "sandbagged" by the prosecution during the trial. In response, Scott gave Schenk the same informa-

> tion that he had related earlier to the police. In addition, however, Scott told Schenk something Scott had not revealed to the police: that he had seen a wallet, as well as the paper bag, on the ground near Wade. Scott said that he picked up the wallet, put it in the paper bag, and placed both behind a parking lot fence. He also said that he later retrieved the bag, took it home, found $100 in the wallet and divided it with Meredith, and then tried to burn the wallet in his kitchen sink. He took the partially burned wallet, Scott told Schenk, placed it in a plastic bag, and threw it in a burn barrel behind his house.
>
> Schenk, without further consulting Scott, retained Investigator Stephen Frick and sent Frick to find the wallet. Frick found it in the location described by Scott and brought it to Schenk.

People v. Meredith, 631 P.2d 46, 49 (Cal.1981).

Wade's credit cards were inside the wallet. Scott and Meredith were charged with the robbery and murder of Wade. What should Schenk do?

See Anderson v. State, 297 So.2d 871 (Fla.Dist.Ct.App.1974). In *Anderson*, the defendant retained a lawyer to defend him against charges of receiving and concealing stolen property. The property in question was subsequently left with the lawyer's receptionist. What should the lawyer do?

In In re Original Grand Jury Investigation, 733 N.E.2d 1135 (Ohio 2000), the court held that an attorney was obligated to turn over to the grand jury an incriminating letter written to a third person by the defendant.

Other similar cases mentioned in the opinion in *Hitch*, p. 1006 above.

518. Investigators of a bank robbery learned immediately after the robbery that one of the suspects had formerly been employed by Genson, a lawyer, and had met with Genson in his office several times shortly after the robbery took place. They learned also that the suspect had given Genson $200 in cash. They told Genson that the cash might be proceeds from the robbery. In re January 1976 Grand Jury, 534 F.2d 719 (7th Cir.1976). What should Genson do? If the money had been given to him as his own (for example, as a fee), was he under an obligation, after the investigators spoke to him, not to dispose of the bills?

519. The attorney-client privilege survives the death of the client. Swidler & Berlin v. United States, 524 U.S. 399 (1998) (6–3). The Office of the Independent Counsel had sought notes of the client, after his death, for use in a criminal investigation.

520. When, if ever, should defense counsel discuss a case with the complaining witness in an effort to persuade him to drop the case? Should he offer to make restitution to the witness for his loss? May defense counsel properly advise a witness that he has the privilege to refuse to testify on grounds of self-incrimination? May he urge the witness to exercise the privilege? See People v. Wolf, 514 N.E.2d 1218 (Ill.App.Ct. 1987). Compare United States v. Smith, 478 F.2d 976 (D.C.Cir.1973), p. 974 note 500 above.

ABA Standards for Criminal Justice, Prosecution Function and Defense Function (3d ed. 1993).

Defense Function Standards

4–7.6 Examination of Witnesses.

. . .

(b) Defense counsel's belief or knowledge that the witness is telling the truth does not preclude cross-examination.

---

521. The defendant is prosecuted for robbery. You are defense counsel. At trial the complaining witness testifies that she was walking along the street and was mugged by the defendant. She testifies that the person who mugged her, whom she has identified as the defendant, was wearing a grey sweater with a pattern of red and white checks. She describes other clothing of her assailant as well. During a recess the defendant tells you that he doesn't own such a sweater; he was wearing such a sweater on the day of the robbery, but he had borrowed it from a friend. The defendant has throughout denied his guilt.

(a) Should you bring out on cross-examination of the complaining witness the fact that she has bad vision? Or that the street on which the robbery took place was dimly lit?

(b) Should you bring out the fact that the complaining witness has in the past made identifications in court which proved to be incorrect?

(c) If you put the defendant on the stand should you ask him whether he owns a sweater of the kind described?

Suppose the defendant has not denied his guilt, nor has he admitted it. The case against him is very strong. You have advised him to plead guilty, which he has declined to do. Are your answers to questions (a)–(c) different?

522. The defendant is prosecuted for robbery. You are defense counsel. He has not denied his guilt, nor has he admitted it. From what he has told you, it is clear that he did commit the robbery and that it occurred at about 5:00 p.m.

(a) The complaining witness mistakenly testifies that the robbery occurred at 3:00 p.m. On cross-examination she sticks to her account of the robbery and says that she is sure that the time is correct because she looked at her watch just after the robbery. Should you call as a witness a respectable, honest friend of the defendant who will testify that the defendant was watching television with him at 3:00 p.m.?

(b) The complaining witness testifies accurately that the robbery occurred at 5:00 p.m. Should you call as a witness a respectable, honest, but mistaken druggist who will testify that at that time the defendant was in his store across town purchasing medicine for his ill wife? From what the defendant and his wife have told you, it is clear that the defendant was in the drug store much later.

523. If defense counsel believes that one of the prosecution witnesses will be unable to identify the defendant, can he seat another person at the defense table and seat the defendant elsewhere in the courtroom, as a means of testing the witness? If he does something of that sort, are there precautions that he should take? See United States v. Thoreen, 653 F.2d 1332 (9th Cir.1981); People v. Simac, 641 N.E.2d 416 (Ill.1994) (bench trial; conviction of defense counsel for criminal contempt upheld). Consider note 216, p. 382 above.

524. How far may a lawyer go in explaining to a client the significance of his responses to the lawyer's questions? In a homicide case, for example, when the lawyer probes for "all legally relevant information," see ABA Standard 4–3.2, p. 1014 above, ought he, on his own initiative or in response to questions from the client, explain the law relating to mitigating or excusing circumstances, such as provocation or self-defense? How ought a lawyer conduct his conversation with a client in order to be sure that he has missed no "legally relevant information," without at the same time influencing "the direction of the client's responses"?

Nix v. Whiteside

475 U.S. 157, 106 S.Ct. 988, 89 L.Ed.2d 123 (1986)

■ CHIEF JUSTICE BURGER delivered the opinion of the Court.

We granted certiorari to decide whether the Sixth Amendment right of a criminal defendant to assistance of counsel is violated when an attorney refuses to cooperate with the defendant in presenting perjured testimony at his trial.

I

A

Whiteside was convicted of second-degree murder by a jury verdict which was affirmed by the Iowa courts. The killing took place on February 8, 1977, in Cedar Rapids, Iowa. Whiteside and two others went to one Calvin Love's apartment late that night, seeking marihuana. Love was in bed when Whiteside and his companions arrived; an argument between Whiteside and Love over the marihuana ensued. At one point, Love directed his girlfriend to get his "piece," and at another point got up, then returned to his bed. According to Whiteside's testimony, Love then started to reach under his pillow and moved toward Whiteside. Whiteside stabbed Love in the chest, inflicting a fatal wound.

Whiteside was charged with murder, and when counsel was appointed he objected to the lawyer initially appointed, claiming that he felt uncomfortable with a lawyer who had formerly been a prosecutor. Gary L. Robinson was then appointed and immediately began investigation. Whiteside gave him a statement that he had stabbed Love as the latter "was pulling a pistol from underneath the pillow on the bed." Upon questioning by Robinson, however, Whiteside indicated that he had not actually seen a gun, but that he was convinced that Love had a gun. No pistol was found on the premises; shortly after the police search following the stabbing, which had revealed no weapon, the victim's family had removed all of the victim's possessions from the apartment. Robinson interviewed Whiteside's companions who were present during the stabbing and none had seen a gun during the incident. Robinson advised Whiteside that the existence of a gun was not necessary to establish the claim of self defense, and that only a reasonable belief that the victim had a gun nearby was necessary even though no gun was actually present.

Until shortly before trial, Whiteside consistently stated to Robinson that he had not actually seen a gun, but that he was convinced that Love had a gun in his hand. About a week before trial, during preparation for direct examination, Whiteside for the first time told Robinson and his associate Donna Paulsen that he had seen something "metallic" in Love's hand. When asked about this, Whiteside responded:

> "[I]n Howard Cook's case there was a gun. If I don't say I saw a gun I'm dead."

Robinson told Whiteside that such testimony would be perjury and repeated that it was not necessary to prove that a gun was available but only that Whiteside reasonably believed that he was in danger. On Whiteside's insisting that he would testify that he saw "something metallic" Robinson told him, according to Robinson's testimony:

> "[W]e could not allow him to [testify falsely] because that would be perjury, and as officers of the court we would be suborning perjury if we allowed him to do it; . . . I advised him that if he did do that it would be my duty to advise the Court of what he was doing and that I felt he was committing perjury; also, that I probably would be allowed to attempt to impeach that particular testimony."

App. to Pet. for Cert. A–85. Robinson also indicated he would seek to withdraw from the representation if Whiteside insisted on committing perjury.

Whiteside testified in his own defense at trial and stated that he "knew" that Love had a gun and that he believed Love was reaching for a gun and he had acted swiftly in self-defense. On cross-examination, he admitted that he had not actually seen a gun in Love's hand. Robinson presented evidence that Love had been seen with a sawed-off shotgun on other occasions, that the police search of the apartment may have been careless, and that the victim's family had removed everything from the apartment shortly after the crime. Robinson presented this evidence to show a basis for Whiteside's asserted fear that Love had a gun.

The jury returned a verdict of second-degree murder, and Whiteside moved for a new trial, claiming that he had been deprived of a fair trial by Robinson's admonitions not to state that he saw a gun or "something metallic." The trial court held a hearing, heard testimony by Whiteside and Robinson, and denied the motion. The trial court made specific findings that the facts were as related by Robinson.

The Supreme Court of Iowa affirmed respondent's conviction. . . . That court held that the right to have counsel present all appropriate defenses does not extend to using perjury, and that an attorney's duty to a client does not extend to assisting a client in committing perjury. Relying on DR 7–102(A)(4) of the Iowa Code of Professional Responsibility for Lawyers, which expressly prohibits an attorney from using perjured testimony, and Iowa Code § 721.2 (now Iowa Code § 720.3 (1985)), which criminalizes subornation of perjury, the Iowa court concluded that not only were Robinson's actions permissible, but were required. The court commended "both Mr. Robinson and Ms. Paulsen for the high ethical manner in which this matter was handled."

B

Whiteside then petitioned for a writ of habeas corpus in the United States District Court for the Southern District of Iowa. In that petition Whiteside alleged that he had been denied effective assistance of counsel and of his right to present a defense by Robinson's refusal to allow him to testify as he had proposed. The District Court denied the writ. Accepting the state trial court's factual finding that Whiteside's intended testimony would have been perjurious, it concluded that there could be no grounds for habeas relief since there is no constitutional right to present a perjured defense.

The United States Court of Appeals for the Eighth Circuit reversed and directed that the writ of habeas corpus be granted. Whiteside v. Scurr, 744 F.2d 1323 (1984). The Court of Appeals accepted the findings of the trial judge, affirmed by the Iowa Supreme Court, that trial counsel believed with good cause that Whiteside would testify falsely and acknowledged that under Harris v. New York, 401 U.S. 222 (1971), a criminal defendant's privilege to testify in his own behalf does not include a right to commit perjury. Nevertheless, the court reasoned that an intent to commit perjury, communicated to counsel, does not alter a defendant's right to effective assistance of counsel and that Robinson's admonition to Whiteside that he would inform the court of Whiteside's perjury constituted a threat to violate the attorney's duty to preserve client confidences. According to the Court of Appeals, this threatened violation of client confidences breached the standards of effective representation set down in Strickland v. Washington, 466 U.S. 668 (1984).[25] The court also concluded that *Strickland*'s prejudice requirement was satisfied by an implication of prejudice from the conflict between Robinson's duty of loyalty to his client and his ethical duties. . . . We . . . reverse.

II

A

The right of an accused to testify in his defense is of relatively recent origin. Until the latter part of the preceding century, criminal defendants in this country, as at common law, were considered to be disqualified from giving sworn testimony at their own trial by reason of their interest as a party to the case. . . . Iowa was among the states that adhered to this rule of disqualification. . . .

By the end of the nineteenth century, however, the disqualification was finally abolished by statute in most states and in the federal courts. . . . Although this Court has never explicitly held that a criminal defendant has a due process right to testify in his own behalf, cases in several Circuits have so held and the right has long been assumed. . . . We have also suggested that such a right exists as a corollary to the Fifth Amendment privilege against compelled testimony. . . .

B

In Strickland v. Washington, we held that to obtain relief by way of federal habeas corpus on a claim of a deprivation of effective assistance of counsel under the Sixth Amendment, the movant must establish both serious attorney error and prejudice. . . .

In *Strickland*, we acknowledged that the Sixth Amendment does not require any particular response by counsel to a problem that may arise. Rather, the Sixth Amendment inquiry is into whether the attorney's conduct was "reasonably effective." To counteract the natural tendency to fault an unsuccessful defense, a court reviewing a claim of ineffective assistance must "indulge a strong presumption that counsel's conduct falls within the wide range of reasonable professional assistance." Id., at 689. . . .

. . .

C

We turn next to the question presented: the definition of the range of "reasonable professional" responses to a criminal defendant client who informs counsel that he will perjure himself on the stand. We must determine whether, in this setting, Robinson's conduct fell within the wide range of professional responses to threatened client perjury acceptable under the Sixth Amendment.

[25] P. 1036 below.

In *Strickland*, we recognized counsel's duty of loyalty and his "overarching duty to advocate the defendant's cause," ibid. Plainly, that duty is limited to legitimate, lawful conduct compatible with the very nature of a trial as a search for truth. Although counsel must take all reasonable lawful means to attain the objectives of the client, counsel is precluded from taking steps or in any way assisting the client in presenting false evidence or otherwise violating the law. This principle has consistently been recognized in most unequivocal terms by expositors of the norms of professional conduct since the first Canons of Professional Ethics were adopted by the American Bar Association in 1908. . . .

. . . Disciplinary Rule 7–102 of the Model Code of Professional Responsibility (1980), entitled "Representing a Client Within the Bounds of the Law," provides:

(A) In his representation of a client, a lawyer shall not:

. . .

(4) Knowingly use perjured testimony or false evidence.

. . .

(7) Counsel or assist his client in conduct that the lawyer knows to be illegal or fraudulent.

This provision has been adopted by Iowa, and is binding on all lawyers who appear in its courts. . . . The more recent Model Rules of Professional Conduct (1983) similarly admonish attorneys to obey all laws in the course of representing a client. . . . Both the Model Code of Professional Responsibility and the Model Rules of Professional Conduct also adopt the specific exception from the attorney-client privilege for disclosure of perjury that his client intends to commit or has committed. . . . Indeed, both the Model Code and the Model Rules do not merely *authorize* disclosure by counsel of client perjury; they *require* such disclosure. . . .

These standards confirm that the legal profession has accepted that an attorney's ethical duty to advance the interests of his client is limited by an equally solemn duty to comply with the law and standards of professional conduct; it specifically ensures that the client may not use false evidence. This special duty of an attorney to prevent and disclose frauds upon the court derives from the recognition that perjury is as much a crime as tampering with witnesses or jurors by way of promises and threats, and undermines the administration of justice. . . .

. . .

It is universally agreed that at a minimum the attorney's first duty when confronted with a proposal for perjurious testimony is to attempt to dissuade the client from the unlawful course of conduct. . . .

The essence of the brief *amicus* of the American Bar Association reviewing practices long accepted by ethical lawyers, is that under no circumstance may a lawyer either advocate or passively tolerate a client's giving false testimony. This, of course, is consistent with the governance of trial conduct in what we have long called "a search for truth." The suggestion sometimes made that "a lawyer must believe his client not judge him" in no sense means a lawyer can honorably be a party to or in any way give aid to presenting known perjury.

D

Considering Robinson's representation of respondent in light of these accepted norms of professional conduct, we discern no failure to adhere to reasonable professional standards that would in any sense make out a deprivation of the Sixth Amendment right to counsel. Whether Robinson's conduct is seen as a successful attempt to dissuade his client from committing the crime of perjury, or whether seen as a "threat" to withdraw from representation and disclose the illegal scheme, Robinson's representation of Whiteside falls well within accepted standards of professional conduct and the range of reasonable professional conduct acceptable under *Strickland.*

The Court of Appeals assumed for the purpose of the decision that Whiteside would have given false testimony had counsel not intervened. . . .

The Court of Appeals' holding that Robinson's "action deprived [Whiteside] of due process and effective assistance of counsel" [744 F.2d at 1328] is not supported by the record since Robinson's action, at most, deprived Whiteside of his contemplated perjury. Nothing counsel did in any way undermined Whiteside's claim that he believed the victim was reaching for a gun. Similarly, the record gives no support for holding that Robinson's action "also impermissibly compromised [Whiteside's] right to testify in his own defense by conditioning continued representation . . . and confidentiality upon [Whiteside's] *restricted* testimony" [744 F.2d at 1329]. The record in fact shows the contrary: (a) that Whiteside did testify, and (b) he was "restricted" or restrained only from testifying falsely and was aided by Robinson in developing the basis for the fear that Love was reaching for a gun. Robinson divulged no client communications until he was compelled to do so in response to Whiteside's post-trial challenge to the quality of his performance. We see this as a case in which the attorney successfully dissuaded the client from committing the crime of perjury.

Paradoxically, even while accepting the conclusion of the Iowa trial court that Whiteside's proposed testimony would have been a criminal act, the Court of Appeals held that Robinson's efforts to persuade Whiteside not to commit that crime were improper, *first,* as forcing an impermissible choice between the right to counsel and the right to testify; and *second,* as compromising client confidences because of Robinson's threat to disclose the contemplated perjury.

Whatever the scope of a constitutional right to testify, it is elementary that such a right does not extend to testifying *falsely.* . . . [T]here is no right whatever—constitutional or otherwise—for a defendant to use false evidence. . . .

. . .

Robinson's admonitions to his client can in no sense be said to have forced respondent into an *impermissible* choice between his right to counsel and his right to testify as he proposed for there was no *permissible* choice to testify falsely. For defense counsel to take steps to persuade a criminal defendant to testify truthfully, or to withdraw, deprives the defendant of neither his right to counsel nor the right to testify truthfully. . . .

On this record, the accused enjoyed continued representation within the bounds of reasonable professional conduct and did in fact exercise his right to testify; at most he was denied the right to have the assistance of counsel in the presentation of false testimony. Similarly, we can discern no breach of professional duty in Robinson's admonition to respondent that he would disclose respondent's perjury to the court. . . . An attorney's duty of confidentiality, which totally covers the client's admission of guilt, does not extend to a client's announced plans to engage in future criminal conduct. . . . In short, the responsibility of an ethical lawyer, as an officer of the court and a key component of a system of justice, dedicated to a search for truth, is essentially the same whether the client announces an intention to bribe or threaten witnesses or jurors or to commit or procure perjury. No system of justice worthy of the name can tolerate a lesser standard.

. . .

E

We hold that, as a matter of law, counsel's conduct complained of here cannot establish the prejudice required for relief under the second strand of the *Strickland* inquiry. . . .

Whether he was persuaded or compelled to desist from perjury, Whiteside has no valid claim that confidence in the result of his trial has been diminished by his desisting from the contemplated perjury. Even if we were to assume that the jury might have believed his perjury, it does not follow that Whiteside was prejudiced.

. . .

Whiteside's attorney treated Whiteside's proposed perjury in accord with professional standards, and since Whiteside's truthful testimony could not have prejudiced the result of his trial, the Court of Appeals was in error to direct the issuance of a writ of habeas corpus and must be reversed.

. . .[26]

---

[26] Justice Brennan and Justice Stevens wrote opinions concurring in the judgment. Justice Blackmun also wrote an opinion concurring in the judgment, which Justice Brennan, Justice Marshall, and Justice Stevens joined. All three opinions expressed the view that it was clear in this case that the defendant had suffered no legally cognizable prejudice, but that the Court should not undertake to prescribe the correct response for an attorney whose client evidently intends to commit perjury at trial.

With respect to the latter issue, Justice Blackmun observed:

ABA Model Rules of Professional Conduct (2004).

Rule 3.3 Candor Toward the Tribunal.

(a) A lawyer shall not knowingly:

. . .

(3) offer evidence, other than the testimony of a defendant in a criminal matter, that the lawyer knows to be false. . . . A lawyer may refuse to offer evidence, other than the testimony of a defendant in a criminal matter, that the lawyer reasonably believes is false.

(b) A lawyer who represents a client in an adjudicative proceeding and who knows that a person intends to engage, is engaging, or has engaged in criminal or fraudulent conduct related to the proceeding shall take reasonable remedial measures, including, if necessary, disclosure to the tribunal.

. . .

---

525. Nix v. Whiteside, p. 1018 above, was distinguished in United States v. Midgett, 342 F.3d 321 (4th Cir.2003), in which the court said that however strong defense counsel's belief that the defendant would commit perjury, in the absence of an admission to that effect, defense counsel has an obligation to go forward with the defense. "Far-fetched as [the defendant's] story might have sounded to a jury, it was not his lawyer's place in these circumstances to decide that [the defendant] was lying and to declare

"Whether an attorney's response to what he sees as a client's plan to commit perjury violates a defendant's Sixth Amendment rights may depend on many factors: how certain the attorney is that the proposed testimony is false, the stage of the proceedings at which the attorney discovers the plan, or the ways in which the attorney may be able to dissuade his client, to name just three. The complex interaction of factors, which is likely to vary from case to case, makes inappropriate a blanket rule that defense attorneys must reveal, or threaten to reveal, a client's anticipated perjury to the court. Except in the rarest of cases, attorneys who adopt 'the role of the judge or jury to determine the facts,' United States ex rel. Wilcox v. Johnson, 555 F.2d 115, 122 (CA3 1977), pose a danger of depriving their clients of the zealous and loyal advocacy required by the Sixth Amendment." 475 U.S. at 188–89.

Justice Stevens observed:

"[B]eneath the surface of this case there are areas of uncertainty that cannot be resolved today. A lawyer's certainty that a change in his client's recollection is a harbinger of intended perjury—as well as judicial review of such apparent certainty—should be tempered by the realization that, after reflection, the most honest witness may recall (or sincerely believe he recalls) details that he previously overlooked. Similarly, the post-trial review of a lawyer's pretrial threat to expose perjury that had not yet been committed—and, indeed, may have been prevented by the threat—is by no means the same as review of the way in which such a threat may actually have been carried out. Thus, one can be convinced—as I am—that this lawyer's actions were a proper way to provide his client with effective representation without confronting the much more difficult questions of what a lawyer must, should, or may do after his client has given testimony that the lawyer does not believe. The answer to such questions may well be colored by the particular circumstances attending the actual event and its aftermath." 475 U.S. at 190–91.

this opinion to the court." Id. at 326. See, to the same effect, State v. McDowell, 669 N.W.2d 204 (Wis.Ct.App.2003).

For other cases presenting the problem of a defendant's false testimony, see, e.g., United States v. Henkel, 799 F.2d 369 (7th Cir.1986) (Nix v. Whiteside applied); Lowery v. Cardwell, 575 F.2d 727 (9th Cir.1978); United States ex rel. Wilcox v. Johnson, 555 F.2d 115 (3d Cir.1977); People v. Johnson, 72 Cal.Rptr.2d 805 (Dist.Ct.App.1998); People v. Schultheis, 638 P.2d 8 (Colo.1981); Shockley v. State, 565 A.2d 1373 (Del.1989); Butler v. United States, 414 A.2d 844 (D.C.1980); Commonwealth v. Mitchell, 781 N.E.2d 1237 (Mass.2003).

526. In Hayes v. Kincheloe, 784 F.2d 1434 (9th Cir.1986), the defendant was prosecuted for murder. He pleaded guilty to second-degree murder. In post-conviction proceedings, he claimed that he had not been informed by his lawyer and had not understood that second-degree murder is an intentional killing, and that his plea was, therefore, involuntary. His lawyer stated that he had thought the state could prove a case of first-degree murder and was surprised that he could negotiate a plea to the lesser offense. He stated also that, although he visited the defendant in jail a number of times, he discussed the defendant's account of the events with him minimally. He said: "[T]he reason for that is that if we went to trial, and [Hayes] had stated certain things to me different than what occurred at the trial, it would cause me difficulty in representing him. So my conversations with Mark as to the actual events as he would state them were very very marginal, not much at all." Id. at 1438 n.3. The conviction was vacated.

Consider *Hayes* in connection with Nix v. Whiteside, above.

Cf. ABA Standards for Criminal Justice, Prosecution Function and Defense Function (3d ed. 1993), Defense Function Standard 4–3.2(b): "Defense counsel should not instruct the client or intimate to the client in any way that the client should not be candid in revealing facts so as to afford defense counsel free rein to take action which would be precluded by counsel's knowing of such facts."

527. The defendant has a constitutional right not to appear before a jury in prison clothes. Estelle v. Williams, 425 U.S. 501 (1976). See note 440, p. 889 above.

Suppose the defendant has no presentable clothing of his own? Is it proper for defense counsel to lend the defendant a clean shirt to wear during the trial? Or a jacket? Or a dark blue suit? (Should the prosecutor advise the complaining witness in a rape case to wear modest clothing during the trial? Suppose she suggests this herself. Should the prosecutor advise her not to change her usual appearance?)

528. Defense strategy.

(1) What factors should defense counsel consider when he decides whether or not to put the defendant on the stand?

(2) How can defense counsel prevent the jury from learning from the prosecutor's questions and defense counsel's objections that there is a statement or other evidence in the case to which counsel believes there are valid legal objections? Suppose, for example, the defendant has made a confession at the police station and defense counsel believes that it is inadmissible because the defendant was not advised of his rights.

(3) What should defense counsel do if the prosecution announces in open court that there are several witnesses available to testify whom he intends not to call but whom defense counsel can call if he chooses? See Artis v. Commonwealth, 191 S.E.2d 190 (Va.1972).

(4) How can defense counsel prevent the prosecutor from claiming surprise and using prior statements of witnesses for the prosecution to impeach their testimony favorable to the defendant? Suppose defense counsel has interviewed the witnesses and they tell her before trial that they did give the prosecutor signed statements incriminating the defendant but that they wish to and will repudiate the statements if called as witnesses at the trial. See Brown v. United States, 411 F.2d 716 (D.C.Cir. 1969); Hooks v. United States, 375 F.2d 212 (5th Cir.1967).

(5) How can defense counsel avoid a missing witness instruction with respect to a witness who is crucial to the defense but whom counsel is unable to locate?

(6) Suppose the defendant has two witnesses who will corroborate his alibi but who themselves have long criminal records. How should defense counsel proceed?

529. ABA Standards for Criminal Justice, The Function of the Trial Judge (3d ed. 2000), Standard 2.5: "Duty of judge to respect privileges. The trial judge should respect the obligation of counsel to refrain from speaking on privileged matters, and should avoid putting counsel in a position where counsel's adherence to the obligation, such as by a refusal to answer, may tend to prejudice the client. Unless the privilege is waived or is otherwise inapplicable, the trial judge should not request counsel to comment on evidence or other matters where counsel's knowledge is likely to be gained from privileged communications."

How should counsel respond if, during the trial, the judge asks a question the answer to which will indicate counsel's belief in the innocence or guilt of his client? See generally United States v. Frazier, 580 F.2d 229 (6th Cir.1978).

Defense Counsel

United States v. Cronic

466 U.S. 648, 104 S.Ct. 2039, 80 L.Ed.2d 657 (1984)

■ JUSTICE STEVENS delivered the opinion of the Court.

Respondent and two associates were indicted on mail fraud charges involving the transfer of over $9,400,000 in checks between banks in Tampa, Fla., and Norman, Okla., during a 4-month period in 1975. Shortly before the scheduled trial date, respondent's retained counsel withdrew. The court appointed a young lawyer with a real estate practice to represent respondent, but allowed him only 25 days for pretrial preparation, even though it had taken the Government over four and one-half years to investigate the case and it had reviewed thousands of documents during that investigation. The two codefendants agreed to testify for the Government; respondent was convicted on 11 of the 13 counts in the indictment and received a 25-year sentence.

The Court of Appeals reversed the conviction because it concluded that respondent did not "have the Assistance of Counsel for his defence" that is guaranteed by the Sixth Amendment to the Constitution. This conclusion was not supported by a determination that respondent's trial counsel had made any specified errors, that his actual performance had prejudiced the defense, or that he failed to exercise "the skill, judgment, and diligence of a reasonably competent defense attorney"; instead the conclusion rested on the premise that no such showing is necessary "when circumstances hamper a given lawyer's preparation of a defendant's case."[27] The question presented by the Government's petition for certiorari is whether the Court of Appeals has correctly interpreted the Sixth Amendment.

I

The indictment alleged a "check kiting" scheme. At the direction of respondent, his codefendant Cummings opened a bank account in the name of Skyproof Manufacturing, Inc. (Skyproof), at a bank in Tampa, Fla., and codefendant Merritt opened two accounts, one in his own name and one in the name of Skyproof, at banks in Norman, Okla. Knowing that there were insufficient funds in either account, the defendants allegedly drew a series of checks and wire transfers on the Tampa account aggregating $4,841,073.95, all of which were deposited in Skyproof's Norman bank account during the period between June 23, 1975, and October 16, 1975; during approximately the same period they drew checks on Skyproof's Norman account for deposits in Tampa aggregating $4,600,881.39. The process of clearing the checks involved the use of the mails. By "kiting" insufficient funds checks between the banks in those two cities, defendants allegedly created false or inflated balances in the accounts. After outlining the overall scheme, Count I of the indictment alleged the mailing of two checks each for less than $1,000 early in May. Each of the additional 12 counts realleged the allegations in Count I except its reference to the two

27. 675 F.2d 1126, 1128 (CA10 1982).

specific checks, and then added an allegation identifying other checks issued and mailed at later dates.

At trial the Government proved that Skyproof's checks were issued and deposited at the times and places, and in the amounts, described in the indictment. Having made plea bargains with defendants Cummings and Merritt, who had actually handled the issuance and delivery of the relevant written instruments, the Government proved through their testimony that respondent had conceived and directed the entire scheme, and that he had deliberately concealed his connection with Skyproof because of prior financial and tax problems.

After the District Court ruled that a prior conviction could be used to impeach his testimony, respondent decided not to testify. Counsel put on no defense. By cross-examination of Government witnesses, however, he established that Skyproof was not merely a sham, but actually was an operating company with a significant cash flow, though its revenues were not sufficient to justify as large a "float" as the record disclosed. Cross-examination also established the absence of written evidence that respondent had any control over Skyproof, or personally participated in the withdrawals or deposits.

The 4-day jury trial ended on July 17, 1980, and respondent was sentenced on August 28, 1980. His counsel perfected a timely appeal, which was docketed on September 11, 1980. Two months later respondent filed a motion to substitute a new attorney in the Court of Appeals, and also filed a motion in the District Court seeking to vacate his conviction on the ground that he had newly discovered evidence of perjury by officers of the Norman bank, and that the Government knew or should have known of that perjury. In that motion he also challenged the competence of his trial counsel. The District Court refused to entertain the motion while the appeal was pending. The Court of Appeals denied the motion to substitute the attorney designated by respondent, but did appoint still another attorney to handle the appeal. Later it allowed respondent's motion to supplement the record with material critical of trial counsel's performance.

The Court of Appeals reversed the conviction because it inferred that respondent's constitutional right to the effective assistance of counsel had been violated. That inference was based on its use of five criteria: "(1) [T]he time afforded for investigation and preparation; (2) the experience of counsel; (3) the gravity of the charge; (4) the complexity of possible defenses; and (5) the accessibility of witnesses to counsel." 675 F.2d 1126, 1129 (CA10 1982) (quoting United States v. Golub, 638 F.2d 185, 189 (CA10 1980)). Under the test employed by the Court of Appeals, reversal is required even if the lawyer's actual performance was flawless. By utilizing this inferential approach, the Court of Appeals erred.

II

An accused's right to be represented by counsel is a fundamental component of our criminal justice system. Lawyers in criminal cases "are necessities, not luxuries."[28] Their presence is essential because they are the means through which the other rights of the person on trial are secured. Without counsel, the right to a trial itself would be "of little avail,"[29] as this Court has recognized repeatedly. "Of all the rights that an accused person has, the right to be represented by counsel is by far the most pervasive, for it affects his ability to assert any other right he may have."[30]

The special value of the right to the assistance of counsel explains why "[i]t has long been recognized that the right to counsel is the right to the effective assistance of counsel." McMann v. Richardson, 397 U.S. 759, 771, n.14 (1970). The text of the Sixth Amendment itself suggests as much. . . .

Thus, in *McMann* the Court indicated that the accused is entitled to "a reasonably competent attorney," 397 U.S., at 770, whose advice is "within the range of competence demanded of attorneys in criminal cases." Id., at 771. . . .

. . .

. . . The right to the effective assistance of counsel is thus the right of the accused to require the prosecution's case to survive the crucible of meaningful adversarial testing. When a true adversarial criminal trial has been conducted—even if defense counsel may have made demonstrable errors—the kind of testing envisioned by the Sixth Amendment has occurred.[31] But if the process loses its character as a confrontation between adversaries, the constitutional guarantee is violated. . . .[32]

III

While the Court of Appeals purported to apply a standard of reasonable competence, it did not indicate that there had been an actual breakdown of the adversarial process during the trial of this case. Instead it concluded that the circumstances surrounding the representation of respondent mandated an inference that counsel was unable to discharge his duties.

28. . . . Gideon v. Wainwright, 372 U.S. 335, 344 (1963).

29. . . . Powell v. Alabama, 287 U.S. 45 (1932). . . .

30. Schaefer, "Federalism and State Criminal Procedure," 70 Harv. L. Rev. 1, 8 (1956).

31. Of course, the Sixth Amendment does not require that counsel do what is impossible or unethical. If there is no bona fide defense to the charge, counsel cannot create one and may disserve the interests of his client by attempting a useless charade. . . . At the same time, even when no theory of defense is available, if the decision to stand trial has been made, counsel must hold the prosecution to its heavy burden of proof beyond reasonable doubt. And, of course, even when there is a bona fide defense, counsel may still advise his client to plead guilty if that advice falls within the range of reasonable competence under the circumstances. . . .

32. Thus, the appropriate inquiry focuses on the adversarial process, not on the accused's relationship with his lawyer as such. If counsel is a reasonably effective advocate, he meets constitutional standards irrespective of his client's evaluation of his performance. . . . It is for this reason that we attach no weight to either respondent's expression of satisfaction with counsel's performance at the time of his trial, or to his later expression of dissatisfaction. . . .

In our evaluation of that conclusion, we begin by recognizing that the right to the effective assistance of counsel is recognized not for its own sake, but because of the effect it has on the ability of the accused to receive a fair trial. Absent some effect of challenged conduct on the reliability of the trial process, the Sixth Amendment guarantee is generally not implicated. . . . Moreover, because we presume that the lawyer is competent to provide the guiding hand that the defendant needs . . . the burden rests on the accused to demonstrate a constitutional violation. There are, however, circumstances that are so likely to prejudice the accused that the cost of litigating their effect in a particular case is unjustified.

Most obvious, of course, is the complete denial of counsel. The presumption that counsel's assistance is essential requires us to conclude that a trial is unfair if the accused is denied counsel at a critical stage of his trial. Similarly, if counsel entirely fails to subject the prosecution's case to meaningful adversarial testing, then there has been a denial of Sixth Amendment rights that makes the adversary process itself presumptively unreliable. . . .

Circumstances of that magnitude may be present on some occasions when although counsel is available to assist the accused during trial, the likelihood that any lawyer, even a fully competent one, could provide effective assistance is so small that a presumption of prejudice is appropriate without inquiry into the actual conduct of the trial. . . .

. . .

But every refusal to postpone a criminal trial will not give rise to such a presumption. . . . Thus, only when surrounding circumstances justify a presumption of ineffectiveness can a Sixth Amendment claim be sufficient without inquiry into counsel's actual performance at trial.

The Court of Appeals did not find that respondent was denied the presence of counsel at a critical stage of the prosecution. Nor did it find, based on the actual conduct of the trial, that there was a breakdown in the adversarial process that would justify a presumption that respondent's conviction was insufficiently reliable to satisfy the Constitution. The dispositive question in this case therefore is whether the circumstances surrounding respondent's representation—and in particular the five criteria identified by the Court of Appeals—justified such a presumption.

IV

The five factors listed in the Court of Appeals' opinion are relevant to an evaluation of a lawyer's effectiveness in a particular case, but neither separately nor in combination do they provide a basis for concluding that competent counsel was not able to provide this respondent with the guiding hand that the Constitution guarantees.

Respondent places special stress on the disparity between the duration of the Government's investigation and the period the District Court allowed to newly appointed counsel for trial preparation. The lawyer was appointed to represent respondent on June 12, 1980, and on June 19, filed a written motion for a continuance of the trial that was then scheduled to begin on June 30. Although counsel contended that he needed at least 30 days for preparation, the District Court reset the trial for July 14—thus allowing 25 additional days for preparation.

Neither the period of time that the Government spent investigating the case, nor the number of documents that its agents reviewed during that investigation, is necessarily relevant to the question whether a competent lawyer could prepare to defend the case in 25 days. The Government's task of finding and assembling admissible evidence that will carry its burden of proving guilt beyond a reasonable doubt is entirely different from the defendant's task in preparing to deny or rebut a criminal charge. Of course, in some cases the rebuttal may be equally burdensome and time consuming, but there is no necessary correlation between the two. In this case, the time devoted by the Government to the assembly, organization, and summarization of the thousands of written records evidencing the two streams of checks flowing between the banks in Florida and Oklahoma unquestionably simplified the work of defense counsel in identifying and understanding the basic character of the defendants' scheme. When a series of repetitious transactions fit into a single mold; the number of written exhibits that are needed to define the pattern may be unrelated to the time that is needed to understand it.

The significance of counsel's preparation time is further reduced by the nature of the charges against respondent. Most of the Government's case consisted merely of establishing the transactions between the two banks. A competent attorney would have no reason to question the authenticity, accuracy, or relevance of this evidence—there could be no dispute that these transactions actually occurred. As respondent appears to recognize, the only bona fide jury issue open to competent defense counsel on these facts was whether respondent acted with intent to defraud. When there is no reason to dispute the underlying historical facts, the period of 25 days to consider the question whether those facts justify an inference of criminal intent is not so short that it even arguably justifies a presumption that no lawyer could provide the respondent with the effective assistance of counsel required by the Constitution.

That conclusion is not undermined by the fact that respondent's lawyer was young, that his principal practice was in real estate, or that this was his first jury trial. Every experienced criminal defense attorney once tried his first criminal case. Moreover, a lawyer's experience with real estate transactions might be more useful in preparing to try a criminal case involving financial transactions than would prior experience in handling, for example, armed robbery prosecutions. The character of a particular lawyer's experience may shed light in an evaluation of his actual performance, but it does not justify a presumption of ineffectiveness in the absence of such an evaluation.

The three other criteria—the gravity of the charge, the complexity of the case, and the accessibility of witnesses—are all matters that may affect what a reasonably competent attorney could be expected to have done under the circumstances, but none identifies circumstances that in themselves make it unlikely that respondent received the effective assistance of counsel.

V

. . . Respondent can therefore make out a claim of ineffective assistance only by pointing to specific errors made by trial counsel. . . .

. . .[33]

---

530. In Bell v. Cone, 535 U.S. 685 (2002) (8–1), the defendant was convicted of capital murder and sentenced to death. At the sentencing hearing, his lawyer cross-examined witnesses for the prosecution but called no witnesses and made no closing argument. On collateral attack, the defendant claimed that he was denied the effective assistance of counsel. The Sixth Circuit upheld his claim and vacated the sentence. It ruled that a showing of prejudice under Strickland v. Washington, p. 1036 below, was not necessary; prejudice, it said, could be presumed because the defendant's lawyer had "entirely fail[ed] to subject the prosecution's case to meaningful adversarial testing," *Cronic*, p. 1028 above. The Supreme Court reversed. The performance of counsel, it said, was not a total failure of representation but was allegedly erroneous in specific respects. As such, it was subject to the cause and prejudice standard of *Strickland*, which the state court had permissibly determined was not met.

See United States v. Russell, 205 F.3d 768 (5th Cir.2000) (continuation of trial during two days when defendant's counsel was absent due to illness and defendant was represented by codefendant's counsel required reversal).

531. In Holloway v. Arkansas, 435 U.S. 475 (1978) (6–3), the Supreme Court reversed the conviction of three codefendants who had been represented by the same lawyer. Before trial and again during trial, the lawyer, a public defender, had moved for assignment of separate counsel on the ground of a possible conflict of interest. The motion was denied. Each of the defendants testified at trial, their lawyer having again advised the court that he could not examine each of them satisfactorily because of the joint defense. The Court declared that while "in some cases multiple defendants can appropriately be represented by one attorney," id. at 482, the failure to appoint separate counsel or to inquire adequately into the need for separate counsel following a timely motion denied the defendants' constitutional right to counsel. Such failure, the Court concluded, required reversal without a showing of specific prejudice.

Holloway was applied in Cuyler v. Sullivan, 446 U.S. 335 (1980). The Court held that ordinarily a defendant must raise the issue of conflict of interest. "Absent special circumstances . . . trial courts may assume either that multiple representation entails no conflict or that the lawyer and his

[33] Justice Marshall concurred in the judgment.

clients knowingly accept such risk of conflict as may exist. . . . Unless the trial court knows or reasonably should know that a particular conflict exists, the court need not initiate an inquiry." Id. at 346–47. The Court held further that the possibility of a conflict of interest from multiple representation is insufficient to show denial of the right to counsel. "In order to establish a violation of the Sixth Amendment, a defendant who raised no objection at trial must demonstrate that an actual conflict of interest adversely affected his lawyer's performance." Id. at 350. An adverse effect must be shown even if the trial judge knew or should have known about the conflict. Mickens v. Taylor, 535 U.S. 162 (2002). See Burger v. Kemp, 483 U.S. 776 (1987) (5–4) (defendants, charged with crimes arising out of joint conduct, represented at separate trials by law partners; *Holloway* claim rejected).

Holloway was applied in somewhat unusual circumstances in Walberg v. Israel, 766 F.2d 1071 (7th Cir.1985). The court concluded that a system whereby appointed counsel for indigents must submit a request for a fee to the appointing judge created a conflict of interest between the defendant and his appointed counsel, whom the judge repeatedly admonished against forcefully urging his client's cause. The consequence, the court said, was that the defendant's right to counsel was denied.

Before sentencing, the defendant made a pro se motion to withdraw his plea of guilty, in which he alleged that his lawyer had coerced him to enter the plea. At a hearing on the motion, he alleged that the lawyer had said he would not investigate the case or file motions on his behalf and was not interested in anything except a guilty plea. Stating that he did not want to be in an "adversarial position" with his client, the lawyer declined to comment at the hearing. The motion to withdraw the plea was denied. The court of appeals held that there was an actual conflict of interest between the defendant and his lawyer at the hearing on the motion to withdraw the plea and remanded for a determination whether the conflict adversely affected the lawyer's conduct. United States v. Davis, 239 F.3d 283 (2d Cir.2001).

In United States v. Henke, 222 F.3d 633 (9th Cir.2000), the defense lawyer had participated in pretrial joint defense meetings with a codefendant who later pleaded guilty and became a government witness. The lawyer was prevented from fully cross-examining the witness because of a joint defense privilege agreement. The court held that the defense motion for a mistrial because of the lawyer's conflict of interest should have been granted.

Fed.R.Crim.P. 44(c), p. 547 above, requires that a judge address the question of conflict of interest when two or more defendants are jointly charged or joined for trial and are represented by the same lawyer or lawyers who are associated in practice. The judge must advise each defendant of his right to effective assistance of counsel and "take appropriate measures" to protect the right.

"[W]here a court justifiably finds an actual conflict of interest, there can be no doubt that it may decline a proffer of waiver [of objection to any conflict of interest of counsel], and insist that defendants be separately represented." Wheat v. United States, 486 U.S. 153, 162 (1988) (5–4). "[A court] must be allowed substantial latitude in refusing waivers of conflicts of interest not only in those rare cases where an actual conflict may be demonstrated before trial, but in the more common cases where a potential for conflict exists which may or may not burgeon into an actual conflict as the trial progresses." Id. at 163.

532. In United States v. Dolan, 570 F.2d 1177 (3d Cir.1978), the court of appeals upheld the trial court's order that an attorney for two codefendants withdraw from the case and represent neither. In view of a clear conflict of interest, the court said, even a defendant's express preference to be represented by that attorney was not sufficient, notwithstanding Faretta v. California, 422 U.S. 806 (1975), p. 1051 below.

533. The defendant, Whitaker, was arrested on a complaint of his wife that he had had sexual intercourse with her daughter by a previous marriage. He admitted the offense. His wife's aunt, Mrs. McElfish, engaged defense counsel, who looked to her for his fee. The wife and the aunt told counsel "that they wanted the case disposed of quickly, quietly and with as little notoriety as possible in order to protect the child involved." The defendant pleaded nolo contendere to a charge of statutory rape and was convicted and sentenced to life imprisonment. After he had served more than ten years in prison, he sought his release on habeas corpus, which the district court, although smelling "foul fish," denied. The court of appeals reversed. "[T]he expressed interest of Mrs. Whitaker and Mrs. McElfish in a speedy, unpublicized disposition of the statutory rape charge and in protecting Mrs. Whitaker's daughter may have materially influenced the nature and extent of counsel's efforts to present a defense. . . . All that we need determine is that [defense counsel] was serving an interest or interests which conflicted with that of Whitaker; we need not delineate any specific prejudice to Whitaker flowing from his representation." Whitaker v. Warden, Maryland Penitentiary, 362 F.2d 838, 839–41 (4th Cir.1966).[34]

534. A defendant represented on appeal by a lawyer who, unknown to the defendant, himself is under indictment and has entered into a plea bargain in the same court from which the appeal is taken is denied the

34. ABA Standards for Criminal Justice, Prosecution Function and Defense Function (3d ed. 1993), Defense Function Standard 4–3.5(e): "In accepting payment of fees by one person for the defense of another, defense counsel should be careful to determine that he or she will not be confronted with a conflict of loyalty since defense counsel's entire loyalty is due the accused. Defense counsel should not accept such compensation unless:

(i) the accused consents after disclosure;

(ii) there is no interference with defense counsel's independence of professional judgment or with the client-lawyer relationship; and

(iii) information relating to the representation of the accused is protected from disclosure as required by defense counsel's ethical obligation of confidentiality.

Defense counsel should not permit a person who recommends, employs, or pays defense counsel to render legal services for another to direct or regulate counsel's professional judgment in rendering such legal services."

effective assistance of counsel. United States v. DeFalco, 644 F.2d 132 (3d Cir.1979).

Strickland v. Washington

466 U.S. 668, 104 S.Ct. 2052, 80 L.Ed.2d 674 (1984)

■ JUSTICE O'CONNOR delivered the opinion of the Court.

This case requires us to consider the proper standards for judging a criminal defendant's contention that the Constitution requires a conviction or death sentence to be set aside because counsel's assistance at the trial or sentencing was ineffective.

I

A

During a 10-day period in September 1976, respondent planned and committed three groups of crimes, which included three brutal stabbing murders, torture, kidnapping, severe assaults, attempted murders, attempted extortion, and theft. After his two accomplices were arrested, respondent surrendered to police and voluntarily gave a lengthy statement confessing to the third of the criminal episodes. The State of Florida indicted respondent for kidnapping and murder and appointed an experienced criminal lawyer to represent him.

Counsel actively pursued pretrial motions and discovery. He cut his efforts short, however, and he experienced a sense of hopelessness about the case, when he learned that, against his specific advice, respondent had also confessed to the first two murders. By the date set for trial, respondent was subject to indictment for three counts of first degree murder and multiple counts of robbery, kidnapping for ransom, breaking and entering and assault, attempted murder, and conspiracy to commit robbery. Respondent waived his right to a jury trial, again acting against counsel's advice, and pleaded guilty to all charges, including the three capital murder charges.

In the plea colloquy, respondent told the trial judge that, although he had committed a string of burglaries, he had no significant prior criminal record and that at the time of his criminal spree he was under extreme stress caused by his inability to support his family. . . . He also stated, however, that he accepted responsibility for the crimes. . . . The trial judge told respondent that he had "a great deal of respect for people who are willing to step forward and admit their responsibility" but that he was making no statement at all about his likely sentencing decision. [App.], at 62.

Counsel advised respondent to invoke his right under Florida law to an advisory jury at his capital sentencing hearing. Respondent rejected the advice and waived the right. He chose instead to be sentenced by the trial judge without a jury recommendation.

In preparing for the sentencing hearing, counsel spoke with respondent about his background. He also spoke on the telephone with respondent's wife and mother, though he did not follow up on the one unsuccessful effort to meet with them. He did not otherwise seek out character witnesses for respondent. . . . Nor did he request a psychiatric examination, since his conversations with his client gave no indication that respondent had psychological problems. . . .

Counsel decided not to present and hence not to look further for evidence concerning respondent's character and emotional state. That decision reflected trial counsel's sense of hopelessness about overcoming the evidentiary effect of respondent's confessions to the gruesome crimes. . . . It also reflected the judgment that it was advisable to rely on the plea colloquy for evidence about respondent's background and about his claim of emotional stress: the plea colloquy communicated sufficient information about these subjects, and by foregoing the opportunity to present new evidence on these subjects, counsel prevented the State from cross-examining respondent on his claim and from putting on psychiatric evidence of its own. . . .

Counsel also excluded from the sentencing hearing other evidence he thought was potentially damaging. He successfully moved to exclude respondent's "rap sheet." . . . Because he judged that a presentence report might prove more detrimental than helpful, as it would have included respondent's criminal history and thereby undermined the claim of no significant history of criminal activity, he did not request that one be prepared. . . .

At the sentencing hearing, counsel's strategy was based primarily on the trial judge's remarks at the plea colloquy as well as on his reputation as a sentencing judge who thought it important for a convicted defendant to own up to his crime. Counsel argued that respondent's remorse and acceptance of responsibility justified sparing him from the death penalty. . . . Counsel also argued that respondent had no history of criminal activity and that respondent committed the crimes under extreme mental or emotional disturbance, thus coming within the statutory list of mitigating circumstances. He further argued that respondent should be spared death because he had surrendered, confessed, and offered to testify against a codefendant and because respondent was fundamentally a good person who had briefly gone badly wrong in extremely stressful circumstances. The State put on evidence and witnesses largely for the purpose of describing the details of the crime. Counsel did not cross-examine the medical experts who testified about the manner of death of respondent's victims.

The trial judge found several aggravating circumstances with respect to each of the three murders. He found that all three murders were especially heinous, atrocious, and cruel, all involving repeated stabbings. All three murders were committed in the course of at least one other dangerous and violent felony, and since all involved robbery, the murders were for pecuniary gain. All three murders were committed to avoid arrest for the accompanying crimes and to hinder law enforcement. In the course of one of the murders, respondent knowingly subjected numerous persons to a grave risk of death by deliberately stabbing and shooting the murder victim's sisters-in-law, who sustained severe—in one case, ultimately fatal—injuries.

With respect to mitigating circumstances, the trial judge made the same findings for all three capital murders. First, although there was no admitted evidence of prior convictions, respondent had stated that he had engaged in a course of stealing. In any case, even if respondent had no significant history of criminal activity, the aggravating circumstances "would still clearly far outweigh" that mitigating factor. Second, the judge found that, during all three crimes, respondent was not suffering from extreme mental or emotional disturbance and could appreciate the criminality of his acts. Third, none of the victims was a participant in, or consented to, respondent's conduct. Fourth, respondent's participation in the crimes was neither minor nor the result of duress or domination by an accomplice. Finally, respondent's age (26) could not be considered a factor in mitigation, especially when viewed in light of respondent's planning of the crimes and disposition of the proceeds of the various accompanying thefts.

In short, the trial judge found numerous aggravating circumstances and no (or a single comparatively insignificant) mitigating circumstance. With respect to each of the three convictions for capital murder, the trial judge concluded: "A careful consideration of all matters presented to the court impels the conclusion that there are insufficient mitigating circumstances . . . to outweigh the aggravating circumstances." See Washington v. State, 362 So.2d 658, 663–64 (Fla.1978) (quoting trial court findings). . . . He therefore sentenced respondent to death on each of the three counts of murder and to prison terms for the other crimes. The Florida Supreme Court upheld the convictions and sentences on direct appeal.

B

Respondent subsequently sought collateral relief in state court on numerous grounds, among them that counsel had rendered ineffective assistance at the sentencing proceeding. Respondent challenged counsel's assistance in six respects. He asserted that counsel was ineffective because he failed to move for a continuance to prepare for sentencing, to request a psychiatric report, to investigate and present character witnesses, to seek a presentence investigation report, to present meaningful arguments to the sentencing judge, and to investigate the medical examiner's reports or cross-examine the medical experts. In support of the claim, respondent submitted 14 affidavits from friends, neighbors, and relatives stating that they would have testified if asked to do so. He also submitted one psychiatric report and one psychological report stating that respondent, though not under the influence of extreme mental or emotional disturbance, was "chronically frustrated and depressed because of his economic dilemma" at the time of his crimes. App. 7. . . .

The trial court denied relief without an evidentiary hearing, finding that the record evidence conclusively showed that the ineffectiveness claim was meritless. . . .

. . .

[W]e granted certiorari to consider the standards by which to judge a contention that the Constitution requires that a criminal judgment be overturned because of the actual ineffective assistance of counsel. . . .

II

In a long line of cases . . . this Court has recognized that the Sixth Amendment right to counsel exists, and is needed, in order to protect the fundamental right to a fair trial. . . .

. . .

[T]he Court has recognized that "the right to counsel is the right to the effective assistance of counsel." McMann v. Richardson, 397 U.S. 759, 771, n.14 (1970). . . .

The Court has not elaborated on the meaning of the constitutional requirement of effective assistance in the . . . class of cases . . . presenting claims of "actual ineffectiveness." In giving meaning to the requirement, however, we must take its purpose—to ensure a fair trial—as the guide. The benchmark for judging any claim of ineffectiveness must be whether counsel's conduct so undermined the proper functioning of the adversarial process that the trial cannot be relied on as having produced a just result.

The same principle applies to a capital sentencing proceeding such as that provided by Florida law. We need not consider the role of counsel in an ordinary sentencing, which may involve informal proceedings and standardless discretion in the sentencer, and hence may require a different approach to the definition of constitutionally effective assistance. A capital sentencing proceeding like the one involved in this case, however, is sufficiently like a trial in its adversarial format and in the existence of standards for decision . . . that counsel's role in the proceeding is comparable to counsel's role at trial—to ensure that the adversarial testing process works to produce a just result under the standards governing decision. For purposes of describing counsel's duties, therefore, Florida's capital sentencing proceeding need not be distinguished from an ordinary trial.

III

A convicted defendant's claim that counsel's assistance was so defective as to require reversal of a conviction or death sentence has two components. First, the defendant must show that counsel's performance was deficient. This requires showing that counsel made errors so serious that counsel was not functioning as the "counsel" guaranteed the defendant by the Sixth Amendment. Second, the defendant must show that the deficient performance prejudiced the defense. This requires showing that counsel's errors were so serious as to deprive the defendant of a fair trial, a trial whose result is reliable. Unless a defendant makes both showings, it cannot be said that the conviction or death sentence resulted from a breakdown in the adversary process that renders the result unreliable.

A

As all the Federal Courts of Appeals have now held, the proper standard for attorney performance is that of reasonably effective assistance. . . . When a convicted defendant complains of the ineffectiveness of counsel's assistance, the defendant must show that counsel's representation fell below an objective standard of reasonableness.

More specific guidelines are not appropriate. The Sixth Amendment refers simply to "counsel," not specifying particular requirements of effective assistance. It relies instead on the legal profession's maintenance of standards sufficient to justify the law's presumption that counsel will fulfill the role in the adversary process that the Amendment envisions. . . . The proper measure of attorney performance remains simply reasonableness under prevailing professional norms.

Representation of a criminal defendant entails certain basic duties. Counsel's function is to assist the defendant, and hence counsel owes the client a duty of loyalty, a duty to avoid conflicts of interest. . . . From counsel's function as assistant to the defendant derive the overarching duty to advocate the defendant's cause and the more particular duties to consult with the defendant on important decisions and to keep the defendant informed of important developments in the course of the prosecution. Counsel also has a duty to bring to bear such skill and knowledge as will render the trial a reliable adversarial testing process. . . .

These basic duties neither exhaustively define the obligations of counsel nor form a checklist for judicial evaluation of attorney performance. In any case presenting an ineffectiveness claim, the performance inquiry must be whether counsel's assistance was reasonable considering all the circumstances. Prevailing norms of practice as reflected in American Bar Association standards and the like . . . are guides to determining what is reasonable, but they are only guides. No particular set of detailed rules for counsel's conduct can satisfactorily take account of the variety of circumstances faced by defense counsel or the range of legitimate decisions regarding how best to represent a criminal defendant. Any such set of rules would interfere with the constitutionally protected independence of counsel and restrict the wide latitude counsel must have in making tactical decisions. . . . Indeed, the existence of detailed guidelines for representation could distract counsel from the overriding mission of vigorous advocacy of the defendant's cause. Moreover, the purpose of the effective assistance guarantee of the Sixth Amendment is not to improve the quality of legal representation, although that is a goal of considerable importance to the legal system. The purpose is simply to ensure that criminal defendants receive a fair trial.

Judicial scrutiny of counsel's performance must be highly deferential. It is all too tempting for a defendant to second-guess counsel's assistance after conviction or adverse sentence, and it is all too easy for a court, examining counsel's defense after it has proved unsuccessful, to conclude that a particular act or omission of counsel was unreasonable. . . . A fair assessment of attorney performance requires that every effort be made to eliminate the distorting effects of hindsight, to reconstruct the circumstances of counsel's challenged conduct, and to evaluate the conduct from counsel's perspective at the time. Because of the difficulties inherent in making the evaluation, a court must indulge a strong presumption that counsel's conduct falls within the wide range of reasonable professional assistance; that is, the defendant must overcome the presumption that, under the circumstances, the challenged action "might be considered sound trial strategy." See Michel v. Louisiana, [350 U.S. 91 (1955)], at 101. There are countless ways to provide effective assistance in any given case. Even the best criminal defense attorneys would not defend a particular client in the same way. . . .

The availability of intrusive post-trial inquiry into attorney performance or of detailed guidelines for its evaluation would encourage the proliferation of ineffectiveness challenges. Criminal trials resolved unfavorably to the defendant would increasingly come to be followed by a second trial, this one of counsel's unsuccessful defense. Counsel's performance and even willingness to serve could be adversely affected. Intensive scrutiny of counsel and rigid requirements for acceptable assistance could dampen the ardor and impair the independence of defense counsel, discourage the acceptance of assigned cases, and undermine the trust between attorney and client.

Thus, a court deciding an actual ineffectiveness claim must judge the reasonableness of counsel's challenged conduct on the facts of the particular case, viewed as of the time of counsel's conduct. A convicted defendant making a claim of ineffective assistance must identify the acts or omissions of counsel that are alleged not to have been the result of reasonable professional judgment. The court must then determine whether, in light of all the circumstances, the identified acts or omissions were outside the wide range of professionally competent assistance. In making that determination, the court should keep in mind that counsel's function, as elaborated in prevailing professional norms, is to make the adversarial testing process work in the particular case. At the same time, the court should recognize that counsel is strongly presumed to have rendered adequate assistance and made all significant decisions in the exercise of reasonable professional judgment.

These standards require no special amplification in order to define counsel's duty to investigate, the duty at issue in this case. As the Court of Appeals concluded, strategic choices made after thorough investigation of law and facts relevant to plausible options are virtually unchallengeable; and strategic choices made after less than complete investigation are reasonable precisely to the extent that reasonable professional judgments support the limitations on investigation. In other words, counsel has a duty to make reasonable investigations or to make a reasonable decision that makes particular investigations unnecessary. In any ineffectiveness case, a particular decision not to investigate must be directly assessed for reasonableness in all the circumstances, applying a heavy measure of deference to counsel's judgments.

The reasonableness of counsel's actions may be determined or substantially influenced by the defendant's own statements or actions. Counsel's actions are usually based, quite properly, on informed strategic choices made by the defendant and on information supplied by the defendant. In particular, what investigation decisions are reasonable depends critically on such information. For example, when the facts that support a certain potential line of defense are generally known to counsel because of what the defendant has said, the need for further investigation may be considerably diminished or eliminated altogether. And when a defendant has given counsel reason to believe that pursuing certain investigations would be fruitless or even harmful, counsel's failure to pursue those investigations may not later be challenged as unreasonable. In short, inquiry into counsel's conversations with the defendant may be critical to a proper assessment of counsel's investigation decisions, just as it may be critical to a proper assessment of counsel's other litigation decisions. . . .

B

An error by counsel, even if professionally unreasonable, does not warrant setting aside the judgment of a criminal proceeding if the error had no effect on the judgment. . . . The purpose of the Sixth Amendment guarantee of counsel is to ensure that a defendant has the assistance necessary to justify reliance on the outcome of the proceeding. Accordingly, any deficiencies in counsel's performance must be prejudicial to the defense in order to constitute ineffective assistance under the Constitution.

In certain Sixth Amendment contexts, prejudice is presumed. Actual or constructive denial of the assistance of counsel altogether is legally presumed to result in prejudice. So are various kinds of state interference with counsel's assistance. . . . Prejudice in these circumstances is so likely that case by case inquiry into prejudice is not worth the cost. . . . Moreover, such circumstances involve impairments of the Sixth Amendment right that are easy to identify and, for that reason and because the prosecution is directly responsible, easy for the government to prevent.

One type of actual ineffectiveness claim warrants a similar, though more limited, presumption of prejudice. In Cuyler v. Sullivan, 446 U.S., at 345–50, the Court held that prejudice is presumed when counsel is burdened by an actual conflict of interest. . . . Even so, the rule is not quite the per se rule of prejudice that exists for the Sixth Amendment claims mentioned above. Prejudice is presumed only if the defendant demonstrates that counsel "actively represented conflicting interests" and that "an actual conflict of interest adversely affected his lawyer's performance." Cuyler v. Sullivan, supra, at 350, 348 (footnote omitted).

Conflict of interest claims aside, actual ineffectiveness claims alleging a deficiency in attorney performance are subject to a general requirement that the defendant affirmatively prove prejudice. . . . Even if a defendant shows that particular errors of counsel were unreasonable, therefore, the defendant must show that they actually had an adverse effect on the defense.

It is not enough for the defendant to show that the errors had some conceivable effect on the outcome of the proceeding. Virtually every act or omission of counsel would meet that test . . . and not every error that conceivably could have influenced the outcome undermines the reliability of the result of the proceeding. . . .

On the other hand, we believe that a defendant need not show that counsel's deficient conduct more likely than not altered the outcome in the case. . . .

. . . The result of a proceeding can be rendered unreliable, and hence the proceeding itself unfair, even if the errors of counsel cannot be shown by a preponderance of the evidence to have determined the outcome.

Accordingly, the appropriate test for prejudice finds its roots in the test for materiality of exculpatory information not disclosed to the defense by the prosecution . . . and in the test for materiality of testimony made unavailable to the defense by Government deportation of a witness. . . . The defendant must show that there is a reasonable probability that, but for counsel's unprofessional errors, the result of the proceeding would have been different. A reasonable probability is a probability sufficient to undermine confidence in the outcome.

. . .

The governing legal standard plays a critical role in defining the question to be asked in assessing the prejudice from counsel's errors. When a defendant challenges a conviction, the question is whether there is a reasonable probability that, absent the errors, the factfinder would have had a reasonable doubt respecting guilt. When a defendant challenges a death sentence such as the one at issue in this case, the question is whether there is a reasonable probability that, absent the errors, the sentencer—including an appellate court, to the extent it independently reweighs the evidence—would have concluded that the balance of aggravating and mitigating circumstances did not warrant death.

In making this determination, a court hearing an ineffectiveness claim must consider the totality of the evidence before the judge or jury. Some of the factual findings will have been unaffected by the errors, and factual findings that were affected will have been affected in different ways. Some errors will have had a pervasive effect on the inferences to be drawn from the evidence, altering the entire evidentiary picture, and some will have had an isolated, trivial effect. Moreover, a verdict or conclusion only weakly supported by the record is more likely to have been affected by errors than one with overwhelming record support. Taking the unaffected findings as a given, and taking due account of the effect of the errors on the remaining findings, a court making the prejudice inquiry must ask if the defendant has met the burden of showing that the decision reached would reasonably likely have been different absent the errors.

IV

. . .

Although we have discussed the performance component of an ineffectiveness claim prior to the prejudice component, there is no reason for a court deciding an ineffective assistance claim to approach the inquiry in the same order or even to address both components of the inquiry if the defendant makes an insufficient showing on one. In particular, a court need not determine whether counsel's performance was deficient before examining the prejudice suffered by the defendant as a result of the alleged deficiencies. The object of an ineffectiveness claim is not to grade counsel's performance. If it is easier to dispose of an ineffectiveness claim on the ground of lack of sufficient prejudice, which we expect will often be so, that course should be followed. Courts should strive to ensure that ineffectiveness claims not become so burdensome to defense counsel that the entire criminal justice system suffers as a result.

. . .

V

Having articulated general standards for judging ineffectiveness claims, we think it useful to apply those standards to the facts of this case in order to illustrate the meaning of the general principles. . . .

Application of the governing principles is not difficult in this case. The facts as described above . . . make clear that the conduct of respondent's counsel at and before respondent's sentencing proceeding cannot be found unreasonable. They also make clear that, even assuming the challenged conduct of counsel was unreasonable, respondent suffered insufficient prejudice to warrant setting aside his death sentence.

With respect to the performance component, the record shows that respondent's counsel made a strategic choice to argue for the extreme emotional distress mitigating circumstance and to rely as fully as possible on respondent's acceptance of responsibility for his crimes. Although counsel understandably felt hopeless about respondent's prospects . . . nothing in the record indicates . . . that counsel's sense of hopelessness distorted his professional judgment. Counsel's strategy choice was well within the range of professionally reasonable judgments, and the decision not to seek more character or psychological evidence than was already in hand was likewise reasonable.

The trial judge's views on the importance of owning up to one's crimes were well known to counsel. The aggravating circumstances were utterly overwhelming. Trial counsel could reasonably surmise from his conversations with respondent that character and psychological evidence would be of little help. Respondent had already been able to mention at the plea colloquy the substance of what there was to know about his financial and emotional troubles. Restricting testimony on respondent's character to what had come in at the plea colloquy ensured that contrary character and psychological evidence and respondent's criminal history, which counsel had successfully moved to exclude, would not come in. On these facts there can be little question, even without application of the presumption of adequate performance, that trial counsel's defense, though unsuccessful, was the result of reasonable professional judgment.

With respect to the prejudice component, the lack of merit of respondent's claim is even more stark. The evidence that respondent says his trial counsel should have offered at the sentencing hearing would barely have altered the sentencing profile presented to the sentencing judge. As the state courts and District Court found, at most this evidence shows that numerous people who knew respondent thought he was generally a good person and that a psychiatrist and a psychologist believed he was under considerable emotional stress that did not rise to the level of extreme disturbance. Given the overwhelming aggravating factors, there is no reasonable probability that the omitted evidence would have changed the conclusion that the aggravating circumstances outweighed the mitigating circumstances and, hence, the sentence imposed. Indeed, admission of the evidence respondent now offers might even have been harmful to his case: his "rap sheet" would probably have been admitted into evidence, and the psychological reports would have directly contradicted respondent's claim that the mitigating circumstance of extreme emotional disturbance applied to his case.

. . .

Failure to make the required showing of either deficient performance or sufficient prejudice defeats the ineffectiveness claim. Here there is a double failure. More generally, respondent has made no showing that the justice of his sentence was rendered unreliable by a breakdown in the adversary process caused by deficiencies in counsel's assistance. Respondent's sentencing proceeding was not fundamentally unfair.

. . .[35]

---

535. Should a defendant's conviction be reversed if, without more, he shows that his counsel was a narcotics addict during the period when he represented the defendant? Does it matter whether or not the defendant knew of his counsel's condition? See United States v. Butler, 167 F.Supp. 102 (E.D.Va.1957). See also Glover v. United States, 531 U.S. 198 (2001) (increased sentence of 6–21 months constitutes prejudice); Williams v. Taylor, 529 U.S. 362 (2000) (6–3) (failure to introduce mitigating evidence

[35] Justice Brennan wrote an opinion concurring in part and dissenting in part. Justice Marshall wrote a dissenting opinion.

at capital sentencing proceeding; ineffective assistance and prejudice shown); Burdine v. Johnson, 262 F.3d 336 (5th Cir.2001) (en banc) (counsel slept through substantial portions of trial; ineffective assistance, prejudice presumed); Tippins v. Walker, 77 F.3d 682 (2d Cir.1996) (same); Vance v. Lehman, 64 F.3d 119 (3d Cir.1995) (shortly after defendant's trial, defense counsel's license to practice law was revoked because of unrelated unprofessional conduct occurring before trial; not ineffective assistance per se); Scarpa v. Dubois, 38 F.3d 1 (1st Cir.1994) (substandard performance of counsel does not warrant conclusive presumption of prejudice); Bellamy v. Cogdell, 974 F.2d 302 (2d Cir.1992) (counsel with mental and physical ailments; not ineffective assistance per se). Cf. Yarborough v. Gentry, 540 U.S. ___ (2003) (state court's determination that defense counsel's performance was not constitutionally deficient was not objectively unreasonable).

Has a defendant who is convicted of possession of heroin been denied the effective assistance of counsel if defense counsel fails to make a sound motion to suppress the heroin seized from the defendant because he does not know the "common-place" state rule "that defendant could challenge the legality of the search and seizure even though he denied that the heroin was taken from him and asserted no proprietary interest in the premises that were entered," People v. Ibarra, 386 P.2d 487, 491 (Cal.1963)? See generally People v. Pope, 590 P.2d 859 (Cal.1979) (en banc) (*Ibarra* rejected).

Should a defendant's conviction be reversed if it is shown that "in order to avoid the appearance of impropriety," defense counsel followed a general policy of not attempting to interview before trial witnesses whose testimony is (apparently) favorable to the prosecution? See Thomas v. Wyrick, 535 F.2d 407 (8th Cir.1976).

536. To what extent must defense counsel who has made a clearly supportable tactical decision about the introduction of evidence or a challenge to the evidence of the prosecution discuss the decision with his client? If he fails to do so, in what circumstances ought his failure be a basis for reversal? See United States v. Moore, 554 F.2d 1086 (D.C.Cir.1976).

537. Should it make any difference to a claim of ineffective assistance of counsel whether defense counsel was retained or appointed? In Cuyler v. Sullivan, 446 U.S. 335 (1980), the Court said not. "A proper respect for the Sixth Amendment disarms petitioner's contention that defendants who retain their own lawyers are entitled to less protection than defendants for whom the State appoints counsel. We may assume with confidence that most counsel, whether retained or appointed, will protect the rights of an accused. But experience teaches that, in some cases, retained counsel will not provide adequate representation. The vital guarantee of the Sixth Amendment would stand for little if the often uninformed decision to retain a particular lawyer could reduce or forfeit the defendant's entitlement to constitutional protection. Since the State's conduct of a criminal trial itself implicates the State in the defendant's conviction, we see no basis for drawing a distinction between retained and appointed counsel that would deny equal justice to defendants who must choose their own lawyers." Id. at 344–45.

538. In Wilson v. Mintzes, 761 F.2d 275 (6th Cir.1985), the court held that the standards applicable to a claim for relief for ineffective assistance of counsel that were elaborated in Strickland v. Washington, above, are not applicable to a request for substitution of retained counsel during the course of a trial. In *Wilson*, the defendant expressed dissatisfaction with his counsel during the trial and asked for a continuance to obtain different counsel. The court distinguished the right to effective assistance of counsel from the right to choose one's counsel. It said: "[I]t is clear that when an accused is financially able to retain an attorney, the choice of counsel to assist him rests ultimately in his hands and not in the hands of the State." Id. at 280. Conceding that the right to a continuance in order to change counsel requires a balance of competing interests, the court said that neither ineffective assistance of counsel nor prejudice need be shown, since the right to counsel of one's choice "is premised on respect for the individual," id. at 286, and not on the fairness of the proceeding or the consequence of the choice. In the circumstances of the case, the court said, a continuance should have been granted.

539. In Lockhart v. Fretwell, 506 U.S. 364 (1993) (7–2), the Court held that defense counsel's failure to make an objection in a state sentencing proceeding, which objection was supported by a decision that was subsequently overruled, is not "prejudice" within the meaning of Strickland v. Washington. To hold otherwise, the Court said, would give criminal defendants "a windfall to which they are not entitled." Id. at 366. "Unreliability or unfairness does not result if the ineffectiveness of counsel does not deprive the defendant of any substantive or procedural right to which the law entitles him." Id. at 372.

See also Wainwright v. Torna, 455 U.S. 586 (1982) (7–1–1). The defendant had been convicted of felonies in state court, and the convictions were affirmed on appeal. The state supreme court dismissed an application for certiorari on the ground that it had not been filed in time. The defendant sought federal habeas corpus, claiming that he had been denied the effective assistance of counsel because of his retained counsel's failure to file the application. The Court held that the district court had correctly denied the petition for habeas corpus. Relying on Ross v. Moffitt, 417 U.S. 600 (1974), it observed that there was not a constitutional right to counsel to pursue discretionary state appeals. Accordingly, it said, the defendant "could not be deprived of the effective assistance of counsel" by his retained counsel's failure. 455 U.S. at 588.

The significance of a failure to appeal is elaborated in Roe v. Flores-Ortega, 528 U.S. 470 (2000) (6–3). The defendant pleaded guilty to murder; his attorney failed to file a notice of appeal. The Court held that the failure was not ineffective assistance per se, as it would be if counsel had consulted with the defendant and failed to follow his instructions or if the defendant had indicated a desire to appeal or a reasonable defendant would want to appeal. To show prejudice, a defendant must show a reasonable probability that, but for counsel's failure, he would have timely appealed. Evidence that there were nonfrivolous grounds for an appeal is often "highly relevant," id. at 485, on the latter point.

Johns v. Smyth

176 F.Supp. 949 (E.D.Va.1959)

[The defendant was convicted of murder and sentenced to life imprisonment. The killing occurred while the defendant and the deceased were inmates at the state penitentiary. The defendant made a statement on the day following the killing to the effect that he killed his victim after the latter took hold of him and suggested an unnatural sexual act; the prison authorities' investigation suggested other motives for the killing. The defendant sought his release by a petition for habeas corpus in the federal district court.]

■ WALTER E. HOFFMAN, DISTRICT JUDGE.

. . .

Little need be said of the trial. The accused did not testify. No proposed instructions were submitted to the trial judge in behalf of the defendant, although under the law of Virginia it was possible for the defendant to have been convicted of involuntary manslaughter and received a sentence of only five years. The defense attorney agreed with the prosecutor that the case would be submitted to the jury without argument of counsel. The instructions given by the court were generally acceptable in covering the categories of first and second degree murder, but failed to mention the possibility of a manslaughter verdict.

Standing alone these complaints would have no merit as they may properly be considered as trial tactics. However, when we look at the motivating force which prompted these decisions of trial counsel, it is apparent that "tactics" gave way to "conscience." In explanation of the agreement not to argue the case before the jury, the court-appointed attorney said:

> "I think an argument to the jury would have made me appear ridiculous in the light of evidence that was offered.
>
> . . .
>
> "I had enough confidence in the judgment of the jury to know that they could have drawn an inference, and I would have been a hypocrite and falsifier if I had gone before the jury and argued in the light of what Johns told me that that statement was accurate.
>
> . . .
>
> "Well, sir, I did not and I wouldn't be dishonest enough to do it in the light of Mr. Johns' statement to me. You can say what the law is and what the record discloses, but if I asked a client, an accused on

> defense, to explain some such statement as this and he gives me the explanation that Johns gave me, I consider it dishonest. You can talk about legal duty to client all you wish, but I consider it dishonest for me to get up before a jury and try to argue that the statement that came out from the Commonwealth was true when Johns had told me that it wasn't. The explanation that he gave me was very vague."

Immediately thereafter, the following occurred:

> Q. That you could not conscientiously argue to the jury that he should be acquitted? A. I definitely could not.
>
> Q. Regardless of what the law is or what your duty to a client is? A. You can talk about law and you can talk about my duty to clients, I felt it was my—that I couldn't conscientiously stand up there and argue that point in the light of what Johns had told me.

The attorney was then asked whether he ever considered requesting permission to withdraw from the case. He replied in the negative.

No attorney should "frame" a factual defense in any case, civil or criminal, and it is not intimated by this opinion that the attorney should plant the seeds of falsehood in the mind of his client. In the instant case, however, the evidence adduced by the prosecution suggested some provocation for the act through the summary of the statement given by the defendant on the day following the killing. When the defendant was interviewed by his court-appointed attorney, the attorney stated that he had reason to doubt the accuracy of the defendant's statement. It was at this time that the attorney's conscience actuated his future conduct which continued throughout the trial. If this was the evidence presented by the prosecution, the defendant was entitled to the faithful and devoted services of his attorney uninhibited by the dictating conscience. The defendant could not be compelled to testify against himself, and if the prosecution saw fit to use the defendant's statement in aid of the prosecution, the attorney was duty bound to exert his best efforts in aid of his client. The failure to argue the case before the jury, while ordinarily only a trial tactic not subject to review, manifestly enters the field of incompetency when the reason assigned is the attorney's conscience. It is as improper as though the attorney had told the jury that his client had uttered a falsehood in making the statement. The right to an attorney embraces effective representation throughout all stages of the trial, and where the representation is of such low caliber as to amount to no representation, the guarantee of due process has been violated. . . .

The entire trial in the state court had the earmarks of an ex parte proceeding. If petitioner had been without the services of an attorney, but had remained mute, it is unlikely that he would have been worse off. The state argues that the defendant may have received a death sentence. Admitting this to be true, it affords no excuse for lack of effective representation.

. . .

[I]t would be a dark day in the history of our judicial system if a conviction is permitted to stand where an attorney, furnished to an indigent defendant, candidly admits that his conscience prevented him from effectively representing his client according to the customary standards prescribed by attorneys and the courts.

Counsel for petitioner will prepare an appropriate order granting the writ of habeas corpus. . . .

---

540. "Except as stated in paragraph (c), a lawyer may withdraw from representing a client if . . . the client insists upon taking action that the lawyer considers repugnant or with which the lawyer has a fundamental disagreement. . . ." ABA Model Rules of Professional Conduct, Rule 1.16(b)(4) (2004). Paragraph (c) has to do with situations requiring notice to or permission of the court to terminate representation.

541. The right to counsel does not guarantee a "meaningful relationship" between an accused and his counsel. Morris v. Slappy, 461 U.S. 1 (1983).

With *Johns*, compare Willis v. United States, 489 F.2d 707 (9th Cir.1973). Counsel was appointed to represent the petitioner in a collateral attack on his conviction. After investigating the petitioner's claims, counsel concluded that they were without legal basis and asked leave of the court to withdraw from the case. The court of appeals observed that counsel had "misconceived his role." Effective representation "requires more than an independent investigation that leads counsel to conclude the client's claim has no legal basis. It is for the court to pass on the legal basis of the claim after its presentation by counsel in as favorable a manner as it permits." 489 F.2d at 708.

The result in *Johns* was questioned in United States ex rel. Wilkins v. Banmiller, 205 F.Supp. 123, 128 n.5 (E.D.Pa.1962).

542. The trial of the defendant is scheduled to begin on Monday morning. After having repeatedly advised the defendant that he would not represent him without having been paid in advance for his services, defense counsel receives a check on the preceding Wednesday. On Friday morning, defense counsel learns that the check has bounced. What should he do? See United States v. Marx, 553 F.2d 874 (4th Cir.1977).

ABA Standards for Criminal Justice, Prosecution Function and Defense Function (3d ed. 1993).

Defense Function Standard

4–3.3: Fees

(a) Defense counsel should not enter into an agreement for, charge, or collect an illegal or unreasonable fee.

(b) In determining the amount of the fee in a criminal case, it is proper to consider the time and effort required, the responsibility assumed by counsel, the novelty and difficulty of the questions involved, the skill requisite to proper representation, the likelihood that other employment will be precluded, the fee customarily charged in the locality for similar services, the gravity of the charge, the experience, reputation and ability of defense counsel and the capacity of the client to pay the fee.

See Winkler v. Keane, 7 F.3d 304 (2d Cir.1993) (agreement that counsel would receive higher fee if defendant were acquitted created conflict of interest, but no effect adverse to defendant was shown).

Faretta v. California

422 U.S. 806, 95 S.Ct. 2525, 45 L.Ed.2d 562 (1975)

■ MR. JUSTICE STEWART delivered the opinion of the Court.

The Sixth and Fourteenth Amendments of our Constitution guarantee that a person brought to trial in any state or federal court must be afforded the right to the assistance of counsel before he can be validly convicted and punished by imprisonment. This clear constitutional rule has emerged from a series of cases decided here over the last 50 years. The question before us now is whether a defendant in a state criminal trial has a constitutional right to proceed *without* counsel when he voluntarily and intelligently elects to do so. Stated another way, the question is whether a State may constitutionally hale a person into its criminal courts and there force a lawyer upon him, even when he insists that he wants to conduct his own defense. It is not an easy question, but we have concluded that a State may not constitutionally do so.

I

Anthony Faretta was charged with grand theft in an information filed in the Superior Court of Los Angeles County, Cal. At the arraignment, the Superior Court Judge assigned to preside at the trial appointed the public defender to represent Faretta. Well before the date of trial, however, Faretta requested that he be permitted to represent himself. Questioning by the judge revealed that Faretta had once represented himself in a criminal prosecution, that he had a high school education, and that he did not want to be represented by the public defender because he believed that that office was "very loaded down with . . . a heavy case load." The judge responded that he believed Faretta was "making a mistake" and emphasized that in further proceedings Faretta would receive no special favors. Nevertheless, after establishing that Faretta wanted to represent himself and did not want a lawyer, the judge, in a "preliminary ruling," accepted

Faretta's waiver of the assistance of counsel. The judge indicated, however, that he might reverse this ruling if it later appeared that Faretta was unable adequately to represent himself.

Several weeks thereafter, but still prior to trial, the judge *sua sponte* held a hearing to inquire into Faretta's ability to conduct his own defense, and questioned him specifically about both the hearsay rule and the state law governing the challenge of potential jurors. After consideration of Faretta's answers, and observation of his demeanor, the judge ruled that Faretta had not made an intelligent and knowing waiver of his right to the assistance of counsel, and also ruled that Faretta had no constitutional right to conduct his own defense. The judge, accordingly, reversed his earlier ruling permitting self-representation and again appointed the public defender to represent Faretta. Faretta's subsequent request for leave to act as cocounsel was rejected, as were his efforts to make certain motions on his own behalf. Throughout the subsequent trial, the judge required that Faretta's defense be conducted only through the appointed lawyer from the public defender's office. At the conclusion of the trial, the jury found Faretta guilty as charged, and the judge sentenced him to prison.

. . .

II

In the federal courts, the right of self-representation has been protected by statute since the beginnings of our Nation. Section 35 of the Judiciary Act of 1789, 1 Stat. 73, 92, enacted by the First Congress and signed by President Washington one day before the Sixth Amendment was proposed, provided that "in all the courts of the United States, the parties may plead and manage their own causes personally or by the assistance of . . . counsel. . . ." The right is currently codified in 28 U.S.C. § 1654.

With few exceptions, each of the several States also accords a defendant the right to represent himself in any criminal case. The Constitutions of 36 States explicitly confer that right. Moreover, many state courts have expressed the view that the right is also supported by the Constitution of the United States.

This Court has more than once indicated the same view. In Adams v. United States ex rel. McCann, 317 U.S. 269, 279, the Court recognized that the Sixth Amendment right to the assistance of counsel implicitly embodies a "correlative right to dispense with a lawyer's help." . . .

The *Adams* case does not, of course, necessarily resolve the issue before us. It held only that "the Constitution does not force a lawyer upon a defendant." Id., at 279. Whether the Constitution forbids a State from forcing a lawyer upon a defendant is a different question. But the Court in *Adams* did recognize, albeit in dictum, an affirmative right of self-representation:

> The right to assistance of counsel and the *correlative right to dispense with a lawyer's help* are not legal formalisms. They rest on

> considerations that go to the substance of an accused's position before the law. . . .
>
> . . . What were contrived as protections for the accused should not be turned into fetters. . . . To deny an accused a choice of procedure in circumstances in which he, though a layman, is as capable as any lawyer of making an intelligent choice, is to impair the worth of great Constitutional safeguards by treating them as empty verbalisms.
>
> . . . When the administration of the criminal law . . . is hedged about as it is by the Constitutional safeguards for the protection of an accused, to deny him in the exercise of his free choice the right to dispense with some of these safeguards . . . is to imprison a man in his privileges and call it the Constitution.

Id. at 279–80 (emphasis added).

In other settings as well, the Court has indicated that a defendant has a constitutionally protected right to represent himself in a criminal trial. . . .

The United States Courts of Appeals have repeatedly held that the right of self-representation is protected by the Bill of Rights. . . .

This Court's past recognition of the right of self-representation, the federal-court authority holding the right to be of constitutional dimension, and the state constitutions pointing to the right's fundamental nature form a consensus not easily ignored. . . . We confront here a nearly universal conviction, on the part of our people as well as our courts, that forcing a lawyer upon an unwilling defendant is contrary to his basic right to defend himself if he truly wants to do so.

III

This consensus is soundly premised. The right of self-representation finds support in the structure of the Sixth Amendment, as well as in the English and colonial jurisprudence from which the Amendment emerged.

A

. . .

The Sixth Amendment does not provide merely that a defense shall be made for the accused; it grants to the accused personally the right to make his defense. It is the accused, not counsel, who must be "informed of the nature and cause of the accusation," who must be "confronted with the witnesses against him," and who must be accorded "compulsory process for obtaining witnesses in his favor." Although not stated in the Amendment in so many words, the right to self-representation—to make one's own defense personally—is thus necessarily implied by the structure of the Amendment. The right to defend is given directly to the accused; for it is he who suffers the consequences if the defense fails.

The counsel provision supplements this design. It speaks of the "assistance" of counsel, and an assistant, however expert, is still an assistant.

The language and spirit of the Sixth Amendment contemplate that counsel, like the other defense tools guaranteed by the Amendment, shall be an aid to a willing defendant—not an organ of the State interposed between an unwilling defendant and his right to defend himself personally. To thrust counsel upon the accused, against his considered wish, thus violates the logic of the Amendment. In such a case, counsel is not an assistant, but a master; and the right to make a defense is stripped of the personal character upon which the Amendment insists. It is true that when a defendant chooses to have a lawyer manage and present his case, law and tradition may allocate to the counsel the power to make binding decisions of trial strategy in many areas. . . . This allocation can only be justified, however, by the defendant's consent, at the outset, to accept counsel as his representative. An unwanted counsel "represents" the defendant only through a tenuous and unacceptable legal fiction. Unless the accused has acquiesced in such representation, the defense presented is not the defense guaranteed him by the Constitution, for, in a very real sense, it is not *his* defense.

B

The Sixth Amendment, when naturally read, thus implies a right of self-representation. This reading is reinforced by the Amendment's roots in English legal history.

. . .

C

In the American Colonies the insistence upon a right of self-representation was, if anything, more fervent than in England.

. . .

In sum, there is no evidence that the colonists and the Framers ever doubted the right of self-representation, or imagined that this right might be considered inferior to the right of assistance of counsel. To the contrary, the colonists and the Framers, as well as their English ancestors, always conceived of the right to counsel as an "assistance" for the accused, to be used at his option, in defending himself. The Framers selected in the Sixth Amendment a form of words that necessarily implies the right of self-representation. That conclusion is supported by centuries of consistent history.

IV

There can be no blinking the fact that the right of an accused to conduct his own defense seems to cut against the grain of this Court's decisions holding that the Constitution requires that no accused can be convicted and imprisoned unless he has been accorded the right to the assistance of counsel. . . . For it is surely true that the basic thesis of those decisions is that the help of a lawyer is essential to assure the defendant a fair trial. And a strong argument can surely be made that the whole thrust of those decisions must inevitably lead to the conclusion that a State may constitutionally impose a lawyer upon even an unwilling defendant.

But it is one thing to hold that every defendant, rich or poor, has the right to the assistance of counsel, and quite another to say that a State may compel a defendant to accept a lawyer he does not want. . . .

It is undeniable that in most criminal prosecutions defendants could better defend with counsel's guidance than by their own unskilled efforts. But where the defendant will not voluntarily accept representation by counsel, the potential advantage of a lawyer's training and experience can be realized, if at all, only imperfectly. To force a lawyer on a defendant can only lead him to believe that the law contrives against him. Moreover, it is not inconceivable that in some rare instances, the defendant might in fact present his case more effectively by conducting his own defense. Personal liberties are not rooted in the law of averages. The right to defend is personal. The defendant, and not his lawyer or the State, will bear the personal consequences of a conviction. It is the defendant, therefore, who must be free personally to decide whether in his particular case counsel is to his advantage. And although he may conduct his own defense ultimately to his own detriment, his choice must be honored out of "that respect for the individual which is the lifeblood of the law." Illinois v. Allen, 397 U.S. 337, 350–51 (Brennan, J., concurring).

V

When an accused manages his own defense, he relinquishes, as a purely factual matter, many of the traditional benefits associated with the right to counsel. For this reason, in order to represent himself, the accused must "knowingly and intelligently" forgo those relinquished benefits. Johnson v. Zerbst, 304 U.S., at 464–65. . . . Although a defendant need not himself have the skill and experience of a lawyer in order competently and intelligently to choose self-representation, he should be made aware of the dangers and disadvantages of self-representation, so that the record will establish that "he knows what he is doing and his choice is made with eyes open." Adams v. United States ex rel. McCann, 317 U.S., at 279.

Here, weeks before trial, Faretta clearly and unequivocally declared to the trial judge that he wanted to represent himself and did not want counsel. The record affirmatively shows that Faretta was literate, competent, and understanding, and that he was voluntarily exercising his informed free will. The trial judge had warned Faretta that he thought it was a mistake not to accept the assistance of counsel, and that Faretta would be required to follow all the "ground rules" of trial procedure. We need make no assessment of how well or poorly Faretta had mastered the intricacies of the hearsay rule and the California code provisions that govern challenges of potential jurors on voir dire. For his technical legal knowledge, as such, was not relevant to an assessment of his knowing exercise of the right to defend himself.

In forcing Faretta, under these circumstances, to accept against his will a state-appointed public defender, the California courts deprived him of his constitutional right to conduct his own defense. . . .

. . .

■ MR. CHIEF JUSTICE BURGER, with whom MR. JUSTICE BLACKMUN and MR. JUSTICE REHNQUIST join, dissenting.

[T]here is nothing desirable or useful in permitting every accused person, even the most uneducated and inexperienced, to insist upon conducting his own defense to criminal charges. Moreover, there is no constitutional basis for the Court's holding, and it can only add to the problems of an already malfunctioning criminal justice system. . . .

I

. . .

As the Court seems to recognize . . . the conclusion that the rights guaranteed by the Sixth Amendment are "personal" to an accused reflects nothing more than the obvious fact that it is he who is on trial and therefore has need of a defense. But neither that nearly trivial proposition nor the language of the Amendment, which speaks in uniformly mandatory terms, leads to the further conclusion that the right to counsel is merely supplementary and may be dispensed with at the whim of the accused. Rather, this Court's decisions have consistently included the right to counsel as an integral part of the bundle making up the larger "right to a defense as we know it." . . .

The reason for this hardly requires explanation. The fact of the matter is that in all but an extraordinarily small number of cases an accused will lose whatever defense he may have if he undertakes to conduct the trial himself. . . .

Obviously, these considerations do not vary depending upon whether the accused actively desires to be represented by counsel or wishes to proceed pro se. Nor is it accurate to suggest, as the Court seems to later in its opinion, that the quality of his representation at trial is a matter with which only the accused is legitimately concerned. . . . Although we have adopted an adversary system of criminal justice . . . the prosecution is more than an ordinary litigant, and the trial judge is not simply an automaton who insures that technical rules are adhered to. Both are charged with the duty of insuring that justice, in the broadest sense of that term, is achieved in every criminal trial. . . . That goal is ill-served, and the integrity of and public confidence in the system are undermined, when an easy conviction is obtained due to the defendant's ill-advised decision to waive counsel. The damage thus inflicted is not mitigated by the lame explanation that the defendant simply availed himself of the "freedom" "to go to jail under his own banner. . . ." United States ex rel. Maldonado v. Denno, 348 F.2d 12, 15 (CA2 1965). The system of criminal justice should not be available as an instrument of self-destruction.

In short, both the "spirit and the logic" of the Sixth Amendment are that every person accused of crime shall receive the fullest possible defense; in the vast majority of cases this command can be honored only by means of the expressly guaranteed right to counsel, and the trial judge is in the best position to determine whether the accused is capable of conducting his defense. True freedom of choice and society's interest in seeing that justice is achieved can be vindicated only if the trial court retains discretion to reject any attempted waiver of counsel and insist that the accused be tried according to the Constitution. This discretion is as critical an element of basic fairness as a trial judge's discretion to decline to accept a plea of guilty. . . .

. . .[36]

---

543. The appointment, over the defendant's objection, of counsel to present mitigating evidence at the sentencing phase of a capital case, violates the right of self-representation. United States v. Davis, 285 F.3d 378 (5th Cir.2002).

A defendant does not have a constitutional right to represent himself on appeal from a conviction. Martinez v. Court of Appeal of California, 528 U.S. 152 (2000). The Court found that the historical evidence on which it had relied in *Faretta* was not applicable to an appeal and that the arguments in *Faretta* based on the Sixth Amendment were also not applicable, because the Amendment does not include a right to appeal. The interest in autonomy, the Court said, grounded in the Due Process Clause, is outweighed by the State's interest in the "fair and efficient administration of justice." The Court noted that a State might base a right of self-representation on its own constitution.

544. *Faretta* does not confer a right to be represented by a lay person who is not qualified to appear as a lawyer. United States v. Wilhelm, 570 F.2d 461 (3d Cir.1978).

See Savage v. Estelle, 924 F.2d 1459 (9th Cir.1990) (defendant with severe speech impediment, who was unable to communicate with jury, did not have right to defend himself).

On waiver of the right to self-representation, see Brown v. Wainwright, 665 F.2d 607 (5th Cir.1982). See also United States v. Flewitt, 874 F.2d 669 (9th Cir.1989) (defendant's pretrial actions did not justify denial of right to self-representation).

545. In McKaskle v. Wiggins, 465 U.S. 168 (1984) (6–3), the Court discussed the role of standby counsel when the defendant elects to defend himself.

> First, the pro se defendant is entitled to preserve actual control over the case he chooses to present to the jury. This is the core of the *Faretta* right. If standby counsel's participation over the defendant's objection effectively allows counsel to make or substantially interfere with any significant tactical decisions, or to control the questioning of witnesses, or to speak instead of the defendant on any matter of improtance, the *Faretta* right is eroded.

[36] Justice Blackmun also wrote a dissenting opinion, which Chief Justice Burger and Justice Rehnquist joined.

UNITED STATES DISTRICT COURT
DISTRICT OF MASSACHUSETTS

UNITED STATES OF AMERICA

V. CRIMINAL NO.___________

____

WAIVER OF COUNSEL BY DEFENDANT

I, the above named defendant, hereby acknowledge that the Court has informed and advised me of my rights under the Constitution of the United States to have the assistance of counsel for my defense.

I hereby waive this constitutional right and elect to proceed without the assistance of counsel.

____
Defendant

____
Witness

Date:____________________

(Waiver of Counsel.wpd - 09/92) [kwvcnsl.]

Second, participation by standby counsel without the defendant's consent should not be allowed to destroy the jury's perception that the defendant is representing himself. The defendant's appearance in the status of one conducting his own defense is important in a criminal trial, since the right to appear pro se exists to affirm the accused's individual dignity and autonomy. . . .

. . .

. . . *Faretta* rights are adequately vindicated in proceedings outside the presence of the jury if the pro se defendant is allowed to address the court freely on his own behalf and if disagreements between counsel and the pro se defendant are resolved in the defendant's favor whenever the matter is one that would normally be left to the discretion of counsel.

. . .

Participation by standby counsel in the presence of the jury is more problematic. It is here that the defendant may legitimately claim that excessive involvement by counsel will destroy the appearance that the defendant is acting pro se. This, in turn, may erode the dignitary values that the right to self-representation is intended to promote and may undercut the defendant's presentation to the jury of his own most effective defense. Nonetheless, we believe that a categorical bar on participation by standby counsel in the presence of the jury is unnecessary.

. . .

Faretta does not require a trial judge to permit "hybrid" representation. . . . But if a defendant is given the opportunity and elects to have counsel appear before the court or jury, his complaints concerning counsel's subsequent unsolicited participation lose much of their force. A defendant does not have a constitutional right to choreograph special appearances by counsel. Once a pro se defendant invites or agrees to any substantial participation by counsel, subsequent appearances by counsel must be presumed to be with the defendant's acquiescence, at least until the defendant expressly and unambiguously renews his request that standby counsel be silenced.

. . .

Faretta rights are also not infringed when standby counsel assists the pro se defendant in overcoming routine procedural or evidentiary obstacles to the completion of some specific task, such as introducing evidence or objecting to testimony, that the defendant has clearly shown he wishes to complete. Nor are they infringed when counsel merely helps to ensure the defendant's compliance with basic rules of courtroom protocol and procedure. In neither case is there any significant interference with the defendant's actual control over the presentation of his defense. . . . A defendant does not have a constitutional right to receive personal instruction from the trial judge on courtroom procedure. Nor does the Constitution require judges to take over chores for a pro se defendant that would normally be attended to by trained counsel as a matter of course. . . .

> Accordingly, we make explicit today what is already implicit in *Faretta*: A defendant's Sixth Amendment rights are not violated when a trial judge appoints standby counsel—even over the defendant's objection—to relieve the judge of the need to explain and enforce basic rules of courtroom protocol or to assist the defendant in overcoming routine obstacles that stand in the way of the defendant's achievement of his own clearly indicated goals. Participation by counsel to steer a defendant through the basic procedures of trial is permissible even in the unlikely event that it somewhat undermines the pro se defendant's appearance of control over his own defense.

Id. at 178–84.

See United States v. Torres, 793 F.2d 436 (1st Cir.1986) (*McKaskle* applied).

---

546. Public trial. "[T]he right to attend criminal trials is implicit in the guarantees of the First Amendment; without the freedom to attend such trials, which people have exercised for centuries, important aspects of freedom of speech and 'of the press could be eviscerated.' Branzburg [v. Hayes], 408 U.S. [665 (1972)], at 681." Richmond Newspapers, Inc. v. Virginia, 448 U.S. 555, 580 (1980).[37] The trial judge in a murder case had granted the defendant's motion, without objection by the prosecution, that the trial be closed to the public. The reasons for closure were to avoid the possibility that the jury would read newspaper reports and to avoid possible distractions during the trial. The Court noted that although the Sixth Amendment gives a defendant the right to a public trial, he has no right to a private trial. It observed that the trial judge had made no findings to support his order; in particular, there had been no inquiry whether other methods would not have sufficed to ensure a fair trial. It concluded: "Absent an overriding interest articulated in findings, the trial of a criminal case must be open to the public." Id. at 581.

A state statute requiring the exclusion of the press and public during the testimony of a minor victim in a sex-offense trial violates the First Amendment. In individual cases, exclusion might be permissible, but a statute requiring exclusion without a particular determination of the need in each case is invalid. Globe Newspaper Co. v. Superior Court, 457 U.S. 596 (1982) (6–3).

During a trial for rape, the judge excluded the press from the voir dire of individual jurors. The press was permitted to attend only the general voir dire. All but about three days of the voir dire, which lasted for six weeks, was held in closed session. The Court held that the right to a public trial was violated. Press-Enterprise Co. v. Superior Court, 464 U.S. 501 (1984). It observed that it was not "crucial" whether the right belongs to the defendant or the public, or is inherent in the system and benefits both. "The presumption of openness may be overcome only by an overriding interest based on findings that closure is essential to preserve higher values

37. In Gannett Co. v. DePasquale, 443 U.S. 368 (1979), the Court had held that the public does not have a right to attend a trial under the Sixth Amendment, which guarantees a public trial for the benefit of the defendant alone. Although there is a "strong societal interest in public trials," such interest "is a far cry . . . from the creation of a constitutional right on the part of the public." Id. at 383.

and is narrowly tailored to serve that interest. The interest is to be articulated along with findings specific enough that a reviewing court can determine whether the closure order was properly entered." Id. at 508, 510. The Court noted that in some cases, a potential juror's compelling interest in privacy might warrant closing the proceedings.

Applying the cases above, the Court concluded that the right of the public to attend criminal trials was violated by an order denying release of the transcript of an extended closed preliminary hearing, which, under state law, is an elaborate proceeding and often the most important stage of the criminal process. Press-Enterprise Co. v. Superior Court, 478 U.S. 1 (1986) (7–2). Denial of public access is permissible, the court said, only if closure is essential to preserve more important values and tailored to that end. "If the interest asserted is the right of the accused to a fair trial, the preliminary hearing shall be closed only if specific findings are made demonstrating that, first, there is a substantial probability that the defendant's right to a fair trial will be prejudiced by publicity that closure would prevent and, second, reasonable alternatives to closure cannot adequately protect the defendant's fair trial rights." Id. at 14.

In Waller v. Georgia, 467 U.S. 39, 46 (1984), the Court said that "there can be little doubt that the explicit Sixth Amendment right of the accused is no less protective of a public trial than the implicit First Amendment right of the press and public." It said that although the right to an open trial "may give way in certain cases to other rights or interests, such as the defendant's right to a fair trial or the government's interest in inhibiting disclosure of sensitive information," such circumstances are rare, and "the balance of interests must be struck with special care." Id. at 45. The Court held that closure of a pretrial hearing on a motion to suppress evidence, in order to avoid disclosure of wiretap material about other persons, was improper.

The court considered the circumstances in which a criminal trial may be closed to the public, in Ayala v. Speckard, 131 F.3d 62 (2d Cir.1997) (en banc). The case involved several drug prosecutions, in each of which an undercover police officer had purchased narcotics from the defendant. The officer testified that he expected to return to work as an undercover agent in the same area in which he had worked previously and that if his identity were known, his life would be in danger. In those circumstances, the court said, closure during the witness's testimony was permissible. "We believe the sensible course is for the trial judge to recognize that open trials are strongly favored, to require persuasive evidence of serious risk to an important interest in ordering any closure, and to realize that the more extensive is the closure requested, the greater must be the gravity of the required interest and the likelihood of risk to that interest." Id. at 70.

---

547. In Nebraska Press Ass'n v. Stuart, 427 U.S. 539 (1976), the Court held that it was improper for a trial judge to issue an order restraining news media from reporting specified categories of highly incriminating evidence in a sensational murder case until after a jury was impaneled. The trial took place in a small Nebraska town. Relying on the First Amendment's protection of freedom of the press, a majority of the Court did not absolutely bar the "extraordinary remedy" of a prior restraint on publication in order to protect the defendant's right to a fair trial, but indicated that it could rarely, if ever, be used. Justice Brennan, Justice Stewart, and Justice Marshall would have imposed an absolute bar to prior restraints; Justice White and Justice Stevens indicated that if they were obliged to address the question they might reach the same conclusion. See United States v. Brown, 218 F.3d 415 (5th Cir.2000) ("gag order" imposed by court, which barred parties, lawyers, and potential witnesses from making any public statements about case during trial was permissible, as least restrictive measure available to ensure fair trial).

548. The Constitution does not absolutely prohibit radio, television, or photographic coverage of a criminal trial over the objection of a defendant. The defendant is entitled to an opportunity to show that in a particular case such coverage was inconsistent with a fair trial, but there is no per se prohibition. Chandler v. Florida, 449 U.S. 560 (1981).

For cases in which the defendant's conviction was reversed because of undue publicity of the trial, see Sheppard v. Maxwell, 384 U.S. 333 (1966) ("carnival atmosphere at trial"), p. 919 above; Estes v. Texas, 381 U.S. 532 (1965).

Motion for Judgment of Acquittal

FEDERAL RULES OF CRIMINAL PROCEDURE

Rule 29

MOTION FOR A JUDGMENT OF ACQUITTAL

(a) Before Submission to the Jury. After the government closes its evidence or after the close of all the evidence, the court on the defendant's motion must enter a judgment of acquittal of any offense for which the evidence is insufficient to sustain a conviction. The court may on its own consider whether the evidence is insufficient to sustain a conviction. If the court denies a motion for a judgment of acquittal at the close of the government's evidence, the defendant may offer evidence without having reserved the right to do so.

(b) Reserving Decision. The court may reserve decision on the motion, proceed with the trial (where the motion is made before the close of all the evidence), submit the case to the jury, and decide the motion either before the jury returns a verdict or after it returns a verdict of guilty or is discharged without having returned a verdict. If the court reserves decision, it must decide the motion on the basis of the evidence at the time the ruling was reserved.

(c) After Jury Verdict or Discharge.

(1) *Time for a Motion.* A defendant may move for a judgment of acquittal, or renew such a motion, within 7 days after a guilty verdict or after the court discharges the jury, whichever is later, or within any other time the court sets during the 7-day period.

(2) *Ruling on the Motion.* If the jury has returned a guilty verdict, the court may set aside the verdict and enter an acquittal. If the jury has failed to return a verdict, the court may enter a judgment of acquittal.

(3) *No Prior Motion Required.* A defendant is not required to move for a judgment of acquittal before the court submits the case to the jury as a prerequisite for making such a motion after jury discharge.

(d) Conditional Ruling on a Motion for a New Trial.

(1) *Motion for a New Trial.* If the court enters a judgment of acquittal after a guilty verdict, the court must also conditionally determine whether any motion for a new trial should be granted if the judgment of acquittal is later vacated or reversed. The court must specify the reasons for that determination.

(2) *Finality.* The court's order conditionally granting a motion for a new trial does not affect the finality of the judgment of acquittal.

(3) *Appeal.*

(A) *Grant of a Motion for a New Trial.* If the court conditionally grants a motion for a new trial and an appellate court later reverses the judgment of acquittal, the trial court must proceed with the new trial unless the appellate court orders otherwise.

(B) *Denial of a Motion for a New Trial.* If the court conditionally denies a motion for a new trial, an appellee may assert that the denial was erroneous. If the appellate court later reverses the judgment of acquittal, the trial court must proceed as the appellate court directs.

United States v. Taylor

464 F.2d 240 (2d Cir.1972)

■ FRIENDLY, CHIEF JUDGE.

The sole question meriting discussion in this opinion is the sufficiency of the evidence to warrant submission to the jury of the question whether Taylor "with intent to defraud" kept in possession and concealed a quantity of counterfeit Federal Reserve notes found in a car which Taylor, accompanied by one MacDonald, was driving from Canada into the United States.

I

Counsel for appellant asks us, as many others have done, to overrule the so-called "Second Circuit rule," first enunciated by Judge Learned Hand in United States v. Feinberg, 140 F.2d 592, 594 (2 Cir.) . . . (1944), and later challenged, at great length but without success, by Judge Jerome Frank in United States v. Masiello, 235 F.2d 279, 285 (2 Cir.) . . . (1956) (concurring opinion). The "rule" in this circuit has been that "the standard of evidence necessary [for the judge] to send a case to the jury is the same in both civil and criminal cases," even though the jury must apply a higher standard before rendering a verdict in favor of the proponent in the latter. United States v. Feinberg, supra, 140 F.2d at 594. Despite our reverence for Judge Hand, perhaps in part because of our desire to remove one of his rare ill-advised opinions from public debate, we agree that the time for overruling the *Feinberg* "single test" standard has arrived.

It is, of course, a fundamental of the jury trial guaranteed by the Constitution that the jury acts, not at large, but under the supervision of a judge. . . . Before submitting the case to the jury, the judge must determine whether the proponent has adduced evidence sufficient to warrant a verdict in his favor. Dean Wigmore considered, 9 Evidence § 2494 at 299 (3d ed. 1940), the best statement of the test to be that of Mr. Justice Brett in Bridges v. Railway Co. [1874] L.R. 7 H.L. 213, 233:

> [A]re there facts in evidence which if unanswered would justify men of ordinary reason and fairness in affirming the question which the Plaintiff is bound to maintain?

It would seem at first blush—and we think also at second—that more "facts in evidence" are needed for the judge to allow men, and now women, "of ordinary reason and fairness" to affirm the question the proponent "is bound to maintain" when the proponent is required to establish this not merely by a preponderance of the evidence but, as all agree to be true in a criminal case, beyond a reasonable doubt. Indeed, the latter standard has recently been held to be constitutionally required in criminal cases. In re Winship, 397 U.S. 358, 361–64 (1970). We do not find a satisfying explanation in the *Feinberg* opinion why the judge should not place this higher burden on the prosecution in criminal proceedings before sending the case to the jury.

After acknowledging "that in their actual judgments the added gravity of the consequences [in criminal cases] makes them [the judges] more exacting," 140 F.2d at 594, Judge Hand based the refusal to require a higher standard of sufficiency in criminal cases on authority and a belief that "[w]hile at times it may be practicable" to "distinguish between the evidence which should satisfy reasonable men, and the evidence which should satisfy reasonable men beyond a reasonable doubt . . . in the long run the line between them is too thin for day to day use." Id.

However the argument from authority may have stood in 1944, that battle has now been irretrievably lost. . . . Almost all the circuits have adopted something like Judge Prettyman's formulation in Curley v. United States, 160 F.2d 229, 232–33 . . . (1947). This, along with its rationale, reads as follows:

> The functions of the jury include the determination of the credibility of witnesses, the weighing of the evidence, and the drawing of justifiable inferences of fact from proven facts. It is the function of the judge to deny the jury any opportunity to operate beyond its province. The jury may not be permitted to conjecture merely, or to conclude upon pure speculation or from passion, prejudice or sympathy. The critical point in this boundary is the existence or non-existence of reasonable doubt as to guilt. If the evidence is such that reasonable jurymen must necessarily have such a doubt, the judge must require acquittal, because no other result is permissible within the fixed bounds of jury consideration. But if a reasonable mind might fairly have a reasonable doubt or might fairly not have one, the case is for the jury, and the decision is for the jurors to make. The law recognizes that the scope of a reasonable mind is broad. Its conclusion is not always a point certain, but, upon given evidence, may be one of a number of conclusions. Both innocence and guilt beyond a reasonable doubt may lie fairly within the limits of reasonable conclusion from given facts. The judge's function is exhausted when he determines that the evidence does or does not permit the conclusion of guilt beyond a reasonable doubt within the fair operation of a reasonable mind.
>
> The true rule, therefore, is that a trial judge, in passing upon a motion for directed verdict of acquittal, must determine whether upon the evidence, giving full play to the right of the jury to determine credibility, weigh the evidence, and draw justifiable inferences of fact, a reasonable mind might fairly conclude guilt beyond a reasonable doubt. If he concludes that upon the evidence there must be such a doubt in a reasonable mind, he must grant the motion; or, to state it another way, if there is no evidence upon which a reasonable mind might fairly conclude guilt beyond a reasonable doubt, the motion must be granted. If he concludes that either of the two results, a reasonable doubt or no reasonable doubt, is fairly possible, he must let the jury decide the matter. (footnotes omitted)

On Judge Hand's second point, while we agree there will be few cases where application of Judge Prettyman's test would produce a different result, we cannot say these are non-existent, as indeed he conceded. The Supreme Court has recognized the feasibility of a standard intermediate between preponderance and proof beyond a reasonable doubt, to wit, clear and convincing evidence. . . . Implicit in the Court's recognition of varying burdens of proof is a concomitant duty on the judge to consider the applicable burden when deciding whether to send a case to the jury.

. . .

---

549. Rule 29(c). Reversing the trial judge's order granting a motion for judgment of acquittal following a verdict of guilty, the court in United States v. Hemphill, 544 F.2d 341, 344 (8th Cir.1976), said: "In passing upon the defendant's post-trial motion for judgment of acquittal notwithstanding the jury's verdict, it was not the prerogative of the district court to resolve conflicts in the testimony, or to pass upon the credibility of witnesses or the weight to be given their testimony; those were jury functions; and the district court was not at liberty to set aside the verdict of the jury simply because the trial judge may have thought that the jury reached the wrong result. The district court was required, and we are required, to view the evidence in the light most favorable to the government, and to give to the government the benefit of all favorable inferences reasonably to be drawn from the evidence. And if the verdict of the jury was sustained by substantial evidence, it should not have been set aside by the district court on factual grounds."

A district court does not have authority to consider a motion for judgment of acquittal made after the jury has returned a verdict, if the motion is made outside the time limit prescribed by Rule 29(c). Carlisle v. United States, 517 U.S. 416 (1996) (7–2). The Court noted that Rule 45(b)(2) expressly prohibits enlargement of the times specified in Rule 29. It held also that the courts' inherent supervisory authority does not include a deviation from the requirements of the Federal Rules.

On the double jeopardy effect of a motion granted before or after the jury returns a verdict, see United States v. Baggett, 251 F.3d 1087 (6th Cir.2001).

Closing Argument

FEDERAL RULES OF CRIMINAL PROCEDURE

Rule 29.1

CLOSING ARGUMENT

Closing arguments proceed in the following order:

(a) the government argues;

(b) the defense argues; and

(c) the government rebuts.

Herring v. New York

422 U.S. 853, 95 S.Ct. 2550, 45 L.Ed.2d 593 (1975)

■ MR. JUSTICE STEWART delivered the opinion of the Court.

A New York law confers upon every judge in a nonjury criminal trial the power to deny counsel any opportunity to make a summation of the evidence before the rendition of judgment. N.Y.Crim.Proc.Law § 320.20(3)(c) (1971). In the case before us we are called upon to assess the constitutional validity of that law.

I

The appellant was brought to trial in the Supreme Court of Richmond County, N.Y., upon charges of attempted robbery in the first and third degrees and possession of a dangerous instrument. He waived a jury.

The trial began on a Thursday, and, after certain preliminaries, the balance of that day and most of Friday were spent on the case for the prosecution. The complaining witness, Allen Braxton, testified that the appellant had approached him outside his home in a Staten Island housing project at about six o'clock on the evening of September 15, 1971, and asked for money. He said that when he refused this demand, the appellant had swung a knife at him. On cross-examination, the appellant's lawyer attempted to impeach the credibility of this evidence by demonstrating inconsistencies between Braxton's testimony and other sworn statements that Braxton had previously made. The only other witness for the prosecution was the police officer who had arrested the appellant upon the complaint of Braxton. The officer testified that Braxton had reported the alleged incident to him, and that the appellant, when confronted by the officer later in the evening, had denied Braxton's story and said that he had been working for a Mr. Taylor at the time of the alleged offense. The officer testified that he had then arrested the appellant and found a small knife in his pocket.

At the close of the case for the prosecution, the court granted a defense motion to dismiss the charge of possession of a dangerous instrument on the ground that the knife in evidence was too small to qualify as a dangerous instrument under state law. The trial was then adjourned for the two-day weekend.

Proceedings did not actually resume until the following Monday afternoon. The first witness for the defense was Donald Taylor, who was the appellant's employer. He testified that he recalled seeing the appellant on the job premises at about 5:30 p.m. on the day of the alleged offense. The appellant then took the stand and denied Braxton's story. He said that he had been working on a refrigerator at his place of employment during the time of the alleged offense, and further testified that Braxton, a former neighbor, had threatened on several occasions to "fix" him for refusing to give Braxton money for wine and drugs.

At the conclusion of the case for the defense, counsel made a motion to dismiss the robbery charges. This motion was denied. The appellant's lawyer then requested to "be heard somewhat on the facts." The trial judge replied: "Under the new statute, summation is discretionary, and I choose not to hear summations." The judge thereupon found the appellant guilty of attempted robbery in the third degree, and subsequently sentenced him to serve an indeterminate term of imprisonment with a maximum of four years. . . .

II

. . .

[T]he right to the assistance of counsel has been understood to mean that there can be no restrictions upon the function of counsel in defending a criminal prosecution in accord with the traditions of the adversary factfinding process that has been constitutionalized in the Sixth and Fourteenth Amendments. . . . The right to the assistance of counsel has thus been given a meaning that ensures to the defense in a criminal trial the opportunity to participate fully and fairly in the adversary factfinding process.

There can be no doubt that closing argument for the defense is a basic element of the adversary factfinding process in a criminal trial. Accordingly, it has universally been held that counsel for the defense has a right to make a closing summation to the jury, no matter how strong the case for the prosecution may appear to the presiding judge. The issue has been considered less often in the context of a so-called bench trial. But the overwhelming weight of authority, in both federal and state courts, holds that a total denial of the opportunity for final argument in a nonjury criminal trial is a denial of the basic right of the accused to make his defense.

. . .

The widespread recognition of the right of the defense to make a closing summary of the evidence to the trier of the facts, whether judge or jury, finds solid support in history. In the 16th and 17th centuries, when notions of compulsory process, confrontation, and counsel were in their infancy, the essence of the English criminal trial was argument between the defendant and counsel for the Crown. Whatever other procedural protections may have been lacking, there was no absence of debate on the factual and legal issues raised in a criminal case. As the rights to compulsory process, to confrontation, and to counsel developed, the adversary system's commitment to argument was neither discarded nor diluted. Rather, the reform in procedure had the effect of shifting the primary function of argument to summation of the evidence at the close of trial, in contrast to the "fragmented" factual argument that had been typical of the earlier common law.

It can hardly be questioned that closing argument serves to sharpen and clarify the issues for resolution by the trier of fact in a criminal case. For it is only after all the evidence is in that counsel for the parties are in a position to present their respective versions of the case as a whole. Only then can they argue the inferences to be drawn from all the testimony, and point out the weaknesses of their adversaries' positions. And for the defense, closing argument is the last clear chance to persuade the trier of fact that there may be reasonable doubt of the defendant's guilt. . . .

The very premise of our adversary system of criminal justice is that partisan advocacy on both sides of a case will best promote the ultimate objective that the guilty be convicted and the innocent go free. In a criminal trial, which is in the end basically a factfinding process, no aspect of such advocacy could be more important than the opportunity finally to marshal the evidence for each side before submission of the case to judgment.

This is not to say that closing arguments in a criminal case must be uncontrolled or even unrestrained. The presiding judge must be and is given great latitude in controlling the duration and limiting the scope of closing summations. He may limit counsel to a reasonable time and may terminate argument when continuation would be repetitive or redundant. He may ensure that argument does not stray unduly from the mark, or otherwise impede the fair and orderly conduct of the trial. In all these respects he must have broad discretion. . . .

But there can be no justification for a statute that empowers a trial judge to deny absolutely the opportunity for any closing summation at all. The only conceivable interest served by such a statute is expediency. Yet the difference in any case between total denial of final argument and a concise but persuasive summation could spell the difference, for the defendant, between liberty and unjust imprisonment.

Some cases may appear to the trial judge to be simple—open and shut—at the close of the evidence. And surely in many such cases a closing argument will, in the words of Mr. Justice Jackson, be "likely to leave [a] judge just where it found him."[38] But just as surely, there will be cases where closing argument may correct a premature misjudgment and avoid an otherwise erroneous verdict. And there is no certain way for a trial judge to identify accurately which cases these will be, until the judge has heard the closing summation of counsel.

The present case is illustrative. This three-day trial was interrupted by an interval of more than two days—a period during which the judge's memory may well have dimmed, however conscientious a note-taker he may have been. At the conclusion of the evidence on the trial's final day, the appellant's lawyer might usefully have pointed to the direct conflict in the trial testimony of the only two prosecution witnesses concerning how and when the appellant was found on the evening of the alleged offense. He might also have stressed the many inconsistencies, elicited on cross-examination, between the trial testimony of the complaining witness and his earlier sworn statements. He might reasonably have argued that the testimony of the appellant's employer was entitled to greater credibility than that of the complaining witness, who, according to the appellant, had

38. R. Jackson, The Struggle for Judicial Supremacy 301 (1941).

threatened to "fix" him because of personal differences in the past. There is no way to know whether these or any other appropriate arguments in summation might have affected the ultimate judgment in this case. The credibility assessment was solely for the trier of fact. But before that determination was made, the appellant, through counsel, had a right to be heard in summation of the evidence from the point of view most favorable to him.

In denying the appellant this right under the authority of its statute, New York denied him the assistance of counsel that the Constitution guarantees. . . .

. . .[39]

Harris v. United States

402 F.2d 656 (D.C.Cir.1968)

■ BURGER, CIRCUIT JUDGE:

Appellant was convicted in the District Court of the unauthorized use of a motor vehicle under 22 D.C.Code § 2204 (1967). His appeal raises only one issue: the propriety of certain remarks made by the prosecutor in his closing argument to the jury.

This claim is raised for the first time on appeal as "plain error" under Rule 52(b) Fed.R.Crim.P. At trial there was no objection—either during the argument or thereafter, at the bench—and no request for a corrective instruction, or motion for a mistrial. In short, Appellant invoked none of several possible methods for bringing these remarks to the attention of the trial judge who was best able to assess their effect on the jury and to undertake corrective measures. The problem of raising objections to improper argument of either counsel presents obvious practical difficulties. Counsel may, of course, object during the argument, but unless the departure from the proprieties is egregious neither the court nor the jury is likely to look favorably upon such an interruption at that stage. The more usual treatment is for counsel to approach the bench at the conclusion of the summing up and request an immediate instruction to correct the impact of objectionable material. In the gravest situation it may be his duty to raise the issue of a mistrial. However, since none of these avenues was pursued here, we find no basis for reversal. . . . The trial judge may also properly stop a lawyer whose summation exceeds permissible grounds; the judge's interruption does not involve the risk that counsel takes when he objects in the midst of a closing argument and such action by the court, while limited to serious transgressions, may avoid declaring a mistrial or reversible error.

[39] Justice Rehnquist wrote a dissenting opinion, which Chief Justice Burger and Justice Blackmun joined.

It is nevertheless clear that the prosecutor's remarks in the present case were of a kind that ought not be made. The defense was based upon Appellant's testimony that he had not stolen the car in question but that someone he presumed to be its owner, and who was unknown to Appellant, had lent him the car. His claim was that when he could not find this person later in the evening in order to return the car he decided to keep it overnight and return it the next morning to the parking lot where he had borrowed it. Before morning, however, he was arrested. The complainant testified that at approximately 10:00 p.m. he had parked his car by the stage door of the theater in whose parking lot Appellant testified the loan was made, and that when he returned the car had been removed. The Appellant testified that the accommodating stranger gave him the car at about 8:30 p.m. Thus complainant's testimony was that he did not arrive at the theater with his car until nearly two hours *after* Appellant said the "Good Samaritan" lender had turned it over to him. It is, of course, not surprising that the jury declined to believe this excessively implausible tale.

But our concern is not with the merits of the case, since the evidence against Appellant—including his own bizarre story—is overwhelming. The prosecutor attacked Appellant's version as an incredible tale. This was, of course, a permissible argument. But he went beyond this and made comments on Appellant's testimony that we consider of questionable propriety. He stated: "I ask you to reject it in toto the defense of John Harris because it reeks of fabrication, it lacks merit, it is not reasonable." He went on: "He would urge upon you that his defense is that he took this car in innocence [*sic*] but mistaken belief that he had the consent of the owner. If you really believe that, then he is pulling the wool over your eyes." And further: "Reasonably, there is a total fabrication. I would submit, ladies and gentlemen, it is a lie."

We address ourselves to these remarks not because we view them as having had significant impact on this case but because of the frequent nonobservance of the prohibition against expressions of personal opinions on the ultimate issue by counsel. The challenged statements are in essence an opinion of counsel as to the veracity of witnesses in circumstances where veracity may determine the ultimate issue of guilt or innocence. Appellant's testimony is a "lie" or "fabrication" only if the jury accepts all of the complainant's testimony and rejects the hypothesis that the claimed third person did intervene and Appellant merely forgot the precise time at which the events in question occurred. Appellant's testimony permitted the prosecutor to ask the jury to consider whether it was implausible, unbelievable, highly suspect, even ridiculous. Many strong adjectives could be used but it was for the jury, and not the prosecutor, to say which witnesses were telling the truth. Neither counsel should assert to the jury what in essence is his opinion on guilt or innocence. Yet this is the effect of remarks such as those of the prosecutor here when the accused gives testimony directly conflicting with that of the government's witnesses.

The precise words here challenged were pointless, if for no other reason, because of the availability of more effective means of characterizing an implausible story.[40] This is more than a matter of semantics; the purpose of the rule forbidding expression of opinion of counsel on the ultimate issue is to keep the focus on the *evidence* and to eliminate the need for opposing counsel to meet "opinions" by urging his own contrary opinion. The impropriety of substituting an attorney's view of the case for the evaluation of the evidentiary facts has been discussed by Drinker in the context of stating one's personal view of his case:

> There are several reasons for the rule, long established, that a lawyer may not properly state his personal belief either to the court or to the jury in soundness of his case. In the first place, his personal belief has no real bearing on the issue; no witness would be permitted so to testify, even under oath, and subject to cross-examination, much less the lawyer without either. Also, if expression of personal belief were permitted, it would give an improper advantage to the older and better known lawyer, whose opinion would carry more weight, and also with the jury at least, an undue advantage to an unscrupulous one. Furthermore, if such were permitted, for counsel to omit to make such a positive assertion might be taken as an admission that he did not believe in his case.

H. Drinker, Legal Ethics 147 (1953) (footnotes omitted).

The First Circuit adopted this reasoning as the basis for a decision that a prosecutor's expression of his "personal opinion of the trustworthiness of the government's evidence and the consequent guilt of the accused" was contrary to Canon 15[41] and merited a reversal. The Court stated:

> To permit counsel to express his personal belief in the testimony (even if not phrased so as to suggest knowledge of additional evidence not known to the jury), would afford him a privilege not even accorded to witnesses under oath and subject to cross-examination. Worse, it creates the false issue of the reliability and credibility of counsel. This is peculiarly unfortunate if one of them has the advantage of official backing.

Greenberg v. United States, 280 F.2d 472, 474–75 (1st Cir.1960) (footnote omitted).

The challenged statements of the prosecutor here do not fall precisely into the prohibitions of Canon 15 or the observations of Drinker but they come disturbingly close to it since they were another way of saying the

40. The prosecutor used the universally accepted and proper form of comment on the contradictions in testimony at one point in his closing statement when he told the jury: "Mr. Harris would urge upon you at the time he got this car it was about 8:00 o'clock, and if you are to believe Mr. Harris, if he got the car at 8:00 o'clock, then you must disbelieve Mr. Gray. . . ."

41. "It is improper for a lawyer to assert in argument his personal belief in his client's innocence or in the justice of his cause." The Code of Professional Responsibility, DR 7–106(C)(4) provides that while appearing before a tribunal a lawyer shall not "assert his personal opinion as to the justness of a cause, as to the credibility of a witness, as to the culpability of a civil litigant, or as to the guilt or innocence of an accused; but he may argue, on his analysis of the evidence, for any position or conclusion with respect to the matters stated herein."

accused was guilty in the prosecutor's opinion. We might add to what others have said on the undesirability of such practices a further comment: lawyers should train themselves to eschew opinions in the course of arguments to juries because this diverts them as well as jurors from their respective functions. By avoiding expressions of personal opinions, the advocates will tend to concentrate on facts, issues and evidence, and make reasoned, even if vigorous, arguments.

The prosecutor is certainly free to strike hard blows at witnesses whose credibility he is challenging. But what he may not do is divert the focus of the jury's consideration of the case from the facts in evidence to the attorney's personal evaluations of the weight of the evidence. The personal evaluations and opinions of trial counsel are at best boring irrelevancies and a distasteful cliche-type argument. At worst, they may be a vague form of unsworn and irrelevant testimony.

. . .

550.

[W]e find that two of the statements which the prosecuting attorney made to the jury were highly prejudicial. At one point he stated:

> "Again, you are supposed to judge the demeanor and the way a witness conducts himself on the stand; whether you would believe or not, that is your job to determine who you can believe and who you can't believe. And, I think Officer McPherson and Agent Stymus [*sic*] showed sincerity. I *firmly believe* what they said is the truth. I *know it is the truth*, and I expect you do, too."

(Tr. 122). (emphasis supplied.)

This type of comment has repeatedly been held to amount to reversible error. . . . The Government's proof was not so clear as to render the error harmless. It is somewhat indiscrete for the prosecutor to comment on his own personal assessment of the credibility of the witnesses, even when that assessment derives solely from what the witnesses have said while on the stand. When he makes a statement which could be construed by the jury as implying that he has additional reasons for knowing that what one witness has said is true, which reasons are not known to the jury, such comment is no longer mere indiscretion but constitutes reversible error. Here, the prosecutor said: "I know it is the truth," the inference being that he had outside knowledge. Put simply, the prosecutor overstepped the bounds of propriety.

Additionally, the prosecutor made the following statement to the jury:

> "The Government is prosecuting Clyde Lamerson in line with what Mr. Koerner [the defense attorney] says. And, Mr. Lamerson,

> had [he] not committed a crime, we would not be doing so. It's as simple as that."

(Tr. 128.) In effect, he stated that the Government prosecutes only the guilty. Even the lesser suggestion that the Government *tries* to prosecute only the guilty has been held reversible error by this Court. In Hall v. United States, 5 Cir.1969, 419 F.2d 582, 587, this Court held:

> The statement "we try to prosecute only the guilty" is not defensible. Expressions of individual opinion of guilt are dubious at best. . . . This statement takes guilt as a pre-determined fact. The remark is, at the least, an effort to lead the jury to believe that the whole governmental establishment had already determined appellant to be guilty on evidence not before them. . . . Or, arguably it may be construed to mean that as a pretrial administrative matter the defendant has been found guilty as charged else he would not have been prosecuted, and that the administrative level determination is either binding upon the jury or else highly persuasive to it. Appellant's trial was held and the jury impaneled to pass on his guilt or innocence, and he was clothed in the presumption of innocence. The prosecutor may neither dispense with the presumption of innocence nor denigrate the function of the trial nor sit as a thirteenth juror.

United States v. Lamerson, 457 F.2d 371, 372 (5th Cir.1972).

551. In Portuondo v. Agard, 529 U.S. 61 (2000) (7–2), the defendant testified. In her closing argument, the prosecutor challenged the defendant's credibility and argued that he had heard the other witnesses testify and had an opportunity to tailor his testimony to theirs. The defendant claimed that the argument infringed his Fifth and Sixth Amendment rights to be present at his trial and to confront his accusers. Rejecting an analogy to Griffin v. California, 380 U.S. 609 (1965), p. 961 above, the Court held that no constitutional right was infringed. The prosecutor's argument, the Court said, treated the defendant as no different from other witnesses, which in this context was sound. In addition to the two dissenting Justices, two Justices, concurring in the judgment, said that comments like those of the prosecutor demeaned the truth-seeking function of the adversary process and "should be discouraged rather than validated." Id. at 16 (Stevens, J., concurring).

552.

> The situation brought before the Court of Appeals was but one example of an all too common occurrence in criminal trials—the defense counsel argues improperly, provoking the prosecutor to respond in kind, and the trial judge takes no corrective action. Clearly two improper arguments—two apparent wrongs—do not make for a right result. Nevertheless, a criminal conviction is not to be lightly overturned on the basis of a prosecutor's comments standing alone, for the statements or conduct must be viewed in context; only by so doing can it be determined whether the prosecutor's conduct affected the

fairness of the trial. To help resolve this problem, courts have invoked what is sometimes called the "invited response" or "invited reply" rule, which the Court treated in Lawn v. United States, 355 U.S. 339 (1958).

The petitioners in *Lawn* sought to have the Court overturn their criminal convictions for income tax evasion on a number of grounds, one of which was that the prosecutor's closing argument deprived them of a fair trial. In his closing argument at trial, defense counsel in *Lawn* had attacked the Government for "persecuting" the defendants. He told the jury that the prosecution was instituted in bad faith at the behest of federal revenue agents and asserted that the Government's key witnesses were perjurers. The prosecutor in response vouched for the credibility of the challenged witnesses, telling the jury that the Government thought those witnesses testified truthfully. In concluding that the prosecutor's remarks, when viewed within the context of the entire trial, did not deprive petitioners of a fair trial, the Court pointed out that defense counsel's "comments clearly invited the reply." Id., at 359–60, n.15.

This Court's holding in *Lawn* was no more than an application of settled law. Inappropriate prosecutorial comments, standing alone, would not justify a reviewing court to reverse a criminal conviction obtained in an otherwise fair proceeding. Instead, as *Lawn* teaches, the remarks must be examined within the context of the trial to determine whether the prosecutor's behavior amounted to prejudicial error. In other words, the Court must consider the probable effect the prosecutor's response would have on the jury's ability to judge the evidence fairly. In this context, defense counsel's conduct, as well as the nature of the prosecutor's response, is relevant. . . . Indeed most Courts of Appeals, applying these holdings, have refused to reverse convictions where prosecutors have responded reasonably in closing argument to defense counsel's attacks, thus rendering it unlikely that the jury was led astray.

In retrospect, perhaps the idea of "invited response" has evolved in a way not contemplated. *Lawn* and the earlier cases cited above should not be read as suggesting judicial approval or—encouragement—[*sic*] of response-in-kind that inevitably exacerbate the tensions inherent in the adversary process. As *Lawn* itself indicates, the issue is not the prosecutor's license to make otherwise improper arguments, but whether the prosecutor's "invited response," taken in context, unfairly prejudiced the defendant.

In order to make an appropriate assessment, the reviewing court must not only weigh the impact of the prosecutor's remarks, but must also take into account defense counsel's opening salvo. Thus the import of the evaluation has been that if the prosecutor's remarks were "invited," and did no more than respond substantially in order to "right the scale," such comments would not warrant reversing a conviction.

> Courts have not intended by any means to encourage the practice of zealous counsel's going "out of bounds" in the manner of defense counsel here, or to encourage prosecutors to respond to the "invitation." Reviewing courts ought not to be put in the position of weighing which of two inappropriate arguments was the lesser. "Invited responses" can be effectively discouraged by prompt action from the bench in the form of corrective instructions to the jury, and when necessary, an admonition to the errant advocate.
>
> Plainly, the better remedy in this case, at least with the accurate vision of hindsight, would have been for the District Judge to deal with the improper argument of the defense counsel promptly and thus blunt the need for the prosecutor to respond. Arguably defense counsel's misconduct could have warranted the judge to interrupt the argument and admonish him . . . thereby rendering the prosecutor's response unnecessary. Similarly, the prosecutor at the close of defense summation should have objected to the defense counsel's improper statements with a request that the court give a timely warning and curative instruction to the jury. Defense counsel, even though obviously vulnerable, could well have done likewise if he thought that the prosecutor's remarks were harmful to his client. Here neither counsel made a timely objection to preserve the issue for review. . . . However, interruptions of arguments, either by an opposing counsel or the presiding judge, are matters to be approached cautiously. At the very least, a bench conference might have been convened out of the hearing of the jury once defense counsel closed, and an appropriate instruction given.

United States v. Young, 470 U.S. 1, 13–14 (1985) (6–2–1). After reviewing the record, the Court concluded that the prosecutor's improper argument did not constitute "plain error" under Rule 52(b) and reversed the judgment of the court of appeals ordering a new trial.

See Darden v. Wainwright, 477 U.S. 168 (1986) (5–4) (improper closing argument did not deprive defendant of fair trial); United States v. Wilson, 135 F.3d 291 (4th Cir.1998) (improper closing argument; conviction reversed); United States v. Shaw, 701 F.2d 367, 390–92 (5th Cir.1983) (improper closing argument did not deprive defendant of fair trial); United States v. Garza, 608 F.2d 659 (5th Cir.1979) (improper closing argument; conviction reversed).

Instructions

FEDERAL RULES OF CRIMINAL PROCEDURE

Rule 30

JURY INSTRUCTIONS

(a) In General. Any party may request in writing that the court instruct the jury on the law as specified in the request. The request must be made at the close of the evidence or at any earlier time that the court reasonably sets. When the request is made, the requesting party must furnish a copy to every other party.

(b) Ruling on a Request. The court must inform the parties before closing arguments how it intends to rule on the requested instructions.

(c) Time for Giving Instructions. The court may instruct the jury before or after the arguments are completed, or at both times.

(d) Objections to Instructions. A party who objects to any portion of the instructions or to a failure to give a requested instruction must inform the court of the specific objection and the grounds for the objection before the jury retires to deliberate. An opportunity must be given to object out of the jury's hearing and, on request, out of the jury's presence. Failure to object in accordance with this rule precludes appellate review, except as permitted under Rule 52(b).

553.

> Because the court failed to clearly inform counsel of its ruling on his requests, counsel's closing argument was based upon a theory of defense which the court rejected, or at least ignored, in its subsequent instructions. We cannot say that this did not impair the effectiveness of counsel's argument and hence of appellant's defense.
>
> . . .
>
> The government asserts that the requested instructions were faulty. But that, if true, is of course irrelevant. It was the court's failure to advise counsel of its ruling prior to closing argument, not the soundness of that ruling, which violated Rule 30 and prejudicially affected counsel's summation.

Wright v. United States, 339 F.2d 578, 580 (9th Cir.1964) (conviction reversed).

554. "It is of course fundamental that as a general rule the failure to object to an instruction during a criminal prosecution on the ground urged on appeal, forecloses the party from raising the question before the reviewing court. . . . The manifest purpose of . . . [Rule 30] is to avoid whenever possible the necessity of a time-consuming new trial by providing the trial judge with an opportunity to correct any mistakes in the charge." United States v. Provenzano, 334 F.2d 678, 690 (3d Cir.1964). "The very purpose of Rule 30 is to require defendant to make timely objection or forfeit all right to later complain." United States v. Jones, 340 F.2d 599, 601 (4th Cir.1965).

Failure to object to errors in the instructions will not, however, bar reversal under Rule 52(b), p. 1169 below, if there has been "plain error" which must be corrected to avoid the possibility of a "miscarriage of justice." Cross v. United States, 347 F.2d 327, 329–30 (8th Cir.1965). See generally Godfrey v. United States, 353 F.2d 456, 458 (D.C.Cir.1965); United States v. Summerour, 279 F.Supp. 407 (E.D.Mich.1968).

United States v. Stephens

486 F.2d 915 (9th Cir.1973)

■ EUGENE A. WRIGHT, CIRCUIT JUDGE.

Stephens appeals from his conviction after a jury trial for robbery of a national bank [18 U.S.C. § 2113(a) and (d)]. He contends that the trial judge's comments to the jury denied him a fair trial. . . . [W]e reverse.

At the close of Stephens' trial in the district court, the judge said:

> Now my comment. If he went out there and looked at that bank with the idea of whether or not to rob it, he certainly had no compunction about whether or not he should rob it, because that is what he was out there for. So if he had no compunction about whether or not he should rob it, I would conclude from what I have heard here that he must have, or that he did rob it. He certainly went out there to look at it for that purpose, he said so himself. That is the way I would calculate what transpired here, putting that together with the rest of the testimony.
>
> Now you are the sole and exclusive judges of the facts. You make the determination as to what the facts are. You are not bound to follow anything I say at all, you can totally disregard anything I say, but I am entitled to express my opinion, and you can differ, and totally disregard it, because as I will tell you again, you are the sole and exclusive judges of the facts. But anyone who goes out and looks a bank over for the purpose of robbing it, and then admits that he robs it and then denies that he robbed it, I would conclude that he actually did rob it.
>
> All right, now again you being the sole and exclusive judges of the fact, it is up to you to make that determination.

. . .

. . . [T]his is not that exceptional case where the evidence against defendant is so overwhelming that his guilt is virtually undisputed.

At the time of the bank robbery, defendant was an escapee from the Washington State Penitentiary. There was evidence that he was involved in other criminal activity near the time and place of the robbery. The evidence of his involvement in this bank robbery, however, was far from overwhelming.

Perhaps the strongest evidence against defendant was his confession of the robbery to an FBI agent, a confession which he later repudiated. In addition, a bank employee recognized defendant as one who had been in the bank about the time of the robbery. His description of the clothing worn by defendant matched the description by one of the tellers of the clothing worn by the robber. However, neither the teller who was robbed, nor the one at the adjoining wicket, could identify defendant as the robber. Moreover, neither the handwriting on the demand note nor the fingerprints on the note were those of the defendant.

In light of the absence of overwhelming evidence of guilt, the judge's comments to the jury may well have tipped the scales against defendant, denying him the fair trial to which he was entitled. The instructions to the jurors advising them that they were not bound by his opinion were not sufficient in this case to cure the error.

It is well settled that a judge presiding at a trial in federal court may make comments on the evidence. He must carefully avoid prejudging the defendant, however, concentrating instead on making a fair effort to clear unanswered issues and point out inconsistencies. . . . Judicial comments must be aimed at aiding the jury's fact finding duties, rather than usurping them.

We note that defense counsel took no exception to the instructions given here. A timely instruction could have come only after the instructions and admonitions to the jury. Since it could not have resulted in an additional, curative instruction, it would have served no useful purpose. The absence of such an exception does not foreclose our consideration of the instructions given. . . .

. . .

555.

There can be no doubt that a federal judge in a criminal case is more than a mere moderator and may assist the jury in arriving at a just conclusion by explaining and commenting upon the evidence and by expressing his opinion upon the facts, provided he clearly states to the jury that all matters of fact are submitted to their determination. . . . However, since a trial judge's influence upon a jury is necessarily of such great magnitude, a trial judge should exercise care and discretion in expressing an opinion so as not to mislead or, in effect, to destroy the jury's right as the sole arbiters of all fact questions. . . .

A survey of cases indicates that reviewing courts are hesitant to reverse a judgment due to an allegedly unfair comment within the charge to the jury unless the trial judge clearly became argumentative and assumed the role of an advocate.

Franano v. United States, 310 F.2d 533, 537 (8th Cir.1962).

A judge may not direct a verdict of guilt. United Brotherhood of Carpenters & Joiners v. United States, 330 U.S. 395, 408 (1947). In an appropriate case, may a judge instruct the jury that an element of the crime with which the defendant is charged has been established as a matter of law?

"[I]n the criminal prosecution of one charged with the commission of a felony, the defendant has an absolute right to a jury determination upon all essential elements of the offense. This right, emanating from the criminal defendant's constitutional right to trial by jury, is neither depleted nor diminished by what otherwise might be considered the conclusive or compelling nature of the evidence against him. This right is personal to the defendant, and, like his right to a jury trial, is one which he, and he alone, may waive; furthermore, in a situation wherein an understandingly tendered waiver is not forthcoming from the defendant, under no circumstances may the trial court usurp this right by ruling as a matter of law on an essential element of the crime charged." United States v. England, 347 F.2d 425, 430 (7th Cir.1965). But see Guy v. United States, 336 F.2d 595, 597 (4th Cir.1964): "There can be no 'issues of fact' where there is no controversy as to the facts. And there can be no issue as to a fact where credible testimony with respect to it is neither denied or impeached."

556. Reasonable doubt. "[W]e explicitly hold that the Due Process Clause protects the accused against conviction except upon proof beyond a reasonable doubt of every fact necessary to constitute the crime with which he is charged." In re Winship, 397 U.S. 358, 364 (1970).

> The reasonable-doubt standard plays a vital role in the American scheme of criminal procedure. It is a prime instrument for reducing the risk of convictions resting on factual error. The standard provides concrete substance for the presumption of innocence—that bedrock "axiomatic and elementary" principle whose "enforcement lies at the foundation of the administration of our criminal law." Coffin v. United States, [156 U.S. 432 (1895)], at 453. . . .
>
> The requirement of proof beyond a reasonable doubt has this vital role in our criminal procedure for cogent reasons. The accused during a criminal prosecution has at stake interests of immense importance, both because of the possibility that he may lose his liberty upon conviction and because of the certainty that he would be stigmatized by the conviction. Accordingly, a society that values the good name and freedom of every individual should not condemn a man for commission of a crime when there is reasonable doubt about his guilt. As we said in Speiser v. Randall, [357 U.S. 513 (1958)] at 525–26: "There is always in litigation a margin of error, representing error in factfinding, which both parties must take into account. Where one party has at stake an interest of transcending value—as a criminal defendant his liberty—this margin of error is reduced as to him by the process of placing on the other party the burden of . . . persuading the factfinder at the conclusion of the trial of his guilt beyond a reasonable doubt. Due process commands that no man shall lose his liberty unless the Government has borne the burden of . . . convincing the factfinder of his guilt." To this end, the reasonable-doubt standard is indispensable, for it "impresses on the trier of fact the necessity of reaching a

> subjective state of certitude of the facts in issue." Dorsen & Rezneck, "In re Gault and the Future of Juvenile Law," 1 Family Law Quarterly, No. 4, pp. 1, 26 (1967).
>
> Moreover, use of the reasonable-doubt standard is indispensable to command the respect and confidence of the community in applications of the criminal law. It is critical that the moral force of the criminal law not be diluted by a standard of proof that leaves people in doubt whether innocent men are being condemned. It is also important in our free society that every individual going about his ordinary affairs have confidence that his government cannot adjudge him guilty of a criminal offense without convincing a proper factfinder of his guilt with utmost certainty.

397 U.S. at 363–64.

In Victor v. Nebraska, 511 U.S. 1 (1994), the Court considered two capital cases in which the trial judge had explained the standard of reasonable doubt to the jury in terms that, the defendants said, improperly lessened the state's burden of proof. In one case, the judge had referred to proof depending on "moral evidence," "an abiding conviction, to a moral certainty, of the truth of the charge," and "not a mere possible doubt." In the other, the judge had referred to "the strong probabilities of the case" and "a moral certainty," "an actual and substantial doubt." In both cases, the Court concluded that in the context of the instructions as a whole, the questioned phrases were not error. See Sullivan v. Louisiana, 508 U.S. 275 (1993) (deficient reasonable-doubt instruction cannot be harmless error). See generally Smith v. United States, 709 A.2d 78 (D.C.App.1998) (en banc), approving a specific jury instruction about reasonable doubt.

After examining the historical development of the law of homicide and concluding that "the presence or absence of the heat of passion on sudden provocation . . . has been, almost from the inception of the common law of homicide, the single most important factor in determining the degree of culpability attaching to an unlawful homicide," the Court held that "the Due Process Clause requires the prosecution to prove beyond a reasonable doubt the absence of the heat of passion on sudden provocation when the issue is properly presented in a homicide case." Mullaney v. Wilbur, 421 U.S. 684, 696, 704 (1975). The Court rejected the contention that the rule of *Winship*, above, did not apply because under Maine law murder and manslaughter were not distinct offenses but only "punishment categories of the single offence of felonious homicide," id. at 689; the importance of the distinction to the defendant, the Court said, was no less.

Mullaney v. Wilbur notwithstanding, in Patterson v. New York, 432 U.S. 197 (1977) (5–3), the Court upheld a state statute requiring the defendant to prove by a preponderance of the evidence the affirmative defense of acting under extreme emotional distress in order to reduce the crime of second-degree murder to manslaughter. The Court said that the Due Process Clause does not require a State to "disprove beyond reasonable doubt every fact constituting any and all affirmative defenses related to the culpability of the accused." Id. at 210. The Court noted in particular that it remained constitutional for a State to require a defendant to prove an insanity defense by a preponderance of the evidence. Id. at 206–207. See also the companion case, Hankerson v. North Carolina, 432 U.S. 233 (1977) (self-defense).

The Court relied heavily on *Patterson* in McMillan v. Pennsylvania, 477 U.S. 79 (1986) (5–4), to uphold a state statute providing that a person convicted of specified crimes is subject to a mandatory minimum sentence of five years' imprisonment, if the sentencing judge finds by a preponderance of the evidence that the person "visibly possessed a firearm" during commission of the offense. The statute provided that possession of a firearm "shall not be an element of the crime." The Court observed that the sentence required by the statute was within the maximum provided for the offenses and that it served only to reduce the judge's sentencing discretion. It said that although there are "constitutional limits," "in determining what facts must be proved beyond a reasonable doubt the state legislature's definition of the elements of the offense is usually dispositive." Id. at 85.

Discussing *Mullaney*, *Patterson*, and *McMillan*, the Court held that a statutory provision authorizing a more severe sentence for an alien who illegally returns to the United States if he was previously deported following conviction of an aggravated felony is a penalty provision and does not define a distinct offense. Almendarez-Torres v. United States, 523 U.S. 224 (1998) (5–4).

Almendarez-Torres is distinguished in Jones v. United States, 526 U.S. 227 (1999) (5–4). It is questioned but not overruled in Apprendi v. New Jersey, 530 U.S. 466 (2000) (7–2), in which the Court applied to the States under the Due Process Clause the same rule that it indicated applied to the Federal Government in *Jones*: "Other than the fact of a prior conviction, any fact that increases the penalty for a crime beyond the prescribed statutory maximum must be submitted to a jury, and proved beyond a reasonable doubt." 530 U.S. at 490.

In Harris v. United States, 536 U.S. 545 (2002) (5–4), the Court considered whether *Apprendi* is consistent with its earlier decision in McMillan v. Pennsylvania. Four Justices concluded that the two cases are consistent. *Apprendi* holds that a fact that extends the maximum sentence that may be imposed must be found by a jury. *McMillan*, on the other hand, holds that a fact that increases the minimum sentence, which remains within the maximum sentence, need not be found by a jury. "Read together, *McMillan* and *Apprendi* mean that those facts setting the outer limits of a sentence, and of the judicial power to impose it, are the elements of the crime for the purposes of the constitutional analysis. Within the range authorized by the jury's verdict, however, the political system may channel judicial discretion—and rely upon judicial expertise—by requiring defendants to serve minimum terms after judges make certain factual findings." 536 U.S. at 567. A fifth Justice (Justice Breyer), expressing his disapproval of *Apprendi* generally and its application to mandatory minimum sentences in particular, concurred.

Again relying on *Patterson*, the Court upheld an Ohio statutory provision requiring the defendant to prove an affirmative defense by a preponderance of the evidence, as it was applied to the defense of self-defense in a prosecution for aggravated murder. The latter crime was defined as " 'purposely, and with prior calculation and design caus[ing] the death of another.' " Martin v. Ohio, 480 U.S. 228 (1987) (5–4). The Court noted that the jury was instructed to consider all the evidence, including evidence bearing on self-defense, when it determined whether the prosecution had met its burden of proving the elements of the crime beyond a reasonable doubt.

A presumption that relieves the prosecution of the burden of proving an element of the offense beyond a reasonable doubt is invalid. Sandstrom v. Montana, 442 U.S. 510 (1979). In *Sandstrom*, the trial judge had instructed the jury in a prosecution for deliberate homicide that a person is presumed to intend the ordinary consequences of his voluntary acts. *Sandstrom* has been applied in a number of cases: Carella v. California, 491 U.S. 263 (1989) (presumption of embezzlement or theft; *Sandstrom* applied); Francis v. Franklin, 471 U.S. 307 (1985) (5–4) (presumption of intent to kill; *Sandstrom* applied); Connecticut v. Johnson, 460 U.S. 73 (1983) (5–4) (presumption about intent). In Rose v. Clark, 478 U.S. 570 (1986) (6–3), the Court held that a violation of *Sandstrom* may be harmless error.

An instruction that witnesses are presumed to speak the truth,[42] in a trial in which the defendant did not testify or call any defense witnesses, was not, when accompanied by full instructions on the government's burden of proof and the presumption of innocence, in conflict with *Winship* and did not deny the defendant due process of law. Cupp v. Naughten, 414 U.S. 141 (1973) (6–3). Such an instruction has, however, been very widely disapproved. See id. at 144 & n.4. An "accomplice instruction" to the effect that the jury should credit the testimony of an accomplice testifying for the defendant only if it believed the testimony beyond a reasonable doubt was impermissible, both because it restricted the defendant's right to present that testimony and because it lowered the government's burden of proof. Cool v. United States, 409 U.S. 100 (1972).

In Taylor v. Kentucky, 436 U.S. 478 (1978) (7–2), the Court held that in the circumstances of the case, the defendant was entitled, on request, to an instruction on the presumption of innocence as well as the requirement of proof beyond a reasonable doubt. In a subsequent case, Kentucky v. Whorton, 441 U.S. 786 (1979) (6–3), the Court said that *Taylor* did not hold that the failure to give a requested instruction on the presumption of innocence is by itself a violation of the Constitution. Such a failure has to be evaluated in light of all the circumstances to determine whether the defendant had a fair trial.

42. "Every witness is presumed to speak the truth. This presumption may be overcome by the manner in which the witness testifies, by the nature of his or her testimony, by evidence affecting his or her character, interest, or motives, by contradictory evidence or by a presumption." 414 U.S. at 142.

It has been held that an instruction that the defendant has the burden of proving an alibi defense violates due process because it undercuts the government's burden of proving guilt beyond a reasonable doubt. "Evidence of alibi should come into a case like any other evidence and must be submitted to the jury for consideration of whether the evidence as a whole on the issue of presence proves the defendant's guilt beyond a reasonable doubt." Smith v. Smith, 454 F.2d 572, 578 (5th Cir.1971). Accord Stump v. Bennett, 398 F.2d 111 (8th Cir.1968). See Johnson v. Bennett, 393 U.S. 253 (1968).

In Jackson v. Virginia, 443 U.S. 307 (1979), the Court relied on *Winship* for its holding that when a state conviction is attacked by habeas corpus in federal court on the ground of insufficiency of evidence, the court must consider "whether there was sufficient evidence to justify a rational trier of the facts to find guilt beyond a reasonable doubt," id. at 313. The previous standard had been that the conviction should be reversed only if there was "no evidence" to support the conviction. The Court emphasized that the relevant question is whether, viewing the evidence in the light most favorable to the prosecution, "*any* rational trier of fact," id. at 319, could believe the defendant guilty beyond a reasonable doubt, not whether the federal court itself was convinced of his guilt beyond a reasonable doubt. See Moore v. Duckworth, 443 U.S. 713 (1979).

The Constitution does not require that the admissibility of evidence that is challenged on constitutional grounds be established beyond a reasonable doubt. In Lego v. Twomey, 404 U.S. 477 (1972) (4–3), the Court held that it was constitutionally sufficient if the voluntariness of a confession was proved "at least by a preponderance of the evidence." Id. at 489. As for *Winship*, the Court said: "Since the purpose that a voluntariness hearing is designed to serve has nothing whatever to do with improving the reliability of jury verdicts, we cannot accept the charge that judging the admissibility of a confession by a preponderance of the evidence undermines the mandate of In re Winship. . . . Our decision in *Winship* was not concerned with standards for determining the admissibility of evidence or with the prosecution's burden of proof at a suppression hearing when evidence is challenged on constitutional grounds. *Winship* went no further than to confirm the fundamental right that protects 'the accused against conviction except upon proof beyond a reasonable doubt of every fact necessary to constitute the crime with which he is charged.' . . . A high standard of proof is necessary, we said, to ensure against unjust convictions by giving substance to the presumption of innocence. . . . A guilty verdict is not rendered less reliable or less consonant with *Winship* simply because the admissibility of a confession is determined by a less stringent standard. Petitioner does not maintain that either his confession or its voluntariness is an element of the crime with which he was charged. He does not challenge the constitutionality of the standard by which the jury was instructed to decide his guilt or innocence; nor does he question the sufficiency of the evidence that reached the jury to satisfy the proper standard of proof. Petitioner's rights under *Winship* have not been violated." Id. at 486–87.

557. Although a defendant may be required to prove by a preponderance of the evidence that he is not competent to stand trial, Medina v. California, 505 U.S. 437 (1992) (7–2), it is a violation of due process to impose a higher burden of proof ("clear and convincing evidence") that would permit a defendant to be tried "even though it is more likely than not that he is incompetent." Cooper v. Oklahoma, 517 U.S. 348, 350 (1996).

558. Applying the general principle that when a jury has no sentencing function it should be instructed to reach its verdict without regard to what sentence might be imposed if the defendant were found guilty, the Court held that a jury in a federal criminal case ordinarily is not required to be and should not be instructed that if the defendant were found not guilty by reason of insanity he would be involuntarily civilly committed. Shannon v. United States, 512 U.S. 573 (1994) (7–2).

559. Lesser included offense. Fed.R.Crim.P. 31(c):

> (c) Lesser Offense or Attempt. A defendant may be found guilty of any of the following:
>
> (1) an offense necessarily included in the offense charged;
>
> (2) an attempt to commit the offense charged; or
>
> (3) an attempt to commit an offense necessarily included in the offense charged, if the attempt is an offense in its own right.

An offense is "necessarily included" in another only if "the elements of the lesser offense are a subset of the elements of the charged offense." Schmuck v. United States, 489 U.S. 705, 716 (1989). "Where the lesser offense requires an element not required for the greater offense, no instruction is to be given under Rule 31(c)." Id. See Carter v. United States, 530 U.S. 255 (2000) (5–4) (*Schmuck* applied; larceny-like offense not a lesser included offense of robbery-like offense, under 18 U.S.C. § 2113).

"[A] lesser-offense charge is not proper where, on the evidence presented, the factual issues to be resolved by the jury are the same as to both the lesser and greater offenses. . . . In other words, the lesser offense must be included within but not, on the facts of the case, be completely encompassed by the greater. A lesser-included offense instruction is only proper where the charged greater offense requires the jury to find a disputed factual element which is not required for conviction of the lesser-included offense." Sansone v. United States, 380 U.S. 343, 349–50 (1965). In United States v. Harary, 457 F.2d 471 (2d Cir.1972), the court concluded that even if the lesser and greater offenses were both charged in the indictment, if there was no disputed factual element to distinguish them, the defendant has a right not to have the jury instructed on both.

If a lesser-included offense instruction is appropriate, the defendant is entitled to have it given. Berra v. United States, 351 U.S. 131 (1956). In Nichols v. Gagnon, 710 F.2d 1267 (7th Cir.1983), the court held that a state court's erroneous failure to give an instruction on a lesser included offense does not require a federal court to set aside the conviction unless there was a "fundamental miscarriage of justice." The court conjectured about the likely impact of a lesser included offense instruction on the jury's deliberations about the more serious offense. See also Beck v. Alabama, 447 U.S. 625 (1980) (7–2), p. 1154 below.

In United States v. Tsanas, 572 F.2d 340 (2d Cir.1978), the court discussed the instructions to be given the jury about its consideration of a lesser offense. The court held that the defendant should have his choice whether the jury should be instructed: (1) that it may consider the lesser offense only after reaching a unanimous verdict of not guilty on the greater, or (2) that it may consider the lesser offense if it cannot agree about the greater. If the defendant expresses no preference, the court can give either instruction.

560. The "*Allen* charge." In Commonwealth v. Tuey, 62 Mass. (8 Cush.) 1, 2–3 (1851), after the jury had deliberated for several hours without reaching agreement, the court instructed them in substance:

> The only mode, provided by our constitution and laws for deciding questions of fact in criminal cases, is by the verdict of a jury. In a large proportion of cases, and perhaps, strictly speaking, in all cases, absolute certainty cannot be attained or expected. Although the verdict to which a juror agrees must of course be his own verdict, the result of his own convictions, and not a mere acquiescence in the conclusion of his fellows, yet, in order to bring twelve minds to a unanimous result, you must examine the questions submitted to you with candor, and with a proper regard and deference to the opinions of each other. You should consider that the case must at some time be decided; that you are selected in the same manner, and from the same source, from which any future jury must be; and there is no reason to suppose that the case will ever be submitted to twelve men more intelligent, more impartial, or more competent to decide it, or that more or clearer evidence will be produced on the one side or the other. And with this view, it is your duty to decide the case, if you can conscientiously do so. In order to make a decision more practicable, the law imposes the burden of proof on one party or the other, in all cases. In the present case, the burden of proof is upon the commonwealth to establish every part of it, beyond a reasonable doubt; and if, in any part of it, you are left in doubt, the defendant is entitled to the benefit of the doubt, and must be acquitted. But, in conferring together, you ought to pay proper respect to each other's opinions, and listen, with a disposition to be convinced, to each other's arguments. And, on the one hand, if much the larger number of your panel are for a conviction, a dissenting juror should consider whether a doubt in his own mind is a reasonable one, which makes no impression upon the minds of so many men, equally honest, equally intelligent with himself, and who have heard the same evidence, with the same attention, with an equal desire to arrive at the truth, and under the sanction of the same oath. And, on the other hand, if a majority are for acquittal, the minority ought seriously to ask themselves, whether they may not reasonably, and ought not to doubt the correctness of a judgment, which is not concurred in by most of those with whom they are associated; and distrust the weight or sufficiency of that evidence which fails to carry conviction to the minds of their fellows.

The jury returned a verdict of guilty. The conviction was affirmed.

In Allen v. United States, 164 U.S. 492, 501–502 (1896), the Court upheld the giving of a similar charge, saying: "While, undoubtedly, the verdict of the jury should represent the opinion of each individual juror, it by no means follows that opinions may not be changed by conference in the jury-room. The very object of the jury system is to secure unanimity by a comparison of views, and by arguments among the jurors themselves. It certainly cannot be the law that each juror should not listen with deference to the arguments and with a distrust of his own judgment, if he finds a large majority of the jury taking a different view of the case from what he does himself. It cannot be that each juror should go to the jury-room with a blind determination that the verdict shall represent his opinion of the case at that moment; or, that he should close his ears to the arguments of men who are equally honest and intelligent as himself."

The so-called "*Allen* charge" has been used regularly since; but it has been criticized with increasing frequency and intensity and has been rejected altogether by some courts. See, e.g., Smalls v. Batista, 191 F.3d 272 (2d Cir.1999) (improper *Allen* charge); United States v. Paniagua-Ramos, 135 F.3d 193 (1st Cir.1998) (same); Potter v. United States, 691 F.2d 1275 (8th Cir.1982) (same). Cases are collected and the *Allen* charge is discussed generally in United States v. Seawell, 550 F.2d 1159 (9th Cir.1977), in which the court concluded that the coercive impact of the charge is such that it should never be repeated a second time in response to a report of further deadlock, unless the jury requests its repetition. But see United States v. Robinson, 560 F.2d 507 (2d Cir.1977) (second *Allen*-type charge is not error per se). Even when the *Allen* charge itself is rejected, supplemental instructions to a jury which is unable to reach a verdict are allowed; the rejected language is that which encourages a dissenting juror to change his mind.

In connection with the giving of *Allen*-type instructions, trial judges have sometimes asked the jury foreman the numerical division among the jurors, a practice that is forbidden in the federal courts. Brasfield v. United States, 272 U.S. 448 (1926). The issue is discussed in Ellis v. Reed, 596 F.2d 1195 (4th Cir.1979).

An *Allen*-type charge accompanied by a poll of the jurors whether further deliberation would be helpful, during the sentencing phase of a capital case, was found not to be coercive and not to deny the defendant's constitutional rights, in Lowenfield v. Phelps, 484 U.S. 231 (1988) (6–3).

Verdict

FEDERAL RULES OF CRIMINAL PROCEDURE

Rule 31

JURY VERDICT

(a) Return. The jury must return its verdict to a judge in open court. The verdict must be unanimous.

(b) Partial Verdicts, Mistrial, and Retrial.

(1) *Multiple Defendants.* If there are multiple defendants, the jury may return a verdict at any time during its deliberations as to any defendant about whom it has agreed.

(2) *Multiple Counts.* If the jury cannot agree on all counts as to any defendant, the jury may return a verdict on those counts on which it has agreed.

(3) *Mistrial and Retrial.* If the jury cannot agree on a verdict on one or more counts, the court may declare a mistrial on those counts. The government may retry any defendant on any count on which the jury could not agree.

(c) Lesser Offense or Attempt. A defendant may be found guilty of any of the following:

(1) an offense necessarily included in the offense charged;

(2) an attempt to commit the offense charged; or

(3) an attempt to commit an offense necessarily included in the offense charged, if the attempt is an offense in its own right.

(d) Jury Poll. After a verdict is returned but before the jury is discharged, the court must on a party's request, or may on its own, poll the jurors individually. If the poll reveals a lack of unanimity, the court may direct the jury to deliberate further or may declare a mistrial and discharge the jury.

---

561. The (apocryphal) request of the foreman of the jury for 11 dinners and a bale of hay is well known. How long and in what circumstances can a jury be required to continue its deliberations after it has become deadlocked? "It is well established that the determination of how long a disagreeing jury will be kept together and required to continue their deliberation is a matter of sound judicial discretion which, in the absence of abuse, will not be disturbed." People v. Presley, 254 N.Y.S.2d 400 (App.Div. 1964), aff'd, 209 N.E.2d 729 (N.Y.1965).

In United States v. Symington, 195 F.3d 1080 (9th Cir.1999), on the eighth day of deliberations, the jury sent a note to the judge complaining about the conduct of a juror. After discussing the matter with counsel and questioning each of the jurors, the judge dismissed the juror who, he concluded, was " 'either unwilling or unable to deliberate with her colleagues.' " The jury subsequently convicted the defendant pursuant to Rule 23(b), which allows a judge to dismiss a juror for "just cause." Concluding that there was a "reasonable possibility" that the impetus for the juror's dismissal was her views on the merits, the court reversed the conviction.

In two cases, the Supreme Court of California discussed at length when a juror may be discharged after deliberations have begun. In People v. Cleveland, 21 P.3d 1225 (Cal.2001), the court held that the juror, who expressed the belief that the evidence was insufficient to prove the charges against the defendant, should not have been discharged. In People v. Williams, 21 P.3d 1209 (Cal.2001), the court held that the juror, who stated that he was unable to follow the judge's instructions about the law, was properly discharged.

AO156 (Rev. 5/85) Verdict

UNITED STATES DISTRICT COURT

_______________ DISTRICT OF _______________

UNITED STATES OF AMERICA
V.

VERDICT

Case Number:

WE, THE JURY, FIND:

____
FOREPERSON'S SIGNATURE

____
DATE

562. It is generally held that the right to a unanimous verdict provided by Rule 31(a) cannot be waived. United States v. Smedes, 760 F.2d 109, 113 (6th Cir.1985). When the jury has not reached a unanimous verdict and the defendant agrees to accept the verdict of 11 jurors, courts have had to distinguish between the unanimous verdict of 11 jurors and the non-unanimous (11–1) verdict of 12 jurors. See *Smedes*, and cases cited.

Distinguishing cases in other circuits, the Court of Appeals for the Eleventh Circuit has held that a defendant can waive the right to a unanimous jury. Such waiver should be allowed, the court said, if the following conditions are met: "(1) the waiver should be initiated by the defendant, not the judge or prosecutor; (2) the jury must have had a reasonable time to deliberate and should have told the court only that it could not reach a decision, but not how it stood numerically; (3) the judge should carefully explain to the defendant the right to a unanimous verdict and the consequences of a waiver of that right; and (4) the judge should question the defendant directly to determine whether the waiver is being made knowingly and voluntarily." Sanchez v. United States, 782 F.2d 928, 934 (11th Cir.1986).

563. In Griffin v. United States, 502 U.S. 46 (1991), the Court upheld the validity of a general verdict of guilty even though the case was submitted to the jury on alternative theories, with respect to one of which there was insufficient evidence to sustain a guilty verdict. The defendant had been prosecuted, along with other defendants, for conspiracy; the evidence implicated her in one alleged conspiratorial objective but not the other. The Court distinguished cases in which a guilty verdict is returned following submission to the jury of theories one of which is constitutionally defective or legally inadequate. The Court also noted that when there is insufficient evidence to sustain one of several theories of the prosecution's case, the preferable practice is for the court to give an instruction removing the theory from the jury's consideration.

The defendant in Schad v. Arizona, 501 U.S. 624 (1991) (5–4), was convicted of first-degree murder on instructions that permitted the jury to convict if it was unanimous for guilt either on a theory of "willfull, deliberate, or premeditated" murder or on a theory of felony murder, without requiring unanimity on one theory or the other. The Court said that a general verdict that did not specify one of several alleged means of committing a crime was permissible. The problem presented, then, was to describe "the point at which differences between means become so important that they may not reasonably be viewed as alternatives to a common end, but must be treated as differentiating what the Constitution requires to be treated as separate offenses." Id. at 633. In order to decide whether a verdict based on alternative theories satisfies the due process requirement of fundamental fairness, a court should "look both to history and wide practice as guides to fundamental values, as well as to narrower analytical methods of testing the moral and practical equivalence" of the theories in question. The Court said also that there is a "threshold presumption of legislative competence" to determine whether there are different but equivalent ways to satisfy an element of a crime. Id. at 637–38. Noting that historically and generally in current law, deliberate murder and felony murder have both been regarded as sufficient to establish the *mens rea* requirement of first-degree murder, the Court affirmed the conviction.

See Richardson v. United States, 526 U.S. 813 (1999) (6–3), involving a *Schad* problem in the application of 21 U.S.C. § 848(a), which requires proof that the defendant committed a "continuing series of violations" of the drug laws. The Court held that the jury must agree not only that the defendant committed a continuing series but also that he committed each of the individual violations that make up the series.

Remmer v. United States

347 U.S. 227, 74 S.Ct. 450, 98 L.Ed. 654 (1954)

■ MR. JUSTICE MINTON delivered the opinion of the Court.

The petitioner was convicted by a jury on several counts charging willful evasion of the payment of federal income taxes. A matter admitted by the Government to have been handled by the trial court in a manner that may have been prejudicial to the petitioner, and therefore confessed as error, is presented at the threshold and must be disposed of first.

After the jury had returned its verdict, the petitioner learned for the first time that during the trial a person unnamed had communicated with a certain juror, who afterwards became the jury foreman, and remarked to him that he could profit by bringing in a verdict favorable to the petitioner. The juror reported the incident to the judge, who informed the prosecuting attorneys and advised with them. As a result, the Federal Bureau of Investigation was requested to make an investigation and report, which was accordingly done. The F.B.I. report was considered by the judge and prosecutors alone, and they apparently concluded that the statement to the juror was made in jest, and nothing further was done or said about the matter. Neither the judge nor the prosecutors informed the petitioner of the incident, and he and his counsel first learned of the matter by reading of it in the newspapers after the verdict.

The above-stated facts were alleged in a motion for a new trial, together with an allegation that the petitioner was substantially prejudiced, thereby depriving him of a fair trial, and a request for a hearing to determine the circumstances surrounding the incident and its effect on the jury. A supporting affidavit of the petitioner's attorneys recited the alleged occurrences and stated that if they had known of the incident they would have moved for a mistrial and requested that the juror in question be replaced by an alternate juror. Two newspaper articles reporting the incident were attached to the affidavit. The Government did not file answering affidavits. The District Court, without holding the requested hearing, denied the motion for a new trial. . . .

In a criminal case, any private communication, contact, or tampering, directly or indirectly, with a juror during a trial about the matter pending before the jury is, for obvious reasons, deemed presumptively prejudicial, if not made in pursuance of known rules of the court and the instructions and directions of the court made during the trial, with full knowledge of the parties. The presumption is not conclusive, but the burden rests heavily upon the Government to establish, after notice to and hearing of the defendant, that such contact with the juror was harmless to the defendant. . . .

We do not know from this record, nor does the petitioner know, what actually transpired, or whether the incidents that may have occurred were harmful or harmless. The sending of an F.B.I. agent in the midst of a trial to investigate a juror as to his conduct is bound to impress the juror and is very apt to do so unduly. A juror must feel free to exercise his functions without the F.B.I. or anyone else looking over his shoulder. The integrity of jury proceedings must not be jeopardized by unauthorized invasions. The trial court should not decide and take final action ex parte on information such as was received in this case, but should determine the circumstances, the impact thereof upon the juror, and whether or not it was prejudicial, in a hearing with all interested parties permitted to participate.

We therefore vacate the judgment of the Court of Appeals and remand the case to the District Court with directions to hold a hearing to determine whether the incident complained of was harmful to the petitioner, and if after hearing it is found to have been harmful, to grant a new trial. . . .

---

564. Relying on *Remmer*, the Court reversed a decision in a federal habeas corpus proceeding that a defendant's conviction should be vacated because one of the jurors was actively seeking a job as an investigator in the district attorney's office while the defendant's trial was in progress. The prosecutor was aware of the facts during the trial and withheld them from the judge and defense counsel until after the trial was complete. In a post-conviction proceeding in the state court, the trial judge had conducted a hearing and denied the motion to vacate the conviction. Such a hearing, the Court concluded, at which the judge found that the verdict had not been affected, was adequate to protect the defendant's rights. Smith v. Phillips, 455 U.S. 209 (1982) (6–3).

See Parker v. Gladden, 385 U.S. 363 (1966) (8–1) (bailiff in charge of jury expressed opinion that defendant was guilty to jurors; conviction reversed); Turner v. Louisiana, 379 U.S. 466 (1965) (8–1) (sequestered jury in constant association with deputy sheriffs, who were principal witnesses for prosecution; conviction reversed).

565. "[T]he testimony of jurors should not be received to show matters which essentially inhere in the verdict itself and necessarily depend upon the testimony of the jurors and can receive no corroboration." Hyde v. United States, 225 U.S. 347, 384 (1912). " '[O]n a motion for a new trial on the ground of bias on the part of one of the jurors, the evidence of jurors as to the motives and influences which affected their deliberations is inadmissible either to impeach or to support the verdict. But a juryman may testify to any facts bearing upon the question of the existence of any extraneous influence, although not as to how far that influence operated upon his mind. So a juryman may testify in denial or explanation of acts or declarations outside of the jury room, where evidence of such acts has been given as ground for a new trial.' " Mattox v. United States, 146 U.S. 140, 149 (1892) (quoting Woodward v. Leavitt, 107 Mass. 453 (1871)). "While this rule can be criticized as forbidding inquiry into the subject most truly pertinent, it represents a pragmatic judgment how best to attempt reconciliation of the irreconcilable. . . . Where an extraneous influence is shown, the court must apply an objective test, assessing for itself the likelihood that the influence would affect a typical juror." Miller v. United States, 403 F.2d 77, 83 n.11 (2d Cir.1968).

Following the defendant's conviction and before he was sentenced, defense counsel made a motion to examine trial jurors to determine whether any juror had consumed alcoholic beverages during the lunch breaks in the course of the trial. The motion was based on unsolicited information from one juror that some jurors had done so. There was also an indication that some jurors had ingested drugs during the trial. Relying on Federal Rule of Evidence 606(b), the Court held that alcohol or drug use was analogous to a juror's physical or mental condition and, as such, a matter "internal" to the jury's deliberations, not subject to inquiry after the verdict. Even if an inquiry might be proper if there were evidence of extreme abuse showing strong evidence of incompetence, the allegations in this case were far less than that. Tanner v. United States, 483 U.S. 107 (1987) (5–4). See United States v. Dioguardi, 492 F.2d 70 (2d Cir.1974) (juror's letter to defendant after trial raised doubt of her competence; conviction affirmed).

566.

> [W]e see no basis for doubting the authority of the trial judge to direct that any interrogation of jurors after a conviction shall be under his supervision. To determine how far such questioning shall be permitted and in what manner it shall be done requires a weighing of two conflicting desiderata. One is the protection of the defendant's right to a fair trial before "an impartial jury." The other is avoidance of the dangers presented by inquiries that go beyond objective facts: inhibition of jury-room deliberations, harassment of jurors, and increased incidence of jury tampering. . . .
>
> . . .
>
> Appellant's assertion that a defendant must be as free to interrogate jurors after a conviction as he is to interrogate prospective witnesses before trial does not require extended answer. Inquiry of jurors after a verdict seeks to impugn the validity of judicial action on the ground of misconduct of a member of the tribunal. The court has a vital interest in seeing that jurors are not harassed or placed in doubt about what their duty is and that false issues are not created. The argument that interviews by a private investigator involve less harassment than such methods as we have outlined is unconvincing. A juror so interviewed often does not know what he is supposed to do or supposed not to do. Moreover, except when the interview yields nothing, it is only the beginning. In any event such considerations go to the exercise of the power, not to its existence.

Miller v. United States, 403 F.2d 77, 81–82 (2d Cir.1968).

567. "All must recognize, of course, that a complete sanitizing of the jury room is impossible. We cannot expunge from jury deliberations the subjective opinions of jurors, their additudinal expositions, or their philosophies. These involve the very human elements that constitute one of the strengths of our jury system, and we cannot and should not excommunicate them from jury deliberations. Nevertheless, while the jury may leaven its deliberations with its wisdom and experience, in doing so it must not bring extra *facts* into the jury room. In every criminal case we must endeavor to see that jurors do not [consider] in the confines of the jury room . . . specific facts about the specific defendant then on trial. . . . To the greatest extent possible all factual [material] must pass through the judicial sieve, where the fundamental guarantees of procedural law protect the rights of those accused of crime." United States v. McKinney, 429 F.2d 1019, 1022–1023 (5th Cir.1970).

"[L]et it once be established that verdicts solemnly made and publicly returned into court can be attacked and set aside on the testimony of those who took part in their publication and all verdicts could be, and many would be, followed by an inquiry in the hope of discovering something which might invalidate the finding. Jurors would be harassed . . . in an effort to secure from them evidence of facts which might establish misconduct sufficient to set aside a verdict. If evidence thus secured could be thus used, the result would be to make what was intended to be a private deliberation, the constant subject of public investigation; to the destruction of all frankness and freedom of discussion and conference." McDonald v. Pless, 238 U.S. 264, 267–68 (1915).

See United States ex rel. Owen v. McMann, 435 F.2d 813 (2d Cir.1970), mediating between these policies.

568. When a jury is polled pursuant to Rule 31(d), each juror is required to state whether the verdict announced by the foreman is in fact his or her verdict. The rule provides that if there is not unanimous concurrence, the judge may declare a mistrial or the jury may be sent back to deliberate further. If a juror indicates doubt about a guilty verdict during a poll, the judge must be careful not to influence the juror to vote for the announced verdict in an effort to resolve any confusion that the juror may have. His best course, unless the juror's doubt is manifestly not about the substance of the verdict, is to send the jury back to deliberate further, without comment. See, e.g., United States v. Sexton, 456 F.2d 961 (5th Cir.1972), in which a variety of cases are described.

569. Inconsistent verdicts. In Dunn v. United States, 284 U.S. 390 (1932), the Court held that inconsistent verdicts of guilty and not guilty on different counts of a single indictment are permissible. Writing for the Court, Justice Holmes relied mistakenly on the proposition that where a defendant is charged with different crimes in separate indictments and tried on each indictment separately, "the same evidence being offered in support of each, an acquittal on one could not be pleaded as *res judicata* of the other," id. at 393. The rule is to the contrary. "*[R]es judicata* may be a defense in a second prosecution. That doctrine applies to criminal as well as civil proceedings . . . and operates to conclude those matters in issue which the verdict determined though the offenses be different." Sealfon v. United States, 332 U.S. 575, 578 (1948).

Holmes's error notwithstanding, *Dunn* was reaffirmed and applied in United States v. Powell, 469 U.S. 57 (1984):

> We believe that the *Dunn* rule rests on a sound rationale that is independent of its theories of res judicata, and that it therefore survives an attack based upon its presently erroneous reliance on such theories. As the *Dunn* Court noted, where truly inconsistent verdicts have been reached, "[t]he most that can be said . . . is that the verdict shows that either in the acquittal or the conviction the jury did not speak their real conclusions, but that does not show that they were not convinced of the defendant's guilt." *Dunn*, [284 U.S.], at 393. The rule that the defendant may not upset such a verdict embodies a prudent acknowledgement of a number of factors. First, as the above quote suggests, inconsistent verdicts—even verdicts that acquit on a predicate offense while convicting on the compound offense—should not necessarily be interpreted as a windfall to the Government at the defendant's expense. It is equally possible that the jury, convinced of guilt, properly reached its conclusion on the compound offense, and then through mistake, compromise, or lenity, arrived at an inconsistent conclusion on the lesser offense. But in such situations the Government has no recourse if it wishes to correct the jury's error; the Government is precluded from appealing or otherwise upsetting such an acquittal by the Constitution's Double Jeopardy Clause. . . .
>
> Inconsistent verdicts therefore present a situation where "error," in the sense that the jury has not followed the court's instructions, most certainly has occurred, but it is unclear whose ox has been gored. Given this uncertainty, and the fact that the Government is precluded from challenging the acquittal, it is hardly satisfactory to allow the defendant to receive a new trial on the conviction as a matter of course. . . . [N]othing in the Constitution would require such a protection, and we therefore address the problem only under our supervisory powers over the federal criminal process. For us, the possibility that the inconsistent verdicts may favor the criminal defendant as well as the Government militates against review of such convictions at the defendant's behest. This possibility is a premise of *Dunn*'s alternative rationale—that such inconsistencies often are a product of jury lenity. Thus, *Dunn* has been explained by both courts and commentators as a recognition of the jury's historic function, in criminal trials, as a check against arbitrary or oppressive exercises of power by the Executive Branch. . . .
>
> The burden of the exercise of lenity falls only on the Government, and it has been suggested that such an alternative should be available for the difficult cases where the jury wishes to avoid an all-or-nothing verdict. . . . Such an act is, as the *Dunn* Court recognized, an "as-

sumption of a power which [the jury has] no right to exercise," but the illegality alone does not mean that such a collective judgment should be subject to review. The fact that the inconsistency may be the result of lenity, coupled with the Government's inability to invoke review, suggests that inconsistent verdicts should not be reviewable.

We also reject, as imprudent and unworkable, a rule that would allow criminal defendants to challenge inconsistent verdicts on the ground that in their case the verdict was not the product of lenity, but of some error that worked against them. Such an individualized assessment of the reason for the inconsistency would be based either on pure speculation, or would require inquiries into the jury's deliberations that courts generally will not undertake. Jurors, of course, take an oath to follow the law as charged, and they are expected to follow it. . . . To this end trials generally begin with voir dire, by judge or counsel, seeking to identify those jurors who for whatever reason may be unwilling or unable to follow the law and render an impartial verdict on the facts and the evidence. But with few exceptions . . . once the jury has heard the evidence and the case has been submitted, the litigants must accept the jury's collective judgment. Courts have always resisted inquiring into a jury's thought processes . . .; through this deference the jury brings to the criminal process, in addition to the collective judgment of the community, an element of needed finality.

Finally, we note that a criminal defendant already is afforded protection against jury irrationality or error by the independent review of the sufficiency of the evidence undertaken by the trial and appellate courts. This review should not be confused with the problems caused by inconsistent verdicts. Sufficiency of the evidence review involves assessment by the courts of whether the evidence adduced at trial could support any rational determination of guilt beyond a reasonable doubt. . . . This review should be independent of the jury's determination that evidence on another count was insufficient. The Government must convince the jury with its proof, and must also satisfy the courts that given this proof the jury could rationally have reached a verdict of guilt beyond a reasonable doubt. We do not believe that further safeguards against jury irrationality are necessary.

469 U.S. at 64–67.

570. On the jury's power to exercise lenity despite the instruction that it is to follow the law, see generally United States v. Dougherty, 473 F.2d 1113 (D.C.Cir.1972). The defendants in *Dougherty* were prosecuted for unlawful entry into Dow Chemical Company offices and for destruction of property, as a protest against the Vietnam War. They requested an instruction that the jury was authorized to "nullify" the judge's instructions and return a verdict of not guilty notwithstanding the law. The court agreed that a jury has such power and that its exercise has been desirable in some instances, but it concluded that the instruction should not be given.

571. The defendant was prosecuted for tax evasion. After being charged that it was the court's duty to determine punishment if the jury found the defendant guilty, the jury returned a verdict of guilty, subscribed to which was a notation that the "[j]ury, however, respectfully request that this court give to J. Sydney Cook, Jr., every degree of leniency possible."

AO 245A (Rev. 12/03) Judgment of Acquittal

UNITED STATES DISTRICT COURT

_______________ DISTRICT OF _______________

UNITED STATES OF AMERICA

V.

JUDGMENT OF ACQUITTAL

CASE NUMBER:

The Defendant was found not guilty. IT IS ORDERED that the Defendant is acquitted, discharged, and any bond exonerated.

____
Signature of Judge

____
Name and Title of Judge

____
Date

On being polled, ten jurors indicated that their verdict of guilty was "based on the note" or "as noted" at the bottom of the verdict. The trial court denied defense counsel's request that the jurors be asked whether their verdict was "qualified" by the request for leniency or whether they would have voted to convict if advised that the request for leniency went beyond their province. Acknowledging that the general rule is that a recommendation of clemency should be treated as surplusage, the court held that the extreme circumstances of the case left a doubt whether the verdict was unqualified, and reversed the conviction. Cook v. United States, 379 F.2d 966 (5th Cir.1967).

See Rogers v. United States, 422 U.S. 35, 38 (1975), in which, citing *Cook* and noting the exception made in that case, the Court said: "Generally, a recommendation of leniency made by a jury without statutory authorization does not affect the validity of the verdict and may be disregarded by the sentencing judge."

572. The defendant moved for a judgment of acquittal under Rule 29 after the close of the government's case and again at the close of the entire case. The trial judge denied both motions. The jury returned a verdict of guilty. Thereafter, the judge imposed sentence (probation and a fine) and signed a judgment of conviction. He then ordered that the indictment be dismissed. As he explained, he did so because although he believed that the government's evidence was legally sufficient to warrant a conviction, for which reason he had denied the motions under Rule 29, he himself believed that the testimony of the main government witness was incredible and that there was danger of a miscarriage of justice. He observed that to have granted a new trial "in the interest of justice" under Rule 33 would have served no purpose. He took the peculiar course he did because he was uncertain of a trial judge's authority to terminate a criminal proceeding in favor of an accused despite the absence of a specific error warranting him to do so.

The court of appeals held that the trial judge had no such authority:

> It is plain that no Rule of Federal Criminal Procedure confers any such power. We have already discussed Rule 29 and shown its inapplicability. The other pertinent provision is Rule 33 relating to the grant of a new trial. We have no doubt that, on [the defendant's] timely motion, the judge had power to grant a new trial if he thought, in the language of the Rule, that this was "required in the interest of justice" even though, in his phrase, "no specific error" warranted this. But admittedly no Rule gives the judge an overriding power to terminate a criminal prosecution in which the Government's evidence has passed the test of legal sufficiency simply because he thinks that course would be most consonant with the interests of justice.
>
> We believe the failure of the Rules to bestow such a power precludes its exercise. . . .
>
> Apart from what we regard as the preclusive effect of the silence of the Rules, we have not been pointed to any precedent for such an inherent power.

United States v. Weinstein, 452 F.2d 704, 715 (2d Cir.1971).

CHAPTER 14

NEW TRIAL

FEDERAL RULES OF CRIMINAL PROCEDURE

Rule 33

NEW TRIAL

(a) Defendant's Motion. Upon the defendant's motion, the court may vacate any judgment and grant a new trial if the interest of justice so requires. If the case was tried without a jury, the court may take additional testimony and enter a new judgment.

(b) Time to File.

(1) *Newly Discovered Evidence.* Any motion for a new trial grounded on newly discovered evidence must be filed within 3 years after the verdict or finding of guilty. If an appeal is pending, the court may not grant a motion for a new trial until the appellate court remands the case.

(2) *Other Grounds.* Any motion for a new trial grounded on any reason other than newly discovered evidence must be filed within 7 days after the verdict or finding of guilty, or within such further time as the court sets during the 7-day period.

United States v. Puco

338 F.Supp. 1252 (S.D.N.Y.), aff'd, 461 F.2d 846 (2d Cir.1972)

■ LASKER, DISTRICT JUDGE. Following conviction in a non-jury trial for selling narcotics and conspiring to do so, defendant has moved (a) pursuant to Rule 33, F.R.Crim.P., to vacate the verdict, authorize the taking of new evidence, and direct "entry of a not guilty verdict on the ground of newly discovered evidence". . . .

(a) The Rule 33 Motion

The critical question at trial was whether or not the defendant attended a meeting on January 11, 1970, with the government's chief witness, Michael Fiore, at which the defendant agreed to procure narcotics. Puco's sole defense was an alibi. He claimed that on the night of January 11, 1970, he was in Baltimore, Maryland, at Louise's Restaurant, and he produced a number of witnesses who testified in support of that claim, although not all of them were able specifically to state that he was at Louise's actually on the evening of January 11th. The present motion offers further testimony to corroborate the alibi. The excuse for not producing these witnesses at trial is that defendant did not know until the first day of the trial that the government would claim that Puco attended a conspiratorial meeting on January 11th and the defendant could not marshal his witnesses in anticipation of such evidence.

The criteria for determination of a motion for a new trial have been ably stated in United States v. Fassoulis, 203 F.Supp. 114, 117 (S.D.N.Y. 1962). A motion for a new trial may not be granted unless the court is "satisfied that the evidence (1) is in fact newly discovered, i.e., discovered since the trial; (2) could not with due diligence have been discovered earlier; (3) is not merely cumulative or impeaching; (4) is material to the issues, and finally, (5) is such, and of such nature, that upon a retrial it will probably produce an acquittal."

. . .

In the instant case, defendant proposes to produce four witnesses to further establish his defense that he was not in New York on the evening of a conspiratorial meeting to arrange the cocaine sale for which he was convicted, but was in Baltimore, Maryland.

Defendant offers first that Clem Florio, a turf analyst and boxing editor for the Baltimore News American, would testify that he was with defendant during the afternoon of January 11th, but has no knowledge of his whereabouts on the evening of the 11th. Defendant's case included testimony that he was present in Baltimore during the day of January 11th, and thus this offer of proof would be merely cumulative and irrelevant, or, at most, of marginal relevance to fixing where defendant was on the night in question.

Next, defendant offers to call Elizabeth Worthington, a former waitress at Louise's Restaurant, where defendant claims he had dinner on the evening involved. In an affidavit she states: "On Monday Jan 11 I worked from 5–12 at the restaurant. I remember Mr. Puco being in the Restaurant that evening and him saying he was leaving in the morning, so I went over and gave him a farewell kiss." (Affidavit of Elizabeth Paule Worthington, sworn to August 11, 1971). This statement, and the balance of the affidavit from which it is taken, are in substance the same as made by defendant's witness Gloria Hicks, a cook at Louise's Restaurant, who testified that she remembered defendant being in the restaurant "all day and all night" on January 11th. Although this evidence is cumulative, it would carry some weight if considered alone in a situation where inconsistent testimony and credibility are at issue. January 11 is the key date here, and this witness does appear to offer valuable testimony, however repetitive it may be of that already in the record. Nonetheless, there is no showing that this testimony could not have been discovered and adduced earlier in the exercise of due diligence. No recess to permit defendant to locate and bring this witness to the trial was requested, and since her affidavit indicates that she spent a fair amount of time with defendant during his stay in

Baltimore prior to the evening in question, it seems unlikely that he would have forgotten her presence and the utility of her testimony to his defense.

Defendant's third offer of new evidence is the testimony of Ralph De Felice, a Philadelphia resident and friend of Joe Di Natale. His affidavit states: "I had dinner with Mr. Puco at Louise's on Sunday Jan 10th and Monday evening Jan 11th," (signed and affirmed August 11, 1971). This evidence suffers from the same deficiency as that of Elizabeth Worthington; it could have been discovered prior to—or during—trial, and as to the alibi it is cumulative. Moreover, the affidavit conflicts with trial testimony of defendant's witness Joe Di Natale, who testified that while De Felice was at dinner at the restaurant on the 10th he was not present on the 11th.

Finally, defendant offers the testimony of Rebecca Fine, a waitress at Louise's Restaurant. Her affidavit (signed and affirmed August 11, 1971) states: "I waited on Mr. Puco and served him meals for a four or five day period during the time Mr. De Natale's horses ran and for several days after. All this was during the second week in January 1971." This, like the offer of evidence of Florio, is cumulative, could have been discovered with due diligence, and is irrelevant or of marginal relevance to determination of where the defendant was on the evening of January 11th.

"It is well settled that motions for new trials are not favored and should be granted only with great caution." United States v. Costello, 255 F.2d 876, 879 (2d Cir.1958). Defendant has contended that he was in Baltimore during the evening of January 11th, and yet at trial called none of the witnesses he now proposes to present. Even if the affidavits of the proposed witnesses are to be believed, the defendant must have known at the time of trial of their presence with him in Maryland on the critical "alibi night" of January 11th. There is no showing that they were unavailable to defendant before or during the trial. "Yet the defense never sought to subpoena [them] or to have the government produce [them], or to have the case adjourned until [they] could be located." United States v. Lanza, 329 F.2d 422, 423 (2d Cir.1964). The fact that some of these "new" witnesses state that they did not know their information was of value to defendant until after his trial is immaterial, for it is not what the witness knows, but what defendant knows about the witnesses which determines whether material evidence could have been discovered with due diligence before or during trial.

Moreover, even if the offers of proof were uniformly material, undiscoverable before trial and not merely cumulative, defendant would fail by the key test, which requires that the evidence "is such, and of such nature, that upon a retrial it will probably produce an acquittal." United States v. Fassoulis, supra. Only the affidavits of De Felice and Worthington could be considered to add anything to the weight of defendant's evidence were they to be admitted. However, the proposed testimony of De Felice has already been contradicted by the testimony of defendant's own witness, Di Natale, to the effect that De Felice was not present at Louise's Restaurant on January 11th. Worthington's testimony might be more important, but, as indicated above, is basically cumulative of that of Gloria Hicks.

But the proposed testimony must be weighed in the total setting of the trial, which includes the astonishing fact that, although all the defense witnesses stated that defendant's son, Steve Puco, Jr., was with him and them at Louise's Restaurant on January 11th, and although Puco Jr. was present in the courtroom throughout the trial (and identified from the witness stand as the defendant's son by Maurice Jacobs in the first instance and other defense witnesses thereafter), he was never called to testify as an alibi witness in support of his own father. It is a reasonable inference that if he had been called he would not have corroborated the story of the other defense witnesses.

The burden of satisfying the requirements of Rule 33 is on the defendant, and he has failed to meet that burden. There is no reason to believe that in this judge-tried case the holding of a hearing could clarify or alter this conclusion. Even taking the facts as here alleged, a new trial would not be warranted. . . . Accordingly, defendant's motion under Rule 33 is denied.

. . .

Jones v. United States

279 F.2d 433 (4th Cir.1960)

■ HAYNSWORTH, CIRCUIT JUDGE.

This is an appeal from the denial of a motion for a new trial based upon after-discovered evidence, the confession of another that he and an accomplice, not the defendants, were the bank robbers.

On a Sunday evening in January 1958, a branch bank in Marlow Heights, Maryland, was robbed. Two armed bandits, wearing "Frankenstein" masks, forced their way into the apartment of the manager of the branch, a Mr. Cranford. They forced Mr. Cranford to accompany one of them to the bank, and, there, to open the night depository. The other, armed with a sawed-off shotgun, remained in the Cranford apartment to guard Mrs. Cranford until receipt of a telephone call from the accomplice to inform him that the accomplice had gained possession of the money.

In May 1958, Jones and Princeler were tried and convicted of the crime. The question was one of identification. The Cranfords had picked the defendants out of lineups and identified them as the bandits, despite the fact that when the crime was committed most of the features of the bandits were concealed by the masks. This identification was strongly supported by circumstantial evidence which connected the defendants with two masks, a sawed-off shotgun and a pair of shoes, identified by the Cranfords as having been used by the bandits, and with a severed piece of a barrel of a shotgun which experts testified had been cut from the sawed-off shotgun. The defendants sought, unsuccessfully, to establish alibis.

Jones and Princeler appealed to this Court. We affirmed their convictions. . . .

From January until June 1958, Jones and Princeler were held in the Baltimore City Jail. From February 14, 1958 until April 24, 1958 one McNicholas was also incarcerated in the Baltimore City Jail upon a charge of robbery of a bank in Sparrows Point, Maryland, on February 12, 1958. There was testimony that Jones, Princeler and McNicholas talked together during exercise periods. One of their fellow prisoners testified he overheard Jones and McNicholas discussing plans for McNicholas to take the blame for the crime with which Jones and Princeler were charged. By the testimony of yet another prisoner, the defendants sought to impeach this testimony upon the ground that the witness sought favor in the hope of parole.

In June 1958, McNicholas, then confined in Lewisburg Penitentiary, sought an interview with FBI agents, to whom on June 16, he gave a written statement in which he said he and an unidentified friend robbed the Marlow Heights bank and that Jones and Princeler were innocent. Some of what little detail there is in this statement was retracted by McNicholas in subsequent statements and testimony.

McNicholas, in August 1958, and Jones, in October, were transferred to the Atlanta Penitentiary. Together there, they discussed their affairs, including the McNicholas confession. They collaborated in the preparation of a written statement, dated December 12, 1958, which McNicholas subsequently signed before a notary. This is the statement which was used to support the motions for new trial.

. . .

At the full hearing held in October [1959], McNicholas testified at length as did Jones, Princeler and a number of other witnesses. McNicholas continued to insist that he and another, whom he still refused to identify, had committed the crime. He testified that the masks and the sawed-off shotgun, introduced as exhibits in the Jones–Princeler trial and identified by the Cranfords, were not those used by him and his accomplice. His testimony contains some detail which counsel contend would support a finding that he was present in the Cranford apartment. It also contains some discrepancies and is contradicted in part by other testimony and his own prior statements. What knowledge of the Cranfords and of their apartment he displayed could have been acquired from Jones and Princeler and from his reading of portions of the transcript of the testimony at the Jones–Princeler trial.

A psychiatrist, who had examined McNicholas in 1958, testified he was a neurotic of above-average intelligence who sought punishment for antisocial conduct. He expressed the opinion that confession of a crime he had not committed would be consistent with his behavior pattern.

At the conclusion of the hearing, the District Judge reviewed the testimony, noted that the attitude of McNicholas was "unappetizing and unpersuasive,'' and found that his story was inherently improbable and unworthy of belief. He denied the motions.

. . .

The principal contention on appeal is that the District Judge, in acting upon the motion, had no right to consider the credibility of the proffered evidence. Essentially, the position is that the inquiry of the trial judge, in considering after-discovered evidence, is limited to the diligence of the movant, the admissibility of the evidence and its materiality if it should be accepted as true. Since the McNicholas testimony would have been admissible if it had been offered at the trial and would have produced a different result if it had been accepted as true by the jury, it is said that however unlikely it may be that a jury would believe such testimony, it was beyond the discretionary power of the trial judge to deny the motion.

Doubtless, it is true that where the after-discovered evidence consists of admitted fact, a court should hesitate to choose between permissible ultimate inferences without regard for the traditional function of the jury. If . . . the fact discovered by the defense after the trial was known to the prosecution and suppressed by it so as to impair to some extent, the fairness of the trial, the area in which the trial judge may exercise his discretion to deny the motion may be further circumscribed.

Where there is a grave question of the credibility of the after-discovered evidence, however, the role of the trial judge is that of the fact-finder, so much so that the Supreme Court has said an appeal from his resolution of the facts should be dismissed as frivolous.[1] The rule has been applied where, as here, a third party confession is the after-discovered evidence upon which the motion for new trial is founded.

This remedial procedure, a motion for new trial based upon after-discovered evidence, is designed to serve the ends of justice. It is made available as a means of relief from manifest injustice. That purpose would hardly be served if the law required the trial judge, who heard all of the evidence and saw all of the witnesses, to assume that a jury would believe testimonial evidence however improbable and unworthy of belief he finds it to be. If the purpose of the remedy is to be served, without subjecting it to undue abuse, the trial judge who approaches the question of the probable effect of the new evidence upon the result, in the event of a new trial, should be vested with a broad discretion in considering matters of credibility as well as of materiality. Stringent or artificial limitations upon the exercise of the discretionary power of the trial judge to grant new trials could only subvert the purpose of the remedy.

The contention is also made that the McNicholas testimony is so persuasive that the District Court could not reasonably conclude that a jury which heard it, with all of the other testimony, would probably convict Jones and Princeler. In an oral opinion, delivered at the conclusion of the hearing on the motion, the District Court reviewed the facts and noted the

1. United States v. Johnson, 327 U.S. 106 (1946).

infirmities in the McNicholas story and its lack of corroboration. In the light of the evidence that Jones and Princeler were the culprits, we think the analysis of the facts by the District Court was entirely reasonable and his conclusion within the range of his discretionary power.

. . .

---

573. The defendant was convicted of entering a store in which he had been employed and stealing $1,125.66. On the night after the crime, he disappeared. Three years later he told a sheriff elsewhere that he was wanted for the theft of $1,175 from the store. At his trial he testified that he had seen the store open on the night of the theft and had become frightened and fled; he had learned of the details of the theft the next day by reading a newspaper story which gave $1,175 as the amount of the theft. The prosecutor ridiculed this testimony; he argued that it was unlikely that such a story would appear in an out-of-town newspaper and that if there had been such a story the amount of the theft would have been reported accurately. Six days after the defendant was convicted, his counsel made a motion for a new trial and offered to show that there had been a newspaper story on the day in question that had reported a theft of $1,175. The crime and the trial occurred in Washington, D.C. Defense counsel had discovered the story in Washington newspapers, which were available in the town where the defendant said he had been on the day following the theft, on file in the Library of Congress. Should the motion for a new trial be granted? See Delbridge v. United States, 262 F.2d 710 (D.C.Cir.1958).

574. The appellant was tried before a judge without a jury and convicted of assault and larceny.

> A government witness working in a filling station testified he saw two men approach an automobile; one of them seized a coat from the car of the complaining witness Carpenter and both men ran when a chase ensued. Carpenter, owner of the coat, followed them into an alley and apprehended one Martin, who was holding the stolen coat. The second man fled.
>
> The day Martin entered a guilty plea in court, appellant came into the courtroom and sat beside Carpenter, who was in court in connection with the case. Carpenter concluded that appellant was Martin's companion at the time of the coat theft and he so informed a detective then present. Appellant explained his presence in court as being there to observe the case of a friend whose case was on the calendar that day. A check showed that the case he described was in fact on the calendar. Later he was arrested and charged.
>
> Appellant's defense was the testimony of his mother, his wife and a neighbor who testified he was in his home 7 or 8 miles from the scene of the crime at the hour of its commission. Appellant denied knowing Martin, his alleged accomplice, and denied being present at

the time of the crime. Carpenter made a positive identification of appellant. He testified that when he caught up with the two men in the alley, appellant brandished a knife but fled when Carpenter grappled with Martin.

On the second day following his conviction, appellant moved for a new trial on the grounds of newly discovered evidence, submitting an affidavit of Martin in which the latter absolved appellant of any part in the crimes. Martin also appeared as a witness at the hearing on the motion and testified he had met appellant when the latter was sent to jail and that he, Martin, volunteered this explanation because he did not want a guiltless man to suffer. Martin named one Tatum as his companion on the day of the offense but absolved Tatum of guilt in the theft saying that he, Martin, had seized the coat on a sudden impulse and that Tatum was not aware that the act was to occur.

Appellant's attorney gave his own affidavit at the hearing in which he recited that he had interviewed Tatum who told him that he, not appellant, was present with Martin on the day in question but had not known Martin was to seize the coat; Tatum was quoted as saying he had run in fright and because Martin ran. Tatum was in the courtroom during the hearing on the new trial motion and presumably heard appellant's attorney read the affidavit identifying him as Martin's companion on the day of the crime. Tatum's presence in court was made known when he was asked by one of the attorneys to stand to compare his height and build with that of appellant. The trial judge noted that there was a substantial difference in height. Carpenter, confronted with both men, again identified appellant as Martin's companion. He said it was 7 p.m. on the day in question (March 28, 1960) and dusk but that he "could see all right."

Brodie v. United States, 295 F.2d 157, 158–59 (D.C.Cir.1961).

Should the motion for a new trial be granted? Suppose it had not been made until after the seven-day period prescribed by Rule 33 for motions on grounds other than newly discovered evidence?

575.

Appellant was convicted by a jury of taking indecent liberties with a child under the age of sixteen years, in violation of § 22–3501(a), D.C.Code (1940, Supp. VII). He resided in an apartment near that of the child and her mother, though under separate roofs. It is not disputed that at the time in question the child, a girl twelve years of age, was in appellant's apartment and did a dance there when only he and she were present. She said he then took the liberties complained of, with his hand upon parts of her person. He denies that this occurred. There is also disagreement in their testimony as to the reason for her coming to his apartment. She says he called to her from his window when she was below on the street. He denies this, saying she came to the apartment inquiring for his daughter, whom she knew and with whom she testified she was on friendly terms. Each claims

> the other was the instigator of the dance. After she had told her mother, the latter called the child's married sister who asked a neighbor across the hall what she should do about it. The police were then called.
>
> Thus it is seen that the testimony upon which the conviction rests came from the child and was denied by the accused. The Government at the close of its case tendered the mother to the defendant if he wished to call her. A short recess was taken, after which the evidence was concluded by the testimony of the defendant and others he called. The mother and married sister were not called. Four days after the verdict a motion for a new trial was made, resting primarily upon an affidavit of the mother. In it she states she was present when the child came home on the evening in question. The child had testified that when she came home she was crying. The affidavit of the mother says her daughter first came in through the living room and there was nothing unusual about her appearance until she came out of the bathroom, went into the kitchen, and, crying bitterly, told the mother of the alleged accident. The affidavit also states, "When I asked Gertrude why she went to Mr. Benton's apartment, she said that she was looking for Barbara Jean, the daughter of Mr. Benton. At the time, Gertrude had been angry for a time with this little girl, Barbara Jean, and had not been on speaking terms with her. . . ." This is at variance in two respects with the testimony of Gertrude on the trial. As we have shown, she testified that she was called by appellant to come, and that she was friendly with his daughter, Barbara Jean. The mother's affidavit concludes, "and in my opinion, my conscience does not allow me to believe that anything happened to my girl on that night, I heard what Mr. Benton said, and I heard what my daughter said."

Benton v. United States, 188 F.2d 625, 626–27 (D.C.Cir.1951).

Should the motion for a new trial be granted? Suppose it had not been made until after the seven-day period prescribed by Rule 33 for motions on grounds other than newly discovered evidence?

576. The defendant was convicted of a narcotics offense largely on the testimony of Challenger, an informer. Two days after the jury returned its verdict and before the defendant was sentenced, Challenger made an affidavit in which he recanted his testimony and expressed his belief that the defendant was innocent. Defense counsel made a motion for a new trial. Soon afterwards, defense counsel sought to withdraw his motion, because Challenger had asked for his affidavit back and had reaffirmed his testimony at trial. Challenger claimed that the affidavit was given under pressure from the defendant's family. Following a hearing, the trial judge concluded that Challenger was "completely irresponsible," and that there was "no reason to believe that on one occasion more than another he was telling the truth." Should the motion for a new trial be granted? See United States v. Troche, 213 F.2d 401 (2d Cir.1954). On the problem of the recanting witness, see United States v. Mackin, 561 F.2d 958 (D.C.Cir.1977); Lindsey

v. United States, 368 F.2d 633 (9th Cir.1966). See generally Sanders v. Sullivan, 863 F.2d 218 (2d Cir.1988).

In United States v. Sanchez, 969 F.2d 1409, 1414 (2d Cir.1992), the court said that a trial judge should ordinarily defer to the jury's assessment of the credibility of witnesses and should grant a new trial on the basis of a conclusion that a witness committed perjury only if she believes that the jury would probably have acquitted without that testimony and "only with great caution and in the most extraordinary circumstances."

577. "[A] defendant's testimony known to the defendant at the time of trial cannot be considered 'newly discovered evidence' under Rule 33, regardless of the codefendant's unavailability during trial because of invocation of his Fifth Amendment privilege." United States v. Jasin, 280 F.3d 355, 368 (3d Cir.2002). The court said that this would "establish a straightforward bright-line rule" and that it followed the plain meaning of Rule 33. Id.

578. Referring to the grant of a new trial "when required in the interest of justice," in a case involving highly unusual circumstances, the court said: "If the complete record, testimonial and physical, leaves a strong doubt as to the defendant's guilt, even though not so strong a doubt as to require a judgment of acquittal, the district judge may be obliged to grant a new trial." United States v. Morales, 910 F.2d 467, 468 (7th Cir.1990).

CHAPTER 15

SENTENCE AND JUDGMENT

579. "[T]he sentencing process, as well as the trial itself, must satisfy the requirements of the Due Process Clause. Even though the defendant has no substantive right to a particular sentence within the range authorized by statute, the sentencing is a critical stage of the criminal proceeding at which he is entitled to the effective assistance of counsel. . . . The defendant has a legitimate interest in the character of the procedure which leads to the imposition of sentence even if he may have no right to object to a particular result of the sentencing process." Gardner v. Florida, 430 U.S. 349, 358 (1977).

The Sentencing Reform Act of 1984, 28 U.S.C. §§ 991–998, provided for a United States Sentencing Commission to promulgate binding Sentencing Guidelines for federal offenses. The principal goals of the guidelines were to eliminate the great variation among sentences for persons similarly situated and convicted of the same offense and to eliminate the uncertainty about the length of time a person would actually spend in prison. In addition, the guidelines were intended to promote sentences the formal terms of which reflected the actual sentences and to promote sentences for different crimes that reflected their relative seriousness.

Sentencing Guidelines were promulgated in 1987. They establish categories of criminal conduct, specific offense characteristics, and "adjustments," which are applied according to a formula to determine the sentence. Parole was eliminated. The Guidelines were upheld against a constitutional challenge that they delegated excessive legislative authority to the Commission and violated the principle of separation of powers. Mistretta v. United States, 488 U.S. 361 (1989) (8–1).

The Court has held that the Sentencing Commission's commentary to the Guidelines is authoritative and binding on the federal courts, unless it violates the Constitution or a federal statute or is a plainly erroneous reading of or plainly inconsistent with the Guideline it interprets. Stinson v. United States, 508 U.S. 36 (1993).

For an extensive review of a sentencing court's authority under the Guidelines to depart from the sentences prescribed therein, see Koon v. United States, 518 U.S. 81 (1996).

18 U.S.C. § 3553(e) empowers a district court to sentence a defendant below the statutory minimum "upon motion of the Government," based on the defendant's "substantial assistance" in the investigation or prosecution of another person. The Sentencing Guidelines contain a similar provision. In Wade v. United States, 504 U.S. 181 (1992), the Court held that a

federal district court has authority to review a prosecutor's refusal to file such a motion for an "unconstitutional motive," such as the defendant's race or religion but not simply on the alleged ground that there was a basis for such a motion. See United States v. Paramo, 998 F.2d 1212 (3d Cir.1993) (prosecutor's refusal to file motion for downward sentencing departure, allegedly to penalize defendant for exercising right to trial, is subject to review).

There have been a very large number of opinions of the federal courts of appeals and district courts construing and applying the Sentencing Guidelines. The front pages of advance sheets of the Federal Reporter System have citations to cases applying the Guidelines arranged according to the provision in issue.

The problem of plea-bargaining in the context of the Sentencing Guidelines is discussed in United States v. Bethancurt, 692 F.Supp. 1427 (D.D.C.1988). Judge Greene concludes: "[I]f the elimination of sentencing disparity was the goal the Congress had in mind when it enacted the new law, it achieved that objective only in the context of judicial sentencing: prosecutorial decisions are likely to result in as much unwarranted sentencing disparity as existed before, if not more so, and they will do so under conditions of decreased fairness." Id. at 1435–36.

FEDERAL RULES OF CRIMINAL PROCEDURE

Rule 32

SENTENCING AND JUDGMENT

(a) Definitions. The following definitions apply under this rule:

(1) "Crime of violence or sexual abuse" means:

(A) a crime that involves the use, attempted use, or threatened use of physical force against another's person or property; or

(B) a crime under 18 U.S.C. §§ 2241–2248 or §§ 2251–2257.

(2) "Victim" means an individual against whom the defendant committed an offense for which the court will impose sentence.

(b) Time of Sentencing.

(1) *In General.* The court must impose sentence without unnecessary delay.

(2) *Changing Time Limits.* The court may, for good cause, change any time limits prescribed in this rule.

(c) Presentence Investigation.

(1) *Required Investigation.*

(A) *In General.* The probation officer must conduct a presentence investigation and submit a report to the court before it imposes sentence unless:

(i) 18 U.S.C. § 3593(c) or another statute requires otherwise; or

(ii) the court finds that the information in the record enables it to meaningfully exercise its sentencing authority under 18 U.S.C. § 3553, and the court explains its finding on the record.

(B) *Restitution.* If the law requires restitution, the probation officer must conduct an investigation and submit a report that contains sufficient information for the court to order restitution.

(2) *Interviewing the Defendant.* The probation officer who interviews a defendant as part of a presentence investigation must, on request, give the defendant's attorney notice and a reasonable opportunity to attend the interview.

(d) Presentence Report.

(1) *Applying the Sentencing Guidelines.* The presentence report must:

(A) identify all applicable guidelines and policy statements of the Sentencing Commission;

(B) calculate the defendant's offense level and criminal history category;

(C) state the resulting sentencing range and kinds of sentences available;

(D) identify any factor relevant to:

(i) the appropriate kind of sentence, or

(ii) the appropriate sentence within the applicable sentencing range; and

(E) identify any basis for departing from the applicable sentencing range.

(2) *Additional Information.* The presentence report must also contain the following information:

(A) the defendant's history and characteristics, including:

(i) any prior criminal record;

(ii) the defendant's financial condition; and

(iii) any circumstances affecting the defendant's behavior that may be helpful in imposing sentence or in correctional treatment;

(B) verified information, stated in a nonargumentative style, that assesses the financial, social, psychological, and medical impact on any individual against whom the offense has been committed;

(C) when appropriate, the nature and extent of nonprison programs and resources available to the defendant;

(D) when the law provides for restitution, information sufficient for a restitution order;

(E) if the court orders a study under 18 U.S.C. § 3552(b), any resulting report and recommendation; and

(F) any other information that the court requires.

(3) *Exclusions*. The presentence report must exclude the following:

(A) any diagnoses that, if disclosed, might seriously disrupt a rehabilitation program;

(B) any sources of information obtained upon a promise of confidentiality; and

(C) any other information that, if disclosed, might result in physical or other harm to the defendant or others.

(e) Disclosing the Report and Recommendation.

(1) *Time to Disclose*. Unless the defendant has consented in writing, the probation officer must not submit a presentence report to the court or disclose its contents to anyone until the defendant has pleaded guilty or nolo contendere, or has been found guilty.

(2) *Minimum Required Notice*. The probation officer must give the presentence report to the defendant, the defendant's attorney, and an attorney for the government at least 35 days before sentencing unless the defendant waives this minimum period.

(3) *Sentence Recommendation*. By local rule or by order in a case, the court may direct the probation officer not to disclose to anyone other than the court the officer's recommendation on the sentence.

(f) Objecting to the Report.

(1) *Time to Object*. Within 14 days after receiving the presentence report, the parties must state in writing any objections, including objections to material information, sentencing guideline ranges, and policy statements contained in or omitted from the report.

(2) *Serving Objections*. An objecting party must provide a copy of its objections to the opposing party and to the probation officer.

(3) *Action on Objections*. After receiving objections, the probation officer may meet with the parties to discuss the objections. The probation officer may then investigate further and revise the presentence report as appropriate.

(g) Submitting the Report. At least 7 days before sentencing, the probation officer must submit to the court and to the parties the presentence report and an addendum containing any unresolved objections, the grounds for those objections, and the probation officer's comments on them.

(h) Notice of Possible Departure from Sentencing Guidelines. Before the court may depart from the applicable sentencing range on a ground not identified for departure either in the presentence report or in a party's prehearing submission, the court must give the parties reasonable notice that it is contemplating such a departure. The notice must specify any ground on which the court is contemplating a departure.

(i) Sentencing.

(1) *In General.* At sentencing, the court:

(A) must verify that the defendant and the defendant's attorney have read and discussed the presentence report and any addendum to the report;

(B) must give to the defendant and an attorney for the government a written summary of—or summarize in camera—any information excluded from the presentence report under Rule 32(d)(3) on which the court will rely in sentencing, and give them a reasonable opportunity to comment on that information;

(C) must allow the parties' attorneys to comment on the probation officer's determinations and other matters relating to an appropriate sentence; and

(D) may, for good cause, allow a party to make a new objection at any time before sentencing is imposed.

(2) *Introducing Evidence; Producing a Statement.* The court may permit the parties to introduce evidence on the objections. If a witness testifies at sentencing, Rule 26.2(a)–(d) and (f) applies. If a party fails to comply with a Rule 26.2 order to produce a witness's statement, the court must not consider that witness's testimony.

(3) *Court Determinations.* At sentencing, the court:

(A) may accept any undisputed portion of the presentence report as a finding of fact;

(B) must—for any disputed portion of the presentence report or other controverted matter—rule on the dispute or determine that a ruling is unnecessary either because the matter will not affect sentencing, or because the court will not consider the matter in sentencing; and

(C) must append a copy of the court's determinations under this rule to any copy of the presentence report made available to the Bureau of Prisons.

(4) *Opportunity to Speak.*

(A) *By a Party.* Before imposing sentence, the court must:

(i) provide the defendant's attorney an opportunity to speak on the defendant's behalf;

(ii) address the defendant personally in order to permit the defendant to speak or present any information to mitigate the sentence; and

(iii) provide an attorney for the government an opportunity to speak equivalent to that of the defendant's attorney.

(B) *By a Victim.* Before imposing sentence, the court must address any victim of a crime of violence or sexual abuse who is present at sentencing and must permit the victim to speak or submit any information about the sentence. Whether or not the victim is present, a victim's right to address the court may be exercised by the following persons if present:

(i) a parent or legal guardian, if the victim is younger than 18 years or is incompetent; or

(ii) one or more family members or relatives the court designates, if the victim is deceased or incapacitated.

(C) *In Camera Proceedings.* Upon a party's motion and for good cause, the court may hear in camera any statement made under Rule 32(i)(4).

(j) Defendant's Right to Appeal.

(1) *Advice of a Right to Appeal.*

(A) *Appealing a Conviction.* If the defendant pleaded not guilty and was convicted, after sentencing the court must advise the defendant of the right to appeal the conviction.

(B) *Appealing a Sentence.* After sentencing—regardless of the defendant's plea—the court must advise the defendant of any right to appeal the sentence.

(C) *Appeal Costs.* The court must advise a defendant who is unable to pay appeal costs of the right to ask for permission to appeal in forma pauperis.

(2) *Clerk's Filing of Notice.* If the defendant so requests, the clerk must immediately prepare and file a notice of appeal on the defendant's behalf.

(k) Judgment.

(1) *In General.* In the judgment of conviction, the court must set forth the plea, the jury verdict or the court's findings, the adjudication, and the sentence. If the defendant is found not guilty or is otherwise entitled to be discharged, the court must so order. The judge must sign the judgment, and the clerk must enter it.

(2) *Criminal Forfeiture.* Forfeiture procedures are governed by Rule 32.2.

---

580. "[I]t is improper for the prosecutor to convey information or to discuss any matter relating to the merits of the case or sentence with the judge in the absence of counsel." Haller v. Robbins, 409 F.2d 857, 859 (1st Cir.1969).

581. Allocution.

> The design of Rule 32(a) [now 32(i)(4)(A)(ii)] did not begin with its promulgation; its legal provenance was the common-law right of allocution. As early as 1689, it was recognized that the court's failure to ask the defendant if he had anything to say before sentence was imposed required reversal. . . . Taken in the context of its history, there can be little doubt that the drafters of Rule 32(a) intended that the defendant be personally afforded the opportunity to speak before imposition of sentence. We are not unmindful of the relevant major changes that have evolved in criminal procedure since the seventeenth century—the sharp decrease in the number of crimes which were punishable by death, the right of the defendant to testify on his own behalf, and the right to counsel. But we see no reason why a procedural rule should be limited to the circumstances under which it arose if reasons for the right it protects remain. None of these modern innovations lessens the need for the defendant, personally, to have the opportunity to present to the court his plea in mitigation. The most persuasive counsel may not be able to speak for a defendant as the defendant might, with halting eloquence, speak for himself. We are buttressed in this conclusion by the fact that the Rule explicitly affords the defendant two rights: "to make a statement in his own behalf," and "to present any information in mitigation of punishment." We therefore reject the Government's contention that merely affording defendant's counsel the opportunity to speak fulfills the dual role of Rule 32(a).
>
> . . . Trial judges before sentencing should, as a matter of good judicial administration, unambiguously address themselves to the defendant. Hereafter trial judges should leave no room for doubt that the defendant has been issued a personal invitation to speak prior to sentencing.

Green v. United States, 365 U.S. 301, 304–305 (1961).

In Hill v. United States, 368 U.S. 424, 428 (1962), however, the Court said that in the absence of any aggravating circumstances, failure to ask a defendant whether he wished to say anything before imposition of sentence "is not a fundamental defect which inherently results in a complete miscarriage of justice, nor an omission inconsistent with the rudimentary demands of fair procedure," and is not a basis for collateral attack of a conviction. Compare United States v. Behrens, 375 U.S. 162 (1963).

In United States v. Adams, 252 F.3d 276 (3d Cir.2001), the court said that the failure of a judge to address the defendant personally at sentencing invalidates the sentence and requires that the case be remanded for resentencing. In United States v. Reyna, 358 F.3d 344 (5th Cir.2004), the court said that failure to give the defendant an opportunity for allocution is subject to plain error review under Rule 52(b).

A defendant has no right to make an unsworn statement to the sentencing jury in a capital case. United States v. Hall, 152 F.3d 381 (5th Cir.1998).

"While it is not error, in some circumstances, for a defendant to be absent during *trial* . . . a defendant *must* be present at sentencing. Only in the most extraordinary circumstances, and where it would otherwise work an injustice, should a court sentence a defendant in absentia, and then only under appropriate safeguards, as where the defendant has expressly waived his right to be present either by sworn affidavit or in open court for the record." United States v. Brown, 456 F.2d 1112, 1114 (5th Cir.1972).

582. Rule 32(i)(4)(A)(iii) provides that the attorney for the government also has an opportunity to speak at sentencing. In United States v. Doe, 655 F.2d 920 (9th Cir.1980), the court held that the *defendant* is entitled to have the court give the prosecutor an opportunity to speak.

583. Before a sentencing court can make an upward departure from the Sentencing Guidelines "on a ground not identified as a ground for upward departure either in the presentence report or in a prehearing submission by the Government, Rule 32(h) requires that the district court give the parties reasonable notice that it is contemplating such a ruling. This notice must specifically identify the ground on which the district court is contemplating an upward departure." Burns v. United States, 501 U.S. 129, 138–39 (1991) (5–4).

584. A district court's failure to advise the defendant at sentencing that he has the right to appeal his sentence, as required by Federal Rule 32(j), is error, but it does not entitle a defendant to collateral relief if he was aware of the right to appeal and was not prejudiced by the failure. Peguero v. United States, 526 U.S. 23 (1999).

FEDERAL RULES OF CRIMINAL PROCEDURE

Rule 32.1

REVOKING OR MODIFYING PROBATION OR SUPERVISED RELEASE

(a) Initial Appearance.

(1) *Person in Custody.* A person held in custody for violating probation or supervised release must be taken without unnecessary delay before a magistrate judge.

(A) If the person is held in custody in the district where an alleged violation occurred, the initial appearance must be in that district.

(B) If the person is held in custody in a district other than where an alleged violation occurred, the initial appearance must be in that district, or in an adjacent district if the appearance can occur more promptly there.

(2) *Upon a Summons.* When a person appears in response to a summons for violating probation or supervised release, a magistrate judge must proceed under this rule.

(3) *Advice.* The judge must inform the person of the following:

(A) the alleged violation of probation or supervised release;

(B) the person's right to retain counsel or to request that counsel be appointed if the person cannot obtain counsel; and

(C) the person's right, if held in custody, to a preliminary hearing under Rule 32.1(b)(1).

(4) *Appearance in the District With Jurisdiction.* If the person is arrested or appears in the district that has jurisdiction to conduct a revocation hearing—either originally or by transfer of jurisdiction—the court must proceed under Rule 32.1(b)–(e).

(5) *Appearance in a District Lacking Jurisdiction.* If the person is arrested or appears in a district that does not have jurisdiction to conduct a revocation hearing, the magistrate judge must:

(A) if the alleged violation occurred in the district of arrest, conduct a preliminary hearing under Rule 32.1(b) and either:

(i) transfer the person to the district that has jurisdiction, if the judge finds probable cause to believe that a violation occurred; or

(ii) dismiss the proceedings and so notify the court that has jurisdiction, if the judge finds no probable cause to believe that a violation occurred; or

(B) if the alleged violation did not occur in the district of arrest, transfer the person to the district that has jurisdiction if:

(i) the government produces certified copies of the judgment, warrant, and warrant application; and

(ii) the judge finds that the person is the same person named in the warrant.

(6) *Release or Detention.* The magistrate judge may release or detain the person under 18 U.S.C. § 3143(a) pending further proceedings. The burden of establishing that the person will not flee or pose a danger to any other person or to the community rests with the person.

(b) Revocation.

(1) *Preliminary Hearing.*

(A) *In General.* If a person is in custody for violating a condition of probation or supervised release, a magistrate judge must promptly conduct a hearing to determine whether there is probable cause to believe that a violation occurred. The person may waive the hearing.

(B) *Requirements.* The hearing must be recorded by a court reporter or by a suitable recording device. The judge must give the person:

(i) notice of the hearing and its purpose, the alleged violation, and the person's right to retain counsel or to request that counsel be appointed if the person cannot obtain counsel;

(ii) an opportunity to appear at the hearing and present evidence; and

(iii) upon request, an opportunity to question any adverse witness, unless the judge determines that the interest of justice does not require the witness to appear.

(C) *Referral.* If the judge finds probable cause, the judge must conduct a revocation hearing. If the judge does not find probable cause, the judge must dismiss the proceeding.

(2) *Revocation Hearing.* Unless waived by the person, the court must hold the revocation hearing within a reasonable time in the district having jurisdiction. The person is entitled to:

(A) written notice of the alleged violation;

(B) disclosure of the evidence against the person;

(C) an opportunity to appear, present evidence, and question any adverse witness unless the court determines that the interest of justice does not require the witness to appear; and

(D) notice of the person's right to retain counsel or to request that counsel be appointed if the person cannot obtain counsel.

(c) Modification.

(1) *In General.* Before modifying the conditions of probation or supervised release, the court must hold a hearing, at which the person has the right to counsel.

(2) *Exceptions.* A hearing is not required if:

(A) the person waives the hearing; or

(B) the relief sought is favorable to the person and does not extend the term of probation or of supervised release; and

(C) an attorney for the government has received notice of the relief sought, has had a reasonable opportunity to object, and has not done so.

(d) Disposition of the Case. The court's disposition of the case is governed by 18 U.S.C. § 3563 and § 3565 (probation) and § 3583 (supervised release).

(e) Producing a Statement. Rule 26.2(a)–(d) and (f) applies at a hearing under this rule. If a party fails to comply with a Rule 26.2 order to produce a witness's statement, the court must not consider that witness's testimony.

Rule 34

ARRESTING JUDGMENT

(a) In General. Upon the defendant's motion or on its own, the court must arrest judgment if:

(1) the indictment or information does not charge an offense; or

(2) the court does not have jurisdiction of the charged offense.

(b) Time to File. The defendant must move to arrest judgment within 7 days after the court accepts a verdict or finding of guilty, or after a plea of guilty or nolo contendere, or within such further time as the court sets during the 7-day period.

Rule 35

CORRECTING OR REDUCING A SENTENCE

(a) Correcting Clear Error. Within 7 days after sentencing, the court may correct a sentence that resulted from arithmetical, technical, or other clear error.

(b) Reducing a Sentence for Substantial Assistance.

(1) *In General.* Upon the government's motion made within one year of sentencing, the court may reduce a sentence if:

(A) the defendant, after sentencing, provided substantial assistance in investigating or prosecuting another person; and

(B) reducing the sentence accords with the Sentencing Commission's guidelines and policy statements.

(2) *Later Motion.* Upon the government's motion made more than one year after sentencing, the court may reduce a sentence if the defendant's substantial assistance involved:

(A) information not known to the defendant until one year or more after sentencing;

(B) information provided by the defendant to the government within one year of sentencing, but which did not become useful to the government until more than one year after sentencing; or

(C) information the usefulness of which could not reasonably have been anticipated by the defendant until more than one year after sentencing and which was promptly provided to the government after its usefulness was reasonably apparent to the defendant.

(3) *Evaluating Substantial Assistance.* In evaluating whether the defendant has provided substantial assistance, the court may consider the defendant's presentence assistance.

(4) *Below Statutory Minimum.* When acting under Rule 35(b), the court may reduce the sentence to a level below the minimum sentence established by statute.

(c) "Sentencing" Defined. As used in this rule, "sentencing" means the oral announcement of the sentence.

---

585. "[T]he narrow function of Rule 35 is to permit correction at any time of an illegal *sentence*, not to re-examine errors occurring at the trial or other proceedings prior to the imposition of sentence." Hill v. United States, 368 U.S. 424, 430 (1962).

Williams v. New York

337 U.S. 241, 69 S.Ct. 1079, 93 L.Ed. 1337 (1949)

■ MR. JUSTICE BLACK delivered the opinion of the Court.

A jury in a New York state court found appellant guilty of murder in the first degree. The jury recommended life imprisonment, but the trial judge imposed sentence of death. In giving his reasons for imposing the death sentence the judge discussed in open court the evidence upon which the jury had convicted stating that this evidence had been considered in the light of additional information obtained through the court's "Probation Department, and through other sources." Consideration of this additional information was pursuant to § 482 of New York Criminal Code which provides:

> Before rendering judgment or pronouncing sentence the court shall cause the defendant's previous criminal record to be submitted to it, including any reports that may have been made as a result of a mental, psychiatric or physical examination of such person, and may seek any information that will aid the court in determining the proper treatment of such defendant.

The Court of Appeals of New York affirmed the conviction and sentence over the contention that as construed and applied the controlling penal statutes are in violation of the due process clause of the Fourteenth Amendment of the Constitution of the United States "in that the sentence of death was based upon information supplied by witnesses with whom the accused had not been confronted and as to whom he had no opportunity for cross-examination or rebuttal. . . ." 83 N.E.2d 698, 699. Because the statutes were sustained over this constitutional challenge the case is here on appeal under 28 U.S.C. § 1257(2).

The narrow contention here makes it unnecessary to set out the facts at length. The record shows a carefully conducted trial lasting more than two weeks in which appellant was represented by three appointed lawyers who conducted his defense with fidelity and zeal. The evidence proved a wholly indefensible murder committed by a person engaged in a burglary. The judge instructed the jury that if it returned a verdict of guilty as charged, without recommendation for life sentence, "The Court must impose the death penalty," but if such recommendation was made, "the Court may impose a life sentence." The judge went on to emphasize that "the Court is not bound to accept your recommendation."

About five weeks after the verdict of guilty with recommendation of life imprisonment, and after a statutory pre-sentence investigation report to the judge, the defendant was brought to court to be sentenced. Asked what he had to say, appellant protested his innocence. After each of his three lawyers had appealed to the court to accept the jury's recommendation of a life sentence, the judge gave reasons why he felt that the death sentence should be imposed. He narrated the shocking details of the crime as shown by the trial evidence, expressing his own complete belief in appellant's guilt. He stated that the pre-sentence investigation revealed many material facts concerning appellant's background which though relevant to the question of punishment could not properly have been brought to the attention of the jury in its consideration of the question of guilt. He referred to the experience appellant "had had on thirty other burglaries in and about the same vicinity" where the murder had been committed. The appellant had not been convicted of these burglaries although the judge had information that he had confessed to some and had been identified as the perpetrator of some of the others. The judge also referred to certain activities of appellant as shown by the probation report that indicated appellant possessed "a morbid sexuality" and classified him as a "menace to society." The accuracy of the statements made by the judge as to appellant's background and past practices was not challenged by appellant or his counsel, nor was the judge asked to disregard any of them or to afford appellant a chance to refute or discredit any of them by cross-examination or otherwise.

The case presents a serious and difficult question. The question relates to the rules of evidence applicable to the manner in which a judge may obtain information to guide him in the imposition of sentence upon an already convicted defendant. Within limits fixed by statutes, New York judges are given a broad discretion to decide the type and extent of punishment for convicted defendants. Here, for example, the judge's discretion was to sentence to life imprisonment or death. To aid a judge in exercising this discretion intelligently the New York procedural policy encourages him to consider information about the convicted person's past life, health, habits, conduct, and mental and moral propensities. The sentencing judge may consider such information even though obtained outside the courtroom from persons whom a defendant has not been permitted to confront or cross-examine. It is the consideration of information obtained by a sentencing judge in this manner that is the basis for appellant's broad constitutional challenge to the New York statutory policy.

Appellant urges that the New York statutory policy is in irreconcilable conflict with the underlying philosophy of a second procedural policy grounded in the due process of law clause of the Fourteenth Amendment. That policy as stated in In re Oliver, 333 U.S. 257, 273, is in part that no person shall be tried and convicted of an offense unless he is given reasonable notice of the charges against him and is afforded an opportunity to examine adverse witnesses. That the due process clause does provide these salutary and time-tested protections where the question for consideration is the guilt of a defendant seems entirely clear from the genesis and historical evolution of the clause. . . .

Tribunals passing on the guilt of a defendant always have been hedged in by strict evidentiary procedural limitations. But both before and since the American colonies became a nation, courts in this country and in England practiced a policy under which a sentencing judge could exercise a wide discretion in the sources and types of evidence used to assist him in determining the kind and extent of punishment to be imposed within limits fixed by law. Out-of-court affidavits have been used frequently, and of course in the smaller communities sentencing judges naturally have in mind their knowledge of the personalities and backgrounds of convicted offenders. A recent manifestation of the historical latitude allowed sentencing judges appears in Rule 32 of the Federal Rules of Criminal Procedure. That rule provides for consideration by federal judges of reports made by probation officers containing information about a convicted defendant, including such information "as may be helpful in imposing sentence or in granting probation or in the correctional treatment of the defendant. . . ."

In addition to the historical basis for different evidentiary rules governing trial and sentencing procedures there are sound practical reasons for the distinction. In a trial before verdict the issue is whether a defendant is guilty of having engaged in certain criminal conduct of which he has been specifically accused. Rules of evidence have been fashioned for criminal trials which narrowly confine the trial contest to evidence that is strictly relevant to the particular offense charged. These rules rest in part on a necessity to prevent a time-consuming and confusing trial of collateral issues. They were also designed to prevent tribunals concerned solely with the issue of guilt of a particular offense from being influenced to convict for that offense by evidence that the defendant had habitually engaged in other misconduct. A sentencing judge, however, is not confined to the narrow issue of guilt. His task within fixed statutory or constitutional limits is to determine the type and extent of punishment after the issue of guilt has been determined. Highly relevant—if not essential—to his selection of an appropriate sentence is the possession of the fullest information possible concerning the defendant's life and characteristics. And modern concepts individualizing punishment have made it all the more necessary that a sentencing judge not be denied an opportunity to obtain pertinent information by a requirement of rigid adherence to restrictive rules of evidence properly applicable to the trial.

Undoubtedly the New York statutes emphasize a prevalent modern philosophy of penology that the punishment should fit the offender and not merely the crime. . . . The belief no longer prevails that every offense in a like legal category calls for an identical punishment without regard to the past life and habits of a particular offender. This whole country has traveled far from the period in which the death sentence was an automatic and commonplace result of convictions—even for offenses today deemed trivial. Today's philosophy of individualizing sentences makes sharp distinctions for example between first and repeated offenders. Indeterminate sentences the ultimate termination of which are sometimes decided by nonjudicial agencies have to a large extent taken the place of the old rigidly fixed punishments. The practice of probation which relies heavily on nonjudicial implementation has been accepted as a wise policy. Execution of the United States parole system rests on the discretion of an administrative parole board. . . . Retribution is no longer the dominant objective of the criminal law. Reformation and rehabilitation of offenders have become important goals of criminal jurisprudence.

Modern changes in the treatment of offenders make it more necessary now than a century ago for observance of the distinctions in the evidential procedure in the trial and sentencing processes. For indeterminate sentences and probation have resulted in an increase in the discretionary powers exercised in fixing punishments. In general, these modern changes have not resulted in making the lot of offenders harder. On the contrary a strong motivating force for the changes has been the belief that by careful study of the lives and personalities of convicted offenders many could be less severely punished and restored sooner to complete freedom and useful citizenship. This belief to a large extent has been justified.

Under the practice of individualizing punishments, investigational techniques have been given an important role. Probation workers making reports of their investigations have not been trained to prosecute but to aid offenders. Their reports have been given a high value by conscientious judges who want to sentence persons on the best available information rather than on guesswork and inadequate information. To deprive sentencing judges of this kind of information would undermine modern penological procedural policies that have been cautiously adopted throughout the nation after careful consideration and experimentation. We must recognize that most of the information now relied upon by judges to guide them in the intelligent imposition of sentences would be unavailable if information were restricted to that given in open court by witnesses subject to cross-examination. And the modern probation report draws on information concerning every aspect of a defendant's life. The type and extent of this information make totally impractical if not impossible open court testimony with cross-examination. Such a procedure could endlessly delay criminal administration in a retrial of collateral issues.

The considerations we have set out admonish us against treating the due process clause as a uniform command that courts throughout the Nation abandon their age-old practice of seeking information from out-of-court sources to guide their judgment toward a more enlightened and just sentence. New York criminal statutes set wide limits for maximum and minimum sentences. Under New York statutes a state judge cannot escape his grave responsibility of fixing sentence. In determining whether a defendant shall receive a one-year minimum or a twenty-year maximum sentence, we do not think the Federal Constitution restricts the view of the sentencing judge to the information received in open court. The due process clause should not be treated as a device for freezing the evidential procedure of sentencing in the mold of trial procedure. So to treat the due process clause would hinder if not preclude all courts—state and federal—from making progressive efforts to improve the administration of criminal justice.

It is urged, however, that we should draw a constitutional distinction as to the procedure for obtaining information where the death sentence is imposed. We cannot accept the contention. Leaving a sentencing judge free to avail himself of out-of-court information in making such a fateful choice of sentences does secure to him a broad discretionary power, one susceptible of abuse. But in considering whether a rigid constitutional barrier should be created, it must be remembered that there is possibility of abuse wherever a judge must choose between life imprisonment and death. And it is conceded that no federal constitutional objection would have been possible if the judge here had sentenced appellant to death because appellant's trial manner impressed the judge that appellant was a bad risk for society, or if the judge had sentenced him to death giving no reason at all. We cannot say that the due process clause renders a sentence void merely because a judge gets additional out-of-court information to assist him in the exercise of this awesome power of imposing the death sentence.

Appellant was found guilty after a fairly conducted trial. His sentence followed a hearing conducted by the judge. Upon the judge's inquiry as to why sentence should not be imposed, the defendant made statements. His counsel made extended arguments. The case went to the highest court in the state, and that court had power to reverse for abuse of discretion or legal error in the imposition of the sentence. That court affirmed. We hold that appellant was not denied due process of law.[1]

. . .[2]

---

586. Look again at Rule 32, p. 1110 above. How much do the provisions of Rule 32 reflect the policies enunciated in *Williams*? In what respect is the rule inconsistent with *Williams*? See also United States v. Burch, 873 F.2d 765 (5th Cir.1989), in which the court said that when Congress approved the Sentencing Guidelines, see p. 1109 above, it abandoned the philosophy of *Williams* that "the punishment should fit the offender and not merely the crime," p. 1122 above. The court said that the sentencing judge should not have considered the defendant's high level of education and socio-economic status as aggravating sentencing factors.

1. What we have said is not to be accepted as a holding that the sentencing procedure is immune from scrutiny under the due process clause. See Townsend v. Burke, 334 U.S. 736.

[2] Justice Murphy wrote a dissenting opinion. Justice Rutledge noted his dissent.

A majority of the Court of Appeals for the Eighth Circuit held, over a dissent, that adoption of the Sentencing Guidelines did not have the effect of making the Confrontation Clause applicable to sentencing proceedings. United States v. Wise, 976 F.2d 393 (8th Cir.1992). Although the Guidelines restricted the sentencing judge's discretion, it "has not so transformed the sentencing phase that it constitutes a separate criminal proceeding." Id. at 401. The dissenting opinion observed that both the philosophy and practice of sentencing had so changed since the decision in *Williams* that the conclusion to the contrary in that case was "obsolete." Id. at 409. The conclusion in *Wise* was upheld in United States v. Silverman, 976 F.2d 1502 (6th Cir.1992) (en banc).

587. Rule 32(e)(1) provides that the presentence report shall not be submitted to the court or its contents disclosed until after the defendant has pleaded guilty or been convicted. "Submission of the report to the court before [the defendant has pleaded guilty or been convicted] constitutes error of the clearest kind. . . . To permit the ex parte introduction of this sort of material to the judge who will pronounce the defendant's guilt or innocence or who will preside over a jury trial would seriously contravene the rule's purpose of preventing possible prejudice from premature submission of the presentence report." Gregg v. United States, 394 U.S. 489, 492 (1969).

588. 18 U.S.C. § 3661: "No limitation shall be placed on the information concerning the background, character, and conduct of a person convicted of an offense which a court of the United States may receive and consider for the purpose of imposing an appropriate sentence."

"[O]nce the guilt of the accused has been properly established, the sentencing judge, in determining the kind and extent of punishment to be imposed, is not restricted to evidence derived from the examination and cross-examination of witnesses in open court but may, consistently with the Due Process Clause of the Fourteenth Amendment, consider responsible unsworn or 'out-of-court' information relative to the circumstances of the crime and to the convicted person's life and characteristics." Williams v. Oklahoma, 358 U.S. 576, 584 (1959).

A sentencing court is not precluded under the federal Sentencing Guidelines from considering conduct of the defendant underlying charges of which he has been acquitted. United States v. Watts, 519 U.S. 148 (1997) (per curiam) (7–2). The Court noted that an acquittal of the criminal charge does not establish that the defendant did not engage in the conduct in question.

589. In Gardner v. Florida, 430 U.S. 349 (1977) (8–1), the court held that a sentence of death imposed in part on the basis of information in a presentence report that the defendant had no opportunity to contest was unconstitutional. Distinguishing its holding in Williams v. New York, p. 1120 above, the Court said that the death penalty had now been recognized by a majority of the Court as "a different kind of punishment than any other which may be imposed in this country." Id. at 357. Furthermore, the

Court said, the application of requirements of due process to the sentencing procedure had been made clearer since *Williams* was decided. Id. at 358.

Specht v. Patterson

386 U.S. 605, 87 S.Ct. 1209, 18 L.Ed.2d 326 (1967)

■ MR. JUSTICE DOUGLAS delivered the opinion of the Court.

We held in Williams v. New York, 337 U.S. 241, that the Due Process Clause of the Fourteenth Amendment did not require a judge to have hearings and to give a convicted person an opportunity to participate in those hearings when he came to determine the sentence to be imposed. . . .

That was a case where at the end of the trial and in the same proceeding the fixing of the penalty for first degree murder was involved—whether life imprisonment or death.

The question is whether the rule of the *Williams* case applies to this Colorado case where petitioner, having been convicted for indecent liberties under one Colorado statute that carries a maximum sentence of 10 years (Colo.Rev.Stat.Ann. § 40–2–32 (1963)) but not sentenced under it, may be sentenced under the Sex Offenders Act, Colo.Rev.Stat.Ann. § 39–19–1 to 10 (1963), for an indeterminate term of from one day to life without notice and full hearing. . . .

The Sex Offenders Act may be brought into play if the trial court "is of the opinion that any . . . person [convicted of specified sex offenses], if at large, constitutes a threat of bodily harm to members of the public, or is an habitual offender and mentally ill." § 1. He then becomes punishable for an indeterminate term of from one day to life on the following conditions as specified in § 2:

> (2) A complete psychiatric examination shall have been made of him by the psychiatrists of the Colorado psychopathic hospital or by psychiatrists designated by the district court; and
>
> (3) A complete written report thereof submitted to the district court. Such report shall contain all facts and findings, together with recommendations as to whether or not the person is treatable under the provisions of this article; whether or not the person should be committed to the Colorado state hospital or to the state home and training schools as mentally ill or mentally deficient. Such report shall also contain the psychiatrist's opinion as to whether or not the person could be adequately supervised on probation.

This procedure was followed in petitioner's case; he was examined as required and a psychiatric report prepared and given to the trial judge prior to the sentencing. But there was no hearing in the normal sense, no right of confrontation and so on.

Petitioner insists that this procedure does not satisfy due process because it allows the critical finding to be made under § 1 of the Sex Offenders Act (1) without a hearing at which the person so convicted may confront and cross-examine adverse witnesses and present evidence of his own by use of compulsory process, if necessary; and (2) on the basis of hearsay evidence to which the person involved is not allowed access.

We adhere to Williams v. New York, supra; but we decline the invitation to extend it to this radically different situation. These commitment proceedings whether denominated civil or criminal are subject both to the Equal Protection Clause of the Fourteenth Amendment . . . and to the Due Process Clause. We hold that the requirements of due process were not satisfied here.

The Sex Offenders Act does not make the commission of a specified crime the basis for sentencing. It makes one conviction the basis for commencing another proceeding under another Act to determine whether a person constitutes a threat of bodily harm to the public, or is an habitual offender and mentally ill. That is a new finding of fact . . . that was not an ingredient of the offense charged. The punishment under the second Act is criminal punishment even though it is designed not so much as retribution as it is to keep individuals from inflicting future harm. . . .

. . .

. . . Under Colorado's criminal procedure, here challenged, the invocation of the Sex Offenders Act means the making of a new charge leading to criminal punishment. The case is not unlike those under recidivist statutes where an habitual criminal issue is "a distinct issue" (Graham v. West Virginia, 224 U.S. 616, 625) on which a defendant "must receive reasonable notice and an opportunity to be heard." Oyler v. Boles, 368 U.S. 448, 452. . . . Due process, in other words, requires that he be present with counsel, have an opportunity to be heard, be confronted with witnesses against him, have the right to cross-examine, and to offer evidence of his own. And there must be findings adequate to make meaningful any appeal that is allowed. . . . None of these procedural safeguards we have mentioned is present under Colorado's Sex Offenders Act. We therefore hold that it is deficient in due process as measured by the requirements of the Fourteenth Amendment. . . .

. . .[3]

---

590. Specht v. Patterson was distinguished in McMillan v. Pennsylvania, 477 U.S. 79 (1986) (5–4), in which the Court upheld a state statute providing that a person convicted of specified felonies is subject to a mandatory minimum sentence of five years' imprisonment, if the sentenc-

[3] Justice Harlan noted his agreement with the Court's conclusions, on different premises.

ing judge finds by a preponderance of the evidence that he "visibly possessed a firearm" while committing the crime. The statute " 'ups the ante' " for the defendant, the Court said, but does not radically alter the sentencing procedure, as did the Colorado procedure at issue in *Specht*. Id. at 89. (The Court concluded also that possession of a firearm was not an element of the offense, requiring proof beyond a reasonable doubt, under In re Winship, p. 1080 note 556 above.)

591. Townsend v. Burke, 334 U.S. 736 (1948), which the Court cited in Williams v. New York, p. 241 above, 337 U.S. at 252 n.18, held that the uncounseled defendant's sentence, based on "assumptions concerning his criminal record which were materially untrue," denied him due process of law. "[I]t is the careless or designed pronouncement of sentence on a foundation so extensively and materially false, which the prisoner had no opportunity to correct by the services which counsel would provide, that renders the proceedings lacking in due process." Id. at 741.

Rule 32(e) requires that a copy of the presentence report be given to the defendant, defense counsel, and an attorney for the government "at least 35 days before sentencing," unless the defendant waives the minimum period.

> [A] defendant must be permitted to state his version of the facts to the court; where the possibility of reliance on misinformation is shown, this right must be extended to permit that presentation by the defendant which will enable the sentencing judge to grasp the relevant facts correctly. . . . In appropriate circumstances, this may mean that a defendant will be permitted to submit affidavits or documents, supply oral statements, or even participate in an evidentiary hearing; alternatively, further corroboration of sentencing data may be required. And while in such cases the procedure to be followed lies within the sound discretion of the sentencing judge, a court's failure to take appropriate steps to ensure the fairness and accuracy of the sentencing process must be held to be plain error and an abuse of that discretion.
>
> Presentence reports, prepared by probation officers for use at sentencing, often call for an exercise of the Court's discretion in this regard. The contents of the reports are not subject to the rules of evidence, and experience has shown that they are heavily relied upon by sentencing judges. Accuracy is therefore of prime concern. . . .

United States v. Robin, 545 F.2d 775, 779–80 (2d Cir.1976).

592. Other criminal conduct. Rule 32(d)(2)(A)(i) provides that the presentence report shall contain the defendant's criminal record. The report commonly includes not only a record of convictions but also information about arrests, pending charges, and criminal activity generally. In United States v. Weston, 448 F.2d 626, 634 (9th Cir.1971), the court held that the sentencing judge had improperly relied on information from the government sources about the defendant's deep involvement in narcotics traffic, which the defendant denied and which had too little indication of dependability. "A rational penal system must have some concern for the probable accuracy of the informational inputs in the sentencing process." Id. at 634.

The court held in United States v. Metz, 470 F.2d 1140 (3d Cir.1972), that pending indictments recited in a presentence report could be considered.

> The fact that the other criminal activity has not been passed on by a court should not be controlling, for "of necessity, much of the information garnered by the probation officer will be hearsay and will doubtless be discounted accordingly, *but the very object of the process is scope*." United States v. Doyle, 348 F.2d [715 (2d Cir.1965)] at 721. (Emphasis added). In fact, the kind of evidence here objected to is more reliable than the hearsay evidence which the sentencing judge can clearly consider, for unlike hearsay, the indictments are based on testimony given under oath and required the existence of probable cause to believe that [the defendant] had committed the other offenses.
>
> We believe that the probable trustworthiness of information concerning other criminal charges is far more significant than the procedural stages of the other charges. United States v. Sweig, 454 F.2d 181 (2d Cir.1972), held that the sentencing judge could properly consider evidence with respect to crimes of which the defendant had been *acquitted. Sweig* turns on the reliability of the evidence considered, for the evidence "was given under oath and was subject to cross-examination and the judge had the opportunity for personal observation of the witnesses." 454 F.2d at 184. . . .
>
> . . . We hold that indictments for other criminal activity are of sufficient reliability to warrant their consideration by a sentencing judge.

470 F.2d at 1142.

A convicted defendant's refusal, without adequate explanation, to cooperate with officials investigating a criminal conspiracy in which he was an admitted participant may properly be considered as a factor in the determination of his sentence. Roberts v. United States, 445 U.S. 552 (1980) (8–1).

A sentence may not be based on prior convictions that are constitutionally invalid because of the denial of counsel. United States v. Tucker, 404 U.S. 443 (1972). A conviction for a misdemeanor without the assistance of counsel that was valid when entered, because no sentence of imprisonment was imposed (see Scott v. Illinois, 440 U.S. 367 (1979), p. 548 note 296 above), may, however, be the basis for sentence enhancement following a subsequent conviction. Nichols v. United States, 511 U.S. 738 (1994) (6–3).

In Curtis v. United States, 511 U.S. 485 (1994) (6–3), the Court held that a defendant sentenced in federal court does not have a constitutional right to attack collaterally the validity of a prior state conviction used as the ground for enhancement of the federal sentence, unless the attack is based on the alleged denial of his right to counsel. *Curtis* involved the sentence-enhancement provision of the Armed Career Criminal Act of 1984,

18 U.S.C. § 924(e). The Court concluded that, unlike some of the other sentence-enhancement provisions that authorize collateral attack on a conviction used for enhancement, the ACCA provision does not, and that the Constitution requires that such attack be allowed only with respect to the right to counsel.

593. In United States v. Grayson, 438 U.S. 41 (1978) (6–3), the Court held that it is permissible for the trial judge, when imposing sentence, to take into account the defendant's observed false testimony at trial. "A defendant's truthfulness or mendacity while testifying on his own behalf, almost without exception, has been deemed probative of his attitudes toward society and prospects for rehabilitation and hence relevant to sentencing." Id. at 50. Responding to the argument that such a rule might inhibit a defendant from testifying truthfully, the Court said that it was not imposing a rigid rule that sentences of defendants who testify falsely be enhanced. "Rather, we are reaffirming the authority of a sentencing judge to evaluate carefully a defendant's testimony on the stand, determine—with a consciousness of the frailty of human judgment—whether that testimony contained willful and material falsehoods, and, if so, assess in light of all the other knowledge gained about the defendant the meaning of that conduct with respect to his prospects for rehabilitation and restoration to a useful place in society." Id. at 55.

Federal Sentencing Guideline § 3C1.1 provides for enhancement of the sentence of a defendant who, by committing perjury, obstructs the administration of justice. In United States v. Dunnigan, 507 U.S. 87 (1993), the Court upheld the provision against the challenge that it undermines a defendant's right to testify. The Court said that "if a defendant objects to a sentence enhancement resulting from her trial testimony, a district court must review the evidence and make independent findings necessary to establish a wilful impediment to or obstruction of justice, or an attempt to do the same." Id. at 95.

A sentencing judge may not draw adverse inferences from a defendant's silence about facts relating to the circumstances and details of the crime. Mitchell v. United States, 526 U.S. 314 (1999) (5–4).

In sentencing proceedings, the Double Jeopardy Clause does not preclude retrial of an issue that had once been resolved against the state. Monge v. California, 524 U.S. 721 (1998) (5–4). The state had alleged grounds for enhancement of the defendant's sentence at the first sentencing proceeding but had offered insufficient evidence to prove it. The Court held that the issue could be relitigated in a subsequent proceeding.

594. Courts have generally held that evidence inadmissible at trial because of a violation of the defendant's Fourth Amendment rights may nevertheless be considered by the trial judge at sentencing. E.g., United States v. Brimah, 214 F.3d 854 (7th Cir.2000) (referring specifically to Sentencing Guidelines); United States v. Lynch, 934 F.2d 1226 (11th Cir.1991). "Both the sentencing court and the post-sentencing administrative agencies are entitled to know all of the facts, including prior alleged offenses that did not result in a conviction. They are, of course, limited to a consideration of information that is accurate, but they are not precluded from considering prior charges that were dismissed or alleged offenses for which charges were not filed because of illegally obtained evidence." United States v. Graves, 785 F.2d 870, 876 (10th Cir.1986) (additional cases cited). Cf. United States v. Hernandez Camacho, 779 F.2d 227 (5th Cir.1985) (sentencing judge may consider defendant's testimony at hearing on motion to suppress evidence). But cf. Verdugo v. United States, 402 F.2d 599 (9th Cir.1968), holding that illegally obtained evidence could not be used at sentencing, where the purpose of the search was to obtain evidence that would increase the defendant's sentence: "[W]here . . . the use of illegally seized evidence at sentencing would provide a substantial incentive for unconstitutional searches and seizures, that evidence should be disregarded by the sentencing judge." Id. at 613. *Verdugo* is discussed and qualified in United States v. Kim, 25 F.3d 1426 (9th Cir.1994).

UNITED STATES DISTRICT COURT FOR THE DISTRICT OF COLUMBIA PRESENTENCE REPORT[4]

I OFFENSE:

On January 29, 1968, at the conclusion of an eight day jury trial, before the Honorable Frank Solomon, defendant Reddish and codefendants Scott A. Scarlet, Albert Maroon, Jr. and Roy Ruby were found guilty of counts one to twelve, inclusive. Count one charges the four defendants with Unauthorized Use of an Automobile, on or about November 15, 1966, which belonged to Richard A. Thomas. Count two charges, on November 22, 1966, the entry of the Brookland Branch of The National Bank of Washington, FDIC insured, with intent to commit a robbery. Counts three, five, seven, nine, and eleven, cite the Federal charge of actual Bank Robbery of monies in the possession of said bank, in the aggregate total of $15,308.32; counts four, six, eight, ten, and twelve cite the D.C. Criminal Code charge of Robbery. Defendant Reddish was named in the thirteenth count of the indictment, charged with Carrying a Dangerous Weapon, pistol, however, this charge was dismissed during trial on the oral motion of the Government.

Official Version:

Your Honor undoubtedly remains familiar with the facts and testimony offered during the jury trial of this case. A brief review, however, is offered. Approximately only minutes to 9:55 a.m., November 22, 1966, three Negro male subjects, wearing masks over their faces, also armed with pistols, entered the Brookland Branch of The National Bank of Washington, D.C., 3006—12th Street, N.E. and announced a bank robbery: "All right folks,

4. This presentence report is based on an actual case; it was prepared for use at an Executive Meeting of the Judicial Council for the District of Columbia Circuit in November 1968. Names have been changed.

this is it, get on the floor!'' Two of the subjects hurdled the counter in front of the teller cages and started grabbing all available monies from the respective teller cages. The aggregate sum of $15,308.02 was seized by subjects and placed in bank money bags. When an automobile horn sounded outside, more or less as a signal, the three original subjects then fled the bank and entered an awaiting 1965 Ford Mustang car, last seen to speed away on Perry Street, N.E. The bank manager and a teller pushed the alarm button; also, they and a private citizen outside of the bank managed to note the license number of the fleeing Mustang, which was later conveyed to responding police officers. The official time of the robbery was established as at 9:55 a.m.

Within minutes of the reported robbery, cruising police officers spotted the aforementioned, aforedescribed Mustang car parked in the 1300 block of Perry Street, N.E., only a few blocks away from the scene of the bank robbery. A black, automatic loaded pistol, plus rolls of coins and paper money, were found and recovered from the aforementioned car. A quick canvass of nearby houses resulted in one witness telling the police officers that a small U–Haul truck had been parked in front of her residence at 1324 Perry Street since about 9:30 a.m.; also, the witness stated that she heard the same truck suddenly speed away at a high rate of speed, at about 10 a.m. A lookout was immediately broadcast for the U–Haul truck; several minutes later, the same truck was observed and stopped by police officers in the 1000 block of Kenilworth Avenue, N.E. After the police officers stopped the aforementioned truck, the driver, later identified as defendant Ernest Reddish, alighted from the driver's side of the truck. As he and the police officers approached one another, the latter observed a pistol handle protruding from subject's pants pocket; also, the officers glimpsed two subjects quickly looking out of the rear window of the truck and suddenly duck down. Defendant Reddish was immediately placed under arrest and a .38 caliber loaded pistol was seized from his pocket. Upon looking into the truck and observing three Negro subjects lying on the floor, the police officers immediately radioed for assistance, at the same time, ordered the three subjects not to move. Upon the arrival of police assistance, the three subjects were ordered from the truck and were immediately placed under arrest. A search of the truck resulted in the recovery of two cloth bank bags containing $14,911.00 in money, also, a (third) pistol, which one of the subjects had dropped as he emerged from the truck; further, a pair of sunglasses, silk handkerchiefs (used to cover their faces as masks) and four pairs of gloves were recovered, all or most of which had been used in the robbery. A personal search of codefendant Ruby's person resulted in the recovery of $320 in bills, which was identified as "bait" money taken during the robbery. A total of $15,297.00 in money was recovered, respectively, from the 1965 Mustang, the truck and from codefendant Ruby; $11.32 apparently was not recovered. After being arrested at 10:19 a.m. and charged with the instant bank robbery-holdup, the four defendants were transported to the Robbery Squad Office, where all four subjects denied the offense. In a subsequent lineup, the bank manager and other witnesses from inside the bank apparently could not be sure of any identification. On the other hand, a private citizen witness, who observed the robbery taking place as she entered the bank but managed to walk outside whereupon she observed the awaiting 1965 Mustang, parked in front of the bank and was able to look at the Negro driver behind the wheel, viewed the same lineup, and identified codefendant, Scott A. Scarlet, as the one she saw behind the wheel and who drove the other subjects away from the hold-up scene.

Intense investigation by both local police and FBI Agents resulted in the uncovering of the fact that the instant truck had been rented by one Alex Alexander, an uncle of defendant Reddish. He informed interrogating officers that he had rented the truck at the request of defendant Reddish and had turned same over to him; the latter had given him $25.00 with which to do so. Mr. Alexander also stated that the license tags found on the instant Mustang had come from a Dodge vehicle which had been given to Reddish and himself to repair and personally use. Alexander denied any knowledge of the intended use of the truck, or about the bank robbery. In subsequent contact with FBI Agents, he identified codefendant Maroon and defendant Reddish as close, long-term friends. As to the pieces of clothing recovered from the floor of the truck—a green raincoat, (2) black kerchiefs, (3) pillow cases, (4) multi-colored scarfs—most were identified by bank tellers-witnesses, as having been worn by the hold-up subjects.

Your Honor is apprised of subsequent aggravating, additional information, that on February 11, 1967, while on bond in CC #000–67, the defendant was arrested in a new case charging assault on two police officers and Carrying a Dangerous Weapon, gun. The new case is represented in CC #500–67, which is scheduled for trial during the week of February 12, 1968. Also, while on bond in CC #000–67, and CC #500–67 the defendant was arrested on November 18, 1967 charged with two counts of Assault with a Dangerous Weapon, gun, now represented in #00–68, for which no trial date has been scheduled. Subject secured his release on bond ($10,000) in CC #00–68, on December 5, 1967.

II DEFENDANT'S VERSION OF OFFENSE:

In the writer's presentence interview with this defendant, he advised that he did not take the witness stand during his trial. He denied any knowledge of the bank robbery. He immediately elaborated that he was planning to move from his residence and was looking for a place to rent, also, a garage to rent to store excess furniture. He stated that he had been searching in the area of Rhode Island Avenue and Monroe Street, N.E., and eventually turned into an alley paralleling 13th and 12th Streets, N.E., off Newton Street, N.E. Here, he says he saw a mattress waiting to be picked up by the trash people. It looked relatively in good condition, and he thought he would examine same closely. He says he left his parked truck, and, after looking at the mattress, picked it up and carried it back to the truck. When he threw the mattress in the back of the truck, he then claimed finding National Bank of Washington bank bags, containing a very large sum of money. After examining the money, also, noting that no one was around, he said he got "hungry" and took off, "asking no questions."

He then indicated coming upon codefendant Maroon, who was standing on a corner with Ruby and Scarlet. He stopped the truck and Maroon and the other two subjects entered the truck. He indicated only that this was on Kenilworth Avenue near the Benning Road viaduct. After pulling away from the curb, the police came up from behind him and pulled him over. "Only I knew what was up front (meaning the money bags) . . . I decided not to say anything to the police." He concluded his version by denying, again, having any knowledge of the bank robbery, or anything else as to how the money bags from the robbery got into his truck.

The defendant offered the foregoing in a very explicit matter-of-fact manner, without any overt concern for his predicament, or remorse for the case itself. What concern was expressed, and perhaps in a manner to entice some sympathy in his behalf, centered around frequent references made to his wife and children and their welfare. He impressed the writer as very sophisticated, also adept at concealing inner feelings of hostility, particularly centered around the police.

III PRIOR RECORD:

3–11–58	Unauthorized Use of Vehicle	Probation, indefinite.

The defendant was apprehended while riding, with three other juveniles, in a stolen car. On March 21, 1958, Judge Wise of D.C. Juvenile Court placed him on indefinite probation supervision.

4–26–58	Unauthorized Use of Vehicle	Sentenced to National Training School for Boys

Within five weeks after being placed on juvenile probation supervision in the above case, the defendant was arrested as the driver of a stolen car which had been rented by a doctor. Facts indicate he led the police on a high speed chase, which ended in a collision and more than $1,000 damages inflicted on the stolen automobile. On April 29, 1958, he was found involved in D.C. Juvenile Court, who immediately ordered him committed to the National Training School for Boys under a minority commitment. . . . The defendant made a satisfactory adjustment while at the National Training School and gained his release on parole on June 20, 1959.

11–7–59(17)	Assault with Dangerous Weapon (Shod foot)	No disposition indicated.

The defendant was arrested with several other youths and charged with assaulting two young victims, one of whom the defendant kicked while lying on the ground. As a result of the arrest and circumstances surrounding same, the Youth Division of the U.S. Board of Parole issued a parole violation warrant, ordering his return to the National Training School.

11–30–59	Parole Violation Warrant	Returned to National Training School for Boys, effective 1–20.
4–8–60	Escape from National Training School	

Adult:

2–2–61	Affray	Consolidated records, Dept. of Prisons, Raleigh, N.C.	30 days jail
9–15–61	Assault with Dangerous Weapon	" "	Two years

Circumstances surrounding this arrest and two year sentence presently remain unknown. The FBI Report, however, indicated the defendant escaped on October 11, 1961, only to be recaptured on the following day, October 12, 1961.

10–25–62	Escape	Consolidated Records, Dept. of Prisons, Raleigh, N.C.	Three months added to the two year sentence.
5–23–66 Washington, D.C.	Carrying a Dangerous Weapon, Pistol		ISS, probation—one year

The arrest facts indicate a man entered a High's Dairy Store in northeast Washington, and announced a robbery by stating, "Give me all the money in your pocket," whereupon he displayed a pistol in his pants pocket. When a second female clerk suddenly emerged from the rear of the store, the man hastily said, "I'm only kidding, I'm not going to shoot you"; he then walked out of the store. The police responded to the scene, obtained a description of the suspect, and shortly afterward, came upon three young adults, including this defendant, one who matched the description of the suspect. All three suspects were searched. Police seized a loaded .38 caliber Empire State revolver, containing five rounds, from the person of defendant Reddish. A .38 caliber revolver was seized from a second subject—Lew E. Wood, who was identified as the suspect who had entered the High's Store and announced the robbery attempt. The third suspect—Pat A. Kidd, was identified as a strong suspect in a different robbery holdup violation. . . . After a presentence investigation the defendant was placed on probation, on August 18, 1967. The writer has reviewed the probation department file in D.C. Court of General Sessions; no indication was reflected in the file as to the issuance of a probation violation warrant in their case, based on the defendant's arrest and/or conviction in CC #000–67.

11–22–66	Bank Robbery (Holdup)	Instant Case CC #000–67
2–11–67	Assault on Police Officers (2) Carrying Dangerous Weapon, Gun	Indicted in CC #500–67

As previously mentioned, while on bond in the instant case, on February 11, 1967, about 4:20 p.m., police officers observed the defendant in a

1966 Chevelle automobile with four other subjects. When the police officer (Moore) approached and asked the defendant for his operator's license, the police officer also observed one subject to push a paper bag under the car seat, but not before the officer had observed a pistol barrel protruding from the bag. When Officer Moore sought to obtain possession of the gun, defendant Reddish is said to have instigated an assault on the officer. When the officer's partner (Flynn) responded, a second occupant of the car, James Jamison, 21, intercepted and yoked Officer Flynn into unconsciousness. When Jamison continued to assault the unconscious officer, Officer Moore shot Jamison, necessitating his removal to a hospital. A third off-duty police officer assisted Officer Moore to subdue and maintain Reddish's arrest. Also, codefendant Maroon, who had been an original occupant of the car, stepped from the gathered crowd and began assaulting both police officers in an attempt to free this defendant Reddish. However, Maroon was subdued and his arrest also effected. Additional facts indicate that four guns (one an automatic pistol), two ski masks, gloves and clotheslines were seized as evidence from the aforementioned car. Reddish, Jamison and codefendant Maroon have been named in a three count indictment in CC #500–67, which is scheduled for trial during the week of February 21, 1968.

11–18–67	Assault with Dangerous Weapon, Gun	Indicted in CC #00–68.

Arrest facts indicate the police responded to a report that Joseph and Jane Johnson, husband and wife, were shot in front of their home at 1000 Curry Avenue, S.E., by means of a gun held in the hands of this defendant. The defendant has now been indicted, however, a trial date has not been scheduled.

IV FAMILY HISTORY:

This defendant was born in Whiteville, Columbus County, North Carolina on August 9, 1942, and was brought to Washington, D.C. by his mother when approximately three or four years of age. He is the oldest of two boys of his natural parents, Ernest and Chellin, nee Redd, Reddish, who are respectively said to be about 50 and 45 years of age. The defendant has advised us he never knew his real father. However, after the birth of his younger brother, James, now 23, and serving in the Army in Vietnam, his mother "took to living in a common-law type marriage" with a Manuel Reddish, 52, whom he calls his stepfather, a chef cook, whom he understands to be his father's natural uncle. Subsequently, four children, two half-brothers and two half-sisters of the defendant, 18 to 13 years of age, resulted from the illicit relationship of the stepfather and mother. About five years ago, the defendant said his stepfather finally separated from his mother, due to the mother's problems with alcoholism. The stepfather now has custody of the four children. The defendant indicated the stepfather's address is known only as a corner house at 8th and W Streets, S.W., his mother is said to be "living with another man," somewhere in the vicinity of 3rd and F Streets, N.E.

The defendant described his early home life, aside from material needs and food being plentiful, as a poor and an unhappy one. He indicated the family frequently moved from one place to another, hardly ever remained in one house for more than one year, and primarily due to his mother's alcoholism problem, wherein she mismanaged financial affairs to cater to her problem. The defendant also indicated his parents argued frequently and became embroiled in actual altercations. The defendant says his relationship with his mother was "only fair" whereas he denied having a satisfactory relationship with the stepfather. From this point, the defendant went on to discuss his past social-legal difficulties and ascribed same as due to the lack of a decent home, the lack of interest and failure to provide proper supervision by his parents, thus, the desire to escape from the "unpleasantness of it all."

Past social, institutional records substantiate a very poor social-familial background, that the parents were seemingly concerned primarily with their own personal pursuits and were inadequate as stable, suitable parental figures. Several of the children have been known to local social-legal agencies; the defendant's half-brother, John Toney, 14, is presently a ward of the local welfare department's child-welfare division, confined at the Cedar Knoll Institution at the D.C. Children's Center.

The defendant has, more or less, been on his own since his initial commitment to the National Training School for Boys at fifteen years of age. While he appeared deliberately guarded about saying anything about leaving the District for North Carolina, or about his confinement period in North Carolina State Penal Institutions, he did claim he entered marriage in 1963 upon his return to the District, and has subsequently sought to live a relatively stable life.

V MARITAL HISTORY:

The defendant married Yvette May Oates, now 22, on September 28, 1963, in a religious ceremony in a private house in the District (verified). The defendant says he met his wife during the period after escaping from the National Training School and before "lighting out for North Carolina," by which time he had caused his future wife to conceive their first child. The two parties now have four children: Chalmers (DOB: 1–22–61); Wanda Pansy (DOB: 6–3–64); Ernest IV (DOB: 3–25–66) and Doretta (DOB: 5–13–67). The defendant professed having great interest in his wife and children and claims his prime concern is the life now centered around providing for his family as to a decent home, something which he missed in his own early background. His wife was interviewed, however, she was not able to talk freely, due to a dental infection. She did, however, profess love for the defendant, claims he is a good father and a good husband. The wife is not employed, nor expects to be. She says she will turn to public assistance should her husband be committed to jail in the instant case. Otherwise, during the writer's discussion of the offense with the defendant, the wife remained silent.

VI HOME AND NEIGHBORHOOD:

Since October 1967, the defendant and his wife and family have been living in a National Capitol Housing Authority row house, which contains three bedrooms, for which they are paying $52 per month rent. From January to October 1967, the family lived in a rented, small crowded one bedroom apartment on Dorchester Lane, S.E.; from December 5, 1964 to January 1967, the family occupied a basement apartment at 3192 Anacostia Avenue, S.E., from which they were evicted when the owner claimed he wanted the entire house for his own family. Prior thereto, it would appear the defendant and his family frequently moved about the southeast and northeast sections of the District, in unstable, crowded living situations, predominantly in lower class neighborhoods noted for high crime rates.

VII EDUCATION:

The defendant last attended Eliot Junior High School, where he was repeating the ninth grade before being committed to the National Training School for Boys. His public school record reflects poor grades, mostly D's and/or failing marks. It is interesting that at the National Training School, the defendant seemingly attended to his academic studies sufficient to have completed eleventh grade level courses. Intelligence examinations at the training school reflected an I.Q. of 83, considered low-average academic intelligence; one psychologist viewed the defendant as having the potential for above-average intellectual performance ability. At the National Training School, the defendant also received some vocational training in auto mechanics, in which field he was described as having favorable potentials. This defendant has impressed the writer as functioning on or about a tenth or eleventh grade social-intellectual level, yet to be highly sophisticated in criminal activities.

VIII RELIGION:

The defendant professes the Baptist faith, but admits he rarely attends church. His conscious concern towards religious values, as a way of life, appears very nil.

IX INTERESTS AND LEISURE TIME ACTIVITIES:

The defendant says his primary leisure time activities and interests center around boxing, swimming and auto drag racing.

X HEALTH:

This defendant stands 5′9″, and says he weighs 200 pounds. He appears very dark brown skinned in complexion and evidences an old vertical scar on his left temple. He claims good physical health; he says he suffered a dislocated right hip while at the National Training School, which resulted in six months hospitalization, however, he denies any subsequent after effects. He describes himself as a social drinker, denies alcohol to be a problem.

During the presentence interview, the defendant was viewed as free from any signs of disturbing personality problems. He evidenced himself to be very fluent and tried to be very persuasive in relating his version of the offense. However, the greater impression is that of a young adult, who, though overtly appearing docile, is quite sophisticated in talking with people in authority. Past impressions of other professional workers and trained specialists describe this defendant as having an extensive suppressed feeling of hostility, particularly towards people in positions of authority. He has also been described as quick to react in antisocial, aggressive behavior. His amenability to personal counselling is questioned by this writer; his response to same would undoubtedly be superficial, without a sincere desire to emotionally integrate counselling.

XI EMPLOYMENT:

October 1967 to December 1967, three months: The defendant says he has been employed as a laborer for the General Construction Company, 1200 Congress Street, S.E. Verification was not made; it is interesting to note that the defendant was confined in the D.C. Jail from November 18, 1967 until December 5, 1967, as a consequence of his arrest in CC #00–68, on the foregoing date. Subsequent employment has been intermittent due to weather conditions.

May 1967 to October 1967, five months: The defendant worked at the Terry Auto Body Shop in the rear of 1450 R. Street, N.W. under a work and training program funded through the D.C. Department of Public Welfare.

March 1964 to November 22, 1966, 32 months: The defendant worked as a truck-driver air-compressor operator for the Bell Air Compressor Rental Company. This company rented out air compressor trucks to construction contractors. His employment earnings varied between $75 to $100 per week, dependent upon the demand for such rental service.

September 1963 to December 1963, four months: Scott General Contractors employed the defendant as a laborer during the foregoing period until the job expired.

Verification of past employment was established at the three latter employers. The writer was advised that the defendant has the ability to be a satisfactory worker, though occasional absenteeism was noted. This writer is impressed with a fairly satisfactory employment record on the part of the defendant. The defendant also indicated he has augmented regular daytime employment, particularly wintertime employment when working conditions are limited, by working part-time and evening jobs, primarily those requiring a delivery truck-driver.

XII MILITARY SERVICE:

The defendant does not have active military service. He has registered with the Selective Service Board No. 24 in Whiteville, Columbus County, North Carolina (SS #00 00 00 000). He says his draft classification is 4–F, due to his criminal record.

XIII FINANCIAL CONDITION:

The defendant denies any assets. He says he possesses a 1965 Pontiac automobile, which he has a time payment contract on, with $1,000 outstanding. The instant car, according to the defendant, was to be surrendered during the week of February 5, 1968. The defendant denied any other outstanding obligations.

XIV EVALUATIVE SUMMARY:

This 25 year old married defendant stands convicted of multiple charges involving a holdup bank robbery, for which he faces sentencing along with three codefendants. Remorse for his actions and/or concern for his present predicament appears lacking. He has established a substantial criminal record, before and subsequent to the instant offense. Such a record portrays an individual who is completely defiant of the law and order and the well-being of others in society. In addition to the instant offense, he still faces trial on multiple charges of assaulting police officers and carrying dangerous weapons (guns); also, a second trial remains pending, which involves an assault with a dangerous weapon, again, a gun.

The defendant is the unfortunate product of parents who were ill-equipped and, least of all, personally-socially adequate for handling the responsibilities of such a role; whose home situation was deprived and least conducive to providing happiness, the proper preparations and motivations for eventually developing into a decent, meaningful member of society. The converse has been the reaction; negative inner feelings of hostility and antisocial, aggressive behavior have developed and long smoldered, finally erupting, within the past year, particularly into acts revealing the severe potential for violence.

The Court is dealing with a defendant who, overtly, appears docile and passive, yet who is now manifesting a manner of sophistication which was concealed or masked, a type of individual society needs least. His amenability for responding to corrective treatment techniques would seemingly offer a poor prognosis. If treatment is to have any potential, corrective measures would certainly have to be employed over a substantial duration in a controlled environmental situation.

Respectfully submitted,

Chief U.S. Probation Officer

By:

U.S. Probation Officer

---

595. Disclosure of the contents of a presentence report to third persons is discussed in United States v. Charmer Indus., Inc., 711 F.2d 1164 (2d Cir.1983). The defendant, a corporation, was convicted in the federal district court in New York of antitrust violations. A presentence report was prepared to assist the court in determining the amount of the fine. The report was later used by an Arizona state agency in connection with a licensing proceeding involving the defendant's subsidiary. Observing that a presentence report has "many of the characteristics—and frailties—of material presented to a grand jury," the court concluded "that the district court should not authorize disclosure of a presentence report to a third person in the absence of a compelling demonstration that disclosure of the report is required to meet the ends of justice." Id. at 1175. Other cases are cited. But see United States v. Schlette, 842 F.2d 1574 (9th Cir.1988) (disclosure of dead defendant's presentence report to newspaper and to estate of person whom defendant had killed was justified).

596. Sentence following retrial. In North Carolina v. Pearce, 395 U.S. 711 (1969), the Court held that a defendant whose conviction is set aside and who is subsequently retried and convicted must be given credit for the portion of the first sentence already served, but that there is no constitutional bar to the imposition of a new sentence more severe than that originally imposed, on the basis of "events subsequent to the first trial."[5]

> To say that there exists no absolute constitutional bar to the imposition of a more severe sentence upon retrial is not, however, to end the inquiry. There remains for consideration the impact of the Due Process Clause of the Fourteenth Amendment.
>
> It can hardly be doubted that it would be a flagrant violation of the Fourteenth Amendment for a state trial court to follow an announced practice of imposing a heavier sentence upon every reconvicted defendant for the explicit purpose of punishing the defendant for his having succeeded in getting his original conviction set aside. Where . . . the original conviction has been set aside because of a

5. The requirement that the defendant be given credit for the portion of the original sentence already served was based on the Double Jeopardy Clause. See p. 1190 note 620 below. With respect to the imposition of a more severe sentence following retrial, the Court rejected arguments based on the Double Jeopardy Clause and the Equal Protection Clause of the Fourteenth Amendment: "The [equal protection] theory advanced is that, since convicts who do not seek new trials cannot have their sentences increased, it creates an invidious classification to impose that risk only upon those who succeed in getting their original convictions set aside. The argument, while not lacking in ingenuity, cannot withstand close examination. In the first place, we deal here not with increases in existing sentences, but with the imposition of wholly new sentences after wholly new trials. Putting that conceptual nicety to one side, however, the problem before us simply cannot be rationally dealt with in terms of 'classifications.' A man who is retried after his first conviction has been set aside may be acquitted. If convicted, he may receive a shorter sentence, he may receive the same sentence, or he may receive a longer sentence than the one originally imposed. The result may depend upon a particular combination of infinite variables peculiar to each individual trial. It simply cannot be said that a State has invidiously 'classified' those who successfully seek new trials, any more than that the State has invidiously 'classified' those prisoners whose convictions are *not* set aside by denying the members of that group the opportunity to be acquitted. To fit the problem of this case into an equal protection framework is a task too Procrustean to be rationally accomplished." 395 U.S. at 722–23.

> constitutional error, the imposition of such a punishment, "penalizing those who choose to exercise" constitutional rights, "would be patently unconstitutional." United States v. Jackson, 390 U.S. 570, 581. And the very threat inherent in the existence of such a punitive policy would, with respect to those still in prison, serve to "chill the exercise of basic constitutional rights." Id., at 582. . . . But even if the first conviction has been set aside for nonconstitutional error, the imposition of a penalty upon the defendant for having successfully pursued a statutory right of appeal or collateral remedy would be no less a violation of due process of law. . . . "This Court has never held that the States are required to establish avenues of appellate review, but it is now fundamental that, once established, these avenues must be kept free of unreasoned distinctions that can only impede open and equal access to the courts. . . ." . . .
>
> Due process of law, then, requires that vindictiveness against a defendant for having successfully attacked his first conviction must play no part in the sentence he receives after a new trial. And since the fear of such vindictiveness may unconstitutionally deter a defendant's exercise of the right to appeal or collaterally attack his first conviction, due process also requires that a defendant be freed of apprehension of such a retaliatory motivation on the part of the sentencing judge.
>
> In order to assure the absence of such a motivation, we have concluded that whenever a judge imposes a more severe sentence upon a defendant after a new trial, the reasons for his doing so must affirmatively appear. Those reasons must be based upon objective information concerning identifiable conduct on the part of the defendant occurring after the time of the original sentencing proceeding. And the factual data upon which the increased sentence is based must be made part of the record, so that the constitutional legitimacy of the increased sentence may be fully reviewed on appeal.

395 U.S. at 723–26.

Discussing *Pearce*, the Court said: "If it was not clear from the Court's holding in *Pearce*, it is clear from our subsequent cases applying *Pearce* that due process does not in any sense forbid enhanced sentences or charges, but only enhancement motivated by *actual vindictiveness* toward the defendant for having exercised guaranteed rights. . . . [W]here the presumption applies, the sentencing authority or the prosecutor must rebut the presumption that an increased sentence or charge resulted from vindictiveness; where the presumption does not apply, the defendant must affirmatively prove actual vindictiveness." Wasman v. United States, 468 U.S. 559, 568–69 (1984). In *Wasman*, the defendant was given an increased sentence on retrial. The sentencing judge explained the sentence as based on an intervening conviction for a crime committed before the first sentence was imposed. The Court held that the presumption of vindictiveness raised by *Pearce* had been rebutted.

There is no presumption of vindictiveness if the first sentence was imposed following conviction on a plea of guilty and, the defendant having successfully appealed from that conviction, the second sentence is imposed following a trial. Alabama v. Smith, 490 U.S. 794 (1989) (8–1). In those circumstances, the Court reasoned, the trial may reveal additional facts about the crime or about the defendant, and the element of plea-bargaining is not present. "[T]here are enough justifications for a heavier second sentence that it cannot be said to be more likely than not that a judge who imposes one is motivated by vindictiveness." Id. at 802.

The reasoning of *Pearce* was held to preclude the state from charging a defendant with a felony based on the same act for which he had been convicted of a misdemeanor, after he had exercised his right to appeal from the latter conviction and have a trial de novo. Blackledge v. Perry, 417 U.S. 21 (1974). See Thigpen v. Roberts, 468 U.S. 27 (1984) (6–3) (*Blackledge* applied). See also United States v. Jamison, 505 F.2d 407 (D.C.Cir.1974) (indictment for first-degree murder barred following mistrial on indictment for second-degree murder, absent justification in intervening circumstances).

Pearce does not preclude imposition of a more severe sentence following a trial de novo, pursuant to a procedure whereby less serious cases may be tried once in an inferior court and the defendant, if convicted, may freely elect to have an entirely independent trial thereafter in a court of general jurisdiction, at which the issues of guilt and penalty are determined without regard to the proceedings in the inferior court. Colten v. Kentucky, 407 U.S. 104 (1972). Nor does *Pearce* preclude a more severe sentence on retrial if sentencing at the second trial is entrusted to the jury, "so long as the jury is not informed of the prior sentence and the second sentence is not otherwise shown to be a product of vindictiveness." Chaffin v. Stynchcombe, 412 U.S. 17, 35 (1973). See also Texas v. McCullough, 475 U.S. 134 (1986), in which at the first trial, sentence was imposed by the jury, the trial judge then granted the defendant's motion for a new trial (on the basis of prosecutorial misconduct), and, at the second trial, the judge imposed sentence at the request of the defendant. The judge entered findings of fact to support the longer sentence. The Court held that in those circumstances, there was no presumption of vindictiveness. It held further that even if such a presumption were applied, the trial judge's findings were sufficient to overcome it.

For a case in which the court found insufficient justification for an increased sentence, see United States v. Jackson, 181 F.3d 740 (6th Cir.1999).

Nature of the Penalty

---

597. "Whatever views may be entertained regarding severity of punishment, whether one believes in its efficacy or its futility . . . these are peculiarly questions of legislative policy." Gore v. United States, 357 U.S. 386, 393 (1958). "[T]he Due Process Clause of the Fourteenth Amendment does not, nor does anything in the Constitution, require a State to fix or impose any particular penalty for any crime it may define or to impose the same or 'proportionate' sentences for separate and independent crimes." Williams v. Oklahoma, 358 U.S. 576, 586 (1959). "Save as limited by constitutional provisions safeguarding individual rights, a State may choose means to protect itself and its people against criminal violation of its laws. The comparative gravity of criminal offenses and whether their consequences are more or less injurious are matters for its determination. . . . It may inflict a deserved penalty merely to vindicate the law or to deter or to reform the offender or for all of these purposes. For the determination of sentences, justice generally requires consideration of more than the particular acts by which the crime was committed and that there be taken into account the circumstances of the offense together with the character and propensities of the offender. His past may be taken to indicate his present purposes and tendencies and significantly to suggest the period of restraint and the kind of discipline that ought to be imposed upon him." Pennsylvania ex rel. Sullivan v. Ashe, 302 U.S. 51, 55 (1937). See Howard v. Fleming, 191 U.S. 126 (1903).

598. "[C]ruel and unusual punishments [shall not be] inflicted." U.S. Constitution amend. VIII.

"Difficulty would attend the effort to define with exactness the extent of the constitutional provision which provides that cruel and unusual punishments shall not be inflicted; but it is safe to affirm that punishments of torture . . . and all others in the same line of unnecessary cruelty, are forbidden by that amendment to the Constitution." Wilkerson v. Utah, 99 U.S. 130, 135–36 (1878) (sentence of death by being publicly shot is not a cruel and unusual punishment for crime of murder). "Punishments are cruel when they involve torture or a lingering death; but the punishment of death is not cruel, within the meaning of that word as used in the Constitution. It implies there something inhuman and barbarous, something more than the mere extinguishment of life." In re Kemmler, 136 U.S. 436, 447 (1890).

The Cruel and Unusual Punishments Clause is discussed at length in Rummel v. Estelle, 445 U.S. 263 (1980) (5–4), in which the Court held that it was not a violation of the Clause for a third felony offender to be sentenced under a recidivist statute to life imprisonment, with eligibility for parole after 12 years. The defendant had argued that the three felonies for which he had been convicted (fraudulent use of a credit card, passing a forged check, and false pretenses) were relatively minor and that the sentence of life imprisonment was therefore excessive. So also, in Ewing v. California, 538 U.S. 11 (2003) (5–4), the Court held that a sentence of 25 years to life for grand theft, under California's three-strikes law, did not violate the Cruel and Unusual Punishments Clause. Relying on Rummel v. Estelle, the Court reversed a ruling below that a 40-year sentence for possession and distribution of less than nine ounces of marijuana was so "grossly disproportionate" to the crime that it violated the Cruel and Unusual Punishments Clause. Hutto v. Davis, 454 U.S. 370 (1982) (6–3).

In Solem v. Helm, 463 U.S. 277, 290 (1983) (5–4), however, the Court held that under the Eighth Amendment, "a criminal sentence must be proportionate to the crime for which the defendant has been convicted." It said: "Reviewing courts, of course, should grant substantial deference to the broad authority that legislatures necessarily possess in determining the types and limits of punishments for crimes as well as to the discretion that trial courts possess in sentencing convicted criminals. But no penalty is per se constitutional. . . . [A] single day in prison may be unconstitutional in some circumstances." Ibid. Among the factors that should be considered are "(i) the gravity of the offense and the harshness of the penalty; (ii) the sentences imposed on other criminals in the same jurisdiction; and (iii) the sentences imposed for commission of the same crime in other jurisdictions." Id. at 292. The defendant in Solem v. Helm had been sentenced as a recidivist to life imprisonment without possibility of parole for passing a bad check, his seventh conviction for a nonviolent felony. The Court concluded that the sentence was prohibited by the Eighth Amendment. *Rummel* and *Hutto* were distinguished.

In Harmelin v. Michigan, 501 U.S. 957 (1991) (5–4), the Court again considered the issue of sentence proportionality. Three Justices (opinion by Justice Kennedy, which Justice O'Connor and Justice Souter joined) adhered to the view that "the Cruel and Unusual Punishments Clause encompasses a narrow proportionality principle," which forbids only "extreme sentences" that are " 'grossly disproportionate.' " Id. at 997, 1001. Two Justices (opinion by Justice Scalia, which Chief Justice Rehnquist joined) concluded that the Clause does not include any principle of proportionality. On those bases, the Court upheld a mandatory sentence of life imprisonment without possibility of parole for possession of more than 650 grams of cocaine. The four dissenting Justices concluded that under Solem v. Helm, the sentence was unconstitutional.

In Weems v. United States, 217 U.S. 349 (1910), the Court held that a statute that prescribed a penalty of not less than 12 years' imprisonment, along with "accessory" penalties and disabilities including wearing a chain, hard labor, and perpetual disabilities after his release, for the crime of falsifying public records violated the constitutional prohibition against cruel and unusual punishments. See also Hope v. Pelzer, 536 U.S. 730 (2002) (6–3), holding that prison discipline of handcuffing a prisoner to a hitching post in conditions that created a risk of physical harm and inflicted unnecessary pain, discomfort, and humiliation violated the Cruel and Unusual Punishments Clause.

Four Justices concluded that expatriation of a native-born American who was convicted by court-martial of deserting during wartime was a cruel and unusual punishment, in Trop v. Dulles, 356 U.S. 86 (1958):

> We believe . . . that use of denationalization as a punishment is barred by the Eighth Amendment. There may be involved no physical mistreatment, no primitive torture. There is instead the total destruction of the individual's status in organized society. It is a form of punishment more primitive than torture, for it destroys for the individual the political existence that was centuries in the development. The punishment strips the citizen of his status in the national and international

AO 245B (Rev. 12/03) Judgment in a Criminal Case
Sheet 1

UNITED STATES DISTRICT COURT

______________________ District of ______________________

UNITED STATES OF AMERICA
V.

JUDGMENT IN A CRIMINAL CASE

Case Number:

USM Number:

____
Defendant's Attorney

THE DEFENDANT:

☐ pleaded guilty to count(s) ______________________

☐ pleaded nolo contendere to count(s) ______________________
which was accepted by the court.

☐ was found guilty on count(s) ______________________
after a plea of not guilty.

The defendant is adjudicated guilty of these offenses:

Title & Section	Nature of Offense	Offense Ended	Count

The defendant is sentenced as provided in pages 2 through ________ of this judgment. The sentence is imposed pursuant to the Sentencing Reform Act of 1984.

☐ The defendant has been found not guilty on count(s) ______________________

☐ Count(s) ______________________ ☐ is ☐ are dismissed on the motion of the United States.

It is ordered that the defendant must notify the United States attorney for this district within 30 days of any change of name, residence, or mailing address until all fines, restitution, costs, and special assessments imposed by this judgment are fully paid. If ordered to pay restitution, the defendant must notify the court and United States attorney of material changes in economic circumstances.

____
Date of Imposition of Judgment

____
Signature of Judge

____
Name and Title of Judge

____
Date

political community. His very existence is at the sufferance of the country in which he happens to find himself. While any one country may accord him some rights, and presumably as long as he remained in this country he would enjoy the limited rights of an alien, no country need do so because he is stateless. Furthermore, his enjoyment of even the limited rights of an alien might be subject to termination at any time by reason of deportation. In short, the expatriate has lost the right to have rights.

> This punishment is offensive to cardinal principles for which the Constitution stands. It subjects the individual to a fate of ever-increasing fear and distress. He knows not what discriminations may be established against him, what proscriptions may be directed against him, and when and for what cause his existence in his native land may be terminated. He may be subject to banishment, a fate universally decried by civilized people. He is stateless, a condition deplored in the international community of democracies. It is no answer to suggest that all the disastrous consequences of this fate may not be brought to bear on a stateless person. The threat makes the punishment obnoxious.
>
> The civilized nations of the world are in virtual unanimity that statelessness is not to be imposed as punishment for crime. It is true that several countries prescribe expatriation in the event that their nationals engage in conduct in derogation of native allegiance. Even statutes of this sort are generally applicable primarily to naturalized citizens. But use of denationalization as punishment for crime is an entirely different matter. The United Nations' survey of the nationality laws of 84 nations of the world reveals that only two countries, the Philippines and Turkey, impose denationalization as a penalty for desertion. In this country the Eighth Amendment forbids this to be done.

Id. at 101–103.

The Court has held that a state statute which made "the 'status' of narcotic addiction a criminal offense" even if the addict "has never touched any narcotic drug within the State or been guilty of any irregular behavior" imposed a cruel and unusual punishment. Robinson v. California, 370 U.S. 660, 666, 667 (1962).

> It is unlikely that any State at this moment in history would attempt to make it a criminal offense for a person to be mentally ill, or a leper, or to be afflicted with a venereal disease. A State might determine that the general health and welfare require that the victims of these and other human afflictions be dealt with by compulsory treatment, involving quarantine, confinement, or sequestration. But, in the light of contemporary human knowledge, a law which made a criminal offense of such a disease would doubtless be universally thought to be an infliction of cruel and unusual punishment in violation of the Eighth and Fourteenth Amendments. . . .
>
> We cannot but consider the statute before us as of the same category. . . . To be sure, imprisonment for ninety days [the statutory minimum sentence, received by the defendant] is not, in the abstract, a punishment which is either cruel or unusual. But the question cannot

be considered in the abstract. Even one day in prison would be a cruel and unusual punishment for the "crime" of having a common cold.

Id. at 666–67. The Court said that the state might establish programs of compulsory treatment and "might impose criminal sanctions, for example, against the unauthorized manufacture, prescription, sale, purchase, or possession of narcotics within its borders." Id. at 664.

A majority of the Court declined to apply the reasoning of *Robinson* to the case of a chronic alcoholic convicted of being drunk in a public place. Powell v. Texas, 392 U.S. 514 (1968). Four Justices said that the "primary purpose" of the cruel and unusual punishment clause "has always been considered, and properly so, to be directed at the method or kind of punishment imposed for the violation of criminal statutes; the nature of the conduct made criminal is ordinarily relevant only to the fitness of the punishment imposed." Id. at 531–32. As for *Robinson*: "The entire thrust of *Robinson*'s interpretation of the Cruel and Unusual Punishments Clause is that criminal penalties may be inflicted only if the accused has committed some act, has engaged in some behavior, which society has an interest in preventing, or perhaps in historical common law terms, has committed some *actus reus*. It thus does not deal with the question of whether certain conduct cannot constitutionally be punished because it is, in some sense, 'involuntary' or 'occasioned by a compulsion.' " Id. at 533.[6]

599. Excessive Fines. The Eighth Amendment's prohibition against "excessive fines" applies to a civil in rem forfeiture, under 21 U.S.C. § 881(a)(4), (7), of property used to facilitate a drug offense, because the forfeiture functions at least partially as punishment. Austin v. United States, 509 U.S. 602 (1993). The Court did not consider what makes a fine excessive. See generally United States v. Bajakajian, 524 U.S. 321 (1998) (5–4) (disproportional punitive forfeiture violates Excessive Fines Clause).

6. Justice White, concurring in the result, said: "If it cannot be a crime to have an irresistible compulsion to use narcotics, Robinson v. California . . . I do not see how it can constitutionally be a crime to yield to such a compulsion. Punishing an addict for using drugs convicts for addiction under a different name. Distinguishing between the two crimes is like forbidding criminal conviction for being sick with flu or epilepsy but permitting punishment for running a fever or having a convulsion. Unless *Robinson* is to be abandoned, the use of narcotics by an addict must be beyond the reach of the criminal law. Similarly, the chronic alcoholic with an irresistible urge to consume alcohol should not be punishable for drinking or for being drunk." 392 U.S. at 548–49. He concurred on the ground that it was not shown that the defendant, albeit compelled to drink, was likewise compelled to be drunk in public, the crime for which he was convicted.

Four Justices dissented. "It is settled that the Federal Constitution places some substantive limitation upon the power of state legislatures to define crimes for which the imposition of punishment is ordered. . . .

"*Robinson* stands upon a principle which, despite its subtlety, must be simply stated and respectfully applied because it is the foundation of individual liberty and the cornerstone of the relations between a civilized state and its citizens: Criminal penalties may not be inflicted upon a person for being in a condition he is powerless to change. . . .

"[The facts of this case] call into play the principle that a person may not be punished if the condition essential to constitute the defined crime is part of the pattern of his disease and is occasioned by a compulsion symptomatic of the disease. This principle, narrow in scope and applicability, is implemented by the Eighth Amendment's prohibition of 'cruel and unusual punishment,' as we construed that command in *Robinson*." Id. at 566–67, 569.

600. Restitution. Federal law provides that as part of a sentence the court may "order, in addition to or, in the case of a misdemeanor, in lieu of any other penalty authorized by law, that the defendant make restitution to any victim of such offense, or if the victim is deceased, to the victim's estate." 18 U.S.C. § 3663(a)(1)(A). In the case of an offense resulting in bodily injury to the victim, restitution may include an amount to cover medical and related expenses, lost income, and funeral and related expenses. § 3663(b)(2)–(3). The statute provides: "To the extent that the court determines that the complication and prolongation of the sentencing process resulting from the fashioning of an order of restitution under this section outweighs the need to provide restitution to any victims, the court may decline to make such an order." § 3663(a)(1)(B)(ii). The procedure for issuing an order of restitution is set forth in 18 U.S.C. § 3664. When it determines whether to order restitution, the court is directed to consider "the amount of the loss sustained by each victim as a result of the offense," and "the financial resources of the defendant, the financial needs and earning ability of the defendant and the defendant's dependents, and such other factors as the court deems appropriate." § 3663(a)(1)(B)(i)(I)–(II). If the defendant is convicted of a crime of violence, an offense against property, an offense relating to tampering with consumer products, or in which an identifiable person or persons suffered a physical injury or pecuniary loss, the court is, generally, directed to order restitution. 18 U.S.C. § 3663A.

In United States v. Fountain, 768 F.2d 790 (7th Cir.1985), the defendants, prison inmates, were convicted in one case of the murder of a prison guard and in the other of the murder of one guard and other crimes including assault on guards, who were injured and one of whom was permanently disabled. The trial judge ordered restitution to the estates of the murdered victims, to the disabled victim, and to the Department of Labor for payments it incurred to the guards or their estates. In one case, the total restitution ordered was nearly $490,000, and in the other it was $70,000. Discussing the restitution order, the court of appeals said:

> The defendants argue that the statute is unconstitutional, because it allows a victim of crime to obtain from the sentencing judge what amounts to a judgment for tort damages, thus thwarting the defendant's Seventh Amendment right to trial by jury in any federal suit at law in which the stakes exceed $20. The argument is unpersuasive when pushed to the extreme of saying that *any* order that a criminal defendant pay a victim money for which the victim could get a judgment in a suit at law is a judgment at law for purposes of the Seventh Amendment. If by "restitution" in criminal law (a distinct concept from civil restitution) we mean simply an order in a criminal case that the criminal restore to his victim what he has taken from him, we are speaking of a form of criminal remedy that predates the Seventh Amendment. Restitution indeed is the earliest criminal remedy. Before there is organized government, criminal misconduct is punished by forcing the criminal to compensate the victim or the

victim's family. . . . Even after the rise of the state we find restitution used as a criminal remedy, as in an English statute of 1529. . . .

The question is, what does restitution as a criminal remedy comprehend? As the word implies and history confirms, the original conception is that of forcing the criminal to yield up to his victim the fruits of the crime. The crime is thereby made worthless to the criminal. This form of criminal restitution is sanctioned not only by history but also by its close relationship to the retributive and deterrent purposes of criminal punishment. The fact that tort law may also have deterrent purposes . . . does not make every payment to the victim of crime a tort sanction; it just shows that tort and criminal law overlap. In fact their differentiation is a relatively modern development. . . .

An order to make restitution of medical and funeral expenses and lost earnings has a weaker connection with the traditional purposes of criminal law. But since medical expenses are restorative, making the criminal reimburse them can be analogized to forcing him to return stolen goods; so can making him restore any earnings that the victim lost as a result of the crime. The analogy is particularly close where, as in the present cases, the criminal wanted to injure his victim, as distinct from injuring him as merely a byproduct of an acquisitive crime. And with regard to all three types of loss—medical, funeral, and earnings—making the criminal bear them serves a useful purpose in the administration of the criminal law. It brings home to him the enormity of his conduct, by forcing him to pay expenses directly related to his victim's suffering.

That forms of criminal restitution other than ordering stolen goods restored to the owner do not have so clear a historical pedigree does not matter. What matters is that criminal restitution is not some newfangled effort to get around the Seventh Amendment but a traditional criminal remedy; its precise contours can change through time without violating the Seventh Amendment. If Congress creates a new cause of action and does not specify the mode of trial, we must look to the nearest historical analogy to decide whether there is a right of trial by jury. . . . Here Congress has made clear that the judge rather than the jury is to determine the facts; and its judgment is entitled to our consideration. Moreover, there is a close historical analogy to restitution in a criminal proceeding of the victim's medical and funeral expenses and lost earnings: restitution of stolen goods, an established criminal remedy when the Seventh Amendment was adopted. Restitution is frequently an equitable remedy, meaning, of course, that there is no right of jury trial. . . . We therefore join those courts that have upheld under the Act orders for restitution of medical bills, lost wages, and the value of personal property destroyed by the criminal. . . .

Restitution as a criminal remedy becomes problematic only where it goes beyond the fruits of the crime or the out-of-pocket expenses of the victim or his lost earnings and includes compensation for earnings . . . that would have been received in the future. Compensation for the loss of future earnings is quintessentially civil. The reason is not merely historical, or conceptual; there is, indeed, no difference of principle between past and future earnings, so far as the purposes of criminal punishment are concerned. To disable a person from working, temporarily or permanently, is to deprive him of his human capital; it is a detail whether the consequence is to deprive him of earnings he would have had in the past or earnings he would have had in the future. The reason for treating past and future earnings differently is practical: the calculation of lost future earnings involves the difficult problem of translating an uncertain future stream of earnings into a present value. . . . It is not a problem meet for solution in a summary proceeding ancillary to sentencing for a criminal offense.

. . .

. . . Obeying the statutory directive that "the imposition of such order . . . not unduly complicate or prolong the sentencing process," 18 U.S.C. § 3579(d), [see 18 U.S.C. § 3663(a)(1)(B)(ii)], we hold that an order requiring a calculation of lost future earnings unduly complicates the sentencing process and hence is not authorized by the Victim and Witness Protection Act—unless, to repeat a vital qualification, the amount is uncontested, so that no calculation is required.

For reasons already stated, we have no difficulty with the portion of the restitution order that relates solely to the medical and funeral expenses of the victims or the past wages of which they were deprived by the defendants' crimes. Nor do we doubt that the Department of Labor is a "person" within the meaning of the third-party payment provision of the statute. . . . [W]e can think of no reason why a federal agency, alone among third-party payors, natural and institutional, should not be reimbursed if it compensates a victim of crime. . . .

The defendants complain, finally, that the judge disregarded their poverty in ordering them to pay amounts which, even as reduced to eliminate the substantial payments for lost future earnings, will far exceed the realistic earning capacity of indigent prisoners unlikely ever to be released from prison. But the statute does not say that indigency is a defense, only that it is a factor the judge is required to take into account . . . and he did that. The judge was worried that such accomplished and audacious murderers might have a story to sell to a publisher or broadcaster, and he wanted to make sure they would never reap any gain from their crimes. This is a proper ground for ordering restitution beyond the defendants' present or foreseeable ability to pay. The prospect that these multiple murderers might someday be cashing royalty checks for the stories of their crimes while their victims remain uncompensated for the losses that the murderers inflicted is an insult to the victims and an affront to the society's moral beliefs. It might be too late then for the victims or their survivors to bring wrongful-death actions; the statute of limitations might have run. They could if they want sue now and get a judgment that they

> could renew till the day (if it ever arrives) when the defendants have money to pay it, but we do not think they should be put to this expense, so likely to be futile.
>
> . . . Everyone knows that [the defendants] cannot *now* make restitution. The point of the order is to make sure that should they ever be able to do so out of earnings from the press or the media, they shall do so. This is a reasonable measure which requires no findings of fact.

768 F.2d at 800–803.

The provision for restitution "to any victim of such offense" authorizes "an award of restitution only for the loss caused by the specific conduct that is the basis of the offense of conviction"; it does not authorize an award of restitution for losses related to other alleged offenses for which the defendant is charged but not convicted. Hughey v. United States, 495 U.S. 411 (1990).

New York's "Son of Sam" law, which provided that proceeds from crime stories written by the criminal be used to compensate the victim of the crime, was struck down by the Court as a violation of the First Amendment, in Simon & Schuster, Inc. v. Members of New York State Crime Victims Board, 502 U.S. 105 (1991). The Court concluded that the statute was a content-based, financial disincentive to speech, which was not justified by a compelling interest of the state. The Court said that a state has a compelling interest in compensating victims from the fruits of a crime, but that the statute was not narrowly tailored to serve that interest.

601. Capital punishment. In three cases involving two defendants who were sentenced to death for rape and one who was sentenced to death for murder, the Court held that "the imposition and carrying out of the death penalty in these cases constitutes cruel and unusual punishment in violation of the Eighth and Fourteenth Amendments." Furman v. Georgia, 408 U.S. 238 (1972). All nine Justices wrote opinions. Justice Brennan and Justice Marshall concluded flatly that capital punishment violated the Eighth Amendment's prohibition against cruel and unusual punishments. Justice Douglas, Justice Stewart, and Justice White concurred on the ground that the death penalty was arbitrarily applied and for that reason was unconstitutional. The other four Justices wrote dissenting opinions. The requirement that the death penalty not be imposed in an "arbitrary and capricious" manner was applied in Woodson v. North Carolina, 428 U.S. 280 (1976) (5–4), and Roberts v. Louisiana, 428 U.S. 325 (1976) (5–4).

A majority of the Court has upheld the death penalty in certain circumstances. In lengthy opinions, the Court upheld capital punishment for murder, imposed under statutory schemes in Georgia, Florida, and Texas, which focused attention on the circumstances of the crime and provided for consideration of aggravating or mitigating factors and which included measures to prevent arbitrary imposition of the penalty. Gregg v. Georgia, 428 U.S. 153 (1976); Proffitt v. Florida, 428 U.S. 242 (1976); Jurek

v. Texas, 428 U.S. 262 (1976). Justice Brennan and Justice Marshall dissented, adhering to their views in *Furman*.

A sentence of death for the crime of rape is "grossly disproportionate and excessive punishment" and is therefore prohibited by the Eighth Amendment. Coker v. Georgia, 433 U.S. 584 (1977). The Court noted that Georgia was the only jurisdiction in the United States that currently authorized capital punishment for rape of an adult woman, and only two others authorized capital punishment if the victim was a child. It noted that in most cases, Georgia juries had not sentenced rapists to death. These facts, four Justices said, confirmed their view that capital punishment for rape was excessive. (Opinion of Justice White, which Justice Stewart, Justice Blackmun, and Justice Stevens joined.) In brief concurring opinions, Justice Brennan and Justice Marshall adhered to their views in *Furman*. Justice Powell, concurring in part and dissenting in part, indicated that he would not foreclose the possibility that capital punishment in cases of aggravated rape might be permissible. Chief Justice Burger and Justice Rehnquist dissented. The Court has held also that imposition of the death penalty for felony murder is inconsistent with the Cruel and Unusual Punishments Clause if the person sentenced did not himself "kill, attempt to kill, or intend that a killing take place or that lethal force . . . be employed," Enmund v. Florida, 458 U.S. 782, 797 (1982) (5–4). Distinguishing *Enmund*, the Court held that the Eighth Amendment does not prohibit capital punishment for a defendant convicted of felony murder, who does not himself kill or intend to kill but whose participation in the felony "is major and whose mental state is one of reckless indifference to the value of human life." Tison v. Arizona, 481 U.S. 137, 152 (1987) (5–4). *Enmund*, the majority said, barred capital punishment for someone like Enmund himself: "[T]he minor actor in an armed robbery, not on the scene, who neither intended to kill nor was found to have had any culpable mental state." Id. at 149.

In Godfrey v. Georgia, 446 U.S. 420 (1980) (6–3), the Court invalidated a sentence of death imposed pursuant to a statute allowing capital punishment for a murder that "was outrageously or wantonly vile, horrible or inhuman in that it involved torture, depravity of mind, or an aggravated battery to the victim." Four Justices (in addition to Justice Brennan and Justice Marshall) concluded that application of the statute to the facts of the case required so broad and vague a construction that it violated the Eighth and Fourteenth Amendments. *Godfrey* was applied in Maynard v. Cartwright, 486 U.S. 356 (1988). But see Lewis v. Jeffers, 497 U.S. 764 (1990) (5–4) (death sentence under similar statute upheld). In Arave v. Creech, 507 U.S. 463 (1993) (7–2), the Court said that an Idaho statute specifying that for purposes of capital punishment sentencing, it is an aggravating circumstance that "[b]y the murder, or circumstances surrounding its commission, the defendant exhibited utter disregard for human life," as construed by the state court, provided adequate guidance for exercise of discretion. The state court had said that the phrase " 'is meant to be reflective of acts or circumstances surrounding the crime which exhibit the highest, the utmost, callous disregard for human life, i.e., the cold-blooded, pitiless slayer.' " Id. at 468. See Tuilaepa v. California, 512 U.S. 967 (1994) (8–1) (sentencing factors having a "common-sense core of meaning" not unconstitutionally vague).

The sentencing authority must be permitted to consider all mitigating factors in the individual case. Lockett v. Ohio, 438 U.S. 586 (1978). Even for a narrowly restricted category of homicide, a mandatory death sentence is not permissible. See Sumner v. Shuman, 483 U.S. 66 (1987) (6–3) (person convicted of murder who is serving sentence of life imprisonment); Roberts v. Louisiana, 431 U.S. 633 (1977) (5–4) (first-degree murder of police officer engaged in performance of his duties).

The Court has considered a wide variety of questions about which aggravating and mitigating factors may or must be considered and the manner in which they are considered. See Wiggins v. Smith, 539 U.S. 510 (2003) (per curiam) (7–2); Ring v. Arizona, 536 U.S. 584 (2002) (7–2); Weeks v. Angelone, 528 U.S. 225 (2000) (5–4); Buchanan v. Angelone, 522 U.S. 269 (1998) (6–3); Tuggle v. Netherland, 516 U.S. 10 (1995); Johnson v. Texas, 509 U.S. 350 (1993) (5–4) (defendant's youth at time of crime); Espinosa v. Florida, 505 U.S. 1079 (1992); Sochor v. Florida, 504 U.S. 527 (1992); Clemons v. Mississippi, 494 U.S. 738 (1990); McKoy v. North Carolina, 494 U.S. 433 (1990) (6–3); Boyde v. California, 494 U.S. 370 (1990) (5–4); Blystone v. Pennsylvania, 494 U.S. 299 (1990) (5–4); Penry v. Lynaugh, 492 U.S. 302 (1989); Franklin v. Lynaugh, 487 U.S. 164 (1988) (6–3); Johnson v. Mississippi, 486 U.S. 578 (1988); Mills v. Maryland, 486 U.S. 367 (1988) (5–4); Lowenfield v. Phelps, 484 U.S. 231 (1988) (7–2); Hitchcock v. Dugger, 481 U.S. 393 (1987); Skipper v. South Carolina, 476 U.S. 1 (1986); Barclay v. Florida, 463 U.S. 939 (1983) (6–3); Zant v. Stephens, 462 U.S. 862 (1983) (7–2); Eddings v. Oklahoma, 455 U.S. 104 (1982) (5–4).

The Constitution does not require that a sentence of death be imposed by a jury. "In light of the facts that the Sixth Amendment does not require jury sentencing, that the demands of fairness and reliability in capital cases do not require it, and that neither the nature of, nor the purpose behind, the death penalty requires jury sentencing, we cannot conclude that placing responsibility on the trial judge to impose the sentence in a capital case is unconstitutional." Spaziano v. Florida, 468 U.S. 447, 464 (1984) (6–3). Accordingly, it is permissible for a state to authorize a judge to override a jury recommendation against capital punishment. The Court noted that 30 out of 37 states that have a capital punishment statute give the decision to the jury; and only three of the remaining seven allow a judge to override a jury's recommendation of life imprisonment. Id. at 463. A capital sentencing statute that requires the sentencing judge to consider a jury's sentencing recommendation but does not specify the weight that the judge is to give the recommendation is constitutional. Harris v. Alabama, 513 U.S. 504 (1995) (8–1).

In Beck v. Alabama, 447 U.S. 625 (1980) (7–2), the Court held that a death sentence was invalid because the jury was not permitted to consider a verdict of guilty of a lesser included, noncapital offense even though the evidence would have supported such a verdict. *Beck* is distinguished in Hopkins v. Reeves, 524 U.S. 88 (1998) (8–1), and Hopper v. Evans, 456 U.S. 605 (1982). Failure to give an instruction on an available lesser-included offense does not require reversal if an instruction on another lesser included offense supported by the evidence was given. Schad v. Arizona, 501 U.S. 624 (1991) (5–4). Nor does *Beck* require that instructions be given on lesser included offenses for which the defendant cannot be convicted because of the statute of limitations. The defendant may choose to waive the statute of limitations in order to have the benefit of the instruction; but if he does not, the jury should not be led to believe that the defendant can be convicted of crimes for which he cannot be convicted. To trick the jury in that way would undermine the public's confidence in criminal justice and disserve the goal of rationality. *Spaziano*, above.

In Caldwell v. Mississippi, 472 U.S. 320 (1985) (5–3), the Court held that the prosecutor's argument to a capital sentencing jury suggesting that responsibility for determining the appropriateness of a death sentence rested not with the jury but with the appellate court on review violated the Eighth Amendment's special requirement of reliability of the judgment that a sentence of death is appropriate in the specific case. Construing *Caldwell*, the Court held that informing a sentencing jury that the defendant was already under sentence of death for another crime did not unconstitutionally undermine the jury's sense of responsibility for determining the appropriateness of capital punishment. Romano v. Oklahoma, 512 U.S. 1 (1994) (5–4). The prior sentence was disclosed as part of the state's proof that the defendant had previously been convicted of a violent felony and would constitute a continuing threat to society, which were aggravating factors bearing on the sentence.

In a capital sentencing proceeding, if the defendant's future dangerousness is in issue and the only alternative to the death penalty is imprisonment without possibility of parole, due process requires that the jury be informed that the defendant, if imprisoned, would not be eligible for parole. Simmons v. South Carolina, 512 U.S. 154 (1994) (7–2). See Kelly v. South Carolina, 534 U.S. 246 (5–4) (*Simmons* applied); Ramdass v. Angelone, 530 U.S. 156 (2000) (5–4) (*Simmons* distinguished); California v. Ramos, 463 U.S. 992 (1983) (5–4) (state court's instruction to jury at penalty hearing that Governor might commute life sentence without parole, without instruction that Governor might also commute death sentence, was not unconstitutional).

A claim that the Constitution prohibits psychiatric testimony about the defendant's future dangerousness at the sentencing hearing was rejected in Barefoot v. Estelle, 463 U.S. 880 (1983) (6–3). Also, a capital sentencing jury is not constitutionally barred from hearing a "victim impact" statement, which provides information about the impact of the crime on the victim and the victim's family. Payne v. Tennessee, 501 U.S. 808 (1991) (6–3). Nor is it impermissible to instruct the jury that it "must not be swayed by mere sentiment, conjecture, sympathy, passion, prejudice, public opinion or public feeling" during the penalty phase of a capital case. California v.

Brown, 479 U.S. 538, 539 (1987) (5–4). In *Brown*, the defendant had contended that the instruction might lead the jury not to give proper attention and weight to mitigating factors bearing on the sentence. See also Jones v. United States, 527 U.S. 373 (1999) (5–4) (jury need not be instructed regarding consequence of failing to agree on sentence recommendation).

In Dawson v. Delaware, 503 U.S. 159 (1992) (8–1), the Court held that the defendant's First Amendment right of association was violated by the admission at a capital sentencing hearing of evidence that he belonged to a white racist prison organization called the Aryan Brotherhood. The Court said that the First Amendment does not absolutely prohibit evidence about a person's associations and beliefs, but that in this case the evidence was altogether irrelevant.

The Eighth Amendment does not require "a state appellate court, before it affirms a death sentence, to compare the sentence in the case before it with the penalties imposed in similar cases if requested to do so by the prisoner." Pulley v. Harris, 465 U.S. 37, 44 (1984) (7–2).

"The Eighth Amendment prohibits the State from inflicting the penalty of death upon a prisoner who is insane." Ford v. Wainwright, 477 U.S. 399, 410 (1986) (7–2). Accordingly, if the sanity of a condemned prisoner is in issue, the state must provide a procedure to determine the issue "with the high regard for truth that befits a decision affecting the life or death of a human being." Id. at 411. Without specifying in detail what constitutes an adequate procedure, the Court said that "the adversary presentation of relevant information [should] be as unrestricted as possible," and "the manner of selecting and using the experts responsible for producing that 'evidence' [should] be conducive to the formation of neutral, sound, and professional judgments as to the prisoner's ability to comprehend the nature of the penalty." Id. at 417. Overruling Penry v. Lynaugh, 492 U.S. 302 (1989) (5–4), the Court held that execution of a person who is mentally retarded violates the Cruel and Unusual Punishments Clause. Atkins v. Virginia, 536 U.S. 304 (2002) (6–3).

Four Justices (Stevens, Brennan, Marshall, Blackmun) have concluded that the Eighth Amendment prohibits the execution of a person who was less than 16 years old at the time of the commission of the offense. Thompson v. Oklahoma, 487 U.S. 815 (1988) (5–4). Justice O'Connor concurred in the judgment vacating the sentence of death, on the ground that the Oklahoma legislature had not specifically addressed the question whether a person could be executed for a crime committed when he was less than 16; the statute in this case specified no minimum age. She declined to decide the more general question.

The Eighth Amendment does not prohibit imposition of capital punishment for a crime committed at the age of 17 or 16. Stanford v. Kentucky, 492 U.S. 361 (1989) (5–4).

In McCleskey v. Kemp, 481 U.S. 279 (1987) (5–4), the Court rejected a claim that the imposition of capital punishment was constitutionally invalid because racial considerations had entered into the decision whether it would be imposed. The defendant was black and was convicted of killing a white person during the course of a robbery. Under Georgia law, a jury recommended that he be sentenced to death following a sentencing hearing, and the judge accepted the jury's recommendation. The claim of racial discrimination was supported by extensive statistical studies of Georgia murder cases, which showed, inter alia, that black defendants who kill white victims have the greatest likelihood of being sentenced to death. According to one statistical model, defendants charged with killing white victims were 4.3 times as likely to be sentenced to death than defendants charged with killing black victims. The Court emphasized that there was no evidence other than the statistical studies that racial discrimination was a factor in this case. It observed that discretion is intended to and does play a large role in capital sentencing proceedings and that were the statistical evidence accepted as proof of racial discrimination in this case, comparable proof of statistical disparities related to any impermissible factor might likewise invalidate a death sentence. "At most," the Court said, "the [statistical] study indicates a discrepancy that appears to correlate with race," but it "does not demonstrate a constitutionally significant risk of racial bias affecting the Georgia capital-sentencing process." 481 U.S. at 312, 313.

In Lankford v. Idaho, 500 U.S. 110 (1991) (5–4), the Court held that imposition of the death penalty violated due process, because the defendant did not have adequate notice at the time of the sentencing hearing that the judge was considering a death sentence.

In Herrera v. Collins, 506 U.S. 390 (1993) (6–3), the Court rejected, in the circumstances of the case, the argument that "the Eighth and Fourteenth Amendments . . . prohibit the execution of a person who is innocent of the crime for which he was convicted." Id. at 398. The petitioner had been convicted of capital murder and sentenced to death. Petitions for state and federal habeas corpus were denied. Ten years later, he filed another petition for federal habeas corpus, in which he alleged that he was innocent of the crimes. The petition was accompanied by four affidavits to the effect that the petitioner was innocent.

The Court said that a claim of innocence based on newly discovered evidence was not and never had been a ground for federal habeas relief, unless it was accompanied by an independent claim of a constitutional error in the underlying state criminal proceeding. The function of habeas, it said, is not to correct errors of fact. The petition here, it said, was in the manner of a motion for a new trial on the basis of newly discovered evidence, which is confined within a two-year time limit by Federal Rule 33. Executive clemency is the "fail safe" for situations outside the rule. Id. at 415.

The Court added: "We may assume, for the sake of argument in deciding this case, that in a capital case a truly persuasive demonstration of 'actual innocence' made after trial would render the execution of a defendant unconstitutional, and warrant federal habeas relief if there were no state avenue open to process such a claim. But because of the very disruptive effect that entertaining claims of actual innocence would have on the need for finality in capital cases, and the enormous burden that having to retry cases based on often stale evidence would place on the States, the threshold showing for such an assumed right would necessarily be extraordinarily high.'' Id. at 417. The Court concluded that the petitioner's showing fell ''far short'' of that threshold. In a concurring opinion, Justice O'Connor said, ''I cannot disagree with the fundamental legal principle that executing the innocent is inconsistent with the Constitution.'' Id. at 419. However, she said, the petitioner ''is not innocent, in any sense of the word.'' Id. She emphasized the overwhelming evidence of his guilt and the weakness of the affidavits accompanying the petition.

Herrera was distinguished in Schlup v. Delo, 513 U.S. 298 (1995) (5–4), in which the defendant coupled his claim of innocence with a claim of constitutional error at trial. The Court said that whereas in Herrera's case, ''the evidence of innocence would have had to be strong enough to make his execution 'constitutionally intolerable' *even if* his conviction was the product of a fair trial,'' the petitioner in this case had only to ''establish sufficient doubt about his guilt to justify the conclusion that his execution would be a miscarriage of justice *unless* his conviction was the product of a fair trial.'' Id. at 853. The test, the Court said, is whether ''it is more likely than not that no reasonable juror would have convicted him in the light of the new evidence.'' Id. at 867.

A defendant who seeks federal habeas corpus to set aside a conviction and capital sentence and who is financially unable to obtain counsel and other necessary services has a statutory right to the appointment of counsel and the furnishing of such services. 21 U.S.C. § 848(q)(4)(B). The right includes a right to assistance in the preparation of the habeas corpus application, which can be claimed by filing a motion requesting the appointment of counsel for the habeas corpus proceeding. McFarland v. Scott, 512 U.S. 849 (1994) (6–3). A district court has jurisdiction to enter a stay of execution where necessary to give effect to the right. Id. (5–4).

''In a capital case the grant of a stay of execution directed to a State by a federal court imposes on that court the concomitant duty to take all steps necessary to ensure a prompt resolution of the matter, consistent with its duty to give full and fair consideration to all of the issues presented in the case.'' In re Blodgett, 502 U.S. 236 (1992). See generally Barefoot v. Estelle, 463 U.S. 880 (1983) (6–3).

The imposition of capital punishment under the Uniform Code of Military Justice was upheld in Loving v. United States, 517 U.S. 748 (1996).

602. Application of the Cruel and Unusual Punishments Clause to the conditions of imprisonment is discussed in Rhodes v. Chapman, 452 U.S. 337 (1981) (8–1), in which the Court reversed a ruling below that the housing of two inmates in a single cell, in all the circumstances of the case, was unconstitutional. The Court observed that ''the Constitution does not mandate comfortable prisons" and that prisons "which house persons convicted of serious crimes, cannot be free of discomfort." Id. at 349. In discharging their responsibility, "courts cannot assume that state legislatures and prison officials are insensitive to the requirements of the Constitution or to the perplexing sociological problems of how best to achieve the goals of the penal function in the criminal justice system: to punish justly, to deter future crime, and to return imprisoned persons to society with an improved chance of being useful, law-abiding citizens." Id. at 353.

In Wilson v. Seiter, 501 U.S. 294 (1991) (5–4), referring to some earlier cases, the Court said that conditions of imprisonment that are not intended as punishment do not violate the Cruel and Unusual Punishment Clause unless they are accompanied by a culpable state of mind of the responsible prison officials. (*Rhodes*, the Court said, had been concerned only with the "objective component" of an Eighth Amendment claim—"Was the deprivation sufficiently serious?"—and did not eliminate the "subjective component"—"Did the officials act with a sufficiently culpable state of mind?" Id. at 298.) The requisite culpable state of mind is at least deliberate indifference to the conditions in question. The Court observed: "*Some* conditions of confinement may establish an Eighth Amendment violation 'in combination' when each would not do so alone, but only when they have a mutually enforcing effect that produces the deprivation of a single identifiable human need such as food, warmth, or exercise—for example, a low cell temperature at night combined with a failure to issue blankets. . . . To say that some prison conditions may interact in this fashion is a far cry from saying that all prison conditions are a seamless web for Eighth Amendment purposes. Nothing so amorphous as 'overall conditions' can rise to the level of cruel and unusual punishment when no specific deprivation of a single human need exists." Id. at 304–305.

In a civil suit by a federal prisoner against prison officials, explaining the meaning of "deliberate indifference," the Court said: "[A] prison official cannot be found liable under the Eighth Amendment for denying an inmate humane conditions of confinement unless the official knows of and disregards an excessive risk to inmate health or safety; the official must both be aware of facts from which the inference could be drawn that a substantial risk of serious harm exists, and he must also draw the inference." Farmer v. Brennan, 511 U.S. 825 (1994). The Court rejected the inmate's argument that an objective standard rather than an official's subjective state of mind should control.

See generally the concurring and dissenting opinion of Judge Posner in Johnson v. Phelan, 69 F.3d 144, 151 (7th Cir.1995).

Rhodes v. Chapman and a generally less favorable attitude toward judicial oversight of the performance of administrative functions substantially reduced, if it did not quite halt, a flow of cases in which the courts had reviewed the administration of prisons and, frequently, required improved conditions on constitutional grounds. See the opinion of Justice Brennan, concurring in the judgment, in Rhodes v. Chapman, in which he states that "individual prisons or entire prison systems in at least 24 States have been declared unconstitutional under the Eighth and Fourteenth Amendments, with litigation underway in many others." Id. at 353–54. The cases to which Justice Brennan referred are cited id. at 353–54 n.1.

603. The Equal Protection Clause prohibits a state from imprisoning an indigent beyond the maximum term of imprisonment fixed by statute because of nonpayment of a fine that he is financially unable to pay. "A statute permitting a sentence of both imprisonment and fine cannot be parlayed into a longer term of imprisonment than is fixed by the statute since to do so would be to accomplish indirectly as to an indigent that which cannot be done directly." Williams v. Illinois, 399 U.S. 235, 243 (1970). The court noted that it was not dealing with "a judgment of confinement for nonpayment of a fine in the familiar pattern of alternative sentence of '$30 or 30 days.' " Id.

Williams was applied in Tate v. Short, 401 U.S. 395 (1971), to the imprisonment of an indigent who was sentenced to be imprisoned because he could not pay accumulated fines for traffic offenses; the court had no other jurisdiction to impose imprisonment. *Williams* and *Tate* were applied in Bearden v. Georgia, 461 U.S. 660 (1983), holding that a state court cannot revoke probation of an indigent convict because of failure to pay a fine and make restitution, unless (1) he wilfully refused to pay or failed to make adequate bona fide efforts to acquire the funds with which to pay, or (2) no alternative sentence will meet the state's interest in punishment and deterrence.

Distinguishing *Williams*, *Tate*, and *Bearden*, the court of appeals held that the defendant was not denied equal protection or due process by the sentencing judge's refusal to credit him for time while he was detained before trial because he was unable to make bail; he was detained for 284 days. Vasquez v. Cooper, 862 F.2d 250 (10th Cir.1988).

604. Consecutive sentences. To what extent can a court extend punishment by imposing consecutive sentences for distinct crimes arising out of the same "transaction"? In Bell v. United States, 349 U.S. 81, 82–84 (1955), the Court said that while "the punishment appropriate for the diverse federal offenses is a matter for the discretion of Congress, subject only to constitutional limitations, more particularly the Eighth Amendment," doubt about congressional intent "should be resolved in favor of lenity" and "against turning a single transaction into multiple offenses." In Gore v. United States, 357 U.S. 386, 389 (1958), the Court held that no rule of lenity was applicable where the defendant was convicted of three different narcotics offenses all based on a single sale of heroin and given consecutive sentences: "The fact that an offender violates by a single transaction several regulatory controls devised by Congress as means for dealing with a social evil as deleterious as it is difficult to combat does not make the several different regulatory controls single and identic. . . . It is one thing for a single transaction to include several units relating to proscribed conduct under a single provision of a statute.[7] It is a wholly

7. In *Bell*, the Court had held that the transportation of two women across state lines on a single trip in violation of the Mann Act, 18 U.S.C. § 2421, was but a single violation of the act.

different thing to evolve a rule of lenity for three violations of three separate offenses created by Congress at three different times, all to the end of dealing more and more strictly with, and seeking to throttle more and more by different legal devices, the traffic in narcotics." Id. at 389, 391. Cumulative punishments for a single offense violate the Double Jeopardy Clause. See note 614, p. 1179 below.

605. Review. "The question of appellate review of sentencing has recently received much advocacy as a needed reform to prevent unjustifiable disparities in the sentences meted to co-defendants. The arguments pro and con for such a review have almost universally been left to the legislative branch of government. Appellate courts have generally refused to disturb the trial court's discretion in this matter unless the punishment is so disproportionate to the offense committed and to the sentences received by co-defendants 'as to be completely arbitrary and shocking to the sense of justice and thus to constitute cruel and unusual punishment in violation of the Eighth Amendment. . . .' " Rodriquez v. United States, 394 F.2d 825, 826 (5th Cir.1968). For cases in which the appellate court found exceptional circumstances not involving cruel and unusual punishment that called for reconsideration of sentence, see, e.g., Thomas v. United States, 368 F.2d 941 (5th Cir.1966); Coleman v. United States, 357 F.2d 563 (D.C.Cir.1965); cf. Leach v. United States, 334 F.2d 945 (D.C.Cir. 1964).

A state procedure that allows a sentence review panel to increase as well as decrease the sentence of a defendant who applied for review was upheld in Robinson v. Warden, 455 F.2d 1172 (4th Cir.1972). Accord Walsh v. Picard, 446 F.2d 1209 (1st Cir.1971). In *Walsh*, the court rejected the argument that the reviewing agency was constitutionally required at least to state its reasons for increasing a sentence.

Enactment of the Sentencing Guidelines, see p. 1109 above, greatly increased the number of appeals from a sentence, both by the defendant and by the government, pursuant to 18 U.S.C. § 3742, below.

---

18 U.S.C. § 3742

Review of a sentence

(a) Appeal by a defendant. A defendant may file a notice of appeal in the district court for review of an otherwise final sentence if the sentence—

(1) was imposed in violation of law;

(2) was imposed as a result of an incorrect application of the sentencing guidelines; or

(3) is greater than the sentence specified in the applicable guideline range to the extent that the sentence includes a greater fine or term of imprisonment, probation, or supervised release than the maximum established in the guideline range, or includes a more limiting condition of probation or supervised release under section 3563(b)(6) or (b)(11) than the maximum established in the guideline range; or

(4) was imposed for an offense for which there is no sentencing guideline and is plainly unreasonable.

(b) Appeal by the Government. The Government may file a notice of appeal in the district court for review of an otherwise final sentence if the sentence—

(1) was imposed in violation of law;

(2) was imposed as a result of an incorrect application of the sentencing guidelines;

(3) is less than the sentence specified in the applicable guideline range to the extent that the sentence includes a lesser fine or term of imprisonment, probation, or supervised release than the minimum established in the guideline range, or includes a less limiting condition of probation or supervised release under section 3563(b)(6) or (b)(11) than the minimum established in the guideline range; or

(4) was imposed for an offense for which there is no sentencing guideline and is plainly unreasonable.

The Government may not further prosecute such appeal without the personal approval of the Attorney General, the Solicitor General, or a deputy solicitor general designated by the Solicitor General.

(c) Plea agreements. In the case of a plea agreement that includes a specific sentence under rule 11(e)(1)(C) of the Federal Rules of Criminal Procedure—

(1) a defendant may not file a notice of appeal under paragraph (3) or (4) of subsection (a) unless the sentence imposed is greater than the sentence set forth in such agreement; and

(2) the Government may not file a notice of appeal under paragraph (3) or (4) of subsection (b) unless the sentence imposed is less than the sentence set forth in such agreement.

(d) Record on review. If a notice of appeal is filed in the district court pursuant to subsection (a) or (b), the clerk shall certify to the court of appeals—

(1) that portion of the record in the case that is designated as pertinent by either of the parties;

(2) the presentence report; and

(3) the information submitted during the sentencing proceeding.

(e) Consideration. Upon review of the record, the court of appeals shall determine whether the sentence—

(1) was imposed in violation of law;

(2) was imposed as a result of an incorrect application of the sentencing guidelines;

(3) is outside of the applicable guideline range, and

(A) the district court failed to provide the written statement of reasons required by section 3553(c);

(B) the sentence departs from the applicable guideline range based on a factor that—

(i) does not advance the objectives set forth in section 3553(a)(2); or

(ii) is not authorized under section 3553(b); or

(iii) is not justified by the facts of the case; or

(C) the sentence departs to an unusual degree from the applicable guidelines range, having regard for the factors to be considered in imposing a sentence, as set forth in section 3553(a) of this title and the reasons for the imposition of the particular sentence, as stated by the district court pursuant to the provisions of section 3553(c); or

(4) was imposed for an offense for which there is no applicable sentencing guideline and is plainly unreasonable.

The court of appeals shall give due regard to the opportunity of the district court to judge the credibility of the witnesses, and shall accept the findings of fact of the district court unless they are clearly erroneous and, except with respect to determinations under subsection (3)(A) or (3)(B), shall give due deference to the district court's application of the guidelines to the facts. With respect to determinations under subsection (3)(A) or (3)(B), the court of appeals shall review de novo the district court's application of the guidelines to the facts.

(f) Decision and disposition. If the court of appeals determines that—

(1) the sentence was imposed in violation of law or imposed as a result of an incorrect application of the sentencing guidelines, the court shall remand the case for further sentencing proceedings with such instructions as the court considers appropriate;

(2) the sentence is outside the applicable guideline range and the district court failed to provide the required statement of reasons in the order of judgment and commitment, or the departure is based on an impermissible factor, or is to an unreasonable degree, or the sentence was imposed for an offense for which there is no applicable sentencing guideline and is plainly unreasonable, it shall state specific reasons for its conclusions and—

(A) if it determines that the sentence is too high and the appeal has been filed under subsection (a), it shall set aside the sentence and remand the case for further sentencing proceedings with such instructions as the court considers appropriate subject to subsection (g);

(B) if it determines that the sentence is too low and the appeal has been filed under subsection (b), it shall set aside the sentence and remand the case for further sentencing proceedings with such instructions as the court considers appropriate, subject to subsection (g);

(3) the sentence is not described in paragraph (1) or (2), it shall affirm the sentence.

(g) Sentencing upon remand. A district court to which a case is remanded pursuant to subsection (f)(1) or (f)(2) shall resentence a defendant in accordance with section 3553 and with such instructions as may have been given by the court of appeals, except that—

(1) in determining the range referred to in subsection 3553(a)(4), the court shall apply the guidelines issued by the Sentencing Commission pursuant to section 994(a)(1) of title 28, United States Code, and that were in effect on the date of the previous sentencing of the defendant prior to the appeal, together with any amendments thereto by any act of Congress that was in effect on such date; and

(2) the court shall not impose a sentence outside the applicable guidelines range except upon a ground that—

(A) was specifically and affirmatively included in the written statement of reasons required by section 3553(c) in connection with the previous sentencing of the defendant prior to the appeal; and

(B) was held by the court of appeals, in remanding the case, to be a permissible ground of departure.

(h) Application to a sentence by a magistrate. An appeal of an otherwise final sentence imposed by a United States magistrate may be taken to a judge of the district court, and this section shall apply (except for the requirement of approval by the Attorney General or the Solicitor General in the case of a Government appeal) as though the appeal were to a court of appeals from a sentence imposed by a district court.

(i) Guideline not expressed as a range. For the purposes of this section, the term "guideline range" includes a guideline range having the same upper and lower limits.

(j) Definitions. For purposes of this section—

(1) a factor is "permissible" ground of departure if it—

(A) advances the objectives set forth in section 3553(a)(2); and

(B) is authorized under section 3553(b); and

(C) is justified by the facts of the case; and

(2) a factor is an "impermissible" ground of departure if it is not a permissible factor within the meaning of subsection (j)(1).

CHAPTER 16

APPEAL

"While bringing this appeal had about the same hope of success as running a three-legged filly in the Kentucky Derby, we commend appellant's attorney for doing his best with what he had." Platts v. United States, 378 F.2d 396, 397 (9th Cir.1967).

606. "[I]t is well settled that there is no constitutional right to an appeal. . . . Indeed, for a century after this Court was established, no appeal as of right existed in criminal cases, and, as a result, appellate review of criminal convictions was rarely allowed. . . . The right of appeal, as we presently know it in criminal cases, is purely a creature of statute; in order to exercise that statutory right one must come within the terms of the applicable statute. . . ." Abney v. United States, 431 U.S. 651, 656 (1977).[1]

A defendant has a right to counsel on his first appeal as of right. Douglas v. California, 372 U.S. 353 (1963). The Due Process Clause guarantees the defendant in a state criminal prosecution the effective assistance of counsel on such an appeal. Evitts v. Lucey, 469 U.S. 387 (1985) (7–2).

A state may not constitutionally deny the appointment of counsel on appeal to defendants who plead guilty. Tesmer v. Granholm, 333 F.3d 683 (6th Cir.2003) (en banc), cert. granted sub nom. Kowalski v. Tesmer, 124 U.S. 1144 (2004).

In Anders v. California, 386 U.S. 738 (1967), the Court required procedures to protect an indigent defendant from dismissal of an appeal as frivolous when it is not in fact frivolous, and it set forth an acceptable procedure. Under the *Anders* procedure, an appointed counsel can request permission to withdraw, accompanying his request with a brief referring to anything in the record that might arguably support an appeal. The brief must be furnished to the indigent and time allowed for him to raise any points he chooses. The appellate court must then examine the record and decide whether the appeal is wholly frivolous and, if it so finds, may then allow counsel to withdraw. In Smith v. Robbins, 528 U.S. 259 (2000) (5–4), the Court upheld a California procedure that differs from that described in *Anders*. The procedure requires both defendant's counsel and the appellate court to find that an appeal is frivolous. The chief difference is that counsel is not required to look for and point out any possibly nonfrivolous arguments.

1. The general statutory basis for appeals from judgments of the federal district courts is 28 U.S.C. § 1291.

UNITED STATES DISTRICT COURT
DISTRICT OF MASSACHUSETTS

____

V. CASE NO. ____________

____

NOTICE OF APPEAL

Notice is hereby given that ___________________ above named, hereby appeals from the _________________________________ entered in the above entitled action on __________________ .

By the Court,

_______________ Date

________________________ Deputy Clerk

(Notice of Appeal.wpd - 12/98) [app., kdapp., kgapp., kcustapp.]

An indigent defendant does not have a constitutional right to have appointed counsel on appeal argue every nonfrivolous issue that the defendant wants to have argued. Counsel's professional judgment may prevail over the defendant's wishes. Jones v. Barnes, 463 U.S. 745 (1983) (7–2). See McCoy v. Court of Appeals of Wisconsin, District 1, 486 U.S. 429 (1988) (5–3), upholding, against the claim that it denied effective assistance of counsel, a state rule providing that a court-appointed counsel who wants to withdraw from an appeal on the ground that it is frivolous must explain why potential issues on appeal lack merit. See also Miller v. Smith, 115 F.3d 1136 (4th Cir.1997) (en banc), holding that a state can limit provision of a free trial transcript for indigents to defendants who are represented on appeal by the public defender's office; it is not required to provide a transcript to an indigent who had secured the services pro bono of a private attorney.

FEDERAL RULES OF APPELLATE PROCEDURE

Rule 4

APPEAL AS OF RIGHT—WHEN TAKEN

. . .

(b) Appeal in a Criminal Case.

(1) *Time for Filing a Notice of Appeal.*

(A) In a criminal case, a defendant's notice of appeal must be filed in the district court within 10 days after the later of:

(i) the entry of either the judgment or the order being appealed; or

(ii) the filing of the government's notice of appeal.

(B) When the government is entitled to appeal, its notice of appeal must be filed in the district court within 30 days after the later of:

(i) the entry of the judgment or order being appealed; or

(ii) the filing of a notice of appeal by any defendant.

(2) *Filing Before Entry of Judgment.* A notice of appeal filed after the court announces a decision, sentence, or order—but before the entry of the judgment or order—is treated as filed on the date of and after the entry.

(3) *Effect of a Motion on a Notice of Appeal.*

(A) If a defendant timely makes any of the following motions under the Federal Rules of Criminal Procedure, the notice of appeal from a judgment of conviction must be filed within 10 days after the entry of the order disposing of the last such remaining motion, or within 10 days after the entry of the judgment of conviction, whichever period ends later. This provision applies to a timely motion:

(i) for judgment of acquittal under Rule 29;

(ii) for a new trial under Rule 33, but if based on newly discovered evidence, only if the motion is made no later than 10 days after the entry of the judgment; or

(iii) for arrest of judgment under Rule 34.

(B) A notice of appeal filed after the court announces a decision, sentence, or order—but before it disposes of any of the motions referred to in Rule 4(b)(3)(A)—becomes effective upon the later of the following:

(i) the entry of the order disposing of the last such remaining motion; or

(ii) the entry of the judgment of conviction.

(C) A valid notice of appeal is effective—without amendment—to appeal from an order disposing of any of the motions referred to in Rule 4(b)(3)(A).

(4) *Motion for Extension of Time.* Upon a finding of excusable neglect or good cause, the district court may—before or after the time has expired, with or without motion and notice—extend the time to file a notice of appeal for a period not to exceed 30 days from the expiration of the time otherwise prescribed by this Rule 4(b).

(5) *Jurisdiction.* The filing of a notice of appeal under this Rule 4(b) does not divest a district court of jurisdiction to correct a sentence under Federal Rule of Criminal Procedure 35(a), nor does the filing of a motion under 35(a) affect the validity of a notice of appeal filed before entry of the order disposing of the motion. The filing of a motion under Federal Rule of Criminal Procedure 35(a) does not suspend the time for filing a notice of appeal from a judgment of conviction.

(6) *Entry Defined.* A judgment or order is entered for purposes of this Rule 4(b) when it is entered on the criminal docket.

---

607. On the meaning of "excusable neglect," Fed.R.App.P. 4(b)(4), see Buckley v. United States, 382 F.2d 611 (10th Cir.1967), in which the court said that the defendant was charged with the inexcusable neglect of his counsel and that "a District Court's ruling as to the presence or absence of excusable neglect should be overturned only if there has been a clear abuse of discretion." Id. at 614. See also Romero v. Peterson, 930 F.2d 1502 (10th Cir.1991) (excusable neglect has "the 'common sense meaning of the two simple words applied to the facts which are developed' ").

608. The defendant Worcester was convicted of filing false income tax returns with intent to evade taxes.

> [T]he district court, in offering to suspend sentence and place Worcester on probation, stated that if he did not "welcome this offer [of probation, but preferred] to run the risk of the 18 months sentence which I originally said I would impose, and to seek by appeal or

> otherwise a complete vindication . . ." he was free to do so. 190 F.Supp. at 553. We can only construe this to mean that if Worcester replied that he was not content to accept probation without appealing, but chose the alternative of appealing, he ran the risk that the sentence he would have to appeal from would be a jail sentence. That Worcester's counsel so understood is clear from his reply, which is part of the record, to the court's offer in which he states that Worcester ". . . agrees to be bound by the conditions contained therein, including the waiver of his right of appeal." The court did not respond that this was an erroneous understanding.
>
> The court was without right to bargain thus with the defendant, or to put a price on an appeal. A defendant's exercise of a right of appeal must be free and unfettered. Just as it is unfair to handicap him because of his poverty . . . it is unfair to use the great power given to the court to determine sentence to place a defendant in the dilemma of making an unfree choice. . . . It is no answer to say that the defendant need not accept the court's "offer." The vice is that vis-a-vis the court he is in an unequal position.
>
> Were the rule otherwise, we can only too readily envisage the possibilities of abuse. A judge who fears he has committed reversible error during the trial, and does not like the thought of being reversed, informs the defendant that he is considering a substantial sentence, but that if the defendant will demonstrate his repentance, or his good citizenship, by waiving appeal, he will suspend it.

Worcester v. Commissioner, 370 F.2d 713, 718 (1st Cir.1966). See North Carolina v. Pearce, 395 U.S. 711 (1969), p. 1141 note 596 above.

FEDERAL RULES OF CRIMINAL PROCEDURE

Rule 52

HARMLESS AND PLAIN ERROR

(a) Harmless Error. Any error, defect, irregularity or variance that does not affect substantial rights must be disregarded.

(b) Plain Error. A plain error that affects substantial rights may be considered even though it was not brought to the court's attention.

---

609. Harmless error. "If, when all is said and done, the conviction is sure that the error did not influence the jury, or had but very slight effect, the verdict and the judgment should stand, except perhaps where the departure is from a constitutional norm or a specific command of Congress. . . . But if one cannot say, with fair assurance, after pondering all that happened without stripping the erroneous action from the whole, that the judgment was not substantially swayed by the error, it is impossible to conclude that substantial rights were not affected. The inquiry cannot be merely whether there was enough to support the result, apart from the phase affected by the error. It is rather, even so, whether the error itself had substantial influence. If so, or if one is left in grave doubt, the conviction cannot stand." Kotteakos v. United States, 328 U.S. 750, 764–65 (1946).

610. Plain error. "The language of the rule implies, and the cases hold, only that while orderly administration of justice requires general adherence to the rule that errors be asserted in the trial court, exceptions must be recognized in unusual circumstances involving seriously prejudicial deficiencies in the trial process." Reisman v. United States, 409 F.2d 789, 791 (9th Cir.1969). "We are not here concerned with technical error or with prejudicial error, or even with our view of what we may deem to be the obvious guilt or innocence of the individual appellants. In the words of Fed.R.Crim.P. 52(b) we are concerned only with any errors 'affecting substantial rights.' As the Supreme Court stated in United States v. Atkinson, 297 U.S. 157, 160 (1936) we may—and we must—notice errors which 'seriously affect the fairness . . . of judicial proceedings.' The circumstances must be 'exceptional' and the error must be such as to prejudice 'in a substantial manner appellant's right to a fair trial.' Polansky v. United States, 332 F.2d 233, 235 (1st Cir.1964)." McMillen v. United States, 386 F.2d 29, 35 (1st Cir.1967). See United States v. Santana-Camacho, 833 F.2d 371 (1st Cir.1987) (prosecutor's misrepresentation of evidence in closing statement constituted plain error).

In Johnson v. United States, 520 U.S. 461 (1997), the Court held that an action of the trial court that was correct at the time of the trial but is plainly erroneous at the time of the appeal, because of a change in the applicable law, satisfies the plain error requirement of Rule 52(b). The error in question was a failure to charge the jury on an element of the offense, which had previously been regarded as a matter of law for the judge. The court nevertheless did not reverse the conviction, because it concluded that the error did not affect the fairness or integrity of the proceedings.

Chapman v. California

386 U.S. 18, 87 S.Ct. 824, 17 L.Ed.2d 705 (1967)

■ MR. JUSTICE BLACK delivered the opinion of the Court.

Petitioners, Ruth Elizabeth Chapman and Thomas LeRoy Teale, were convicted in a California state court upon a charge that they robbed, kidnaped, and murdered a bartender. She was sentenced to life imprisonment and he to death. At the time of the trial, Art. I, § 13, of the State's Constitution provided that "in any criminal case, whether the defendant testifies or not, his failure to explain or to deny by his testimony any evidence or facts in the case against him may be commented upon by the court and by counsel, and may be considered by the court or the jury." Both petitioners in this case chose not to testify at their trial, and the

State's attorney prosecuting them took full advantage of his right under the State Constitution to comment upon their failure to testify, filling his argument to the jury from beginning to end with numerous references to their silence and inferences of their guilt resulting therefrom. The trial court also charged the jury that it could draw adverse inferences from petitioners' failure to testify. Shortly after the trial, but before petitioners' cases had been considered on appeal by the California Supreme Court, this Court decided Griffin v. California, 380 U.S. 609, in which we held California's constitutional provision and practice invalid on the ground that they put a penalty on the exercise of a person's right not to be compelled to be a witness against himself, guaranteed by the Fifth Amendment to the United States Constitution and made applicable to California and the other States by the Fourteenth Amendment. . . . On appeal, the State Supreme Court . . . admitting that petitioners had been denied a federal constitutional right by the comments on their silence, nevertheless affirmed, applying the State Constitution's harmless-error provision, which forbids reversal unless "the court shall be of the opinion that the error complained of has resulted in a miscarriage of justice." We granted certiorari limited to these questions:

"Where there is a violation of the rule of Griffin v. California, 380 U.S. 609, (1) can the error be held to be harmless, and (2) if so, was the error harmless in this case?" 383 U.S. 956–57.

In this Court petitioners contend that both these questions are federal ones to be decided under federal law; that under federal law, we should hold that denial of a federal constitutional right, no matter how unimportant, should automatically result in reversal of a conviction, without regard to whether the error is considered harmless; and that, if wrong in this, the various comments on petitioners' silence cannot, applying a federal standard, be considered harmless here.

I

Before deciding the two questions here—whether there can ever be harmless constitutional error and whether the error here was harmless—we must first decide whether state or federal law governs. . . .

[The Court concluded that federal law governs.]

II

We are urged by petitioners to hold that all federal constitutional errors, regardless of the facts and circumstances, must always be deemed harmful. Such a holding, as petitioners correctly point out, would require an automatic reversal of their convictions and make further discussion unnecessary. We decline to adopt any such rule. All 50 States have harmless-error statutes or rules, and the United States long ago through its Congress established for its courts the rule that judgments shall not be reversed for "errors or defects which do not affect the substantial rights of the parties." 28 U.S.C. § 2111. None of these rules on its face distinguishes between federal constitutional errors and errors of state law or federal statutes and rules. All of these rules, state or federal, serve a very useful purpose insofar as they block setting aside convictions for small errors or defects that have little, if any, likelihood of having changed the result of the trial. We conclude that there may be some constitutional errors which in the setting of a particular case are so unimportant and insignificant that they may, consistent with the Federal Constitution, be deemed harmless, not requiring the automatic reversal of the conviction.

III

In fashioning a harmless-constitutional-error rule, we must recognize that harmless-error rules can work very unfair and mischievous results when, for example, highly important and persuasive evidence, or argument, though legally forbidden, finds its way into a trial in which the question of guilt or innocence is a close one. What harmless-error rules all aim at is a rule that will save the good in harmless-error practices while avoiding the bad, so far as possible.

The federal rule emphasizes "substantial rights" as do most others. The California constitutional rule emphasizes "a miscarriage of justice," but the California courts have neutralized this to some extent by emphasis, and perhaps overemphasis, upon the court's view of "overwhelming evidence." We prefer the approach of this Court in deciding what was harmless error in our recent case of Fahy v. Connecticut, 375 U.S. 85. There we said: "The question is whether there is a reasonable possibility that the evidence complained of might have contributed to the conviction." Id., at 86–87. Although our prior cases have indicated that there are some constitutional rights so basic to a fair trial that their infraction can never be treated as harmless error,[2] this statement in *Fahy* itself belies any belief that all trial errors which violate the Constitution automatically call for reversal. At the same time, however, like the federal harmless-error statute, it emphasizes an intention not to treat as harmless those constitutional errors that "affect substantial rights" of a party. An error in admitting plainly relevant evidence which possibly influenced the jury adversely to a litigant cannot, under *Fahy*, be conceived of as harmless. Certainly error, constitutional error, in illegally admitting highly prejudicial evidence or comments, casts on someone other than the person prejudiced by it a burden to show that it was harmless. It is for that reason that the original common-law harmless-error rule put the burden on the beneficiary of the error either to prove that there was no injury or to suffer a reversal of his erroneously obtained judgment. There is little, if any, difference between our statement in Fahy v. Connecticut about "whether there is a reasonable possibility that the evidence complained of might have contributed to the conviction" and requiring the beneficiary of a constitutional error to prove beyond a reasonable doubt that the error complained of did not contribute to the verdict obtained. We, therefore, do no more than adhere to the

2. See, e.g., Payne v. Arkansas, 356 U.S. 560 (coerced confession); Gideon v. Wainwright, 372 U.S. 335 (right to counsel); Tumey v. Ohio, 273 U.S. 510 (impartial judge).

meaning of our *Fahy* case when we hold, as we now do, that before a federal constitutional error can be held harmless, the court must be able to declare a belief that it was harmless beyond a reasonable doubt. While appellate courts do not ordinarily have the original task of applying such a test, it is a familiar standard to all courts, and we believe its adoption will provide a more workable standard, although achieving the same result as that aimed at in our *Fahy* case.

. . .

[The Court concluded that the error in this case had not been harmless.]

. . .[3]

---

611. Reversing what had previously been understood to be the rule, see *Chapman*, p. 1170 above, the Court held that the erroneous admission of a coerced confession may be harmless error, in Arizona v. Fulminante, 499 U.S. 279 (1991) (5–4). The Court said:

> It is evident from a comparison of the constitutional violations which we have held subject to harmless error, and those which we have held not, that involuntary statements or confessions belong in the former category. The admission of an involuntary confession is a "trial error," similar in both degree and kind to the erroneous admission of other types of evidence. The evidentiary impact of an involuntary confession, and its effect upon the composition of the record, is indistinguishable from that of a confession obtained in violation of the Sixth Amendment—of evidence seized in violation of the Fourth Amendment—or of a prosecutor's improper comment on a defendant's silence at trial in violation of the Fifth Amendment. When reviewing the erroneous admission of an involuntary confession, the appellate court, as it does with the admission of other forms of improperly admitted evidence, simply reviews the remainder of the evidence against the defendant to determine whether the admission of the confession was harmless beyond a reasonable doubt.
>
> Nor can it be said that the admission of an involuntary confession is the type of error which "transcends the criminal process." This Court has applied harmless-error analysis to the violation of other constitutional rights similar in magnitude and importance and involving the same level of police misconduct. For instance, we have previously held that the admission of a defendant's statements obtained in violation of the Sixth Amendment is subject to harmless-error analysis. . . . We have also held that the admission of an out-of-court statement by a nontestifying codefendant is subject to harmless-error

[3] Justice Stewart wrote an opinion concurring in the result. Justice Harlan wrote a dissenting opinion.

> analysis. . . . The inconsistent treatment of statements elicited in violation of the Sixth and Fourteenth Amendments, respectively, can be supported neither by evidentiary or deterrence concerns nor by a belief that there is something more "fundamental" about involuntary confessions. This is especially true in a case such as this one where there are no allegations of physical violence on behalf of the police. A confession obtained in violation of the Sixth Amendment has the same evidentiary impact as does a confession obtained in violation of a defendant's due process rights. Government misconduct that results in violations of the Fourth and Sixth Amendments may be at least as reprehensible as conduct that results in an involuntary confession. . . . Indeed, experience shows that law enforcement violations of these constitutional guarantees can involve conduct as egregious as police conduct used to elicit statements in violation of the Fourteenth Amendment. It is thus impossible to create a meaningful distinction between confessions elicited in violation of the Sixth Amendment and those in violation of the Fourteenth Amendment.

Id. at 310–12. A majority of the Court held, however, that the admission of the confession in *Fulminante* was not harmless error.

Discussing which constitutional errors may be harmless error and which are never harmless error, the Court held that constitutionally inadequate instructions about the prosecution's burden of proof beyond a reasonable doubt are in the latter category. Sullivan v. Louisiana, 508 U.S. 275 (1993). Without adequate instructions on the burden of proof, the Court said, there has effectively been no jury verdict of guilt; so it is meaningless to ask whether a jury would have returned the same verdict had there been no error. The error in this case, it said, was a "structural error," to which harmless-error analysis does not apply.

In determining whether a jury instruction stating a presumption that unconstitutionally shifts the burden of proof to the defendant is harmless error (see Rose v. Clark, 478 U.S. 570 (1986) (6–3)), a reviewing court should first "ask what evidence the jury actually considered in reaching its verdict" and "then weigh the probative force of that evidence as against the probative force of the presumption standing alone." Yates v. Evatt, 500 U.S. 391, 405 (1991) (7–2). In order to find that the erroneous instruction was harmless error, the court must conclude that "the force of the evidence presumably considered by the jury in accordance with the instructions is so overwhelming as to leave it beyond a reasonable doubt that the verdict resting on that evidence would have been the same in the absence of the presumption." Id. at 405.

See Connecticut v. Johnson, 460 U.S. 73 (1983) (5–4), in which the Court said that an instruction (referring to a "conclusive presumption") that may have removed an issue of fact from the jury's consideration is never harmless error, except perhaps in "rare situations," such as when the issue is conceded by the defendant or is not relevant to the charge on which he is convicted.

See also Neder v. United States, 527 U.S. 1 (1999) (6–3) (failure to instruct jury on element of offense may be harmless error); Delaware v. Van Arsdall, 475 U.S. 673 (1986) (erroneous restriction of cross-examination may be harmless error); Rushen v. Spain, 464 U.S. 114 (1983) (ex parte communication between judge and juror; harmless error); Milton v. Wainwright, 407 U.S. 371 (1972) (5–4) (admission of confession, if error, was harmless); Harrington v. California, 395 U.S. 250 (1969) (6–3) (violation of *Bruton*, p. 776 note 395 above; harmless error).

612. In United States v. Hasting, 461 U.S. 499 (1983), the court of appeals had reversed the convictions of five defendants for kidnapping and other crimes arising out of the brutal abduction and rape of three women, on the ground that in his closing argument the prosecutor had violated defendants' right under Griffin v. California, 380 U.S. 609 (1965), p. 961 above. Assuming that the court of appeals's action had been an exercise of its supervisory power, intended to enforce its admonitions to prosecutors not to make impermissible comments at trial, the Court said that the harmless-error rule of *Chapman* cannot be evaded by an assertion of supervisory power.

> Supervisory power to reverse a conviction is not needed as a remedy when the error to which it is addressed is harmless since, by definition, the conviction would have been obtained notwithstanding the asserted error. Further, in this context, the integrity of the process carries less weight, for it is the essence of the harmless-error doctrine that a judgment may stand only when there is no "reasonable possibility that the [practice] complained of might have contributed to the conviction." Fahy v. Connecticut, 375 U.S. 85, 86–87 (1963). Finally, deterrence is an inappropriate basis for reversal where, as here, the prosecutor's remark is at most an attenuated violation of *Griffin* and where means more narrowly tailored to deter objectionable prosecutorial conduct are available.
>
> To the extent that the values protected by supervisory authority are at issue here, these powers may not be exercised in a vacuum. Rather, reversals of convictions under the court's supervisory power must be approached "with some caution," [United States v.] *Payner*, 447 U.S. [727 (1980)], at 734, and with a view toward balancing the interests involved, id., at 735–36, and n.8. . . . [T]he Court of Appeals failed in this case to give appropriate—if, indeed, any—weight to these relevant interests. It did not consider the trauma the victims of these particularly heinous crimes would experience in a new trial, forcing them to relive harrowing experiences now long past, or the practical problems of retrying these sensitive issues more than four years after the events. . . . The conclusion is inescapable that the Court of Appeals focused exclusively on its concern that the prosecutors within its jurisdiction were indifferent to the frequent admonitions of the court. The court appears to have decided to deter future similar comments by the drastic step of reversal of these convictions. But the interests preserved by the doctrine of harmless error cannot be so lightly and

> casually ignored in order to chastise what the court viewed as prosecutorial overreaching.
>
> . . .
>
> . . . In holding that the harmless-error rule governs even constitutional violations under some circumstances, the Court recognized that, given the myriad safeguards provided to assure a fair trial, and taking into account the reality of the human fallibility of the participants, there can be no such thing as an error-free, perfect trial, and that the Constitution does not guarantee such a trial. . . . *Chapman* [v. California, 386 U.S. 18 (1967)] reflected the concern, later noted by Chief Justice Roger Traynor of the Supreme Court of California, that when courts fashion rules whose violations mandate automatic reversals, they "retrea[t] from their responsibility, becoming instead 'impregnable citadels of technicality.'" R. Traynor, The Riddle of Harmless Error 14 (1970) (quoting Kavanagh, Improvement of Administration of Criminal Justice by Exercise of Judicial Power, 11 A.B.A.J. 217, 222 (1925)).
>
> Since *Chapman*, the Court has consistently made clear that it is the duty of a reviewing court to consider the trial record as a whole and to ignore errors that are harmless, including most constitutional violations. . . . The goal, as Chief Justice Traynor has noted, is "to conserve judicial resources by enabling appellate courts to cleanse the judicial process of prejudicial error without becoming mired in harmless error." Traynor, supra, at 81.
>
> Here, the Court of Appeals, while making passing reference to the harmless-error doctrine, did not apply it. Its analysis failed to strike the balance between disciplining the prosecutor on the one hand, and the interest in the prompt administration of justice and the interests of the victims on the other.

461 U.S. at 506–509. Examining the record, the Court concluded that the prosecutor's comment was harmless error and reversed the judgment below ordering a new trial. See, to the same effect, Bank of Nova Scotia v. United States, 487 U.S. 250 (1988) (8–1).

In Rose v. Clark, 478 U.S. 570 (1986) (6–3), the Court said that circumstances in which the doctrine of harmless error does not apply are exceptional. "Harmless-error analysis . . . presupposes a trial at which the defendant, represented by counsel, may present evidence and argument before an impartial judge and jury." Id. at 578. Beyond that, "if the defendant had counsel and was tried by an impartial adjudicator, there is a strong presumption that any other errors that may have occurred are subject to harmless-error analysis. The thrust of the many constitutional rules governing the conduct of criminal trials is to ensure that those trials lead to fair and correct judgments. Where a reviewing court can find that the record developed at trial establishes guilt beyond a reasonable doubt, the interest in fairness has been satisfied and the judgment should be affirmed." Id. at 579.

FEDERAL RULES OF CRIMINAL PROCEDURE

Rule 38

STAYING A SENTENCE OR A DISABILITY

(a) Death Sentence. The court must stay a death sentence if the defendant appeals the conviction or sentence.

(b) Imprisonment.

(1) *Stay Granted.* If the defendant is released pending appeal, the court must stay a sentence of imprisonment.

(2) *Stay Denied; Place of Confinement.* If the defendant is not released pending appeal, the court may recommend to the Attorney General that the defendant be confined near the place of the trial or appeal for a period reasonably necessary to permit the defendant to assist in preparing the appeal.

(c) Fine. If the defendant appeals, the district court, or the court of appeals under Federal Rule of Appellate Procedure 8, may stay a sentence to pay a fine or a fine and costs. The court may stay the sentence on any terms considered appropriate and may require the defendant to:

(1) deposit all or part of the fine and costs into the district court's registry pending appeal;

(2) post a bond to pay the fine and costs; or

(3) submit to an examination concerning the defendant's assets and, if appropriate, order the defendant to refrain from dissipating assets.

(d) Probation. If the defendant appeals, the court may stay a sentence of probation. The court must set the terms of any stay.

(e) Restitution and Notice to Victims.

(1) *In General.* If the defendant appeals, the district court, or the court of appeals under Federal Rule of Appellate Procedure 8, may stay—on any terms considered appropriate—any sentence providing for restitution under 18 U.S.C. § 3556 or notice under 18 U.S.C. § 3555.

(2) *Ensuring Compliance.* The court may issue any order reasonably necessary to ensure compliance with a restitution order or a notice order after disposition of an appeal, including:

(A) a restraining order;

(B) an injunction;

(C) an order requiring the defendant to deposit all or part of any monetary restitution into the district court's registry; or

(D) an order requiring the defendant to post a bond.

(f) Forfeiture. A stay of a forfeiture is governed by Rule 32.2(d).

(g) Disability. If the defendant's conviction or sentence creates a civil or employment disability under federal law, the district court, or the court of appeals under Federal Rule of Appellate Procedure 8, may stay the disability pending appeal on any terms considered appropriate. The court may issue any order reasonably necessary to protect the interest represented by the disability pending appeal, including a restraining order or an injunction.

FEDERAL RULES OF APPELLATE PROCEDURE

Rule 9

RELEASE IN A CRIMINAL CASE

(a) Release Before Judgment of Conviction.

(1) The district court must state in writing, or orally on the record, the reasons for an order regarding the release or detention of a defendant in a criminal case. A party appealing from the order must file with the court of appeals a copy of the district court's order and the court's statement of reasons as soon as practicable after filing the notice of appeal. An appellant who questions the factual basis for the district court's order must file a transcript of the release proceedings or an explanation of why a transcript was not obtained.

(2) After reasonable notice to the appellee, the court of appeals must promptly determine the appeal on the basis of the papers, affidavits, and parts of the record that the parties present or the court requires. Unless the court so orders, briefs need not be filed.

(3) The court of appeals or one of its judges may order the defendant's release pending the disposition of the appeal.

(b) Release After Judgment of Conviction. A party entitled to do so may obtain review of a district-court order regarding release after a judgment of conviction by filing a notice of appeal from that order in the district court, or by filing a motion in the court of appeals if the party has already filed a notice of appeal from the judgment of conviction. Both the order and the review are subject to Rule 9(a). The papers filed by the party seeking review must include a copy of the judgment of conviction.

(c) Criteria for Release. The court must make its decision regarding release in accordance with the applicable provisions of 18 U.S.C. §§ 3142, 3143, and 3145(c).

CHAPTER 17

DOUBLE JEOPARDY

"[N]or shall any person be subject for the same offense to be twice put in jeopardy of life or limb. . . ." U.S. Constitution amend. V.

613.

> [W]e today find that the double jeopardy prohibition of the Fifth Amendment represents a fundamental ideal in our constitutional heritage, and that it should apply to the States through the Fourteenth Amendment. . . .
>
> . . .
>
> The fundamental nature of the guarantee against double jeopardy can hardly be doubted. Its origins can be traced to Greek and Roman times, and it became established in the common law of England long before this Nation's independence. . . . As with many other elements of the common law, it was carried into the jurisprudence of this Country through the medium of Blackstone, who codified the doctrine in his Commentaries. "[T]he plea of *autrefoits acquit*, or a former acquittal," he wrote, "is grounded on this universal maxim of the common law of England, that no man is to be brought into jeopardy of his life more than once for the same offence." Today, every State incorporates some form of the prohibition in its constitution or common law.

Benton v. Maryland, 395 U.S. 784, 794–95 (1969).

In Crist v. Bretz, 437 U.S. 28 (1978) (6–3), the Court held explicitly that the federal rule that jeopardy attaches when the jury is empaneled and sworn is an integral part of the guarantee against double jeopardy and is binding on the states.

614. "[T]he Fifth Amendment guarantee against double jeopardy . . . has been said to consist of three separate constitutional protections. It protects against a second prosecution for the same offense after acquittal. It protects against a second prosecution for the same offense after conviction. And it protects against multiple punishments for the same offense." North Carolina v. Pearce, 395 U.S. 711, 717 (1969).

See Sanabria v. United States, 437 U.S. 54 (1978) (7–2), applying, in unusual circumstances, the rule that there can be no retrial after an acquittal. See also Smalis v. Pennsylvania, 476 U.S. 140 (1986) (grant of demurrer challenging sufficiency of the evidence at close of prosecution's case was an acquittal under the Double Jeopardy Clause, appeal from which is barred).

The Double Jeopardy Clause bars a government appeal from a judgment of acquittal under Rule 29(c), p. 1063 above, entered after the jury, having failed to reach a verdict, has been discharged. United States v. Martin Linen Supply Co., 430 U.S. 564 (1977). See United States v. Baggett, 251 F.3d 1087 (6th Cir.2001), discussing the double jeopardy effect of a motion for a judgment of acquittal granted before or after the jury returns a verdict.

In Serfass v. United States, 420 U.S. 377 (1975) (8–1), the Court held that the Double Jeopardy Clause did not bar an appeal by the government from pretrial dismissal of an indictment based on a legal ruling that the trial judge made after examining records and an affidavit containing evidence to be presented at trial. Notwithstanding the trial judge's reliance on such material, jeopardy had *not* attached, since the defendant had not been put to trial before the trier of the facts. See United States v. Sanford, 429 U.S. 14 (1976).

In United States v. Wilson, 420 U.S. 332 (1975) (7–2), after the jury returned a verdict of guilty at the defendant's trial, the trial judge reconsidered his pretrial motion to dismiss the indictment for undue delay before indictment and granted it; the delay, the judge concluded, had prejudiced his right to a fair trial. The government appealed. The court of appeals dismissed the appeal on the ground that since the trial court had relied on facts brought out at trial for its conclusion that the defendant had been prejudiced, the dismissal was equivalent to an acquittal; the appeal, therefore, violated the Double Jeopardy Clause.

The Court held that the appeal was proper. It said that "where there is no threat of either multiple punishment or successive prosecutions, the Double Jeopardy Clause is not offended. . . . Although review of any ruling of law discharging a defendant obviously enhances the likelihood of conviction and subjects him to continuing expense and anxiety, a defendant has no legitimate claim to benefit from an error of law when that error could be corrected without subjecting him to a second trial before a second trier of fact." Id. at 344–45. Since reversal on appeal of the order of dismissal would simply reinstate the jury's verdict, an appeal was permissible.

Reversing a ruling it had made only three terms before (United States v. Jenkins, 420 U.S. 358 (1975)), the Court held that if the defendant successfully moves to have the trial terminated before submission of the question of his guilt to judge or jury, the government is not barred from an appeal and, if it is successful on the appeal, a retrial. United States v. Scott, 437 U.S. 82 (1978) (5–4). The defendant's motion for a dismissal because of pretrial delay had been granted at the close of the evidence. The Court said: "We think that in a case such as this the defendant, by deliberately choosing to seek termination of the proceedings against him on a basis unrelated to factual guilt or innocence of the offense of which he is accused, suffers no injury cognizable under the Double Jeopardy Clause if the

Government is permitted to appeal from such a ruling of the trial court in favor of the defendant. We do not thereby adopt the doctrine of 'waiver' of double jeopardy rejected in *Green* [v. United States, 355 U.S. 184 (1957), p. ___ below]. Rather, we conclude that the Double Jeopardy Clause, which guards against Government oppression, does not relieve a defendant from the consequences of his voluntary choice. In *Green* the question of defendant's factual guilt or innocence of murder in the first degree was actually submitted to the jury as a trier of fact; in the present case, respondent successfully avoided such a submission of the first count of the indictment by persuading the trial court to dismiss it on a basis which did not depend on guilt or innocence. He was thus neither acquitted nor convicted, because he himself successfully undertook to persuade the trial court not to submit the issue of guilt or innocence to the jury which had been empaneled to try him." 437 U.S. at 98–99.

615. A defendant may not be prosecuted for an offense after having been tried and convicted of a lesser included offense. It "is invariably true of a greater and lesser included offense [that] the lesser offense . . . requires no proof beyond that which is required for conviction of the greater. . . . The greater offense is therefore by definition the 'same' for purposes of double jeopardy as any lesser offense included in it." Brown v. Ohio, 432 U.S. 161, 168 (1977) (6–3). "[W]hatever the sequence may be, the Fifth Amendment forbids successive prosecution and cumulative punishment for a greater and lesser included offense." Id. at 169. Accord Harris v. Oklahoma, 433 U.S. 682 (1977) (prosecution for underlying felony after conviction for felony murder). See Illinois v. Vitale, 447 U.S. 410 (1980) (5–4) (*Brown* applied). In *Brown*, the Court noted that "an exception may exist where the State is unable to proceed on the more serious charge at the outset because the additional facts necessary to sustain that charge have not occurred or have not been discovered despite the exercise of due diligence." 432 U.S. at 169 n.7.

Brown was distinguished in Montana v. Hall, 481 U.S. 400 (1987) (6–2), in which the defendant was indicted for sexual assault on his stepdaughter. He moved to dismiss on the ground that under state law the offense was incest, not sexual assault. The motion was granted. He was then convicted of incest. He appealed successfully, on the ground that the incest statute at the time of the offense did not apply to sexual assault on a stepchild. The Court held that a retrial was not barred. The case, it said, "falls squarely within the rule that retrial is permissible after a conviction is reversed on appeal." Id. at 404. *Brown* was distinguished also in Garrett v. United States, 471 U.S. 773 (1985) (5–3), holding that the Double Jeopardy Clause does not prohibit a prosecution for a "continuing criminal enterprise" (21 U.S.C. § 848) after the defendant has been convicted of one of the underlying predicate offenses. See also Jeffers v. United States, 432 U.S. 137 (1977) (defendant, having objected to trial together of greater and lesser charges, convicted of lesser charge at first trial).

In Ohio v. Johnson, 467 U.S. 493 (1984) (7–2), the defendant was charged in a single indictment with involuntary manslaughter, grand theft, murder, and aggravated robbery, all four counts arising out of the same events involving a killing and theft. He pleaded guilty to the first two counts over the state's objection, and was sentenced. The trial court then granted his motion to dismiss the latter two counts on the ground that the conviction of the lesser included offenses precluded further prosecution of the more serious offenses arising out of the same acts. The Court reversed. The joinder of the greater and lesser charges in a single prosecution is permissible. Here, the state never sought to try the charges separately. Nor were the guilty pleas an implied acquittal of the more serious offenses. The defendant's guilty pleas do not bar the state from one full opportunity to prove the crimes charged in the indictment. *Johnson* was applied in Gilmore v. Zimmerman, 793 F.2d 564 (3d Cir.1986), in which, at the sentencing hearing, the trial judge on his own motion struck a guilty plea that he had previously accepted. The plea to the lesser offense had been worked out by the prosecutor and defense counsel and was acceptable to both sides. The judge's reason for rejecting it was that there was an insufficient factual basis.

See Whalen v. United States, 445 U.S. 684 (1980) (7–2). The defendant was convicted of rape and of killing the same victim in the perpetration of rape. Construing federal statutory law, the Court concluded that the imposition of consecutive sentences for the two offenses was impermissible. *Whalen* was distinguished in Missouri v. Hunter, 459 U.S. 359 (1983) (7–2), in which the Court, finding a clear legislative intent to permit the imposition of cumulative sentences under two statutes proscribing the same conduct, held that the Double Jeopardy Clause does not prohibit the imposition of consecutive sentences under the statutes in a single trial. The Court observed that the Clause's protection against multiple prosecutions was not involved because the charges were joined in a single trial.

After the defendant had been convicted of the lesser offense of aggravated robbery, he was charged with aggravated murder and convicted following a jury verdict. On appeal, concluding that the charge of aggravated murder violated the Double Jeopardy Clause, the state court substituted a conviction for murder and reduced the defendant's sentence accordingly. It concluded that the jury's verdict necessarily supported the conviction for murder, all the elements of the lesser offense being excluded. On habeas corpus, the federal court of appeals held that the substituted conviction was invalid; it said that the defendant had only to show a "reasonable possibility" that he was prejudiced by the barred charge. The Court reversed. It held that "when a jeopardy-barred conviction is reduced to a conviction for a lesser included offense which is not jeopardy-barred, the burden shifts to the defendant to demonstrate a reasonable probability that he would not have been convicted of the non-jeopardy-barred offense absent the presence of the jeopardy-barred offense." Morris v. Mathews, 475 U.S. 237, 246–47 (1986) (7–2). The Court stated that the case was not one for application of the harmless error standard. Rather, it was a case in which there was error that was not harmless. The question, it said, was whether substitution of the lesser conviction was an adequate remedy. Cf. Jones v. Thomas, 491 U.S. 376 (1989) (5–4) (defendant improperly sentenced cumulatively in single trial for felony murder and underlying felony could be made to serve balance of longer sentence for murder after shorter sentence for felony, already fully served, was vacated.)

616. The defendant in Witte v. United States, 515 U.S. 389 (1995), was convicted on a plea of guilty to drug offenses. The presentence report described additional drug offenses during the same period, which were not included among those to which he pleaded guilty. Over the objection of the defendant and the government, the court considered the latter offenses as "relevant conduct" for sentencing purposes, which resulted in an increase in his sentence under the Sentencing Guidelines. On the basis of a downward departure from the prescribed sentence, the final sentence was much less than the minimum prescribed standard sentence. Thereafter, the defendant was indicted for uncharged offenses that had been considered at the prior sentencing. He moved to dismiss the indictment on the ground that punishment for those offenses was prohibited by the Double Jeopardy Clause as multiple punishments for the same offense. The Court rejected his claim. Referring to prior cases, it said that "use of evidence of related criminal conduct to enhance a defendant's sentence for a separate crime within the authorized statutory limits does not constitute punishment for that conduct within the meaning of the Double Jeopardy Clause." Id. at 399.

617. Reviewing a wavering line of prior decisions, the Court held that a civil forfeiture is not a punishment for purposes of the Double Jeopardy Clause and, therefore, that punishing a defendant for an offense and, in a separate civil proceeding, declaring the forfeiture of his property for the same offense is not prohibited. United States v. Ursery, 518 U.S. 267 (1996) (8–1).

The Court returned to the general issue of when a penalty imposed in a noncriminal proceeding bars a subsequent prosecution in Hudson v. United States, 522 U.S. 93 (1997). The petitioners were bankers who were assessed money penalties for violations of banking laws and regulations and barred from banking activities, in proceedings of the Office of the Comptroller of the Currency. They were subsequently indicted for the same conduct that was involved in the prior proceedings. The Court held that the Double Jeopardy Clause did not prohibit their prosecution, because the prior penalties were noncriminal. It said that whether "a particular punishment is criminal or civil is, at least initially, a matter of statutory construction." Id. at 493. Even if the legislature intended the punishment as civil, however, if it had too many indicia of criminality it might be treated as criminal for purposes of the Double Jeopardy Clause. Quoting from Kennedy v. Mendoza-Martinez, 372 U.S. 144, 168–69 (1963), the Court said that among such indicia were:

> (1) "[w]hether the sanction involves an affirmative disability or restraint"; (2) "whether it has historically been regarded as a punishment"; (3) "whether it comes into play only on a finding of *scienter*"; (4) "whether its operation will promote the traditional aims of punishment—retribution and deterrence"; (5) "whether the behavior to

which it applies is already a crime"; (6) "whether an alternative purpose to which it may rationally be connected is assignable for it"; and (7) "whether it appears excessive in relation to the alternative purpose assigned."

A conclusion that a statutory civil sanction is in effect criminal is permissible only if there is " 'the clearest proof,' " United States v. Ward, 448 U.S. 242, 249 (1980), that it is criminal in nature.

See Kansas v. Hendricks, 521 U.S. 346 (1997) (5–4), in which the Court held that the Double Jeopardy Clause was not violated by provisions of the Kansas Sexually Violent Predator Act establishing procedures for the civil commitment of persons who are likely to engage in "predatory acts of sexual violence" because of a "mental abnormality" or a "personality disorder." After serving nearly ten years of a sentence for a sexual offense against two boys, the petitioner was scheduled for release. The state filed civil commitment proceedings under the statute. Following a jury trial at which he was found beyond a reasonable doubt to be a sexually violent predator, he was civilly committed. Applying tests like those stated in *Mendoza-Martinez*, above, the court concluded that the commitment was noncriminal.

618. Denial of a motion to dismiss an indictment on the ground of double jeopardy is a "final decision" under 28 U.S.C. § 1291 and is, therefore, immediately appealable. Abney v. United States, 431 U.S. 651 (1977). Such a ruling, the Court said, constitutes "a final rejection of a criminal defendant's double jeopardy claim." Furthermore, the claim "is collateral to, and separable from the principal issue at the accused's impending criminal trial," and postponement of the appeal would undermine the right not to be put to trial twice for the same offense. Id. at 659. See Richardson v. United States, 468 U.S. 317 (1984) (8–1), applying *Abney* to an appeal from the denial of a motion for a judgment of acquittal on the ground of insufficient evidence, which, if granted, would have barred retrial because of the Double Jeopardy Clause.

Green v. United States

355 U.S. 184, 78 S.Ct. 221, 2 L.Ed.2d 199 (1957)

■ Opinion of the Court by MR. JUSTICE BLACK, announced by MR. JUSTICE DOUGLAS.

This case presents a serious question concerning the meaning and application of that provision of the Fifth Amendment to the Constitution which declares that no person shall ". . . be subject for the same offence to be twice put in jeopardy of life or limb. . . ."

The petitioner, Everett Green, was indicted by a District of Columbia grand jury in two counts. The first charged that he had committed arson by maliciously setting fire to a house. The second accused him of causing the death of a woman by this alleged arson which if true amounted to murder in the first degree punishable by death. Green entered a plea of not guilty to both counts and the case was tried by a jury. After each side had presented its evidence the trial judge instructed the jury that it could find Green guilty of arson under the first count and of either (1) first degree murder or (2) second degree murder under the second count. The trial judge treated second degree murder, which is defined by the District Code as the killing of another with malice aforethought and is punishable by imprisonment for a term of years or for life, as an offense included within the language charging first degree murder in the second count of the indictment.

The jury found Green guilty of arson and of second degree murder but did not find him guilty on the charge of murder in the first degree. Its verdict was silent on that charge. The trial judge accepted the verdict, entered the proper judgments and dismissed the jury. Green was sentenced to one to three years' imprisonment for arson and five to twenty years' imprisonment for murder in the second degree. He appealed the conviction of second degree murder. The Court of Appeals reversed that conviction because it was not supported by evidence and remanded the case for a new trial. . . .

On remand Green was tried again for first degree murder under the original indictment. At the outset of this second trial he raised the defense of former jeopardy but the court overruled his plea. This time a new jury found him guilty of first degree murder and he was given the mandatory death sentence. Again he appealed. Sitting en banc, the Court of Appeals rejected his defense of former jeopardy . . . and affirmed the conviction. . . . We granted certiorari. . . .

The constitutional prohibition against "double jeopardy" was designed to protect an individual from being subjected to the hazards of trial and possible conviction more than once for an alleged offense. In his Commentaries, which greatly influenced the generation that adopted the Constitution, Blackstone recorded: ". . . the plea of *autrefois acquit*, or a former acquittal, is grounded on this universal maxim of the common law of England, that no man is to be brought into jeopardy of his life more than once for the same offence." Substantially the same view was taken by this Court in Ex parte Lange, 18 Wall. 163, at 169: "The common law not only prohibited a second punishment for the same offence, but it went further and forbid a second trial for the same offence, whether the accused had suffered punishment or not, and whether in the former trial he had been acquitted or convicted." The underlying idea, one that is deeply ingrained in at least the Anglo-American system of jurisprudence, is that the State with all its resources and power should not be allowed to make repeated attempts to convict an individual for an alleged offense, thereby subjecting him to embarrassment, expense and ordeal and compelling him to live in a continuing state of anxiety and insecurity, as well as enhancing the possibility that even though innocent he may be found guilty.

In accordance with this philosophy it has long been settled under the Fifth Amendment that a verdict of acquittal is final, ending a defendant's jeopardy, and even when "not followed by any judgment, is a bar to a subsequent prosecution for the same offence." United States v. Ball, 153 U.S. 662, 671. Thus it is one of the elemental principles of our criminal law that the Government cannot secure a new trial by means of an appeal even though an acquittal may appear to be erroneous. . . .

Moreover it is not even essential that a verdict of guilt or innocence be returned for a defendant to have once been placed in jeopardy so as to bar a second trial on the same charge. This Court, as well as most others, has taken the position that a defendant is placed in jeopardy once he is put to trial before a jury so that if the jury is discharged without his consent he cannot be tried again. . . . This prevents a prosecutor or judge from subjecting a defendant to a second prosecution by discontinuing the trial when it appears that the jury might not convict. At the same time jeopardy is not regarded as having come to an end so as to bar a second trial in those cases where "unforeseeable circumstances . . . arise during [the first] trial making its completion impossible, such as the failure of a jury to agree on a verdict." Wade v. Hunter, 336 U.S. 684, 688–89.

At common law a convicted person could not obtain a new trial by appeal except in certain narrow instances. As this harsh rule was discarded courts and legislatures provided that if a defendant obtained the reversal of a conviction by his own appeal he could be tried again for the same offense. Most courts regarded the new trial as a second jeopardy but justified this on the ground that the appellant had "waived" his plea of former jeopardy by asking that the conviction be set aside. Other courts viewed the second trial as continuing the same jeopardy which had attached at the first trial by reasoning that jeopardy did not come to an end until the accused was acquitted or his conviction became final. But whatever the rationalization, this Court has also held that a defendant can be tried a second time for an offense when his prior conviction for that same offense had been set aside on appeal. . . .

In this case, however, we have a much different question. At Green's first trial the jury was authorized to find him guilty of either first degree murder (killing while perpetrating a felony) or, alternatively, of second degree murder (killing with malice aforethought). The jury found him guilty of second degree murder, but on his appeal that conviction was reversed and the case remanded for a new trial. At this new trial Green was tried again, not for second degree murder, but for first degree murder, even though the original jury had refused to find him guilty on that charge and it was in no way involved in his appeal. For the reasons stated hereafter, we conclude that this second trial for first degree murder placed Green in jeopardy twice for the same offense in violation of the Constitution.

Green was in direct peril of being convicted and punished for first degree murder at his first trial. He was forced to run the gantlet once on that charge and the jury refused to convict him. When given the choice between finding him guilty of either first or second degree murder it chose the latter. In this situation the great majority of cases in this country have regarded the jury's verdict as an implicit acquittal on the charge of first degree murder. But the result in this case need not rest alone on the assumption, which we believe legitimate, that the jury for one reason or another acquitted Green of murder in the first degree. For here, the jury was dismissed without returning any express verdict on that charge and without Green's consent. Yet it was given a full opportunity to return a verdict and no extraordinary circumstances appeared which prevented it from doing so. Therefore it seems clear, under established principles of former jeopardy, that Green's jeopardy for first degree murder came to an end when the jury was discharged so that he could not be retried for that offense. . . . In brief, we believe this case can be treated no differently, for purposes of former jeopardy, than if the jury had returned a verdict which expressly read: "We find the defendant not guilty of murder in the first degree but guilty of murder in the second degree."

After the original trial, but prior to his appeal, it is indisputable that Green could not have been tried again for first degree murder for the death resulting from the fire. A plea of former jeopardy would have absolutely barred a new prosecution even though it might have been convincingly demonstrated that the jury erred in failing to convict him of that offense. And even after appealing the conviction of second degree murder he still could not have been tried a second time for first degree murder had his appeal been unsuccessful.

Nevertheless the Government contends that Green "waived" his constitutional defense of former jeopardy to a second prosecution on the first degree murder charge by making a *successful* appeal of his improper conviction of second degree murder. We cannot accept this paradoxical contention. "Waiver" is a vague term used for a great variety of purposes, good and bad, in the law. In any normal sense, however, it connotes some kind of voluntary knowing relinquishment of a right. . . . When a man has been convicted of second degree murder and given a long term of imprisonment it is wholly fictional to say that he "chooses" to forego his constitutional defense of former jeopardy on a charge of murder in the first degree in order to secure a reversal of an erroneous conviction of the lesser offense. In short, he has no meaningful choice. And as Mr. Justice Holmes observed, with regard to this same matter in Kepner v. United States, 195 U.S. 100, at 135: "Usually no such waiver is expressed or thought of. Moreover, it cannot be imagined that the law would deny to a prisoner the correction of a fatal error, unless he should waive other rights so important as to be saved by an express clause in the Constitution of the United States."

It is true that in *Kepner*, a case arising in the Philippine Islands under a statutory prohibition against double jeopardy, Mr. Justice Holmes dissented from the Court's holding that the Government could not appeal an acquittal in a criminal prosecution. He argued that there was only one continuing jeopardy until the "case" had finally been settled, appeal and all, without regard to how many times the defendant was tried, but that view was rejected by the Court. The position taken by the majority in *Kepner* is completely in accord with the deeply entrenched principle of our criminal law that once a person has been acquitted of an offense he cannot be prosecuted again on the same charge. This Court has uniformly adhered to that basic premise. For example, in United States v. Ball, 163 U.S. 662, 671, a unanimous Court held: "The verdict of acquittal was final, and could not be reviewed, on error or otherwise, without putting [the defendant] twice in jeopardy, and thereby violating the Constitution." . . .

Using reasoning which purports to be analogous to that expressed by Mr. Justice Holmes in *Kepner*, the Government alternatively argues that Green, by appealing, prolonged his original jeopardy so that when his conviction for second degree murder was reversed and the case remanded he could be tried again for first degree murder without placing him in new jeopardy. We believe this argument is also untenable. Whatever may be said for the notion of continuing jeopardy with regard to an offense when a defendant has been convicted of that offense and has secured reversal of the conviction by appeal, here Green was not convicted of first degree murder and that offense was not involved in his appeal. If Green had only appealed his conviction of arson and that conviction had been set aside surely no one would claim that he could have been tried a second time for first degree murder by reasoning that his initial jeopardy on that charge continued until every offense alleged in the indictment had been finally adjudicated.

Reduced to plain terms, the Government contends that in order to secure the reversal of an erroneous conviction of one offense, a defendant must surrender his valid defense of former jeopardy not only on that offense but also on a different offense for which he was not convicted and which was not involved in his appeal. Or stated in the terms of this case, he must be willing to barter his constitutional protection against a second prosecution for an offense punishable by death as the price of a successful appeal from an erroneous conviction of another offense for which he has been sentenced to five to twenty years' imprisonment. As the Court of Appeals said in its first opinion in this case, a defendant faced with such a "choice" takes a "desperate chance" in securing the reversal of the erroneous conviction. The law should not, and in our judgment does not, place the defendant in such an incredible dilemma. Conditioning an appeal of one offense on a coerced surrender of a valid plea of former jeopardy on another offense exacts a forfeiture in plain conflict with the constitutional bar against double jeopardy.

. . .

. . . The right not to be placed in jeopardy more than once for the same offense is a vital safeguard in our society, one that was dearly won and one that should continue to be highly valued. If such great constitutional protections are given a narrow, grudging application they are deprived of much of their significance. We [conclude] that the second trial of Green for first degree murder was contrary to both the letter and spirit of the Fifth Amendment.

. . .[1]

---

619. *Green* was applied to a case in which, after reversal of his conviction for the lesser offense, the defendant was again prosecuted for the more serious offense and again convicted of the *lesser* offense, in Price v. Georgia, 398 U.S. 323 (1970).

In Cichos v. Indiana, 385 U.S. 76 (1966), the defendant was charged with reckless homicide and involuntary manslaughter. He was convicted of reckless homicide on a jury verdict reciting only that he was guilty of that crime. He appealed successfully and was retried on both counts. He was again convicted of reckless homicide and sentenced. Under Indiana law, involuntary manslaughter was punishable more severely than reckless homicide, but the elements of the two crimes were the same, so that proof of reckless homicide necessarily established "an unlawful killing that amounts to involuntary manslaughter." Id. at 78. The Supreme Court accepted the conclusions of the Indiana Supreme Court that the effect of charging the two crimes was to give the jury discretion on the issue of sentencing and that its verdict did not constitute an acquittal of the more serious offense. On that basis, the Court concluded that the issue presented in *Green* was not present in the case.

Compare Pacelli v. United States, 588 F.2d 360 (2d Cir.1978), in which the defendant was convicted of a conspiracy charge and related substantive charges. The conspiracy charge was later found to have been barred by the Double Jeopardy Clause. The court upheld the convictions of the substantive counts, on the basis that the defendant's trial on the substantive counts had not been prejudiced by the joinder.

The defendant in United States ex rel. Jackson v. Follette, 462 F.2d 1041 (2d Cir.1972), was convicted of first-degree murder for the killing of a police officer after an armed robbery. At trial, the jury was instructed with respect to premeditated murder and felony murder, both constituting murder in the first degree, and told that if it found the defendant guilty of one, it should say nothing about the other. The conviction was for premeditated murder. The conviction was reversed on collateral attack. The defendant was tried again on both theories of murder. This time he was convicted for felony murder. After discussing *Green*, *Price*, and *Cichos* and observing that the case was sui generis, the court concluded that there had been no "substantial unfairness" to the defendant, since he would have been subject to retrial for premeditated murder in any event and the same evidence would have been admissible, and that "fairness to the public" demanded that the conviction be affirmed. Id. at 1050. In analogous circumstances, the court found that *Green* was applicable and that the defendant could not be put to trial a second time on the count on which the

[1] Justice Frankfurter wrote a dissenting opinion, which Justice Burton, Justice Clark, and Justice Harlan joined.

jury had not returned a verdict. Terry v. Potter, 111 F.3d 454 (6th Cir.1997).

620. The Double Jeopardy Clause requires that a person who has been convicted and sentenced, whose conviction is subsequently set aside, and who is convicted and sentenced a second time be given credit toward the second sentence for any portion of the first sentence that he served.

> We think it is clear that this basic constitutional guarantee is violated when punishment already exacted for an offense is not fully "credited" in imposing sentence upon a new conviction for the same offense. The constitutional violation is flagrantly apparent in a case involving the imposition of a maximum sentence after reconviction. Suppose, for example, in a jurisdiction where the maximum allowable sentence for larceny is 10 years imprisonment, a man succeeds in getting his larceny conviction set aside after serving three years in prison. If, upon reconviction, he is given a 10-year sentence, then, quite clearly, he will have received multiple punishments for the same offense. For he will have been compelled to serve separate prison terms of three years and 10 years, although the maximum single punishment for the offense is 10 years imprisonment. Though not so dramatically evident, the same principle obviously holds true whenever punishment already endured is not fully subtracted from any new sentence imposed.
>
> We hold that the constitutional guarantee against multiple punishments for the same offense absolutely requires that punishment already exacted must be fully "credited" in imposing sentence upon a new conviction for the same offense. If, upon a new trial, the defendant is acquitted, there is no way the years he spent in prison can be returned to him. But if he is reconvicted, those years can and must be returned—by subtracting them from whatever new sentence is imposed.

North Carolina v. Pearce, 395 U.S. 711, 718–19 (1969).

The Double Jeopardy Clause does not, however, bar imposition of a more severe sentence following the second conviction than that originally imposed if the second sentence is based on "events subsequent to the first trial." Id. at 723.

> Long-established constitutional doctrine makes clear that, beyond the requirement [of "credit"] already discussed, the guarantee against double jeopardy imposes no restrictions upon the length of a sentence imposed upon reconviction. . . .
>
> Although the rationale for this "well-established part of our constitutional jurisprudence" has been variously verbalized, it rests ultimately upon the premise that the original conviction has, at the defendant's behest, been wholly nullified and the slate wiped clean. As to whatever punishment has actually been suffered under the first conviction, that premise is, of course, an unmitigated fiction. . . . But, so far as the conviction itself goes, and that part of the sentence that

> has not yet been served, it is no more than a simple statement of fact to say that the slate *has* been wiped clean. The conviction *has* been set aside, and the unexpired portion of the original sentence will never be served. A new trial may result in an acquittal. But if it does result in a conviction, we cannot say that the constitutional guarantee against double jeopardy of its own weight restricts the imposition of an otherwise lawful single punishment for the offense in question. To hold to the contrary would be to cast doubt upon the whole validity of the basic principle . . . and upon the unbroken line of decisions that have followed that principle for almost 75 years. We think those decisions are entirely sound, and we decline to depart from the concept they reflect.

Id. at 719–21. See note 596, p. 1141 above.

621. Is the holding of *Green*, p. 1184 above, consistent with the holding of North Carolina v. Pearce, note 620 above, that a defendant may be given a more severe sentence on a second conviction than was imposed on a prior conviction of the same offense? In Stroud v. United States, 251 U.S. 15 (1919), on which the Court relied in *Pearce*, the defendant, having been convicted of first-degree murder on a jury verdict specifying "without capital punishment," was subsequently retried and convicted of first-degree murder without a recommendation dispensing with capital punishment and was sentenced to death. The Court affirmed the judgment. The opinion for the Court in *Green* stated that *Stroud* is "clearly distinguishable," the defendant in *Stroud* having been retried for first-degree murder "after he had successfully asked an appellate court to set aside a prior conviction for that same offense." 355 U.S. at 195 n.15. The dissenting opinion in *Green* stated that *Stroud* is "of special relevance." Id. at 213. "As a practical matter, and on any basis of human values, it is scarcely possible to distinguish a case in which the defendant is convicted of a greater offense from one in which he is convicted of an offense that has the same name as that of which he was previously convicted but carries a significantly different punishment, namely death rather than imprisonment." Id.[2] The majority in *Pearce* appears to concede that conceptually the problems of the two cases are closely related.

Justice Harlan, in *Pearce*, concluded that *Green* had discarded *Stroud* and should control the solution to the problem of resentencing:

> Every consideration enunciated by the Court in support of the decision in *Green* applies with equal force to the situation at bar. In each instance, the defendant was once subjected to the risk of receiving a maximum punishment, but it was determined by legal process that he should receive only a specified punishment less than the maximum. . . . And the concept or fiction of an "implied acquittal" of the greater offense . . . applies equally to the greater sentence: in each

2. *Stroud* is not mentioned in the Court's opinion in Cichos v. Indiana, 385 U.S. 76 (1966), p. 1189 note 619 above.

case it was determined at the former trial that the defendant or his offense was of a certain limited degree of "badness" or gravity only, and therefore merited only a certain limited punishment. . . .

If, as a matter of policy and practicality, the imposition of an increased sentence on retrial has the same consequences whether effected in the guise of an increase in the degree of offense or an augmentation of punishment, what other factors render one route forbidden and the other permissible under the Double Jeopardy Clause? It cannot be that the provision does not comprehend "sentences"—as distinguished from "offenses"—for it has long been established that once a prisoner commences service of sentence, the Clause prevents a court from vacating the sentence and then imposing a greater one. . . .

The Court does not suggest otherwise, but in its view, apparently, when the conviction itself and not merely the consequent sentence has been set aside, or when either has been set aside at the defendant's behest, the "slate has been wiped clean," and the Double Jeopardy Clause presents no bar to the imposition of a sentence greater than that originally imposed. . . .

. . .

[United States v.] *Ball* [163 U.S. 662 (1896)] held, simply, that a defendant who succeeds in getting his first conviction set aside may thereafter be retried for the same offense of which he was formerly convicted. This is, indeed, a fundamental doctrine in our criminal jurisprudence, and I would be the last to undermine it. But *Ball* does not speak to the question of what *punishment* may be imposed on retrial. I entirely fail to understand the Court's suggestion, unless it assumes that *Ball* must stand or fall on the question-begging notion that, to quote the majority today, "the original conviction has, at the defendant's behest, been wholly nullified and the slate wiped clean." . . .

In relying on this conceptual fiction, the majority forgets that Green v. United States prohibits the imposition of an increased punishment on retrial precisely *because* convictions are usually set aside only at the defendant's behest, and not in spite of that fact . . . the defendant's choice to appeal an erroneous conviction is protected by the rule that he may not again be placed in jeopardy of suffering the greater punishment not imposed at the first trial. Moreover, in its exaltation of form over substance and policy, the Court misconceives, I think, the essential principle of *Ball* itself:

> While different theories have been advanced to support the permissibility of retrial, of greater importance than the conceptual abstractions employed to explain the *Ball* principle are the implications of that principle for the sound administration of justice. Corresponding to the right of an accused to be given a fair trial is the societal interest in punishing one whose guilt is clear after he

> has obtained such a trial. It would be a high price indeed for society to pay were every accused granted immunity from punishment because of any defect sufficient to constitute reversible error in the proceedings leading to conviction.

United States v. Tateo, 377 U.S. 463, 466 (1964).

> To be sure, this societal interest is compromised to a degree if the second judge is forbidden to impose a greater punishment on retrial than was meted out at the first trial. For example, new facts may develop between the first and second trial which would, as an initial matter, be considered in aggravation of sentence. By the same token, however, the prosecutor who was able to prove only second degree murder at the former trial might improve his case in the interim and acquire sufficient evidence to prove murder in the first degree. In either instance, if one views the second trial in a vacuum, the defendant has received less punishment than is his due. But in both cases, the compromise is designed to protect other societal interests, and it is, after *Green*, a compromise compelled by the Double Jeopardy Clause.

395 U.S. at 746–50 (concurring and dissenting opinion).

Justice Harlan's argument in *Pearce* was rejected again in United States v. DiFrancesco, 449 U.S. 117 (1980) (5–4). The Court there concluded that the Double Jeopardy Clause does not prohibit an appeal from a sentence by the government, on the ground that the sentence is too lenient. *DiFrancesco* was applied in Pennsylvania v. Goldhammer, 474 U.S. 28 (1985) (5–4).

In Bullington v. Missouri, 451 U.S. 430 (1981) (5–4), however, a majority of the Court distinguished *Stroud*. The defendant was convicted of murder. At a separate sentencing hearing at which the two possible sentences were death and life imprisonment, the jury chose the latter penalty. The defendant's conviction was reversed and he was retried and again found guilty. The Court concluded that the first jury's sentencing decision precluded a sentence of death after the second trial. Acknowledging that the Court generally had not interpreted the Double Jeopardy Clause to bar imposition of a harsher sentence at retrial after an original conviction has been set aside, the majority concluded that the procedures followed in this case were more like those followed at a trial to determine guilt or innocence than those followed at a typical sentencing proceeding. The opinion noted particularly that the jury was given only two choices of sentence, that the prosecutor sought to establish facts to justify the death sentence, that the jury was required to find such facts beyond a reasonable doubt, and that it was required to reach a decision to impose the death sentence unanimously. See Arizona v. Rumsey, 467 U.S. 203 (1984) (7–2) (*Bullington* applied). *Bullington* does not apply to noncapital sentencing proceedings. Monge v. California, 524 U.S. 721 (1998) (5–4) (retrial of sentence enhancement provision).

Bullington was distinguished in Poland v. Arizona, 476 U.S. 147 (1986) (6–3). In *Poland*, the defendants were sentenced to death on the basis of an "aggravating circumstance," the evidence for which the reviewing court found to be insufficient. The defendants were convicted a second time and again sentenced to death, on the basis of aggravating circumstances not considered at the first sentencing hearing. Failure to consider the latter circumstances, the Court said, was not an "acquittal" for purposes of the Double Jeopardy Clause. Construing *Stroud*, *Bullington*, and *Poland*, the Court held that the Double Jeopardy Clause does not bar imposition of capital punishment at a second trial for murder after a defendant's successful appeal from a conviction, if at the sentencing phase of the first trial the sentencing jury was deadlocked and, as required by law, the judge imposed a life sentence. The first sentence, the Court said, does not count as an "acquittal" of capital punishment in those circumstances. Sattazahn v. Pennsylvania, 537 U.S. 101 (2003) (5–4). See Schiro v. Farley, 510 U.S. 222 (1994) (7–2), in which the Court held that it did not violate the prohibition against successive prosecutions for the state to present evidence that a killing was intentional as an aggravating factor at the sentencing hearing, after a jury had returned a verdict of guilty on a count of felony murder without reaching a verdict on a count of "knowingly" killing the victim.

In Ricketts v. Adamson, 483 U.S. 1 (1987) (5–4), the defendant was charged with first-degree murder. As part of the plea agreement, he agreed to testify against two other persons allegedly involved in the murder. The agreement provided that if he did not testify, the entire agreement would be void and the original charge would be reinstated. He testified as agreed. While the other defendants' convictions were on appeal, he was sentenced and began service of the sentence. The other defendants' convictions were reversed. The defendant agreed to testify at their retrial only if certain conditions, including his release from custody afterwards, were met. Upon his refusal to testify, the original charge was reinstated, and he was convicted of first-degree murder. In those circumstances, the Court said, in view of the explicit terms of the plea agreement, the Double Jeopardy Clause was not violated. The Court concluded that it was immaterial that there was a disagreement about the construction of the plea agreement (concerning the defendant's obligation to testify at the second trial), which was resolved by a court or that, following the adverse resolution of that issue, the defendant offered to testify and, the original charge having been reinstated, the state rejected the offer.

In United States v. Whitley, 734 F.2d 994 (4th Cir.1984), the defendant pleaded guilty to one count of a four-count indictment and was sentenced. The other three counts were dismissed. Thereafter, the defendant filed a motion to vacate the conviction and sentence. The motion was granted, and the case was remanded for trial. The defendant was retried on the original indictment and convicted on all four counts. He was sentenced to a substantially longer term of imprisonment than that of the first sentence. The court held that the increased sentence was prohibited by *Pearce*, since "absent a reasoned explanation to justify increased punishment, to uphold the sentence would create a reasonable apprehension of vindictiveness which would have a chilling effect on defendants' exercise of their rights to appeal." Id. at 997. The original sentence was for a lesser included offense of the original charges, and the sentencing judge was aware of the facts of the crime. Had the original sentence been for one of several distinct charges, rather than for crimes arising out of a single transaction, and the second sentence for distinct crimes not covered by the first sentence, the result would have been different.

622. The defendant was charged in a three-count indictment with (1) bank robbery by force and violence, (2) larceny, and (3) armed bank robbery. The maximum penalty for each count was, respectively, imprisonment for (1) 20 years, (2) 10 years, and (3) 25 years. At trial the jury, following an erroneous instruction that if it found the defendant guilty of one count it need not consider the other counts, returned a verdict, "Guilty as charged," without specifying which count it had in mind. A sentence of 20 years imprisonment was imposed. The conviction was reversed because of the error in the instructions. On what counts can the defendant be retried? See United States v. Schmidt, 376 F.2d 751 (4th Cir.1967).

623. "It is elementary in our law that a person can be tried a second time for an offense when his prior conviction for that same offense has been set aside by his appeal." Forman v. United States, 361 U.S. 416, 425 (1960). See United States v. Tateo, 377 U.S. 463 (1964). "From the standpoint of a defendant, it is at least doubtful that appellate courts would be as zealous as they now are in protecting against improprieties at the trial or pretrial stage if they knew that reversal of a conviction would put the accused irrevocably beyond the reach of further prosecution." Id. at 466.

Overruling a previous decision, the Court held in Burks v. United States, 437 U.S. 1 (1978), that the prohibition against double jeopardy does *not* permit retrial of a defendant who successfully appeals from denial of a motion for judgment of acquittal on the ground that the evidence is insufficient to sustain the verdict. Distinguishing a reversal for trial error from a reversal for insufficient evidence, the Court said that in the latter case, the "appellate reversal means that the Government's case was so lacking that it should not have even been *submitted* to the jury. Since we necessarily afford absolute finality to a jury's *verdict* of acquittal—no matter how erroneous its decision—it is difficult to conceive how society has any greater interest in retrying a defendant when, on review, it is decided as a matter of law that the jury could not properly have returned a verdict of guilty." Id. at 16. See Hudson v. Louisiana, 450 U.S. 40 (1981) (*Burks* applied).

Burks was distinguished in Tibbs v. Florida, 457 U.S. 31 (1982) (5–4). There, the Court contrasted reversal of a conviction on a finding that the verdict was against the weight of the evidence with a holding that the evidence was not legally sufficient to support the verdict, and held that in the former situation retrial was permissible. The distinction between *Burks* and *Tibbs* is explored in Carter v. Estelle, 691 F.2d 777 (5th Cir.1982) (*Burks* applied).

Burks was distinguished also in Justices of the Boston Municipal Court v. Lydon, 466 U.S. 294 (1984), in which the defendant was convicted at a bench trial and was entitled thereafter to a de novo jury trial. He had claimed at the bench trial that he should be acquitted because insufficient evidence of guilt had been introduced. In this case, the Court said, unlike *Burks*, there had been no judicial determination that the evidence was insufficient to convict. *Burks* does not entitle the defendant to a ruling on his claim before he can be retried under the two-tier system.

Burks does not bar retrial for a lesser included offense after reversal of a conviction for a greater offense because of insufficient evidence of an element required for the greater but not for the lesser offense. Anderson v. Mullin, 327 F.3d 1148 (10th Cir.2003).

Burks does not require that, after a mistrial has been declared because of a hung jury, an appellate court review the denial of the defendant's motion for a judgment of acquittal on the ground that the government had failed to introduce sufficient evidence to sustain a verdict of guilty. Richardson v. United States, 468 U.S. 317 (1984) (7–2). The Court said that *Burks* does not "extend beyond the procedural setting in which it arose," that is, "once a defendant obtained an unreversed appellate ruling that the Government had failed to introduce sufficient evidence to convict him at trial, a second trial was barred by the Double Jeopardy Clause." Id. at 323. There having been no such ruling, retrial was not barred. Nor is *Burks* applicable when a conviction is set aside on appeal because of the erroneous admission of evidence. The Double Jeopardy Clause does not prohibit a retrial, provided that all the evidence admitted at the first trial, including that which was erroneously admitted, was sufficient to sustain a conviction. Lockhart v. Nelson, 488 U.S. 33 (1988) (6–3).

Mistrial

See Rule 26.3, p. 1003 above.

United States v. Jorn

400 U.S. 470, 91 S.Ct. 547, 27 L.Ed.2d 543 (1971)

■ MR. JUSTICE HARLAN delivered the judgment of the Court in an opinion joined by THE CHIEF JUSTICE, MR. JUSTICE DOUGLAS, and MR. JUSTICE MARSHALL.

The Government directly appeals the order of the United States District Court for the District of Utah dismissing, on the ground of former jeopardy, an information charging the defendant-appellee with willfully assisting in the preparation of fraudulent income tax returns, in violation of 26 U.S.C. § 7206(2).

Appellee was originally charged in February 1968 with 25 counts of violating § 7206(2). He was brought to trial before Chief Judge Ritter on August 27, 1968. After the jury was chosen and sworn, 14 of the counts were dismissed on the Government's motion. The trial then commenced, the Government calling as its first witness an Internal Revenue Service agent in order to put in evidence the remaining 11 allegedly fraudulent income tax returns the defendant was charged with helping to prepare. At the trial judge's suggestion, these exhibits were stipulated to and introduced in evidence without objection. The Government's five remaining witnesses were taxpayers whom the defendant allegedly had aided in preparation of these returns.

After the first of these witnesses was called, but prior to the commencement of direct examination, defense counsel suggested that these witnesses be warned of their constitutional rights. The trial court agreed, and proceeded, in careful detail, to spell out the witness' right not to say anything that might be used in a subsequent criminal prosecution against him and his right, in the event of such a prosecution, to be represented by an attorney. The first witness expressed a willingness to testify and stated that he had been warned of his constitutional rights when the Internal Revenue Service first contacted him. The trial judge indicated, however, that he did not believe the witness had been given any warning at the time he was first contacted by the IRS, and refused to permit him to testify until he had consulted an attorney.

The trial judge then asked the prosecuting attorney if his remaining four witnesses were similarly situated. The prosecutor responded that they had been warned of their rights by the IRS upon initial contact. The judge, expressing the view that any warnings that might have been given were probably inadequate, proceeded to discharge the jury; he then called all the taxpayers into court, and informed them of their constitutional rights and of the considerable dangers of unwittingly making damaging admissions in these factual circumstances. Finally, he aborted the trial so the witnesses could consult with attorneys.

The case was set for retrial before another jury, but on pretrial motion by the defendant, Judge Ritter dismissed the information on the ground of former jeopardy. The Government filed a direct appeal to this Court, and we noted probable jurisdiction. . . .

. . .

II

The Fifth Amendment's prohibition against placing a defendant "twice in jeopardy" represents a constitutional policy of finality for the defendant's benefit in federal criminal proceedings. A power in government to subject the individual to repeated prosecutions for the same offense would cut deeply into the framework of procedural protections which the Constitution establishes for the conduct of a criminal trial. And society's awareness of the heavy personal strain which a criminal trial represents for the individual defendant is manifested in the willingness to limit the Government to a single criminal proceeding to vindicate its very vital interest in enforcement of criminal laws. Both of these considerations are expressed in Green v. United States, 355 U.S. 184, 187–88 (1957), where the Court noted that the policy underlying this provision "is that the State with all its resources and power should not be allowed to make repeated attempts to convict an individual for an alleged offense, thereby subjecting him to embarrassment, expense and ordeal and compelling him to live in a continuing state of anxiety and insecurity, as well as enhancing the possibility that even though innocent he may be found guilty." These considerations have led this Court to conclude that a defendant is placed in jeopardy in a criminal proceeding once the defendant is put to trial before the trier of the facts, whether the trier be a jury or a judge. . . .

But it is also true that a criminal trial is, even in the best of circumstances, a complicated affair to manage. The proceedings are dependent in the first instance on the most elementary sort of considerations, e.g., the health of the various witnesses, parties, attorneys, jurors, etc., all of whom must be prepared to arrive at the courthouse at set times. And when one adds the scheduling problems arising from case overloads, and the Sixth Amendment's requirement that the single trial to which the double jeopardy provision restricts the Government be conducted speedily, it becomes readily apparent that a mechanical rule prohibiting retrial whenever circumstances compel the discharge of a jury without the defendant's consent would be too high a price to pay for the added assurance of personal security and freedom from governmental harassment which such a mechanical rule would provide. As the Court noted in Wade v. Hunter, 336 U.S. 684, 689 (1949), "a defendant's valued right to have his trial completed by a particular tribunal must in some circumstances be subordinated to the public's interest in fair trials designed to end in just judgments."

Thus the conclusion that "jeopardy attaches" when the trial commences expresses a judgment that the constitutional policies underpinning the Fifth Amendment's guarantee are implicated at that point in the proceedings. The question remains, however, in what circumstances retrial is to be precluded when the initial proceedings are aborted prior to verdict without the defendant's consent.

In dealing with that question, this Court has, for the most part, explicitly declined the invitation of litigants to formulate rules based on categories of circumstances which will permit or preclude retrial. Thus, in United States v. Perez, 9 Wheat. 579 (1824), this Court held that a defendant in a capital case might be retried after the trial judge had, without the defendant's consent, discharged a jury that reported itself unable to agree. Mr. Justice Story's opinion for the Court in *Perez* expressed the following thoughts on the problem of reprosecution after a mistrial had been declared without the consent of the defendant:

> We think, that in all cases of this nature, the law has invested Courts of justice with the authority to discharge a jury from giving any verdict, whenever, in their opinion, taking all the circumstances into consideration, there is a manifest necessity for the act, or the ends of

> public justice would otherwise be defeated. They are to exercise a sound discretion on the subject; and it is impossible to define all the circumstances, which would render it proper to interfere. To be sure, the power ought to be used with the greatest caution, under urgent circumstances, and for very plain and obvious causes; and, in capital cases especially, Courts should be extremely careful how they interfere with any of the chances of life, in favour of the prisoner. But, after all, they have the right to order the discharge; and the security which the public have for the faithful, sound, and conscientious exercise of this discretion, rests, in this, as in other cases, upon the responsibility of the Judges, under their oaths of office.

Id., at 580.

The *Perez* case has since been applied by this Court as a standard of appellate review for testing the trial judge's exercise of his discretion in declaring a mistrial without the defendant's consent. . . .

But a more recent case—Gori v. United States, 367 U.S. 364 (1961)—while adhering in the main to the *Perez* theme of a "manifest necessity" standard of appellate review—does suggest the possibility of a variation on that theme according to a determination by the appellate court as to which party to the case was the beneficiary of the mistrial ruling. In *Gori*, the Court was called upon to review the action of a trial judge in discharging the jury when it appeared to the judge that the prosecution's questioning of a witness might lead to the introduction of evidence of prior crimes. We upheld reprosecution after the mistrial in an opinion which, while applying the principle of *Perez*, appears to tie the judgment that there was no abuse of discretion in these circumstances to the fact that the judge was acting "in the sole interest of the defendant." 367 U.S., at 369. . . .

In the instant case, the Government, relying principally on *Gori*, contends that even if we conclude the trial judge here abused his discretion, reprosecution should be permitted because the judge's ruling "benefited" the defendant and also clearly was not compelled by bad-faith prosecutorial conduct aimed at triggering a mistrial in order to get another day in court. If the judgment as to who was "benefited" by the mistrial ruling turns on the appellate court's conclusion concerning which party the trial judge was, in point of personal motivation, trying to protect from prejudice, it seems reasonably clear from the trial record here that the judge's insistence on stopping the trial until the witnesses were properly warned was motivated by the desire to protect the witnesses rather than the defendant. But the Government appears to view the question of "benefit" as turning on an appellate court's post hoc assessment as to which party would in fact have been aided in the hypothetical event that the witnesses had been called to the stand after consulting with their own attorneys on the course of conduct that would best serve to insulate them personally from criminal and civil liability for the fraudulent tax returns. That conception of benefit, however, involves nothing more than an exercise in pure speculation. In sum, we are unable to conclude on this record that this is a case of a mistrial made "in the sole interest of the defendant." . . .

Further, we think that a limitation on the abuse-of-discretion principle based on an appellate court's assessment of which side benefited from the mistrial ruling does not adequately satisfy the policies underpinning the double jeopardy provision. Reprosecution after a mistrial has unnecessarily been declared by the trial court obviously subjects the defendant to the same personal strain and insecurity regardless of the motivation underlying the trial judge's action. The Government contends, however, that the policies evinced by the double jeopardy provision do not reach this sort of injury; rather the unnecessarily inflicted second trial must, in the Government's view, appear to be the result of a mistrial declaration which "unfairly aids the prosecution or harasses the defense." Govt. Brief 8.

Certainly it is clear beyond question that the Double Jeopardy Clause does not guarantee a defendant that the Government will be prepared, in all circumstances, to vindicate the social interest in law enforcement through the vehicle of a single proceeding for a given offense. Thus, for example, reprosecution for the same offense is permitted where the defendant wins a reversal on appeal of a conviction. . . . The determination to allow reprosecution in these circumstances reflects the judgment that the defendant's double jeopardy interests, however defined, do not go so far as to compel society to so mobilize its decisionmaking resources that it will be prepared to assure the defendant a single proceeding free from harmful governmental or judicial error. But it is also clear that recognition that the defendant can be reprosecuted for the same offense after successful appeal does not compel the conclusion that double jeopardy policies are confined to prevention of prosecutorial or judicial overreaching. For the crucial difference between reprosecution after appeal by the defendant and reprosecution after a sua sponte judicial mistrial declaration is that in the first situation the defendant has not been deprived of his option to go to the first jury and, perhaps, end the dispute then and there with an acquittal. On the other hand, where the judge, acting without the defendant's consent, aborts the proceeding, the defendant has been deprived of his "valued right to have his trial completed by a particular tribunal." See Wade v. Hunter, 336 U.S. 684, 689 (1949).

If that right to go to a particular tribunal is valued, it is because, independent of the threat of bad-faith conduct by judge or prosecutor, the defendant has a significant interest in the decision whether or not to take the case from the jury when circumstances occur which might be thought to warrant a declaration of mistrial. Thus, where circumstances develop not attributable to prosecutorial or judicial overreaching, a motion by the defendant for mistrial is ordinarily assumed to remove any barrier to reprosecution, even if the defendant's motion is necessitated by prosecutorial or judicial error. In the absence of such a motion, the *Perez* doctrine of manifest necessity stands as a command to trial judges not to foreclose the defendant's option until a scrupulous exercise of judicial discretion leads to the conclusion that the ends of public justice would not be served by a continuation of the proceedings. . . .

The conscious refusal of this Court to channel the exercise of that discretion according to rules based on categories of circumstances . . . reflects the elusive nature of the problem presented by judicial action foreclosing the defendant from going to his jury. But that discretion must still be exercised; unquestionably an important factor to be considered is the need to hold litigants on both sides to standards of responsible professional conduct in the clash of an adversary criminal process. Yet we cannot evolve rules based on the source of the particular problem giving rise to a question whether a mistrial should or should not be declared, because, even in circumstances where the problem reflects error on the part of one counsel or the other, the trial judge must still take care to assure himself that the situation warrants action on his part foreclosing the defendant from a potentially favorable judgment by the tribunal.

In sum, counsel for both sides perform in an imperfect world; in this area, bright-line rules based on either the source of the problem or the intended beneficiary of the ruling would only disserve the vital competing interests of the Government and the defendant. The trial judge must recognize that lack of preparedness by the Government to continue the trial directly implicates policies underpinning both the double jeopardy provision and the speedy trial guarantee. . . . Alternatively, the judge must bear in mind the potential risks of abuse by the defendant of society's unwillingness to unnecessarily subject him to repeated prosecutions. Yet, in the final analysis, the judge must always temper the decision whether or not to abort the trial by considering the importance to the defendant of being able, once and for all, to conclude his confrontation with society through the verdict of a tribunal he might believe to be favorably disposed to his fate.

III

Applying these considerations to the record in this case, we must conclude that the trial judge here abused his discretion in discharging the jury. Despite assurances by both the first witness and the prosecuting attorney that the five taxpayers involved in the litigation had all been warned of their constitutional rights, the judge refused to permit them to testify, first expressing his disbelief that they were warned at all, and then expressing his views that any warnings that might have been given would be inadequate. . . . In probing the assumed inadequacy of the warnings that might have been given, the prosecutor was asked if he really intended to try a case for willfully aiding in the preparation of fraudulent returns on a theory that would not incriminate the taxpayers. When the prosecutor started to answer that he intended to do just that, the judge cut him off in midstream and immediately discharged the jury. . . . It is apparent from the record that no consideration was given to the possibility of a trial continuance; indeed, the trial judge acted so abruptly in discharging the jury that, had the prosecutor been disposed to suggest a continuance, or the defendant to object to the discharge of the jury, there would have been no opportunity to do so. When one examines the circumstances surrounding the discharge of this jury, it seems abundantly apparent that the trial judge made no effort to exercise a sound discretion to assure that, taking all the circumstances into account, there was a manifest necessity for the sua sponte declaration of this mistrial. . . . Therefore, we must conclude that in the circumstances of this case, appellee's reprosecution would violate the double jeopardy provision of the Fifth Amendment.

. . .[3]

Illinois v. Somerville

410 U.S. 458, 93 S.Ct. 1066, 35 L.Ed.2d 425 (1973)

■ MR. JUSTICE REHNQUIST delivered the opinion of the Court.

We must here decide whether declaration of a mistrial over the defendant's objection, because the trial court concluded that the indictment was insufficient to charge a crime, necessarily prevents a State from subsequently trying the defendant under a valid indictment. We hold that the mistrial met the "manifest necessity" requirement of our cases, since the trial court could reasonably have concluded that the "ends of public justice" would be defeated by having allowed the trial to continue. Therefore, the Double Jeopardy Clause of the Fifth Amendment, made applicable to the States through the Due Process Clause of the Fourteenth Amendment, Benton v. Maryland, 395 U.S. 784 (1969), did not bar retrial under a valid indictment.

I

On March 19, 1964, respondent was indicted by an Illinois grand jury for the crime of theft. The case was called for trial and a jury impaneled and sworn on November 1, 1965. The following day, before any evidence had been presented, the prosecuting attorney realized that the indictment was fatally deficient under Illinois law because it did not allege that respondent intended to permanently deprive the owner of his property. Under the applicable Illinois criminal statute, such intent is a necessary element of the crime of theft, and failure to allege intent renders the indictment insufficient to charge a crime. But under the Illinois Constitution, an indictment is the sole means by which a criminal proceeding such as this may be commenced against a defendant. Illinois further provides that only formal defects, of which this was not one, may be cured by amendment. The combined operation of these rules of Illinois procedure and substantive law meant that the defect in the indictment was "jurisdictional"; it could not be waived by the defendant's failure to object, and

[3] Chief Justice Burger wrote a brief concurring opinion. Justice Black and Justice Brennan filed a statement that they believed that the court lacked jurisdiction over the case, but that they joined the judgment of the court. Justice Stewart wrote a dissenting opinion which Justice White and Justice Blackmun joined.

could be asserted on appeal or in a post-conviction proceeding to overturn a final judgment of conviction.

Faced with this situation, the Illinois trial court concluded that further proceedings under this defective indictment would be useless and granted the State's motion for a mistrial. On November 3, the grand jury handed down a second indictment alleging the requisite intent. Respondent was arraigned two weeks after the first trial was aborted, raised a claim of double jeopardy which was overruled, and the second trial commenced shortly thereafter. The jury returned a verdict of guilty, sentence was imposed, and the Illinois courts upheld the conviction. Respondent then sought federal habeas corpus, alleging that the conviction constituted double jeopardy contrary to the prohibition of the Fifth and Fourteenth Amendments. . . . [T]he Seventh Circuit held that respondent's petition for habeas corpus should have been granted because, although he had not been tried and *acquitted* . . . jeopardy had attached when the jury was impaneled and sworn, and a declaration of mistrial over respondent's objection precluded a retrial under a valid indictment. For the reasons stated below, we reverse that judgment.

II

The fountainhead decision construing the Double Jeopardy Clause in the context of a declaration of a mistrial over a defendant's objection is United States v. Perez, 9 Wheat. 579 (1824). . . . [The opinion quotes the passage from *Perez* quoted in United States v. Jorn, 400 U.S. 470 (1971), p. 1196 above.]

This formulation, consistently adhered to by this Court in subsequent decisions, abjures the application of any mechanical formula by which to judge the propriety of declaring a mistrial in the varying and often unique situations arising during the course of a criminal trial. The broad discretion reserved to the trial judge in such circumstances has been consistently reiterated in decisions of this Court. . . .

In reviewing the propriety of the trial judge's exercise of his discretion, this Court, following the counsel of Mr. Justice Story, has scrutinized the action to determine whether, in the context of that particular trial, the declaration of a mistrial was dictated by "manifest necessity" or the "ends of public justice." The interests of the public in seeing that a criminal prosecution proceed to verdict, either of acquittal or conviction, need not be forsaken by the formulation or application of rigid rules that necessarily preclude the vindication of that interest. This consideration, whether termed the "ends of public justice," United States v. Perez, supra, at 580, or, more precisely, "the public's interest in fair trials designed to end in just judgments," Wade v. Hunter, [336 U.S. 684 (1949)] at 689, has not been disregarded by this Court.

. . .

While virtually all of the cases turn on the particular facts and thus escape meaningful categorization . . . it is possible to distill from them a general approach, premised on the "public justice" policy enunciated in United States v. Perez, to situations such as that presented by this case. A trial judge properly exercises his discretion to declare a mistrial if an impartial verdict cannot be reached, or if a verdict of conviction could be reached but would have to be reversed on appeal due to an obvious procedural error in the trial. If an error would make reversal on appeal a certainty, it would not serve "the ends of public justice" to require that the Government proceed with its proof when, if it succeeded before the jury, it would automatically be stripped of that success by an appellate court. . . . While the declaration of a mistrial on the basis of a rule or a defective procedure that would lend itself to prosecutorial manipulation would involve an entirely different question . . . such was not the situation in the above cases or in the instant case.

. . .

III

. . .

We believe that in light of the State's established rules of criminal procedure, the trial judge's declaration of a mistrial was not an abuse of discretion. Since this Court's decision in Benton v. Maryland, supra, federal courts will be confronted with such claims that arise in large measure from the often diverse procedural rules existing in the 50 States. Federal courts should not be quick to conclude that simply because a state procedure does not conform to the corresponding federal statute or rule, it does not serve a legitimate state policy. . . .

In the instant case, the trial judge terminated the proceeding because a defect was found to exist in the indictment that was, as a matter of Illinois law, not curable by amendment. The Illinois courts have held that even after a judgment of conviction has become final, the defendant may be released on habeas corpus, because the defect in the indictment deprives the trial court of "jurisdiction." The rule prohibiting the amendment of all but formal defects in indictments is designed to implement the State's policy of preserving the right of each defendant to insist that a criminal prosecution against him be commenced by the action of a grand jury. The trial judge was faced with a situation . . . in which a procedural defect might or would preclude the public from either obtaining an impartial verdict or keeping a verdict of conviction if its evidence persuaded the jury. If a mistrial were constitutionally unavailable in situations such as this, the State's policy could only be implemented by conducting a second trial after verdict and reversal on appeal, thus wasting time, energy, and money for all concerned. Here, the trial judge's action was a rational determination designed to implement a legitimate state policy, with no suggestion that the implementation of that policy in this manner could be manipulated so as to prejudice the defendant. . . . Here, the delay was minimal, and the mistrial was, under Illinois law, the only way in which a defect in the indictment could be corrected. Given the established standard of discretion set forth in *Perez*, *Gori* [v. United States, 367 U.S. 364 (1961)], and *Hunter*, we cannot say that the declaration of a mistrial was not required by "manifest necessity" and the "ends of public justice."

Our decision in *Jorn*, relied upon by the court below and respondent, does not support the opposite conclusion. While it is possible to excise various portions of the plurality opinion to support the result reached below, divorcing the language from the facts of the case serves only to distort its holdings. That opinion dealt with action by a trial judge that can fairly be described as erratic. The Court held that the lack of apparent harm to the defendant from the declaration of a mistrial did not itself justify the mistrial, and concluded that there was no "manifest necessity" for the mistrial, as opposed to less drastic alternatives. The Court emphasized that the absence of any manifest need for the mistrial had deprived the defendant of his right to proceed before the first jury, but it did not hold that that right may never be forced to yield, as in this case, to "the public's interest in fair trials designed to end in just judgments." The Court's opinion in *Jorn* is replete with approving references to Wade v. Hunter, supra, which latter case stated:

> The double-jeopardy provision of the Fifth Amendment, however, does not mean that every time a defendant is put to trial before a competent tribunal he is entitled to go free if the trial fails to end in a final judgment. Such a rule would create an insuperable obstacle to the administration of justice in many cases in which there is no semblance of the type of oppressive practices at which the double-jeopardy prohibition is aimed. There may be unforeseeable circumstances that arise during a trial making its completion impossible, such as the failure of a jury to agree on a verdict. In such event the purpose of law to protect society from those guilty of crimes frequently would be frustrated by denying courts power to put the defendant to trial again. And there have been instances where a trial judge has discovered facts during a trial which indicated that one or more members of the jury might be biased against the Government or the defendant. It is settled that the duty of the judge in this event is to discharge the jury and direct a retrial. *What has been said is enough to show that a defendant's valued right to have his trial completed by a particular tribunal must in some instances be subordinated to the public's interest in fair trials designed to end in just judgments.*

Wade v. Hunter, 336 U.S., at 688–89 (footnote omitted; emphasis added).

The determination by the trial court to abort a criminal proceeding where jeopardy has attached is not one to be lightly undertaken, since the interest of the defendant in having his fate determined by the jury first impaneled is itself a weighty one. . . . Nor will the lack of demonstrable additional prejudice preclude the defendant's invocation of the double jeopardy bar in the absence of some important countervailing interest of proper judicial administration. . . . But where the declaration of a mistrial implements a reasonable state policy and aborts a proceeding that at best would have produced a verdict that could have been upset at will by one of the parties, the defendant's interest in proceeding to verdict is outweighed by the competing and equally legitimate demand for public justice. . . .

. . .[4]

---

624. In Wade v. Hunter, 336 U.S. 684 (1949), on which the Court relied in *Somerville*, above, the defendant was an American soldier who was tried for rape before a general court-martial in Germany during World War II. Before the first trial ended, the charges were withdrawn; they were transmitted to another command which convened a new court-martial at which the defendant was convicted. The Court found that "the tactical situation brought about by a rapidly advancing army was responsible for withdrawal of the charges from the first court-martial," id. at 691, and rejected the petitioner's claim that he had been subjected to double jeopardy. See also Armstrong v. United States, 367 F.2d 821 (7th Cir.1966) (assassination of President Kennedy during trial).

625. Gori v. United States, 367 U.S. 364 (1961). The defendant was brought to trial before a jury on a charge of receiving stolen goods. On the first day of trial, during presentation of the government's case, the trial judge on his own motion declared a mistrial; the defendant's counsel neither approved nor objected to the action, the apparent reason for which was that the trial judge believed that the prosecutor's questions "presaged inquiry calculated to inform the jury of other crimes by the accused, and [the judge] took action to forestall it," id. at 366. The court of appeals affirmed the petitioner's conviction at a subsequent trial, although it thought the mistrial was not required by the prosecutor's conduct; it found, and the Court agreed, "that the order was the product of the trial judge's extreme solicitude . . . in favor of the accused," id. at 367. The Court affirmed, saying: "Judicial wisdom counsels against anticipating hypothetical situations in which the discretion of the trial judge may be abused and so call for the safeguard of the Fifth Amendment—cases in which the defendant would be harassed by successive, oppressive prosecutions, or in which a judge exercises his authority to help the prosecution, at a trial in which its case is going badly, by affording it another, more favorable opportunity to convict the accused. Suffice that we are unwilling, where it clearly appears that a mistrial has been granted in the sole interest of the defendant, to hold that its necessary consequence is to bar all retrial. It would hark back to the formalistic artificialities of seventeenth century criminal procedure so to confine our federal trial courts by compelling them to navigate a narrow compass between Scylla and Charybdis. We would not thus make them unduly hesitant conscientiously to exercise their most sensitive judgment—according to their own lights in the immediate exigencies of trial—for the more effective protection of the criminal accused." Id. at 369–70.

[4] Justice White wrote a dissenting opinion, which Justice Douglas and Justice Brennan joined. Justice Marshall also wrote a dissenting opinion.

In Arizona v. Washington, 434 U.S. 497 (1978) (6–3), the defendant had been convicted of murder and a new trial ordered because the prosecutor withheld exculpatory evidence. At the second trial, defense counsel in his opening statement referred to the previous trial and the suppression of evidence. The prosecutor moved for a mistrial, on the basis that the reasons for the order of a new trial were inadmissible and defense counsel's remarks were incurably prejudicial to the prosecution, so that a mistrial was a "manifest necessity." Over the defendant's objection, the judge granted the motion for a mistrial, without expressly considering alternatives or expressly finding that there was manifest necessity.

The Court concluded that the defendant's subsequent retrial did not violate the Double Jeopardy Clause. The standard of manifest necessity, it said, required a "high degree" of need. Id. at 506. When a mistrial is granted because the prosecutor wants to improve his case or for the purpose of harassment or a tactical advantage, "the strictest scrutiny" of the need for a new trial is warranted. Id. at 508. At the other extreme are cases in which a mistrial follows a jury deadlock; there, the trial judge's judgment that a mistrial is appropriate is "accorded great deference." The Court concluded that on the facts of this case also, the trial judge's ruling was "entitled to special respect." Id. at 510. Otherwise, a trial judge's effort to protect an orderly, impartial procedure might be impaired by fear that if he declared a mistrial erroneously, a retrial would be barred. Accordingly, in this case the public interest in a fair trial prevailed over the defendant's right to have a trial concluded by the first jury impaneled. The Court added that the failure to make the finding of manifest necessity explicit was immaterial.

For additional cases applying the test of manifest necessity, see, e.g., Johnson v. Karnes, 198 F.3d 589 (6th Cir.1999) (defense counsel improperly introduced evidence of defendant's prior acquittal on related charge; no manifest necessity); United States v. Stevens, 177 F.3d 579 (6th Cir.1999) (witness, without whom government could not convict, refused to testify; no manifest necessity); United States v. Gantley, 172 F.3d 422 (6th Cir. 1999) (judge's display of anger at defendant; manifest necessity); Gilliam v. Foster, 75 F.3d 881 (4th Cir.1996) (en banc) (jury saw unadmitted but relevant, nonprejudicial photographs; no manifest necessity); United States v. Sloan, 36 F.3d 386 (4th Cir.1994) (defendant failed to testify after counsel had stated that defendant would testify; no manifest necessity); United States v. Ruggiero, 846 F.2d 117 (2d Cir.1988) (possibility of jury tampering; manifest necessity); United States ex rel. Clauser v. McCevers, 731 F.2d 423 (7th Cir.1984) (indictment invalid; manifest necessity); United States v. Sartori, 730 F.2d 973 (4th Cir.1984) (judge recused himself; no manifest necessity); United States v. Mastrangelo, 662 F.2d 946 (2d Cir. 1981) (trial judge believed that defendant was responsible for murder of key prosecution witness; manifest necessity); Harris v. Young, 607 F.2d 1081 (4th Cir.1979) (prosecutor failed to comply fully with discovery order; no manifest necessity); United States ex rel. Stewart v. Hewitt, 517 F.2d 993 (3d Cir.1975) (court official responsible for care of jury was defendant's father-in-law; manifest necessity).

626. Downum v. United States, 372 U.S. 734 (1963). The defendant was brought to trial for mail theft and forging and uttering stolen checks. Both sides had announced that they were ready to proceed and a jury was selected and sworn. After a noon recess the prosecution asked that the jury be discharged because a key witness on some counts was not present. Despite the defendant's objection the jury was discharged. Two days later the case proceeded to trial over the defendant's plea of former jeopardy, a new jury was sworn, and the defendant was convicted. Noting that the prosecutor proceeded to trial without ensuring that the witness would be present and elected not to dismiss the counts for which the witness was essential and try the remaining counts, the Court accepted the defendant's claim of double jeopardy and reversed the conviction. Compare Brock v. North Carolina, 344 U.S. 424 (1953) (mistrial on state's motion to secure testimony of witness not a violation of Due Process Clause).

627. In United States v. Dinitz, 424 U.S. 600 (1976) (6–2), the trial judge excluded one of the defendant's lawyers after the lawyer had repeatedly violated the judge's instructions about his opening statement. The defendant moved for a mistrial, which was granted. Before his second trial, he moved to dismiss the indictment on the ground that the Double Jeopardy Clause barred a retrial. The Court held that in the absence of bad faith, the judge's action even if erroneous did not bar another trial following a mistrial on the defendant's motion. See Lee v. United States, 432 U.S. 23 (1977) (8–1), in which, relying on *Dinitz*, the Court said that retrial was permissible after the trial court, having already heard the evidence, granted the defendant's motion to dismiss the information because it failed to allege an essential element of the offense; the dismissal, the Court concluded, was functionally the same as a mistrial. See also United States v. DiPietro, 936 F.2d 6 (1st Cir.1991) (defense counsel's failure to object to mistrial due to prosecutor's statements in closing argument bars claim of double jeopardy).

628. "Prosecutorial conduct that might be viewed as harassment or overreaching, even if sufficient to justify a mistrial on defendant's motion . . . does not bar retrial absent intent on the part of the prosecutor to subvert the protections afforded by the Double Jeopardy Clause. . . . Only where the governmental conduct in question is intended to 'goad' the defendant into moving for a mistrial may a defendant raise the bar of Double Jeopardy to a second trial after having succeeded in aborting the first on his own motion." Oregon v. Kennedy, 456 U.S. 667, 675–76 (1982). See United States v. Catton, 130 F.3d 805 (7th Cir.1997) (discussing application of *Kennedy* to error leading to reversal of conviction; insufficient proof that prosecutor committed error deliberately to avoid likely acquittal); United States v. Doyle, 121 F.3d 1078 (7th Cir.1997) (same; insufficient proof that prosecutor intended to abort trial).

629. The defendants were indicted for second-degree murder. At trial, defense counsel obtained a mistrial on grounds not involving prosecutorial or judicial misconduct. Defendants were then indicted and convicted of first-degree murder. The court held that *Pearce* and later cases, see note

596, p. 1141 above, barred an indictment for the more serious offense without justification in the intervening circumstances. United States v. Jamison, 505 F.2d 407 (D.C.Cir.1974).

630. It is clear that a defendant can be brought to trial a second time after a mistrial because the jury is unable to reach a verdict. United States v. Perez, 22 U.S. (9 Wheat.) 579 (1824). If the jury is unable to reach a verdict at the second trial, can the defendant be tried a third time? Or a fourth? Cases are reviewed in State v. Witt, 572 S.W.2d 913 (Tenn.1978), in which the court concluded that although no constitutional provision precluded a fourth trial after a third hung jury, "trial judges have the inherent authority to terminate a prosecution in the exercise of a sound judicial discretion, where, as here, repeated trials, free of prejudicial error, have resulted in genuinely deadlocked juries and where it appears that at future trials substantially the same evidence will be presented and that the probability of continued hung juries is great." Id. at 917.

To the same effect, see State v. Abbati, 493 A.2d 513 (N.J.1985). The court said: "We hold that a trial court may dismiss an indictment with prejudice after successive juries have failed to agree on a verdict when it determines that the chance of the State's obtaining a conviction upon further retrial is highly unlikely. The trial court must carefully and expressly consider the following factors, which shall govern its ultimate decision whether to dismiss the indictment: (1) the number of prior mistrials and the outcome of the juries' deliberations, so far as is known; (2) the character of prior trials in terms of length, complexity, and similarity of evidence presented; (3) the likelihood of any substantial difference in a subsequent trial, if allowed; (4) the trial court's own evaluation of the relative strength of each party's case; and (5) the professional conduct and diligence of respective counsel, particularly of the prosecuting attorney. The court must also give due weight to the prosecutor's decision to reprosecute, assessing the reasons for that decision, such as the gravity of the criminal charges and the public's concern in the effective and definitive conclusion of criminal prosecutions. Conversely, the court should accord careful consideration to the status of the individual defendant and the impact of a retrial upon the defendant in terms of untoward hardship and unfairness." Id. at 521–22.

In State v. Simmons, 752 A.2d 724 (N.J.Super.2000), the defendant was convicted and sentenced on separate counts of robbery and murder. After serving 19 years in prison, the convictions were vacated and he was retried. He was convicted of robbery, but the jury was unable to agree on the count of murder. He was tried a second time and the jury was unable to agree. Applying *Abbati*, the court ruled that the defendant could not be retried.

On the problem of repetitive trials, see generally Robinson v. Wade, 686 F.2d 298 (5th Cir.1982), in which, after the defendant had been convicted and sentenced to death three times and the convictions reversed on appeal, the court held that a fourth trial was not barred.

Collateral Estoppel (Issue Preclusion)

Ashe v. Swenson

397 U.S. 436, 90 S.Ct. 1189, 25 L.Ed.2d 469 (1970)

■ MR. JUSTICE STEWART delivered the opinion of the Court.

. . .

Sometime in the early hours of the morning of January 10, 1960, six men were engaged in a poker game in the basement of the home of John Gladson at Lee's Summit, Missouri. Suddenly three or four masked men, armed with a shotgun and pistols, broke into the basement and robbed each of the poker players of money and various articles of personal property. The robbers—and it has never been clear whether there were three or four of them—then fled in a car belonging to one of the victims of the robbery. Shortly thereafter the stolen car was discovered in a field, and later that morning three men were arrested by a state trooper while they were walking on a highway not far from where the abandoned car had been found. The petitioner was arrested by another officer some distance away.

The four were subsequently charged with seven separate offenses—the armed robbery of each of the six poker players and the theft of the car. In May 1960 the petitioner went to trial on the charge of robbing Donald Knight, one of the participants in the poker game. At the trial the State called Knight and three of his fellow poker players as prosecution witnesses. Each of them described the circumstances of the holdup and itemized his own individual losses. The proof that an armed robbery had occurred and that personal property had been taken from Knight as well as from each of the others was unassailable. The testimony of the four victims in this regard was consistent both internally and with that of the others. But the State's evidence that the petitioner had been one of the robbers was weak. Two of the witnesses thought that there had been only three robbers altogether, and could not identify the petitioner as one of them. Another of the victims, who was the petitioner's uncle by marriage, said that at the "patrol station" he had positively identified each of the other three men accused of the holdup, but could say only that the petitioner's voice "sounded very much like" that of one of the robbers. The fourth participant in the poker game did identify the petitioner, but only by his "size and height, and his actions."

The cross-examination of these witnesses was brief, and it was aimed primarily at exposing the weakness of their identification testimony. Defense counsel made no attempt to question their testimony regarding the holdup itself or their claims as to their losses. Knight testified without contradiction that the robbers had stolen from him his watch, \$250 in cash, and about \$500 in checks. His billfold, which had been found by the police in the possession of one of the three other men accused of the robbery, was admitted in evidence. The defense offered no testimony and waived final argument.

The trial judge instructed the jury that if it found that the petitioner was one of the participants in the armed robbery, the theft of "any money" from Knight would sustain a conviction. He also instructed the jury that if the petitioner was one of the robbers, he was guilty under the law even if he had not personally robbed Knight. The jury—though not instructed to elaborate upon its verdict—found the petitioner "not guilty due to insufficient evidence."

Six weeks later the petitioner was brought to trial again, this time for the robbery of another participant in the poker game, a man named Roberts. The petitioner filed a motion to dismiss, based on his previous acquittal. The motion was overruled, and the second trial began. The witnesses were for the most part the same, though this time their testimony was substantially stronger on the issue of the petitioner's identity. For example, two witnesses who at the first trial had been wholly unable to identify the petitioner as one of the robbers, now testified that his features, size, and mannerisms matched those of one of their assailants. Another witness who before had identified the petitioner only by his size and actions now also remembered him by the unusual sound of his voice. The State further refined its case at the second trial by declining to call one of the participants in the poker game whose identification testimony at the first trial had been conspicuously negative. The case went to the jury on instructions virtually identical to those given at the first trial. This time the jury found the petitioner guilty, and he was sentenced to a 35-year term in the state penitentiary.

. . . The petitioner then brought the present habeas corpus proceeding in the United States District Court for the Western District of Missouri, claiming that the second prosecution had violated his right not to be twice put in jeopardy. Considering itself bound by this court's decision in Hoag v. New Jersey, 356 U.S. 464, the District Court denied the writ. . . .

[T]he operative facts here are virtually identical to those of Hoag v. New Jersey, supra. In that case the defendant was tried for the armed robbery of three men who, along with others, had been held up in a tavern. The proof of the robbery was clear, but the evidence identifying the defendant as one of the robbers was weak, and the defendant interposed an alibi defense. The jury brought in a verdict of not guilty. The defendant was then brought to trial again, on an indictment charging the robbery of a fourth victim of the tavern holdup. This time the jury found him guilty. After appeals in the state courts proved unsuccessful, Hoag brought his case here.

Viewing the question presented solely in terms of Fourteenth Amendment due process—whether the course that New Jersey had pursued had "led to fundamental unfairness," 356 U.S., at 467—this Court declined to reverse the judgment of conviction, because "in the circumstances shown by this record, we cannot say that petitioner's later prosecution and conviction violated due process." 356 U.S., at 466. The Court found it unnecessary to decide whether "collateral estoppel"—the principle that bars relitigation between the same parties of issues actually determined at a previous trial—is a due process requirement in a state criminal trial, since it accepted New Jersey's determination that the petitioner's previous acquittal did not in any event give rise to such an estoppel. . . . And in the view the Court took of the issues presented, it did not, of course, even approach consideration of whether collateral estoppel is an ingredient of the Fifth Amendment guarantee against double jeopardy.

The doctrine of Benton v. Maryland, 395 U.S. 784, puts the issues in the present case in a perspective quite different from that in which the issues were perceived in Hoag v. New Jersey, supra. The question is no longer whether collateral estoppel is a requirement of due process, but whether it is a part of the Fifth Amendment's guarantee against double jeopardy. And if collateral estoppel is embodied in that guarantee, then its applicability in a particular case is no longer a matter to be left for state court determination within the broad bounds of "fundamental fairness," but a matter of constitutional fact we must decide through an examination of the entire record. . . .

"Collateral estoppel" is an awkward phrase, but it stands for an extremely important principle in our adversary system of justice. It means simply that when an issue of ultimate fact has once been determined by a valid and final judgment, that issue cannot again be litigated between the same parties in any future lawsuit. Although first developed in civil litigation, collateral estoppel has been an established rule of federal criminal law at least since this court's decision more than 50 years ago in United States v. Oppenheimer, 242 U.S. 85. As Mr. Justice Holmes put the matter in that case, "It cannot be that the safeguards of the person, so often and so rightly mentioned with solemn reverence, are less than those that protect from a liability in debt." 242 U.S., at 87. As a rule of federal law, therefore, "[i]t is much too late to suggest that this principle is not fully applicable to a former judgment in a criminal case, either because of lack of 'mutuality' or because the judgment may reflect only a belief that the Government had not met the higher burden of proof exacted in such cases for the Government's evidence as a whole although not necessarily as to every link in the chain." United States v. Kramer, 289 F.2d 909, 913.

The federal decisions have made clear that the rule of collateral estoppel in criminal cases is not to be applied with the hypertechnical and archaic approach of a 19th century pleading book, but with realism and rationality. Where a previous judgment of acquittal was based upon a general verdict, as is usually the case, this approach requires a court to "examine the record of a prior proceeding, taking into account the pleadings, evidence, charge, and other relevant matter, and conclude whether a rational jury could have grounded its verdict upon an issue other than that which the defendant seeks to foreclose from consideration."[5] The inquiry

5. Mayers & Yarbrough, "*Bis Vexari*: New Trials and Successive Prosecutions," 74 Harv. L. Rev. 1, 38–39. . . .

"must be set in a practical frame and viewed with an eye to all the circumstances of the proceedings." Sealfon v. United States, 332 U.S. 575, 579. Any test more technically restrictive would, of course, simply amount to a rejection of the rule of collateral estoppel in criminal proceedings, at least in every case where the first judgment was based upon a general verdict of acquittal.

Straightforward application of the federal rule to the present case can lead to but one conclusion. For the record is utterly devoid of any indication that the first jury could rationally have found that an armed robbery had not occurred, or that Knight had not been a victim of that robbery. The single rationally conceivable issue in dispute before the jury was whether the petitioner had been one of the robbers. And the jury by its verdict found that he had not. The federal rule of law, therefore, would make a second prosecution for the robbery of Roberts wholly impermissible.

The ultimate question to be determined, then, in the light of Benton v. Maryland, supra, is whether this established rule of federal law is embodied in the Fifth Amendment guarantee against double jeopardy. We do not hesitate to hold that it is. For whatever else that constitutional guarantee may embrace . . . it surely protects a man who has been acquitted from having to "run the gantlet" a second time. Green v. United States, 355 U.S. 184, 190.

The question is not whether Missouri could validly charge the petitioner with six separate offenses for the robbery of the six poker players. It is not whether he could have received a total of six punishments if he had been convicted in a single trial of robbing the six victims. It is simply whether, after a jury determined by its verdict that the petitioner was not one of the robbers, the State could constitutionally hale him before a new jury to litigate that issue again.

After the first jury had acquitted the petitioner of robbing Knight, Missouri could certainly not have brought him to trial again upon that charge. Once a jury had determined upon conflicting testimony that there was at least a reasonable doubt that the petitioner was one of the robbers, the State could not present the same or different identification evidence in a second prosecution for the robbery of Knight in the hope that a different jury might find that evidence more convincing. The situation is constitutionally no different here, even though the second trial related to another victim of the same robbery. For the name of the victim, in the circumstances of this case, had no bearing whatever upon the issue of whether the petitioner was one of the robbers.

In this case the State in its brief has frankly conceded that following the petitioner's acquittal, it treated the first trial as no more than a dry run for the second prosecution: "No doubt the prosecutor felt the state had a provable case on the first charge and, when he lost, he did what every good attorney would do—he refined his presentation in light of the turn of events at the first trial." But this is precisely what the constitutional guarantee forbids.

. . .[6]

---

631. *Ashe* was applied to other sets of facts in Harris v. Washington, 404 U.S. 55 (1971), and Turner v. Arkansas, 407 U.S. 366 (1972), both involving collateral estoppel on the issue of the identity of the person who committed the crimes charged in successive prosecutions.

In United States v. Nash, 447 F.2d 1382 (4th Cir.1971), the defendant testified at her trial for mail theft, was acquitted, and was subsequently prosecuted for perjury at the first trial. The court held that collateral estoppel barred reconsideration of the truthfulness of her testimony at the first trial since, on the facts of the case, "it is inconceivable that there would have been an acquittal if the jury had not accorded truth to her testimony." Id. at 1385. Accord United States v. Hernandez, 572 F.2d 218 (9th Cir.1978). Cf. United States v. Bailey, 34 F.3d 683 (8th Cir.1994) (dismissal of prior indictment alleging facts contained in subsequent indictment; *Hernandez* distinguished). In Cardillo v. Zyla, 486 F.2d 473 (1st Cir.1973), a convicted defendant sought damages against witnesses at his trial who, he alleged, had committed perjury. The court said that his claim for damages was "inseparable from the issues at the heart of the criminal prosecution" and that "to litigate them would inevitably be to relitigate to greater or lesser degree the nine-day criminal trial," id. at 475, and held that collateral estoppel applied.

In United States v. Gugliaro, 501 F.2d 68 (2d Cir.1974), however, the defendant testified at his trial for conspiracy, mail fraud, and other offenses and ultimately (after a second trial on the conspiracy count) was acquitted on all counts. He was then prosecuted for perjury at the first trial and convicted. The court of appeals reviewed the application of collateral estoppel in such circumstances and, concluding that the jury in the prior trials had not necessarily concluded that the facts stated in the defendant's testimony were true when it acquitted him, affirmed the conviction. Accord United States v. Dipp, 581 F.2d 1323 (9th Cir.1978).

Prosecution of the defendant for perjury after he is acquitted at a criminal trial is not barred if the state establishes by clear and convincing evidence that it obtained substantial new evidence after the trial and was not negligent in failing to discover it sooner. State v. Canon, 622 N.W.2d 270 (Wis.2001).

See Nichols v. Scott, 69 F.3d 1255 (5th Cir.1995), discussing generally whether the government is estopped to assert a set of facts different from those it had asserted at the prior trial of a codefendant. The defendant and

[6] Justice Black and Justice Harlan wrote brief concurring opinions. Justice Brennan wrote a concurring opinion, which Justice Douglas and Justice Marshall joined, in which he argued that "the Double Jeopardy Clause requires the prosecution, except in most limited circumstances, to join at one trial all the charges against a defendant that grow out of a single criminal act, occurrence, episode, or transaction." 397 U.S. at 453–54. Chief Justice Burger wrote a dissenting opinion.

the codefendant were indicted for the murder of the victim of a robbery that they had committed together. The medical evidence was that the victim had died from a single gunshot wound. At the sentencing hearing of the codefendant, who had pleaded guilty, the prosecutor urged that he had fired the fatal shot. Subsequently, at the defendant's trial, the same prosecutor argued that the defendant had fired the fatal shot, but that even if the codefendant had fired the shot, the defendant also was guilty of capital murder. At the sentencing hearing also, the prosecutor argued that the defendant had fired the fatal shot, but did not emphasize that aspect of the case. The court held that collateral estoppel was not applicable because the defendant was not a party in the prior proceedings; nor was there an affirmative finding by the jury in the prior proceedings that the codefendant had fired the fatal shot. Nor would the court invoke the doctrine of "judicial estoppel," which would bar the state from taking a position inconsistent with that it had taken previously. The court said that the doctrine was not constitutionally based and that it had "apparently never been applied against the government in a criminal case." Id. at 1272.

632. Neither the Double Jeopardy Clause nor the Due Process Clause bars the prosecution from introducing otherwise admissible evidence of criminal conduct having to do with a crime of which the defendant has been acquitted. The acquittal establishes only that the defendant was not guilty beyond a reasonable doubt. The admission of the evidence at a subsequent trial is not subject to so high a standard. Dowling v. United States, 493 U.S. 342 (1990) (6–3). In *Dowling*, the defendant had been acquitted of burglary and robbery charges. At a subsequent trial for a bank robbery, the victim of the earlier crimes testified that he was the person who had entered the house and committed them. Her testimony was admitted to strengthen his identification as the bank robber and to link him with another person who was involved in both crimes. The jury was told that the defendant had been acquitted of the earlier crimes. Aside from the different quanta of proof, the Court said, the jury at the first trial might have acquitted the defendant on some basis other than his identification as the person involved in the earlier incident. *Dowling* was applied in United States v. Felix, 503 U.S. 378 (1992).

633. Ciucci v. Illinois, 356 U.S. 571 (1958). The defendant was charged in separate indictments with murdering his wife and three children. In successive trials, he was convicted of the murder of his wife and two of the children. Penalties of imprisonment were imposed at the first two trials and the death penalty at the third. To the claim that the prosecutor had "announced a determined purpose to prosecute petitioner until a death sentence was obtained," the Supreme Court responded: "The State was constitutionally entitled to prosecute these individual offenses singly at separate trials and to utilize therein all relevant evidence [in this case, evidence of all four deaths], in the absence of proof establishing that such a course of action entailed fundamental unfairness." Id. at 573.[7]

7. Following the decision in *Ciucci*, in 1961, the Illinois legislature enacted as part of the criminal code a requirement that, when the defendant may be prosecuted for

Ciucci was decided on the authority of Hoag v. New Jersey, 356 U.S. 464 (1958), which was overruled by *Ashe*, above. The difference between *Ciucci* and *Ashe* is that the defendant in the former case was *convicted* at each of the successive trials. Unless a theory similar to Justice Brennan's "single transaction" theory, see page 1214 n.6 above, is adopted, *Ciucci* is not disturbed by *Ashe*. The issue is discussed in Moton v. Swenson, 488 F.2d 1060 (8th Cir.1973).

634. Does the Double Jeopardy Clause or the Due Process Clause require that collateral estoppel be applied to a pretrial ruling that evidence be suppressed?

"A hypothetical case may help in the consideration of this problem. Defendant X is the subject of two indictments in two counties, one for bank robbery, the other for having stolen an automobile to be used as the getaway car. He pleads not guilty to both charges and notifies the state that he proposes to prove an alibi, which will exonerate him of both offenses, and for which he has strong support. The state's reliance will be on weak identification evidence and a confession to both crimes. The bank robbery charge is to be tried first. X moves to suppress the confession on a number of grounds—use of physical violence; deprivation of food, water, and rest; promises of immunity, etc. Both sides recognize that determination of the motion will very likely decide the case. After a hearing of several days, a judge suppresses the confession. The state elects not to exercise a right to appeal, drops the bank robbery indictment, and indicates its intention to press the stolen car indictment. X moves again to suppress the confession. The state insists on a hearing, saying it has new evidence to rebut X's claims. Does due process permit it to be given one?" United States ex rel. DiGiangiemo v. Regan, 528 F.2d 1262, 1265 (2d Cir.1975). The court concluded that the state should not be given a second hearing on the motion to suppress.

Cf. United States ex rel. Hubbard v. Hatrak, 588 F.2d 414 (3d Cir. 1978), in which the defendant claimed the benefit of collateral estoppel with respect to a finding at the prior separate trial of a cofelon for the same crimes. The court concluded that a nonparty collateral estoppel rule is not required by due process.

635. For the purpose of deciding when there is a sufficient "identity of offenses" to support a claim of double jeopardy, how is it determined whether successive prosecutions are for a single offense or for multiple offenses?

more than one offense arising out of the same conduct, the offenses must be prosecuted in a single prosecution if the prosecutor knows of the offenses at the beginning of the prosecution and the offenses are within the jurisdiction of a single court, unless justice requires otherwise. 720 Ill.Comp.Stat.Ann. § 5/3–3(b). This requirement was applied, e.g., in People v. Golson, 207 N.E.2d 68 (Ill. 1965). A similar rule has been adopted by some courts. See, e.g., State v. Gregory, 333 A.2d 257 (N.J.1975) (additional cases and comment cited).

" 'A conviction or acquittal upon one indictment is no bar to a subsequent conviction and sentence upon another, unless the evidence required to support a conviction upon one of them would have been sufficient to warrant a conviction upon the other. The test is not whether the defendant has already been tried for the same act, but whether he has been put in jeopardy for the same offense. A single act may be an offense against two statutes; and if each statute requires proof of an additional fact which the other does not, an acquittal or conviction under either statute does not exempt the defendant from prosecution and punishment under the other.' " Gavieres v. United States, 220 U.S. 338, 342 (1911) (quoting Morey v. Commonwealth, 108 Mass. 433, 434 (1871)). Blockburger v. United States, 284 U.S. 299 (1932), is the case most frequently cited. See Garrett v. United States, 471 U.S. 773 (1985) (5–3) (distinct statutory offenses); Albernaz v. United States, 450 U.S. 333 (1981) (same). See also Ball v. United States, 470 U.S. 856 (1985) (simultaneous prosecution under overlapping statutes is permissible, but not conviction and punishment under different statutes for the same conduct).

The *Blockburger* test, as it is called, was expanded in Grady v. Corbin, 495 U.S. 508 (1990) (5–4). The defendant was convicted of traffic offenses. Thereafter, he was indicted for homicide, arising out of the death of a person injured in the accident caused by the traffic offenses. The prosecution filed a bill of particulars specifying the traffic offenses as the basis of the homicide charges. The Court held that the homicide prosecution was barred. "[T]he Double Jeopardy Clause bars any subsequent prosecution in which the government, to establish an essential element of an offense charged in that prosecution, will prove conduct that constitutes an offense for which the defendant has already been prosecuted." Id. at 521. Distinguishing *Dowling*, p. 1215 note 632 above, the Court said: "The critical inquiry is what conduct the State will prove, not the evidence the State will use to prove that conduct. . . . [T]he presentation of specific evidence in one trial does not forever prevent the government from introducing that same evidence in a subsequent proceeding." Id. at 521–22. (The Court noted also that the person injured in the accident had died before the defendant was convicted of the traffic offenses, avoiding the problem suggested in Brown v. Ohio, 432 U.S. 161, 169 n.7 (1977) (6–3), discussed in note 615, p. 1181 above. 495 U.S. at 516 n.7.) Cf. United States v. Felix, 503 U.S. 378 (1992) (*Grady* not followed). Three years later, Grady v. Corbin was overruled, and the *Blockburger* test was restored. United States v. Dixon, 509 U.S. 688 (1993) (5–4).

In Rutledge v. United States, 517 U.S. 292 (1996), the Court held that under the *Blockburger* test, a conspiracy to distribute a controlled substance (21 U.S.C. § 846) was a lesser included offense of conducting a continuing criminal enterprise (21 U.S.C. § 848), because the "in concert" element of the latter offense was based on the § 846 conspiracy. The petitioner had been sentenced to a concurrent life sentence and was assessed $50 (under 18 U.S.C. § 3013) for each offense. Without ruling on other aspects of the case, the Court concluded that at least the double assessment amounted to cumulative punishment and was barred by the Double Jeopardy Clause.

636. The Department of Justice has announced as a general policy " 'that several offenses arising out of a single transaction should be alleged and tried together and should not be made the basis of multiple prosecutions, a policy dictated by considerations both of fairness to defendants and of efficient and orderly law enforcement.' " Petite v. United States, 361 U.S. 529, 530 (1960). See Thompson v. United States, 444 U.S. 248 (1980); Rinaldi v. United States, 434 U.S. 22 (1977).

637. The prosecution of a defendant as an adult after an adjudicatory hearing in the Juvenile Court and a determination that he had violated a criminal statute and a subsequent finding that he was unfit for treatment as a juvenile violates the Double Jeopardy Clause. Breed v. Jones, 421 U.S. 519 (1975). The Court observed that its holding would not interfere with the flexibility of juvenile proceedings; the decision whether to transfer a juvenile for proceedings as an adult could be made prior to an adjudicatory hearing on the merits.

Breed v. Jones was distinguished in Swisher v. Brady, 438 U.S. 204 (1978) (6–3). In that case, the Court upheld a Maryland procedure by which the state can file exceptions in the juvenile court to a master's proposed finding of nondelinquency and the court can accept, reject, or modify the finding, but only on the basis of the record before the master or additional evidence to which the parties do not object. The Court concluded that the entire procedure was a unitary one and that the juvenile court's review of the master's finding did not place a juvenile in jeopardy a second time.

638. Successive prosecutions by the federal government and a state or by different states for crimes arising out of the same transaction and proved by the same evidence are not constitutionally impermissible double jeopardy. "In applying the dual sovereignty doctrine . . . the crucial determination is whether the two entities that seek successively to prosecute a defendant for the same course of conduct can be termed separate sovereigns. This determination turns on whether the two entities draw their authority to punish the offender from distinct sources of power." Heath v. Alabama, 474 U.S. 82, 88 (1985) (7–2). In *Heath*, the defendant was convicted of murder in Georgia and sentenced to life imprisonment. He was then convicted of murder for the same act in Alabama and sentenced to death. See also Abbate v. United States, 359 U.S. 187 (1959) (state–federal); Bartkus v. Illinois, 359 U.S. 121 (1959) (federal–state). Successive prosecutions by a municipality and the same state violate the Double Jeopardy Clause. Waller v. Florida, 397 U.S. 387 (1970).

The Department of Justice has a policy against duplicating a state prosecution. *Petite*, note 636 above, 361 U.S. at 531. See United States v. Fritz, 580 F.2d 370 (10th Cir.1978) (*Petite* policy is an internal rule of government that does not confer a right on the defendant).

CHAPTER 18

COLLATERAL ATTACK

Sunal v. Large

332 U.S. 174, 67 S.Ct. 1588, 91 L.Ed. 1982 (1947)

■ MR. JUSTICE DOUGLAS delivered the opinion of the Court.

Sunal and Kulick registered under the Selective Training and Service Act of 1940, 54 Stat. 885, 57 Stat. 597, 50 U.S.C.App. § 301, et seq. Each is a Jehovah's Witness and each claimed the exemption granted by Congress to regular or duly ordained ministers of religion. § 5(d). The local boards, after proceedings unnecessary to relate here, denied the claimed exemptions and classified these registrants as I–A. They exhausted their administrative remedies but were unable to effect a change in their classifications. Thereafter they were ordered to report for induction—Sunal on October 25, 1944, Kulick on November 9, 1944. Each reported but refused to submit to induction. Each was thereupon indicted, tried and convicted under § 11 of the Act for refusing to submit to induction. Sunal was sentenced on March 22, 1945, Kulick on May 7, 1945, each to imprisonment for a term of years. Neither appealed.

At the trial each offered evidence to show that his selective service classification was invalid. The trial courts held, however, that such evidence was inadmissible, that the classification was final and not open to attack in the criminal trial. On February 4, 1946, we decided Estep v. United States and Smith v. United States, 327 U.S. 114. These cases held on comparable facts that a registrant, who had exhausted his administrative remedies and thus obviated the rule of Falbo v. United States, 320 U.S. 549, was entitled, when tried under § 11, to defend on the ground that his local board exceeded its jurisdiction in making the classification—for example, that it had no basis in fact. 327 U.S. pp. 122–123.

It is plain, therefore, that the trial courts erred in denying Sunal and Kulick the defense which they tendered. Shortly after the *Estep* and *Smith* cases were decided, petitions for writs of habeas corpus were filed on behalf of Sunal and Kulick. In each case it was held that habeas corpus was an available remedy. In Sunal's case the Circuit Court of Appeals for the Fourth Circuit held that there was a basis in fact for the classification and affirmed a judgment discharging the writ. . . . In Kulick's case the Circuit Court of Appeals for the Second Circuit reversed a District Court holding that there was evidence to support the classification . . . and ruled, without examining the evidence, that since Kulick had been deprived of the defense he should be discharged from custody without prejudice to further prosecution. . . . The cases are here on petitions for writs of certiorari, which we granted because of the importance of the questions presented.

The normal and customary method of correcting errors of the trial is by appeal. Appeals could have been taken in these cases, but they were not. It cannot be said that absence of counsel made the appeals unavailable as a practical matter. . . . Defendants had counsel. Nor was there any other barrier to the perfection of their appeals. . . . Moreover, this is not a situation where the facts relied on were dehors the record and therefore not open to consideration and review on appeal. . . . The error was of record in each case. It is said, however, that the failure to appeal was excusable, since under the decisions as they then stood—March 22, 1945, and May 7, 1945—the lower courts had consistently ruled that the selective service classification could not be attacked in a prosecution under § 11. . . . It is also pointed out that on April 30, 1945, we had denied certiorari in a case which sought to raise the same point, and that Estep v. United States, supra, and Smith v. United States, supra, were brought here and decided after Sunal's and Kulick's time for appeal had passed. The argument is that since the state of the law made the appeals seem futile, it would be unfair to those registrants to conclude them by their failure to appeal.

We put to one side comparable problems respecting the use of habeas corpus in the federal courts to challenge convictions obtained in the state courts. . . . So far as convictions obtained in the federal courts are concerned, the general rule is that the writ of habeas corpus will not be allowed to do service for an appeal. . . . There have been, however, some exceptions. That is to say, the writ has at times been entertained either without consideration of the adequacy of relief by the appellate route or where an appeal would have afforded an adequate remedy. Illustrative are those instances where the conviction was under a federal statute alleged to be unconstitutional, where there was a conviction by a federal court whose jurisdiction over the person or the offense was challenged, where the trial or sentence by a federal court violated specific constitutional guaranties. It is plain, however, that the writ is not designed for collateral review of errors of law committed by the trial court—the existence of any evidence to support the conviction, irregularities in the grand jury procedure, departure from a statutory grant of time in which to prepare for trial, and other errors in trial procedure which do not cross the jurisdictional line. . . .

Yet the latter rule is not an absolute one; and the situations in which habeas corpus has done service for an appeal are the exceptions. Thus where the jurisdiction of the federal court which tried the case is challenged or where the constitutionality of the federal statute under which conviction was had is attacked, habeas corpus is increasingly denied in case an appellate procedure was available for correction of the error. Yet, on the other hand, where the error was flagrant and there was no other remedy available for its correction, relief by habeas corpus has sometimes been granted. As stated by Chief Justice Hughes in Bowen v. Johnston, 306 U.S. 19, 27, the rule which requires resort to appellate procedure for the correction of errors "is not one defining power but one which relates to the appropriate exercise of power." That rule is, therefore, "not so inflexible that it may not yield to exceptional circumstances where the need for the remedy afforded by the writ of habeas corpus is apparent." Id. p. 27. That case was deemed to involve "exceptional circumstances" by reason of the fact that it indicated "a conflict between state and federal authorities on a question of law involving concerns of large importance affecting their respective jurisdictions." Id. p. 27. The Court accordingly entertained the writ to examine into the jurisdiction of the court to render the judgment of conviction.

The same course was followed in Ex parte Hudgings, 249 U.S. 378, where petitioner was adjudged guilty of contempt for committing perjury. The Court did not require the petitioner to pursue any appellate route but issued an original writ and discharged him, holding that perjury without more was not punishable as a contempt. That situation was deemed exceptional in view of "the nature of the case, of the relation which the question which it involves bears generally to the power and duty of courts in the performance of their functions, of the dangerous effect on the liberty of the citizen when called upon as a witness in a court which might result if the erroneous doctrine upon which the order under review was based were not promptly corrected. . . ." Id. p. 384. . . .

The Circuit Courts of Appeals thought that the facts of the present cases likewise presented exceptional circumstances which justified resort to habeas corpus though no appeals were taken. In their view the failure to appeal was excusable, since relief by that route seemed quite futile.

But denial of certiorari by this Court in the earlier case imported no expression of opinion on the merits. . . . The same chief counsel represented the defendants in the present cases and those in the *Estep* and *Smith* cases. At the time these defendants were convicted the *Estep* and *Smith* cases were pending before the appellate courts. The petition in the *Smith* case was, indeed, filed here about two weeks before Kulick's conviction and about a month after Sunal's conviction. The same road was open to Sunal and Kulick as the one *Smith* and *Estep* took. Why the legal strategy counseled taking appeals in the *Smith* and *Estep* cases and not in these we do not know. Perhaps it was based on the facts of these two cases. For the question of law had not been decided by the Court; and counsel was pressing for a decision here. The case, therefore, is not one where the law was changed after the time for appeal had expired. . . . It is rather a situation where at the time of the convictions the definitive ruling on the question of law had not crystallized. Of course, if Sunal and Kulick had pursued the appellate course and failed, their cases would be quite different. But since they chose not to pursue the remedy which they had, we do not think they should now be allowed to justify their failure by saying they deemed any appeal futile.

We are dealing here with a problem which has radiations far beyond the present cases. The courts which tried the defendants had jurisdiction over their persons and over the offense. They committed an error of law in excluding the defense which was tendered. That error did not go to the jurisdiction of the trial court. Congress, moreover, has provided a regular, orderly method for correction of all such errors by granting an appeal to the Circuit Court of Appeals and by vesting us with certiorari jurisdiction. It is not uncommon after a trial is ended and the time for appeal has passed to discover that a shift in the law or the impact of a new decision has given increased relevance to a point made at the trial but not pursued on appeal. . . . If in such circumstances, habeas corpus could be used to correct the error, the writ would become a delayed motion for a new trial, renewed from time to time as the legal climate changed. Error which was not deemed sufficiently adequate to warrant an appeal would acquire new implications. Every error is potentially reversible error; and many rulings of the trial court spell the difference between conviction and acquittal. If defendants who accept the judgment of conviction and do not appeal can later renew their attack on the judgment by habeas corpus, litigation in these criminal cases will be interminable. Wise judicial administration of the federal courts counsels against such course, at least where the error does not trench on any constitutional rights of defendants nor involve the jurisdiction of the trial court.

An endeavor is made to magnify the error in these trials to constitutional proportions by asserting that the refusal of the proffered evidence robbed the trial of vitality by depriving defendants of their only real defense. But as much might be said of many rulings during a criminal trial. Defendants received throughout an opportunity to be heard and enjoyed all procedural guaranties granted by the Constitution. Error in ruling on the question of law did not infect the trial with lack of procedural due process. As stated by Mr. Justice Cardozo in Escoe v. Zerbst, 295 U.S. 490, 494, "When a hearing is allowed but there is error in conducting it or in limiting its scope, the remedy is by appeal. When an opportunity to be heard is denied altogether, the ensuing mandate of the court is void, and the prisoner confined thereunder may have recourse to habeas corpus to put an end to the restraint."

. . .

■ MR. JUSTICE RUTLEDGE, dissenting.

. . .

The writ should be available whenever there clearly has been a fundamental miscarriage of justice for which no other adequate remedy is presently available. Beside executing its great object, which is the preservation of personal liberty and assurance against its wrongful deprivation, considerations of economy of judicial time and procedures, important as they undoubtedly are, become comparatively insignificant. This applies to situations involving the past existence of a remedy presently foreclosed, as well as to others where no such remedy has ever been afforded.

In the prevailing state of our criminal law, federal and state, there are few errors, either fundamental or of lesser gravity, which cannot be corrected by appeal timely taken, unless the facts disclosing or constituting them arise after the time has expired. If the existence of a remedy by appeal at some stage of the criminal proceedings is to be taken for the criterion, then in very few instances, far less than the number comprehended by our decisions, will the writ be available. Taken literally, the formula so often repeated, that the writ is not a substitute for appeal, is thus in conflict with every case where the ground upon which the writ has been allowed either was or might have been asserted on appeal. The formula has obvious validity in the sense that the writ is not readily to be used for overturning determinations made on appeal or for securing review where no specification has been made or no appeal has been taken of matters not going to make the conviction a gross miscarriage of justice.

But any effort to shut off the writ's functioning merely because appeal has not been taken in a situation where, but for that fact alone, the writ would issue, seems to me to prescribe a system of forfeitures in the last area where such a system should prevail. Certainly a basic miscarriage of justice is no less great or harmful, either to the individual or to the general cause of personal liberty, merely because appeal has not been taken, than where appeal is taken but relief is wrongfully denied.

These considerations apply with special force, though not exclusively, where good reason existed, as I think did here, for failure to note the appeal in the brief time allowed. Whether or not the inferior federal courts were justified in taking the *Falbo* [v. United States, 320 U.S. 549 (1944)] decision for more than its specific ruling, the fact remains that their broadly prevailing view was that that case had cut off all right to make such defenses as Sunal and Kulick tendered.

In that prevailing climate of opinion in those courts, there was hardly any chance that appeal to the federal circuit courts of appeals would bring relief by their action. The chances for reversal therefore hung almost exclusively upon the doubtful, not to say slender,[1] chance that this Court in the exercise of its discretionary power would grant certiorari.

The deprivation here was of the right to make any substantial defense. I do not think a trial which forecloses the basic right to defend, upon the only valid ground available for that purpose, is any less unfair or conclusive as against the office of habeas corpus than one which takes place when the court is without jurisdiction to try the offense, as when the charge is made under an unconstitutional statute or for other reason sets forth no lawfully prescribed offense, or when the court loses jurisdiction by depriving the accused of his constitutional right to counsel. That right is no more and no

1. Although denial of certiorari is not to be taken as expression of opinion in any case, it would be idle to claim that it has no actual or reasonable influence upon the practical judgment of lawyers whether appeal should be noted and taken upon the chance that in a case substantially identical this Court's discretion would be exercised, in the absence of conflict, in a contrary manner at the stage of application for certiorari.

less than an important segment of the right to have any valid defense advanced and considered. It becomes almost meaningless if the larger right to defend is itself cut off.

. . .[2]

---

639. Fiore v. White, 531 U.S. 225 (2001) (per curiam). After the defendant's conviction had become final, in another case the state supreme court interpreted the statute pursuant to which he was convicted and determined that his conduct was not covered by the statute. The Court relied on In re Winship, 397 U.S. 358 (1970), p. 1080 above, to hold that the defendant's conviction violated the Due Process Clause. See Bunkley v. Florida, 538 U.S. 835 (2003) (6–3) (*Fiore* applied).

640. "The writ of habeas corpus is the fundamental instrument for safeguarding individual freedom against arbitrary and lawless state action. Its pre-eminent role is recognized by the admonition in the Constitution that: 'The Privilege of the Writ of Habeas Corpus shall not be suspended. . . .' U.S. Const., Art. I, § 9, cl. 2. The scope and flexibility of the writ—its capacity to reach all manner of illegal detention—its ability to cut through barriers of form and procedural mazes—have always been emphasized and jealously guarded by courts and lawmakers. The very nature of the writ demands that it be administered with the initiative and flexibility essential to insure that miscarriages of justice within its reach are surfaced and corrected." Harris v. Nelson, 394 U.S. 286, 290–91 (1969). "[T]he basic purpose of the writ is to enable those unlawfully incarcerated to obtain their freedom." Johnson v. Avery, 393 U.S. 483, 485 (1969).

For important steps in the expansion of habeas corpus from a remedy narrowly available to test the jurisdiction of the sentencing court to a means for asserting the denial of a constitutional right at trial, see Frank v. Mangum, 237 U.S. 309 (1915); Moore v. Dempsey, 261 U.S. 86 (1923); Mooney v. Holohan, 294 U.S. 103 (1935); and Brown v. Allen, 344 U.S. 443 (1953). The development of the writ is traced in Fay v. Noia, 372 U.S. 391, 399–426 (1963) (6–3), and, with different significance, in Wainwright v. Sykes, 433 U.S. 72, 77–85 (1977). (That portion of the opinion is partially omitted below, p. 1231.) See also Justice Harlan's dissenting opinion in Fay v. Noia, 372 U.S. at 449–63.

641. Collateral attack in the federal courts on state and federal convictions is covered generally by 28 U.S.C. §§ 2241–2255. Applications for writs of habeas corpus by state prisoners in particular are covered by § 2254; motions under § 2255 replace applications for habeas corpus by federal prisoners. The background of § 2255 is discussed in United States v. Hayman, 342 U.S. 205 (1952). The statute does not limit the remedy of habeas corpus; it "was intended simply to provide in the sentencing court a remedy exactly commensurate with that which had previously been available by habeas corpus in the court of the district where the prisoner was

[2] Justice Burton concurred in the result. Justice Frankfurter wrote a dissenting opinion. Justice Murphy noted that he joined Justice Rutledge's dissenting opinion and added a further note.

confined.'' Hill v. United States, 368 U.S. 424, 427 (1962). See Davis v. United States, 417 U.S. 333 (1974).

The availability of relief under §§ 2254 and 2255 was narrowed in 1996 by the Antiterrorism and Effective Death Penalty Act of 1996, 110 Stat. 1214. Among the important provisions are that a state prisoner cannot obtain habeas relief solely because a state court misapplied constitutional principles to the facts, but only if the state court's ''decision was contrary to, or involved an unreasonable application of, clearly established Federal law, as determined by the Supreme Court of the United States.'' § 2254(d)(1). There is also a one-year statute of limitations, applicable to federal and state prisoners, which ordinarily begins to run on the date on which the conviction becomes final. Special, largely technical, provisions are applicable to capital cases. See Felker v. Turpin, 518 U.S. 651 (1996). See also Stewart v. Martinez-Villareal, 523 U.S. 637 (1998) (7–2); Calderon v. Thompson, 523 U.S. 538 (1998) (5–4).

In [Terry] Williams v. Taylor, 529 U.S. 362 (2000) (5–4), construing § 2254(d)(1), the Court said that a decision is ''contrary to . . . clearly established Federal law'' if it is ''opposite to that reached by this Court on a question of law or if the state court decides a case differently than this Court has on a set of materially indistinguishable facts.'' 529 U.S. at 413. A state decision involves an ''unreasonable application of clearly established Federal law'' if the state court ''identifies the correct governing principle from this Court's decisions but unreasonably applies that principle to the facts.'' Id. at 413. The standard of reasonableness, the Court said, is an objective one. It noted that an ''*unreasonable* application'' is different from an ''*incorrect* application.'' Id. at 365. The Court concluded that the defendant had satisfied both of those tests. See Lockyer v. Andrade, 538 U.S. 63 (2003) (state court decision not objectively unreasonable); Mitchell v. Esparza, 540 U.S. ___ (2003) (same); Yarborough v. Gentry, 540 U.S. ___ (2003) (same); Price v. Vincent, 538 U.S. 634 (2003), applying 28 U.S.C. § 2254(d).

In [Michael Wayne] Williams v. Taylor, 529 U.S. 420 (2000), the Court construed 28 U.S.C. § 2254(e)(2), as amended by the AEDPA, which bars an evidentiary hearing on constitutional claims pursuant to an application for habeas corpus if the defendant ''has failed to develop the factual basis'' of his claims in state court proceedings, except under stringent conditions. The Court said that the failure in question is not established ''unless there is lack of diligence, or some greater fault,'' attributable to the defendant or his counsel. 529 U.S. at 432. Diligence ''depends on whether the prisoner made a reasonable attempt, in light of the information available at the time, to investigate and pursue claims in state court.'' Id. at 435. The Court concluded that the defendant had not been diligent with respect to one of his claims but that he had been diligent with respect to the other two.

Further provisions of the AEDPA, having to do with appeal from dismissal of a habeas petition on procedural grounds, are construed in Slack v. McDaniel, 529 U.S. 473 (2000) (7–2).

In Washington v. Smith, 219 F.3d 620 (7th Cir.2000), the AEDPA is applied to a claim of ineffective assistance of counsel. The claim was upheld.

On the AEDPA statute of limitations, see Carey v. Saffold, 536 U.S. 214 (2002) (5–4), holding that the statute is tolled during the entire period during which the state's post-conviction review process is unresolved.

The Court has promulgated rules governing cases under both sections and model forms to be used in an application to the district court for relief under them. In addition, the Federal Rules of Civil Procedure are generally applicable to cases under § 2254, see Fed.R.Civ.P 81(a)(2). The Federal Rules of Civil Procedure or Criminal Procedure may be applied to motions under § 2255, see Rule 12 of the Rules Governing Section 2255 Proceedings.

The requirement that state remedies be exhausted before a petition for habeas corpus is brought in federal court for relief from a state conviction is discussed at length in Rose v. Lundy, 455 U.S. 509 (1982) (8–1). A majority of the Court held that a petition containing some claims the state remedies for which have been exhausted and some claims the state remedies for which have not must be dismissed in its entirety; a minority thought that the federal court should consider the former claims. A person convicted in a state court must present his claims to the state supreme court in a petition for discretionary review, if that is possible, before seeking federal habeas corpus. O'Sullivan v. Boerckel, 526 U.S. 838 (1999) (6–3). See generally Anderson v. Harless, 459 U.S. 4 (1982) (6–3).

On federal habeas corpus review, a state conviction is reversible for constitutional error of the "trial type" (errors occurring in the presentation of evidence to the jury) only if the error "had substantial and injurious effect or influence in determining the jury's verdict," Kotteakos v. United States, 328 U.S. 750, 776 (1946). Such error is not subject on collateral review to the standard of Chapman v. California, 386 U.S. 18, 24 (1967), requiring reversal unless the error "was harmless beyond a reasonable doubt." Brecht v. Abrahamson, 507 U.S. 619 (1993) (6–3). In *Brecht*, the error was the prosecution's references to the defendant's post-*Miranda* silence, in violation of Doyle v. Ohio, 426 U.S. 610 (1976), p. 481 note 268 above. *Brecht* was applied in California v. Roy, 519 U.S. 2 (1996) (per curiam).

"When a federal judge in a habeas proceeding is in grave doubt about whether a trial error of federal law had 'substantial and injurious effect or influence in determining the jury's verdict,' that error is not harmless. And the petitioner must win." O'Neal v. McAninch, 513 U.S. 432, 436 (1995) (6–3). The Court observed that treating the error in such circumstances as not harmless will "at least often" avoid holding someone in custody in violation of the Constitution, whereas treating the error as harmless "would virtually guarantee that many, *in fact*, will be held in unlawful custody." Id. at 442.

The Court has held that the rule of Stone v. Powell, 428 U.S. 465 (1976), see p. 877 note 434 above, is *not* applicable to a claim that the conviction was based on statements obtained in violation of Miranda v. Arizona, 384 U.S. 436 (1966). Withrow v. Williams, 507 U.S. 680 (1993) (5–4). The Court observed that, unlike the exclusion of evidence that was involved in Stone v. Powell, the *Miranda* rules safeguard a fundamental trial right and are related to the fairness of the trial itself and the accuracy of the result.

On the standard for federal collateral review of state determinations of fact, see 28 U.S.C. § 2254(e)(1), providing that a state court's determination shall be "presumed to be correct" and that the defendant has the burden of rebutting the presumption "by clear and convincing evidence."

642. The defendants in United States v. Chambers, 291 U.S. 217 (1934), were indicted for violations of the federal prohibition law. Before their trial the Twenty-First Amendment to the Constitution, which repealed the Eighteenth Amendment, was ratified. The district court dismissed the indictment, and the government appealed. The Court affirmed, saying: "The National Prohibition Act, to the extent that its provisions rested upon the grant of authority to the Congress by the Eighteenth Amendment, immediately fell with the withdrawal by the people of the essential constitutional support. The continuance of the prosecution of the defendants after the repeal of the Eighteenth Amendment, for a violation of the National Prohibition Act alleged to have been committed in North Carolina, would involve an attempt to continue the application of the statutory provisions after they had been deprived of force. This consequence is not altered by the fact that the crimes in question were alleged to have been committed while the National Prohibition Act was in effect. The continued prosecution necessarily depended upon the continued life of the statute which the prosecution seeks to apply. In case a statute is repealed or rendered inoperative, no further proceedings can be had to enforce it in pending prosecutions unless competent authority has kept the statute alive for that purpose." Id. at 222–23. See also Massey v. United States, 291 U.S. 608 (1934) (conviction of violation of prohibition law affirmed on appeal but no final judgment rendered before ratification of Twenty-First Amendment; conviction vacated). If a judgment of conviction has become final before repeal of the statute on which the conviction is based, however, the repeal does not preclude execution of sentence. E.g., United States ex rel. Randall v. United States Marshall, 143 F.2d 830 (2d Cir.1944). See generally Bell v. Maryland, 378 U.S. 226 (1964).

643. The Court has struggled with the problem of when and how far to give retroactive effect to changes favorable to the defendant in the constitutional requirements of criminal procedure. For steps along the way, see, e.g., Linkletter v. Walker, 381 U.S. 618 (1965) (7–2), and Solem v. Stumes, 465 U.S. 638 (1984) (6–3). In Teague v. Lane, 489 U.S. 288 (1989) (7–2), four members of the Court expressed the view that "unless they fall within an exception to the general rule, new constitutional rules of criminal procedure will not be applicable to those cases which have become final before the new rules are announced." Id. at 310. "In general . . . a case announces a rule when it breaks new ground or imposes a new obligation on the States or the Federal Government. . . . To put it differently, a case announces a new rule if the result was not *dictated* by precedent existing at the time the defendant's conviction became final." Id. at 301. There are exceptions to the general rule against retroactivity if the newly announced constitutional rule places " 'certain kinds of primary, private individual conduct beyond the power of the criminal law-making authority to proscribe' " (quoting Mackey v. United States, 401 U.S. 667, 692 (1971) (opinion of Harlan, J.)) or if it is one of those "watershed rules of criminal procedure," those "new procedures without which the likelihood of an accurate conviction is seriously diminished." The opinion adds that "we believe it unlikely that many such components of basic due process have yet to emerge." Id. at 311, 313.

The analysis of *Teague* has been adopted by the Court and was applied in O'Dell v. Netherland, 521 U.S. 151 (1997) (5–4) (*Simmons*, p. 1155 above; new rule principle applied); Lambrix v. Singletary, 520 U.S. 518 (1997) (5–4) (*Espinosa*, p. 1154 above; new rule principle applied); Gray v. Netherland, 518 U.S. 152 (1996) (5–4) (evidentiary notice requirement; new rule principle applied); Caspari v. Bohlen, 510 U.S. 383 (1994) (8–1) (*Bullington*, p. 1193 above, extended to noncapital sentencing procedure; new rule principle applied); Graham v. Collins, 506 U.S. 461 (1993) (5–4) (capital sentencing procedure; new rule principle applied); Stringer v. Black, 503 U.S. 222 (1992) (6–3) (capital sentencing procedure; new rule principle not applied); Butler v. McKellar, 494 U.S. 407 (1990) (5–4) (*Roberson*, p. 443 above; new rule principle applied); Saffle v. Parks, 494 U.S. 484 (1990) (5–4) (capital sentencing procedure; new rule principle applied); Penry v. Lynaugh, 492 U.S. 302 (1989) (capital sentencing procedure; new rule principle not applied). In Butler v. McKellar, the Court said that the " 'new rule' principle validates reasonable good-faith interpretations of existing precedents made by state courts even though they are shown to be contrary to later decisions." 494 U.S. at 414. It indicated that an interpretation is reasonable if the correct interpretation was "susceptible to debate among reasonable minds." Id. at 415. In Bousley v. United States, 523 U.S. 614 (1998) (7–2), the Court held that *Teague* is not applicable to a ruling that modified the scope of a federal criminal statute; the ruling was made after the defendant had pleaded guilty on the basis of the prior statutory construction.

Wainwright v. Sykes

433 U.S. 72, 97 S.Ct. 2497, 53 L.Ed.2d 594 (1977)

■ MR. JUSTICE REHNQUIST delivered the opinion of the Court.

We granted certiorari to consider the availability of federal habeas corpus to review a state convict's claim that testimony was admitted at his trial in violation of his rights under Miranda v. Arizona, 384 U.S. 436 (1966), a claim which the Florida courts have previously refused to consider on the merits because of noncompliance with a state contemporaneous-objection rule. Petitioner Wainwright, on behalf of the State of Florida, here challenges a decision of the Court of Appeals for the Fifth Circuit ordering a hearing in state court on the merits of respondent's contention.

Respondent Sykes was convicted of third-degree murder after a jury trial in the Circuit Court of DeSoto County. He testified at trial that on the evening of January 8, 1972, he told his wife to summon the police because he had just shot Willie Gilbert. Other evidence indicated that when the police arrived at respondent's trailer home, they found Gilbert dead of a shotgun wound, lying a few feet from the front porch. Shortly after their arrival, respondent came from across the road and volunteered that he had shot Gilbert, and a few minutes later respondent's wife approached the police and told them the same thing. Sykes was immediately arrested and taken to the police station.

Once there, it is conceded that he was read his *Miranda* rights, and that he declined to seek the aid of counsel and indicated a desire to talk. He then made a statement, which was admitted into evidence at trial through the testimony of the two officers who heard it, to the effect that he had shot Gilbert from the front porch of his trailer home. There were several references during the trial to respondent's consumption of alcohol during the preceding day and to his apparent state of intoxication, facts which were acknowledged by the officers who arrived at the scene. At no time during the trial, however, was the admissibility of any of respondent's statements challenged by his counsel on the ground that respondent had not understood the *Miranda* warnings. Nor did the trial judge question their admissibility on his own motion or hold a factfinding hearing bearing on that issue.

Respondent appealed his conviction, but apparently did not challenge the admissibility of the inculpatory statements. He later filed in the trial court a motion to vacate the conviction and, in the State District Court of Appeals and Supreme Court, petitions for habeas corpus. These filings, apparently for the first time, challenged the statements made to police on grounds of involuntariness. In all of these efforts respondent was unsuccessful.

Having failed in the Florida courts, respondent initiated the present action under 28 U.S.C. § 2254, asserting the inadmissibility of his statements by reason of his lack of understanding of the *Miranda* warnings. The United States District Court for the Middle District of Florida ruled that Jackson v. Denno, 378 U.S. 368 (1964), requires a hearing in a state criminal trial prior to the admission of an inculpatory out-of-court statement by the defendant. It held further that respondent had not lost his right to assert such a claim by failing to object at trial or on direct appeal, since only "exceptional circumstances" of "strategic decisions at trial" can create such a bar to raising federal constitutional claims in a federal habeas action. The court stayed issuance of the writ to allow the state court to hold a hearing on the "voluntariness" of the statements.

Petitioner warden appealed this decision to the United States Court of Appeals for the Fifth Circuit. That court first considered the nature of the right to exclusion of statements made without a knowing waiver of the right to counsel and the right not to incriminate oneself. It noted that Jackson v. Denno, supra, guarantees a right to a hearing on whether a defendant has knowingly waived his rights as described to him in the *Miranda* warnings, and stated that under Florida law "[t]he burden is on the State to secure [a] prima facie determination of voluntariness, not upon the defendant to demand it." 528 F.2d 522, 525 (1976).

The court then directed its attention to the effect on respondent's right of Florida Rule Crim.Proc. 3.190(i), which it described as "a contemporaneous objection rule" applying to motions to suppress a defendant's inculpatory statements. It focused on this Court's decisions in Henry v. Mississippi, 379 U.S. 443 (1965); Davis v. United States, 411 U.S. 233 (1973); and Fay v. Noia, 372 U.S. 391 (1963), and concluded that the failure to comply with the rule requiring objection at the trial would only bar review of the suppression claim where the right to object was deliberately bypassed for reasons relating to trial tactics. . . . Concluding that "[t]he failure to object in this case cannot be dismissed as a trial tactic, and thus a deliberate by-pass," the court affirmed the District Court order that the State hold a hearing on whether respondent knowingly waived his *Miranda* rights at the time he made the statements.

The simple legal question before the Court calls for a construction of the language of 28 U.S.C. § 2254(a), which provides that the federal courts shall entertain an application for a writ of habeas corpus "in behalf of a person in custody pursuant to the judgment of a state court only on the ground that he is in custody in violation of the Constitution or laws or treaties of the United States." But, to put it mildly, we do not write on a clean slate in construing this statutory provision. . . . For more than a century . . . this Court has grappled with the relationship between the classical common-law writ of habeas corpus and the remedy provided in 28 U.S.C. § 2254. Sharp division within the Court has been manifested on more than one aspect of the perplexing problems which have been litigated in this connection. Where the habeas petitioner challenges a final judgment of conviction rendered by a state court, this Court has been called upon to decide no fewer than four different questions, all to a degree interrelated with one another: (1) What types of federal claims may a federal habeas court properly consider? (2) Where a federal claim is cognizable by a federal habeas court, to what extent must that court defer to a resolution of the claim in prior state proceedings? (3) To what extent must the petitioner who seeks federal habeas exhaust state remedies before resorting to the federal court? (4) In what instances will an adequate and independent state ground bar consideration of otherwise cognizable federal issues on federal habeas review?

Each of these four issues has spawned its share of litigation. . . .

. . .

. . . Only the fourth area—the adequacy of state grounds to bar federal habeas review—is presented in this case. The foregoing discussion of the other three is pertinent here only as it illustrates this Court's historic willingness to overturn or modify its earlier views of the scope of the writ, even where the statutory language authorizing judicial action has remained unchanged.

As to the role of adequate and independent state grounds, it is a well-established principle of federalism that a state decision resting on an adequate foundation of state substantive law is immune from review in the federal courts. . . . The application of this principle in the context of a federal habeas proceeding has therefore excluded from consideration any questions of state *substantive* law, and thus effectively barred federal habeas review where questions of that sort are either the only ones raised by a petitioner or are in themselves dispositive of his case. The area of controversy which has developed has concerned the reviewability of federal claims which the state court has declined to pass on because not presented in the manner prescribed by its *procedural* rules. The adequacy of such an independent state procedural ground to prevent federal habeas review of the underlying federal issue has been treated very differently than where the state-law ground is substantive. . . .

In *Brown* [v. Allen, 344 U.S. 443 (1953)], petitioner Daniels' lawyer had failed to mail the appeal papers to the State Supreme Court on the last day provided by law for filing, and hand delivered them one day after that date. Citing the state rule requiring timely filing, the Supreme Court of North Carolina refused to hear the appeal. This Court . . . held that federal habeas was not available to review a constitutional claim which could not have been reviewed on direct appeal here because it rested on an independent and adequate state procedural ground. 344 U.S., at 486–87.

In Fay v. Noia, supra, respondent Noia sought federal habeas to review a claim that his state-court conviction had resulted from the introduction of a coerced confession in violation of the Fifth Amendment to the United States Constitution. While the convictions of his two codefendants were reversed on that ground in collateral proceedings following their appeals, Noia did not appeal and the New York courts ruled that his subsequent *coram nobis* action was barred on account of that failure. This Court held that petitioner was nonetheless entitled to raise the claim in federal habeas, and thereby overruled its decision 10 years earlier in Brown v. Allen, supra:

> [T]he doctrine under which state procedural defaults are held to constitute an adequate and independent state law ground barring direct Supreme Court review is not to be extended to limit the power granted the federal courts under the federal habeas statute.

372 U.S., at 399.

As a matter of comity but not of federal power, the Court acknowledged "a limited discretion in the federal judge to deny relief . . . to an applicant who had deliberately by-passed the orderly procedure of the state courts and in so doing has forfeited his state court remedies." Id., at 438. In so stating, the Court made clear that the waiver must be knowing and actual—" 'an intentional relinquishment or abandonment of a known right or privilege.' " Id., at 439, quoting Johnson v. Zerbst, 304 U.S., at 464. Noting petitioner's "grisly choice" between acceptance of his life sentence and pursuit of an appeal which might culminate in a sentence of death, the Court concluded that there had been no deliberate bypass of the right to have the federal issues reviewed through a state appeal.

A decade later we decided Davis v. United States, supra, in which a federal prisoner's application under 28 U.S.C. § 2255 sought for the first time to challenge the makeup of the grand jury which indicted him. The Government contended that he was barred by the requirement of Fed.Rule Crim.Proc. 12(b)(2) providing that such challenges must be raised "by motion before trial." The Rule further provides that failure to so object constitutes a waiver of the objection, but that "the court for cause shown may grant relief from the waiver." We noted that the Rule "promulgated by this Court and, pursuant to 18 U.S.C. § 3771, 'adopted' by Congress, governs by its terms the manner in which the claims of defects in the institution of criminal proceedings may be waived," 411 U.S., at 241, and held that this standard contained in the Rule, rather than the Fay v. Noia concept of waiver, should pertain in federal habeas as on direct review. Referring to previous constructions of Rule 12(b)(2), we concluded that review of the claim should be barred on habeas, as on direct appeal, absent a showing of cause for the noncompliance and some showing of actual prejudice resulting from the alleged constitutional violation.

Last Term, in Francis v. Henderson, 425 U.S. 536 (1976), the rule of *Davis* was applied to the parallel case of a state procedural requirement that challenges to grand jury composition be raised before trial. The Court noted that there was power in the federal courts to entertain an application in such a case, but rested its holding on "considerations of comity and concerns for the orderly administration of criminal justice. . . ." 425 U.S., at 538–39. While there was no counterpart provision of the state rule which allowed an exception upon some showing of cause, the Court concluded that the standard derived from the federal rule should nonetheless be applied in that context since " '[t]here is no reason to . . . give greater preclusive effect to procedural defaults by federal defendants than to similar defaults by state defendants.' " Id., at 542, quoting Kaufman v. United States, 394 U.S. 217, 228 (1969). As applied to the federal petitions of state convicts, the *Davis* cause-and-prejudice standard was thus incorporated directly into the body of law governing the availability of federal habeas corpus review.

To the extent that the dicta of Fay v. Noia may be thought to have laid down an all-inclusive rule rendering state timely objection rules ineffective to bar review of underlying federal claims in federal habeas proceedings—absent a "knowing waiver" or a "deliberate bypass" of the right to so object—its effect was limited by *Francis*, which applied a different rule and barred a habeas challenge to the makeup of a grand jury. Petitioner

Wainwright in this case urges that we further confine its effect by applying the principle enunciated in *Francis* to a claimed error in the admission of a defendant's confession.

. . .

We . . . conclude that Florida procedure did, consistently with the United States Constitution, require that respondent's confession be challenged at trial or not at all, and thus his failure to timely object to its admission amounted to an independent and adequate state procedural ground which would have prevented direct review here. . . . We thus come to the crux of this case. Shall the rule of Francis v. Henderson supra, barring federal habeas review absent a showing of "cause" and "prejudice" attendant to a state procedural waiver, be applied to a waived objection to the admission of a confession at trial? We answer that question in the affirmative.

As earlier noted in the opinion, since Brown v. Allen, 344 U.S. 443 (1953), it has been the rule that the federal habeas petitioner who claims he is detained pursuant to a final judgment of a state court in violation of the United States Constitution is entitled to have the federal habeas court make its own independent determination of his federal claim, without being bound by the determination on the merits of that claim reached in the state proceedings. This rule of Brown v. Allen is in no way changed by our holding today. Rather, we deal only with contentions of federal law which were *not* resolved on the merits in the state proceeding due to respondent's failure to raise them there as required by state procedure. We leave open for resolution in future decisions the precise definition of the "cause"-and-"prejudice" standard, and note here only that it is narrower than the standard set forth in dicta in Fay v. Noia, 372 U.S. 391 (1963), which would make federal habeas review generally available to state convicts absent a knowing and deliberate waiver of the federal constitutional contention. It is the sweeping language of Fay v. Noia going far beyond the facts of the case eliciting it, which we today reject.

The reasons for our rejection of it are several. The contemporaneous-objection rule itself is by no means peculiar to Florida, and deserves greater respect than *Fay* gives it, both for the fact that it is employed by a coordinate jurisdiction within the federal system and for the many interests which it serves in its own right. A contemporaneous objection enables the record to be made with respect to the constitutional claim when the recollections of witnesses are freshest, not years later in a federal habeas proceeding. It enables the judge who observed the demeanor of those witnesses to make the factual determinations necessary for properly deciding the federal constitutional question. While the 1966 amendment to § 2254 requires deference to be given to such determinations made by state courts, the determinations themselves are less apt to be made in the first instance if there is no contemporaneous objection to the admission of the evidence on federal constitutional grounds.

A contemporaneous-objection rule may lead to the exclusion of the evidence objected to, thereby making a major contribution to finality in criminal litigation. Without the evidence claimed to be vulnerable on federal constitutional grounds, the jury may acquit the defendant, and that will be the end of the case; or it may nonetheless convict the defendant, and he will have one less federal constitutional claim to assert in his federal habeas petition. If the state trial judge admits the evidence in question after a full hearing, the federal habeas court pursuant to the 1966 amendment to § 2254 will gain significant guidance from the state ruling in this regard. Subtler considerations as well militate in favor of honoring a state contemporaneous-objection rule. An objection on the spot may force the prosecution to take a hard look at its hole card, and even if the prosecutor thinks that the state trial judge will admit the evidence he must contemplate the possibility of reversal by the state appellate courts or the ultimate issuance of a federal writ of habeas corpus based on the impropriety of the state court's rejection of the federal constitutional claim.

We think that the rule of Fay v. Noia, broadly stated, may encourage "sandbagging" on the part of defense lawyers, who may take their chances on a verdict of not guilty in a state trial court with the intent to raise their constitutional claims in a federal habeas court if their initial gamble does not pay off. The refusal of federal habeas courts to honor contemporaneous-objection rules may also make state courts themselves less stringent in their enforcement. Under the rule of Fay v. Noia, state appellate courts know that a federal constitutional issue raised for the first time in the proceeding before them may well be decided in any event by a federal habeas tribunal. Thus, their choice is between addressing the issue notwithstanding the petitioner's failure to timely object, or else face the prospect that the federal habeas court will decide the question without the benefit of their views.

The failure of the federal habeas courts generally to require compliance with a contemporaneous-objection rule tends to detract from the perception of the trial of a criminal case in state court as a decisive and portentous event. A defendant has been accused of a serious crime, and this is the time and place set for him to be tried by a jury of his peers and found either guilty or not guilty by that jury. To the greatest extent possible all issues which bear on this charge should be determined in this proceeding: the accused is in the courtroom, the jury is in the box, the judge is on the bench, and the witnesses, having been subpoenaed and duly sworn, await their turn to testify. Society's resources have been concentrated at that time and place in order to decide, within the limits of human fallibility, the question of guilt or innocence of one of its citizens. Any procedural rule which encourages the result that those proceedings be as free of error as possible is thoroughly desirable, and the contemporaneous-objection rule surely falls within this classification.

We believe the adoption of the *Francis* rule in this situation will have the salutary effect of making the state trial on the merits the "main event," so to speak, rather than a "tryout on the road" for what will later be the determinative federal habeas hearing. There is nothing in the Constitution or in the language of § 2254 which requires that the state trial on the issue of guilt or innocence be devoted largely to the testimony of fact witnesses directed to the elements of the state crime, while only later will there occur in a federal habeas hearing a full airing of the federal constitutional claims which were not raised in the state proceedings. If a criminal defendant thinks that an action of the state trial court is about to deprive him of a federal constitutional right there is every reason for his following state procedure in making known his objection.

The "cause"-and-"prejudice" exception of the *Francis* rule will afford an adequate guarantee, we think, that the rule will not prevent a federal habeas court from adjudicating for the first time the federal constitutional claim of a defendant who in the absence of such an adjudication will be the victim of a miscarriage of justice. Whatever precise content may be given those terms by later cases, we feel confident in holding without further elaboration that they do not exist here. Respondent has advanced no explanation whatever for his failure to object at trial,[3] and, as the proceeding unfolded, the trial judge is certainly not to be faulted for failing to question the admission of the confession himself. The other evidence of guilt presented at trial, moreover, was substantial to a degree that would negate any possibility of actual prejudice resulting to the respondent from the admission of his inculpatory statement.

We accordingly conclude that the judgment of the Court of Appeals for the Fifth Circuit must be reversed, and the cause remanded to the United States District Court for the Middle District of Florida with instructions to dismiss respondent's petition for a writ of habeas corpus.

■ MR. CHIEF JUSTICE BURGER, concurring.

I concur fully in the judgment and in the Court's opinion. I write separately to emphasize one point which, to me, seems of critical importance to this case. In my view, the "deliberate bypass" standard enunciated in Fay v. Noia, 372 U.S. 391 (1963), was never designed for, and is inapplicable to, errors—even of constitutional dimension—alleged to have been committed during trial.

In Fay v. Noia, the Court applied the "deliberate bypass" standard to a case where the critical procedural decision—whether to take a criminal appeal—was entrusted to a convicted defendant. Although Noia, the habeas petitioner, was represented by counsel, he himself had to make the decision whether to appeal or not; the role of the attorney was limited to giving advice and counsel. In giving content to the new deliberate-bypass standard, *Fay* looked to the Court's decision in Johnson v. Zerbst, 304 U.S. 458

3. In Henry v. Mississippi, 379 U.S., at 451, the Court noted that decisions of counsel relating to trial strategy, even when made without the consultation of the defendant, would bar direct federal review of claims thereby foregone, except where "the circumstances are exceptional."

Last Term in Estelle v. Williams [425 U.S. 501 (1976)], the Court reiterated the burden on a defendant to be bound by the trial judgments of his lawyer.

"Under our adversary system, once a defendant has the assistance of counsel the vast array of trial decisions, strategic and tactical, which must be made before and during trial rests with the accused and his attorney." 425 U.S., at 512.

(1938), a case where the defendant had been called upon to make the decision whether to request representation by counsel in his federal criminal trial. Because in both *Fay* and *Zerbst*, important rights hung in the balance of the *defendant's own decision*, the Court required that a waiver impairing such rights be a knowing and intelligent decision by the defendant himself. As *Fay* put it:

> If a habeas applicant, after consultation with competent counsel or otherwise, understandingly and knowingly forewent the privilege of seeking to vindicate his federal claims in the state courts . . . then it is open to the federal court on habeas to deny him all relief. . . .

372 U.S., at 439.

The touchstone of *Fay* and *Zerbst*, then, is the exercise of volition by the defendant himself with respect to his own federal constitutional rights. In contrast, the claim in the case before us relates to events during the trial itself. Typically, habeas petitioners claim that unlawfully secured evidence was admitted . . . or that improper testimony was adduced, or that an improper jury charge was given . . . or that a particular line of examination or argument by the prosecutor was improper or prejudicial. But unlike *Fay* and *Zerbst*, preservation of this type of claim under state procedural rules does not generally involve an assertion by the defendant himself; rather, the decision to assert or not to assert constitutional rights or constitutionally based objections at trial is necessarily entrusted to the defendant's attorney, who must make on-the-spot decisions at virtually all stages of a criminal trial. As a practical matter, a criminal defendant is rarely, if ever, in a position to decide, for example, whether certain testimony is hearsay and, if so, whether it implicates interests protected by the Confrontation Clause; indeed, it is because " '[e]ven the intelligent and educated layman has small and sometimes no skill in the science of law' " that we held it constitutionally required that every defendant who faces the possibility of incarceration be afforded counsel. Argersinger v. Hamlin, 407 U.S. 25 (1972); Gideon v. Wainwright, 372 U.S. 335, 345 (1963).

Once counsel is appointed, the day-to-day conduct of the defense rests with the attorney. He, not the client, has the immediate—and ultimate—responsibility of deciding if and when to object, which witnesses, if any, to call, and what defenses to develop. Not only do these decisions rest with the attorney, but such decisions must, as a practical matter, be made without consulting the client. The trial process simply does not permit the type of frequent and protracted interruptions which would be necessary if it were required that clients give knowing and intelligent approval to each of the myriad tactical decisions as a trial proceeds.

Since trial decisions are of necessity entrusted to the accused's attorney, the *Fay–Zerbst* standard of "knowing and intelligent waiver" is simply inapplicable. The dissent in this case, written by the author of Fay v. Noia, implicitly recognizes as much. According to the dissent, *Fay* imposes the knowing-and-intelligent-waiver standard "where possible" during the course of the trial. In an extraordinary modification of *Fay*, Mr. Justice Brennan would now require "that the lawyer actually exercis[e] his expertise and judgment in his client's service, and with his client's knowing and intelligent participation *where possible*"; he does not intimate what guidelines would be used to decide when or under what circumstances this would actually be "possible." Post, at 116. (Emphasis supplied.) What had always been thought the standard governing the *accused's* waiver of his own constitutional rights the dissent would change, in the trial setting, into a standard of conduct imposed upon the defendant's *attorney*. This vague "standard" would be unmanageable to the point of impossibility.

. . .

■ MR. JUSTICE BRENNAN, with whom MR. JUSTICE MARSHALL joins, dissenting.

. . .

I

I begin with the threshold question: What is the meaning and import of a procedural default? If it could be assumed that a procedural default more often than not is the product of a defendant's conscious refusal to abide by the duly constituted, legitimate processes of the state courts, then I might agree that a regime of collateral review weighted in favor of a State's procedural rules would be warranted. *Fay*, however, recognized that such rarely is the case; and therein lies *Fay*'s basic unwillingness to embrace a view of habeas jurisdiction that results in "an airtight system of [procedural] forfeitures." 372 U.S., at 432.

. . .

[A]ny realistic system of federal habeas corpus jurisdiction must be premised on the reality that the ordinary procedural default is born of the inadvertence, negligence, inexperience, or incompetence of trial counsel. . . . The case under consideration today is typical. . . . [A]ny realistic reading of the record demonstrates that we are faced here with a lawyer's simple error.

Fay's answer thus is plain: the bypass test simply refuses to credit what is essentially a lawyer's mistake as a forfeiture of constitutional rights. . . .

II

What are the interests that Sykes can assert in preserving the availability of federal collateral relief in the face of his inadvertent state procedural default? Two are paramount.

As is true with any federal habeas applicant, Sykes seeks access to the federal court for the determination of the validity of his federal constitutional claim. . . .

. . .

[U]ndue deference to local procedure can only serve to undermine the ready access to a federal court to which a state defendant otherwise is entitled. But federal review is not the full measure of Sykes' interest, for there is another of even greater immediacy: assuring that his constitutional claims can be addressed to *some* court. For the obvious consequence of barring Sykes from the federal courthouse is to insulate Florida's alleged constitutional violation from any and all judicial review because of a lawyer's mistake. From the standpoint of the habeas petitioner, it is a harsh rule indeed that denies him "any review at all where the state has granted none," Brown v. Allen, 344 U.S. [443 (1953)], at 552 (Black, J., dissenting)—particularly when he would have enjoyed both state and federal consideration had his attorney not erred.

. . .

. . . I believe that *Fay*'s commitment to enforcing intentional but not inadvertent procedural defaults offers a realistic measure of protection for the habeas corpus petitioner seeking federal review of federal claims that were not litigated before the State. The threatened creation of a more "airtight system of forfeitures" would effectively deprive habeas petitioners of the opportunity for litigating their constitutional claims before any forum and would disparage the paramount importance of constitutional rights in our system of government. Such a restriction of habeas corpus jurisdiction should be countenanced, I submit, only if it fairly can be concluded that *Fay*'s focus on knowing and voluntary forfeitures unduly interferes with the legitimate interests of state courts or institutions. The majority offers no suggestion that actual experience has shown that *Fay*'s bypass test can be criticized on this score. And, as I now hope to demonstrate, any such criticism would be unfounded.

III

A regime of federal habeas corpus jurisdiction that permits the reopening of state procedural defaults does not invalidate any state procedural rule as such; Florida's courts remain entirely free to enforce their own rules as they choose, and to deny any and all state rights and remedies to a defendant who fails to comply with applicable state procedure. The relevant inquiry is whether more is required—specifically, whether the fulfillment of important interests of the State necessitates that federal courts be called upon to impose additional sanctions for inadvertent noncompliance with state procedural requirements such as the contemporaneous-objection rule involved here.

Florida, of course, can point to a variety of legitimate interests in seeking allegiance to its reasonable procedural requirements, the contemporaneous-objection rule included. . . . As *Fay* recognized, a trial, like any organized activity, must conform to coherent process, and "there must be sanctions for the flouting of such procedure." 372 U.S., at 431. The strict enforcement of procedural defaults, therefore, may be seen as a means of deterring any tendency on the part of the defense to slight the state forum, to deny state judges their due opportunity for playing a meaningful role in the evolving task of constitutional adjudication, or to mock the needed finality of criminal trials. All of these interests are referred to by the Court in various forms.

The question remains, however, whether any of these policies or interests are efficiently and fairly served by enforcing both intentional and inadvertent defaults pursuant to the identical stringent standard. I remain convinced that when one pierces the surface justifications for a harsher rule posited by the Court, no standard stricter than *Fay*'s deliberate-bypass test is realistically defensible.

Punishing a lawyer's unintentional errors by closing the federal courthouse door to his client is both a senseless and misdirected method of deterring the slighting of state rules. It is senseless because unplanned and unintentional action of any kind generally is not subject to deterrence; and, to the extent that it is hoped that a threatened sanction addressed to the defense will induce greater care and caution on the part of trial lawyers, thereby forestalling negligent conduct or error, the potential loss of all valuable state remedies would be sufficient to this end. And it is a misdirected sanction because even if the penalization of incompetence or carelessness will encourage more thorough legal training and trial preparation, the habeas applicant, as opposed to his lawyer, hardly is the proper recipient of such a penalty. Especially with fundamental constitutional rights at stake, no fictional relationship of principal-agent or the like can justify holding the criminal defendant accountable for the naked errors of his attorney. This is especially true when so many indigent defendants are without any realistic choice in selecting who ultimately represents them at trial. Indeed, if responsibility for error must be apportioned between the parties, it is the State, through its attorney's admissions and certification policies, that is more fairly held to blame for the fact that practicing lawyers too often are ill-prepared or ill-equipped to act carefully and knowledgeably when faced with decisions governed by state procedural requirements.

Hence, while I can well agree that the proper functioning of our system of criminal justice, both federal and state, necessarily places heavy reliance on the professionalism and judgment of trial attorneys, I cannot accept a system that ascribes the absolute forfeiture of an individual's constitutional claims to situations where his lawyer manifestly exercises *no* professional judgment at all—where carelessness, mistake, or ignorance is the explanation for a procedural default. Of course, it is regrettable that certain errors that might have been cured earlier had trial counsel acted expeditiously must be corrected collaterally and belatedly. I can understand the Court's wistfully wishing for the day when the trial was the sole, binding and final "event" of the adversarial process—although I hesitate to agree that in the eyes of the criminal defendant it has ever ceased being the "main" one. . . . But it should be plain that in the real world, the interest in finality is repeatedly compromised in numerous ways that arise with far greater frequency than do procedural defaults. . . . Indeed, the very existence of the well-established right collaterally to reopen issues previously litigated before the state courts . . . represents a congressional policy choice that is inconsistent with notions of strict finality—and probably more so than authorizing the litigation of issues that, due to inadvertence, were never addressed to any court. Ultimately, all of these limitations on the finality of criminal convictions emerge from the tension between justice and efficiency in a judicial system that hopes to remain true to its principles and ideals. Reasonable people may disagree on how best to resolve these tensions. But the solution that today's decision risks embracing seems to me the most unfair of all: the denial of any judicial consideration of the constitutional claims of a criminal defendant because of errors made by his attorney which lie outside the power of the habeas petitioner to prevent or deter and for which, under no view of morality or ethics, can he be held responsible.

In short, I believe that the demands of our criminal justice system warrant visiting the mistakes of a trial attorney on the head of a habeas corpus applicant only when we are convinced that the lawyer actually exercised his expertise and judgment in his client's service, and with his client's knowing and intelligent participation where possible. This, of course, is the precise system of habeas review established by Fay v. Noia.

IV

. . .

One final consideration deserves mention. Although the standards recently have been relaxed in various jurisdictions, it is accurate to assert that most courts, this one included, traditionally have resisted any realistic inquiry into the competency of trial counsel. There is nothing unreasonable, however, in adhering to the proposition that it is the responsibility of a trial lawyer who takes on the defense of another to be aware of his client's basic legal rights and of the legitimate rules of the forum in which he practices his profession. If he should unreasonably permit such rules to bar the assertion of the colorable constitutional claims of his client, then his conduct may well fall below the level of competence that can fairly be expected of him. For almost 40 years it has been established that inadequacy of counsel undercuts the very competence and jurisdiction of the trial court and is always open to collateral review. Johnson v. Zerbst, 304 U.S. 458 (1938). Obviously, as a practical matter, a trial counsel cannot procedurally waive his own inadequacy. If the scope of habeas jurisdiction previously governed by Fay v. Noia is to be redefined so as to enforce the errors and neglect of lawyers with unnecessary and unjust rigor, the time may come when conscientious and fairminded federal and state courts, in adhering to the teaching of Johnson v. Zerbst, will have to reconsider whether they can continue to indulge the comfortable fiction that all lawyers are skilled or even competent craftsmen in representing the fundamental rights of their clients.[4]

---

[4] Justice Stevens wrote a concurring opinion. Justice White wrote an opinion concurring in the judgment.

644. In Engle v. Isaac, 456 U.S. 107 (1982) (7–2), several respondents who had been convicted in the Ohio state courts of homicide or assault sought habeas corpus in the federal district court. Each claimed that the trial judge had erroneously instructed the jury that the defendant had the burden of proving self defense by a preponderance of the evidence. State law required contemporaneous objection to jury instructions. Defense counsel had made no objection.

The defendant's constitutional claim was that under prior cases, notably Mullaney v. Wilbur, 421 U.S. 684 (1975), p. 1081 above, absence of self defense was an element of the crimes charged against them, which the Due Process Clause required the state to prove beyond a reasonable doubt. This claim, the Court said, was "colorable." Neither "futility" of pressing a claim in the state court (because Ohio courts had long ruled to the contrary) nor "novelty" of the claim constituted cause for the failure to press the claim in the state courts. While *Sykes* did not necessarily require defense counsel "to exercise extraordinary vision or to object to every aspect of the proceedings in the hope that some aspect might mask a latent constitutional claim," the respondents' claims in these cases "were far from unknown at the time of their trials," and they did not lack "the tools to construct their constitutional claim." 456 U.S. at 130–32. "Where the basis of a constitutional claim is available, and other defense counsel have perceived and litigated that claim, the demands of comity and finality counsel against labeling alleged unawareness of the objection as cause for a procedural default." Id. at 134.

Two years after the decision in Engle v. Isaac, the Court decided Reed v. Ross, 468 U.S. 1 (1984) (5–4). In that case also, the defendant's claim was that the jury had been instructed, contrary to *Mullaney*, that the defendant had the burden of proof on an element of the offense. As in the earlier case, defense counsel did not raise the issue at trial. Nor did he raise the issue on appeal. A state rule of procedure barred relief on the latter ground. The Court held that Ross's claim was cognizable by habeas corpus in federal court.

The difference between the two cases, the court said, was that Ross's trial and appeal occurred in 1969 and the trial of the defendants in Engle v. Isaac in 1975. In the intervening years, the Court's decision in In re Winship, 397 U.S. 358 (1970), and other federal court decisions had laid the basis for the *Mullaney* argument (*Mullaney* itself having been decided in 1975, after the trial of two of the defendants and before the trial of the third). Therefore, defense counsel in Engle v. Isaac had had more reason to object to the jury instructions than had defense counsel in *Ross*. The novelty of the claim in Ross's case satisfied the requirement of "cause" for the procedural default.

> Because of the broad range of potential reasons for an attorney's failure to comply with a procedural rule, and the virtually limitless array of contexts in which a procedural default can occur, this Court has not given the term "cause" precise content. . . . Nor do we attempt to do so here. Underlying the concept of cause, however, is at

> least the dual notion that, absent exceptional circumstances, a defendant is bound by the tactical decisions of competent counsel . . . and that defense counsel may not flout state procedures and then turn around and seek refuge in federal court from the consequences of such conduct. . . . A defense attorney, therefore, may not ignore a State's procedural rules in the expectation that his client's constitutional claims can be raised at a later date in federal court. . . . Similarly, he may not use the prospect of federal habeas corpus relief as a hedge against the strategic risks he takes in his client's defense in state court. . . . In general, therefore, defense counsel may not make a tactical decision to forgo a procedural opportunity—for instance, an opportunity to object at trial or to raise an issue on appeal—and then, when he discovers that the tactic has been unsuccessful, pursue an alternative strategy in federal court. The encouragement of such conduct by a federal court on habeas corpus review would not only offend generally accepted principles of comity, but would also undermine the accuracy and efficiency of the state judicial systems to the detriment of all concerned. Procedural defaults of this nature are, therefore, "inexcusable," Estelle v. Williams, 425 U.S. 501, 513 (1976) (Powell, J., concurring), and cannot qualify as "cause" for purposes of federal habeas corpus review.
>
> On the other hand, the cause requirement may be satisfied under certain circumstances when a procedural failure is not attributable to an intentional decision by counsel made in pursuit of his client's interests. And the failure of counsel to raise a constitutional issue reasonably unknown to him is one situation in which the requirement is met. If counsel has no reasonable basis upon which to formulate a constitutional question . . . it is safe to assume that he is sufficiently unaware of the question's latent existence that we cannot attribute to him strategic motives of any sort.
>
> . . .
>
> Accordingly, we hold that where a constitutional claim is so novel that its legal basis is not reasonably available to counsel, a defendant has cause for his failure to raise the claim in accordance with applicable state procedures.

468 U.S. at 13–16. Confining its discussion to the facts of the particular case and distinguishing Engle v. Isaac on the basis noted above, the Court concluded that "Ross' claim was sufficiently novel in 1969 to excuse his attorney's failure to raise the *Mullaney* issue at that time." Id. at 20.

Four Justices dissented. The dissenting opinion called the majority's basis for distinguishing Engle v. Isaac a "bizarre line of reasoning," 468 U.S. at 25. It said further: "[T]his equating of novelty with cause pushes the Court into a conundrum which it refuses to recognize. The more 'novel' a claimed constitutional right, the more unlikely a violation of that claimed right undercuts the fundamental fairness of the trial. To untie this knot in logic, the Court proposes a definition of novelty that makes a claim novel if the legal basis for asserting the claim is not reasonably available. . . . This standard, of course, has no meaningful content independent of the factual setting in which it is applied. The Court's attempt to give content to this novelty standard, however, is simply too facile; under its application, virtually any new constitutional claim can be deemed 'novel.' " Id. at 22.

The standard of cause for a procedural default is elaborated further in Murray v. Carrier, 477 U.S. 478 (1986) (7–2). The Court said that an inadvertent failure of competent counsel to raise a substantive claim of error on appeal does not constitute cause that permits federal collateral attack on a state conviction. "[T]he existence of cause for a procedural default must ordinarily turn on whether the prisoner can show that some objective factor external to the defense impeded counsel's efforts to comply with the State's procedural rule." Examples of such "objective impediments," the Court said, are "a showing that the factual or legal basis for a claim was not reasonably available to counsel" (citing Reed v. Ross) or that " 'some interference by officials' . . . made compliance impracticable." Id. at 488. See Amadeo v. Zant, 486 U.S. 214 (1988) (cause for procedural default established by officials' concealment of factual basis for challenge to jury composition that was subject of default).

In Murray v. Carrier, the Court noted that the cause-and-prejudice test applied to procedural defaults on appeal as well as at trial. A procedural default on appeal is found not to satisfy the cause standard, in Smith v. Murray, 477 U.S. 527 (1986) (5–4). Defense counsel had deliberately not raised an objection to the admission of certain evidence at the sentencing hearing, because he concluded that the objection would probably fail; it later appeared that the objection had merit. Concluding that the legal issue did not meet the novelty standard of Reed v. Ross, the Court said that a deliberate procedural default "is the very antithesis of the kind of circumstance that would warrant excusing a defendant's failure to adhere to a State's legitimate rules for the fair and orderly disposition of its criminal cases." Id. at 534.

The cause and prejudice standard does not apply to a failure to raise a claim of ineffective assistance of counsel on direct appeal. Massaro v. United States, 538 U.S. 500 (2003). The Court concluded that such claims are unlikely to be made if counsel at trial and on appeal are the same and that even if they are not the same, the record on direct appeal is likely to be inadequate to consider such a claim, so that efficient administration dictated that it be considered in collateral proceedings in the district court. Accordingly a claim of ineffective assistance of counsel need not be raised on direct appeal.

See generally United States v. Frady, 456 U.S. 152 (1982) (6–1), declaring that the cause-and-prejudice standard and not the plain error standard is applicable on collateral attack of a federal conviction. "[T]o obtain collateral relief a prisoner must clear a significantly higher hurdle than would exist on direct appeal." Id. at 166. Engle v. Isaac, above, similarly rejects the plain error standard for federal collateral attack of a state conviction.

645. Wainwright v. Sykes and succeeding cases applying the cause-and-prejudice standard effectively replaced Fay v. Noia's "deliberate by-pass" test, see pp. 1231–32 above, without rejecting it altogether. (*Sykes* had left open the question whether *Fay* remained applicable to its own facts, the failure to take any appeal at all. 433 U.S. at 88 n.12. See, to the same effect, Murray v. Carrier, p. 1243 note 644 above, 477 U.S. at 492.) In Coleman v. Thompson, 501 U.S. 722 (1991) (6–3), the Court interred the *Fay* rule for all purposes: "We now make it explicit: In all cases in which a state prisoner has defaulted his federal claims in state court pursuant to an independent and adequate state procedural rule, federal habeas review of the claims is barred unless the prisoner can demonstrate cause for the default and actual prejudice as a result of the alleged violation of federal law, or demonstrate that failure to consider the claims will result in a fundamental miscarriage of justice. *Fay* was based on a conception of federal/state relations that undervalued the importance of state procedural rules. The several cases after *Fay* that applied the cause and prejudice standard to a variety of state procedural defaults represent a different view. We now recognize the important interest in finality served by state procedural rules, and the significant harm to the States that results from the failure of federal courts to respect them." Id. at 750. The *Coleman* opinion reviews the cases after *Sykes* leading up to this result.

646. As Justice Brennan observed in his dissenting opinion in Wainwright v. Sykes, see p. 1240 above, the requirement of cause for a procedural default can have no application when the constitutional claim is ineffective assistance of counsel. The Court made that explicit in Murray v. Carrier, 477 U.S. 478, 488 (1986) (7–2): "[I]f the procedural default is the result of ineffective assistance of counsel, the Sixth Amendment itself requires that responsibility for the default be imputed to the State. . . . Ineffective assistance of counsel, then, is cause for a procedural default." The Court added, however, that the doctrine of exhaustion of state remedies, see p. 1226 above, "generally requires that a claim of ineffective assistance be presented to the state courts as an independent claim before it may be used to establish cause for a procedural default. The question whether there is cause for a procedural default does not pose any occasion for applying the exhaustion doctrine when the federal habeas court can adjudicate the question of cause—a question of federal law—without deciding an independent and unexhausted constitutional claim on the merits. But if a petitioner could raise his ineffective assistance claim for the first time on federal habeas in order to show cause for a procedural default, the federal habeas court would find itself in the anomalous position of adjudicating an unexhausted constitutional claim for which state court review might still be available." Id. at 489. See generally Kimmelman v. Morrison, 477 U.S. 365 (1986). The test of ineffective assistance of counsel is that elaborated in Strickland v. Washington, p. 1036 above. See, e.g., Frey v. Fulcomer, 974 F.2d 348 (3d Cir.1992) (capital sentencing proceeding).

An ineffective assistance of counsel claim, asserted as the cause for procedural default of another constitutional claim, can itself be procedurally defaulted. Edwards v. Carpenter, 529 U.S. 446 (2000). That is to say, if an ineffective assistance claim was not considered by a state court because of a procedural default for which there is not adequate cause, that claim may not serve as adequate cause for the procedural default of another constitutional claim.

In Coleman v. Thompson, 501 U.S. 722 (1991) (6–3), the Court noted that a claim of ineffective assistance of counsel is a constitutional claim only if the defendant has a Sixth Amendment right to counsel in the first place. Accordingly, ineffective assistance of counsel in state collateral proceedings, in which the state has no constitutional obligation to provide counsel, is not cause for a procedural default. "[W]here the State has no responsibility to ensure that the petitioner was represented by competent counsel . . . the petitioner bears the risk in federal habeas for all attorney errors made in the course of representation." Id. at 754.

647. The Court has established a number of rules to assist federal courts in determining whether a state court's decision rests on a federal ground or a state procedural ground. "[W]hen . . . a state court decision fairly appears to rest primarily on federal law, or to be interwoven with federal law, and when the adequacy and independence of any possible state law ground is not clear from the face of the opinion, we will accept as the most reasonable explanation that the state court decided the case the way it did because it believed that federal law required it to do so. . . . If the state court decision indicates clearly and expressly that it is alternatively based on bona fide separate, adequate, and independent grounds, we, of course, will not undertake to review the decision." Michigan v. Long, 463 U.S. 1032, 1040–41 (1983) (6–3) (direct review). See Harris v. Reed, 489 U.S. 255 (1989) (8–1) (*Long* applicable in habeas corpus proceedings). Even though federal issues were presented to the state court, the presumption stated in *Long* does not apply unless its factual premise—that the state decision "appears to rest primarily on federal law, or to be interwoven with federal law"—is met. Coleman v. Thompson, 501 U.S. 722 (1991) (6–3). If the state court's opinion denying relief is unexplained, the presumption is that "where there has been one reasoned state judgment rejecting a federal claim, later unexplained orders upholding that judgment or rejecting the same claim rest upon the same ground. . . . [W]here . . . the last reasoned opinion on the claim explicitly imposes a procedural default [it is presumed] that a later decision rejecting the claim did not silently disregard that bar and consider the merits." Ylst v. Nunnemaker, 501 U.S. 797, 803 (1991) (6–3). See Lee v. Kemna, 534 U.S. 362 (2002) (6–3) (state ground, failure to make motion for continuance in writing and in proper form, inadequate).

648. In James v. Kentucky, 466 U.S. 341 (1984) (7–1), the trial judge did not give the instruction to the jury required by Carter v. Kentucky, p. 961 note 490 above. On appeal, the state court held that the failure to give the instruction was not reversible error because the defendant had called it an "admonition" rather than an "instruction" in his request. The Court reversed, holding that there was not a procedural fault providing an adequate and independent state ground for denying the constitutional claim. The "distinction between admonitions and instructions," it said, "is not the sort of firmly established and regularly followed state practice that can prevent implementation of federal constitutional rights." Id. at 348–49.

649. In Engle v. Isaac, 456 U.S. 107, 135 (1982) (7–2), the Court said that the cause-and-prejudice test was adequate to correct miscarriages of justice. "The terms 'cause' and 'actual prejudice' are not rigid concepts; they take their meaning from the principles of comity and finality. . . . In appropriate cases those principles must yield to the imperative of correcting a fundamentally unjust incarceration." In Murray v. Carrier, 477 U.S. 478, 495–96 (1986) (7–2), quoting Engle v. Isaac, 456 U.S. at 135, it reiterated its confidence "that, for the most part, 'victims of a fundamental miscarriage of justice will meet the cause-and-prejudice standard.' " It went on to say: "But we do not pretend that this will always be true. Accordingly, we think that in an extraordinary case, where a constitutional violation has probably resulted in the conviction of one who is actually innocent, a federal habeas court may grant the writ even in the absence of a showing of cause for the procedural default." Id. at 496. The case was remanded for a determination whether that standard had been met. See also Bousley v. United States, 523 U.S. 614 (1998) (7–2) (remand for determination of actual innocence); Kuhlmann v. Wilson, 477 U.S. 436, 454 (1986) (6–3) (no miscarriage of justice); Smith v. Murray, 477 U.S. 527, 537–38 (5–4) (same).

In Sawyer v. Whitley, 505 U.S. 333 (1992), the defendant challenged the exclusion of certain evidence at a sentencing hearing, at which he was sentenced to death. The cause-and-prejudice test was not met. In the context of capital punishment, the Court said, the "actual innocence" test means that a petitioner "must show by clear and convincing evidence that but for a constitutional error, no reasonable juror would have found him eligible for the death penalty" under the applicable state law. Id. at 350. The Court concluded that that test had not been met in this case. *Sawyer* was distinguished in Schlup v. Delo, 513 U.S. 298 (1995) (5–4), in which the defendant's claim of innocence was accompanied by a claim of constitutional error at trial.

650. Second or successive applications for habeas corpus under 28 U.S.C. § 2254 are severely restricted. It is provided flatly "that a claim that was presented in a prior application shall be dismissed." § 2244(b)(1). A claim that was not presented in a prior application is also to be dismissed unless the claim relies on a new, retroactive rule of constitutional law "that was previously unavailable"; "the factual predicate for the claim could not have been discovered previously through the exercise of due diligence"; or "the facts underlying the claim, if proved and viewed in light of the evidence as a whole, would be sufficient to establish by clear and convincing evidence that, but for constitutional error, no reasonable factfinder would have found the applicant guilty of the underlying offense." 28 U.S.C. § 2244(b)(2). A second or successive motion under § 2255 is similarly restricted. For applications of these provisions, see Slack v. McDaniel, 529 U.S. 473 (2000); Stewart v. Martinez-Villareal, 523 U.S. 637 (1998).

651. The defendant, represented by competent counsel, pleaded guilty to four counts of an indictment charging that he committed four burglaries on a day when, it later appeared, he was in jail. Should the conviction be set aside on collateral attack? Does it matter (1) that the pleas in question were accompanied by a plea to another count charging a burglary which the defendant could have and presumably did commit; (2) that he received consecutive sentences of five years' imprisonment on each count; (3) that the prosecuting attorney asserts that the date specified in the indictment was incorrect because of a typographical error? See Quarles v. Dutton, 379 F.2d 934 (5th Cir.1967).

652. Custody. In the federal courts, the writ of habeas corpus is available only to a person in "custody." 28 U.S.C. § 2241.[5] At one time, under the traditional principle that the writ tested the legality of detention, if a favorable answer to the questions the petitioner sought to raise would not require his release, the writ was not available. A prisoner could not attack a judgment pursuant to which he was not currently in custody. McNally v. Hill, 293 U.S. 131 (1934). In Peyton v. Rowe, 391 U.S. 54 (1968), *McNally* was overruled. The Court concluded that a prisoner serving consecutive sentences could use habeas corpus to attack not only the sentence he was then serving but also any sentence he was to serve thereafter. The Court observed that postponement of a hearing would make the determination of factual issues more difficult. It noted also that the statute, while requiring that the prisoner be in custody, did not limit relief to release from custody but authorized the courts to dispose of the case "as law and justice require," 28 U.S.C. § 2243. See Garlotte v. Fordice, 515 U.S. 39 (1995) (7–2) (*Peyton* applied; prisoner is in custody for purpose of attacking conviction already served, if conviction affects eligibility for parole under sentence currently being served); Maleng v. Cook, 490 U.S. 488 (1989) (*Peyton* applied to state sentence consecutive to federal sentence presently being served). Parole is sufficient "custody" to make the writ available, Jones v. Cunningham, 371 U.S. 236 (1963) (writ available to test restraints on a "petitioner's liberty to do those things which in this country free men are entitled to do," 371 U.S. at 243). It has been held that probation is sufficient custody, e.g., Olson v. Hart, 965 F.2d 940 (10th Cir.1992), as also is a requirement of community service, Barry v. Bergen County Probation Dept, 128 F.3d 152 (3d Cir.1997).

In Hensley v. Municipal Court, 411 U.S. 345 (1973), the Court held that a defendant who had been convicted and sentenced to imprisonment and was at large on his own recognizance pending execution of his sentence was in custody for purposes of habeas corpus. The holding presumably applies to all defendants who are released on any form of bail; but the

5. A federal court may in exceptional cases grant relief in the nature of *coram nobis* to a person who is not in custody, under the "all-writs provision," 28 U.S.C. § 1651(a): "The Supreme Court and all courts established by Act of Congress may issue all writs necessary or appropriate in aid of their respective jurisdictions and agreeable to the usages and principles of law." United States v. Morgan, 346 U.S. 502 (1954). See Mathis v. United States, 369 F.2d 43 (4th Cir.1966).

Court indicated that the doctrine of exhaustion of state remedies would preclude federal habeas corpus for defendants before trial or a final appeal. See Justices of Municipal Court v. Lydon, 466 U.S. 294 (1984) (*Hensley* applied). See also Lillios v. State of New Hampshire, 788 F.2d 60 (1st Cir.1986) (fine and suspension of driver's license not custody); Harts v. Indiana, 732 F.2d 95 (7th Cir.1984) (one-year suspension of driver's license; same).

The custody requirement for federal habeas corpus is not met when the only punishment imposed is a fine, even though the conviction may be attended by "the ordinary collateral consequences or civil disabilities flowing from a fine-only conviction." Hanson v. Circuit Court of First Judicial Circuit, 591 F.2d 404, 407 (7th Cir.1979). Cases to the same effect in other circuits are cited id. at 405 n.1.

The petitioner in Parker v. Ellis, 362 U.S. 574 (1960), completed service of his sentence and was released from state prison after his petition had been dismissed by the district court, the court of appeals had affirmed, and the Court had granted certiorari, but before it heard the case. The Court dismissed the writ of certiorari on the ground that the case had become moot: "[I]t is a condition upon this Court's jurisdiction to adjudicate an application for habeas corpus that the petitioner be in custody when that jurisdiction can become effective," id. at 576. *Parker* was overruled in Carafas v. LaVallee, 391 U.S. 234 (1968) (petition for certiorari filed and granted after petitioner released from custody): "[U]nder the statutory scheme, once the federal jurisdiction has attached in the District Court, it is not defeated by the release of the petitioner prior to completion of proceedings on such application," id. at 238. The Court added: "Petitioner is entitled to consideration of his application for relief on its merits. He is suffering, and will continue to suffer, serious disabilities because of the law's complexities and not because of his fault, if his claim that he has been illegally convicted is meritorious." Id. at 239. Among the consequences of his conviction mentioned by the Court were that "he cannot engage in certain businesses; he cannot serve as an official of a labor union for a specified period of time; he cannot vote in any election held in New York State; he cannot serve as a juror." Id. at 237. In Maleng v. Cook, above, the Court observed that its decision in *Carafas* depended not on the collateral consequences of the conviction but on "the fact that the petitioner had been in physical custody under the challenged conviction at the time the petition was filed." 490 U.S. at 492. "The negative implication of this holding," it said, "is . . . that once the sentence for a conviction has completely expired, the collateral consequences of that conviction are not themselves sufficient to render an individual 'in custody' for the purposes of a habeas attack on it." Id. See Spencer v. Kemna, 523 U.S. 1 (1998) (8–1).

Are any or all of the consequences mentioned by the Court in *Carafas* sufficient to warrant collateral proceedings to determine the validity of a conviction if the proceedings are not commenced until after the prisoner has been released from custody? See Cappetta v. Wainwright, 406 F.2d

1238 (5th Cir.1969) (invalidation of conviction and sentence fully served would effect reduction of sentence presently being served).

653. Does a State have any constitutional obligation to afford an avenue for collateral attack on a conviction on federal constitutional grounds? If so, why? In Young v. Ragen, 337 U.S. 235 (1949), the Supreme Court referred to "the requirement that prisoners be given some clearly defined method by which they may raise claims of denial of federal rights." Id. at 239.[6] The question was raised in Case v. Nebraska, 381 U.S. 336 (1965), but the subsequent enactment of adequate state legislation made a decision of the question unnecessary. Compare Testa v. Katt, 330 U.S. 386 (1947).

---

6. The Court may have had in mind only the narrower question whether the requirement of exhaustion of state remedies could be invoked when the existence of any such remedy was problematic.

*

INDEX

References are to pages.

1-58778-738-5
90000
9 781587 787386